DALLAS 2000

Proceedings of the 2000 ACM SIGMOD

International Conference on Management of Data
May 16-18, 2000

Dallas, Texas

Edited by Weidong Chen, Jeffrey Naughton and Philip A. Bernstein

SIGMOD Record, Volume 29, Issue 2, June 2000

D1456401

FOREWORD

The 2000 ACM SIGMOD International Conference on Management of Data was held May 16-18, 2000, in Dallas, Texas. The SIGMOD Conference is an annual international forum for the presentation, discussion, and dissemination of new results on database technology and application, and for the demonstration of prototype implementations of this technology. It is sponsored by the Association for Computing Machinery (ACM) and its Special Interest Group on Management of Data (SIGMOD). This year, as in preceding years, two days of the conference were overlapped with the Symposium on Principles of Database Systems(PODS).

Once again, acceptance into the conference proceedings was extremely competitive. From the 248 research program submissions, the program committee selected 42 papers for inclusion into the proceedings. We received papers on a wide range of topics, ranging from "traditional" topics such as query optimization and evaluation, to data mining, to a new emphasis on the web and XML. Needless to say, to accept only 42 papers we were forced to reject many high quality papers. We would like to thank all the authors for submitting to SIGMOD.

In addition to the research program, the conference featured an excellent industrial program, thought provoking panels, illuminating tutorials, and 20 software prototype demonstrations.

Producing this proceedings took a great deal of work. The program committee members each reviewed a daunting pile of papers. We are extremely indebted to Surajit Chaudhuri and the Microsoft Conference Management Tool team for developing the software and hosting the site that handled the submission, distribution, and reviewing of the papers.

Phil Bernstein chaired an industrial program committee that assembled the strong industrial program. Jiawei Han did the same for the demo program. Svein-Olaf Hvasshovd solicited and selected the tutorials, while Alon Levy organized the panels.

The conference would not have been a success without help from so many people. Leo Fegaras organized and planned the local arrangments. Mario Nascimento served as publicity chair and acted as webmaster. Vijay Kumar was in charge of finances. Alex Delis ensured the successful registration. Masaru Kitsuregawa, Christian S. Jensen, and Claudia Bauzer Medeiros served as our Asian, European, and South American coordinators. As corporate sponsor's chair, Sharma Chakravarthy successfully raised enough support to keep our registration fees low. David Levine ensured the successful operation of demos by serving as our local demo chair. This year we began a new undergraduate scholarship program with Le Gruenwald in charge, and awarded scholarships to support the attendance to SIGMOD by five undergraduate students.

Maggie Dunham - General Chair
Jeffrey Naughton - Program Chair
Weidong Chen - Proceedings Chair
Nick Koudas - Electronic Proceedings Chair

ASSOCIATION FOR COMPUTING MACHINERY
SPECIAL INTEREST GROUP on MANAGEMENT OF DATA
2000 ANNUAL CONFERENCE
CONFERENCE ORGANIZING COMMITTEE

SIGMOD GENERAL CHAIR: Margaret H. Dunham, Southern Methodist University
PROGRAM CHAIR: Jeffrey F. Naughton, University of Wisconsin-Madison
INDUSTRIAL PROGRAM CHAIR: Philip A. Bernstein, Microsoft
DEMONSTRATIONS CHAIR: Jiawei Han, Simon Fraser University
PANELS CHAIR: Alon Levy, University of Washington
TUTORIALS CHAIR: Svein-Olaf Hvasshovd, Clustra Systems
ASIAN COORDINATOR: Masaru Kitsuregawa, University of Tokyo
EUROPEAN COORDINATOR: Christian S. Jensen, Aalborg University
SOUTH AMERICAN COORDINATOR: Claudia Bauzer Medeiros, University of Campinas
REGISTRATION CHAIR: Alex Delis, Polytechnic University
PUBLICITY CHAIR: Mario A. Nascimento, University of Alberta
TREASURER: Vijay Kumar, University of Missouri-Kansas City
LOCAL ARRANGEMENTS CHAIR: Leonidas Fegaras, University of Texas at Arlington
CORPORATE SPONSORS CHAIR: Sharma Chakravarthy, University of Florida
PROCEEDINGS CHAIR: Weidong Chen, Southern Methodist University
ELECTRONIC PROCEEDINGS CHAIR: Nick Koudas, AT & T Labs - Research
LOCAL DEMO CHAIR: David Levine, University of Texas at Arlington
UNDERGRADUATE SCHOLARSHIP CHAIR: Le Gruenwald, University of Oklahoma

PROGRAM COMMITTEE:

Serge Abiteboul, INRIA
Divyakant Agrawal, University of California, Santa Barbara
Gustavo Alonso, ETH Zurich
Paolo Atzeni, Universita' di Roma Tre
Daniel Barbar, George Mason University
Yuri Breitbart, University of Kentucky
Michael Carey, IBM Almaden Research Center
Surajit Chaudhuri, Microsoft Research
Sophi Cluet, INRIA
Umesh Dayal, Hewlett-Packard Labs
Lois Delcambre, Oregon Graduate Institute
Leonidas Fegaras, University of Texas at Arlington
Mary Fernandez, AT & T Labs
Michael Franklin, University of Maryland
Phillip Gibbons, Bell Labs
Goetz Graefe, Microsoft

v

EXTERNAL REFEREES

Serge Abiteboul
Atul Adya
Bernd Amann
Sihem Amer-Yahia
Periklis Andritsos
Sunil Arya
Roger Barga
Roberto Bayardo
Jeff Bernhardt
Stephen Blott
Philipp Bohannon
Reinhard Braumandl
Kurt Brown
Adam Buchsbaum
Luca Cabibbo
K. Selcuk Candan
Chee-Yong Chan
Sharat Chandran
Hae-Don Chon
Jiang-Hsing Chu
Bobbie Cochrane
Kevin Compton
Gautam Das
Claude Delobel
Dan Duchamp
Susan Dumais
Brian Dunkel
Hakan Ferhatosmanoglu
Daniela Florescu
Irini Fundulaki
Minos Garofalakis
Aris Gionis
Parke Godfrey
Jonathan Goldstein
Goetz Graefe
Jarek Gryz
Jayant Haritsa

Mauricio A. Hernandez
JoAnne Holliday
Arvind Hulgeri
Matt Huras
Carlos Hurtado
David Hutchinson
Piotr Indyk
H. V. Jagadish
Theodore Johnson
H. Kang
Markus Keidl
Tasos Kementsietsidis
Hyoung-Joo Kim
Christian Koenig
Hank Korth
Paul Larson
Alon Levy
Daniel Lieuwen
Bruce Lindsay
Ling Liu
Nikos Mamoulis
Gianni Mecca
Paolo Merialdo
George Mihaila
Wai Yin Mok
Lynn Monson
Srinivasa Narayanan
Svetlozar Nestorov
Zaiqing Nie
Andrew Nierman
Liadan O'Callaghan
Kevin O'Gorman
Sriram Padmanabhan
Themistoklis Palpanas
Jignesh M. Patel
Jian Pei
Viswanath Poosala

Magda Procopiuc
Davood Rafiei
Krithi Ramamritham
Rajeev Rastogi
Corey Reina
Mirek RiedeWald
Keri Romanufa
Prasan Roy
Ralf Schenkel
Stefan Seltzsam
Jayavel Shanmugasundaram
Kyuseok Shim
Richard Sidle
Jerome Simeon
Spiros Skiadopoulos
Don Slutz
Peter Spiro
Ioana Stanoi
Subbu N. Subramanian
Dan Suciu
Toby J. Teorey
Anja Theobald
Dimitri Theodoratos
Yannis Theodoridis
Riccardo Torlone
Jim Trevor
Alejandro Vaisman
Yannis Velegrakis
Pierangelo Veltri
Quan Wang
Fanny Wattez
PHock-Shan Wong
William Wright
Xintao Wu
Yi-Leh Wu
Jeffrey X. Yu
Ning Zhong

RESEARCH SESSIONS

DEMONSTRATIONS

Mining Frequent Patterns without Candidate Generation *

Jiawei Han, Jian Pei, and Yiwen Yin
School of Computing Science
Simon Fraser University
{han, peijian, yiweny}@cs.sfu.ca

Abstract

Mining frequent patterns in transaction databases, time-series databases, and many other kinds of databases has been studied popularly in data mining research. Most of the previous studies adopt an Apriori-like candidate set generation-and-test approach. However, candidate set generation is still costly, especially when there exist prolific patterns and/or long patterns.

In this study, we propose a novel frequent pattern tree (FP-tree) structure, which is an extended prefix-tree structure for storing compressed, crucial information about frequent patterns, and develop an efficient FP-tree-based mining method, FP-growth, for mining *the complete set of frequent patterns* by pattern fragment growth. Efficiency of mining is achieved with three techniques: (1) a large database is compressed into a highly condensed, much smaller data structure, which avoids costly, repeated database scans, (2) our FP-tree-based mining adopts a pattern fragment growth method to avoid the costly generation of a large number of candidate sets, and (3) a partitioning-based, divide-and-conquer method is used to decompose the mining task into a set of smaller tasks for mining confined patterns in conditional databases, which dramatically reduces the search space. Our performance study shows that the FP-growth method is efficient and scalable for mining both long and short frequent patterns, and is about an order of magnitude faster than the Apriori algorithm and also faster than some recently reported new frequent pattern mining methods.

---

* The work was supported in part by the Natural Sciences and Engineering Research Council of Canada (grant NSERC-A3723), the Networks of Centres of Excellence of Canada (grant NCE/IRIS-3), and the Hewlett-Packard Lab, U.S.A.

1 Introduction

Frequent pattern mining plays an essential role in mining associations [3, 12], correlations [6], causality [19], sequential patterns [4], episodes [14], multidimensional patterns [13, 11], max-patterns [5], partial periodicity [9], emerging patterns [7], and many other important data mining tasks.

Most of the previous studies, such as [3, 12, 18, 16, 13, 17, 20, 15, 8], adopt an Apriori-like approach, which is based on an *anti-monotone Apriori heuristic* [3]: *if any length k pattern is not frequent in the database, its length $(k + 1)$ super-pattern can never be frequent.* The essential idea is to iteratively generate the set of candidate patterns of length $(k + 1)$ from the set of frequent patterns of length k (for $k \geq 1$), and check their corresponding occurrence frequencies in the database.

The Apriori heuristic achieves good performance gain by (possibly significantly) reducing the size of candidate sets. However, in situations with prolific frequent patterns, long patterns, or quite low minimum support thresholds, an Apriori-like algorithm may still suffer from the following two nontrivial costs:

- It is costly to handle a huge number of candidate sets. For example, if there are 10^4 frequent 1-itemsets, the Apriori algorithm will need to generate more than 10^7 length-2 candidates and accumulate and test their occurrence frequencies. Moreover, to discover a frequent pattern of size 100, such as $\{a_1, \ldots, a_{100}\}$, it must generate more than $2^{100} \approx 10^{30}$ candidates in total. This is the inherent cost of candidate generation, no matter what implementation technique is applied.

- It is tedious to repeatedly scan the database and check a large set of candidates by pattern matching, which is especially true for mining long patterns.

Is there any other way that one may reduce these costs in frequent pattern mining? May some novel data structure or algorithm help?

After some careful examination, we believe that the bottleneck of the Apriori-like method is at the *candidate set generation and test*. If one can avoid generating a huge set of candidates, the mining performance can be substantially improved.

This problem is attacked in the following three aspects.

First, a novel, compact data structure, called *frequent pattern tree*, or FP-tree for short, is constructed, which is an extended prefix-tree structure storing crucial, quantitative information about frequent patterns. Only frequent length-1 items will have nodes in the tree, and the tree nodes are arranged in such a way that more frequently occurring nodes will have better chances of sharing nodes than less frequently occurring ones.

Second, an FP-tree-based pattern fragment growth mining method, is developed, which starts from a frequent length-1 pattern (as an initial *suffix pattern*), examines only its *conditional pattern base* (a "sub-database" which consists of the set of frequent items co-occurring with the suffix pattern), constructs its (*conditional*) FP-tree, and performs mining recursively with such a tree. The pattern growth is achieved via concatenation of the suffix pattern with the new ones generated from a conditional FP-tree. Since the frequent itemset in any transaction is always encoded in the corresponding path of the frequent pattern trees, pattern growth ensures the completeness of the result. In this context, our method is not Apriori-like *restricted generation-and-test* but *restricted test only*. The major operations of mining are count accumulation and prefix path count adjustment, which are usually much less costly than candidate generation and pattern matching operations performed in most Apriori-like algorithms.

Third, the search technique employed in mining is a *partitioning-based, divide-and-conquer method* rather than Apriori-like *bottom-up generation of frequent itemsets combinations*. This dramatically reduces the size of *conditional pattern base* generated at the subsequent level of search as well as the size of its corresponding *conditional* FP-tree. Moreover, it transforms the problem of finding long frequent patterns to looking for shorter ones and then concatenating the suffix. It employs the least frequent items as suffix, which offers good selectivity. All these techniques contribute to substantial reduction of search costs.

A performance study has been conducted to compare the performance of FP-growth with Apriori and TreeProjection, where TreeProjection is a recently proposed efficient algorithm for frequent pattern mining [2]. Our study shows that FP-growth is at least an order of magnitude faster than Apriori, and such a margin grows even wider when the frequent patterns grow longer, and FP-growth also outperforms the TreeProjection algorithm. Our FP-tree-based mining method has also been tested in large transaction databases in industrial applications.

The remaining of the paper is organized as follows. Section 2 introduces the FP-tree structure and its construction method. Section 3 develops an FP-tree-based frequent pattern mining algorithm, FP-growth . Section 4 presents our performance study. Section 5 discusses the issues on scalability and improvements of the method. Section 6 summarizes our study and points out some future research issues.

2 Frequent Pattern Tree: Design and Construction

Let $I = \{a_1, a_2, \ldots, a_m\}$ be a **set of items**, and a **transaction database** $DB = \langle T_1, T_2, \ldots, T_n \rangle$, where T_i ($i \in [1..n]$) is a transaction which contains a set of items in I. The **support**[1] (or occurrence frequency) of a **pattern** A, which is a set of items, is the number of transactions containing A in DB. A, is a **frequent pattern** if A's support is no less than a predefined *minimum support threshold*, ξ.

Given a transaction database DB and a minimum support threshold, ξ, the problem of *finding the complete set of frequent patterns* is called the **frequent pattern mining problem**.

2.1 Frequent Pattern Tree

To design a compact data structure for efficient frequent pattern mining, let's first examine an example.

Example 1 Let the transaction database, DB, be (the first two columns of) Table 1 and $\xi = 3$.

A compact data structure can be designed based on the following observations.

1. Since only the frequent items will play a role in the frequent pattern mining, it is necessary to perform one scan of DB to identify the set of frequent items (with *frequency count* obtained as a by-product).

---

[1]Notice that *support* is defined here as *absolute* occurrence frequency, not the *relative* one as in some literature.

2. If we store the *set* of frequent items of each transaction in some compact structure, it may avoid repeatedly scanning of *DB*.

3. If multiple transactions share an identical frequent item set, they can be merged into one with the number of occurrences registered as *count*. It is easy to check whether two sets are identical if the frequent items in all of the transactions are sorted according to a fixed order.

4. If two transactions share a common prefix, according to some sorted order of frequent items, the shared parts can be merged using one prefix structure as long as the *count* is registered properly. If the frequent items are sorted in their *frequency descending order*, there are better chances that more prefix strings can be shared.

TID	Items Bought	(Ordered) Frequent Items
100	f, a, c, d, g, i, m, p	f, c, a, m, p
200	a, b, c, f, l, m, o	f, c, a, b, m
300	b, f, h, j, o	f, b
400	b, c, k, s, p	c, b, p
500	a, f, c, e, l, p, m, n	f, c, a, m, p

Table 1: A transaction database as running example.

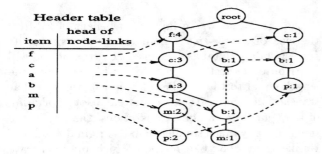

Figure 1: The **FP-tree** in Example 1.

With these observations, one may construct a frequent pattern tree as follows.

First, a scan of *DB* derives a *list* of frequent items, $\langle (f{:}4), (c{:}4), (a{:}3), (b{:}3), (m{:}3), (p{:}3) \rangle$, (the number after ":" indicates the support), in which items ordered in frequency descending order. This ordering is important since each path of a tree will follow this order. For convenience of later discussions, the frequent items in each transaction are listed in this ordering in the rightmost column of Table 1.

Second, one may create the root of a tree, labeled with "*null*". Scan the *DB* the second time. The scan of the first transaction leads to the construction of the first branch of the tree: $\langle (f{:}1), (c{:}1), (a{:}1), (m{:}1), (p{:}1) \rangle$. Notice that the frequent items in the transaction is ordered according to the order in the *list* of frequent items. For the second transaction, since its (ordered) frequent item list $\langle f, c, a, b, m \rangle$ shares a common prefix $\langle f, c, a \rangle$ with the existing path $\langle f, c, a, m, p \rangle$, the count of each node along the prefix is incremented by 1, and one new node $(b{:}1)$ is created and linked as a child of $(a{:}2)$ and another new node $(m{:}1)$ is created and linked as the child of $(b{:}1)$. For the third transaction, since its frequent item list $\langle f, b \rangle$ shares only the node $\langle f \rangle$ with the f-prefix subtree, f's count is incremented by 1, and a new node $(b{:}1)$ is created and linked as a child of $(f{:}3)$. The scan of the fourth transaction leads to the construction of the second branch of the tree, $\langle (c{:}1), (b{:}1), (p{:}1) \rangle$. For the last transaction, since its frequent item list $\langle f, c, a, m, p \rangle$ is identical to the first one, the path is shared with the count of each node along the path incremented by 1.

To facilitate tree traversal, an item header table is built in which each item points to its occurrence in the tree via a **head of node-link**. Nodes with the same item-name are linked in sequence via such **node-links**. After scanning all the transactions, the tree with the associated node-links is shown in Figure 1. □

This example leads to the following design and construction of a *frequent pattern tree*.

Definition 1 (FP-tree) A frequent pattern tree (or FP-tree in short) is a tree structure defined below.

1. It consists of one root labeled as "*null*", a set of item prefix subtrees as the children of the root, and a frequent-item header table.

2. Each node in the item prefix subtree consists of three fields: *item-name*, *count*, and *node-link*, where *item-name* registers which item this node represents, *count* registers the number of transactions represented by the portion of the path reaching this node, and *node-link* links to the next node in the FP-tree carrying the same item-name, or null if there is none.

3. Each entry in the frequent-item header table consists of two fields, (1) *item-name* and (2) *head of node-link*, which points to the first node in the FP-tree carrying the *item-name*. □

Based on this definition, we have the following FP-tree construction algorithm.

Algorithm 1 (FP-tree construction)

Input: A transaction database DB and a minimum support threshold ξ.

Output: Its frequent pattern tree, FP-tree

Method: The FP-tree is constructed in the following steps.

1. Scan the transaction database DB once. Collect the set of frequent items F and their supports. Sort F in support descending order as L, the *list of frequent items*.

2. Create the root of an FP-tree, T, and label it as "null". For each transaction $Trans$ in DB do the following.

   Select and sort the frequent items in $Trans$ according to the order of L. Let the sorted frequent item list in $Trans$ be $[p|P]$, where p is the first element and P is the remaining list. Call $insert\_tree([p|P], T)$.

   The function $insert\_tree([p|P], T)$ is performed as follows. If T has a child N such that $N.item\text{-}name = p.item\text{-}name$, then increment N's count by 1; else create a new node N, and let its count be 1, its parent link be linked to T, and its node-link be linked to the nodes with the same *item-name* via the node-link structure. If P is nonempty, call $insert\_tree(P, N)$ recursively.

Analysis. From the FP-tree construction process, we can see that one needs exactly two scans of the transaction database, DB: the first collects the set of frequent items, and the second constructs the FP-tree. The cost of inserting a transaction $Trans$ into the FP-tree is O($|Trans|$), where $|Trans|$ is the number of frequent items in $Trans$. We will show that the FP-tree contains the complete information for frequent pattern mining. □

2.2 Completeness and Compactness of FP-tree

Several important properties of FP-tree can be observed from the FP-tree construction process.

Lemma 2.1 *Given a transaction database DB and a support threshold ξ, its corresponding* FP-tree *contains the complete information of DB in relevance to frequent pattern mining.*

Rationale. Based on the FP-tree construction process, each transaction in the DB is mapped to one path in the FP-tree, and the frequent itemset information in each transaction is completely stored in the FP-tree. Moreover, one path in the FP-tree may represent frequent itemsets in multiple transactions without ambiguity since the path representing every transaction must start from the root of each item prefix subtree. Thus we have the lemma. □

Lemma 2.2 *Without considering the (null) root, the size of an FP-tree is bounded by the overall occurrences of the frequent items in the database, and the height of the tree is bounded by the maximal number of frequent items in any transaction in the database.*

Rationale. Based on the FP-tree construction process, for any transaction T in DB, there exists a path in the FP-tree starting from the corresponding item prefix subtree so that the set of nodes in the path is exactly the same set of frequent items in T. Since no frequent item in any transaction can create more than one node in the tree, the root is the only extra node created not by frequent item insertion, and each node contains one node-link and one count information, we have the bound of the size of the tree stated in the Lemma. The height of any p-prefix subtree is the maximum number of frequent items in any transaction with p appearing at the head of its frequent item list. Therefore, the height of the tree is bounded by the maximal number of frequent items in any transaction in the database, if we do not consider the additional level added by the root. □

Lemma 2.2 shows an important benefit of FP-tree: the size of an FP-tree is bounded by the size of its corresponding database because each transaction will contribute at most one path to the FP-tree, with the length equal to the number of frequent items in that transaction. Since there are often a lot of sharing of frequent items among transactions, the size of the tree is usually much smaller than its original database. Unlike the Apriori-like method which may generate an exponential number of candidates in the worst case, under no circumstances, may an FP-tree with an exponential number of nodes be generated.

FP-tree is a highly compact structure which stores the information for frequent pattern mining. Since a single path "$a_1 \rightarrow a_2 \rightarrow \cdots \rightarrow a_n$" in the a_1-prefix subtree registers all the transactions whose maximal frequent set is in the form of "$a_1 \rightarrow a_2 \rightarrow \cdots \rightarrow a_k$" for any $1 \leq k \leq n$, the size of the FP-tree is substantially smaller than the size of the database and that of the candidate sets generated in the association rule mining.

The items in the frequent item set are ordered in the support-descending order: More frequently occurring items are arranged closer to the top of the FP-tree and thus are more likely to be shared. This indicates that FP-tree structure is usually highly compact. Our experiments also show that a small FP-trees is resulted by compressing some quite large database. For example, for the database *Connect-4* used in MaxMiner [5], which contains 67,557 transactions with 43 items in each transaction, when the support threshold is 50% (which is used in the MaxMiner experiments [5]), the total number of occurrences of frequent items is 2,219,609, whereas the total number of nodes in the FP-tree is 13,449 which represents a reduction ratio of 165.04, while it withholds hundreds of thousands of frequent patterns! (Notice that for databases with mostly short transactions, the reduction ratio is not that high.)

Nevertheless, one cannot assume that an FP-tree can always fit in main memory for any large databases. Methods for highly scalable FP-growth mining will be discussed in Section 5.

3 Mining Frequent Patterns using FP-tree

Construction of a compact FP-tree ensures that subsequent mining can be performed with a rather compact data structure. However, this does not automatically guarantee that it will be highly efficient since one may still encounter the combinatorial problem of candidate generation if we simply use this FP-tree to generate and check all the candidate patterns.

In this section, we will study how to explore the compact information stored in an FP-tree and develop an efficient mining method for mining *the complete set of frequent patterns* (also called *all patterns*).

We observe some interesting properties of the FP-tree structure which will facilitate frequent pattern mining.

Property 3.1 (Node-link property) *For any frequent item a_i, all the possible frequent patterns that contain a_i can be obtained by following a_i's node-links, starting from a_i's head in the FP-tree header.*

This property is based directly on the construction process of FP-tree. It facilitates the access of all the pattern information related to a_i by traversing the FP-tree once following a_i's node-links.

Example 2 Let us examine the mining process based on the constructed FP-tree shown in Figure 1. Based on Property 3.1, we collect all the patterns that a node a_i participates by starting from a_i's head (in

the header table) and following a_i's node-links. We examine the mining process by starting from the bottom of the header table.

For node p, it derives a frequent pattern $(p{:}3)$ and two paths in the FP-tree : $\langle f{:}4, c{:}3, a{:}3, m{:}2, p{:}2 \rangle$ and $\langle c{:}1, b{:}1, p{:}1 \rangle$. The first path indicates that string "(f, c, a, m, p)" appears twice in the database. Notice although string $\langle f, c, a \rangle$ appears three times and $\langle f \rangle$ itself appears even four times, they only appear twice **together** with p. Thus to study which string appear together with p, only p's prefix path $\langle f{:}2, c{:}2, a{:}2, m{:}2 \rangle$ counts. Similarly, the second path indicates string "(c, b, p)" appears once in the set of transactions in DB, or p's prefix path is $\langle c{:}1, b{:}1 \rangle$. These two prefix paths of p, "$\{(f{:}2, c{:}2, a{:}2, m{:}2), (c{:}1, b{:}1)\}$", form p's sub-pattern base, which is called p's **conditional pattern base** (i.e., the sub-pattern base under the condition of p's existence). Construction of an FP-tree on this conditional pattern base (which is called p's **conditional FP-tree**) leads to only one branch $(c{:}3)$. Hence only one frequent pattern $(cp{:}3)$ is derived. (Notice that a pattern is an itemset and is denoted by a string here.) The search for frequent patterns associated with p terminates.

For node m, it derives a frequent pattern $(m{:}3)$ and two paths $\langle f{:}4, c{:}3, a{:}3, m{:}2 \rangle$ and $\langle f{:}4, c{:}3, a{:}3, b{:}1, m{:}1 \rangle$. Notice p appears together with m as well, however, there is no need to include p here in the analysis since any frequent patterns involving p has been analyzed in the previous examination of p. Similar to the above analysis, m's conditional pattern base is, $\{(f{:}2, c{:}2, a{:}2), (f{:}1, c{:}1, a{:}1, b{:}1)\}$. Constructing an FP-tree on it, we derive m's conditional FP-tree, $\langle f{:}3, c{:}3, a{:}3 \rangle$, a single frequent pattern path. Then one can call FP-tree-based mining recursively, i.e., call $mine(\langle f{:}3, c{:}3, a{:}3 \rangle | m)$.

Figure 2 shows "$mine(\langle f{:}3, c{:}3, a{:}3 \rangle | m)$" involves mining three items (a), (c), (f) in sequence. The first derives a frequent pattern $(am{:}3)$, and a call "$mine(\langle f{:}3, c{:}3 \rangle | am)$"; the second derives a frequent pattern $(cm{:}3)$, and a call "$mine(\langle f{:}3 \rangle | cm)$"; and the third derives only a frequent pattern $(fm{:}3)$. Further recursive call of "$mine(\langle f{:}3, c{:}3 \rangle | am)$" derives $(cam{:}3)$, $(fam{:}3)$, and a call "$mine(\langle f{:}3 \rangle | cam)$", which derives the longest pattern $(fcam{:}3)$. Similarly, the call of "$mine(\langle f{:}3 \rangle | cm)$", derives one pattern $(fcm{:}3)$. Therefore, the whole set of frequent patterns involving m is $\{(m{:}3), (am{:}3), (cm{:}3), (fm{:}3), (cam{:}3), (fam{:}3), (fcam{:}3), (fcm{:}3)\}$. This indicates *a single path* FP-tree *can be mined by outputting all the combinations of the items in the path*.

Similarly, node b derives $(b{:}3)$ and three paths: $\langle f{:}4, c{:}3, a{:}3, b{:}1 \rangle$, $\langle f{:}4, b{:}1 \rangle$, and $\langle c{:}1, b{:}1 \rangle$. Since b's

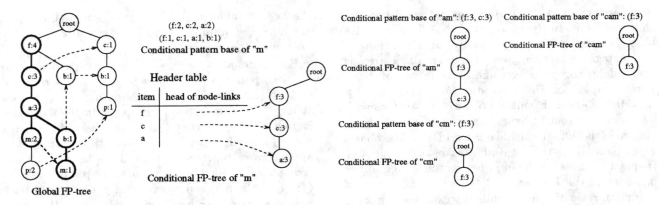

Figure 2: A conditional **FP-tree** built for m, i.e, "**FP-tree** $\mid m$"

conditional pattern base: $\{(f{:}1, c{:}1, a{:}1), (f{:}1), (c{:}1)\}$ generates no frequent item, the mining terminates. Node a derives one frequent pattern $\{(a{:}3)\}$, and one subpattern base, $\{(f{:}3, c{:}3)\}$, a single path conditional **FP-tree**. Thus, its set of frequent patterns can be generated by taking their combinations. Concatenating them with $(a{:}3)$, we have $\{(fa{:}3), (ca{:}3), (fca{:}3)\}$. Node c derives $(c{:}4)$ and one subpattern base, $\{(f{:}3)\}$, and the set of frequent patterns associated with $(c{:}3)$ is $\{(fc{:}3)\}$. Node f derives only $(f{:}4)$ but no conditional pattern base.

item	conditional pattern base	conditional FP-tree
p	$\{(f{:}2, \quad c{:}2, \quad a{:}2, \quad m{:}2),$ $(c{:}1, b{:}1)\}$	$\{(c{:}3)\}\mid p$
m	$\{(f{:}4, c{:}3, a{:}3, m{:}2),$ $(f{:}4, c{:}3, a{:}3, b{:}1, m{:}1)\}$	$\{(f{:}3, \quad c{:}3,$ $a{:}3)\}\mid m$
b	$\{(f{:}4, c{:}3, a{:}3, b{:}1), (f{:}4, b{:}1),$ $(c{:}1, b{:}1)\}$	$\emptyset$
a	$\{(f{:}3, c{:}3)\}$	$\{(f{:}3, c{:}3)\}\mid a$
c	$\{(f{:}3)\}$	$\{(f{:}3)\}\mid c$
f	$\emptyset$	$\emptyset$

Table 2: Mining of all-patterns by creating conditional (sub)-pattern bases

The conditional pattern bases and the conditional **FP-trees** generated are summarized in Table 2. □

The correctness and completeness of the process in Example 2 should be justified. We will present a few important properties related to the mining process.

Property 3.2 (Prefix path property) *To calculate the frequent patterns for a node a_i in a path P, only the* prefix subpath *of node a_i in P need to be accumulated, and the frequency count of every node in the prefix path should carry the same count as node a_i.*

Rationale. Let the nodes along the path P be labeled as $a_1, \ldots, a_n$ in such an order that a_1 is the root of the prefix subtree, a_n is the leaf of the subtree in P, and a_i $(1 \le i \le n)$ is the node being referenced. Based on the process of construction of **FP-tree** presented in Algorithm 1, for each prefix node a_k $(1 \le k < i)$, the prefix subpath of the node a_i in P occurs together with a_k exactly $a_i.count$ times. Thus every such prefix node should carry the same count as node a_i. Notice that a postfix node a_m (for $i < m \le n$) along the same path also co-occurs with node a_i. However, the patterns with a_m will be generated at the examination of the postfix node a_m, enclosing them here will lead to redundant generation of the patterns that would have been generated for a_m. Therefore, we only need to examine the prefix subpath of a_i in P. □

For example, in Example 2, node m is involved in a path $\langle f{:}4, c{:}3, a{:}3, m{:}2, p{:}2 \rangle$, to calculate the frequent patterns for node m in this path, only the prefix subpath of node m, which is $\langle f{:}4, c{:}3, a{:}3 \rangle$, need to be extracted, and the frequency count of every node in the prefix path should carry the same count as node m. That is, the node counts in the prefix path should be adjusted to $\langle f{:}2, c{:}2, a{:}2 \rangle$.

Based on this property, the prefix subpath of node a_i in a path P can be copied and transformed into a count-adjusted prefix subpath by adjusting the frequency count of every node in the prefix subpath to the same as the count of node a_i. The so transformed prefix path is called the **transformed prefixed path** of a_i for path P.

Notice that the set of transformed prefix paths of a_i form a small database of patterns which co-occur with a_i. Such a database of patterns occurring with a_i is called a_i's **conditional pattern base**, and is denoted as "$pattern\_base \mid a_i$". Then one can compute all the frequent patterns associated with

6

a_i in this a_i-conditional pattern_base by creating a small FP-tree, called a_i's **conditional FP-tree** and denoted as "FP-tree $| a_i$". Subsequent mining can be performed on this small, conditional FP-tree. The processes of construction of conditional pattern bases and conditional FP-trees have been demonstrated in Example 2.

This process is performed recursively, and the frequent patterns can be obtained by a pattern growth method, based on the following lemmas and corollary.

Lemma 3.1 (Fragment growth) *Let α be an itemset in DB, B be α's conditional pattern base, and β be an itemset in B. Then the support of $\alpha \cup \beta$ in DB is equivalent to the support of β in B.*

Rationale. According to the definition of conditional pattern base, each (sub)transaction in B occurs under the condition of the occurrence of α in the original transaction database DB. If an itemset β appears in B ψ times, it appears with α in DB ψ times as well. Moreover, since all such items are collected in the conditional pattern base of α, $\alpha \cup \beta$ occurs exactly ψ times in DB as well. Thus we have the lemma. $\square$

From this lemma, we can easily derive an important corollary.

Corollary 3.1 (Pattern growth) *Let α be a frequent itemset in DB, B be α's conditional pattern base, and β be an itemset in B. Then $\alpha \cup \beta$ is frequent in DB if and only if β is frequent in B.*

Rationale. This corollary is the case when α is a frequent itemset in DB, and when the support of β in α's conditional pattern base B is no less than ξ, the minimum support threshold. $\square$

Based on Corollary 3.1, mining can be performed by first identifying the frequent 1-itemset, α, in DB, constructing their conditional pattern bases, and then mining the 1-itemset, β, in these conditional pattern bases, and so on. This indicates that the process of mining frequent patterns can be viewed as first mining frequent 1-itemset and then progressively growing each such itemset by mining its conditional pattern base, which can in turn be done similarly. Thus we successfully transform a frequent k-itemset mining problem into a sequence of k frequent 1-itemset mining problems via a set of conditional pattern bases. What we need is just pattern growth. There is no need to generate any combinations of candidate sets in the entire mining process.

Finally, we provide the property on mining all the patterns when the FP-tree contains only a single path.

Lemma 3.2 (Single FP-tree path pattern generation) *Suppose an FP-tree T has a single path P. The complete set of the frequent patterns of T can be generated by the enumeration of all the combinations of the subpaths of P with the support being the minimum support of the items contained in the subpath.*

Rationale. Let the single path P of the FP-tree be $\langle a_1:s_1 \rightarrow a_2:s_2 \rightarrow \cdots \rightarrow a_k:s_k \rangle$. The support frequency s_i of each item a_i (for $1 \leq i \leq k$) is the frequency of a_i co-occurring with its prefix string. Thus any combination of the items in the path, such as $\langle a_i, \cdots, a_j \rangle$ (for $1 \leq i, j \leq k$), is a frequent pattern, with their co-occurrence frequency being the minimum support among those items. Since every item in each path P is unique, there is no redundant pattern to be generated with such a combinational generation. Moreover, no frequent patterns can be generated outside the FP-tree. Therefore, we have the lemma. $\square$

Based on the above lemmas and properties, we have the following algorithm for mining frequent patterns using FP-tree.

Algorithm 2 (FP-growth: Mining frequent patterns with FP-tree by pattern fragment growth)

Input: FP-tree constructed based on Algorithm 1, using DB and a minimum support threshold ξ.

Output: The complete set of frequent patterns.

Method: Call FP-growth (FP-tree, $null$).

Procedure FP-growth $(Tree, \alpha)$
{
(1) **if** $Tree$ contains a single path P
(2)   **then for each** combination (denoted as β) of the nodes in the path P **do**
(3)   generate pattern $\beta \cup \alpha$ with $support = minimum\ support\ of\ nodes\ in\ \beta$;
(4) **else for each** a_i in the header of $Tree$ **do** {
(5)   generate pattern $\beta = a_i \cup \alpha$ with $support = a_i.support$;
(6)   construct β's conditional pattern base and then β's conditional FP-tree $Tree_\beta$;
(7)   **if** $Tree_\beta \neq \emptyset$
(8)   **then** call FP-growth $(Tree_\beta, \beta)$ }
}

Analysis. With the properties and lemmas in Sections 2 and 3, we show that the algorithm correctly finds the complete set of frequent itemsets in transaction database DB.

7

As shown in Lemma 2.1, FP-tree of DB contains the complete information of DB in relevance to frequent pattern mining under the support threshold ξ.

If an FP-tree contains a single path, according to Lemma 3.2, its generated patterns are the combinations of the nodes in the path, with the support being the minimum support of the nodes in the sub-path. Thus we have lines (1)-(3) of the procedure. Otherwise, we construct conditional pattern base and mine its conditional FP-tree for each frequent itemset a_i. The correctness and completeness of prefix path transformation are shown in Property 3.2, and thus the conditional pattern bases store the complete information for frequent pattern mining. According to Lemmas 3.1 and its corollary, the patterns successively grown from the conditional FP-trees are the set of sound and complete frequent patterns. Especially, according to the fragment growth property, the support of the combined fragments takes the support of the frequent itemsets generated in the conditional pattern base. Therefore, we have lines (4)-(8) of the procedure. □

Let's now examine the efficiency of the algorithm. The FP-growth mining process scans the FP-tree of DB once and generates a small pattern-base B_{a_i} for each frequent item a_i, each consisting of the set of transformed prefix paths of a_i. Frequent pattern mining is then recursively performed on the small pattern-base B_{a_i} by constructing a conditional FP-tree for B_{a_i}. As reasoned in the analysis of Algorithm 1, an FP-tree is usually much smaller than the size of DB. Similarly, since the conditional FP-tree, "FP-tree $\mid a_i$", is constructed on the pattern-base B_{a_i}, it should be usually much smaller and never bigger than B_{a_i}. Moreover, a pattern-base B_{a_i} is usually much smaller than its original FP-tree, because it consists of the transformed prefix paths related to only one of the frequent items, a_i. Thus, each subsequent mining process works on a set of usually much smaller pattern bases and conditional FP-trees. Moreover, the mining operations consists of mainly prefix count adjustment, counting, and pattern fragment concatenation. This is much less costly than generation and test of a very large number of candidate patterns. Thus the algorithm is efficient.

From the algorithm and its reasoning, one can see that the FP-growth mining process is a divide-and-conquer process, and the scale of shrinking is usually quite dramatic. If the shrinking factor is around 20~100 for constructing an FP-tree from a database, it is expected to be another hundreds of times reduction for constructing each conditional FP-tree from its already quite small conditional frequent pattern base.

Notice that even in the case that a database may generate an exponential number of frequent patterns, the size of the FP-tree is usually quite small and will never grow exponentially. For example, for a frequent pattern of length 100, "$a_1, \ldots, a_{100}$", the FP-tree construction results in only one path of length 100 for it, such as "$\langle a_1, \to \cdots \to a_{100} \rangle$". The FP-growth algorithm will still generate about 10^{30} frequent patterns (if time permits!!), such as "$a_1, a_2, \ldots, a_1 a_2, \ldots, a_1 a_2 a_3, \ldots, a_1 \ldots a_{100}$". However, the FP-tree contains only one frequent pattern path of 100 nodes, and according to Lemma 3.2, there is even no need to construct any conditional FP-tree in order to find all the patterns.

4 Experimental Evaluation and Performance Study

In this section, we present a performance comparison of FP-growth with the classical frequent pattern mining algorithm Apriori, and a recently proposed efficient method TreeProjection.

All the experiments are performed on a 450-MHz Pentium PC machine with 128 megabytes main memory, running on Microsoft Windows/NT. All the programs are written in Microsoft/Visual C++6.0. Notice that we do not directly compare our absolute number of runtime with those in some published reports running on the RISC workstations because different machine architectures may differ greatly on the absolute runtime for the same algorithms. Instead, we implement their algorithms to the best of our knowledge based on the published reports on the same machine and compare in the same running environment. Please also note that *run time* used here means the total execution time, i.e., the period between input and output, instead of *CPU time* measured in the experiments in some literature. Also, all reports on the runtime of FP-growth include the time of constructing FP-trees from the original databases.

The synthetic data sets which we used for our experiments were generated using the procedure described in [3].

We report experimental results on two data sets. The first one is T25.I10.D10K with 1K items, which is denoted as $\mathcal{D}_1$. In this data set, the average transaction size and average maximal potentially frequent itemset size are set to 25 and 10, respectively, while the number of transactions in the dataset is set to 10K. The second data set, denoted as $\mathcal{D}_2$, is T25.I20.D100K with 10K items. There are exponentially numerous frequent itemsets in both data sets, as the support threshold goes down. There are pretty long frequent itemsets as well as a large number of short frequent itemsets in them. They contain abundant mixtures of short and long frequent itemsets.

4.1 Comparison of FP-growth and Apriori

The scalability of FP-growth and Apriori as the support threshold decreases from 3% to 0.1% is shown in Figure 3.

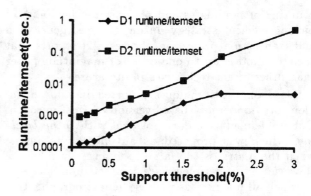

Figure 4: Run time of FP-growth per itemset versus support threshold.

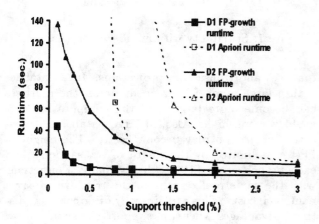

Figure 3: Scalability with threshold.

FP-growth scales much better than Apriori. This is because as the support threshold goes down, the number as well as the length of frequent itemsets increase dramatically. The candidate sets that Apriori must handle becomes extremely large, and the pattern matching with a lot of candidates by searching through the transactions becomes very expensive.

Figure 4 shows that the run time per itemset of FP-growth. It shows that FP-growth has good scalability with the reduction of minimum support threshold. Although the number of frequent itemsets grows exponentially, the run time of FP-growth increases in a much more conservative way. Figure 4 indicates as the support threshold goes down, the run time per itemset decreases dramatically (notice rule time in the figure is in exponential scale). This is why the FP-growth can achieve good scalability with the support threshold.

To test the scalability with the number of transactions, experiments on data set $\mathcal{D}_2$ are used. The support threshold is set to 1.5%. The results are presented in Figure 5.

Both FP-growth and Apriori algorithms show linear scalability with the number of transactions from

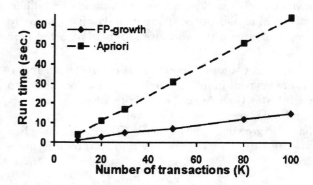

Figure 5: Scalability with number of transactions.

10K to 100K. However, FP-growth is much more scalable than Apriori. As the number of transactions grows up, the difference between the two methods becomes larger and larger. Overall, FP-growth is about an order of magnitude faster than Apriori in large databases, and this gap grows wider when the minimum support threshold reduces.

4.2 Comparison of FP-growth and TreeProjection

TreeProjection is an efficient algorithm recently proposed in [2]. The general idea of TreeProjection is that it constructs a lexicographical tree and projects a large database into a set of reduced, item-based subdatabases based on the frequent patterns mined so far. The number of nodes in its lexicographic tree is exactly that of the frequent itemsets. The efficiency of TreeProjection can be explained by two main factors: (1) the transaction projection limits the support counting in a relatively small space; and (2) the lexicographical tree facilitates the management and counting of candidates and provides the flexibility of picking efficient strategy during the tree generation and transaction projection phrases. [2] reports that their method is up to one order of magnitude faster than other recent techniques in literature.

Based on the techniques reported in [2], we implemented a memory-based version of TreeProjection. Our implementation does not deal with *cache blocking*, which was proposed as an efficient technique when the matrix is too large to fit in main memory. However, our experiments are conducted on data sets in which all matrices as well as the lexicographic tree can be held in main memory (with our 128 megabytes main memory machine). We believe that based on such constraints, the performance data are in general comparable and fair. Please note that the experiments reported in [2] use different datasets and different machine platforms. Thus it makes little sense to directly compare the absolute numbers reported here with [2].

According to our experimental results, both methods are efficient in mining frequent patterns. Both run much faster than Apriori, especially when the support threshold is pretty low. However, a close study shows that FP-growth is better than TreeProjection when support threshold is very low and database is quite large.

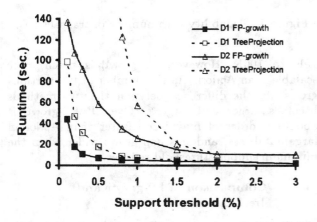

Figure 6: Scalability with support threshold.

As shown in Figure 6, both TreeProjection and FP-growth have good performance when the support threshold is pretty low, but FP-growth is better. As shown in Figure 7, in which the support threshold is set to 1%, both FP-growth and TreeProjection have linear scalability with the number of transactions, but FP-growth is more scalable.

The main costs in TreeProjection are computing of

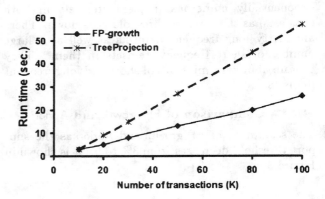

Figure 7: Scalability with number of transactions.

matrices and transaction projections. In a database with a large number of frequent items, the matrices can become quite large, and the computation cost could become high. Also, in large databases, transaction projection may become costly. The height of FP-tree is limited by the length of transactions, and each branch of an FP-tree shares many transactions with the same prefix paths in the tree, which saves nontrivial costs. This explains why FP-growth has distinct advantages when the support threshold is low and when the number of transactions is large.

5   Discussions

In this section, we discuss several issues related to further improvements of the performance and scalability of FP-growth.

1. Construction of FP-trees for projected databases.

When the database is large, and it is unrealistic to construct a main memory-based FP-tree, an interesting alternative is to first partition the database into a set of projected databases and then construct an FP-tree and mine it in each projected database.

The partition-based projection can be implemented as follows: Scan DB to find the set of frequent items and sort them into a *frequent item list* L in frequency descending order. Then scan DB again and project the set of frequent items (except i) of a transaction T into the i-projected database (as a transaction), where i is in T and there is no any other item in T ordered after i in L. This ensures each transaction is projected to at most one projected database and the total size of the project databases is smaller than the size of DB.

Then scan the set of projected databases, in the reverse order of L, and do the following. For the j-projected databases, construct its FP-tree and project the set of items (except j and i) in each transaction T_j in the j-projected database into i-projected database as a transaction, if i is in T_j and there is no any other item in T_j ordered after i in L.

By doing so, an FP-tree is constructed and mined for each frequent item, which is much smaller than the whole database. If a projected database is still too big to have its FP-tree fit in main memory, its FP-tree construction can be postponed further.

2. Construction of a disk-resident FP-tree.

Another alternative at handling large databases is to construct a disk-resident FP-tree.

The B+-tree structure has been popularly used in relational databases, and it can be used to index FP-tree as well. The top level nodes of the B+tree can be split based on the roots of item prefix sub-trees, and the second level based on the common prefix paths, and so on. When more than one page are needed to store a prefix sub-tree, the information related to the shared prefix paths need to be registered as page header information to avoid extra page access to fetch such frequently used crucial information.

To reduce the I/O costs by following node-links, *mining should be performed in a group accessing mode*, i.e., when accessing nodes following node-links, one should exhaust the node traversal tasks in main memory before fetching the nodes on disks.

Notice that one may also construct *node-link-free* FP-trees. In this case, when traversing a tree path, one should project the prefix subpaths of *all the nodes* into the corresponding conditional pattern bases. This is feasible if both FP-tree and one page of each of its one-level conditional pattern bases can fit in memory. Otherwise, additional I/Os will be needed to swap in and out the conditional pattern bases.

3. Materialization of an FP-tree.

Although an FP-tree is rather compact, its con-struction needs two scans of a transaction database, which may represent a nontrivial overhead. It could be beneficial to materialize an FP-tree for regular fre-quent pattern mining.

One difficulty for FP-tree materialization is how to select a good minimum support threshold ξ in materialization since ξ is usually query-dependent. To overcome this difficulty, one may use a low ξ that may usually satisfy most of the mining queries in the FP-tree construction. For example, if we notice that 98% queries have $\xi \geq 20$, we may choose $\xi = 20$ as the FP-tree materialization threshold: that is, only 2% of queries may need to construct a new FP-tree. Since an FP-tree is organized in the way that less frequently occurring items are located at the deeper paths of the tree, it is easy to select only the upper portions of the FP-tree (or drop the low portions which do not satisfy the support threshold) when mining the queries with higher thresholds. Actually, one can directly work on the materialized FP-tree by starting at an appropriate header entry since one just need to get the prefix paths no matter how low support the original FP-tree is.

4. Incremental updates of an FP-tree.

Another issue related to FP-tree materialization is how to incrementally update an FP-tree, such as when adding daily new transactions into a database containing records accumulated for months.

If the materialized FP-tree takes 1 as its minimum support (i.e., it is just a compact version of the origi-nal database), the update will not cause any problem since adding new records is equivalent to scanning additional transactions in the FP-tree construction. However, a full FP-tree may be an undesirably large.

In the general case, we can register the occurrence frequency of every items in F_1 and track them in updates. This is not too costly but it benefits the incremental updates of an FP-tree as follows. Suppose an FP-tree was constructed based on a validity support threshold (called "watermark") $\psi = 0.1\%$ in a DB with 10^8 transactions. Suppose an additional 10^6 transactions are added in. The frequency of each item is updated. If the highest relative frequency among the originally infrequent items (i.e., not in the FP-tree) goes up to, say 12%, the watermark will need to go up accordingly to $\psi > 0.12\%$ to exclude such item(s). However, with more transactions added in, the watermark may even drop since an item's relative support frequency may drop with more transactions added in. Only when the FP-tree watermark is raised to some undesirable level, the reconstruction of the FP-tree for the new DB becomes necessary.

6 Conclusions

We have proposed a novel data structure, *frequent pattern tree* (FP-tree), for storing compressed, crucial information about frequent patterns, and developed a pattern growth method, FP-growth, for efficient mining of frequent patterns in large databases.

There are several advantages of FP-growth over other approaches: (1) It constructs a highly com-pact FP-tree, which is usually substantially smaller than the original database, and thus saves the costly database scans in the subsequent mining processes. (2) It applies a pattern growth method which avoids costly candidate generation and test by successively concatenating frequent 1-itemset found in the (conditional) FP-trees : In this context, mining is not Apriori-like (*restricted*) *generation-and-test* but *frequent pattern* (*fragment*) *growth only*. The major operations of mining are count accumulation and prefix path count adjustment, which are usually much less costly than candidate generation and pattern matching operations performed in most Apriori-like algorithms. (3) It applies a partitioning-based divide-and-conquer method which dramatically reduces the size of the subsequent conditional pattern bases and conditional FP-trees. Several other optimization techniques, including direct pattern generation for single tree-path and employing the least frequent events as suffix, also contribute to the efficiency of the method.

We have implemented the FP-growth method, studied its performance in comparison with several influential frequent pattern mining algorithms in large databases. Our performance study shows that the method mines both short and long patterns efficiently in large databases, outperforming the current candidate pattern generation-based algorithms. The FP-growth method has also been implemented in the new version of DBMiner system and been tested in large industrial databases, such as in London Drugs databases, with satisfactory performance

There are a lot of interesting research issues related to FP-tree-based mining, including further study and implementation of SQL-based, highly scalable FP-tree structure, constraint-based mining of frequent patterns using FP-trees, and the extension of the FP-tree-based mining method for mining sequential patterns [4], max-patterns [5], partial periodicity [10], and other interesting frequent patterns.

Acknowledgements

We would like to express our thanks to Charu Aggarwal and Philip Yu for promptly sending us the IBM Technical Reports [2, 1], and to Runying Mao and Hua Zhu for their implementation of several variations of FP-growth in the DBMiner system and for their testing of the method in London Drugs databases.

References

[1] R. Agarwal, C. Aggarwal, and V. V. V. Prasad. Depth-first generation of large itemsets for association rules. *IBM Tech. Report RC21538*, July 1999.

[2] R. Agarwal, C. Aggarwal, and V. V. V. Prasad. A tree projection algorithm for generation of frequent itemsets. In *J. Parallel and Distributed Computing*, 2000.

[3] R. Agrawal and R. Srikant. Fast algorithms for mining association rules. In *VLDB'94*, pp. 487–499.

[4] R. Agrawal and R. Srikant. Mining sequential patterns. In *ICDE'95*, pp. 3–14.

[5] R. J. Bayardo. Efficiently mining long patterns from databases. In *SIGMOD'98*, pp. 85–93.

[6] S. Brin, R. Motwani, and C. Silverstein. Beyond market basket: Generalizing association rules to correlations. In *SIGMOD'97*, pp. 265–276.

[7] G. Dong and J. Li. Efficient mining of emerging patterns: Discovering trends and differences. In *KDD'99*, pp. 43–52.

[8] G. Grahne, L. Lakshmanan, and X. Wang. Efficient mining of constrained correlated sets. In *ICDE'00*.

[9] J. Han, G. Dong, and Y. Yin. Efficient mining of partial periodic patterns in time series database. In *ICDE'99*, pp. 106–115.

[10] J. Han, J. Pei, and Y. Yin. Mining partial periodicity using frequent pattern trees. In *CS Tech. Rep. 99-10*, Simon Fraser University, July 1999.

[11] M. Kamber, J. Han, and J. Y. Chiang. Metarule-guided mining of multi-dimensional association rules using data cubes. In *KDD'97*, pp. 207–210.

[12] M. Klemettinen, H. Mannila, P. Ronkainen, H. Toivonen, and A.I. Verkamo. Finding interesting rules from large sets of discovered association rules. In *CIKM'94*, pp. 401–408.

[13] B. Lent, A. Swami, and J. Widom. Clustering association rules. In *ICDE'97*, pp. 220–231.

[14] H. Mannila, H Toivonen, and A. I. Verkamo. Discovery of frequent episodes in event sequences. *Data Mining and Knowledge Discovery*, 1:259–289, 1997.

[15] R. Ng, L. V. S. Lakshmanan, J. Han, and A. Pang. Exploratory mining and pruning optimizations of constrained associations rules. In *SIGMOD'98*, pp. 13–24.

[16] J.S. Park, M.S. Chen, and P.S. Yu. An effective hash-based algorithm for mining association rules. In *SIGMOD'95*, pp. 175–186.

[17] S. Sarawagi, S. Thomas, and R. Agrawal. Integrating association rule mining with relational database systems: Alternatives and implications. In *SIGMOD'98*, pp. 343–354.

[18] A. Savasere, E. Omiecinski, and S. Navathe. An efficient algorithm for mining association rules in large databases. In *VLDB'95*, pp. 432–443.

[19] C. Silverstein, S. Brin, R. Motwani, and J. Ullman. Scalable techniques for mining causal structures. In *VLDB'98*, pp. 594–605.

[20] R. Srikant, Q. Vu, and R. Agrawal. Mining association rules with item constraints. In *KDD'97*, pp. 67–73.

Data Mining on an OLTP System (Nearly) for Free

Erik Riedel[1], Christos Faloutsos, Gregory R. Ganger, David F. Nagle

School of Computer Science
Carnegie Mellon University
Pittsburgh, PA 15213
{riedel,christos,ganger,nagle}@cs.cmu.edu

Abstract

This paper proposes a scheme for scheduling disk requests that takes advantage of the ability of high-level functions to operate directly at individual disk drives. We show that such a scheme makes it possible to support a Data Mining workload on an OLTP system almost for free: there is only a small impact on the throughput and response time of the existing workload. Specifically, we show that an OLTP system has the disk resources to consistently provide one third of its sequential bandwidth to a background Data Mining task with close to zero impact on OLTP throughput and response time at high transaction loads. At low transaction loads, we show much lower impact than observed in previous work. This means that a production OLTP system can be used for Data Mining tasks without the expense of a second dedicated system. Our scheme takes advantage of close interaction with the on-disk scheduler by reading blocks for the Data Mining workload as the disk head "passes over" them while satisfying demand blocks from the OLTP request stream. We show that this scheme provides a consistent level of throughput for the background workload even at very high foreground loads. Such a scheme is of most benefit in combination with an Active Disk environment that allows the background Data Mining application to also take advantage of the processing power and memory available directly on the disk drives.

This research was sponsored by DARPA/ITO through ARPA Order D306, and issued by Indian Head Division, NSWC under contract N00174-96-0002. Partial funding was provided by the National Science Foundation under grants IRI-9625428, DMS-9873442, IIS-9817496, and IIS-9910606. Additional funding was provided by donations from NEC and Intel. We are indebted to generous contributions from the member companies of the Parallel Data Consortium. At the time of this writing, these companies include Hewlett-Packard Laboratories, LSI Logic, Data General, Compaq, Intel, 3Com, Quantum, IBM, Seagate Technology, Hitachi, Siemens, Novell, Wind River Systems, and Storage Technology Corporation. The views and conclusions contained in this document are those of the authors and should not be interpreted as representing the official policies, either expressed or implied, of any supporting organization or the U.S. Government.

1 Introduction

Query processing in a database system requires several resources, including 1) memory, 2) processor cycles, 3) interconnect bandwidth, and 4) disk bandwidth. Performing additional tasks, such as data mining, on a transaction processing system without impacting the existing workload would require there to be "idle" resources in each of these four categories. A system that uses Active Disks [Riedel98] contains additional memory and compute resources at the disk drives that are not utilized by the transaction processing workload. Using Active Disks to perform highly-selective scan and aggregation operations directly at the drives keeps the interconnect requirements low. This leaves the disk arm and media rate as the critical resources. This paper proposes a scheduling algorithm at the disks that allows a background sequential workload to be satisfied essentially for free while servicing random foreground requests. We first describe a simple priority-based scheduling scheme that allows the background workload to proceed with a small impact on the foreground work and then extend this system to read additional blocks completely "for free" by reading blocks during the otherwise idle rotational delay time. We also show that these benefits are consistent at high foreground transaction loads and as data is striped over a larger number of disks.

2 Background and Motivation

The use of data mining to elicit patterns from large databases is becoming increasingly popular over a wide range of application domains and datasets [Fayyad98, Chaudhuri97, Widom95]. One of the major obstacles to starting a data mining project within an organization is the high initial cost of purchasing the necessary hardware. This means that someone must "take a chance" on the up-front investment simply on the suspicion that there may be interesting "nuggets" to be mined from the organization's existing databases.

The most common strategy for data mining on a set of transaction data is to purchase a second database system, duplicate the transaction records from the OLTP system in the decision support system each evening, and perform mining tasks only on the second system, i.e. to use a "data warehouse" separate from the production system. This strategy not only requires the expense of a second system, but requires the management cost of maintaining two com-

[1] now with Hewlett-Packard Laboratories, Palo Alto, California, riedel@hpl.hp.com

system	# of CPUs	memory (GB)	# of disks	storage (GB)	live data (GB)	cost ($)
NCR WorldMark 4400 (TPC-C)	4	4	203	1,822	1,400	$839,284
NCR TeraData 5120 (TPC-D 300)	104	26	624	2,690	300	$12,269,156

Table 1: Comparison of an OLTP and a DSS system from the same vendor. Data from *www.tpc.org*, May and June 1998.

plete copies of the data. Table 1 compares a transaction system and a decision support system from the same manufacturer. The decision support system contains a larger amount of compute power, and higher aggregate I/O bandwidth, even for a significantly smaller amount of live data. In this paper, we argue that the ability to operate close to the disk makes it possible for a significant amount of data mining to be performed using the transaction processing system, without requiring a second system at all. This provides an effective way for an organization to "bootstrap" its mining activities.

Active Disks provide an architecture to take advantage of the processing power and memory resources available in future generation disk drives to perform application-level functions. Next generation drive control chips have processing rates of 150 and 200 MHz and use standard RISC cores, with the promise of up to 500 MIPS processors in two years [Cirrus98, Siemens98]. This makes it possible to perform computation directly on commodity disk drives, offloading server systems and network resources by computing at the edges of the system. The core advantages of this architecture are 1) the parallelism in large systems, 2) the reduction in interconnect bandwidth requirements by filtering and aggregating data directly at the storage devices, before it is placed onto the interconnect and 3) closer integration with on-disk scheduling and optimization. Figure 1 illustrates the architecture of such a system.

Previous work has shown that highly parallel and selective operations such as aggregation, selection, or selective joins can be profitably offloaded to Active Disks or similar systems [Riedel98, Acharya98, Keeton98]. Many data mining operations including nearest neighbor search, association rules [Agrawal96], ratio and singular value decomposition [Korn98], and clustering [Zhang97, Guha98] eventually translate into a few large sequential scans of the entire data. If these selective, parallel scans can be performed directly at the individual disks, then the limiting factor will be the bandwidth available for reading data from the disk media. This paper offers one example of a scheduling optimization that can be performed only with application-level knowledge available directly at the disk drives.

3 Proposed System

The performance benefits of Active Disks are most dramatic with the highly-selective parallel scans that form a core part of many data mining applications. The scheduling system we propose assumes that a mining application can be specified abstractly as:

```
(1) foreach block(B) in relation(X)
(2) filter(B) -> B'
(3) combine(B') -> result(Y)
```

assumption: ordering of blocks does not affect the result of the computation

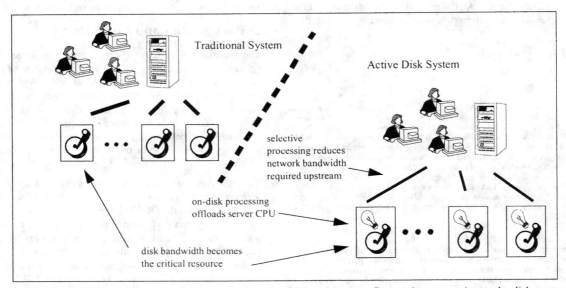

Figure 1: Diagram of a traditional server and an Active Disk architecture. By moving processing to the disks, the amount of data transferred on the network is reduced, the computation can take advantage of the parallelism provided by the disks and benefit from closer integration with on-disk scheduling. This allows the system to continue to support the same transaction workload with additional mining functions operating at the disks.

Action in Today's Disk Drive

| foreground demand request | seek from A to B | wait for rotation | read block |

Modified Action With "Free" Block Scheduling

| background requests | seek from A to C | read "free" block at C, seek from C to B | wait for rotation | read block |

Figure 2: Illustration of 'free' block scheduling. In the original operation, a request to read or write a block causes the disk to seek from its current location (A) to the destination cylinder (B). It then waits for the requested block to rotate underneath the head. In the modified system, the disk has a set of potential blocks that it can read "at its convenience". When planning a seek from A to B, the disk will consider how long the rotational delay at the destination will be and, if there is sufficient time, will plan a shorter seek to C, read a block from the list of background requests, and then continue the seek to B. This additional read is completely 'free' because the time waiting for the rotation to complete at cylinder B is completely wasted in the original operation.

where steps (1) and (2) can be performed directly at the disk drives in parallel, and step (3) combines the results from all the disks at the host once the individual computations complete.

Applications that fit this model - low computation cost for the `filter` function and high selectivity (large data reduction) from B to B' - will be limited by the raw bandwidth available for sequential reads from the disk media. In a dedicated mining system, this bandwidth would be the full sequential bandwidth of the individual disks. However, even in a system running a transaction processing workload, a significant amount of the necessary bandwidth is available in the idle time between and during disk seek and rotational latency for the transaction workload.

The key insight is that while positioning the disk mechanism for a foreground transaction processing (OLTP) workload, disk blocks passing under the disk head can be read "for free". If the blocks are useful to a background application, they can be read without any impact on the OLTP response time by completely hiding the read within the request's rotational delay. In other words, while the disk is moving to the requested block, it opportunistically reads blocks that it passes over and provides them to the data mining application. If this application is operating directly at the disk drive, then the block can be immediately processed, without ever having to be transferred to the host. As long as the data mining application - or any other background application - can issue a large number of requests at once and does not depend on the order of processing the requested background blocks, the background application can read a significant portion of its data without any cost to the OLTP workload. The disk can ensure that only blocks of a particular application-specific size (e.g. database pages) are provided and that all the blocks requested are read exactly once, but the order of blocks will be determined by the pattern of the OLTP requests.

Figure 2 shows the basic intuition of the proposed scheme. The drive maintains two request queues: 1) a queue of *demand* fore-

ground requests that are satisfied as soon as possible; and 2) a list of the background blocks that are satisfied when convenient. Whenever the disk plans a seek to satisfy a request from the foreground queue, it checks if any of the blocks in the background queue are "in the path" from the current location of the disk head to the desired foreground request. This is accomplished by comparing the delay that will be incurred by a direct seek and rotational latency at the destination to the time required to seek to an alternate location, read some number of blocks and then perform a second seek to the desired cylinder. If this "detour" is shorter than the rotational delay, then some number of background blocks can be read without increasing the response time of the foreground request. If multiple blocks satisfy this criteria, the location that satisfies the largest number of background blocks is chosen. Note that in the simplest case, the drive will continue to read blocks at the current location, or seek to the destination and read some number of blocks before the desired block rotates under the head.

4 Experiments

All of our experiments were conducted using a detailed disk simulator [Ganger98], synthetic traces based on simple workload characteristics, and traces taken from a server running a TPC-C transaction workload. The simulation models a closed system with a think time of 30 milliseconds which approximates that seen in our traces. We vary the multiprogramming level (MPL) of the OLTP workload to illustrate increasing foreground load on the system. Multiprogramming level is specified in terms of disk requests, so a multiprogramming level of 10 means that there are ten disk requests active in the system at any given point (either queued at one of the disks or waiting in think time).

In the synthetic workloads, the OLTP requests are evenly spaced across the entire surface of the disk with a read to write ratio of 2:1 and a request size that is a multiple of 4 kilobytes chosen from an

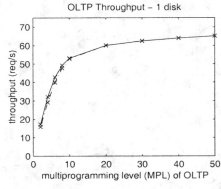

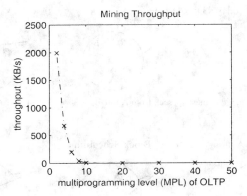

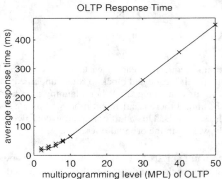

Figure 3: Throughput comparison for a single disk using Background Blocks Only. The first chart shows the throughput of the OLTP workload both with and without the Mining workload. Using the Background Blocks Only approach, we see that the addition of the Mining workload has a small impact on OLTP throughput that decreases as the OLTP load increases and the Mining workload "backs off". This trend is visible in the chart on the upper right which shows the Mining throughput trailing off to zero as the OLTP load increases. Finally, the bottom chart shows the impact of the Mining workload on the response time of the OLTP. This impact is as high as 30% at low load, and decreases to zero as the load increases.

exponential distribution with a mean of 8 kilobytes. The background data mining (Mining) requests are large sequential reads with a minimum block size of 8 kilobytes. In the experiments, Mining is assumed to occur across the entire database, so the background workload reads the entire surface of the disk. Reading the entire disk is a pessimistic assumption and further optimizations are possible if only a portion of the disk contains data (see Section 4.5).

All simulations run for one hour of simulated time and complete between 50,000 and 250,000 foreground disk requests and up to 900,000 background requests, depending on the load.

There are several different approaches for integrating a background sequential workload with the foreground OLTP requests. The simplest only performs background requests during disk idle times (i.e. when the queue of foreground requests is completely empty). The second uses the "free blocks" technique described above to read extra background blocks during the rotational delay of an OLTP request, but does nothing during disk idle times. Finally, a scheme that integrates both of these approaches allows the drive to service background requests whenever they do not interfere with the OLTP workload. This section presents results for each of these three approaches followed by results that show the effect is consistent as data is striped over larger numbers of disks. Finally, we present results for the traced workload that correspond well with those seen for the synthetic workload.

4.1 Background Blocks Only, Single Disk

Figure 3 shows the performance of the OLTP and Mining workloads running concurrently as the OLTP load increases. Mining requests are handled at low priority and are serviced only when the foreground queue is empty. The first chart shows that increasing the OLTP load increases throughput until the disk saturates and queues begin to build. This effect is also clear in the response time chart below, where times grow quickly at higher loads. The second chart shows the throughput of the Mining workload at about 2 MB/s for low load, but decreases rapidly as the OLTP load increases, forcing out the low priority background requests. The third chart shows the impact of Mining requests on OLTP response time. At low load, when requests are already fast, the OLTP response time increases by 25 to 30%. This increase occurs because new OLTP requests arrive while a Mining request is being serviced. As the load increases, OLTP request queueing grows, reducing the chance that an OLTP request would wait behind a Mining request in service and eliminating the increase in OLTP response time as the Mining work is forced out.

4.2 'Free' Blocks Only, Single Disk

Figure 4 shows the effect of reading 'free' blocks while the drive performs seeks for OLTP requests. Low OLTP loads produce low Mining throughput because little opportunity exists to exploit 'free' block on OLTP requests. As the foreground load increases, the opportunity to read 'free' blocks improves, increasing Mining throughput to about 1.7 MB/s. This is a similar level of throughput seen in the Background Blocks Only approach, but occurs under high OLTP load where the first approach could sustain significant

16

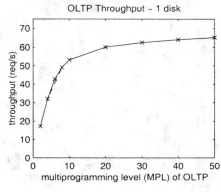

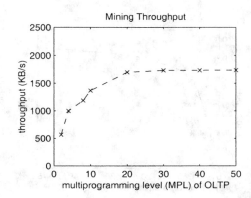

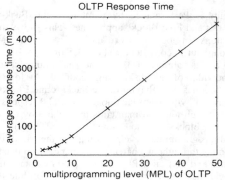

Figure 4: Performance of the Free Blocks Only approach. When reading exclusively 'free' blocks, the Mining throughput is limited by the rate of the OLTP workload. If there are no OLTP requests being serviced, there are also no 'free' blocks to pick up. One advantage of using only the 'free' blocks is that the OLTP response time is completely unaffected, even at low loads. The true benefit of the 'free' blocks comes as the OLTP load increases. Where the Background Blocks Only approach rapidly goes to zero at high loads, the Free Blocks Only approach reaches a steady 1.7 MB/s of throughput that is sustained even at very high OLTP loads.

Mining throughput only under light load, rapidly dropping to zero for loads above 10. Since Mining does not make requests during completely idle time in the 'Free' Blocks Only approach, OLTP response time does not increase at all. The only shortcoming of the 'Free' Blocks Only approach is the low Mining throughput under light OLTP load.

4.3 Combination of Background and 'Free' Blocks, Single Disk

Figure 5 shows the effect of combining these two approaches. On each seek caused by an OLTP request, the disk reads a number of 'free' blocks as described in Figure 2. This models the behavior of a query that scans a large portion of the disk, but does not care in which order the blocks are processed. Full table scans in the TPC-D queries, aggregations, or the association rule discovery application [Riedel98] could all make use of this functionality. Figure 5 shows that Mining throughput increases to between 1.4 and 2.0 MB/s at low load. At high loads, when the Background Blocks Only approach drops to zero, the combined system continues to provide a consistent throughput at about 2.0 MB/s without any impact on OLTP throughput or response time. The full sequential bandwidth of the modeled disk (if there were no foreground requests) is only 5.3 MB/s to read the entire disk[1], so this repre-

---

[1] Note that reading the entire disk is pessimistic since reading the inner tracks of modern disk drives is significantly slower than reading the outer tracks. If we only read the beginning of the disk (which is how "maximum bandwidth" numbers are determined in manufacturer spec sheets), the bandwidth would be as high as 6.6 MB/s, but our scheme would also perform proportionally better.

sents more than 1/3 of the raw bandwidth of the drive completely "in the background" of the OLTP load.

4.4 Combination Background and 'Free' Blocks, Multiple Disks

Systems optimized for bandwidth rather than operations per second will usually have more disks than are strictly required to store the database (as illustrated by the decision support system of Table 1). This same design choice can be made in a combined OLTP/Mining system.

Figure 6 shows that Mining throughput using our scheme increases linearly as the workloads are striped across a multiple disks. Using two disks to store the same database (i.e. increasing the number of disks used to store the data in order to get higher Mining throughput, while maintaining the same OLTP load and total amount of "live" data) provides a Mining throughput above 50% of the maximum drive bandwidth across all load factors, and Mining throughput reaches more than 80% of maximum with three disks.

We can see that the performance of the multiple disk systems is a straightforward "shift" of the single disk results, where the Mining throughput with n disks at a particular multiprogramming level is simply n times the performance of a single disk at $1/n$ that MPL. The two disk system at 20 MPL performs twice as fast as the single disk at 10 MPL, and similarly with 3 disks at 30 MPL. This predictable scaling in Mining throughput as disks are added bodes well for database administrators and capacity planners designing these hybrid systems. Additional experiments indicate that these

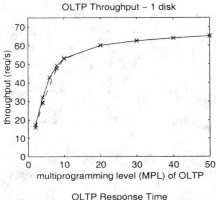

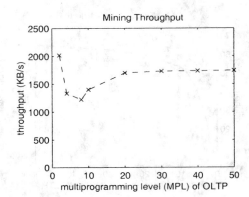

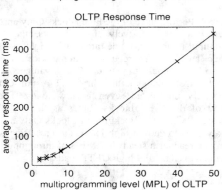

Figure 5: Performance by combining the Background Blocks and Free Blocks approaches. This shows the best portions of both performance curves. The Mining throughput is consistently about 1.5 or 1.7 MB/s, which represents almost 1/3 of the maximum sequential bandwidth of the disk being modeled. At low OLTP loads, it has the behavior of the Background Blocks Only approach, with a similar impact on OLTP response time and at high loads, it maintains throughput by the use of 'free' blocks. Also note that at even lower multiprogramming levels (going to the right on the Mining throughput chart), performance would be even better and that an MPL of 10 requests outstanding at a single disk is already a relatively high absolute load in today's systems.

benefits are also resilient in the face of load imbalances ("hot spots") among disks in the foreground workload.

4.5 'Free' Blocks, Details

Figure 7 shows the performance of the 'free' block system at a single, medium foreground load (an MPL of 10 as shown in the previous charts). The rate of handling background requests drops steadily as the fraction of unread background blocks decreases and more and more of the unread blocks are at the "edges" of the disk

(i.e. the areas not often accessed by the OLTP workload and the areas that are expensive to seek to). This means that if data can be kept near the "front" or "middle" of the disk, overall 'free' block performance would improve (staying to the right of the second chart in Figure 7). Extending our scheduling scheme to "realize" when only a small portion of the background work remains and issue some of these background requests at normal priority (with the corresponding impact on foreground response time) should also improve overall throughput. The challenge is to find an appro-

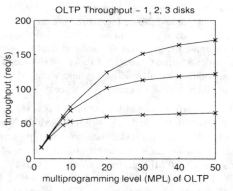

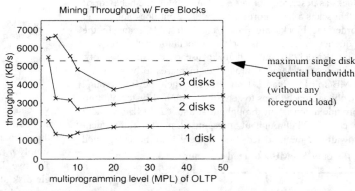

Figure 6: Throughput of 'free' blocks as additional disks are used for the same OLTP workload. If we stripe the same amount of data over a larger number of disks while maintaining a constant OLTP load, we see that the total Mining throughput increases as expected. It "shifts" up and to the right in proportion to the number of disks used.

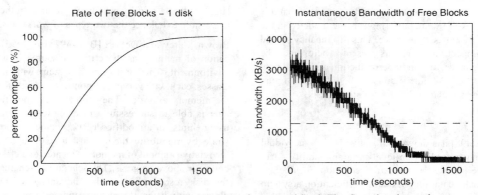

Figure 7: Details of 'free' block throughput with a particular foreground load. The first plot shows the amount of time needed to read the entire disk in the background at a multiprogramming level of 10. The second plot shows the instantaneous bandwidth of the background workload over time. We see that the bandwidth is significantly higher at the beginning, when there are more background blocks to choose from. As the number of blocks still needed falls, less of them are "within reach" of the 'free' algorithm and the throughput decreases. The dashed line shows the average bandwidth of the entire operation.

priate trade-off of impact on the foreground against improved background performance.

Finally, note that even with the basic scheme as described here, it is possible to read the entire 2 GB disk for 'free' in about 1700 seconds (under 28 minutes), allowing a disk to perform over 50 "scans per day" [Gray97] of its entire contents completely unnoticed.

4.6 Workload Validation

Figure 8 shows the results of a series of traces taken from a real system running TPC-C with varying loads. The traced system is a 300 MHz Pentium II with 128 MB of memory running Windows NT and Microsoft SQL Server on a one gigabyte TPC-C test database striped across two Quantum Viking disks. When we add a background sequential workload to this system, we see results similar to those of the synthetic workloads. At low loads, several MB/s of Mining throughput are possible, with a 25%

impact on the OLTP response time. At higher OLTP loads, the Mining workload is forced out, and the impact on response time is reduced unless the 'free' block approach is used. The Mining throughput is a bit lower than the synthetic workload shown in Figure 6, but this is most likely because the OLTP workload is not evenly spread across the disk while the Mining workload still tries to read the entire disk.

The disk being simulated and the disk used in the traced system is a 2.2 GB Quantum Viking 7,200 RPM disk with a (rated) average seek time of 8 ms. We have validated the simulator against the drive itself and found that read requests come within 5% for most of the requests and that writes are consistently under-predicted by an average of 20%. Extraction of disk parameters is a notoriously complex job [Worthington95], so a 5% difference is a quite reasonable result. The under-prediction for writes could be the result of several factors and we are looking in more detail at the disk param-

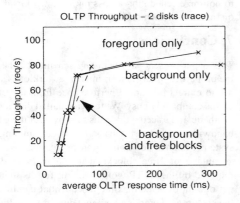

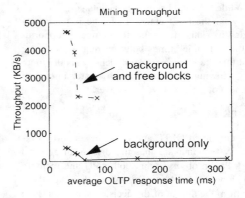

Figure 8: Performance for the traced OLTP workload in a two disk system. The numbers are more variable than the synthetic workload, but the basic benefit of the 'free' block approach is clear. We see that use of the 'free' block system provides a significant boost above use of the Background Blocks Only approach. Note that since we do not control the multiprogramming level of the traced workload, the *x* axes in these charts are the average OLTP response time, which combines the three charts given in the earlier figures into two and makes the MPL a hidden parameter.

19

eters to determine the cause of the mismatch. It is possible that this is due to a more aggressive write buffering scheme modeled in the simulator than actually exists at the drive. This discrepancy should have only a minor impact on the results presented here, since the focus is on seeks and reads, and an underprediction of service time would be pessimistic to our results. The demerit figure [Ruemmler94] for the simulation is 37% for all requests.

5 Discussion

Previous work [Riedel98] has shown that Active Disks - individual disk drives that provide application-level programmability - can provide the compute power, memory, and reduction in interconnect bandwidth to make data mining queries efficient on a system designed for a less demanding workload. This paper illustrates that there is also sufficient disk bandwidth in such a system to make a combined transaction processing and data mining workload possible. We show that a significant amount of data mining work can be accomplished with only a small impact on the existing transaction processing performance. This means that if the "dumb" disks in a traditional system are replaced with Active Disks, there will be sufficient resources in compute power, memory, interconnect bandwidth, and disk bandwidth to support both workloads. It is no longer necessary to buy an expensive second system with which to perform decision support and basic data mining queries.

Alternatively, one could design a backup system that would be able to read the entire contents of a 2 GB disk in 30 minutes with minimal impact on a running OLTP workload. It would no longer be necessary to run backups in the middle of the night, stop the system in order to back it up, or endure reduced performance during backups.

The results in Section 4.5 indicate that our current scheme is pessimistic because it requires the background workload to read every last block on the disk, even at much lower bandwidth. There are a number of optimizations in data placement and the choice of which background blocks to "go after" to be explored, but our simple scheme shows that significant gains are possible.

The prevailing trends in disk drive technology are also promising for this approach. While rotational speeds are increasing and seek times decreasing, by far the most dramatic change is the steady increase in media density. This means that the number of opportunities and the duration of "idle" times between requests is being slowly reduced, but that the rapid increase in density should more than compensate by allowing us to read a much greater amount of data for a given amount of disk area we "pass over".

6 Related Work

Previous studies of combined OLTP and decision support workloads on the same system indicate that the disk is the critical resource [Paulin97]. Paulin observes that both CPU and memory utilization is much higher for the Mining workload than the OLTP, which is also clear from the design of the decision support system shown in Table 1 in our introduction. In his experiments, all system resources are shared among the OLTP and decision support workloads with an impact of 36%, 70%, and 118% on OLTP response time when running decision support queries against a heavy, medium, and light transaction workload, respectively. The author concludes that the primary performance issue in a mixed workload is the handling of I/O demands on the data disks, and

suggests that a priority scheme is required in the database system as a whole to balance the two types of workloads.

Brown, Carey and DeWitt [Brown92, Brown93] discuss the allocation of memory as the critical resource in a mixed workload environment. They introduce a system with multiple workload classes, each with varying response time goals that are specified to the memory allocator. They show that a modified memory manager is able to successfully meet these goals in the steady state using 'hints' in a modified LRU scheme. The modified allocator works by monitoring the response time of each class and adjusting the relative amount of memory allocated to a class that is operating below or above its goals. The scheduling scheme we propose here for disk resources also takes advantage of multiple workload classes with different structures and performance goals. In order to properly support a mixed workload, a database system must manage all system resources and coordinate performance among them.

Existing work on disk scheduling algorithms [Denning67, Worthington94] shows that dramatic performance gains are possible by dynamically reordering requests in a disk queue. One of the results in this previous work indicates that many scheduling algorithms can be performed equally well at the host [Worthington94]. The scheme that we propose here takes advantage of additional flexibility in the workload (the fact that requests for the background workload can be handled at low priority and out of order) to expand the scope of reordering possible in the disk queue. Our scheme also requires detailed knowledge of the performance characteristics of the disk (including exact seek times and overhead costs such as settle time) as well as detailed logical-to-physical mapping information to determine which blocks can be picked up for free. This means that this scheme would be difficult, if not impossible, to implement at the host without close feedback on the current state of the disk mechanism. This makes it a compelling use of additional "smarts" directly at the disk.

With the advent of Storage Area Networks (SANs), storage devices are being shared among multiple hosts performing different workloads [HP98, IBM99, Seagate98, Veritas99]. As the amount and variety of sharing increases, the only central location to optimize scheduling across multiple workloads will be directly on the devices themselves.

7 Conclusions

This paper presents a scheduling scheme that takes advantage of the properties of large, scan-intensive workloads such as data mining to extract additional performance from a system that already seems completely busy. We used a detailed disk simulator and both synthetic and traced workloads to show that there is sufficient disk bandwidth to support a background data mining workload on a system designed for transaction processing. We propose to take advantage of 'free' blocks that can be read during the seeks required by the OLTP workload. Our results indicate that we can get one third of the maximum sequential bandwidth of a disk for the background workload without any effect on the OLTP response times. This level of performance is possible even at high transaction loads. At low transaction loads, it is possible to achieve an even higher level of background throughput if we allow a small impact (between 25 and 30% impact on transaction response time) on the OLTP performance.

The use of such a scheme in combination with Active Disks that also provide parallel computational power directly at the disks makes it possible to perform a significant amount of data mining without having to purchase a second, dedicated system or maintain two copies of the data.

8 Acknowledgements

The authors wish to thank Jiri Schindler for help extracting disk parameters, Khalil Amiri for many valuable discussions, and all the other members of the Parallel Data Lab for their invaluable support. We thank Jim Gray, Charles Levine, Jamie Reding and the rest of the SQL Server Performance Engineering group at Microsoft for allowing us to use their TPC-C Benchmark Kit. We thank Pat Conroy of MTI, as well as the anonymous SIGMOD reviewers for comments on earlier drafts of this paper.

9 References

[Acharya98]   Acharya, A., Uysal, M. and Saltz, J. "Active Disks" *ASPLOS*, October 1998.

[Agrawal96]   Agrawal, R. and Schafer, J. "Parallel Mining of Association Rules" *IEEE Transactions on Knowledge and Data Engineering* 8 (6), December 1996.

[Brown92]   Brown, K., Carey, M., DeWitt, D., Mehta, M. and Naughton, J. "Resource Allocation and Scheduling for Mixed Database Workloads" *Technical Report*, University of Wisconsin, 1992

[Brown93]   Brown, K., Carey, M. and Livny, M. "Managing Memory to Meet Multiclass Workload Response Time Goals" *VLDB*, August 1993.

[Chaudhuri97]   Chaudhuri, S. and Dayal, U. "An Overview of Data Warehousing and OLAP Technology" *SIGMOD Record* 26 (1), March 1997.

[Cirrus98]   Cirrus Logic, Inc. "New Open-Processor Platform Enables Cost-Effective, System-on-a-chip Solutions for Hard Disk Drives" *www.cirrus.com/3ci*, June 1998.

[Denning67]   Denning, P.J. "Effects of Scheduling on File Memory Operations" *AFIPS Spring Joint Computer Conference*, April 1967.

[Fayyad98]   Fayyad, U. "Taming the Giants and the Monsters: Mining Large Databases for Nuggets of Knowledge" *Database Programming and Design*, March 1998.

[Ganger98]   Ganger, G.R., Worthington, B.L. and Patt, Y.N. "The DiskSim Simulation Environment Version 1.0 Reference Manual" *Technical Report*, University of Michigan, February 1998.

[Gray97]   Gray, J. "What Happens When Processing, Storage, and Bandwidth are Free and Infinite?" *IOPADS Keynote*, November 1997.

[Guha98]   Guha, S., Rastogi, R. and Shim, K. "CURE: An Efficient Clustering Algorithm for Large Databases" *SIGMOD*, June 1998.

[HP98]   Hewlett-Packard Company "HP to Deliver Enterprise-Class Storage Area Network Management Solution" *News Release*, October 1998.

[IBM99]   IBM Corporation and International Data Group "Survey says Storage Area Networks may unclog future roadblocks to e-Business" *News Release*, December 1999.

[Keeton98]   Keeton, K., Patterson, D.A. and Hellerstein, J.M. "A Case for Intelligent Disks (IDISKs)" *SIGMOD Record* 27 (3), August 1998.

[Korn98]   Korn, F., Labrinidis, A., Kotidis, Y. and Faloutsos, C. "Ratio Rules: A New Paradigm for Fast, Quantifiable Data Mining" *VLDB*, August 1998.

[Paulin97]   Paulin, J. "Performance Evaluation of Concurrent OLTP and DSS Workloads in a Single Database System" *Master's Thesis*, Carleton University, November 1997.

[Riedel98]   Riedel, E., Gibson, G. and Faloutsos, C. "Active Storage For Large-Scale Data Mining and Multimedia" *VLDB*, August 1998.

[Ruemmler94]   Ruemmler, C. and Wilkes, J. "An Introduction to Disk Drive Modeling" *IEEE Computer* 27 (3), March 1994.

[Seagate98]   Seagate Technology, Inc. "Storage Networking: The Evolution of Information Management" *White Paper*, November 1998.

[Siemens98]   Siemens Microelectronics, Inc. "Siemens Announces Availability of TriCore-1 For New Embedded System Designs" *News Release*, March 1998.

[Veritas99]   Veritas Software Corporation "Veritas Software and Other Industry Leaders Demonstrate SAN Solutions" *News Release*, May 1999.

[Widom95]   Widom, J. "Research Problems in Data Warehousing" *CIKM*, November 1995.

[Worthington94]   Worthington, B.L., Ganger, G.R. and Patt, Y.N. "Scheduling Algorithms for Modern Disk Drives" *SIGMETRICS*, May 1994.

[Worthington95]   Worthington, B.L., Ganger, G.R., Patt, Y.N., Wilkes, J. "On-Line Extraction of SCSI Disk Drive Parameters" *SIGMETRICS*, May 1995.

[Zhang97]   Zhang, T., Ramakrishnan, R. and Livny, M. "BIRCH: A New Data Clustering Algorithm and Its Applications" *Data Mining and Knowledge Discovery* 1 (2), 1997.

Turbo-charging Vertical Mining of Large Databases

Pradeep Shenoy[†§]   Jayant R. Haritsa[††*]   S. Sudarshan[§]
Gaurav Bhalotia[§]   Mayank Bawa[§]   Devavrat Shah[§]

[†]Database Systems Lab, SERC   [‡]Lucent Bell Labs   [§]Computer Science and Engg.
Indian Institute of Science   600 Mountain Avenue   Indian Institute of Technology
Bangalore 560012, INDIA   Murray Hill, NJ 07974, USA   Mumbai 400076, INDIA

Abstract

In a vertical representation of a market-basket database, each *item* is associated with a column of values representing the transactions in which it is present. The association-rule mining algorithms that have been recently proposed for this representation show performance improvements over their classical horizontal counterparts, but are either efficient only for certain database sizes, or assume particular characteristics of the database contents, or are applicable only to specific kinds of database schemas. We present here a new vertical mining algorithm called **VIPER**, which is general-purpose, making no special requirements of the underlying database. VIPER stores data in compressed bit-vectors called "snakes" and integrates a number of novel optimizations for efficient snake generation, intersection, counting and storage. We analyze the performance of VIPER for a range of synthetic database workloads. Our experimental results indicate significant performance gains, especially for large databases, over previously proposed vertical and horizontal mining algorithms. In fact, there are even workload regions where VIPER outperforms an optimal, but practically infeasible, horizontal mining algorithm.

1 Introduction

The need for efficiently mining "association rules" from large historical "market-basket" databases has been well established in the literature. Most of the algorithms developed for this purpose (e.g. [1, 2, 7]) are designed for use on databases where the data layout is *horizontal*. In a horizontal layout, the database is organized as a set of rows, with each row representing a customer transaction in terms of the items that were purchased in the transaction.

Of late, there has been considerable interest in alternative *vertical* data representations wherein each *item* is associated with a column of values representing the transactions in which it is present. Since association rule mining's objective is to discover correlated items, the vertical layout appears to be a *natural* choice for achieving this goal.

Further, as explained later, vertical partitioning opens up possibilities for fast and simple support counting, for reducing the effective database size, for compact storage of the database, for better support of dynamic databases, and for asynchrony in the counting process. Based on these observations, a variety of "vertical mining" algorithms have been proposed recently [3, 4, 6, 9, 11]. Performance evaluations of these algorithms has indicated that they can provide significantly faster mining times as compared to their horizontal counterparts.

While the above-mentioned algorithms have served to highlight the utility of the vertical approach, they all suffer from a common limitation in that they are rather "specialized" – that is, they are either efficient only for certain database sizes, or assume specific characteristics of the database contents, or are applicable only to special kinds of database schemas, or place restrictions on future mining activities. For example, the ColumnWise algorithm in [3] is designed primarily for relations that are "wide" rather than "long", that is, where the number of items (i.e. columns) is significantly more than the number of transactions (i.e. rows) in the database. Similarly, the MaxEclat and MaxClique algorithms of [11] assume that users will be able to provide a lower bound on the minimum support used in all future mining activities. Finally, the performance studies have mostly been evaluated on databases that completely fit into main memory. Therefore, the ability of these algorithms to scale with database size, an important requirement for mining applications, has not been conclusively shown.

1.1 Contributions

We present here a new vertical mining algorithm called **VIPER** (Vertical Itemset Partitioning for Efficient Rule-extraction) that aims to address the above-mentioned limitations. No assumptions about the underlying database or the mining cycle are made in its design – that is, VIPER is as "general-purpose" as the classical horizontal mining algorithms. VIPER stores data in compressed bit-vectors called "snakes" and integrates a number of novel optimizations for efficient snake generation, intersection, counting and storage – these optimizations exploit the vertical data layout to a significantly greater degree as compared to the prior algorithms.

Using a synthetic database generator, we compare the response time performance of VIPER against a representative set of previously proposed vertical and horizontal mining algorithms. An important feature of our experiments

---

*Contact Author: haritsa@dsl.serc.iisc.ernet.in

is that they include workloads where the database is large enough that the working set of the database cannot be completely stored in memory. This situation may be expected to frequently arise in data mining applications since they are typically executed on huge historical databases.

Our experimental results indicate that VIPER provides significant performance gains, especially for large databases. Further, it shows close to linear scaleup with database size. Very interestingly, VIPER's performance improvement is to the extent that there are workload regions where it can outperform even an *idealized* horizontal mining algorithm that has *complete apriori* knowledge of the identities of all the frequent itemsets and only needs to find their counts. This is a new result that clearly establishes the power of vertical mining.

2 Background

2.1 Data Layout Alternatives

Conceptually, a market-basket database is a two-dimensional matrix where the rows represent individual customer purchase transactions and the columns represent the items on sale. This matrix can be implemented in the following four different ways, which are pictorially shown in Figure 1:

Horizontal item-vector (HIV): The database is organized as a set of rows with each row storing a transaction identifier (TID) and a bit-vector of 1's and 0's to represent for each of the items on sale, its presence or absence, respectively, in the transaction (Figure 1a).

Horizontal item-list (HIL): This is similar to HIV, except that each row stores an ordered list of item-identifiers (IID), representing only the items *actually* purchased in the transaction (Figure 1b).

Vertical tid-vector (VTV): The database is organized as a set of columns with each column storing an IID and a bit-vector of 1's and 0's to represent the presence or absence, respectively, of the item in the set of customer transactions (Figure 1c). Note that a VTV database occupies exactly the same space as an HIV representation.

Vertical tid-list (VTL): This is similar to VTV, except that each column stores an ordered list of only the TIDs of the transactions in which the item was purchased (Figure 1d). Note that a VTL database occupies exactly the same space as an HIL representation.

Virtually all the prior association rule mining algorithms, both vertical and horizontal, have opted for a *list-based* layout since this format takes much less space than the bit-vector approach (which has the overhead of explicitly representing *absence*) in sparse databases. We make the case in this paper, however, that a special form of the bit-vector-based VTV layout results in both significant performance improvements *and* reduced space requirements.

2.2 Merits of Vertical Mining

As mentioned in the Introduction, the vertical layout appears to be a natural choice for achieving association rule mining's objective of discovering correlated items. More specifically, it has the following major advantages over the horizontal layout:

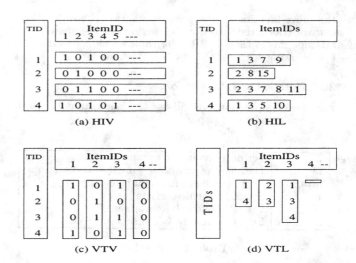

Figure 1: Comparison of Data Layouts

Firstly, computing the supports of itemsets is simpler and faster with the vertical layout since it involves only the *intersections* of tid-lists or tid-vectors, operations that are well-supported by current database systems. In contrast, complex hash-tree data structures and functions are required to perform the same function for horizontal layouts (e.g. [2]).

Secondly, with the vertical layout, there is an automatic "reduction" of the database before each scan in that only those itemsets that are *relevant* to the following scan of the mining process are accessed from disk. In the horizontal layout, however, extraneous information that happens to be part of a row in which useful information is present is *also transferred* from disk to memory. This is because database reductions are comparatively hard to implement in the horizontal layout. Further, even if reduction were possible, the extraneous information can be removed only in the scan *following the one* in which its irrelevance is discovered. Therefore, there is always a *reduction lag* of at least one scan in the horizontal layout.

Thirdly, bit-vector formats, due to their sequences of 0's and 1's, offer scope for *compression*. From this perspective also, the vertical layout is preferred since a VTV format results in higher compression ratios than the equivalent HIV format. This is because compression techniques typically perform better with larger datasets since there is greater opportunity for identifying repeating patterns – in a VTV, the length of the dataset is proportional to the number of customer transactions, whereas for HIV, it is limited to the number of items in the database, usually a fixed quantity that is small relative to the number of tuples in the database.

Finally, the vertical layout permits *asynchronous* computation of the frequent itemsets. For example, given a database with items A, B, C, once the supports of items A and B are known, counting the support of their combination AB can commence even if item C has not yet been fully counted. This is in marked contrast to the horizontal approach where the counting of all itemsets has to proceed synchronously with the scan of the database. We believe that asynchrony will prove to be an especially important advantage in *parallel* implementations of the mining process.

A careful algorithmic design is required to ensure that

the above-mentioned inherent advantages of the vertical layout are translated into tangible performance benefits – we attempt this in the VIPER algorithm, which is described in the following sections.

2.3 Notation and Assumptions

For ease of exposition, we will use the following notation in the remainder of this paper:

$\mathcal{I}$	Set of items in the database
$\mathcal{D}$	Database of customer purchase transactions
$minSup$	User-specified minimum rule support
F	Set of frequent itemsets in $\mathcal{D}$
F_k	Set of frequent k-itemsets in $\mathcal{D}$
C_k	Set of candidate k-itemsets in $\mathcal{D}$

Table 1: Notation

Without loss of generality, we assume that each itemset is always represented as a lexicographically ordered sequence of items. Similarly, a set of itemsets is also always maintained in lexicographic order.

3 The VIPER Algorithm

In this section, we overview the main features and the flow of execution of the VIPER algorithm – detailed descriptions of its internal components are deferred to the following sections.

VIPER uses the vertical tid-vector (VTV) format for representing an item's occurrence in the tuples of the database. The bit-vector is stored in a *compressed* form, taking advantage of the sparseness that is typically exhibited in large databases. Exactly the same format is also used for storing the *itemsets* that are dynamically constructed and evaluated during the mining process. While this format is consistently used for disk storage, it is converted on-the-fly into alternative representations during main-memory operations, for efficiency reasons.

We will hereafter refer to an itemset and its associated compressed tid-vector as a **"Snake"**. Further, we use the term "frequent snake" to mean that the corresponding itemset is frequent, and the term "i-snake" to refer to a snake corresponding to an itemset comprised of i items.

At a macro level, VIPER is a multi-pass algorithm, wherein data (in the form of snakes) is read from and written to the disk in each pass. It proceeds in a bottom up manner and at the end of the data mining, the supports of all frequent itemsets are available. Each pass involves the simultaneous counting of *several levels* of candidates via intersections of the input snakes. A variety of techniques, described below, are implemented to improve the efficiency of this mining process.

3.1 Efficiency Features

To minimize the computational costs, VIPER implements a new candidate generation scheme called **FORC** (Fully ORganized Candidate-generation), partly based on the technique of *equivalence class* clustering [11]. The FORC scheme avoids the expensive searching associated with Apriori-Gen [2], the predominant candidate generation algorithm for both horizontal and vertical mining.

VIPER also incorporates a novel snake intersection and counting scheme called **FANGS** (Fast ANding Graph for Snakes). The FANGS scheme is based on a simple DAG structure that has a small footprint and efficiently supports *concurrent* intersection of multiple snake-pairs by using a *pipelined* strategy.

At first glance, VIPER's writing of intermediate results to disk may appear to represent an additional overhead, especially since virtually all the prior horizontal and vertical mining algorithms are "read-only". However, we claim that this is a *positive tradeoff* since the data that is written is utilized to significantly speed up the subsequent mining process. Moreover, the disk traffic is minimized in a variety of ways – with these optimizations, VIPER turns out to have, in our experiments, *less overall disk traffic* than the read-only algorithms. The optimizations include ensuring that each processed snake is read *only once*; counting the support for candidates of several levels in a single pass, resulting in a *logarithmic* reduction in the number of passes over the database; writing only a carefully chosen *subset* of processed snakes to disk; and snake *compression* through a process called **Skinning**.

Finally, the space reduction resulting from the snake compression is augmented by automatically and immediately deleting snakes that are no longer relevant to the remainder of the mining process.

3.2 The Mining Process

We now move on to discuss the flow of execution in the VIPER mining process, whose pseudocode is shown in Figure 2. Assuming the most general case where the original database is stored in the standard *horizontal item-list* (HIL) format, the following sequence of passes (over continually shrinking databases) is executed.

3.2.1 Pass 1

In the first pass over the database, the snakes for all the individual items are created and stored on the disk. That is, the database is converted from the HIL layout to the snake format. During this process, the supports of these items are counted and F_1 is determined.

3.2.2 Pass 2

In the second pass, an obvious mechanism to compute F_2 is to intersect and count the supports of all $\binom{|F_1|}{2}$ snake pairs. However, this would be prohibitively expensive as it requires numerous snake intersections. Therefore, F_2 is determined using the following alternative approach, suggested in [11]: Temporary *horizontal* tuples (in list format) are sequentially created *in main memory* from the disk-resident collection of frequent 1-snakes. To make this clear, assume that A, B and C are the frequent 1-snakes and that the first bit (after decompression) in each of them is a 0, 1 and 1, respectively. Then, the equivalent horizontal tuple is "{TID=1},{IID of B},{IID of C}". Now, given this effectively horizontal database, for each tuple, all pairs of items in the tuple are enumerated, and their counts are simply updated in a 2-D triangular array (dimension F_1) of counters.

An important point to note in the above process is that *no snakes are constructed* during this pass. This is because writing out the snakes of all the pair-wise combinations would not only be extremely expensive, but also quite

```
Algorithm VIPER(𝒟, ℐ, minSup){
    Input: Horizontal Database (𝒟), Set of items (ℐ),
           Minimum Support (minSup)
    Output: Set of Frequent Itemsets with Supports (F)

    // Pass 1: Write all 1-snakes to disk and identify F₁
    F = countLevelOne(𝒟);
    // Pass 2: Identify F₂
    F = F ∪ countPairs(F₁);
    // Subsequent Passes
    i = 2 ; until (isEmpty(Fᵢ)) {
        // Create a new DAG for this level
        candDAG = createDAG(level = i);
        Cᵢ = Fᵢ;
        // Candidate Generation for levels k+1 to 2k
        for k in i to 2i do {
            C_{k+1} = FORC(C_k);
            if (isEmpty(C_{k+1})) break;
            candDAG = candDAG ∪ C_{k+1};
        }
        if (isEmpty(candDAG)) break;  // Terminate

        // List of snakes to be read
        readList[i] = findReadList(candDAG);
        // Trim the list of snakes to be written
        writeList[i] = writePrune(candDAG);

        // Snake intersection, counting and writing
        FANGS(candDAG, readList[i], writeList[i]);

        // Update F from levels i+1 to 2i
        for k in i + 1 to 2i do
            F = F ∪ frequentItems(candDAG,k);

        // Delete the snakes written in previous pass
        DeleteSnakes(writeList[i/2]);

        // Increment the mining level
        i = i * 2;
    }
}
```

Figure 2: The VIPER Algorithm

wasteful given that many of the combinations may eventually turn out to be infrequent. Generalizing this observation, there are two features of VIPER's snake writing (after the first pass):

- The only snakes ever written to disk are *frequent* snakes; further, only a *useful* subset of the identified frequent snakes, that is, those snakes that are potentially relevant for future passes, are written to disk.

- The writing of a frequent snake always *lags* one pass behind the pass in which the snake is identified to be frequent. Therefore, the "unwritten" snakes that are required as inputs to the current pass are *dynamically generated* using the snakes written out in the previous pass.

3.2.3 Subsequent Passes

In each subsequent pass P $(P > 2)$, the first step is to generate the candidate itemsets of the current level, based on the immediately previous level's frequent itemsets, using the FORC candidate generation procedure. That is, $C_{i+1} = FORC(F_i)$. The candidate itemsets of levels $i + 2, i + 3, \ldots, 2i$ are then computed using the same FORC procedure, except that now the *candidate set* of each level is used to generate the candidate set of the next level. That is, $C_{k+1} = FORC(C_k)$ for $i + 1 \le k \le 2i - 1$.

We note here that our counting scheme is capable of counting candidates of length $i+1$ to $i+k$ for any k, $1 \le k \le i$. This is useful in the last pass when there may not remain any candidates beyond level $i + k$ $(k < i)$, or in case the number of candidates turns out to be unmanageably large. In the latter case, the counting is *truncated* to consider only candidates upto length $i + k$ $(k < i)$ – the appropriate value of k depends on the amount of available memory.

The generated list of candidates is inserted into the DAG structure which is the basis of the FANGS snake intersection and counting scheme. After employing a variety of pruning techniques, the set of snakes to be read (*ReadList*) and to be written (*WriteList*) in this pass are identified. The snakes in *ReadList* are then sequentially scanned into memory and the counts of all the candidate itemsets generated in this pass $(C_{i+1}, \ldots, C_{2i})$ are concurrently computed using the FANGS procedure. Simultaneously, the snakes in *WriteList* are written out to disk. When the database scan is over, all frequent itemsets F_{i+1} through F_{2i} will have been identified.

The last operation of the pass is to *delete* all the snakes that were written out in the *previous* pass since they are no longer required, thereby minimizing the disk space overhead.

3.2.4 Termination

The above process is repeated until there are no more candidate itemsets. Finally, the complete set of frequent itemsets, F, is returned along with the support of each of its elements. With this information, the desired association rules can be easily determined [2].

In the following sections, the details of the main components of VIPER – Skinning for snake compression, FORC for candidate generation, and FANGS for snake merging – are described.

4 Snake Generation and Compression

The snake generation process operates in the following manner: During each pass, a (page-sized) buffer is maintained in main memory for each itemset whose snake is currently being "materialized". The snake portions corresponding to these itemsets are first accumulated in these buffers – when a buffer is full, it is written to a disk-resident *common* file.[1] Within the file, the pages associated with each individual snake are chained together using a linked list of pointers. The specific set of operations in each pass is given below:

First Pass: In the first pass, the original HIL database is sequentially scanned and for each item that occurs in a transaction, the associated TID is passed to a routine which first generates 0 bits for all the tuples between the last TID in which the item occurred and

---

[1] The option of writing each snake into a separate file is presently not feasible since current operating systems do not permit applications to have more than a limited number of file descriptors simultaneously open. Further, there may be an actual *advantage* to writing them to a common file in that *correlated* frequent snakes may tend to have their data blocks close to each other since their buffers would fill up during similar time periods.

the current TID and then adds a 1 bit for the current TID. This bit-sequence is then compressed (using the Skinning technique described below) and added to the buffer associated with the item.

Second Pass: In the second pass, the frequent 1-snakes are decompressed to dynamically create horizontal tuples in memory, but no output snakes are constructed (as described earlier in Section 3).

Subsequent Passes: In subsequent passes, where the vertical format is exclusively used, new snakes are generated by "ANDing" of existing snakes. For example, the snake for the itemset ABC may be generated by intersecting the AB and AC snakes. This process requires decompression of the input snakes but is computationally inexpensive since it only requires simple arithmetic. For ANDing, a straightforward option is to decompress the snakes into tid-vectors and then to AND these vectors. However, as discussed later in this section, tid-vectors typically take more space than tid-lists. So, as the tid-vectors are being produced in memory, they are converted on-the-fly into tid-lists. Therefore, the ANDing reduces to "joining" tid entries, and the output is a tid-list. This tid-list is, as for the first pass described above, converted on-the-fly into a bit-vector and then a snake.

We emphasize again here that all of the above transformations between snakes, tid-vectors, and tid-lists are done only *in memory* – what is stored on disk is always a snake.

4.1 Skinning

At first glance it may seem that the classical and simple to implement *Run-Length Encoding (RLE)* would be the appropriate choice to compress the bit-vectors. However, we expect that while there may be long runs of 0's, runs of 1's which imply a *consecutive* sequence of customers purchasing the same item may be uncommon in transactional databases. In the worst-case, where all the 1's occur in an isolated manner, the RLE vector will output *two* words for each occurrence of a 1 – one word for the preceding 0 run and one for the 1 itself. This means that the resulting database will be *double* the size of the original HIL database, which would have only one word associated with each 1 (since 0's are not explicitly represented). In short, it would result in an *expansion*, rather than compression.

We have, therefore, developed an alternative snake compression technique called **Skinning**, based on the classical Golomb encoding scheme [5]. Here, runs of 0's and runs of 1's are divided into groups of size W_0 and W_1, respectively – the W's are referred to as "weights". Each such full group is represented in the encoded vector by a single "weight" bit set to 1. The last partial group (of length $R \bmod W_i$, where R is the total length of the run) is represented by a count field that stores the binary equivalent of the remainder length, expressed in $log_2 W_i$ bits. Finally, a "field separator" 0 bit is placed between the last weight-bit and the count field to indicate the transition from the former to the latter. Note that a "run separator" for distinguishing between a run of 0's and a run of 1's, is *not* required since it is implicitly known that the run symbol changes after the count field and the number of bits used for the count field ($log_2 W_i$) is fixed.[2]

With appropriate choices of W_0 and W_1, Skinning results in close to an *order of magnitude* compression from the VTV format to the snake format for the databases considered in our experiments. Further, this high degree of compression is sufficient to ensure that although a VTV usually takes much more space than a VTL (or HTL) representation for sparse matrices, the snake database itself is only about *one-third* of the size obtained with these formats.

4.1.1 Frequent Snake Compression Bounds

While the above compression ratios have been empirically observed, we can go a step further in assessing the compression ratio for *frequent* snakes. Note that these are exactly the snakes of interest since, as mentioned before, VIPER is designed to only store frequent snakes.[3] Using the fact that a frequent snake, by definition, has a minimum proportion (equal to $minSup$) of 1's, we derive in [8] lower bounds on the compression ratio which show that, for realistic mining environments, a frequent snake *always* occupies less than *half* its corresponding size in a list-based format.

5 The FORC Candidate Generation Algorithm

We present here a new algorithm called **FORC** (Fully ORganized Candidate-generation) for efficiently generating candidate itemsets. FORC is based on the powerful technique of *equivalence class* clustering described in [11], but adds important new optimizations of its own.

The FORC algorithm operates as follows: Given a set S_k (which can be either a set of frequent itemsets or a set of candidate itemsets) from which to generate C_{k+1}, the itemsets in S_k are first grouped into clusters called "equivalence classes". The grouping criterion is that all itemsets in an equivalence class should share a common prefix of length $k-1$.[4] For each class, its prefix is stored in a hash table and the last element of every itemset in the class is stored in a lexicographically ordered list, called the extList.

With this framework, a straightforward mechanism of generating candidates is the following: For each prefix in the hash table, take the union of the prefix with all *ordered pairs* of items from the extList of the class (the ordering ensures that duplicates are not generated). For each of these potential candidates, check whether all its k-subsets are also present in S_k, the necessary condition for an itemset to be a candidate. This searching is simple since the $k-1$ prefix of the subset that is being searched for indicates which extList is to be searched. Finally, include those which survive the test in C_{k+1}.

5.1 Simultaneous Search Optimization

We can optimize the above-mentioned process by recognizing that since the unions are taken with ordered pairs, the prefix of the subsets of the candidates thus formed *will not* depend on the second extension item, which in turn means that all these subsets are shared and the same for each element in the extList. Hence, repeated searches for the same subsets can be avoided and they can be searched for *simultaneously*, as shown in the following example.

Example 5.1 Consider a set S_4 in which the only itemsets that begin with the prefix ABC are $ABCD$, $ABCH$,

---

[2] Without loss of generality, we assume that every bit vector starts with a run of 1's, possibly of zero length.

[3] With the sole exception, of course, that all 1-snakes are stored during the first pass.

[4] As mentioned earlier, an itemset is always represented as a lexicographically ordered sequence of items.

ABCM and *ABCR*. These itemsets are grouped into a common equivalence class g, with the class prefix being $P_g = ABC$ and the associated extension list being $extList_g = D, H, M, R$. We now need to find all the candidates associated with each of the itemsets in g, and we illustrate this process by showing it for *ABCH* – the others are processed similarly.

To find the candidates associated with *ABCH*, we first identify the items that are lexicographically greater than H in $extList_g$, namely, M and R. Now, the potential candidates are *ABCHM* and *ABCHR*, and we need to check whether all their 4-subsets are also in S_4. That means we have to search for *ABHi*, *ACHi* and *BCHi*, where i is either M or R (we do not have to search for *ABCi* although it is a 4-subset because its prefix is the same as P_g and therefore, by definition, will be present in S_k).

Now, to search for *ABHM*, for example, we access its group, say h, with prefix $P_h = ABH$ and then check $extList_h$ – if M exists, it means *ABHM* exists in S_k. The important point to note now is that, having come this far, we can trivially *also determine* whether *ABHR*, which corresponds to the *other* candidate *ABCHR*, exists in S_k by verifying whether R is present in $extList_h$. ꞯndBox

Generalizing the above instance, we can *overlap* the subset status determination of multiple candidates by ensuring that all subsets across these candidates that belong to a common group are checked for with only one access of the associated *extList*. This is in marked contrast to the standard practice of subset status determination on a sequential (one candidate after another) basis, resulting in high computational cost.

5.2 Implementation of Simultaneous Search

```
SetOfItemsets FORC (S_k){
    Input: Set of k-itemsets (S_k)
    Output: Set of candidate k + 1-itemsets (C_{k+1})

    for each itemset i in S_k do
        insert (i.prefix) into hashTable;
        insert (i.lastelement) into i.prefix →extList;

    C_{k+1} = φ ;
    for each prefix P in the hashTable do {
        E = P →extList ;
        for each element t in E do {
            newP = P ∪ t ;
            remList = {i | i ∈ E and i > t} ;
            for each (k − 1) subset subP of newP do
                remList = remList ∩ (subP →extList);
            for each element q in remList do {
                newCand = newP ∪ {q} ;
                C_{k+1} = C_{k+1} ∪ newCand ;
            }
        }
    }
    return C_{k+1} ;
}
```

Figure 3: Candidate Generation with FORC

FORC implements the simultaneous search optimization as shown in the pseudocode of Figure 3: For each (P, e)

combination, where P is a prefix in the hash table and e is an element in its extList, P is extended with e to obtain the *newP* itemset. The items in the extList that are greater than e are copied into another list called the "remnant" list, remList. The $k − 1$-length subsets of *newP* are enumerated and the associated equivalence class of each of these subsets is determined from its prefix. For each of these classes, the associated subset exists only if its last item is present in their own extList. Hence, intersecting remList with extList gives the survivors after searching in this class and the survivors are reassigned to remList. This remList updation process is executed across all the $k − 1$ classes, and after completion, the *newP* is extended with each of the elements in remList to obtain candidates of size $k + 1$.

All operations in the above implementation are done in lexicographic order. It is easy to see that this feature ensures that an equivalence class, once processed, will never have to be referred to again while processing the remaining classes.

5.3 Discussion

As described above, while FORC is based on the equivalence class clustering technique proposed in [11], it adds important optimizations for efficient representation and searching. Further, although we use FORC as part of our new vertical mining algorithm, note that it can be used equally well for *horizontal mining* too since there are no format-specific features in the generation process. That is, like AprioriGen[2], it can be used for *both* vertical and horizontal mining. However, it scores over AprioriGen on the following counts:

In AprioriGen, a *hash-tree* data structure is used for storing candidate itemsets and their running counts. This results in *scattering* "joinable" itemsets (i.e. itemsets with a common prefix upto their last element) across the hashtree, making identification of such itemsets a computationally intensive task since all combinations have to be explicitly examined.

Another drawback of the AprioriGen approach is that it traverses the hashtree afresh even when multiple candidates either have common subsets or have subsets with a common prefix. So, for example, if {ABCDE}, {ABCDF} and {ABCDG} are potential candidates, then their subsets {BCDE}, {BCDF} and {BCDG} are searched for by traversing from the root in every instance although the {BCD} initial segment of the hash route is the same for all of them.

6 The FANGS Snake Processing Algorithm

The FANGS (Fast ANding Graph for Snakes) algorithm is based on the observation that any candidate of length between $i + 1$ and $2i$ can be represented as the union of *some pair* of frequent i-itemsets. That is, its support can be calculated by intersecting the corresponding i-snakes. Hence, given the set of frequent i-snakes as input, the support for all candidates of length $i + 1$ to $2i$ can be computed in a single pass by simultaneously intersecting all the associated pairs.

6.1 The Graph Structure

In each pass over the database, a DAG of the candidate itemsets (generated by the FORC algorithm described in the previous section) is first created. The "leaves" of the DAG are the frequent itemsets at level i. Each intermediate node at height r is a candidate of length $i + r$, and is pointed to by some pair of its subsets at height $r-1$. This is easy to arrange since if an itemset is a candidate, all its subsets are also either candidates or frequent itemsets. Finally, each of the candidate snakes in the DAG has an associated "latest TID" (LTID) variable and a "currentCount" (CCNT) variable, both of which are initialized to zero (the functions of these variables are explained later).

The intuition behind the DAG structure is as follows: We know that the union of any two $i+r-1$-subsets of a $i+r$-candidate is the candidate itself. In this sense, the pair of child nodes "covers" the candidate itemset in that these nodes can be intersected to generate (and count) the candidate. Further, an itemset has to be counted only if its immediate subsets are also present in the transaction. Hence, for an $i+r$-length candidate, we choose a pair of $i+r-1$-subsets to cover it, instead of other smaller subsets.

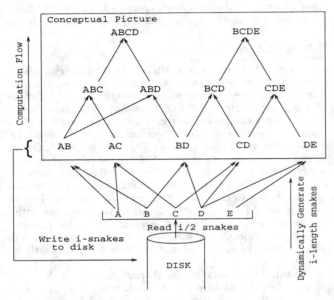

Figure 4: The DAG of Candidate Snakes

The above concepts are illustrated in the "conceptual picture" box of Figure 4, which shows a sample portion of the complete DAG structure. Here, the leaves of the DAG are the frequent 2-itemsets AB, AC, BD, CD and DE. At the next level, each of the 3-candidates is pointed to by some pair of leaves – for example, ABC and BCD are pointed to by (AB, AC) and (BD, CD), respectively. Similarly, pairs of the 3-candidates point to the candidates at level 4, namely, $ABCD$ and $BCDE$.

6.2 The Counting Process

With the above structure, the counting scheme is simple: The snakes corresponding to all the leaf itemsets are concurrently read, a page at a time, from disk into memory. During this process, as mentioned earlier in Section 4, they are dynamically converted into equivalent tid-lists. Each of these lists is processed a single TID at a time, and the processing is co-ordinated so that the TIDs are processed in *sorted* order. During the course of counting, the LTID and CCNT variables of the candidate itemsets are continuously updated.

The counting starts from the tid-lists of the leaves, and when a TID is read for a leaf, the LTID variable of its immediate parents are updated with this information. If a

parent's current marking is a smaller TID, then it is simply marked with the new TID instead. However, if it is already marked with the same TID, its CCNT is incremented, and its parents are in turn updated with this TID. Intuitively, this corresponds to generating the subset-snakes of a candidate *on-the-fly*, and intersecting them at the node. The upward propagation of the updates at a node correspond to that node's participation in further intersections.

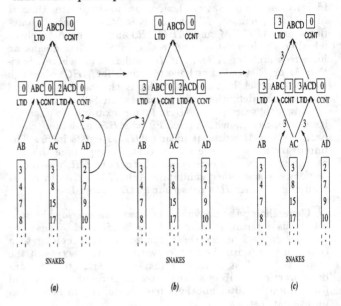

Figure 5: Snake Intersection and Counting

A pictorial example of the counting scheme is shown in Figure 5a-c.[5] Here, the snakes AB, AC and AD are being read from disk. They are read in a TID at a time, and in sorted order. The first update is from the snake AD upwards – all its parents are marked with the TID 2. In the next step, AB is read, and the candidate ABC updated with the TID 3. The third step involves reading in AC's TID, and updating the candidates ABC and ACD with this TID. At this step, since ABC has already been marked with the TID 3, its counter is incremented, and the update is propagated to the candidate $ABCD$. At the same time, since ACD is marked with a smaller TID (2), it is simply marked with 3.

The above mechanism for counting reduces the number of updates and performs them in an *on-demand* manner, thereby mitigating the expense of completely computing several intersections. This makes the overall cost of FANGS much lower than other complete-intersection-based vertical algorithms. Further, it opens up possibilities for a variety of optimizations – in the remainder of this section, we describe a few such optimizations that are currently implemented in VIPER.

6.3 Lazy Snake Writes

FANGS implements a *lazy snake write* optimization that substantially reduces the number of snakes written to disk – in fact, the only snakes that are written are those that are potentially useful in subsequent computations.

More concretely, while counting the candidates in the DAG using i-snakes, we do not know which among the top-level $2i$-candidates will turn out to be frequent, and which

---

[5]The DAG is, again, only partially shown.

snakes will be used to generate subsequent itemsets. Writing out all the 2*i*-candidate snakes to disk can be very expensive and wasteful. Therefore, we do not write *any* 2*i*-snake, but instead *dynamically regenerate* only the required snakes in the next pass. For this purpose, we associate with each 2*i*-candidate a "generator cover", that is, a pair of *i*-snakes that can be used to dynamically generate it in the next pass. These *i*-snakes are written in the current pass for use in the subsequent pass. In turn, these *i*-snakes are regenerated in the current pass using a pair of *i*/2-snakes that had been written out in the previous pass.

Dynamic regeneration is easily incorporated into the counting process by adding an *additional* level to the DAG corresponding to the *i*/2-snakes. The modified DAG now looks like the entire picture of Figure 4, with the leaves being the *i*/2-snakes that generate the *i*-snakes. Specifically, though the conceptual picture shows the DAG leaves as the 2-snakes AB, AC, BD, CD and DE, in reality each of these snakes are being generated dynamically from the 1-snakes A, B, C, D and E; the 2-snakes are written to disk only during the current pass. Note that this modification does not require any changes in the counting scheme except for including an additional level of updates.

6.4 Generator Cover Selection and Writing

A simple mechanism for selecting the generator covers described above is the following: During the pass, write out *all* the *i*-snakes to disk. After the pass is over, which means that the frequent itemsets among the top-level 2*i*-candidates have now been identified, for each of these frequent itemsets choose any pair of *i*-snakes whose union gives the itemset.

This simple process can be optimized, however, by observing that generator covers can be identified *prior* to performing the intersections. That is, we can associate a pair of *i*-snakes for each top-level candidate even before counting it. This results in a substantial benefit in that *only* those *i*-snakes that could *potentially* be used for re-generating a top-level candidate during the next pass need to be written to disk.

The second optimization in the generator cover identification step utilizes the fact that *several* generator cover choices may exist for a top-level candidate. For example, in Figure 4, both (AB, CD) and (AC, BD) are generator covers for $ABCD$. We can exploit this by choosing the covers in an *overlapped* fashion – that is, for each new top-level candidate, try as far as possible to use the *i*-snakes that have *already* been identified to cover previous itemsets. This will result in a further reduction of the number of the snakes that are written to disk.

The final optimization is related to the *order* in which the top-level candidates are processed for identifying generator covers. Note that, given the above "overlap" heuristic, the order has a bearing on the eventual assignment of generator covers. We therefore choose to process the candidates in decreasing order of their *estimated supports*.[6] Within this processing order, preference is given to generator covers comprised of leaves with higher support – the idea here is that high support leaves will be common to a larger fraction of the candidates, and therefore choosing them "early on" will eventually result in a smaller set of snakes in the global cover.

Note that a plausible alternative to the above ordering is to do exactly *the opposite* – give preference to covers com-

---
[6]The estimated support is computed using the scheme presented in [1].

prised of leaves with *low supports*, based on the observation that such snakes will be more highly compressed, resulting in less computational effort and disk traffic. Of course, this may result in having a larger number of snakes represented in the cover.

In short, the choice is between "a small cover of high-frequency snakes" and "a bigger cover of low-frequency snakes". We evaluated both possibilities in our experiments and found that the former approach yields better results.

6.5 Snake Trimming through Top-Down Writes

We have outlined above the techniques for choosing and minimizing the number of snakes to be written to disk. We now move on to presenting an additional optimization that "trims" the chosen snakes by increasing their *sparseness*, resulting in higher compression ratios.

The key idea here is that the *i*-snakes that are written to disk are used *only* for regenerating the top-level candidates in the following pass. Therefore, only those TIDs which *completely* contain the top-level itemset need to be included in the leaf-snake. To make this clear, consider the following example: Suppose that snakes AB and CD are being written to disk in order to generate $ABCD$ in the next pass. Now, if a transaction has the items A, B, D, E, we would normally add this transaction to the snake AB, but not to the snake CD. However, we can exploit the information that the snake AB is being used only to generate the snake $ABCD$, and hence this transaction is useless for that purpose. Therefore, there is *no need* to add this particular transaction to the AB snake as well.

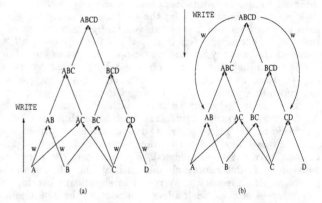

Figure 6: Bottom-up and Top-Down Approaches to Snake Writing

The above optimization is easily incorporated into the counting process described earlier in this section: Instead of the bottom-up approach of updating the *i*-snakes when they are detected in a transaction, adopt a *top-down* approach wherein these updates are made only when the top-level 2*i*-candidate is detected in the transaction. That is, the writes are "focussed" with regard to the ultimate objective.

These contrasting approaches are shown pictorially in Figure 6. In the bottom-up approach of Figure 6a, the snakes AB and CD are appended to for all successful intersections of A, B and C, D, respectively. With the top-down approach of Figure 6b, however, these snakes are updated only when the top-level itemset $ABCD$ is detected in a transaction (through intersections of its subsets).

Note that this does *not* mean that the trimmed snake AB is identical to the snake $ABCD$ because writes to AB

may be made from all of the different top-level candidates for which it forms part of the cover. It is, of course, ensured that a particular TID is added only once to a snake.

7 Related Work

Algorithms for (sequential) vertical mining have been previously presented in [6, 9, 11, 4, 3]. We restrict our attention here to the most recent among these, namely MaxClique[11], ColumnWise[3] and Hierarchical BitMap[4].

The **MaxClique** algorithm, which is a pioneering effort in the development of the vertical mining approach, is based on a vertical tid-list (VTL) format. It first generates the equivalence classes of frequent itemsets (as described for VIPER) and then refines these classes into smaller *cliques*. For each clique, the mining process operates in two phases: In the first phase, beginning with a *support-ordered* list of the itemsets of the clique, the first itemset is repeatedly intersected with each of the following itemsets in the list until an infrequent itemset is generated. In the second phase, each of the remaining itemsets in the list are combined with each of the itemsets in the first set and the supports of all these combinations are counted to identify all the additional frequent itemsets.

While cliques are more refined than equivalence classes, identifying them is computationally expensive, especially when the class graph is not sparse. Secondly, the algorithm assumes that the TID-lists of an *entire* clique can be completely stored in memory – this may not always be feasible for large databases. Thirdly, since the cliques may share individual items, the same item may have to be read in from disk *multiple* times. Finally, the problem of computing L_2 mentioned in Section 3 is circumvented by assuming an off-line "pre-processing" step that gathers the counts of *all* 2-itemsets that qualify against a user-specified *lower bound* on the minimum support. It is not clear how realistic it is to expect users to be able to choose such a bound across all future mining activities. Moreover, the pre-processing step has to be repeated every time the database is augmented.

Extensions to the basic MaxClique algorithm have been proposed in [10, 11] to address some of the above problems, but the feasibility and performance impact of these modifications have not been assessed. For example, the proposal to recursively decompose cliques until all the TID-lists in a clique fit into memory, may result in significant overlap of items across cliques, with adverse impact on the disk traffic.

The **ColumnWise (CW)** algorithm is designed for "wide and short" databases, where the number of items is significantly more than the number of transactions. For such databases it may not be possible to store the counters of all the candidates in memory and therefore using the traditional horizontal mining approach may result in significant disk traffic for paging the counters between memory and disk. To address this issue, the CW algorithm assumes a VTL format and does the counting *sequentially*, a candidate at a time, by merging the tid-lists of the individual items featured in the candidate. The rest of the algorithm is identical to Apriori. Their experimental study only considers the I/O traffic but not the total execution time of the mining process. Also, CW does not feature any special optimizations for taking advantage of the vertical format.

Finally, the **Hierarchical BitMap (HBM)** algorithm uses a VTV representation that is augmented with an *auxiliary index* indicating which "groups" (every consecutive set of 16 bits forms a group) contain only 0's. This identification helps, during the intersection process, to skip the groups for which either vector has a 0 in the auxiliary index. While this makes the intersection more efficient, it is at the cost of having to maintain auxiliary structures that are proportional to the size of the database.

From the above discussion, we conclude that the state-of-the-art in vertical mining algorithms is subject to various restrictions on the underlying database size, shape, contents or the mining process. Further, and very importantly, their ability to scale with database size has not been conclusively evaluated since their experiments have focussed on environments where the *entire database* is smaller than the main memory of their experimental platforms. A comparative summary of the algorithms, as also VIPER, is given in Table 2.

8 Performance Study

We have conducted a detailed study to assess VIPER's performance against representative vertical and horizontal mining algorithms. In particular, we compare it with MaxClique[7] and Apriori. We also include in the evaluation suite an idealized, but practically infeasible, horizontal mining algorithm, called **ORACLE**, which "magically" knows the identities of all the frequent itemsets in the database and only needs to gather the actual supports of these itemsets. Note that this algorithm represents the absolute minimal amount of processing that is necessary and therefore represents a lower bound on the execution time of horizontal mining algorithms.[8]

Our experiments cover a range of database and mining workloads, and include *all* the experiments described in [11] – the only difference is that we also consider database sizes that are *significantly larger* than the available main memory. A range of rule support threshold values between 0.25% and 2% are considered in these experiments. The primary performance metric in all the experiments is the *total execution time* taken by the mining operation. (This total execution time includes the pre-processing time in the case of the MaxClique algorithm.) Due to space limitations, we show only a few representative experiments here – the others are available in [8].

The databases used in our experiments were synthetically generated using the technique described in [2] and attempt to mimic the customer purchase behavior seen in retailing environments. The parameters used in the synthetic generator and their default values are described in Table 3.

Parameter Symbol	Parameter Meaning	Default Value
N	No. of items	1000
T	Mean transaction length	10
L	No. of frequent itemsets	2000
I	Mean frequent itemset length	4
D	No. of transactions	2M – 25M

Table 3: Parameter Table

Our experiments were conducted on a SGI Octane 225 MHz workstation running Irix 6.5, configured with a 128 MB main memory and a local 4 GB SCSI disk. For the databases with parameters $T = 10$ and $I = 4$, (see Table 3),

---

[7]The code for MaxClique was supplied to us by its authors.

[8]The bound applies, of course, only within the framework of the horizontal mining data and storage structures used in our study.

Mining Algorithm	Database Format	Compressed	Candidate Generation	Single/Multiple Scans of a Column	Main Restrictions
MaxClique	Tid-list	no	Clique	Multiple	Pre-processing / Small db
ColumnWise	Tid-list	no	AprioriGen	Multiple	Short-Wide Tables / Small db
HBM	Bit-vector	no	AprioriGen	Multiple	Memory-intensive / Small db
VIPER	Bit-vector	yes	FORC	Single	

Table 2: Comparison of Vertical Mining Algorithms

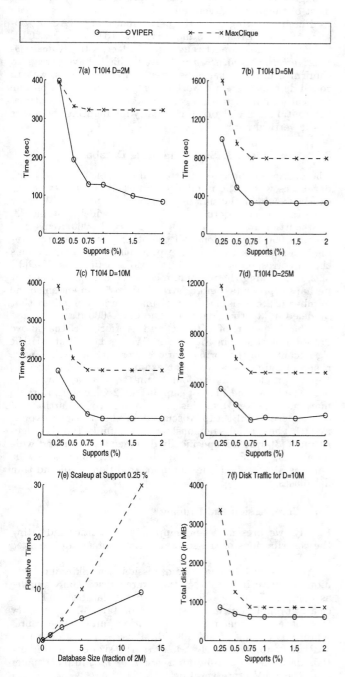

Figure 7: Comparison of VIPER and MaxClique

the associated database sizes are approximately 100MB (2M tuples), 250MB (5M tuples), 500MB (10M tuples) and 1.25 GB (25M tuples). Finally, the weights used in VIPER's skinning scheme to create compressed snakes from tid-vectors are $W_0 = 256$ and $W_1 = 1$ (the rationale for these choices is given in [8]).

8.1 Experiment 1: Comparison with MaxClique

In our first experiment, we evaluated the performance of the VIPER and MaxClique algorithms for the T10I4 database across a range of database sizes. The results of this experiment are shown in Figures 7a–d, which correspond to databases with 2M, 5M, 10M and 25M transactions, respectively. As is shown in these graphs, VIPER consistently performs better than MaxClique. Also, the difference in performance shows a marked increase with the size of the database. For example, while their performance at $minSup = 0.25\%$ is comparable for the 2M database (Figure 7a), we see for the same support a performance ratio of over 3 in favor of VIPER in the database with 25M transactions (Figure 7d).

8.1.1 Performance Scalability

In Figure 7e, the results of Figures 7a–d are combined to compare the *scalability*, with respect to database size, of VIPER and MaxClique. In this figure, which is evaluated for $minSup = 0.25\%$, the database size is shown relative to the 2M database, while the running times have been normalized with respect to the corresponding running times for the 2M database.

The results show that VIPER has excellent scalability with database size – the ratios of time taken versus database sizes are nearly equal. This conforms to our expectation – since the computation cost in VIPER is on a per-transaction basis, it should scale linearly with an increase in the number of transactions. In contrast, MaxClique shows significant degradation with increasing database size.

8.1.2 Resource Usage

The disk activity of VIPER and MaxClique for the T10I4D10M database is shown in Figure 7f over the range of support values. We see here that VIPER's disk traffic is consistently *less* than that of MaxClique, highlighting the effect of the several optimizations that VIPER incorporates to reduce disk I/O.

MaxClique, on the other hand, reads in a TID-list corresponding to a single item multiple times, depending upon the number of cliques in which it is present. As a result, the disk reads increase dramatically at low supports where there is considerable overlap between clusters. In this situation, VIPER's strategy of a single scan per snake in conjunction with lazy snake writes, appears to be the preferred choice.

Another feature of VIPER is that its main memory usage is effectively independent of the database size. This is because it only needs to store the data structures associated with the FORC and FANGS algorithms (apart from, of course, the read and write snake buffers), and the size of these data structures is dependent only on the density of patterns in the database, *not* the database size. For example, VIPER's peak memory usage across all the workloads considered in the baseline experiment is 4 MB. In contrast, MaxClique's memory usage depends on the lengths of the TID-lists and the number of TID-lists in each clique. Accordingly, MaxClique uses close to 2.5 MB for the database with 2M transactions, and as much as 23 MB for the 10M database.

8.2 Experiment 2: Comparison with Apriori and ORACLE

We now move on to compare VIPER's performance with that of the Apriori and ORACLE *horizontal* mining algorithms. The performance for all the database sizes considered in the baseline T10I4 experiment was evaluated and a representative graph for the 10M database is shown in Figure 8.1.

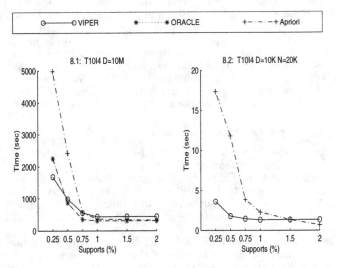

Figure 8: (.1) **Comparison with Apriori and ORACLE** (.2) **Short and Wide Database**

In Figure 8.1, we first notice that Apriori's performance, steeply degrades at lower supports and is considerably worse than that of VIPER. This is because it has to make several scans over the entire database at these lower supports. At high supports, Apriori appears to perform marginally better than VIPER. However, this is an artifact of our experimental setup wherein the original database is in horizontal format and VIPER has the overhead of converting this database to the vertical format – in particular, writing out of *all* the 1-snakes. This overhead is the predominant mining cost at high supports – when it is factored out, VIPER performs better than Apriori. In practice, we might expect that applications using vertical mining algorithms would store their databases in the vertical format itself.

Another interesting observation here is that if we compare the results with those in Figure 7c, Apriori actually outperforms MaxClique over the entire higher support region. This might seem to be at odds with the results reported

in [11], wherein MaxClique always beat Apriori by substantial margins. The difference here is that the pre-processing times are included in our execution time computations – these times were ignored (for all algorithms) in [11]. However, the pre-processing step takes different amounts of time for different algorithms – in Apriori, only the "join" of F_1 is counted in the second pass, whereas in MaxClique the "join" of $\mathcal{I}$ (the set of all items in the database) is counted in the second pass, and typically $\mathcal{I} \gg F_1$ – this has a major impact at higher supports, where the preprocessing step takes up most of the overall execution time.

Finally, moving on to the performance of ORACLE, observe that VIPER's performance is close to that of ORACLE for most of the support range and, in fact, VIPER *does noticeably better* at $minSup = 0.25\%$! This behavior was also confirmed in our other experiments. Based on this, we can conclude that there are workload regions where "an on-line vertical mining algorithm can outperform even the optimal horizontal mining algorithm", clearly highlighting the power of the vertical approach.

8.3 Experiment 3: Short and Wide Database

The previous experiments were evaluated on "tall and thin" databases where the number of transactions (rows) significantly exceeded the number of items (columns). We now move on to considering a "short and wide" database[3] – in particular, a database with $N = 20,000$ items and $D = 10,000$ transactions, all the other parameters remaining the same as those of the previous experiments. This choice corresponds to a "width-ratio" (defined as N/D[3]) of 2.0, matching the maximum considered in [3]. In fact, it perhaps represents a more "stressful" environment since the number of items is an order of magnitude more than that modeled in [3] (their database had only 1000 items).

The behavior of VIPER and Apriori for the above database is shown in Figure 8.2. We see here that VIPER significantly outperforms Apriori over virtually the entire range of support values – for example, at 0.25% support, Viper completes in one-fourth the time taken by Apriori. (Only at the highest support of 2% does Apriori do marginally better, and this again is due to the artifact of our experimental setup, discussed in the previous experiment.) These results demonstrate that, unlike the CW algorithm of [3], which is specifically designed for short-and-wide databases, VIPER applies equally to both short-and-wide databases, as well as the the more traditional tall-and-thin databases.

8.4 Compression and Pruning

Finally, we present a few supporting statistics indicating the contributions of the several optimizations implemented in VIPER.

With regard to snake compression, the Skinning technique resulted in databases that were substantially smaller as compared to the original horizontal database. This is clearly brought out in the statistics of Table 4, which show the space requirements for the various alternative representations of the T10I4D10M database – here we see that VIPER is approximately *one-third* the size of the original HIL database and almost an *order of magnitude* smaller than the VTV representation.

The pruning mechanisms for reducing the number of snakes written to disk resulted in considerable savings, as demonstrated in the following extract from VIPER's output for the second pass over the T10I4D10M database:

Representation Format	Disk Space
HIL	392 MB
VTL	392 MB
VTV	1.2 GB
Snakes	135 MB

Table 4: Database Format Sizes (T10I4D10M)

```
Database:  t10i4d10m, supp:  0.25,
Starting level = 2
Candidates at level3:   3458
Candidates at level4:   2402
# 2-snakes generated:   2504
# 2-snakes written:   1474
```

What this extract means is that during this pass a total of 2504 2-snakes were dynamically regenerated while counting the supports of C_3 and C_4. Only 1474 of them were written back to disk as potential covers for the 2402 C_4 candidates, to be used in regenerating the frequent 4-snakes which are the leaves of the DAG during the following pass.

8.5 Other Experiments

We evaluated the sensitivity of the above results obtained for the T10I4 database to the choice of database parameters – these results were similar to those described here and are available in [8]. An interesting observation was that for a T20I4D10M database, wherein the transactions are longer, the 0.25% support evaluation *could not* be conducted for MaxClique since the number of TID-lists in a clique is very large in this environment, and the combined memory requirement to store the TID-lists of a clique (approximately 500 MB) heavily exceeded the available physical memory (128 MB). This result highlights the fact that MaxClique does not scale easily to databases whose active segment exceeds the available memory.

9 Conclusions

In this paper, we have addressed the problem of designing a "general-purpose" vertical mining algorithm whose applicability or efficiency, unlike previously proposed algorithms, is not subject to restrictions on the underlying database size, shape, contents, or the mining process. We presented VIPER, a new algorithm that uses a compressed bit-vector representation of itemsets, called snakes, and aggressively materializes the benefits offered by the vertical data layout. It features a novel DAG-based snake intersection scheme that permits the candidates of multiple levels to be efficiently counted in a single pass. Other optimizations include cluster-based candidate generation, single scan per snake, lazy snake writes, generator cover selection and snake trimming, all of which together result in significant savings in both computation and disk traffic.

Our experimental results demonstrate that VIPER consistently performs better than MaxClique, which represents the state-of-the-art in vertical mining – further, VIPER has the added advantage of excellent scalability, an important requirement for a viable mining algorithm. Finally, we also showed that VIPER is capable of not only outperforming Apriori, but also ORACLE, the idealized horizontal mining algorithm – this is a new result establishing the power of the vertical approach.

In our future work, we propose to explore the development of *parallel* vertical mining algorithms that can effectively exploit vertical mining's attractive feature of supporting asynchrony in the counting process.

Acknowledgments

We are very grateful to Mohammed Zaki for providing us with the MaxClique program. We thank Vikram Pudi for his insightful comments and assistance in the coding of the algorithms. The work of J. R. Haritsa was supported in part by research grants from the Dept. of Science and Technology and the Dept. of Bio-technology, Govt. of India.

References

[1] R. Agrawal, T. Imielinski, and A. Swamy. Mining association rules between sets of items in large databases. In *Proc. of ACM SIGMOD Intl. Conf. on Management of Data*, May 1993.

[2] R. Agrawal and R. Srikant. Fast algorithms for mining association rules. In *Proc. of 20th Intl. Conf. Very Large Databases (VLDB)*, September 1994.

[3] B. Dunkel and N. Soparkar. Data organization and access for efficient data mining. In *Proc. of 15th Intl. Conf. on Data Engineering (ICDE)*, 1999.

[4] G. Gardarin, P. Pucheral, and F. Wu. Bitmap based algorithms for mining association rules. Technical report 1998-18, University of Versailles, 1998. (http://www.prism.uvsq.fr/rapports/1998/document_1998_18.ps.gz)

[5] S.W. Golomb. Run-length encoding. *IEEE Trans. on Information Theory*, 12(3), July 1966.

[6] M. Holsheimer, M. Kersten, H. Mannila, and H. Toivonen. A perspective on databases and data mining. In *Proc. of 1st Intl. Conf. on Knowledge Discovery and Data Mining (KDD)*, August 1995.

[7] A. Savasere, E. Omiecinski, and S. Navathe. An efficient algorithm for mining association rules in large databases . In *Proc. of 21st Intl. Conf. on Very Large Databases (VLDB)*, 199 5.

[8] P. Shenoy, J. Haritsa, S. Sudarshan, M. Bawa, G. Bhalotia, and D. Shah. Turbo-charging vertical mining of large databases. Technical Report TR-2000-02, DSL, Indian Institute of Science, 2000. (http://dsl.serc.iisc.ernet.in/pub/TR/TR-2000-02.ps)

[9] S-J. Yen and A.L.P. Chen. An efficient approach to discovering knowledge from large databases. In *Proc. of 4th Intl. Conf. on Parallel and Distributed Information Systems (PDIS)*, 1996.

[10] M. J. Zaki. *Scalable Data Mining for Rules*. PhD thesis, Dept. of Computer Science, University of Rochester, July 1998.

[11] M. J. Zaki, S. Parthasarathy, M. Ogihara, and W. Li. New algorithms for fast discovery of association rules. In *Proc. of 3rd Intl. Conf. on Knowledge Discovery and Data Mining (KDD)*, August 1997.

High Speed On-line Backup When Using Logical Log Operations

David B. Lomet
Microsoft Research
One Microsoft Way, Redmond, WA 98052
email: lomet@microsoft.com

Abstract

Media recovery protects a database from failures of the stable medium by maintaining an extra copy of the database, called the backup, and a media recovery log. When a failure occurs, the database is "restored" from the backup, and the media recovery log is used to roll forward the database to the desired time, usually the current time. Backup must be both fast and "on-line", i.e. concurrent with on-going update activity. Conventional on-line backup sequentially copies from the stable database, almost independent of the database cache manager, but requires page-oriented log operations. But results of logical operations must be flushed to a stable database (a backup is a stable database) in a constrained order to guarantee recovery. This order is not naturally achieved for the backup by a cache manager concerned only with crash recovery. We describe a **"full speed"** backup, only loosely coupled to the cache manager, and hence similar to current on-line backups, but effective for general logical log operations. This requires additional logging of cached objects to guarantee media recoverability. We then show how logging can be greatly reduced when log operations have a constrained form which nonetheless provides very useful additional logging efficiency for database systems.

1   Introduction

Crash recovery requires that the stable database S be accessible and correct. Media recovery provides recovery from failures involving data in S. It is also a last resort to cope with erroneous applications that have corrupted S. To guard against stable database failures, the media recovery system provides (i) an additional copy of the database (called a backup B) and (ii) a media recovery log that is applied to the backup to roll its state forward to the desired state, usually the most recent committed state. To recover from failures, the media recovery system first *restores* S by copying B, perhaps stored on tertiary storage, to the usual secondary storage that contains S. Then the media recovery log operations are applied to the restored S to "roll forward" the state to the time of the last committed transaction (or to some designated earlier time).

Backing up the stable database is on-line if it is concurrent with normal database activity, "off-line" if concurrent activity is precluded. High availability requires on-line backup. Hence on-line backup is our focus, and in particular, on-line backup when logical operations, those that involve more than a single object or page, are logged. Other elements of media recovery do not necessarily require new techniques.

- Restoring the erroneous (part of) S with a copy from B is usually done off-line because media failure frequently precludes database activity. Off-line restore has little impact on availability as it occurs after media failure, a low frequency event. Off-line restore poses no technical problems unique to logical operations.

- Maintaining the media recovery log is conventional and is not impacted by the choice of log operations.

- Rolling forward the restored S involves redo recovery, which, for logical operations, has been described in our earlier work [10, 11].

1.1   Log Operations

Traditional Forms

Traditionally, database systems exploit two kinds of log operations.

Physical: A physical operation updates exactly one database object. No objects are read. Data values to be used in the update come from the log record itself. An example of this is a physical page write, where the value of the target page is to be set to a value stored in the log record.

Physiological: A physiological operation [4] also updates a single object, but also reads it. Hence, a physiological operation denotes a change in the object's value (a state transition). This avoids the need to store the entire new value for a target object in the log record. An example is the insert of a record onto a page. The page is read, the new record (whose value is stored in the log record) is inserted, and the result is written back to the page.

These two forms of log operations (also called page-oriented operations) make cache management particularly simple. Updated (dirty) objects in the cache can be flushed to S in any order, so long as the write ahead log (WAL) protocol is obeyed. For databases, pages are the recoverable objects and records are frequently the unit of update. Both are small. Thus, the importance of simple cache management can be allowed to control the form of log operation, restricting operations to the traditional varieties.

Logical Operations

When extending recovery to new domains, the cost of logging becomes a major consideration. Logical log operations can greatly reduce the amount of data written to the log, and hence reduce the normal execution cost of providing recovery. A log operation is logical [11], as opposed to page-oriented, if the operation can read one or more objects (pages) and write (potentially different) multiple objects.

Some examples of how logical logging can substantially reduce the logging required during normal execution are:

Application Recovery: Logical log operations for recovering application A's state [8] are:

$R(X, A)$: A reads X into its input buffer, transforming its state to a new state A'. Unlike page-oriented operations, the values of X and A' are not logged.

$W_l(A, X)$: A writes X from its output buffer. A's state is unchanged. Unlike page-oriented operations, we do not log the new value of X.

$Ex(A)$: The execution of A between resource manager calls is a physiological operation that reads and writes A's state. Execution begins when control is returned to A, and results in the new state when A next calls the resource manager.

File System Recovery: Logical operations can reduce logging cost for file system recovery. A copy operation copies file X to file Y. This same operation form describes a sort, where X is the unsorted input and Y is the sorted output. With logical operations, only source and target file identifiers are logged. With page oriented operations, one can't avoid logging the value of Y (or X).

Database Recovery: Logical operations are useful for, e.g., B-tree splits. A split operation moves index entries with keys greater than the split key from the old page to the new page. A logical split operation avoids logging the initial contents of the new page, which is unavoidable when using page-oriented operations.

The key to the logging economy of logical operations is that we can log operand identifiers instead of operand data values because the data values can come from many objects in the stable state. Since operand values can be large (applications or files may be several megabytes), logging an identifier (unlikely to be larger than 16 bytes) is a great saving.

Logical operations complicate cache management because cached objects can have flush order dependencies. As an example, for the operation *copy(X,Y)*, copying the value of object X to the object Y, we must ensure that the updated value of Y is flushed to S before we permit object X (if it has been subsequently updated) to be flushed to S, overwriting its old value. If an updated X is flushed before Y is flushed, a system failure will lose the old value of X needed to make replay of the copy operation possible. Hence, a subsequent redo of the copy operation will not produce the correct value for Y. These flush dependencies complicate the task of high speed on-line backup.

1.2 Existing Database Backup Techniques

In early database systems, the database was taken off-line while a backup was taken. This permitted a transaction or operation consistent view of the database to be copied at high speed from the "stable" medium of the database. Such off-line techniques work for all log-based recovery schemes and permit high speed backup. But the system is then unavailable during the backup process. Current availability requirements usually preclude this approach.

Backup is mentioned in [2, 5, 1, 4, 12, 13]. Gray [2] has the earliest discussion of "fuzzy dumps" and how to optimize media recovery by preprocessing the media recovery log. Haerder and Reuter [5] describe "archive recovery" but do not provide detail on how the on-line "fuzzy dump" is actually created or used. Bernstein et al [1] note that "The techniques used to cope with media failures are conceptually similar to those used to cope with system failures." Gray and Reuter [4] describe the "fuzzy dump" by reference to "fuzzy checkpoints", as used with system failures. The ARIES paper [12] describes this as "fuzzy image copying (archive dumping)". The high speed of these backup techniques depends upon constructing the backup by copying directly from the stable database S to the backup database B, independent of the cache manager.

There are other, incremental approaches to the backup problem. We have previously suggested [9] that a temporal index structure can be managed to ensure there is adequate redundancy so that recovery can restore the current state. But this non-conventional approach cannot currently be exploited because database systems lack temporal index support. Mohan and Narang [13] describe a method that works in a more conventional setting, and we return to this topic in the last section of the paper.

Our interest here is in conventional on-line database backup that copies data at high speed from the active S

to the backup B while update activity continues. Hence the state captured in B is fuzzy with respect to transaction boundaries. Coordination between backup process and active updating when traditional log operations are used occurs at the disk arm. That is, backup captures the state of an object either before or after some disk page write (we assume I/O page atomicity). B remains recoverable because page-oriented operations permit the flushing of pages to a stable database in any order. Since logged operations are all page-oriented, B is (i) *operation consistent*, i.e., results of an operation are either entirely in B, or are entirely absent; and (ii) selective redo of logged operations whose results are absent from B will recover the current database S.

The media recovery log must, of course, include all operations needed to bring objects up-to-date. The on-line system, which is updating S and logging the update operations, does not know precisely when an object is copied to B, and so needs to be "synchronized" with the backup process to make sure the log will contain the needed operations. For page-oriented log operations, synchronization between backup and cache manager only occurs at the begining of the backup. (Data contention during backup to read or write pages is resolved by disk access order.) The media recovery log scan start point can be the crash recovery log scan start point at the time backup begins. B will include all operation results currently in S at this point, plus some that are posted during the backup. Hence, this log, as subsequently updated by later updates, can provide recovery to the current state from B as well as from S. Subsequently, backup is independent of the cache manager, and can exploit any technique that it wishes to effect a high speed copy. This usually involves sweeping through S copying pages in a convenient order, e.g., based on physical location of the data. Different parts can be copied in parallel as well.

1.3 The Problem

Existing database backup methods do not work with logical operations and cannot support an on-line backup involving high speed copying while update activity continues. The fuzzy backup technique described above depends on logged operations being page-oriented. But logical log operations [10, 11] can involve multiple pages (or objects) and updated objects (e.g. pages) must be flushed to S in a careful order for S to remain recoverable. **Objects updated by logical operations have the same ordering constraints when "flushed" (copied) to the backup database B to ensure correct media recovery.**

The fundamental problem here is that we have two databases, S and B, upon which flush dependencies must be enforced. A "logical" solution to this problem is to stage all copying from S to B through the cache manager, and flush dirty data synchronously (a "linked" flush) to both S and B. (That is, dirty data flushed to S is also flushed to B such that the next flush of dirty data does not commence until the prior

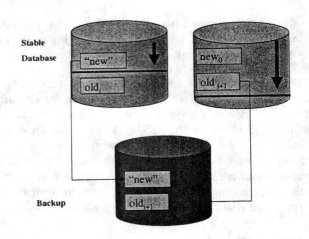

Figure 1: A B-tree backup problem arises for the sequence: backup("new") to B; flush(new_0) to S; flush(old_{i+1}) to S; backup(old_{i+1} to B). Backup B has the new version old_{i+1} of old, but not new_0 for new, even though new_0 was flushed to S prior to old_{i+1}
.

"linked" flush to both S and B has completed.) Of course this is a completely unrealistic solution. Copying from S to B via the database cache is unrealistic for page-oriented operations because of the performance impact. Pursuing this for logical log operations, where "linked" flushes are required is even less realistic.

To efficiently create an on-line backup requires an "asynchronous" copy process that does not "go through the cache manager". But the task of keeping B recoverable so that media failure recovery is possible is the same task as with crash recovery and the stable database S. We must constrain flushing so that the flush dependencies we enforce for S are also enforced for B. **Unfortunately, when an asynchronous on-line backup is in progress, flush dependencies enforced for S can be violated for B.** And because of that, the fuzzy dumps of section 1.2 are not guaranteed to be recoverable.

The B-tree split example of Figure 1 illustrates the problem. The old node is updated and half of its contents moved to a new node. A logical split $MovRec(old, key, new)$ identifies the source old (in state old_i) and the target new (updated to state new_0). The log operation does not include the data moved. A second operation $RmvRec(old, key)$ deletes the copied records from old, producing state old_{i+1}. Should the $MovRec$ operation need to be replayed during recovery because new is not in state new_0 in S, old must be available in its pre-split state old_i containing the copied records. Hence, our write graph requires that new be flushed to S prior to old being overwritten with old_{i+1}, which lacks the copied records. This sequence ensures that S is recoverable should the system crash.

Consider now that a backup is in progress, indicated by the large arrow in the stable database of Figure 1. The part of the database in which new resides has already been copied to B by an in-progress backup before this flushing activity occurs, but the part in which *old* resides has not. At completion of the backup, *old* has updated value old_{i+1} in B, but *new*'s updated new_0 value is not present. This violates the required flush order for B. Indeed, the records moved from *old* to *new* are nowhere in B. Since a logical operation $MovRec$ was used to log the split, its log record does not include these records either. Hence, B cannot be successfully recovered to the current state to support media recovery.

1.4 Our Contribution: Backup with Logical Ops

So the situation that confronts us is that the "linked flush" approach has unrealistic performance, and the traditional fuzzy dump of S to B doesn't work.

We show how to backup a database system that logs logical operations by taking a high-speed backup in a manner that is similar to but subtly different from a fuzzy dump for a database using only page-oriented operations. Like the best of the prior fuzzy dump algorithms, the database cache manager is bypassed. Our method ensures that the results of logged logical operations are "flushed" to B in the correct order, and hence that B remains recoverable [10], without tight coupling with the cache manaer. We exploit three insights:

1. an object can be written to the log as a substitute for being flushed to S or B. The object version needed for media recovery is then available from the (media) log.

2. knowledge of the order in which objects in S are copied to B can avoid some of the extra logging described above, hence improving backup efficiency.

3. limiting the forms of logical operations can limit the flush ordering, and exploiting this can further reduce the logging required to keep the backup recoverable.

1.5 Organization of Paper

In section two, we describe the redo recovery framework [10] that defines the requirements for redo recovery: installation graph, write graphs, unexposed objects, redo test, etc. Section three describes how to provide high speed, on-line backup when general logical operations are logged. This incurs extra cost for writing extra data to the log, however. So in section four, we limit ourselves to "tree" operations [10], a restricted class of logical operation which is nonetheless more general than the class of page-oriented operations. They permit, for example, the logging of B-tree splits without logging any data records. The tree operation class greatly reduces the need for extra logging. In section five, we provide a simple analysis to quantify the extra logging required for both general and tree operations. The analysis almost surely overstates the amount of extra logging, but suggests that this cost is quite modest. We end with a brief discussion of issues and directions in section six.

Operations	
$Ex(A)$	Application Execute: reads and writes A
$R(A,X)$	Application Read: reads A,X and writes A
$W_P(X,log(v))$	Physical Write: writes X with v *from log*
$W_{PL}(X)$	Physiological Write: reads and writes X
$W_L(A,X)$	Application Logical Write: reads A, writes X
$W_{IP}(X,log(X))$	CM Identity Write of X with its current value
Operation	***Op* Attributes**
$readset(Op)$	Read set of operation Op
$writeset(Op)$	Write set of operation Op
Write Graph	**Node n Attributes**
$ops(n)$	Set of operations associated with node n
$vars(n)$	Subset of $Writes(n)$ flushed to install $ops(n)$
$Reads(n)$	$\cup \{readset(Op)\|\ Op\ in\ ops(n)\}$
$Writes(n)$	$\cup \{writeset(Op)\|\ Op\ in\ ops(n)\}$
W	Write graph – intersecting writes
rW	Refined write graph – exploiting unexposed

Table 1: Introduced notation

2 Flush Dependencies and Recoverability

Here we describe informally the important elements of redo recovery [10]. We focus on how logical operations give rise to flush dependencies among cached objects, i.e., careful ordering of the flushes in order to keep the S recoverable. We introduce some notation, summarized in Table 1, to make the subsequent exposition more concise and precise.

2.1 Overview

There are three key elements of redo recovery:

an installation graph prescribes the order in which the effects of operations must be "placed" into S in order for recovery to be possible. An installed operation is one that needn't be replayed during recovery because its effects do not need to be regenerated. An uninstalled operation is one that needs to be replayed for recovery to succeed. It is sometimes possible to install operations without changing S.

a write graph translates installation order on operations to flush order on updated objects. If updated objects are flushed to S in write graph order, then their updating operations are installed into the S in installation order. We focus here on write graphs, which manifest the flush dependencies with which we need to deal.

a redo test that is used during recovery to determine which operations to replay. Clearly, all operations considered uninstalled by the cache manager during normal execution will require replay. Redo tests can be relatively crude, and result in the replay of additional operations, and recovery can still succeed.

If the cache manager flushes updated objects to S in write graph order, installation order is enforced and recovery, exploiting a redo test, will recover S.

2.2 Installation Graph

The installation graph resembles the conflict graph of serializability theory, but is weaker. Installation graph nodes are log operations and edges are conflicts between operations. A log operation Op reads objects $readset(Op)$ and writes $writeset(Op)$. There are two kinds of installation edges from operation O to P for $O < P$ in conflict order:

read-write: $(readset(O) \cap writeset(P) \neq \phi)$ This order is violated when P's updates are installed in the stable database before O's updates. A crash immediately after P's updates are installed would require that O be replayed to produce the missing effects. But this would be impossible because $readset(O)$ has changed. Hence, the database will not be recoverable.

write-write: When recovery is LSN-based (the usual case, and what we assume here), database state is never reset (rolled back to an earlier state) during recovery, and hence write-write edges($writeset(O) \cap writeset(P) \neq \phi$) are usually implicitly enforced.

Write-read conflicts ($writeset(O) \cap readset(P) \neq \phi$) are not installation graph edges. Installing an operation B that reads X before an earlier operation A that wrote X does not impair our ability to replay A. Only subsequent updates of objects in A's read set makes A's replay impossible. Of course, during the normal execution, B will see A's updates, so B's updates will correctly serializes after A, even when A is not installed before B.

2.3 Explainable States, Recovery, and Redo Test

After a crash, we must identify a set I of installed operations that *explain* S. We require that I be a prefix of the installation graph, so that installation order is enforced. (A prefix I is a subset such that if P is in I, then any $O < P$ is also in I.) Then a prefix I of the installation graph *explains* S if for each object X in S, either:

exposed: X's value is needed for recovery. Then it equals the value written by the last operation (in conflict order) in I that wrote to X; or

unexposed: X will be overwritten during recovery before it is read by an uninstalled operation. We do not care what X's value is since recovery does not depend on it.

After a crash, S is recoverable if it is explainable and the log contains all uninstalled operations (those that need to be redone). The recovery task of cache management is to guarantee that there is always an I that explains S. A redo test, REDO, ensures that replayed operations keep S explainable. A fundamental result from [10] is that if I explains S and O is a minimal (in conflict graph order)

uninstalled operation, then O is indeed applicable (it finds its inputs in the same state as during normal execution) and the resulting extension of I to $I \cup \{O\}$ explains the new state of S and hence permits recovery to continue.

2.4 Write Graphs

A cache manager (**CM**) divides volatile state (cache) into "dirty" part (objects whose cached version is not in S) and "clean" part (objects whose cached version is in S, hence already installed and not discussed here). The cache manager manages the cache contents by reading new objects into and purging ojbects from the cache. Flushing a dirty object to S, thus installing its update operations, is one way to enable an object to be purged from the cache.

The CM must ensure that there is at least one I that explains the stable state S to ensure that S remains recoverable. It exploits a write graph WG for this [10]. Each WG node v represents a set $ops(v)$ of uninstalled operations and a set $vars(v)$ of the objects (variables) these operations write. There is an edge from node v to node w in WG if there is an installation graph edge from an operation P in $ops(v)$ to an operation Q in $ops(w)$. Operations of $ops(v)$ are installed by flushing the last values written to the objects of $vars(v)$ (making them a part of S). The objects of $vars(v)$ are flushed together atomically to guarantee operation atomicity. The $vars(v)$ sets must be flushed in write graph order to enforce installation order.

Many write graphs can be derived from an installation graph. A single node WG that calls for atomically flushing the entire cache is always sufficient to ensure recovery regardless of installation graph. However, the more nodes into which the uninstalled operations and the objects that they write can be divided, the more flexibility the cache manager has. Page-oriented operations can have degenerate write graphs, each node v having $|vars(v)| = 1$, and with no edges between nodes and hence no restrictions on flush order. Not so for logical operations. Logical operations can result both in nodes where $|vars(v)| > 1$ and with a required flush order between nodes.

The "Intersecting Writes" Write Graph

The "intersecting-writes" write graph W of [10] usually has several nodes. The algorithm for generating W uses the idea of collapsing a graph A with respect to a partition P of its nodes. The result is a graph B where each node w corresponds to a class in the partition P. An edge exists between nodes v and w of B if there is an edge between nodes a and b of A contained respectively in v and w. There are two "collapses". During the first collapse, each partition class of P represents nodes corresponding to operations with write sets that intersect. In the second collapse, which makes the graph acyclic and hence a feasible flush order, each class of P denotes a strongly connected region of the graph.

In addition to the problem of flush dependencies, a write graph can require that multiple objects be flushed together atomically. Multi-object flush sets arise in two ways:

- op O updates several objects ($|writeset(O)| > 1$) or

- when cycles are removed during the second collapse of strongly connected regions R to node m, requiring the atomic flushing of $vars(m) = \cup\{vars(n)|n \in R\}$.

There is no way to remove objects from $vars(n)$ for any node n of W. $|vars(n)|$ increases monotonically, resulting in ever larger atomic flushes, until $vars(n)$ is finally flushed. This is highly unsatisfactory.

A Write Graph Exploiting Unexposed Objects

We need a WG that permits objects to be removed from $vars(n)$ of a node n when appropriate operations occur. This can be attained by exploiting objects that are unexposed. We alter the initial collapse of W above to construct a new "refined" write graph rW [11]. (We still need the second collapse to make rW acyclic.) The result is a write graph with more nodes n and fewer objects in $vars(n)$.

Only exposed objects need values from the last(in conflict order) installed operations that write them. Because of this, a "blind write" of X, which does not read the prior values of X, can remove X from $vars(n)$ of an existing node. The simplest blind write is a physical write $W_P(X, log(v))$ that reads no objects in the stable database (the value v comes from the log record) and writes X. Because a blind write does not require the prior value of X, this value is not needed for future recovery of X itself. To ensure that v is not needed for recovery, all operations that read X's v are installed prior to installing node n. We introduce an extra write graph edge from a node m, with an operation in $ops(m)$ that reads X's v, to node n (called an inverse write-read edge) that causes m to be purged from the cache before n. No uninstalled operation's recovery then depends upon the old value of X when n has no write graph predecessors and can be purged (via flushing $vars(n)$). X has become unexposed and we do not need to flush it. Hence we can remove X from $vars(n)$.

There are two salient differences between W and rW:

- In W, $vars(n) = Writes(n)$. In rW, not all objects in $Writes(n)$ are in $vars(n)$. Nonetheless, we install all operations in $ops(n)$ by flushing only $vars(n)$.

- There may be extra edges between nodes n and m in rW to ensure that certain objects are not exposed, and these need not be installation graph edges between operations in $ops(n)$ and $ops(m)$.

The example of Figure 2 illustrates how a blind write operation removes objects from a multi-object atomic flush set in rW. Multiple objects written by operation A are in node 1's atomic flush set, i.e., $vars(1) = \{X,Y\}$. After operation C, $vars(1) = \{Y\}$.

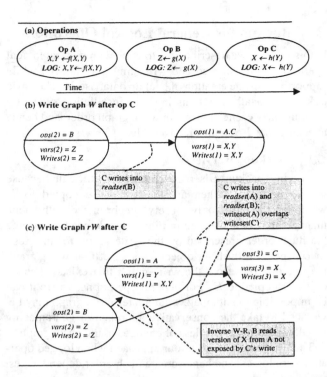

Figure 2: Write graphs rW and W when an X becomes unexposed. W has one node for X and Y, requiring their atomic flushing. rW has separate nodes for X and Y, the unexposed X being removed from $vars(1)$.

2.5 Cache Manager Identity Writes

rW only **makes possible** the shrinkage of flush sets $vars(n)$. To remove objects from a $vars(n)$ requires an operation of the appropriate form, and such an operation might not arise. However, the cache manager can itself remove objects from $vars(n)$ without atomically flushing them. It initiates an identity write operation $W_{IP}(X)$ that "writes" an object of $vars(n)$ without changing it and that is logged as a physical operation by writing the value of X to the log. This operation results in a new node m with $ops(m) = \{W_{IP}(X)\}$ and $vars(m) = X$. Importantly, it removes X from $vars(n)$. When n has no predecessors, $vars(n)$ (now not including X) can be atomically flushed, installing all operations of $ops(n)$. This technique works with arbitrary log operations. Later values for unexposed objects removed from $vars(n)$, which are not flushed, are recovered via the values logged for them as a result of their identity writes.

We have resorted here to logging physical writes to effectively manage the cache when $|vars(n)| > 1$. This approach was shown in [11] to be lower cost and have less impact on system operation than atomic flush transactions. Further, multiple updates can accumulate in each object before we log or flush it. Hence, as is common in database systems, the cost of flushing (and logging) is amortised over several updating operations, a substantial saving.

39

3 Backup for General Logical Operations

In this section, we describe how to cope with general logical operations that can read and write multiple objects, while supporting on-line creation of backup database B. The basic task is to install operations in B in installation order, by flushing dirty cached objects in write graph order, and hence to ensure that B remains recoverable.

3.1 Backup Overview

Preserving backup B's recoverability is difficult because we do not know when an object will be copied to B when the backup is only loosely synchronized with cache management, as illustrated in Figure 1. We need to enforce the flush order prescribed by the write graph for the flush to B when we flush an object to S. But that write graph may be different from the write graph that exists when an object is copied to B. For general operations, where it can be impossible to anticipate what a later write graph may be, we need to take the conservative approach of guaranteeing installation order regardless of changes to the write graph.

There are two aspects to our approach when logged operations are logical and hence create flush order dependencies.

Backup Progress We define a backup order (total or partial) that constrains when objects in S will be copied to B. Each recoverable object is in this ordering. We track the progress of backup in terms of how far it has gone in this ordering. While this constrains the backup process, backup retains great flexibility in how it sequences the copying of S to B. We characterize the backup process in terms of whether a backup is active and its progress in terms of the backup order. The testing of this characterization represents the synchronization required between the backup process and cache management. This is similar to the conventional fuzzy dump process, but we need added synchronization to reduce backup costs.

Cache Management The backup progress relative to the objects that we wish to flush from the cache determines how we manage the cache. Either we can flush objects from the cache normally to install operations, or we inject cache manager identity writes that ensure that object values are present on the log when they are needed and might not end up in B. This is installation without flushing (Iw/oF)into B, which we describe in the next subsection.

3.2 Installing Without Flushing

We saw in section 2.5 how cache manager identity writes could be used to avoid having to flush multiple objects to the stable database atomically. We can, when attempting to effect the installation of operations in a backup, reduce the number of objects requiring flushing (i.e. in $vars(n)$) to zero. We call this *"Installing without Flushing"* or **Iw/oF**. Every object in $vars(n)$ for a write graph node n whose $ops(n)$ we wish to install is updated via a cache manager identity write. Each of these operations removes its target object from $vars(n)$ and writes its value to the log. At the end, there are no objects in $vars(n)$. When n has no write graph predecessor node and $vars(n)$ is empty, $ops(n)$ is installed in the stable database, without any of the objects in $vars(n)$ having been flushed.

What has happened is that the logged values for objects in $vars(n)$ permit us to recover the stable database without having actually written these values to the stable database, in our case, the backup. Logging the identity operations is just as effective for recovery as flushing because these log records permit the truncation of the log in the same way that flushing does. This log truncation was described in [11] where we showed how this permitted us to advance the $rLSN$ of each object so written. Intuitively, this ensures that objects not captured in the backup are captured in the media recovery log and hence are available for media recovery.

3.3 Dealing with Write Graph Nodes

We need to understand when a backup is under way and the state of its progress. We then know how to deal with write graph nodes. Assume write graph node n has no predecessor write graph nodes. To keep S recoverable from a system crash, we atomically flush the objects in $vars(n)$ to S. If backup is not in progress, this suffices. If backup is in progress, we also want to simultaneously install $ops(n)$ into B. (This permits us to rely on only a single write graph.) There are two cases.

Pending : The objects of $vars(n)$ (usually, there will only be a single object so that atomic flushing can be ensured by disk write atomicity) are known to have not yet been backed up. Hence, their new values will become part of B if we write them to S. Therefore, this flush effectively installs (eventually) the operations of $ops(n)$ in B. Write graph nodes that must follow the current node to maintain installation order, in fact do so correctly for B as well as for S.

$\neg Pending$: An object of $vars(n)$ *may* already have been copied to B. Hence flushing $vars(n)$ now to S does not necessarily install $ops(n)$ in B. However, we can install $ops(n)$ into B without flushing any objects. We introduce cache manager identity write log operations (W_{IP}) for $vars(n)$, as we have described above. These log operations are in the media recovery log for B because we are writing them to the log after backup has begun. (Of course, we can flush pending objects to S, and log only the non-pending objects.)

In both cases above, we have installed the operations $ops(n)$ of write graph node n into the active backup at the "same time" that we install them into the stable database. What we have not described is how we record the progress of the backup, how we use backup order to determine whether objects have already been backed up, and exactly how the cache manager coordinates with the backup process to guarantee that the assumptions we are exploiting are valid during the cache manager process of handling write graph nodes. We consider these aspects below. We then describe a specific cache management algorithm.

3.4 Backup Progress

We need to discuss two things in this subsection, the backup ordering, and how backup progress is tracked relative to this order. It is this ordering that tells us whether an object being flushed to S will appear in B.

Backup Order

With each object X, we associate a value $\#X$ in the backup [partial] order such that for any other object $\#Y$, if $\#X < \#Y$, then X is guaranteed to be copied to B before Y. Where these values are not ordered, no knowledge exists about the relative order of copying the objects to B. We track the progress of a backup in terms of these values, which can be derived from the physical locations of data on disk.

It is possible to divide the database into disjoint partitions, and to independently track backup progress in each partition. This permits us to back up partitions in parallel. If no single operation can read or write objects from more than a single partition, we can independently track backup progress for each partition and hence arbitrarily interleave the copying of the partitions from S to B. (The degenerate case where each object is a partition is produced when operations are page-oriented, and backing up a partition is an atomic action.)

Tracking Backup Progress

To permit backup to proceed with little synchronization between it and the cache manager, we deliberately introduce some fuzziness in how we track its progress. Thus backup reports its progress only from time to time. Depending on system tuning considerations, the reporting can be made more or less precise. We control this by varying the granularity of the steps in which we report backup progress.

For each partition in which backup progress is to be tracked independently (there may be one or several), we maintain two values, D (Done) and P (Pending), in the backup order, that divides objects in the partition into three sets, as described below and as shown in Figure 3.

$Done(X)$: When $\#X < D$, X has been copied to B. Hence, X, if flushed now, will not appear in B.

$Pend(X)$; When $\#X > P$, X has not yet been copied to B. Hence, X, if flushed now, will appear in B.

$Doubt(X)$: When $D < \#X < P$, we do not know whether or not X has been copied to B. Hence, if X is flushed now, we do not know whether it will appear in B or not.

If $\#X$ is not ordered relative to P or D, then we do not know whether it has been backed up or not, and hence treat it as if it were in doubt ($Doubt$).

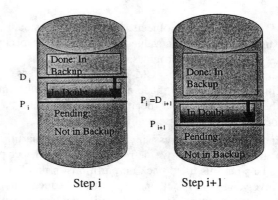

Figure 3: **Tracking backup progress.** At each step, the previously "in-doubt" part of S becomes part of S known to be copied to B. The "pending" part, previously known to not be in B, is partitioned into "in doubt" and still "pending". The values of P and D track this.

We require that there be maximum value Max and minimum value Min such that for all X, $Min < \#X < Max$. These permit us to initiate, terminate, and track the progress of the backup. Between backups, we set $D = P = Min$. This tells us that no object has been copied to a current backup B, and that all objects are pending for B, whenever it starts. When backup starts, we set P to some higher value P_1, leaving $D = Min$. Objects X with $\#X < P$ are in doubt as we do not track progress between $D = Min$ and $P = P_1$, the boundary for the first step. When backup has copied all objects less than P, it sets $D = P$, indicating that all the objects below P (i.e. in the first step) are done. It then sets $P = P_2$, the boundary for the second step. Now, only objects above P_2 are pending and hence guaranteed not yet to be in the current backup. Objects between $D = P_1$ and $P = P_2$ are in doubt.

Backup completes when P is set to Max, the highest value possible. This is the last step. At that point, there are no longer any pending objects and hence no objects, if now flushed, that are guaranteed to have their values for those objects appear in B. When backup completes this step, it resets to $D = P = Min$.

Our technique for charting backup progress reduces to a one step process when the only steps of backup progress are $D = P = Min$ and $D = Min, P = Max$. The only information then is whether backup is in progress or not. Backup need only synchronize with the CM when it changes the values of D and P. Hence, we can vary the granularity of synchronization (see below) from twice per backup (delimiting the duration of the backup) to many times, depending on the urgency to reduce the additional logging activity required to keep B recoverable.

Synchronization

While the CM is flushing objects to the stable database, it must know the state of backup progress. So it checks D

and P prior to flushing objects. However, unless additional measures are taken, the values for D and P can change while flushing is in progress. To prevent this requires synchronization between CM and backup process. This synchronization can be made at a granularity (in terms of number of steps) that is deemed appropriate for backup performance, but it is essential for correctness.

Since backup progress in each database partition is tracked independently, we define a backup latch per partition. This permits us to back up partitions in parallel. (Alternatively, we could back up the partitions sequentially, thus ordering the partitions, i.e. resulting in one large partition.) The backup latch protects D and P for a partition, hence synchronizing backup with the flushing activity of the cache manager.

When the backup process updates its progress, it requests the partition backup latch in exclusive mode. When granted, backup can update D and P. When updating is complete, backup releases the backup latch. When the cache manager flushes objects in $vars(n)$ of write graph node n, it requests the backup latch in share mode. This prevents backup from changing D and P while the CM is flushing objects. The CM then compares $\#X$ in $vars(n)$ with D and P, safe in the knowledge that these quantities will not change until it has completed its flushing activity and releases the backup latch for the partition. Share mode enables a multi-threaded CM to flush objects concurrently.

3.5   Cache Management Algorithm

Putting the above together yields the following algorithm. First, request the backup latch in share mode for the partition containing X in $vars(n)$, where n has no write graph predecessors. (We assume here that X is the only object in $vars(n)$, to enforce operation atomicity.) When granted, proceed, based on backup progress, as follows:

$Done(X)$: Install $ops(n)$ in B and S via Iw/oF. The value needed for X for media recovery will be on the media recovery log. We flush X to S before X is dropped from the cache in order to have the latest value of X available to us. Thus we both log and flush X before dropping it from the cache.

$Doubt(X)$: We proceed as for $Done(X)$. This may be unnecessary, but we cannot determine this, and this guarantees that B is recoverable.

$Pend(X)$: Merely flush X to S to install $ops(n)$ not only in the S, but also in B. The value for X needed for media recovery will be in B.

When the CM has completed flushing objects, it releases the backup latch.

4   Backup for Tree Operations

4.1   Description

In this section, we explore how to perform backup for a constrained set of log operations called "tree" operations [10]. These are more flexible than page-oriented operations and require less logging of data values. Like page-oriented operations, a tree operation can read and write an existing object, but it can also write an object not previously updated (a **new** object) in the same operation. Here, we modify this definition slightly. We include page-oriented operations ("physiological" operations denoted by W_{PL}) in the tree operation definition. But we do not permit an operation to update multiple objects. Instead, a "logical" write operation (W_L) writing the new object cannot update the old (read) object. Hence tree operations are of two forms:

1. Page-oriented: Possibly read an existing object old and write old, i.e. $W_{PL}(old)$ or $W_P(old, log(v))$

2. Write-new: Read an existing object old and write a new object new, i.e. $W_L(old, new)$

Tree operations are useful as we can initialize a new object without logging its initial value. For example, B-tree node split operations can be very efficiently logged compared to page-oriented operations.

Page-oriented operations: The update of old is logged as $RmvRec(old, key)$ that removes records with keys larger than key from old. The update of new is logged as a physical write with records needed to initialize new in the log record, i.e. as $W_P(new, log(value_{new}))$.

Tree operations: We log the update of new, moving the high records from old to new, as $MovRec(old, key, new)$. The update of old is logged as before. $MovRec$ must precede $RmvRec$ because the updated old will not contain the moved records.

For tree operation write graphs, the only edges are between node n where $vars(n) = \{new\}$ and m with $vars(m) = \{old\}$ for which an operation reads old and writes new. This can produce a "branching" of the write graph. However, no joining of write graph paths, and no cycles requiring a collapse are introduced. This results in a write graph where each node n has $|vars(n)| = 1$. Hence, as with page-oriented operations, we can identify a write graph node with its updated object, e.g. new can identify both an object and the write graph node n with $vars(n) = \{new\}$. Thus, new is a predecessor of old (and old is a successor of new) in WG.

Successors for any object X in the cache are on at most one path of write graph nodes. A successor node may, however, have more than one predecessor as a single old object can spawn edges to multiple new objects. Tree operations are so-named because their write graph (when only tree operations are logged) is a set of trees.

We call *old* a potential successor of *new* if there has been an operation that reads *old* and writes *new* but *old* has not yet been updated, and we denote the union of successors and potential successors of a cached object X by $S(X)$. With only tree operations, $S(X)$ never increases for any X in the cache. $S(X)$ is fixed at the time that an object is first updated in the cache. Subsequent operations may add predecessors, but not successors because an object can only be a *new* object the first time it is updated.

4.2 Backup

We identify when to use Iw/oF to install operations of $ops(n)$ into B. Recall that the set $S(X)$ for each X in $vars(n)$ is fixed when n is added to the write graph. The properties of $S(X)$ and n together help determine how to install the operations in $ops(n)$. The most important factor in whether Iw/oF logging is needed when we flush X is how backup progress compares with the position of X and its successors, $S(X)$. To help us with that, we maintain $MAX(X) = max(\{\#y | y \in S(X)\})$ with each cached object X. When an operation $W_L(Y,X)$, reading Y and writing X, appears, we incrementally compute for the new object X, $MAX(X) = max(\#Y, MAX(Y))$. ($MAX(Y) = 0$ if Y has no successors.) Then we say that $S(X)$ is "done", "pending", or "in doubt" directly based on that state of $MAX(X)$. If $Max(X) \leq D$, then $Done(S(X))$ and no successor y of X will appear in B. Otherwise, when $Max(X) > D$, then $\neg Done(S(X))$, and some successor y of X might appear in B.

Our case analysis for when we can avoid Iw/oF logging depends on the state of backup progress. The cases are graphically shown in Figure 4.

$Pend(X) or Done(S(X))$: Either X will definitely appear in B ($Pend(X)$); or no y in $S(X)$ will be included in B (i.e. $Done(S(X))$). We can flush X without extra logging because flush order cannot be violated.

$(Done(X) \& \neg Done(S(X)))$ or $(\neg Pend(X) \& Pend(S(X)))$: We know that either X will not get to B and are unsure about $S(X)$ or $S(X)$ will get to B but we are unsure about X. Hence, to guarantee that X gets to B should any of $S(X)$ get to B, we use Iw/oF and write X to the log.

$Doubt(X) \& Doubt(S(X))$: When X and $S(X)$ are both in the region where backup is active, we are "in doubt" as to whether they will get to B. In this region, we exploit the † property which holds about half the time.

  † **if** (any y in $S(X)$ gets to B when flushed to S) **then** (any earlier flush of X to S gets to B)

When † holds, flush order to the backup will not be compromised. If X does not get into B (which is the dangerous case), then neither will all of $S(X)$.

Consider first the case where $S(X) = \{y\}$, i.e. there is a single successor to X. X needs to be installed not later than

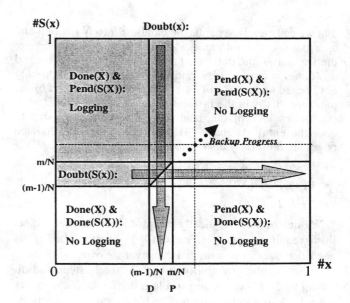

Figure 4: The regions of $< \#X, \#S(X) >$ space as to whether or not additional logging is required to ensure that flush order dependencies for S are enforced for B. The shaded area requires the extra Iw/oF logging.

y, i.e. if y is in the backup, X must also be in the backup. This is so when $\#y < \#X$.

When $|S(X)| > 1$, it is tempting to think that if $\#X > Max(X)$, then X can be flushed without extra logging. But this is not so. If there is an order violation between any pair of successors (i.e. † does not hold), then we must use Iw/oF for that successor. That ensures that there is a successor to X that is guaranteed to be installed in B. But we are unsure whether X will get to B. Hence we must use Iw/oF to ensure that X will also be installed in B. Thus, once an order violation appears among $S(X)$, any subsequently added predecessors of X also have an order violation and must likewise be installed in B using Iw/oF. Thus, each write graph node n has a $violation(n)$ flag. The $violation(X)$ flag is set if $\#X \leq \#y$ where y is an immediate successor resulting from an operation that read y and wrote X or if $violation(y)$ is set. This incrementally maintains $violation(X)$ for all X.

5 Logging Performance

In this section, we present a comparative analysis of how much extra logging is required by the cache manager when a backup is in progress. This extra logging is a function of how many steps there are in the backup- and hence of how frequently the backup process synchronizes with the cache manager to report its progress. We treat both general operations and tree operations, and quantify the added logging costs of going from physiological operations to tree operations to completely general operations.

We assume that a backup is done in N equal steps and

that we can clearly separate the database into N disjoint and approximately equal pieces. When we are at the mth step, the fraction of the database that has been definitely backed up (done) is $(m-1)/N$, and the fraction that is definitely not backed up yet ($Pend$) is $1 - m/N$, while the part of the database that is in the process of being backed up ($Doubt$) constitutes $1/N$ of the database. (These fractions sum to one, the entire database.) Hence, assuming that updated pages are uniformly distributed, we have:

- $Prob\{Done(X)\} = Prob\{\#X \le D\} = \frac{m-1}{N}$
- $Prob\{Pend(X)\} = Prob\{\#X > P\} = 1 - \frac{m}{N}$
- $Prob\{Doubt(X)\} = \frac{1}{N}$

We determine analytically the probability that an object flush requires logging ($Prob_m\{log\}$) because Iw/oF is needed at backup step m, and then average over the N steps by summing the probability at each of the N steps and dividing by N. (There is no extra logging for media recovery when backup is not in progress.) This overall probability is
$$Prob\{log\} = \frac{1}{N}\sum_{m=1}^{N} Prob_m\{log\}$$

Now we need to determine $Prob_m\{log\}$.

5.1   General Logical Operations

For general operations, we must do extra logging for Iw/oF whenever we are not sure that the object X being flushed will be included in the current active backup. The probability of this is
$$Prob_m\{\neg Pend(X)\} = Prob\{\#X < P\} = \frac{m}{N}.$$

The cost averaged over all steps is
$$Prob\{log\} = \frac{1}{N}\sum_{m=1}^{N}\frac{m}{N} = \frac{1}{N^2}\sum_{m=1}^{N} m = \frac{1}{2}(1 + \frac{1}{N})$$

For example, when $N = 1$, and we merely know when a backup is in progress, we must always do the extra logging. For high N, this cost approaches $\frac{1}{2}$.

5.2   Tree Operations

For tree operations, we assume that $|S(X)| = 1$, i.e. each cached object has exactly one successor. This is not realistic. First, an object might have no successors and be flushed without extra logging. (If X has one successor y, then y cannot have any successors.) Second, an object may have more than one successor. Nonetheless, this analysis provides some insight into the logging requirements. It surely overstates the logging cost relative to general log operations. For tree operations, we may find that an object has no successors, permitting us to frequently avoid any logging- while we get no such information for general operations, where successors can emerge at any time.

Subject to the preceding qualifications, the cost in extra logging at step m to flush an object X is
$$Prob_m\{log\} = Prob\{\neg Pend(X)\&\neg Done(S(X))\}$$
$$- Prob\{Doubt(X)\&Doubt(S(X))\&Prob\{\#S(X) < \#X\})$$

Substituting prior values for $Pend$, $Done$, and $Doubt$, logging cost at step m becomes
$$Prob_m\{log\} = \frac{m}{N}(1 - \frac{m-1}{N}) - \frac{1}{2N^2} = \frac{N+1}{N^2}m - \frac{1}{N^2}m^2 - \frac{1}{2N^2}$$

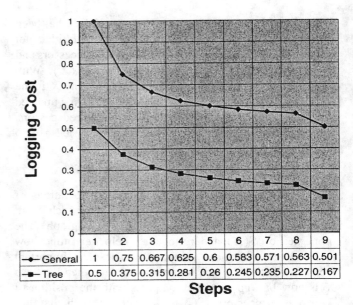

Steps	1	2	3	4	5	6	7	8	9
General	1	0.75	0.667	0.625	0.6	0.583	0.571	0.563	0.501
Tree	0.5	0.375	0.315	0.281	0.26	0.245	0.235	0.227	0.167

Figure 5: The frequency (probability) with which extra logging is required for general and tree operations as a function of the number of backup steps.

Averaging over all steps, we get
$$Prob\{log\} = \frac{1}{N}\sum_{m=0}^{N}(\frac{N+1}{N^2}m - \frac{1}{N^2}m^2 - \frac{1}{2N^2}) = \frac{1}{6} + \frac{1}{2N} - \frac{1}{6N^2}$$
Asymptotically, as the number of steps in the backup process increase, only one flush in six needs extra logging.

5.3   Assessing Results

Figure 5 contrasts the extra logging costs for general operations versus tree operations as the number of backup steps that are synchronized with the cache manager increases.

General operations require that an object be logged (Iw/oF over half the time to flush it to the stable database. The more backup steps, the closer to 50% this is. If we only know that backup is active (one step), we must log all flushed variables.

Tree operations reduce logging (compared with general ops) by between half and two thirds, to about about one object flush in six. This fractional reduction increases as the number of backup steps increases, i.e the more steps, the fewer times that Iw/oF logging is needed.

In both cases, most of the reduction in logging (almost 90%) has been achieved with an eight step backup, so there is little incentive to further increase the number of backup steps.

Our analysis surely overstates the extra costs of supporting logical operations for high speed backups.

- Extra logging only ocurs during backup. Usually a database backup is only active a small part of the time, frequently during periods of low database activity. Hence, extra logging, when averaged over total time, is much less than what is reported here. Further, this extra logging merely reduces somewhat the very substantial gain that comes from using logical operations.

- Extra logging can also substitute for flushing. Should X be dirty in the cache, but hot, such that we do not drop it from the cache, logging it to install its update operations in S treats S the way we have been treating B. To drop X from the cache requires a flush to S, but this may well be greatly delayed by further updates.

This demonstrates that a high performance, asynchronous, on-line backup is possible while logging logical operations.

6   Discussion

6.1   Incremental Backups

By identifying the portion of the database state S that has changed since the last backup, we need only back up that changed portion. This is called an "incremental backup". Many database systems support a form of this. A clever way to do it while supporting high speed full backup and avoiding the cache manager is described in [13]. A natural question is whether our approach lends itself also to such incremental backup. There are two aspects of incremental backup.

1. Identify the set of database objects updated since the last backup. Schemes that do this for page-oriented log operations can be adapted for our more powerful operations. Adaptation is required because recovery checkpointing and how the log truncation point is identified are different, at least in detail.

2. Copy the identified objects to the backup. This is essentially the same problem that we have for full backup. Its solution should be similar as well, involving Iw/oF logging and tracking backup progress.

Hence, much of the efficiency of [13] also holds for backup with logical log operations.

6.2   Application Read Operations and Backup

In [8], we introduced log operations that permit efficient logging for application recovery. The only logical log operation we pursued there was "application read"($R(X, A)$). This avoided physically logging the value of X or A, but required that A be flushed before a change to X was flushed. In all resulting write graphs, only applications are predecessors. If applications are the last objects included in a backup, we guarantee that the † property holds (if X is included in the backup when X is flushed, so is any earlier flush of A), and **no Iw/oF logging** is incurred for backup. This is yet another example of how constraining operations can increase efficiency.

6.3   Some Future Directions

Three areas for further research seem interesting to pursue.

1. Tree operations reduce the logged data, avoid cyclic dependencies, and update only a single page. Are there other more general operation classes that avoid substantial logging during a backup?

2. Media failure might affect only a small part of the database. With logical operations, it may not be easy to determine the database part upon which its recovery depends. Preventing operations from having operands from more than one partition makes a partition the unit of media recovery. Are there other simple techniques?

3. Media recovery can protect against some application errors that corrupt the database. In this case, we may not recover the latest database state, but a state that excludes the effects of the corrupting application. This is difficult now. Can we support this in a general way?

References

[1] Bernstein, P., Hadzilacos, V. Goodman, N. *Concurrency Control and Recovery in Database Systems*. Addison Wesley (1987).

[2] Gray, J. Notes on Data Base Operating Systems. IBM Tech Report RJ2188 (Feb. 1978), IBM Corp., San Jose, CA

[3] Gray, J., McJones, P., et al. The Recovery Manager of the System R Database Manager. ACM Computing Surveys, 13,2 (June 1981) 223-242.

[4] Gray, J. and Reuter, A. *Transaction Processing: Concepts and Techniques*. Morgan Kaufmann (1993) San Mateo, CA

[5] Haerder, T. and Reuter, A. Principles of transaction-oriented database recovery. ACM Comp. Surveys 15,4 (Dec. 1983) 287-317.

[6] King, R. P., Halim, N., Garcia-Molina, H. Polyzois, C. A. Management of a remote backup copy for disaster recovery. ACM Trans. on Database Systems 16, 2 (June 1991) 338-368

[7] Kumar, V. and Hsu, M. (eds.) *Recovery Mechanisms in Database Systems*. Prentice Hall, NJ 1998

[8] Lomet, D. Application recovery using generalized redo recovery. Intl. Conf. on Data Eng., Orlando (Feb. 1998) 154-163.

[9] Lomet, D. and Salzberg, B. Exploiting a History Database for Backup, VLDB Conference, Dublin (Sept. 1993) 380-390.

[10] Lomet, D. and Tuttle, M. Redo recovery from system crashes. VLDB Conference, Zurich (Sept. 1995) 457-468.

[11] Lomet, D. and Tuttle, M. Logical logging to extend recovery to new domains. ACM SIGMOD Conference, Philadelphia (May 1999) 73-84.

[12] Mohan, C., Haderle, D., Lindsay, B., Pirahesh, H., and Schwarz, P. ARIES: A transaction recovery method supporting fine-granularity locking and partial rollbacks using write-ahead logging. ACM Trans. On Data. Sys. 17,1 (Mar. 1992) 94-162.

[13] Mohan, C. and Narang, I. An Efficient and Flexible Method for Archiving a Data Base. ACM SIGMOD Conference, Washington, DC (May 1993) 139-146.

Efficient Resumption of Interrupted Warehouse Loads*

Wilburt Juan Labio† Janet L. Wiener‡ Hector Garcia-Molina
Stanford University
{wilburt, wiener, hector}@db.stanford.edu

Vlad Gorelik
Sagent Technologies
vgorelik@sagenttech.com

Abstract

Data warehouses collect large quantities of data from distributed sources into a single repository. A typical load to create or maintain a warehouse processes GBs of data, takes hours or even days to execute, and involves many complex and user-defined transformations of the data (e.g., find duplicates, resolve data inconsistencies, and add unique keys). If the load fails, a possible approach is to "redo" the entire load. A better approach is to resume the incomplete load from where it was interrupted. Unfortunately, traditional algorithms for resuming the load either impose unacceptable overhead during normal operation, or rely on the specifics of transformations. We develop a resumption algorithm called *DR* that imposes no overhead and relies only on the high-level properties of the transformations. We show that *DR* can lead to a ten-fold reduction in resumption time by performing experiments using commercial software.

1   Introduction

Data warehouses collect large quantities of data from distributed sources into a single repository. A typical load to create or maintain a warehouse processes 1 to 100 GB and takes hours to execute. For example, Walmart's maintenance load averages 16 GB per day [3]. Typical maintenance loads of Sagent customers process 6 GB per week and initial loads process up to 100 GB.

Warehouse loads are usually performed when the system is off-line (e.g., overnight), and must be completed within a fixed period. A failure during the load creates havoc:

This research was funded by Rome Laboratories under Air Force Contract F30602-94-C-0237, by the Massive Digital Data Systems (MDDS) Program sponsored by the Advanced Research and Development Committee of the Community Management Staff, and by Sagent Technologies, Inc.

†Currently at Gigabeat, Inc. Palo Alto CA; wilburt@gigabeat.com

‡Currently at Compaq SRC, Palo Alto, CA; wiener@pa.dec.com.

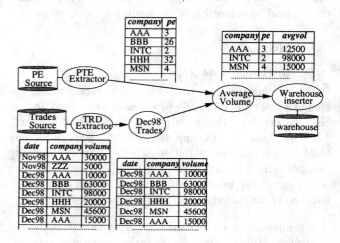

Figure 1: Load Workflow

Current commercial systems abort the failed load, and the administrator must restart the load from scratch and hope a second failure does not occur. If there is not enough time for the new load, it may be skipped, leaving the database out of date or incomplete, and generating an even bigger load for the next period. Load failures are not unlikely due to the complexity of the warehouse load. For instance, Sagent customers report that one out of every thirty loads fails [10].

Traditional recovery techniques described below could be used to save partial load states, so that not all work is lost when a failure occurs. However, these techniques are shunned in practice because they generate high overheads during normal processing and because they may require modification of the load processing. In this paper we present a new, low-overhead technique for *resuming* failed loads. Our technique exploits high-level "properties" of the workflow used to load the warehouse, so that work is not repeated during a resumed load.

To illustrate the type of processing performed during a load, consider the simple load workflow of Figure 1. In this load workflow, *extractors* obtain data from the stock Trades and the price-to-earnings ratio (PE) sources. Figure 1 shows a sample prefix of the tuples extracted from each source. The Trades data is first processed by the *Dec98Trades transform*,

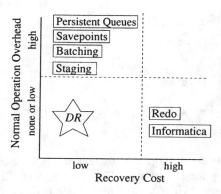

Figure 2: Applicability of Algorithms

which only outputs trades done in December 1998. Thus, the first two trades are removed since they happened in November 1998. Then, the *AverageVolume* transform groups the trades by company and finds the average trade volume of the companies whose *pe* is less than or equal to 4. For instance, companies BBB and HHH are discarded since they have high *pe*'s. The output of *AverageVolume* is then sent to the *inserter*, which stores the tuples in the warehouse.

In practice, load workflows can be much more complex than what we have illustrated, often having tens to hundreds of transforms [10]. Transforms include not only conventional database operations (e.g., join) but also arbitrary processing (e.g., data scrubbing, byte reordering) coded by application specialists. To maximize pipelining and load speed, the output tuples of each component are sent to the next as soon as they are generated. With all this complexity, load failures occur.

There are many ways to recover a failed warehouse load. The fundamental features of various techniques are informally contrasted with our technique, called *DR*, in Figure 2. The vertical axis represents the *normal-operation overhead* of a technique, while the horizontal axis indicates the *recovery cost* of a technique. In the lower right quadrant of Figure 2 are two techniques that have very low normal-operation overhead. One is to simply redo the entire load over again. Clearly, this technique can suffer from high recovery cost. Informatica's solution [6] is similar: After a failure, Informatica reprocesses all the data, but filters out already stored tuples when they reach the warehouse for the second time (i.e., just before the inserter).

Other techniques, shown in the upper left quadrant of Figure 2, attempt to minimize the recovery cost by aggressively modifying the load workflow or load processing. Staging divides the workflow into consecutive stages, and saves intermediate results between stages. All input data enters the first stage. All of the first stage's output is saved. The saved output is input to the second stage, and so on. The second stage can then be restarted after a failure from the saved input, without redoing the first stage.

Input batching divides the input to the load workflow into sequentially processed batches. Other techniques are to take periodic savepoints [5] of the workflow state, or save tuples in transit in persistent queues [1, 2]. When a failure occurs, the *modified* transforms cooperate to revert to the latest savepoint, and proceed from there.

In general, techniques that modify the load workflow suffer from two disadvantages: (1) the normal-operation overhead is potentially high, as confirmed by our experiments; and (2) the specific details of the load processing need to be known.

The *DR* technique we propose in this paper has no normal-operation overhead, and does not modify the load workflow. Yet, its recovery cost can be much lower than Informatica's technique or redoing the entire load. Unlike them, *DR* avoids reprocessing input tuples and uses filters to intercept tuples much earlier than Informatica's technique. *DR* relies on simple and high-level transform properties (e.g., are tuples processed in order?). These properties can either be declared by the transform writer or can usually be inferred from the basic semantics of the transform, without needing to know exactly how it is coded. After a failure, the load is restarted, except that portions that are no longer needed are "skipped." To illustrate, suppose that after a failure we discover that tuples AAA through MSN are found in the warehouse (Figure 1. If we know that tuples are processed in alphabetical order by the *PTE Extractor* and by the *AverageVolume* transform, the *PTE Extractor* can retrieve tuples starting with the one that follows MSN. If tuples are not processed in order, it may still be possible to generate a list of company names that are no longer needed, and that can be skipped. During the reload, transforms operate as usual, except that they only receive the input tuples needed to generate what is missing in the warehouse. In summary, our strategy is to exploit some high-level semantics of the load workflow, and to be selective when resuming a failed load.

We note that there are previous techniques that are similar to *DR* in that they incur low normal-operation overhead but still have a low recovery cost. However, these techniques are applicable to very specific workflows for disk-based sorting [8], object database loading [11], and loading a flat file into the warehouse [9, 12]. Our technique can handle more general workflows.

We do not claim that *DR* always recovers a load faster than other techniques. For instance, techniques that modify the normal load workflow may have slower normal operation loads but faster resumed loads. However, our experiments show that *DR* is competitive if not better than these techniques for many workflows. In particular, *DR* is better for workflows that make heavy use of pipelining. Even if a workflow does not have a natural pipeline, our experiments show that a hybrid algorithm that combines *DR* and staging (or batching) can lower recovery cost.

We make the following contributions toward the efficient resumption of failed warehouse loads.

- We develop a framework for describing successful warehouse loads, and load failures. Within this framework, we identify basic properties that are useful in resuming loads.

- We develop *DR*, which minimizes recovery cost while imposing no overhead during normal operation. *DR* does not require knowing the specifics of a transform, but only its basic, high-level properties. *DR* is presented here in the context of warehousing, but is really a generic solution for resuming any long-duration, process intensive, task.

- We show experimentally that *DR* can significantly reduce recovery cost, as compared to traditional techniques. In our experiments we use Sagent's warehouse load package to load TPC-D tables and materialized views containing answers to TPC-D queries.

Outline: We describe a warehouse load in Section 2, and discuss warehouse load failure in Section 3. We develop the *DR* algorithm in Sections 4 and 5. Experiments are presented in Section 6.

2   Normal Operation

When data is loaded into the warehouse, tuples are transferred from one *component* (*extractor*, *transform*, or *inserter*) to another. The order of the tuples is important to the resumption algorithm, so we define sequences as ordered lists of tuples with the same attributes.

Definition 2.1 (Sequence) A sequence of tuples $\mathcal{T}$ is an ordered list of tuples $[t_1..t_n]$, and all the tuples in $\mathcal{T}$ have the attributes $[a_1..a_m]$.   □

We next discuss how a component tree represents a load workflow. In [7], we show how our *DR* algorithm can be extended to handle a component directed acyclic graph.

2.1   Component Tree Design

Figure 3 illustrates the same component tree as Figure 1, with abbreviations for the component names. Constructing a component tree involves several important design decisions. First, the data obtained by the extractors is specified. Second, the transforms that process the extracted data are chosen. Moreover, if a desired transformation is not available, a user may construct a new custom-made transform. Finally, the warehouse tables into which the inserter loads the data are specified. The extractors, transforms, and inserter comprise the *nodes* of the component tree.

Each transform and inserter expects certain *input parameter* sequences at load time. Similarly, each transform and extractor generates an output sequence to its *output parameter*. The input and output parameters are specified by connecting the extractors, transforms, and the inserter together with *edges* in the component tree. In the design, the "properties" that hold for each node or edge are declared for use by our resumption algorithm, as detailed in Section 4. Commercial load packages already declare basic properties like the key attributes of an input parameter.

In some cases, different components of a tree may be assigned to different machines. Hence, during a load, data transfers between components may represent data transfers over the network. We now illustrate a component tree.

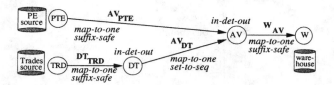

Figure 3: Component Tree with Properties

Example 2.1 In Figure 3, the extractors are denoted PTE for the price-to-earnings (PE) source, and TRD for the Trades source. The transforms are denoted DT (for $Dec98$-$Trades$), and AV (for $AverageVolume$). The inserter is denoted W. The input parameters of each component are denoted by the component that produces the input. For instance, AV_{DT} is an input parameter of AV that is produced by DT.   □

In our notation, Y_X denotes the input parameter of component Y produced by component X, and Y_O is the output parameter of Y. We use Attrs(Y_X) to denote the attributes of the Y_X tuples. Similarly, KeyAttrs(Y_X) specifies their key attributes. W denotes the warehouse inserter.

We note that the component trees designed for warehouse creation and maintenance are different [7]. However, our resumption algorithm applies equally well to both creation and maintenance component trees. We therefore use the term "load" to mean either one.

2.2   Successful Warehouse Load

When a component tree is used to load data, the extractors produce sequences that are inputs to the transforms. That is, each input parameter is "instantiated" with a tuple sequence. Each transform then produces an output sequence that is sent to subsequent components. Finally, the inserter receives a tuple sequence and inserts the tuples in committed batches. To maximize pipelined parallelism, each output sequence is received as the next component's input as it is generated. More specifically, at each point in time, a component Y has produced a prefix of its entire output sequence and shipped the prefix tuples to the next component. The next example illustrates a warehouse load during normal operation, i.e., no failures occur.

Example 2.2 Consider Figure 3. The extractors fill their output parameters PTE_O and TRD_O with the sequences $\mathcal{PTE}_O$ and $\mathcal{TRD}_O$. (The calligraphy font denotes sequences.) Input parameter AV_{PTE} is instantiated with the sequence $\mathcal{AV}_{PTE} = \mathcal{PTE}_O$. Note that PTE does not need to produce $\mathcal{PTE}_O$ in its entirety before it can ship a prefix of $\mathcal{PTE}_O$ to AV. Similarly, DT_{TRD} is instantiated with $\mathcal{DT}_{TRD} = \mathcal{TRD}_O$, and so on. Finally, W_{AV} of the inserter is instantiated with $\mathcal{W}_{AV} = \mathcal{AV}_O$. W inserts the tuples in $\mathcal{W}_{AV}$ in order and issues a commit periodically. In the absence of failures, $\mathcal{W}_{AV}$ is eventually stored in the warehouse.   □

To summarize our notation, $\mathcal{Y}_X$ and $\mathcal{Y}_O$ denote the sequences used for input parameter Y_X and output parameter Y_O during a warehouse load. When Y produces $\mathcal{Y}_O$ by processing $\mathcal{Y}_X$ (and possibly other input sequences), we say $Y(...\mathcal{Y}_X...) = \mathcal{Y}_O$. $\mathcal{W}$ denotes the sequence that is loaded into the warehouse in the absence of failures.

3 Warehouse Load Failure

In this paper, we only consider system-level load failures, e.g., RDBMS or software crashes, hardware crashes, lack of disk space. We do not consider load failures due to invalid data. Furthermore, we consider system-level failures that do not affect information stored in stable storage. Any of the components can suffer from such a system-level failure. Even though various components may fail, the effect of any failure on the warehouse is the same. That is, only a prefix of the normal operation input sequence $\mathcal{W}$ is loaded into the warehouse.

Observation In the event of a failure, only a prefix of $\mathcal{W}$ is stored in the warehouse. □

In [7], we discuss in detail why the observation holds when an extractor, a transform, an inserter or the network fails.

3.1 Data for Resumption

When a component Y fails, the warehouse load eventually halts due to lack of input. Once Y recovers, the load can be resumed. The only data available for resumption is the portion of $\mathcal{W}$ in the warehouse, plus the source data. An extractor E may offer some of the following procedures to re-extract data. We use $\mathcal{E}_O$ to denote the sequence that would have been extracted by E had there been no failures. More details are in Section 5.3.

GetAll() extracts the same set of tuples as are in $\mathcal{E}_O$. The order of the tuples may be different. (Many sources, such as commercial RDBMS, do not guarantee order.) We assume that all extractors provide GetAll(), that is, that the original data is still available. If $\mathcal{E}_O$ cannot be reproduced, then $\mathcal{E}_O$ must be logged.

GetAllInorder() extracts the same sequence $\mathcal{E}_O$. This procedure may be supported, e.g., by a commercial RDBMS extractor that uses an SQL ORDER BY clause.

GetSubset(...) provides the $\mathcal{E}_O$ tuples that are not in the subset indicated by GetSubset's parameters. Sources that can selectively filter tuples typically provide GetSubset.

GetSuffix(...) provides a suffix of $\mathcal{E}_O$ that excludes the prefix indicated by GetSuffix's parameters. Sources that can filter and order tuples typically provide GetSuffix.

In this paper, we assume that the re-extraction procedures only produce tuples that were in the original sequence $\mathcal{E}_O$. However, our algorithms also work when additional tuples appear only in the suffix of $\mathcal{E}_O$ that was not processed before the failure.

3.2 Redoing the Warehouse Load

When the warehouse load fails, only a prefix $\mathcal{C}$ of $\mathcal{W}$ is in the warehouse. The goal of a resumption algorithm is to load the remaining tuples of $\mathcal{W}$ in any order (since the warehouse is an RDBMS). The simplest resumption algorithm, called *Redo*, simply repeats the load. First $\mathcal{C}$ is deleted, and then for each extractor in the component tree, the re-extraction procedure GetAll() is invoked.

Although *Redo* is very simple, it still requires that if the same set of tuples are obtained by the extractors, the same set of tuples are inserted into the warehouse. Since this property pertains to an entire workflow, it can be hard to test. A *singular property* that pertains to a single transform is much easier to test. The following singular property, set-to-set, is sufficient to enable *Redo*. That is, if all extractors use GetAll or GetAllInorder, and all transforms are set-to-set, then *Redo* can be used. Definition 3.1 tests this condition.

Property 3.1 (set-to-set(Y)) If given the same set of input tuples, Y produces the same set of output tuples, then set-to-set(Y) = true. Otherwise, set-to-set(Y) = false. □

Definition 3.1 (Same-set(Y)) If Y is an extractor and Y uses GetAllInorder or GetAll during resumption then Same-set(Y) = true. Otherwise, if $\forall Y_X$: Same-set(X) and set-to-set(Y) then Same-set(Y) = true. Otherwise, Same-set(Y) = false. □

4 Properties for Resumption

In this section, we identify singular properties of transforms or input parameters that *DR* combines into "transitive properties" to avoid reprocessing some of the input tuples.

To illustrate, consider the simple component tree in Figure 4. Suppose that the sequence $\mathcal{W}_Y$ to be inserted into the warehouse is $[y_1 y_2 y_3]$, and $[x_1 x_2 x_3 x_4]$ is the $\mathcal{Y}_X$ input sequence that yields $\mathcal{W}_Y$ (Figure 5). An edge $x_i \rightarrow y_j$ indicates that x_i "contributes" in the computation of y_j. (We define contributes formally in Definition 4.1.) Also suppose that after a failure, only y_1 is in the warehouse. Clearly, it is safe to filter $\mathcal{Y}_X$ tuples that contribute only to $\mathcal{W}_Y$ tuples, such as y_1, already in the warehouse. Thus in Figure 5, x_1 and x_2 can be filtered. We need to be careful with y_1 contributors that also contribute to other $\mathcal{W}_Y$ tuples. For example, if x_2 contributes to y_2 as well, then we cannot filter x_2, since it is still needed to generate y_2.

In general, we need to answer the following questions to avoid reprocessing input tuples:

Question (1): For a given warehouse tuple, which tuples in $\mathcal{Y}_X$ contribute to it?

Question (2): When is it safe to filter those tuples from $\mathcal{Y}_X$?

The challenge is that we must answer these questions using limited information. In particular, we can only use the tuples stored in the warehouse before the failure, and the singular properties, attributes and key attributes declared when the component tree was designed.

In Section 4.1, we identify four singular properties to answer Question (2). We then define three *transitive properties* that apply to sub-trees of the component tree. *DR* will

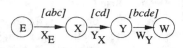

Figure 4: Component tree

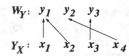

Figure 5: Map-to-one

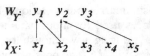

Figure 6: Suffix-safe

derive the transitive properties based on the declared singular properties. In Section 4.2, we define two more singular properties. Using these properties, we define *identifying attributes* of the tuples to answer Question (1). *DR* will derive the identifying attributes based on the declared singular properties and key attributes. We also show that the singular properties hold for many commercial transforms, such those in Sagent's DataMart 3.0 for warehouse creation and maintenance, in Section 6. Since singular properties pertain to a transform or an input parameter and not to a whole workflow, they are easy to grasp and can often be deduced easily from the transform manuals. Henceforth, we refer to singular properties as "properties" for conciseness.

Before proceeding, we formalize the notion of contributing input tuples. An input tuple x_i in an input sequence $\mathcal{Y}_X$ of transform Y *contributes* to a tuple y_j in a resulting output sequence $\mathcal{Y}_O$ if y_j is only produced when x_i is in $\mathcal{Y}_X$. The definition of "contributes" uses the function IsSubsequence($\mathcal{S}$, $\mathcal{T}$), which returns true if $\mathcal{S}$ is a subsequence of $\mathcal{T}$, and false otherwise.

Definition 4.1 (Contributes, Contributors) Given transform Y, let $Y(...\mathcal{Y}_X...) = \mathcal{Y}_O$ and $Y(...\mathcal{Y}'_X...) = \mathcal{Y}'_O$. Also let $\mathcal{Y}_X = [x_1..x_{i-1}x_ix_{i+1}..x_n]$ and $\mathcal{Y}'_X = [x_1..x_{i-1}x_{i+1}..x_n]$. Contributes($x_i,y_j$) = true, if $y_j \in \mathcal{Y}_O$ and $y_j \notin \mathcal{Y}'_O$. Otherwise, Contributes(x_i,y_j) = false. Contributors($\mathcal{Y}_X$, y_j) = $\mathcal{T}$, where IsSubsequence($\mathcal{T}$, $\mathcal{Y}_X$) and ($\forall x_i \in \mathcal{T}$: Contributes(x_i, y_j)) and ($\forall x_i \in \mathcal{Y}_X$: Contributes(x_i,y_j) $\Rightarrow$ $x_i \in \mathcal{T}$). $\square$

We extend Definition 4.1 in a transitive fashion in [7] to define when a tuple contributes to a warehouse tuple. For instance, if x_i contributes to y_j, which in turn contributes to a warehouse tuple w_k, then x_i contributes to w_k.

Some tuples may not contribute to any output tuple. For instance, if a transform computes the sum of its input tuples then an input tuple $t = \langle 0 \rangle$ does not contribute to the sum. Such tuples are called *inconsequential input tuples* and are candidates for filtering.

4.1 Safe Filtering

During resumption, a transform Y may not need to produce all of its normal operation output $\mathcal{Y}_O$. Therefore, Y may not need to reprocess some of its input tuples. In this section, we identify properties that ensure safe filtering of input tuples.

The *map-to-one* property holds for Y_X whenever every input tuple x_i contributes to at most one Y_O output tuple y_j (as in Figure 5). For instance, the input parameters of selection, projection, union, aggregation and some join transforms are map-to-one. Nearly all of Sagent's input parameters are map-to-one.

Property 4.1 (map-to-one(Y_X)) Given transform Y with input parameter Y_X, Y_X is *map-to-one* if $\forall \mathcal{Y}_X, \forall \mathcal{Y}_O, \forall x_i \in$

$\mathcal{Y}_X$: ($Y(...\mathcal{Y}_X...) = \mathcal{Y}_O$) $\Rightarrow$ ($\neg \exists y_j, y_k \in \mathcal{Y}_O$ such that Contributes(x_i,y_j) and Contributes(x_i,y_k) and $j \neq k$). $\square$

If Y_X is map-to-one, and some tuples in $\mathcal{Y}_O$ are not needed, then their contributing tuples in $\mathcal{Y}_X$ can be safely filtered at resumption time. For example, in Figure 5, if tuples y_1 and y_2 are not needed in $\mathcal{Y}_O$, then the subset $\{x_1, x_2, x_4\}$ of Y_X can be filtered.

Subset-feasible(Y_X) is a transitive property that states that it is feasible to filter some subset of the Y_X input tuples. Subset-feasible(Y_X) holds when all of the input parameters in the path from Y_X to the warehouse are map-to-one. In this case, we can safely filter the Y_X tuples that contribute to some warehouse tuple because these Y_X tuples contribute to no other warehouse tuples.

Definition 4.2 (Subset-feasible(Y_X)) Given transform Y with input parameter Y_X, Subset-feasible(Y_X) = true if Y is the warehouse inserter. Otherwise, Subset-feasible(Y_X) = true if Y_X is map-to-one and Subset-feasible(Z_Y). Otherwise, Subset-feasible(Y_X) = false. $\square$

While the map-to-one and subset-feasible properties allow a *subset* of the input sequence to be filtered, the *suffix-safe* property allows a *prefix* of the input sequence to be filtered. The suffix-safe property holds when any prefix of the output can be produced by some prefix of the input sequence. Moreover, any suffix of the output can be produced from some suffix of the input sequence. For instance, the input parameters of transforms that perform selection, projection, union, and aggregation over sorted input are suffix-safe.

Property 4.2 (suffix-safe(Y_X)) Given $\mathcal{T} = [t_1..t_n]$, let First($\mathcal{T}$) = t_1, Last($\mathcal{T}$) = t_n, and $t_i \leq_{\mathcal{T}} t_j$ if t_i is before t_j in $\mathcal{T}$ or $i = j$. Given transform Y with input parameter Y_X, Y_X is *suffix-safe* if $\forall \mathcal{Y}_X, \forall \mathcal{Y}_O, \forall y_j, y_{j+1} \in \mathcal{Y}_O$: ($Y(...\mathcal{Y}_X...) = \mathcal{Y}_O$) $\Rightarrow$ (Last(Contributors($\mathcal{Y}_X$, y_j)) $\leq_{\mathcal{Y}_X}$ First(Contributors($\mathcal{Y}_X$, y_{j+1}))). $\square$

Figure 6 illustrates conceptually how suffix-safe can be used. If only $[y_3]$ of $\mathcal{Y}_O$ in Figure 6 needs to be produced, processing the suffix $[x_5]$ of $\mathcal{Y}_X$ will produce $[y_3]$. Conversely, if $[y_1y_2]$ does not need to be produced, the prefix $[x_1x_2x_3x_4]$ can be filtered from Y_X at resumption time. Notice that when the suffix-safe property is used, inconsequential input tuples like x_3 can be filtered. Filtering such tuples is not possible using the map-to-one property. 78% of Sagent's transforms' input parameters are suffix-safe.

Prefix-feasible(Y_X) is a transitive property that states that it is feasible to filter some prefix of the Y_X input sequence. This property is true if all of the input parameters from Y_X to the warehouse are suffix-safe. (The reasoning is similar to that for Subset-feasible(Y_X) and map-to-one.)

Definition 4.3 (Prefix-feasible(Y_X)) Given transform Y with input parameter Y_X, Prefix-feasible(Y_X) = true if Y is the warehouse inserter. Otherwise, Prefix-feasible(Y_X) = true if Y_X is suffix-safe and Prefix-feasible(Z_Y). Otherwise, Prefix-feasible(Y_X) = false. □

Filtering a prefix of the Y_X input sequence is possible only if Y_X receives the same sequence during load resumption as it did during normal operation. For instance, in Figure 6, even if Prefix-feasible(Y_X) holds, we cannot filter out any prefix of the Y_X input if the input sequence is $[x_5 x_4 x_3 x_2 x_1]$ during resumption. We now define some properties that guarantee that an input parameter Y_X receives the same sequence at resumption time.

We say that a transform Y is *in-det-out* if Y produces the same output sequence $\mathcal{Y}_O$ whenever it processes the same input sequences. All of Sagent's transforms are *in-det-out*.

Property 4.3 (in-det-out(Y)) Transform Y is *in-det-out* if Y produces the same output sequence whenever it processes the same input sequences. □

The in-det-out property guarantees that if a transform Y and all of the transforms preceding Y are in-det-out, and the data extractors produce the same sequences at resumption time, then Y will produce the same sequence, too. Hence, Z_Y receives the same sequence.

The requirement that all of the preceding transforms are in-det-out can be relaxed if some of the input parameters are *set-to-seq*. That is, if the order of the tuples in Y_X does not affect the order of the output tuples in Y_O, then Y_X is set-to-seq. For example, the same output sequence is produced by a sorting transform as long it processes the same set of input tuples.

Property 4.4 (set-to-seq(Y_X)) Given transform Y with input parameter Y_X, Y_X is *set-to-seq* if Y is in-det-out and $\forall \mathcal{Y}_X, \mathcal{Y}'_X$: ($\mathcal{Y}_X$ and $\mathcal{Y}'_X$ have the same set of tuples and all other input parameters of Y receive the same sequence) $\Rightarrow$ $Y(...\mathcal{Y}_X...) = Y(...\mathcal{Y}'_X...)$. □

Same-seq(Y_X) is a transitive property based on in-det-out and set-to-seq that holds if Y_X is guaranteed to receive the same sequence at resumption time. A weaker guarantee that sometimes allows for prefix filtering is that Y_X receives a suffix of the normal operation input $\mathcal{Y}_X$. We do not develop this weaker guarantee here.

Definition 4.4 (Same-seq(Y_X)) If X is an extractor then Same-seq(Y_X) = true if X uses the GetAllInorder re-extraction procedure. Otherwise, Same-seq(Y_X) = true if X is in-det-out and $\forall X_V$: Same-seq(X_V) or (X_V is set-to-seq and Same-set(V)). Otherwise, Same-seq(Y_X) = false. □

4.2 Identifying Contributors

To determine which $\mathcal{Y}_X$ tuples contribute to a warehouse tuple w_k, we are only provided with the value of w_k after the failure. Since transforms are black boxes, the only way to identify the contributors to w_k is to match the attributes that the $\mathcal{Y}_X$ tuples and w_k have in common. (If a transform

changes an attribute value, e.g., reorders its bytes, we assume that it also changes the attribute name.)

We now define properties that, when satisfied, guarantee that we can identify exactly the $\mathcal{Y}_X$ contributors to w_k by matching certain *identifying attributes*, denoted IdAttrs(Y_X). In practice, some inconsequential $\mathcal{Y}_X$ input tuples may also match w_k on IdAttrs(Y_X). However, these tuples can be safely filtered since they do not contribute to the output. If the contributors cannot be identified, IdAttrs(Y_X) is set to [ ].

We define the *no-hidden-contributor* property to hold for Y_X if all of the $\mathcal{Y}_X$ tuples that contribute to some output tuple y_j match y_j on Attrs(Y_X) $\cap$ Attrs(Y_O). Selection, projection, aggregation, and union transforms have input parameters with no hidden contributors, as do all of Sagent's input parameters.

Property 4.5 (no-hidden-contributor(Y_X)) Given transform Y with input parameter Y_X, if $\forall \mathcal{Y}_X, \forall \mathcal{Y}_O, \forall y_j \in \mathcal{Y}_O$, $\forall x_i \in$ Contributors($\mathcal{Y}_X, y_j$), $\forall a \in$ (Attrs(Y_X) $\cap$ Attrs(Y_O)): $(Y(...\mathcal{Y}_X...) = \mathcal{Y}_O) \Rightarrow (x_i.a = y_j.a)$ then *no-hidden-contributors*(Y_X) = true. □

If Y_X has no hidden contributors, we can identify a set of input tuples that contains all of the contributors to an output tuple y_j. This set is called the *potential contributors* of y_j. Shortly, we will use keys and other properties to verify that the set of potential contributors of y_j contains only tuples that do contribute to y_j. We now illustrate how the potential contributors are found.

Example 4.1 In the tree in Figure 4, the labels above the edges give the attributes of the input tuples, e.g., Attrs(Y_X) = $[cd]$. If Y_X has no hidden contributors, then all of the $\mathcal{Y}_X$ contributors to warehouse tuple w_k, denoted S_k, match w_k on $[cd]$ (i.e., Attrs(Y_X) $\cap$ Attrs(Y_O)). If X_E has no hidden contributors, then the $\mathcal{X}_E$ contributors to $x_i \in S_k$ match x_i on $[c]$ (i.e., Attrs(X_E) $\cap$ Attrs(X_O)). Therefore, the potential contributors of w_k in $\mathcal{X}_E$ are exactly the ones that match w_k on $[c]$. □

We call attributes that identify the $\mathcal{Y}_X$ potential contributors the *candidate identifying attributes* (CandAttrs) of Y_X.

Definition 4.5 (CandAttrs(Y_X)) There are three possibilities for CandAttrs(Y_X): (1) If Y is the warehouse inserter, CandAttrs(Y_X) = Attrs(Y_X). (2) If Y_X has hidden contributors, CandAttrs(Y_X) = [ ]. (3) Otherwise, CandAttrs(Y_X) = CandAttrs(Z_Y) $\cap$ Attrs(Y_X). □

In summary, CandAttrs(Y_X) is the set of attributes that are present throughout the path from Y_X to the warehouse, unless some input parameters has hidden contributors.

CandAttrs(Y_X) may identify both tuples that do and do not contribute to w_k. To isolate the actual contributors of w_k, we need to use key attributes and the *no-spurious-output* property. The no-spurious-output property holds for transform Y if each output tuple y_j has at least one contributor from each input parameter Y_X. While this property holds for many transforms, including all but one of Sagent's, union transforms do not satisfy it.

Property 4.6 (no-spurious-output(Y)) A transform Y produces *no spurious output* if $\forall$ input parameters Y_X, $\forall \mathcal{Y}_X$, $\forall \mathcal{Y}_O$, $\forall y_j \in \mathcal{Y}_O$: $Y(...\mathcal{Y}_X...) = \mathcal{Y}_O \Rightarrow$ Contributors($\mathcal{Y}_X$, $y_j) \neq [\,]$. □

We now illustrate how key attributes, candidate attributes, and the no-spurious-output property combine to determine the identifying attributes (IdAttrs).

Example 4.2 In Figure 4, CandAttrs(X_E) = [c] if X_E, Y_X, and W_Y have no hidden contributors. There are three possibilities for IdAttrs(X_E): (1) IdAttrs(X_E) = KeyAttrs(X_E) if KeyAttrs(X_E) $\subseteq$ CandAttrs(X_E) and both X and Y satisfy the no-spurious-output property. (2) IdAttrs(X_E) = KeyAttrs(W_Y) if KeyAttrs(W_Y) $\subseteq$ CandAttrs(X_E). (3) IdAttrs(X_E) = IdAttrs(Y_X) if IdAttrs(Y_X) $\subseteq$ CandAttrs(X_E).

To illustrate (1), suppose KeyAttrs(X_E) is [c]. If $w_k.c = 1$, any $\mathcal{X}_E$ tuple that contributes to w_k must have $c = 1$ since CandAttrs(X_E) = [c]. Since neither X nor Y has spurious output tuples, there is at least one $\mathcal{X}_E$ tuple that contributes to w_k. c is the key for X_E, so the one $\mathcal{X}_E$ tuple with $c = 1$ must be the contributor.

To illustrate (2), suppose KeyAttrs(W_Y) = [c]. If $w_k.c = 1$, any $\mathcal{X}_E$ tuple that contributes to w_k must have $c = 1$ since CandAttrs(X_E) = [c]. Since c is the key of W_Y, all $\mathcal{X}_E$ tuples with $c = 1$ must contribute to either w_k or to no warehouse tuples.

To illustrate (3), suppose IdAttrs(Y_X) = [c]. Then given a warehouse tuple w_k with $w_k.c = 1$, we can identify the $\mathcal{Y}_X$ contributors to w_k, denoted S_k, by matching their c attribute with 1. Since X_E has no hidden contributors (because CandAttrs(X_E) $\neq [\,]$), a $\mathcal{X}_E$ tuple with $c = 1$ must contribute to a tuple $x_j \in S_k$ or to no tuple in $\mathcal{Y}_X$. Hence, we can identify exactly the $\mathcal{X}_E$ contributors to w_k by matching their c attribute values.

In summary, the key attributes of X_E, Y_X (or any other input parameter in the path from X_E to W_Y), or W_Y can serve as IdAttrs(X_E). These key attributes must be a subset of CandAttrs(X_E) to ensure that matching can be performed between the warehouse tuples and the $\mathcal{X}_E$ tuples. □

The example above provides the intuition for our definition of IdAttrs.

Definition 4.6 (**IdAttrs(Y_X)**) Let P be the the path from Y_X to the warehouse. There are three possibilities for IdAttrs(Y_X). (1) If (KeyAttrs(Y_X) $\subseteq$ CandAttrs(Y_X) and $\forall Z_V \in P$: Z_V has no spurious output tuples), then IdAttrs(Y_X) = KeyAttrs(Y_X). (2) Let $Z_V \in P$ but $Z_V \neq Y_X$. If IdAttrs(Z_V) $\neq [\,]$ and IdAttrs(Z_V) $\subseteq$ CandAttrs(Y_X), then IdAttrs(Y_X) = IdAttrs(Z_V). (3) Otherwise IdAttrs(Y_X) = [\,]. □

Case (1) in Definition 4.6 uses the key attributes of Y_X as IdAttrs(Y_X). Case (2) checks if the IdAttrs of each input parameter can be used as IdAttrs(Y_X). In [7], we discuss heuristics for choosing the input parameter in P whose identifying attribute is used for IdAttrs(Y_X).

4.3 The Trades Example Revisited

In Table 1, we provide SQL definitions for the transform functions in our main example. These definitions are not

available to *DR*, and in general, cannot be written in SQL. Here, however, we use SQL to help illustrate the properties satisfied by the input parameters and transforms. Both transforms in Table 1 are in-det-out.

Transform	Function computed by transform
DT	`select *` `from` DT_{TRD} `where` $date \geq$ 12/1/98 `and` $date \leq$ 12/31/98

AV	`select` $AV_{PTE}.company$, $AV_{PTE}.pe$,
	   `avg`($AV_{DT}.volume$) `as` $avgvol$
	`from` AV_{PTE}, AV_{DT}
	`where` $AV_{PTE}.company = AV_{DT}.company$
	   `and` $AV_{PTE}.pe \leq 4$
	`group by` $AV_{PTE}.company$, $AV_{PTE}.pe$

Table 1: Properties and functions of transforms.

The first four columns of Table 2 show the attributes, keys, and properties declared for each input parameter. We now explain why the properties hold. DT reads each tuple in DT_{TRD} and only outputs the tuple if it has a date in December 1998. Therefore, DT_{TRD} is suffix-safe, since DT outputs tuples in the input tuple order. It is map-to-one because each input tuple contributes to zero or one output tuple. It is not set-to-seq, since a different order of input tuples will produce a different order of output tuples.

Transform AV reads each tuple in AV_{PTE} and, if its *pe* attribute is ≤ 4, it finds all of the trade tuples for the same company in AV_{DT}, which are probably not in order by company. AV then groups the AV_{DT} tuples and computes the average trade volume for each company. Then it processes the next tuple in AV_{PTE}. AV_{PTE} is map-to-one since each tuple contributes to zero or one output tuple. the same reason it is suffix-safe: AV processes tuples from AV_{PTE} in order. AV_{DT} is map-to-one since each trade tuple contributes to the average volume tuple of only one company. However, AV_{DT} is not suffix-safe, e.g., the trade tuple needed to join with the first tuple in AV_{PTE} may be the last tuple in AV_{DT}. Similarly, it is set-to-seq because the order of trades tuples is not relevant to AV. Finally, since the warehouse inserter stores its input tuples in order, W_{AV} is map-to-one and suffix-safe but not set-to-seq.

The last two columns of Table 2 show the identifying attributes and the transitive properties. None of the input parameters has hidden contributors. The identifying attribute of W_{AV}, AV_{DT}, DT_{TRD} and AV_{PTE} is [*company*] because it is the key of W_{AV}. The transitive properties (e.g., Subset-feasible) are computed (by *DR*) using Definitions 4.2 and 4.3. Note that Same-seq and Same-set are not computed since the re-extraction procedures have not been determined yet.

5 The *DR* Resumption Algorithm

We now present the *DR* resumption algorithm, which uses the properties developed in Section 4. *DR* is actually two algorithms, *Design* and *Resume*, hence the name. After a component tree G is designed, *Design* constructs a

Input Y_X	Attrs(Y_X)	KeyAttrs(Y_X)	Y_X Properties	IdAttrs(Y_X)	Y_X Transitive Properties
DT_{TRD}	[date,company,volume]	[date,company]	map-to-one suffix-safe	[company]	Subset-feasible
AV_{PTE}	[company,pe]	[company]	map-to-one suffix-safe	[company]	Subset-feasible, Prefix-feasible
AV_{DT}	[date,company,volume]	[date,company]	map-to-one set-to-seq	[company]	Subset-feasible
W_{AV}	[company,pe,avgvol]	[company]	map-to-one suffix-safe	[company]	Subset-feasible, Prefix-feasible

Table 2: Declared and inferred properties of input parameters.

component tree G' that *Resume* uses to resume any failed warehouse load on G. The component tree G' is the same as G except: (1) re-extraction procedures are assigned to the extractors in G'; and (2) filters are assigned to some of the input parameters in G'.

Design constructs G' using only the declared attributes, keys, and properties of G. When a warehouse load that uses G fails, *Resume* initializes the filters and re-extraction procedures in G' based on the tuples that were stored in the warehouse. *Resume* then uses G' to resume the warehouse load. Since neither *Design* nor *Resume* runs during normal operation, *DR* does not incur any normal operation overhead!

5.1 Example using *DR*

We first illustrate *DR* on our running example. *Design* first computes the Subset-feasible and Prefix-feasible transitive properties and the IdAttrs of each input parameter, as shown in Figure 7.

Design then constructs G'. First, it assigns re-extraction procedures to the extractors based on their computed properties and identifying attributes. Since IdAttrs(AV_{PTE}) = [company], company can identify contributor source PE tuples. Since both Prefix-feasible(AV_{PTE}) and Subset-feasible(AV_{PTE}) hold, *Design* can assign either GetSuffix or GetSubset to PTE to avoid re-extracting all the PE tuples. Suppose PTE supports neither GetSuffix nor GetSubset. *Design* assigned GetAllInorder to PTE instead.

Design can assign GetSubset to TRD since Subset-feasible(DT_{TRD}) holds and IdAttrs(DT_{TRD}) = [company]. However, suppose TRD only supports GetAll, so it is assigned instead.

For each input parameter, *Design* then chooses whether to discard a prefix of the input ("prefix filter"), or to discard a subset of the input ("subset filter"). Since discarding a prefix requires the Same-seq property, *Design* computes the Same-seq property as it assigns filters to each input parameter, as follows.

DT_{TRD}: Same-seq(DT_{TRD}) does not hold because TRD is assigned GetAll, so it is not possible to filter a prefix of the DT_{TRD} input sequence. Since DT_{TRD} is Subset-feasible and IdAttrs(DT_{TRD}) = [company], it is possible to assign a subset filter, denoted DT_{TRD}^f, to remove a subset of the DT_{TRD} input sequence. When a failed load is resumed,

DT_{TRD}^f removes the subset of tuples in DT_{TRD} whose *company* attribute value matches some warehouse tuple.

AV_{PTE}: Same-seq(AV_{PTE}) holds because PTE is assigned GetAllInorder. AV_{PTE} is also Prefix-feasible. Therefore, a prefix filter AV_{PTE}^f is assigned to AV_{PTE}. When a failed load is resumed, AV_{PTE}^f removes the prefix of the AV_{PTE} input sequence that ends with the tuple whose *company* attribute matches the last warehouse tuple.

AV_{DT}: AV_{DT} is Subset-feasible and IdAttrs(AV_{DT}) = [company], so a subset filter can also be assigned to AV_{DT}. It is not assigned, however, since *Design* determines that this filter is redundant with the DT_{TRD}^f filter.

Figure 8 shows G'. G' is constructed in two "passes" over G: a backward pass to compute IdAttrs, Prefix-feasible, and Subset-feasible, and a forward pass to compute Same-seq and assign filters. Hence, the time to construct G' is negligible compared to the time to design and debug G, which is on the order of weeks or months [10]. Algorithm *Design* is done and G' is set aside.

Now suppose that a load using G fails, and the tuple sequence that made it into the warehouse is $\mathcal{C} = [\langle AAA, 3, 12500 \rangle, \langle INTC, 2, 98000 \rangle, \langle MSN, 4, 15000 \rangle]$, where the three attributes are *company*, *pe*, and *avgvol*, respectively. Based on $\mathcal{C}$, *Resume* instantiates the filters and procedures (i.e., GetSuffix, GetSubset) of G' that are sensitive to $\mathcal{C}$.

Subset filter DT_{TRD}^f is instantiated to remove all DT_{TRD} tuples whose company is AAA, $INTC$ or MSN. Prefix filter AV_{PTE}^f is instantiated to remove the prefix of its AV_{PTE} input that ends with the tuple whose *company* attribute is MSN. Then the load is resumed by calling the re-extraction procedures of G'. Because of the filters, the input tuples that contribute to the tuples in $\mathcal{C}$ are filtered and are not processed again by DT, AV and W.

In summary, *DR* avoids re-processing many of the input tuples using filters. Also, if the extractors PTE and TRD had supported GetSubset or GetSuffix, *DR* could have even avoided re-extracting tuples from the sources.

5.2 Filters

In the example, we mentioned subset filters and prefix filters. There are two types of subset filters and two types of prefix filters that may be assigned to Y_X. In each case, the filter

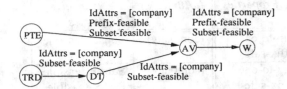

Figure 7: IdAttrs and transitive properties of G

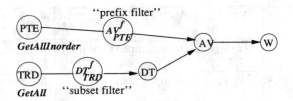

Figure 8: G' with procedures and filters assigned

receives X's output sequence as input, and the filter sends its output to Y as the Y_X input sequence.

Clean-Prefix Filter: The clean-prefix filter $CP[s, A]$ is instantiated with a tuple s and a set of attributes A. CP discards tuples from its input sequence until it finds a tuple t that matches s on A. CP discards t, and continues discarding until an input tuple t' does *not* match s on A. All tuples starting with t' are output by CP. We use CP on Y_X when Y_X is Subset-feasible, Prefix-feasible, and Same-seq, and IdAttrs(Y_X) is not empty. In this case, all input tuples up to and including the contributors of the last $\mathcal{C}$ tuple, denoted Last($\mathcal{C}$), can be safely filtered. So CP is instantiated as $CP[\text{Last}(\mathcal{C}), \text{IdAttrs}(Y_X)]$, where $\mathcal{C}$ is the tuple sequence in the warehouse after the crash. We call CP a clean filter because no $\mathcal{C}$ contributors emerge from it.

Dirty-Prefix Filter: The dirty-prefix filter $DP[s, A]$ is a slight modification to CP that begins its output sequence with t instead of t'. We use DP on Y_X when Y_X is Prefix-feasible and Same-seq, but not Subset-feasible. DP is instantiated as $DP[\text{Last}(\mathcal{C}), \text{IdAttrs}(Y_X)]$.

Clean-Subset Filter: The clean-subset filter $CS[\mathcal{S}, A]$, is instantiated with a tuple sequence $\mathcal{S}$ and a set of attributes A. For each tuple t in its input sequence $\mathcal{I}$, if t matches any $\mathcal{S}$ tuple on the A attributes, then t is discarded. Otherwise, t is output. In other words, CS performs an anti-semijoin between $\mathcal{I}$ and $\mathcal{S}$ ($\mathcal{I} \bar{\ltimes}_A \mathcal{S}$). We use CS on Y_X when Y_X is Subset-feasible and IdAttrs(Y_X) is not empty. CS is instantiated as $CS[\mathcal{C}, \text{IdAttrs}(Y_X)]$.

Dirty-Subset Filter: The dirty-subset filter $DS[\mathcal{C}, A]$, is a slight modification to CS that applies when Y_X is Prefix-feasible but not Same-seq. Unlike CS, DS removes a suffix $\mathcal{C}_s$ of $\mathcal{C}$ before performing the anti-semijoin. $\mathcal{C}_s$ contains the tuples that share Y_X contributors with Last($\mathcal{C}$) and can be obtained by matching $\mathcal{C}$ tuples with the Last($\mathcal{C}$) tuple on IdAttrs(Y_X). DS then acts like the clean-subset filter $CS[\mathcal{C} - \mathcal{C}_s, \text{IdAttrs}(Y_X)]$.

In summary, the properties that hold for an input parameter Y_X determine the types of filters that can be assigned to Y_X. When more than one filter type can be assigned, we assign the filter that removes the most input tuples. When filter type f removes more tuples than g, we say $f \succ g$. The relationships among the filter types are as follows: $CP \succ DP \succ DS$, $CP \succ CS \succ DS$.

Hence, we try to assign the clean-prefix filter first, and the dirty-subset filter last. In DR, we assign the dirty-prefix filter before the clean-subset filter for two reasons. First, it is much cheaper to match each input tuple to a single filter tuple s than to a sequence of tuple filters $\mathcal{S}$. Second, the

prefix filters can remove tuples that do not contribute to any warehouse tuple, simply because they precede a contributing tuple. The subset filters can only remove contributors. The second advantage is especially apparent in our experimental results in Section 6.

The procedure *AssignFilter* is shown in Figure 9. Observe that *AssignFilter* assigns a filter to Y_X whenever possible. *Design* uses a subsequent procedure to remove redundant filters.

Algorithm 5.1 *AssignFilter*
Input: Component trees G, G', input parameter Y_X
Output: Input parameter Y_X in G' is assigned a filter whenever possible
 If (Prefix-feasible(Y_X) and Subset-feasible(Y_X) and Same-seq(Y_X) and IdAttrs(Y_X) $\neq$ [ ])
  Insert $Y_X^f = CP[\text{Last}(\mathcal{C}), \text{IdAttrs}(Y_X)]$ between Y and X (in G')
 Else If (Prefix-feasible(Y_X) and Same-seq(Y_X) and IdAttrs(Y_X) $\neq$ [ ])
  Insert $Y_X^f = DP[\text{Last}(\mathcal{C}), \text{IdAttrs}(Y_X)]$ between Y and X
 Else if (Subset-feasible(Y_X) and IdAttrs(Y_X) $\neq$ [ ])
  Insert $Y_X^f = CS[\mathcal{C}, \text{IdAttrs}(Y_X)]$ between Y and X
 Else if (Prefix-feasible(Y_X) and IdAttrs(Y_X) $\neq$ [ ])
  Insert $Y_X^f = DS[\mathcal{C}, \text{IdAttrs}(Y_X)]$ between Y and X

Figure 9: AssignFilter algorithm

5.3 Re-extraction Procedures

The re-extraction procedures are now defined in terms of the filters.

Definition 5.1 (Re-extraction procedures)
 GetAllInorder() = $\mathcal{E}_O$, the output of E during normal operation.
 GetAll() = $\mathcal{T}$: $\mathcal{T}$ and $\mathcal{E}_O$ have the same set of tuples.
 GetSuffix(s,A) = $\mathcal{T}$: $CP[s,A] = \mathcal{T}$.
 GetDirtySuffix(s,A) = $\mathcal{T}$: $DP[s, A] = \mathcal{T}$.
 GetSubset($\mathcal{S}$,A) = $\mathcal{T}$: $CS[\mathcal{S}, A] = \mathcal{T}$.
 GetDirtySubset($\mathcal{S}$,A) = $\mathcal{T}$: $DS[\mathcal{S}, A] = \mathcal{T}$. □

The procedure *AssignReextraction*, which is shown in [7], is similar to *AssignFilter*. It tries to push the filters into the re-extraction. For example, the same properties that allow CP to be assigned to $\mathcal{E}_O$ also allow GetSuffix to be assigned to E instead.

Algorithm 5.2 *Design*
Input: Component tree G
Output: Component tree G'
    1. Copy G to G'
    2. Compute IdAttrs(Y_X), Subset-feasible(Y_X),
       Prefix-feasible(Y_X) for each input
       parameter Y_X in reverse topological order.
    3. For each extractor E
       AssignReextraction(G,G',E)
    4. For each input parameter Y_X in topological order
       Compute Same-seq(Y_X)
       AssignFilter(G,G',Y_X)
       If Y_X is assigned a filter,
          Set Same-seq(Y_X) to false.
    5. *RemoveRedundantFilters*(G, G')
    6. Save G' persistently and return G'

Algorithm 5.3 *Resume*
Input: Component tree G'
Side Effect: Resumes failed warehouse load
    Let $\mathcal{C}$ be the tuples in the warehouse
    1. Instantiate each re-extraction procedure in G'
       and each filter in G' with actual value of $\mathcal{C}$
    2. For each extractor E in G'
       Invoke re-extraction procedure assigned to E

Figure 10: *DR* algorithm

Transforms:
100% (19/19) are in-det-out.
95% (18/19) have no spurious output.
Input Parameters:
91% (21/23) are map-to-one.
78% (18/23) are suffix-safe.
17% (4/23) are set-to-seq (i.e., perform sorting).
100% (23/23) have no hidden contributors.

Figure 11: Properties of Sagent transforms and input parameters

5.4 The *Design* and *Resume* Algorithms

Figure 10 shows algorithms *Design* and *Resume* of *DR*. *Design* constructs G' by processing the component tree G in two passes. In reverse topological order, *Design* computes IdAttrs, Prefix-feasible and Subset-feasible. It then uses *AssignReextraction* to assign procedures to the extractors. Finally, in topological order, it computes Same-seq and uses *AssignFilters* to assign filters to the input parameters. In [7], we show how *Design* removes redundant filters. After a failure, *Resume* simply instantiates the re-extraction procedures and filters in G' with the actual value of the warehouse tuple sequence $\mathcal{C}$. The warehouse load is then resumed by invoking the re-extraction procedures.

The worst-case complexity of *DR* is $O(n^2 \cdot |\mathcal{C}| + n^3)$, assuming that n^2 filters are assigned. However, in practice, few filters are assigned by *DR*, but those filters lead to significant performance improvements. Furthermore, our experiments show that the overhead in instantiating the filters is reasonable.

6 Experiments

In this section, we compare *DR* to other recovery algorithms. We performed experiments using Sagent's Data Mart 3.0. The software ran on a Dell XPS D300 with a Pentium II 300 MHz processor and 64 MB of RAM. More details of the experiments are in [7].

We first examined the extractors and transforms offered by Sagent. All of the extractors support GetAll and GetAllInorder, but only the "SQL" extractor support GetSuffix, GetDirtySuffix, GetSubset, and GetDirtySubset. The properties of the 19 basic Sagent transforms (selection, projection, union, aggregation, join, etc.) are summarized in Figure 11, and show that the properties we have defined are fairly common in practice.

We then constructed two different component trees. The first tree loads the TPC-D fact table *Lineitem*. Fact tables typically extract transactional data from a single table, massage it, in this case with four transforms, and store it in the warehouse. The second tree loads the materialized view corresponding to TPC-D query Q3, which uses five transforms to join three source tables and perform a GROUP BY and a SUM of revenue estimates.

6.1 *DR* versus no-overhead algorithms

In the first set of experiments, we compared *DR* to the algorithms that impose no normal operation overhead (i.e., the lower right quadrant of Figure 2). We compared three variants of *DR* to *Redo* and *Inf*. *Inf* is the algorithm used by Informatica [6], and uses only one filter just before the inserter. DR_{src} pushes filtering to the extractors. DR_{pre} uses a prefix filter right after each extractor, while DR_{sub} uses a subset filters there. Normally, *DR* would produce DR_{src}.

Figure 12 plots resumption time for the fact table load against the number of tuples already loaded in the warehouse, which we varied from 0–95%. As expected, *DR* performs better than *Redo* when 20% (or more) of the tuples are in the warehouse. For instance, when the warehouse is 95% loaded, DR_{src} completes a resumed load 10 times faster than *Redo*, and and DR_{sub} is 2.3 times faster. *DR* is also faster than *Inf*. On the other hand, when the warehouse is empty at the time of failure, *DR* performs 10–12% worse than *Redo* because of the filter overhead. Among the three *DR* variants, DR_{src} performs the best because it filters the tuples the earliest. DR_{sub} performs worse than DR_{pre} because of the expensive anti-semijoin operation employed by DR_{sub}'s filters.

Figure 13 shows similar results for the view load. However, DR_{sub} and *Inf* perform worse than *Redo* regardless of how many tuples are loaded: the view query is very selective, and many of the source tuples extracted do not contribute to any warehouse tuple. Since subset filters can only remove tuples that contribute to a warehouse tuple, the filters used by

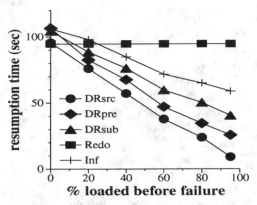

Figure 12: Fact table load resumption

# Savepoints	Load Time (s)	% Increase
0	94.7	0%
1	166.4	75.7%
2	245.9	159.7%
3	314.0	231.6%

Table 3: Fact table savepoint overhead

# Batches	Load Time (s)	% Increase
1	94.7	0%
2	97.6	3.1%
3	104.8	7.4%
4	107.0	13.0%
5	113.0	19.3%
10	150.6	59.0%

Table 4: Fact table batching overhead

DR_{sub} and *Inf* do not remove enough tuples to compensate for the cost of their filters.

6.2 *DR* versus Savepoints and Batching

In the second set of experiments, we compared *DR* to "staging" (with savepoints) and "batching," two algorithms in the upper left quadrant of Figure 2.

Table 3 compares the normal operation overhead of loading the fact table as savepoints are added. Without savepoints, the fact table loads in 94.7 seconds. Each savepoint slows down the load by 70-80%! In contrast, *DR* has no overhead.

We also introduced up to three savepoints to the view load. However, even with three savepoints, the load is only 7% slower because the "*Join*" transforms are very selective and occur before the first savepoint. Hence, few tuples are recorded in the savepoints.

Table 4 shows the normal operation overhead of batching. As the load is divided into more batches, pipelining decreases and there is more overhead for starting batches, so the total load time increases.

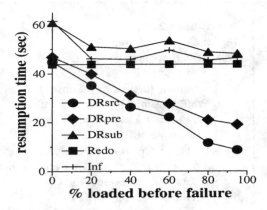

Figure 13: View table load resumption

We then measured the resumption times of *DR*, using DR_{src}, versus *Save*, which used two savepoints, and *Batch*, which used three batches. We loaded the warehouse and stopped the load after t_{fail} seconds. We then resumed the load and recorded the resumption time.

Figures 14 and 15 plot the resumption times of *DR*, *Save*, and *Batch* as t_{fail} increases. The graphs show that *Save*'s resumption time improves in discrete steps that occur as each savepoint completes. For the fact table load, *DR* is more efficient than *Save* because the warehouse table is populated early in the load, and *DR* can use the warehouse tuples to make resumption efficient. *DR*'s resumption time for the view load is relatively slower because the first output tuples are not produced until the load is nearly complete. Unfortunately, neither *Save* nor *DR* performs well. The two savepoints *Save* uses essentially partition the view tree into three "sub-trees." Although *Save* does not use incomplete savepoints to improve resumption, *DR* can treat an incomplete savepoint and the "sub-tree" that produced it as a warehouse table and a component tree. The performance of this hybrid algorithm, denoted *Hybrid*, is better than either *Save* or *DR*.

Batch's resumption time also improves in discrete steps, as each batch completes. *DR* is surprisingly more efficient than *Batch* on the fact table load, given that *DR* imposes no normal operation overhead. However, *DR* can use any completed subset of the load to reduce resumption time. On the view load, *Batch* resumes faster than *DR*: *Batch*'s resumption speed is its payback for "manual" modification of the workflow and much slower normal operation loads.

6.3 Discussion

We can draw a number of conclusions from the previous experiments. First, *DR* resumes a failed load much more efficiently than *Redo* and *Inf*. *DR* is also flexible in that the more properties exist, the more choices *DR* has and the better *DR* performs.

Second, there is a need for a "cost-based" analysis of when to use *DR*. For instance, if the warehouse table is empty, *Redo* is better than both *DR* and *Inf*. However, as more tuples are loaded, using *DR* becomes more beneficial. A "cost-based" analysis can also determine when to use subset

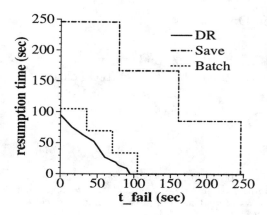

Figure 14: Savepoints and Batching vs DR (Fact table)

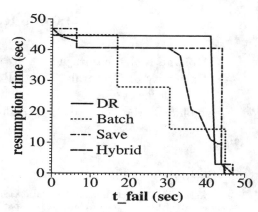

Figure 15: Savepoints and Batching vs DR (View table)

filters, which may not remove enough tuples to justify their cost (e.g., the cost of performing an anti-semijoin).

Third, savepoints (or snapshots) result in significant normal operation overhead. However, if certain transforms of a component tree are very selective (i.e., few output tuples compared to input tuples), the overhead of savepoints may be tolerable. When a batching algorithm is used, a careful selection of the number of input batches is required: More batches can result in significant normal operation overhead. On the other hand, fewer batches result in longer resumption times.

7 Conclusions

We developed a resumption algorithm *DR* that performs most of its analysis during "design time," and imposes no overhead during normal operation. The *Design* portion of *DR* only needs to be invoked once, when the warehouse load component tree is designed, no matter how many times the *Resume* portion is called to resume a load failure. *DR* is novel because it uses only properties that describe how complex transforms process their input at a high level (e.g., are the tuples processed in order?). These properties can be deduced easily from the transform specifications, and some of them (e.g., keys, ordering) are already declared in current warehouse load packages. By performing experiments under various TPC-D scenarios using Sagent's load facility, we showed that *DR* leads to very efficient resumption.

Although we have developed *DR* to resume warehouse loads, *DR* is useful for many applications. In particular, if an application performs complex and distributed processing, *DR* is a prime recovery algorithm candidate when minimal normal operation overhead is required. Since previous algorithms either require heavy overhead during normal operation, or incur high recovery cost, *DR* fills the need for an efficient lightweight recovery algorithm.

References

[1] P. A. Bernstein, M. Hsu, and B. Mann. Implementing Recoverable Requests Using Queues. In *SIGMOD*, pp. 112–122, 1990.

[2] P. A. Bernstein and E. Newcomer. *Principles of Transaction Processing*. Morgan-Kaufman, 1997.

[3] F. Carino. High-performance, parallel warehouse servers and large-scale applications, Oct. 1997. Talk about Teradata given in Stanford Database Seminar.

[4] TPC Committee. Transaction Processing Council. Available at: http://www.tpc.org/.

[5] J. Gray and A. Reuter. *Transaction Processing: Concepts and Techniques*. Morgan-Kaufman, 1993.

[6] Informatica. Powermart 4.0 overview. Available at: http://www.informatica.com/pm_tech_over.html.

[7] W. J. Labio, J. L. Wiener, H. Garcia-Molina, and V. Gorelik. Resumption algorithms. Technical report, Stanford University, 1998. Available at http://www-db.stanford.edu/pub/papers/resume.ps.

[8] C. Mohan and I. Narang. Algorithms for Creating Indexes for Very Large Tables Without Quiescing Updates. In *SIGMOD*, pp. 361–370, 1992.

[9] R. Reinsch and M. Zimowski. Method for Restarting a Long-Running, Fault-Tolerant Operation in a Transaction-Oriented Data Base System Without Burdening the System Log. U.S. Patent 4,868,744, IBM, 1989.

[10] Sagent Technologies. Personal correspondence with customers.

[11] J. L. Wiener and J. F. Naughton. OODB Bulk Loading Revisited: The Partitioned-List Approach. In *VLDB*, pp. 30–41, Zurich, Switzerland, 1995.

[12] A. Witkowski, F. Cariño, and P. Kostamaa. NCR 3700 — The Next-Generation Industrial Database Computer. In *VLDB*, pp. 230–243, 1993.

On-line Reorganization in Object Databases

Mohana K. Lakhamraju
University of California,
Berkeley CA
mohan@cs.berkeley.edu

Rajeev Rastogi,   S. Seshadri
Bell Labs, Murray Hill, NJ
rastogi@research.bell-labs.com
seshadri@research.bell-labs.com

S. Sudarshan
Indian Institute of Technology,
Bombay, India
sudarsha@cse.iitb.ernet.in

Abstract

Reorganization of objects in an object databases is an important component of several operations like compaction, clustering, and schema evolution. The high availability requirements (24×7 operation) of certain application domains requires reorganization to be performed on-line with minimal intereference to concurrently executing transactions.

In this paper, we address the problem of on-line reorganization in object databases, where a set of objects have to be migrated from one location to another. Specifically, we consider the case where objects in the database may contain physical references to other objects. Relocating an object in this case involves finding the set of objects (parents) that refer to it, and modifying the references in each parent. We propose an algorithm called the Incremental Reorganization Algorithm (IRA) that achieves the above task with minimal interference to concurrently executing transactions. The IRA algorithm holds locks on at most two distinct objects at any point of time. We have implemented IRA on Brahma, a storage manager developed at IIT Bombay, and conducted an extensive performance study. Our experiments reveal that IRA makes on-line reorganization feasible, with very little impact on the response times of concurrently executing transactions and on overall system throughput. We also describe how the IRA algorithm can handle system failures.

1   Introduction

Globalization requires that corporate information systems be available twenty four hours a day, seven days a week (24×7 operations). Very high availability of database systems is also required for mission-critical applications such as telecommunications, process monitoring systems etc. For example, telecom switches typically have down time requirements of atmost three minutes in a year. A major technical challenge for architects of such highly available systems is to devise and implement *on-line* utilties for periodic and routine maintenance of the systems [ZS98, Edi96].

In this paper, we consider the problem of on-line reorganization in object databases, in which a set of objects have to be migrated from one location to another with minimal interference to concurrently executing transactions. On-line reorganization is a fundamental component of many utility operations such as:

Compaction: Continuous allocation and deallocation of

space for variable length objects can result in fragmentation. Compaction gets rid of fragmentation by migrating objects to a different location and packing them closely [NOPH92].

Copying Garbage Collection: One approach to garbage collection is to copy all the live objects from a given region to a new region and then reclaim the given region [NOPH92, YNY94].

Clustering and Partitioning: The clustering of related objects within the same disk block or adjacent disk blocks greatly improves the performance of a transaction that accesses those set of objects within a small time frame. The partitioning of objects across several disks (also referred to as declustering) to enable concurrently accessed objects to be fetched in parallel can also enhance performance significantly. Based on changes in workload and updates to objects, new clustering and partitioning decisions are made, which require the system to migrate a set of objects from one location to another [WMK94, TN91].

Schema Evolution: Schema Evolution could cause an increase in object size. Such objects may have to be moved since they no longer fit in their current location. This requires reorganization of objects [BKKK87].

Performing the above operations in an online fashion requires that object references be maintained consistently while a set of objects are relocated from one place to another. Object references could be logical or physical and we consider the two cases in turn.

On-line reorganization is quite simple if the object references are logical. In this case, migrating an object O does not require the object references to O in other objects to be modified. Instead, it suffices to update the data structure that contains the mapping from the logical reference of an object to the physical location of the object. Thus, the objects can be migrated one at a time, with minimal interference to concurrent transactions, by locking out other concurrent transactions from the above mapping for an object while it is being migrated.

However, logical references typically entail one extra level of indirection for every access of the object. In disk resident databases, this could result in an additional I/O for every object access. In a memory resident database, this increases the access path length to an object by a factor of two, and may also increase main-memory requirements considerably. These overheads are unacceptable in a number of scenarios such as call setup in telecommunications, which require response times to be in the order of tens of microseconds [JLR+94].

On the other hand, if object references are physical, they point to the actual disk or memory address of the object. Consequently, since physical object references result in more direct access to data and shorter access path lengths, main-memory database systems like DataBlitz [JLR+94, BLR+97] and TimesTen use physical instead of logical references [1]. Physical object references, however, complicate object migration since migrating an object O requires finding the set of referencers of O, $\mathcal{R}_O$, and updating the references in each object in $\mathcal{R}_O$. To find the set $\mathcal{R}_O$, we could maintain back pointers from every object in the database. However, doing so increases storage overheads greatly, and causes lock contention in back pointer lists of "popular" objects, which are pointed to from many objects. Thus, maintaining back pointers is unacceptable in many applications.

Another alternative for finding $\mathcal{R}_O$ is to traverse the object graph, and find parents of objects that need to be migrated. Performing a consistent traversal of the object graph concurrently with ongoing transactions is a non-trivial task. The naive way of doing so is to block out all transactions and perform the traversal on a quiescent database. Since this has been the only alternative available, conventional wisdom says object migration can be very disruptive to normal processing if physical references are used. This is perhaps the most important reason for the use of logical object identifiers by some vendors.

In this paper, we address the problem of on-line reorganization using object graph traversals, in an object database where references are physical[2]. Prior work [KW93] on on-line reorganization of an object-oriented database with physical references requires an action-quiescent state and *some low level support from the hardware and the operating system*. In addition, the proposed algorithms use forwarding addresses and require use of a complicated failure recovery technique. The problem of reorganization has been studied extensively in the context of relational databases [ZS98, Edi96, ZS96a, SD92, Omi96, AON96]. Although the references in a relational database are physical, they are stored only in the index structures. Thus, discovering the set of references to a record is a much simpler task in relational databases. Research into reorganization in relational databases has mainly concentrated on minimizing the number of locks being held and the amount of I/O necessary for reorganization. The work most closely related to ours is work on on-line garbage collection [YNY94, AFG95, ARS+97]. Though not the subject of this paper, our reorganization algorithm is also capable of performing garbage collection using an approach similar to that of a copying garbage collector [NOPH92, YNY94]. Thus, our algorithm can perform both garbage collection and reorganization and yet allow references to be physical, an ability that to the best of our knowledge, no previous algorithm in the literature possesses. We explore this and other relationships to related work in detail in Section 4.6 and Section 6.

---

[1] The original motivation for this work came from the memory fragmentation problem in the Dali Object Storage Manager [BLR+97]. Dali is the research prototype for the DataBlitz main memory database system.

[2] Note that the algorithms presented are applicable whereever a set of objects have to be reorganized while being concurrently accessed, e.g. a stable heap [KW93]

1.1 Our contribution

We present a novel algorithm, the *Incremental Reorganization Algorithm* (IRA) which performs on-line reorganization with minimal interference to concurrently executing transactions. The crucial and complex part of IRA lies in how it efficiently determines the set of objects, $\mathcal{R}_O$, that reference an object O, with minimal interference to concurrent transactions. IRA uses a single fuzzy traversal (which uses only latches, and no locks) to determine an approximate $\mathcal{R}_O$ for all objects O being migrated; then for each O, one at a time, an exact $\mathcal{R}_O$ is found, locked, and the object is migrated. Thereby, very few locks are held at any time by IRA, thus minimizing interference with concurrent transactions. Moreover, The IRA is tolerant to failures in the sense that it tries to minimize the amount of wasted work.

For large databases, traversing the entire database in order to carry out a reorganization could be very expensive. IRA deals effectively with this problem by partitioning the database. IRA can be run on one partition at a time, thereby restricting traversal performed. Partitioning has been used in the past for garbage collection in object-oriented databases [YNY94, AFG95], and for reorganization of relational databases [Edi96].

The basic version of IRA requires transactions to follow *strict two-phase locking* (2PL), that is, all locks are held until the end of the transaction. This may be too restrictive in some high performance situations. We present two extensions to IRA, which improve concurrency further:

1. The first extension relaxes the strict two-phase locking requirement. Instead, transactions are only required to hold short duration locks on objects while accessing them.

2. The second extension does not require IRA to lock all objects in $\mathcal{R}_O$ simultaneously. Instead, it allows objects in $\mathcal{R}_O$ to be locked one at a time, while holding a lock on O, the object being migrated. Thus, at most two locks are held at any point in time by this extension.

We have implemented IRA and its extensions in Brahmā, a storage manager developed at IIT Bombay. We compare the performance of IRA to that of a system not running any reorganization. Our experiments demonstrate that for a wide range of workloads, the response times and throughput of the system while running IRA only degrade marginally. The maximum degradation in the average response time is around 5% while the maximum degradation in throughput is about 10%. We also compare IRA with a naive reorganization algorithm (which locks a significant portion of the database during reorganization). The average response times of transactions with the naive reorganization algorithm are significantly higher, and the throughput is correspondingly lower. More importantly, the variance in response times is several orders of magnitude higher with the naive algorithm, than with IRA. Thus, IRA is much better than the naive algorithm in ensuring that transactions are not adversely impacted by reorganization.

The rest of the paper is organized as follows: We outline our system model and assumptions in Section 2. Section 3 discusses the IRA algorithm in detail. The extensions and optimizations to IRA are discussed in Section 4. In the same section, we also discuss the failure handling and garbage collection aspects of our algorithm. We present the results of our performance evaluation in Section 5. We survey related work in Section 6 and present our conclusions and explore future directions for research in Section 7.

2   System Model

In this section, we describe the system model on which our on-line reorganization algorithm is based. The system model is very similar to the one used by Amsaleg et. al. [AFG95] and Roy et. al. [ARS+97] in their garbage collection work.

In our model, the objects in the database form a directed graph called the *object graph*. The nodes of the graph are the objects in the database, and an edge $R \rightarrow O$ exists in the graph if and only if R contains a reference to O. We assume that all references are physical. We use the term *reference* to mean the object identifier of an object, as well as to refer to an edge in the object graph, i.e., a reference from some object R to an object O. The intended usage will be clear from the context.

We shall refer to the objects R that reference an object O as the *parents* of O, and to O as a *child* of R. In our model, there exists a special object called the *persistent root*[3]. All objects in the object graph that are reachable either from the persistent root, or from an object whose reference is in the local memory of an active transaction are *live* objects; the rest of the objects in the database are not reachable (i.e, they are garbage). To traverse the entire graph, one can start at the persistent root, and follow references from one object to another.

We assume that the database is divided into units called *partitions*. We also assume that given an object identifier, we can inexpensively find the partition to which the object belongs[4]. The idea of partitioning has also been used by on-line garbage collection algorithms [YNY94, AFG95] and reorganization algorithms in relational databases [Edi96], to focus the problem on small units of the database.

The goal of partitioning is to be able to reorganize one partition at a time, and in particular, to be able to avoid traversing the entire database in order to find parents. Specifically, we wish to traverse only the objects in a partition, yet find all parents of objects that are to be migrated.

In order to do so, each partition $\mathcal{P}$ contains an *External Reference Table* (ERT), which stores all references $R \rightarrow O$ such that O belongs to $\mathcal{P}$ and R does not belong to $\mathcal{P}$. Thus, the ERT for partition $\mathcal{P}$ stores back pointers for references that come into $\mathcal{P}$ from other partitions. Objects O belonging to $\mathcal{P}$ that are noted in the ERT are called the *referenced objects of the ERT*. For simplicity, we assume that the persistent root is in a separate partition of its own, so that references from the persistent root to an object in any partition, is in the corresponding partition's ERT. We postpone for now the issue of how the ERT is maintained, and return to it in Section 3.3.

In this paper, for concreteness, we focus on the following specific reorganization problem: Given a partition $\mathcal{P}$, migrate all the objects in $\mathcal{P}$ to their specified new locations. This does not compromise the generality of our solutions; they can easily be extended if i) objects from multiple partitions have to be migrated and/or ii) only certain specific objects in the partition need to be migrated. We do not consider the problems of when to reorganize, which partition to reorganize and where the objects of the partition should be migrated. This is an orthogonal problem and the driving operation (e.g., compaction, clustering) makes these decisions.

We assume that transactions follow strict 2PL, i.e., all locks are held until the transaction commits or aborts (the algorithm is extended to relax this assumption in Section 4.1)[5]. A transaction can obtain a reference to an object only by following a sequence of references from the persistent root, unless it created the object. Once a transaction has locked an object O (in the appropriate mode), it can i) copy into its local memory any reference out of O, ii) delete a reference out of O and iii) insert a reference into O (i.e., store into O a reference to some object), copying it from the transaction's local memory. In all of the above, the transaction is not required to hold a lock on the referenced object.

For clarity of presentation we assume that objects are not created in the partition being reorganized after our reorganization algorithm starts execution[6].

We assume that the transactions follow the Write Ahead Logging Protocol **WAL**, i.e., they log the undo value before actually performing an update, but the redo value may be logged anytime before the lock on the object in question is released.

3   The Incremental Reorganization Algorithm (IRA)

In this section, we describe our *Incremental Reorganization Algorithm* (IRA), for reorganizing a partition. Before delving into the details of IRA, we outline a simple off-line algorithm for reorganizing a partition which assumes that the database is quiescent.

3.1   Reorganizing A Quiescent Database

We first consider how to reorganize a quiescent database, i.e., one on which no transactions are executing concurrently with reorganization. Reorganizing a partition $\mathcal{P}$ involves migrating each object O that belongs to $\mathcal{P}$. The basic steps in migrating an object O are i) find the parents of O, ii) move O to the new location, and iii) update the references to O in the parents of O.

In non-partitioned databases, finding the parents of an object requires a traversal of the object graph starting from the persistent root. However, in the case of partitioned databases, we do not have to traverse the entire graph; rather, we only traverse objects in the partition $\mathcal{P}$ that is being reorganized.

Traversal starts from all the objects that are referenced by objects external to the partition — these are exactly those objects referenced in the External Reference Table (ERT) of the partition. Whenever we traverse an edge from R to O, we add R to the list of parents of O. In addition to the parents found by traversing edges within the partition, we must add all parents from other partitions; these can be found in the ERT of partition $\mathcal{P}$.

---

[3]For ease of presentation, we assume there exists only one persistent root. Our algorithms can handle multiple persistent roots also.

[4]For example, the partition could be inferred from a fixed number of left most bits of the object identifier or some other hash function on the object identifier.

[5]We do not require locks to be held for transaction duration on schema level objects like index structures and collections. Updates to references, due to object migration, within these objects can be handled similar to relational databases.

[6]Our algorithms work correctly even if this assumption does not hold except it will not migrate objects created after the reorganization process starts execution. We outline how to extend our algorithm to migrate all objects created until some point of time after the reorganization process begins execution in [LRSS99]. Obviously objects created after the reorganization process completes can not be migrated.

Rather than performing a traversal of the partition once for each object, a single traversal is used to find the parents of all objects being migrated. As we perform the traversal, we construct multiple parent lists, one for each object we encounter in the course of traversal.

The assumption of the database being quiescent is important for the above algorithm, since concurrently executing transactions may update the object graph while traversal is going on. This could lead to the traversal missing some objects, or finding edges that get deleted later.

3.2   Outline of the IRA Algorithm

The above solution based on quiescing all database activity is too stringent for many applications. In contrast, the IRA algorithm allows transactions to execute on the partition all times during reorganization.

```
Incremental_Reorganization(P) {
    (Objects, Parent_Lists) =
        Find_Objects_And_Approx_Parents(P)
    For (each object O_old in the set Objects) do
        Find_Exact_Parents(O_old, Parent_Lists)
        Move_Object_And_Update_References(O_old,
            Parent_Lists)
}
```

Figure 1: Incremental Reorganization Algorithm

We now outline how the IRA algorithm is able to allow transactions to execute on the partition being reorganized. Figure 1 outlines the top level idea underlying IRA. As can be seen from Figure 1, the algorithm consists of two broad steps. The first step, implemented by the function Find_Objects_And_Approx_Parents finds the set of objects in the partition, and an approximation of the set of parents of these objects, by performing a fuzzy traversal of the partition. The objects, and the set of their corresponding parent lists are returned by the above function.

The fuzzy traversal does not obtain locks on the objects being traversed; instead, only a short term latch is obtained on the object for the duration of examining the references out of the object. The reason the traversal obtains only an approximation of the set of parents of an object is that parents of an object are constantly changing since other transactions execute concurrently. This step is explained in detail in Section 3.4.

The second step of IRA iterates over the set of objects discovered in the first step, and for each object, i) finds and locks the exact parents and then, ii) moves the object to its new location and updates references to the object. The second step is explained in detail in Section 3.5.

To help find the exact set of parents of an object, we collect all pointer inserts and deletes since the reorganization process started, in a data structure called the Temporary Reference Table (TRT). The TRT structure and its maintenance are described in Section 3.3.

3.3   Temporary Reference Table (TRT)

The *Temporary Reference Table* (TRT) of a partition P, is a transient data structure, in which the deletion and addition of a reference to an object O in P are logged. The TRT structure is similar to the TRT used in [AFG95, ARS+97].

The TRT contains tuples of the form $(O, R, tid, action)$, where R is the referencer (parent) from which a reference to object O has been deleted or added by transaction tid;

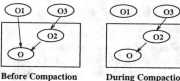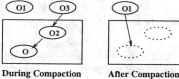

Figure 2: Motivating pointer delete logging in TRT

and *action* denotes whether the reference was inserted or deleted. We will call O above as the *referenced object* of the above tuple in the TRT, and the set of all such objects as the *referenced objects of the TRT*. A pointer delete must be noted in the TRT *before* the pointer is actually deleted by the transaction. Pointer inserts can be noted after the actual operation is done, but they should be made before the lock on the object in question is released.

A simple mechanism to maintain the TRT and the ERT, as pointers are updated, is to process the system logs (as in [AFG95, ARS+97]) by a separate process called log analyzer[7] as soon as they are handed over to the logging subsystem. The log analyzer updates the TRT/ERT if the update log it is processing has caused a reference pointer to be inserted or deleted. Updates to the TRT itself are not logged, while updates to the ERT can be logged as in [AFG95]. Alternately, if the logging overheads for the ERT are perceived to be excessive, one can choose not to log updates to the ERT; however, in this case, we would then have to reconstruct the ERT at restart recovery.

We will now motivate the need for recording each of the above actions based on the high level description of IRA presented in Figure 1 and via the following examples:

Pointer Deletes: In the absence of the TRT, the following scenario is possible: Before IRA begins, a transaction T deletes a pointer from object $O1$ to an object O, but retains the reference to O in its local memory. When IRA runs, it would not find $O1$ to be a parent of O (and not try to lock $O1$ either, as a result).

After IRA migrates O, T may insert back the reference (either explicitly or due to an abort of T) to O; however, the reference would still point to the old location of O, which is now garbage. This scenario is illustrated in Figure 2. The TRT helps handle such cases by recording that a reference to O has been cut; IRA will wait for T (by attempting to lock $O1$ which is found by consulting the TRT) to complete before migrating O.

Another reason for logging pointer deletes, is to ensure that the fuzzy traversal does not miss out on some live objects in the partition. For example, if the only reference to O is deleted by a transaction T, O (and some of its descendants) may never be encountered during the fuzzy traversal. If T inserts a reference to O back after the traversal, IRA may not migrate O, although O is a valid object of the partition.

To fix this problem, IRA additionally performs a traversal from all objects in the TRT to which a reference has been deleted, as we will see. Thus, O (and all of its de-

---

[7]The TRT and ERT can also be maintained by other mechanisms like modifying the functions that perform pointer updates etc. For purposes of isolating this function, and to demonstrate that this kind of analysis can be added very easily to an existing system without disturbing existing user code, we have chosen to introduce a separate process for the TRT/ERT maintenance. The actual mechanism for maintaining the TRT/ERT is of no consequence to our algorithms.

scendants) will be encountered during the traversal, and migrated.

Pointer Inserts: As we mentioned earlier, IRA performs a fuzzy traversal and therefore may not encounter some pointer inserts that take place while IRA is in progress. However, these pointer inserts create new parents. Before migrating an object O, IRA consults the TRT to check if O has any new parents that IRA did not encounter during the traversal.

3.4 Finding Objects and their Approximate Set of Parents

As the first step towards reorganization of objects in a partition, we identify the set of all live objects in the partition, and for each object we identify an approximate set of its parents (3). To do so we perform a fuzzy traversal of objects in the partition, starting from objects referenced from the ERT.

```
Find_Objects_And_Approx_Parents(P) {
/* Find the set of objects in the partition and their
approximate set of parents */
L1: (Traversed_objects, Parent_lists) =
        Fuzzy_Traversal(referenced objects in ERT of P)
L2: While (∃ a referenced object O in the TRT
    that is not in Traversed_objects)
        (Traversed_objects, Parent_lists) =
            Fuzzy_Traversal({O})
        return (Traversed_Objects, Parent_Lists)
}
```

Figure 3: Find Objects and Approximate Parents

The fuzzy traversal of the object graph is performed by Algorithm Fuzzy_Traversal, the pseudo code for which is not explicitly shown. Algorithm Fuzzy_Traversal starts traversal from the set of objects passed to it as its first argument and restricts the traversal to objects of the partition being reorganized. It adds the new set of objects encountered in a particular call to Traversed_Objects and adds the set of parents of these objects encountered in a particular call to Parent_Lists.

During the traversal, locks are not acquired on the objects encountered; instead, a latch is obtained to ensure physical consistency of the object while it is being read. The latch is released after the object has been read and all references out of the object have been noted. Thereby, the traversal is fuzzy, and does not return a transaction consistent view of the object graph within the partition. Note that even though not explicitly shown in the algorithm, latches on the shared data structures, ERT and TRT, need to be obtained whenever they are accessed. For clarity of presentation, we have omitted the actual latching details but note that the latch on TRT and ERT is not held while the Fuzzy_Traversal procedure executes.

The initial starting points for the traversal are the objects in ERT. The loop at line L2 is required to guarantee that no object in the partition is missed during the traversal. We will illustrate this with an example. Suppose the only reference to an object O is from R and this reference is cut before R is encountered by the Fuzzy_Traversal algorithm. This would result in O not being visited by the traversal and therefore not being recognised as a live object. Clearly, the transaction that cut the reference to O could reinsert it.

The following lemma states that all live objects are encountered by Find_Objects_And_Approx_Parents. This also enables IRA to detect and delete garbage objects (objects that are not live) simultaneously with reorganization. We will explore this connection in detail in Section 6.

Lemma 3.1 *When Algorithm Find_Objects_And_Approx_Parents completes, all live objects in the partition $\mathcal{P}$ are in Traversed_Objects.*

See [LRSS99] for the proof; due to space constraints, we omit it here.

An alternative to traversal from the ERT is to use object allocation information to find all objects in the partition, and visit all of them during traversal; doing so would not enable us to detect garbage objects, but would be otherwise the same.

3.5 Finding the Exact Set of Parents and Migrating an Object

We now explain the second step of the incremental reorganization algorithm. In this step, for each live object in the partition, we obtain the exact set of parents and then migrate the object. As we mentioned before, the set of parents of an object identified by the fuzzy traversal need not be exact. Function Find_Exact_Parents (pseudo code presented in Figure 4) makes this exact.

```
Find_Exact_Parents(O_old, Parent_Lists) {
S1: Get Write Locks on all the objects in the parent
    list of O_old
    For each object R in the parent list of O_old
        If R is not a parent of O_old
            Unlock R, and remove R from
            parent list of O_old
S2: While (∃ a tuple t in the TRT which has O_old
    as the referenced object)
        Write lock the parent object R of O_old in t
        Delete t from TRT
        If R is a parent of O_old
            Add R to the parent list of O_old
        else Unlock R
}
```

Figure 4: Find Exact Parents

Find_Exact_Parents first obtains locks on the approximate parents of O_{old}, identified by the fuzzy traversal. If an object R is not a parent of O_{old} any longer (the reference was deleted after R was encountered during the fuzzy traversal), then R can be unlocked and removed from the parent list of O_{old}. Find_Exact_Parent next checks the TRT for the existence of a tuple containing O_{old} as the referenced object. If a tuple exists, then a reference to O_{old} from an object R has either been added or deleted. If a reference from R to O_{old} has been deleted, the transaction that deleted the reference has completed when IRA obtains a lock on R (by strict 2PL). Therefore, that transaction can no longer introduce a reference to O_{old} (any references introduced by it already will be in the TRT). If a reference from R to O_{old} has been added and R still contains that reference after a lock on R is obtained, then R is added to the parent list of O_{old}.

The while loop in Find_Exact_Parents terminates when there is no tuple in the TRT that contains O_{old} as the referenced object. The following two lemmas together guarantee that all parents of O_{old} have been locked and there is no fear of a pointer to O_{old} reappearing in the database after O_{old} has been migrated.

Note that there is no need to obtain a lock on O_{old} itself, since the only way to access it is via a parent, and due to the strict 2PL requirement, no transaction can have a lock on O_{old} once all its parents are locked.

Lemma 3.2 *All live objects that have a reference to O_{old} at the time Find_Exact_Parents completes are locked by IRA.*

Proof: We provide an proof sketch here. A more formal proof can be found in [LRSS99]. Let t be the time instant at which Find_Exact_Parents completes. Let us assume that there exists a live object R containing a reference to O_{old} at time t that has not been locked by IRA. We will consider two cases:

Case 1: *The reference was added before the reorganization algorithm started*
By Lemma 3.1, R would have been encountered by the fuzzy traversal. Therefore, the reference also would have been encountered at the time R was encountered and therefore R is in the parent list of O_{old} at t. Therefore, R would have been locked by IRA at statement S1 of Find_Exact_Parents – a contradiction.

Case 2: *The reference was added after the reorganization algorithm started*
Let T be the transaction that added the reference. If T has completed at t, then the insertion would be logged in the TRT and the loop at S2 would have caught this and locked R. Therefore, T has still not completed at t. Since, we do not allow creation of objects after the reorganization process starts, T should have obtained a reference to O_{old} from some other object. Let R' be the object in which T first found a reference to O_{old}. If the reference from R' to O_{old} is not present at time t, then T must have deleted it, and by WAL, this deletion must be in TRT at time t. Therefore, IRA must have obtained a lock on R' in the loop at S2, which is impossible since T has a lock on R' at t. Therefore, the reference from R' to O_{old} is present at time t. Without loss of generality, we can assume IRA has a lock on R' (otherwise we can keep repeating the proof of this lemma for the reference from R' to O_{old} and this will push back the time of addition of the reference being considered in the proof until the time of addition of the reference satisfies Case 1). However, T holds a lock on R' at t – a contradiction.

Lemma 3.3 *There does not exist an active transaction that has a reference to O_{old} in its local memory at the time Find_Exact_Parents completes.*

The proof is similar to the proof of Lemma 3.2; see [LRSS99] for details.

It now follows that no transaction in the future can obtain a reference to O_{old} and so O_{old} can be safely moved. The move is performed by Move_Object_And_Update_Ref, the pseudo code for which is presented in Figure 5. This is essentially a bookkeeping function that actually effects the migration of O_{old} and ensures all references to the object at the old location refer to the new location and that all the ERTs are consistent with the migration. O_{new} is made visible to other transactions after this function completes since the locks on the parents of O_{old} are released at the end. We treat the migration of each object as a transaction (see section 4.3). In other words, the calls to Find_Exact_Parents and Move_Object_and_Update_Refs for a particular object

```
Move_Object_And_Update_Refs(O_old, Parent Lists) {
    Copy O_old to the new location, say O_new
    For each parent R in the parent list of O_old
        Change the reference in R to point to O_new
        Update ERTs of the partitions where O_old
        and O_new reside to reflect the change
    For each child C of O_old that is in the partition
    being reorganized
        If C is not yet migrated
            Replace O_old by O_new in the parent list of C
    For each child C of O_new
        Update the ERT of the partition corresponding
        to C to reflect the migration
    delete O_old
    Unlock all the parents of O_old (O_new)
}
```

Figure 5: Move Object and Update References

O_{old} in Figure 1 are together executed in the context of a transaction. As a result, system failures will not undo the migration of objects, if the transaction in whose context the object was migrated has completed. The migration of an object which was in progress at the time of failure (if any) will be undone. The reorganization process has to be started afresh to migrate the objects yet to be migrated. Alternatively, the reorganization process can log information about its execution state, to ensure that it does not have to be started afresh in case of a system failure. The impact of failures is further explored in section 4.4.

4   Extensions and Optimizations

In this section, we consider two important extensions to IRA. The first does away with the assumption that transactions follow strict 2PL. The second reduces the number of concurrent locks held by IRA. We then describe how to aggressively reclaim space occupied by the TRT and limit the amount of logging to the TRT.

4.1   Relaxing Strict 2PL Assumption

In this section, we show how the assumption that transactions follow strict 2PL can be relaxed. We assume, however, that before accessing an object, a short duration lock is obtained; the lock may be released after the object has been accessed.

For the reorganization process to work correctly when transactions do not follow strict 2PL, we augment the lock manager to keep track of which active transactions had acquired short duration locks on which objects. Whenever the IRA locks an object, it must additionally wait for all active transactions that have ever acquired a lock on this object to complete. Thus, the IRA waits for transactions that may have copied a reference into its local memory but may not currently hold a lock on the source of the reference. This results in transactions behaving as though they were following strict 2PL with respect to the reorganization process.

4.2   Reducing the Number of Concurrent Locks

The algorithm proposed in the previous section requires all parents of an object to be locked before it can be relocated. However, for objects with a large number of parents, this could prove to be restrictive since a substantial portion of the database may end up getting locked.

In this section, we show how to reduce the number of concurrent locks held by IRA. Rather than obtaining a lock on all the parents of an object, and then migrating the object and updating references in the parents, we lock the object being migrated (in both the old and the new locations) and then lock the parents one at a time, releasing the lock on a parent before obtaining a lock on the next parent. The reference in the parent is updated to the new location of the object while the parent is locked. As a result, each parent update is now done within the context of a transaction as opposed to each object migration in a transaction as described in section 3.5 (also see section 4.3). Please refer to [LRSS99] for the pseudo code for this extension.

No transaction can obtain a lock on the object being migrated since it is locked by the IRA while the object is being migrated. Transactions can however copy references to both O_{new} and O_{old} into other objects. We can ignore new references to O_{new} since they are correct after relocation. New references to O_{old} will be detected using the TRT as described earlier. Thus, it is correct to obtain locks on one parent at a time. This extension is a very powerful optimization since locks are held on at most two distinct objects at any point of time.

However, the algorithm can lead to the following situation: For an object O being migrated, there may exist a parent R which references O_{old} and another parent R' which references O_{new}. This has the following repercussions:

- In the event of a system failure, after restart recovery, the database may have two different objects, one pointing to O_{old}, and the other pointing to O_{new}. In this case, both O_{old} and O_{new} need to be locked before allowing transactions to start execution. The Reorganization process can then be restarted.

- The references to O out of R and R' do not match. Therefore, any transaction that attempts to compare references will obtain an erroneous result. Thus, this optimization is valid only if either (1) transactions do not compare references without obtaining locks on the referenced objects, or (2) the comparison operation does an additional check to see if the two referenced objects are old and new versions of an object being migrated – if so, the two references are considered to be equal.

Note that this optimization can be used in conjunction with the extension of Section 4.2.

4.3 Transaction context for Object Migration

In section 3.5, we noted that each object migration is done within the context of a transaction. In the extended version of the algorithm in section 4.2, each parent update is done in the context of a transaction. As mentioned earlier, this will ensure that work completed once will not be lost on a failure and will not have to be repeated upon recovery. To keep the descriptions of the algorithms simple, we used a seperate transaction for each object (or each parent in the extension). In practice, this could impose a high logging and IO overhead. To address this problem, we note that it is not required for correctness that each operation be a seperate transaction. Multiple object migrations can be grouped into a transaction (similarly, multiple parent updates can be grouped in the extension) to reduce the logging overhead. The trade-off here is between the size of the transaction and the amount of work that may need to be repeated after a failure. In the next section, we look at some other optimizations related to failure handling.

4.4 Handling Failures

In this section, we consider the effect of failures on the ERT, and on the two steps of the IRA algorithm, in turn.

1. If the ERT is to be persistent, the updates made by the log analyzer to the ERT should also be logged. This logging is performed as though these updates were made by the original transaction whose log is being analyzed. This ensures that aborts of transactions and restart recovery do not have to do anything special to keep the ERT consistent. This was the approach taken in [AFG95].

   Alternatively, if the logging overheads for the ERT are perceived to be excessive, one can choose not to log updates to ERT; however, in this case, we would then have to reconstruct ERT at restart recovery, which requires a complete scan of the database. An intermediate solution is to checkpoint ERT periodically and use the logs for pointer deletes and inserts during restart recovery to bring the ERT up to date.

2. Algorithm Find_Objects_And_Approx_Parents which is the first step of IRA does not obtain any locks. Therefore, it can never be involved in a deadlock. A system failure during Find_Objects_And_Approx_Parents would however result in the loss of the work performed until the failure.

   A simple solution to system failures during Find_Objects_And_Approx_Parents is to restart the IRA algorithm on restart recovery. However, if the loss of work is unacceptable, the data structures Traversed_Objects and Parent Lists can be checkpointed periodically. In the event of a failure, the TRT is reconstructed on the basis of the logs generated after the IRA started.

   Optionally, the TRT could also be checkpointed and then only the logs after the checkpoint need to be considered during the TRT reconstruction. In any case, after the TRT is reconstructed, the last checkpoint of the data structures can then be used to reduce the work of Find_Objects_And_Approx_Parents (by not traversing parts of the graph which have already been traversed).

3. The second step of IRA is to invoke Find_Exact_Parents and Migrate_Object for each object in the partition – we perform this within a transaction. Therefore, once a call to these functions succeed for an object O, the migration of O is complete.

   Migrate_Object does not obtain any locks and can not be involved in a deadlock. Find_Exact_Parents has to be reinvoked if it fails due to a deadlock.

   After a system failure during the second step, the objects that have not yet been migrated need to be migrated. If Traversed_Objects and Parents Lists are checkpointed after the completion of the first step, then the TRT can be reconstructed after a system failure by performing a scan of the system logs and the second step (to migrate remaining objects) can be started right away after recovery from failure. If the work done in the first step is lost during a system failure, IRA is started afresh from the beginning for the objects yet to be migrated.

4.5 Minimizing Space and Time Overhead of TRT

In this section, we describe methods to reduce the time and space overheads of the TRT. First, note that the TRT on a partition is required only if a reorganization process is in progress and does not exist otherwise. Once the reorganization process starts, the log analyzer starts noting relevant updates in the TRT. The reorganization process waits for all transactions that are active at the time it started, to complete, before starting the fuzzy traversal. This ensures that all relevant updates are indeed present in the TRT.

If transactions follow strict 2PL, the tuples corresponding to pointer deletes in the TRT can be deleted as soon as the transaction that logged them completes (aborts or commits). The main reason pointer deletes are logged is to ensure that any reinsertion of the reference by the transaction that deleted the pointer is seen by the reorganization process. Since insertions of pointers are logged separately in the TRT and pointers cannot be cached (in local memory) across transaction boundaries, this deletion of the tuple from the TRT does not compromise correctness. We assume here that if the abort of a transaction reintroduced a deleted reference, it is treated as an insertion of a reference, so the insertion remains in the TRT. Moreover, when a transaction that deleted a reference from R to O commits, we can also delete any tuple (if it exists) in the TRT that corresponds to the insertion of the reference from R to O.

Note that if transactions do not follow strict 2PL, a reference deleted by a transaction T may have been seen by another transaction T' which may reinsert the reference after T commits. Thus, for the non-2PL case, we do not allow the TRT tuples corresponding to deleted pointers to be purged after the transaction that deleted the pointer completes.

4.6 Relationship to Garbage Collection

One of the advantages of performing a traversal of the object graph is that the live objects of the partition can be detected. If we were only performing garbage collection, then a sweep through the partition would have identified the garbage objects. This is essentially the partitioned Mark and Sweep algorithm [AFG95]. The other option for garbage collection is to migrate all the live objects of a partition to a new partition and reclaim the entire space in the old partition. This is essentially the partitioned copying collector algorithm [YNY94]. However, the copying collector algorithm of [YNY94] assumes the object references are logical. Migrating objects when references are physical is hard – the focus of this paper is to attack this problem. However, as a side effect, we also have a partitioned copying collector algorithm even if the references are physical. The authors in [YNY94], in fact, advocated this algorithm over Mark and Sweep due to the ability of the algorithm to recluster the database. Thus, a system that implements our reorganization utility does not require a separate garbage collection utility.

5 Performance Evaluation

In this section, we investigate the impact of IRA on the performance of concurrent transactions. We consider the following: (a) a system running the basic version of IRA (without the extensions described in Section 4), (b) a system that is not running a reorganization utility, henceforth called NR, for No Reorganization, and (c) a system that runs a reorganization utility which quiesces the entire partition being reorganized (described in Section 5.1). The reorganization utilities were added to Brahmā, a storage manager developed at IIT Bombay. Brahmā provides support for the strict 2PL protocol and supports WAL through an implementation of ARIES. Brahmā also supports extendible hash indices which were used to implement the TRT and the ERT. A lock timeout mechanism was used to handle deadlocks and was set to one second throughout the experiments. Our experiments were conducted on a standalone 167 Mhz Sun UltraSparc-1 machine running Solaris 2.6 and equipped with 128 MB of RAM.

5.1 Partition Quiesce Reorganization (PQR)

We now outline the Partition Quiesce Reorganization Algorithm (PQR), which quiesces the partition being reorganized before performing the reorganization. By quiescing a partition, we mean that no reference to an object in the partition can be added or deleted. This is essentially a scaled down version of the off-line algorithm of Section 3.1.

However, while it is trivial to ensure no transaction is active in the off-line algorithm, it is bit more complex to ensure the partition being reorganized is quiescent. To quiesce a partition, we need to locks all objects not in the partition, that have a reference to an object in the partition. This ensures that no transaction can obtain a reference to an object in the partition.

Like in the IRA a TRT is maintained to detect insertion of new references while other parents are being locked. The following pseudo code outlines how a partition is quiesced. Once a partition is quiesced, reorganization is straightforward.

```
Quiesce_Partition(P)
    while (∃ a parent object R in ERT which is not locked)
        Lock R
    while (∃ a parent object R in TRT which is not locked)
        Lock R
```

Note that as in the case for IRA there is no need to lock the objects in the partition, since any transaction that accesses these objects must have come in through some external parent (possibly the persistent root). The external parent would be locked above, so with strict 2PL no transaction could be accessing any object in the partition.

5.2 Workload

We now describe the workload we consider in our experiments. This includes how the object graph is structured, and the access pattern of transactions. Table 1 shows the parameters used in the experiments.

Parameter	Meaning	Default
NUMPARTITIONS	partitions in the database	10
NUMOBJS	objects per partition	4080
MPL	multi programming level	30
OPSPERTRANS	length of random walk per transaction	8
UPDATEPROB	probability of exclusive access	0.5
GLUEFACTOR	fraction of inter-partition references	0.05

Table 1: Parameters of the implementation

Object Graph Structure The object database is made of NUMPARTITIONS number of partitions, each containing NUMOBJS number of objects. In each partition, the objects are organized into clusters, where each cluster is a tree with 85 objects. The roots of these clusters are treated as persistent roots. One edge from each node in the cluster refers to a node in another cluster C; C is chosen to be in another partition with probability GLUEFACTOR; thus controlling the number of inter-partition references.

Transaction Access Pattern The multi programming level (MPL) determines the number of concurrent transactions in the system at any given time. The multi programming level is fixed by spawning MPL threads that submit transactions to the system. When a transaction submitted by a thread completes, the thread submits the next transaction.

A typical transaction performs a random walk through the object graph. All the transactions in a particular thread start their random walk in a specific "home" partition and the threads are uniformly assigned to all the partitions. For the transactions in a particular thread, the starting points of the random walks are chosen randomly from among the persistent roots in the partition assigned to that thread.

The random walk chooses the next object to be accessed randomly from the references out of the current object. The number of objects accessed during the random walk is given by the OPSPERTRANS parameter which is fixed at 8. At each stage in the walk, the transaction may get a lock on the next object in shared or exclusive mode. This is determined by a parameter called the UPDATEPROBABILITY which represents the probability that an access performed by the transaction is an update access.

5.3 Results of Experiments

Previous studies [YNY94, AFG95, ARS+97] have studied the I/O overhead of partition traversal and found it to be reasonable. Therefore, we do not address this issue in our experiments. They have also studied the impact on normal processing of maintaining the TRT and ERT (and shown it to be reasonable) and therefore we do not address that issue either in this section.

In all our experiments, the database was kept memory resident for two reasons: i) In many high performance situations like telecommunications applications which require physical references, the database is indeed memory resident and ii) The goal of the experiments were to stress on the concurrency and data contention aspects of our algorithms, and not the I/O aspects as we mentioned above. We plan to investigate the performance in a disk-based setting in the future.

We evaluated the algorithms based mainly on the two performance metrics: i) Throughput and ii) Average Response Time. Transactions were run until the reorganization operation completed in the case of IRA and the PQR algorithm. In all cases, IRA takes longer to complete the reorganization than the PQR algorithm. Measuring the throughput and the response time of the transactions while reorganization is being performed is a direct measure of the impact of these algorithms on concurrent transactions. In the case of the system where there was no compaction, we ran 10,000 transactions in each thread. Since our experiments were on a real system, all times are measured as the wall clock elapsed time.

In the following sections, we report the results of the experiments in which we varied one parameter while others were fixed at the default values shown in Table 1. All the times are in milliseconds and throughput is measured in transactions per second (tps) unless otherwise mentioned.

5.3.1 MPL

In this section, we evaluate the performance of the algorithms as the MPL is varied. The purpose of these experiments is to examine in detail the difference in throughput for a range of system load.

Figure 6 shows the throughput of the algorithms as the MPL is varied. The NR system has consistently the best throughput as would be expected. The throughput of IRA is very close to the NR system for all the MPL values, while the throughput of the PQR algorithm is significantly lower.

Note that the throughput of the NR system peaks around an MPL of 5 since resource contention set in around that value. Recall that the entire database is memory resident; therefore CPU gets saturated very soon. The reason the throughput does not peak at an MPL of one is that logs have to be flushed to disk at commit time; therefore, there is some CPU I/O parallelism to be exploited. The throughput of IRA also peaks around the same value for similar reasons.

The throughput of the PQR algorithm peaks much later, around an MPL value of 30. The reason PQR algorithm peaks later is it causes severe data contention and underutilizes the resources at low MPL values. In fact, at some point of time during the reorganization, even at an MPL of 30, all threads get blocked by the reorganization process. To understand this, note that all the external parents of the objects in the partition are locked. Clearly, the threads that originate their walk in the partition being reorganized (there are three of them at an MPL of 30 since there are 10 partitions), cannot proceed since the persistent roots of this partition are considered to be external to the partition and therefore locked. Moreover, some transaction in the other threads may eventually need to lock one of the external parents (which could be in any partition). Thus, over a period of time some transaction of each thread ends up waiting for the reorganization process in the PQR algorithm.

The above effect will get amplified dramatically in a system with plenty of resources like a multi-processor environment. The throughput of NR and IRA would scale with additional resources as we increase the MPL while the throughput of PQR would stagnate due to the excessive data contention which essentially locks out all transactions from the system.

Figure 7 shows the average response times of the respective algorithms. The average response times reflect the throughput curves. We now analyze the response times of transactions, at an MPL of 30, where the PQR algorithm achieves its peak throughput, a bit more carefully.

	Throughput	Avg. Resp. Time (msec)	Max Resp. Time (msec)	Std. Devn. of Resp. Times
NR	35.0	819	1503	127
IRA	33.7	861	1935	135
PQR	28.0	1030	100040	4113

Table 2: Analysis of Response Times

Table 2, in addition to the throughput and the average response time, shows the maximum[8] of the response times of the transactions and the standard deviation of the response times of the transactions. The standard deviation and the maximum of the response times of transactions in the NR system and the system with IRA are very close. This is a very desirable behavior of a utility, since this implies that concurrent transactions in effect do not see the utility. Predictability of response times is also very important in real time systems and IRA scores on this count too. In contrast, the PQR algorithm affects concurrent transactions severely,

---

[8]Though, we have shown only the maximum response time, the trend remains the same even when we consider the 10 highest response times or the average of the top 10 response times

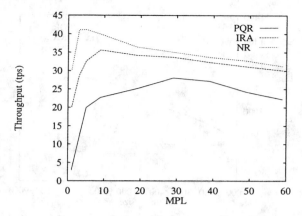

Figure 6: MPL scaleup - Throughput

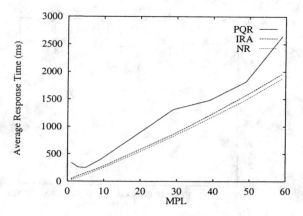

Figure 7: MPL scaleup - ART

and in fact, brings the system to a grinding halt, eventually, as explained above.

5.3.2 Number of Objects in a Partition

In this section, we compare the algorithms when the size of the partitions is scaled up. Figures 8 and 9 show the relative performance of the algorithms. As the partition size increases, the number of objects that need to be relocated and hence the number of parent pointers that need to be updated and the number of locks that need to be obtained increases. Because of this, the reorganization takes a longer time as partition size increases.

First, we observe from Figure 8 that the throughput is quite steady[9] both in the IRA case and the NR case, as the number of objects in the partition grows. On the other hand, the throughput of the PQR algorithm drops consistently as the number of objects in the partition is increased. In locking the entire partition, for the duration of the reorganization, which takes a longer time as partition size increases, PQR blocks transactions for a longer time. Thus, it monopolizes system resources for a longer time and also causes greater wasted work due to aborts (as a result of timeouts) of transactions.

Coming to the average response time, we can observe from Figure 9 that the increase in case of PQR is much more dramatic than that in case of IRA. This can be attributed again to the increased amount of time transactions have to wait for the reorganization process to complete.

5.3.3 Update Probability

Next, we studied the effects of varying the update probability. Figures 10 and 11 show the throughput and the average response time of transactions as the update probability is varied. In fact, this experiment is the final confirmation that the default values chosen by us were more than fair to the PQR algorithm. MPL values lower than 30 (running experiments beyond an MPL of 30 is pointless since we are examining areas of very high contention which is not reflective of normal processing), partition sizes larger than 4080 (with an average object size of 100 bytes a partition is around 400K which is very small), update probability smaller than 0.5 (which is much more normal) would only skew the results even more in favor of IRA.

_____
[9]There is a very small variation of less than 2% which is within the experimental noise since we were measuring wall clock time on a real system

The PQR algorithm is relatively less affected by an increase in update probability since the data contention is severe even at low update probability. Therefore, an incremental increase in update probability has a much higher impact on IRA and NR. The performance of PQR algorithm still remains lower than IRA even for very high update probability values.

5.3.4 Other Experiments

We also examined the performance of the algorithms as the other performance metrics like the gluefactor, the transaction path length and the number of partitions were varied. Due to space constraints we skip the details of these experiments and refer the reader to the full version of the paper [LRSS99].

Finally, we repeated all our experiments while measuring throughput and response time of the PQR algorithm for the duration of IRA rather than just the duration of the PQR algorithm. The motivation for this study is the following observation: While it is true that the PQR algorithm affects concurrent transactions severely for the duration of reorganization, it brings back normalcy much faster. Thus, for the extra duration that IRA requires to complete reorganization, a system with PQR algorithm would have throughput as though there were no reorganization. Thus, a natural question is what is the loss in throughput of IRA compared to PQR if throughput is measured for the duration of IRA for both algorithms. We found the difference in throughputs never exceeded 3%. Note that the throughput of PQR can never exceed that of NR and since the difference between IRA and NR was never big in the first place, the difference between IRA and PQR could never have been big.

6 Related work

The only prior work [KW93] we know of for on-line reorganization of objects with physical references requires an action-quiescent state during which all objects that are in the memory of active transactions and persistent roots are copied into a new space. This could cause severe intereference to concurrent transactions. Apart from the above, their model is very different from ours and requires low level support from the hardware and the operating system. For example, they require, that they be able to change references in the registers and stacks of active transactions and trap certain pointer dereferences using memory protection. Finally, they use forwarding addresses, which may cause an extra I/O and require complicated

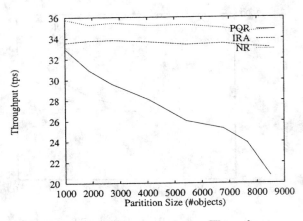

Figure 8: Partition size scaleup - Throughput

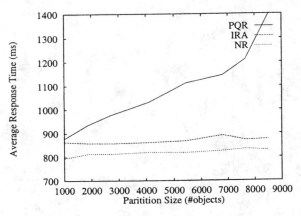

Figure 9: Partition size scaleup - ART

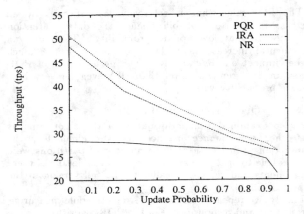

Figure 10: Update Probability - Throughput

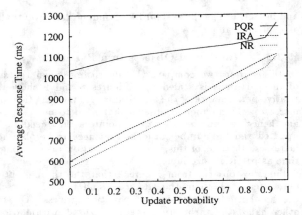

Figure 11: Update Probability - ART

recovery mechanisms to ensure consistency of the disk version of the database.

On-line reorganization is a well studied topic in relational databases [AON96, Omi96, SD92, ZS96a, ZS96b, ZS98]. In a relational database, references to a record are restricted to be from the indexes on the table. Thus, discovering the set of references to a record is a much simpler task in relational databases. Research into reorganization in relational databases has therefore concentrated on minimizing the number of locks being held and the amount of I/O necessary for reorganization.

The motivation for the problem of reorganization of object-oriented databases when references are physical arises from the fact that logical references impose an overhead on every access of the object. In [EGK95], three alternatives for the implementation of logical object identifiers are compared. The best technique based on direct mapping, often requires one extra I/O per object access which is unacceptable in situations where low response times are desired. Moreover, the very motivation for the work in [EGK95] is the inability to perform reorganization efficiently when references are physical which is exactly the focus of this paper. Finally, while it is true that if references are physical, quite a few object references have to be changed during the reorganization, it is important to note that reorganization is an infrequent occurrence, that can be performed at lean times, whereas, using a logical identifier would mean the price of the extra level of indirection is paid for *every* access.

There are several problems other than reorganization with an on-line flavor. On-line index construction algorithms [SC92b, MN92] build an index on a relation while the relation is being updated. The concurrent updates are collected in a side file and applied later. The entire relation is locked for a very short duration to enable the on-line operation to catch up. This idea was also extended to the execution of large queries [SC92a].

The problem most related to on-line reorganization in object-oriented databases is on-line garbage collection [YNY94, AFG95, ARS+97] in object-oriented databases. The system model is very similar in both the problems. There are two broad classes of garbage collection algorithms. The first consists of algorithms that migrate live objects elsewhere. The partitioned copying collector algorithm of [YNY94], where all the live objects of a partition are migrated out of the partition, is an example. These algorithms however assume object references are logical. Migrating objects when references are physical is much more difficult since it requires the references in all parents to be updated correctly. The focus of this paper is exactly on this problem. Since, our reorganization algorithm also detects all live objects in a partition, it can easily be augmented to copy all objects out of the partition, similar to the partitioned copying collector algorithm. However, our reorganization algorithm works correctly even when references are physical. The second class consists of algorithms that do not migrate live objects but perform garbage collection in place. Reference Counting and Mark and Sweep based algorithms belong to this class.

[AFG95] is a partitioned mark and sweep algorithm while [ARS+97] is a combination of reference counting and mark and sweep. These algorithms can handle physical references but do not perform any reorganization. Therefore, they do not perform the crucial step of finding and locking all parents of an object. In fact, our algorithm holds locks on atmost two distinct objects at any point of time and in contrast to [YNY94, AFG95, ARS+97], does not require transactions to follow strict 2PL. In summary, our algorithm can perform garbage collection and reorganization and yet allow references to be physical, an ability that to the best of our knowledge, no previous algorithm in literature possesses.

The notion of TRT has been used in previous work on garbage collection and reorganization in relational databases (called side files in this context). However, the space optimization measures we present in Section 4.5 are novel to this paper. The orthogonal issue of how to choose the partition size to minimize the overhead of the partition traversal has been addressed in [CWZ94].

7   Conclusions and Future Work

We have considered the problem of on-line reorganization in an object oriented database where object references are physical, and presented the IRA algorithm, and several variants of it to improve concurrency. One of the variants holds locks on only two distinct objects at any point of time, and does not require transactions to follow strict 2PL. The experiments we conducted confirmed that the IRA algorithm interferes very little with concurrently executing transactions. Thus, for database systems that employ physical object references for higher performance (e.g., main-memory database systems), IRA ensures that they do not pay a very high penalty during object reorganization.

In the future, we plan to address the issue of improving the I/O efficiency of the reorganization process. Even if the partition being reorganized fits in memory, the external parents of the objects in the partition may not. An object external to the partition being reorganized may have to be fetched multiple times as it may be the parent of multiple objects in the partition. A natural question that arises is in what order to we migrate objects so that the number of I/O's required is minimized. In a main memory database, the same order could be relevant since it may minimize the number of times locks have to be obtained on an external object. In the near future, we plan to carry out a detailed performance study of our algorithms in a disk-based setting.

References

[AFG95]   L. Amsaleg, M. Franklin, and O. Gruber. Efficient incremental garbage collection for client-server object database systems. In *Proceedings of the 21st VLDB Conference*, September 1995.

[AON96]   K. Achyutuni, E. Omiecinski, and S. Navathe. Two techniques for on-line index modification in shared nothing parallel databases. In *Proceedings of ACM SIGMOD Conference*, pages 125–136, Montreal, June 1996.

[ARS+97]   S. Ashwin, P. Roy, S. Seshadri, A. Silberschatz, and S. Sudarshan. Garbage collection in object oriented databases using transactional cyclic reference counting. In *Proceedings of the 23rd VLDB Conference*, Athens, Greece, August 1997.

[BKKK87]   J. Banerjee, W. Kim, H. Kim, and H. F. Korth. Semantics and implementation of schema evolution in object-oriented databases. In *Proceedings of ACM SIGMOD Conference*, pages 311–322, 1987.

[BLR+97]   P. Bohannon, D. Lieuwen, R. Rastogi, S. Seshadri, A. Silberschatz, and S. Sudarshan. The architecture of the dali storage manager. *Journal of Multi-Media Tools and Applications*, 4(2), March 1997.

[CWZ94]   J.E. Cook, A.L. Wolf, and B.G. Zorn. Partition selection policies in object database garbage collection. In *Proceedings of ACM SIGMOD Conference*, pages 371–382, Minneapolis, USA, May 1994.

[Edi96]   B. Salzberg (Special Issue Editor). Special issue on online reorganization. *IEEE Data Engineering Bulletin*, 19(2), June 1996.

[EGK95]   A. Eickler, C. A. Gerlhof, and D. Kossman. A performance evaluation of oid mapping techniques. In *Proceedings of the 21st VLDB Conference*, September 1995.

[JLR+94]   H.V. Jagadish, D. Lieuwen, R. Rastogi, A. Silberschatz, and S. Sudarshan. Dali: A high performance main-memory storage manager. In *Proceedings of the 20th VLDB Conference*, 1994.

[KW93]   E.K. Kolodner and W. E. Weihl. Atomic incremental garbage collection and recovery of a large stable heap. In *Proceedings of ACM SIGMOD Conference*, pages 177–186, Washington, DC, May 1993.

[LRSS99]   M.K. Lakhamraju, R. Rastogi, S. Seshadri, and S. Sudarshan. On-line reorganization of objects. In *Technical Report, Bell-labs*, February 1999.

[MN92]   C. Mohan and I. Narang. Algorithms for creating very large tables without quiescing updates. In *Proceedings of ACM SIGMOD Conference*, pages 361–370, San Diego, USA, May 1992.

[NOPH92]   S. Nettles, J. O'Toole, D. Pierce, and N. Haines. Replication-based incremental copying collection. In *International Workshop on Memory Management*, pages 357–364, St. Malo, France, September 1992.

[Omi96]   E. Omiecinski. Concurrent file reorganization: Clustering, conversion and maintenance. *IEEE Data Engineering Bulletin*, 19(2), 1996.

[SC92a]   V. Srinivasan and M. Carey. Compensation based online query processing. In *Proceedings of ACM SIGMOD Conference*, San Diego, CA, 1992.

[SC92b]   V. Srinivasan and M. Carey. Performance of on-line index construction algorithms. In *3rd International Conferance on Extending Database Technology*, pages 292–309, Vienna, Austria, March 1992.

[SD92]   B. Salzberg and A. Dimock. Principles of transaction-based on-line reorganization. In *Proceedings of 18th VLDB Conference*, pages 511–520, 1992.

[TN91]   M. M. Tsangaris and J. F. Naughton. A stochastic approach for clustering in object bases. In *Proceedings of the ACM SIGMOD Conference*, Denver, Colorado, May 1991.

[WMK94]   Jr W.J. Mciver and R. King. Self-adaptive, on-line reclustering of complex object data. In *Proceedings of ACM SIGMOD Conference*, pages 407–418, Minneapolis, USA, May 1994.

[YNY94]   V. Yong, J. Naughton, and J. Yu. Storage reclamation and reorganization in client-server persistent object stores. In *Proceedings of the Data Engineering International Conference*, pages 120–133, February 1994.

[ZS96a]   C. Zou and B. Salzberg. On-line reorganization of sparesely-populated B^+-trees. In *Proceedings of ACM SIGMOD Conference*, pages 115–124, Montreal, June 1996.

[ZS96b]   C. Zou and B. Salzberg. Towards efficient online database reorganization. *IEEE Data Engineering Bulletin*, 19(2):33–40, June 1996.

[ZS98]   C. Zou and B. Salzberg. Safely and efficiently updating references during on-line reorganization. In *Internation Conference on Very Large Databases*, New York, USA, August 1998.

Finding Generalized Projected Clusters in High Dimensional Spaces

Charu C. Aggarwal, Philip S. Yu
IBM T. J. Watson Research Center
Yorktown Heights, NY 10598
{ charu, psyu }@watson.ibm.com

Abstract

High dimensional data has always been a challenge for clustering algorithms because of the inherent sparsity of the points. Recent research results indicate that in high dimensional data, even the concept of proximity or clustering may not be meaningful. We discuss very general techniques for projected clustering which are able to construct clusters in arbitrarily aligned subspaces of lower dimensionality. The subspaces are specific to the clusters themselves. This definition is substantially more general and realistic than currently available techniques which limit the method to only projections from the original set of attributes. The generalized projected clustering technique may also be viewed as a way of trying to redefine clustering for high dimensional applications by searching for hidden subspaces with clusters which are created by inter-attribute correlations. We provide a new concept of using extended cluster feature vectors in order to make the algorithm scalable for very large databases. The running time and space requirements of the algorithm are adjustable, and are likely to tradeoff with better accuracy.

1   Introduction

The problem of clustering data points is defined as follows: Given a set of points in multidimensional space, find a partition of the points into *clusters* so that the points within each cluster are similar to one another. Various distance functions may be used in order to make a quantitative determination of similarity. In addition, an objective function may be defined with respect to this distance function in order to measure the overall quality of a partition. The method has been studied in considerable detail [5, 8, 15, 11, 17, 18] by both the statistics and database communities because of its applicability to many practical problems such

as customer segmentation, pattern recognition, trend analysis and classification. An overview of clustering methods may be found in [11].

A common class of methods in clustering are *partitioning methods* in which a set of seeds (or representative objects) are used in order to partition the points implicitly [11]. Several variations of this technique exist such as the k-means and k-medoid algorithms [11]. In medoid-based techniques, the points from the database are used as seeds, as the algorithm tries to search for the optimal set of k seeds which results in the best clustering. An effective practical technique in this class called CLARANS [15] uses a restricted search space in order to improve efficiency.

Another well known class of techniques are *hierarchical clustering methods* in which the database is decomposed into several levels of partitioning which are represented by a dendogram [11]. Such methods are qualitatively effective, but practically infeasible for large databases since the performance is at least quadratic in the number of database points.

In density-based clustering methods [5], the neighborhood of a point is used in order to find dense regions in which clusters exist. Other related techniques for large databases include condensation and grid based methods in conjunction with spatial and hierarchical structures [8, 18]. The BIRCH method [18] uses a hierarchical data structure called the CF-Tree in order to incrementally build clusters. This is one of the most efficient approaches for low dimensional data, and it requires only one scan over the database. Another hierarchical method called CURE [8] was recently proposed, which tends to show excellent quality because it uses robust methods in order to measure distances between clusters. Therefore, it adjusts well to different shapes of clusters. An interesting grid-partitioning technique called *Optigrid* [9] has recently been proposed which is designed to perform well for high dimensional data.

In spite of these improved techniques, high dimensional data continues to pose a challenge to clustering algorithms at a very fundamental level. Most clustering algorithms do not work efficiently in higher dimensional

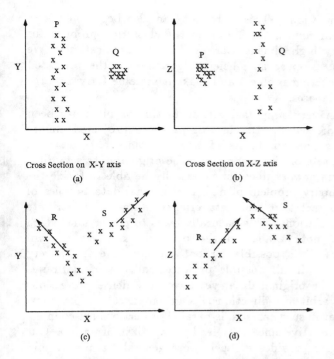

Cross Section on X-Y axis
(a)

Cross Section on X-Z axis
(b)

(c)

(d)

Figure 1: Illustrations of projected clustering

spaces because of the inherent sparsity of the data. This problem has been traditionally referred to as the *dimensionality curse* and is the motivation for a significant amount of work in high-dimensional clustering and similarity search [7, 9, 10, 13]. Recent theoretical results [3] have shown that in high dimensional space, the distance between every pair of points is almost the same for a wide variety of data distributions and distance functions. Under such circumstances, even the meaningfulness of proximity or clustering in high dimensional data may be called into question. One solution to this problem is to use feature selection in order to reduce the dimensionality of the space [14], but the correlations in the dimensions are often specific to data locality; in other words, some points are correlated with respect to a given set of features and others are correlated with respect to different features. Thus it may not always be feasible to prune off too many dimensions without at the same time incurring a substantial loss of information. We demonstrate this with the help of an example.

In Figure 1, we have illustrated four figures. The top two Figures 1(a) and 1(b) correspond to one set of points, while the bottom two Figures 1(c) and 1(d) correspond to another set. Figure 1(a) represents the X-Y cross-section of the first set of points, whereas Figure 1(b) represents the X-Z cross-section. There are two patterns of points labeled P and Q. The pattern P corresponds to a set of points which are close to one another in the X-Z plane. The second pattern Q corresponds to a set of points which are

very close in the X-Y plane. Note that traditional feature selection does not work in this case, as each dimension is relevant to at least one of the clusters. At the same time, clustering in the full dimensional space will not discover the two patterns, since each of them is spread out along one of the dimensions. Figures 1(a) and (b) illustrate a simple case when the clusters are aligned along a particular axis system. Methods for finding such projected clusters have been discussed in [1]. Related methods for finding locally dense subspaces have also been discussed in [2, 4]. These are not really clustering methods, since they return dense rectangular projections with huge point overlaps. In reality, none of the above methods may be general enough in order to find the true clusters. The clusters could exist in arbitrarily oriented subspaces of lower dimensionality. The examples in Figures 1(c) and (d) illustrate these cases wherein the projected clusters could exist in arbitrarily oriented subspaces. The two such patterns are labeled by R and S. In this case, the planes on which the projection should take place are the normals to the arrows illustrated in the Figures 1(c) and 1(d). Often the examination of real data shows that points may tend to get aligned along arbitrarily skewed and elongated shapes in lower dimensional space because of correlations in the data. Clearly, the choice of axis parallel projections cannot find such clusters effectively.

In this context, we shall now define what we call a *generalized projected cluster*. A generalized projected cluster is a set $\mathcal{E}$ of vectors together with a set $\mathcal{C}$ of data points such that the points in $\mathcal{C}$ are closely clustered in the subspace defined by the vectors $\mathcal{E}$. The subspace defined by the vectors in $\mathcal{E}$ may have much lower dimensionality than the full dimensional space. The Figures 1(c) and (d) contain two clusters in arbitrarily oriented subspaces.

In this paper we focus on an algorithm to find clusters in lower dimensional projected subspaces for data of high dimensionality. We assume that the number k of clusters to be found is an input parameter. In addition to the number of clusters k the algorithm will take as input the dimensionality l of the subspace in which each cluster is reported. The output of the algorithm will be twofold:
• A $(k+1)$-way partition $\{\mathcal{C}_1, ..., \mathcal{C}_k, \mathcal{O}\}$ of the data, such that the points in each partition element except the last form a cluster. (The points in the last partition element are the *outliers*, which by definition do not cluster well.)
• A possibly different orthogonal set $\mathcal{E}_i$ of vectors for each cluster $\mathcal{C}_i$, $1 \leq i \leq k$, such that the points in $\mathcal{C}_i$ cluster well in the subspace defined by these vectors. (The vectors for the outlier set $\mathcal{O}$ can be assumed to be the empty set.) For each cluster $\mathcal{C}_i$, the cardinality of the corresponding set $\mathcal{E}_i$ is equal to the user defined parameter l.

In order to describe our algorithm we shall introduce a few notations and definitions. Let N denote the total number of data points. Assume that the dimensionality of the overall space is d. Let $\mathcal{C} = \{\overline{x_1}, \overline{x_2}, \ldots, \overline{x_t}\}$ be the set of points in a cluster. The *centroid* of a cluster is the algebraic average of all the points in the cluster. Thus, the centroid of the cluster $\mathcal{C}$ is given by $\overline{X}(\mathcal{C}) = \sum_{i=1}^{t} \overline{x_i}/t$. We will denote the distance between two points $\overline{x_1}$ and $\overline{x_2}$ by $dist(\overline{x_1}, \overline{x_2})$. In this paper, we will work with the euclidean distance metric.

Let $\overline{y} = (y_1, \ldots y_d)$ be a point in the d-dimensional space, and let $\mathcal{E} = \{\overline{e_1} \ldots \overline{e_l}\}$ be a set of $l \leq d$ orthonormal vectors in this d-dimensional space. These orthonormal vectors define a subspace. The projection $\mathcal{P}(\overline{y}, \mathcal{E})$ of point $\overline{y}$ in subspace $\mathcal{E}$ is an l-dimensional point given by $(\overline{y} \cdot \overline{e_1}, \ldots, \overline{y} \cdot \overline{e_l})$. Here $\overline{y} \cdot \overline{e_i}$ denotes the dot-product of $\overline{y}$ and $\overline{e_i}$.

Let $\overline{y_1}$ and $\overline{y_2}$ be two points in the original d-dimensional space. Then, the *projected distance* between the points $\overline{y_1}$ and $\overline{y_2}$ in subspace $\mathcal{E}$ is denoted by $Pdist(\overline{y_1}, \overline{y_2}, \mathcal{E})$ and is equal to the euclidean distance between the projections $\mathcal{P}(\overline{y_1}, \mathcal{E})$ and $\mathcal{P}(\overline{y_2}, \mathcal{E})$ in the l-dimensional space represented by $\mathcal{E}$. The *projected energy* of the cluster $\mathcal{C} = \{\overline{x_1}, \overline{x_2}, \ldots, \overline{x_t}\}$ in subspace $\mathcal{E}$ is denoted by $R(\mathcal{C}, \mathcal{E})$ and is given by the mean square distance of the points to the centroid of the cluster, when all points in $\mathcal{C}$ are projected to the subspace $\mathcal{E}$. Thus, we have:

$$R(\mathcal{C}, \mathcal{E}) = \sum_{i=1}^{t} \{Pdist(\overline{x_i}, \overline{X}(\mathcal{C}), \mathcal{E})\}^2/t$$

Note that the projected energy[1] of a cluster in a subspace is always less than that in the full dimensional space. For certain good choices of subspaces the projected energy is likely to be significantly smaller than that in full dimensional space. For example, for the case of Figures 1(c) and (d), the 2-dimensional subspaces in which the projected energy is likely to be small for clusters R and S are the planes normal to the arrows illustrated. It is the aim of the algorithm to discover clusters with small projected energy in subspaces of user-specified dimensionality l, where the subspace for each cluster could be different. Providing l as an input parameter gives the user considerable flexibility in discovering clusters in different dimensionalities. We will also discuss methods for providing the user guidance in finding a good value of l for which meaningful clusters may be found.

In this paper, we will examine this very general concept of using arbitrarily projected subspaces for finding clusters. Since dense full dimensional clusters cannot be found in very high dimensional data sets, this method searches for hidden subspaces in which points cluster well because of correlations among the

dimensions. This technique can also be considered a meaningful re-definition of the clustering problem for very high dimensional data mining applications. We also propose an efficient algorithm for the projected clustering problem and make it scalable for vary large databases.

A very simplified version of this problem has been addressed in [1]. In this paper, a projected cluster is defined in terms of sets of points together with subsets of dimensions from the original data set. Such a framework may not necessarily be able to tackle the sparsity problem of high dimensional data because of the fact that real data often contains inter-attribute correlations. This naturally leads to projections which are not parallel to the original axis system. In fact, it is possible for data to continue to be very sparse in all possible projected subsets of attributes of the original data, yet have very dense projections in arbitrary directions. Our empirical results show that in such cases, axis-parallel projections are counter-productive since they lead to loss of information. Our paper provides a much more general framework and algorithms in which clusters can be represented in any arbitrarily projected space.

This paper is organized as follows. Section 2 describes our clustering algorithm in detail. The algorithm is known as ORCLUS (arbitrarily ORiented projected CLUSter generation). We discuss several improvements to the basic algorithm, and introduce the concept of *extended* cluster feature vectors (ECF) which are used to make the algorithm scale to very large databases. We also show how to use a progressive random sampling approach in order to improve the scalability with database size. In Section 3, we discuss the empirical results, whereas Section 4 discusses the conclusions and summary.

1.1 Projected Clusters and Skews

Most real data contains different kinds of skews in the data in which some subsets of dimensions are related to one another. Furthermore, these subsets of correlated dimensions may be different in different localities of the data. Correlated sets of dimensions lead to points getting aligned along arbitrary shapes in lower dimensional space. Such distributions of points which are far from the uniform distribution are referred to as skews. Projected clusters in lower dimensional subspaces are closely connected to the problem of finding skews in the data. Each orthogonal set of vectors which defines a subspace for a projected cluster provides a very good idea of the nature of skews and correlations in the data. For example, in the Figures 1(c) and (d), the arrows represent the directions of sparsity (greatest elongations because of correlated sets of dimensions). Coincidentally, the

---
[1] We have chosen the term energy, since this is a metric which is invariant on rotation of the axis system, and can be expressed as the sum of the energies of the individual axis directions.

direction of projection in which the points in the clusters are most similar are the normal planes to these arrows. In general, the subspace in which the maximum sparsity of point distribution occurs is the complementary subspace to the one in which the points are most similar to one another. For such distributions of points in very high dimensional space, the data is likely to continue to be very sparse in *full* dimensionality (thereby ruling out the use of full dimensional clustering algorithms such as those discussed in [17]), whereas the only realistic way of detecting regions of similarity would be to use lower dimensional projections for each cluster.

1.2 A Related Method

Singular Value Decomposition (SVD) [6, 16] is a well known technique in order to represent the data in a lower dimensional subspace by pruning away those dimensions which result in the least loss of information. Since the projected clustering method also projects the data into a lower dimensional subspace, it is interesting to examine the relationship between the two techniques. We will first give a brief overview of the methodology of singular value decomposition. The idea is to transform the data into a new coordinate system in which the (second order) correlations in the data are minimized. This transformation is done by using a two step process.

In the first step, the $d * d$ covariance matrix is constructed for the data set. Specifically, the entry (i, j) in the matrix is equal to the covariance between the dimensions i and j. The diagonal entries correspond to the variances of the individual dimension attributes. In the second step, the eigenvectors of this positive semi-definite matrix are found. These eigenvectors define an orthonormal system along which the second order correlations in the data are removed. The corresponding eigenvalues denote the spread (or variance) along each such newly defined dimension in this orthonormal system. Therefore, the eigenvectors for which the corresponding eigenvalues are the largest can be chosen as the subspace in which the data is represented. This results in only a small loss of information, since the data does not show much variance along the remaining dimensions.

The problem of dimensionality reduction is concerned with removing the dimensions in the *entire* data set so that the least amount of information is lost. On the other hand, the focus here is to find the best projection for each cluster in such a way that the greatest amount of *similarity* among the points in that cluster can be detected. Therefore, in the dimensionality reduction problem one chooses the eigenvectors with the *maximum* spread in order to retain the most information which distinguishes the points from one another. On the other hand, in the novel approach

discussed in this paper, we pick the directions with the least spread for *each specific cluster*, so as to retain the information about the similarity of the points with one another in that cluster. Obviously, the directions with least spread are different for different clusters. The subspace which is complementary to the projection subspace for a given cluster is not useless information, since it may be used in order to retain the maximum information which distinguishes the points *within that cluster* from one another, if our technique is to be used for applications such as indexing.

The projected clustering problem is much more complex than the dimensionality reduction problem, because we are faced with the simultaneous problem of partitioning the data set as well as finding the directions with most similarity in each partition.

1.3 Covariance Matrix Diagonalization

In this section, we will discuss some properties of covariance matrix diagonalization which are useful for our clustering algorithm. We mention all the below properties as fact, which may be verified from [12]. Let C be the covariance matrix for the set of points $\mathcal{C}$. The matrix C is positive semidefinate and can be expressed in the format $C = P \Delta P^T$.

Here Δ is a diagonal matrix with non-negative entries. The columns in P are the (orthonormal) eigenvectors of C. The diagonal entries $\lambda_1 \ldots \lambda_d$ of Δ are the eigenvalues of C. The orthonormal eigenvectors define a new axis system and the matrix Δ is the covariance matrix of the original set of points when represented in this system. Since all non-diagonal entries are zero, it means that all second-order correlations have been removed. This also means that the eigenvalues correspond to the variances along each of the new set of axes. The trace $\sum_{i=1}^{d} \lambda_i$ is invariant under the axis-transformation defined by the eigensystem P and is equal to the trace of the original covariance matrix C. This is also equal to the energy of the cluster $\mathcal{C}$ in full dimensional space. It can also be shown that picking the $l \leq d$ smallest eigenvalues results in the l-dimensional subspace $\mathcal{E}$ of eigenvectors, in which sum of the variances along the l-directions is the least among all possible transformations. This is the same as the projected energy of the cluster $\mathcal{C}$ in subspace $\mathcal{E}$. *Thus, the diagonalization of the covariance matrix provides information about the projection subspace of a cluster which minimizes the corresponding energy.*

2 Generalized Projected Clustering

We decided on a variant of hierarchical merging methods for our algorithm. Unfortunately, the class of hierarchical methods is prohibitively expensive for very large databases, since the algorithms scale at least quadratically with the number of points. One solution is to run the method on only a random sample of points, but this can lead to a loss of accuracy. Consequently, we decided on the compromise solution of applying the technique to a small number k_0 of initial points, but using techniques from partitional clustering in order to always associate a current cluster with each of the points. The current clusters are then used in order to make more robust merging decisions. In effect, information from the entire database is used in the hierarchical merging process, even though the number of merges is greatly reduced. We will refer to the initial set of points as the *seeds*. At each stage of the algorithm, the following are associated with each seed s_i:

(1) **Current Cluster** C_i: This is the set of points from the database which are closest to seed s_i in some subspace $\mathcal{E}_i$ associated with cluster C_i. We assume that at each stage of the algorithm, the number of current clusters is denoted by k_c.

(2) **Current Subspace** $\mathcal{E}_i$: This is the subspace in which the points from C_i cluster well. The dimensionality l_c of $\mathcal{E}_i$ is at least equal to the user-specified dimensionality l. Initially, l_c is equal to the full dimensionality, and the value of l_c is reduced gradually to the user-specified dimensionality l. The idea behind this gradual reduction is that in the first few iterations the clusters may not necessarily correspond very well to the natural lower-dimensional subspace clusters in the data; and so a larger subspace is retained in order to avoid loss of information. (Only the most noisy subspaces are excluded.) In later iterations, the clusters are much more refined, and therefore subspaces of lower rank may be extracted.

The overall algorithm consists of a number of iterations, in each of which we apply a sequence of merging operations in order to reduce the number of current clusters by the factor $\alpha < 1$. We also reduce the dimensionality of current cluster C_i by $\beta < 1$ in a given iteration. Thus, the significance of dividing up the merging process over different iterations, is that each iteration corresponds to a certain dimensionality of the subspace in which the clusters are discovered. The first few iterations correspond to a higher dimensionality, and each successive iteration continues to peel off more and more noisy subspaces for the different clusters. The values of α and β need to be related in such a way that the reduction from k_0 to k clusters occurs in the same number of iterations as the reduction from $l_0 = |\mathcal{D}|$ to l dimensions. Therefore, the relationship $\log_{(1/\alpha)}(k_0/k) = \log_{(1/\beta)}(l_0/l)$ must be satisfied.

In the description of the algorithm ORCLUS, we have chosen $\alpha = 0.5$ and calculated the value of β according to the above relationship. The overall description of the algorithm is illustrated in Figure 2, and consists of a number of iterations in which each of the following three steps are applied:

```
Algorithm ORCLUS(Number of Clusters: k,
                 Number of Dimensions: l)
{ C_i is the current cluster i }
{ E_i is the set of vectors defining subspace for cluster C_i }
{ k_c ⇒ current number of seeds; l_c ⇒ current
                dimensionality associated with each seed }
{ S = {s_1, s_2 ... s_{k_c}} is the current set of seeds }
{ k_0 is the number of seeds that we begin with }
begin
  Pick k_0 > k points from the database and denote by
    S; { S = (s_1, ... s_{k_c}) }
  k_c = k_0; l_c = d;
  for each i set E_i = D;
  { Initially, E_i is the original axis-system }
  α = 0.5; β = e^{-log(d/l)·log(1/α)/log(k_0/k)};
  while (k_c > k) do
  begin
    { Find partitioning induced by the seeds }
    (s_1, ... s_{k_c}, C_1, ... C_{k_c}) = Assign( s_1, ... s_{k_c}, E_1, ... E_{k_c});
    { Determine current subspace associated with
                each cluster C_i }
    for i = 1 to k_{new} do E_i = FindVectors(C_i, l_{new});
    { Reduce number of seeds and dimensionality
                associated with each seed }
    k_{new} = max{k, k_c · α}; l_{new} = max{l, l_c · β};
    (s_1 ... s_{k_{new}}, C_1, ... C_{k_{new}}, E_1 ... E_{k_{new}}) =
                Merge(C_1, ... C_{k_c}, k_{new}, l_{new});
    k_c = k_{new}; l_c = l_{new};
  end;
  (s_1, ... s_k, C_1, ... C_k) = Assign( s_1, ... s_k, E_1, ... E_k);
  return(C_1 ... C_{k_c});
end;
```

Figure 2: The Clustering Algorithm

```
Algorithm Assign(s_1, ... s_{k_c}, E_1 ... E_{k_c})
begin
  for each i ∈ {1, ..., k_c} do C_i = φ;
  for each data point p do begin
    Determine Pdist(p, s_i, E_i) for each i ∈ {1, ..., k_c}
    { Distance of point p to s_i in subspace E_i};
    Determine the seed s_i with the least value of
    Pdist(p, s_i, E_i) and add p to C_i;
  end
  for each i ∈ {1, ..., k_c} do s_i = X̄(C_i);
  return(s_1, ... s_{k_c}, C_1 ... C_{k_c});
end
```

Figure 3: Creating the Cluster Partitions

```
Algorithm FindVectors(Cluster of points:C,
                Dimensionality of projection:q)
begin
  Determine the d * d covariance matrix M for C;
  Determine the eigenvectors of matrix M;
  E = Set of eigenvectors corresponding to
                smallest q eigenvalues;
  return(E);
end
```

Figure 4: Finding the Best Subspace for a Cluster

Algorithm $Merge(s_1 \ldots s_{k_c}, k_{new}, l_{new})$
begin
    for each pair $i, j \in \{1, \ldots k_c\}$ satisfying $i < j$ **do begin**
        $\mathcal{E}'_{ij} = FindVectors(\mathcal{C}_i \cup \mathcal{C}_j, l_{new})$;
        { Defined by eigenvectors for l_{new} smallest eigenvalues }
        $s'_{ij} = \overline{X}(\mathcal{C}_i \cup \mathcal{C}_j)$ { Centroid of $\mathcal{C}_i \cup \mathcal{C}_j$ };
        $r_{ij} = R(\mathcal{C}_i \cup \mathcal{C}_j, \mathcal{E}'_{ij})$
        { Projected energy of $\mathcal{C}_i \cup \mathcal{C}_j$ in subspace $\mathcal{E}'_{ij}$ }
    end
    while $(k_c > k_{new})$ **do begin**
        Find the smallest value of $r_{i'j'}$ among
            all pairs $i, j \in \{1, \ldots k_c\}$ satisfying $i < j$;
        { Merge the corresponding clusters $\mathcal{C}_{i'}$ and $\mathcal{C}_{j'}$; }
        $s_{i'} = s'_{i'j'}$; $\mathcal{C}_{i'} = \mathcal{C}_{i'} \cup \mathcal{C}_{j'}$; $\mathcal{E}_{i'} = \mathcal{E}'_{i'j'}$;
        Discard seed $s_{j'}$ and $\mathcal{C}_{j'}$ and renumber the
            seeds/clusters indexed larger than j' by subtracting 1;
        Renumber the values s'_{ij}, $\mathcal{E}_{ij}$, r_{ij} correspondingly
            for any $i, j \geq j'$;
        { Since cluster i' is new, the pairwise recomputation
        for $r_{i'j}$ for different j needs to be done }
        for each $j \neq i' \in \{1, \ldots k_c - 1\}$ **do begin**
            Recompute $\mathcal{E}'_{i'j} = FindVectors(\mathcal{C}_{i'} \cup \mathcal{C}_j, l_{new})$;
            $s'_{i'j} = \overline{X}(\mathcal{C}_{i'} \cup \mathcal{C}_j)$; { Centroid of $\mathcal{C}_{i'} \cup \mathcal{C}_j$ }
            $r_{i'j} = R(\mathcal{C}_{i'} \cup \mathcal{C}_j, \mathcal{E}'_{i'j})$ { Proj. En. of $\mathcal{C}_{i'} \cup \mathcal{C}_j$ in $\mathcal{E}'_{i'j}$; }
        end
        $k_c = k_c - 1$;
    end
    return$(s_1, \ldots s_{k_{new}}, \mathcal{C}_1, \ldots \mathcal{C}_{k_{new}}, \mathcal{E}_1, \ldots \mathcal{E}_{k_{new}})$
end

Figure 5: The Merging Algorithm

(1) **Assign:** The database is partitioned into k_c current clusters by assigning each point to its closest seed. In the process of partitioning, the distance of a database point to seed s_i is measured in the subspace $\mathcal{E}_i$. In other words, for each database point p, the value of $Pdist(p, s_i, \mathcal{E}_i)$ is computed, and the point p is assigned to the current cluster $\mathcal{C}_i$ for which this value is the least. At the end of this procedure each seed is replaced by the centroid of the cluster which was just created. The procedure serves to refine both the set of clusters in a given iteration and the set of seeds associated with these clusters. This method is illustrated in Figure 3.

(2) **FindVectors:** In this procedure we find the subspace $\mathcal{E}_i$ of dimensionality l_c for each current cluster $\mathcal{C}_i$. This is done by computing the covariance matrix for the cluster $\mathcal{C}_i$ and picking the l_c orthonormal eigenvectors with the least spread (eigenvalues). This finds the least energy subspace of rank l_c for cluster $\mathcal{C}_i$. The value of l_c reduces from iteration to iteration. The overall process is illustrated in Figure 4.

(3) **Merge:** During a given iteration, the *Merge* phase reduces the number of clusters from k_c to $k_{new} = (1 - \alpha) \cdot k_c$. In order to do so, closest pairs of current clusters need to be merged successively. This is easy to do in full dimensional algorithms, since the goodness of the merge can be easily quantified in full dimensionality.

This case is somewhat more complex. Since each current cluster $\mathcal{C}_i$ exists in its own (possibly different) subspace $\mathcal{E}_i$, how do we decide the suitability of merging "closest" pairs? Since, the aim of the algorithm is to discover clusters with small projected energy, we design a measure for testing the suitability of merging two clusters by examining the projected energy of the union of the two clusters in the corresponding least spread subspace. The quantitative measure for the suitability of merging each pair of seeds $[i, j]$ is calculated using a two step process.

In the first step, use singular value decomposition on the points in $\mathcal{C}_i \cup \mathcal{C}_j$ and find the eigenvectors corresponding to the smallest l_{new} eigenvalues. (l_{new} is the projected dimensionality in that iteration.) These eigenvectors define the least spread subspace for the points in the union of the two segmentations. Let us denote this subspace by $\mathcal{E}'_{ij}$. In the second step, we find the centroid s'_{ij} of $\mathcal{C}_i \cup \mathcal{C}_j$ and use the energy $r_{ij} = R(\mathcal{C}, \mathcal{E}'_{ij})$ of this cluster in the subspace $\mathcal{E}'_{ij}$ as the indicator of how well the points for the two clusters combine into a single cluster. Note that the points for the two clusters are likely to combine well using this method, if the least spread directions for the individual clusters were similar to begin with. In this case, $\mathcal{E}'_{ij}$, $\mathcal{E}_i$, and $\mathcal{E}_j$ are all likely to be similarly oriented subspaces with small (projected) energies. The overall idea here is to measure how well the two current clusters can be fit into a single pattern of behavior. For example, in the Figure 1(c), two current clusters $\mathcal{C}_i$ and $\mathcal{C}_j$ which consist of points from the same data pattern (say R) are likely to result in similar planes of 2-dimensional projection (normal plane to the direction of the arrows for R). Consequently, the points in $\mathcal{C}_i \cup \mathcal{C}_j$ are likely to be projected to a similar plane. The value of the energy r_{ij} when measured in this plane is likely to be small.

The above two-step process is repeated for each pair of seeds, and the pair of seeds $[i', j']$ is found for which $r_{i'j'}$ is the least. If the seeds are merged, then the centroid $s'_{i'j'}$ of the combined cluster is added to the set of seeds, whereas seeds $s_{i'}$ and $s_{j'}$ are removed. The current cluster associated with this new seed $s_{i'j'}$ is $\mathcal{C}_{i'} \cup \mathcal{C}_{j'}$, and the current subspace is $\mathcal{E}'_{ij}$. This agglomeration procedure is repeated multiple times, so that the number of clusters is reduced by a factor of α. The overall merging procedure is described in Figure 5.

The algorithm terminates when the merging process over all the iterations has reduced the number of clusters to k. At this point, the dimensionality l_c of the subspace $\mathcal{E}_i$ associated with each cluster $\mathcal{C}_i$ is also equal to l. The algorithm performs one final pass over the database in which it uses the *Assign* procedure in order to partition the database. If desired, the *FindVectors()* procedure may be used in order to determine the optimum subspace associated with each cluster at termination.

One of the aspects of this merging technique is that it needs to work explicitly with the set of current clusters $C_1 \ldots C_{k_c}$. Since the database size may be very large, it would be extremely cumbersome to maintain the sets $C_1 \ldots C_{k_c}$ explicitly. Furthermore, the covariance matrix calculation is also likely to be very I/O intensive, since each set of covariance matrix calculations is likely to require a pass over the database. Since the covariance matrix may be calculated $O(k_0^2)$ times by the *Merge* operation (see analysis later), this translates to $O(k_0^2)$ passes over the database. The value of k_0 is likely to be several times the number of clusters k to be determined. This level of I/O is unacceptable. We introduce the concept of *extended cluster feature vectors*, so that all of the above operations can be performed by always maintaining certain summary information about the clusters. This provides considerable ease in calculation of the covariance matrices. Details of this technique will be provided in a later section.

2.1 Picking the Projected Dimensionality

An important input parameter to the algorithm is the projected dimensionality l. To give some guidance to the user in picking this parameter, we design a measure which is motivated by the reason we have defined the concept of generalized projected clustering in the first place. It has been proved in [3], that with increasing dimensionality the distance between every pair of points is almost the same under certain conditions on the data distributions. This means that if a cluster of points C is compared to the universal set of points U in very high dimensional space D, then we have $\frac{R(C,D)}{R(U,D)} \approx 1$.

This is a very undesirable situation because it indicates that the average spread (energy) for a cluster is almost the same as the average spread for the points in the entire database in full dimensional space. This is also the reason for the instability of randomized clustering algorithms in high dimensional space: different runs lead to different clusters, all of which are almost equally good according to this or other measures.

However, in subspaces of D, this ratio may be much smaller than 1. In general a ratio which is significantly smaller than 1 is desirable, because it indicates a tightly knit cluster in the corresponding projected subspace. We define the following quality measure called *cluster sparsity coefficient*: $S(C_1 \ldots C_k, \mathcal{E}_1 \ldots \mathcal{E}_k) = (1/k) \cdot \sum_{i=1}^{k} \frac{R(C_i, \mathcal{E}_i)}{R(U, \mathcal{E}_i)}$. The lower the value of l, the smaller the fraction is likely to be, because $\mathcal{E}_i$ may be picked in a more optimum way in lower dimensionality so as to reduce the energy $R(C_i, \mathcal{E}_i)$ for the particular distribution of points in C_i, whereas the aggregate set of points in U may continue to have high energy $R(U, \mathcal{E}_i)$. At termination, the algorithm may return the cluster sparsity coefficient. If this value is almost 1,

then it is clear that a smaller value of the projected dimensionality needs to be picked. In fact the user may define a minimum threshold for this (intuitively interpretable) quality measure and pick the largest value of l at which the cluster sparsity coefficient returned at termination is less than the threshold.

2.2 Outlier Handling

In order to take into account the fact that some of the points are outliers, we may need to make some modifications to the algorithm. Let δ_i be the projected distance of the nearest other seed to the seed s_i in subspace $\mathcal{E}_i$ for each $i \in \{1, \ldots k_c\}$. Consider an arbitrary point P in the database during the assignment phase. Let s_r be the seed to which the database point P is assigned during the assignment phase. The point P is an outlier, if its projected distance to seed s_r in subspace E_r is larger than δ_r.

In addition, some of the seeds which were initially chosen may also be outliers. These need to be removed during the execution of the algorithm. A simple modification which turns out to be quite effective is the discarding of a certain percentage of the seeds in each iteration, for which the corresponding clusters contain very few points. When the outlier handling option is implemented, the value of the seed reduction factor α is defined by the percentage reduction in each iteration due to either merges or discards.

2.3 Scalability for Very Large Databases

As discussed above, the times for calculating covariance matrices can potentially be disastrously large (especially in terms of I/O times), if the covariance matrix is calculated from scratch for each $FindVectors(\cdot)$ operation. Therefore, we use a concept similar to the use of the Cluster Feature vector (CF-vector) [18] in order to find the covariance matrix efficiently. We shall refer to this as the extended CF-vector (or ECF-vector).

The ECF-vector is specific to a given cluster C, and contains $d^2 + d + 1$ entries. These entries are of three kinds:

(1) There are d^2 entries corresponding to each pair of dimensions (i, j). For each pair of dimensions (i, j), we sum the products of the ith and jth components for each point in the cluster. In other words, of x_i^k denotes the ith component of the kth point in the cluster, then for a cluster C and pair of dimensions (i, j), we maintain the entry $\sum_{k \in C} x_i^k \cdot x_j^k$. Thus there are d^2 entries of this type. For a cluster C, we will refer to this entry as $ECF1_{ij}^C$ for each pair of dimensions i and j. We will refer to the entire set of such entries as $\overline{ECF1^C}$.

(2) There are d entries corresponding to each dimension i. We sum the ith components for each point in the cluster. Thus, we maintain the entry $\sum_{k \in C} x_i^k$. For a cluster C, we shall refer to this entry as $ECF2_i^C$. The corresponding set of entries is referred to as $\overline{ECF2^{C}}$. **(3)** The number of points in the cluster C is denoted by $ECF3^{C}$.

Note that the first set of d^2 entries are not included in the standard definition of CF-vector as introduced in [18]. The entire cluster feature vector is denoted by $\overline{ECF^{C}} = (\overline{ECF1^{C}}, \overline{ECF2^{C}}, ECF3^{C})$. Two important features of the ECF-vector are as follows:

Observation 2.1 *The covariance matrix can be derived directly from the ECF-vector. Specifically, the covariance between the dimensions i and j for a set of points C is equal to $ECF1_{ij}^{C}/ECF3^{C} - ECF2_{i}^{C} \cdot ECF2_{j}^{C}/(ECF3^{C})^2$.*

Proof: The average of the product of the ith and jth attribute is given by $ECF1_{ij}^{C}/ECF3^{C}$, whereas the average of the ith attribute is given by $ECF2_{i}^{C}/ECF3^{C}$. Since the covariance between the ith and jth attributes is given by the subtraction of the product of averages from the average product, the result follows. ∎
It has been established by Zhang et. al. [18] that the CF-vector may be used in order to calculate the centroid, and radius of a cluster. Since the ECF-vector is a superset of the CF-vector, these measures may also be calculated from the ECF-vector. Our use of the extended CF-vector provides the ability to calculate the covariance matrix as well. The usefulness of the above result is that the covariance matrix can be calculated very efficiently from the ECF-vector. The use of the summary characteristics of a cluster is so useful because of the fact that it satisfies the additive property.

Observation 2.2 *The ECF-vector satisfies the additive property. The ECF-vector for the union of two sets of points is equal to the sum of the corresponding ECF-vectors.*

The proof of the above trivially follows from the fact that the ECF-vector for a set of points can be expressed as the sum of the ECF-vectors of the individual points. The additive property ensures that while constructing a ECF-vector for the union of two clusters, it is not necessary to recalculate everything from scratch, but that it is sufficient to add the ECF-vectors of the two clusters.

The ECF-vectors are used in order to modify OR-CLUS in the following way. *During the entire operation of the algorithm, the current clusters $C_1 \ldots C_{k_c}$ associated with each seed are not maintained explicitly.* Instead, the extended CF-vectors for the seeds are maintained. The ECF-vector for a cluster is sufficient to calculate the radius, centroid [18], and covariance matrix for each cluster. In each iteration, the seeds are defined by the centroids of the current clusters for the last iteration. In addition, the additive property of the ECF-vectors ensures that during a *Merge* operation, the

ECF-vector for the merged cluster may be calculated easily. The ECF-vectors need to be recalculated in each iteration only during the *Assign(·)* phase; a simple additive process which does not affect the overall time-complexity of the algorithm.

2.4 Running Time Requirements

The running time of the algorithm depends upon the initial number of seeds k_0 chosen by the algorithm. The skeletal structure for the algorithm contains the two basic process of merging and assignment of points to seeds. (The addition of the outlier handling option only reduces the running time of the algorithm since merges are replaced by simple discards. Therefore the analysis presented below is an overestimate on the running time of the algorithm.) The running time for the various procedures of the algorithm are as below:

(1) Merge: The time for merging is asymptotically controlled by the time required in the first iteration of reducing the value of the number of current clusters from k_0 to $\alpha \cdot k_0$. To start off, the eigenvectors for each of the k_0^2 pairs of current clusters are calculated. This requires a running time of $O(d^3)$ for each pair. Furthermore, for each of the subsequent (at most) $(1-\alpha) \cdot k_0 - k$ merges, the eigenvectors for $O(k_0)$ pairs of clusters need to be re-calculated. Since, each eigenvector calculation is $O(d^3)$, it follows that the total time for eigenvector calculations during the merge operation of the algorithm is given by $O(k_0^2 \cdot d^3)$. Furthermore, for each merge operation, $O(k_0^2)$ time is required in order to pick the cluster with the least energy. Therefore, the total running time for all merges is given by $O(k_0^2(k_0 + d^3))$.
(2) Assign: The running time for assignment of the N points in d-dimensional space to the k_0 clusters in the first iteration is given by $O(k_0 \cdot N \cdot d)$. In the second iteration, the time is given by $O((k_0 \cdot \alpha) \cdot N \cdot d)$, and so on. Therefore the overall running time for the assignment process is given by $O(k_0 \cdot N \cdot d/(1 - \alpha))$.
(3) Subspace Determination: The time for eigenvector calculations (or subspace determinations) during the *Merge* phase has already been included in the analysis above. It now only remains to calculate the time for subspace determinations during each iterative phase (the *FindVectors* procedure after the *Assign*) of the algorithm. During the first iteration of the algorithm, there are k_0 subspace determinations, during the second iteration, there are $k_0 \cdot \alpha$ subspace determinations and so on. Therefore, during the entire algorithm, there are at most $k_0/(1 - \alpha)$ subspace determinations. This running time is strictly dominated by the subspace determinations during the *Merge* phase, and can hence be ignored asymptotically.

Upon summing up the various components of the running time, the total time required is given by $O(k_0^3 + k_0 \cdot N \cdot d + k_0^2 \cdot d^3)$. Note that this running time is dependent upon the choice of the initial parameter k_0. A choice of a larger value of k_0 is likely to increase the running time, but also improve the quality of clustering.

2.5 Space Requirements

The use of the ECF vector cuts down the space requirements of the algorithm considerably, since the current clusters associated with each seed need not be maintained. During each iteration of the algorithm, at most k_c extended CF-vectors need to be maintained. The space requirement for this is given by $k_c \cdot (d^2+d+1)$. Since $k_c \leq k_0$, the overall space requirement of the algorithm is $O(k_0 \cdot d^2)$. This is independent of database size, and may very easily fit in main memory for reasonable values of k_0 and d.

2.6 Progressive Sampling Techniques

It is possible to speed up the assignment phase of the algorithm substantially by using a progressive type of random sampling. Note that the component in the running time which is dependent on N is caused by the $Assign(\cdot)$ procedure of the algorithm. This component of the running time can be the bottleneck when the database is very large. Another observation is that the CPU time for performing the $Assign(\cdot)$ procedure reduces by the factor α in each iteration, as the number of seeds reduces by the same factor. The purpose of the $Assign(\cdot)$ procedure is to keep correcting the seeds in each iteration so that each seed is a more central point of the current cluster that is associated with it. It is possible to achieve the same results by using a progressive kind of random sampling. Thus, only a randomly sampled subset of the points are assigned to the seeds in each iteration. This random sample can be different over multiple iterations and can change in size. (If the size of the random sample increases by a factor of α in each iteration, then the time for the assignment phase is the same in each iteration.) Thus, one possibility is to start off with a random sample of size $N \cdot k/k_0$ and increase by a factor of α in each iteration, so that in the final iteration all the database points are used. Thus, the time for the assignment phase in each iteration would be $N \cdot k \cdot d$, and over all iterations would be $N \cdot k \cdot d \cdot \log_\alpha(k_0/k)$. This kind of progressive sampling can provide considerable savings in CPU time in the first few iterations, if k_0 is substantially larger than k. Furthermore, it is unlikely to lose much in terms of accuracy because when the seeds become more refined in the last few iterations, then larger sample sizes are used.

3 Empirical Results

The simulations were performed on a 233-MHz IBM RS/6000 computer with 128 M of memory, 2GB SCSI drive, and running AIX 4.1.4. We tested the following accuracy and performance measures:

1. Accuracy of the clustering with respect to matching of points in Input and Output Clusters.
2. Scaling of running times with database size.
3. Scaling of the I/O performance with initial number of seeds.

In order to test the accuracy results, we determined the *Confusion Matrix* which indicated how well the output clusters matched with the input points. The entry (i, j) of the confusion matrix indicates the number of points belonging to the output cluster i, which were generated as a part of the input cluster j. If the clustering algorithm performs well, then each row and column is likely to have one entry which is significantly larger than the others. On the other hand, in the case when the clustering technique is so bad as to be completely random, then the points are likely to be evenly distributed among the different clusters.

3.1 Synthetic Data Generation

The first stage of synthetic data generation was to find the arbitrarily oriented subspaces associated with each cluster. In order to generate the subspace associated with each cluster, we generated random matrices, such that the (i, j)th entry of the matrix was a random real number in the range $(-1, 1)$. In addition, the matrix was made to be symmetric so that the (i, j)th entry was equal to the (j, i)th entry. Since, this is a symmetric matrix, the eigenvalues are all real, and an orthonormal eigenvector system exists. This orthonormal axis system will be used to generate the input orientation for the corresponding cluster. We used a different matrix for each of the clusters in order to generate the corresponding orientation.

The number of points in each cluster was determined by using the following method to determine the number of points in each cluster: We first determined the constant of proportionality r_i which found how many points were present in each cluster i. The constant of proportionality r_i was determined by the formula $r_i = p + R \cdot q$. Here p and q are constants, and R is a random number which is drawn from a uniform distribution in the range $(0, 1)$. (Thus, the resulting number will be drawn from the uniform distribution in the range $(p, p+q)$.) For the purpose of our experiments, we used $p = 1$ and $q = 5$. Thus, if $r_1, r_2, \ldots r_k$ be the proportionality constants for the entire space, then the number of points N_i in the cluster i was determined by using the formula $N_i = N \cdot r_i / \sum_{i=1}^{k} r_i$.

The next step was to generate the anchor points (an approximation of the central point) of each cluster. The anchor points were chosen from a uniform distribution of points in the space. Once the anchor points were determined, they were used to generate the clusters of points. We have already discussed how the axes orientations for each cluster are determined by using the eigenvectors of the randomly generated symmetric matrices. Now it remains to distribute the points in each cluster corresponding to this axis system. Since this axis system corresponds to one in which the correlations of the points are zero, we generate the coordinates with respect to this transformed subspace independently from one another. (The generated points can then be transformed back to their original space.) For each cluster, we picked the l eigenvectors which defined the subspace in which it was hidden. The points were distributed in a uniform random distribution along the other $d - l$ axes directions.

It now remains to explain how the point distribution for the hidden axes directions was accomplished. The first step was to determine the spread along each of the l eigenvectors. This was determined by a pair of spread parameters μ_s and γ. The spread along the eigenvector i was determined to be proportional to $(Q_i)^\gamma$, where Q_i was drawn from an exponential distribution with mean μ_s, and γ was a parameter which determined the level of disproportionality that we wished to create in the various axes directions. This is because when the value of γ is increased, the amount of disproportionality in the values of $(Q_i)^\gamma$ increased for different values of i. Thus, the ith coordinate for the point with respect to the transformed subspace was drawn from a normal distribution with its mean at the anchor point and its variance equal to $(Q_i)^\gamma$. For our experiments, we used $d = 20$, $\mu_s = 0.1$, $\gamma = 2$, $p = 1$, $q = 5$, $k = 5$ and $l = 6$.

The resulting clusters were very sparse in full dimensional space. The cluster sparsity coefficient when measured in full dimensional space for the input clusters for this choice of parameters was 0.85. Furthermore, we checked the sparsity coefficient of *each individual input cluster for each 1-dimensional [2] axis parallel projection*, and found that in each case, the cluster sparsity coefficient was at least as high as 0.7, and averaged at 0.83. The high sparsity coefficients indicate that the generated data is one on which either full-dimensional or axis-parallel projected clustering would be meaningless.

3.2 Failure of axis-parallel projections

We tested an axis-parallel version[3] of this algorithm

---

[2] Cluster sparsity coefficients for higher dimensional projections would always be at least as large as the minimum sparsity coefficient of some 1-dimensional subset, and will be at most as large as the maximum sparsity coefficient of any 1-dimensional subset. This can be proved from the additive property of the energy metric over different dimensions. A formal proof is omitted.

[3] We have another axis-parallel projected clustering algorithm called PROCLUS [1] which also could not match input to output clusters well. In addition, PROCLUS would classify an unusually large number of input points as outliers. We found that the axis-parallel version of ORCLUS was slightly more stable and accurate than PROCLUS.

Input Clusters / Output Clusters	A	B	C	D	E
1	639	178	0	0	131
2	0	931	549	465	29
3	121	35	851	265	90
4	50	225	135	2889	408
5	135	133	201	128	1412

Table 1: Axis Parallel projections: Confusion Matrix -[User-specified $l = 14$]

Input Clusters / Output Clusters	A	B	C	D	E
1	367	202	261	208	263
2	70	835	631	1331	241
3	169	101	604	103	73
4	108	180	99	2001	128
5	231	184	141	104	1365

Table 2: Axis Parallel projections: Confusion Matrix -[User-specified $l = 6$]

on the data set. This was done by ensuring that the $FindVectors(\cdot)$ procedure returned the least spread axis parallel directions. We will state the salient observations very briefly:

• The axis parallel projected version found very poor matching between the input and output clusters. The method was not significantly better than a random clustering technique for some of the runs. We have illustrated two runs on the same data set of 10,000 points, with varying values of the projected dimensionality and illustrated the results in Tables 1 and 2. The Confusion Matrix in Table 1 ($l = 14$) is slightly better than the confusion matrix in Table 2 ($l = 6$), though neither of them can be considered very clean partitionings, since each input cluster is split into several output clusters and vice-versa. This was part of an interesting trend that we observed: *reducing the user-specified value of projected dimensionality l always worsened the quality of clustering by the axis-parallel version.* When the clusters exist in arbitrary subspaces, then forcing particular kinds of projections on the clusters leads to loss of information; the greater the projection, the greater the loss.

• The axis-parallel version was unstable. Slight changes in initialization conditions (such as changing the random seed) significantly changed the the matrices obtained in Tables 1 and 2.

The above results are quite expected; our observations on the sparsity coefficients indicate the unsuitability of the class of axis-parallel projection methods.

3.3 Results for ORCLUS

Input Clusters / Output Clusters	A	B	C	D	E
1	898	0	0	0	2
2	0	1401	0	124	0
3	23	0	1703	0	0
4	0	40	0	3623	59
5	24	61	33	0	2009

Table 3: ORCLUS: Confusion Matrix (Case 1) [User-specified $l = 6$]

Input Clust. / Output Clust.	A	B	C	D	E
1	9201	103	12	0	0
2	122	16144	7	24	0
3	0	0	29821	0	22
4	3	0	0	20451	24
5	15	101	0	0	23950

Table 4: ORCLUS: Confusion Matrix (Case 2) [User-specified $l = 6$]

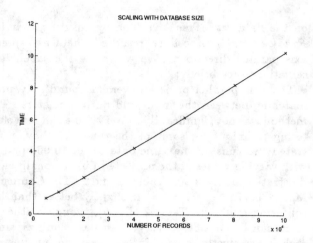

Figure 6: Scaling of running time with database size

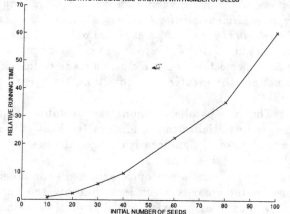

Figure 7: Scaling of running time with k_0

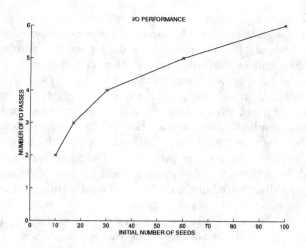

Figure 8: Scaling of I/O passes with k_0

For the purpose of our tests, we always used $k_0 = 15 \cdot k$, unless mentioned otherwise. We generated several input data sets and computed the Confusion Matrix for each of the cases. We will present some of the confusion matrices which are very representative of the general trend that we observed. First we ran the algorithm for different values of the projected dimensionality l and tested the corresponding cluster sparsity coefficient. In each case, we found that the output cluster sparsity coefficient dropped significantly from $l = 7$ to $l = 6$ (Case 1- 0.081 to 0.003; Case 2- 0.09 to 0.0024), whereas the drop from $l = 6$ to $l = 5$ was relatively small (Case 1- 0.003 to 0.0025; Case 2- 0.0024 to 0.0022). In fact, the percentage drop in sparsity coefficient was always the highest from $l = 7$ to $l = 6$ which was the dimensionality of the subspace in which the input clusters were hidden. We used this criterion to pick the projected dimensionality $l = 6$ in both the cases that we illustrate below. The first data set (Case 1) contained 10,000 points, and the results are indicated in Table 3. This is the same data set which was used in Tables 1 and 2. As we can see from the table one of the entries in each column is clearly much larger than the rest of the entries. This indicates that each input cluster gets directed into one output cluster with the exception of some points, which get distributed to other clusters. Table 4 (Case 2) illustrates another example containing 100,000 points. The trends are very similar to Table 3. These results are generally indicative of a very clean mapping from the input to output clusters. We also tested the sensitivity of this clustering to variations in the value of the input parameter l. We found in each case that a good confusion matrix was obtained in the range of $l = 2$ to $l = 8$, and was only slightly worse than the confusion matrix for the optimized value $l = 6$. This is also an indication of the stability of this technique.

We also present the computational scalability results

for the algorithm here. The results were averaged over five runs in each case in order to smooth the curve. The scaling of running time with the number of points N in the database is illustrated in Figure 6. As we see, the algorithm performance is practically linear with database size. Note that the curve is interesting only for the case when N is substantially larger than k_0, the initial number of seeds.

Figure 7 illustrates the CPU performance when the initial number of seeds k_0 was increased. We know that the quality of the clusters is likely to be better when starting with a larger number of seeds, because each cluster is then likely to be covered by at least one seed. Correspondingly, the running time of the algorithm also increases, because of the contribution of the subspace determination operations during the *Merge* phase. The I/O requirements varied less dramatically with the initial number of seeds. This is because the total number of iterations is $\log_\alpha(k/k_0)$, in each of which at most one I/O pass is performed. Figure 8 illustrates the corresponding trend. This curve remains the same irrespective of database size, dimensionality, or the final number of projected dimensions. These results indicate that when a larger number of initial seeds are picked in the interest of greater accuracy, the method is unlikely to be I/O bound.

4   Conclusions and Summary

In this paper we discussed the concept of finding arbitrarily oriented projected clusters in high dimensional spaces, a definition of clustering which is a practical and effective solution to the dimensionality curse for the traditional version of this problem. The idea of eliminating the most sparse subspaces for each cluster, and projecting the points into those subspaces in which the greatest similarity occurs is a very generalized notion of clustering of which the full dimensional case is a special one. Since the sparsity of high dimensional data prevents the detection of natural clusters for full-dimensional problems, this modified definition of clustering is best likely to redefine our understanding of the notion of high dimensional clustering. In future research, we will show how to use this technique for effective high dimensional data visualization.

References

[1] C. C. Aggarwal et. al. Fast algorithms for projected clustering. *ACM SIGMOD Conference*, 1999.

[2] R. Agrawal et. al. Automatic Subspace Clustering of High Dimensional Data for Data Mining Applications. *ACM SIGMOD Conference*, 1998.

[3] K. Beyer et. al. When is nearest neighbor meaningful? *ICDT Conference*, 1999.

[4] C. Cheng, A. W. Fu, Y. Zhang. Entropy-based Subspace Clustering for Mining Numerical Data. *ACM SIGKDD Conference*, 1999.

[5] M. Ester et. al. A Density Based Algorithm for Discovering Clusters in Large Spatial Databases with Noise. *KDD Conference*, 1996.

[6] C. Faloutsos, K.-I. Lin. FastMap: A Fast Algorithm for Indexing, Data-Mining and Visualization of Traditional and Multimedia Datasets. *ACM SIGMOD Conference*, 1995.

[7] A. Gionis, P. Indyk, R. Motwani. Similarity Search in High Dimensions via Hashing. *VLDB Conference*, 1999.

[8] S. Guha, R. Rastogi, K. Shim. CURE: An Efficient Clustering Algorithm for Large Databases. *ACM SIGMOD Conference*, 1998.

[9] A. Hinneburg, D. Keim. Optimal Grid-Clustering: Towards Breaking the Curse of Dimensionality in High-Dimensional Clustering. *VLDB Conference*, 1999.

[10] P. Indyk, R. Motwani. Approximate Nearest Neighbors: Towards Removing the Curse of Dimensionality. *STOC*, 1998.

[11] A. Jain, R. Dubes. *Algorithms for Clustering Data*. Prentice Hall, New Jersey, 1998.

[12] I. T. Jolliffe. *Principal Component Analysis*. Springer-Verlag, New York, 1986.

[13] J. Kleinberg. Two algorithms for nearest-neighbor search in high dimensional space. *STOC*, 1997.

[14] R. Kohavi, D. Sommerfield. Feature Subset Selection Using the Wrapper Method: Overfitting and Dynamic Search Space Topology. *KDD*, 1995.

[15] R. Ng, J. Han. Efficient and Effective Clustering Methods for Spatial Data Mining. *VLDB Conference*, 1994.

[16] K. Ravi Kanth, D. Agrawal, A. Singh. Dimensionality Reduction for Similarity Searching in Dynamic Databases. *ACM SIGMOD Conference*, 1998.

[17] X. Xu et. al. A Distribution-Based Clustering Algorithm for Mining in Large Spatial Databases. *ICDE Conference*, 1998.

[18] T. Zhang, R. Ramakrishnan, M. Livny. BIRCH: An Efficient Data Clustering Method for Very Large Databases. *ACM SIGMOD Conference*, 1996.

Density Biased Sampling: An Improved Method for Data Mining and Clustering *

Christopher R. Palmer
Computer Science Department
Carnegie Mellon University
Pittsburgh, PA
crpalmer@cs.cmu.edu

Christos Faloutsos
Computer Science Department
Carnegie Mellon University
Pittsburgh, PA
christos@cs.cmu.edu

Abstract

Data mining in large data sets often requires a sampling or summarization step to form an in-core representation of the data that can be processed more efficiently. Uniform random sampling is frequently used in practice and also frequently criticized because it will miss small clusters. Many natural phenomena are known to follow Zipf's distribution and the inability of uniform sampling to find small clusters is of practical concern. Density Biased Sampling is proposed to probabilistically under-sample dense regions and over-sample light regions. A weighted sample is used to preserve the densities of the original data. Density biased sampling naturally includes uniform sampling as a special case. A memory efficient algorithm is proposed that approximates density biased sampling using only a single scan of the data. We empirically evaluate density biased sampling using synthetic data sets that exhibit varying cluster size distributions finding up to a factor of six improvement over uniform sampling.

1 Introduction

Uniform sampling is often used in database and data mining applications and Olken provides an excellent argument for the need to include sampling primitives in databases [17]. Whether or not uniform sampling is the "best" sampling technique must be evaluated on an application by application basis. Some records may be of more value in the sample than others. If we knew the value of each record, we could sample by assigning a probability proportional to the importance of the record. It is unlikely that we can define the value of each record in the database and, worse yet, it may be difficult to generalize results obtained from such a sample because the sample is no longer representative of the database. Instead, we'll consider applications in which it is possible to define sets of equivalent records and use the size of these sets to bias our sample while ensuring that the sample is still representative. Data mining applications on spatial data are a natural application because we have a simple notion of equivalent points: points that are close. To show the applicability of using groups of equivalent points to bias the sample, we will concentrate on clustering a database.

Clustering can be generally defined as the following problem. Given N points in d dimensional feature space, find interesting groups of points. There is no definitive way to quantify "interesting" but many algorithms assume that the number of clusters, k, is known a priori and find the k clusters that minimize some error metric. Other algorithms look at areas of space that are denser than some threshold parameter and then form clusters from these dense regions. Clustering is of practical importance in many settings. For example, clustering can be used for classification problems in machine learning [16], in information retrieval to identify concepts [4] or to improve the presentation of web search results [22], by physicists to find the spatial grouping of stars into galaxies [15] and in general to find relationships in the data and to succinctly model the data distribution. Interesting problems for all of these applications involve data sets that have at least a million points.

A typical clustering algorithm will initialize the parameters of the model (randomly or based on a sample) and iteratively use the model to assign the data to group(s). According to this assignment, a new model is constructed. This iterative process involves the entire data set at each step and take an unbounded number

*This material is based upon work supported by the National Science Foundation under Grants No. IRI-9625428, DMS-9873442, IIS-9817496, IIS-9910606, and REC-9729374, and by the Defense Advanced Research Projects Agency under Contract No. N66001-97-C-8517. Additional funding was provided by donations from NEC and Intel. Any opinions, findings, and conclusions or recommendations expressed in this material are those of the author(s) and do not necessarily reflect the views of the National Science Foundation, DARPA, or other funding parties.

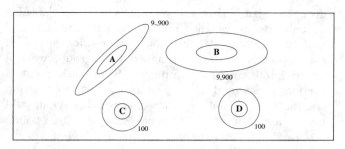

Figure 1: Four clusters with skewed sizes

of steps to converge. It is essential that we reduce the data size. One solution is to summarize the data and create a new representation that is more compact. The best algorithms based on data summarization use the current model to summarize a subset of the data [2, 3]. As such, it is imperative that the initial model for a summarizing clustering algorithm be representative of the data.

Alternatively, many people use a p-uniform sample (a sample in which each element has probability p of being selected). A sample is selected from the database and clustered. Provided that the sample was representative of the data, the clustering is expected to generalize to the entire data set. Once the sample has been clustered, a single pass over the database to correct for small errors (due to sampling) is recommended. To see why uniform sampling is not necessarily ideal, consider the example in Figure 1. This example and much of the discussion is based on data generated by the "mixture model." The mixture model assumes that the data is generated by a mixture of k Gaussian distributions. Each distribution has a corresponding mean and covariance matrix and points are assumed to have been generated by one of these Gaussians. Our example contains 4 clusters and the distribution of points between clusters has been dramatically skewed: clusters A and B each contain 9,900 points while clusters C and D each contain only 100 points. The shaded area contains most of the points of each cluster (the dense core of the Gaussian distribution). A 1% sample of this data set would be expected to draw around 99 points from each of A and B and a single point from each of C and D. For any given sample, if one or more points are actually selected from the C and D clusters, they will likely be treated as noise by the clustering algorithm. That is, we expect that clusters C and D will be completely missed!

Let us consider what has happened with this uniform sample to see what properties are needed by a good sampling technique. First, it is important that the sample contain many points from the shaded region because they will be the best representatives of the cluster. Uniform sampling has this property since the shaded area is the dense core of the Gaussian. But,

as we saw, the uniform sample fails because it is not representative of all the groups of points. We want to sample more evenly from all the different groups. For example, if we already knew the clusters, we'd rather randomly pick 50 points from each cluster to form the sample. Using the size of the groups to bias the sample is the heart of our proposed method and we call this a *Density Biased Sample*. Since we pick the points uniformly from each cluster, the density biased sample here will still contain more points from the shaded regions. But, it is not necessarily a good sample because it is no longer representative of the data (it makes A and C appear to be the same size). Instead, we notice that each sampled point from clusters A and B is representing $\frac{9,900}{50} = 198$ points, while each sampled point from cluster C and D is only representing 2 points. Augmenting the sample with a weighting of the points is called a *Weighted Sample*.

Cluster sizes are not actually expected to be skewed as dramatically as was shown in the example. Instead, it seems more likely that cluster sizes will follow a Zipf distribution. Zipf distributions occur extremely frequently in practice: they have been found in the frequency distribution of vocabulary words in text (English and Latin works of literature [24]; the Bible [6]); the distribution of city populations [24]; distribution of first and last names of people [5]; sales patterns [6]; income distributions (the "Pareto law" [20]); and distribution of website hits [13].

The main contribution of this paper is to introduce a new sampling technique and an efficient algorithm that improves on uniform sampling when cluster sizes are skewed. The rest of the paper is organized as follows. First, we present density biased sampling in general terms, parameterized to form a set of sampling techniques that includes uniform sampling as a special case. We then comment on related work. Next, we develop a one-pass algorithm that produces an approximate density biased sample and informally characterize its behaviour. Experimental results follow which demonstrate that density biased sampling is more effective than uniform sampling when the size of the clusters is skewed.

2 Density Biased Sampling

Suppose that we have N values $x_1, x_2, \cdots, x_N$ that are partitioned into g groups that have sizes $n_1, n_2, \cdots, n_g$ and we want to generate a sample with expected size M in which the probability of point x_i is dependent on the group sizes (particularly dependent on the size of the group containing x_i). The groups in the motivating example were defined to be the clusters. This is obviously computationally infeasible. We will define a simple algorithm for group assignments in section 4 and proceed to define Density Biased Sampling in terms of arbitrary groups.

Our example from Figure 1 suggested the criteria that we want our sampling to satisfy. We will define a probability function and a corresponding weighting of the sample points that satisfies:

i) Within a group, points are selected uniformly.

ii) The sample is density preserving.

iii) The sample is biased by group size.

iv) Expected sample size is M.

We define *density preserving* to mean that the expected sum of the weights of the sampled points for each group is proportional to the group's size. That is, if group i contains the points $\{x_1, x_2, \cdots, x_{n_i}\}$, point x_j is included in the sample (with weight w_j) with probability $P(x_j)$, then

$$\sum_{j=1}^{n_i} w_j \cdot P(x_j) = \kappa n_i$$

for some constant κ. This formalizes the notion of "representative of the data distribution." Uniform sampling satisfies this definition. A p-uniform sample has $\kappa = p$.

To satisfy criterion i), we define P(selecting point $x \mid x$ in group i) $= f(n_i)$. Each point in the group then has the same probability of being selected and we assign each point from the group equal weight $w(n_i) = 1/f(n_i)$. The expected weight of the points in group i is:

$$\sum_{j=1}^{n_i} P(\text{point } x_i) \cdot w(n_i) = \sum_{j=1}^{n_i} f(n_i) \cdot 1/f(n_i) = n_i$$

which satisfies property ii). To bias the sample by group size, we define $f(n_i) = \frac{\alpha}{n_i^e}$ for any constant e. Notice that for $e = 0$, we have simply defined a uniform sample (independent of group assignments) and for $e = 1$ we expect to select the same number of points per group (as in the example). We define α such that the expected sample size is M (requirement iv):

$$
\begin{aligned}
E(\text{sample size}) &= \sum_{i=1}^{g} E(\text{size of group } i) \\
M &= \sum_{i=1}^{g} n_i f(n_i) = \sum_{i=1}^{g} n_i \frac{\alpha}{n_i^e} \\
\Rightarrow \alpha &= \frac{M}{\sum_{i=1}^{g} n_i^{1-e}}
\end{aligned}
$$

The following observations apply in general and will be useful when we discuss an implementation of density biased sampling. First, if there are g groups of size $\frac{n}{g}$ then every point is assigned the same probability and weight. That is, we have implemented uniform sampling. The second observation is that if each point is randomly assigned to a group, we will approximate uniform sampling. Since each point is randomly assigned to a group, the expected group size is n/g. That is, the expected behaviour will be to approximate a uniform sample when points are randomly assigned to groups. These first two observations will be important when we define a simple algorithm for group assignments. We will be able to see that poor parameter choices will gracefully degrade to a uniform sample.

The final observation relates to a sample of data generated by a mixture model in which each cluster has equal size. The ideal groups for such a dataset are the clusters (as we saw in the motivating example). That is, in this special case, uniform sampling is equivalent to Density Biased Sampling with ideal groups. We will use this observation in our experiments to quantify the effects of a much simpler definition of group assignments.

3   Related Work

Sampling has attracted much interest in databases: Olken et al. give algorithms for uniform sampling from hash tables and index trees [17]; Hellerstein et al. use sampling to give approximate answers to aggregation queries [12]; Haas et al. use sampling to make estimates for the number of distinct values of an attribute for query optimization [10].

Sampling is also used extensively for data mining: Commercial vendors of statistical packages (e.g., SAS, at http://www.sas.com/) typically use uniform sampling to handle large datasets.

Clustering is one of the typical operations in data mining. There is a *huge* literature on clustering for Information Retrieval (see [18] for a recent survey), with additional interest in social and biological sciences (see [11]). Clustering for large datasets has attracted a lot of interest in the database field.

Zhang et al. proposed the BIRCH algorithm which was the first to explicitly use a data summarization step [23]. A tree of spherical groups of points (a CF-tree) is built and the size of spheres is grown as memory is exhausted. The assumption that the points may be summarized as spheres is often criticized and more recently Bradley, Fayyad and Reina have used the current model of the data to select points that should be summarized by their sufficient statistics [2, 3]. They show that this model based summarization is more effective than the BIRCH CF tree summarization. To produce good clustering results, they assume that the data is randomized (or at least the initial portion of the data is a random sample). It seems that a density biased

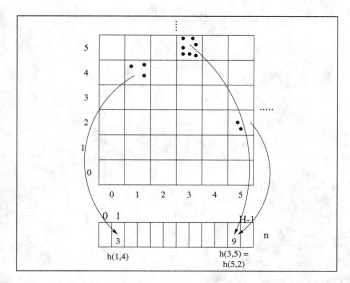

Figure 2: Density approximation by hashing

$$hash(< v_1, ..., v_d >) =$$
$$\text{FOR } i = 1 \text{ TO } d \text{ DO } h = h * 65,599 + v_i$$
$$\text{RETURN } h \text{ MOD } H$$

Figure 3: Hash function

FOR each input vector x
    DO $n[h(x)] = n[h(x)] + 1$
Reset the input and compute α
FOR each input vector x
    DO with prob. $\alpha/n[h(x)]^e$
        output $< n[h(x)]^e/\alpha, x >$

Figure 4: Two-pass hash approximation to density biased sampling

sample would be ideal to "seed" their initial model.

Uniform sampling has also been used directly for clustering. CURE uses a uniform random sample and a new hierarchical clustering algorithm that out-performs BIRCH in experiments using non-spherical clusters that are unevenly sized with noise in the data [9]. They ensure that the sample is large enough to adequately cover all clusters. Salem directly compares uniform sampling against CF-tree summarization finding the uniform sampling is as good a representation for sufficiently large samples [14]. Sampling in both papers is done using Vitter's reservoir sampling [21].

Density Biased Sampling (DBS) is related to previous sampling techniques. In particular, Probability Proportional to Size (PPS) sampling has similarities to DBS. PPS sampling is a multi-stage sampling technique. The data is grouped and then some subset of the groups are chosen. From the chosen groups, elements are added to the sample. In PPS sampling, the selection of groups is biased proportionally to their size. DBS will be inversely biased by group size and is a one stage sampling technique. PPS sampling would be difficult if not impossible to implement as a one pass algorithm. Stratified sampling is used for spatial analysis (for example, [19]). Stratified sampling is another form of two stage sampling.

4   Approximating Density Biased Sampling

Density biased sampling requires that the data be partitioned into "groups." We have no a priori knowledge of how the data will be distributed and adopt the obvious technique for grouping the points. Numerical attributes are divided into G bins and categorical attributes have a bin for each category.

When dealing entirely with d-dimensional numerical data, the space is divided into bins by placing a d-dimensional grid over the data. If the data is drawn from a low dimensional space and the number of occupied bins, B, is small, we can compute the bin counts using $O(d \times B)$ bytes. We call this an *exact density biased sample*. If too many of the bins are occupied, an approximate histogram algorithm can be used [8]. But, in higher dimensions, it becomes prohibitively expensive to merely represent the occupied bins.

Those potential implementations suffer from the lack of available memory. We propose a hashing based approach where all available memory is used to create an array of bin counts. Call this array n (then $n[i]$ corresponds to n_i in the previous section) and assume that it has H entries (indexed from 0). To index into this array, we will use a hash function from the bin label to array index (see Figure 2). The bin labels are integers (either in the range $0, \cdots, G - 1$ for numerical data or $0, \cdots, c - 1$ for categorical data with c categories). Hashing bin labels should be similar to hashing strings since each element is expected to be drawn from a relatively small range and we expect values to frequently differ in only one position (adjacent bins). Aho, Sethi and Ullman suggest that the hash function shown in Figure 3 is appropriate for the symbol table of a compiler [1]. For simplicity, assume that $h(x)$ is a function that takes value x, quantizes it and then invokes *hash* on the quantized version. Then the two pass algorithm using a hash function to approximate density biased sampling is trivial and shown in Figure 4.

The second pass over the data makes this an unappealing algorithm. If $0 \leq e \leq 1$, this algorithm can be converted into a one pass reservoir style algorithm.

```
α_D = 0
FOR each input point x DO
    IF n[h(x)] ≠ 0 THEN α_D = α_D − n[h(x)]^{1−e}          (*)
    n[h(x)] = n[h(x)] + 1
    α_D = α_D + n[h(x)]^{1−e}                              (*)
    WITH prob.  P = min{M/(α_D * n[h(x)]^e), 1} DO
        IF the output buffer is full THEN reduce()
        add  < P, x >  to the output buffer
reduce()
FOR each output buffer entry  < P_i, x_i >  DO output  < 1/P_i, x_i >


reduce() is
    FOR each output buffer entry  < P_i, x_i >  DO
        Let P'_i = min{M/(α_D * n[h(x)]^e), 1}
        WITH prob.  P'_i/P_i replace this entry with  < P'_i, x_i >
        OTHERWISE remove this entry
```

Figure 5: One pass hash approximation to density biased sampling

That is, to eliminate this second pass over the data, we need to build the densities and the sample in parallel. To do so, we will build a sample of the first j items and then show how this can be used to build a sample of the first $j + 1$ items. The following lemma is needed to show that the sample of the first j items is a superset of the sample of the first $j + 1$ items.

Lemma 1 If, when the data is restricted to the first j records, the probability of outputting some record x is P_j. Then for $j \leq j'$, $P_j \geq P_{j'}$.

Proof 1 (Sketch) n^e and n^{1-e} are monotone increasing functions and the probability function that we use is of the form

$$P = \frac{M}{n_x^e \sum_{i=1}^{g} n_g^{1-e}}$$

As more data is processed the number of terms in the summation will never decrease nor will any value of n decrease and consequently the denominator of the probability function will be monotone increasing and the probabilities will be monotone decreasing.

A buffer of points that have some chance of being in the sample will be maintained. The buffer contains elements $\{< P_i, x_i >\}$ to indicate that x_i was added to the buffer with probability P_i. Suppose that at some later point, x_i would have probability P'_i of being output. We can convert the current output buffer into a buffer that is a density biased sample of the currently processed data. The lemma tells us that $P'_i \leq P_i$ and consequently we will never erroneously discard a point due to an underestimate of its probability. If we

keep $< P'_i, x_i >$ in the buffer with probability P'_i/P_i (otherwise, remove this entry from the buffer), then x_i is in the buffer with probability P'_i. The weight of a point is just $1/P'_i$ which means that we can output the weighted sample from the reduced buffer. The one pass algorithm is shown in detail in Figure 5

Assuming that **reduce** always removes at least one entry, this algorithm is equivalent to the 2-pass version. It is equivalent because the current output buffer is always a superset of a density biased sample and the reduce operation converts it to a density biased sample of the data process to this point. When reduce fails to remove any entries, we randomly select an entry to evict. This happens quite rarely in practice[1]. In our experiments, the output buffer is of size $1.1 \times M$ to generate a sample of expected size M. The two lines marked with (*) compute the current denominator of α in constant time (instead of time proportional to the number of bins).

Obviously this one pass algorithm can be used for any representation of the bin densities. Hashing is only used to map from input point to group size and any other mapping could be used here instead.

Collisions are a possible problem for this algorithm. It seems that the ideal value of e would be 1 because the sample will always be density preserving. If bins g and $g + 1$ collided to form bin g then the expected

---

[1] This approach, of course, creates a small bias toward points later in the database. It is trivial to correct this problem by recording the number of times that each point in the buffer "survived" one of the random evictions and using this to weight the selection of the point to evict. But, since this does appear to be insignificant, it is not developed further.

weight of the points from bin $g+1$ in the sample is:

$$n_{g+1} \cdot P(\text{select } x \mid x \text{ in } g+1) \cdot (\text{weight in} g+1)$$
$$= n_{g+1} \cdot \frac{M/g}{n_g + n_{g+1}} \cdot (n_g + n_{g+1})$$
$$= \frac{M}{g} n_{g+1}$$

This computation is particularly interesting because it illustrates why collisions will not be a serious problem in practice. If $n_g >> n_{g+1}$ then any points in bin $g+1$ will be heavily over-weighted in the sample. But, the probability of selecting one of the incorrectly weighted points will be very small. This means that with high probability we will not output any points from bin $g+1$. If two bins of about equal size collide, an exact density biased sample would be expected to output more points from each of these bins. Collisions perturb the sample but we see that a relatively small number of collisions will not tend to dramatically change the sample.

Finally, a few words about the sensitivity of this algorithm to the parameters. For very small values of H (the hash table size), the bins will be essentially randomly distributed to the various elements of n and this will generate an approximation of a uniform sample (by our observation of random group assignments). Similarly, if G is too large and each bin has occupancy 1 or 0 then this algorithm outputs a uniform sample (because each occupied bin will be of equal size). For very poor choices of the hash table size or the number of bins per attribute, hash based density biased sampling will reduce to a uniform sample. That is, the algorithm is expected to be quite robust to poor parameter choices.

5 Experiments

There are several unknowns that will be explored in our experiments. First, and foremost, we wish to see that density biased sampling provides better clustering results than uniform sampling and BIRCH when the cluster sizes follow a Zipf distribution. The Zipf data set will constitute an average case and we explore a very skewed distribution of cluster sizes and a data set in which cluster sizes are all equal to observe a range of behaviours.

We have chosen to represent groups by binning the data. This will have some effectiveness implications. Using equal sized clusters makes uniform sampling equivalent to ideal density biased sampling. We can measure the effect of the binning by looking at this extreme case. We will find that binning introduces a small error that is acceptable given the significant improvements seen for realistic cluster size distributions.

Our approximation uses hashing to map bins to their respective counts. This introduces an error resulting from collisions. We will measure the effects of collisions

and find that they make little to no difference in the effectiveness of the sample.

5.1 Methodology

Several sampling or summarizing algorithms are compared experimentally. An experiment consists of selecting a data distribution, a clustering algorithm and then varying the amount of available memory to measure performance for various sample sizes. All the contending methods use a single pass over the data to generate a sample, weighted sample, or a summarized representation of the data. The algorithms used are:

i) BIRCH. Summarization is done with CF-trees and the maximum available memory will be limited to 2x the space needed to hold the sample [23].

ii) Uniform random sampling. A reservoir sampling algorithm is used and requires only the amount of memory needed to represent the sample [21].

iii) Hash based approximation to density biased sampling. The amount of memory used is twice the amount of memory needed to represent the sample. We will use two values for e for density biased sampling. Using $e = 1$ is *Inverse Biased Sampling* (IBS) and $e = .5$ is *Inverse Root Biased Sampling* (IRBS).

iv) Exact density biased sampling. The occupied bins are represented explicitly and the memory needed is not restricted. The only difference between iii) and iv) are collisions in the hash table. For $e = 1$, call this *Exact IBS* and, for $e = .5$, call this *Exact IRBS*.

BIRCH is included because it is extensively studied and has recently been directly compared to uniform sampling for equal sized clusters in low dimensional space [14]. Our experiments extend the cases in which BIRCH and uniform sampling have been directly compared. The hash based algorithm requires auxiliary memory. The hierarchical clustering algorithm uses about twice the memory needed to represent the sample and thus the decision to allow BIRCH and the hash based algorithm the opportunity to use this memory is reasonable.

BIRCH is provided with a default configuration that uses the framework shown in Figure 6. The sampling and the refinement step will be those used by BIRCH and are considered to be "off the shelf" components that are beyond our control. In BIRCH, the sampling step builds the CF-trees, the clustering step uses a simple hierarchical clustering algorithm and the refinement step implements a single iteration of the k-means algorithm (the output clusters are the center of mass of all the points that are included in the cluster). This framework is used by all our competing algorithms and consequently any differences in performance are directly attributable to the sampling/summarizing technique.

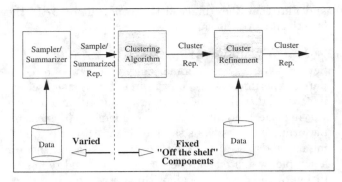

Figure 6: Clustering framework

Param.	Value(s)	Interpretation
N	200,000	# of points
d	20 or 50	# of dimensions
k	500	# of clusters
σ	.05	Standard deviation
$p_1, \cdots, p_k$	Varies	Prob. of cluster membership

Table 1: Parameters for data generation

5.2 Evaluation Metrics

The natural evaluation metric for the BIRCH algorithm is the root mean square (RMS) distance to cluster centers. If we assign each point $x_i = (x_i^1, \cdots, x_i^d)$ to the closest cluster center, $c_i = (c_i^1, \cdots, c_i^d)$, then the distance from the center is the standard Euclidean distance

$$\| x_i - c_i \|_2 = \sqrt{\sum_{a=1}^{d} (x_i^a - c_i^a)^2}$$

and the root mean square error is defined to be

$$\sqrt{\frac{\sum_{i=1}^{n} \| x_i - c_i \|_2^2}{n}}$$

RMS distance does not provide all of the information that we need. We are particularly concerned with the number of clusters that are actually found by the respective algorithms. RMS distance does not provide this information and we introduce a very simple metric to count the number of clusters that are "found."

Suppose that we knew that the true cluster centers were $\{c_1, c_2, \cdots, c_k\}$ and we wish to evaluate a system that found cluster centers $\{\hat{c}_1, \hat{c}_2, \cdots, \hat{c}_{k'}\}$. We say that cluster c_i is found if $\exists \hat{c}_j$ with $\| c_i - \hat{c}_j \|_2 < \epsilon$. We select $\epsilon = 0.001$ and define the metric *Number of Clusters found* (NC) to be the number of the true clusters that are "found." Notice that algorithms are not rewarded for finding the same cluster more than once nor are they rewarded for merging clusters.

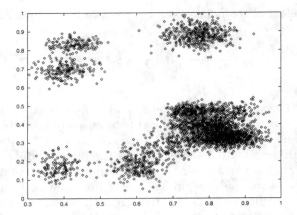

Figure 7: Sample synthetic data: $n = 4,000$, $d = 2$, $k = 10$, $\sigma = .05$

5.3 Data Generation

We randomly generate data based on the parameters in Table 1 using a mixture model. There are k clusters and N points in the d-dimensional unit hypercube. Each of the d attributes for a cluster center are generated in the range $[.1, .9]$. A diagonal covariance matrix is generated by computing a variance in the range $[0, \sigma^2]$ and using the square root of the variance. Covariances computed in this fashion are in the range $[0, \sigma]$ but will have very few small values. Since $\sigma = .05$ and the centers are generated in the range $[.1, .9]$, the majority of the points will be in the unit hypercube. For simplicity we discard the few points that are outside the hypercube. To generate the data, each point is randomly assigned to a cluster using the the probability distribution $P(\text{cluster } i) = p_i$. Once assigned to a cluster, the appropriate mean and covariance is used to generate a point according to a Gaussian distribution.

The center of mass of each cluster is recorded for future use in computing NC. By using the center of mass and not the randomly generated mean, any clustering that correctly classifies all the points will be guaranteed to "find" the cluster.

Three different cluster membership distributions are used:

i) *Even*: All clusters are equally likely ($p_i = 1/k$).

ii) *Zipf*: Cluster sizes follow a Zipf distribution ($p_i = 1/(H_k \cdot i)$ where H_k is the kth harmonic number).

iii) *OneBig*: One cluster has most of the points, all other clusters have 100 points ($p_1 = (n - 100(k - 1))/n$ and $p_i = 100/n$ for $2 \leq i \leq k$).

Figure 7 shows a very small example of the data that is generated. This data was generated with Zipf sizes, $k = 10$, $n = 2000$ and all other parameters unchanged. The clusters are fairly well separated but we see that

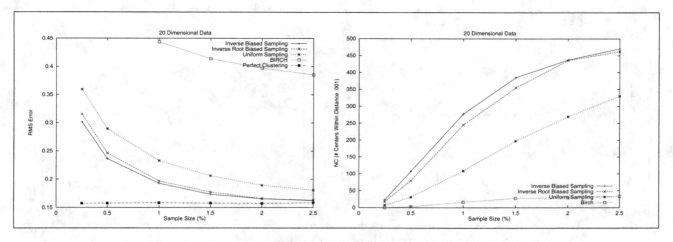

Figure 8: Zipf sizes (d=20): RMS Error predicted and NC for the same experiment

6   Results

Figure 8 shows performance for the algorithms for various sample sizes (equivalently memory size) for 20-dimensional data with Zipf cluster sizes. We see that the relative orderings of the contending algorithms is identical for the two metrics and we can see similar relative performance. This relationship is true for all the experiments reported. Either metric could be used to draw similar conclusions. Due to space limitations, we can only present one metric and use NC because it is easier to unambiguously interpret.

BIRCH performs quite poorly in these experiments. BIRCH appears to require memory that is 10% of the total database size to perform well in our 20 and 50 dimensional experiments. BIRCH tends to do slightly better under the RMS distance metric than NC metric but is generally still quite poor.

In the average case, IBS and IRBS are much better than uniform sampling. Figure 10 shows NC for various sample sizes for 20 and 50 dimensional data with Zipf cluster sizes. For 1% samples, IBS and IRBS find approximately 2.3 times as many clusters as uniform sampling in 20 dimensions and more than twice as many clusters in 50 dimensions. A 2.5% IRBS or IBS sample finds 90% of the clusters while a 2.5% uniform sample finds fewer than 70% of the clusters.

As the cluster sizes become more skewed, this difference in performance increases. Figure 9 shows the same information for data sets in which the OneBig cluster sizes are used. For 1% sample sizes, IBS and IRBS find between 4 and 6 times as many clusters as uniform sampling. A 2.5% IBS or IRBS sample finds more than 95% of the clusters while a 2.5% uniform

sample still finds fewer than 70% of the clusters.

Figure 11 shows that binning is a good approximation to the ideal groups for IRBS but not as good for IBS. In 20 dimensions, IRBS is typically within 7.5% of uniform and in 50 dimensions generally within 16%. On the other hand, IBS is only within 20% and 43% in 20 and 50 dimensions respectively. We see that IBS is sensitive to the quality of the groupings generated by binning the data but that IRBS is hardly affected by our grid-based choice of group assignments.

Finally, Figure 12 shows that collisions have essentially no effect on clustering the Zipf cluster sizes data set. In both 20 and 50 dimensions, the approximation is typically within 10 clusters of exact IBS and exact IRBS.

To summarize:

- IRBS and IBS are much better than uniform sampling for clustering data sets with skewed cluster sizes.

- Using bins is a reasonable choice for IRBS.

- Collisions do not reduce the effectiveness of IBS or IRBS.

We generally conclude that IRBS gives the best performance of any of the algorithms considered.

The running time of all the algorithms is linear in the database size and completely dominated by the cost of reading the data. Table 2 shows the wall clock running time to generate a 1% sample for a 20 dimensional data set with Zipf cluster sizes. "Read-only" is the time is takes to read the data and perform no other processing. The third row is the wall clock time less the time that it takes to read the data. This is the time attributed to the sampling algorithm. We see that all algorithms are quite efficient and do not contribute undue overhead.

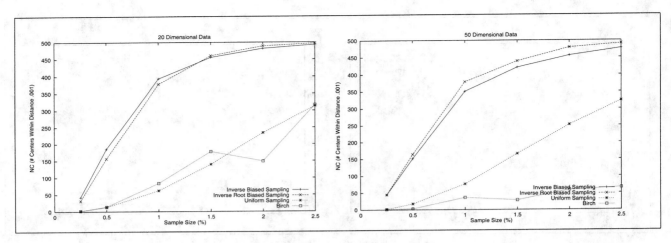

Figure 9: OneBig sizes (d=20/50): Ideal case for density biased sampling

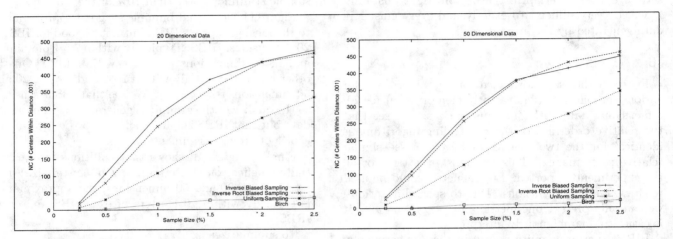

Figure 10: Zipf sizes (d=20/50): Data moderately skewed, density biased sampling excellent

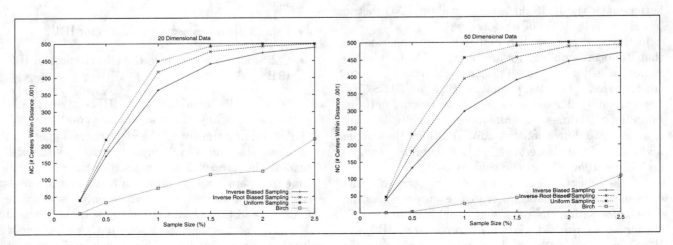

Figure 11: Even sizes (d=20/50): Ideal case for uniform sampling

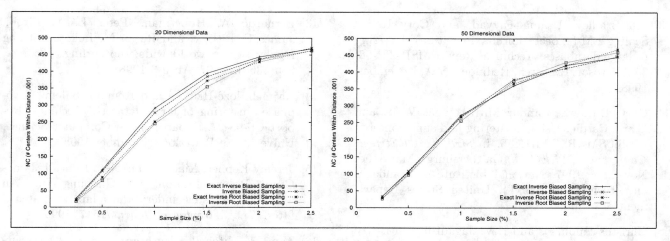

Figure 12: Zipf sizes (d=20/50): Collisions only cause minor differences

Method	Read-only	Sample	BIRCH	IRBS
Time	16.7	17.7	18.1	18.1
- Read	-16.7	-16.7	-16.7	-16.7
Actual		1.0	1.4	1.4

Table 2: Zipf sizes (d=20): Wall clock execution times

7   Applications and Further Research

We have used density biased sampling as a preprocessing step for clustering. Good summarization algorithms assume that the data appears in a random order and that the first component is representative of the data [2, 3]. Using a density biased sample is more likely to satisfy these assumptions than a uniform sample of equal size (in bytes). So, not only can IRBS be used to cluster, it can also be used to improve summarization based algorithms (such as [2, 3]) and to develop better initial models (as done with uniform sampling in [7]).

More generally, density biased sampling offers a representative sample of the data that includes more of the unexpected points. Any algorithm that does not require that all inputs be distinct can be trivially extended to support a weighted sample. Many statistical algorithms use multiple samples to reduce variability. Density biased samples should reduce the variability of the algorithms because we can include more of the "unusual" points (i.e., the points that are likely to induce variability) while ensuring a representative sample.

Finally, it appears that it should be possible to efficiently construct a density biased sample using an R-tree index by descending in the R-tree only as far as needed to compute the bin sizes. Using an existing index may make it possible to construct samples without reading the entire database.

8   Conclusions

We proposed a new sampling technique: *Density Biased Sampling*. Density biased sampling naturally includes uniform sampling as a special case. We implemented density biased sampling using a hashing function to map bins in space to a linear ordering, allowing it to work with very limited memory. The hash based approximation to density biased sampling with $e = .5$ (IRBS) is more effective for clustering than either a uniform sample or a CF-tree summarization (for realistic data). We found that binning is particular appropriate for IRBS and that collisions had little to no impact on the effectiveness of the sample generated by IRBS and IBS.

The method favours clusters containing fewer points. Uniform sampling tends to miss these smaller clusters. These clusters are the most likely to contain interesting results because the domain experts are likely aware of the very large clusters. Using a Zipf distribution of cluster sizes (an "average" case) and taking a 1% sample, IBS and IRBS find more than twice as many clusters as uniform sampling. As the cluster sizes become even more skewed, this increases to between 4 times and 6 times for 20 and 50 dimensions respectively.

References

[1] Alfred V. Aho, Ravi Sethi, and Jeffrey D. Ullman. *Compilers. Principles, Techniques and Tools.* Addison–Wesley, 1986. Pages 433–438.

[2] P.S Bradley, Usama Fayyad, and Cory Reina. Scaling clustering algorithms to large databases. In *Proceedings of the Fourth International Conference on Knowledge Discovery and Data Mining (KDD-98)*, pages 9–15, New York City, New York, August 1998. AAAI Press.

[3] P.S Bradley, Usama Fayyad, and Cory Reina. Scaling EM (expectation maximization) clustering to large databases. Technical Report MSR-TR-98-35, Microsoft Research, Redmond, WA, November, 1998.

[4] Chris Buckley, Mandar Mitra, Janet Walz, and Clarie Cardie. Using clustering and superconcepts within SMART: TREC 6. In *Sixth Text REtrieval Conference (TREC-6)*, Gaithersburg, Maryland, November 1997. National Institute of Standards and Technology (NIST), United States Department of Commerce.

[5] Christos Faloutsos and H.V. Jagadish. On B-tree indices for skewed distributions. In *18th VLDB Conference*, pages 363–374, Vancouver, British Columbia, Aug. 23-27 1992.

[6] Christos Faloutsos, Yossi Matias, and Avi Silberschatz. Modeling skewed distributions using multifractals and the '80-20 law'. *VLDB*, September 1996.

[7] Usama M. Fayyad, Cory A. Reina, and Paul S. Bradley. Initialization of iterative refinement clustering algorithms. In *Proceedings of the Fourth International Conference on Knowledge Discovery and Data Mining (KDD–98)*, pages 194–198, New York City, New York, August 1998. AAAI Press.

[8] Phillip B. Gibbons and Yossi Matias. New sampling-based summary statistics for improving approximate query answers. In *Proceedings of the ACM SIGMOD International Conference on Management of Data (SIGMOD-98)*, volume 27,2 of *ACM SIGMOD Record*, pages 331–342, New York, June1–4 1998. ACM Press.

[9] Sudipto Guha, Rajeev Rastogi, and Kyuseok Shim. CURE: An efficient clustering algorithm for large databases. In *Proceedings of the ACM SIGMOD International Conference on Management of Data (SIGMOD-98)*, volume 27,2 of *ACM SIGMOD Record*, pages 73–84, New York, June1–4 1998. ACM Press.

[10] Peter J. Haas, Jeffrey F. Naughton, S. Seshadri, and Lynne Stokes. Sampling-based estimation of the number of distinct values of an attribute. In *Proc. of VLDB*, pages 311–322, Zurich, Switzerland, September 1995.

[11] John A. Hartigan. *Clustering Algorithms*. John Wiley & Sons, 1975.

[12] Joseph M. Hellerstein, Peter J. Haas, and Helen Wang. Online aggregation. In *SIGMOD Conference*, pages 171–182, 1997.

[13] Bernardo A. Huberman, Peter L. T. Pirolli, James E. Pitkow, and Rajan M. Lukose. Strong regularities in world wide web surfing. *Science*, 280(5360):95–97, April 3 1998.

[14] Najmeh Joze-Hkajavi and Kenneth Salem. Two-phase clustering of large datasets. Technical Report CS-98-27, Department of Computer Science, University of Waterloo, November 1998.

[15] Jeremy Kepner, Xiaohui Fan, Neta Buhcall, James Gunn, Robert Lupton, and Ghohung Xu. An automated cluster finder: the adaptive matched filter. *The Astrophysics Journal*, 517, 1999.

[16] Tom M. Mitchell. *Machine Learning*. McGraw-Hill, 1997.

[17] Frank Olken, Doron Rotem, and Ping Xu. Random sampling from hash files. In *Proceedings of the 1990 ACM SIGMOD International Conference on Management of Data*, volume 19,2 of *ACM SIGMOD Record*, pages 375–386. ACM Press, June1–4 1990.

[18] Edie Rasmussen. Clustering algorithms. In William B. Frakes and Ricardo Baeza-Yates, editors, *Information Retrieval: Data Structures and Algorithms*, pages 419–442. Prentice Hall, 1992.

[19] Brian D. Ripley. *Spatial Statistics*. John Wiley & Sons, 1981.

[20] Manfred Schroeder. *Fractals, Chaos, Power Laws: Minutes from an Infinite Paradise*. W.H. Freeman and Company, New York, 1991.

[21] Jeffrey Scott Vitter. Random sampling with a reservoir. *ACM Transactions on Mathematical Software*, 11(1):37–57, March 1985.

[22] Oren Zamir and Oren Etzioni. Web document clustering: A feasibility demonstration. In *Proceedings of the 21st Annual International ACM SIGIR Conference on Research and Development in Information Retrieval*, pages 46–54, 1998.

[23] Tian Zhang, Raghu Ramakrishnan, and Miron Livny. BIRCH: an efficient data clustering method for very large databases. In *Proceedings of the ACM SIGMOD International Conference on Management of Data*, volume 25, 2 of *ACM SIGMOD Record*, pages 103–114, New York, June4–6 1996. ACM Press.

[24] G.K. Zipf. *Human Behavior and Principle of Least Effort: An Introduction to Human Ecology*. Addison Wesley, Cambridge, Massachusetts, 1949.

LOF: Identifying Density-Based Local Outliers

Markus M. Breunig[†], Hans-Peter Kriegel[†], Raymond T. Ng[‡], Jörg Sander[†]

† Institute for Computer Science	‡ Department of Computer Science
University of Munich	University of British Columbia
Oettingenstr. 67, D-80538 Munich, Germany	Vancouver, BC V6T 1Z4 Canada
{ breunig | kriegel | sander } @dbs.informatik.uni-muenchen.de	rng@cs.ubc.ca

ABSTRACT

For many KDD applications, such as detecting criminal activities in E-commerce, finding the rare instances or the outliers, can be more interesting than finding the common patterns. Existing work in outlier detection regards being an outlier as a binary property. In this paper, we contend that for many scenarios, it is more meaningful to assign to each object a *degree* of being an outlier. This degree is called the *local outlier factor* (LOF) of an object. It is *local* in that the degree depends on how isolated the object is with respect to the surrounding neighborhood. We give a detailed formal analysis showing that LOF enjoys many desirable properties. Using real-world datasets, we demonstrate that LOF can be used to find outliers which appear to be meaningful, but can otherwise not be identified with existing approaches. Finally, a careful performance evaluation of our algorithm confirms we show that our approach of finding local outliers can be practical.

Keywords
Outlier Detection, Database Mining.

1. INTRODUCTION

Larger and larger amounts of data are collected and stored in databases, increasing the need for efficient and effective analysis methods to make use of the information contained implicitly in the data. *Knowledge discovery in databases* (KDD) has been defined as the non-trivial process of identifying valid, novel, potentially useful, and ultimately understandable knowledge from the data [9].

Most studies in KDD focus on finding patterns applicable to a considerable portion of objects in a dataset. However, for applications such as detecting criminal activities of various kinds (e.g. in electronic commerce), rare events, deviations from the majority, or exceptional cases may be more interesting and useful than the common cases. Finding such exceptions and outliers, however, has not yet received as much attention in the KDD community as some other topics have, e.g. association rules.

Recently, a few studies have been conducted on outlier detection for large datasets (e.g. [18], [1], [13], [14]). While a more detailed discussion on these studies will be given in section 2, it suffices to point out here that most of these studies consider being an outlier as a binary property. That is, either an object in the dataset is an outlier or not. For many applications, the situation is more complex. And it becomes more meaningful to assign to each object a *degree* of being an outlier.

Also related to outlier detection is an extensive body of work on clustering algorithms. From the viewpoint of a clustering algorithm, outliers are objects not located in clusters of a dataset, usually called noise. The set of noise produced by a clustering algorithm, however, is highly dependent on the particular algorithm and on its clustering parameters. Only a few approaches are directly concerned with outlier detection. These algorithms, in general, consider outliers from a more global perspective, which also has some major drawbacks. These drawbacks are discussed in detail in section 2 and section 3. Furthermore, based on these clustering algorithms, the property of being an outlier is again binary.

In this paper, we introduce a new method for finding outliers in a multidimensional dataset. We introduce a local outlier (*LOF*) for each object in the dataset, indicating its degree of outlier-ness. This is, to the best of our knowledge, the first concept of an outlier which also quantifies how outlying an object is. The outlier factor is local in the sense that only a restricted neighborhood of each object is taken into account. Our approach is loosely related to density-based clustering. However, we do not require any explicit or implicit notion of clusters for our method. Specifically, our technical contributions in this paper are as follow:

- After introducing the concept of *LOF*, we analyze the formal properties of *LOF*. We show that for most objects in a cluster their *LOF* are approximately equal to 1. For any other object, we give a lower and upper bound on its *LOF*. These bounds highlight the local nature of *LOF*. Furthermore, we analyze when these bounds are tight. We identify classes of objects for which the bounds are tight. Finally, for those objects for which the bounds are not tight, we provide sharper bounds.

- The *LOF* of an object is based on the single parameter of *MinPts*, which is the number of nearest neighbors used in defining the local neighborhood of the object. We study how this parameter affects the *LOF* value, and we present practical guidelines for choosing the *MinPts* values for finding local outliers.

- Last but not least, we present experimental results which show both the capability and the performance of finding local outliers. We conclude that finding local outliers using *LOF* is meaningful and efficient.

The paper is organized as follows. In section 2, we discuss related work on outlier detection and their drawbacks. In section 3 we discuss in detail the motivation of our notion of outliers, especially, the advantage of a local instead of a global view on outliers. In section 4 we introduce *LOF* and define other auxiliary notions. In section 5 we analyze thoroughly the formal properties of *LOF*. Since *LOF* requires the single parameter *MinPts*, in section 6 we analyze the impact of the parameter, and discuss ways to choose *MinPts* values for *LOF* computation. In section 7 we perform an extensive experimental evaluation.

2. RELATED WORK

Most of the previous studies on outlier detection were conducted in the field of statistics. These studies can be broadly classified into two categories. The first category is *distribution-based*, where a standard distribution (e.g. Normal, Poisson, etc.) is used to fit the data best. Outliers are defined based on the probability distribution. Over one hundred tests of this category, called discordancy tests, have been developed for different scenarios (see [5]). A key drawback of this category of tests is that most of the distributions used are univariate. There are some tests that are multivariate (e.g. multivariate normal outliers). But for many KDD applications, the underlying distribution is unknown. Fitting the data with standard distributions is costly, and may not produce satisfactory results.

The second category of outlier studies in statistics is *depth-based*. Each data object is represented as a point in a *k*-d space, and is assigned a depth. With respect to outlier detection, outliers are more likely to be data objects with smaller depths. There are many definitions of depth that have been proposed (e.g. [20], [16]). In theory, depth-based approaches could work for large values of *k*. However, in practice, while there exist efficient algorithms for $k = 2$ or 3 ([16], [18], [12]), depth-based approaches become inefficient for large datasets for $k \geq 4$. This is because depth-based approaches rely on the computation of *k*-d convex hulls which has a lower bound complexity of $\Omega(n^{k/2})$ for *n* objects.

Recently, Knorr and Ng proposed the notion of *distance-based* outliers [13], [14]. Their notion generalizes many notions from the distribution-based approaches, and enjoys better computational complexity than the depth-based approaches for larger values of *k*. Later in section 3, we will discuss in detail how their notion is different from the notion of local outliers proposed in this paper. In [17] the notion of distance based outliers is extended by using the distance to the *k*-nearest neighbor to rank the outliers. A very efficient algorithms to compute the top *n* outliers in this ranking is given, but their notion of an outlier is still distance-based.

Given the importance of the area, fraud detection has received more attention than the general area of outlier detection. Depending on the specifics of the application domains, elaborate fraud models and fraud detection algorithms have been developed (e.g. [8], [6]).

In contrast to fraud detection, the kinds of outlier detection work discussed so far are more exploratory in nature. Outlier detection may indeed lead to the construction of fraud models.

Finally, most clustering algorithms, especially those developed in the context of KDD (e.g. CLARANS [15], DBSCAN [7], BIRCH [23], STING [22], WaveCluster [19], DenClue [11], CLIQUE [3]), are to some extent capable of handling exceptions. However, since the main objective of a clustering algorithm is to find clusters, they are developed to optimize clustering, and not to optimize outlier detection. The exceptions (called "noise" in the context of clustering) are typically just tolerated or ignored when producing the clustering result. Even if the outliers are not ignored, the notions of outliers are essentially binary, and there are no quantification as to how outlying an object is. Our notion of local outliers share a few fundamental concepts with density-based clustering approaches. However, our outlier detection method does not require any explicit or implicit notion of clusters.

3. PROBLEMS OF EXISTING (NON-LOCAL) APPROACHES

As we have seen in section 2, most of the existing work in outlier detection lies in the field of statistics. Intuitively, outliers can be defined as given by Hawkins [10].

Definition 1: (Hawkins-Outlier)

An outlier is an observation that deviates so much from other observations as to arouse suspicion that it was generated by a different mechanism.

This notion is formalized by Knorr and Ng [13] in the following definition of outliers. Throughout this paper, we use o, p, q to denote objects in a dataset. We use the notation $d(p, q)$ to denote the distance between objects p and q. For a set of objects, we use C (sometimes with the intuition that C forms a cluster). To simplify our notation, we use $d(p, C)$ to denote the minimum distance between p and object q in C, i.e. $d(p,C) = min\{ d(p,q) \mid q \in C \}$.

Definition 2: (DB(*pct, dmin*)-Outlier)

An object p in a dataset D is a *DB(pct, dmin)*-outlier if at least percentage *pct* of the objects in D lies greater than distance *dmin* from p, i.e., the cardinality of the set $\{q \in D \mid d(p, q) \leq dmin\}$ is less than or equal to $(100 - pct)\%$ of the size of D.

The above definition captures only certain kinds of outliers. Because the definition takes a global view of the dataset, these outliers can be viewed as "global" outliers. However, for many interesting real-world datasets which exhibit a more complex structure, there is another kind of outliers. These can be objects that are outlying

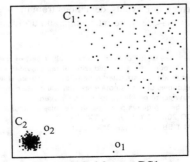

Figure 1: 2-*d* dataset DS1

relative to their local neighborhoods, particularly with respect to the densities of the neighborhoods. These outliers are regarded as "local" outliers.

To illustrate, consider the example given in Figure 1. This is a simple 2-dimensional dataset containing 502 objects. There are 400 objects in the first cluster C_1, 100 objects in the cluster C_2, and two additional objects o_1 and o_2. In this example, C_2 forms a denser cluster than C_1. According to Hawkins' definition, both o1 and o2 can be called outliers, whereas objects in C_1 and C_2 should not be. With our notion of a "local" outlier, we wish to label both o_1 and o_2 as outliers. In contrast, within the framework of distance-based outliers, only o_1 is a reasonable DB(*pct,dmin*)-outlier in the following sense. If for every object q in C_1, the distance between q and its nearest neighbor is greater than the distance between o_2 and C_2 (i.e., $d(o_2,C_2)$), we can in fact show that there is no appropriate value of *pct* and *dmin* such that o_2 is a DB(*pct,dmin*)-outlier but the the objects in C_1 are not.

The reason is as follows. If the *dmin* value is less than the distance $d(o_2,C_2)$, then all 501 objects (*pct* = 100*501/502) are further away from o_2 than *dmin*. But the same condition holds also for every object q in C_1. Thus, in this case, o_2 and all objects in C_1 are DB(*pct, dmin*)-outliers.

Otherwise, if the *dmin* value is greater than the distance $d(o_2, C_2)$, then it is easy to see that: o_2 is a DB(*pct,dmin*)-outlier implies that there are many objects q in C_1 such that q is also a DB(*pct,dmin*)-outlier. This is because the cardinality of the set $\{p \in D \mid d(p,o_2) \leq dmin\}$ is always bigger than the cardinality of the set $\{p \in D \mid d(p,q) \leq dmin\}$. Thus, in this case, if o_2 is a DB(*pct,dmin*)-outlier, so are many objects q in C_1. Worse still, there are values of *pct* and *dmin* such that while o_2 is not an outlier, some q in C_1 are.

4. FORMAL DEFINITION OF LOCAL OUTLIERS

The above example shows that the global view taken by DB(*pct, dmin*)-outliers is meaningful and adequate under certain conditions, but not satisfactory for the general case when clusters of different densities exist. In this section, we develop a formal definition of local outliers, which avoids the shortcomings presented in the previous section. The key difference between our notion and existing notions of outliers is that being outlying is *not a binary property*. Instead, we assign to each object an *outlier factor*, which is the degree the object is being outlying.

We begin with the notions of the *k-distance* of object p, and, correspondingly, the *k-distance neighborhood* of p.

Definition 3: (*k*-distance of an object p)

For any positive integer k, the *k*-distance of object p, denoted as *k-distance*(p), is defined as the distance $d(p,o)$ between p and an object $o \in D$ such that:

(i)   for at least k objects o'$\in D \setminus \{p\}$ it holds that $d(p,o') \leq d(p,o)$, and

(ii)   for at most k-1 objects o'$\in D \setminus \{p\}$ it holds that $d(p,o') < d(p,o)$.

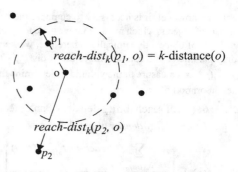

Figure 2: *reach-dist(p_1,o)* and *reach-dist(p_2,o)*, for *k*=4

Definition 4: (*k*-distance neighborhood of an object p)

Given the *k*-distance of p, the *k-distance neighborhood of p* contains every object whose distance from p is not greater than the *k*-distance, i.e. $N_{k\text{-}distance(p)}(p) = \{ q \in D \setminus \{p\} \mid d(p, q) \leq k\text{-}distance(p) \}$.

These objects q are called the *k*-nearest neighbors of p.

Whenever no confusion arises, we simplify our notation to use $N_k(p)$ as a shorthand for $N_{k\text{-}distance(p)}(p)$. Note that in definition 3, the *k*-distance(p) is well defined for any positive integer k, although the object o may not be unique. In this case, the cardinality of $N_k(p)$ is greater than k. For example, suppose that there are: (i) 1 object with distance 1 unit from p; (ii) 2 objects with distance 2 units from p; and (iii) 3 objects with distance 3 units from p. Then 2-distance(p) is identical to 3-distance(p). And there are 3 objects of 4-distance(p) from p. Thus, the cardinality of $N_4(p)$ can be greater than 4, in this case 6.

Definition 5: (reachability distance of an object p w.r.t. object o)

Let k be a natural number. The *reachability distance* of object p with respect to object o is defined as

$$reach\text{-}dist_k(p, o) = \max \{ k\text{-}distance(o), d(p, o) \}.$$

Figure 2 illustrates the idea of reachability distance with $k = 4$. Intuitively, if object p is far away from o (e.g. p_2 in the figure), then the reachability distance between the two is simply their actual distance. However, if they are "sufficiently" close (e.g., p_1 in the figure), the actual distance is replaced by the *k*-distance of o. The reason is that in so doing, the statistical fluctuations of $d(p,o)$ for all the p's close to o can be significantly reduced. The strength of this smoothing effect can be controlled by the parameter k. The higher the value of k, the more similar the reachability distances for objects within the same neighborhood.

So far, we have defined *k*-distance(p) and *reach-dist$_k$*(p) for any positive integer k. But for the purpose of defining outliers, we focus on a specific instantiation of k which links us back to density-based clustering. In a typical density-based clustering algorithm, such as [7], [3], [22], or [11], there are two parameters that define the notion of density: (i) a parameter *MinPts* specifying a minimum number of objects; (ii) a parameter specifying a volume. These two parameters determine a density *threshold* for the clustering algorithms to operate. That is, objects or regions are connected if their neighborhood densities exceed the given density threshold. To detect density-based outliers, however, it is necessary to compare the densities of different sets of objects, which means that we have to determine the density of sets of objects dynamically. Therefore, we keep *MinPts* as the only parameter and use the values reach-dist$_{MinPts}(p, o)$, for $o \in N_{MinPts}(p)$, as a measure of the volume to determine the density in the neighborhood of an object p.

Definition 6: (local reachability density of an object p)

The *local reachability density* of p is defined as

$$lrd_{MinPts}(p) = 1 / \left(\frac{\sum_{o \in N_{MinPts}(p)} reach\text{-}dist_{MinPts}(p, o)}{|N_{MinPts}(p)|} \right)$$

Intuitively, the local reachability density of an object p is the inverse of the average reachability distance based on the *MinPts*-nearest neighbors of p. Note that the local density can be ∞ if all the reachability distances in the summation are 0. This may occur for an object p if there are at least *MinPts* objects, different from p, but sharing the same spatial coordinates, i.e. if there are at least *MinPts* duplicates of p in the dataset. For simplicity, we will not handle this case explicitly but simply assume that there are no duplicates. (To deal with duplicates, we can base our notion of neighborhood on a k-distinct-distance, defined analogously to k-distance in definition 3, with the additional requirement that there be at least k objects with different spatial coordinates.)

Definition 7: ((local) outlier factor of an object p)

The *(local) outlier factor* of p is defined as

$$LOF_{MinPts}(p) = \frac{\sum_{o \in N_{MinPts}(p)} \frac{lrd_{MinPts}(o)}{lrd_{MinPts}(p)}}{|N_{MinPts}(p)|}$$

The outlier factor of object p captures the degree to which we call p an outlier. It is the average of the ratio of the local reachability density of p and those of p's *MinPts*-nearest neighbors. It is easy to see that the lower p's local reachability density is, and the higher the local reachability densities of p's *MinPts*-nearest neighbors are, the higher is the *LOF* value of p. In the following section, the formal properties of *LOF* are made precise. To simplify notation, we drop the subscript *MinPts* from *reach-dist*, *lrd* and *LOF*, if no confusion arises.

5. PROPERTIES OF LOCAL OUTLIERS

In this section, we conduct a detailed analysis on the properties of *LOF*. The goal is to show that our definition of *LOF* captures the spirit of local outliers, and enjoys many desirable properties. Specifically, we show that for most objects p in a cluster, the *LOF* of p is approximately equal to 1. As for other objects, including those outside of a cluster, we give a general theorem giving a lower and upper bound on the *LOF*. Furthermore, we analyze the tightness of our bounds. We show that the bounds are tight for important classes of objects. However, for other classes of objects, the bounds may not be as tight. For the latter, we give another theorem specifying better bounds.

5.1 *LOF* for Objects Deep in a Cluster

In section 3, we motivate the notion of a local outlier using figure 1. In particular, we hope to label o_2 as outlying, but label all objects in the cluster C_1 as non-outlying. Below, we show that for most objects in C_1 its *LOF* is approximately 1, indicating that they cannot be labeled as outlying.

Lemma 1: Let C be a collection of objects. Let *reach-dist-min* denote the minimum reachability distance of objects in C, i.e., *reach-dist-min* = *min* {*reach-dist(p, q)* | $p, q \in C$}. Similarly, let *reach-dist-max* denote the maximum reachability distance of objects in C. Let ε be defined as (*reach-dist-max/reach-dist-min* $- 1$). Then for all objects $p \in C$, such that:

    (i)   all the *MinPts*-nearest neighbors q of p are in C, and

    (ii)   all the *MinPts*-nearest neighbors o of q are also in C,

it holds that $1/(1 + \varepsilon) \leq LOF(p) \leq (1 + \varepsilon)$.

Proof (Sketch): For all *MinPts*-nearest neighbors q of p, *reach-dist(p, q)* $\geq$ *reach-dist-min*. Then the local reachability density of p, as per definition 6, is $\leq 1/$*reach-dist-min*. On the other hand, *reach-dist(p, q)* $\leq$ *reach-dist-max*. Thus, the local reachability density of p is $\geq 1/$*reach-dist-max*.

Let q be a *MinPts*-nearest neighbor of p. By an argument identical to the one for p above, the local reachability density of q is also between $1/$*reach-dist-max* and $1/$*reach-dist-min*.

Thus, by definition 7, we have *reach-dist-min/reach-dist-max* $\leq LOF(p) \leq$ *reach-dist-max/reach-dist-min*. Hence, we establish $1/(1 + \varepsilon) \leq LOF(p) \leq (1 + \varepsilon)$. ∎

The interpretation of lemma 1 is as follows. Intuitively, C corresponds to a "cluster". Let us consider the objects p that are "deep" inside the cluster, which means that all the *MinPts*-nearest neighbors q of p are in C, and that, in turn, all the *MinPts*-nearest neighbors of q are also in C. For such deep objects p, the *LOF* of p is bounded. If C is a "tight" cluster, the ε value in lemma 1 can be quite small, thus forcing the *LOF* of p to be quite close to 1.

To return to the example in figure 1, we can apply lemma 1 to conclude that the *LOF*s of most objects in cluster C_1 are close to 1.

5.2 A General Upper and Lower Bound on *LOF*

Lemma 1 above shows a basic property of *LOF*, namely that for objects deep inside a cluster, their *LOF*s are close to 1, and should not be labeled as a local outlier. A few immediate questions come to mind. What about those objects that are near the periphery of the cluster? And what about those objects that are outside the cluster, such as o_2 in figure 1? Can we get an upper and lower bound on the *LOF* of these objects?

Theorem 1 below shows a general upper and lower bound on *LOF(p)* for *any* object p. As such, theorem 1 generalizes lemma 1 along two dimensions. First, theorem 1 applies to any object p, and is not restricted to objects deep inside a cluster. Second, even for objects deep inside a cluster, the bound given by theorem 1 can be tighter than the bound given by lemma 1, implying that the epsilon defined in lemma 1 can be made closer to zero.. This is because in lemma 1, the values of *reach-dist-min* and *reach-dist-max* are obtained based on a larger set of reachability distances. In contrast, in theorem 1, this minimum and maximum are based on just the *MinPts*-nearest neighborhoods of the objects under consideration,

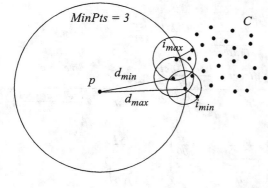

$$d_{min} = 4*i_{max} \qquad\qquad d_{max} = 6*i_{min}$$
$$\Rightarrow LOF_{MinPts}(p) \geq 4 \qquad \Rightarrow LOF_{MinPts}(p) \leq 6$$

Figure 3: Illustration of theorem 1

giving rise to tighter bounds. In section 5.3, we will analyze in greater details the tightness of the bounds given in theorem 1.

Before we present theorem 1, we define the following terms. For any object p, let $direct_{min}(p)$ denote the minimum reachability distance between p and a $MinPts$-nearest neighbor of p, i.e.,
$$direct_{min}(p) = \min \{ \text{reach-dist}(p, q) \mid q \in N_{MinPts}(p) \}.$$
Similarly, let $direct\_max(p)$ denote the corresponding maximum, i.e. $direct_{max}(p) = \max \{ \text{reach-dist}(p, q) \mid q \in N_{MinPts}(p) \}$.

Furthermore, to generalize these definitions to the $MinPts$-nearest neighbor q of p, let $indirect_{min}(p)$ denote the minimum reachability distance between q and a $MinPts$-nearest neighbor of q, i.e.,
$$indirect_{min}(p) = \min \{ \text{reach-dist}(q, o) \mid q \in N_{MinPts}(p) \text{ and } o \in N_{MinPts}(q) \}.$$
Similarly, let $indirect_{max}(p)$ denote the corresponding maximum. In the sequel, we refer to p's $MinPts$-nearest neighborhood as p's *direct* neighborhood, and refer to q's $MinPts$-nearest neighbors as p's *indirect* neighbors, whenever q is a $MinPts$-nearest neighbor of p.

Figure 3 gives a simple example to illustrate these definitions. In this example, object p lies some distance away from a cluster of objects C. For ease of understanding, let $MinPts = 3$. The $direct_{min}(p)$ value is marked as d_{min} in the figure; the $direct_{max}(p)$ value is marked as d_{max}. Because p is relatively far away from C, the 3-distance of every object q in C is much smaller than the actual distance between p and q. Thus, from definition 5, the reachability distance of p w.r.t. q is given by the actual distance between p and q. Now among the 3-nearest neighbors of p, we in turn find their minimum and maximum reachability distances to their 3-nearest neighbors. In the figure, the $indirect_{min}(p)$ and $indirect_{max}(p)$ values are marked as i_{min} and i_{max} respectively.

Theorem 1: Let p be an object from the database D, and $1 \leq MinPts \leq |D|$.
Then, it is the case that
$$\frac{direct_{min}(p)}{indirect_{max}(p)} \leq LOF(p) \leq \frac{direct_{max}(p)}{indirect_{min}(p)}$$

Proof (Sketch): (a) $\frac{direct_{min}(p)}{indirect_{max}(p)} \leq LOF(p)$:

$\forall o \in N_{MinPts}(p): \text{reach-dist}(p, o) \geq direct_{min}(p)$, by definition of $direct_{min}(p)$.

$$\Rightarrow 1 / \frac{\sum_{o \in N_{MinPts}(p)} \text{reach-dist}(p, o)}{|N_{MinPts}(p)|} \leq \frac{1}{direct_{min}(p)}, \text{ i.e.}$$

$$lrd(p) \leq \frac{1}{direct_{min}(p)}$$

$\forall q \in N_{MinPts}(o): \text{reach-dist}(o, q) \leq indirect_{max}(p)$, by definition of $indirect_{max}(p)$.

$$\Rightarrow 1 / \frac{\sum_{q \in N_{MinPts}(o)} \text{reach-dist}(o, q)}{|N_{MinPts}(o)|} \geq \frac{1}{indirect_{max}(p)}, \text{i.e.}$$

$$lrd(o) \geq \frac{1}{indirect_{max}(p)}$$

Thus, it follows that

$$LOF(p) = \frac{\sum_{o \in N_{MinPts}(p)} \frac{lrd(o)}{lrd(p)}}{|N_{MinPts}(p)|} \geq$$

$$\frac{\sum_{o \in N_{MinPts}(p)} \frac{\left(\frac{1}{indirect_{max}(p)}\right)}{\left(\frac{1}{direct_{min}(p)}\right)}}{|N_{MinPts}(p)|} = \frac{direct_{min}(p)}{indirect_{max}(p)}$$

(b) $LOF(p) \leq \frac{direct_{max}(p)}{indirect_{min}(p)}$: analogously. ∎

To illustrate the theorem using the example in figure 3, suppose that d_{min} is 4 times that of i_{max}, and d_{max} is 6 times that of i_{min}. Then by theorem 1, the LOF of p is between 4 and 6. It should also be clear from theorem 1 that $LOF(p)$ has an easy-to-understand interpretation. It is simply a function of the reachability distances in p's direct neighborhood relative to those in p's indirect neighborhood.

5.3 The Tightness of the Bounds

As discussed before, theorem 1 is a general result with the specified upper and lower bounds for LOF applicable to any object p. An immediate question comes to mind. How good or tight are these bounds? In other words, if we use LOF_{max} to denote the upper bound $direct_{max}/indirect_{min}$, and use LOF_{min} to denote the lower bound $direct_{min}/indirect_{max}$, how large is the spread or difference between LOF_{max} and LOF_{min}? In the following we study this issue. A key part of the following analysis is to show that the spread $LOF_{max}-LOF_{min}$ is dependent on the ratio of $direct/indirect$. It turns out that the spread is small under some conditions, but not so small under other conditions.

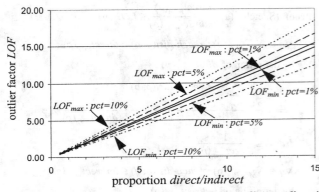

Figure 4: Upper and lower bound on *LOF* depending on *direct/indirect* for different values of *pct*

$$\frac{LOF_{max} - LOF_{min}}{\frac{direct}{indirect}} = \frac{indirect}{direct} \cdot$$

$$\left(\frac{direct + \frac{direct \cdot pct}{100}}{indirect - \frac{indirect \cdot pct}{100}} - \frac{direct - \frac{direct \cdot pct}{100}}{indirect + \frac{indirect \cdot pct}{100}} \right) =$$

$$= \left(\frac{1 + \frac{pct}{100}}{1 - \frac{pct}{100}} - \frac{1 - \frac{pct}{100}}{1 + \frac{pct}{100}} \right) = \frac{4 \times \frac{pct}{100}}{1 - \left(\frac{pct}{100} \right)^2}$$

Given $direct_{min}(p)$ and $direct_{max}(p)$ as defined above, we use $direct(p)$ to denote the mean value of $direct_{min}(p)$ and $direct_{max}(p)$. Similarly, we use $indirect(p)$ to denote the mean value of $indirect_{min}(p)$ and $indirect_{max}(p)$. In the sequel, whenever no confusion arises, we drop the parameter p, e.g., $direct$ as a shorthand of $direct(p)$.

Now to make our following analysis easier to understand, we simplify our discussion by requiring that $(direct_{max} - direct_{min})/direct = (indirect_{max} - indirect_{min})/indirect$. That is, we assume that the reachability distances in the direct and indirect neighborhoods fluctuate by the same amount. Because of this simplification, we can use a single parameter pct in the sequel to control the fluctuation. More specifically, in figure 4, $pct = x\%$ corresponds to the situation where $direct_{max} = direct*(1+x\%)$, $direct_{min} = direct*(1-x\%)$, $indirect_{max} = indirect*(1+x\%)$ and $indirect_{min} = indirect*(1-x\%)$. Figure 4 shows the situations when pct is set to 1%, 5% and 10%. The spread between LOF_{max} and LOF_{min} increases as pct increases.

More importantly, figure 4 shows that, for a fixed percentage $pct=x\%$, the spread between LOF_{max} and LOF_{min} grows linearly with respect to the ratio $direct/indirect$. This means that the relative span $(LOF_{max} - LOF_{min})/(direct/indirect)$ is constant. Stated differently, the relative fluctuation of the LOF depends only on the *ratios* of the underlying reachability distances and not on their *absolute* values. This highlights the spirit of local outliers.

To be more precise, in fact, the whole situation is best captured in the 3-dimensional space where the three dimensions are: $(LOF_{max} - LOF_{min})$, $(direct/indirect)$, and pct. Figure 4 then represents a series of 2-D projections on the first two dimensions. But figure 4 does not show the strength of the dependency between the relative fluctuation of the LOF and the relative fluctuation of pct. For this purpose, figure 5 is useful. The y-axis of the figure shows the ratio between the two dimensions $(LOF_{max} - LOF_{min})$ and $(direct/indirect)$ in the 3-dimensional space mentioned above, and the x-axis corresponds to the other dimension pct. To understand the shape of the curve in figure 5, we have to take a closer look at the ratio $(LOF_{max} - LOF_{min})/(direct/indirect)$:

Figure 5 shows that $(LOF_{max} - LOF_{min})/(direct/indirect)$ is only dependent on the percentage value pct. Its value approaches infinity if pct approaches 100, but it is very small for reasonable values of pct. This also verifies that the relative fluctuation of the LOF is constant for a fixed percentage pct, as we have seen in figure 4.

To summarize, if the fluctuation of the average reachability distances in the direct and indirect neighborhoods is small (i.e., pct is low), theorem 1 estimates the LOF very well, as the minimum and maximum LOF bounds are close to each other. There are two important cases for which this is true.

- The percentage pct is very low for an object p, if the fluctuation of the reachability distances is rather homogeneous, i.e., if the $MinPts$-nearest neighbors of p belong to the same cluster. In this case, the values $direct_{min}$, $direct_{max}$, $indirect_{min}$ and $indirect_{max}$ are almost identical, resulting in the LOF being close to 1. This is consistent with the result established in lemma 1.

- The argument above can be generalized to an object p which is not located deep inside a cluster, but whose $MinPts$-nearest neighbors all belong to the same cluster (as depicted in figure 3). In this case, even though LOF may not be close to 1, the bounds on LOF as predicted by theorem 1 are tight.

5.4 Bounds for Objects whose Direct Neighborhoods Overlap Multiple Clusters

So far we have analyzed the tightness of the bounds given in theorem 1, and have given two conditions under which the bounds are tight. An immediate question that comes to mind is: under what

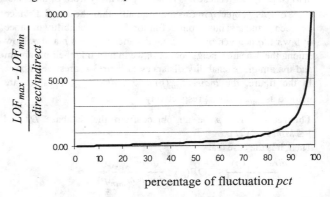

Figure 5: Relative span for *LOF* depending on percentage of fluctuation for *d* and *w*

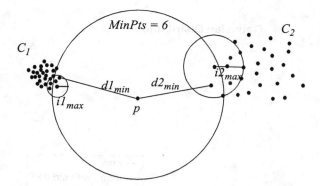

Figure 6: Illustration of theorem 2

condition are the bounds not tight? Based on figure 5, if the *MinPts*-nearest neighbors of an object p belong to different clusters having different densities, the value for *pct* may be very large. Then based on figure 5, the spread between LOF_{max} and LOF_{min} value can be large. In this case, the bounds given in theorem 1 do not work well.

As an example, let us consider the situation shown in figure 1 again. For object o_2, because all its *MinPts*-nearest neighbors come from the same cluster C_2, the bounds given by theorem 1 on the *LOF* of o_2 is expected to be tight. In contrast, the *MinPts*-nearest neighbors of o_1 come from both clusters C_1 and C_2. In this case, the given bounds on the *LOF* of o_1 may not be as good.

Theorem 2 below intends to give better bounds on the LOF of object p when p's *MinPts*-nearest neighborhood overlaps with more than one cluster. The intuitive meaning of theorem 2 is that, when we partition the *MinPts*-nearest neighbors of p into several groups, each group contributes proportionally to the *LOF* of p.

An example is shown in figure 6 for *MinPts*=6. In this case, 3 of object p's 6-nearest neighbors come from cluster C_1, and the other 3 come from cluster C_2. Then according to theorem 2, LOF_{min} is given by $(0.5*d1_{min} + 0.5*d2_{min})/(0.5/i1_{max} + 0.5/i2_{max})$, where $d1_{min}$ and $d2_{min}$ give the minimum reachability distances between p and the 6-nearest neighbors of p in C_1 and C_2 respectively, and $i1_{max}$ and $i2_{max}$ give the maximum reachability distances between q and q's 6-nearest neighbors, where q is a 6-nearest neighbor of p from C_1 and C_2 respectively. For simplicity, figure 6 does not show the case for the upper bound LOF_{max}.

Theorem 2: Let p be an object from the database D, $1 \leq MinPts \leq |D|$, and C_1, C_2, ..., C_n be a partition of $N_{MinPts}(p)$, i.e. $N_{MinPts}(p) = C_1 \cup C_2 \cup ... \cup C_n \cup \{p\}$ with $C_i \cap C_j = \varnothing$, $C_i \neq \varnothing$ for $1 \leq i,j \leq n, i \neq j$.

Furthermore, let $\xi_i = |C_i|/|N_{MinPts}(p)|$ be the percentage of objects in p's neighborhood, which are also in C_i. Let the notions $direct^i_{min}(p)$, $direct^i_{max}(p)$, $indirect^i_{min}(p)$, and $indirect^i_{max}(p)$ be defined analogously to $direct_{min}(p)$, $direct_{max}(p)$, $indirect_{min}(p)$, and $indirect_{max}(p)$ but restricted to the set C_i (e.g., $direct^i_{min}(p)$ denotes the minimum reachability distance between p and a *MinPts*-nearest neighbor of p in the set C_i). Then, it holds that (a)

$$LOF(p) \geq \left(\sum_{i=1}^{n} \xi_i \cdot direct^i_{min}(p) \right) \left(\sum_{i=1}^{n} \frac{\xi_i}{indirect^i_{max}(p)} \right)$$

and (b)

$$LOF(p) \leq \left(\sum_{i=1}^{n} \xi_i \cdot direct^i_{max}(p) \right) \left(\sum_{i=1}^{n} \frac{\xi_i}{indirect^i_{min}(p)} \right)$$

■

We give a proof sketch of theorem 2 in the appendix. Theorem 2 generalizes theorem 1 in taking into consideration the ratios of the *MinPts*-nearest neighbors coming from multiple clusters. As such, there is the following corollary.

Corollary 1: If the number of partitions in theorem 2 is 1, then LOF_{min} and LOF_{max} given in theorem 2 are exactly the same corresponding bounds given in theorem 1.■

6. THE IMPACT OF THE PARAMETER *MINPTS*

In the previous section, we have analyzed the formal properties of *LOF*. For objects deep inside a cluster, we have shown that the *LOF* is approximately equal to 1. For other objects, we have established two sets of upper and lower bounds on the *LOF*, depending on whether the *MinPts*-nearest neighbors come from one or more clusters. It is important to note that all the previous results are based on a given *MinPts* value. In this section, we discuss how the *LOF* value is influenced by the choice of the *MinPts* value, and how to determine the right *MinPts* values for the *LOF* computation.

6.1 How *LOF* Varies according to Changing *MinPts* Values

Given the analytic results established in the previous section, several interesting questions come to mind. How does the *LOF* value change when the *MinPts* value is adjusted? Given an increasing sequence of *MinPts* values, is there a corresponding *monotonic* sequence of changes to *LOF*? That is, does *LOF* decrease or increase monotonically?

Unfortunately, the reality is that *LOF* neither decreases nor increases monotonically. Figure 7 shows a simple scenario where all the objects are distributed following a Gaussian distribution. For each *MinPts* value between 2 and 50, the minimum, maximum and mean *LOF* values, as well as the standard deviation, are shown.

Let us consider the maximum *LOF* as an example. Initially, when the *MinPts* value is set to 2, this reduces to using the actual inter-object distance $d(p,o)$ in definition 5. By increasing the *MinPts* value, the statistical fluctuations in reachability distances and in *LOF* are weakened. Thus, there is an initial drop on the maximum *LOF* value. However, as the *MinPts* value continues to increase, the maximum *LOF* value goes up and down, and eventually stabilizes to some value.

If the *LOF* value changes non-monotonically even for such a pure distribution like the Gaussian distribution, the *LOF* value changes more wildly for more complex situations. Figure 8 shows a two-dimensional dataset containing three clusters, where S_1 consists of 10

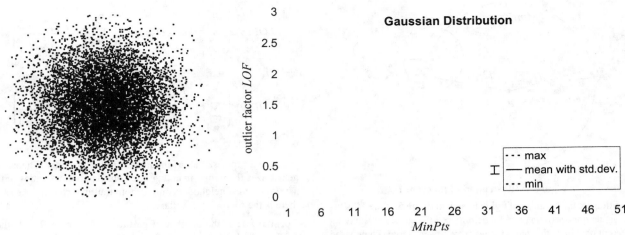

Figure 7: Fluctuation of the outlier-factors within a Gaussian cluster

objects, S_2 of 35 objects and S_3 of 500 objects. On the right side are representative plots for one object from each of these clusters. The plots show the *LOF* over *MinPts* for the range from 10 to 50. While the *LOF* of an object in S_3 is very stable around 1, the *LOF*s of the objects in S_1 and S_3 change more wildly.

6.2 Determining a Range of *MinPts* Values

Because the *LOF* value can go up and down, we propose as a heuristic that we use a range of *MinPts* values. In the following, we provide guidelines as to how this range can be picked. We use *MinPtsLB* and *MinPtsUB* to denote the "lower bound" and the "upper bound" of the range.

Let us first determine a reasonable value of *MinPtsLB*. Clearly, *MinPtsLB* can be as small as 2. However, as explained above and before definition 5, it is wise to remove unwanted statistical fluctuations due to *MinPts* being too small. As an example, for the Gaussian distribution shown in figure 7, the standard deviation of *LOF* only stabilizes when *MinPtsLB* is at least 10. As another extreme example, suppose we turn the Gaussian distribution in figure 7 to a uniform distribution. It turns out that for *MinPts* less than 10, there can be objects whose *LOF* are significant greater than 1. This is counter-intuitive because in a uniform distribution, no object should be labeled as outlying. Thus, the first guideline we provide for picking *MinPtsLB* is that it should be at least 10 to remove unwanted statistical fluctuations.

The second guideline we provide for picking *MinPtsLB* is based on a more subtle observation. Consider a simple situation of one object p and a set/cluster C of objects. If C contains fewer than *MinPtsLB* objects, then the set of *MinPts*-nearest neighbors of each object in C will include p, and vice versa. Thus, by applying theorem 1, the *LOF* of p and all the objects in C will be quite similar, thus making p indistinguishable from the objects in C.

If, on the other hand, C contains more than *MinPtsLB* objects, the *MinPts*-nearest neighborhoods of the objects deep in C will not contain p, but some objects of C will be included in p's neighborhood. Thus, depending on the distance between p and C and the density of C, the *LOF* of p can be quite different from that of an object in C. The key observation here is that *MinPtsLB* can be regarded as the *minimum* number of objects a "cluster" (like C above) has to contain, so that other objects (like p above) can be local outliers

relative to this cluster. This value could be application-dependent. For most of the datasets we experimented with, picking 10 to 20 appears to work well in general.

Next, we turn to the selection of a reasonable value of *MinPtsUB*, the upper bound value of the range of *MinPts* values. Like the lower bound *MinPtsLB*, the upper bound also has an associated meaning. Let C be a set/cluster of "close by" objects. Then *MinPtsUB* can be regarded as the *maximum* cardinality of C for all objects in C to potentially be local outliers. By "close by" we mean, that the *direct$_{min}$*, *direct$_{max}$*, *indirect$_{min}$* and *indirect$_{max}$* values are all very similar. In this case, for *MinPts* values exceeding *MinPtsUB*, theorem 1 requires that the *LOF* of all objects in C be close to 1. Hence, the guideline we provide for picking *MinPtsUB* is the maximum number of "close by" objects that can potentially be local outliers.

As an example, let us consider the situation shown in figure 8 again. Recall that S_1 consists of 10 objects, S_2 of 35 objects and S_3 of 500 objects. From the plots, it is clear that the objects in S_3 are never outliers, always having their *LOF* values close to 1. In contrast, the objects in S_1 are strong outliers for *MinPts* values between 10 and 35. The objects in S_2 are outliers starting at *MinPts* = 45. The reason for the last two effects is that, beginning at *MinPts* = 36, the *MinPts*-nearest neighborhoods of the objects in S_2 start to include some object(s) from S_1. From there on, the objects in S_1 and S_2 exhibit roughly the same behavior. Now at *MinPts* = 45, the members of this "combined" set of objects S_1 and S_2 start to include object(s) from S_3 in their neighborhoods, and thus starting to become outliers relative to S_3. Depending on the application domain, we may want to consider a group of 35 objects (like S_2) a cluster or a bunch of "close by" local outliers. To facilitate this, we can choose a *MinPtsUB* value accordingly, that is either smaller than 35 or larger than 35. A similar argument can be made for *MinPtsLB* with respect to the minimum number of objects relative to which other objects can be considered local outliers.

Having determined *MinPtsLB* and *MinPtsUB*, we can compute for each object its *LOF* values within this range. We propose the heuristic of ranking all objects with respect to the maximum *LOF* value within the specified range. That is, the ranking of an object p is based on: $\max\{LOF_{MinPts}(p) \mid MinPtsLB \le MinPts \le MinPtsUB\}$.

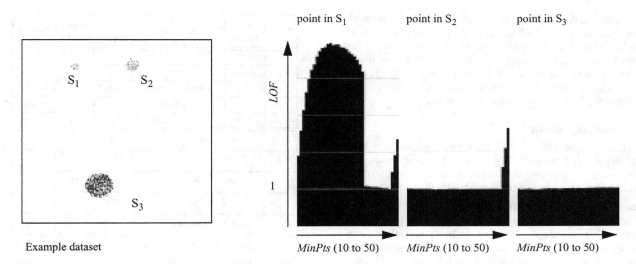

Example dataset

Figure 8: Ranges of *LOF* values for different objects in a sample dataset

Given all the *LOF* values within the range, instead of taking the maximum, we could take other aggregates, such as the minimum or the mean. The situation in figure 8 shows that taking the minimum could be inappropriate as the minimum may erase the outlying nature of an object completely. Taking the mean may also have the effect of diluting the outlying nature of the object. We propose to take the maximum to highlight the instance at which the object is the most outlying.

7. EXPERIMENTS

In this section, with the proposed heuristic of taking the maximum *LOF* value within the range, we show that our ideas can be used to successfully identify outliers which appear to be meaningful but cannot be identified by other methods. We start with a synthetical 2-dimensional dataset, for which we show the outlier factors for all objects, in order to give an intuitive notion of the *LOF* values computed. The second example uses the real-world dataset that has been used in [KN98] to evaluate the *DB(pct, dmin)* outliers. We repeat their experiments to validate our method. In the third example, we identify meaningful outliers in a database of german soccer

players, for which we happen to have a "domain expert" handy, who confirmed the meaningfulness of the outliers found. The last subsection contains performance experiments showing the practicability of our approach even for large, high-dimensional datasets.

Additionally, we conducted experiments with a 64-dimensional dataset, to demonstrate that our definitions are reasonable in very high dimensional spaces. The feature vectors used are color histograms extracted from tv snapshots [2]. We indentified multiple clusters, e.g. a cluster of pictures from a tennis match, and reasonable local outliers with *LOF* values of up to 7.

7.1 A Synthetic Example

The left side of figure 9 shows a 2-dimensional dataset containing one low density Gaussian cluster of 200 objects and three large clusters of 500 objects each. Among these three, one is a dense Gaussian cluster and the other two are uniform clusters of different densities. Furthermore, it contains a couple of outliers. On the right side of figure 9 we plot the *LOF* of all the objects for *MinPts* = 40 as a third dimension. We see that the objects in the uniform clusters all have their *LOF* equal to 1. Most objects in the Gaussian clusters

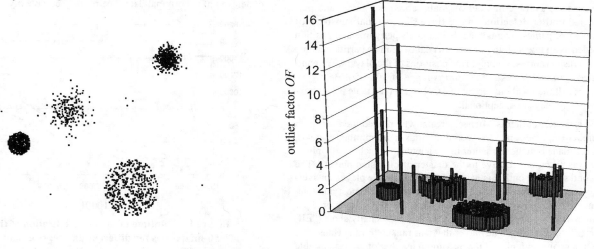

Figure 9: Outlier-factors for points in a sample dataset (*MinPts*=40)

101

also have 1 as their *LOF* values. Slightly outside the Gaussian clusters, there are several weak outliers, i.e., those with relatively low, but larger than 1, *LOF* values. The remaining seven objects all have significantly larger *LOF* values. Furthermore, it is clear from the figure that the value of the *LOF* for each of these outliers depends on the density of the cluster(s) relative to which the object is an outlier, and the distance of the outlier to the cluster(s).

7.2 Hockey Data

In [13], the authors conducted a number of experiments on historical NHL player data; see [13] for a more detailed explanation of the attributes used. We repeat their experiments on the NHL96 dataset, computing the maximum *LOF* in the *MinPts* range of 30 to 50.

For the first test, on the 3-dimensional subspace of points scored, plus-minus statistics and penalty-minutes, they identified Vladimir Konstantinov as the only *DB*(0.998, 26.3044) outlier. He was also our top outlier with the *LOF* value of 2.4. The second strongest local outlier, with the *LOF* of 2.0, is Matthew Barnaby. For most outliers found, we do not explain why they are outliers from a domain-expert standpoint here; the interested reader can find this information in [13]. The point here is that by ranking outliers with their maximum *LOF* value, we get almost identical results. In the next subsection, we show how this approach can identify some outliers that [13] cannot find.

In the second test, they identified the *DB*(0.997, 5) outliers in the 3-dimensional subspace of games played, goals scored and shooting percentage, finding Chris Osgood and Mario Lemieux as outliers. Again, they are our top outliers, Chris Osgood with the *LOF* of 6.0 and Mario Lemieux with the *LOF* of 2.8. On our ranked list based on *LOF*, Steve Poapst, ranked third with the *LOF* of 2.5, played only three games, scored once and had a shooting percentage of 50%.

7.3 Soccer Data

In the following experiment, we computed the local outliers for a database of soccer-player information from the "Fußball 1. Bundesliga" (the German national soccer league) for the season 1998/99. The database consists of 375 players, containing the name, the number of games played, the number of goals scored and the position of the player (goalie, defense, center, offense). From these we derived the average number of goals scored per game, and performed outlier detection on the three-dimensional subspace of number of games, average number of goals per game and position (coded as an integer). In general, this dataset can be partitioned into four clusters corresponding to the positions of the players. We computed the *LOF* values in the *MinPts* range of 30 to 50. Below we discuss all the local outliers with *LOF* > 1.5 (see table 3), and explain why they are exceptional.

The strongest outlier is Michael Preetz, who played the maximum number of games and also scored the maximum number of goals, which made him the top scorer in the league ("Torschützenkönig"). He was an outlier relative to the cluster of offensive players. The second strongest outlier is Michael Schjönberg. He played an average number of games, but he was an outlier because most other defense players had a much lower average number of goals scored per game. The reason for this is that he kicked the penalty shots ("Elfmeter") for his team. The player that was ranked third is Hans-Jörg Butt, a goalie who played the maximum number of games possible

Rank	Outlier Factor	Player Name	Games Played	Goals Scored	Position
1	1.87	Michael Preetz	34	23	Offense
2	1.70	Michael Schjönberg	15	6	Defense
3	1.67	Hans-Jörg Butt	34	7	Goalie
4	1.63	Ulf Kirsten	31	19	Offense
5	1.55	Giovane Elber	21	13	Offense
minimum			0	0	
median			21	1	
maximum			34	23	
mean			18.0	1.9	
standard deviation			11.0	3.0	

Table 3: Results of the soccer player dataset

and scored 7 goals. He was the only goalie to score *any* goal; he too kicked the penalty shots for his team. On rank positions four and five, we found Ulf Kirsten and Giovane Elber, two offensive players with very high scoring averages.

7.4 Performance

In this section, we evaluate the performance of the computation of *LOF*. The following experiments were conducted on an Pentium III-450 workstation with 256 MB main memory running Linux 2.2. All algorithms were implemented in Java and executed on the IBM JVM 1.1.8. The datasets used were generated randomly, containing different numbers of Gaussian clusters of different sizes and densities. All times are wall-clock times, i.e. include CPU-time and I/O.

To compute the *LOF* values within the range between *MinPtsLB* and *MinPtsUB*, for all the *n* objects in the database *D*, we implemented a two-step algorithm. In the first step, the *MinPtsUB*-nearest neighborhoods are found, and in the second step the *LOF*s are computed. Let us look at these two steps in detail.

In the first step, the *MinPtsUB*-nearest neighbors for every point *p* are materialized, together with their distances to *p*. The result of this step is a materialization database *M* of size *n**MinPtsUB distances. Note that the size of this intermediate result is independent of the dimension of the original data. The runtime complexity of this step

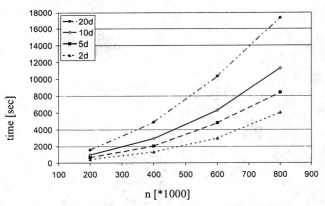

Figure 10: Runtime of the materialization of the 50-nn queries for different dataset sizes and different dimensions using an index

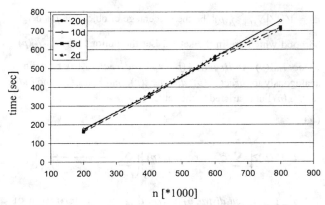

Figure 11: Runtime for the computation of the LOFs for different dataset sizes

is $O(n*$time for a *k-nn* query). For the *k-nn* queries, we have a choice among different methods. For low-dimensional data, we can use a grid based approach which can answer *k-nn* queries in constant time, leading to a complexity of $O(n)$ for the materialization step. For medium to medium high-dimensional data, we can use an index, which provides an average complexity of $O(\log n)$ for *k-nn* queries, leading to a complexity of $O(n \log n)$ for the materialization. For extremely high-dimensional data, we need to use a sequential scan or some variant of it, e.g. the VA-file ([21]), with a complexity of $O(n)$, leading to a complexity of $O(n^2)$ for the materialization step. In our experiments, we used a variant of the X-tree ([4]), leading to the complexity of $O(n \log n)$. Figure 10 shows performance experiments for different dimensional datasets and *MinPtsUB*=50. The times shown do include the time to build the index. Obviously, the index works very well for 2-dimensional and 5-dimensional dataset, leading to a near linear performance, but degenerates for the 10-dimensional and 20-dimensionsal dataset. It is a well known effect of index structures, that their effectivity decreases with increasing dimension.

In the second step, the *LOF* values are computed using the materialization database *M*. The original database *D* is not needed for this step, as *M* contains sufficient information to compute the *LOFs*. The database *M* is scanned twice for every value of *MinPts* between *MinPtsLB* and *MinPtsUB*. In the first scan, the local reachability densities of every object are computed. In the second step, the final *LOF* values are computed and written to a file. These values can then be used to rank the objects according to their maximum *LOF* value in the interval of *MinPtsLB* and *MinPtsUB*. The time complexity of this step is $O(n)$. This is confirmed by the graph shown in figure 11, where the *LOF* values for *MinPtsLB*=10 to *MinPtsUB*=50 were computed.

8. CONCLUSIONS

Finding outliers is an important task for many KDD applications. Existing proposals consider being an outlier as a binary property. In this paper, we show that for many situations, it is meaningful to consider being an outlier not as a binary property, but as the degree to which the object is isolated from its surrounding neighborhood. We introduce the notion of the local outlier factor *LOF*, which captures exactly this relative degree of isolation. We show that our definition of *LOF* enjoys many desirable properties. For objects deep

inside a cluster, the *LOF* value is approximately 1. For other objects, we give tight lower and upper bounds on the *LOF* value, regardless of whether the *MinPts*-nearest neighbors come from one or more clusters. Furthermore, we analyze how the *LOF* value depends on the *MinPts* parameter. We give practical guidelines on how to select a range of *MinPts* values to use, and propose the heuristic of ranking objects by their maximum *LOF* value within the selected range. Experimental results demonstrate that our heuristic appears to be very promising in that it can identify meaningful local outliers that previous approaches cannot find. Last but not least, we show that our approach of finding local outliers is efficient for datasets where the nearest neighbor queries are supported by index structures and still practical for very large datasets.

There are two directions for ongoing work. The first one is on how to describe or explain why the identified local outliers are exceptional. This is particularly important for high-dimensional datasets, because a local outlier may be outlying only on some, but not on all, dimensions (cf. [14]). The second one is to further improve the performance of *LOF* computation. For both of these directions, it is interesting to investigate how *LOF* computation can "handshake" with a hierarchical clustering algorithm, like OPTICS [2]. On the one hand, such an algorithm may provide more detailed information about the local outliers, e.g., by analyzing the clusters relative to which they are outlying. On the other hand, computation may be shared between *LOF* processing and clustering. The shared computation may include *k-nn* queries and reachability distances.

References

[1] Arning, A., Agrawal R., Raghavan P.: "A Linear Method for Deviation Detection in Large Databases", Proc. 2nd Int. Conf. on Knowledge Discovery and Data Mining, Portland, OR, AAAI Press, 1996, p. 164-169.

[2] Ankerst M., Breunig M. M., Kriegel H.-P., Sander J.: "OPTICS: Ordering Points To Identify the Clustering Structure", Proc. ACM SIGMOD Int. Conf. on Management of Data, Philadelphia, PA, 1999.

[3] Agrawal R., Gehrke J., Gunopulos D., Raghavan P.: "Automatic Subspace Clustering of High Dimensional Data for Data Mining Applications", Proc. ACM SIGMOD Int. Conf. on Management of Data, Seattle, WA, 1998, pp. 94-105.

[4] Berchthold S., Keim D. A., Kriegel H.-P.: "The X-Tree: An Index Structure for High-Dimensional Data", 22nd Conf. on Very Large Data Bases, Bombay, India, 1996, pp. 28-39.

[5] Barnett V., Lewis T.: "Outliers in statistical data", John Wiley, 1994.

[6] DuMouchel W., Schonlau M.: "A Fast Computer Intrusion Detection Algorithm based on Hypothesis Testing of Command Transition Probabilities", Proc. 4th Int. Conf. on Knowledge Discovery and Data Mining, New York, NY, AAAI Press, 1998, pp. 189-193.

[7] Ester M., Kriegel H.-P., Sander J., Xu X.: "A Density-Based Algorithm for Discovering Clusters in Large Spatial Databases with Noise", Proc. 2nd Int. Conf. on Knowledge Discovery and Data Mining, Portland, OR, AAAI Press, 1996, pp. 226-231.

[8] Fawcett T., Provost F.: "Adaptive Fraud Detection", Data Mining and Knowledge Discovery Journal, Kluwer Academic Publishers, Vol. 1, No. 3, 1997, pp. 291-316.

[9] Fayyad U., Piatetsky-Shapiro G., Smyth P.: "Knowledge

Discovery and Data Mining: Towards a Unifying Framework", Proc. 2nd Int. Conf. on Knowledge Discovery and Data Mining, Portland, OR, 1996, pp. 82-88.

[10] Hawkins, D.: "*Identification of Outliers*", Chapman and Hall, London, 1980.

[11] Hinneburg A., Keim D. A.: "*An Efficient Approach to Clustering in Large Multimedia Databases with Noise*", Proc. 4th Int. Conf. on Knowledge Discovery and Data Mining, New York City, NY, 1998,pp. 58-65.

[12] Johnson T., Kwok I., Ng R.: "*Fast Computation of 2-Dimensional Depth Contours*", Proc. 4th Int. Conf. on Knowledge Discovery and Data Mining, New York, NY, AAAI Press, 1998, pp. 224-228.

[13] Knorr E. M., Ng R. T.: "*Algorithms for Mining Distance-Based Outliers in Large Datasets*", Proc. 24th Int. Conf. on Very Large Data Bases, New York, NY, 1998, pp. 392-403.

[14] Knorr E. M., Ng R. T.: "*Finding Intensional Knowledge of Distance-based Outliers*", Proc. 25th Int. Conf. on Very Large Data Bases, Edinburgh, Scotland, 1999, pp. 211-222.

[15] Ng R. T., Han J.: "*Efficient and Effective Clustering Methods for Spatial Data Mining*", Proc. 20th Int. Conf. on Very Large Data Bases, Santiago, Chile, Morgan Kaufmann Publishers, San Francisco, CA, 1994, pp. 144-155.

[16] Preparata F., Shamos M.: "*Computational Geometry: an Introduction*", Springer, 1988.

[17] Ramaswamy S., Rastogi R., Kyuseok S.: "*Efficient Algorithms for Mining Outliers from Large Data Sets*", Proc. ACM SIDMOD Int. Conf. on Management of Data, 2000.

[18] Ruts I., Rousseeuw P.: "Computing Depth Contours of Bivariate Point Clouds, Journal of Computational Statistics and Data Analysis, 23, 1996, pp. 153-168.

[19] Sheikholeslami G., Chatterjee S., Zhang A.: "*WaveCluster: A Multi-Resolution Clustering Approach for Very Large Spatial Databases*", Proc. Int. Conf. on Very Large Data Bases, New York, NY, 1998, pp. 428-439.

[20] Tukey J. W.: "*Exploratory Data Analysis*", Addison-Wesley, 1977.

[21] Weber R., Schek Hans-J., Blott S.: "*A Quantitative Analysis and Performance Study for Similarity-Search Methods in High-Dimensional Spaces*", Proc. Int. Conf. on Very Large Data Bases, New York, NY, 1998, pp. 194-205.

[22] Wang W., Yang J., Muntz R.: "*STING: A Statistical Information Grid Approach to Spatial Data Mining*", Proc. 23th Int. Conf. on Very Large Data Bases, Athens, Greece, Morgan Kaufmann Publishers, San Francisco, CA, 1997, pp. 186-195.

[23] Zhang T., Ramakrishnan R., Linvy M.: "*BIRCH: An Efficient Data Clustering Method for Very Large Databases*", Proc. ACM SIGMOD Int. Conf. on Management of Data, ACM Press, New York, 1996, pp.103-114.

Appendix

Proof of Theorem 2 (Sketch): Let p be an object from the database D, $1 \leq MinPts \leq |D|$, and $C_1, C_2, ..., C_n$ be a partition of $N_{MinPts}(p)$, i.e. $N_{MinPts}(p) = C_1 \cup C_2 \cup ... \cup C_n \cup \{p\}$ with $C_i \cap C_j = \emptyset$, $C_i \neq \emptyset$ for $1 \leq i,j \leq n$, $i \neq j$. Furthermore, let

$\xi_i = |C_i|/|N_{MinPts}(p)|$ be the percentage of objects in p's neighborhood which are in the set C_i. Let the notions $direct^i_{min}(p)$, $direct^i_{max}(p)$, $indirect^i_{min}(p)$, and $indirect^i_{max}(p)$ be defined analogously to $direct_{min}(p)$, $direct_{max}(p)$, $indirect_{min}(p)$, and $indirect_{max}(p)$ but restricted to the set C_i.

(a)

$$LOF(p) \geq \left(\sum_{i=1}^{n} \xi_i \cdot direct^i_{min}(p) \right) \left(\sum_{i=1}^{n} \frac{\xi_i}{indirect^i_{max}(p)} \right)$$

$\forall o \in C_i: reach\text{-}dist(p, o) \geq direct^i_{min}(p)$, by definition of $direct^i_{min}(p)$. $\Rightarrow$

$$\frac{\sum_{o \in N_{MinPts}(p)} reach\text{-}dist(p,o)}{|N_{MinPts}(p)|} = \left(\sum_{i=1}^{n} \sum_{o \in C_i} \frac{reach\text{-}dist(p,o)}{|N_{MinPts}(p)|} \right)^{-1}$$

$$\leq \left(\sum_{i=1}^{n} \sum_{o \in C_i} \frac{direct^i_{min}(p)}{|N_{MinPts}(p)|} \right)^{-1} =$$

$$= \left(\sum_{i=1}^{n} \frac{|C_i| \cdot direct^i_{min}(p)}{|N_{MinPts}(p)|} \right)^{-1} = \left(\sum_{i=1}^{n} \xi_i \cdot direct^i_{min}(p) \right)^{-1}$$

i.e. $lrd(p) \leq \left(\sum_{i=1}^{n} \xi_i \cdot direct^i_{min}(p) \right)^{-1}$

$\forall q \in N_{MinPts}(o): reach\text{-}dist(o,q) \leq indirect^i_{max}(p)$

$\Rightarrow lrd(o) \geq \frac{1}{indirect^i_{max}(p)}$ .Thus, it follows that

$$LOF(p) = \frac{\sum_{o \in N_{MinPts}(p)} \frac{lrd(o)}{lrd(p)}}{|N_{MinPts}(p)|} = \frac{1}{lrd(p)} \cdot \sum_{o \in N_{MinPts}(p)} \frac{lrd(o)}{|N_{MinPts}(p)|}$$

$$\geq \left(\sum_{i=1}^{n} \xi_i \cdot direct^i_{min}(p) \right) \cdot \left(\sum_{i=1}^{n} \sum_{o \in C_i} \frac{\frac{1}{indirect^i_{max}(p)}}{|N_{MinPts}(p)|} \right)$$

$$= \left(\sum_{i=1}^{n} \xi_i \cdot direct^i_{min}(p) \right) \cdot \left(\sum_{i=1}^{n} \frac{\xi_i}{indirect^i_{max}(p)} \right)$$

(b)

$$LOF(p) \leq \left(\sum_{i=1}^{n} \xi_i \cdot direct^i_{max}(p) \right) \left(\sum_{i=1}^{n} \frac{\xi_i}{indirect^i_{min}(p)} \right)$$

: analogously. ∎

Answering Complex SQL Queries Using Automatic Summary Tables

Markos Zaharioudakis, Roberta Cochrane, George Lapis, Hamid Pirahesh, Monica Urata

IBM Almaden Research Center
San Jose, CA 95120
{markos, bobbiec, lapis, pirahesh}@almaden.ibm.com, monicau@us.ibm.com

ABSTRACT

We investigate the problem of using materialized views to answer SQL queries. We focus on modern decision-support queries, which involve joins, arithmetic operations and other (possibly user-defined) functions, aggregation (often along multiple dimensions), and nested subqueries. Given the complexity of such queries, the vast amounts of data upon which they operate, and the requirement for interactive response times, the use of materialized views (MVs) of similar complexity is often mandatory for acceptable performance. We present a novel algorithm that is able to rewrite a user query so that it will access one or more of the available MVs instead of the base tables. The algorithm extends prior work by addressing the new sources of complexity mentioned above, that is, complex expressions, multidimensional aggregation, and nested subqueries. It does so by relying on a graphical representation of queries and a bottom-up, pair-wise matching of nodes from the query and MV graphs. This approach offers great modularity and extensibility, allowing for the rewriting of a large class of queries.

1. INTRODUCTION

Recent years have seen rapid growth in the area of decision-support queries. Such queries typically operate over huge amounts of data (many Terabytes), performing multiple joins and complex aggregation. Furthermore, they are becoming increasingly more interactive, requiring response times in the order of seconds. Traditional optimization techniques often fail to meet these new requirements. In such cases, a solution often used in practice is to create a number of *materialized views* (MVs) that contain the pre-computed results of the common operations in a set of user queries; individual user queries can then be optimized by accessing the MVs instead of the raw data.

In this paper, we present an algorithm that is able to take advantage of MVs by proving that the contents of an MV and a user query overlap, and compensating for the non-overlapping parts. When an overlap exists, we say that the query and the MV *match*. After discovering a match, the query can be rewritten so that it will access the MV instead of one or more of the base tables. We consider MVs that are expressed as SQL queries with aggregation. Given their transparent (automatic) use in optimization, and the fact that they summarize the raw data via aggregation, we refer to such MVs as *Automatic Summary Tables* (ASTs). Experience with the TPC-D benchmark and several customer applications has shown that ASTs can often improve the response time of decision-support queries by orders of magnitude. Such performance advantages have made ASTs indispensable in data warehousing environments. Of course, for a complete AST solution, the following related problems must also be addressed: (a) finding the best set of ASTs for each workload under space and/or update overhead constraints, (b) deciding whether an AST should actually be used in answering a query, and (c) maintaining the ASTs efficiently when the base tables are updated. Examples of existing work on these problems include [7], [2], and [10] for (a), (b), and (c), respectively.

In the remainder of this section we describe a sample DB schema, give an example of matching, and list our main contributions. In Section 2, we briefly explain the query graph model. In Section 3, we describe a general matching infrastructure, and then, in Sections 4 and 0 we present a number of specific matching "patterns". In Section 6, we give the details of how individual expressions from a query are matched with (or derived from) the expressions of an AST. In Section 7, we review related work. Finally, in Section 8 we summarize the main points of the paper.

1.1 Sample Database and Example

Figure 1 shows the sample DB schema that we have used for the examples in this paper. The schema contains a single fact table (Trans), which records credit card transactions. Each transaction corresponds to the purchase of one product, and records the product group (fpgid), the location (flid) and date of the purchase, the credit card id (faid), the number of items purchased (qty), and the price and discount rate for the product. The product groups, locations, and credit card accounts comprise three of the schema's dimensions. The product dimension consists of a single level recorded in the PGroup table. The location dimension contains city, state, and country levels, and is represented by a single, de-normalized table (Loc). The account dimension contains two levels, represented by the Cust and Acct tables. The schema contains a Time dimension as well, which is encoded in the date field of the Trans table. The Time levels (day, month, and year) are extracted from the date field using built-in functions. The arrows in Figure 1 represent referential integrity (RI) constraints connecting the fact table to the dimensions.

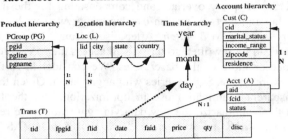

Figure 1: Simplified credit card schema

```
Q1: select faid, state, year(date) as year,     AST1: select faid, flid, year(date) as year,
        count(*) as cnt                                   count(*) as cnt
    from Trans, Loc                                   from Trans
    where flid = lid and country = 'USA'              group by faid, flid, year(date)
    group by faid, state, year(date)
    having count(*) > 100


NewQ1: select faid, state, year, sum(cnt) as cnt
        from AST1, Loc
        where flid = lid and country = 'USA'
        group by faid, state, year
        having sum(cnt) > 100
```

Figure 2: Example of query rewrite

An analyst of such an application will be interested in aggregating the transaction data along different dimensions and levels. For example, query Q1 in Figure 2 counts the number of transactions performed in USA per each account, state, and year and returns the counts that are greater than 100. If AST1 is defined as in Figure 2, then Q1 can be rewritten as NewQ1, which accesses AST1 instead of the Trans table. Given that the average customer performs a few hundred transactions per year, most of them within the same city, AST1 is about hundred times smaller than Trans. Therefore, NewQ1 should perform much better than Q1.

1.2 Our Contributions

The problem of query matching has received considerable attention before. However, previous work has focused on certain simple query patterns only. In our work, we have build on such simple patterns in order to design a powerful algorithm that extends prior art in the following ways.
1. Modern SQL applications make heavy use of subqueries. Today, scalar subqueries can be used

wherever a scalar is expected, and subqueries that return tables can be used wherever a table is expected. This flexibility leads to complex multi-block queries. In the best scenario, existing algorithms can rewrite only the innermost query blocks using single-block ASTs. In contrast, the algorithm described here can match multi-block queries with multi-block ASTs.
2. Even in the context of single-block queries, existing algorithms cannot handle complex expressions very well. Often, SELECT and GROUP-BY lists are restricted to base table columns only or aggregate functions of base table columns. Here, we extend the existing work to include arbitrary expressions.
3. Multidimensional aggregation (expressed via *supergroup functions* like cube, rollup, and grouping sets) is fundamental in decision-support applications. Nevertheless, it has not been considered before in the context of matching. Here, we present matching conditions for queries and ASTs that perform multidimensional aggregation.
4. Previous algorithmic descriptions have often been rather abstract. Sometimes the emphasis is on theoretical results, and at other times, important details are omitted. In contrast, here we describe in detail a practical algorithm, a substantial portion of which has been implemented inside DB2 UDB. Furthermore, the algorithm is modular and extensible; it consists of a generic matching infrastructure and a collection of matching conditions for specific query patterns.

2. BACKGROUND: THE QGM MODEL

In this section, we give a brief overview of the Query Graph Model (QGM), which serves as the basis for our matching algorithm. In QGM, a query is represented as a rooted directed acyclic graph[1] in which the leaf nodes (boxes) represent base tables, internal nodes represent table operations, and edges represent a flow of records from a child (producer) box to a parent (consumer) box. Each non-leaf box produces a relational table after performing its operation on its input, which is a set of relational tables. The root QGM box produces the final query result.

QGM boxes are labeled by the *type* of their operation. The two most common types are SELECT and GROUP-BY. SELECT boxes represent the select-project-join portions of queries; they apply the WHERE or HAVING predicates, and compute all of the scalar expressions that appear in SELECT and GROUP-BY clauses. GROUP-BY boxes perform grouping and compute the aggregate functions. For example, the QGM graph for query Q1 is shown in Figure 3. The bottom SELECT box in the figure performs a join

---

[1] In this paper, we will not consider correlated or recursive queries whose QGM graphs contain cycles.

between the Trans and Loc tables, as specified by the flid = lid join predicate, applies the selection predicate country = USA to the records coming from the Loc table, computes the year(date) grouping expression, and passes on the values of this expression as well the values of the faid and state columns to the parent GROUP-BY box. The GROUP-BY box groups its input records by faid, state, and year, computes the number of records per group, and passes on the grouping columns and the counts to its parent. Finally, the top SELECT box applies the HAVING predicate cnt > 10 and exports the final result. It should be emphasized that QGM represents the query semantics and not any particular execution plan. For example, the bottom SELECT box in Figure 3 does not dictate whether the join is performed before or after the selection of the USA locations.

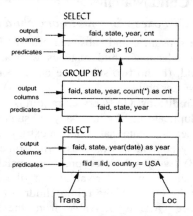

Figure 3: QGM graph for query Q1

As indicted by Figure 3 and the above discussion, a QGM box is described by its type and by its *input columns*, *output columns*, and *predicates*. The predicates and the output columns are computed by *expressions* that are built using input columns. In the remainder of this section, we define these constructs in greater detail.

The *input columns* (or *QNCs*, in QGM terminology) of a box are the columns consumed by the box; their values are produced by the children of the box and flow along the edges that connect the box to its children. QNCs are used, together with functions, operators, and constants, to build *expressions*. Expressions that consist of a single QNC or constant are considered *simple*; otherwise, they are *complex*. Expressions specify the computations for the output columns and the predicates of a box. *Predicates* are found in both SELECT and GROUP-BY boxes. SELECT predicates may be simple selection predicates, join predicates, or selection predicates with subqueries. As a result, a SELECT box may have multiple children, which are join operands or subqueries. GROUP-BY predicates describe the groups to be created. Such grouping predicates are either simple QNCs (like faid, state, and year in Figure 3) or supergroup functions over simple QNCs. GROUP-BY

boxes have a single child always. The *output columns* (or *QCLs*, in QGM terminology) of a box are the columns produced by the box itself. For SELECT boxes, QCL expressions can be arbitrarily complex as long as they do not contain any aggregate functions. The reverse is true for GROUP-BY boxes; their QCLs include all of the grouping input columns, plus aggregate functions over simple input columns. (Given that all of the grouping QNCs are QCLs as well, we refer to such columns simply as *grouping columns*. The set of these grouping columns is the *grouping set* of the box.) It should be noted that a given QCL may be consumed by multiple parent boxes, and hence, there is a 1:N relationship between QCLs and QNCs.

3. THE MATCHING FRAMEWORK

As explained below, the matching algorithm is based on the idea of matching pairs of QGM boxes. In general, a box E *matches* with another box R, if and only if a QGM graph G(E,R) can be constructed such that G(E,R) contains the subgraph G(R) rooted at R, and G(E,R) is semantically equivalent to the subgraph G(E) rooted at E, i.e., G(E,R) and G(E) always produce the same result. If box E matches with box R, then G(E,R) – G(R) is the *compensation*, that is, the set of operations that have to be performed on the output of R in order to get the same output as E. A graphical representation of this definition is shown in Figure 4. If the compensation is empty, the match is *exact* and boxes E and R are equivalent; otherwise, box E is equivalent to the root box of the compensation. Obviously, a non-exact match relationship is asymmetric; to distinguish the different roles of the two boxes in such a relationship, we call E the *subsumee* and R the *subsumer*.

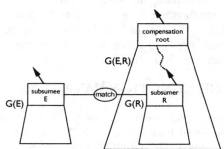

Figure 4: The matching relationship

Having defined the match relationship, we can now present the matching algorithm, starting with its two main components: the *match function* and the *navigator*. The match function takes as input two QGM boxes and determines whether they match. Ideally, the match function should implement the match relationship defined above. However, this definition is too general for practical use. In reality, the match function tries to approximate the match definition in meaningful and practical ways. It does so by considering certain simple, but general graph *patterns*, which consist of the given subsumee and subsumer, as well as the compensation boxes for the matches between the children of the subsumee and subsumer. For each pattern, the match function tests a number of sufficient conditions to determine if a match is possible. Two such conditions that are common for every pattern are the following:

1. At least one of the subsumee's children must match with some subsumer child.
2. The subsumee and subsumer must be of the same type.

The first condition makes sure that there is some minimum overlap between the two boxes. The second condition serves as a quick test, although it is somewhat restrictive[2].

The match function is driven by the navigator. The navigator scans the query and AST graphs in a bottom-up fashion, identifying potential pairs of matching boxes (where the subsumee comes from the query graph and the subsumer comes from the AST graph), and invoking the match function, until the root AST box is matched (if possible) with one or more query boxes. To perform its task, the navigator initializes a set of candidate subsumee/subsumer pairs by forming all of the pairs between the leaves of the graphs. During each iteration, the navigator removes a pair from this set and passes it to the match function. If a match is established, the navigator forms all of the pairs between the parents of the subsumee and the subsumer. The navigator processes its set of candidate box pairs in an order that guarantees that during each invocation of the match function, the children of the two input boxes have been matched already, i.e., the match function has been invoked on each pair-wise combination of the children. Furthermore, the match function knows the compensations for the matches between the children. As a result, it does not have to look at the whole subgraphs of its input boxes; it needs to concentrate on the subsumee, the subsumer, and the child compensation boxes only.

4. MATCH FUNCTION PATTERNS

In this section, we present a list of patterns for matching. The patterns listed here consist of SELECT and/or *simple GROUP-BY* boxes, i.e., GROUP-BYs with no supergroup functions. We start by considering patterns where all of the matches among the children of a candidate subsumee/subsumer pair are exact. Then we present patterns where the child matches have compensation. In each case, we first state the matching conditions, then describe the compensation, and finish with an example. It should be noted that the matching conditions are sufficient only, and

as a result, they are correct only when viewed together with the associated compensation. Due to space, correctness proofs are not included here; instead, some intuitive justification is given in the context of the examples.

Before we proceed, some more terminology must be established regarding the children of two SELECT boxes in a candidate match. As we will see, it is possible to have a subsumee child that does not match with any of the subsumer children; such a subsumee child is called a *rejoin* child. It is also possible to have a subsumer child with no matching subsumee child; such a subsumer child is called an *extra* child and a join between an extra child and the rest of the subsumer is called an *extra join*.

4.1 Exact Child Matches

4.1.1 SELECT boxes with one-to-one child matches

Pattern: The subsumee and subsumer are SELECT boxes and (a) each subsumee child matches with at most one subsumer child, (b) no two subsumee children match with the same subsumer child[3].

Matching Conditions: (1) Every extra join is lossless, i.e., it does not duplicate or eliminate any subsumer rows. (2) Every subsumer predicate that is not an extra join predicate is semantically equivalent (matches) with some subsumee predicate[4]. (3) Every subsumee predicate matches with a subsumer predicate or is derivable from the subsumer's QCLs and/or the QCLs of the rejoin children (if any). (4) Each subsumee QCL is derivable from the subsumer's QCLs and/or the QCLs of the rejoin children. (A subsumee expression (predicate or QCL) is derivable, if it can be written as a function of the subsumer and/or the rejoin QCLs. The details about expression equivalence and derivability are given in Section 6.)

Compensation: The compensation consists of the rejoin children (if any) and a SELECT box that (a) rejoins the subsumer with the rejoin children, (b) applies all of the subsumee's predicates that do not have matching subsumer predicates, and (c) derives all of the subsumee's QCLs from the subsumer's QCLs and/or the rejoin QCLs.

Example: Figure 5 shows a match between query Q2 and AST2. The QGM graphs for Q2 and AST2 consist of one SELECT box joining three base tables. As explained below, the two SELECT boxes satisfy all of the above conditions, and hence they match with a compensation that consists of a SELECT box (Sel-1C1) and the PGroup table. The rewritten query is NewQ2 in Figure 5. In this example,

---

[2] For example, a SELECT DISTINCT box may match with a GROUP-BY box, as they both eliminate duplicates. A way to match SELECT DISTINCT and GROUP-BY without violating condition 2 is presented in [13].

[3] These assumptions are not always true. (Usually, they are violated when self-joins are involved.) A method for relaxing these assumptions is described in [13].

[4] More generally, every subsumer predicate must "subsume" some subsumee predicate, where p1 subsumes p2 if every row eliminated by p1 is also eliminated by p2. For example, x > 10 subsumes x > 20.

PGroup is a rejoin child and Loc is an extra child. Condition 1 is satisfied, as the RI constraint between columns flid and lid makes the join between Trans and Loc lossless. For condition 2, the relevant subsumer predicates are faid = aid and disc > 0.1, both of which appear in the subsumee as well. As a result, the AST does not eliminate any rows that are needed by the query. For condition 3, the relevant subsumee predicates are fpgid = pgid, price > 100, and pgname = TV, all of which are derivable. As shown in Figure 5, these predicates become part of the compensation. With respect to QCL derivability (condition 4), two things are worth observing. First, the compensation derives Q2's aid column from the AST's faid column. Although aid and faid originate from different base tables, they are equivalent because of the faid = aid join predicate. Our algorithm is able to recognize such column equivalence and thus derive aid from faid. Second, the amt column can be derived from the AST using the qty, price, and disc QCLs, or the disc and value QCLs. As shown in Figure 5, when alternative derivations are possible, we choose the one that involves the minimum number of subsumer QCLs.

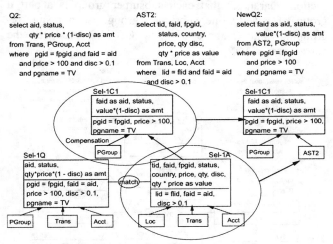

Figure 5: SELECT boxes with exact child matches.

4.1.2 GROUP-BY boxes

Pattern: The subsumee and subsumer are simple GROUP-BY boxes whose children match exactly.

Matching Conditions: (1) Every subsumee grouping column is semantically equivalent (matches) with some subsumer grouping column. (2) If the subsumee's and subsumer's grouping sets match exactly, i.e., every subsumee grouping column matches with a subsumer grouping column and vice-versa, then every aggregate subsumee QCL matches with some subsumer aggregate QCL; otherwise, every aggregate subsumee QCL is derivable from the subsumer's QCLs.

Compensation: No compensation is required if the subsumee and subsumer grouping sets match exactly. Otherwise, the compensation consists of a GROUP-BY box

that re-groups by the subsumee's grouping columns, and derives the subsumee's QCLs from the subsumer's QCLs. For aggregate functions, special derivation rules must be observed; these are listed below for the most common aggregates. (The rules can be combined to derive any other aggregate that is an algebraic expression of the listed functions.) Throughout this list we assume that x is a subsumee QNC, y and z are subsumer QNCs, z is non-nullable, and x and y are semantically equivalent.

a. COUNT(*) is derived as SUM(cnt), where cnt is the COUNT(*) subsumer QCL or the COUNT(z) subsumer QCL.

b. COUNT(x) is derived as SUM(cnt), where cnt is the COUNT(y) subsumer QCL. If x is non-nullable, then cnt might also be the COUNT(z) subsumer QCL.

c. SUM(x) is derived as SUM(sm), where sm is the SUM(y) subsumer QCL. If y is a grouping column, then SUM(x) can also be derived as SUM(y*cnt), where cnt is the COUNT(*) subsumer QCL; in this case, the compensation includes a SELECT box as well to compute the y*cnt expression before regrouping.

d. MAX(x) is derived as MAX(max) or MAX(y). In the first derivation, max is the MAX(y) subsumer QCL; in the second derivation, y must be a grouping column.

e. MIN(x) is similar to MAX(x).

f. COUNT(distinct x) is derived as COUNT(y), if y is a grouping column.

g. SUM(distinct x) is derived as SUM(y), if y is a grouping column.

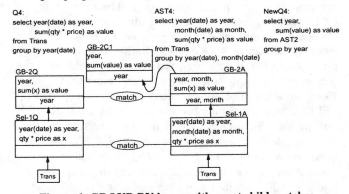

Figure 6: GROUP-BY boxes with exact child matches

Example 1: In Figure 6 the two SELECT boxes (Sel-1Q and Sel-1A) are matched first using the conditions from Section 4.1.1. Sel-1Q and Sel-1A match exactly[5]. As a result, the two GROUP-BY boxes (GB-2Q and GB-2A)

---

[5] Strictly speaking, the match is not exact because Sel-1A produces more columns than Sel-1Q. However, if the only difference is that the subsumer produces more columns than the subsumee, then we consider the match to be exact, unless the subsumee is the top query box in which case compensation is required to project out the extra subsumer columns.

comply with the current pattern, and are matched using the current conditions. This match requires re-grouping compensation (box GB-2C1) in order to compute the query's yearly groups from the AST's monthly groups. Additionally, the compensation derives the yearly sums by re-summing the monthly sums, using rule (c) above. This derivation is correct because the AST's monthly sums are partial sums for the query's yearly sums.

4.2 Non-Exact Child Matches

When the children of a given subsumee/subsumer pair do not match exactly, then, in addition to the subsumee and subsumer, we must also consider the boxes that comprise the compensations for the non-exact child matches. Usually, these child compensation boxes have to be included in the compensation for the parent match. This is called *pulling up* the child compensation boxes.

4.2.1 GROUP-BY boxes with SELECT-only child compensation

Pattern: The subsumee and subsumer are GROUP-BY boxes whose children match with compensation that is a single[6] SELECT box, which may perform rejoins. Furthermore, we assume here that if AGG(x) is a subsumee aggregate function, then QNC x originates from non-rejoin columns only (this assumption is relaxed in [13]).

Matching Conditions: (1) Every subsumee grouping column is derivable from the subsumer grouping columns and/or the rejoin QCLs (if any). (2) If no regrouping compensation is required, then every subsumee aggregate QCL matches with some subsumer aggregate QCL. Otherwise, every subsumee aggregate QCL is derivable from the subsumer's QCLs. (3) Pullup condition: every predicate in the child compensation is derivable from the subsumer's grouping columns and/or the rejoin QCLs.

Compensation: The compensation includes the pulled up SELECT box, potentially followed above by a GROUP-BY box. If the child compensation does not perform rejoins, then the rule for including or not the GROUP-BY box is the same as in Section 4.1.2. Otherwise, regrouping can be avoided only if the two grouping sets are the same **and** the rejoin is 1:N with the rejoin tables being the "1" side. If regrouping is required, then the aggregate functions are derived using the rules of Section 4.1.2 again.

Example1 (no rejoins): In Figure 7, the two SELECT boxes (Sel-1Q and Sel-1A) are matched first, creating the Sel-1C1 compensation box, which comprises the child compensation for the next match between the two GROUP-BY boxes. GB-2Q and GB-2A satisfy all the conditions of the current section, and as a result, they match with a

---

[6] The assumption that the child compensation consists of a single SELECT box is not restrictive because consecutive SELECT boxes can (almost) always be merged into a single SELECT.

compensation that consists of boxes Sel-2C1 and GB-2C2. Sel-2C1 is the pulled-up version of Sel-1C1. It is worth observing that Sel-1C1 is not pulled up "as is"; as indicated by the pullup condition, only the predicates are pulled up. In contrast, the QCLs that appear in Sel-2C1 are created there as a side effect of deriving the subsumee's expressions (see Section 6). The reasoning behind this tactic of not pulling up the QCLs can be explained in the context of the "x" QCL: x is needed in Sel-1C1 to make that box equivalent to Sel-1Q. However, x is not preserved at the output of the parent GB-2Q box; it is used there internally only, to compute the sums. Furthermore, sum(x) is derived from the AST as sum(value). As a result, what we need in Sel-2C1 is value, not x. This pullup tactic is not unique to this pattern; it is used whenever compensation is pulled up. With respect to predicate pullup, we notice that the AST rows eliminated by the month > 6 predicate in Sel-2C1 are exactly the same rows (modulo duplicates) that are eliminated by the same predicate in Sel-1Q. As a result, the predicates in Sel-2C1 and Sel-1Q have the same effect. Finally, as in Section 4.1.2, condition 1 of the current section guarantees that each subsumer group is a partial group of exactly one subsumee group. As a result, re-grouping and re-aggregating in GB-2C2 produces the correct result.

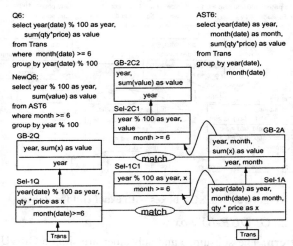

Figure 7: GROUP-BY boxes with simple SELECT child compensation

Example2 (with rejoin): Figugre 8 shows an example with rejoins. Let's assume, for the moment, that the join between Loc and Trans in Q7 is an N:M join. Then, according to the above rules, the compensation between the two GROUP-BY boxes (GB-2Q and GB-2A) must include a GROUP-BY box (GB-2C2). To see why this compensation is correct, we first observe that Q7 joins Trans with Loc, whereas NewQ7 joins AST7 with Loc. Given that AST7 is a summarization of Trans, the outputs of Sel-1Q and Sel-2C1 differ only in the multiplicity of their rows; Sel-1Q produces more duplicates than Sel-2C1. Other than duplicates, however, Sel-1Q and Sel-2C1 produce the same rows. Furthermore, Sel-2C1 "remembers" the number of the lost duplicates in its cnt QCL. As a result, Sel-2C1 does not lose any information, and the counts computed by the query can be derived in GB-2C2 by re-grouping and summing over the AST's cnt column. If we take into account the fact that the join between Loc and Trans is 1:N, then GB-2C2 is not needed because the join does not affect the multiplicity of the Trans rows. Furthermore, the effect of the country = USA predicate is to eliminate some whole groups, but it does not affect the number of Trans rows that fall into each group. Hence, the counts produced by Q7 are the same as the counts produced by AST7.

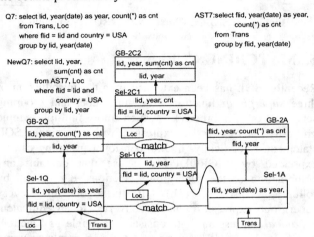

Figugre 8: GROUP-BY boxes with rejoin child compensation

4.2.2 GROUP-BY boxes with GROUP-BY child compensation

Pattern: The general form for this pattern is shown in Figure 9. The subsumee and subsumer are GROUP-BY boxes (GB-Q and GB-A) and the child compensation contains at least one GROUP-BY box and a number (possibly zero) of SELECT boxes. In Figure 9, GB-cC2 is the lowest GROUP-BY box in the child compensation.

Matching Condition: To handle this pattern, the match function calls itself recursively, trying to match GB-cC2 with the subsumer (GB-A). This recursive invocation of the match function conforms to patterns 4.1.2 or 4.2.1: GB-cC2 plays the role of the subsumee, GB-A is the subsumer, and Sel-cC1, if present, is the child compensation. If this intermediate match succeeds, then the original match (between GB-Q and GB-A) succeeds as well.

Compensation: To build the compensation, we start with the intermediate compensation for the match between GB-cC2 and GB-A. Then, all the child-compensation boxes above GB-cC2 are copied above GB-pC2 in the parent compensation. For example, Box-pCN is an exact copy of Box-cCN. Finally, the original subsumee (GB-Q) is also copied at the top of the parent compensation (GB-pC(N+1)). To see why this construction is correct, we first

notice that if GB-cC2 and GB-A match, then, by the match definition, GB-cC2 and GB-pC2 are equivalent. As a result, all boxes above GB-cC2 in the child compensation are equivalent to their copies in the parent compensation. In particular, Box-cCN is equivalent to Box-pCN. However, Box-cCN is also equivalent to child-Q, due to the match between child-Q and child-A. We conclude that child-Q is equivalent to Box-pCN. As a result, boxes GB-Q and GB-pC(N+1) are equivalent as well, because they are copies of each other and their children are equivalent.

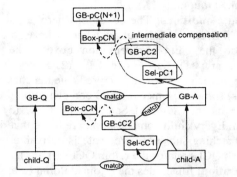

Figure 9:GROUP-BY boxes with GROUP-BY child compensation (general form)

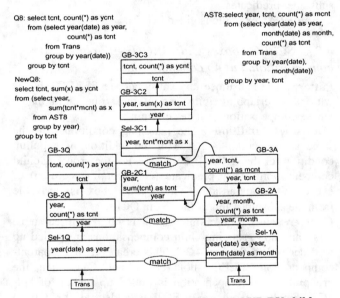

Figure 10: GROUP-BY boxes with GROUP-BY child compensation

Example: In the example of Figure 10, Q8 and AST8 are histogram queries; Q8 prints out all of the yearly transaction counts, and for each such value it gives the number of different years during which that count was achieved. AST8 performs the same computation but for monthly transaction counts. In Figure 10, box GB-2C1 is the compensation for the match between the two inner GROUP-BYs. Boxes GB-3C2 and Sel-3C1 is the compensation for the match between GB-2C1 and GB-3A, where the conditions and rules of Section 4.1.2 were used. Finally, box GB-3C3 is a copy of GB-3Q that completes the compensation for the match between GB-3Q and GB-3A.

4.2.3 SELECT boxes with SELECT-only child compensation

Pattern: The subsumee and subsumer are SELECT boxes whose children match with compensations that do not include any grouping.

Matching Conditions: The conditions here are similar to the ones in Section 4.1.1, but adjustments have to be made to include the child compensation boxes. The revised conditions are: (1) Same as in 4.1.1 (2) Every subsumer predicate that is not an extra join predicate matches with (or subsumes) some subsumee or child compensation predicate. (3) Same as in 4.1.1. (4) Same as in 4.1.1. (5) Pullup condition: Every child compensation predicate that does not have a matching subsumer predicate is derivable from the subsumer's QCLs and/or the rejoin QCLs (if any).

Compensation: It includes the rejoin children (if any) and a single SELECT box that contains all the subsumee and/or child-compensation predicates that do not have matching subsumer predicates.

Example: An example is given in [13].

4.2.4 SELECT boxes with GROUP-BY child compensation, but no common joins

Pattern: The subsumee and subsumer are SELECT boxes with no overlapping joins and at most one child match whose compensation includes grouping.

Matching Conditions: The matching conditions are the same as in Section 4.2.3, with the addition of a pullup condition for the GROUP-BY box(es) of the grouping child compensation: every predicate (i.e., grouping column) of every child-compensation GROUP-BY box is derivable from the subsumer and/or the rejoin QCLs.

Compensation: The compensation is built in three steps. First, any non-grouping child compensations are pulled up as described in Section 4.2.3. This creates a single parent-compensation SELECT box (call it Sel-pC1). Then, the grouping child compensation is pulled up on top of Sel-pC1. Finally, another SELECT is added at the top to compensate the subsumee's predicates and QCLs.

Example: Figure 11 shows an example for this pattern (the bottom SELECT boxes have been omitted to save space). In this example, the two top SELECT boxes (Sel-3Q and Sel-3A) are matched using the conditions for the current pattern. Compensation boxes GB-3C2 and Sel-3C1 are the pulled-up versions of GB-2C2 and Sel-2C1, respectively. Box Sel-3C3 is the additional SELECT box inserted to compensate the subsumee's cnt > 2 predicate and derive its QCLs. This example is discussed further in Section 6.

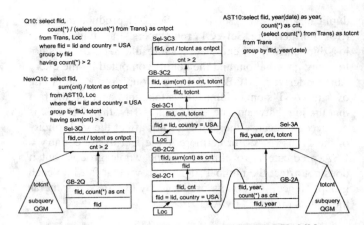

Figure 11: SELECT boxes with GROUP-BY child compensation

5. MATCHING CUBES

Recently, SQL has been extended with the introduction of three *supergroup* functions – rollup, cube, and grouping sets (or "gs" for brevity) – which allow multiple simple group-by queries to be expressed within a single SQL statement. Specifically, multidimensional grouping can be expressed by a GROUP-BY clause that contains any combination of the supergroup functions, e.g., group by rollup(a,b), gs((f,g), (f,h)). It turns out that every supergroup expression can be converted to an equivalent *canonical* expression that consists of a single gs function: $gs(GS_1, GS_2, ..., GS_k)$, where each GS_i is a simple grouping set [9]. In this section, we present matching conditions for such canonical expressions only[7]. We start by explaining the precise semantics of the gs function. Then, we present two patterns with multidimensional group-by's.

Let Q be a query block with the following GROUP-BY clause: group by $gs(GS_1, GS_2, ..., GS_k)$, where $GS_i = \{ A_1^i, A_2^i, ..., A_{ni}^i \}$. Let $GS = \bigcup_1^k GS_i$, and N be the number of elements in GS. Then Q is equivalent to the union of k simple group-by query blocks, known as *cuboids*, and Q is said to be a *cube query*. Each cuboid Q_i groups by GS_i and produces N columns – one column for each grouping item in GS_i, plus $N - n_i$ NULL-valued columns, that is, one NULL-valued column for each grouping item that belongs to GS but not to GS_i. An example of a cube query is shown in Figure 12. For simplicity, we assume that all of the base table columns are non-nullable, and as a result, the only NULL values appearing at the output are the ones added to represent the grouped-out columns of each cuboid.

---

[7] For efficiency, our algorithm matches cubes and rollups directly, without expanding them to grouping sets. However, the basic matching ideas are the same in every case.

112

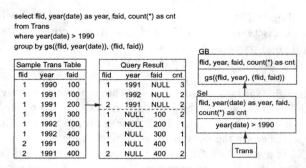

```
select flid, year(date) as year, faid, count(*) as cnt
from Trans
where year(date) > 1990
group by gs((flid, year(date)), (flid, faid))
```

Sample Trans Table			Query Result			
flid	year	faid	flid	year	faid	cnt
1	1990	100	1	1991	NULL	3
1	1991	100	1	1992	NULL	2
1	1991	200	2	1991	NULL	2
1	1991	300	1	NULL	100	2
1	1992	300	1	NULL	200	1
1	1992	400	1	NULL	300	1
2	1991	400	1	NULL	400	1
2	1991	400	2	NULL	400	2

Figure 12: Cube query with sample result and QGM graph

5.1 Simple GROUP-BY query with cube AST

Pattern: The subsumee is a simple GROUP-BY box whereas the subsumer is a multidimensional GROUP-BY box. The child compensation may be empty or consist of a single SELECT box with or without rejoins. (Child compensations with GROUP-BY boxes are handled in exactly the same manner as in Section 4.2.2.) Let GS^E be the subsumee's grouping set, and GS_i^R, i = 1, 2, …, k be the subsumer's grouping sets.

Matching Conditions: The approach taken here is to match the subsumee with one of the cuboids that comprise the subsumer. Care must be taken, however, so that the NULL columns of a cuboid will not participate in the matching. Specifically, a match is possible if there is at least one subsumer grouping set GS_i^R such that the conditions and derivation rules of 4.1.2 or 4.2.1 are satisfied when restricted to the grouping columns of GS_i^R only (rather than all of the subsumer's grouping columns).

Compensation: If more than one of the subsumer's cuboids satisfy the matching conditions, then, to minimize the amount of regrouping in the compensation, the cuboid with the smallest number of grouping columns is selected. Let GS_{min}^R be the selected cuboid. The compensation consists of a SELECT box potentially followed above by a GROUP-BY box. The inclusion rule for the GROUP-BY box is the same as the rules in 4.1.2 or 4.2.1 restricted to the grouping columns of GS_{min}^R. The SELECT box applies the pulled-up predicates from the child compensation (if any), as well as a *slicing predicate*, which selects the cuboid corresponding to GS_{min}^R out of the other cuboids. The slicing predicate is a conjunction of IS NULL and IS NOT NULL conditions over the subsumer's grouping columns: if a grouping column belongs to GS_{min}^R, then it must not be NULL; otherwise it must be NULL.

Example: In Figure 13, the grouping set of Q11.1 matches exactly with the (flid, year) grouping set of AST11. In addition, rule (a) from 4.1.2 and the pullup condition from 4.2.1, restricted to (flid, year), are also satisfied. As a result,

Q11.1 can be rewritten as NewQ11.1, which simply selects the (flid, year) cuboid without regrouping. In contrast, matching Q11.2 with AST11 requires regrouping, even though Q11.2 has the same grouping set as Q11.1. The reason is that the pullup condition is not satisfied in (flid, year), as this set does not include the month column. As a result, we have to use the (flid, year, month) cuboid from the AST and regroup. Finally, no match exists for Q11.3, because rule (f) from 4.1.2 requires that faid be a grouping column, and as a result, AST11 should have a grouping set with at least faid, flid, year, and month.

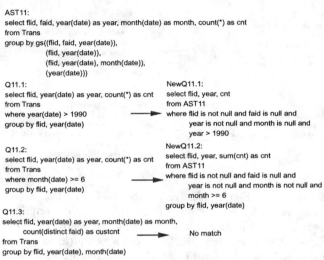

```
AST11:
select flid, faid, year(date) as year, month(date) as month, count(*) as cnt
from Trans
group by gs((flid, faid, year(date)),
            (flid, year(date)),
            (flid, year(date), month(date)),
            (year(date)))
```

```
Q11.1:
select flid, year(date) as year, count(*) as cnt
from Trans
where year(date) > 1990
group by flid, year(date)
```
→
```
NewQ11.1:
select flid, year, cnt
from AST11
where flid is not null and faid is null and
      year is not null and month is null and
      year > 1990
```

```
Q11.2:
select flid, year(date) as year, count(*) as cnt
from Trans
where month(date) >= 6
group by flid, year(date)
```
→
```
NewQ11.2:
select flid, year, sum(cnt) as cnt
from AST11
where flid is not null and faid is null and
      year is not null and month is not null and
      month >= 6
group by flid, year(date)
```

```
Q11.3:
select flid, year(date) as year, month(date) as month,
       count(distinct faid) as custcnt
from Trans
group by flid, year(date), month(date)
```
→ No match

Figure 13: Simple GROUP-BY query with Cube AST

5.2 Cube Query with Cube AST.

Pattern: Both the subsumee and subsumer are multidimensional GROUP-BYs. Let GS_i^E, i = 1, 2, …, m be the subsumee's grouping sets, $GS^E = \bigcup_1^m GS_i^E$, and GS_i^R, i = 1, 2, …, k be the subsumer's grouping sets.

Matching Conditions: A match is possible if every subsumee cuboid can be independently matched with the subsumer using the conditions from Section 5.1. Otherwise, if any of these sub-matches fails, the entire match fails.

Compensation: If none of the sub-matches requires regrouping compensation, then the final compensation is a single SELECT box, which contains the pulled-up predicates from the child compensation (if any) and the slicing predicate. In this case, the slicing predicate is the disjunction of the slicing predicates for each sub-match. If, however, any of the sub-matches requires regrouping compensation, then the subsumee is treated as if it were a simple GROUP-BY, whose grouping set is GS^E. GS^E is then matched with the subsumer using the conditions from Section 5.1. In this case, the SELECT portion of the compensation is the same as in Section 5.1, i.e., it contains the pulled-up predicates (if any) and a slicing predicate that selects the smallest subsumer cuboid that matches with GS^E. Regrouping, however, is performed not by GS^E, but by a multidimensional GROUP-BY box that has the same gs function as the subsumee.

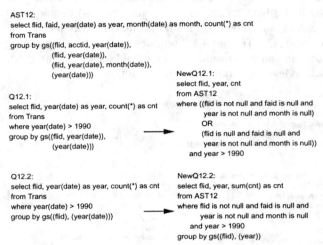

AST12:
select flid, faid, year(date) as year, month(date) as month, count(*) as cnt
from Trans
group by gs((flid, acctid, year(date)),
            (flid, year(date)),
            (flid, year(date), month(date)),
            (year(date)))

Q12.1:
select flid, year(date) as year, count(*) as cnt
from Trans
where year(date) > 1990
group by gs((flid, year(date)),
            (year(date)))

NewQ12.1:
select flid, year, cnt
from AST12
where ((flid is not null and faid is null and
        year is not null and month is null)
       OR
       (flid is null and faid is null and
        year is not null and month is null))
and year > 1990

Q12.2:
select flid, year(date) as year, count(*) as cnt
from Trans
where year(date) > 1990
group by gs((flid), (year(date)))

NewQ12.2:
select flid, year, sum(cnt) as cnt
from AST12
where flid is not null and faid is null and
      year is not null and month is null
and year > 1990
group by gs((flid), (year))

Figure 14: Matching Cubes

Example: In Figure 14, every cuboid of Q12.1 matches with AST12. None of these sub-matches requires regrouping, and hence, no regrouping is performed by NewQ12.1 either; NewQ12.1 just extracts the (locid, year) and (year) cuboids out of the AST and re-applies the year > 1990 predicate. In contrast, the match between Q12.2 and AST12 requires regrouping because the query's (locid) grouping set does not match exactly with any of the AST's grouping sets. As a result, Q12.2 is temporarily viewed as a simple group-by query, which matches with the (locid, year) AST cuboid. That cuboid is selected out of the AST in NewQ12.2, which then regroups by gs((locid), (year)).

6. EXPRESSION MATCHING AND DERIVATION

So far, we have often required that some subsumee expression E_{exp} (predicate or QCL) be semantically equivalent with some subsumer expression R_{exp}. A method is therefore required to test for expression equivalence. The first step of such a method should be to translate E_{exp} into an equivalent expression E'_{exp} that is valid within the subsumer's context, i.e., uses subsumer QNCs. This is very important because what might appear as column X inside E_{exp} may not be a direct reference to a base table column, but rather a complex sub-expression produced by a nested subquery. As a result, it is not possible to directly compare the QNCs in E_{exp} with those in R_{exp}, as they originate from different subgraphs. Once the translation is done, any expression-matching algorithm can be used to compare the parse trees of E'_{exp} and R_{exp}. However, expression matching

is orthogonal to the rest of the matching algorithm, and will not be discussed further. Instead, our focus here is on the expression-translation method, which is a crucial component of our matching infrastructure.

When the subsumee and subsumer children match exactly, translation is easy. Specifically, for each QCL X produced by a non-rejoin subsumee child, there is an equivalent QCL Y produced by the subsumer's matching child. As a result, if X_E is a subsumee QNC that consumes X and appears in E_{exp}, and the subsumer consumes Y (i.e., the subsumer has a QNC Y_R), then we can replace X_E in E_{exp} with its equivalent Y_R QNC. By replacing each non-rejoin QNC in E_{exp} with its equivalent subsumer QNC (if it exists), we get E'_{exp}. Translation is more complicated when the children do not match exactly. This is best illustrated by an example. In particular, consider the example in Figure 11, but with a modified AST10 that has a HAVING predicate: count(*) > 2. Adding this predicate to AST10 makes a match between the two top SELECT boxes impossible because their predicates are not semantically equivalent, even though they are syntactically equivalent. The problem is illustrated in Table 1, which shows the query and AST results for a sample Trans table. We see that the HAVING predicate eliminates the group (1, 1991), which is necessary to produce the correct query result.

	Locid	Date	Cnt
Sample Trans Table (flid and date columns)	1	01/03/1990	
	1	02/10/1990	
	1	04/12/1990	
	1	10/20/1991	
AST Result	1	1990	3
Query Result	1		4

Table 1

Our method detects this semantic inequivalence between the two HAVING predicates by appropriately translating the query predicate. The steps taken during the translation are shown in Figure 15, where each QNC name has been annotated with the name of the box that contains the QNC. The translation begins by creating a copy of the whole expression (step 1). Then, each QNC is translated in turn. To translate a QNC, we first find the child box that produces the QNC and replace the QNC with the associated QCL expression; in our example, cnt-3Q is produced by count(*) in box GB-2Q (step 2). The next step is to replace count(*) with its equivalent QCL expression at the top of the child compensation. Thus, count(*) is translated to sum(cnt-2C2) (step 3). Then, we recursively translate each new QNC (except QNCs produced by rejoin children) until we reach the bottom of the child compensation. This way, sum(cnt-2C2) becomes sum(cnt-2C1) (step 4). Finally, we notice that cnt-2C1 and cnt-3A are equivalent, as they are both produced by the cnt QCL of the subsumer's child. As a result, we can replace cnt-2C1 with cnt-3A (step 5). The translated predicate is sum(cnt-3A) > 2, which is obviously not the same as the subsumer's predicate cnt-3A > 2.

The translation method described above is also the first step in deriving a subsumee expression E_{exp} from the subsumer's QCLs. After translating E_{exp} to E'_{exp}, derivability can be established by making sure that the subsumer computes at its output certain necessary subexpressions of E'_{exp} (or even the entire E'_{exp}). The problem that arises, however, is to determine the parts of E'_{exp} that can/should be computed by the subsumer. In general, translation causes an expression to expand by replacing individual QNCs with equivalent subexpressions. For example, cnt-3Q > 2 is translated to sum(cnt-3A) > 2. Derivation is the reverse operation, where pieces of the translated expression are collapsed as they are computed along the derivation path. For example, sum(cnt-3A) > 2 is derived as cnt-3C3 > 2 at the top of the compensation. The next paragraph explains the derivation method in more detail in the context of the cnt / totcnt expression that computes the cntpct QCL of query Q10.

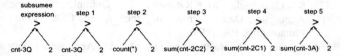

Figure 15: Expression translation

The expression is first translated as sum(cnt-3A) / totcnt-3A. During this translation, our method determines that the division operator and the sum function should be computed by the Sel-3C3 and GB-3C2 boxes, respectively. Given that those are they only internal nodes of the expression tree, and that neither of them should be computed by the subsumer, we conclude that for the expression to be derivable, the subsumer must preserve the cnt-3A and totcnt-3A QNCs at its output, which it does. As a result, the expression can be pulled up inside Sel-3C1 as sum(cnt-3C1) / totcnt-3C1. Next, the expression is pulled up one box further and becomes sum(cnt-3C2) / totcnt-3C2 within the context of GB-3C2. During this pullup, the totcnt QCL is created inside Sel-3C1 and consumed by the totcnt-3C2 QNC. The last step is to pull the expression from GB-3C2 up to Sel-3C3. To do so, the totcnt and cnt QCLs, as well as the totcnt-3C2 predicate, are created inside GB-3C2. (In fact, cnt should already be there, because it was created earlier during the derivation of the query's HAVING predicate). Notice that the cnt QCL in GB-3C2 actually computes the sum function. As a result, the expression is pulled up as cnt-3C3 / totcnt-3C3, which becomes the expression that computes the original cntpct QCL.

7. RELATED WORK

In this paper, we have presented a practical algorithm for real SQL queries with aggregation. Previous work most closely related to ours includes [6], [12], and [1]. In all three cases, the domain of the algorithms presented consists of simple, single-block select-where-groupby-having SQL statements. In [6], matching is performed by applying a set of rewrite rules to the query until a portion of it is syntactically identical to the AST. To handle multi-block queries, [6] proposed the use of similar rewrite rules for transforming multi-block queries to single-block ones. However, such a transformation is often impossible.

Another limitation of [6] is its reliance on syntactic matching, which cannot, for example, derive a query expression from the AST expressions. This limitation is also recognized in [12], where semantic matching conditions are proposed. For example, if P_Q and P_A are the sets of WHERE predicates in the query and the AST respectively, [12] requires that P_Q is equivalent to P_A & P_C, where P_C is a set of predicates that involve only AST and rejoin columns, i.e., P_C are the compensation predicates. Although this condition is more general than our conditions 2 and 3 in Section 4.1.1, no algorithm is presented in [12] for finding the P_C predicates. As we argued in Section 6, such an algorithm is orthogonal to a general matching infrastructure and should rely on first translating the query predicates into the context of the AST.

Neither [6] nor [12] make use of database semantics that are specified via constraints. Such semantics are exploited [1]. In addition to RI constraints, which have helped us handle extra AST tables, [1] considers other functional dependencies as well in order to derive query columns that are not present at the AST. Furthermore, [1] presents matching conditions for outer-join operations. In general, however, the algorithm description in [1] is rather sketchy.

Using our algorithm (or any of [1], [6], [12]), a query may be rerouted towards multiple ASTs by an iterative process where, at each iteration, the result of the previous rewrite is matched with the next available AST. A different approach is taken in [2], where, for each aggregate function, the general format of the rewritten query is determined in advance. Many candidate rewritings can be derived from the general format by simultaneously combining the aggregation results of different ASTs (e.g. sum(x) might be derived as sum(sum_x_i*cnt_j*cnt_k), where sum_x_i, cnt_j, and cnt_k are computed by the ith, j^{th}, and k^{th} ASTs respectively). The candidate rewritings are then tested for equivalence with the original user query using the equivalence theory developed in [2] and [11]. Although such a global approach should, in general, be more powerful (but also less efficient) that an iterative approach, it is not clear that this is indeed the case with [2]. In particular, all of the examples presented there can be handled by our algorithm as well. Furthermore, HAVING clauses were not allowed in [2].

Another interesting problem, from a theoretical perspective, is the discovery of *complete* rewriting algorithms, which, given a query and a set of MVs, guarantee that a rewriting will be found, if one exists. The existence and complexity of complete rewriting algorithms depends on the complexity of the queries and MVs considered and the language used to construct the rewritings. In general, finding a complete algorithm is a hard problem, and existing ones are limited to restricted classes of queries. [7] presents a complete algorithm for simple conjuctive queries without constants, comparisons, or aggregation, using set semantics. This algorithm is adapted for bag semantics in [2]. Finally, a more powerful algorithm for simple conjuctive queries and MVs that may also contain counts is developed in [4] using bag-set semantics.

8. SUMMARY

All of the related work reviewed in Section 7 applies to user and AST queries that are single block and do not contain complex expressions. In this context, queries can be described as sets of base table columns (e.g., predicate, grouping, select-list, and aggregation columns). Previous matching algorithms typically operate by comparing such sets of base table columns from the query and the AST. This approach, however, cannot handle multi-block queries and/or complex expressions, for two reasons. First, as their semantics become more complicated, queries cannot be described as single units anymore; instead they must be broken into smaller pieces, and matching should be done in a piece-by-piece fashion. Second, columns that appear in various parts of a query are not, in general, base table columns anymore; instead they are computed as complex expressions over other columns, potentially produced by nested query blocks. As a result, a translation mechanism is required before query and AST columns can be compared.

In this paper, we have presented a matching algorithm that addresses the above issues by relying on a general matching infrastructure, consisting of the QGM model, the navigator, the match function, and the translation mechanism. This infrastructure offers great modularity and extensibility by breaking the matching task into many smaller sub-matches, each involving only a small subset of QGM boxes in isolation (i.e., a subsumee, a subsumer, and their child-compensation boxes). In addition to the generic matching infrastructure, we have also presented matching conditions

and compensation rules for several specific query patterns. Overall, our experience of implementing the matching algorithm inside IBM's DB2 UDB DBMS and testing its performance benefits has been very positive. Using a small number of ASTs in each case, we have seen dramatic improvements in query response times both with TPC-D queries and with a number of customer applications.

9. REFERENCES

[1] R.G. Bello, K. Dias, A. Downing, J. Feenan, J. Finnerty, W.D. Norcott, H. Sun, A. Witkowski, M. Ziauddin, "Materialized Views In Oracle", Proc. of the 24th VLDB Conf., New York, NY, 1998.

[2] S. Chaudhuri, S. Krishnamurthy, S. Potamianos, K. Shim, "Optimizing queries with materialized views", Proc. of the 11th Data Engineering Conf., Taipei, 1995.

[3] S. Cohen, W. Nutt, A. Serebrenik, "Rewriting Aggregate Queries Using Views", Proc. of the ACM-PODS Conf., Philadelphia, PA, 1999.

[4] J. Gray, A. Bosworth, A. Layman, H. Pirahesh, "Data Cube: A Relational Aggregation Operator Generalizing Group-By, Cross-Tab, and Sub-Totals", Proc. of the 12th Data Engineering Conf., 1996.

[5] S. Grumbach, M. Rafanelli, L. Tininini, "Querying Aggregate Data", Proc. of the ACM-PODS Conf., Philadelphia, PA, 1999.

[6] A. Gupta, V. Harinarayan, D. Quass, "Aggregate Query Processing in Data Warehousing Environments", Proc. of the 21th VLDB Conf., Zurich, Switzerland, 1995.

[7] V. Harinarayan, A. Rajaraman, J. D. Ullman, "Implementing Data Cubes Efficiently", Proc. of the ACM-SIGMOD Conf., Montreal, Canada, 1996.

[8] A. Y. Levy, A. O. Mendelzon, Y. Sagiv, D. Srivastava, "Answering queries using views", Proc. of the ACM-PODS Conf., San Jose, CA, 1995.

[9] J. Melton (ed.), "Final Committee Draft – Database Language SQL – Part 2: Foundation (SQL/Foundation)", H2-98-519/DBL FRA-017, 1998.

[10] I. S. Mumick, D. Quass, B. S. Mumick, " Maintenance of Data Cubes and Summary Tables in a Warehouse", Proc. Of the ACM-SIGMOD Conf., Tuscon, AZ, 1997

[11] W. Nutt, Y. Sagiv, S. Shurin, "Deciding equivalence among aggregate queries", Proc. of the ACM-PODS Conf., Seattle, WA, 1998.

[12] D. Srivastava, S. Dar, H.V. Jagadish, A.Y. Levi "Answering Queries with Aggregation Using Views", Proc. of the 22nd VLDB Conf., Mumbai, India, 1996.

[13] Zaharioudakis, R. Cochrane, G. Lapis, H. Pirahesh, M. Urata, "Answering Complex SQL Queries Using Automated Summary Tables", available upon request from the authors.

Synchronizing a database to Improve Freshness

Junghoo Cho   Hector Garcia-Molina
Stanford University
{cho, hector}@cs.stanford.edu

Abstract

In this paper we study how to refresh a local copy of an autonomous data source to maintain the copy up-to-date. As the size of the data grows, it becomes more difficult to maintain the copy "fresh," making it crucial to synchronize the copy effectively. We define two freshness metrics, change models of the underlying data, and synchronization policies. We analytically study how effective the various policies are. We also experimentally verify our analysis, based on data collected from 270 web sites for more than 4 months, and we show that our new policy improves the "freshness" very significantly compared to current policies in use.

1 Introduction

Local copies of remote data sources are frequently made to improve performance or availability. For instance, a data warehouse may copy remote sales and customer tables for local analysis. Similarly, a web search engine copies portions of the web, and then indexes them to help users navigate the web. In many cases, the remote source is updated independently without pushing updates to the client that has a copy, so the client must periodically poll the source to detect changes and refresh its copy. This scenario is illustrated in Figure 1.

Clearly, a portion of the local copy may get temporarily out-of-date, due to the delay between source updates and the refresh of the local copy. In many applications it may be important to control how out-of-date information becomes, and to perform the refresh process so that data "freshness" is improved. In this paper we address some important questions regarding this refresh or synchronization process. For instance, how often should we synchronize the copy to maintain, say, 80% of the copy up-to-date? How much fresher does the copy get if we synchronize it twice as often? In what order should data items be synchronized? For instance, would it be better to synchronize a data item more often when we

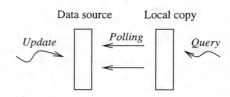

Figure 1: Conceptual diagram of the problem

believe that it changes more often than the other items? (Surprisingly, the answer to this last question is *no* in some cases!)

Although the synchronization and freshness problem arises in various contexts, our work is driven by the need to manage web data. At Stanford, we maintain a local repository called WebBase, containing a significant portion of the web (currently 42 million pages), that supports researchers experimenting with web searching and mining [10, 5]. (The Google search engine used this repository before it became a commercial product [1].) Web search engines and services, such as Alexa, AltaVista and Infoseek, also maintain similar copies of the web, or indexes based on the web data collected. To maintain the repository and/or index up-to-date, the web pages must be periodically revisited. This work is done by a program called a *web crawler*.

As the size of the web grows rapidly, it becomes crucial to synchronize the data more effectively. A recent study shows that it takes up to 6 months for a new page to be indexed by popular web search engines [9]. Also, a lot of users express frustration, when a search engine returns obsolete links, and the users follow the links in vain. According to the same study, up to 14% of the links in the search engines are broken. By tuning the synchronization policy, we believe we can reduce the wasted resources and time significantly.

The effective synchronization of a local copy introduces many interesting challenges. First of all, measuring the freshness of the copy is not trivial. Intuitively, the copy is considered fresh when it is not different from the "real-world" remote data. Therefore, we can measure its freshness only when we know the *current status* of the real-world data. But how can we know the current status of the real-world data, when it is spread across thousands of web sites? Second, we do not know exactly when a particular data item will change, even if it changes at a certain average rate. For instance, the pages in the CNN web site are updated about once a day, but the update of a particular page depends on how the news related to that page develops over time. Therefore, visiting the page once a day does not guarantee its freshness.

In this paper, we will formally study how to synchronize the data to maximize its freshness. The main contributions we make are:

- We present a formal framework to study the synchronization problem, and we define the notions of freshness and age of a copy. While our study focuses on the web environment, we believe our analysis can be applied to other contexts, such as a *data warehouse*. In a warehouse, *materialized views* are maintained on top of *autonomous* databases, and again, we need to *poll* the underlying database periodically to guarantee some level of freshness.

- We present several synchronization policies that are currently employed, and we compare how effective they are. Our study will show that some policies that may be intuitively appealing might actually perform *worse* than a naive policy.

- We also propose a new synchronization policy which may improve the freshness by orders of magnitude in certain cases.

- We validate our analysis using experimental data collected from 270 web sites over 4 months. The data will show that our new policy is indeed better than any of the current policies.

The rest of this paper is organized as follows. In Section 2, we present a framework for the synchronization problem. Then in Section 3, we explain what options exist for synchronizing the local copy, and we compare these options in Section 4 and 5. In Section 6, we verify our analysis using data collected from the world wide web.

2 Framework

To study the synchronization problem, we first need to understand the meaning of "freshness," and we need to know how the data change over time. In this section we present our framework to address these issues. In our discussion, we refer to the data source that we monitor as the *real-world database* and its local copy as the *local database* when we need to distinguish them. Similarly, we refer to their data items as the *real-world elements* and as the *local elements*.

In Section 2.1, we start our discussion with the definition of two freshness metrics, *freshness* and *age*. Then in Section 2.2, we discuss how we model the evolution of individual real-world elements. Finally in Section 2.3 we discuss how we model the real-world database as a whole.

2.1 Freshness and age

Intuitively, we consider a database "fresher" when the database has more up-to-date elements. For instance, when database A has 10 up-to-date elements out of 20 elements, and when database B has 15 up-to-date elements, we consider B to be fresher than A. Also, we have a notion of "age:" Even if all elements are obsolete, we consider database A "more current" than B, if A was synchronized 1 day ago, and B was synchronized 1 year ago. Based on this intuitive notion, we define *freshness* and *age* as follows:

1. **Freshness:** Let $S = \{e_1, \ldots, e_N\}$ be the local database with N elements. Ideally, all N elements will be maintained up-to-date, but in practice, only $M(< N)$ elements will be up-to-date at a specific time. (By up-to-date we mean that their values equal those of their real-world counterparts.) We define the *freshness* of S at time t as $F(S; t) = M/N$. Clearly, the *freshness* is the fraction of the local database that is up-to-date. For instance, $F(S; t)$ will be one if all local elements are up-to-date, and $F(S; t)$ will be zero if all local elements are out-of-date. For mathematical convenience, we reformulate the above definition as follows:

Definition 1 The *freshness* of a local element e_i at time t is
$$F(e_i; t) = \begin{cases} 1 & \text{if } e_i \text{ is up-to-date at time } t \\ 0 & \text{otherwise.} \end{cases}$$

Then, the *freshness* of the local database S at time t is
$$F(S; t) = \frac{1}{N} \sum_{i=1}^{N} F(e_i; t).$$
□

Note that freshness is hard to measure exactly in practice, since we need to "instantaneously" compare the real-world data to the local copy. But as we will see, it is possible to estimate freshness (and age) given some information about how the real-world data changes.

2. **Age:** To capture "how old" the database is, we define the metric *age* as follows:

Definition 2 The *age* of the local element e_i at time t is
$$A(e_i; t) = \begin{cases} 0 & \text{if } e_i \text{ is up-to-date at time } t \\ (t - \text{modification time of } e_i) & \text{otherwise.} \end{cases}$$

Then the *age* of the local database S is
$$A(S; t) = \frac{1}{N} \sum_{i=1}^{N} A(e_i; t).$$
□

The *age* of S tells us the average "age" of the local database. For instance, if all real-world elements changed one day ago and we have not synchronized them since, $A(S; t)$ is one day.

In Figure 2, we show the evolution of $F(e_i; t)$ and $A(e_i; t)$ of an element e_i. In this graph, the horizontal axis represents time, and the vertical axis shows the value of $F(e_i; t)$ and $A(e_i; t)$. We assume that the real-world element changes at the dotted lines and the local element is synchronized at the dashed lines. The *freshness* drops to zero when the real-world element

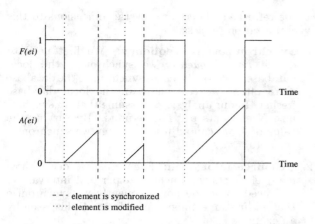

Figure 2: An example of the time evolution of $F(e_i; t)$ and $A(e_i; t)$

changes, and the *age* increases linearly from that point on. When the local element is synchronized to the real-world element, its *freshness* recovers to one, and its *age* drops to zero.

Obviously, the freshness (and age) of the local database may change over time. For instance, the freshness might be 0.3 at one point of time, and it might be 0.6 at another point of time. To compare different synchronization methods, it is important to have a metric that fairly considers freshness over a period of time, not just at one instant. In this paper, we use the freshness *averaged over time* as this metric.

Definition 3 We define the freshness of element e_i averaged over time, $\bar{F}(e_i)$, and the freshness of database S averaged over time, $\bar{F}(S)$, as

$$\bar{F}(e_i) = \lim_{t \to \infty} \frac{1}{t} \int_0^t F(e_i; t) dt$$

$$\bar{F}(S) = \lim_{t \to \infty} \frac{1}{t} \int_0^t F(S; t) dt.$$

The time average of age can be defined similarly. □

From the definition, we can prove that $\bar{F}(S)$ is the sum of $\bar{F}(e_i)$: $\bar{F}(S) = \frac{1}{N} \sum_{i=1}^{N} \bar{F}(e_i)$. For detailed proof, see [3].

2.2 Poisson process and probabilistic evolution of an element

To study how effective different synchronization methods are, we need to know how the real-world element changes. In this paper, we assume that the elements are modified by a *Poisson process*. A Poisson process is often used to model a sequence of events that happen *randomly* and *independently* with a *fixed rate* over time. For instance, the occurrences of fatal auto accidents, or the arrivals of customers at a service center, are usually modeled by *Poisson processes*. Under a Poisson process, it is well-known that the time to the next event is exponentially distributed [11].

Lemma 1 *Let T be the time when the next event occurs in a Poisson process with change rate λ. Then the probability density function for T is*

$$f_T(t) = \begin{cases} \lambda e^{-\lambda t} & \text{for } t > 0 \\ 0 & \text{for } t \leq 0. \end{cases}$$

□

In this paper, we assume that each element e_i is modified by the Poisson process with change rate λ_i. That is, each element changes at its own rate λ_i, and this rate may differ from element to element. For example, one element may change once a day, and another element may change once a year. Later in Section 6, we will experimentally verify that the Poisson process describes well the changes of *real* web pages.

Under the Poisson process model, we can analyze the freshness and age of the element e_i over time. More precisely, let us compute the *expected value* of *freshness* and *age* of e_i at time t. For the analysis, we assume that we synchronize e_i at $t = 0$ and at $t = I$.

By integrating the probability density function of Lemma 1, we can obtain the probability that e_i changes in the interval $(0, t]$:

$$\Pr\{T \leq t\} = \int_0^t f_T(t) dt = 1 - e^{-\lambda t}$$

Since e_i is not synchronized in the interval $(0, I)$, the local element e_i may get out-of-date with probability $\Pr\{T \leq t\} = 1 - e^{-\lambda t}$ at time $t \in (0, I)$. Hence, the *expected freshness* is

$$\mathrm{E}[F(e_i; t)] = 0 \cdot (1 - e^{-\lambda t}) + 1 \cdot e^{-\lambda t} = e^{-\lambda t} \quad \text{for } t \in (0, I).$$

Note that the expected freshness is 1 at time $t = 0$ and that the expected freshness approaches 0 as time passes.

We can obtain the *expected value* of age of e_i similarly. If e_i is modified at time $s \in (0, I)$, the age of e_i at time $t \in (s, I)$ is $(t - s)$. From Lemma 1, e_i changes at time s with probability $\lambda e^{-\lambda s}$, so the expected age at time $t \in (0, I)$ is

$$\mathrm{E}[A(e_i; t)] = \int_0^t (t - s)(\lambda e^{-\lambda s}) ds = t(1 - \frac{1 - e^{-\lambda t}}{\lambda t})$$

Note that $\mathrm{E}[A(e_i; t)] \to 0$ as $t \to 0$ and that $\mathrm{E}[A(e_i; t)] \approx t$ as $t \to \infty$; the expected age is 0 at time 0 and the expected age is approximately the same as the elapsed time when t is large. In Figure 3, we show the graphs of $\mathrm{E}[F(e_i; t)]$ and $\mathrm{E}[A(e_i; t)]$. Note that when we resynchronize e_i at $t = I$, $\mathrm{E}[F(e_i; t)]$ recovers to one and $\mathrm{E}[A(e_i; t)]$ goes to zero.

2.3 Evolution model of database

In the previous subsection we modeled the evolution of an element. Now we discuss how we model the database as a whole. Depending on how its elements change over time, we can model the real-world database by one of the following:

- **Uniform change-frequency model:** In this model, we assume that all real-world elements

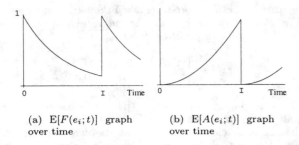

(a) $E[F(e_i; t)]$ graph over time

(b) $E[A(e_i; t)]$ graph over time

Figure 3: Time evolution of $E[F(e_i; t)]$ and $E[A(e_i; t)]$

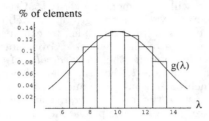

Figure 4: Histogram of the change frequencies

change at the *same* frequency λ. This is a simple model that could be useful when:

— we do not know how often the *individual* element changes over time. We only know how often the entire database changes *on average*, so we may assume that all elements change at the same *average* rate λ.

— the elements change at *slightly* different frequencies. In this case, this model will work as a good approximation.

- **Non-uniform change-frequency model:** In this model, we assume that the elements change at *different* rates. We use λ_i to refer to the the change frequency of the element e_i. When the λ_i's vary, we can plot the histogram of λ_i's as we show in Figure 4. In the figure, the horizontal axis shows the range of change frequencies (e.g., $9.5 < \lambda_i \leq 10.5$) and the vertical axis shows the fraction of elements that change at the given frequency range. We can approximate the discrete histogram by a continuous distribution function $g(\lambda)$, when the database consists of many elements. We will adopt the continuous distribution model whenever convenient.

For the reader's convenience, we summarize our notation in Table 1. As we continue our discussion, we will explain some of the symbols that have not been introduced yet.

3 Synchronization policy

So far we discussed how the real-world database changes over time. In this section we study how the local copy can be refreshed. There are several dimensions to this synchronization process:

1. **Synchronization frequency:** We first need to decide *how frequently* we synchronize the local database. Obviously, as we synchronize the database more often, we can maintain the local database fresher. In our analysis, we assume that we synchronize N elements per I time-units. By varying the value of I, we can adjust how often we synchronize the database.

2. **Resource allocation:** Even after we decide how many elements we synchronize per unit interval, we still need to decide how frequently we synchronize *each individual* element. We illustrate this issue by an example.

   Example 1 The database consists of three elements, e_1, e_2 and e_3. It is known that the elements change at the rates $\lambda_1 = 4$, $\lambda_2 = 3$, and $\lambda_3 = 2$ (times/day). We have decided to synchronize the database at the *total* rate of 9 elements/day. In deciding how frequently we synchronize each element, we consider the following options:

   - Synchronize all elements uniformly at the same rate. That is, synchronize e_1, e_2 and e_3 at the same rate of 3 (times/day).

   - Synchronize an element proportionally more often when it changes more often. In other words, synchronize the elements at the rates of $f_1 = 4$, $f_2 = 3$, $f_3 = 2$ (times/day). □

   Based on how the fixed synchronization-resource is allocated to the individual elements, we can classify synchronization policies as follows. We study these policies later in Section 5.

   (a) **Uniform allocation policy:** We synchronize all elements at the same rate, regardless of how often they change. That is, each element e_i is synchronized at the fixed frequency f. In Example 1, the first option corresponds to this policy.

   (b) **Non-uniform allocation policy:** We synchronize elements at different rates. In particular, with a **proportional allocation policy** we synchronize element e_i at a frequency f_i that is proportional to its change frequency λ_i. Thus, the frequency ratio λ_i/f_i, is the same for any i under the proportional allocation policy. In Example 1, the second option corresponds to this policy.

3. **Synchronization order:** Now we need to decide in *what order* we synchronize the elements in the database.

   Example 2 We maintain a local database of 10,000 web pages from site A. In order to maintain the local copy up-to-date, we continuously update our local database by revisiting the pages in the site. In performing the update, we may adopt one of the following options:

symbol	meaning
(a) $\bar{F}(S)$, $\bar{F}(e_i)$	Freshness of database S (and element e_i) averaged over time
(b) $\bar{A}(S)$, $\bar{A}(e_i)$	Age of database S (and element e_i) averaged over time
(c) $\bar{F}(\lambda_i, f_i)$, $\bar{A}(\lambda_i, f_i)$	Freshness (and age) of element e_i averaged over time, when the element changes at the rate λ_i and is synchronized at the frequency f_i
(i) λ_i	Change frequency of element e_i
(j) $f_i \ (= 1/I_i)$	Synchronization frequency of element e_i
(k) λ	Average change frequency of database elements
(l) $f \ (= 1/I)$	Average synchronization frequency of database elements

Table 1: The symbols that are used throughout this paper and their meanings

- We maintain an explicit list of all URLs in the site, and we visit the URLs repeatedly in the same order. Notice that if we update our local database at a fixed rate, say 10,000 pages/day, then we synchronize a page, say p_1, at the fixed interval of one-day.

- We only maintain the URL of the root page of the site, and whenever we crawl the site, we start from the root page, following links. Since the link structure (and the order) at a particular crawl determines the page visit order, the synchronization order may change from one crawl to the next. Notice that under this policy, we synchronize a page, say p_1, at variable intervals. For instance, if we visit p_1 at the end of one crawl and at the beginning of the next crawl, the interval is close to zero, while in the opposite case it is close to two days.

- Instead of actively synchronizing pages, we synchronize pages on demand, as they are *requested* by a user. Since we do not know which page the user will request next, the synchronization order may appear random. Under this policy, the synchronization interval of p_1 is not bound by any value. It may range from zero to infinity. □

We can summarize the above options as follows:

(a) **Fixed order:** We synchronize all elements in the database in the *same* order repeatedly. Therefore, a particular element is synchronized at a *fixed interval* under this policy. This policy corresponds to the first option of the above example.

(b) **Random order:** We synchronize all elements repeatedly, but the synchronization order may be different in each iteration. This policy corresponds to the second option in the example.

(c) **Purely random:** At each synchronization point, we select an arbitrary element from the database and synchronize it. Therefore, an element is synchronized at intervals of arbitrary length. This policy corresponds to the last option in the example.

In Section 4 we will compare how effective these synchronization order policies are.

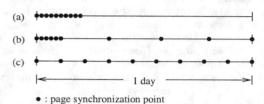

$\bullet$: page synchronization point

Figure 5: Several options for the synchronization points

4. **Synchronization points:** In some cases, we may need to synchronize the database only in a limited time-window. For instance, if a web site is heavily accessed during day-time, it might be desirable to crawl the site only in the night, when it is less frequently visited. We illustrate several options due to this constraint by an example.

Example 3 We maintain a local database of 10 pages from site A. The site is heavily accessed during day-time. We consider several synchronization policies, including the following:

- **Figure 5(a):** We synchronize all 10 pages in the beginning of the day, say midnight.

- **Figure 5(b):** We synchronize most pages in the beginning of the day, but we still synchronize some pages during the rest of the day.

- **Figure 5(c):** We synchronize 10 pages uniformly over a day. □

In this paper, we assume that we synchronize the database uniformly over time. We believe this assumption is valid especially for the web environment. Because the web sites are located in many different time zones, it is not easy to identify which time zone a particular web site resides in. Also, the access pattern to a web site varies widely. For example, some web sites are heavily accessed during day time, while others are accessed mostly in the evening, when users are at home. Since crawlers cannot guess the best time to visit each site, they typically visit sites at a uniform rate that is convenient to the crawler.

policy	Freshness $\bar{F}(S)$	Age $\bar{A}(S)$
Fixed-order	$\frac{1-e^{-r}}{r}$	$I(\frac{1}{2} - \frac{1}{r} + \frac{1-e^{-r}}{r^2})$
Random-order	$\frac{1}{r}(1 - (\frac{1-e^{-r}}{r})^2)$	$I(\frac{1}{3} + (\frac{1}{2} - \frac{1}{r})^2 - (\frac{1-e^{-r}}{r^2})^2)$
Purely-random	$\frac{1}{1+r}$	$I(\frac{r}{1+r})$

Table 2: Freshness and age formula for various synchronization-order policies

4 Comparison of synchronization-order policies

Clearly, we can increase the database freshness by synchronizing more often. But exactly how often should we synchronize, for the freshness to be, say, 0.8? Conversely, how much freshness do we get if we synchronize 100 elements per second? In this section, we will address these questions by analyzing synchronization order policies. Through the analysis, we will also learn which synchronization-order policy is the best in terms of freshness and age.

In this section we assume that all real-world elements are modified at the same average rate λ. That is, we adopt the *uniform change-frequency* model (Section 2.3). When the elements change at the same rate, it does not make sense to synchronize the elements at different rates, so we also assume the *uniform allocation* policy (Item 2a in Section 3). These assumptions significantly simplify our analysis, while giving us solid understanding on the issues that we address.

Based on these assumptions, we analyze different synchronization-order policies in detail in [3], and we summarize the result in Table 2. In the table, we use r to represent the frequency ratio λ/f, where λ is the frequency at which a real-world element changes and $f(= 1/I)$ is the frequency at which a local element is synchronized. When $r < 1$, we synchronize the elements more often than they change, and when $r > 1$, the elements change more often than we synchronize them.

To help readers interpret the formulas, we show the freshness and the age graphs in Figure 6. In the figure, the horizontal axis is the frequency ratio r, and the vertical axis shows the freshness and the age of the local database. Notice that as we synchronize the elements more often than they change ($\lambda \ll f$, thus $r = \lambda/f \to 0$), the freshness approaches 1 and the age approaches 0. Also, when the elements change more frequently than we synchronize them ($r = \lambda/f \to \infty$), the freshness becomes 0, and the age increases. Finally, notice that the freshness is not equal to 1, even if we synchronize the elements as often as they change ($r = 1$). This result comes for two reasons. First, an element changes at random points of time, even if it changes at fixed *average* rate. Therefore, the element may not change between some synchronizations, and it may change more than once between other synchronizations. For this reason, it cannot be always up-to-date. Second, some delay may exist between the change of an element and its synchronization, so some elements may be

"temporarily obsolete," decreasing the freshness of the database.

The graphs of Figure 6 have many practical implications. For instance, we can answer all of the following questions by looking at the graphs.

- **How can we measure how fresh the local database is?** By measuring how frequently the real-world elements change,[1] we can estimate how fresh the local database is. For instance, when the real-world elements change once a day, and when we synchronize the local elements also once a day ($\lambda = f$ or $r = 1$), the freshness of the local database is $(e-1)/e \approx 0.63$, under the fixed-order policy.

  Note that we derived the equations in Table 2 assuming that the real-world elements change at the *same* rate λ. Therefore, the equations may not be true when the real-world elements change at *different* rates. However, we can still interpret λ as the *average* rate at which the whole database change, and we can use the formulas as approximations. Later in Section 5, we derive exact formula when the elements change at different rates.

- **How can we guarantee a certain freshness of the local database?** From the graph, we can find how frequently we should synchronize the local elements in order to achieve a certain freshness. For instance, if we want at least 0.8 freshness, the frequency ratio r should be less than 0.46 (fixed-order policy). That is, we should synchronize the local elements at least $1/0.46 \approx 2$ times as frequently as the real-world elements change.

- **Which synchronization-order policy is the best?** The fixed-order policy performs best by both metrics. For instance, when we synchronize the elements as often as they change ($r = 1$), the freshness of the fixed-order policy is $(e-1)/e \approx 0.63$, which is 30% higher than that of the purely-random policy. The difference is more dramatic for age. When $r = 1$, the age of the fixed-order policy is only one fourth of the random-order policy. In general, as the variability in the time between visits increases, the policy gets less effective.

5 Comparison of resource-allocation policies

In the previous section, we addressed various questions, assuming that all elements in the database change at the same rate. But what can we do if the elements change at *different* rates and we know how often each element changes? Is it better to synchronize the element more often when it changes more often? In this section, we address this question by analyzing different resource-allocation policies (Item 2 in Section 3). For the analysis, we model the real-world database by the *non-uniform* change-frequency model (Section 2.3), and we

---

[1] In Section 6, we briefly discuss how we can measure the frequency of change. To learn more on this topic, please refer to [4].

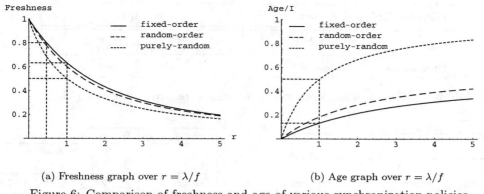

(a) Freshness graph over $r = \lambda/f$ (b) Age graph over $r = \lambda/f$

Figure 6: Comparison of freshness and age of various synchronization policies

assume the *fixed-order* policy for the synchronization-order policy (Item 3 in Section 3), because the fixed-order policy is the best synchronization-order policy. In other words, we assume that the element e_i changes at the frequency λ_i (λ_i's may be different from element to element), and we synchronize e_i at the *fixed interval* $I_i(= 1/f_i,\ f_i$: synchronization frequency of e_i). Remember that we synchronize N elements in $I(= 1/f)$ time units. Therefore, the average synchronization frequency ($\frac{1}{N}\sum_{i=1}^{N} f_i$) should be equal to f.

In Section 5.1, we start our discussion by comparing the uniform allocation policy with the proportional allocation policy. Surprisingly, the uniform policy turns out to be *always* more effective than the proportional policy. Then in Section 5.2 we try to understand why this happens by studying a simple example. Finally in Section 5.3 we study how we should allocate resources to the elements to achieve the optimal freshness or age.

5.1 Uniform and proportional allocation policy

In this subsection, we first assume that change frequencies of real-world elements follow the *gamma distribution* and compare how effective the *proportional* and the *uniform* policies are. In [3], we prove that the conclusion of this section is valid for *any* distribution.

The gamma distribution is often used to model a random variable whose domain is non-negative numbers. Also, the distribution is known to cover a wide array of distributions. For instance, the exponential and the chi-square distributions are special instances of the gamma distribution, and the gamma distribution is close to the normal distribution when the variance is small. This mathematical property and versatility makes the gamma distribution a desirable one for describing the distribution of the change frequency.

Under these assumptions, we analyzed the uniform and proportional allocation policies for a database S [3], and we summarize the result in Table 3. In the table, r represents the frequency ratio λ/f, where λ is the average rate at which elements change (the mean of the gamma distribution), and f is the average rate at which we synchronize them ($1/I$). Also, δ represents the standard deviation of change frequencies

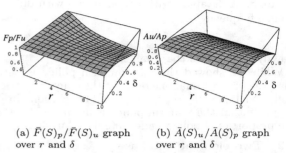

(a) $\bar{F}(S)_p/\bar{F}(S)_u$ graph over r and δ (b) $\bar{A}(S)_u/\bar{A}(S)_p$ graph over r and δ

Figure 7: $\bar{F}(S)_p/\bar{F}(S)_u$ and $\bar{A}(S)_u/\bar{A}(S)_p$ graphs over r and δ

(more precisely, $\delta^2 =$ (variance)/(mean)^2 of the gamma distribution).

To help the discussion, we use the subscript p to refer to the proportional allocation policy and the subscript u to refer to the uniform allocation policy. Then, the uniform policy is better than the proportional one, when $\bar{F}(S)_p < \bar{F}(S)_u$ and $\bar{A}(S)_u < \bar{A}(S)_p$. To compare the two policies, we plot $\bar{F}(S)_p/\bar{F}(S)_u$ and $\bar{A}(S)_u/\bar{A}(S)_p$ graphs in Figure 7. Note that when the uniform policy is better, the ratios are below 1 ($\bar{F}(S)_p/\bar{F}(S)_u < 1$ and $\bar{A}(S)_u/\bar{A}(S)_p < 1$), and when the proportional policy is better, the ratios are above 1 ($\bar{F}(S)_p/\bar{F}(S)_u > 1$ and $\bar{A}(S)_u/\bar{A}(S)_p > 1$).

Surprisingly, we can clearly see that the ratios are below 1 for any r and δ values: The uniform policy is always better than the proportional policy! In fact, the uniform policy gets more effective as the elements change at more different frequencies. That is, when the variance of change frequencies is zero ($\delta = 0$), all elements change at the same frequency, so two policies give the same result ($\bar{F}(S)_p/\bar{F}(S)_u = 1$ and $\bar{A}(S)_u/\bar{A}(S)_p = 1$). But as δ increases (i.e., as the elements change at more different frequencies), $\bar{F}(S)_u$ grows larger than $\bar{F}(S)_p$ ($\bar{F}(S)_p/\bar{F}(S)_u \to 0$) and $\bar{A}(S)_u$ gets smaller than $\bar{A}(S)_p$ ($\bar{A}(S)_u/\bar{A}(S)_p \to 0$). Interestingly, we can observe that the age *ratio* does not change much as r increases, while the freshness *ratio*

123

allocation policy	Freshness $\bar{F}(S)$	Age $\bar{A}(S)$
Uniform	$\frac{1-(1+r\delta^2)^{1-\frac{1}{\delta^2}}}{r(1-\delta^2)}$	$\frac{I}{(1-\delta^2)}\left[\frac{1-\delta^2}{2} - \frac{1}{r} + \frac{1-(1+r\delta^2)^{2-\frac{1}{\delta^2}}}{r^2(1-2\delta^2)}\right]$
Proportional	$\frac{1-e^{-r}}{r}$	$\frac{I}{(1-\delta^2)}\left[\frac{1}{2} - \frac{1}{r} + \frac{1-e^{-r}}{r^2}\right]$

Table 3: Freshness and age formula for various resource-allocation policies

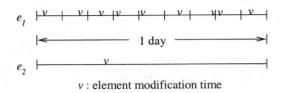

v : element modification time

Figure 8: A database with two elements with different change frequency

row	f_1+f_2	f_1	f_2	benefit	best
(a)	1	1	0	$\frac{1}{2}\times\frac{1}{18}=\frac{1}{36}$	0 1
(b)		0	1	$\frac{1}{2}\times\frac{1}{2}=\frac{9}{36}$	
(c)	2	2	0	$\frac{1}{2}\times\frac{1}{18}+\frac{1}{2}\times\frac{1}{18}=\frac{2}{36}$	0 2
(d)		1	1	$\frac{1}{2}\times\frac{1}{18}+\frac{1}{2}\times\frac{1}{2}=\frac{10}{36}$	
(e)		0	2	$\frac{1}{3}\times\frac{2}{3}+\frac{1}{3}\times\frac{1}{3}=\frac{12}{36}$	
(f)	5	3	2	$\frac{3}{36}+\frac{12}{36}=\frac{30}{72}$	2 3
(g)		2	3	$\frac{2}{36}+\frac{6}{16}=\frac{31}{72}$	
(h)	10	9	1	$\frac{9}{36}+\frac{1}{4}=\frac{36}{72}$	7 3
(i)		7	3	$\frac{7}{36}+\frac{6}{16}=\frac{41}{72}$	
(j)		5	5	$\frac{5}{36}+\frac{15}{36}=\frac{40}{72}$	

Table 4: Estimation of benefits for different choices

heavily depends on the r value.

While we showed that the uniform policy is better than the proportional one only for the gamma distribution model, it is in fact very general conclusion. In [3], we prove that the uniform policy is *always* better than the proportional policy under *any* distribution.

5.2 Two element database

Intuitively, we expected that the proportional policy would be better than the uniform policy, because we allocate more resources to the elements that change more often, which may need more of our attention. But why is it the other way around? In this subsection, we try to understand why we get the unintuitive result, by studying a very simple example: a database consisting of two elements. The analysis of this simple example will let us understand the result more concretely, and it will reveal some intuitive trends. We will confirm the trends more precisely when we study the optimal synchronization policy later in Section 5.3.

Now we analyze a database consisting of two elements: e_1 and e_2. For the analysis, we assume that e_1 changes at 9 times/day and e_2 changes at once/day. We also assume that our goal is to maximize the freshness of the database averaged over time. In Figure 8, we visually illustrate our simple model. For element e_1, one day is split into 9 intervals, and e_1 changes *once and only once* in each interval. However, we do not know exactly when the element changes in one interval. For element e_2, it changes *once and only once* per day, and we do not know when it changes. While this model is not exactly a Poisson process model, we adopt this model due to its simplicity and concreteness.

Now let us assume that we decided to synchronize only *one* element per day. Then what element should we synchronize? Should we synchronize e_1 or should we synchronize e_2? To answer this question, we need to compare how the freshness changes if we pick one element over the other. If the element e_2 changes in the middle of the day and if we synchronize e_2 right after it changed, it will remain up-to-date for the remaining half of the day. Therefore, by synchronizing element e_2 we get 1/2 day "benefit"(or freshness increase). However, the probability that e_2 changes before the middle of the day is 1/2, so the "expected benefit" of synchronizing e_2 is $1/2 \times 1/2$ day = 1/4 day. By the same reasoning, if we synchronize e_1 in the middle of an interval, e_1 will remain up-to-date for the remaining half of the interval (1/18 of the day) with probability 1/2. Therefore, the expected benefit is $1/2 \times 1/18$ day = 1/36 day. From this crude estimation, we can see that it is more effective to select e_2 for synchronization!

Table 4 shows the expected benefits for several other scenarios. The second column shows the total synchronization frequencies ($f_1 + f_2$) and the third column shows how much of the synchronization is allocated to f_1 and f_2. In the fourth column we estimate the expected benefit, and in the last column we show the f_1 and f_2 values that give the *highest* expected benefit. To save space, when $f_1 + f_2 = 5$ and 10, we show only some interesting (f_1, f_2) pairs. Note that since $\lambda_1 = 9$ and $\lambda_2 = 1$, row (h) corresponds to the proportional policy ($f_1 = 9, f_2 = 1$), and row (j) corresponds to the uniform policy ($f_1 = f_2 = 5$). From the table, we can observe following interesting trends:

1. **Rows (a)-(e):** When the synchronization frequency ($f_1 + f_2$) is much smaller than the change frequency ($\lambda_1 + \lambda_2$), it is better to give up synchronizing the elements that change too fast. In other words, when it is not possible to keep up with everything, it is better to focus on what we can track.

2. **Rows (h)-(j):** Even if the synchronization frequency is relatively large ($f_1 + f_2 = 10$), the uniform allocation policy (row (j)) is more effective than the proportional allocation policy (row (h)). The opti-

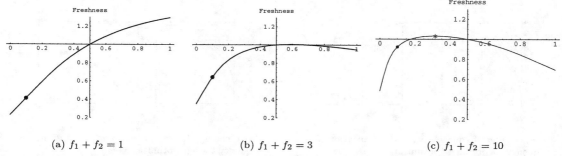

(a) $f_1 + f_2 = 1$	(b) $f_1 + f_2 = 3$	(c) $f_1 + f_2 = 10$

Figure 9: Series of freshness graphs for different synchronization frequency constraints. In all of the graphs, $\lambda_1 = 9$ and $\lambda_2 = 1$.

mal point (row (i)) is located somewhere between the proportional policy and the uniform policy.

We can verify this trend using our earlier analysis based on a Poisson process. We assume that the changes of e_1 and e_2 are Poisson processes with change frequencies $\lambda_1 = 9$ and $\lambda_2 = 1$. To help the discussion, we use $\bar{F}(\lambda_i, f_i)$ to refer to the time average of freshness of e_i when it changes at λ_i and is synchronized at f_i. Then, the freshness of the database is

$$\bar{F}(S) = \frac{1}{2}(\bar{F}(e_1) + \bar{F}(e_2)) = \frac{1}{2}(\bar{F}(\lambda_1, f_1) + \bar{F}(\lambda_2, f_2))$$
$$= \frac{1}{2}(\bar{F}(9, f_1) + \bar{F}(1, f_2)).$$

When we fix the value of $f_1 + f_2$, the above equation has only one degree of freedom, and we can plot $\bar{F}(S)$ over, say, f_2. In Figure 9, we show a series of graphs obtained this way. The horizontal axis here represents the fraction of the synchronization allocated to e_2. That is, when $x = 0$, we do not synchronize element e_2 at all ($f_2 = 0$), and when $x = 1$ we synchronize only element e_2 ($f_1 = 0$ or $f_2 = f_1 + f_2$). Therefore, the middle point ($x = 0.5$) corresponds to the uniform policy ($f_1 = f_2$), and $x = 0.1$ point corresponds to the proportional policy (Remember that $\lambda_1 = 9$ and $\lambda_2 = 1$). The vertical axis in the graph shows the *normalized* freshness of the database. We normalized the freshness so that $\bar{F}(S) = 1$ at the uniform policy ($x = 0.5$). To compare the uniform and the proportional policies more clearly, we indicate the freshness of the proportional policy by a dot, and the x and the y axes cross at the uniform policy.

From these graphs, we can clearly see that the uniform policy is always better than the proportional policy, since the dots are always below the origin. Also note that when the synchronization frequency is small (graph (a)), it is better to give up on the element that changes too often (We get the highest freshness when $x = 1$ or $f_1 = 0$). When $f_1 + f_2$ is relatively large (graph (c)), the optimal point is somewhere between the uniform policy and the proportional policy. The freshness is highest when $x \approx 0.3$ in Figure 9(c) (the star in the graph).

5.3 The optimal resource-allocation policy

From the previous discussion, we learned that the uniform policy is indeed better than the proportional policy. Also, we learned that the optimal policy is neither the uniform policy nor the proportional policy. For instance, we get the highest freshness when $x \approx 0.3$ for Figure 9(c). Then, what is the best way to allocate the resource to elements for a general database S? In this section, we will address this question. More formally, we will study how often we should synchronize individual elements when we know how often they change, in order to maximize the freshness or age. Mathematically, we can formulate our goal as follows:

Problem 1 Given λ_i's ($i = 1, 2, \ldots, N$), find the values of f_i's ($i = 1, 2, \ldots, N$) which maximize

$$\bar{F}(S) = \frac{1}{N}\sum_{i=1}^{N}\bar{F}(e_i) = \frac{1}{N}\sum_{i=1}^{N}\bar{F}(\lambda_i, f_i)$$

when f_i's satisfy the constraints

$$\frac{1}{N}\sum_{i=1}^{N}f_i = f \quad \text{and} \quad f_i \geq 0 \quad (i = 1, 2, \ldots, N)$$

□

Because we can derive the closed form of $\bar{F}(\lambda_i, f_i),^2$ we can solve the above problem by the *method of Lagrange multipliers* [12]. To illustrate the property of its solution, we use the following example.

Example 4 The real-world database consists of five elements, which change at the frequencies of 1, 2, ..., 5 (times/day). We list the change frequencies in row (a) of Table 5 (We explain the meaning of rows (b) and (c) later, as we continue our discussion.). We decided to synchronize the local database at the rate of 5 elements/day total, but we still need to find out how often we should synchronize each element.

For this example, we can solve the above problem numerically, and we show the graph of its solution

---

[2]For instance, $\bar{F}(\lambda_i, f_i) = (1 - e^{-\lambda_i/f_i})/(\lambda_i/f_i)$ for the fixed-order policy.

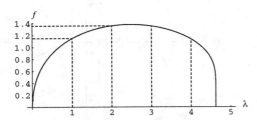

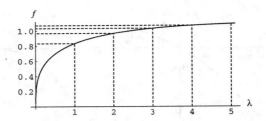

(a) change frequency vs. synchronization frequency for freshness optimization

(b) change frequency vs. synchronization frequency for age optimization

Figure 10: Solution of the freshness and age optimization problem of Example 4

	e_1	e_2	e_3	e_4	e_5
(a) change frequency	1	2	3	4	5
(b) synchronization frequency (freshness)	1.15	1.36	1.35	1.14	0.00
(c) synchronization frequency (age)	0.84	0.97	1.03	1.07	1.09

Table 5: The optimal synchronization frequencies of Example 4

in Figure 10(a). The horizontal axis of the graph corresponds to the change frequency of an element, and the vertical axis shows the optimal synchronization frequency of the element with that given change frequency. For instance, the optimal synchronization frequency of e_1 is 1.15 ($f = 1.15$), because the change frequency of element e_1 is 1 ($\lambda = 1$). Similarly from the graph, we can find the optimal synchronization frequencies of other elements, and we list them in row (b) of Table 5.

Notice that while e_4 changes twice as often as e_2, we need to synchronize e_4 less frequently than e_2. Furthermore, the synchronization frequency of e_5 is zero, while it changes at the highest rate. This result comes from the shape of Figure 10(a). In the graph, when $\lambda > 2.5$, f decreases as λ increases. Therefore, the synchronization frequencies of the elements e_3, e_4 and e_5 gets smaller and smaller. □

While we obtained Figure 10(a) by solving Example 4, we can prove that the shape of the graph is the same for *any* distributions of λ_i's [3]. That is, the optimal graph for *any* database S is *exactly the same* as Figure 10(a), except that the graph of S is scaled by a constant factor from Figure 10(a). Since the shape of the graph is always the same, the following statement is true in any scenario: *To improve freshness, we should penalize the elements that change too often.*

Similarly, we can compute the optimal *age* solution for Example 4, and we show the result in Figure 10(b). The axes in this graph are the same as before. Also, we list the optimal synchronization frequencies in row (c) of Table 5. Contrary to the freshness, we can observe that we should synchronize the element more often when it changes more often ($f_1 < \cdots < f_5$). However,

notice that the difference between the synchronization frequencies is marginal: All f_i's are approximately close to one. In other words, the optimal solution is rather close to the uniform policy than to the proportional policy. Similarly for age, we can prove that the shape of the optimal age graph is always the same as Figure 10(b). Therefore, the trend we observed here is very general and holds for *any* database.

6 Experiments

Throughout this paper we modeled database changes as a Poisson process. In this section, we first verify the Poisson process model using experimental data collected from 270 sites for more than 4 months. Then, using the observed change frequencies on the web, we compare the effectiveness of our various synchronization policies. The experimental results will show that our optimal policy performs significantly better than the current policies used by crawlers.

6.1 Experimental setup

To collect the data on how often web pages change, we crawled around 720,000 pages from 270 "popular" sites every day, from February 17th through June 24th, 1999. This was done with the Stanford WebBase crawler, a system designed to create and maintain large web repositories. The system is capable of high indexing speeds (about 60 pages per second), and can handle relatively large data repositories (currently 300GB of HTML is stored). In this section we briefly discuss how the particular sites were selected for our experiments.

To select the sites for our experiment, we used the snapshot of the web in our WebBase repository. Currently, WebBase maintains the snapshot of 42 million web pages, and based on this snapshot we identified the top 400 "popular" sites as the candidate sites. To measure the popularity of sites, we essentially counted how many pages in our repository have a link to each site, and we used the count as the popularity measure of a site.[3]

Then, we contacted the webmasters of all candidate sites asking their permission for our experi-

---

[3]More precisely, we used PageRank as the popularity measure, which is similar to the link count. To learn more about PageRank, please refer to [10, 5].

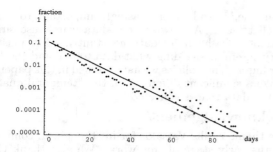

Figure 11: Change intervals for pages with the average change interval of 10 days

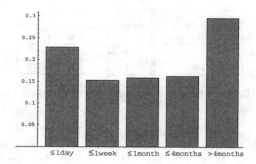

Figure 12: Percentage of pages with given average interval of change

ment. After this step, 270 sites remained, including sites such as Yahoo (`http://yahoo.com`), Microsoft (`http://microsoft.com`), and Stanford (`http://www.stanford.edu`). Obviously, focusing on the "popular" sites biases our results to a certain degree, but we believe this bias is toward what most people are interested in.

From each site chosen this way, we selected around 3,000 pages and crawled them every day. From this daily update information, we can measure how often a page changes. For instance, when we detected 4 changes during our 4 month experiment, we can reasonably infer that the page changes every month on average. Later, we also briefly talk about the limitation of our experiment when we present the result of our experiment.

6.2 Verification of Poisson process

In this subsection, we verify whether the Poisson process adequately models web page changes. In Lemma 1, we computed how long it takes for a page to change under the Poisson process. According to the lemma, the time between changes follow the exponential distribution $\lambda e^{-\lambda t}$. We can use this result to verify our assumption. That is, if we plot the time between changes of a page p_i, the time should be distributed as $\lambda_i e^{-\lambda_i t}$, if changes of p_i follow a Poisson process.

In Figure 11, we show that the changes of a web page can indeed be modeled by the Poisson process. To plot this graph, we first selected only those pages whose *average* change intervals were 10 days and measured the time between changes in those pages. (We also plotted graphs for the pages with other average change intervals, and got similar results when we had sufficient data.) From this data we could get the distribution of the change intervals, which is shown in Figure 11. The horizontal axis represents the interval between changes, and the vertical axis shows the fraction of changes with that interval. The vertical axis in the graph is logarithmic to emphasize that the distribution is exponential. The line in the graph is what a Poisson process would predict. While there exist small variations, we can clearly see that Poisson process predicts very well the observed data.

While this result strongly indicates that a Poisson process is a good model for the web page changes, our result is also limited. Since we crawled pages on a daily basis, we could not obtain detailed change histories for the pages that change very often, and because we conducted our experiment only for 4 months, we could not detect changes to the pages that rarely change. Also, there may exist a set of pages that are updated at regular intervals, which may not necessarily follow a Poisson process.

However, we believe that it is safe to use the Poisson model for the following reasons. First, crawlers rarely can visit a page every day,[4] so most crawlers do not particularly care exactly how often a page changes if the page changes very often (say, more than once every day). Also, when the crawler manages hundreds of millions of pages, it is very difficult to identify the pages that are updated regularly, so we may assume that the set of pages managed by the crawler are modified by a random process *on average*.

6.3 Frequency of change and its implication

Based on the data that we collected, we report how many pages change how often, in Figure 12. In the figure, the horizontal axis represents the average change interval of pages, and the vertical axis shows the fraction of pages changed at the given average interval. For instance, we can see that about 23% of pages changed more than once a day from the first bar of Figure 12.

From this data, we can estimate how much improvement we can get, if we adopt the optimal-allocation policy. For the estimation, we assume that we maintain 100 million pages locally and that we synchronize all pages every month.[5] Also based on Figure 12, we assume that 23% of pages change every day, 15% of pages change every week, etc. For the pages that did not change in 4 months, we assume that they change every year. While it is a crude approximation, we believe we can get some idea on how effective different policies are.

In Table 6, we show the predicted freshness and age for various resource-allocation policies. To compute the numbers, we assumed the fixed-order policy (Item 3a in Section 3) as the synchronization-order policy. We can

---

[4]Crawlers should not abuse web sites. Otherwise, the site administrators sometimes block accesses.

[5]Many popular search engines report numbers similar to these.

policy	Freshness	Age
Proportional	0.12	400 days
Uniform	0.57	5.6 days
Optimal	0.62	4.3 days

Table 6: Freshness and age prediction based on the real web data

clearly see that the optimal policy is significantly better than any other policies. For instance, the freshness increases from 0.12 to 0.62 (500% increase!), if we use the optimal policy instead of the proportional policy. Also, the age decreases by 23% from the uniform policy to the optimal policy. From these numbers, we can also learn that we need to be very careful when we optimize the policy based on the frequency of change. For instance, the proportional policy, which people may intuitively prefer, is significantly worse than any other policies: The age of the proportional policy is 100 times worse than that of the optimal policy!

7 Related work

References [5] and [2] also study how to improve a web crawler. However, these references focus on how to *select* the pages to *initially* crawl, in order to improve the "quality" of the local collection. Contrary to these works, we studied how to *maintain* the collection up-to-date. Reference [6] studies how to schedule the web crawler to improve the freshness. The model used for web pages is similar to ours; however, the model for the crawler and freshness is very different. In data warehousing context, a lot of work has been done to efficiently maintain the local copy, or the *materialized view* [7, 8, 13]. However, most of the work focused on different issues, such as minimizing the size of the view while reducing the query response time [8].

8 Conclusion

In this paper we studied how to synchronize a local database to improve its freshness and age. We presented a formal framework, which provides a theoretical foundation for this problem, and we studied the effectiveness of various refresh policies. In our study we identified a potential pitfall (proportional synchronization), and proposed an optimal policy that can improve freshness and age very significantly. Finally, we investigated the changes of real web pages and validated our analysis based on this experimental data.

In our current framework, we assumed that for users the freshness or age of every element is equally important. But what if the elements have different "importance"? For example, if the database S consists of two elements (e_1 and e_2), and if e_1 is twice as important as e_2 ($F(S) = \frac{1}{3}[2F(e_1) + F(e_2)]$), how should we synchronize them to maximize the freshness? While we need more thorough analysis to answer this question, our preliminary result indicates that we need to synchronize e_1 more often than e_2, but not necessarily twice as often.

As more and more digital information becomes available, it will be increasingly important to collect it effectively. A crawler or a data warehouse simply cannot refresh all its data constantly, so it must be very careful in deciding what data to poll and check for freshness. The policies we have studied in this paper can make a significant difference in the "temporal quality" of the data that is collected.

Acknowledgement

We thank Vasilis Vassalos for his thoughtful comments at the early stage of this work. We also thank Chris Jihye Won for her constant support and encouragement.

References

[1] Google Inc. http://www.google.com.

[2] S. Chakrabarti, M. van den Berg, and B. Dom. Focused crawling: A new approach to topic-specific web resource discovery. In *The 8th International World Wide Web Conference*, 1999.

[3] J. Cho and H. Garcia-Molina. Synchronizing a database to improve freshness. Technical report, Stanford University, 1999. http://www-db.stanford.edu/~cho/papers/cho-synch.ps.

[4] J. Cho and H. Garcia-Molina. Estimating frequency of change. Technical report, Stanford University, 2000.

[5] J. Cho, H. Garcia-Molina, and L. Page. Efficient crawling through URL ordering. *Computers networks and ISDN systems*, 30:161–172, 1998.

[6] E. Coffman, Jr., Z. Liu, and R. R. Weber. Optimal robot scheduling for web search engines. Technical report, INRIA, 1997.

[7] J. Hammer, H. Garcia-Molina, J. Widom, W. J. Labio, and Y. Zhuge. The Stanford data warehousing project. *IEEE Data Engineering Bulletin*, June 1995.

[8] V. Harinarayan, A. Rajaraman, and J. D. Ullman. Implementing data cubes efficiently. In *ACM SIGMOD Conference*, 1996.

[9] S. Lawrence and C. L. Giles. Accessibility of information on the web. *Nature*, 400:107–109, 1999.

[10] L. Page and S. Brin. The anatomy of a large-scale hypertextual web search engine. *Computers networks and ISDN systems*, 30:107–117, 1998.

[11] H. M. Taylor and S. Karlin. *An Introduction To Stochastic Modeling*. Academic Press, 3rd edition, 1998.

[12] G. B. Thomas, Jr. *Calculus and analytic geometry*. Addison-Wesley, 4th edition, 1969.

[13] Y. Zhuge, H. Garcia-Molina, J. Hammer, and J. Widom. View maintenance in a warehousing environment. In *ACM SIGMOD Conference*, 1995.

How To Roll a Join: Asynchronous Incremental View Maintenance

Kenneth Salem
Dept. of Computer Science
University of Waterloo
kmsalem@uwaterloo.ca

Kevin Beyer
Computer Sciences Dept.
University of Wisconsin
beyer@cs.wisc.edu

Bruce Lindsay
Roberta Cochrane
IBM Almaden Research Center
{bruce,bobbiec}@almaden.ibm.com

Abstract

Incremental refresh of a materialized join view is often less expensive than a full, non-incremental refresh. However, it is still a potentially costly atomic operation. This paper presents an algorithm that performs incremental view maintenance as a series of small, asynchronous steps. The size of each step can be controlled to limit contention between the refresh process and concurrent operations that access the materialized view or the underlying relations. The algorithm supports point-in-time refresh, which allows a materialized view to be refreshed to any time between the last refresh and the present.

1 Introduction

In a relational database, a view is a relation that is derived from other relations. Views, like other relations, can be queried, and new views may be derived from them. A view may be materialized by storing the view's tuples in the database. In many cases, a materialized view can be queried more efficiently than a non-materialized view because its tuples need not be re-derived. The more complex the view, and the more often that view is queried, the more benefit materialization can provide. Materialized views have many applications.[6]

Unless it is updated, a materialized view becomes stale when its underlying relations are modified. Updating a stale materialized view so that it reflects the current state of its underlying tables is called *refreshing* the view. Another option is *point-in-time* refresh, which updates the stale view to a specified intermediate time between its old state and the state reflected by the current underlying tables. Point-in-time refresh is valuable in many applications. However, when point-in-time refresh is performed, care must be taken to leave

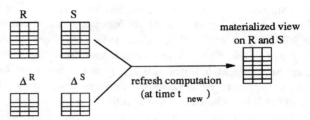

Figure 1: Incremental View Maintenance

the materialized view in a transaction-consistent intermediate state.

Unless the underlying tables are very small, or change very quickly, it is usually desirable to refresh a materialized view incrementally. That is, rather than completely recomputing the view in the desired state, the change from the old state to the desired state is computed and then used to modify the old materialized view. For various classes of views, it is well-understood how to calculate an incremental change.[3, 7, 4] Figure 1 illustrates a refresh operation that updates a materialized view from time t_{old} to time t_{new}. The refresh operation uses the view's underlying tables, R and S, and the deltas (incremental changes) for those tables from t_{old} to t_{new} to refresh the view from t_{old} to t_{new}.

There are several problems with the incremental view maintenance technique of Figure 1. First, the incremental refresh operation needs to be executed as an atomic transaction. It must see a consistent snapshot of the underlying tables. The transaction may be long-lived, resulting in contention between the refresh process and concurrent updates to the underlying tables, and between the refresh operation and concurrent reads of the materialized view. As the *refresh interval* (the amount of time between t_{old} and t_{new}) gets longer, as the view definition becomes more complex, and as the number of views to be maintained increases, this problem becomes worse.

Second, the refresh transaction needs to be *synchronous* with the refresh interval. That is, the transac-

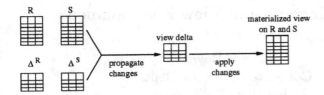

Figure 2: Propagate and Apply

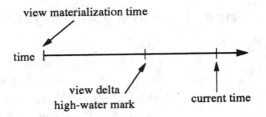

Figure 3: The Contents of the View Delta Table

tion must be performed at a specific time, usually t_{new}, because it needs to see R and S as they exist at that time. This precludes point-in-time refresh. It is not possible to decide at 8:00pm to refresh a materialized view from its 4:00pm state to its 5:00pm state, because at 8:00pm the underlying tables may no longer be as they were at 5:00pm. The decision to refresh the view must be made at 5:00pm and the refresh cost must be paid at 5:00pm, even though more resources may be available later when the load is lighter.

The long transaction problem can be addressed by using very small refresh intervals. For example, the materialized view can be refreshed within every transaction. However, this forces the materialized view to track the current time very closely. For some applications such close tracking is required, but for others it either impractical or undesirable, e.g., when the materialized view represents daily results. The use of short refresh intervals also does not address the synchronization problem. View maintenance costs are paid by each update transaction.

An orthogonal technique involves splitting the refresh computation into a *propagation* phase and an *apply* phase.[4] This is shown in Figure 2. During the propagation phase, changes to the view are computed and stored. Later, during the apply phase, the stored changes (the *view delta*) are used to update the materialized view. This approach breaks a single refresh transaction into separate propagate and apply transactions. It also partially addresses the synchronization problem: the application phase can be delayed, since the view delta can be stored. However, the propagation phase, which includes multiple join queries among the underlying tables and their changes, is still synchronous and atomic.

This paper's contribution is an incremental view maintenance technique called *rolling join propagation* that address both the long transaction problem and the synchronization problem. It has three significant features. First, view delta propagation is asynchronous. That is, the computation of the view delta for a time interval ending at time t_{new} takes place at some time after t_{new}. Second, view delta propagation is treated as a continuous process. The view delta is propagated using a series of small transactions, rather than a single large transaction. The size of

each transaction can be be controlled. This control provides a means of limiting the contention between the propagation process and concurrent updates to the underlying tables. Third, the changes recorded in the view delta are *timestamped* to indicate when they should be applied to the view. Timestamps facilitate the control of propagation transaction sizes and enable point-in-time incremental maintenance.

The rolling propagation technique uses separate propagation and apply processes, as was shown in Figure 2. Aside from the usual producer/consumer synchronization, the two processes are completely independent. Either process, or both, can be suspended during periods of high system load, or for other reasons. At any given time, the view delta table contains a complete, timestamped view delta covering the interval from the view's current materialization time to a view delta high-water mark time. This is shown in Figure 3. The view delta may contain additional tuples as well. For example, it may contain partially-computed changes for the time between the high-water mark and the current time. However, the apply process can easily distinguish (and avoid) such tuples using their timestamps. Because the tuples are timestamped, the apply process can, at any time, use the view delta to roll the materialized view forward to any time point up to the view delta's high-water mark. This provides for point-in-time refresh of the materialized view.

2 Definitions and Assumptions

The database consists of a set of tables, which are multisets of tuples. Transactions cause the database to evolve over time. Transactions may insert, delete, and update tuples. An update is modeled as an insertion and a deletion.

A *delta table* describes changes made to another table (possibly a view). We will refer to the non-delta tables as *base tables* when it is necessary to distinguish them from delta tables. If R is a base table, Δ^R will be used to represent the delta table that describes R's changes. Δ^R has the same attributes as R plus two additional attributes: count and timestamp. A count value of $+n$ is used to represent the insertion of n copies of its associated tuple. A value of $-n$ represents the deletion of n copies of the tuple. The `timestamp` represents the time of the insertion or deletion.

To maintain a uniform notation, each base table is considered to have implicit `count` and `timestamp` attributes. The implicit `count` associated with each tuple in the base table is +1. (Thus, a base table is represented as the insertion of one copy of each of its tuples into an empty table.) The implicit `timestamp` value is null. The `count` and `timestamp` attributes in base tables exist only for notational convenience. They are not represented explicitly in the database.

The rolling propagation algorithm is presented for select-project-join views, i.e., for views of the form $\pi(\sigma(R^1 \bowtie R^2 \bowtie \ldots \bowtie R^n))$. When it is convenient to do so, the explicit relational operators will be dropped, and the view definition will simply be denoted by $R^1 R^2 \ldots R^n$. Although rolling propagation is presented for select-project-join views, it can be extended easily to accommodate views involving union. It can also be extended to accommodate select-project-join views with aggregation by using *summary delta tables*, as described in [8].

In addition to select, project, and join, the algorithm makes use of union and negation operators. The multiset union of tables R^1 and R^2 will be written $R^1 + R^2$. The negation operation, written $-R$, changes the sign of every count in R. The notation $R^1 - R^2$ is used as a shorthand for $R^1 + (-R^2)$.

The transaction history is assumed to be serializable, and the order of transaction commits is assumed to be consistent with the serialization order. This would be the case, for example, in any system that used strict two-phase locking as its concurrency control mechanism. The notation R_a is used to denote the state of table R at time t_a. R_a includes the effects of all transactions that have committed at or before t_a, and does not include any effects from transactions that commit after t_a.

In delta tables, the value of a tuple's `timestamp` attribute is the commit time of the transaction that inserted or most recently updated the tuple. The operation $\sigma_{a,b}$ selects all tuples having timestamps greater than t_a and less than or equal to t_b. The notation $R_{a,b}$ is a shorthand for $\sigma_{a,b}(\Delta^R)$.

The algorithms presented in this paper compute view deltas using *propagation queries*. In general, a computed view delta will be the union of the results of one or more such queries. The propagation queries for a view V have the same form as V's definition, except that one or more of the base tables are replaced by their corresponding delta tables. For example, if V is defined by $\pi(\sigma(R^1 \bowtie R^2 \bowtie \ldots \bowtie R^n))$, a possible propagation query is $\pi(\sigma(R^1 \bowtie R^2_{a,b} \bowtie \ldots \bowtie R^n))$. In this case, R^2 has been replaced by R^2's delta over the time interval from t_a to t_b. The notation $Q^V[i]$ is used to represent

the ith relation in a propagation query Q^V for view V. $Q^V[i]$ is either R^i or $R^i_{x,y}$, depending on whether or not R^i has been replaced by its delta table in the query.

Propagation queries produce delta tables. The `timestamp` and `count` attributes for these tables are computed from the `timestamp` and `count` attributes of the tables on which the query is defined. The `count` of a view delta tuple is the product of the `count`s of the tuples from which it is derived. The `timestamp` of a view delta tuple is the minimum of the `timestamp`s of the tuples from which it is derived. Section 3.3 describes why the minimum `timestamp` value is chosen.

The notation Q^V_b is used to represent the result of evaluating query Q^V at time t_b. Thus, if $Q^V = R^1 R^2_{a,b} \ldots R^n$, then $Q^V_b = R^1_b R^2_{a,b} \ldots R^n_b$. (Similarly, V_b is the state of view V at time t_b.) At times it will be necessary to consider query results such as $R^1_a R^2_{a,b} \ldots R^N_b$, in which different base tables are seen at different times. Such a query will be denoted by $Q^V_{[a,,b]}$, i.e., by explicitly listing the vector of relation times, or by defining $\tau = [a,,b]$ and writing Q^V_τ. Note that $\tau = [a,,b]$ specifies that R^1 is seen at t_a and R^3 is seen at t_b, but it does not specify a time for R^2, which appears as a delta table in Q^V. It is not necessary to specify times for delta tables because they do not evolve over time.

Suppose that V is a three-way join view, Q^V is a propagation query for V, and τ is a vector timestamp. The query result Q^V_τ is said to be *realizable* at time t_x iff the following two conditions hold for all $1 \le i \le n$:

- if $Q^V[i] = R^i$, then $\tau[i] = t_x$

- if $Q^V[i] = R^i_{a,b}$, then $t_b \le t_x$.

For example $R^1_b R^2_{a,b} R^n_b$ $(t_a < t_b)$ is realizable at time t_b, and only at time t_b. The query result $R^1_b R^2_{a,b} R^3_c$ $(t_a < t_b < t_c)$ is not realizable at any time, since R^1 and R^3 are seen at different times. Unless historical snapshots of base relations are maintained or updates to R_1 are prevented between times t_b and t_c (so that $R^1_b = R^1_c$), no serializable transaction can generate this result. Similarly, the query result $R^1_a R^2_{a,b} R^3_a$ $(t_a < t_b)$ is not realizable at any time. In this case, the result uses changes to R^2 up through time t_b, but R^1 and R^3 need to be seen at an earlier time t_a. Note that results of queries that involve only delta tables are realizable at any time after the end of the latest delta time interval in the query.

3 The Rolling Join Propagation Algorithm

This section starts with a presentation of a simple, synchronous algorithm for view delta propagation. The asynchronous, rolling propagation algorithm is arrived at by successive refinement of the original algorithm. Each refinement addresses a shortcoming of its predecessor.

3.1 Synchronous Propagation

Several techniques for generating view deltas for SPJ views have been described in the literature.[3, 7, 4] For example, if V is $R^1 R^2 R^3$, then $V_{a,b}$ can be calculated as:

$$
\begin{aligned}
V_{a,b} = \ & R^1_{a,b} R^2_b R^3_b + R^1_b R^2_{a,b} R^3_b + R^1_b R^2_b R^3_{a,b} \quad (1) \\
& - R^1_{a,b} R^2_{a,b} R^3_b - R^1_{a,b} R^2_b R^3_{a,b} - R^1_b R^2_{a,b} R^3_{a,b} \\
& + R^1_{a,b} R^2_{a,b} R^3_{a,b}
\end{aligned}
$$

The view delta is computed as the union of the results of seven propagation queries. This approach is easily generalized to n-way join views. In the general case, the view delta is computed as the union of $2^n - 1$ query results, one query for each possible combination of base and delta tables that includes at least one delta table.

Except for the all-delta query, all of the queries of Equation 1 are realizable only time t_b, i.e., all of the queries must see the base tables as they exist at t_b. That is, the queries must be executed together as an atomic transaction at time t_b. A propagation query used to compute a view delta $V_{a,b}$ is *synchronous* if it cannot be realized later than t_b. All of the queries of Equation 1 (except the last) are synchronous.

A synchronous propagation technique that requires only n query results to propagate a delta for an n-way join view is described in [7]. For the case $n = 3$, this technique computes $V_{a,b}$ using:

$$
V_{a,b} = R^1_{a,b} R^2_b R^3_b + R^1_a R^2_{a,b} R^3_b + R^1_a R^2_a R^3_{a,b} \quad (2)
$$

Note that in each propagation query, base tables to the left of the delta table must be seen at the beginning of the propagation interval (at t_a), and those to the right of the delta table must be seen at the end of the interval, at t_b. Although this technique uses fewer queries to produce the view delta, two of the query results ($R^1_a R^2_{a,b} R^3_b$ and $R^1_a R^2_a R^3_{a,b}$) are not realizable. For this reason, Equation 2 may be less useful in practice that Equation 1. For the purposes of this paper, however, Equation 2 serves as a useful starting point since it involves fewer propagation queries.

3.2 Asynchronous Propagation

The computation described by Equation 1 must be performed atomically at time t_b. Thus, the cost of propagating the view delta from 4:00pm to 5:00pm must incurred in the form of a transaction that runs at 5:00pm. The propagation transaction cannot be delayed. Furthermore, it may be long-lived, particularly if the propagation interval is long or the view is complex.

Long-lived propagation transactions can lead to data contention at the base tables from which the view is derived.

The goal of asynchronous propagation is to break the propagation computation into smaller pieces, each of which is performed after the propagation interval. Thus, view delta for the period from 4:00pm to 5:00pm would be computed by a series of smaller transactions that might not begin running until well after 5:00pm.

Asynchronous propagation can be achieved using *compensation.*[12, 13] Consider the query result $Q^V_b = R^1_{a,b} R^2_b R^3_b$ from Equation 1. Suppose that Q^V is evaluated at some later time t_c rather than t_b, resulting in $Q^V_c = R^1_{a,b} R^2_c R^3_c$. Since R^2 and R^3 may have evolved between t_b and t_c, Q^V_b and Q^V_c will, in general, not be the same. However, this problem can be fixed by compensating for any errors caused by changes to R^2 and R^3 made between t_b and time t_c. Compensation involves adding extra changes to the view delta. For example, if Q^V_c includes extra view tuple insertions not found in Q^V_b, they are compensated for by the addition of matching deletions to the view delta.

The difference between Q^V_b and Q^V_c is $Q^V_{b,c}$. That is, the query Q^V can be treated as a view definition and its incremental change from t_b to t_c can be calculated. The compensation required to correct for this difference is exactly $-Q^V_{b,c}$ since every insertion in $Q^V_{b,c}$ becomes a matching deletion in $-Q^V_{b,c}$, and deletions become matching insertions. Since Q^V has the same form as the view V, $Q^V_{b,c}$ (and hence $-Q^V_{b,c}$) can be calculated using the same method used to calculate the view delta, e.g., Equation 2 or Equation 1.

Consider the following example for $V = R^1 R^2$. Using the method illustrated in Equation 2, the view delta $V_{a,b}$ can be calculated using

$$
V_{a,b} = R^1_{a,b} R^2_b + R^1_a R^2_{a,b}
$$

The first query can be moved to time t_c and the second to time t_d, and compensation can be added for each query to correct any errors introduced by the moves. This leads to

$$
V_{a,b} = R^1_{a,b} R^2_c - (\mathbf{R^1_{a,b} R^2})_{\mathbf{b,c}} + R^1_d R^2_{a,b} - (\mathbf{R^1 R^2_{a,b}})_{\mathbf{a,d}}
$$

The compensation queries are shown in bold face, and the asynchronous *forward* queries are not.[1] The first compensation can be calculated by another application of the method of Equation 2:

$$
(R^1_{a,b} R^2)_{b,c} = (R^1_{a,b})_{b,c} R^2_c + (R^1_{a,b})_b R^2_{b,c}
$$

---

[1] The term *forward* query will be used to describe propagation queries that involve only a single delta table. The term *compensation* query is used for queries that involve more than one delta table.

```
ComputeDelta(Q, τ_old, t_new) {
    for each i from 1 to n do
        // generate one query for each base relation in Q
        if (Q[i] = R^i) ∧ (τ_old[i] < t_new)
            // Q' is the query to be executed
            let Q' ← Q[1]...Q[i-1]R^i_{old[i],new}Q[i+1]...Q[n]
            // t_exec holds the execution time of the query, which is returned by Execute
            t_exec ← Execute(Q')
            if Q' has any base tables then
                // using the method of Equation 2, tables left of i should be seen at τ_old,
                // tables right of i should be seen at t_new
                let τ_intended ← [old[1],...,old[i-1],,new,...,new]
                // tables were actually seen at t_x, so recursively compensate back to the intended time
                ComputeDelta(-Q', τ_intended, t_exec)
            fi
        fi
    od
}
```

Figure 4: Asynchronous Propagation Using Recursive Compensation

Since $R^1_{a,b}$ does not evolve, $(R^1_{a,b})_{b,c}$ is empty, and the compensation expression can be simplified to:

$$(R^1_{a,b}R^2)_{b,c} = R^1_{a,b}R^2_{b,c}$$

Using the same approach, the compensation term $(R^1 R^2_{a,b})_{a,d}$ can be found to be $R^1_{a,d}R^2_{a,b}$, which gives the following asynchronous calculation of $V_{a,b}$:

$$V_{a,b} = R^1_{a,b}R^2_c - R^1_{a,b}R^2_{b,c} + R^1_d R^2_{a,b} - R^1_{a,d}R^2_{a,b} \quad (3)$$

Figure 4 shows an asynchronous propagation algorithm called ComputeDelta that generalizes this approach to views defined over n base relations. The algorithm takes an n-way propagation query Q an initial vector timestamp $τ_{old}$ and a new time t_{new}. It computes $Q_{old,new}$, i.e., the delta for Q from time $τ_{old}$ to time t_{new}. It can be used to compute a view delta $V_{a,b}$ by setting $Q = V$, $τ_{old} = [a, a, ..., a]$, and $t_{new} = t_b$. For example, execution of ComputeDelta($R^1 R^2, [a, a, ..., a], t_b$) will produce the asynchronous calculation shown in Equation 3.

ComputeDelta uses a function Execute to execute queries. Each Execute call is assumed to insert its results into a view delta table in which the view delta is being accumulated. The view delta table itself is not indicated explicitly in Figure 4. Each call to Execute performs its query as a separate transaction and returns the commit time of that transaction. Section 5 describes how this is accomplished in our implementation.

3.3 Timestamps

The algorithm of Figure 4 performs asynchronous propagation of the view delta for a propagation interval whose endpoints are defined by the parameters $τ_{old}$ and t_{new}. Over which propagation intervals should a view delta be propagated? There are two conflicting answers to this question.

The length of the propagation interval determines the cost of the propagation queries. Choosing small intervals leads to many small propagation queries. Choosing larger intervals leads to fewer, larger queries. Thus, the interval acts as a parameter that can be tuned to balance query execution overhead against data contention. In addition, the propagation interval determines the time points to which the materialized view can be rolled. If the view is materialized at time t_a and the view delta $V_{a,b}$ is propagated, then it is possible to roll the view forward from t_a to t_b. However, it is not possible to roll the view to any time $t_{b'}$, where $t_a < t_{b'} < t_b$.

Ideally, the propagation and apply processes should be as independent as possible. The choice of a propagation interval can be made independent of the apply process by generating a *timestamp* for each tuple in the propagated view delta. The timestamp indicates commit time of transaction that generated the change. To roll a view from time t_a to time $t_{b'}$, the apply process selects view delta tuples with timestamps in that interval and applies those tuples (only) to the materialized view. With this change, the propagation process can proceed independently of apply. The propagation interval can be used solely as a tuning parameter for the propagation process, allowing size of the propagation queries to be controlled. The propagation process can be implemented as a loop that continuously generates timestamped view delta tuples

```
Propagate(V, t_initial) {
    t_cur ← t_initial
    do forever
        choose a propagation interval length δ
        ComputeDelta(V, [cur, ..., cur], t_cur + δ)
        t_cur ← t_cur + δ
    od
}
```

Figure 5: A Continuous, Asynchronous Propagation Process

for successively later time intervals. Such a process, called Propagate is shown in Figure 5. Propagate generates a view delta starting at a specified time $t_{initial}$. The variable t_{cur} tracks the view delta high-water mark, which was illustrated in Figure 3. At the conclusion of every iteration of Propagate, the view delta is accurate for the interval from $t_{initial}$ to t_{cur}.

Each base table's delta includes a timestamp attribute indicating the commit times of the changes it records. As was noted in Section 2, a view delta tuple's timestamp is the *minimum* of the timestamps of the tuples that joined to produce it.[2] That the minimum timestamp is the correct one to choose may be counter-intuitive. In Section 4 this choice is shown to be correct. However, the following examples may provide some intuituion.

Suppose that $V = R^1 R^2$ and that V_0 contains a tuple $r^1 r^2$, where r^1 is a tuple found in R_0^1 and r^2 is a tuple found in R_0^2. At time t_a, where $t_0 < t_a < t_1$, tuple r^1 is deleted from R^1. At time t_b, where $t_a < t_b < t_1$, tuple r^2 is deleted from R^2. The effect of these deletions should be the deletion of $r^1 r^2$ from the view at time t_a.

The execution of ComputeDelta($V, [0, ..., 0], t_1$) (see Figure 4) calculates $V_{0,1}$ as

$$V_{0,1} = R_{0,1}^1 R_c^2 - R_{0,1}^1 R_{1,c}^2 + R_d^1 R_{0,1}^2 - R_{0,d}^1 R_{0,1}^2$$

where t_c and t_d are query execution times later than t_1. Query $R_{0,1}^1 R_c^2$ will produce an empty result, since r^2 has already been deleted from R^2 at time t_c. Query $R_d^1 R_{0,1}^2$ will also produce an empty result for a similar reason. Query $-R_{0,1}^1 R_{1,c}^2$ will be empty because R^2 does not change between t_1 and t_c in this example. Query $-R_{0,d}^1 R_{0,1}^2$ will find the tuple $(t_a, -1, r^1)$ in $R_{0,d}^1$ and the tuple $(t_b, -1, r^2)$ in $R_{0,1}^2$. (The -1's are the values of the count attribute.). The compensation query will join those tuples and add $(t_a, -1, r^1 r^2)$ to the view delta, since the minimum timestamp (t_a) and the negated

---

[2]Recall that base tables are considered have implicit null timestamps, so only timestamps from the delta tables are considered when choosing the minimum. Every maintenance query involves at least one delta table.

product of the counts will be used. This is the desired result.

Now consider an insertion scenario. Suppose that tuple x^1 is inserted into R^1 at time t_a and tuple x^2 is inserted into R^2 at time t_b. If x^1 and x^2 join, the effect should be the insertion of $x^1 x^2$ into V at time t_b. ComputeDelta($V, [0, ..., 0], t_1$) calculates the view delta as follows. Query $R_{0,1}^1 R_c^2$ will find the tuple $(t_a, +1, x^1)$ in $R_{0,1}^1$, and it will find x^2 in R_c^2. Thus, it will add $(t_a, +1, x^1 x^2)$ into the view delta. For a similar reason, $R_d^1 R_{0,1}^2$ will add $(t_b, +1, x^1 x^2)$ to the view delta. Query $-R_{0,1}^1 R_{1,c}^2$ is empty, but $-R_{0,d}^1 R_{0,1}^2$ will find insertion tuples in $R_{0,1}^2$ and $R_{0,d}^1$. Since it chooses the minimum timestamp, it will add $(t_a, -1, x^1 x^2)$ to the view delta. In net effect, the insertion and deletion at t_a cancel each other out, leaving only the insertion at time t_b. Again, this is the desired result.

3.4 Rolling Propagation

The Propagate algorithm from Figure 5, together with timestamps, addresses the incremental view maintenance issues discussed in Section 1. The rolling propagation algorithm is a refinement of Propagate. The principal difference between the two is that rolling propagation provides more control over the sizes of the propagation queries.

The ComputeDelta procedure, on which Propagate is based, provides one tunable parameter: the length of the propagation interval. All forward queries use the same interval. However, in many cases the base tables from which a view is derived will be updated at different rates. For example, consider a star schema in which the central fact table is frequently updated and the surrounding dimension tables are rarely updated. If the propagation interval is the same for all forward queries, the forward queries for the fact table will be much larger than the forward queries for the dimension tables. The rolling propagation algorithm allows a different interval to be used for each base table. Thus, rolling propagation provides n independent tunable parameters, rather than one.

Rolling propagation also tends to generate fewer, larger propagation queries than Propagate does. Although both algorithms are based on ComputeDelta, rolling propagation defers the compensations for some forward queries and combines them with compensations for later queries. As it result, it makes fewer calls to ComputeDelta than Propagate does.

Figures 6,7,8, and 9 constitute a graphical explanation of the rolling propagation algorithm and its relationship to ComputeDelta and Propagate. Suppose that $V = R^1 R^2$. Figure 6 shows a coordinate space with one time axis for R^1 and one for R^2. The point t_a on the R^1 axis represents R_a^1, i.e., R_1 as it exists at t_a. Time t_0 on each axis represents the relation cre-

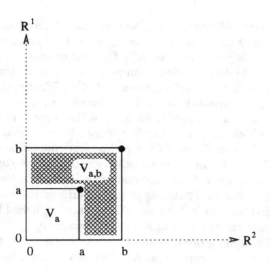

Figure 6: Graphical Representation the Evolution of R^1R^2

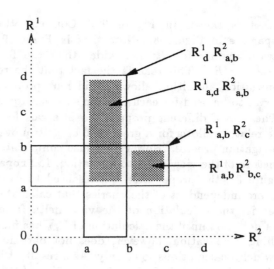

Figure 7: ComputeDelta(R^1R^2, $[a, \ldots, a]$, t_b)

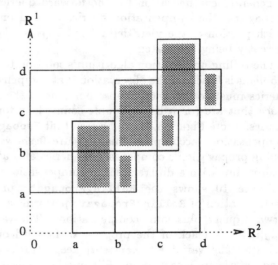

Figure 8: Three Iterations of Propagate(R^1R^2, t_a)

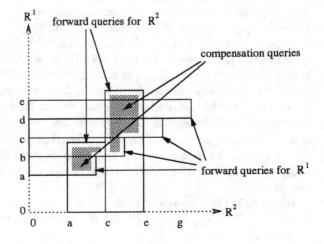

Figure 9: Rolling Propagation

ation times. The region below and to the left of the point (a, a) represents the join $R_a^1 R_a^2 = V_a$. Similarly, the region below and to the left of (b, b) represents V_b, and the view delta $V_{a,b}$ is the L-shaped cross-hatched region.[3]

ComputeDelta(V, $[a, \ldots, a]$, t_b) generates $V_{a,b}$ using the four propagation queries shown in Equation 3. In Figure 7, each of these queries is represented diagrammatically by a rectangular region. For example, $R_{a,b}^1 R_{b,c}^2$ is represented by the region bounded by t_a and t_b on the R^1 axis and by t_b and t_c on the R^2 axis. Similarly $R_d^1 R_{a,b}^2$ is bounded by t_0 and t_d on the R^1 axis and t_a and t_b on the R^2 axis. The forward queries are represented by unshaded rectangles, and the shaded regions are the compensation queries. Note that the net effect of these four queries is exactly the L-shaped region representing $V_{a,b}$ that was shown in Figure 6. The portion of $R_d^1 R_{a,b}^2$ that protrudes above the line R_b^1, which is not part of the L-shaped region, is compensated for. So is the portion of $R_{a,b}^1 R_c^2$ that protrudes beyond the line R_b^2. The compensation of the region $R_{a,b}^1 R_{a,b}^2$ corrects for the double counting of that region by the two forward queries, which overlap there.

The Propagate process from Figure 5 generates consecutive view deltas by repeated application of ComputeDelta. This is illustrated graphically in Figure 8, which shows the sequential calculation of $V_{a,b}$, $V_{b,c}$, and $V_{c,d}$ by three iterations of Propagate. Each of these three calculations is identical in form to the calculation shown in Figure 7.

Finally, the behavior of the rolling propagation

---

[3]It may be helpful to think of a relation like R^1 as consisting of a log of changes since t_0. In net effect, the portion of this log from t_0 to t_a is the same as R_a^1.

process is shown in Figure 9. Compare this to Propagate in Figure 8. Note that in Figure 9, the forward queries for R^2 are wider than the forward queries for R^1. This reflects the fact that the rolling propagation algorithm allows a different propagation interval to be used for each relation's forward queries.

The use of different propagation intervals for each base relation allows for a great deal of control over the propagation process. However, it also complicates the structure of the view delta computation. In Propagate (Figure 8), the propagation queries used to calculate $V_{a,b}$ are independent of the queries that calculate $V_{b,c}$. That is, the calculation of the view delta from $V_{b,c}$ does not start until the calculation of $V_{a,b}$ has finished. Rolling propagation, however, does not partition the view delta calculations so cleanly. As a result, it is less obvious when the calculation of any portion of the view delta has been completed. It is also less obvious how to generate compensation for the forward queries. In Propagate, the compensation queries depend only on which portion of the view delta (e.g., $V_{a,b}$ vs. $V_{b,c}$) is currently being calculated.

The rolling propagation algorithm's solution to these problems is based on the observation that compensation queries must cover exactly those portions of the $R^1 R^2$ space that are (or will be) double-counted by forward queries. From Figure 8, it can be seen that Propagate's compensations accomplish this. Figure 9 shows that rolling propagation's compensation queries also accomplish it, but with a different set of compensations.

Figure 10 shows the RollingPropagate process. Each iteration of RollingPropagate performs a single forward query plus some compensations. The variable $t_{fwd}[i]$ keeps track of the progress of forward queries for R^i. The variable $querylist[i]$ keeps track of the progress of compensation for R^i's queries. Specifically, $querylist[i]$ lists the forward queries for R^i that have not yet been completely compensated for.[4] The variable $t_{comp}[i]$ tracks the oldest uncompensated query in $querylist[i]$ (or $t_{fwd}[i]$ if $querylist[i]$ is empty). For example, after the queries shown in Figure 9, both $t_{fwd}[1]$ and $t_{fwd}[2]$ would be t_e. $querylist[2]$ would be empty, and $t_{comp}[2] = t_{fwd}[2] = t_e$, since both of R^2's forward queries have been compensated for. However, $querylist[1]$ would include the two most recent forward queries for R^1 (those with propagation intervals $R^1_{c,d}$ and $R^1_{d,e}$), since portions of these queries that require compensation have not yet been compensated for. $t_{comp}[1] = t_c$, the beginning of the oldest query in $querylist[1]$.

When RollingPropagate performs a forward query $Q = R^1 \ldots R^{i-1} R^i_{x,y} R^{i+1} \ldots R^n$ for R^i, it compensates

_____
[4] A forward query has been completely compensated for if every region of the query that will overlap another forward query has been compensated for.

for forward queries of lower-numbered relations with which Q overlaps. Thus, when $V = R^1 R^2$, no compensation is performed for R^1's forward queries, and R^2's forward queries perform compensation that accounts for overlap between R^2's queries and R^1's. Ideally, the necessary compensation can be accomplished with a single call to ComputeDelta. In general, however, the region for which compensation is required is not rectangular. This is true of both of the compensation queries shown in Figure 9. In these cases, the region to be compensated is divided into rectangular sub-regions, and one call to ComputeDelta is used to perform the compensation for each sub-region. This is accomplished by the repeat/until loop in RollingPropagate.

The rolling propagation computation is more flexible that that of Propagate. An obvious question, however, is how to determine the view delta high-water mark. (Recall from Figure 3 that the view delta high-water mark indicates which portion of the view delta has been completely calculated.) For example, given the state of the computation shown in Figure 9, how far forward from t_a can the apply process roll the materialized view?

RollingPropagate(V, t_a) will have completely calculated the view delta from t_a to t_b once all of the forward queries that overlap with that interval have been completely compensated. The RollingPropagate algorithm tracks the compensation of forward queries through the $t_{comp}[i]$ variables. After any iteration of the algorithm, the view delta high water mark is determined by the minimum value of $t_{comp}[i]$ over all of the relations R^i. Thus, after the computation in Figure 9, $t_{comp}[1] = t_c$, $t_{comp}[2] = t_e$, and the view delta high water mark is at t_c.

4 Correctness

There are many equivalent ways to represent a view delta. For example, a insertion can be represented using a single tuple with a count of $+1$, as two tuples, one with a count of $+2$ and another with a count of -1, and so on. The *net effect* operator, ϕ, maps equivalent tables into a canonical form.

Definition 4.1
The net effect *of a table R, written $\phi(R)$, is the table obtained from R by the following steps. First, R is grouped on all attributes except* count *and* timestamp. *Within each group,* count *values are aggregated using addition, and the group's* timestamp *becomes null. Finally, tuples for which* count *is equal to zero are eliminated.*

Note that, when applied to a base table, the net effect operation turns a multiset into a set, with tuple multiplicity in the original multiset represented by count values in the net effect. The net effect operation

```
RollingPropagate(V, t_initial) {
    // t_fwd[i] tracks the progress of forward queries for R^i
    // querylist[i] lists forward queries for R^i that have not been fully compensated
    // t_comp[i] tracks oldest query in querylist[i]
    for each 1 ≤ i ≤ n : t_fwd[i] ← t_initial, t_comp[i] ← t_initial, querylist[i] ← ∅
    do forever
        choose a base relation R^i with the smallest t_fwd[i]
        PruneQueryLists(t_fwd[i])
        choose a propagation interval length δ for R^i
        // perform forward query for R^i. t_e holds the execution time, which is returned by Execute
        t_e ← Execute(R^1 ... R^{i-1} R^i_{fwd[i],fwd[i]+δ} R^{i+1} ... R^n)
        if i < n then insert R^1_e ... R^{i-1}_e R^i_{fwd[i],fwd[i]+δ} R^{i+1}_e ... R^n_e into querylist[i]
        // generate call(s) to ComputeDelta to compensate for the forward query
        if i > 1 // no need to compensate for R^1's forward queries
            repeat
                δ' ← min(δ, CompInterval(R^i, t_fwd[i]))
                // compensate for overlap with forward queries for R^1 through R^{i-1}.
                τ_d ← [CompTime(R^1, t_fwd[i]), ..., CompTime(R^{i-1}, t_fwd[i]), , t_e, ..., t_e]
                ComputeDelta(R^1 ... R^{i-1} R^i_{fwd[i],fwd[i]+δ'} R^{i+1} ... R^n, τ_d, t_e)
                t_fwd[i] ← t_fwd[i] + δ'
                δ ← δ - δ'
            until δ = 0
        fi
    od
}


// determine how wide a compensation for R^i can be, starting at t,
// without becoming non-rectangular
CompInterval(R^i, t) {
    let t_e be the smallest execution time greater than t of all queries appearing in
        querylist[1] ∪ ... ∪ querylist[i - 1]
    return(t_e - t)
}


// determine how far back a compensation query at t should compensate R^i
CompTime(R^i, t) {
    let R^1_e ... R^{i-1}_e R^i_{x,y} R^{i+1}_e ... R^n_e be the query from any querylist[i]
        with the smallest execution time t_e that is greater than t
    return(t_x)
}


// remove fully-compensated queries from the query lists, and update t_comp[i]
PruneQueryLists(t) {
    for each R^i do
        remove from querylist[i] all queries with execution times less than or equal to t
        if querylist[i] is empty
            t_comp[i] ← t_fwd[i]
        else
            let R^1_e ... R^{i-1}_e R^i_{x,y} R^{i+1}_e ... R^n_e have the smallest execution time in querylist[i]
            t_comp[i] ← t_x
    od
}
```

Figure 10: The Rolling Propagation Process

has the following properties:

$$\phi(\phi(R)) = \phi(R)$$
$$\phi(R + S) = \phi(\phi(R) + S) = \phi(R + \phi(S))$$
$$= \phi(\phi(R) + \phi(S))$$
$$\phi(RS) = \phi(R)\phi(S)$$

Provided that the selection condition does not involve **count** or **timestamp** and that a projection does not eliminate **count** or **timestamp**, the net effect operation also has the following properties:

$$\phi(\sigma(R)) = \sigma(\phi(R))$$
$$\phi(\pi(R)) = \phi(\pi(\phi(R)))$$

Intuitively, a table Δ is a delta table for R if it can be used to "roll" the state of R from one time to another. That is, if $\phi(R_i + \Delta) = \phi(R_j)$, then Δ is a delta table for R from time t_i to time t_j. However, the delta tables used by the rolling compensation algorithm are more flexible than this because they include timestamps. With such a delta table, it is possible to select tuples having timestamps within a particular time window and then use the selected tuples as a view delta over that window. This is captured by the following definition:

Definition 4.2
The table Δ is a timed delta table *for R from t_i to t_j $(t_i < t_j)$ iff for all times t_a and t_b such that $t_i \leq t_a < t_b \leq t_j$ it satisfies the following condition:*

$$\phi(\sigma_{a,b}(\Delta) + R_a) = \phi(R_b)$$

Timed delta tables can be split to produce timed delta tables over smaller time intervals. Consecutive timed delta tables can also be combined to produce a single timed delta table over a larger interval.

Lemma 4.1 *If Δ is a timed delta table for R from t_i to t_j, and t_x is a time between t_i and t_j, then $\sigma_{i,x}(\Delta)$ is a timed delta table for R from t_i to t_x, and $\sigma_{x,j}(\Delta)$ is a timed delta table for R from t_x to t_j.*

Lemma 4.2 *If Δ is a delta table for R from t_i to t_x, and Δ' is a delta table for R from t_x to t_j, then $\Delta + \Delta'$ is a timed delta table for R from t_i to t_j.*

The following theorems state that the **ComputeDelta**, **Propagate**, and **RollingPropagate** procedures are correct. Because of space limitations, they are presented here without proof. Proofs can be found in the extended version of this paper.[11]

Theorem 4.1 *Let Δ be the result of executing* **ComputeDelta***(V,τ_a,t_b) for a view V. Δ is a timed delta table for V from time τ_a to time t_b.*

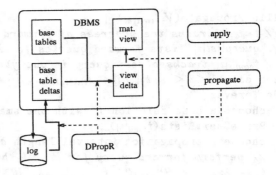

Figure 11: View Maintenance Architecture

Theorem 4.2 *Let Δ be the delta table that has been produced by* **Propagate***(V,t_a) after some number of complete iterations, and let t_b be the value of t_{cur} in* **Propagate***. Δ is a timed delta table for V from time t_a to time t_b.*

Theorem 4.3 *Let Δ be the table produced by* **RollingPropagate***(V,t_a) and let t_b be the minimum value (over all i) of $t_{comp}[i]$. At all times, $\sigma_{a,b}(\Delta)$ is a timed view delta for V from t_a to t_b.*

5   Implementation Issues

A prototype of the rolling propagation algorithm has been implemented using a set of external drivers around the DB2 relational database engine. Figure 11 gives a high-level view of the prototype's architecture. Solid lines represent data flow. The dashed lines are used to indicate which driver controls each data flow.

The external drivers use a set of control tables maintained in the database engine. The control tables identify the tables associated with each materialized view, including the view delta table, the underlying base tables, and their delta tables. The control tables also record the current view materialization time and the view delta high-water mark. The **propagate** driver implements the rolling propagation algorithm to populate view delta tables. The **apply** driver implements incremental point-in-time refresh by applying changes recorded in the view delta table.

One issue that arose during the design of the prototype was the method of populating the base table deltas. There are two options. One is to define triggers on each base table R, so that updates, insertions, and deletions will trigger the insertion of change records into Δ^R. The other option is to populate Δ^R by extracting changes from the database engine's transaction log.

The trigger method is simpler to implement and it does not require knowledge of the database engine's log format. However, it has several disadvantages. One is that it expands the update footprint of any transaction that modifies R to include Δ^R. Thus, the transaction

138

can conflict with propagation queries (initiated by the **propagate** driver) that read the delta table. Note that if a materialized view depends on R, every propagation transaction will read either R or Δ^R. A more serious problem for the trigger-based approach is the generation of timestamps for the tuples in Δ^R. As was noted in Section 2, the timestamp of a delta tuple is supposed to identify the serialization order of the transaction that performed the change. In many systems (e.g., those that use two-phase locking for concurrency control), the serialization order of a transaction is not known until it commits. This means that a trigger that fires at the time of an insertion or deletion into R will not be able to attach an appropriate timestamp.

The prototype view maintenance implementation uses a tool called DB2 DataPropagator (DPropR) to populate the base delta tables directly from the transaction log. DPropR tags each delta tuple with a unique transaction identifier. In addition, DPropR maintains a separate global table, called the *unit-of-work* table, which maps the identifier of each relevant transaction to its commit sequence number and commit timestamp. Both the sequence number and the timestamp are consistent with the transaction serialization order, but the sequence numbers are unique, while commit timestamps may not be. DPropR populates the unit-of-work table as it encounters commit records of relevant transactions in the log. A transaction is relevant if it has made a change to one of the view's underlying tables.

The **propagate** process obtains commit sequence numbers and timestamps for the tuples in Δ^R by joining Δ^R with the unit-of-work table on the unique transaction identifier. Internally, **propagate** uses commit sequence numbers as "times". However, it records both a sequence number and a timestamp in each view delta tuple so that real times can be used to specify propagation intervals and materialized view states.

A similar approach might be possible in a trigger-based system if the database engine provides commit triggers. A commit trigger could potentially be used to record each transaction's serialization point in a unit-of-work table, provided that the trigger has some means of determining the serialization order. However, unless relevant transactions could somehow be identified, the unit-of-work table would have to record serialization times for all update transactions.

A related issue that must be addressed by the **propagate** process is how to determine the evaluation time of a propagation query. The function **Evaluate** used by **ComputeDelta** and **RollingPropagate** is expected to return the serialization time of the transaction in which the propagation query is evaluated. In the prototype, **propagate** determines the commit sequence number of such a transaction by forcing it to write a unique value into a special global table. The special table has an associated delta table, which is populated by DPropR. Once the transaction has completed, **propagate** waits for DPropR to capture its special table update. From the captured update, **propagate** can determine the maintenance query's transaction identifier. The unit-of-work table can then be used to determine its serialization time.

6 Related Work

Many view maintenance algorithms have been described. An overview of this work can be found in [6], which also discusses applications. The algorithms described in [3, 7, 4] are probably most closely related to the rolling propagation algorithm. The algorithms in [3] handle select/project/join views only, and require pre-update snapshots of the base table. Those of [7] handle a broader class of view definitions, including views with union, recursion, and negation, but they require both pre-update and post-update snapshots of the base tables. [4] presents algorithms for deferred maintenance of views that may involve union and difference operations in addition to select, project and join. All of these approaches are synchronous: incremental maintenance queries must see base tables either at the beginning of the propagation interval or at the end. [4] also proposes the decomposition of the view maintenance problem into separate propagate and apply phases. Another technique, based on multi-versioning, for reducing contention between materialized view updates and concurrent reads is presented in [10]. A description of the implementation of incremental view maintenance in a commercial relational database system can be found in [2].

The summary-delta table method was proposed in [8] for incremental maintenance of relational views that involve aggregation. A summary-delta table records the net change to an aggregate over a particular time window. The rolling propagation technique can be extended to support views with aggregation by using summary-delta tables.

Compensation as a view maintenance technique was proposed in [12]. The Eager Compensation Algorithm described in [12] operates in a warehousing environment in which the base tables and the materialized views are located in different systems. The warehouse (where the view is located) is notified explicitly of each update to the base tables. The warehouse responds to an update notification by issuing a maintenance query to compute incremental change necessary to reflect the update in the materialized view. If further updates occur while the maintenance query is pending, the warehouse modifies the maintenance queries for those updates so that the updates' effects on the pending queries will be compensated for. Compensation is also used in [13] and [1] in a more general environment in which the base tables may be distributed across several systems.

Self-maintainable views are views that can be incrementally maintained using only the base deltas, and not the base tables themselves. Self-maintainable views were introduced in [5], and [9] presents techniques for expanding materialized views so that they become self-maintainable.

7 Conclusion

Most incremental view maintenance techniques are synchronous. They tie the incremental refresh effort to the refresh time, since the base tables must be seen in a particular state. Compensation can be used to decouple the refresh effort from the refresh time, while the database continues to evolve.

Rolling propagation is a compensation-based technique for asynchronous incremental view maintenance. Unlike other compensation-based techniques, it provides explicit control over the granularity of the view maintenance transactions. Rolling propagation also completely decouples the propagation of a view changes from the application of those changes to the materialized view. Applications can control point-in-time refresh of the materialized view, while view delta propagation is tuned independently to suit the requirements of the underlying database system.

8 Acknowledgements

The authors would like to thank Beth Hamel, Hamid Pirahesh, Jay Shanmugasundaram, and Richard Sidle for their help and comments.

References

[1] D Agrawal, A. El Abbadi, A. Singh, and T. Yurek. Efficient view maintenance at data warehouses. In *Proceedings of the ACM SIGMOD International Conference on Management of Data*, pages 417–427, 1997.

[2] Randall Bello, Karl Dias, Alan Downing, James Feenan, Jim Finnerty, William Norcott, Harry Sun, Andrew Witkowski, and Mohamed Ziauddin. Materialized views in Oracle. In *Proceedings of the International Conference on Very Large Data Bases*, pages 659–664, 1998.

[3] José A. Blakeley, Per-Åke Larson, and Frank Wm. Tompa. Efficiently updating materialized views. In *Proceedings of the ACM SIGMOD International Conference on Management of Data*, pages 61–71, 1986.

[4] Latha S. Colby, Timothy Griffin, Leonid Libkin, Inderpal Singh Mumick, and Howard Trickey. Algorithms for deferred view maintenance. In *Proceedings of the ACM SIGMOD International Conference on Management of Data*, pages 469–480, 1996.

[5] Ashish Gupta, H. V. Jagadish, and Inderpal Singh Mumick. Data integration using self-maintainable views. In *International Conference on Extending Database Technology*, pages 140–144, 1996.

[6] Ashish Gupta and Inderpal Singh Mumick. Maintenance of materialized views: Problems, techniques, and applications. *Bulletin of the IEEE Technical Committee on Data Engineering*, 18(2):3–19, 1995.

[7] Ashish Gupta, Inderpal Singh Mumick, and V. S. Subrahmanian. Maintaining views incrementally. In *Proceedings of the ACM SIGMOD International Conference on Management of Data*, pages 157–167, 1993.

[8] Inderpal Singh Mumick, Dallan Quass, and Barinderpal Singh Mumick. Maintenance of data cubes and summary tables in a warehouse. In *Proceedings of the ACM SIGMOD International Conference on Management of Data*, pages 100–111, 1997.

[9] Dallan Quass, Ashish Gupta, Inderpal Singh Mumick, and Jennifer Widom. Making views self-maintainable for data warehousing. In *Conference on Parallel and Distributed Information Systems*, pages 158–169, 1996.

[10] Dallan Quass and Jennifer Widom. On-line warehouse view maintenance. In *Proceedings of the ACM SIGMOD International Conference on Management of Data*, pages 393–404, 1997.

[11] K. Salem, K. Beyer, B. Lindsay, and R. Cochrane. How to roll a join: Asynchronous incremental view maintenance. Technical Report CS-2000-6, Dept. of Computer Science, University of Waterloo, February 2000.

[12] Yue Zhuge, Hector Garcia-Molina, Joachim Hammer, and Jennifer Widom. View maintenance in a warehousing environment. In *Proceedings of the ACM SIGMOD International Conference on Management of Data*, pages 316–327, 1995.

[13] Yue Zhuge, Hector Garcia-Molina, and Janet Wiener. The strobe algorithms for multi-source warehouse consistency. In *Conference on Parallel and Distributed Information Systems*, 1996.

On Wrapping Query Languages and Efficient XML Integration*

Vassilis Christophides
Institute of Computer Science
FORTH, P.O. Box 1385
Heraklion, Greece
christop@csi.forth.gr

Sophie Cluet
INRIA Rocquencourt
BP 105, 78153
Le Chesnay Cedex, France
Sophie.Cluet@inria.fr

Jérôme Siméon
Bell Laboratories
600 Mountain Avenue
Murray Hill, NJ, USA
simeon@research.bell-labs.com

Abstract

Modern applications (Web portals, digital libraries, etc.) require integrated access to various information sources (from traditional DBMS to semistructured Web repositories), fast deployment and low maintenance cost in a rapidly evolving environment. Because of its flexibility, there is an increasing interest in using XML as a middleware model for such applications. XML enables fast wrapping and declarative integration. However, query processing in XML-based integration systems is still penalized by the lack of an algebra with adequate optimization properties and the difficulty to understand source query capabilities. In this paper, we propose an algebraic approach to support efficient XML query evaluation. We define a general purpose algebra suitable for semistructured or XML query languages. We show how this algebra can be used, with appropriate type information, to also wrap more structured query languages such as OQL or SQL. Finally, we develop new optimization techniques for XML-based integration systems.

1 Introduction

XML [6] is becoming widely used for the development of Web applications that require data integration (Web portals, e-commerce, etc). Although fashion surely accounts for some of XML's popularity, it is also justified on technical grounds. XML enables easy wrapping of external sources and declarative integration, thus allowing fast deployment and cheap maintenance of applications. Still, XML-based systems are not yet as efficient as traditional integration software [39, 8, 40, 26, 22, 7]. In this paper, we address this issue.

Let us consider an example to motivate the use of XML technology and the improvements we propose. In this example, we plan to build a Web site providing

*Project supported by OPAL (Esprit IV project 20377) and AQUARELLE (Telematics Application Program IE-2005).

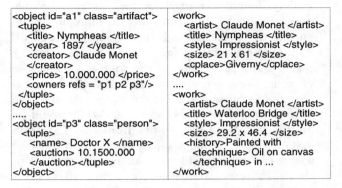

Figure 1: Sample XML Data for Cultural Goods

access to commercial information about cultural goods (e.g., www.christies.com). For this application, we need to integrate two sources: one, highly structured, is an object database containing trading information; the other is a partially structured document repository supporting full-text queries, that contains descriptive information about artistic work. Figure 1 shows some sample XML data exported from our sources.

There are several advantages in building this application with XML. First, due to its flexible data model, XML can represent both structured and semistructured information (see Figure 1). Second, it is easy to convert any data into XML, and to do so in a generic fashion (i.e., independently of the source schema). Third, several languages support declarative integration of XML data (e.g., MSL [31], StruQL [17] or YAT_L [13]). Finally, being a standard, XML facilitates interoperability. Yet, query processing in XML-based integration systems raises some hard issues.

- *Wrapping type information.* There are certainly many reasons why preserving type information is useful, but it is particularly important for query optimization [20]. Although most data management systems can now export data in XML, they usually don't provide the corresponding type information. This is mostly because XML's current form of typing (i.e., DTDs [6]) is not sufficient to capture rich type systems (e.g., an object database schema) or, conversely, partially structured documents (e.g., in Figure 1, `work`s might come with mandatory elements as well as elements not known in advance, like `history` or `cplace`). Several recent proposals (notably XML Schema [38]) are studying this issue, but no definitive standard is available yet. In [13], we introduced a type system, suitable to represent any mix of well-formed and valid XML data, that we will use in the rest of paper.

- *Wrapping source query capabilities.* Internet sources usually do not export data but, instead, provide query facilities. Thus, in order to integrate them, one needs to understand their "query language". This is also important for performance reasons: by pushing the processing to the sources as much as possible, the application avoids massive data transfers and reduces XML conversion overhead. The only technique proposed so far and that would be appropriate for XML, comes from the TSIMMIS system: query templates [33] are used to describe source capabilities. However, an exhaustive description of sources capabilities (i.e., find all possible queries given a schema) is not feasible with such templates. Moreover these imply a costly *ad hoc* development, in order to wrap an appropriate set of queries for each application.

- *Processing XML queries efficiently* in an integration context remains an open problem. A well-understood algebra that supports the peculiarities of XML languages is missing. Moreover, we need the ability to exploit partial type information and heterogeneous source capabilities.

In this paper, we propose an algebraic framework and optimization techniques to address the last two issues. More precisely, we make the following contributions:

An algebra for XML. We introduce an operational model based on a general-purpose algebra for XML. This algebra is expressive enough to capture most of the semantics of existing semistructured/XML or structured query languages.

A source description language. We show how this algebra can be used to wrap full text queries but also structured query languages such as OQL or SQL in a complete (i.e., as a query language and not as a set of queries) and generic (i.e., with no effort required from the application developer) way.

Query processing techniques. We show that our algebra is appropriate to optimize integration applications. Notably, we introduce new rewriting techniques for query composition, investigate the impact of type information during query processing and illustrate how query evaluation can take advantage of source query capabilities.

```
------------------------------------------------
logos{simeon}: o2-wrapper -server gringos.inria.fr \
                          -system cultural         \
                          -base art                \
                          -port 6066
  o2-wrapper is running at logos.inria.fr:6066
logos{simeon}:
------------------------------------------------
sappho{christop}: xmlwais-wrapper                  \
   -directory ~christop/wais-sources/museum.src \
   -port 6060
  xmlwais-wrapper is running at sappho.ics.forth.gr:6060
sappho{christop}:
------------------------------------------------
cosmos{cluet}: yat-mediator -port 6666
  yat-mediator is running at cosmos.inria.fr:6666
yat> connect o2artifact logos.inria.fr:6066;
yat> connect xmlartwork sappho.ics.forth.gr:6060;
yat> import o2artifact;
yat> import xmlartwork;
yat> load "/u/cluet/YAT/view1.yat";
```

Figure 2: Installing Wrappers and Mediators

The paper is organized as follows. Section 2 illustrates the advantages of XML integration by explaining the different steps required to build our example application with YAT, our home-brewed integration system. This section also recalls the specifics of the type system we are using. Section 3 introduces our algebra. The description language to wrap source query languages is presented in Section 4. We present the optimization techniques in Section 5 and conclude in Section 6.

2   XML integration with YAT

The YAT System is a semistructured data conversion system [13, 36] that we are currently turning in to a full-fledged XML integration system. It relies on a library of generic wrappers and a declarative integration language called YAT_L. Figure 2 illustrates the three steps required to setup our application example with YAT:

- *simeon* wraps the O_2 object database. For this, he simply needs to run the `o2-wrapper` program that can export structural information from any O_2 database (e.g., the `art` database) as well as the system query capabilities (i.e., it wraps OQL, as we will see in Section 4).

- *christop* wraps the cultural source with another generic wrapper. The `xmlwais` wrapper understands XML data, typed with our type system and full-text indexed by Wais [34]. It expects as parameter a standard Wais source configuration file (e.g., `museum.src`).

- *cluet* runs a `yat` mediator, connects both wrappers using the port numbers given by her fellow developers, imports the structural and query capabilities of the two connected system and loads her favorite integration program (e.g., `view1.yat`).

142

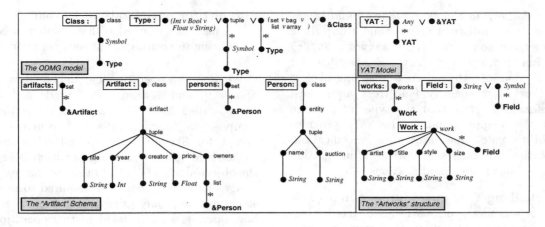

Figure 3: O_2, XML-Wais and YAT mediator structural metadata

Before taking a closer look at the integration program, we first give the structural information exported by each wrapper. Note that for interoperability reasons, wrappers and mediators communicate data, structures and operations in XML.

The YAT type system can represent structural information at various levels of genericity (model, schema, data). The relationship between these levels is captured through an *instantiation* mechanism that we recall here briefly (see [13] for more details). Figure 3 shows a graphical representation of the YAT model along with the type information imported by our wrappers.

The left hand-side of the figure represent the O_2 data model, that conforms to the ODMG standard [9], and the schema of our **art** database example. Note that (i) bold fonts denote pattern (i.e., tree) identifiers, (ii) the **&** symbol denotes references, (iii) the ⋆ and ∨ symbols denote respectively multiple occurrences and alternatives. Thus, an O_2 type is either an atomic type, a tuple, a collection or a reference to a class pattern. A tuple pattern is in turn a collection of sub-patterns, each associating an attribute name (*Symbol*) to its value. Below, the class **Artifact** is a concrete instantiation of a **Class**, whose value is a tuple with attributes **title**, **year**, etc. The lower right part of the figure represents the information exported by the **xmlwais** wrapper. Each document contains mandatory information (**artist**, etc), possibly followed by any additional **Field**s. This illustrates the ability of YAT type system to capture partially structured information.

Last, the top right part of Figure 3 shows a representation of YAT (meta)model, that captures all patterns. One important property is that the O_2 model, **Artifacts** schema, and **Artworks** structure are recognized as instances of this almighty model (in fact, we have **Artifact <: ODMG <: YAT**). We will see in Section 4 that query languages wrapping will also take advantage of this mechanism.

Integration programs in declarative languages are usually composed of a sequence of rules or queries [31, 17, 13], whose partial results are connected together through Skolem functions. We give bellow an example of a YAT_L query [19, 37], from our integration program **view1.yat**. This query construct a collection of documents (**artworks**), one per known artwork, each combining the information available in our two sources.

```
artworks() :=
    MAKE doc * &artwork($t,$c) :=
        work [ title: $t, artist: $a,
               year: $y, price: $p,
               style: $s, size: $si,
               owners *$o, more: $fields ]
    MATCH artifacts WITH
        set *class: artifact:
            tuple [ title: $t, year: $y,
                    creator: $c, price: $p,
                    owners: list *class: person:
                        tuple [ name: $o,
                                auction: $au] ],
        works WITH
            works *work [ artist: $a,
                    title: $t', style: $s,
                    size: $si, *($fields) ]
    WHERE $y > 1800 AND $c = $a AND $t = $t'
```

This query consists of three clauses. The **MATCH** clause performs pattern-matching: filters are used to navigate through the structure of data and to bind variables to information of interest (e.g., the artifact's title to variable $t, the list of optional XML elements to **$fields**). YAT_L's filtering mechanism relies on instantiation: if a tree is instance of a filter, then one can deduce a mapping between node values and variables. Otherwise, a type error occurs. Note that for unambiguous filters (i.e., involving unambiguous regular expressions), this can be done in polynomial time [4]. The **WHERE** clause fulfills the usual function. The **MAKE** clause constructs the result by creating a new pattern with the values returned by the previous clauses. In the example, we build a new `artwork` tree for each distinct artifact and group these subtrees under the `doc` node. Here, `artwork($t,$c)` is a Skolem function, creating a new tree identifiers for each distinct values of title and creator. Using Skolem functions allow us to identify (sub)trees and, thus, to create references. Note that the type information provided by the wrappers and by the YAT$_L$ program can be used to guide the integration specification, check application consistency or notify the integration administrator about source modifications.

Technical challenges in query processing. This illustrates the simplicity of XML-based integration. Apart from the quality of structural descriptions provided by YAT, other semistructured/XML systems (like TSIMMIS [32] or MIX [3]) would offer similar functionalities. Still, we have to evaluate user queries in an efficient way. As an invitation to proceed further, assume a user, after noticing some artworks with a creation place (`cplace`), issues the following query:

Q1: *What are the artifacts created at "Giverny"?*

MAKE $t
MATCH artworks **WITH** doc.work.[title.$t,
                                    more.cplace.$cl]
WHERE $cl = "Giverny"

In order to process **Q1**, we need to address several problems: how to compose it with the view definition (note that **Q1** accesses the semistructured fields of artwork documents), how to understand that only the XML-Wais source is needed to answer the query and how to exploit the Wais textual queries to avoid downloading all the documents.

3   YAT operational model and algebra

The choice of the operational model is essential: in the remainder of the paper, it will be used for the description of source capabilities as well as for query optimization. Moreover, it must support the following requirements:

Expressive power. It must capture the evaluation of existing languages, along with their XML-specific features. Notably complex pattern matching primitives with ordered navigation (like in XQL [35] or YAT$_L$), recursion and object creation.

Support for flexible typing. XML favors flexibility and most XML query languages are not typed. Yet, we also need to wrap structured languages. Thus, the operational model must support both flexible type filtering (for Lorel[1] or XML-QL[16]) and more strict forms of typing (for OQL [9]).

Support for optimization. Of course, we also need an algebra equipped with a number of equivalences offering interesting optimization opportunities.

We propose a operational model based on a functional approach, and a fixed set of predefined functions – the so-called YAT XML algebra. The model allows composition, function calls, and recursion. Note that except for Skolem functions, all other functions are without side-effects. The algebra itself is inspired from the object algebra of [14]. In this section, we present the newly introduced operators, required to deal with tree structures, and only briefly recall the others. We show how queries are translated in this operational model. Finally, we give an overview of alternative algebras.

3.1   YAT XML algebra

One of the main characteristics of XML data is that, like objects, it can be arbitrarily nested. Thus, we adopt a technique similar to that used for object-oriented algebras. Starting from an arbitrary XML structure, we apply an operator, called *Bind*, whose purpose is to extract the relevant information and produce a structure, called *Tab*, comparable to a ¬1NF relation. On these *Tab* structures, we can then apply the classical operators, such as *Join*, *Select*, *Project*, etc. Finally, an inverse operation to *Bind*, called *Tree*, can be used to generate a new nested XML structure.

The Bind operator extracts data from an input tree according to a given filter (i.e., a tree with distinct variables). It produces a table that contains the variable bindings resulting from the pattern-matching. On Figure 4, the *Bind* operation is applied on the tree representing the XML collection of works, with a filter that binds for each work its title (`$t`), artist (`$a`), style (`$s`), size (`$si`) and optional elements (note that, being on the edge, variable `$fields` will contain the *collection* of such elements). Note the similarity between the *Tab* structure and a ¬1NF relation. The *Bind* operator supports type filtering, vertical and horizontal navigation (through regular expressions – see `$fields` in our example). It can be expensive to evaluate, but we will see in Section 5.1 how to rewrite a *Bind* into more simple operations.

The Tree operator is applied on *Tab* structures and returns a collection of trees conforming to some input pattern. On Figure 4, the *Tree* operation is applied on the result of the previous *Bind* (where `F[$t,$a,$s,$si,$fields]` denotes the corresponding filter). The works are grouped according to the artists' names (with the grouping primitive `*($a)`), with each subtree containing the titles of their works.

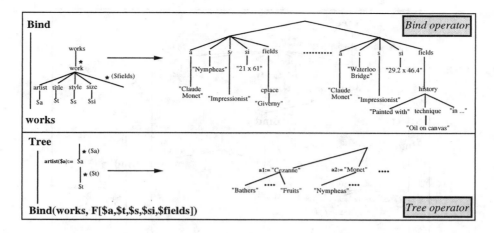

Figure 4: Bind and Tree operators

Skolem functions are used to create new identifiers and perform value assignment. In the previous example, `artist($a):=` creates an identifier for each artist name. Skolem functions do not create values but have side effects on the integrated view (as in [2]) and are somehow orthogonal to the rest of the algebra.

The other operators are those of the object algebra of [14]. *Select, Project, Join, Union, Intersection* come from relational. Classical object operations are: *Group, Sort, Map* and *D-Join* (for dependency join) which is used to navigate within nested collections. Their definition on *Tab* structures rather than collections of tuples is straightforward. We do not recall their definition here, but will explain their use whenever necessary. Except for the *Map*, these operators are always applied on the top level of a *Tab* structure (in a manner similar to the relational algebra). If one needs to go deeper, an extra *Bind* has to be applied.

As most of the algebra is composed of standard operators, we can take advantage of their well-known optimization properties and reuse rewriting techniques proposed in the object context (including relational ones or those for nested queries [14]). We can remark that *Bind* and *Tree* are two frontier operations that isolate XML-specific processing from more standard one. Last, by allowing recursive calls in the algebra (which was not the case of [14]), we can capture generalized path expressions (GPE) [11, 1]. The optimization of GPE is not addressed here (see [12, 20]).

An important aspect is that the YAT algebra is independent of any underlying physical access structure and can be used to reason about the evaluation of XML queries, whether the corresponding XML data are locally stored (e.g., in a document management system or an XML repository) or virtually accessed (e.g., through wrappers as in our context). In Section 5 we will present useful rewritings for both cases.

3.2 YAT$_L$ algebraic translation

Figure 5 shows the algebraic translation of the YAT$_L$ view definition presented in Section 2 and of query **Q1** (translation of other XML query languages would be performed in a similar manner[1]). It has been obtained using the following translation steps:

1. Named documents (e.g., `artifacts`) are the input operations of the algebraic expression.

2. Each **MATCH** statement translates into a *Bind* operation that captures its filtering/binding semantics, and creates a *Tab* structure for further processing.

3. Predicates involving various inputs translate into *Join* operations.

4. Other predicates in the **WHERE** clause translate into *Select* operations.

5. The **MAKE** clause translates into a *Tree* operation.

3.3 Related work

The Lore algebra [27] is a physical algebra, aimed at the optimization involving indexes. SAL [5] is a logical XML algebra, but it does not provide the appropriate expressive power either. The algebra of [18] is both logical and is sufficiently expressive. Yet, the relationship with our algebra is still unclear. For instance, they provide a simpler version of the Bind operator in terms of regular expression matching, while we will see that our more complex Bind can serve in exploiting source capabilities. Compared to object algebras, the *Bind* resembles the *Scan* operator of [15] (minus the condition, plus potentially complex patterns). An object algebra with side-effects operations similar to Skolem functions is presented in [2].

---

[1] Note that translating some particular features, like recursive structure preservation in XQL, would be more involved.

145

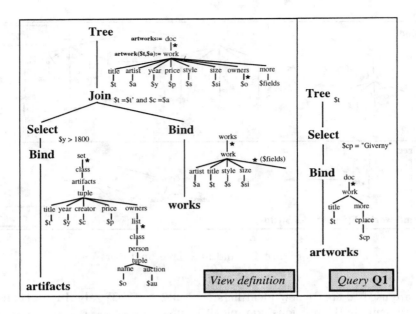

Figure 5: Algebraization of YAT$_L$ queries

4 Wrapping query capabilities

As we explained in Section 2, each wrapper exports its source capabilities. In this section, we explain how this information is communicated to the mediator. Moreover, we show how the combination of our operational model and type system allows to do it at the appropriate level of genericity: from full query languages (e.g., OQL on the ODMG model) to sets of queries (e.g., methods of an O$_2$ schema, textual predicates on XML elements).

Wrapping source operations in YAT is performed in two steps that concern (i) their signature and (ii) their semantics. The first step is necessary to be able to access the operation. For instance, let us assume that our O$_2$ schema features a specific method: `current_price` on class Artifact. It can be imported by the O$_2$ wrapper using the following XML syntax:

```
1    <operation kind="external" name="current_price">
2      <input><value model="Artifact_Schema"
3                    pattern="Artifact"/></input>
4      <output><leaf label=Float /></output>
5    </operation>
```

The **input** and **output** elements contain the signature: `current_price` takes an **Artifact** and returns a **Float**. This declaration is performed automatically by the O$_2$ wrapper with the help of the O$_2$ schema manager. Once the method is wrapped, it can be made available at the mediator.

The second step is only required for optimization purposes. In most cases, the wrapper performs both steps automatically. However, for the sources featuring operations not captured by the core operational model, the second step must be done manually. This issue is discussed in Section 5. Now, let us explain more precisely how to use all this to capture OQL and Wais.

4.1 Describing OQL capabilities

We consider here the description of OQL [9]. Obviously, SQL [28] can be described in a similar manner (even-though the wrapper's implementation is more complex due to the non-functional nature of SQL).

Capturing binding capabilities. YAT operational model borrows a large part of OQL algebra [14]. But if YAT captures OQL, the opposite is not true mostly for one reason: OQL binding capabilities are more restricted (e.g., it cannot query schema information). In order to take this restriction into account, we need to distinguish between *Bind* operations that can be actually evaluated by OQL and those that cannot, i.e., we need to understand which are the acceptable filters for OQL. Figure 6 (lines 2 to 33) shows such a specification of valid filters (that we call a *Fmodel*). The O$_2$ *Fpatterns* are nothing but an XML serialization of the type patterns of Figure 3, possibly annotated with flags (attributes **bind** and **inst**). When present, flags correspond to filter restrictions. A **bind** flag can be used to indicate that the corresponding node cannot contain a variable, or only a tree or label variable. A **inst** flag can be used to indicate that the corresponding label or edge must be completely instantiated (**ground** value) or left unchanged (**none** value). For instance, the filter for O$_2$ classes (**Fclass**, line 3) imposes that (i) only subtrees corresponding to actual O$_2$ objects or values can be bound (**bind="tree"**, line 4) (ii) extraction of class schema information is prevented (**bind="none"**,

```
1   <interface name="o2artifact">
2    <fmodel name="o2fmodel">
3     <fpattern name="Fclass">
4      <node label="class" bind="tree">
5      <node label="Symbol" bind="none" inst="ground">
6      <value pattern="Ftype"/></node></node>
7     </fpattern>
8     <fpattern name="Ftype">
9      <union>
10      <leaf label="Int"/>
11      <leaf label="Bool"/>
12      <leaf label="Float"/>
13      <leaf label="String"/>
14      <node label="tuple" col="set" bind="tree">
15       <star inst="ground">
16        <node label="Symbol" bind="none">
17        <value label="Ftype"/></node></star></node>
18      <node label="set" col="set" bind="tree">
19       <star inst="none"><value label="Ftype"/>
20       </star></node>
21      <node label="bag" col="bag" bind="tree">
22       <star inst="none"><value label="Ftype"/>
23       </star></node>
24      <node label="list" bind="tree">
25       <star inst="none"><value label="Ftype"/>
26       </star></node>
27      <node label="array" bind="tree">
28       <star inst="none"><value label="Ftype"/>
29       </star></node>
30      <ref pattern="Fclass"/>
31      </union>
32     </fpattern>
33    </fmodel>
34
35    <operation name="bind" kind="algebra">
36     <input>
37      <value model="o2model" pattern="Type"/>
38      <filter model="o2fmodel" pattern="Ftype"/></input>
39     <output><value model="yat" pattern="Tab"/></output>
40    </operation>
41    <operation name="select" kind="algebra"></operation>
42    <operation name="map" kind="algebra"></operation>
43    <operation name="eq" kind="boolean"></operation>
44   </interface>
```

Figure 6: O_2 Filter patterns and operational interface

line 5) and (iii) the name of the class in a schema specific filter has to be instantiated (`inst="ground"`, line 5).

OQL operations. Figure 6 also shows a large part of the operational interface exported by the O_2 wrapper (lines 35 to 43). Each operation has a **name** (**bind**, **eq**, etc) and a **kind** (**algebra**, **boolean**, **external**, etc).

The first declared algebraic operation is the *Bind* (line 35). Its signature has been *specialized* using the already exported *Fpattern* **Ftype** (line 8). The other algebraic operators that O_2 can evaluate follow (**select**, **map**, etc). We do not need to specialize their signatures as these operations are always applied on a *Tab* structure resulting from a *Bind*, i.e., on collection of tuples containing valid ODMG data. Note that an operation can be pushed only on some data imported by the source or on the result of a previously

pushed operation. Furthermore, all the arguments of the operation must be pushable. For instance, a selection can be pushed only with the predicates (e.g., =, <=, etc.)) or functions (e.g., the method **current_price**) that are understood by O_2. In the case of our integration example, the *Bind* and *Select* operations on the left-hand side of Figure 5 can be pushed to O_2 and translated by the wrapper into the following equivalent OQL query:

select t: A.title, y: A.year, c: A.creator, p: A.price,
          n: O.name, au: O.auction,
from A in artifacts, O in A.owners
where A.year > 1800

4.2 Describing Wais capabilities

For most sources, one of the basic operation is to ask for an entry point (a relation, a named object, a document, etc). However, even this seemingly simple operation is not always supported. For instance, many Web sites (e.g., search engines) are only accessible through form-based query interfaces and do not export their full content. For these sources, it is capital to understand the operations they supported even if these are not captured by the original YAT algebra.

Another apparently straightforward assumption is that you can retrieve what you query. Again, this is not always true. The Z39.50 [41] protocol (underlying the Wais retrieval engine and which is widely used for digital libraries) is based on attribute/value textual queries. This protocol establishes a clear separation between what you may retrieve and what you may query. For instance, one could specify that only the **artist** and **style** elements can be exported from our XML documents while allowing queries only on the optional fields [29]. This can be captured, thanks to the extensibility of our operational model, by declaring a predicate for each queried field and exporting them to the mediator.

Importing the query capabilities of an XML-Wais source. We now show how to wrap the full-text capabilities of our XML-Wais source ("signature" step), and how to declare a source-specific equivalence ("semantic" step). For the first step, we need to: (i) specify the source *Fpattern*s, (ii) declare support for *Bind* and *Select* operations, and (iii) declare the full-text predicate **contains** supplied by Wais. We give below the corresponding part of the interface:

```
1   <fmodel name="waisfmodel">
2    <fpattern name="Fworks">
3     <node label="works" bind="none" inst="ground">
4      <star inst="none">
5      <value pattern="work" bind="tree"/>
6      </star></node>
7     </fpattern>
```

```
8    </fmodel>
9
10   <operation name="bind" kind="algebra">
11    <input>
12     <value model="Artworks_Structure" pattern="works"/>
13     <filter model="waisfmodel" pattern="Fworks"/>
14    </input>
15    <output>
16     <value model="yat" pattern="Tab"/></output>
17   </operation>
18   <operation name="select" kind="algebra"></operation>
19   <operation name="contains" kind="external">
20    <input>
21     <value model="Artworks_Structure" pattern="Work"/>
22     <leaf label=String /></input>
23    <output><leaf label="Bool"/></output>
24   </operation>
```

Note that, as opposed to the O_2 interface, the *Fpattern* here is very restrictive: it only permits to bind subtrees corresponding to full documents (i.e., only **work** elements). Yet, not much has been achieved since the mediator does not know the semantics of the **contains** predicate, the only one that can be pushed to this source. Hopefully, some connection exists between **contains** and the equality predicate that exists in our algebra. More precisely, a query asking for works by impressionist artists could be evaluated by (i) a full-text search for works containing the string "impressionist" followed by (ii) a standard evaluation of the equality predicate within the mediator. This is expressed with the following equivalence, that we give here in a more readable form than its original in XML:

```
Select($x=$y, Bind(works, works*work[F($x)]))==
Select($x=$y,Select(contains($w,$y),
      Bind(works, works*work($w)[F($x)])))
```

As expected, the equivalence states that starting from a selection with equality over the result of a Bind (F($x) denotes here an arbitrary sub-filter with a variable **x**), one can add a more general **contains** predicate over the root of the document ($w).

4.3   Related work

In Garlic [24], source capabilities are coded by the programmer within the corresponding wrapper. They remain unknown to the optimizer, that must communicate with the wrappers at optimization/evaluation time to know what part of the query has been accepted and what remains to be processed. In Disco [39, 25], the description of source operations is not typed, which entails extra work for the optimizer in order to match the generated plans against the imported query descriptions. In TSIMMIS [33], optimization opportunities are reduced since the interface language is capable of describing only sets of queries rather than full query languages. To the best of our knowledge, YAT is the only system allowing a generic and complete description of query capabilities for structured sources in such an heterogeneous environment.

5   Optimizing with query capabilities

As pointed out earlier in the paper, optimization techniques from relational and object databases [23, 14] can be applied directly on the corresponding operations in our algebra. In this section, we introduce rewriting techniques for the new *Bind* and *Tree* operators.

5.1   XML queries and Bind rewriting

The *Bind* operation captures some of the most powerful features of XML query languages, like vertical and horizontal navigation, and type filtering. As it is a potentially expensive operation, it is crucial to understand how to simplify and/or rewrite a *Bind*. First, a simpler *Bind* has a better chance to be pushed to a source. Moreover, *Bind* entails navigation that can be costly and should be transformed into more traditional associative access.

Bind and vertical navigation

The upper left part of Figure 7 shows the binding operation over **artifacts**, taken out from the algebraic translation of our view definition (Figure 5). This *Bind* corresponds to a vertical navigation from the set of artifacts down to their local attributes (e.g., **title**) and further down to the information contained in their associated set of owners. Navigation through nested collections is usually captured in object algebras by a join whose right input depends on the left (i.e., *DJoin* in our algebra [14]). Hence, the equivalence between *Bind* and *Djoin* shown in the upper middle part of the figure is not surprising: we can see how *Bind* can be split into more elementary ones, connected through a *DJoin*[2]. As a reward, we can apply classic *DJoin* rewritings and transform navigation into associative access: for instance, in the upper right part of the figure we exploit the **persons** extent to transform the *DJoin* into a standard *Join* supporting more efficient evaluation algorithms.

A complex *Bind* can always be splitted into elementary *Bind*s (i.e., with only one-level deep filters), connected together through *DJoin*s. Another possibility is to split a complex *Bind* into a linear sequence of elementary ones, each one navigating down the result of the previous one. The lower left part of Figure 7 illustrates this rewriting on the *Bind* operation over **artworks** (part of the **Q1** algebraic expression given in Figure 5). Among other things, this rewriting is useful to simplify query compositions or push some evaluation to a source.

Bind, horizontal navigation and type filtering

The absence of type information is usually bad news. Indeed, when a *Bind* operation features a complex filter and no structural information is available, the only

---

[2]Note the introduction of the new variable **$x** that is removed afterwards by a projection.

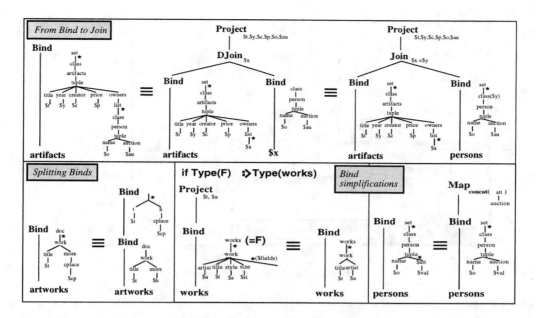

Figure 7: Algebraic Equivalences

evaluation strategy is to navigate through the whole data graph. This is usually what happens in purely semistructured systems. In this case, adding specialized indexes, like in [27], is the only way to achieve reasonable performances. Hopefully, we often have more interesting opportunities, using type information about the data (coming from the source) or the filter (coming from the query). This is particularly useful for queries mixing structured and semistructured data.

Semistructured queries over structured data

By semistructured queries, we mean queries that access both structure and content, e.g., by using tag variables or flexible type filtering. To illustrates this scenario, the lower right part of Figure 7 retrieves the attribute names of **person** objects. Because we have precise type information (see Figure 3), we can simplify the filter, as shown on Figure 7. Note this resembles rewriting techniques for generalized path expressions [12, 20]. This rewriting has several benefits, the most obvious of which being that the *Bind* operation can now be pushed to O₂!

Structured queries over semistructured data

Consider the partially structured XML artworks of our example and assume a user is only interested in the **title** and **artist** elements of artifacts. As illustrated on the lower middle part of Figure 7, this corresponds to a projection that can be used to rewrite the *Bind* operation and simplify the query. Doing so, we must be careful not to change the type filtering semantics of the *Bind*: a sufficient condition for the equivalence to hold is for the type of **works** to be an instance of the type of the filter.

5.2 XML views and Tree-Bind rewriting

The *Tree* operation captures the restructuring semantics of a query or view definition: it features grouping and sorting which are typically expensive operations. A *Tree* can be rewritten as sequence of *Group*, *Sort* and nested *Map* operations, on which existing optimization techniques can be used [14, 10]. Nevertheless, the evaluation of a *Tree* will remain costly if applied on a large amount of data. This is usually not the case with user queries, but may occur when constructing the view. Thus, it is very important to eliminate intermediate *Tree* operations resulting from the composition of queries with the view definition.

It is now time to go back to the evaluation of query **Q1** (see page 4). The left part of Figure 8 presents the algebraic translation of **Q1** composed with the view definition. This complex expression corresponds to a naive evaluation strategy in which the view is materialized, then the query evaluated on the result. Fortunately, our XML algebra comes equipped with all the equivalences we need to rewrite it into the expression on the right part of the figure. Due to space limitations, we only sketch the optimization process here (see [36] for more details).

The first essential step, illustrated by arrows in Figure 8, is to get rid of the *Bind-Tree* sequence that appears at the frontier between view definition and query. To do so, we first use *Bind*-Split equivalence given in Figure 7: this introduces an instantiation relationship between the filters of the lower *Bind* and of the *Tree*. Given this relationship, a second equivalence can be used to rewrite the *Bind-Tree* sequence in a simple projection with renaming. We are now mostly dealing with operations on which standard rewritings

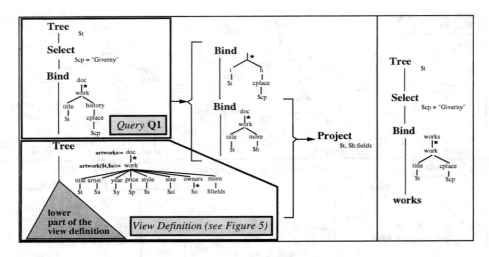

Figure 8: Optimization of Q1

apply. Because all artifacts are available in the XML source, we can push the projection down and: (i) eliminate the branch corresponding to the O_2 source, (ii) simplify the *Bind* on the XML source. Finally, using the *Bind*-Split equivalence in the other way, we can merge the remaining filters to obtain the final expression. Note that we could further optimize the query by using the XML source full text capabilities: this is the subject of the next section.

5.3   Capability-based rewriting

Exploiting source capabilities during query processing is definitely the most important technique in a distributed context. Indeed, pushing some of the query evaluation to an external source allows: to reduce the processing time by using source specific indexes or similar fast access structures; to minimize the communication costs between the sources and the mediator, as well as the conversion costs to the middleware model; to limit the system resources (e.g., memory) required by the mediator; and to benefit from possible parallelism introduced by remote query execution. The next example shows how description of source capabilities from Section 4 can be used during optimization.

Q2: *Which impressionist artworks are sold for less than 200,000.00?*

MAKE   *answer [title:$t, artist:$a, price:$p]
MATCH works **WITH** doc *work [title:$t,artist:$a,
                                   price: $p,style: $s]
WHERE $p < 200000 **AND** $s = "Impressionist"

The algebraic translation of the query is shown on the left-hand side of Figure 9, along with the equivalence that transforms the *Bind-Tree* sequence into a *Project* operation. The optimized version, shown on the right-hand side, would be evaluated in the following way: first, the XML-Wais source (lower left

part) is asked for all artworks containing the string "Impressionist". Next, a second *Bind* is applied to extract the `title`, `artist` and `style` elements from the selected artworks. Then, *for each* pair of title and artist, the O_2 source is called to retrieve the corresponding artifact information. This aspect is due to the *Djoin* operation that corresponds to a nested loop evaluation with values of variables `$t` and `$a` passed from the left-hand side to the right-hand side. Such "information passing" is a classical technique in distributed query optimization [30, 21].

Now, to obtain this plan, the optimizer performs several rounds of rewritings. The first round is quite similar to the one we gave for query **Q1**: after the *Bind-Tree* simplification, the projection is used to simplify the *Bind* on each source and selections are pushed. The goal of the second round of rewritings is to push as much evaluation as possible to the sources. On the O_2 side, little work is required since, as explained in Section 4.1, both *Bind* and selection can be trivially transformed into an OQL query. On the XML-Wais side, the optimizer tries to match the *Bind* operation with the Wais capabilities that have been declared. As, the only possibility is to push a simple *Bind* on XML documents along with a `contains` predicate, the optimizer: (i) introduces a *Select* with `contains` and (ii) splits the *Bind* to match the Wais capabilities description. The first step requires the equivalence declared in Section 4.2, connecting the selection with equality and the selection with `contains`. The second step simply uses the *Bind*-Split equivalence given in Figure 7. Finally, a last round of optimization determines possible information passing between sources and it is based on standard rewritings between *Joins* and *Djoins*.

6   Summary

We have presented a framework for efficient query evaluation in XML integration systems. It relies on

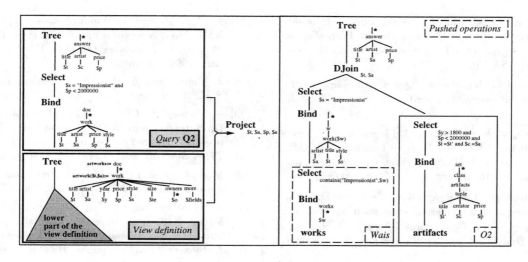

Figure 9: Algebraic translation and optimization of **Q2**

a general purpose XML algebra that captures the expressive power of semistructured or XML query languages and that can be used to wrap structured languages such as OQL or SQL. This algebra comes with equivalences to optimize of query compositions, to exploit type information and to push query evaluation to the external source. This work takes place within the context of the YAT System [36], currently developed at Bell Labs and INRIA[3]. The new XML version of the system, with its algebraic evaluation engine, is running and stable. The implementation of the optimizer is still on-going, based on heuristics and a simple linear search strategy consisting of the three rewriting rounds presented in last section.

References

[1] S. Abiteboul, D. Quass, J. McHugh, J. Widom, and J. L. Wiener. The lorel query language for semistructured data. *International Journal on Digital Libraries*, 1(1):68–88, Apr. 1997.

[2] S. Amer-Yahia, S. Cluet, and C. Delobel. Bulk loading techniques for object databases and an application to relational data. In *Proceedings of International Conference on Very Large Databases (VLDB)*, New York, Aug. 1998.

[3] C. K. Baru, A. Gupta, B. Ludäscher, R. Marciano, Y. Papakonstantinou, P. Velikhov, and V. Chu. XML-based information mediation with MIX. In *Proceedings of ACM SIGMOD Conference on Management of Data*, pages 597–599, Philadelphia, Pennsylvania, June 1999. Demonstration.

[4] C. Beeri and T. Milo. Schemas for integration and translation of structured and semi-structured data. In *Proceedings of International Conference on Database Theory (ICDT)*, Lecture Notes in Computer Science, Jerusalem, Israel, Jan. 1999.

[5] C. Beeri and Y. Tzaban. SAL: An algebra for semistructured data and XML. In *International Workshop on the Web and Databases (WebDB'99)*, Philadelphia, Pennsylvania, June 1999.

[6] T. Bray, J. Paoli, and C. M. Sperberg-McQueen. Extensible markup language (XML) 1.0. W3C Recommendation, Feb. 1998. http://www.w3.org/TR/REC-xml/.

[7] P. Buneman, S. B. Davidson, K. Hart, G. C. Overton, and L. Wong. A data transformation system for biological data sources. In *Proceedings of International Conference on Very Large Databases (VLDB)*, pages 158–169, Zurich, Switzerland, Sept. 1995.

[8] M. J. Carey, L. M. Haas, P. M. Schwarz, M. Arya, W. F. Cody, R. Fagin, M. Flickner, A. Luniewski, W. Niblack, D. Petkovic, J. Thomas II, J. H. Williams, and E. L. Wimmers. Towards heterogeneous multimedia information systems: The garlic approach. In *Research Issues in Data Engineering*, pages 124–131, Los Alamitos, California, Mar. 1995.

[9] R. G. Cattell. *The Object Database Standard: ODMG 2.0*. Morgan Kaufmann, 1997.

[10] S. Chaudhuri and K. Shim. Including group-by in query optimization. In *Proceedings of International Conference on Very Large Databases (VLDB)*, pages 354–366, Santiago de Chile, Chile, Sept. 1994.

[11] V. Christophides, S. Abiteboul, S. Cluet, and M. Scholl. From structured documents to novel query facilities. In *Proceedings of ACM SIGMOD Conference on Management of Data*, pages 313–324, Minneapolis, Minnesota, May 1994.

[12] V. Christophides, S. Cluet, and G. Moerkotte. Evaluating queries with generalized path expressions. In *Proceedings of ACM SIGMOD Conference on Management of Data*, pages 413–422, Montreal, Canada, June 1996.

[13] S. Cluet, C. Delobel, J. Siméon, and K. Smaga. Your mediators need data conversion! In *Proceedings of ACM SIGMOD Conference on Management of Data*, pages 177–188, Seattle, Washington, June 1998.

---

[3]http://www-rocq.inria.fr/~simeon/YAT/

[14] S. Cluet and G. Moerkotte. Nested queries in object bases. In *Proceedings of International Workshop on Database Programming Languages*, pages 226–242, New York City, USA, Aug. 1993.

[15] S. Cluet and G. Moerkotte. Query processing in the schemaless and semistructured context. unpublished, 1996.

[16] A. Deutsch, M. F. Fernandez, D. Florescu, A. Y. Levy, and D. Suciu. XML-QL: A query language for XML. Submission to the World Wide Web Consortium, Aug. 1998. http://www.w3.org/TR/NOTE-xml-ql/.

[17] M. F. Fernandez, D. Florescu, A. Y. Levy, and D. Suciu. Warehousing and incremental evaluation for web site management. In *Proceedings of 14^{ièmes} Journées Bases de Données Avancées*, Hammamet, Tunisie, Oct. 1998.

[18] M. F. Fernandez, J. Siméon, D. Suciu, and P. Wadler. A data model and algebra for XML query. Communication to the W3C, Jan. 2000.

[19] M. F. Fernandez, J. Siméon, and P. Wadler (editors). XML query languages: Experiences and exemplars. Communication to the W3C, Sept. 1999.

[20] M. F. Fernandez and D. Suciu. Optimizing regular path expressions using graph schemas. In *Proceedings of IEEE International Conference on Data Engineering (ICDE)*, Orlando, Florida, Feb. 1998.

[21] D. Florescu, A. Y. Lévy, I. Manolescu, and D. Suciu. Query optimization in the presence of limited access patterns. In *Proceedings of ACM SIGMOD Conference on Management of Data*, Philadelphia, Pennsylvania, May 1999. to appear.

[22] G. Gardarin, S. Gannouni, B. Finance, P. Fankhauser, W. Klas, D. Pastre, R. Legoff, and A. Ramfos. IRO-DB : A distributed system federating object and relational databases. In *Object Oriented Multibase Systems : A Solution for Advanced Applications*. Prentice Hall, 1995.

[23] G. Graefe. Query evaluation techniques for large databases. *ACM Computing Surveys*, 25(2):73–170, June 1993.

[24] L. M. Haas, D. Kossmann, E. L. Wimmers, and J. Yang. Optimizing queries across diverse data sources. In *Proceedings of International Conference on Very Large Databases (VLDB)*, pages 276–285, Athens, Greece, Aug. 1997.

[25] O. Kapitskaia, A. Tomasic, and P. Valduriez. Dealing with discrepancies in wrapper functionality. In *Actes des 13^{ièmes} Journées Bases de Données Avancées (BDA'97)*, pages 327–349, Grenoble, France, Sept. 1997.

[26] L. Liu, C. Pu, and Y. Lee. An adaptive approach to query mediation across heterogeneous information sources. In *Proceedings of International Conference on Cooperative Information Systems (CoopIS)*, pages 144–156, Brussels, Belgium, June 1996.

[27] J. McHugh and J. Widom. Query optimization for XML. In *Proceedings of International Conference on Very Large Databases (VLDB)*, Edinburgh, Scotland, Aug. 1999. to appear.

[28] J. Melton and A. R. Simon. *Understanding the New SQL: A complete Guide*. Morgan Kaufmann, 1993.

[29] A. Michard, V. Christophides, M. Scholl, M. Stapleton, D. Sutcliffe, and A.-M. Vercoustre. The aquarelle resource discovery system. *Computer Networks and ISDN Systems*, 30(13):1185–1200, Aug. 1998.

[30] M. T. Özsu and P. Valduriez. *Principles of Distributed Database Systems*. Prentice Hall, 1991.

[31] Y. Papakonstantinou, S. Abiteboul, and H. Garcia-Molina. Object fusion in mediator systems. In *Proceedings of International Conference on Very Large Databases (VLDB)*, pages 413–424, Bombay, India, Sept. 1996.

[32] Y. Papakonstantinou, H. Garcia-Molina, and J.Widom. Object exchange across heterogeneous information sources. In *Proceedings of IEEE International Conference on Data Engineering (ICDE)*, pages 251–260, Taipei, Taiwan, Mar. 1995.

[33] Y. Papakonstantinou, A. Gupta, H. Garcia-Molina, and J. D. Ullman. A query translation scheme for rapid implementation of wrappers. In *Proceedings International Conference on Deductive and Object-Oriented Databases (DOOD)*, volume 1013 of *Lecture Notes in Computer Science*, pages 97–107. Springer-Verlag, Singapore, Dec. 1995.

[34] U. Pfeifer. *freeWAIS-sf*. University of Dortmund, 0.5 edition, Oct. 1995.

[35] J. Robie, J. Lapp, and D. Schach. XML query language (XQL). Workshop on XML Query Languages, Dec. 1998. W3C.

[36] J. Siméon. *Intégration de sources de données hétérogènes (Ou comment marier simplicité et efficacité)*. PhD thesis, Université de Paris XI, Jan. 1999.

[37] J. Siméon and S. Cluet. Design issues in XML languages: A unifying perspective. Draft manuscript, Oct. 1999.

[38] H. S. Thompson, D. Beech, M. Maloney, and N. Mendelsohn. XML schema parts 1: Structures. W3C Working Draft, Sept. 1999.

[39] A. Tomasic, L. Raschid, and P. Valduriez. Scaling heterogeneous databases and the design of disco. In *Proceedings of the 16th International Conference on Distributed Computing Systems*, pages 449–457, Hong Kong, May 1996.

[40] L.-L. Yan, M. T. Özsu, and L. Liu. Accessing heterogeneous data through homogenization and integration mediators. In *Proceedings of International Conference on Cooperative Information Systems (CoopIS)*, Charleston, South Carolina, June 1997.

[41] Information retrieval (z39.50): Application service definition and protocol specification. NISO Press, Bethesda, MD, 1995. ANSI/NISO Z39.50-1995.

XMill: an Efficient Compressor for XML Data

Hartmut Liefke*
Univ. of Pennsylvania
liefke@seas.upenn.edu

Dan Suciu
AT&T Labs
suciu@research.att.com

Abstract

We describe a tool for compressing XML data, with applications in data exchange and archiving, which usually achieves about twice the compression ratio of gzip at roughly the same speed. The compressor, called XMill, incorporates and combines existing compressors in order to apply them to heterogeneous XML data: it uses zlib, the library function for gzip, a collection of datatype specific compressors for simple data types, and, possibly, user defined compressors for application specific data types.

1 Introduction

We have implemented a compressor/decompressor for XML data, to be used in data exchange and archiving, that achieves about twice the compression rate of general-purpose compressors (gzip), at about the same speed. The tool can be downloaded from www.research.att.com/sw/tools/xmill/.

XML is now being adopted by many organizations and industry groups, like the healthcare, banking, chemical, and telecommunications industries. The attraction in XML is that it is a self-describing data format, using tags to mark individual data items. However, there are some serious concerns about exporting one's data into XML. Since XML data is irregular and verbose, it can impact both query processing and data exchange. Many applications (e.g. Web logs, biological data, etc) use other, specialized data formats to archive and exchange data, which are much more economical than XML. As a self-describing format XML brings flexibility, but compromises efficiency.

In this paper we show how to exploit XML's self describing nature to gain in compression. We describe

---

*This work was done while the author was visiting AT&T Labs.

a compressor (XMill) and a decompressor (XDemill) whose architecture leverages existing compressing algorithms and tools to XML data: XMill uses zlib (the library function version of gzip), a few simple, data type specific compressors, and can be further extended with user-defined compressors for complex, application specific data types. The idea in XMill is that it uses the XML tags to decide which compression algorithm to apply.

While experimenting with XMill we made a striking discovery. By migrating data from other, more space-efficient formats to XML, the size of the compressed data decreases. Many such formats are in use today, for biological data, for Web logs, etc. In each case the data is stored in a simple (but application specific) format, usually designed to be reasonably space-efficient for the application at hand. When translated into XML the data expands, mainly because XML tags are verbose and must be repeated; gzip compresses the XML data pretty well, but it is still larger than the original gzipped data. With XMill however, the XML data is compressed better than the original gzipped data, almost to half the size. Thus, by making the data self-describing, one improves compression. Of course, the same kind of compression could be applied to the original format, but one has to write a specific compressor for each format. In summary, by converting to XML, one gains both flexibility and efficiency (when compression is used).

Our compressor, XMill, applies **three principles** to compress XML data:

Separate structure from data The *structure*, consisting of XML tags and attributes, is compressed separately from the *data*, which consists of a sequence of data items (strings) representing element contents and attribute values.

Group related data items Data items are grouped into *containers*, and each container is compressed separately. For example, all <name> data items form one container, while all <phone> items form a second container. This is a generalization of *column-wise compression* in relational databases (see e.g. [10]).

Apply semantic compressors Some data items are text or numbers, while others may be DNA sequences. XMill applies specialized compressors (*semantic compressors*) to different containers.

An original component of XMill are the *container expressions*, a concise language used for grouping data items in containers, and for choosing the right combination of semantic compressors.

Applicability and limitations The compressor described here has two limitations. The first is that it is not designed to work in conjunction with a query processor. Our targeted applications are data exchange, where compression is used to better utilize network bandwidth, and data archiving, where compression is used to reduce space requirement. A second limitation of XMill is that it wins over existing techniques only if the data set is large, typically over 20KB, because of the additional bookkeeping overhead and the fact that small data containers are poorly compressed by gzip. Hence it is of limited or no use in XML messaging, where many small-sized XML messages are exchanged between applications.

Contributions In this paper, we make the following contributions.

- We describe an extensible architecture for an XML compressor that leverages existing compression techniques and semantic compressors to XML data.

- We describe container expressions, a brief yet powerful language for grouping data items according to their semantics, and specifying combined semantic compressors. We present an efficient implementation technique for the path language, which dramatically improves performance for deeply nested data.

- We evaluate XMill on several real data sets and show that it achieves best overall compression rates among several popular compressors. Furthermore, we show that by using XMill one decreases the size of the compressed data by migrating from other data formats to XML.

The paper is organized as follows. Sec. 2 describes two motivating examples. Sec. 3 provides background about compression techniques and gives an information-theoretic justification for our approach to XML compression. The architecture of XMill, the container expression language and semantic compressors are described in Sec. 4. In Sec. 5 we show how to make XMill scalable and to achieve compression/decompression times competitive with gzip. Sec. 6 describes experimental results, which we discuss in Sec. 7. We describe related work in Sec. 8 and conclude in Sec. 9.

2 Motivating Example

We start by illustrating with a very simple, but quite useful example: Web Log files. Virtually every Web server logs its traffic, for security purposes, and this data can be (and often is) analyzed. Each line in the log file represents an HTTP request. A typical entry in such a log file is[1]:

```
202.239.238.16|GET / HTTP/1.0|text/html|200|
1997/10/01-00:00:02|-|4478|-|-|http://www.net.jp/|
Mozilla/3.1[ja](I)
```

Different formats are currently in use: in our example we use a variation on Apache's *Custom Log Format*[2]. Each line is a record with eleven fields delimited by |: host, request line, content type, etc. Hence, the file's structure is very simple, with records with a fixed number of variable-length fields[3].

Collected over long periods of time, Web logs can take huge amounts of space. In our example we only considered a file with 100000 entries as the one above. Its size is almost 16MB, and gzip shrinks it to 1.6MB:

weblog.dat: **15.9MB**   weblog.dat.gz: **1.6MB**

Applications processing such Web logs are brittle, and in general not portable, since different vendors use different formats. To gain flexibility, we may consider converting the Web log into XML with the following format:

```
<apache:entry>
 <apache:host>202.239.238.16</apache:host>
 <apache:requestLine>GET / HTTP/1.0</apache:requestLine>
 <apache:contentType>text/html</apache:contentType>
 <apache:statusCode>200</apache:statusCode>
 <apache:date>1997/10/01-00:00:02</apache:date>
 <apache:byteCount>4478</apache:byteCount>
 <apache:referer>http://www.net.jp/</apache:referer>
 <apache:userAgent>Mozilla/3.1[ja](I)</apache:userAgent>
</apache:entry>
```

Applications are now easier to write. However the size increases substantially:

weblog.xml: **24.2MB**   weblog.xml.gz: **2.1MB**

Our goal is to gain from XML's flexibility without using more space. An obvious idea is to assign integer codes (1, 2, 3, ...) to the XML tags, and use a single character for closing tags. A more interesting idea is to separate the XML tags (encoded as numbers) from the data values, and compress with gzip independently the tags and the data values. We save space, because the XML tags are the same for each record, and gzip can encode this very efficiently (see Sec. 3.2). With XMill this effect is accomplished by command line:[4] xmill -p // weblog.xml. This brings the size down to:

---

[1]This is one line in the log file.
[2]http://www.apache.org/docs/mod/mod_log_config.html
[3]Missing values are common and are indicated by -.
[4]Sec. 4.2 describes XMill's command line.

```
                        ...
-p//apache:host=>seq(u8 "." u8 "." u8 "." u8)
-p//apache:byteCount=>u
-p//apache:contentType=>e
-p//apache:requestLine=>seq("GET " rep("/" e) " HTTP/1.0")
                        ...
```

Figure 1: Semantic compressor settings `settings.pz`.

weblog1.xmi: **1.75MB**

The next idea is to compress data values separately, based on their tags: that is, all host values are compressed together, all request lines are compressed together, etc.

This behavior is the default and is achieved using the command line `xmill weblog.xml`. Since gzip achieves better compression when applied to values of similar types, this reduces the size even further:

weblog2.xmi: **1.33MB**

We now use less space than the original gzipped file.

We can do quite a lot better than that. The idea is to inspect carefully each field and use a specialized compressor for it. For example the `<apache:host>` is usually (or always) an IP address, hence can be stored as four unsigned bytes; most entries in `<apache:requestLine>` start with GET and end in HTTP/1.0 (some in HTTP/1.1): these substrings can be factored out. Other improvements are also possible. We analyzed eight of the eleven fields and applied specialized compressors available in `XMill`. The corresponding `XMill` command line is:

```
xmill -f settings.pz weblog.xml
```

where some parts of file `settings.pz` are shown in Fig. 1 (specialized compressors are described in Sec. 4.3). This reduces the compressed size to:

weblog3.xmi: **0.82MB**

Note that this is about half the original gzipped file. This achieves our goal: the compressed XML-ized data can be stored in less space than the compressed original data, while applications gain in flexibility[5].

The Web log is a simple example illustrating column-wise compression applied to XML. The second example is much more complex. SwissProt is a well-maintained database for representing protein structure [6]. It uses a specific data format, called EMBL [8], for representing information about genes and proteins (not shown here for lack of space). We converted the original EMBL data into XML as shown in Fig. 2.

We repeated the experiments above on a fragment of the SwissProt data[7]. The original file had 98MB and

---

[5]Of course, an application has to decompress the data first.
[6]http://www.expasy.ch/sprot/
[7]We omitted comments and the actual DNA sequence, which can be compressed using specialized compressors.

```
<Entry id="108_LYCES" mtype="PRT" seqlen="102">
 <AC>Q43495</AC>
 <Mod dat="15-JUL-1999" Rel="38" typ="Created"></Mod>
 <Mod dat="15-JUL-1999" Rel="38" typ="Last SeqUpd"></Mod>
 <Mod dat="15-JUL-1999" Rel="38" typ="Last AnnUpd"></Mod>
 <Descr>PROTEIN 108 PRECURSOR</Descr>
 <Species>Lycopersicon esculentum (Tomato)</Species>
 <Org>Eukaryota</Org> ... <Org>Solanum</Org>
 <Ref num="1" pos="SEQUENCE FROM N.A">
  <Comment>STRAIN=CV. VF36</Comment>
  <MedlineID>94143497</MedlineID>
  <Author>CHEN R</Author> <Author>SMITH A.G</Author>
  <Cite>Plant Physiol. 101:1413-1413(1993)</Cite>
 </Ref>
...
<EMBL prim_id="Z14088" sec_id="CAA78466"></EMBL>
<MENDEL prim_id="8853" sec_id="LYCes"></MENDEL>
<Keyword>Signal</Keyword>
<Features>
 <SIGNAL from="1" to="30">  <Descr>POTENTIAL</Descr>
 </SIGNAL>
 <CHAIN from="31" to="102">  <Descr>PROTEIN 108</Descr>
 </CHAIN>
  ...
</Features>
</Entry>
```

Figure 2: XML Representation of SwissProt entry

the XML-ized version had 165MB. gzip reduces the files to 16MB and 19MB, respectively:

sprot.dat:	**98MB**	sprot.xml:	**165MB**
sprot.dat.gz:	**16MB**	sprot.xml.gz:	**19MB**

Repeating the three steps above we obtained the following improvements in size:

sprot1.xmi:	**15MB**
sprot2.xmi:	**11MB**
sprot3.xmi:	**8.6MB**

Note that the last file is obtained after fine-tuning `XMill` on the SwissProt data.

In both examples the three steps correspond precisely to the compression principles spelled out in Sec. 1. As the examples suggests, each principle contributes with a significant improvement.

3 Background

3.1 XML

For the purpose of this paper, an XML document consists of three kinds of tokens: tags, attributes, and data values. As usual we model an XML document as a tree: nodes are labeled with tags or attributes, and leaves are labeled with data values. The *path* to a data value is the sequence of tags (and, possible one attribute) from the root to the data value node.

3.2 Compressors

General Purpose Compressors Most practical dictionary compressors are derived from the LZ (Ziv and Lempel) family of compressors. The idea in the original

LZ77 [20] is to replace repeating sequences in the input text with a pointer to a previous occurrence. We refer the reader to [2] for a good introduction, but only mention here one important property of LZ77 that we exploited in XMill. Namely a large number of repetitions of the same sequence, like A B C A B C ...A B C are compressed extremely well, essentially as a run length encoding storing only one copy of A B C, its length, and a repetition count.

The popular general-purpose compression tool gzip uses LZ77 in combination with other techniques. A function library, zlib, makes its functionality available to applications. We used zlib in XMill, and will refer to zlib and gzip interchangeably in the paper.

Special Purpose Compressors A variety of special-purpose compressors exists, ranging from ad-hoc to highly complex ones [2, 16]. Special data types can be encoded in binary, e.g. *integer* or *date*. A *dictionary encoding* assigns an integer to each new word in the input, and stores the mapping from codes to strings in a dictionary. Specialized compressors exist for a variety of data types, e.g. images, sound or DNA sequences [2, 7].

3.3   Information Theory

In his classic paper [18] introducing information theory Claude Elwood Shannon describes an *information source*, a *channel*, and a *destination*, and studies how much information can be sent by the source to the destination. This is given precisely by how well the source can be compressed. A source S generates a message $x_1, x_2, \ldots, x_m$, symbol by symbol, with each symbol drawn from a fixed, finite alphabet $A = \{a_1, \ldots, a_n\}$. Shannon modeled a source as a Markov Process, and defined its *entropy*, H. The most popular formula for the entropy is for the special case of order 0 Markov Processes, where each symbol a_i has a fixed probability p_i:

$$H \stackrel{\text{def}}{=} p_1 \log \frac{1}{p_1} + \ldots + p_n \log \frac{1}{p_n}$$

Shannon proved in his paper the *fundamental theorem for a noiseless channel*, which essentially says that a message of m symbols cannot be compressed to less than mH bits on average, and that almost optimal compressors exists. Dictionary compressors, discussed at the beginning of this section, have been shown to achieve almost optimal compression [2].

Optimal compression of heterogeneous sources Unlike Shannon's information sources, XML data is heterogeneous. We define a *heterogeneous information source* S to be a collection of $k+1$ sources $S_0, S_1, \ldots, S_k$, over alphabets $A, B_1, \ldots, B_k$. The first alphabet has k symbols, $A = \{a_1, \ldots, a_k\}$, called *tags*, while the others can have an arbitrary number of symbols. The heterogeneous source emits messages of the following shape:

$$x_1, y_1, x_2, y_2, \ldots, x_m, y_m \tag{1}$$

where $x_1, \ldots, x_m \in A$, and, whenever $x_j = a_i$, then the next symbol y_j belongs to B_i.

We prove that the three compression principles in Sec. 1 lead to an optimal compression for heterogeneous sources. Heterogeneous sources are a simplification of XML since they don't model nesting: nesting can be modeled by probabilistic grammars [2].

If all $k + 1$ sources are of order 0, then the heterogeneous source S is equivalent to a (homogeneous) source modeled by a Markov Process with $k + 1$ states over the alphabet $A \cup B_1 \cup \ldots \cup B_k$ (details omitted).

Consider the following compression of a heterogeneous source in three steps: (1) separate the tags $x_1, x_2, \ldots$ from the data items $y_1, y_2, \ldots$, (2) further separate the data items according to their source $S_i, i = 1, k$, (3) apply an optimal compressor for each source $S_0, \ldots, S_k$. Let $H_0, H_1, \ldots, H_k$ be the entropies of the $k + 1$ sources, and let $p_1, \ldots, p_k$ be the probabilities of source S_0. Then the compression just described uses:

$$mH_0 + mp_1H_1 + mp_2H_2 + \ldots mp_kH_k \tag{2}$$

bits for the message (1) of length $2m$. This is because it needs mH_0 bits for $x_1, x_2, \ldots, x_m$; then there are, on average mp_1 symbols from source S_1, etc. Our theorem below proves that this is optimal:

Theorem 3.1 *The entropy of the heterogeneous source S is:* $\frac{1}{2}(H_0 + p_1H_1 + \ldots + p_kH_k)$. *Hence the number of bits used in (2) is optimal on average.*

4   The Architecture of XMill

The architecture of XMill is based on the three principles described in Sec. 1 and is shown in Fig. 3. The XML file is parsed by a SAX[8] parser that sends tokens to the path processor. Every XML token (tag, attribute, or data value) is assigned to a container. Tags and attributes, forming the XML structure, are sent to the structure container. Data values are sent to various data containers, according to the container expressions, and containers are compressed independently.

The core of XMill is the *path processor* that determines how to map data values to containers. The user can control this mapping by providing a series of *container expressions* on the command line. For each XML data value the path processor checks its *path* against each container expression, and determines either that the value has to be stored in an existing container, or creates a new container for that value.

---

[8]Simple API for XML, http://www.megginson.com/SAX/.

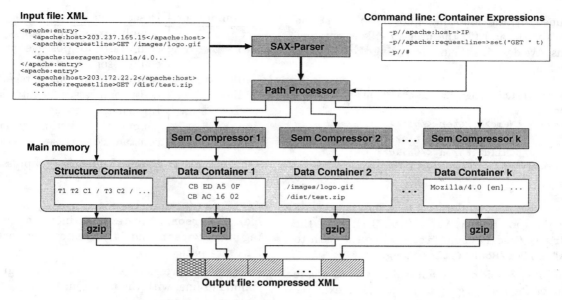

Figure 3: Architecture of the Compressor

Users can associate semantic compressors with containers. A few *atomic* semantic compressors are predefined in `XMill`, like binary encoding of integers, differential compressors, etc. Users can also *combine* semantic compressors into more complex ones or can write new semantic compressors and *link* them into `XMill`. The default *text* "compressor" simply copies its input to the container, without any semantic compression.

Containers are kept in a main memory window of fixed size (the default is 8MB). When the window is filled, all containers are gzipped, stored on disk, and the compression resumes. In effect this splits the input file into independently compressed blocks.

The decompressor `XDemill` is simpler, and its architecture is not shown. After loading and unzipping the containers, the decompressor parses the structure container, invokes the corresponding semantic decompressor for the data items and generates the output.

4.1 Separating Structure from Content

The *structure* of an XML file consists of its tags and attributes, and is tokenized in `XMill` as follows. Start-tags are dictionary-encoded, i.e. assigned an integer value, while all end-tags are replaced by the token `/`. Data values are replaced with their container number. To illustrate, consider the following small XML file:

```
<Book> <Title lang="English"> Views </Title>
       <Author> Miller </Author>
       <Author> Tai </Author>
</Book>
```

Tags, such as `Book`, `Title`, ... are dictionary encoded as T1, T2, etc. Data values (e.g. `English`, `Views`, `Miller`, and `Tai`) are assigned containers C3, C4, and C5 depending on their parent tag:

```
Book = T1, Title = T2, @lang = T3, Author = T4
Structure = T1 T2 T3 C3 / C4 / T4 C5 / T4 C5 / /
```

In practice all tokens are encoded as integers (with 1, 2, or 4 bytes, see Sec. 4.3): tags/attributes are positive integers, `/` is 0, and container numbers are negative integers. The structure above needs 14 bytes.

So far we have ignored white spaces between tags, e.g. between `<Book>` and `<Title>`, and the decompressor produces a canonical indentation. Optionally, `XMill` can preserve white spaces: in that case it stores them in container[9] 1. In our example, the structure becomes T1 C1 T2 C1 T3 C3 / C4 / C1 T4 ....

The size of the compressed file typically increases only slightly when white spaces are preserved: around 4%. We observed a higher increase (30%) only for Treebank, a linguistic database (see Sec. 6), because of its deeply nested structure. In the rest of the paper we will assume that white spaces are ignored.

We observed that, in practice, our simple encoding scheme compresses extremely well. Since many data sources tend to have repeated or similar structures (e.g. many books with one Title, one `@lang` attribute and two Authors), `gzip`'s algorithm (Sec. 3.2) can reduce the size dramatically. In our experiments the compressed structure was typically around 1%-3% of the compressed file for data with regular structure and 20% for data with highly irregular structure (Treebank).

4.2 Grouping Data Values

Each data value is uniquely assigned to one data container. The mapping from data values to containers

---

[9]Container 0 holds the structure while container 2 holds the PI's, DTD's, and comments.

is determined by the following information: (1) the data value's path, and (2) the user-specified container expressions. We describe them next, using the following running example:

```
<Doc> <Book> <Title lang="English"> Views </Title>
      </Book>
      <Person> <Name>  Peter </Name>
               <Title> Mr. </Title>
               <Child> Karen </Child>
      </Person>
</Doc>
```

Recall that the *path* to a data value is the sequence of tags from the root to that value (Sec. 3.1): e.g. the path to Mr. is /Doc/Person/Title, while the path to "English" is /Doc/Book/Title/@lang.

Container Expressions A natural idea is to create one container for each tag or attribute. For example all Title data values go to one container, all @lang attribute values go to a different container, etc.

This simple mapping typically performs well in practice, but sometimes it is too restrictive. The context may change the tag's semantics: /Doc/Book/Title has a different meaning from /Doc/Person/Title, hence the two Title's are best compressed separately. Conversely, different tags may have the same meaning, like Name and Child.

Our approach is to describe mappings from paths to containers with container expressions. Consider the following regular expressions derived from XPath [4]:

$$e ::= label \mid * \mid \# \mid e_1/e_2 \mid e_1//e_2 \mid (e_1|e_2) \mid (e)+$$

Except for $(e)+$ and $\#$, all are XPath constructs: *label* is either a *tag* or an *@attribute*, $*$ denotes any tag or attribute, e_1/e_2 is concatenation, $e_1//e_2$ is concatenation with any path in between, and $(e_1|e_2)$ is alternation. To these constructs we added $(e)+$, the strict Kleene closure.

The interesting novel construct is $\#$. It stands for any tag or attribute (much like $*$), but each match of $\#$ will determine a new container. The formal semantics of container expressions is described in [12].

A *container expression* has the form $c ::= /e \mid //e$, where $/e$ matches e starting from the root of the XML tree while $//e$ matches e at arbitrary depth in the tree. We abbreviate $//*$ with $//$.

Example 4.1 //Name creates one container for all data values whose path ends in Name. //Person/Title creates a container for all Person's titles. // places all data items into a single container.

Example 4.2 //# creates a family of containers: one for each ending tag or attribute. It is a concise way to express a whole collection of container expressions:

Compressor	Description
t	default text compressor
u	compressor for positive integers
i	compressor for integers
u8	compressor for pos. integers < 256
di	delta compressor for integers
rl	run-length encoder
e	enumeration (dictionary) encoder
"..."	constant compressor

Table 1: Atomic Semantic Compressors

//Title, //@lang, etc. (one for each tag in the XML file). //Person/# creates a distinct container for each tag under Person, and (#)+ creates a distinct container for every path.

Container expressions $c_1, \ldots, c_n$ are given in the command line, with the p switch:

```
xmill -p c1 -p c2 ... -p cn  file.xml
```

For each data value, the path processor matches its path against $c_1, c_2, \ldots$, in that order. Assuming the first match is found at c_i, the processor computes the "values" of the #'s in c_i which made the match possible. These values, together with i, uniquely determine the data value's container.

Example 4.3 Consider the following command line:

```
xmill -p //Person/Title  -p //(Name|Child)
      -p //#  file.xml
```

This command line compresses all Person's titles together, all Names and Childs together. All other data values are compressed based on their ending tag. In particular .../Book/Title will be compressed separately from .../Person/Title.

Default Behavior The expression -p //# is always inserted at the end of the command line. In particular, the command line xmill file.xml is equivalent to xmill -p //# file.xml. This ensures that every data value is stored in at least one container and it provides a reasonable default behavior.

4.3 Semantic Compressors

XML data often comes with a variety of specialized data types like integers, dates, US states, airport codes, which are best compressed by specialized semantic compressors. XMill supports three kinds of semantic compressors: atomic, combined, and user-defined.

Atomic semantic compressors: There are eight such compressors in XMill, shown in Table 1. We explain here just a few and refer the reader to [16] or standard textbooks [17] for a general discussion.

The text compressor t does not compress, but rather copies the string to the container unchanged (it will be compressed later by gzip). Positive integers (compressor u) are binary encoded as follows: numbers less than 128 use one byte, those less than 16384 use two bytes, otherwise they use four bytes. The most significant one or two bits determine the length. The last entry is a constant compressor that does not produce any output (the best compression of all !), but checks that the input is the given constant. Some semantic compressor-decompressor pairs may be lossy, e.g. u, u8, i do not preserve leading zeros.

Semantic compressors are optionally specified on the command line using the syntax c=>s where c is a container expression (Sec. 4.2) and s is a semantic compressor. When missing, the default semantic compressor is text. For a simple illustration, consider the example:

```
xmill -p //price=>i  -p //state=>e  file.xml
```

The price data items are compressed as integers, states as enumeration values, and all remaining data items are grouped based on their tag (recall that the default -p //# is added at the end), with no semantic compression.

A semantic compressor may reject its input string. In the example above, a price value which does not parse as an integer will be rejected by the i compressor. In that case XMill tries the next path expression: eventually, the last -p //# will match. One can exploit this behavior by specifying alternative compressors, like in xmill -p //price=>i -p //price=>e ... to capture price values like 1450, low, 55, high, ...

Combined compressors: Often data values have structure. For example an IP address consists of four integers separated by dots (e.g. 104.44.29.21); a request value (Sec. 2) consists of GET followed by a variable string. XMill has three compressor combinators for compressing such values:

- *Sequence Compressor* seq(s1 s2 ...). For example, seq(u8 "." u8 "." u8 "." u8) compresses an IP address as four integers.

- *Alternate Compressor* or(s1 s2 ...). For example, consider page references in a bibliography file. These can be either like 145-199, or single pages like 145. The composite compressor is or(seq(u "-" u) u).

- *Repetition Compressor* rep(d s). Here d is the delimiter and s another semantic compressor. For example, a sequence of comma separated keywords can be compressed by rep("," e).

Fig. 1 illustrates the use of combined semantic compressors for the Weblog data.

User-defined Compressors Some applications require highly specialized compressors, like for DNA sequences [7]. Users can write their own compressors/decompressors and link them into XMill and XDemill, conforming to a specified API, called SCAPI (Semantic Compressor API [11]). Semantic compressors can be used in the command line, like in xmill -p //DNAseq=>dna file.xml, where dna is the compressor's name. The extended XMill becomes application specific, since a file compressed with such an extended XMill can only be decompressed by an XDemill with the corresponding decompressor.

5   Implementation

XMill and XDemill are implemented in C++, and have together about 18,000 of code. We wrote our own SAX parser for XML, which parses the XML file and translates it into a stream of events: one event for each start-tag, end-tag, data value, etc. Every XML event (token) is sent to the path processor, which is described next.

5.1   Path Processor

The path processor keeps track of the current path for each data value and evaluates successively each container expression on the path: the latter involves evaluating a regular expression, and, if successful, evaluating the semantic compressor on that data value. This is the most time-critical piece in the compressor and we tried three different evaluation methods. They are described in detail in [12].

Direct Evaluation of Regular Expressions Each container expression is preprocessed into a minimized, deterministic automaton (DFA)[9], and for each of them we maintain its current state while parsing the XML file. This method becomes inefficient when we have more than one container expression, since we need to evaluate several DFAs for each XML tag.

Evaluation using DataGuides Here we use a cache: if $p_1, p_2, \ldots$ are all the XML paths seen so far, then the cache consists of a trie for $p_1, p_2, \ldots$. This trie becomes equivalent to a DataGuide [5] at the end of the XML document. We keep a list of corresponding DFA states at each DataGuide node, and only need to advance a single pointer in the DataGuide while parsing XML tags. An exception is when we encounter a new path p: then we expand the DataGuide with a new node and we need to compute its associated DFA states. The size of the DataGuides ranges from a few nodes (for regular data) to very large (for irregular data). We found DataGuides efficient except for the most irregular and deeply nested data.

Evaluation using Reversed DataGuides Irregular and deeply nested data causes the DataGuide to grow out of proportions. An example of such data is the XML-ized *TreeBank* linguistic database[10] [13], which contains annotated sentences from the Wall Street Journal. The DataGuide had 340000 nodes, which translated into about 16MB of main memory (depending on the number of DFAs), far exceeding our 8MB memory window.

Our third strategy uses a *reversed DataGuides*, which is just the DataGuide structure for the *reverse* paths, and working in conjunction with reversed DFA's. The reversed DataGuide in our example has 1.1 million nodes (in contrast to 340000 nodes). However it is possible to *prune* the reversed DataGuide much better than the direct DataGuide, because container expressions usually discriminate based on the last few tags in the path: e.g. `//Person/Name` and `//#` only look at the last one or two tags. In all our examples the reversed DataGuide were pruned after one or two tags. For the Treebank data, pruning was done after one tag, reducing the reversed DataGuide to approx. 250 nodes (the number of distinct leaf tags).

6 Experimental Evaluation

We evaluated XMill on several data sets. Our goal was to validate XMill for XML data archiving and data exchange and to test XMill as a compensatory tool for migrating other data formats to XML.

Data sources We report the evaluation of XMill on six data sources, whose characteristics are shown in Fig. 6. The Weblog and the SwissProt data were described in Sec. 2. Treebank [13] is a large collection of parsed English sentences from the Wall Street Journal stored in a Lisp like notation, which we converted to XML. TPC-D(XML) is an XML representation of the TPC-D benchmark database, using two levels of nesting[11]. We deleted from the TPC-D data the `Comment` field, which takes about 30% of the space, and consists of randomly generated characters. DBLP is the popular database bibliography database[12]. Finally, Shakespeare is a corpus of marked-up Shakespeare plays, and it is stored directly in XML.

Fig. 6 shows the size of the original data sources, the size of their XML representation, and four characteristic measures: our assessment of the data's regularity (yes/no), the maximal depth of the XML tree, the number of distinct tags, and the number of nodes in the DataGuide (another measure of (i)regularity).

Classes of experiments We performed three classes of experiments. First, we compared the compression ratios of `gzip` and XMill under various settings. We

also tested the variation of the compression ratio as a function of the data size, and its sensitivity to the memory window. Second, we measured the compression and decompression times of XMill and `gzip`. Third, we measured the total effect of XMill in an XML data exchange application over the network.

Platform We ran the first two sets of experiments on a Windows NT, 300Mhz PII machine with 128MB main memory. The data exchange experiment was performed by sending data from AT&T Labs, running an SGI Challenge L (4 x 270MHz MIPS R12000, Irix 6.5.5m) to two places: the University of Pennsylvania, running a Sun Enterprise 3000 (4 x 250Mhz UltraSPARC) with 1024MB of memory, and a home PC (100MHz, Linux, 32MB) connected to a cable modem. We transfered files with `rcp`, for which we measured a transfer rate of 8.08MBits/s (AT&T to Penn) and 1.25MBits/s (AT&T to home PC via cable modem).

Experimental Methodology The *compression ratio* is expressed as "bits per bytes", e.g. 2 bits/bytes means 25% of the uncompressed file size. The *running time* represents the elapsed time in seconds. We run each experiment eight times and take the average of the last five runs. For the data exchange experiment, we measured the compression and decompression times separately (at AT&T) from the data transfer; each was executed eight times, as explained.

In comparing the running time of XMill with `gzip` we noticed differences in the (time and space) efficiency of `gzip` (the stand-alone tool) and `zlib` (the library used in XMill). For meaningful comparisons, we replaced `gzip` with `minigzip`, a stand-alone program in `zlib`, and compiled it with the same options as XMill. In all experiments below, "gzip" actually means `minigzip`.

6.1 Compression Ratio

Fig. 5 shows the compression ratios for different data sources and compressors. For each data set, the four connected bars represent `gzip`, and XMill run with three settings (as in Sec. 2): no grouping (XMill //), grouping based on parent tag (XMill //#; the default), and user-defined grouping with semantic compression (abbreviated XMill <u>). In XMill <u> we used the best combination container expressions we could find for each data set. For the first four data sets, the bar on the left represents the relative size of the gzipped original file (i.e. the height of the bar is `size(gzip(orig))/(8*size(XML))`).

For the first four data sets (which had more data and less text), XMill's compressed under the default setting to 45%-60% the size of `gzip`. Using semantic compressors, XMill reduced the size to 35%-47% of `gzip`'s. For the more text-like data sets, XMill performs only slightly better than `gzip`. Note that with the

---

[10]More information about TreeBank is available under `http://www.cis.upenn.edu/~treebank/`.

[11]We tried other XML representations too, and observed no significant change in the experimental results.

[12]`http://www.informatik.uni-trier.de/~ley/db`

Data Source	Original Size	Size in XML	Regular?	Depth	Tags	DataGuide Size
Weblog Data	57.7MB	172MB	yes	1	10	11
SwissProt	98.5MB	158MB	yes	3	92	58
Treebank	39.6MB	53.8MB	no	35	251	339920
TPC-D	34.6MB	119MB	yes	2	43	60
DBLP	-	47.2MB	yes	3	10	145
Shakespeare	-	7.3MB	no	5	21	58

Figure 4: Data sources for performance evaluation

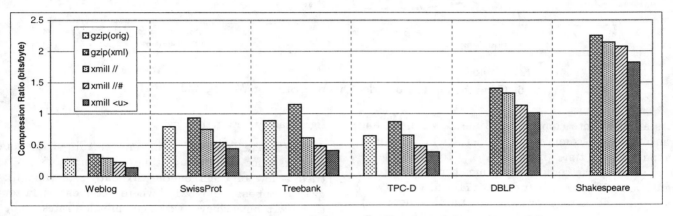

Figure 5: Compression Results

default setting, XMill already compressed the XML file better than gzip compressed the original file.

Fig. 6 shows the compression ratio as a function of the XML data size for Weblog and SwissProt. On small files, XMill performs worse than gzip because it splits the data into too many small containers. The crossing point for both data sets was at about 20KB.

Fig. 7(a) shows the sensitivity of XMill's compression ratio on the memory window size. The compression ratio is normalized with respect to the default of 8MB. The results show that a smaller memory window size substantially degrades the compression rate, again because a small window implies small containers, on which the compression rate is poor. Beyond 8MB, both data sets were compressed in only a few blocks, and the compression rate did not improve too much.

6.2 Compression/Decompression Time

We measured the (de)compression time for Weblog, SwissProt, and Treebank and considered three compression strategies: gzip, XMill //#, and XMill <u>. Fig. 8(a) shows the compression time for each data source and compressor. For XMill, the time is split into two parts: (1) parsing and applying semantic compressors, and (2) applying gzip. XMill is generally as fast as gzip, since XMill saves time by applying gzip to a smaller data size and spends the time on regrouping. For the same reason, XMill <u> is faster

than XMill //#, because the semantic compressors pre-compress the data, hence gzip spends less time.

Fig. 8(b) shows the decompression time for each of the data sources and compressors, broken down according to the decompression step. There are four such steps: (1) gunzip the containers, (2) interpret the XML structure and merge the data values, applying the appropriate semantic decompressors: this results in a stream of SAX events, (3) generate the XML string (start-tags, end-tags, data values, etc), (4) output the file. For gunzip we only have steps (1) and (4). Note that the time fragmentation into parts (1)-(4) is not completely accurate, because of caching interferences.

For a complete decompression (written to a file) XDemill's speed is comparable to gunzip. If we remove the output step (4) for on-the-fly decompression, then XDemill is about twice slower than gunzip. We pay here the price of having to merge data from different containers. However, an application could do even better by consuming SAX events directly, rather than having to re-parse the XML string: such applications only need XMill to perform steps (1) and (2) (gunzip's output always needs to be parsed).

6.3 Data Exchange

Fig. 9 shows the results of exchanging Weblog data from AT&T to the Univ. of Pennsylvania (a) and to a home computer via a cable modem (b). The

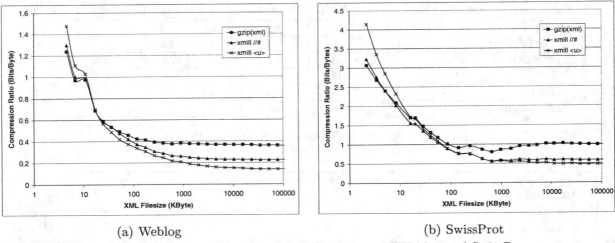

(a) Weblog   (b) SwissProt

Figure 6: Compression Ratio under Different Sizes of Weblog and SwissProt

bars are split into compression time (lower bar), and transmission+decompression (upper bar). The end-to-end transfer time (from XML file to XML file) is dominated by the compression time: here there are no significant differences between XMill and gzip (with some slight advantage for XMill on the slow network). If the file is already compressed, then XMill shows detectable improvements over gzip; again, better so in the case of a slow network. Furthermore, if the decompressed data is used directly in an application (via a SAX interface), then only the transfer and decompress+decode time matters, and XMill takes only about 60% of the time of gzip. We obtained similar results for SwissProt, which are omitted.

7 Discussion and Future Work

Benefits of XMill The experiments show that XMill clearly achieves better compression rates than gzip (around a factor of 2, for data-like XML, less for text-like XML), without sacrificing speed. This makes XMill a clear winner for data archiving. For data exchange however, the improvement depends on two factors: the type of exchange application, and the relative processor v.s. network speed. For a slow network, XMill's improvements are always detectable, because of its better compression rate. For a fast network, one has to look at all three exchange steps: compression, network transfer, and decompression. Compression is consistently the most expensive, and is about the same in gzip and XMill. Hence, the relative advantage depends on the type of application. For an end-to-end file transfer, there is no clear winner. In XML publishing, the file is compressed only once, and only network transfer and decompression matters: XMill is consistently, but only modestly faster than gzip. If, moreover, the data is imported directly into applications, then the decompression does not need to produce an output XML file: here XMill can become

significantly better than gzip.

Time/Space Tradeoff Different general-purpose compressors offer a variety of time/space tradeoffs. We tried a few of them on our six data sets (Fig. 6): gzip, compress, and bzip, where compress is faster than gzip but achieves worse compression rates, while bzip achieves better compression rates but is excessively slow. The results are shown in Fig. 7(b), where all compression rates and compression times are normalized with respect to that of gzip. The blobs highlight the "data-like" XML data sets (Weblog, SwissProt, Treebank, and TPC-D). The diagram shows that XMill offers the best overall time/space tradeoff for XML data. Given bzip's impressive performance, we replaced gzip with bzip in XMill. Interestingly, while the resulting compressor (called xbmill) compresses better than XMill, the compression times did not increase as badly as between gzip and bzip: this is because xbmill applies bzip to a smaller amount of data.

Schema Extraction All container expressions in XMill have to be specified manually. They were designed keeping the XML-Schema in mind [19], and it is relatively straightforward to generate them from a given XML-Schema. However, it would be more useful to extract them automatically from a given XML data set. Unlike previous work on schema extraction for semistructured data [14], the critical part is choosing the right semantic compressor for each container. An automatic datamining tool must recognize integers, dates or structured fields and cluster data correspondingly.

8 Related Work

General Compression General compression methods are described in textbooks [2, 17]. A more recent method is block-sorting compression described in [3], which is used in bzip. It sorts the characters in a block first before applying other compression.

162

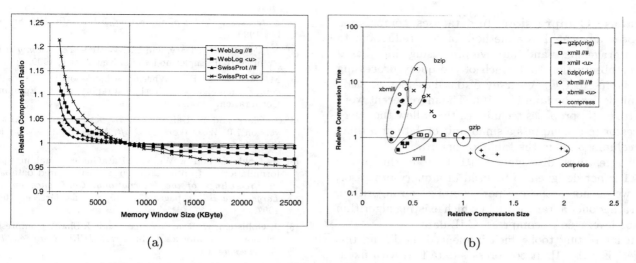

(a)

(b)

Figure 7: (a) Compression under Varying Memory Windows, (b) Compression Rate vs. Time

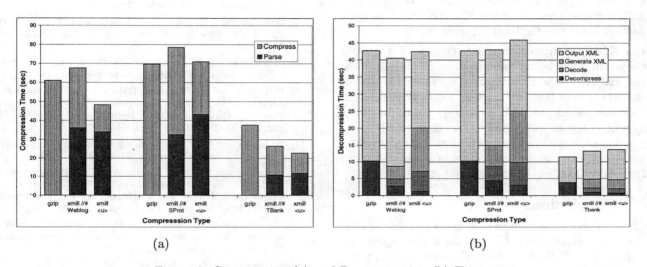

(a)

(b)

Figure 8: Compression (a) and Decompression (b) Time

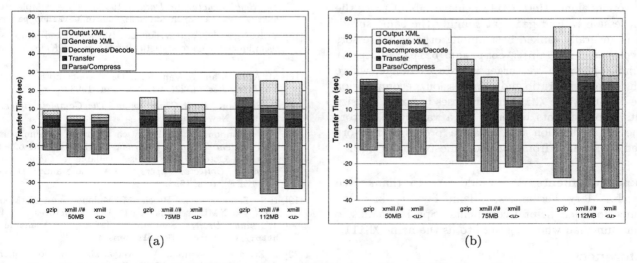

(a)

(b)

Figure 9: Network Transfer Time from AT&T Labs to Penn (a) and to a home PC (b)

Database Compression In databases, compression has been advocated as a method for cost reduction: to save storage space and improve processing time, based on the observation that much of the query processing time is due to I/O. A survey of database compression techniques can be found in [16]. The more recent work in [10, 6, 15] proposes techniques that allow the query processor to decompress a small unit of data at a time: one column value in the table, or one row.

Two features distinguish XMill from this work: XMill is not designed to be used in a query processor, and we do not propose a new compression algorithm, but rather offer a framework in which existing algorithm can be leveraged to compress XML data.

An interesting tool which influenced us during this project is pzip [1]. It compresses data files with fixed-length records very efficiently by first applying run-length encoding on mostly blank character columns and by gouping the remaining columns using its schema extraction tool before submitting it to zlib.

Other XML Compressors At the time of writing, a single product has been announced, by XML Solutions, called xmlzip (www.xmlzip.com). Implemented in Java, xmlzip cuts the XML tree at a certain depth and compresses the upper part separately from the lower part, both using gzip. Tested on our data sets (Fig 6), it ran out of memory on all sets except Shakespeare. There, it achieves a compression ratio between that of gzip's and XMill, but at much lower speed.

9 Conclusions

We have described a compressor for XML data called XMill, which is an extensible tool for applying existing compressors to XML data. Its main engine is zlib, the library function variant for gzip. One of our targeted applications is XML data archiving, where compression rate counts alone. Here XMill achieves about twice the compression rate of gzip, at roughly the same speed, and is generally ranked best among other compressors we compared it against: compress, bzip, xmlzip. A second application we target is data exchange, where both compression ratio and compression/decompression time count. While XMill never looses to gzip, the size of its improvements depends on a variety of factors (type of application and relative processor/network speed), and range from none to almost a factor of 2.

Acknowledgments We would like to thank Ken Church, Mary Fernandez, Glenn Fowler, and Val Tannen for their helpful comments. Special thanks to Peter Buneman who suggested to us the name XMill.

References

[1] D. Belanger and K. Church. Data flows with examples from telecommunications. In *Proceedings of 1999 Workshop on Databases in Telecommunication*, Edinburgh, UK, September 1999.

[2] T.C. Bell, J.G. Cleary, and I.H. Witten. *Text Compression*. Prentice Hall, Englewood Cliffs, New Jersey, 1990.

[3] M. Burrows and D. J. Wheeler. A block-sorting lossless data compression algorithm. Technical report, Digital Equipment Corporation, May 1994.

[4] J. Clark and S. DeRose. XML path language (XPath), version 1.0. *W3C Working Draft*, August 1999. Available as http://www.w3.org/TR/xpath.

[5] R. Goldman and J. Widom. DataGuides: enabling query formulation and optimization in semistructured databases. In *Proceedings of the International Conference on Very Large Data Bases*, pages 436–445, Athens, Greece, August 1997.

[6] J. Goldstein, R. Ramakrishnan, and U. Shaft. Compressing relations and indexes. In *Proc. IEEE Conf on Data Engineering*, 1998.

[7] S. Grumbach and F. Tahi. A new challenge for compression algorithms: genetic sequences. *Information Processing and Management*, 30(6):875–886, 1994.

[8] D. G. Higgins, R. Fuchs, P. J. Stoehr, and G. N. Cameron. The EMBL data library. *Nucleic Acids Research*, 20:2071–2074, 1992.

[9] J. Hopcroft and J. Ullman. *Introduction to automata theory, languages, and computation*. Addison-Wesley, 1979.

[10] B.R. Iyer and D. Wilhite. Data compression support in databases. In *VLDB'94, Proceedings of 20th International Conference on Very Large Data Bases*, pages 695–704, Santiago de Chile, Chile, September 1994.

[11] H. Liefke and S.B. Davidson. An extensible compressor for XML data. *SIGMOD Record*, 29(1), March 2000.

[12] H. Liefke and D. Suciu. XMill: An efficient compressor for XML data. Technical Report MS-CIS-98-06, Department of Computer and Information Science, University of Pennsylvania, Philadelphia, PA 19104, October 1999.

[13] M.P. Marcus, B. Santorini, and M. Marcinkiewicz. Building a large annotated corpus of english: the penn treebank. *Computational Linguistics*, 19, 1993.

[14] S. Nestorov, S. Abiteboul, and R. Motwani. Inferring structure in semistructured data. In *Proceedings of the Workshop on Management of Semi-structured Data*, 1997. Available from http://www.research.att.com/~suciu/workshop-papers.html.

[15] W.K. Ng and C.V. Ravishankar. Block-oriented compression techniques for large statistical databases. *TKDE*, 9(2):314–328, 1997.

[16] M. A. Roth and S. Van Horn. Database compression. *ACM SIGMOD Record*, 22(3):31–39, Sept. 1993.

[17] D. Salomon. *Data Compression. The Complete Reference*. Springer, New York, 1997.

[18] C.E. Shannon. A mathematica theory of communication. *Bell System Technical Journal*, 27:379–423 and 623–656, July and October 1948. Also available in *Claude Elwood Shannon, Collected Papers*, N.J.A.Sloane and A.D.Wyner eds, IEEE Press, 1993.

[19] H.S. Thompson, D. Beech, M. Maloney, and N. Mendelsohn. XML schema part 1: Structures. *W3C Working Draft*, September 1999. Available as http://www.w3.org/TR/xmlschema-1.

[20] J. Ziv and A. Lempel. A universal algorithm for sequential data compression. *IEEE Transactions on Information Theory*, 23(3):337–343, 1977.

XTRACT: A System for Extracting Document Type Descriptors from XML Documents

Minos Garofalakis
Bell Laboratories
minos@bell-labs.com

Aristides Gionis*
Stanford University
gionis@cs.stanford.edu

Rajeev Rastogi
Bell Laboratories
rastogi@bell-labs.com

S. Seshadri
Bell Laboratories
seshadri@bell-labs.com

Kyuseok Shim†
KAIST and AITrc
shim@cs.kaist.ac.kr

Abstract

XML is rapidly emerging as the new standard for data representation and exchange on the Web. An XML document can be accompanied by a *Document Type Descriptor* (DTD) which plays the role of a schema for an XML data collection. DTDs contain valuable information on the structure of documents and thus have a crucial role in the efficient storage of XML data, as well as the effective formulation and optimization of XML queries. In this paper, we propose XTRACT, a novel system for inferring a DTD schema for a database of XML documents. Since the DTD syntax incorporates the full expressive power of *regular expressions*, naive approaches typically fail to produce concise and intuitive DTDs. Instead, the XTRACT inference algorithms employ a sequence of sophisticated steps that involve: (1) finding patterns in the input sequences and replacing them with regular expressions to generate "general" candidate DTDs, (2) factoring candidate DTDs using adaptations of algorithms from the logic optimization literature, and (3) applying the Minimum Description Length (MDL) principle to find the best DTD among the candidates. The results of our experiments with real-life and synthetic DTDs demonstrate the effectiveness of XTRACT's approach in inferring concise and semantically meaningful DTD schemas for XML databases.

1   Introduction

Motivation and Background. The genesis of the Extensible Markup Language (XML) was based on the thesis that structured documents can be freely exchanged and manipulated, if published in a standard, open format. Indeed, as a corroboration of the thesis, XML today promises to enable a suite of next-generation Web applications ranging from intelligent web searching to electronic commerce.

In many respects, XML data is an instance of *semistructured data* [1]. XML documents comprise hierarchically nested collections of *elements*, where each element can be either atomic (i.e., raw character data) or composite (i.e., a sequence of nested subelements). Further, *tags* stored with elements in an XML document describe the semantics of the data rather than simply specifying how the element is to be displayed (as in HTML). Thus, XML data, like semistructured data, is hierarchically structured and self-describing.

A characteristic, however, that distinguishes XML from semistructured data models is the notion of a *Document Type Descriptor* (DTD) that may optionally accompany an XML document. A document's DTD serves the role of a schema specifying the internal structure of the document. Essentially, a DTD specifies for every element, the *regular expression* pattern that subelement sequences of the element need to conform to. DTDs are critical to realizing the promise of XML as the data representation format that enables free interchange of electronic data (EDI) and integration of related news, products, and services information from disparate data sources. This is because, in the absence of DTDs, tagged documents have little meaning. However, once the major software vendors and corporations agree on domain-specific standards for DTD formats, it would become possible for inter-operating applications to extract, interpret, and analyze the contents of a document based on the DTD that it conforms to.

In addition to enabling the free exchange of electronic documents through industry-wide standards, DTDs also provide the basic mechanism for defining the structure of the underlying XML data. As a consequence, DTDs play a crucial role in the efficient storage of XML data as well as the formulation, optimization, and processing of queries over a collection of XML documents. For instance, in [23], DTD information is exploited to generate effective relational schemas, which are subsequently employed to efficiently store and query entire XML documents in a relational database. In [7], frequently occurring portions of XML documents are stored in a relational system, while the remainder is stored in an overflow graph; once again, the DTD is exploited to simplify overflow mappings. Similarly, DTDs can be used to devise efficient plans for queries and thus speed up query evaluation in XML databases by restricting the search to only relevant portions of the data (see, for example, [8, 13]). The basic idea is to use the knowledge of the structure of the data captured by the DTD to prune elements that cannot potentially satisfy the path expression in the query. Finally, by shedding light on how the underlying data is structured, DTDs aid users in forming

---

*Work done while visiting Bell Laboratories.
†Work done while visiting Bell Laboratories.

165

meaningful queries over the XML database.

Despite their importance, however, DTDs are *not mandatory* and an XML document may not always have an accompanying DTD. In fact, several recent papers (e.g., [12, 25]) claim that it is frequently possible that only specific portions of XML databases will have associated DTDs, while the overall database is still "schema-less". This may be the case, for instance, when large volumes of XML documents are automatically generated from data stored in relational databases, flat files (e.g., HTML pages, bibliography files), or other semistructured data repositories. Since very little data is in XML format today, it is very likely that, at least initially, the majority of XML documents will be automatically generated from pre-existing data sources by a new generation of software tools. In most cases, such automatically-created document collections will not have an accompanying DTD.

Therefore, based on the above discussion on the virtues of a DTD, it is important to devise algorithms and tools that can infer an accurate, meaningful DTD for a given collection of XML documents (i.e., *instances* of the DTD). This is *not* an easy task. Since the DTD syntax incorporates the full specification power of regular expressions, manually deducing such a DTD schema for even a small set of XML documents created by a user could prove to be a process of daunting complexity. Furthermore, as we show in this paper, naive approaches fail to deliver meaningful and intuitive DTD descriptions of the underlying data. Both problems are, of course, exacerbated for *large* XML document collections. In light of the several benefits of DTDs, we can motivate a myriad of potential applications for efficient, automated DTD discovery tools. For example, consider an employment web site that integrates information on job openings from thousands of different web sites including company home pages, newspaper classified sites, and so on. These XML documents, although related, may not all have the same structure and, even if some of the documents are accompanied by DTDs, the DTDs may not be identical. An alternative to manually transforming all the XML documents to conform to a single format would be to simply store the documents in their original formats and use DTD discovery tools to derive a single DTD description for the entire database. This inferred DTD can then help in the formulation, optimization, and processing of queries over the database of stored XML documents. Further, the ability to extract DTDs for a range of XML formats supported by the major participants in a specific industrial setting can also aid in the DTD standardization process for the industry.

Our Contributions. In this paper, we describe the architecture of XTRACT, a novel system for inferring an accurate, meaningful DTD schema for a repository of XML documents. A naive and straightforward solution to our DTD extraction problem would be to infer as the DTD for an element, a "concise" expression which describes *exactly* all the sequences of subelements nested within the element in the entire document collection. As we demonstrate in Section 3,

however, the DTDs generated by this approach tend to be voluminous and unintuitive (especially for large XML document collections). In fact, we discover that accurate and meaningful DTD schemas that are also intuitive and appealing to humans (i.e., resemble what a human expert is likely to come up with) tend to *generalize*. That is, "good" DTDs are typically regular expressions describing subelement sequences that *may not actually occur* in the input XML documents. (Note that this, in fact, is always the case for DTD regular expressions that correspond to infinite regular languages, e.g., DTDs containing one or more Kleene stars "*" [15].) In practice, however, there are numerous such candidate DTDs that generalize the subelement sequences in the input, and choosing the DTD that best describes the structure of these sequences is a non-trivial task. In the inference algorithms employed in the XTRACT system, we propose the following novel combination of sophisticated techniques to generate DTD schemas that effectively capture the structure of the input sequences.

●**Generalization.** As a first step, the XTRACT system employs novel heuristic algorithms for finding patterns in each input sequence and replacing them with appropriate regular expressions to produce more general candidate DTDs. The main goal of the generalization step is to judiciously introduce metacharacters (like Kleene stars "*") to produce regular subexpressions that generalize the patterns observed in the input sequences. Our generalization heuristics are based on the discovery of frequent, neighboring occurrences of subsequences and symbols within each input sequence. In their effort to introduce a sufficient amount of generalization while avoiding an explosion in the number of resulting patterns, our techniques are inspired by practical, real-life DTD examples.

●**Factoring.** As a second step, the XTRACT system *factors* common subexpressions from the generalized candidate DTDs obtained from the generalization step, in order to make them more concise. The factoring algorithms applied are appropriate adaptations of techniques from the logic optimization literature [4, 24].

●**Minimum Description Length (MDL) Principle.** In the final and most important step, the XTRACT system employs Rissanen's *Minimum Description Length* (MDL) principle [21, 22] to derive an elegant mechanism for composing a near-optimal DTD schema from the set of candidate DTDs generated by the earlier two steps. (Our MDL-based notion of optimality will be defined formally later in the paper.) The MDL principle has its roots in information theory and, essentially, provides a principled, scientific definition of the optimal "theory/model" that can be inferred from a set of data examples [20]. Abstractly, in our problem setting, MDL ranks each candidate DTD depending on the number of bits required to describe the input collection of sequences *in terms of the DTD* (DTDs requiring fewer bits are ranked higher). As a consequence, the optimal DTD according to the MDL principle is the one that is general enough to cover a large subset of the input sequences but, at the same time, captures the structure of the input sequences with a fair amount of detail, so that they can be described easily (with few additional bits) using the DTD. Thus, the MDL principle provides a formal notion of "best DTD" that exactly matches our intuition. Using MDL essentially allows XTRACT to control the amount of generalization introduced in the inferred DTD in a principled, scientific and, at the same time, intuitively appealing fashion. We demonstrate that selecting the optimal DTD based on the MDL principle has a direct and natural mapping to the *Facility Location Problem* (FLP), which is known to be NP-complete [14]. Fortunately, efficient approximation algorithms with guaranteed performance ratios have been proposed for the FLP in the literature [6], thus allowing us to efficiently compose the final DTD in a near-optimal manner.

We have implemented our XTRACT DTD derivation algorithms and conducted an extensive experimental study with both real-life and synthetic DTDs. Our findings show that, for a set of random inputs that conform to a predetermined DTD, XTRACT always produces a DTD that is either identical or very close to the original DTD. We also observe that the quality of the DTDs returned by XTRACT is far superior compared to those output by the IBM Alphaworks DDbE (Data Descriptors by Example) DTD extraction tool[1], which is unable to identify a majority of the DTDs. Further, a number of the original DTDs correctly inferred by XTRACT contain several regular expressions terms, some nested within one another. Thus, our experimental results clearly demonstrate the effectiveness of XTRACT's methodology for deducing fairly complex DTDs.

Several extensions to DTDs, e.g., Document Content Descriptors (DCDs) and XML Schemas, are being evolved by the Web community. These extensions aim to add typing information, since DTDs treat all data as strings. Therefore, XTRACT, can be used with little or no changes for inferring DCDs and XML Schemas in conjunction with other mechanisms for inferring the types. However, these proposals are still evolving – therefore, we do not concentrate on these extensions in this paper.

The work reported in this paper has been done in the context of the $\mathcal{SERENDIP}$ data mining project at Bell Laboratories (www.bell-labs.com/projects/serendip).

2   Related Work

The problem of mining DTDs from a collection of XML documents is, to the best of our knowledge, novel and has not been previously addressed in the literature. A few DTD extraction software tools can be found on the Web (e.g., the IBM Alphaworks DDbE product) – however, it has been our experience that these tools are somewhat naive in their approach and the quality of the DTDs inferred by them is poor (see Section 7).

---

[1] www.alphaworks.ibm.com/formula/xml/

The problem of extracting a schema from semistructured data has been addressed in [8, 13, 18]. Although, XML can be viewed as an instance of semistructured data, the kinds of schema considered in [8, 13, 18] are very different from a DTD. The schemas extracted by [8, 13, 18] attempt to find a typing for semistructured data. Assuming a graph-based model for semistructured data (nodes denote objects and labels on edges denote relationships between them), finding a typing is tantamount to grouping objects that have similarly labeled edges to and from similarly typed objects. The typing then describes this grouping in terms of the labels of the edges to (from) this type of objects and the types of the objects at the other end of the edge. In contrast, one can perhaps view the DTD as having already grouped all objects based on their incoming edges (tag of the element) into the same type and then describing the possible sequence of outgoing edges (subelements) as a regular expression. It is the fact that the outgoing edges from a type can be described by an arbitrary regular expression that distinguishes DTDs from the schemas in semistructured databases. Since the schemas in semistructured databases are expressed using plain sequences or sets of edges, they cannot be used to infer DTDs corresponding to arbitrary regular expressions.

The inference of formal languages from examples has a long and rich history in the field of computational learning theory, and more related to our work is the extensive study of the inference of *Deterministic Finite Automata* (DFAs) [2, 10, 11] (see also [19] for a detailed survey of the topic). The above line of work is purely theoretical and focuses on investigating the computational complexity of the language inference problem, while we are mainly interested in devising practical algorithms for real-world applications. In this sense, our research is more closely related to the work in [5] which addresses the problem of approximating *roughly equivalent* regular expressions from a long enough string, and the work in [16] where *MDL* principle is used to infer a *pattern language* from positives examples. However, the problem tackled in [16] is much simpler than ours, since it assumes that the set of simple patterns whose subset is to be computed is available. Furthermore, the patterns considered in [16] are simple sequences that are permitted to contain single symbol wildcards. In our problem setting, unlike [16], patterns are general regular expressions and are not known apriori.

3   Problem Formulation and Overview

In this section, we present a precise definition of the problem of inferring a DTD from a collection of XML documents and then present an overview of the steps performed by the XTRACT system. Briefly, an XML document consists of nested element structures starting with a root element. Subelements of an element can either be elements or simple character data. A DTD is a grammar for describing the structure of an XML document. A DTD constrains the structure of an element by specifying a regular expression that its subelement sequences have to conform to. Figure 1 illustrates an example XML document, in which the root element (`article`) has two nested subelements (`title` and `author`), and the `author` element in turn has two nested subelements. Figure 2 illustrates a DTD that our example XML document conforms to. More details on the XML specification can be found in [3]. For brevity, in the remainder of the paper, we denote elements of an XML document by a single letter from the lower-case alphabet.

```
<article>
  <title>
    A Relational Model for Large Shared
    Data Banks
  </title>
  <author>
    <name> E. F. Codd </name>
    <affiliation> IBM Research </affiliation>
  </author>
</article>
```

Figure 1: An Example XML Document

```
<!ELEMENT article(title, author*)>
<!ELEMENT title (#PCDATA)>
<!ELEMENT author(name, affiliation)>
<!ELEMENT name (#PCDATA)>
<!ELEMENT affiliation (#PCDATA)>
```

Figure 2: An Example DTD

3.1 Problem Definition

Our primary focus in this paper is to infer a DTD for a collection of XML documents. Thus, for each element that appears in the document collection, our goal is to derive a regular expression that subelement sequences for the element (in the XML documents) conform to. Note that an element's DTD is completely independent of the DTD for other elements, and only restricts the sequence of subelements nested within the element. Therefore, for simplicity of exposition, in the remainder of the paper, we concentrate on the problem of extracting a DTD for a single element. We do not address the problem of computing attribute lists for an element – since these are simple lists, their computation is not particularly challenging.

Let e be an element that appears in the XML documents for which we want to infer a DTD. It is straightforward to compute the sequence of subelements nested within each `<e> </e>` pair in the XML document collection. Let I denote the set of N such sequences, one sequence for every occurrence of element e in the data. The problem we address in this paper can be stated as follows.

Problem Statement. Given a set I of N input sequences nested within element e, compute a DTD for e such that every sequence in I conforms to the DTD.□

As stated, an obvious solution to the problem is to find the most "concise" regular expression R whose language is I. One mechanism to find such a regular expression is to factor as much as possible, the expression corresponding to the *or* of sequences in I. Factoring a regular expression makes it "concise" without changing the language of the expression. For example, $ab|ac$ can be factored into $a(b|c)$. An alternate method for computing the most concise regular expression is to first find the automaton with the smallest number of states that accepts I and then derive the regular expression from the automaton. (Note, however, that the obtained regular expression may not be the shortest regular expression for I.) In any case, such a concise regular expression whose language is I, is unfortunately not a "good" DTD in the sense it tends to be voluminous and unintuitive. We illustrate this using the DTD of Figure 2. Suppose we have a collection of XML documents that conform to this DTD. Abbreviating the `title` tag by t, and the `author` tag by a, it is reasonable to expect the following sequences to be the subelement sequences of the `article` element in the collection of XML documents: t, ta, taa, $taaa$, $taaaa$. Clearly, the most concise regular expression for the above language is $t|t(a|a(a|a(a|aa)))$ which is definitely much more voluminous and much less intuitive than a DTD such as ta^*.

In other words, the obvious solution above never "generalizes" and would therefore never contain metacharacters like * in the inferred DTD. Clearly, a human expert would at most times want to use such metacharacters in a DTD to succinctly convey the constraints he/she wishes to impose on the structure of XML documents. Thus, the challenge is to infer for the set of input sequences I, a "general" DTD which is similar to what a human would come up with. However, as the following example illustrates, there can be several possible "generalizations" for a given set of input sequences and thus we need to devise a mechanism for choosing the one that best describes the sequences.

Example 3.1 Consider $I = \{ab, abab, ababab\}$. A number of DTDs match sequences in I – (1) $(a \mid b)^*$, (2) $ab \mid abab \mid ababab$, (3) $(ab)^*$, (4) $ab \mid ab(ab \mid abab)$, and so on. DTD (1) is similar to ANY in that it allows any arbitrary sequence of as and bs, while DTD (2) is simply an *or* of all the sequences in I. DTD (4) is derived from DTD (2) by factoring the subsequence ab from the last two disjuncts of DTD (2). The problem with DTD (1) is that it represents a gross over-generalization of the input, and the inferred DTD completely fails to capture any structure inherent in the input. On the other hand, DTDs (2) and (4) accurately reflect the structure of the input sequences but do not generalize or learn any meaningful patterns which make the DTDs smaller or simpler to understand. Thus, none of the DTDs (1), (2) or (4) seem "good". However, of the above DTDs, (3) has great intuitive appeal since it is succinct and it generalizes the set of input sequences without losing too much information about the structure of the sequences. □

Based on the discussion in the above example, we can characterize the set of desirable DTDs by placing the following two qualitative restrictions on the inferred DTD.

R1: The DTD should be *concise* (i.e., small in size).

R2: The DTD should be *precise* (i.e, not cover too many sequences not contained in I).

Restriction R1 above ensures that the inferred DTD is easy to understand and succinct, thus eliminating, in many cases, concise regular expressions whose language is I. Restriction R2, on the other hand, attempts to ensure that the DTD is not too general and captures the structure of input sequences, thus eliminating a DTD such as ANY. While the above restrictions seem reasonable at an intuitive level, in general, there is a tradeoff between a DTD's "conciseness" and its "preciseness", and a good DTD is one that strikes the right balance between the two. The problem here is that conciseness and preciseness are qualitative notions – in order to resolve the tradeoff between the two, we need to devise quantitative measures for mathematically capturing these two qualitative notions.

3.2 Using the MDL Principle to Define a Good DTD

We use the MDL principle [21, 22] to define an information-theoretic measure for quantifying and thereby resolving the tradeoff between the conciseness and preciseness properties of DTDs. The MDL principle has been successfully applied in the past in a variety of situations ranging from constructing good decision tree classifiers [17, 20] to learning common patterns in sets of strings [16].

Roughly speaking, the MDL principle states that the best theory to infer from a set of data is the one which minimizes the sum of

(A) the length of the theory, in bits, and

(B) the length of the data, in bits, when encoded with the help of the theory.

We will refer to the above sum for a theory, as the *MDL cost* for the theory. The MDL principle is a general one and needs to be instantiated appropriately for each situation. In our setting, the theory is the DTD and the data is the sequences in I. Thus, the MDL principle assigns each DTD an MDL cost and ranks the DTDs based on their MDL costs (DTDs with lower MDL costs are ranked higher). Furthermore, parts (A) and (B) of the MDL cost for a DTD depend directly on its conciseness and preciseness, respectively. Part (A) is the number of bits required to describe the DTD and is thus a direct measure of its conciseness. Further, since a DTD that is more precise captures the structure of the input sequences more accurately, fewer bits are required to describe the sequences in I in terms of a more precise DTD. As a result, Part (B) of the MDL cost captures a DTD's preciseness. The MDL cost for a DTD thus provides us with an elegant and principled mechanism (rooted in information theory) for quantifying (and combining) the conflicting concepts of conciseness and preciseness in a single unified framework.

Note that the actual encoding scheme used to specify a DTD as well as the data (with the help of the DTD) plays a critical role in determining the actual values for the two components of the MDL cost. We defer the details of the actual encoding scheme to Section 4. However, in the following example, we employ a simple encoding scheme (a coarser version of the scheme in Section 4) to illustrate how ranking DTDs based on their MDL cost closely matches our intuition of their "goodness".

Example 3.2 Consider the input set I and DTDs from Example 3.1. We compute the MDL cost of each DTD, which, as mentioned earlier, is the cost of encoding the DTD itself and the sequences in I in terms of the DTD. We then rank the DTDs based on their MDL costs (DTDs with smaller costs are considered better). In our simple encoding scheme, we assume a cost of 1 unit for each character.

DTD (1), $(a \mid b)^*$, has a cost of 6 for encoding the DTD. In order to encode the sequence $abab$ using the DTD, we need one character to specify the number of repetitions of the the term $(a \mid b)$ that precedes the $*$ (in this case, this number is 4), and 4 additional characters to specify which of a or b is chosen from each repetition. Thus, the total cost of encoding $abab$ using $(a \mid b)^*$ is 5 and the MDL cost of the DTD is $6 + 3 + 5 + 7 = 21$. Similarly, the MDL cost of DTD (2) can be shown to be 14 (to encode the DTD) + 3 (to encode the input sequences; we need one character to specify the position of the disjunct for each sequence) = 17. The cost of DTD (3) is 5 (to encode the DTD) + 3 (to encode the input sequences – note that we only need to specify the number of repetitions of the term ab for each sequence) = 8. Finally, DTD (4) has a cost of 14 + 5 (1 character to encode sequence ab and 2 characters for each of the other two input sequences) = 19. Thus, since DTD (3) has the least MDL cost, it would be considered the best DTD by the MDL principle – which matches our intuition. □

3.3 Overview of the XTRACT System

The architecture of the XTRACT system is illustrated in Figure 3(a). As shown in the figure, the system consists of three main components: the generalization module, the factoring module, and the MDL module. Input sequences in I are processed by the three subsystems one after another, the output of one subsystem serving as input to the next. We denote the outputs of the generalization and factoring modules by S_G and S_F, respectively. Observe that both S_G and S_F contain the initial input sequences in I. This is to ensure that the MDL module has a wide range of DTDs to choose from that includes the obvious DTD which is simply an *or* of all the input sequences in I. In the following, we provide a brief description of each subsystem; we defer a more detailed description of the algorithms employed by each subsystem to later sections.

The Generalization Subsystem. For each input sequence, the generalization module generates zero or more candidate

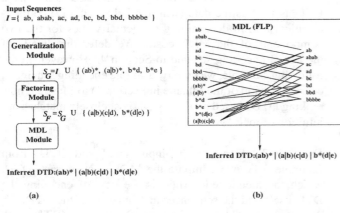

Input Sequences
$I = \{$ ab, abab, ac, ad, bc, bd, bbd, bbbbe $\}$

Generalization Module

$S_G = I \quad \cup \quad \{ (ab)^*, (a|b)^*, b^*d, b^*e \}$

Factoring Module

$S_F = S_G \quad \cup \quad \{ (a|b)(c|d), b^*(d|e) \}$

MDL Module

Inferred DTD: $(ab)^* | (a|b)(c|d) | b^*(d|e)$

(a)

MDL (FLP)

ab
abab
ac
ad
bc
bd
bbd
bbbbe
$(ab)^*$
$(a|b)^*$
b^*d
b^*e
$b^*(d|e)$
$(a|b)(c|d)$

ab
abab
ac
ad
bc
bd
bbd
bbbbe

Inferred DTD: $(ab)^* | (a|b)(c|d) | b^*(d|e)$

(b)

Figure 3: Architecture of the XTRACT System

DTDs that are derived by replacing patterns in the input sequence with regular expressions containing metacharacters like $*$ and $|$ (e.g., $(ab)^*$, $(a \mid b)^*$). Note that the initial input sequences do not contain metacharacters and so the candidate DTDs introduced by the generalization module are more general. For instance, in Figure 3(a), sequences *abab* and *bbbe* result in the more general candidate DTDs $(ab)^*$, $(a \mid b)^*$ and b^*e being output by the generalization subsystem. Also, observe that each candidate DTD produced by the generalization module may cover only a subset of the input sequences. Thus, the final DTD output by the MDL module may be an *or* of multiple candidate DTDs.

Ideally, in the generalization phase, we should consider all DTDs that cover one or more input sequences as candidates, so that the MDL step can choose the best among them. However, the number of such DTDs can be enormous. For example, the sequence *ababaabb* is covered by the following DTDs in addition to many more – $(a \mid b)^*$, $(a \mid b)^*a^*b^*$, $(ab)^*(a \mid b)^*$, $(ab)^*a^*b^*$. Therefore, in this paper, we outline several novel heuristics, inspired by real-life DTDs[2], for limiting the set of candidate DTDs S_G output by the generalization module.

The Factoring Subsystem. The factoring component factors two or more candidate DTDs in S_G into a new candidate DTD. The length of the new DTD is smaller than the sum of the sizes of the DTDs factored. For example, in Figure 3(a), candidate DTDs b^*d and b^*e representing the expression $b^*d \mid b^*e$, when factored, result in the DTD $b^*(d \mid e)$; similarly, the candidates ac, ad, bc and bd are factored into $(a \mid b)(c \mid d)$ (the pre-factored expression is $ac \mid ad \mid bc \mid bd$). Although factoring leaves the semantics of candidate DTDs unchanged, it is nevertheless an important step. The reason being that factoring reduces the size of the DTD and thus the cost of encoding the DTD, without seriously impacting the cost of encoding input sequences

---

[2]The DTDs are available at Robin Cover's SGML/XML web page (www.oasis-open.org/cover/).

using the DTD. Thus, since the DTD encoding cost is a component of the MDL cost for a DTD, factoring can result in certain DTDs being chosen by the MDL module that may not have been considered earlier. We appropriately modify factoring algorithms for boolean functions in the logic optimization area [4, 24] to meet our needs. However, even though every subset of candidate DTDs can, in principle, be factored, the number of these subsets can be huge and only a few of them result in good factorizations. We propose novel heuristics to restrict our attention to subsets that can be factored effectively.

The MDL Subsystem. The MDL subsystem finally chooses from among the set of candidate DTDs S_F generated by the previous two subsystems, a set of DTDs that cover all the input sequences in I and the sum of whose MDL costs is minimum. The final DTD is then an *or* of the DTDs in the set. For the input sequences in Figure 3(a), we illustrate (using solid lines) in Figure 3(b), the input sequences (in the right column) covered by the candidate DTDs in S_F (in the left column).

The above cost minimization problem naturally maps to the *Facility Location Problem* (FLP) for which polynomial-time approximation algorithms have been proposed in the literature [6, 14]. We adapt the algorithm from [6] for our purposes, and using it, the XTRACT system is able to infer the DTD shown at the bottom of Figure 3(b).

4   The MDL Subsystem

The MDL subsystem constitutes the core of the XTRACT system – it is responsible for choosing a set S of candidate DTDs from S_F such that the final DTD $\mathcal{D}$ (which is an *or* of the DTDs in S) (1) covers all sequences in I, and (2) has minimum MDL cost. Consequently, we describe this module first, and postpone the presentation of the generalization and factoring modules to Sections 5 and 6, respectively.

Recall that the MDL cost of a DTD that is used to explain a set of sequences, comprises (A) the length, in bits, needed to describe the DTD; and (B) the length of the sequences (in bits) when encoded in terms of the DTD. In the following subsection, we first present the encoding schemes for computing parts (A) and (B) of the MDL cost of a DTD. Subsequently, in Section 4.2, we present the algorithm for computing the set $S \subseteq S_F$ of candidate DTDs whose *or* yields the final DTD $\mathcal{D}$ with minimum MDL cost. Note that the candidate DTDs in S_F can be complex regular expressions (containing $*$, $|$, etc.) output by the generalization and factoring subsystems.

4.1   The Encoding Scheme

We begin by describing the procedure for estimating the number of bits required to encode the DTD itself (part (A) of the MDL cost). Let Σ be the set of subelement symbols that appear in sequences in I. Let $\mathcal{M}$ be the set of metacharacters $|, *, +, ?, (,)$. Let the length of a DTD viewed as a string

(A) $seq(D, s) = \epsilon$ if $D = s$. In this case, the DTD D is a sequence of symbols from the alphabet Σ and does not contain any metacharacters.

(B) $seq(D_1 \ldots D_k, s_1 \ldots s_k) = seq(D_1, s_1) \ldots seq(D_k, s_k)$; that is, D is the concatenation of regular expressions $D_1 \ldots D_k$ and the sequence s can be written as the concatenation of the subsequences $s_1 \ldots s_k$, such that each subsequence s_i matches the corresponding regular expression D_i.

(C) $seq(D_1| \ldots |D_m, s) = i\ seq(D_i, s)$; that is, D is the exclusive choice of regular expressions $D_1 \ldots D_m$, and i is the index of the regular expression that the sequence s matches. Note that we need $\lceil \log m \rceil$ bits to encode the index i.

(D) $seq(D^*, s_1 \ldots s_k) = \begin{cases} k\ seq(D, s_1) \ldots seq(D, s_k) & \text{if } k > 0 \\ 0 & \text{otherwise} \end{cases}$

In other words, the sequence $s = s_1 \ldots s_k$ is produced from D^* by instantiating the repetition operator k times, and each subsequence s_i matches the i-th instantiation. In this case, since there is no simple and inexpensive way to bound apriori the number of bits required for the index k, we first specify the number of bits required to encode k in unary (that is, a sequence of $\lceil \log k \rceil$ 1s, followed by a 0) and then the index k using $\lceil \log k \rceil$ bits. The 0 in the middle serves as the delimiter between the unary encoding of the length of the index and the actual index itself.

Figure 4: The Encoding Scheme

in $\Sigma \cup \mathcal{M}$, be n. Then, the length of the DTD in bits is $n\lceil \log(| \Sigma | + | \mathcal{M} |) \rceil$. As an example, let Σ consist of the elements a and b. The length in bits of the DTD a^*b^* is $4 * \lceil \log(2 + 6) \rceil = 12$. Similarly, the length in bits of the DTD $(ab|abb)(aa|ab^*)$ is $16 * 3 = 48$.

We next describe the scheme for encoding a sequence using a DTD (part (B) of the MDL cost). Our encoding scheme constructs a sequence of integral indices (which forms the encoding) for expressing a sequence in terms of a DTD. The following simple examples illustrate the basic building blocks on which our encoding scheme for more complex DTDs is built:

1. The encoding for the sequence a in terms of the DTD a is the empty string ϵ.

2. The encoding for the sequence b in terms of the DTD $a \mid b \mid c$ is the integral index 1 (denotes that b is at position 1, counting from 0, in the above DTD).

3. The encoding for the sequence bbb in terms of the DTD b^* is the integral index 3 (denotes 3 repetitions of b).

We now generalize the encoding scheme for arbitrary DTDs and arbitrary sequences. Let us denote the sequence of integral indices for a sequence s when encoded in terms of a DTD D by $seq(D, s)$. We define $seq(D, s)$ recursively in terms of component DTDs within D as shown in Figure 4. Thus, $seq(D, s)$ can be computed using a recursive procedure based on the encoding scheme of Figure 4. Note that we have not provided the definitions

of the encodings for operators $^+$ and ? since these can be defined in a similar fashion to * (for $^+$, k is always greater than 0, while for ?, k can only assume values 1 or 0). We now illustrate our encoding scheme using the following example.

Example 4.1 Consider the DTD $(ab|c)^*(de|fg^*)$ and the sequence $abccabfggg$ to be encoded in terms of the DTD. Below, we list how steps (A), (B), (C) and (D) in Figure 4 are recursively applied to derive the encoding $seq((ab|c)^*(de|fg^*), abccabfggg)$.

1. **Apply Step (B):** $seq((ab|c)^*, abccab)\ seq((de|fg^*), fggg)$
2. **Apply Step (D):** $4\ seq(ab|c, ab)\ seq(ab|c, c)\ seq(ab|c, c)$ $seq(ab|c, ab)\ seq((de|fg^*), fggg)$
3. **Apply Step (C):** $4\ 0\ seq(ab, ab)\ 1\ seq(c, c)\ 1\ seq(c, c)\ 0$ $seq(ab, ab)\ 1\ seq(fg^*, fggg)$
4. **Apply Step (A):** $4\ 0\ 1\ 1\ 0\ 1\ seq(fg^*, fggg)$
5. **Apply Steps (A), (B) and (D):** $4\ 0\ 1\ 1\ 0\ 1\ 3$

In order to derive the final bit sequence corresponding to the above indices, we need to include in the encoding the unary representation for the number of bits required to encode the indices 4 and 3. Thus, we obtain the following bit encoding for the sequence (we have inserted blanks in between the encoding for successive indices for clarity).

$seq((ab|c)^*(de|fg^*), abccabfggg) = 1110100\ 0\ 1\ 1\ 0\ 1\ 11011$

$\square$

In steps (B), (C) and (D), we need to be able to determine if a sequence s matches a DTD D. Since a DTD is a regular expression, well-established techniques for finding out if a sequence is covered by a regular expression can be used for this purpose [15] and have a complexity of $O(|D| \cdot |s|)$ ($|s|$ denotes the length of sequence s). These methods involve constructing a non-deterministic finite automaton for D and can also be used to decompose the sequence s into subsequences such that each subsequence matches the corresponding sub-part of the DTD D, thus enabling us to come up with the encoding.

Note that there may be multiple ways of partitioning the sequence s such that each subsequence matches the corresponding sub-part of the DTD D. In such a case, we can extend the above procedure to enumerate every decomposition of s that match sub-parts of D, and then select from among the decompositions the one that results in the minimum length encoding of s in terms of D. The complexity of considering all possible decompositions, however, is much higher and therefore not included in our XTRACT implementation.

4.2 Computing the DTD with Minimum MDL Cost

We now turn our attention to the problem of computing the final DTD $\mathcal{D}$ (which is an *or* of a subset $\mathcal{S}$ of candidate DTDs in $\mathcal{S}_\mathcal{F}$) that covers all the input sequences in I and whose MDL cost for encoding sequences in I is minimum. The above minimization problem maps naturally to the *Facility*

Location Problem (FLP) [6, 14]. The FLP is formulated as follows: Let C be a set of clients and J be a set of facilities such that each facility "serves" every client. There is a cost $c(j)$ of "choosing" a facility $j \in J$ and a cost $d(j,i)$ of serving client $i \in C$ by facility $j \in J$. The problem definition asks to choose a subset of facilities $F \subset J$ such that the sum of costs of the chosen facilities plus the sum of costs of serving every client by its closest chosen facility is minimized, that is

$$\min_{F \subset J} \{ \sum_{j \in F} c(j) + \sum_{i \in C} \min_{j \in F} d(j,i) \}. \qquad (1)$$

The problem of inferring the minimum MDL cost DTD can be reduced to FLP as follows: Let C be the set I of input sequences and J be the set of candidate DTDs in $\mathcal{S}_{\mathcal{F}}$. The cost of choosing a facility is the length of the corresponding candidate DTD. The cost of serving client i from facility j, $d(j,i)$, is the length of the encoding of the sequence corresponding to client i using the DTD corresponding to facility j. If a DTD j does not cover a sequence i, then we set $d(j,i)$ to ∞. Thus, the set F computed by the FLP corresponds to our desired set S of candidate DTDs.

The FLP is NP-hard; however, it can be reduced to the *set cover problem* and then approximated within a logarithmic factor as shown in [14]. In our implementation, we employ the randomized algorithm from [6] which approximates the FLP within a constant factor if the distance function is a metric. Even though our distance function is not a metric, we have found the FLP approximations produced by [6] for our problem setting to be very good in practice. Furthermore, the time complexity of [6] for computing the approximate solution is $O(N^2 \cdot \log N)$, where $N = |I|$.

5 The Generalization Subsystem

The quality of the DTD computed by the MDL module is very dependent on the set of candidate DTDs $\mathcal{S}_{\mathcal{F}}$ input to it. In case $\mathcal{S}_{\mathcal{F}}$ were to contain only input sequences in I, then the final DTD output by the MDL subsystem would simply be the *or* of all the sequences in I. However, as we observed earlier, this is not a desirable DTD since it is neither concise nor intuitive. Thus, in order to infer meaningful DTDs, it is crucial that the candidate DTDs in $\mathcal{S}_{\mathcal{F}}$ be *general*. The goal of the generalization component is to achieve this objective by inferring a set $\mathcal{S}_G$ of general DTDs which are then input to the factorization step. As we mentioned before, the factorization step infers additional factored DTDs and generates $\mathcal{S}_{\mathcal{F}}$ which is a superset of $\mathcal{S}_G$.

The generalization component in XTRACT infers a number of regular expressions which we have found to frequently appear in real-life DTDs. Some of the most common regular expressions from real-life DTDs are a^*bc^*, $(abc)^*$, $(a|b|c)^*$, and $((ab)^*c)^*$. These are examples that appear in the Newspaper Association of America (NAA) Classified Advertizing Standards XML DTD[3]. (A detailed description of the NAA

[3]www.naa.org/technology/clsstdtf/Adex010.dtd

data can be found in the full version of this paper [9].)

Although our algorithms can infer regular expressions that are more complex than the above, we do not infer certain complex expressions such as $(ab?c^*d?)^*$ that are less likely to occur in practice. We defer further discussion of this topic to Section 7.

We now discuss our generalization algorithm which is outlined in Figure 5. Procedure GENERALIZE infers several DTDs for each input sequence in I independently and adds them to the set $\mathcal{S}_G$. Therefore, it may over-generalize in some cases (since we are inferring DTDs based on a single sequence); however, our MDL step will ensure that such overly general DTDs are not chosen as part of the final inferred DTD, if there are better alternatives. Recall that the generalization step is merely trying to provide several alternate candidates to the MDL step. In particular, $\mathcal{S}_G \supseteq I$, and therefore, the DTD corresponding to the *or*'s of the input will always be considered during the MDL step.

The essence of procedure GENERALIZE lies in the two procedures DISCOVERSEQPATTERN and DISCOVEROR-PATTERN, which are repeatedly called with various parameter values. We discuss the details of these procedures and the roles of their parameters next.

5.1 Discovering Sequencing Patterns

Procedure DISCOVERSEQPATTERN, shown in Figure 5, takes as input an input sequence s and returns a candidate DTD that is derived from s by replacing sequencing patterns of the form $xx \cdots x$, for a subsequence x in s, with the regular expression $(x)^*$. In addition to s, the procedure also accepts as input a threshold parameter $r > 1$ which is the minimum number of contiguous repetitions of subsequence x in s required for the repetitions to be replaced with $(x)^*$. In case there are multiple subsequences x with the maximum number of repetitions in Step 2, the longest among them is chosen, and subsequent ties are resolved arbitrarily.

Note that instead of introducing the regular expression term $(x)^*$ into the sequence s, we choose to introduce an *auxiliary* symbol that serves as a representative for the term. The auxiliary symbols enable us to keep the description of our algorithms simple and clean, since their input is always a simple sequence of symbols. We ensure that there is a one-to-one correspondence between auxiliary symbols and regular expression terms throughout the XTRACT system; thus, if the auxiliary symbol, A denotes $(bc)^*$ in one candidate DTD, then it represents $(bc)^*$ in every other candidate DTD. Also, observe that procedure DISCOVERSEQPATTERN may perform several iterations and thus new sequencing patterns may contain auxiliary symbols corresponding to patterns replaced in previous iterations. For example, invoking procedure DISCOVERSEQPATTERN with the input sequence $s = abababcababc$ and $r = 2$ yields the sequence A_1cA_1c after the first iteration, where A_1 is an auxiliary symbol for the term $(ab)^*$. After the second iteration, the procedure returns the candidate DTD A_2, where A_2 is the auxiliary sym-

procedure GENERALIZE(I)
begin
1. **for each** sequence s in I
2.   add s to $\mathcal{S}_G$
3.   **for** $r := 2, 3, 4$
4. $s' :=$ DISCOVERSEQPATTERN(s, r)
5.   **for** $d := 0.1 \cdot |s'|, 0.5 \cdot |s'|, |s'|$
6. $s'' :=$ DISCOVERORPATTERN(s', d)
7.   add s'' to $\mathcal{S}_G$
end

procedure DISCOVERSEQPATTERN(s, r)
begin
1. **repeat**
2.   let x be a subsequence of s with the maximum
3.   number ($\geq r$) of contiguous repetitions in s
4.   replace all ($\geq r$) contiguous occurrences of
5. x in s with a new auxiliary symbol $A_i = (x)^*$
6. **until** (s no longer contains $\geq r$ contiguous
7.   occurrences of any subsequence x)
8. **return** s
end

procedure DISCOVERORPATTERN(s, d)
begin
1. $s_1, s_2, \ldots, s_n :=$ PARTITION(s, d)
2.   **for each** subsequence s_j in $s_1, s_2, \ldots, s_n$
3.   let the set of distinct symbols in s_j
4.   be $a_1, a_2, \ldots, a_m$
5.   **if** $(m > 1)$
6.   replace subsequence s_j in sequence s by a
7.   new auxiliary symbol $A_i = (a_1 | \cdots | a_m)^*$
8. **return** s
end

procedure PARTITION(s, d)
begin
1. $i := start := end := 1$
2. $s_i = s[start, end]$
3. **while** $(end < |s|)$
4.   **while** $(end < |s|$ **and** a symbol in s_i occurs to
5.   the right of s_i within a distance d)
6. $end := end + 1$;
7. $s_i := s[start, end]$;
8.   **if** $(end < |s|)$
9. $i := i + 1$;
10. $start := end + 1$;
11. $end := end + 1$;
12. $s_i := s[start, end]$;
13. **return** $s_1, s_2, \cdots, s_i$
end

Figure 5: The Generalization Algorithm

bol corresponding to $((ab)^*c)^*$. Thus, the resulting candidate DTD returned by procedure DISCOVERSEQPATTERN can contain *'s nested within other *'s. Finally, we have chosen to invoke DISCOVERSEQPATTERN (from GENERALIZE) with three different values for the parameter r to control the eagerness with which we generalize. For example, for the sequence $aabbb$, DISCOVERSEQPATTERN with $r = 2$ would infer a^*b^*, while with $r = 3$, it would infer aab^*. In the MDL step, if many other sequences are covered by aab^*, then a DTD of aab^* may be preferred to a DTD of a^*b^*, since it more accurately describes sequences in I.

The time complexity of the procedure is dominated by the first step that involves finding the subsequence x with the maximum number of contiguous repetitions. Since s contains at most $O(|s|^2)$ possible subsequences and computing the number of repetitions for each subsequence takes $O(|s|)$ steps, the complexity of the first step is $O(|s|^3)$ per iteration, in the worst case.

5.2 Discovering Or Patterns

Procedure DISCOVERORPATTERN infers patterns of the form $(a_1|a_2|\ldots|a_m)^*$ based on the locality of these symbols within a sequence s. It discovers such localities by first partitioning (using procedure PARTITION) the input sequence s into the smallest possible subsequences $s_1, s_2, \ldots, s_n$, such that for any occurrence of a symbol a in a subsequence s_i, there does not exist another occurrence of a in some other subsequence s_j within a distance d (which is a parameter to DISCOVERORPATTERN). Each subsequence s_i in s is then replaced by the pattern $(a_1|a_2|\ldots|a_m)^*$ where $a_1, \ldots, a_m$ are the distinct symbols in the subsequence s_i. The intuition here is that if s_i contains frequent repetitions of the symbols $a_1, a_2, \ldots, a_m$ in close proximity, then it is very likely that s_i originated from a regular expression of the form $(a_1|a_2|\ldots|a_m)^*$. As an illustration, on the input sequence $abcbac$, procedure DISCOVERORPATTERN returns

- aA_1ac for $d = 2$, where $A_1 = (b \mid c)^*$,
- aA_2 for $d = 3$, where $A_2 = (a \mid b \mid c)^*$, and
- A_2 for $d = 4$, where $A_2 = (a \mid b \mid c)^*$.

A critical component for discovering *or* patterns is procedure PARTITION, which we now discuss in more detail. Before that, we define the following notation for sequences. For a sequence s, $s[i, j]$ denotes the subsequence of s starting at the ith symbol and ending at the jth symbol of s. Procedure PARTITION constructs subsequences of s in the order s_1, s_2, and so on. Assuming that s_1 through s_j have been generated, it constructs s_{j+1} by starting s_{j+1} immediately after s_j ends and expanding the subsequence s_{j+1} to the right as long as required to ensure that there is no symbol in s_{j+1} that occurs within a distance d to the right of s_{j+1}. By construction, there cannot exist such a symbol to the left of s_{j+1}. Note that the condition of whether a symbol in s_i occurs within a distance d outside s_i can be checked in $O(|s|)$ time if we keep track of the next occurrence outside s_i

of every symbol in s_i – this can be achieved by initially constructing for every symbol, the locations of its occurrences in s sorted order. Therefore, the time complexity of procedures PARTITION and DISCOVERORPATTERN can be easily shown to be $O(|s|^2)$.

Note that procedure GENERALIZE invokes DISCOVEROR-PATTERN on the DTDs that result from calls to DISCOVER-SEQPATTERN and therefore it is possible to infer more complex DTDs of the form $(a|(bc)^*)^*$ in addition to DTDs like $(a|b|c)^*$. For instance, for the input sequence $s = abcbca$, procedure DISCOVERSEQPATTERN invoked with $r = 2$ would return $s' = aA_1a$, where $A_1 = (bc)^*$, which when input to DISCOVERORPATTERN returns $s'' = A_2$ for $d = |s'|$, where $A_2 = (a|A_1)^*$. Further, observe that DISCOVEROR-PATTERN is invoked with various values of d (expressed as a fraction of the length of the input sequence) to control the degree of generalization. Small values of d lead to conservative generalizations while larger values result in more liberal generalizations.

6   The Factoring Subsystem

In a nutshell, the factoring step derives factored forms for expressions consisting of an *or* of a subset of the candidate DTDs in S_G. For example, for candidate DTDs ac, ad, bc and bd in S_G, the factoring step would generate the factored form $(a \mid b)(c \mid d)$. Note that since the final DTD is an *or* of candidate DTDs in S_F, factored forms are candidates, too. Further, a factored candidate DTD, because of its smaller size, has a lower MDL cost, and is thus more likely to be chosen in the MDL step. Thus, since factored forms (due to their compactness) are more desirable (see restriction **R1** in Section 3), factoring can result in better-quality DTDs. In this section, we describe the algorithms used by the factoring module to derive factored forms of the candidate DTDs in S_G produced by the generalization step.

Factored DTDs are common in real life, when there are several choices to be made. For example, in the DTD in Figure 2, an article may be categorized based on whether it appeared in a workshop, conference, or journal; it may also be classified according to its area as belonging to either computer science, physics, chemistry, etc. As a consequence, the DTD (in factored form) for the element `article` could be as follows:

```
<!ELEMENT article(title, author*,
(workshop | conference | journal),
(computer science | physics | chemistry | ...))
```

In addition to the factored forms generated from candidates in S_G, the set of candidate DTDs output by the factorization module, S_F, also contains all the DTDs in S_G. Ideally, factored forms for every subset of S_G should be added to S_F to be considered by the MDL module. However, this is clearly impractical, since S_G could be very large. We have devised a heuristic strategy for selecting sets of candidates in S_G that when factored yield "good" factored DTDs. Intuitively, our heuristic greedily selects DTDs from S_G that

(1) share common prefixes or suffixes, and (2) have minimal overlap with other selected DTDs. Due to space constraints, we omit the detailed description of our heuristic as well as the factoring algorithm itself (which is an adaptation of factoring algorithms for boolean expressions from the logic optimization literature [24]). The details can be found in the full version of this paper [9].

7   Experimental Results

To determine the effectiveness of XTRACT's methodology for inferring the DTD of a database of XML documents, we conducted a study with both synthetic and real-life DTDs. We also compared the DTDs produced by XTRACT with those generated by the IBM Alphaworks DTD extraction tool, DDbE[4], for XML data. Our results indicate that XTRACT outperforms DDbE over a wide range of DTDs, and accurately finds almost every original DTD while DDbE fails to do so for most DTDs. Thus, our results clearly demonstrate the effectiveness of XTRACT's approach that employs generalization and factorization to derive a range of general and concise candidate DTDs, and then uses the MDL principle as the basis to select amongst them.

7.1   Algorithms

In the following, we describe the two DTD extraction algorithms that we considered in our experimental study.
XTRACT: Our implementation of XTRACT includes all three modules as described in Sections 4, 5, and 6. In the generalization step, we discover both sequencing and *or* patterns using procedure GENERALIZE. In the factoring step, $k = \frac{N}{10}$ subsets are chosen for factoring and the parameter δ is set to 0 in the procedure FACTORSUBSETS. Finally, in the MDL step, we employ the algorithm from [6] to compute an approximation to the FLP solution.
DDbE: We used Version 1.0 of the DDbE DTD extraction tool in our experiments. DDbE is a Java component library for inferring a DTD from a data set consisting of well-formed XML instances. DDbE offers parameters that allow the user to control the structure of the content models and the types used for attribute declarations. Two important parameters of DDbE are (1) the maximum number of consecutive identical tokens that should not be replaced by a list, and (2) the number of applications of factoring. For our experiments we used the default values of these parameters, which are 1 and 2, respectively [9].

7.2   Data Sets

In order to evaluate the quality of DTDs retrieved by XTRACT, we used both synthetic as well as real-life DTD schemas. For each DTD for a single element, we generated an XML file containing 1000 instantiations of the element. These 1000 instantiations were generated by randomly sampling from the DTD for the element. Thus, the initial set of input sequences I to both XTRACT and DDbE contained

---

[4]www.alphaworks.ibm.com/formula/xml/

No.	Original DTD
1	$abcde\|efgh\|ij\|klm$
2	$(a\|b\|c\|d\|f)^*gh$
3	$(a\|b\|c\|d)^*\|e$
4	$(abcde)^*f$
5	$(ab)^*\|cdef\|(ghi)^*$
6	$abcdef(g\|h\|i\|j)(k\|l\|m\|n\|o)$
7	$(a\|b\|c)d^*e^*(fgh)^*$
8	$(a\|b)(cdefg)^*hijklmnopq(r\|s)^*$
9	$(abcd)^*\|(e\|f\|g)^*\|h\|(ijklm)^*$
10	$a^*\|(b\|c\|d\|e\|f)^*\|gh\|(i\|j\|k)^*\|(lmn)^*$

Table 1: Synthetic DTD Data Set

No	Original DTD	Simplified DTD

1	`<!ENTITY included-elements`
	`(audio-clip|blind-box-reply|`
	`link|pi-char|video-clip)>`
		$a\|b\|c\|d\|e$

2	`<!ELEMENT communications-contacts` `(phone|fax|email|pager|web-page)*>`	$(a\|b\|c\|d\|e)^*$

3	`<!ELEMENT employment-services`
	`(employment-service.type,`
	`employment-service.location*`
	`(e.zz-generic-tag)*)>`
		ab^*c^*

4	`<!ENTITY location (addr*,area?,` `city?,state?,zip-code?,country?)>`	$a^*b?c?d?$

5	`<!ELEMENT transfer-info`
	`(transfer-number,(from-to,co-id)+,`
	`contact-info)*>`
		$(a(bc)^+d)^*$

6	`<!ELEMENT real-estate-services`
	`(r-e.type,r-e.location?,`
	`r-e.response-modes*,r-e.comment?)*>`
		$(ab?c^*d?)^*$

Table 2: Real-life DTD Data Set

somewhere between 500 and 1000 sequences (after the elimination of duplicates) conforming to the original DTD.
Synthetic DTD Data Set. We used a synthetic data generator to generate the synthetic data sets. Each DTD is randomly chosen to have one of the following two forms: $A_1\|A_2\|A_3\|\cdots\|A_n$ and $A_1A_2A_3\cdots A_n$. Thus, a DTD has n building blocks with n randomly chosen between 1 and mb, where mb is an input parameter to the generator that specifies the maximum number of building blocks in a DTD. Each building block A_i further consists of n_i symbols, where n_i is randomly chosen to be between 1 and ms (the parameter ms specifies the maximum number of symbols that can be contained in a building block). Each building block A_i has one of the following four forms, each of which has an equal probability of occurrence: (1) $(a_1\|a_2\|a_3\|\ldots\|a_{n_i})$, (2) $a_1a_2a_3\ldots a_{n_i}$, (3) $(a_1\|a_2\|a_3\|a_4\|\ldots\|a_{n_i})^*$; and (4) $(a_1a_2a_3a_4\ldots a_{n_i})^*$. Here, the a_i's denote subelement symbols. Thus, our synthetic data generator essentially generates DTDs containing one level of nesting of regular expression terms.

In Table 1, we show the synthetic DTDs that we considered in our experiments. Note that, in the figure, we only include the regular expression corresponding to the DTD. The DTDs were produced using our generator with the input parameters mb and ms both set to 5. (We use letters from the alphabet as subelement symbols.)

The ten synthetic DTDs vary in complexity with later DTDs being more complex than earlier ones. For instance, DTD 1 does not contain any metacharacters, while DTDs 2 through 5 contain simple sequencing and *or* patterns. DTD 6 represents a DTD in factored form, while in DTDs 7 through 10 factors are combined with sequencing and *or* patterns.
Real-life DTD Data Set. We obtained our real-life DTDs from the Newspaper Association of America (NAA) Classified Advertising Standards XML DTD produced by the NAA Classified Advertising Standards Task Force[5]. We examined this real-life DTD data and collected six representative DTDs that are shown in Table 2. Of the DTDs shown in the table, the last three DTDs are quite interesting.

---

[5]www.naa.org/technology/clsstdtf/Adex010.dtd

DTD 4 contains the metacharacter ? in conjunction with the metacharacter *, while DTDs 5 and 6 contain two regular expressions with *'s, one nested within the other.

7.3 Quality of Inferred DTDs

Synthetic DTD Data Set. For the synthetic data set, XTRACT infers *each* of the original DTDs correctly. In contrast, DDbE computes the accurate DTD only for DTD 1, which is the simplest DTD containing no metacharacters. Even for the simple DTDs 2–5, not only is DDbE unable to correctly deduce the original DTD, but it also infers a DTD that does not cover the set of input sequences. In addition, DDbE is not very good at factoring DTDs and, unlike XTRACT, it is unable to derive the final factored form for DTD 6. Finally, DDbE infers an extremely complex DTD for the simple DTD 7 and overly general DTDs for the more complex DTDs 8–10. (The exact DTDs inferred by DDbE can be found in the full version of this paper [9].) Our results for synthetic data clearly demonstrate the superiority of XTRACT's approach (based on the combination of generalization, factoring, and the MDL principle) compared to that of DDbE for the DTD inference problem.
Real-life DTD Data Set. The DTDs generated by the two algorithms for the real-life data set are shown in Table 3. Of the six DTDs, XTRACT is able to infer the first five correctly. In contrast, DDbE is able to derive the accurate DTD only for DTDs 1 and 2, and an approximate DTD for DTD 3. Basically, with an additional factoring step, DDbE could obtain the original DTD for DTD 3. Note, however, that DDbE is unable to infer the simple DTD 4 that contains the metacharacter ?. In contrast, XTRACT is able to deduce this DTD because its factorization step takes into account the identity element "1" and simplifies expressions

No	Simplified DTD	DTD Obtained by XTRACT	DTD obtained by DDbE
1	$a\|b\|c\|d\|e$	$a\|b\|c\|d\|e$	$a\|b\|c\|d\|e$
2	$(a\|b\|c\|d\|e)^*$	$(a\|b\|c\|d\|e)^*$	$(a\|b\|c\|d\|e)^*$
3	(ab^*c^*)	ab^*c^*	$(ab^+c^*)\|(ac^*)$
4	$a^*b?c?d?$	$a^*b?c?d?$	$(a^+b(c\|(c?d))?)\|$ $((b\|a^+)?cd)\|((a^+\|b)?d)\|$ $((a^+\|b)?c)\|a^+\|b)$
5	$(a(bc)^+d)*$	$(a(bc)^*d)^*$	$(a\|b\|c\|d)^+$
6	$(ab?c^*d?)*$	$-$	$(a\|b\|c\|d)+$

Table 3: DTDs generated for Real-life Data Set

of the form $1|a$ to $a?$. DTD 5 represents an interesting case where XTRACT is able to mine a DTD containing regular expressions containing nested *'s. This is due to our generalization module that iteratively looks for sequencing patterns. On the other hand, DDbE simply over-generalizes DTD 5 by *or*-ing all the symbols in it and enclosing them within the metacharacter $^+$. Finally, neither XTRACT nor DDbE is able to correctly infer DTD 6. (The approximate DTD derived by XTRACT for DTD 6 is rather complex and, therefore, we chose to omit it from Table 3.) The reason for XTRACT's failure is that our generalization subsystem does not detect patterns containing the optional symbol ?. Finding such patterns requires a more sophisticated analysis of symbol occurrences within and across sequences, and we plan to pursue this further as part of our future work.

8 Conclusions

We have presented the architecture of the XTRACT system for inferring a DTD for a database of XML documents. The problem of automated DTD derivation is complicated by the fact that the DTD syntax incorporates the full expressive power of regular expressions. Specifically, as we have shown, naive approaches that do not "generalize" beyond the input element sequences fail to deduce concise and semantically meaningful DTDs. Instead, XTRACT applies sophisticated algorithms to compute a DTD that is more along the lines of what a human expert would infer. We compared the quality of the DTDs inferred by XTRACT with those returned by the IBM Alphaworks DDbE tool on synthetic and real-life DTDs. In our experiments, XTRACT outperformed DDbE by a wide margin; for most of our test cases, XTRACT was able to accurately infer the DTD whereas DDbE completely failed to do so. A number of the DTDs which were correctly identified by XTRACT were fairly complex and contained factors, metacharacters and nested regular expression terms. Thus, our results clearly demonstrate the effectiveness of the XTRACT approach that employs generalization and factorization to derive a range of general and concise candidate DTDs, and then uses the MDL principle as the basis to select amongst them.

References

[1] S. Abiteboul. Querying semi-structured data. In *Proc. of the Intl. Conf. on Database Theory (ICDT)*, 1997.

[2] D. Angluin. On the complexity of minimum inference of regular sets. *Information and Control*, 39(3):337–350, 1978.

[3] T. Bray, J. Paoli, and C. M. Sperberg-McQueen. Extensible markup language (XML). (www.w3.org/TR/REC-xml)

[4] R. K. Brayton and C. McMullen. The decomposition and factorization of boolean expressions. In *Proc of the Intl. Symp. on Circuits and Systems*, 1982.

[5] A. Brazma. Efficient identification of regular expressions from representative examples. In *Proc. of the Ann. Conf. on Computational Learning Theory (COLT)*, 1993.

[6] M. Charikar and S. Guha. Improved combinatorial algorithms for the facility location and k-median problems. In *Proc. of the Ann. Symp. on Foundations of Computer Science (FOCS)*, 1999.

[7] A. Deutsch, M. Fernandez, and D. Suciu. Storing semi-structured data with stored. In *Proc. of the ACM SIGMOD Intl. Conf. on Management of Data*, 1999.

[8] M. Fernandez and D. Suciu. Optimizing regular path expressions using graph schemas. In *Proc. of the Intl. Conf. on Database Theory (ICDT)*, 1997.

[9] M. Garofalakis, A. Gionis, R. Rastogi, S. Seshadri, and K. Shim. XTRACT: A System for Extracting Document Type Descriptors from XML Documents. Bell Labs Tech. Memorandum, 1999.

[10] E. Mark Gold. Language identification in the limit. *Information and Control*, 10(5):447–474, 1967.

[11] E. Mark Gold. Complexity of automaton identification from given data. *Information and Control*, 37(3):302–320, 1978.

[12] R. Goldman, J. McHugh, and J. Widom. From semistructured data to XML: Migrating the lore data model and query language. In *Proc. of the Intl. Workshop on the Web and Databases (WebDB)*, 1999.

[13] R. Goldman and J. Widom. DataGuides: Enabling query formulation and optimization in semistructured databases. In *Proc. of the Intl. Conf. on Very Large Data Bases (VLDB)*, 1997.

[14] D. S. Hochbaum. Heuristics for the fixed cost median problem. *Mathematical Programming*, 22:148–162, 1982.

[15] J. E. Hopcroft and J. D. Ullman. *Introduction to Automaton Theory, Languages, and Computation*. Addison-Wesley, Reading, Massachusetts, 1979.

[16] P. Kilpeläinen, H. Mannila, and E. Ukkonen. MDL learning of unions of simple pattern languages from positive examples. In *Proc. of the European Conf. on Computational Learning Theory (EuroCOLT)*, 1995.

[17] M. Mehta, J. Rissanen, and R. Agrawal. MDL-based decision tree pruning. In *Proc. of the Intl. Conf. on Knowledge Discovery and Data Mining (KDD)*, 1995.

[18] S. Nestorov, S. Abiteboul, and R. Motwani. Extracting schema from semistructured data. In *Proc. of the ACM SIGMOD Intl. Conf. on Management of Data*, 1998.

[19] L. Pitt. "Inductive inference, DFAs, and computational complexity". *Analogical and Inductive Inference*, pp. 18–44, 1989.

[20] J. R. Quinlan and R. L. Rivest. Inferring Decision Trees Using the Minimum Description Length Principle. *Information and Computation*, 80:227–248, 1989.

[21] J. Rissanen. Modeling by shortest data description. *Automatica*, 14:465–471, 1978.

[22] J. Rissanen. *Stochastic Complexity in Statistical Inquiry*. World Scientific Publ. Co., 1989.

[23] J. Shanmugasundaram, G. He, K. Tufte, C. Zhang, D. DeWitt, and J. Naughton. Relational databases for querying XML documents: Limitations and opportunities. In *Proc. of the Intl. Conf. on Very Large Data Bases (VLDB)*, 1999.

[24] A. R. R. Wang. *Algorithms for Multi-level Logic Optimization*. PhD thesis, Univ. of California, Berkeley, 1989.

[25] J. Widom. Data management for XML: research directions. *IEEE Data Engineering Bulletin*, 1991.

Spatial Join Selectivity Using Power Laws

Christos Faloutsos[1]
¹Computer Science Department
Carnegie Mellon University - USA
christos@cs.cmu.edu

Bernhard Seeger[2]
²Fachbereich Mathematik und Informatik
Universität Marburg - Germany
seeger@mathematik.uni-marburg.de

Agma Traina[3]   Caetano Traina Jr.[4]
³,⁴Computer Science Department
University of São Paulo at São Carlos - Brazil
{agmalcaetano}@icmc.sc.usp.br

Abstract

We discovered a surprising law governing the spatial join selectivity across two sets of points. An example of such a spatial join is *"find the libraries that are within 10 miles of schools"*. Our law dictates that the number of such qualifying pairs follows a power law, whose exponent we call "pair-count exponent" (PC). We show that this law also holds for self-spatial-joins (*"find schools within 5 miles of other schools"*) in addition to the general case that the two point-sets are distinct. Our law holds for many real datasets, including diverse environments (geographic datasets, feature vectors from biology data, galaxy data from astronomy).

In addition, we introduce the concept of the Box-Occupancy-Product-Sum (BOPS) plot, and we show that it can compute the pair-count exponent in a timely manner, reducing the run time by orders of magnitude, from quadratic to linear. Due to the pair-count exponent and our analysis (Law 1), we can achieve accurate selectivity estimates in constant time (O(1)) without the need for sampling or other expensive operations. The relative error in selectivity is about 30% with our fast BOPS method, and even better (about 10%), if we use the slower, quadratic method.

[1] This material is based upon work supported by the National Science Foundation under Grants No. IRI-9625428, DMS-9873442, IIS-9817496, and IIS-9910606, and by the DARPA under Contract No. N66001-97-C-8517. Additional funding was provided by donations from NEC and Intel. Any opinions, findings, and conclusions or recommendations expressed in this material are those of the author(s) and do not necessarily reflect the views of the National Science Foundation, DARPA, or other funding parties.
[2] Research supported by Grant No. SE 553/2-1 from DFG (Deutsche Forschungsgemeinschaft).
[3,4] Research supported by FAPESP (Fundação de Amparo à Pesquisa do Estado de São Paulo - Brazil, under Grants 98/0559-7 and 98/05556-5.

The names of the authors are in alphabetical order.

1. INTRODUCTION

Multi-dimensional and spatial database management systems (DBMS) have attracted a lot of interest. One of the most important operations in a spatial DBMS [GÜT94] is the spatial join, which is the counterpart to the equi-join in a relational DBMS.

The typical query is also called the 'all pairs' query or 'spatial distance join', as in the example, *'Estimate the number of schools that are within 5 miles from libraries'*. Spatial distance joins are considered to be among the most exxential joins in application areas, like data mining [CMN 99] [NH 94]. They are useful in multiple settings, such as the following.

- In geographic information systems (GIS) under the name of overlay queries: for example, *'Find all houses within 2 miles of a river'*.
- In urban planning, business planning, commercial intelligence: *'How many households are within 1 mile of our branches and from our competition's branches'*.
- In spatial data mining to detect correlations and test hypotheses: for example, *'Find 4-bedroom houses that are within 5 miles of a school'*, or *'How many luxury apartments are within 2 miles of a lake'* [NH94].
- In temporal data mining: *'Find economic embargos that were followed by war within a year'*, or *'Find network-switch failures that were within 5 seconds of a power surge'* [MTV 95] [HKM+96].
- In multimedia and traditional databases: *'Find pairs of stock price changes that are within $10 of each other'* [FRM 94].

The **spatial distance join** is defined using two spatial data sets, A and B, and a distance function L. For a given radius r, the spatial distance join computes $\{<a,b> \mid a \in A$ and $b \in B, L(a,b) \le r\}$. A special case arises when the two datasets, A and B are identical. Such joins will be qualified as '**self** spatial joins'. We will use the term '**cross** spatial joins', when we need to emphasize that the two point sets are distinct. Otherwise, we will simply use the term 'spatial join' to denote a spatial distance join between two distinct datasets.

The goal of this work is to estimate the selectivity of spatial joins among two datasets as opposed to only one. The join selectivity represents the size of the resultant set of the spatial distance join divided by the size of the Cartesian product of the whole data. Estimation of the join selectivity is important for the following two reasons.

• An accurate estimation is necessary to optimize complex queries. Though there has been quite a lot of work done on how to estimate the selectivity of equi-joins, the problem of estimating the size of spatial joins has received only minimal attention up to now.

• In application areas like the ones mentioned earlier, the size of the spatial distance join (as a function of the radius) is important for evaluating the correlation between datasets. Note that it is generally too costly to obtain the size of the spatial join by simply computing the spatial distance join itself. Therefore, an accurate and inexpensive method is required to estimate the size of spatial distance joins.

Our main contribution is that we observe a 'power law', which holds for many pairs of real datasets. We show how to use this power law to accurately estimate the spatial join selectivities efficiently (in constant time, O(1)).

The rest of the paper is organized as follows. Section 2 presents the related work. Section 3 describes our main contribution, the pair-count exponent $\mathcal{P}$ and the fast way to estimate it, through the proposed box-occupancy-product-sum (BOPS). Section 4 discusses implementation and speed issues of the proposed methods. Section 5 gives experimental results, and Section 6 discusses issues for practitioners. Section 7 presents the conclusions.

2. RELATED WORK

There has been quite a lot of work on spatial joins recently. See, for example [ORE86], [BKS93], [LR94], [PD96], [KS97], [APR+98] and [MP99]. Most of the mentioned work has dealt with developing efficient methods to process spatial intersection joins for two-dimensional data sets [BSW99] [DNS91] [SK96] with little emphasis on the estimation of selectivity. Recently, methods have also been examined and developed for processing spatial distance joins on multidimensional point sets [SSA97], [KS98]. The term *"similarity join"* has frequently also been used for spatial distance joins in the literature. For one-dimensional data, the spatial distance join corresponds to the 'band-join' [DNS91]. Although not directly related to our spatial join selectivity, we mention earlier attempts to estimate the selectivity of range queries. Typical methods include the

milestone 'uniformity and independence' assumptions [SAC+79]. Although simple to use in a query optimizer, these assumptions are pessimistic and unrealistic [CHR84]. Modern methods include histograms [POO97], kernel estimators [BKS99], wavelets [VW99], and hybrid methods using query feedback [KW99]. Methods for selectivity estimation of range queries in spatial datasets use multi-dimensional histograms [TS96], or arguments from the theory of fractals [BF95]. It should be noted that most of these methods are susceptible to the 'dimensionality curse' [SIL96] [SCO92].

Analytical estimates of spatial distance join selectivities are few. The very recent work presented in [PMT99] assumed the data are uniformly distributed in the address space. As mentioned earlier, the uniformity assumption was discredited long ago [CHR84], [FK94] as unrealistic and unfeasible. Our experiments in Section 5 indeed show that it is unrealistic. The cost model presented [TSS98] was built for datasets not uniformly distributed datasets using R-tree-based structures.

In the next sections we proceed with our proposed solution. The major observation is that the selectivity of spatial distance joins follows a power law surprisingly well.

3. PROPOSED METHOD

Our main contribution and its corollaries are discussed below. The problem to be solved is the following.

Given: two point-sets A and B and a radius r

Find: the distribution of the count of pairs, as a function of the radius r.

That is, is this distribution Gaussian? Is it Poisson? Is it Weibul? It turns out that real datasets do not follow any of the traditional statistical distributions. Instead, we show that the distribution of the pair-wise distances follows a *power law*. Table 1 lists symbols used in this document. Next, we describe our power law, as well as several useful properties of its exponent.

Symbol	Definition
N	population of the first point-set
M	the population of the second point-set
E	embedded dimensionality of the point-set (# of attributes/axis)
$\mathcal{P}$	pair-count exponent
r	radius in the queries
r_{min}	smallest distance between the two point-sets
r_{max}	largest distance
s	side of grid cells
l	number of points in BOPS-plot

Table 1: Symbols and definitions

3.1. Pair-count function and the PC exponent

We propose to study the probability distribution function of the number of pairs as a function of the distance between those pairs. Specifically, we define and study the pair-count function $PC_{A,B}(r)$, or simply $PC(r)$, of two point-sets A and B used in a spatial join query. It is defined as follows.

Definition 1: For two point-sets A and B, we define $PC_{A,B}(r)$ as the **pair-count function**, that is, the count of pairs within distance r or less. The first member of the pair should belong to point set A, and the second member to point set B.

$PC_{A,B}(r)$ = count(of A-B pairs, within distance $\leq r$)

Some observations are helpful:

• Our $PC(r)$ function roughly corresponds to the 'cumulative probability density function' from statistics.
• We typically omit the subscripts A, B for simplicity.
• The implied distance function can be any L_p norm. We use the $L_{infinity}$ norm unless otherwise specified. The reason is that all the upcoming results hold for any L_p norm, but the formulas are simpler for the $L_{infinity}$ norm.
• For a self spatial join (i.e., A== B) we *omit* the self-pairs, and we count each pair only *once*. That is, if there are N points in the set, we consider $N*(N-1)/2$ pairs. Again, the upcoming results can be easily adapted to handle any of the omitted cases.

For reasons that will soon be obvious, we define the concept of the pair-count plot:

Definition 2: The **pair-count plot**, or simply **PC-plot**, for two point sets A and B is the plot of $PC_{A,B}(r)$ versus r, in log-log scales.

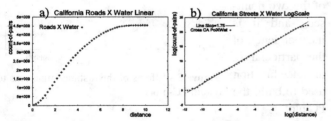

Figure 1 - The Pair-count plot of California datasets (CA-str cross joined with CA-wat) (a) linear scales, and (b) log-log scales

Figure 1 presents (a) a pair-count plot for real datasets in linear scales, and (b) the same pair-count plot in log-log scales (b). The datasets are explained in Section 5. The question is whether functions obey any rules? It turns out that many of them indeed follow a law, specifically a power law, as we discuss next. The experiments we have done with many real datasets show that many of them result in a PC-plot that is almost linear (within 1.5% MLS error and typically less) for a suitable range of distances r (radius from r_1 to r_2). Considering this, we present our major result.

Law 1 (PAIR-COUNT): For several real datasets and for a usable range of scales, the pair-count $PC(r)$ of pairs within distance r or less follows a power law:

$$PC(r) = K \cdot r^{\mathscr{P}} \qquad (1)$$

where K is a proportionality constant. Equivalently Definition 3 follows.

Definition 3: The exponent of the law is defined as the **pair-count exponent** $\mathscr{P}$ as

$$\mathscr{P} = \frac{\partial(\log(PC(r)))}{\partial\log(r)} \qquad (2)$$

Figure 1(b) shows the pair-count plot for the same pair of datasets as Figure 1(a) in log-log scales. The plots are clearly linear, for a significant range of scales. This range is usually most sought after for queries; we are not interested in radii much smaller or larger than the typical distances involved in the dataset.

Figure 2 shows PC-Plots and fitting lines for two cross-joins of California datasets, **a** streets cross joined with railroads and **b** streets cross joined with water. The description of these datasets and additional $PC(r)$ plots are shown later in Section 5, which deals with our experiments.

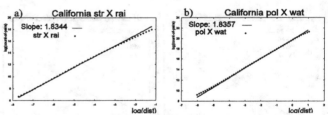

Figure 2 - PC-Plots and slopes of the fitting lines and the pair-count exponent $\mathscr{P}$ for two pairs of California datasets: **(a)** streets cross joined with railroads; **(b)** streets cross joined with water.

3.2. Properties of the pair-count exponent $\mathscr{P}$

The following observations show some of the interesting properties of the pair-count exponent $\mathscr{P}$.

Observation 1: *The pair-count exponent $\mathscr{P}$ includes the "correlation fractal dimension" D_2 as a special case.*

Justification: When the second dataset is identical to the first, the PC exponent is, by definition, equal to the "correlation fractal dimension" [BELUSSI_95]. Intuitively, this is the 'intrinsic' dimensionality of the dataset.

Observation 2: *The pair-count exponent $\mathcal{P}$ is invariant to affine transformations, namely to translation, rotation, and uniform scaling.*

Justification: By 'uniform scaling' we mean that all the axes are scaled by the same amount. Translation and rotation do not affect the distances and thus leave the plots unchanged. Uniform scaling scales all the distances, and thus shifts the plot to the left or the right. Its slope, however, remains the same.

Observation 3: *The pair-count exponent $\mathcal{P}$ is invariant to sampling.*

Justification: Sampling is useful when we deal with large datasets, although our upcoming BOPS algorithm can handle huge datasets even better. It is useful that our power law holds for subsets of our data. The intuitive argument is as follows. Consider a dataset A with N points and a sampling rate p_a ($0 \leq p_a \leq 1$), that is the sample has $N*p_a$ points. Similarly, let M be the number of points in dataset B, and let p_b be its sampling rate. Consider a point a_1 from the dataset A and let $a_1(r)$ be the number of its B-type neighbors within distance r. After sampling, it will have $p_a(r)*p_b$ neighbors on the average. Thus, the total number of pairs in the two samples within distance r will be the original $PC(r)$ times p_a*p_b on the average. This will not change the slope of the PC-plot: it will only lower the position of the plot, by $\log(p_a*p_b)$.

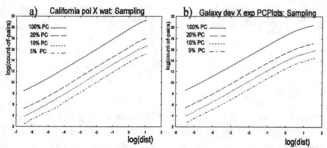

Figure 3 - Illustration of the effects of sampling on the pair-count exponent $\mathcal{P}$. The PC-plots for the full datasets and for 20%, 10% and 5% samples. (a) California pol X wat and (b) Galaxy dev and X exp.

Figure 3 shows the $PC(r)$ plots for two pairs of datasets. In (a) it shows California political cross joined with California water and in (b) it shows Galaxy-dev cross-joined with Galaxy-exp, as well as their 20%, 10% and 5% samples. Notice that the plots are linear, and those corresponding to samples are parallel to the full dataset. Tables 3 and 4

summarize their $\mathcal{P}$ values.

Observation 4: *The pair-count exponent $\mathcal{P}$ is invariant to the L_p distance used.*

Justification: Consider the 'sphere' that each L_p metric defines (see Figure 4). Let $vol(p,r)$ be the volume of an n-dimensional L_p-'sphere' of radius r. For $p=2$, this is indeed a sphere; for p=infinity this is an n-dimensional cube, etc. Our power law states that the

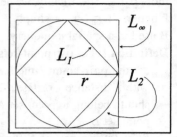

Figure 4 - The shapes of L_∞ L_1 and L_2 norms in 2-d.

number of type-B neighbors of a type-A point grows as $r^{\mathcal{P}}$ or, equivalently it grows as volume$^{\mathcal{P}/E}$. Then, if $PC_p(r)$ denotes the number of neighbors within L_p distance r, we have:

$$PC_{AB}(r, L_P) = PC(r, L_\infty) \cdot \left(vol(p,r) / vol(p,r)\right)^{\mathcal{P}/E} \quad (3)$$

therefore, the number of pairs will only differ by a multiplicative constant for different values of p in the L_p metric. Figure 5 shows the effect of norm invariance on the cross join of two California datasets (political and water). It is clear that the three L_p metrics chosen result in parallel lines. Therefore, for the rest of this work, we will only focus on the L_{inf} metric.

We can conclude that the pair-count exponent shows an intrinsic property of the two point-sets, and it is independent of the particular L_p distance function used to build the PC plot.

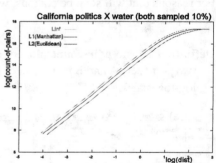

Figure 5 - Effects of the distance functions to obtain PC-plots.

4. IMPLEMENTATION AND SPEED ISSUES

By the definition of the 'pair-count exponent', we need to estimate the pair-counts for several distances r. Each of them requires $O(N*M)$ operations, which are quadratic on the size of the input datasets. This is prohibitive for large datasets. The question becomes: how we can accelerate the computation of $\mathcal{P}$. This is precisely the topic of this section.

4.1. A faster way to compute the 'pair-count exponent' $\mathscr{P}$

Here we give a Lemma, which computes of the pair-count exponent $O(N+M)$ and thus performs dramatically faster for huge datasets. A crucial concept that we introduce is the *Box-Occupancy- Product-Sum* (BOPS), which is defined as follows. Consider the address space of two point-sets in a *n*-dimensional space, and impose an *n*-grid with grid-cells of side s (or, equivalently, radius $r=s/2$). Focusing on the *i*-th cell, let $C_{A,i}$, $C_{B,i}$ be the counts ('occupancies') of points from the first and from the second point-set, respectively, as illustrated in Figure 6.

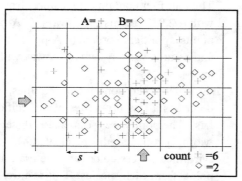

Figure 6 - A grid superimposed over a point-set to count C_{Ai} and C_{Bi}

Definition 2: The **"Box-Occupancy-Product-Sum" (BOPS)** of a grid with cell side s is defined as the sum of products of occupancies as

$$BOPS(s) = \sum_i C_{A,i} * C_{B,i} \qquad (4)$$

and the **BOPS plot** is the plot of *BOPS(s)* as a function of the grid side s, in log-log scales.

Lemma 1 (BOPS): The pair-count exponent $\mathscr{P}$ for a given radius is equal to the box-occupancy- product-sum (BOPS) for the doubled radius; that is

$$PC(s/2) \approx BOPS(s) \qquad (5)$$

Proof: The fundamental assumption is that the densities of points are smooth functions. Thus, if a point p_1 of set A has x neighbors from the set B within radius r, so does a close-by neighbor p_2 that also belongs to set A.

Thus, for a given cell side s and another given cell (say, the *i*-th one), consider one of the points of the set A. This point has a number of neighbors proportional to $C_{B,i}$ neighbors from the set B within radius $s/2$. Thus, the *i*-th cell contributes with

$$C_{A,i} * C_{B,i} \qquad (6)$$

pairs. Adding up the contributions of all the cells, we have

$$PC(s/2) = \sum_i C_{A,i} \cdot C_{B,i} \qquad (7)$$

which completes the proof.

QED

Corollary: The BOPS follows a power law with its exponent equal to the "pair-count exponent".

$$BOPS(s) = s^P \qquad (8)$$

Proof: Trivial, from Lemma 1 and Law 1.

QED

We are going to use the estimation $PC(r) = BOPS(2r)$ for the rest of this work. The 'BOPS' Lemma has important efficiency implications which are vital for large datasets. Next we show how to use this Lemma for fast selectivity estimations.

4.2. Algorithms

The problem is defined as follows.

Given two point-sets A and B in *n*-dimensional space,

Estimate their pair-count exponent $\mathscr{P}$ and the proportionality constant K.

We developed a *single-pass* algorithm to obtain the BOPS plot. Specifically, the algorithm is linear $O(N+M)$ over the total number of points in both datasets. If l is the number of points that we want in the BOPS plot (ie., number of grid-sizes), then the complexity of our algorithm is

---

Without loss of generality, due to Observation 2,
Normalize the address space of the datasets to the unit hyper-cube;
For each desirable grid-size $s=1/2^j$, j= 1, 2, ..., *l*,
    For each point *a* of dataset A
        Decide which grid cell it falls in (say, the i-th cell);
        Increment the count $C_{A,i}$;
    For each point *b* of dataset B
        Decide which grid cell it falls in (say, the i-th cell);
        Increment the count $C_{B,i}$;
    Compute the sum of product occupancies ;
        $BOPS(s) = \sum C_{A,i} * C_{B,i}$
    Print the values of log(*s*/2) and log(BOPS(*s*)) as the BOPS-plot;
Perform a linear interpolation and report the slope P and the; proportionality constant K.

Figure 7 - Algorithm for calculating BOPS plots.

$O((N+M)*l*n)$, where n is the dimensionality of the input point-sets. Below is a brief algorithm to generate the BOPS-plot and the estimate of the pair-count exponent.

4.3. Estimation of selectivity

Here we describe exactly how to estimate the spatial join selectivities, exploiting our two major observations, the pair-count law and the BOPS lemma. More specifically, the problem is as follows.

> **Given** two point-sets A and B, and a radius r,
> **Estimate** the count of pairs $PC(r)$.

We distinguish the following methods, depending on what else we are given:

- **PC plot estimation**: Through previously kept statistics on the PC plot, suppose that we already know the pair-count exponent $\mathscr{P}$ and the proportionality constant K. Then we estimate immediately the PC plot as
$PC(r) = K * r^{\mathscr{P}}$

- **BOPS plot estimation**: We assume that we are given only the dataset, without any statistics about the data. Then, we generate the BOPS plot for several values of grid-side s, and we estimate the slope $\mathscr{P}$ and the constant K, as explained in the algorithm in Figure 7. Notice that we not only obtain our estimate, but we also provide $\mathscr{P}$ and K for future upcoming queries.

An obvious trick to approximate the BOPS plot is to do sampling first. We discuss its relative merit in Section 5.

5. EXPERIMENTS

We implemented our method and checked whether the power law holds for different data sets. For the sake of clarity we named the datasets used in the experiments. Point-sets come in groups; thus, each dataset is characterized by its group name, a dash '-' and the dataset name. Their characteristics are as follows.

- **California** - Two-dimensional sets of points, they refer to geographical coordinates in California (see Figure 8(a)). The four files contain data features from streets (CA-str with 62,933 points), railways (CA-rai with 31,059 points), political borders (CA-pol with 46,850 points), and natural water systems (CA-wat, with 72,066 points) [CEN 89].

- **Iris** - This set contains three files, each of which describes a few properties of a specific flower type of Iris. The points are 4-dimensional (sepal length, sepal width, petal length, petal width); the species are 'virginica', 'versicolor' and 'setosa', and there are 50 points from each species. This is a well-known dataset in the literature of machine learning and statistics, which we obtained from the UC-Irvine Repository (see Figure 8(b)).

- **Galaxy** - Galaxies come from the SLOAN telescope: (x,y) coordinates, plus class label (see Figure 8(c)). There are 82,277 in the 'dev' class (deVaucouleurs), and 70,405 in the 'exp' class (exponential).

- **Eigenfaces** - Two datasets ('lyf' with 11,900 points; and 'tyf' with 3,456 points) come from the Informedia project [WKS+96] at Carnegie Mellon University. Each face was processed with the eigenfaces method [TP 91], resulting in 16-dimensional points.

Our experiments are designed to answer the following questions.

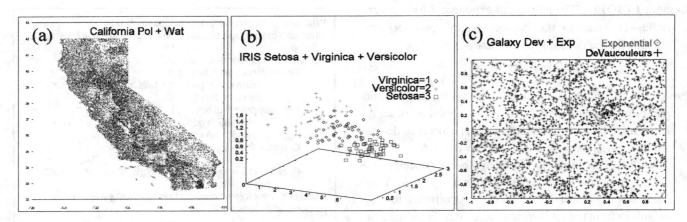

Figure 8 - Real data used in the experiments. **(a)** California: CA-pol and CA-wat, (2-dimensional point-sets), **(b)** Iris: setosa, versicolor and virginica (4-dimensional point-sets) and **(c)** Galaxy: class dev and exp (2-dimensional point-sets).

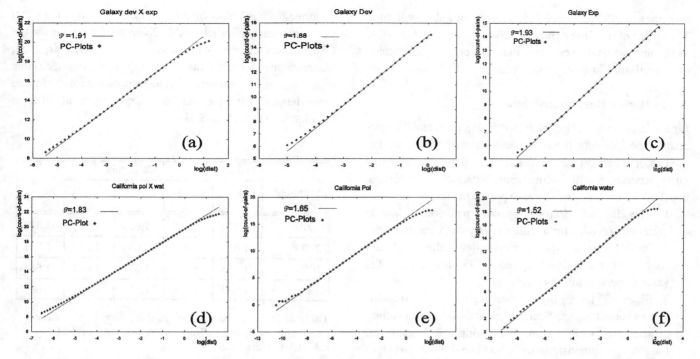

Figure 9 - PC plots and the pair-count exponents $\wp$ of geographical data. First row: Galaxy datasets (a) cross join of 'dev' and 'exp', (b) self join of 'dev', (c) self join of 'exp'. Second row California datasets (d) cross join of CA-pol and CA-wat, (e) self join of CA-pol, (f) self join of CA-wat.

- How often do real datasets follow the proposed power law?
- How good is the linear fit?
- How accurate is our 'box-occupancy-product-sum' Lemma?
- What are the effects on sampling and affine transformations on them ?
- How fast is the BOPS method, compared to other estimations of *PC(r)*?

Due to lack of space, we present here mainly the graphs of some of the datasets used in the experiments.

5.1. Accuracy of '*PC*' Law

We present our experiments in two groups, two-dimensional geographical datasets (California and Galaxy data), and higher-dimensionality ones (Iris, Eigenfaces).

5.1.1 - Geographical datasets

The immediate application for the pair-count exponent is to estimate the selectivities for cross spatial joins. Thus, the natural candidates to show that this method works are geographical datasets. Figure 9 shows the pair-count exponent for California and Galaxy datasets, and it can be

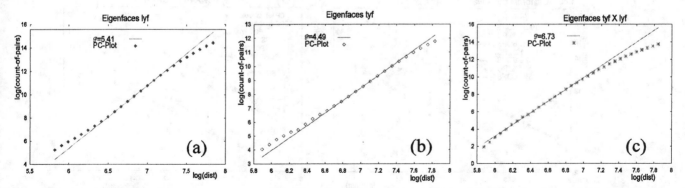

Figure 10 - PC Plots and the pair-count exponent $\wp$ of the Eigenfaces datasets, (a) self join of 'lyf' dataset, (b) self join of 'tyf' dataset, (c) cross join of 'lyf' and 'tyf' datasets.

seen that the PC plots are linear for a suitable range of r. The slopes of the fitting lines are also shown, and these give us the proportionality constant that will be used to estimate the selectivities in cross or self joins.

5.1.2 - Higher Dimensional datasets

Figure 10 presents the PC-plots, the fitting lines and the pair-count exponent $\mathcal{P}$ for the Eigenfaces datasets which are 16-dimensional data. It can be seen that our power law remains quite accurate for high-dimensional datasets. Recurring conclusions from all the above experiments are:

1. The linear fit implied by our 'pair-count' law is extremely precise, for a wide variety of diverse datasets.
2. For self-joins, as well as for cross-joins, the correlation coefficient of the fit is at least 0.995 (where '1' is the value of perfect linear correlation).
3. Especially for the high-dimensional datasets, the self-join exponent is significantly lower than the embedding dimensionality of the data. For example, in Eigenfaces, the intrinsic dimensionality is between 4.5 to 6.7 (values of $\mathcal{P}$ varies from 4.49 for self-join of 'lyf' to 6.73 for the cross-join of 'tyf' and 'lyf'), while the embedding dimensionality E was 16. This implies that these n-dimensional points are not even close to being uniformly distributed (if they were, then $\mathcal{P} = 16$). Thus, any analysis making the uniform assumption will be very inaccurate, since the dimensionality of the data ($\mathcal{P}$ or E) is in the exponent!

5.2. Sampling

We present further experiments in order to illustrate Observation 3, which states that PC plots are invariant to sampling. Figure 11 presents the pair-count exponents

obtained from PC plots (points) and BOPS plots (lines). All plots are clearly parallel. Table 2 shows the results for the Galaxy and California datasets when the pair-count exponent was calculated for self-joins. Sampling clearly has negligible effects on the PC exponent. Table 3 shows the results for the same datasets using the pair-count exponent obtained from PC plots and from BOPS plots.

Sampling rate	Galaxy		California		
	dev	exp	pol	wat	str
100%	1.876	1.928	1.650	1.529	1.838
20%	1.875	1.932	1.643	1.562	1.701
10%	1.873	1.952	1.631	1.694	1.661
5%	1.880	2.146	1.515	1.711	1.623

Table 2: The pair-count exponents $\mathcal{P}$ for samples of Galaxy ('dev' and 'exp') and California (CA_pol, CA_wat and CA_str) datasets for self-joins.

Sampling rate	Galaxy dev x exp		California pol x wat		California pol x str	
	$\mathcal{P}$ from PC	$\mathcal{P}$ from BOPS	$\mathcal{P}$ from PC	$\mathcal{P}$ from BOPS	$\mathcal{P}$ from PC	$\mathcal{P}$ from BOPS
100%	1.915	1.963	1.835	1.819	1.783	1.743
20%	1.915	1.963	1.833	1.825	1.776	1.759
10%	1.902	1.965	1.839	1.816	1.783	1.715
5%	1.918	1.736	1.856	1.786	1.752	1.725

Table 3: The pair-count exponent $\mathcal{P}$ values (PC and BOPS) for joins on sampled data from Galaxy ('dev' and 'exp') datasets and also on California_pol, California_wat, California_str datasets.

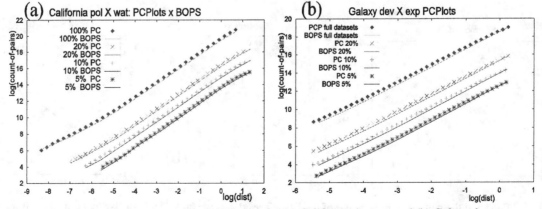

Figure 11 - PC-plots and corresponding BOPS plots for (a) California datasets and (b) Galaxy datasets. Both plots are shown for the full datasets and three levels of sampling.

Conclusions from the above experiments are as follows.

1). The pair-count exponent $\mathcal{P}$ is practically unaffected by sampling, for reasonable sample sizes (e.g., equal or higher than 10%).

2). Whatever the sampling rate, the corresponding BOPS plot on the samples is very close to the pair-count plot of the samples. This means that whatever the time that sampling can save, BOPS applied on the samples will outperform, with practically the same accuracy.

The estimation of $\mathcal{P}$ obtained from BOPS results on relative error practically always less than 5%. Only when the sampled size of a dataset is very small, the BOPS plot results in a 9% error; indeed, 9% of error is also a reasonable value.

5.3. Accuracy of Selectivity Estimations

We see that the pair-count Law is obeyed (Figures 9 and 10). We also have just seen (Figure 11 and Table 3) that our BOPS Lemma leads to very close approximations for the pair-count exponent. The question now becomes how precise the selectivity estimation $PC(r)$ can be by using,

(a) our Law 1 and
(b) our estimates from BOPS.

	Galaxy			California		
	dev x exp	dev x dev	exp x exp	pol x wat	pol x pol	wat x wat
PC plot estimation	0.02	0.01	0.02	0.02	0.02	0.06
BOPS plot estimation	0.13	0.24	0.25	0.16	0.30	0.34

Table 4 - Geometric average of the relative error of selectivity estimation.

Table 4 shows the relative error for the selectivities calculated by $\frac{PC(r) - \hat{PC}(r)}{PC(r)}$, and we report the geometric average values for several values of r. The top row estimates $\hat{PC}(r)$ as follows.

Step (a): Compute the PC plot.
Step (b): Fit the line to obtain the estimation.

In order to measure the relative error in estimating the selectivities of queries, we compared pair-count exponent methods to the real prediction given by Law 1. Table 4 presents the geometric average of the relative error of the PC plot by the pair-count exponents $\mathcal{P}$ when we compare the values obtained from PC and BOPS plots with the actual figures given by Law 1.

5.4. Timing results

The question now becomes: (a) how long it takes to estimate the PC exponent with the PC plot and (b) how long it takes to obtain the estimation from the BOPS plot. Table 5 reports the wall clock times for each plot on an Intel Pentium II 450 MHz, running Windows NT. Both methods were implemented in C++ language.

We can see in Table 5 that there is a huge difference in the CPU time when calculating the PC plots and BOPS plots. Calculating the pair-count exponent using BOPS method save orders of magnitude. Moreover, BOPS plots give a fast and accurate approximation of $\mathcal{P}$. Sampling also gives a close approximation of $\mathcal{P}$, but is much more time-consuming because all the dataset must be scanned in order to generate the sample before to apply the PC plot. When we compare the time needed to obtain the pair-count exponent for a dataset sampled to 10% of the data (a limit to preserve the accuracy of the estimation), BOPS still remains much faster than sampling technique, from 5.27 seconds for the whole dataset for BOPS to 2.11 minutes for a 10% sampling for

Datasets		PC-Plot (time in sec.)	BOPS (time in sec.)
California	pol x wat (100% of data)	7,752.50	3.44
	pol x wat (10% of data)	73.36	0.5
	str x rai (100% of data)	4,434.27	2.55
	str x rai (10% of data)	42.64	0.47
	pol x str (100 % of data)	7,664.28	3.44
	pol x str (10% of data)	66.58	0.53
Galaxy	dev x exp (100% of data)	13,078.38	5.27
	dev x exp (10% of data)	126.98	0.72
Iris	setosa x virginica	5.32	0.01
	virginica x versicolor	4.98	0.01

Table 5 - Clock time in seconds to obtain the pair-count exponent by PC-plots and BOPS-plots.

the PC plot.

Table 5 reports the times needed to build each plot for several pairs of datasets. It also shows the times, when only samples are fed into the two algorithms. The sampling rate is reported on each row, and it is the same for both datasets. The observations are the following:

1). Our BOPS method is up to four order of magnitude faster.

2). In fact, BOPS on the full sets is still faster than the PC plots on the samples (10% sampling rate), up to 20 times!

TThus, we conclude that the BOPS plot is a fast and accurate tool for selectivity estimation of spatial joins.

6. DISCUSSION

Our discussion addresses two questions, which are

a) How often should we expect the 'pair-count' law to hold?

b) How can we use it to do other extrapolations?

6.1. How often?

We mention that power laws regularly occur in real datasets. In fact, our 'pair- count' law is obeyed by the self-join of any self-similar dataset, in which case the 'pair-count' exponent is exactly the correlation fractal dimension D_2 of that dataset. It is well-known that vast majority of real datasets are self-similar [BF95], coastlines, with fractal dimension 1.1-1.3, stock prices (fractal dimension = 1.5), rain patches (fractal dimension = 1.3), brain surface of mammals (fractal dimension = 2.6-2.7). As we have just seen, the same is true for the self-joins of our real datasets (1.9 for the GALAXY datasets, 1.5-1.8 for the CA datasets, 1.9-2.9 for the 4-dimensional IRIS datasets, and 4.5-5.4 for the 16-dimensional Eigenfaces datasets).

6.2. Other extrapolations

There is a wealth of estimations that we can perform whenever a pair of real datasets obeys the pair-count law, and the invariant properties of the pair-count exponent $\mathcal{P}$. One extrapolation is to estimate the minimum distance r_{min} between the closest pair of points. The formula is

$$PC(r_{min}) = 1 = Kr_{min}^{\mathcal{P}}$$
$$r_{min} = K^{-1/\mathcal{P}}$$
(11)

The justification comes straightforward from Law 1. We can also estimate the distance r_c of the c-th closest pair and the formula is

$$PC(r_c) = Kr_c^{\mathcal{P}}$$
(12)

Additional extrapolations can be performed for subsets and supersets of the two original datasets since the pair-count exponent $\mathcal{P}$ is not affected by sampling.

7. CONCLUSIONS

The main contribution of this work is the identification of a power law, namely the 'pair-count' law. This is the *first and only* published law that governs the distribution of pair-wise distances between two real, n-dimensional point-sets. This law leads to the estimation of spatial join selectivities through a simple formula, which is extremely accurate, less than 9% of error. Given the pair-count exponent $\mathcal{P}$, the selectivity estimations can be performed in constant time ($O(1)$) without the need for sampling or any other costly operations. Additional contributions include the following:

- The identification of several invariant properties of the pair-count exponent $\mathcal{P}$. It is invariant to rotation, translation, scaling, sampling. Moreover, this holds for any L_p norm.
- Efficiency issues: the introduction of the BOPS concept (box-occupancy-product-sum). It allows a fast estimation of the pair-count exponent $\mathcal{P}$. Its response time is *orders of magnitude* better than the straightforward estimation using the pair-count function $PC(r)$. Thanks to the BOPS plot, the whole concept of the pair-count exponent becomes practical. In fact, our method used on the full sets, is still significantly faster than the PC plots on samples.
- Experiments on many, diverse datasets. The experiments show that (a) the pair-count law holds for a surprisingly large number of real datasets and (b) that our BOPS approximation is highly accurate. The error is less than 9% for the pair-count exponent $\mathcal{P}$ and less than 35% for the selectivity estimation.

Future research could focus on the discovery of additional power laws in real, spatial datasets, as well as on explaining the reasons why these laws hold.

8. ACKNOWLEDGMENTS

We are grateful for the use of Iris datasets from the UC-Irvine Repository. We would like also to thank Bob Nichol for the Galaxy datasets and the Informedia research group at Carnegie Mellon Univeristy for the Eigenfaces datasets used in this paper.

9. REFERENCES

[APR+98] L. Arge, O. Procopiuc, S. Ramaswamy, T. Suel, J.S. Vitter - *"Scalable Sweeping-Based Spatial Join"*. VLDB 1998, pp. 570-581.

[BF 95] A.Belussi and C. Faloutsos - *"Estimating the Selectivity of Spatial Queries Using the 'Correlation' Fractal Dimension"*. VLDB 1995, pp. 299-310.

[BKS 93] T. Brinkhoff, H. P. Kriegel, B. Seeger - *"Efficient Processing of Spatial Joins using R-trees"*, SIGMOD 1993. pp. 237-246.

[BSW 99] J. Van den Bercken, B. Seeger, P. Widmayer - *"The Bulk Index Join: A Generic Approach to Processing Non-Equijoins"*. ICDE 1999, pp. 257.

[CEN 89] Bureau of the Census - *Tiger/Line Precensus Files: 1990 technical documentation*. Bureau of the Census. Washington, D.C. 1989.

[CHR 84] S. Christodoulakis - *"Implications of Certain Assumptions in Database Performance Evaluation"*. TODS 9(2), 1984, pp. 163-186.

[CMN 99] S. Chaudhuri, R. Motwani, V. R. Narasayya - *"On Random Sampling over Joins"*. SIGMOD 1999, pp. 263-274.

[DNS 91] D. J. DeWitt, J. F. Naughton, D. A. Schneider - *"An Evaluation of Non-Equijoin Algorithms"*. VLDB 1991, pp. 443-452.

[FJS 97] C. Faloutsos, H.V. Jagadish and N. Sidiropoulos - *"Information Recovery from Partial data"*. Tech. Report ISR-TR-97-7, Inst. For Systems Research, Univ. of Maryland, College Park, MD, 1997.

[FK 94] C. Faloutsos, I. Kamel - "Beyond Uniformity and Independence: Analysis of R-trees Using the Concept of Fractal Dimension". PODS 1994, pp. 4-13.

[FRM 94] C. Faloutsos, M. Ranganathan, Y. Manolopoulos - *"Fast Subsequence Matching in Time-Series Databases"*. SIGMOD 1994, pp. 419-429.

[GÜN 93] O. Günther - *"Efficient Computation of Spatial Joins"*. ICDE 1993, pp. 50-59.

[GÜT 94] R. H. Güting - *"An Introduction to Spatial Database Systems"*. The VLDB Journal. 3(4). October 1994. pp. 357-399.

[HKMRT 96] K. Hätönen, M. Klemettinen, H. Mannila, P. Ronkainen, H. Toivonen - *"Knowledge Discovery from Telecommunication Network Alarm Databases"*. ICDE 1996, pp.115-122.

[KS 97] N. Koudas, K.C. Sevcik, - *"Size Separation Spatial Join"*. SIGMOD 1997, 324-335.

[KS 98] N. Koudas, K. C. Sevcik, - *"High Dimensional Similarity Joins: Algorithms and Performance Evaluation"*. ICDE 1998, pp. 466-475.

[KW 99] A. Christian Kvnig, G. Weikum - *"Combining Histograms and Parametric Curve Fitting for Feedback-Driven Query Result-size Estimation"*.VLDB 1999, pp.423-434.

[LR 94] M.-L.Lo, C. V. Ravishankar - *"Spatial Joins using Seeded Trees"*. SIGMOD 1994, pp. 209-220.

[MP 99] N. Mamoulis, D. Papadias - *"Integration of Spatial Join Algorithms for Processing Multiple Inputs"*. SIGMOD 1999. pp.1-12.

[MTV 95] H. Mannila, H. Toivonen, A. I. Verkamo - *"Discovering Frequent Episodes in Sequences"*. KDD 1995, pp.210-215.

[NH 94] R. T. Ng, J, Han - *"Efficient and Effective Clustering Methods for Spatial Data Mining"*. VLDB 1994, pp. 144-155.

[ORE 86] J. Orenstein, - *"Spatial Query Processing in an Object-Oriented Database System"*. SIGMOD 1986, pp. 326-33.

[PD 96] J. M. Patel, D. J. DeWitt, - *"Partition Based Spatial-Merge Join"*. SIGMOD 1996, pp. 259-270.

[POO 97] V. Poosala - *"Histogramm-based estimation techniques in databases"*. PhD thesis, Univ. of Wisconsin-Madison, 1997.

[PMT 99] D. Papadias, N. Mamoulis, Y. Theodoridis - *"Processing and Optimization of Multiway Spatial Joins Using R-Trees"*. PODS 1999, pp 44-55.

[SAC+ 79] P. G. Selinger, M. M. Astrahan, D. D. Chamberlin, R. A. Lorie, T. T. Price, - *"Access Path Selection in a Relational Database Management System"*. SIGMOD 1979, pp. 23-34.

[SCO 92] D. W. Scott - *Multivariate Density Estimation*, Wiley & Sons 1992.

[SIL 96] B. W. Silverman - *Density Estimation for Statistics and Data Analysis*. Chapman & Hall 1986.

[SK 96] K. C. Sevcik, N. Koudas - *"Filter Trees for Managing Spatial Data over a Range of Size Granularities"*. VLDB 1996, pp.16-27.

[SSA 97] K. Shim, R. Srikant, R.Agrawal - *"High-Dimensional Similarity Joins"*. ICDE 1997. pp. 301-311.

[TP 91] M. Turk and A. Pentland - "Eigenfaces for Recognition". Journal of cognitive Neuroscience, vol 3(1), 1991, pp. 71-86.

[TS 96] Y. Theodoridis, T. K. Sellis - *"A Model for the Prediction of R-tree Performance"*. PODS 1996, pp.161-171.

[TSS 98] Y. Theodoridis, E. Stefanakis, T. K. Sellis - *"Cost Models for Join Queries in Spatial Databases"*. ICDE 1998, pp. 476-483.

[WKS+ 96] H. D. Wactlar, T. Kanade, M.A. Smith and S. M. Stevens - *"Intelligente Access to Digital Video: Informedia Project"*. IEEE Computer, vol 29(3), pp. 46-52, May 1996.

[VW 99] J. S. Vitter, M. Wang - *"Approximate Computation of Multidimensional Aggregates of Sparse Data Using Wavelets"*. SIGMOD 1999, pp. 193-204.

Closest Pair Queries in Spatial Databases *

Antonio Corral   Yannis Manolopoulos   Yannis Theodoridis   Michael Vassilakopoulos

Dept. of Languages &
Computation,
University of Almeria,
04120 Almeria,
Spain.

Data Eng. Lab,
Dept. of Informatics,
Aristotle University
of Thessaloniki,
GR-54006 Greece.

Computer Technology
Institute,
P.O. Box 1122,
GR-26110 Patras,
Greece.

Data Eng. Lab,
Dept. of Informatics,
Aristotle University
of Thessaloniki,
GR-54006 Greece.

acorral@ualm.es   manolopo@csd.auth.gr   ytheod@cti.gr   mvass@computer.org

Abstract

This paper addresses the problem of finding the K closest pairs between two spatial data sets, where each set is stored in a structure belonging in the R-tree family. Five different algorithms (four recursive and one iterative) are presented for solving this problem. The case of 1 closest pair is treated as a special case. An extensive study, based on experiments performed with synthetic as well as with real point data sets, is presented. A wide range of values for the basic parameters affecting the performance of the algorithms, especially the effect of overlap between the two data sets, is explored. Moreover, an algorithmic as well as an experimental comparison with existing incremental algorithms addressing the same problem is presented. In most settings, the new algorithms proposed clearly outperform the existing ones.

1 Introduction

The role of spatial databases is continuously increasing in many modern applications during last years. Mapping, urban planning, transportation planning, resource management, geomarketing, archeology and environmental modeling are just some of these applications.

The key characteristic that makes a spatial database a powerful tool is its ability to manipulate spatial data, rather than simply to store and represent them. The most basic form of such a manipulation is answering queries related to the spatial properties of data. Some typical spatial queries are the following:

- a "Point Location Query" seeks for the spatial objects that fall on a given point.

- a "Range Query" seeks for the spatial objects that are contained within a given region (usually expressed as a rectangle).

- a "Join Query" may take many forms. It involves two or more spatial data sets and discovers pairs (or tuples, in case of more than two data sets) of spatial objects that satisfy a given predicate. For example, a join query that acts on two data sets, may discover all pairs of spatial objects that intersect each other.

- Finally, a very common spatial query is the "Nearest Neighbor Query" that seeks for the spatial objects residing more closely to a given object. In its simplest form, it discovers one such object (the Nearest Neighbor). Its generalization discovers K such objects (K Nearest Neighbors), for a given K.

In this paper, a spatial query that combines join and nearest neighbor queries is examined. It is called "K Closest Pairs Query" (K-CPQ) and it discovers the K pairs of spatial objects formed from two data sets that have the K smallest distances between them, where $K \geq 1$. Like a join query, all pairs of objects are candidates for the result. Like a nearest neighbor query, the K nearest neighbor property is the basis for the final ordering. In the degenerate case of $K = 1$, the closest pair of spatial objects is discovered. This problem is a rather novel one. Although, the CP problem is well honored in Computational Geometry, to the authors knowledge, there is only one paper in the literature that has addressed it in the context of spatial databases [11] by presenting a number of incremental algorithms for its solution. A similar problem is the "all nearest neighbor" problem which has been investigated in [9].

K-CPQs are very useful in many applications that use spatial data for decision making and other demanding data handling operations. For example, consider a case where one data set represents the locations of the numerous archeological sites of Greece, while the second set stands for the most important holiday resorts. A K-CPQ will discover the K pairs of sites and holiday resorts that have the K smaller distances so that tourists accommodated in a resort can easily visit the

*Research performed under the European Union's TMR Chorochronos project, contract number ERBFMRX-CT96-0056 (DG12-BDCN).

archeological site of each pair of the result. This information could be utilized by the tourist authorities for advertising purposes. The value of K is dependent on the advertising budget of the tourist authorities.

The fundamental assumption is that the two spatial data sets are stored in structures belonging in the family of R-trees [10]. R-trees and their variants (see [8, 15]), are considered an excellent choice for indexing various kinds of spatial data (like points, polygons, 2-d objects, etc) and have already been adopted in commercial systems (Informix, Oracle, etc). In this paper we focus on sets of point data. Five different algorithms are presented for solving the problem of K-CPQ. Four of these algorithms are recursive and one is iterative. The problem of 1-CPQ is treated as a special case, since increased performance can be achieved by making use of properties holding for this case. Moreover, an extensive performance study, based on experiments performed with synthetic as well as with real point data sets, is presented. A wide range of values for the basic parameters affecting the performance of the algorithms is examined. In addition, an algorithmic as well as a comparative performance study with the incremental algorithms of [11] is presented. The finding of the above studies is the determination of the algorithm outperforming all the others for each set of parameter values. As it turns out, the new (non-incremental) algorithms outperform the existing incremental algorithms, under various settings.

The organization of this paper is the following. In Section 2 the problem of K-CPQ, a brief description of the family of R-trees and some useful metrics between R-tree nodes and distances of closest pairs are presented. In Section 3 the five new algorithms are introduced and they are compared algorithmically with the algorithm of [11]. Sections 4 and 5 exhibit a detailed performance study of all the algorithms for 1- and K-CPQs, respectively. Moreover, in Section 5 a comparative performance study between the newly introduced algorithms and the algorithm of [11] is presented. In Section 6 conclusions on the contribution of this paper and related future research plans are presented.

2 Closest Pair Queries and R-trees

2.1 Definition of Problem

Let two point sets, $P = \{p_1, p_2, \ldots, p_{NP}\}$ and $Q = \{q_1, q_2, \ldots, q_{NQ}\}$, be stored in two R-trees, R_P and R_Q, respectively. As 1-CP (One Closest Pair) of these two point sets we define a pair

$$(p_z, q_l), \quad p_z \in P \wedge q_l \in Q$$

such that

$$\text{dist}(p_i, q_j) \geq \text{dist}(p_z, q_l), \quad \forall p_i \in P \wedge \forall q_j \in Q$$

In other words, an 1-CP of P and Q is a pair that has the smallest distance between all pairs of points that can be formed by choosing one point of P and one point of Q.[1] As K-CPs (K Closest Pairs) of P and Q we define a collection of K ordered pairs

$$(p_{z_1}, q_{l_1}), (p_{z_2}, q_{l_2}), \ldots, (p_{z_K}, q_{l_K}),$$

$$p_{z_1}, p_{z_2}, \ldots, p_{z_K} \in P \wedge q_{l_1}, q_{l_2}, \ldots q_{l_K} \in Q$$

such that

$$\text{dist}(p_i, q_j) \geq \text{dist}(p_{z_K}, q_{l_K}) \geq$$
$$\text{dist}(p_{z_{(K-1)}}, q_{l_{(K-1)}}) \geq \cdots \geq \text{dist}(p_{z_1}, q_{l_1}),$$

$$\forall (p_i, q_j) \in (P \times Q - \{(p_{z_1}, q_{l_1}), (p_{z_2}, q_{l_2}), \ldots, (p_{z_K}, q_{l_K})\})$$

In other words, K-CPs of P and Q are K pairs that have the K smallest distances between all pairs of points that can be formed by choosing one point of P and one point of Q. K must be smaller than $|P| \cdot |Q|$, i.e. the number of pairs that can be formed from P and Q.

Note that, due to ties of distances, the result of 1-CPQ or the K-CPQ may not be unique for a specific pair of P and Q. The aim of the presented algorithms is to find one of the possible instances. Note also that in the context of this paper "dist" stands for Euclidean Distance, although the presented methods can be easily adapted to any Minkowski metric. We also focus on 2-dimensional space, but the extension to k-dimensional space is straightforward.

2.2 R-trees

R-trees are hierarchical data structures based on B^+-trees. They are used for the dynamic organization of a set of k-dimensional geometric objects representing them by the minimum bounding k-dimensional rectangles. Each R-tree node corresponds to the MBR that contains its children. The tree leaves contain pointers to the objects of the database, instead of pointers to children nodes. The nodes are implemented as disk pages.

Many variations of R-trees have appeared in the literature (an exhaustive survey can be found in [8]). One of the most popular variations is the R*-tree [1]. The R*-tree follows a node split technique that is more sophisticated than that of the simple R-tree and is considered the most efficient variant of the R-tree family, since, as far as searches are concerned, it can be used in exactly the same way as simple R-trees. In this paper, we choose R*-trees to perform our experimental study.

---

[1]The 1-CP problem addressed in this paper is an extension of the popular closest pair problem that appears in computational geometry [20] for two point sets.

2.3 Useful Metrics

Since the different algorithms for CPQs act on pairs of R-trees, some metrics between MBRs (that can be used to increase performance of the algorithms) will be defined. Let N_P and N_Q be two internal nodes of R_P and R_Q, respectively. Each of these nodes has an MBR that contains all the points that reside in the respective subtree. In order for this rectangle to be the minimum bounding one, at least one point is located at each edge of the rectangle. Let M_P and M_Q represent the MBRs of N_P and N_Q, respectively. Let r_1, r_2, r_3 and r_4 be the four edges of M_P and s_1, s_2, s_3 and s_4 be the four edges of M_Q. By MINDIST(r_i, s_i) we denote the minimum distance between two points falling on r_i and s_i. Accordingly, by MAXDIST(r_i, s_i) we denote the maximum distance between two points falling on r_i and s_i. In the sequel, we extend definitions of metrics between a point and an MBR that appear in [21] and define a set of useful metrics between two MBRs. In case M_P and M_Q are disjoint we can define a metric that expresses the minimum possible distance of two points contained in different MBRs:

$$\text{MINMINDIST}(M_P, M_Q) = \min_{i,j}\{\text{MINDIST}(r_i, s_j)\}$$

In case the MBRs of the two nodes intersect, then MINMINDIST(M_P, M_Q) equals 0. In any case (intersecting or disjoint MBRs) we can define the metrics

$$\text{MINMAXDIST}(M_P, M_Q) = \min_{i,j}\{\text{MAXDIST}(r_i, s_j)\}$$

and

$$\text{MAXMAXDIST}(M_P, M_Q) = \max_{i,j}\{\text{MAXDIST}(r_i, s_j)\}$$

MAXMAXDIST expresses the maximum possible distance of any two points contained in different MBRs. MINMAXDIST expresses an upper bound of distance for at least one pair of points. More specifically, there exists at least one pair of points (contained in different MBRs) with distance smaller than or equal to MINMAXDIST. In Figure 1, two MBRs and their MINMINDIST, MINMAXDIST and MAXMAXDIST distances are depicted. Recall that at least one point is located on each edge of each MBR. To summarize, for each pair (p_i, q_j) of points, p_i enclosed by M_P and q_j enclosed by M_Q, it holds that

$$\text{MINMINDIST}(M_P, M_Q) \le \text{dist}(p_i, q_j) \le \text{MAXMAXDIST}(M_P, M_Q) \tag{1}$$

Moreover, there exists at least one pair (p_i, q_j) of points, p_i enclosed by M_P and q_j enclosed by M_Q, such that

$$\text{dist}(p_i, q_j) \le \text{MINMAXDIST}(M_P, M_Q) \tag{2}$$

These metrics can be calculated by formulae analogous to the ones presented in [18, 21], where metrics between a point and an MBR are defined.

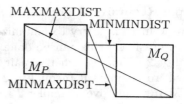

Figure 1: Two MBRs and their MINMINDIST, MIN-MAXDIST and MAXMAXDIST.

3 Algorithms for CPQs

In the following, a number of different algorithmic approaches for discovering the 1-CP and the K-CPs between points stored in two R-trees are presented. Since the height of an R-tree depends on the number of points inserted (as well as in the order of insertions), the two R-trees may have the same, or different heights. Besides, an algorithm for such a problem may be recursive or iterative. All these different possibilities are examined in the next sections. For the ease of exposition, we proceed from simpler to more complicated material.

3.1 Naive Algorithm

The simplest approach to the problem of Closest Pair Queries is to follow a recursive naive solution for the 1-CP subproblem and for two R-trees of the same height. Such an algorithm consists of the following steps.

CP1 Start from the roots of the two R-trees and set the minimum distance found so far, T, to ∞.

CP2 If you access a pair of internal nodes, propagate downwards recursively for every possible pair of MBRs.

CP3 If you access two leaves, calculate the distance of each possible pair of points. If this distance is smaller that T, update T.

The desired 1-CP is the one that corresponds to the final value of T.

3.2 Exhaustive Algorithm

An improvement of the previous algorithm is to make use of the left part of Inequality 1 and prune some paths in the two trees that are not likely to lead to a better solution. That is, to propagate downwards only for those pairs of MBRs that satisfy this property. The CP2 step of the previous algorithm would now be:

CP2 If you access a pair of internal nodes, calculate MINMINDIST for each possible pair of MBRs. Propagate downwards recursively only for those pairs that have MINMINDIST $\le T$.

3.3 Simple Recursive Algorithm

A further improvement is to try to minimize the value of T as soon as possible. This can be done by making use of Inequality 2. That is, when a pair of internal nodes is visited, to examine if Inequality 2 applied to every pair of MBRs, can give a smaller T value. Since Inequality 2 holds for at least one pair of points, this improvement is sound for the 1-CP problem. The CP2 step would now be:

CP2 If you access a pair of internal nodes, calculate the minimum of MINMAXDIST for all possible pairs of MBRs. If this minimum is smaller than T, update T. Calculate MINMINDIST for each possible pair of MBRs. Propagate downwards recursively only for those pairs that have MINMINDIST $\leq T$.

3.4 Sorted Distances Recursive Algorithm

Pairs of MBRs that have smaller MINMINDIST are more likely to contain the 1-CP and to lead to a smaller T. A heuristic that aims at improving our algorithms even more when two internal nodes are accessed, is to sort the pairs of MBRs according to ascending order of MINMINDIST and to obey this order in propagating downwards recursively. This order of processing is expected to improve pruning of paths. The CP2 step of the previous algorithm would be:

CP2 If you access a pair of internal nodes, calculate the minimum of MINMAXDIST for all possible pairs of MBRs. If this minimum is smaller than T, update T. Calculate MINMINDIST for each possible pair of MBRs and sort these pairs in ascending order of MINMINDIST. Following this order, propagate downwards recursively only for those pairs that have MINMINDIST $\leq T$.

3.5 Heap Algorithm

Unlike the previous ones, this algorithm is non recursive. In order to overcome recursion and to keep track of propagation downwards while accessing the two trees, a heap is used. This heap holds pairs of MBRs according to their MINMINDIST. The pair with the smallest value resides on top of the heap. This pair is the next candidate for visiting. The overall algorithm is as follows.

CP1 Start from the roots of the two R-trees, set T to ∞ and initialize the heap.

CP2 If you access a pair of internal nodes, calculate the minimum of MINMAXDIST for all possible pairs of MBRs. If this minimum is smaller than T, update T. Calculate MINMINDIST for each possible pair of MBRs. Insert into the heap those pairs that have MINMINDIST $\leq T$.

CP3 If you access two leaves, calculate the distance of each possible pair of points. If this distance is smaller that T, update T.

CP4 If the heap is empty then stop.

CP5 Get the pair on top of the heap. If this pair has MINMINDIST $> T$, then stop. Else, repeat the algorithm from CP2 for this pair.

The 1-CP is the pair that has distance T.

3.6 Treatment of Ties

In the algorithms where ties of MINMINDIST values may appear (the Sorted Distances and the Heap algorithms), it is possible to get a further improvement by choosing the next pair in case of a tie using some heuristic (and not following the order produced by the sorting or the heap handling algorithm). The following list presents five criteria that are likely to improve performance. Thus, in case of a tie of two or more pairs, choose the pair that has:

1. as one of its elements the largest MBR (the area of an MBR is expressed as a percentage of the area of the relevant root),

2. the smallest MINMAXDIST between its two elements,

3. the largest sum of the areas of its two elements,

4. the smallest difference of areas between the MBR that embeds both its elements and these elements,

5. the largest area of intersection between its two elements.

In case the criterion we use can not resolve the tie (provide a winner), another criterion may be used at a second stage.

3.7 Treatment of different heights

When the two R-trees storing the two point sets have different heights the algorithms are slightly more complicated. In recursive algorithms, there are two approaches for treating different heights.

- The first approach is called "fix-at-root". The idea is, when the algorithm is called with a pair of internal nodes at different levels, downwards propagation stops in the tree of the lower level node, while propagation in the other tree continues, until a pair of nodes at the same level is reached. Then, propagation continues in both subtrees as usual.

- The second approach is called "fix-at-leaves" and works in the opposite way. Recursion propagates downwards as usual. When the algorithm is called with a leaf node on the one hand and an internal node on the other hand, downwards propagation stops in the tree of the leaf node, while propagation in the other tree continues as usual.

For example, for the Simple algorithm, application of the "fix-at-leaves" strategy results in the following extra step:

CP2.1 If you access a pair with one leaf and one internal node, calculate the minimum of MINMAXDIST for all possible pairs of MBRs that consist of the MBR of this leaf and an MBR contained in the internal node. If this minimum is smaller than T, update T. Calculate also MINMINDIST for all these pairs. For each pair that has MINMINDIST $\leq T$, make a recursive call with node parameters the nodes corresponding to the MBRs of the pair (note that the one parameter will be the leaf node and the other parameter will be a child of the internal node).

While application of the "fix-at-root" strategy, for the same algorithm results in the following extra step:

CP2.1 If you access two nodes residing at different levels, calculate the minimum of MINMAXDIST for all possible pairs of MBRs that consist of an MBR contained in the higher level node and the MBR of the lower level node. If this minimum is smaller than T, update T. Calculate also MINMINDIST for all these pairs. For each pair that has MINMINDIST $\leq T$, make a recursive call with node parameters the nodes corresponding to the MBRs of the pair (note that the one parameter will be the node residing at the lower level).

The Heap algorithm can be easily modified to deal with different heights by the "fix-at-leaves" or the "fix-at-root" strategy. The extra steps that needs to be added to the Heap algorithm is analogous to one of the steps presented above (depending on the strategy). The only difference is that a recursive call is replaced by an insertion in the heap.

3.8 Extending to K Closest Pairs

In order to solve the K-CPs problem an extra structure that holds the K Closest Pairs is necessary. This structure is organized as a max heap (called K-heap) and holds pairs of points according to their distance. The pair of points with the largest distance resides on top of the heap.

- Initially the K-heap is empty.
- The pairs of points discovered in step CP3 are inserted in the K-heap until it gets full.
- Then, when a new pair of points is discovered in step CP3 and if its distance is smaller than the top of the K-heap, the top is deleted and this pair is inserted in the K-heap.

The above additions are the only ones needed for the Naive and the Exhaustive algorithms to solve the K-CPs problem and were used in the implementation of the K-CP versions of these algorithms.

However, these additions are not sufficient for the Simple, the Sorted Distances and the Heap algorithms. These algorithms make use of Inequality 2 that, in general, does not hold for more than one pairs of points. This means that updating of T based on MINMAXDIST values must be discarded. A simple modification that can make these three algorithms suitable for solving the K-CPs problem is to use the distance of the top of the K-heap as the value of T, after the K-heap has become full. While the K-heap has empty slots, infinity should be used as T. An alternative, although more complicated, modification (used in the implementation of the K-CP versions of the three algorithms) is to make use of the right part of Inequality 1, while pruning unnecessary paths in the two trees. That is, among a number of pairs of MBRs to find the one with MAXMAXDIST that might update the value of T. Details are outlined in [5].

3.9 Related Work

Hjaltason and Samet [11] also presented algorithms for closest pair queries in spatial databases (called "distance join algorithms" in [11]). These algorithms are based on a priority queue and resemble the functionality of the Heap algorithm. However, there are significant differences between the algorithms of [11], the Heap and the other algorithms presented in the present paper. The key differences are outlined in the following paragraphs.

The algorithms of [11] store in the priority queue item pairs of the following types: node/node, node/obr, obr/node and object/object (where "node" is an R-tree node, "obr" is an object bounding rectangle and "object" is an actual data item). The Heap algorithm stores pair items that are of internal-node/internal-node type (where with "node" an R-tree node is referred). While processing a pair of subtrees between the two data sets, the algorithms of [11] are likely to insert in the priority queue a significant portion of all the above four types of item pairs that can be formed from these subtrees. On the contrary, while processing the same pair of subtrees, the Heap algorithm inserts only a portion of the internal-node pairs that can be formed from these subtrees (a small fraction of the pairs that are likely to be inserted in the priority queue of [11]). This fact advocates for the creation of a significantly larger priority queue for [11] in comparison to the structure of our Heap algorithm.

Due to its expected large size, the priority queue of [11] is stored partially in main memory (with one part as a heap and another part as an unordered list) and partially in secondary memory (as a number of linked lists). The distinction of the size of each part is crucial for performance (since pairs that are unlikely to be accessed should be stored on disk) and depends on the arbitrary choice of a constant called D_T. As the authors of [11] state, a policy for choosing D_T is a subject for further investigation. On the contrary, the queue of the Heap algorithm is completely stored in main memory, since its size is significantly smaller.

The basic algorithm of [11] is incremental, in the sense that an unlimited number of closest pairs is produced in ascending order of distance. To reduce the size of the priority queue and increase the performance of the algorithm, in [11], an extra structure is introduced and an upper bound K is set for the number of closest pairs that can be produced. After this modification, the algorithm becomes incremental up to K, only. The algorithms of the present paper calculate all K closest pairs together. The main idea behind them is to increase performance by achieving the highest pruning possible, while tree paths are followed.

The algorithms of [11] solve ties of distances using one of two approaches: depth-first (a pair with a node at a deeper level has priority) and breadth-first (the opposite). Moreover, the algorithms of [11] traverse trees according to one of three policies: basic (priority is given to one of the trees, arbitrarily), even (priority is given to the node at shallower depth) and simultaneous (all possible pairs of nodes are candidates for traversal). On the other hand, all our algorithms follow the simultaneous approach.

Finally, in the algorithms of [11], there is no distinction for the 1-CPQ (1-CPQ is just a case of K-CPQ). In our algorithms, the 1-CPQ is a special case and the use of Inequality 2 increases pruning and performance.

After presenting our proposals for efficient CPQ processing as well as related work, an extensive experimentation follows for 1- and K-CPQs. The goal of the experiments is to trace the pros and cons of each alternate solution and provide guidelines for query optimization purposes. Due to space limitations, in the presentation to follow some charts are omitted; interested readers can refer to [5] for the complete performance study.

4   1-CPQs Performance Comparison

This section provides the results of an extensive experimentation study aiming at measuring and evaluating the efficiency of the four CP algorithms (the Naive one excluded) proposed in Section 3 for 1-CP queries, namely the Exhaustive, the Simple, the Sorted Distances,[2] and the Heap algorithm (in the sequel, de-

---

[2]We have experimented with six sorting methods (Bubble-, Selection-, Insertion-, Heap-, Quick-, MergeSort) and chosen MergeSort because it obtained the best performance in terms of both I/O and CPU cost.

noted by EXH, SIM, STD, and HEAP, respectively). As already discussed, two parameters that need to be further evaluated deal with (i) the treatment of ties when STD and HEAP need to choose among several node pairs with equal MINMINDIST and (ii) the treatment of R-trees with different heights. After fixing these two techniques, we proceed with an extensive comparison of the proposed algorithms. A major part of the experimentation consists of detecting and evaluating the effect of two crucial factors involved: (i) the portion of overlapping between the two data sets and (ii) the size of the underlying buffering scheme. For our experiments we have built several R*-trees using the following data sets:

- a group of random data sets of cardinality 20K, 40K, 60K, and 80K points following a uniform-like distribution,

- a real data set from the Sequoia database [22] consisting of 62,536 points that represent sites in California, and

- a uniformly distributed data set consisting of 62,536 points, too.

All experiments have run on a workstation of 64 Mbytes RAM and several Gbytes of secondary storage. The page size was set to 1 Kbyte thus resulting to R*-tree node capacity $M = 21$ (minimum occupancy was set to $m = M/3 = 7$, a reasonable choice according to [1]).

4.1   Treatment of ties

According to the discussion in Subsection 3.6, five alternative techniques are presented to deal with ties between two or more node/node pairs that are likely to appear during the sorting phase of the STD or the HEAP algorithm. We call them T1 - T5 and evaluate them in Figures 2.a and 2.b for the STD algorithm and the HEAP algorithms, respectively. 60K/60K data sets have been used. By fixing the performance of T1 to 100% we present the relative gain or loss of the other alternatives. Several other combinations were also tested but the trends are similar and thus are not presented here. For this set of experiments

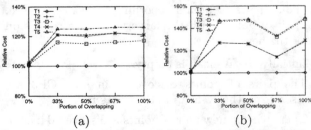

(a)   (b)

Figure 2: Comparison of Different Tie Treatment Approaches in the (a) STD and (b) HEAP Algorithms with Random Data Sets (60K/60K).

the buffer was disabled. The conclusion is that T1 is the clear winner. It always outperforms all other alternatives since the other techniques lead to a performance deterioration of up to 50% with respect to T1. Obviously, the differences are clear for overlapping data sets since for disjoint ones (overlapping = 0%) ties appear rarely and thus almost all alternatives appear to be equivalent.

4.2 R-trees with different heights

The "classic" join procedure propagates the two R-trees and fixes the level of the shorter tree when it reaches the leaves ("fix-at-leaves") [3, 14, 16, 23]. In Subsection 3.7 we presented an alternative, called "fix-at-root", where the level of the shorter tree is fixed at the root as long as the algorithm propagates downwards in the taller tree until both reach the same level. We compare the two approaches and the results are illustrated in Figures 3.a and 3.b for the STD and HEAP algorithms, respectively. The cardinality of the taller R-tree was fixed to 80K random data (height $h = 5$) while the shorter R-tree consisted of 20K - 60K random data (all with $h = 4$). Three configurations were considered: 0%, 50%, and 100% overlapping between the two data sets. The buffer size was again set to zero.[3] Although

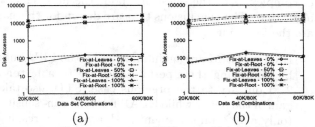

| | |
| (a) | (b) |

Figure 3: Comparison of Different Height Treatment Approaches in the (a) STD and (b) HEAP Algorithms. Log Scale.

neglected in the literature of spatial join processing, the "fix-at-root" approach turns out to be very efficient for the purposes of closest-pair algorithms. After many experiments we concluded that within the SIM and HEAP algorithms, it always performs better than the traditional "fix-at-leaves" approach with a relative performance gain usually ranging from 10% up to 40%. On the other hand, in the STD algorithm, the two are more or less equivalent except the case of 0% overlapping where "fix-at-leaves" performs much better than the "fix-at-root" approach. This is explained by the fact that pruning with "fix-at-root" is likely to appear at higher levels in the taller tree than the "fix-at-leaves", thus excluding larger subtrees from further processing.

---

[3] We have run the same experiments for several buffer sizes and the conclusions were similar.

4.3 Comparison of 1-CP algorithms

We now proceed with the performance comparison of the four algorithms, which were proposed as improvements to the naive solution. We first assume zero buffer (Subsection 4.3.1). As intuitively shown in Section 2, closest pair queries are very sensitive to the relative location of the two data sets involved, especially the portion of overlapping. In other words, the higher the overlap between the two workspaces the more expensive the query, in terms of disk accesses. To measure that, we track the sensitivity of the algorithms on that parameter (Subsection 4.3.2) and then we introduce a buffer of predefined size following the least-recently-used (LRU) policy (Subsection 4.3.3).

4.3.1 The effect of zero buffer capacity

All four algorithms were evaluated with respect to the cardinality of the data sets, the distribution of data and the portion of overlapping between the two data sets. For this set of experiments the buffer was set to zero. Figure 4 illustrates the performance of each algorithm on 1-CPQ between real Sequoia data set and random data of varying cardinality and (a) 0% and (b) 100% overlapping workspaces. Based on these experimental

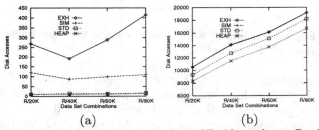

| | |
| (a) | (b) |

Figure 4: Comparison of the four CP Algorithms: Real vs. Random Data in (a) 0% and (b) 100% Overlapping Workspaces.

outcomes (for more outcomes see [5]) we conclude that for 0% overlapping, the cost of HEAP and STD is one order of magnitude lower than that of SIM and EXH. Also, for overlapping workspaces, HEAP and STD are the winners with an average relative gap of 20% and 10%, respectively. In general, we derive that STD and HEAP appear to be the most promising ones, since they almost always outperform the other two. Another conclusion is that the overlap factor should be further investigated since all 1-CP algorithms are very sensitive to this parameter. In other words, the key question that needs to be addressed is the following: is there a threshold (if yes, which) that makes the performance of the three algorithms distinct enough?

4.3.2 The effect of the overlap

This sensitivity is quantitatively measured in the set of experiments that follow. In particular, we measured the relative cost of the three algorithms (SIM, STD, and HEAP) with respect to the cost of EXH, with the portion of overlapping ranging from 0% to 100%. For each experiment, on the one hand, it was the real data set, denoted by "R", consisting of 62,536 entries (Figure 5) and, on the other hand, a random data set of 40K or 80K cardinality. Especially for the R/80K experiments where the two R*-trees have different heights, we adopted the "fix-at-root" treatment which was shown to be efficient in Subsection 4.2. Indeed and in accordance to our intuition, overlap between the data sets is crucial for the performance of all 1-CP algorithms. The cost for a query involving fully overlapping data sets is orders of magnitude higher than that involving disjoint workspaces. The behavior of the three algorithms is

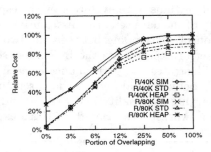

Figure 5: Finding a Threshold on the Overlap Factor: Real vs. Random Data.

surprisingly similar. For small overlap (at most 5%), they all achieve a significant improvement being 2-20 times faster than EXH when a real data set is joined with a uniform one. A justification for this huge improvement when real data is involved is the fact that node rectangles between the two R*-trees are likely to be disjoint (or low overlapping) even for high overlapping data sets. As a conclusion, zero or low overlap gives a serious advantage to the three non-exhaustive algorithms. It also turns out that this parameter must be taken into account very seriously when performing experimentation on CP algorithms.

4.3.3 Introducing the LRU-buffer

Cache policies considerably affect the performance of the algorithms dealing with secondary storage. [13, 4] have already studied the effect of the LRU-buffer size in spatial selection, spatial join and spatial join between different kinds of data, respectively. In this subsection we present how the LRU buffer affects the performance of each algorithm. We used LRU buffer varying from B = 0 ... 256 pages (dedicated to each R-tree as two equal portions of B/2 pages). For each experiment, on the one hand, it was the real data set, denoted by "R", and, on the other hand, a random data set (of cardinality 40K or 80K). Figure 6 illustrates the

results for the two configurations considered between the two data sets (0% and 100% overlapping). As before, for the R/80K experiment where the two R-trees have different heights, it was the "fix-at-root" approach adopted. Case (a) is clear: although EXH

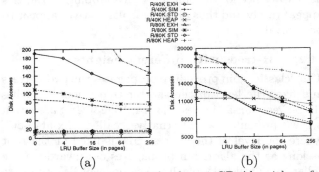

(a)   (b)

Figure 6: Comparison of the four 1-CP Algorithms for Varying LRU Buffer Size: Real vs. Random Data in (a) 0% and (b) 100% Overlapping Workspaces.

and SIM are getting improved (by a factor that reaches up to 2-3 for B = 256 pages) as long as the buffer size grows, they never come close to STD and HEAP. Interestingly, the latter ones are not sensitive to the buffer size. On the other hand, overlapping adds a lot of complexity to the question about the most efficient algorithm. The conclusions that are drawn for this case are the following:

- EXH and SIM are again affected by the LRU buffer by improving their performance up to a factor of 2. Contrary to the previous case, STD also takes gain of the buffer while HEAP remains non-sensitive (only a 10% improvement is shown). The result of that behavior is that HEAP quickly loses its relative advantage and, after the threshold of B = 4 pages, the others outperform it.

- For large LRU buffer sizes, the three recursive algorithms (EXH, SIM, and STD) show interesting similarities. First, the degree of improvement is similar as the buffer grows (5%-10% for each duplication of buffer size). Second, their behavior is independent from the cardinality of the data sets.

Regarding sensitivity to buffer size, the non-recursive HEAP algorithm is quite stable because it processes the nodes from each R-tree in a simultaneous way. On the other hand, the recursive EXH, SIM and STD algorithms are more sensitive to the capacity of the LRU buffer because they process a 1-CP query by following a depth-first traversal pattern.

4.4 General guidelines

General guidelines that arise through this experimentation are the following:

- STD and HEAP are the most efficient, since they usually outperform the other two up to one order of magnitude (for zero buffer size).

- The overlap factor between joined data sets deserves serious consideration when performing experimentation on CP algorithms since the cost for fully overlapping workspaces is several orders of magnitude higher than that for disjoint workspaces. According to our experiments, zero or small (at most 5%) overlap gives a serious advantage to the three non-exhaustive algorithms since they turn out to be 2-20 times faster than the exhaustive one.

- Although HEAP is the winner for zero buffer, it quickly loses its relative advantage as buffer size increases and, after the threshold of B = 4, the other three algorithms outperform it.

5 K-CPQs Performance Comparison

We proceed with evaluating the performance of the four algorithms for K-CPQs also taking into consideration several parameters that affect performance (Subsection 5.1). A comparison with an incremental approach, already found in the literature [11], is also included (Subsection 5.2).

5.1   Comparison of the four algorithms

In correspondence to Section 4, we first assume zero buffer (Subsection 5.1.1) and then measure the sensitivity of the algorithms on the overlap (Subsection 5.1.2) and the buffer size (Subsection 5.1.3).

5.1.1   Experiments with zero buffer

For this set of experiments, we have chosen to run K-CPQs between the real and the uniform data set, with K varying from 1 up to 100,000. Figure 7 illustrates the performance of each algorithm assuming (a) 0% and (b) 100% overlapping workspaces. Obviously, the

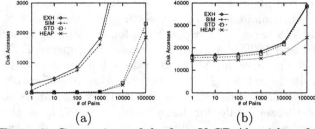

(a)   (b)

Figure 7: Comparison of the four K-CP Algorithms for Varying K: Real vs. Uniform Data in (a) 0% and (b) 100% Overlapping Workspaces.

cost of each algorithm gets higher as K increases. Interestingly, the deterioration is not smooth; after a threshold the cost increases exponentially. This threshold is usually between $K = 100$ and 1,000. Another observation is that the portion of overlapping

again plays an important role in the ranking of the four algorithms, as already detected in Section 4 (for $K = 1$). For non-overlapping data sets (Figure 7a), STD and HEAP are 10 - 50 times faster than EXH, whereas SIM cannot achieve a significant improvement. On the other hand, for overlapping workspaces (Figure 7b), it is only HEAP that clearly improves performance with respect to EXH (although less than before: 10%-30%). Since the overlap factor again turns out to be crucial for the relative performance of the K-CP algorithms we further investigate it in the sequel.

5.1.2   The effect of the overlap

The goal of this set of experiments is to detect a threshold (if such exists) that would be used as a guideline for an effective choice among the four algorithms. To reach such a conclusion, we illustrate in Figure 8 the relative cost of the STD and HEAP algorithms with respect to the cost of EXH. For each experiment, it was again the real and the uniform data sets chosen, with K varying from 1 up to 100,000. The results detect the winner for each configuration:

- SIM cannot improve the performance more than 20% except the case where $K = 1$ and overlap less than 25% (see also [5]).

- STD and HEAP are almost equivalent for overlap less than 10% (being from 5 up to 50 times faster than EXH) and, then, HEAP clearly outperforms STD with a relative gap increasing with K. For overlap more than 50%, HEAP achieves 15% (for small K values) up to 35% (for large K values) savings in I/O compared with the rest algorithms.

As a guideline, for disjoint workspaces STD and HEAP are both very efficient while for overlapping workspaces HEAP is the algorithm to be preferred, and this holds for an arbitrary K value.

5.1.3   The effect of the LRU-buffer

Similar to Subsection 4.3.3, an LRU buffer varying from B = 0 up to 256 pages was dedicated to the two R-trees in two equal portions of B/2 pages. For each experiment, it was again, on the one hand, the real data set and, on the other hand, the uniform data set. Part of the results is illustrated in Figure 9 (for the (a) STD and (b) HEAP algorithms). The charts correspond to overlap 0% between the two data sets. According to these results (appearing in more detail in [5]), for 0% overlap between two data sets, SIM and STD take advantage of the buffer and their cost is significantly reduced as the buffer size increases (up to one order of magnitude for $K = 100,000$ and B = 256 pages). On the other hand, HEAP is sensitive to the buffer size only for large K values saving more than half of its cost when $K \geq 10,000$ and B > 16 pages. When comparing

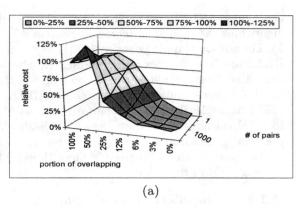
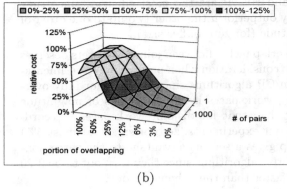

Figure 8: Finding a Threshold on the Overlap Factor for Varying K in (a) STD, and (b) HEAP.

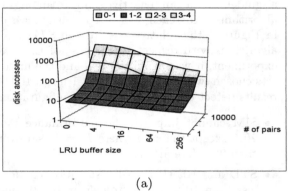
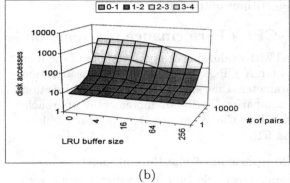

Figure 9: The Effect of the LRU Buffer Size for Varying K in (a) STD and (b) HEAP. Log Scale.

it with the other two algorithms, it turns out that the superiority of HEAP (as already shown in Figure 7) is overcome by its lack of sensitivity to the existence of the LRU buffer. Thus, STD quickly outperforms HEAP, i.e., for B > 4 pages. We have also run this set of experiments for overlapping workspaces as well and reached to similar conclusions, therefore they are not illustrated. A remark that deserves more attention and does not appear for 0% overlap, concerns the behavior of SIM with respect to STD and HEAP: for large buffer sizes SIM competes both of them and, in some cases, even outperforms them, although marginally. Overall, as a general hint, we suggest that HEAP (respectively, STD) is the algorithm to be preferred when the LRU buffer is small enough (respectively, medium to large).

5.2 Comparison with the incremental approach

In [11] three alternative tree traversal policies were presented: basic, even, and simultaneous tree traversals (in the sequel, BAS, EVN, and SML, respectively), as already discussed in Section 3. We have implemented all three alternatives and, although our algorithms are not incremental, in this subsection we provide

a performance comparison in order to extract useful conclusions about the behavior of each one. In the rest of the section, we compare the performance of STD and HEAP, on the one hand, with EVN and SML, on the other hand, since BAS turned out to be inefficient for most settings of our experiments (included in [5]). Figure 10 illustrates the performance of two algorithms (STD and HEAP) proposed in Section 3 and two algorithms (EVN and SML) proposed in [11] for all combinations of two settings for buffer size (0 and 128 pages) and two settings for overlapping factor (0% and 100%). According to these experiments, EVN is competitive for small K values but turns out to be inefficient for $K \geq 10,000$. For zero buffer size, it is HEAP and SML that outperform the others in most cases while for large buffer size, STD is the most efficient. The advantage of STD due to large buffer has been also mentioned in Subsection 5.1.3. It is also worth mentioning that for disjoint workspaces HEAP and SML appear to have identical behavior.[4]

---

[4]Both algorithms work in a simultaneous way. Apart from their policy in filling the heap structure, a major difference consists of the policy in treatment of ties. However, this is not reflected in the overall I/O cost when the workspaces are disjoint, since ties are rare in that case.

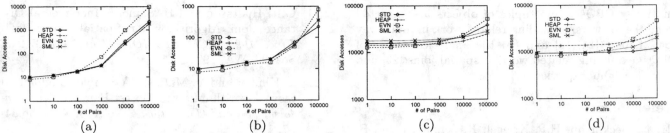

Figure 10: Comparison of two Incremental and two Non-incremental Algorithms: (a) No Buffer, Overlap = 0%, (b) 128 Page Buffer, Overlap = 0%, (c) No Buffer, Overlap = 100%, (d) 128 Page Buffer, Overlap = 100%. Log Scale.

Additional results, exploring the effect of the buffer size in the relative performance of SML, STD and HEAP, are presented in [5].

5.3 General guidelines

Overall, processing K-CPQs is a very expensive operation. Among the four proposed algorithms we can choose the most robust ones following some guidelines:

- Assuming no buffer, STD and HEAP are both very efficient when the workspaces of the two data sets do not overlap while, for overlapping workspaces, HEAP is the most efficient choice.

- When assuming a buffer of reasonable size (e.g., B > 4 pages), STD outperforms HEAP, since the latter one turned out to be insensitive to the existence of the LRU buffer.

Regarding the incremental algorithms proposed in [11], although SML is a competitive approach for several configurations, it is again HEAP (for zero or small buffer) and STD (for large buffer) that usually outperform SML with a gap reaching up to 20% and 50%, respectively. On the other hand, unlike the three competitors (SML, STD, and HEAP), EVN is not stable to the variety of K values we experimented with.

6 Conclusions

CPQs are important in spatial databases; [19] includes a variation of this query in a benchmark for Paradise [6]. However, unlike in computational geometry literature [7, 12], efficient processing of the CP problem has not gained special attention in spatial database research. Certain other problems of computational geometry, including the "all nearest neighbor" problem (that is related to the CP problem), have been solved for external memory systems [9]. To the authors' knowledge, [11] is the only reference to this type of queries in the spatial database literature. In this paper, we presented a naive and four improved algorithms to process both 1- and K-CPQs. Three out of them are recursive (the exhaustive, the simple, and the sorted distances) and one is iterative (heap). An extensive experimentation

was also included, which resulted to several conclusions about the efficiency of each algorithm with respect to K, the size of the underlying buffer and the portion of overlapping between the workspaces of the two data sets. They are listed as follows:

- Sorted distances and Heap are the most promising algorithms, since they perform well in the vast majority of different configurations.

- Buffer size plays an important role, as presented in detail, since it gives bonus to simple and sorted distances rather than heap.

- K does not radically affect the relative performance and the previous conclusions generally hold even for large K values.

We have also presented the novel "fix-at-root" technique for treating R-trees with different heights as an efficient, as turned out to be, alternative of the popular "fix-at-leaves" technique. In comparison with the algorithms proposed in [11], our algorithms are more stable with K and (especially, sorted distances) usually outperform them by 10% - 50%. Our work is also the first that addresses and evaluates the effect of the portion of overlapping in the performance of CP algorithms ([11] considered fully overlapping workspaces only). As presented through the experiments, a small increase in the overlap between the data sets may cause performance deterioration of orders of magnitude, in terms of I/O cost and this is a key issue for effective query optimization. Moreover, this behavior raises the issue of the 'meaning' of CPQs under some conditions. Following [2], we plan to explore the effect of overlap on the CP problem, taking into account the (geometric) distinction between the closest and the most remote pairs.

One direction of future work is to study two special cases of CPQs: "self-CPQ" and "Semi-CPQ". In the first case, both data sets actually refer to the same entity ($P \equiv Q$) [5]. In the second case, a set of point pairs is produced, where the first point of each pair appears only once in the result (i.e. for each point in P, the nearest point in Q is discovered) [11]. Other directions of future work also include (a) the study of multi-way CPQs where tuples of objects are expected to be the answers, extending related work in multi-way spatial joins [14, 16] and (b) the analytical study of CPQs, extending related work in spatial joins [23] and nearest-neighbor queries [17].

References

[1] N. Beckmann, H.P. Kriegel, R. Schneider and B. Seeger: "The R*-tree: an Efficient and Robust Access Method for Points and Rectangles", *Proc. 1990 ACM SIGMOD Conf.*, pp.322-331, Atlantic City, NJ, 1990.

[2] K.S. Beyer, J. Goldstein, R. Ramakrishnan and U. Shaft: "When Is 'Nearest Neighbor' Meaningful?", *Proc. 7th Int. Conf. on Database Theory (ICDT'99)*, pp.217-235, Jerusalem, Israel, 1999.

[3] T. Brinkhoff, H.-P. Kriegel and B. Seeger: "Efficient Processing of Spatial Joins Using R-trees", *Proc. 1993 ACM SIGMOD Conf.*, pp.237-246, Washington, DC, 1993.

[4] A. Corral, M. Vassilakopoulos and Y. Manolopoulos: "Algorithms for Joining R-trees and Linear Region Quadtrees", *Proc. 6th Int. Symp. on Spatial Databases (SSD'99)*, pp.251-269, Hong Kong, China, 1999.

[5] A. Corral, Y. Manolopoulos, Y. Theodoridis and M. Vassilakopoulos: "Closest Pair Queries in Spatial Databases", Technical Report, Data Engineering Lab, Dept. of Informatics, Aristotle Univ. of Thessaloniki, Greece, 1999 (available from URL: http://delab.csd.auth.gr/~michalis/cpq.html).

[6] D.J. DeWitt, N. Kabra, J. Luo, J.M. Patel and J.-B. Yu: "Client-Server Paradise", *Proc. 20th VLDB Conf.*, pp. 558-569, Santiago, Chile, 1994.

[7] M. Dietzfelbinger, T. Hagerup, J. Katajainen and M. Penttonen: "A Reliable Randomized Algorithm for the Closest-Pair Problem", *Journal of Algorithms*, Vol.25, No.1, pp.19-51, 1997.

[8] V. Gaede and O. Guenther: "Multidimensional Access Methods", *ACM Computer Surveys*, Vol.30, No.2, pp.170-231, 1998.

[9] M.T. Goodrich, J.-J. Tsay, D.E. Vengroff and J.S. Vitter: "External-Memory Computational Geometry", *Proc. 34th Annual IEEE Symp. on Foundations of Comp. Science (FOCS'93)*, pp.714-723, Palo Alto, CA, 1993.

[10] A. Guttman: "R-trees - a Dynamic Index Structure for Spatial Searching", *Proc. 1984 ACM SIGMOD Conf.*, pp.47-57, Boston, MA, 1984.

[11] G.R. Hjaltason and H. Samet: "Incremental Distance Join Algorithms for Spatial Databases", *Proc. 1998 ACM SIGMOD Conf.*, pp.237-248, Seattle, WA, 1998.

[12] S. Khuller and Y. Matias: "A Simple Randomized Sieve Algorithm for the Closest-Pair Problem", *Information and Computation*, Vol.118, No.1, pp.34-37, 1995.

[13] S.T. Leutenegger and M.A. Lopez: "The Effect of Buffering on the Performance of R-Trees", *Proc. 14th IEEE Int. Conf. on Data Engineering (ICDE'98)*, pp.164-171, Orlando, FL, 1998.

[14] N. Mamoulis and D. Papadias: "Integration of Spatial Join Algorithms for Processing Multiple Inputs", *Proc. 1999 ACM SIGMOD Conf.*, pp.1-12, Philadelphia, PA, 1999.

[15] Y. Manolopoulos, Y. Theodoridis and V. Tsotras: *Advanced Database Indexing*, Kluwer Academic Publishers, 1999.

[16] D. Papadias, N. Mamoulis and Y. Theodoridis: "Processing and Optimization of Multi-way Spatial Joins Using R-trees", *Proc. 18th ACM PODS Symp. (PODS'99)*, pp.44-55, Philadelphia, PA, 1999.

[17] A.N. Papadopoulos and Y. Manolopoulos: "Performance of Nearest Neighbor Queries in R-Trees", *Proc. 6th Int. Conf. on Database Theory (ICDT'97)*, pp.394-408, Delphi, Greece, 1997.

[18] A.N. Papadopoulos and Y. Manolopoulos: "Nearest Neighbor Queries in Shared-Nothing Environments", *Geoinformatica*, Vol.1, No.4, pp.369-392, 1997.

[19] J.M. Patel et al.: "Building a Scalable Geo-Spatial DBMS: Technology, Implementation, and Evaluation", *Proc. 1997 ACM SIGMOD Conf.*, pp.336-347, Tucson, AZ, 1997

[20] F.P. Preparata and M.I. Shamos: *Computational Geometry: an Introduction*, Springer-Verlag, 1985.

[21] N. Roussopoulos, S. Kelley and F. Vincent: "Nearest Neighbor Queries", *Proc. 1995 ACM SIGMOD Conf.*, pp.71-79, San Hose, CA, 1995.

[22] M. Stonebraker, J. Frew, K. Gardels and J. Meredith: "The Sequoia 2000 Benchmark", *Proc. 1993 ACM SIGMOD Conf.*, pp.2-11, Washington, DC, 1993.

[23] Y. Theodoridis, E. Stefanakis and T. Sellis: "Cost Models for Join Queries in Spatial Databases", *Proc. 14th IEEE Int. Conf. on Data Engineering (ICDE'98)*, pp.476-483, Orlando, FL, 1998.

Influence Sets Based on
Reverse Nearest Neighbor Queries

Flip Korn
AT&T Labs-Research
flip@research.att.com

S. Muthukrishnan
AT&T Labs-Research
muthu@research.att.com

Abstract

Inherent in the operation of many decision support and continuous referral systems is the notion of the "influence" of a data point on the database. This notion arises in examples such as finding the set of customers affected by the opening of a new store outlet location, notifying the subset of subscribers to a digital library who will find a newly added document most relevant, *etc.* Standard approaches to determining the influence set of a data point involve range searching and nearest neighbor queries.

In this paper, we formalize a novel notion of influence based on reverse neighbor queries and its variants. Since the nearest neighbor relation is not symmetric, the set of points that are closest to a query point (*i.e.*, the nearest neighbors) differs from the set of points that have the query point as their nearest neighbor (called the reverse nearest neighbors). Influence sets based on reverse nearest neighbor (RNN) queries seem to capture the intuitive notion of influence from our motivating examples.

We present a general approach for solving RNN queries and an efficient R-tree based method for large data sets, based on this approach. Although the RNN query appears to be natural, it has not been studied previously. RNN queries are of independent interest, and as such should be part of the suite of available queries for processing spatial and multimedia data. In our experiments with real geographical data, the proposed method appears to scale logarithmically, whereas straightforward sequential scan scales linearly. Our experimental study also shows that approaches based on range searching or nearest neighbors are ineffective at finding influence sets of our interest.

1   Introduction

A fundamental task that arises in various marketing and decision support systems is to determine the "influence" of a data point on the database, for example, the influence of a new store outlet or the influence of a new document to a repository. The concept of influence depends on the application at hand and is often difficult to formalize. We first develop an intuitive notion of influence sets through examples to motivate our formalization of it. The following two examples are drawn from spatial domains.

Example 1 (Decision Support Systems): There are many factors that may contribute to a clientele adopting one outlet over another, but a simple premise is to base it on the geographical proximity to the customers. Consider a marketing application in which the issue is to determine the business impact of opening an outlet of Company A at a given location. A simple task is to determine the segment of A's customers who would be likely to use this new facility. Alternatively, one may wish to determine the segment of customers of Company B (say A's competitor) who are likely to find the new facility more convenient than the locations of B. Such segments of customers are loosely what we would like to refer to as *influence sets*.   □

Example 2 (Continuous Referral Systems): Consider a referral service wherein a user can specify a street address, and the system returns a list of the five closest FedEx^{TM} drop-off locations.[1] A responsible referral service may wish to give the option (*e.g.*, by clicking a button) to make this a *continuous query*, that is, to request the system to notify the user when this list changes. The referral service will then notify those users whose list changes due to the opening of a closer FedEx drop-off location or the closing of an existing one. When such an event happens, the users who need to be updated correspond to our notion of the influence set of the added or dropped location.   □

Both examples above reinforce the notion of the influence set of a data point in terms of geographical proximity. This concept of influence sets is inherent

---

[1]See http://www.fedex.com/us/dropoff for a realization of this.

in many other decision support situations and referral services for which there is no underlying spatial or geographical distance, but for which there is a notion of similarity based on the vector space model (in which "distance" between vectors is taken as a measure of dissimilarity). The following two examples provide illustration.

Example 3 (Profile-based Marketing): A company may wish to keep profiles of its customers' interests so that it can gear a new service towards most customers. For example, suppose AT&T launches a new wireless service. The service may be abstracted a feature vector (*e.g.*, covers New England area, free local calling on weekends, best for $100-per-month users). The issue is which customers will find this the most suitable plan for their calling patterns; these customers form the influence set of the new service. One approach is to identify such users based on the distance between their profiles and the feature vector representing the new service. □

Example 4 (Maintaining Document Repositories): Consider a repository of technical reports. When a new report is filed, it may be desirable to alert the authors of other TRs who would likely find the document interesting based on similarity to their publications; the set of all such authors corresponds to the notion of influence set we have been developing so far. Here, the influence set is defined based on the similarity between text documents which has been well-explored in the Information Retrieval community. Other similar scenarios abound, such as in a repository of Web pages, precedent legal cases, *etc.* □

Let us now make the notion of an influence set more precise. We start with a data set S, some suitable definition of distance between points in S, and a query point q; the goal is to find the subset of points in S influenced by q. Two suggestions present themselves immediately. The first is to use range queries wherein one specifies a threshold radius ϵ from q, and all points within ϵ are returned. The second is to use the well known concept of *nearest neighbors* (NN), or, more generally, k-nearest neighbors wherein one specifies k, and the k closest points to q are returned.

Both of these suggestions fall short of capturing the intuitive notion of influence we have so far developed. In both cases, parameters have to be engineered to yield an appropriate result size, and it is not obvious how to choose a value without *a priori* knowledge of the local density of points. Range queries may be appropriate for other notions of influence (*e.g.*, the opening of a toxic waste dump on its surrounding population) but not for what is required in the examples given above. NN queries are commonly used in domains

which call for searching based on proximity; however, they are not appropriate in this context for similar reasons. Consider Example 1, in which one wants to find potential customers for a new store outlet q. The deciding factor is not how close a customer is to q, but rather if the customer is further from every *other* store than from q. Thus, it may very well be the case that potential customers lie outside a small radius from q, or are further from q than the first few nearest neighbors. Expanding the search radius will not necessarily work around this problem. Although it may encompass more customers who are likely to be influenced by q, it may do so at the trade-off of introducing many customers who are not in the influence set (*i.e.*, customers whose closest store is *not* q). Later, we will make these discussions more concrete and present quantitative measures of comparison (see Section 6).

We address these shortcomings and develop a notion of influence set with broad applications. A fundamental observation which is the basis for our work here is that the nearest neighbor relation is *not symmetric*. For example, if p is the nearest neighbor of q, then q need not be the nearest neighbor of p (see Figure 1).[2] Note that this is the case even though the underlying distance function is Euclidean and, hence, symmetric. Similarly, the k-nearest neighbor relation is not symmetric. It follows that, for a given query point q, the nearest neighbors of q may differ substantially from the set of all points for which q is a nearest neighbor. We call these points the *reverse nearest neighbors* of q.

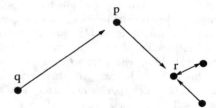

Figure 1: Nearest neighbors need not be symmetric: the NN of q is p, whereas the NN of p is r. (An arrow from point i to point j indicates that j is the nearest neighbor of i.)

We now summarize our contributions:

- We identify a natural and broadly applicable notion for the "influence" of a data point on the database (namely, the *influence set*), and formalize it based on reverse nearest neighbors (RNN) and its variants (such as reverse k-nearest neighbors, reverse furthest neighbor, *etc.*);

---

[2]That is, provided there are other points in the collection.

- We present a general approach for determining reverse nearest neighbors. Our approach is geometric, reducing the problem to that of testing the enclosure of points in geometric objects; it works for different distance functions and variants of RNNs. Although the RNN query appears to be natural, it has not been studied previously. RNN queries are of independent interest, and as such should be part of the suite of available queries for processing spatial and multimedia data;

- Based on our approach, we propose efficient and scalable R-tree based methods for implementing reverse nearest neighbor queries. We also perform an experimental study of the I/O-efficiency of the proposed R-tree based methods. Using our approach, we show in terms of standard precision and recall measures to assess the output quality, that well known database queries (range and nearest neighbor queries) are *not* effective in finding influence sets.

The structure of the paper is as follows. Section 2 defines RNN queries and describes its relationship to NN queries. Section 3 presents an approach and algorithmic framework for answering RNN queries; we also propose a scalable method for implementating this framework using R-trees in Section 4. Section 5 gives empirical results from experiments for RNN queries. In Section 6, we formalize the basic notion of influence sets based on RNN queries and give results from a qualitative study of the effectiveness of well known queries to substitute for RNN queries. Then we develop the variants of RNN queries needed for generalized notions of influence sets. Section 7 reviews the related work. Section 8 lists the conclusions and gives directions for future work.

2   Reverse Nearest Neighbor Queries

Reverse nearest neighbor (RNN) queries are the basis for influence sets, and are also of independent interest. We define and develop them in this section. We start from the definition of the nearest neighbor (NN) query, a standard query in spatial and multimedia databases and define the RNN query and its variants based on this. We will develop the underlying concepts in two dimensions for simplicity; there will be no difficulty in extending them to higher dimensions. In our discussion, we shall assume the distance between any two points $p = (p_x, p_y)$ and $q = (q_x, q_y)$ is $d(p, q) = (q_x - p_x)^2 + (q_y - p_y)^2$, known as the Euclidean, or L_2, distance.[3]

2.1   Formal Definitions

Suppose we have a collection S of points in the plane. For a nearest neighbor query, we are given a query point q, and the goal is to determine the nearest neighbor set $\mathcal{NN}(q)$ defined as

$$\mathcal{NN}(q) = \{r \in S \mid \forall p \in S : d(q, r) \leq d(q, p)\}.$$

Our focus here is on the inverse relation among the points. Given any query point q, we need to determine the set $\mathcal{RNN}(q)$ of reverse nearest neighbors, defined as

$$\mathcal{RNN}(q) = \{r \in S \mid \forall p \in S : d(r, q) \leq d(r, p)\}.$$

$\mathcal{RNN}(q)$ may be empty, or have one or more elements, and we may wish to return any one of them, or the entire list.

2.2   Variants

There are two variants of this basic scenario that are of interest to us. We will define only the variants for RNN queries, although the corresponding variants of NN queries may also be of interest.

- *Monochromatic vs Bichromatic.* In some applications, the points in S are of two different categories, such as clients and servers; the points may therefore be thought of as being colored *red* or *blue*. The RNN query now consists of a point in one of the categories, say blue, and must determine the red points for which the query point is the closest blue point. Formally, let B denote the set of blue points and R the set of red points. Consider a blue query point q. We have,

$$\mathcal{RNN}(q) = \{r \in R \mid \forall p \in B : d(r, q) \leq d(r, p)\}.$$

We call this the *bichromatic* version; in contrast, the basic scenario above wherein all points were of the same category is the *monochromatic* version. Both versions of the problem are of interest.

At first look, the mono and bichromatic versions of the RNN problem seem very similar. For a blue query point, we consider only the red points and their distance to the closest blue point (vice versa for the red query points). However, at a deeper level, there is a fundamental difference. Let us focus on the L_2 case.

Proposition 1 *For any query point, $\mathcal{RNN}(q)$ may have at most 6 points in the monochromatic case; in the bichromatic case, the size of the set $\mathcal{RNN}(q)$ may be unbounded.*

A proof of this may be found in [17]. From a combinatorial viewpoint, the output of RNN queries is bounded; this in turn affects the efficiency because a RNN query is output-sensitive. This entire phenomenon is not restricted to the plane (*e.g.*, in three dimensions, the

---

[3]Other L_p distances may also be interest, for example L_1 where $d(p, q) = |q_x - p_x| + |q_y - p_y|$ or L_∞ where $d(p, q) = \max\{|q_x - p_x|, |q_y - p_y|\}$.

$\mathcal{RNN}(q)$ contains at most 12 points under L_2 distance and so on), or the distance function (*e.g.*, in the L_∞ case, the cardinality of $\mathcal{RNN}(q)$ is at most $3^d - 1$ in d dimensions).

- *Static vs Dynamic*. Sometimes we wish to insert or delete points from the set S and still support the RNN query; we refer to this as the *dynamic* case. In contrast, the case when set S is not modified is called the *static* case. The dynamic case is relevant in most applications. The crux here, as in all dynamic problems, is to be able to handle insertions and deletions efficiently without rebuilding the entire data structure.

3 Our Approach to RNN Queries

Our approach for solving the reverse nearest neighbors query problem is quite general, and it applies also to its variants as we shall see.

3.1 Static Case

For exposition, let us consider a basic version of the problem. We are given a set S of points which is not updated, and the distance between any two points is measured using Euclidean distance. Our approach involves two steps.

Step 1. For each point $p \in S$, determine the distance to the nearest neighbor of p in S, denoted $N(p)$. Formally, $N(p) = \min_{q \in S - \{p\}} d(p, q)$. For each $p \in S$, generate a circle $(p, N(p))$ where p is its center and $N(p)$ its radius. (See Figure 2(a) for an illustration.)

Step 2. For any query q, determine all the circles $(p, N(p))$ that contain q and return their centers p.

We have not yet described how to perform the two steps above, but we will first prove that they suffice.

Lemma 1 *Step 2 determines precisely all the reverse nearest neighbors of q.*

Proof. If point p is returned from Step 2, then q falls within the circle $(p, N(p))$. Therefore, the distance $d(p, q)$ is smaller than the radius $N(p)$. In other words, $d(p, q) \leq N(p)$ and hence q is the nearest neighbor of p (equivalently, p is a reverse nearest neighbor of q). Conversely, if p is the reverse nearest neighbor of q, $d(p, q) \leq N(p)$ and, therefore, q lies within the circle $(p, N(p))$. Hence, p will be found in Step 2. $\square$

What our approach has achieved is to reduce the problem of answering the reverse nearest neighbor query to the problem of finding all nearest neighbors (Step 1) and then to what is known in the literature as *point enclosure problems* wherein we need to determine all the objects that contain a query point (Step 2).

Our approach is attractive for two reasons. First, both steps are of independent interest and have been studied in the literature. They have efficient solutions, as we will see later. Second, our approach extends to the variants of our interest as we show below.

Other distance functions. If the distance function is L_∞ rather than L_2, we generate squares $(p, N(p))$ in Step 1 with center p and sides $2N(p)$. (See Figure 2(b) for an illustration.) Similarly, for other L_p distance functions, we will have suitable geometric shapes.

Bichromatic version. Consider only blue query points for now. We perform the two steps above only for the red points in set S. For each red point $p \in S$, we determine $N(p)$, the distance to the nearest blue neighbor. The rest of the description above remains unchanged. We also process for red query points analogously.

3.2 Dynamic Case

Our description above was for the static case only. For the dynamic case, we need to make some modifications. Below we assume the presence of a (dynamically maintained) data structure for answering NN queries. Recall the definition of $N(p)$ for point p from the previous section. Consider an insertion of a point q (as illustrated in Figure 3(a)):

1. Determine the reverse nearest neighbors p of q. For each such point p, we replace circle $(p, N(p))$ with $(p, d(p, q))$, and update $N(p)$ to equal $d(p, q)$;

2. Find $N(q)$, the distance of q from its nearest neighbor, and add $(q, N(q))$ to the collection of circles.

Lemma 2 *The insertion procedure is correct.*

Proof. It suffices to argue that, for each point p, $N(p)$ is the correct distance of p to its nearest neighbor after an insertion. This clearly holds for the inserted point q from Step 2. Among the rest of the points, the only ones which will be affected are those which have q as their nearest neighbor, in other words, the reverse nearest neighbors of q. For all such points p, we update their $N(p)$'s appropriately in Step 1. The remaining points p do not change $N(p)$ as a result of inserting q. Hence, all points p have the correct value of $N(p)$. $\square$

Step 1 is shown in Figure 3(b) where we shrink all circles $(p, N(p))$ for which q is the nearest neighbor of p to $(p, d(p, q))$. Step 2 is shown in Figure 3(c).

Now consider an deletion of a point q (as illustrated in Figure 4(a)):

1. We need to remove the circle $(q, N(q))$ from the collection of circles (see Figure 4(b));

2. Determine all the reverse nearest neighbors p of q. For each such point p, determine its current $N(p)$ and replace its existing circle with $(p, N(p))$.

We can argue much as before that the deletion procedure is correct. The crucial observation is that

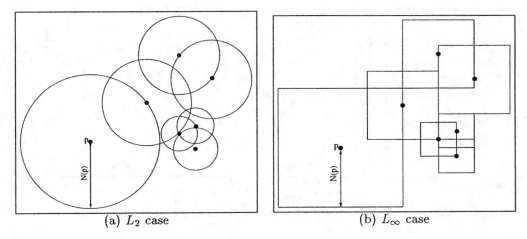

(a) L_2 case   (b) L_∞ case

Figure 2: A point set and its nearest neighborhoods.

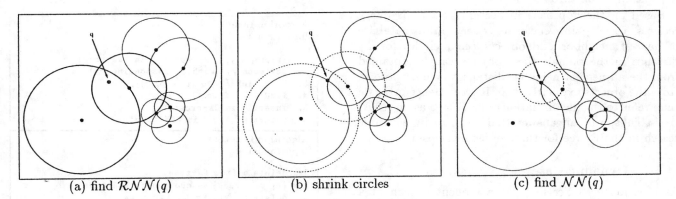

(a) find $\mathcal{RNN}(q)$ (b) shrink circles   (c) find $\mathcal{NN}(q)$

Figure 3: A geometrical illustration of the insertion algorithm.

the only existing circles $(p, N(p))$ that get affected are those that have q on the circumference, that is, those associated with the reverse nearest neighbors of q; their circles get expanded in Step 1 (see Figure 4(c)). The details for how to extend these algorithms to other distance functions and to the bichromatic version are similar to those given in the previous section.

4   Scalable RNN Queries

In this section we propose a scalable method for implementing RNN queries on large, out-of-core data sets, based on our approach from Section 3. Like NN queries, RNN queries are I/O-bound (as opposed to, *e.g.*, spatial joins which are CPU-bound), and thus the focus is on I/O performance. Because R-trees [7, 2, 16] have been successfully deployed in spatial databases and because of their generality to support a variety of norms via bounding boxes, we use them in the proposed method. However, note that any spatial access method could be employed (see [6] for a recent

survey of spatial access methods). Our deployment of R-trees is standard, but requires some elaboration. First we describe static RNN search; we then present details of the algorithms and data structures for the dynamic case.

4.1   Static Case

The first step in being able to efficiently answer RNN queries is to precompute the nearest neighbor for each and every point. The problem of efficiently computing all-nearest neighbors in large data sets has been studied in [3, 8], and thus we do not investigate it further in this paper.[4]

Given a query point q, a straightforward but naive approach for finding reverse nearest neighbors is to sequentially scan through the entries $(p_i \to p_j)$ of a precomputed all-NN list in order to determine which points p_i are closer to q than to p_i's current nearest

---

[4] All-nearest neighbors is a special case of a spatial join.

205

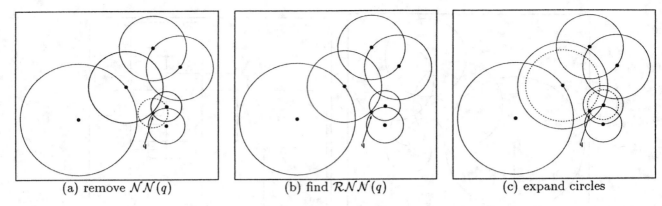

| (a) remove $\mathcal{NN}(q)$ | (b) find $\mathcal{RNN}(q)$ | (c) expand circles |

Figure 4: A geometrical illustration of the deletion algorithm.

neighbor p_j. Ideally, one would like to avoid having to sequentially scan through the data.

Based on the approach in Section 3, a RNN query reduces to a point enclosure query in a database of nearest neighborhood objects (*e.g.*, circles for L_2 distance in the plane); these objects can be obtained from the all-nearest neighbor distances. We propose to store the objects explicitly in an R-tree. Henceforth, we shall refer to this instantiation of an R-tree as an *RNN-tree*. Thus, we can answer RNN queries by a simple search in the R-tree for those objects enclosing q.

4.2 Dynamic Case

As mentioned in Section 4.1, a sequential scan of a precomputed all-NN list can be used to determine the reverse nearest neighbors of a given point query q. Insertion and deletion can be handled similarly. Even if this list were inverted, enabling deletion to be achieved in constant time by looking up the corresponding entry $(p_j \rightarrow \{p_{i_1}, p_{i_2}, \ldots, p_{i_k}\})$, queries and insertions would still require a pass over the data. We would like to avoid having to do this.

We describe how to incrementally maintain the RNN-tree in the presence of insertions and deletions. To do this will require a supporting access method that can find nearest neighbors of points efficiently. At this point, one may wonder if a single R-tree will suffice for finding reverse nearest neighbors as well as nearest neighbors, in other words, if our RNN-tree can be used for this purpose, This turns out to be not the case since geometric objects rather than points are stored in the RNN-tree, and thus the bounding boxes are not optimized for nearest neighbor search performance on points. Therefore, we propose to use a separate R-tree for NN queries, henceforth referred to as an *NN-tree*. Note that the NN-tree is *not* needed for static RNN queries, only for insertions and deletions, and that, in addition to the RNN-tree, it must be dynamically maintained.

```
Algorithm Insert:
Input: point q

1.   {p1,p2,...,pk} ← query q in RNN-tree;
2.   for each pi (with corresponding Ri) do
3.      shrink Ri to (pi,d(pi,q));
4.   find N(q) from NN-tree;
5.   insert q in NN-tree;
6.   insert (q,N(q)) in RNN-tree;
```

```
Algorithm Delete:
Input: point q

1.   delete q from NN-tree;
2.   {p1,p2,...,pk} ← query q in RNN-tree;
3.   delete (q,N(q)) from RNN-tree;
4.   for each pi (with corresponding Ri) do
5.      find N(pi) from NN-tree;
6.      grow Ri to (pi,N(pi));
```

Figure 5: Proposed Algorithms for Insertion and Deletion.

Figure 5 presents pseudocode for insertion and deletion. The algorithm for insertion retrieves (from the RNN-tree) the reverse nearest neighbors p_i of q, and their corresponding neighborhood objects R_i, without having to scan; each R_i is then reduced in size to $(p_i, d(p_i, q))$. The algorithm for deletion works similarly, using the RNN-tree to find the points p_i affected by the deletion; each corresponding R_i is then expanded to $(p_i, d(p_i, N(p_i))$.

5 Experiments on RNN queries

We designed a set of experiments to test the I/O performance of our proposed method on large data sets. Our goal was to determine the scale-up trend of both static and dynamic queries. We also examined the performance of bichromatic versus monochromatic data. Below we present results from two batches of experiments, for static and dynamic RNN queries.

Methods: We compared the proposed algorithms given in Section 4 to the basic scanning approach. In the static case, the scanning approach precomputes an all-NN list and makes a pass through it to determine the reverse nearest neighbors. In the dynamic case, the scanning approach precomputes and maintains an inverted all-NN list. Each entry in the all-NN list corresponds to a point in the data set, and thus requires storing two items for nearest neighbor information: the point coordinates and nearest neighbor distances. Similarly, the RNN-tree used in the proposed method requires storing each point and its associated nearest neighborhood. Both also use an NN-tree for nearest neighbor search. Thus, the methods require the same storage space.

Data Sets: Our testbed includes two real data sets. The first is mono and the second is bichromatic:

- `cities1` - Centers of 100K cities and small towns in the USA (chosen at random from a larger data set of 132K cities), represented as latitude and longitude coordinates;

- `cities2` - Coordinates of 100K red cities (*i.e.*, clients) and 400 black cities (*i.e.*, servers). The red cities are mutually disjoint from the black cities, and points from both colors were chosen at random from the same source.

Queries: We assume the so-called 'biased' query model, in which queries are more likely to come from dense regions [13]. We chose 500 query points at random (without replacement) from the same source that the data sets were chosen; note that these points are external to the data sets. For dynamic queries, we simulated a mixed workload of insertions by randomly choosing between insertions and deletions. In the case of insertions, one of the 500 query points were inserted; for deletions, an existing point was chosen at random. We report the average I/O per query, that is, the cumulative number of page accesses divided by the number of queries.

Software: The code for our experiments was implemented in C on a Sun SparcWorkstation. To implement RNN queries, we extended DR-tree, a disk-resident R*-tree package; to implement NN queries (which were used for the second batch of experiments), we used the DR-tree as is.[5] The page size was set to 4K.

---

[5]available at `ftp://ftp.olympos.umd.edu`.

5.1 Static Case

We uniformly sampled the `cities1` data set to get subsets of varying sizes, between 10K and 100K points. Figure 6(a) shows the I/O performance of the proposed method compared to sequential scan. Each query took roughly between 9-28 I/Os for the data sets we tried with our approach; in contrast, the performance of the scanning approach increased from 40 to 400 I/Os with increasing data set size (n). The gap between the two curves clearly widens as n increases, and the proposed method appears to scale logarithmically, whereas the scanning approach scales linearly.

We performed the same experiment for `cities2`. Figure 6(b) plots the I/O performance. It is interesting to note that the performance degrades more with increasing n (from 12-65 I/Os) with bichromatic data; this is primarily because the output size is larger in bichromatic case than in the monochromatic case as remarked earlier. However, this increase again appears to be logarithmic.

5.2 Dynamic Case

Again, we used the `cities1` data set and uniformly sampled it to get subsets of varying sizes, between 10K and 100K points. As shown in Figure 7, the I/O cost for an even workload of insertions and deletions appears to scale logarithmically, whereas the scanning method scales linearly. It is interesting to note that the average I/O is up to four times worse than in the static case, although this factor decreases for larger data sets. We broke down the I/O into four categories – RNN queries, NN queries, insertions and deletions – and found that each took approximately the same number of I/Os. Thus, the maintenance of the NN-tree accounts for the extra I/O compared to the static queries.

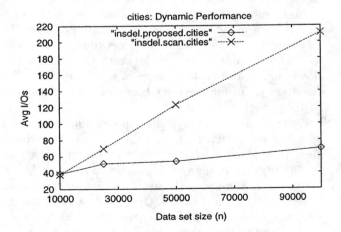

Figure 7: The I/O performance of dynamic RNN queries (proposed method vs. scanning) in the presence of an even mix of insertions and deletions.

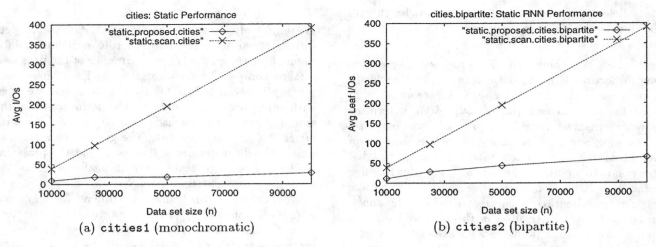

(a) `cities1` (monochromatic)　　　　(b) `cities2` (bipartite)

Figure 6: The I/O performance of static RNN queries (proposed method vs. scanning) for (a) `cities1` (monochromatic) and (b) `cities2` (bipartite).

6   Influence Sets

6.1   Basic notion and applications

Our first, and most basic, definition of the influence set of a point q is simply that it is the set of all reverse nearest neighbors of q, that is, $\mathcal{RNN}(q)$. This may be mono or bichromatic reverse nearest neighbors, depending on the application.

Before exploring this notion further, let us briefly reexamine the motivating examples from Section 1. In Examples 1 and 2, the influence set of the new location of a store outlet is indeed the set of customers who find the new location the closest amongst all locations of stores. This is an instance of bichromatic RNN. In Example 3, the customers who are influenced by a new service are those whose profiles have the feature vector of the new service closest amongst all service feature vectors. Again, the influence set of the new service corresponds to our basic definition above. In Example 4, the influence set of a new document is the set of all documents in the database that find it the closest under a suitable measure of similarity; here, the definition of an influence set based on monochromatic RNNs applies.

We can think of many other applications where the basic notion of influence set arises. What is perhaps more interesting is that this notion of influence sets *implicitly* arises in many computational tasks.

For example, many problems of interest in Operations Research and Combinatorial Optimization have greedy solutions with good performance. One such example is the *facility location* problem. Here we are given many points and the goal is to designate some as facilities and others as non-facilities. There is a cost to designating a point as a facility, and a cost for non-

facilities which equals the cost of accessing the closest facility. This problem is known to be NP-hard, and thus the focus is on designing approximation algorithms for this problem. The method of choice in practice for this problem is the greedy method – it is simple, and is a provably small approximation [14].[6] The greedy algorithm involves repeatedly adding a facility, deleting one, or swapping a facility with a non-facility. In order to implement this algorithm, we need to determine the enhanced cost when a new facility is added which involves looking at precisely those locations whose NN distance is changed when a new facility is added (or deleted, swapped). The set of all such locations is indeed our basic definition of a influence set; these have been implicitly computed in this context for a long time. Another example is that of computing the shortest path from a single point to every other point in the database. When a point is added to a partial solution that greedy algorithms maintain, the distance of remaining points to the partial solution has to be updated and this will again be given by the influence set of the point added to the partial solution. Many other implicit uses of influence sets exist in Combinatorial Optimization.

6.2   Using existing methods

There are two potential problems with the effectiveness of any approach to finding influence sets. One is the *precision* problem wherein a large portion of the retrieved set contains irrelevant points. Conversely, there is the *recall* problem wherein the retrieved set misses some of the relevant points. An effective approach would achieve high precision at high recall

---

[6]Better approximations exist, but they are based on Linear Programming [10].

(ideally, 100% precision at 100% recall). In this section we present results from an experiment to demonstrate that nearest neighbor queries and range queries are not effective "engineering" substitutes for RNN queries in finding influence sets; we use standard precision and recall metrics from information retrieval to assess their quality.

The first issue that arises in finding influence sets is what region to search in. Two possibilities immediately present themselves: find the closest points (i.e., the k-nearest neighbors) or all points within some radius (i.e., ϵ-range search). Of course, there are many variants of these basic queries, such as searching with weighted distances, searching over polygonal or elliptical regions, etc. To demonstrate the ineffectiveness of these approaches, it shall suffice to consider the most basic version. The question then is how to engineer the parameter value (namely k or ϵ) that will contain the desired information. Without a priori knowledge of the density of points near the query point q, it is not clear how to choose these values. Regardless, we show that any clever strategy to engineer parameter values (be it from histograms, etc.) would still fall short.

Figure 8 illustrates this concept. The black points represent servers and the white points represent clients. In this example, we wish to find all the clients for which q is their closest server. The example illustrates that a ϵ-range (alternatively, k-NN) query cannot find the desired information in this case, regardless of which value of ϵ (or k) is chosen. Figure 8(a) shows a 'safe' radius ϵ_l in which all points are reverse nearest neighbors of q; however, there exist reverse nearest neighbors of q outside ϵ_l. Figure 8(b) shows a wider radius ϵ_h that includes all of the reverse nearest neighbors of q but also includes points which are not. In this example, it is possible to achieve 100% precision or 100% recall, but not both simultaneously.

We ran an experiment to investigate how often this trade-off occurs in practice. The experiment was carried out as follows. Suppose we had an oracle to suggest the largest radius ϵ_l admitting no false-positives, i.e., whose neighborhood contains only points in the influence set. For this scenario, we assess the quality of the retrieved set from the number of false-negatives within this radius. More specifically, we measured the recall at 100% precision, that is, the cardinality of the retrieved set divided by that of the influence set. Further suppose we had an oracle to suggest the smallest radius ϵ_h allowing no false-negatives, i.e., whose neighborhood contains the full influence set (equivalently, reverse nearest neighbors). For this scenario, we assess the quality of the retrieved set from the number of false-positives within this radius. More specficially, we measured the precision at 100% recall, that is, the cardinality of the influence set divided by that of the retrieved set.

We used the cities2 data set in the our experiment and averaged over 100 queries. The results are summarized in Table 1. The quality of the retrieved set at radius ϵ_l is poor, containing a small fraction of the full influence set. The quality of the retrieved set at radius ϵ_h is also poor, containing a lot of 'garbage' in addition to the influenced points.

measure	radius	value
precision (at 100% recall)	ϵ_h	44.3%
recall (at 100% precision)	ϵ_l	40.2%

Table 1: The effectiveness of range queries in finding influence sets. Quality is measured by precision at 100% recall and recall at 100% precision.

6.3 Extended notions of influence sets

In this section, we extend the notion of influence sets from the previous section. We do not explore these notions in depth here using experiments; instead we focus on sketching how our approach for finding the basic influence sets can be modified to find these extended influence sets. Some of these modifications will be straightforward, others less so.

Reverse k-nearest neighbors. A rather simple extension of the influence set of point q is to define it to be the set of all points that have q as one of their k nearest neighbors. Here, k is fixed and specified a priori. For static queries, the only difference in our solution is that we store the neighborhood of kth neighbor rather than nearest neighbor. (Note that we do not explicitly store the k nearest neighbors.) Each query is an enclosure problem on these objects as in the basic case. For insertions and deletions, we update the neighborhood of the kth nearest neighbor of each affected point as follows. When inserting or deleting q, we first find the set of affected points using the enclosure problem as done for answering queries. For insertion, we perform a range query to determine the k nearest neighbors of each such affected point and do necessary updates. For deletion, the neighborhood radius of the affected points is expanded to the distance of the $(k + 1)$th neighbor, which can be found by a modified NN search on R-trees.

Influence sets with predicates. The basic notion of influence sets can be enhanced with predicates. Some examples of predicates involve bounding the search distance (find reverse nearest neighbors within a specified region of interest) and providing multiple facilities (find the reverse nearest neighbors to any, some, or all of multiple points in the set $\{q_1, \ldots, q_m\}$).

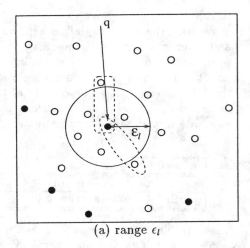

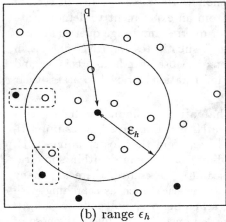

| (a) range ϵ_l | (b) range ϵ_h |

Figure 8: In many cases, any ϵ-range query or k-NN query will be either (a) too small or (b) too big.

For such queries, we can push the predicates inside the R-tree search.

Reverse furthest neighbors. An interesting variation of influence sets is to base it on dissimilarity rather than similarity, in other words, on furthest neighbors rather than nearest neighbors. More formally, define the influence set of a point q to be the set of all points r such that q is farther from r than any other point of the database is from r. This notion of influence has a solution that differs from the basic notion in an interesting way. We sketch the solution here only for the static case, but all modifications to convert this into a dynamic solution are based on ideas we already described before. We will also only describe the solution for the two dimensional case, but extending it to the multi-dimensional case is straightforward.

Say S is the set of points which will be fixed. A query point is denoted q. For simplicity, we will first describe our solution for the L_∞ distance.

Preprocessing: We first determine the furthest point for each point $p \in S$ and denote it as $f(p)$. We will put a square with center p and sides $2d(p, f(p))$ for each p; say this square is R_p.

Query processing: The simple observation is that for any query q, the reverse furthest neighbors r are those for which the R_r does *not* include q. Thus the problem we have is *square non-enclosure* problem. (Recall that, in contrast, the reverse nearest neighbors problem led to square enclosure problem.)

The following observation is the key to solving the square non-enclosure problem.

Lemma 3 *Consider the intervals x_r and y_r obtained by projecting the square R_r on x and y axis respectively. A point $q = (x, y)$ is not contained in R_r if and only if either x_r does not contain x or y_r does not contain y.*

Therefore, if we return all the x_r's that do not contain x as well as those y_r's that do not contain y's, each square r in the output is repeated atmost twice. So the problem can be reduced to a one dimensional problem on intervals without losing much efficiency. Let us restate the one dimensional problem formally: we are given a set of intervals, say N of them. Each query is a one dimensional point, say p, and the goal is to return all interval that do not contain p.

For solving this problem, we maintain two sorted arrays, one of the right endpoints of the intervals and the other of their left endpoints. The following observation is easy:

Proposition 2 *Any interval with its right endpoint to the left of p does not contain p. Likewise, any interval with its left endpoint to the right of p does not contain it.*

Hence, it suffices to perform two binary searches with p in the two arrays, to determine the intervals that do not contain p. Notice that from a practical viewpoint, the only data structure we need is a B-tree to keep these two arrays.

Theorem 1 *There exists an $\Theta(\log_B N + t)$ time algorithm to answer each query in the square non-enclosure problem, where t is the output size, $N = n/B$ is the number of disk blocks, and B is the block size; space used is $\Theta(N)$.*

Although the solution above is simple, we are not aware of any published claim of this result for square non-disclosure problem. As mentioned before, this immediately gives a solution for finding the set of all reverse furthest neighbors for a query point under the L_∞ distance. While a R-tree may be used to solve this

210

problem, our solution above shows that the only data structure we need is to a B-tree. Hence, the solution is very efficient. For other distance functions, we still have non-enclosure problem, but with different shapes (*e.g.*, circles for Euclidean distance). Practical approaches for solving such problems would be to either use bounding boxes to reduce the problem to square non-enclosure with some false positives, or to use R-tree based search.

7 Related Work

There has been a lot of work on nearest neighbor queries [5, 11, 4, 15, 9]. NN queries are useful in many applications: GIS (*'Find the k nearest hospitals from the place of an accident.'*), information retrieval (*'Find the most similar web page to mine.'*), multimedia databases (*'Find the tumor shape that looks the most similar to the query shape.'* [12]), *etc.* Conceptually, a RNN query is different from a NN query; it is the inverse.

There has been work in the area of spatial joins, and more specifically with all-nearest neighbor queries [8]. To the best of our knowledge, none of the previous work has addressed the issue of incremental maintenance. While reverse nearest neighbors is conceptually different, RNN queries provide an efficient means to incrementally maintain all-nearest neighbors.

Both incremental and random incremental Delaunay triangulations could be used for answering RNN queries, as the update step involves identifying points (and their circumcircles) local to the query point whose edges are affected by insertion/deletion, a superset of reverse nearest neighbors.[7] However, these algorithms rely on being able to efficiently locate the simplex containing the query point, a problem for which there is no efficient solution in large data sets. In addition, the algorithms make the general position assumption and do not work well for the bipartite case.

Our approach for RNN queries relied on solving point enclosure problems with different shapes. Point enclosure problems with n rectangles can be solved after $O(n \log^{d-1} n)$ time preprocessing in $O(\log^{d-1} n + t)$ time per query where t is the output size [1]. Such efficient algorithms are not known for other shapes, for dynamic cases, or for external memory datasets. Our R-tree approach is simple and applies to all the variants of RNN queries.

8 Conclusions and Future Work

The "influence" of a point in a database is a useful concept. In this paper, we introduce an intuitive notion of influence based on reverse nearest neighbors, and illustrate through examples that it has broad

---

[7] Alternatively, one could use the dual data structure, Voronoi diagrams.

appeal in many application domains. The basic notion of influence sets depends on *reverse nearest neighbor* queries, which are also of independent interest. We provide the first solution to this problem, and validate its I/O-efficiency through experiments. We also demonstrate using experiments that standard database queries such as range searching and NN queries are ineffective at finding influence sets. Finally, we further extend the notion of influence based on variants of RNN queries and provide efficient solutions for these variants as well.

We have initiated the study of influence sets using reverse nearest neighbors. Many issues remain to be explored, for example, the notion of influence outside of the typical query-response context, such as in data mining. It is often desirable to process the data set to suggest a region in which a query point should lie so as to exert maximal influence. What is the appropriate notion of influence sets in this context? From a technical point of view, efficient solutions for RNN queries are needed in high dimensions. Extensions of our approach to higher dimensions is straightforward; however, in very high dimensions, alternative approaches may be needed, as is the case for high dimensional NN queries. Also, the role of RNN queries can be explored further, such as in other proximity-based problems. It is our belief that the RNN query is a fundamental query, deserving to be a standard tool for data processing.

Acknowledgements

The authors wish to thank Christos Faloutsos, Dimitris Gunopoulos, H.V. Jagadish, Nick Koudas, and Dennis Shasha for their comments.

References

[1] P. Agrawal. Range searching. In E. Goodman and J. O'Rourke, editors, *Handbook of Discrete and Computational Geometry*, pages 575–598. CRC Press, Boca Raton, FL, 1997.

[2] N. Beckmann, H.-P. Kriegel, R. Schneider, and B. Seeger. The R*-tree: An efficient and robust access method for points and rectangles. *ACM SIGMOD*, pages 322–331, May 23-25 1990.

[3] T. Brinkhoff, H.-P. Kriegel, and B. Seeger. Efficient processing of spatial joins using R-trees. In *Proc. of ACM SIGMOD*, pages 237–246, Washington, D.C., May 26-28 1993.

[4] B. Chazelle and L. J. Guibas. Fractional cascading: I. A data structuring technique. *Algorithmica*, 1:133–162, 1986.

[5] K. Fukunaga and P. M. Narendra. A branch and bound algorithm for computing k-nearest

neighbors. *IEEE Trans. on Computers (TOC)*, C-24(7):750–753, July 1975.

[6] V. Gaede and O. Gunther. Multidimensional access methods. *ACM Computing Surveys*, 30(2):170–231, June 1998.

[7] A. Guttman. R-trees: A dynamic index structure for spatial searching. In *Proc. ACM SIGMOD*, pages 47–57, Boston, Mass, June 1984.

[8] G. R. Hjaltason and H. Samet. Incremental distance join algorithms for spatial databases. *ACM SIGMOD '98*, pages 237–248, June 1998.

[9] G. R. Hjaltason and H. Samet. Distance browsing in spatial databases. *ACM TODS*, 24(2):265–318, June 1999.

[10] K. Jain and V. Vazirani. Primal-dual approximation algorithms for metric facility location and k-median problems. *Proc. 40th IEEE Foundations of Computer Science (FOCS '99)*, pages 2–13, 1999.

[11] D. G. Kirkpatrick. Optimal search in planar subdivisions. *SIAM J. Comput.*, 12:28–35, 1983.

[12] F. Korn, N. Sidiropoulos, C. Faloutsos, E. Siegel, and Z. Protopapas. Fast nearest-neighbor search in medical image databases. *Conf. on Very Large Data Bases (VLDB)*, pages 215–226, September 1996.

[13] B. Pagel, H. Six, H. Toben, and P. Widmayer. Towards an analysis of range query performance. In *Proc. of ACM SIGACT-SIGMOD-SIGART Symposium on Principles of Database Systems (PODS)*, pages 214–221, Washington, D.C., May 1993.

[14] R. Rajaraman, M. Korupolu, and G. Plaxton. Analysis of a local search heuristic for facility location problems. *Proceedings of ACM-SIAM Symposium on Discrete Algorithms (SODA '98)*, pages 1–10, 1998.

[15] N. Roussopoulos, S. Kelley, and F. Vincent. Nearest neighbor queries. In *Proc. of ACM-SIGMOD*, pages 71–79, San Jose, CA, May 1995.

[16] T. Sellis, N. Roussopoulos, and C. Faloutsos. The R+ tree: A dynamic index for multi-dimensional objects. In *Proc. 13th International Conference on VLDB*, pages 507–518, England,, September 1987.

[17] M. Smid. Closest point problems in computational geometry. In J.-R. Sack and J. Urrutia, editors, *Handbook on Computational Geometry*. Elsevier Science Publishing, 1997.

MOCHA: A Self-Extensible Database Middleware System for Distributed Data Sources*

Manuel Rodríguez-Martínez
Department of Computer Science
University of Maryland, College Park
manuel@cs.umd.edu

Nick Roussopoulos
Department of Computer Science
University of Maryland, College Park
nick@cs.umd.edu

Abstract

We present MOCHA, a new self-extensible database middleware system designed to interconnect distributed data sources. MOCHA is designed to scale to large environments and is based on the idea that some of the user-defined functionality in the system should be deployed by the middleware system itself. This is realized by shipping Java code implementing either advanced data types or tailored query operators to remote data sources and have it executed remotely. Optimized query plans push the evaluation of powerful *data-reducing* operators to the data source sites while executing *data-inflating* operators near the client's site. The Volume Reduction Factor is a new and more explicit metric introduced in this paper to select the best site to execute query operators and is shown to be more accurate than the standard selectivity factor alone. MOCHA has been implemented in Java and runs on top of Informix and Oracle. We present the architecture of MOCHA, the ideas behind it, and a performance study using scientific data and queries. The results of this study demonstrate that MOCHA provides a more flexible, scalable and efficient framework for distributed query processing compared to those in existing middleware solutions.

1 Introduction

Database middleware systems are used to integrate collections of data sources distributed over a computer network. Typically, these type of systems follow an architecture centered around a *data integration server*, which provides client applications with a uniform view and access mechanism to the data available in each source. Such an uniform view of the data is realized by imposing a global data model on top of the local data model used by each source. There are two main choices for deploying an integration server: a commercial database server or a mediator system. In the first approach, a commercial database server is configured to access a remote data source through a *database gateway*, which provides an access method mechanism to the remote data. In the second approach, a mediator server specially designed and tailored

for distributed query processing is used as the integration server. The mediator utilizes the functionality of *wrappers* to access and translate the information from the data sources into the global data model. In both of these existing types of middleware solutions the user-defined, application-specific data types and query operators defined under the global data model are contained in libraries which must be linked to the clients, integration servers, gateways or wrappers deployed in the system. There are numerous examples of systems that follow this architecture, some of which are Oracle8i [Ora99], Informix Universal Server [Inf97], TSIMMIS [CGMH+94], DISCO [TRV96] and Garlic [RS97].

Most of the research on database middleware systems carried out during the past years has focused on the problems of translation and semantic integration of the distinct data collections. In this paper, however, we deal with two important problems which have received little attention from the research community: (1) the deployment of the application-specific functionality[1], and (2) the efficient processing of queries with user-defined operators. These are critical problems since they affect the scalability, ease-of-use, efficiency and evolution of the system. Nevertheless, we are not aware of any work that has effectively addressed the first issue, and the second one is just beginning to receive more attention from the community [RS97, HKWY97, GMSvE98, MS99].

In order to effectively address these two important issues we have designed and implemented **MOCHA** (**M**iddleware **B**ased **O**n a **C**ode **SH**ipping **A**rchitecture), a novel database middleware system designed to interconnect hundreds of data sources. MOCHA is built around the notion that the middleware for a large-scale distributed environment should be *self-extensible*. A self-extensible middleware system is one in which new application-specific functionality needed for query processing is deployed to remote sites in **automatic fashion** by the middleware system itself. In MOCHA, this is realized by shipping Java code containing new capabilities to the remote sites, where it can be used to manipulate the data of interest. A major goal behind this idea of automatic code deployment is to fill-in the need for application-

---

*This research was sponsored by DOD/Lucite Contract CG9815.

---

[1]These are complex data types and query operators not generally provided by general purpose commercial systems, but rather custom-built for a particular application by third-party developers.

specific processing components at remote sites that do not provide them. These components are migrated on demand by MOCHA from site to site and become available for immediate use. This approach sharply contrasts with existing solutions in which administrators need to manually install all the required functionality throughout the system.

MOCHA capitalizes on its ability to automatically deploy code in order to provide an efficient query processing service. By shipping code for query operators, MOCHA can generate efficient plans that place the execution of powerful *data-reducing* operators ("filters") on the data sources. Examples of such operators are aggregates, predicates and data mining operators, which return a much smaller abstraction of the original data. On the other hand, *data-inflating* operators that produce results larger that their arguments are evaluated near the client. Since in many cases, the code being shipped is much more smaller than the data sets, automatic code deployment facilitates query optimization based on data movement reduction, which can greatly reduce query execution time. Again, this is very different from the existing middleware solutions, which perform expensive data movement operations since either all data processing occurs at the integration server, or a data source evaluates only those operators that exist **a priori** in its environment [RS97].

In this paper we describe a prototype implementation of MOCHA which has been operational at the University of Maryland since the early Spring of 1998. MOCHA is currently been considered as a middleware solution for the NASA Earth Science Information Partnership (ESIP) Federation. MOCHA is written in Java and supports major database servers, such as Oracle and Informix, file servers and XML repositories. We argue that MOCHA provides users with a more flexible, scalable and efficient framework to deploy new application-specific functionality than those used in existing middleware solutions. Our experiments show that when compared with the processing schemes used in previous solutions, the query processing framework proposed in MOCHA can substantially improve query performance by a factor of 4-1 in the case of aggregates and 3-1 in the case of projections, predicates, and distributed joins. These experiments were carried out on the MOCHA prototype using data and queries from the Sequoia 2000 Benchmark [Sto93].

The remainder of this paper is organized as follows. Section 2 further describes the shortcomings in existing middleware solutions and motivates the need for MOCHA. Section 3 presents the architecture of MOCHA and our solutions to the problems presented in section 2. Section 4 describes the proposed query processing framework for MOCHA. Section 5 contains a performance study of the MOCHA prototype. Finally, our conclusions are presented in section 6.

2 Motivation for MOCHA

Given the immense popularity of the World Wide Web, the continuous growth of the Internet, and the ever increasing number of corporate intranets, database middleware will be required to interconnect hundreds of data sites deployed over these networks. The data sets stored by many of these sites will be based on complex data types such as images, audio, text, geometric objects and even programs. Given this scenario, we argue that middleware solutions for these kind of environments will be successful only if they can provide: (1) scalable, efficient and cost-effective mechanisms to deploy and maintain the application-specific functionality used throughout the system, and (2) adequate query processing capabilities to efficiently execute the queries posed by the users. We argue that the existing middleware solutions fall short from providing adequate support for these two requirements, and we now proceed to justify this argument.

2.1 Deployment of Functionality

In order to deploy new application-specific functionality into a system based on mediators, or database servers (using either gateways or a client/server scheme), the data structures, procedures, and configuration files that contain the implementation of the new types and query operators are collected into libraries which must be installed at each site where a participating integration server, gateway, wrapper or client application resides. This is the scheme followed by Oracle 8i [Ora99], Informix [Inf97], Predator [SLR97], Jaguar [GMSvE98], TSIMMIS [CGMH+94], DISCO [TRV96] and Garlic [RS97]. We argue that as the number of sites in the system increases, such an approach becomes impractical because of the complexity and cost incurred in maintaining the software throughout the system.

To illustrate this point, consider an Earth Science application that manipulates data stored and maintained in sites distributed across the United States. Suppose there is one data site per state, which holds data scientists gathered from specific regions within that state. As part of its global schema, the system contains the following relation:

```
Rasters(time : Integer, band : Integer,
        location : Rectangle, image : Raster);
```

Table `Rasters` stores raster images containing weekly energy readings gathered from satellites orbiting the Earth. Attribute `time` is the week number for the reading, `band` is the energy band measured, `location` is the rectangle covering the region under study and `image` is the raster image itself.

To implement the schema for relation `Rasters` in existing middleware solutions, it would be necessary to install the libraries containing the code, mostly C/C++ code, for the `Rectangle` and `Raster` data types on each site where a client, integration server, wrapper or gateway interested in using table `Rasters` resides. This translates into at least fifty installations for the wrappers and gateways, plus as many more as are necessary for the integration servers and clients. The administrators of the system will have to access all these sites and manually perform these installations. Moreover, it is often the case that the functionality has to be *ported* to different hardware and operating system platforms. As a result, developers must invest extra effort in making the functionality work **consistently** across platforms. Furthermore, scientists are frequently experimenting with new or improved methods to compute properties about their data, such as averages on the amount of energy absorption. Therefore, many users will not be satisfied with some of the code that has been already deployed, and will require for existing operators to be upgraded or replaced by new ones. Thus, it becomes necessary to have a scalable and efficient mechanism to keep track of and maintain the deployed code base in the system. Clearly, the logistics in such a large-scale system are formidable for an approach based on manual installations and upgrades of application-specific functionality to be feasible.

2.2 Efficient Query Processing

In the context of large-scale distributed environments, it is unrealistic to assume that every site has the same query execution capabilities. Therefore, many existing middleware solutions use a query processing framework in which most operators in a query are completely evaluated by the integration server [Ora99, Inf97, CGMH+94, TRV96]. The wrappers and gateways are mainly used to extract data items from the sources, and translate them into the middleware schema for further processing at the integration site. This approach for query processing is often called *data shipping* [FJK96] because data is moved from the source to the query processing site. In the alternative approach, called *query shipping* [FJK96], one or more of the query operators are evaluated at the data sources, and only the results are sent back to the integration server. A third approach, called *hybrid shipping* [FJK96], combines query and data shipping, and is shown to be the superior alternative. Garlic [RS97] exploits this latter approach in a powerful framework in which the evaluation of some of the query operators is "pushed" to the data source. However, this framework is somewhat limited since it can only be applied to those operators that are **already implemented** at the data source, and the integration server must evaluate any remaining operator(s) in the query. Thus, in all these middleware solutions, query operator placement is severely restricted by the availability of the code implementing the operators used in a query. In many situations, this can easily lead to worst-case scenarios in which a query plan dictates the transfer of very large amounts of data (megabytes or more!) over the communications network, making data transmission a severe performance bottleneck.

We illustrate this point with the Earth Science application introduced in section 2.1. Let the data site in the State of Maryland contain 200 entries in table `Rasters`. For this table, attributes `time` and `band` are 4-byte integers, attribute `location` is a 16-byte record and attribute `image` is a 1MB byte array. A user at the State of Virginia poses the following query for the data site at the State of Maryland:

```
SELECT   time,location,AvgEnergy(image)
FROM     Rasters
WHERE    AvgEnergy(image) < 100
```

This query will retrieve the time, location and average energy reading for all entries whose average energy reading is less than the constant 100. Function `AvgEnergy()` returns a 8-byte double precision floating point number, so the size of the records in the result is just 28 bytes. Clearly, the best way to execute this query is to let the data source at Maryland read every tuple from table `Rasters`, evaluate function `AvgEnergy()`, evaluate the qualification clause, and perform all the projections in the query, returning only the final results to the integration site in Virginia. Notice that even if all tuples in table `Rasters` satisfy the qualification clause, data movement still is negligible since 200 tuples × 28 bytes is approximately 5KB! However, this efficient approach is feasible **only if** the code for `AvgEnergy()` exists at the Maryland data site. Otherwise, this query must be evaluated by first shipping the attributes `time`, `location` and `image`, contained in every tuple in table `Rasters` from the data site in Maryland to the integration site in Virginia, and then performing the operations as mentioned before. Now, consider the cost of the operation just described. The system is moving roughly 200MB worth of data over a wide area network, an operation that will take minutes or even hours to complete since the bandwidth available to an application in most wide area links is very limited, often under 1Mbps. Clearly, the lack of adequate query processing functionality can easily lead to poor performance because a middleware system might be **restricted** to use an inefficient query processing strategy simply because the functionality required to use a superior one is not available where it is needed. Since it is highly improbable that all the functionality needed to process every query posed will be available everywhere, existing solutions are of limited use in large-scale environments. Notice that although many systems indeed provide the capabilities to manually add the code for user-defined types and operators into the wrappers [CGMH+94], gateways [Inf97], or remote data servers [SLR97, GMSvE98, MS99], this approach simply cannot scale for the reasons already discussed in section 2.1. Thus, the query processing framework used in existing solutions is limited and ill-suited for a large-scale environment in which users have diverse needs for processing data.

3 MOCHA Architecture

We have designed MOCHA around two fundamental principles that will enable it to overcome the shortcomings of previous middleware solutions. The first principle is that all application-specific functionality needed to process any given query is to be delivered by MOCHA to all interested sites in **automatic** fashion, and this is realized by shipping the Java classes containing the required functionality. The second principle is that each query operator is to be evaluated at the site that results in minimum data movement. The goal is to ship the code and the computation of operators around the system in order to minimize the effects of the network bottleneck. We argue that this framework provides the foundation for a more scalable, robust and efficient middleware solution. Figure 1 depicts the organization of the major components in the architecture for MOCHA. These are the **Client Application**, the **Query Processing Coordinator (QPC)**, the **Data Access Provider (DAP)** and the **Data Server**. We now elaborate on the principles and design choices for MOCHA which form the basis for our arguments. A more detailed description can be found in [RMR00b].

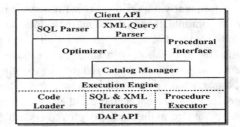

Figure 2: Organization of the QPC

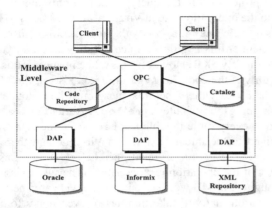

Figure 1: MOCHA Architecture

3.1 Client Application

MOCHA supports three kinds of client applications: 1) applets, 2) servlets, and 3) stand-alone Java applications. We expect applets to be the most commonly deployed clients in the system, used as the GUI for the users to pose queries against the data collections and visualize their results. Servlets can be used to interact with users that do not use applets with their Web browsers. The servlet receives the requests from the browser, interacts with MOCHA to query the data sources, and formats all results as either HTML or XML data. Finally, stand-alone Java applications will likely be used by administrators or software developers, who will need to carry out complex tasks such as system configuration and tuning, catalog management or distributed software debugging, to name a few. MOCHA provides a set of Java libraries with the APIs necessary for the client to easily interact with the system. These APIs contain all the required infrastructure to load the code containing the application-specific components necessary to manipulate the query results.

3.2 Query Processing Coordinator (QPC)

The Query Processing Coordinator (QPC) is the middle-tier component that controls the execution of all the queries and commands received from the client applications. QPC provides services such as query parsing, query optimization, query operator scheduling, query execution and monitoring of the entire execution process. QPC also provides access to the metadata in the system and to the repository containing the Java classes with application-specific functionality needed for query processing. During query execution, the QPC is responsible for deploying all the necessary functionality to the client application and to those remote sites from which data will be extracted.

The internal components of the QPC are depicted in Figure 2. The Client API serves as the entry point to accept the requests from a client application. The QPC offers three main data processing services. The first one provides access to distributed data sites which are modeled as object-relational sources. QPC provides the infrastructure to perform operations such as distributed joins and transactions over these sources. The requests for these kind of services are encoded as SQL queries, which are first pre-processed by the *SQL parser* in the QPC. The second data processing service provided by QPC allows users to directly query the content of XML repositories. XML is rapidly becoming a very important technology and we felt that MOCHA should support native access to XML repositories without the burden of first mapping them to another data model. We are currently developing the infrastructure that will enable the QPC to process queries over the XML repositories. Finally, since many sources, such as Web servers or file systems, do not provide a query language abstraction, the QPC provides a procedural interface through which operations such as HTTP requests, ftp downloads or proprietary file system access requests can be issued to access these data sources.

One of the most important components of the QPC is its query optimizer, which generates the best strategy to solve the queries over the distributed sources. The optimizer follows a dynamic programming model for query optimization similar to those in System-R [SAC+79] and R* [ML86]. We will defer further details on query optimization until section 4. For now, it suffices to say that the plan generated by the optimizer explicitly indicates which are the operators to be evaluated by the QPC and those to be evaluated at the remote data sites. In addition, the plan indicates which Java classes need to be dynamically deployed to each of the participants in the query execution process. All plans are encoded and exchanged as XML documents, and the interested reader can find examples of their structure in [RMR00a]. The QPC uses the services of the *Catalog Manager* module to retrieve from the catalog all relevant metadata for query optimization and code deployment. Section 3.5 briefly describes the organization of this catalog. The QPC also contains an extensible query execution engine based on iterators [Gra93]. There are iterators to perform local selections, local joins, remote selections, distributed joins, semi-joins, transfers of files and sorting, among others. The execution engine also provides a series of methods used to issue procedural commands (i.e. ftp requests) and to deploy the application-specific code. The

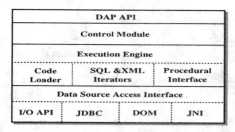

DAP API		
Control Module		
Execution Engine		
Code Loader	SQL &XML Iterators	Procedural Interface
Data Source Access Interface		

I/O API	JDBC	DOM	JNI

Figure 3: DAP Organization

Code Loader module in the execution engine is used to extract the required code from the code repository, and prepare it for deployment. The DAP API provides the facilities to communicate with the remote data sources.

3.3 Data Access Provider (DAP)

The role of a Data Access Provider (DAP) is to provide the QPC with a uniform access mechanism to a remote data source. In this regard, the DAP might seem similar to a wrapper or a gateway. However, the DAP has an extensible query execution engine capable of loading and using application-specific code obtained from the network with the help of the QPC. Since a DAP is run at the data source site or in close proximity to it, MOCHA exploits this capability to push down to the DAP the code and computation of certain operators that "filter" the data been queried, and minimize the amount of data sent back to the QPC. This is a feature unique to MOCHA. Figure 3 shows the internal organization of a DAP. Query and procedural requests issued by the QPC are received through the DAP API, and routed to the *Control Module*, where they are decoded and prepared for execution. Each request contains information for the *Execution Engine* in the DAP that includes the kind of task to be performed (i.e. a query plan), the code that must be loaded, and the access mechanism necessary to extract the data. The execution engine first calls the *Code Loader* to load the required application-specific code, which is delivered to the DAP by the QPC through a mechanism that will be described in section 3.6. Then, it creates iterators for SQL or XML query requests, or prepares a procedural call to execute operations such as reading a file from a file system, requesting a Web page, etc. Notice that the iterators to access a source are built on top of standard Java packages such as JDBC, DOM (for XML repositories), Java Native Interface (JNI) and the I/O routines. Once the DAP has extended its query execution capabilities, it retrieves the data from the source, maps them into the middleware schema, and then filters them with the operators (if any) specified by the QPC in the query plan. The DAP then sends back to the QPC all values that it produced so they can be further processed to generate final results.

3.4 Data Server

The Data Server is the server application that stores the data sets for a particular data site. This element can be a full-fledged database server, a Web server or even a file server providing access to flat files. In the current MOCHA prototype, we provide support for object-relational database servers such as Informix and Oracle8i, XML repositories and file systems, since these are among the most commonly used servers to store the emerging complex data sets.

3.5 Catalog Organization

Query optimization and automatic code deployment are driven by the metadata in the catalog. The catalog contains metadata about views defined over the data sources, user-defined data types, user-defined operators, and any other relevant information such as selectivity of various operators. The views, data types and operators are generically referred to as "resources" and are uniquely identified by a Uniform Resource Identifier (URI). The metadata for each resource is specified in a document encoded with the Resource Description Framework (RDF), an XML-based technology used to specify metadata for resources available in networked environments. In MOCHA, for each resource there is a catalog entry of the form (URI, RDF File), and this is used by the system to understand the behavior and proper utilization of each resource. The reader is referred to [RMR00a] for more details about the structure of the URIs, the RDF metadata schema and other catalog management issues in MOCHA.

3.6 Automatic Code Deployment

In MOCHA, deploying code with application-specific components is done by shipping the compiled Java classes containing the implementation of data types and query operators. To simplify this discussion, we assume that each type or operator is entirely defined in only one Java class; but in general, their implementation can span several classes. When a system administrator needs to incorporate a new or updated data type or query operator into the system, he/she first stores the Java class for that resource into a well-known *code repository* (see Figure 4). Next, the administrator registers the new type or operator by adding entries into the system catalog that indicate the name of the type or operator, its associated URI, its RDF file, and any other relevant information such as version number, user privileges, etc. Once the code has been registered, the new functionality is ready for use in the queries posed by the users.

The automatic deployment of code starts after QPC receives a new query request from a client. The first task for the QPC is to generate a list with the data types and operators needed to process the query. QPC then accesses the metadata in the catalog to map each type or operator into the specific class implementing it. Each class is then retrieved from the code repository by the QPC's code loader and prepared for distribution. Before the actual execution of the query starts, QPC distributes the pieces of the plan to be executed by each of the DAPs running on the targeted data sites. Afterwards, the QPC starts the *code deployment phase* in which it first ships the classes for the data types to the client and to the DAPs, and then ships the classes for the query operators to be executed by each DAP. Figure 4 depicts how the class `AvgEnergy.class`, which implements function `AvgEnergy()`, would be shipped to a remote DAP. Once the code deployment phase is completed, QPC signals each DAP to activate its piece of the query plan, and only then, QPC and the DAPs start processing the data and generating results, all of which are gathered by QPC and sent back to the client for visualization purposes.

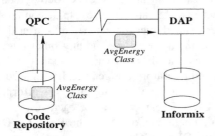

Figure 4: Shipping code for `AvgEnergy()`

It is important to emphasize that the code deployment phase occurs **on-line** as an automatic process carried out completely by the QPC without any human involvement. There is no need to restart any element in MOCHA before it can start using the functionality received during the code deployment phase. Instead, each of the QPC, DAPs and client application contain the necessary logic to load the classes into their Java run time systems and start using them immediately. Therefore, the capabilities of each element in MOCHA can be **extended** at run time in a dynamic fashion. Notice that the tasks for the administrators are simplified since they only need to deal with one or a few repositories where all the code resides. Upgrades or new functionality are simply added to the repository, and from there, they are deployed as needed by MOCHA. To the best of our knowledge, no other system implements this unique approach in which the middleware is self-extensible.

One very interesting issue that we are going to address in depth in the near future, is the possibility for a DAP to cache frequently used code so it can be reused many times without the need for repeated delivery. One simple solution is to have the QPC and DAP exchange information about the last known modification dates for the classes for types and operators already imported into a DAP. The DAP informs the QPC of all instances in which dates do not match, and the QPC only delivers the code for these cases.

3.7 Organization of Data Types

In MOCHA, the attributes in a tuple are implemented as Java objects. MOCHA provides a set of well-known Java type interfaces with the methods needed by the QPC, DAPs and client applications to handle the classes for data types correctly. Figure 5 shows the hierarchical structure of the type system for the MOCHA prototype. The dark rectangles represent type interfaces and the white ones represent Java classes for a particular type. At the root of the type hierarchy is the `MWObject` interface which identifies a class as one implementing a MOCHA data type, and also specifies the methods to be used to read/write each data value into the network.

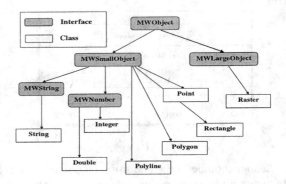

Figure 5: MOCHA Type System

The `MWLargeObject` and `MWSmallObject` interfaces extend `MWObject`, partitioning all types into two groups: large objects and small objects. Large objects are used for large sized types such as images, audio or text documents. Small objects are used for smaller types such as numbers, strings, points or rectangles. Additionally, interfaces for character and numeric types are derived from `MWSmallObject`. Any new type added to the system must implement one of the interfaces below `MWObject`.

3.8 Organization of Query Operators

MOCHA groups query operators into two categories: 1) projections and predicates, and 2) aggregates. The complex functions present in projections and predicates are implemented as static methods in a Java class. Figure 6(a) shows how such functions are evaluated in the executor module contained by either QPC or a DAP. The query plan created by QPC indicates the class name and the method name associated with each function. The executor module uses this information to create a *function evaluation object*, which executes the body of the method and hence the query operator. The executor successively passes tuples to the function evaluation object and collects the resulting attributes for further processing or adds them into the result.

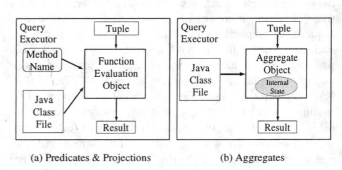

(a) Predicates & Projections   (b) Aggregates

Figure 6: Operator Evaluation in MOCHA

Aggregates are implemented as Java objects, as shown in Figure 6(b). The Java class for any aggregate operator implements the interface `Aggregate` provided by MOCHA. This interface specifies three methods that are used to compute the aggregate value: `Reset()`, `Update()` and `Summarize()`. For each aggregate operator, the executor creates one aggregate object for each of the different groups found during the aggregation process. The internal state in an aggregate object is first set to an initial state by calling `Reset()`. Then, the executor successively calls `Update()` to modify the internal state in each object using the next tuple at hand and the current internal state. Once all the tuples are processed, the final value for each aggregate is extracted from the internal state in each aggregate object by calling `Summarize()`.

3.9 Implementation Issues

We now discuss three important implementation issues for MOCHA: memory management, communications over the network and security.

3.9.1 Memory Management

In Java, most of the memory management is done by the Java run time system, the so called Java Virtual Machine (JVM), and programmers do not need to worry about all the intricate low-level details regarding object allocation/deallocation. Unfortunately, these advantages are often offset by programming practices in which objects are excessively created, and then discarded after just one use! We found such practices in some JDBC drivers and proprietary Java database access APIs in which new objects are created to store column values each time a new tuple is read from the data source. Our experience with MOCHA proved that this paradigm is extremely inefficient for most database applications. The main reason is that object allocation involves calls to expensive synchronized methods in the JVM. Since possibly thousands of tuples are read from a data source during a query, the overhead of such calls has a devastating effect on performance. Moreover, as the number of objects allocated increases, the garbage collector might perform more work each time is called to dispose of the unused memory. Therefore, in MOCHA we adopted an aggressive policy of object preallocation and re-use. When an iterator is created by the execution engine, the constructor for the iterator creates one structure to read the columns from the database, and one structure to store the results to be returned by each call of the method `Next()` in the iterator. Thus, our implementation only creates these objects once and continuously re-uses them during the course of query processing.

3.9.2 Communications Over the Network

In our initial implementation of MOCHA we used the Java Remote Method Invocation (RMI) mechanism for the communications between the DAPs and the QPC. RMI is very similar to CORBA since it provides a communications interface based on method calls to remote object instances. RMI certainly made our implementation easy and elegant, but it proved too unstable and slow, specially when tuples containing complex and large types, such as images, where exchanged. RMI relies on stubs and skeletons to generate the remote method calls, and we found the data serialization protocol to be unstable, occasionally sending incorrect signals

to the receivers, thus causing exceptions when the stubs attempted to unmarshall the data been exchanged. We also found that at the receiver's end, multiple objects were allocated each time a new tuple was read, an approach that is simply too inefficient, as we already discussed in section 3.9.1. We dealt with these problems by building our own communications infrastructure on top of the network sockets provided by Java. As result of this decision we needed to incorporate several methods in the `MWObject` interface to specify a generic mechanism to serialize the data in each tuple across the network. Although this required more effort on our part, we felt it was an essential task to guarantee that communications in MOCHA were stable, reliable and efficient.

3.9.3 Security

Since a client, QPC or DAP can dynamically load and execute compiled Java code, it is necessary to have a security mechanism to guarantee that the code does not executes dangerous operations on the host machines. In most object-relational engines, user-defined code is assumed to be "trusted", and it is the responsibility of the programmer to guarantee that the code is safe. In a large-scale environment, this kind of policy is unreasonable, and therefore, MOCHA leverages on the security architecture provided by Java. Administrators can configure the clients, QPC and DAPs to implement fine-grained security policies as supported by the `SecurityManager` class provided by Java. These policies include restrictions on the access to local file systems, allocation of network sockets, creation of threads, etc. Notice also that since the DAP is run as a process independent of the Data Server, a crash in a DAP will likely go unnoticed by the Data Server. It is important to realize, however, that security comes at the price of extra overhead. Each time an operation which the administrator defines as dangerous is attempted, a call to the security manager will be made to determine if the operation can proceed or not. Therefore, care must be taken to avoid a situation in which, for example, every call to an user-defined predicate triggers multiple calls to the security manager. In our view, security is a very important and complex issue in itself, deserving more careful exploration and done in close collaboration with the programming languages community, since the run time system must efficiently support the implementation of the security mechanisms.

4 Query Processing Framework

We have designed MOCHA to capitalize on its ability to ship code in order to generate query plans that minimize data movement. Following a cost-based approach, MOCHA pushes the evaluation of *data-reducing* operators to the DAPs running on the data sites and the evaluation of *data-inflating* operators to the QPC. The philosophy behind this scheme is that data movement typically is the major performance bottleneck in large-scale environments because network bandwidth is a shared resource, relatively expensive to upgrade, and the applications aggressively compete to obtain a fraction of it. Notice that problems with heavy user loads on remote servers can be alleviated with replication, caching or even by upgrading to better server hardware since CPUs, memory and disks are becoming more powerful and less expensive. Therefore, MOCHA takes the pragmatic approach of first optimizing to minimize network costs.

In MOCHA, *data-reducing* operators are those operators that reduce the number and/or the size of the tuples in the result. Under this category we include: a) predicates with low selectivity, which filter out unnecessary tuples, b) predicates whose arguments are large-sized attributes that are not part of the result, c) projections that map large-sized attributes into scalars or smaller values, d) aggregates that map sets of tuples into a few distilled values and e) semi-joins which eliminate tuples that do not participate in a join. For example, the projection operator `AvgEnergy(image)` presented in section 2.2 is data-reducing because it maps a 1MB image into a 8-byte floating-point number. Whenever possible, data-reducing operators are evaluated by the DAPs, using a new query processing policy that we call **code shipping**. This policy specifies that a query operator and its code will be **shipped** to and executed by the DAP for a given data source. Code shipping can be viewed as query shipping enhanced with the capability to *materialize* the code for an operator remotely, as described in section 3.6.

On the other hand, *data-inflating* operators are those that inflate the data values and/or present them in many forms, projections, rotations, sizes and levels of detail. Recall the Earth Science application from section 2.1. Suppose a user from the State of Virginia now poses the following query to the data site in the State of Maryland:

```
SELECT  time, location, IncrRes(image, 2X)
FROM    Rasters
```

This query retrieves all images from the table `Rasters` in Maryland, but function `IncrRes()` increases the resolution of each image by a factor 2X. Therefore, the projection `IncrRes(image, 2X)` is data-inflating since it synthesizes a new image that is four times larger than the original one. Other kinds of data-inflating operators are those used to visualize the same data value from many perspectives, for example, an operator that rotates an image by a certain degree θ without changing its size or one that allows a user to visualize a three-dimensional solid from different orientations (i.e. top, bottom or sideways). In these operators, the same data value is repeatedly transformed, and therefore, these transformations are more efficiently done near the client. For that reason, MOCHA executes data-inflating operators at the QPC using a data shipping strategy.

In MOCHA, each complex aggregate, predicate or projection operator Ω has an associated execution cost which has the general form:

$$Cost(\Omega) = CompCost(\Omega) + NetworkCost(\Omega)$$

Here $CompCost(\Omega)$ is the total cost of computing Ω over an input relation R. The $NetworkCost(\Omega)$ is total cost

of data movement incurred while executing Ω on R. If Ω is evaluated at the DAP, then this component is the cost of sending to the QPC the results generated after applying Ω to all tuples in R. Otherwise, when Ω is evaluated at the QPC, this component is the cost of moving to the QPC each of the arguments to Ω in each of the tuples in R. The interested read can find more specific details and some of the exact cost formulas for each kind of operators in [RMR00b].

The cost of each operator Ω is used in the proposed optimization algorithm for MOCHA in order to find its proper execution placement. Before going into further details about the algorithm we need to introduce a new cost metric, the *Volume Reduction Factor* for an operator, which is used in the optimization process.

Definition 4.1 The **Volume Reduction Factor**, VRF, for an operator Ω over an input relation R is defined as:

$$VRF(\Omega) = \frac{VDT}{VDA} \qquad (0 \leq VRF(\Omega) < \infty),$$

where VDT is the total data volume to be transmitted after applying Ω to R, and VDA is the total data volume originally present in R.

Therefore, an operator Ω is *data-reducing* **if and only if** its VRF is less than 1; otherwise, it is *data-inflating*. In a similar fashion, we can define the *Cumulative Volume Reduction Factor* for a query plan P.

Definition 4.2 The **Cumulative Volume Reduction Factor**, $CVRF$, for a query plan P to answer query Q over input relations $R_1, ..., R_n$ is defined as:

$$CVRF(P) = \frac{CVDT}{CVDA} \qquad (0 \leq CVRF(P) < \infty),$$

where $CVDT$ is the total data volume to be transmitted over the network after applying all the operators in P to $R_1, ..., R_n$ and $CVDA$ is the total data volume in $R_1, ..., R_n$.

The intuition here is that the smaller the $CVRF$ of the plan, the less data it sends over the network, and the better performance the plan provides. This observation is validated by the results in sections 5.3-5.4.

Figure 7(a) shows the pseudo-code for the proposed System R-style optimizer for MOCHA. Consider, for example, the query: $\sigma_g(A) \bowtie \pi_f(\sigma(B))$, where predicate g is data-reducing and projection f is data-inflating. The algorithm first runs steps (1)-(3) to build selection plans for each of the expressions $\sigma_g(A)$ and $\pi_f(\sigma(B))$. Step (2) builds an initial plan with two nodes, one to be executed by the QPC (a QPC node), and one to be executed by the DAP (a DAP node) associated with the particular relation (A or B). At this point, the QPC node only has annotations that indicate the output to be returned, and the DAP node has annotations that indicate the attributes to be extracted. This initial plan is then modified in step (3) to add the user-defined operators that the middleware must execute. Figure 7(b) shows the algorithm used to place these complex operators, given as input a relation R and a plan P. First, the set of complex operators $\mathcal{O}$

```
procedure MOCHA_Optimizer(R_1, ..., R_n):
/* find best join plan */
1. for i = 1 to n do
2.     P ← selectPlan(R_i)
3.     optPlan(R_i) ← PlaceComplex(P, R_i)
4. for i = 2 to n do
5.     for all S ⊆ {R_1, ..., R_n} s.t. |S| = i do
6.         bestPlan ← dummy plan with infinite cost
7.         for all R_j, S_j s.t. S = {R_j} ∪ S_j do
8.             P ← joinPlan(optPlan(S_j), optPlan(R_j))
9.             P ← PlaceComplex(P, R_j)
10.            if cost(P) ≤ cost(bestPlan)
11.                bestPlan ← P
12.        optPlan(S) ← bestPlan
13. return optPlan({R_1, ..., R_n})
```

(a) System R-style Optimizer

```
procedure PlaceComplex(P, R):
/* find best operator placement */
1. O ← getComplexOps(P, R)
2. nDAP ← findDAP(P, R)
3. nQPC ← findAncestorQPC(P, nDAP)
4. for all Ω ∈ O do {
5.     if VRF(Ω) < 1
6.         insert(Ω, nDAP)
7.     else
8.         insert(Ω, nQPC)}
9. sortRank(nDAP)
10. sortRank(nQPC)
```

(b) Operator Placement

Figure 7: MOCHA Optimization Algorithm

that can be applied to the input relation is found with function $getComplexOps()$. Next, the DAP node used to access the relation R in plan P is found with function $findDAP()$. This DAP node is then used to find its nearest ancestor node in the plan P which also is a QPC node. Then, each operator Ω in the set O is placed at its best execution location based on its VRF value. Those operators with VRF less than 1 are placed at the DAP node, and the rest are placed at the QPC node. These heuristics serve to minimize the $CVRF$ of the plan P, and hence, its data movement and cost. In particular, they are used to produce plans with $CVRF$ less or equal to 1. Finally, the complex predicates added to each node are sorted based on increasing value of the metric: $rank(p) = (SF_p - 1)/CompCost(p)$, where SF_p is the selectivity of predicate p, as proposed in [HS93]. The result of this process on expressions $\sigma_g(A)$ and $\pi_f(\sigma(B))$ is shown on the left hand side of Figure 8. The gray nodes are QPC nodes, and the white ones are DAP nodes.

Once the single table access plans have been built, the algorithm in Figure 7(a) runs through steps (4)-(13) to explore all different possibilities to perform the join, incrementally building a left-deep plan in which a new relation R_j is added into an already existing join plan S_j for a subset of the relations. This task is done by function $joinPlan()$ in step (8). After the join plan is built, the algorithm again places complex operators in step (9). These are operators whose arguments come from more than one relation. Finally, the plan

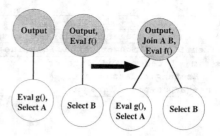

Figure 8: Optimization in MOCHA

P with smallest cost is selected. Here the cost of the plan includes the join cost and the evaluation costs of all complex operators. The final join plan for our example is shown on the right hand side of Figure 8. Notice that our algorithm is not exhaustive in terms of possible alternatives for complex operator placement (as is [CS96] for predicates). This is an intentional compromise done to avoid the extra combinatorial explosion of such an exhaustive search. At present, we have not completed the implementation of the cost-based query optimizer for the QPC although the major building blocks, such as query plans and search procedures, are in place. Since we have to deal not only with complex predicates, but also with complex projections and aggregates, we are exploring a series of pruning heuristics to reduce the search space of the optimizer, and speed up the optimization process.

5 Performance Evaluation

To validate our design choices and performance expectations for MOCHA, we benchmarked our prototype to characterize its behavior and show: a) the feasibility of using Java to implement types and operators, b) the benefits obtained by using code shipping, c) the need to use data shipping for data-inflating operators and d) that VRF is an accurate cost estimator for choosing the best query plan.

5.1 Benchmark Data and Queries

We used scientific data sets and queries from the Sequoia 2000 Benchmark [Sto93] to test our MOCHA prototype. Typically, these type of data sets are stored at different sites, and the applications manipulating them are inherently distributed. We used the regional version of the benchmark with data sets corresponding to the State of California, and Table 1 depicts the schema and other relevant information about these data sets. Similarly, Table 2 shows the queries used in our experiments, and each one is explained in the follow up sections. We derived these queries from the ones in Sequoia by adding and combining several new complex operators.

5.2 Experimental Methodology

We implemented the MOCHA prototype using Sun's Java Developers Kit 1.2, and all middleware data types and operators were implemented in classes containing 100% Java code. We used the Informix Universal Server and our own spatial *datablade* to provide support at the DBMS level for

Relation	Description	Cardinality	Size
`Polygons(landuse: Integer, location: Polygon)`	Polygons enclosing different types of land regions.	77,643	18.8MB
`Graphs(identifier: Integer, graph: Polyline)`	Graphs representing water drainage networks.	201,650	31MB
`Rasters(time: Integer, band: Integer, location: Rectangle, data: Raster, lines: Integer, samples: Integer)`	Satellite raster images made from weekly energy readings from Earth's surface regions. Each sample (pixel) represents a point on the surface region.	200	200MB

Table 1: Datasets

```
Q1: SELECT landuse,
        TotalArea(location),
        TotalPerimeter(location)
    FROM Polygons
    GROUP BY landuse;

Q3: SELECT time, band, location,
        IncrRes(data,lines,samples,2X)
    FROM Rasters;

Q5: SELECT R1.location, R1.time, R2.time,
        (AvgEnergy(R1.data) - AvgEnergy(R2.data))
    FROM Rasters1 R1, Rasters2 R2
    WHERE Equal(R1.location,R2.location);

Q2: SELECT time, band, location,
        Clip(data,lines,samples,WIN)
    FROM Rasters;

Q4: SELECT identifier
    FROM Graphs
    WHERE NumVertices(graph) > N
    AND ArcLength(graph) > S;
```

Table 2: Benchmark Queries

the data sets described in section 5.1. To provide connectivity between Informix and the DAP, we developed a JDBC-like library with support for the retrieval of complex types. In all the experiments discussed in this paper, we ran QPC on a Sun Ultra SPARC 60 with 128MB of memory. For the experiments in section 5.3, one DAP and Informix ran on a Sun Ultra SPARC 1 with 256MB of memory. In addition, for the experiment in section 5.4 we added a Sun Ultra SPARC 5 with 128 MB of memory, to run a second pair of DAP and Informix server. All machines ran Solaris 2.6 and were connected to a 10Mbps Ethernet network, and this choice of network was made mainly to obtain reproducible results. But in practice, we expect MOCHA to be run on wide area environments over which the available bandwidth would be much smaller, making MOCHA's benefits even more pronounced.

The main objective of this study is to clearly show the substantial performance benefits provided by a system that uses code shipping, such as MOCHA, over one that lacks this capability, and must rely heavily on data shipping. We configured QPC to use query plans that place all operators on either the DAP (with code shipping) or the QPC (with data shipping), which permits the study of each operator under each strategy. In each experiment, we ran the query plan on the MOCHA prototype and measured execution time from the time QPC starts deploying code to the time it receives the last tuple in the result. We present these results using graphs, in which the x-axis shows the query been tested and the y-axis gives its execution time under each strategy. Execution time was divided into four components: 1) **DB Time**- time spent reading tuples from the data source by DAP; 2) **CPU Time**- time spent evaluating all complex operators; 3) **Net Time**- time spent sending data from a DAP to QPC; and 4) **Misc Time**- time spent on all initialization and cleanup tasks. The **Net Time** component includes both network transmission time and the communications software overhead. All values reported as execution time are averages obtained from

five independent measurements. In addition, we measured the total volume of data accessed by each plan ($CVDA$), the total volume of data transmitted by each plan ($CVDT$) and the volume of data in the query result. In each case, the $CVRF$ for each plan was computed from these measured values. We ran all experiments late at night, when all machines and the network were unloaded.

5.3 Queries Over a Single Data Source

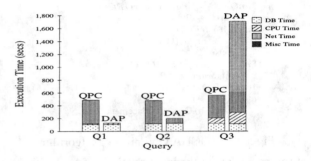

(a) Execution Times

Query	Site	CVDA	CVDT	Volume in Result	CVRF
Q_1	DAP	18.8MB	740B	740B	4×10^{-5}
	QPC	18.8MB	18.8MB	740B	1
Q_2	DAP	200MB	40MB	40MB	0.20
	QPC	200MB	200MB	40MB	1
Q_3	DAP	200MB	800MB	800MB	4
	QPC	200MB	200MB	800MB	1

(b) Data Volumes

Figure 9: Performance for Q_1, Q_2 and Q_3

We used queries Q_1, Q_2 and Q_3 from Table 2 to measure the effect of complex aggregates and projections on the volume of data transmitted during query processing. Queries Q_1 and Q_2 contain data-reducing operators; query Q_1 is an aggregation query that computes the total area and total perimeter of all the polygons covering each type of land region. In Q_2, each image in table `Rasters` is clipped into an image whose size is determined by the clipping box `WIN`, which we chose so as to generate an image five times smaller than the original. On the other hand, Q_3 contains a data-inflating projection implemented by function `IncrRes()`. In this case, each image is transformed into a new image with twice the resolution and four times the size of the original. Figure 9(a) demonstrates that operator evaluation at the DAP with code shipping is the best option to execute Q_1 and Q_2, as it results in performance improvements of 4-1 and 3-1, respectively. In each case, the performance gain is achieved by capitalizing on code shipping to run the data-reducing operators close to the data source and only send to the QPC a few result values. Figure 9(b) shows the large savings in the volume of data movement that can be obtained by using code shipping to evaluate these operators at the data site. However, code shipping is totally inadequate to run Q_3 at the DAP since this query contains a data-inflating operator. The evaluation of projection IncrRes(data, lines, samples, 2X) at the DAP results in the transmission of tuples four times larger than those sent when QPC executes it, and the network cost is increased by a factor of 4. Notice, however, that MOCHA will not use code shipping in this case, since any data-inflating operator will be evaluated at the QPC using data shipping. The results in Figure 9(b) emphasize the accuracy of the VRF in selecting the best operator placement, because in each case the best alternative is the one with the smallest $CVRF$.

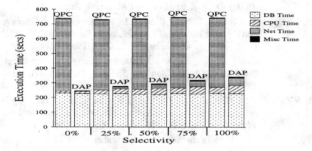

(a) Execution Times

Selectivity	Site	CVDA	CVDT	Volume in result	CVRF
0	DAP	31MB	0B	0B	0
	QPC	31MB	31MB	0B	1
0.25	DAP	31MB	200KB	200KB	0.01
	QPC	31MB	31MB	200KB	1
0.50	DAP	31MB	400KB	400KB	0.01
	QPC	31MB	31MB	400KB	1
0.75	DAP	31MB	600KB	600KB	0.02
	QPC	31MB	31MB	600KB	1
1	DAP	31MB	790KB	790KB	0.02
	QPC	31MB	31MB	790KB	1

(b) Data Volumes

Figure 10: Performance for Q_4

Query Q_4 contains two complex predicates which compare the number of vertices and the total length of each drainage network against two constants. The execution times for Q_4 under various selectivity values are shown in Figure 10(a). As we can see, execution at the DAP outperforms execution at the QPC in all cases regardless of selectivity, with performance improved by a factor of 3-1 for the first three selectivity values and 2-1 for the remaining ones. By pushing the code and evaluation of the predicates in Q_4 to the DAP, the system avoids shipping the large-sized attribute graph over the network, as seen from Figure 10(b), thus provid-

ing substantial performance gains. Figure 10(b) shows that again the VRF is an accurate metric for determining the best plan for a query with complex predicates. One important concept emerging from the results in Figures 10(a)-10(b) is that an operator placement metric based on selectivity and result cardinality is not the best metric for cost estimation because it fails to take into account the volume of transmitted data, as happens in Q_4. Consider the case of 50% selectivity in Q_4. From Figure 10(b), we can see that code shipping only moves 400KB (1% of the original data volume) from the DAP to QPC, not 15MB or half of the volume in the Graphs table. In fact, for Q_4 the percentage of data transmitted is always much smaller than what would be expected if selectivity alone were used to make the estimate. The full set of results in [RMR00b] shows that selectivity might also under estimate the actual amount of data transferred. As a result, a query operator placement scheme based on selectivity and result cardinality might produce plans with poor performance for distributed queries because of these inaccuracies since these plans might transfer a larger (smaller) data volume than expected. In contrast, the VRF combines the selectivity information, cardinality and the size of the attributes in the tuples been transmitted to make a better estimate of the cost of a query operator and determine its proper placement.

5.4 Queries Over Multiple Data Sources

For this category we used query Q_5, from Table 2, which performs a distributed join between two tables, Rasters1 and Rasters2. The schema for these tables is the same as the one for table Raster but the images where reduced to 128KB in size, and there are only three locations common to both of these tables. Table Rasters1 was stored on a Sun Ultra SPARC 1, which we call Site1, while Rasters2 was stored on a Sun Ultra SPARC 5, which we call Site2. Q_5 joins all tuples that coincide on the location attribute, and projects the location, the week number for each reading and the difference in the average energy between the readings.

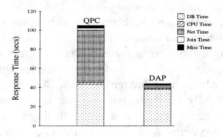

Figure 11: Execution Time for Q_5

Figure 11 shows the execution time for Q_5 for the alternatives in which complex operators in the join are executed at the QPC or at the DAP; the join itself is performed at the QPC. When complex operators must be executed at the QPC, attributes time, location and data in all tuples from each of the relations have to be moved to QPC. As tuples arrive, function AvgEnergy() is evaluated to perform the projections, and then the tuples are stored to disk, from which they are later read to perform a hash join operation. In this figure, the **Join Time** component indicates the cost of accessing disk to perform this join operation. Notice that performance is dominated by the cost of transferring the images over the network. On the other hand, the join performs over two and a half times better when the DAP evaluates the complex operators. In this case, a 2-way semi-join can be performed by computing, at each DAP, the semi-joins `Rasters1`⋉`Rasters2` (at Site1) and `Rasters2`⋉`Rasters1` (at Site2), using the *complex predicate* in Q_5 for both of them. After each semi-join operation is performed, function `AvgEnergy()` is evaluated and all projections are taken. Thus, only attributes `time`, `location` and `AvgEnergy(data)` are moved from a DAP to QPC, where they are first materialized to disk and then joined. By using this strategy the network cost is minimized and the overall execution time of the query is substantially reduced. In terms of data movement, both plans access 30.6MB worth of data from the data sources, and produce a result of size 49.2KB. However, the first approach moves 30.6MB worth of data over the network, while the second approach only moves 3.8KB. This translates into a $CVRF$ values of 1 and 0.0001, respectively. Hence, experimental evidence confirms that the VRF can be used to determine the best operator placement in the plan for a distributed join.

6 Conclusions

We have proposed MOCHA as an alternative database middleware solution to the problem of integrating data sources distributed over a network. We have argued that the schemes used in existing middleware solutions, where user-defined functionality for data types and query operators is manually deployed, is inadequate and will not scale to environments with hundreds of data sources. The high cost and complexity involved in having administrators installing and maintaining the necessary software libraries into every site in the system makes such approach impractical. MOCHA, on the other hand, is a self-extensible middleware system written in Java, in which user-defined functionality is automatically deployed by the system to the sites that do not provide it. This is realized by shipping Java classes implementing the required functionality to the remote sites. Code shipment in MOCHA is fully automatic with no user involvement and this reduces the complexity and cost of deploying functionality in large systems. MOCHA classifies operators as data-reducing ones, which are evaluated at the data sources, and data-inflating ones, which are evaluated near the client. Data shipping is used for data-inflating operators, and a new policy named code shipping is used for the data-reducing ones. The selection between code shipping and data shipping is based on a new metric, the Volume Reduction Factor, which measures the amount of data movement in distributed queries. Our experiments with the MOCHA prototype show that selecting the right strategy and the right site to execute the operators can increase query performance by a factor of 4-1,

in the case of aggregates, or 3-1, in the case of projections, predicates and joins. These experiments also demonstrated that the Volume Reduction Factor (VRF) is a more accurate cost metric for distributed processing than the standard metric based on selectivity factor and result cardinality because VRF also considers the volume of data movement.

References

[CGMH+94] S. Chawathe, H. Garcia-Molina, J. Hammer, K. Ireland, Y. Papakonstantinou, J. Ullman, and J. Widom. The TSIMMIS Project: Integration of Heterogeneous Information Sources. In *Proc. of IPSJ Conf.*, Tokyo, Japan, 1994.

[Inf97] Informix Corporation. Virtual Table Interface Programmer's Guide, September 1997.

[Ora99] Oracle Corporation. Oracle Transparent Gateways, 1999. http://www.oracle.com/gateways/html/transparent.html.

[CS96] S. Chaudhuri and K. Shim. Optimization of Queries with User-defined Predicates. In *Proc. 22nd VLDB Conf.*, pp. 87–98, Bombay, India, 1996.

[FJK96] M.J. Franklin, B.T. Jónsson, and D. Kossmann. Performance Tradeoffs for Client-Server Query Processing. In *Proc. ACM SIGMOD Conf.*, pp. 149–160, Montreal, Canada, 1996.

[GMSvE98] M. Godfrey, T. Mayr, P. Seshadri, and T. von Eicken. Secure and Portable Database Extensibility. In *Proc. ACM SIGMOD Conf.*, pp. 390–401, Seattle, WA, USA, 1998.

[Gra93] Goetz Grafe. Query Evaluation Techniques for Large Databases. *ACM Computer Surveys*, 25(2):73–170, June 1993.

[HKWY97] L.M. Haas, D. Kossmann, E.L. Wimmers, and J. Yans. Optimizing Queries Across Diverse Data Sources. In *Proc. 23rd VLDB Conf.*, pp. 276–285, Athens, Greece, 1997.

[HS93] J.M. Hellerstein and M. Stonebraker. Predicate Migration: Optimizing Queries with Expensive Predicates. In *Proc. ACM SIGMOD Conf.*, pp. 267–276, Washington, D.C., USA, 1993.

[ML86] L.F. Mackert and G.M. Lohman. R* Optimizer Validation and Performance Evaluation for Distributed Queries. In *Proc. 12th VLDB Conf.*, Kyoto, Japan, 1986.

[MS99] T. Mayr and P. Seshadri. Optimization of client-site user-defined functions. In *Proc. ACM SIGMOD Conf.*, Philadelphia, PA, USA, 1999.

[RMR00a] M. Rodríguez-Martínez and N. Roussopoulos. Automatic Deployment of Application-Specific Metadata and Code in MOCHA. In *Proc. 7th EDBT Conf.*, Konstanz, Germany, 2000.

[RMR00b] M. Rodríguez-Martínez and N. Roussopoulos. MOCHA: A Self-Extensible Database Middleware System For Distributed Data Sources. Technical Report UMIACS-TR 2000-05, CS-TR 4105, University of Maryland, January 2000.

[RS97] M.T. Roth and P. Schwarz. Don't Scrap It, Wrap It! A Wrapper Architecture for Legacy Data Sources. In *23rd VLDB Conf.*, Athens, Greece, 1997.

[SAC+79] P.G. Selinger, M.M. Astrahan, D.D. Chamberlin, R.A. Lorie, and T.G. Price. Access Path Selection in a Relational Database Management System. In *Proc. ACM SIGMOD Conf.*, pp. 23–34, Boston, MA, USA, 1979.

[SLR97] P. Seshadri, M. Livny, and R. Ramakrishnan. The Case for Enhanced Abstract Data Types. In *Proc. 23rd VLDB Conf.*, pp. 66–75, Athens, Greece, 1997.

[Sto93] M. Stonebraker. The SEQUOIA 2000 Storage Benchmark. In *Proc. ACM SIGMOD Conf.*, Washington, D.C., 1993.

[TRV96] A. Tomasic, L. Rashid, and P. Valduriez. Scaling Heterogeneous Databases and the Design of DISCO. In *Proc. 16th ICDCS Conf.*, Hong Kong, 1996.

Towards Self-Tuning Data Placement in Parallel Database Systems

Mong Li Lee[1][*]   Masaru Kitsuregawa[2]   Beng Chin Ooi[1][†]

Kian-Lee Tan[1][†]   Anirban Mondal[1]

[1] Department of Computer Science
National University of Singapore, SINGAPORE
{leeml,ooibc,tankl,anirbanm}@comp.nus.edu.sg

[2] Institute of Industrial Science
University of Tokyo, JAPAN
kitsure@tkl.iis.u-tokyo.ac.jp

ABSTRACT

Parallel database systems are increasingly being deployed to support the performance demands of end-users. While declustering data across multiple nodes facilitates parallelism, initial data placement may not be optimal due to skewed workloads and changing access patterns. To prevent performance degradation, the placement of data must be reorganized, and this must be done on-line to minimize disruption to the system.

In this paper, we consider a dynamic self-tuning approach to reorganization in a shared nothing system. We introduce a new index-based method that faciliates fast and efficient migration of data. Our solution incorporates a globally height-balanced structure and load tracking at different levels of granularity. We conducted an extensive performance study, and implemented the methods on the Fujitsu AP3000 machine. Both the simulation and empirical results demonstrate that our proposed method is indeed scalable and effective in correcting any deterioration in system throughput.

1. INTRODUCTION

Given the explosive growth of data on the Internet and prevalence of web-based applications such as e-commerce, the issues of managing huge volumes of data and providing fast and timely answers to queries have assumed paramount importance. The WWW is a dynamic environment where the number of users grows rapidly and changing access patterns may exhibit high skew. Web-sites of stock trading database and many other data-intensive applications which

---

[*]Contact author is currently a visiting faculty at the University of Wisconsin-Madison.

[†]The work of these two authors were resulted from the exchange programme funded by the Japan Society for the Promotion of Science (JSPS).

are inherently dynamic in nature have unpredictable workload patterns: they may see heavy access to some particular blocks of data just yesterday, but has low access frequency today.

Shared-nothing parallel computing infrastructure such as clusters of WWW servers and network of workstations [2, 13, 17] has become increasingly widespread because they are built from high performance, low-cost commodity hardware. The availability and scalability of these systems are important for entrepreneurs in the e-commerce business as it implies that they can build their system gradually depending upon the workload. Such a computing cluster comprises a number of processing elements (PEs), each of which has its own memory and disk. Data is typically partitioned across all the PEs to exploit the I/O bandwidth of the PEs. To further facilitate efficient query and update evaluation, data at each PE is indexed.

While the initial data placement can be effective for static databases, changes in access patterns can cause the performance of the system to degrade rapidly as some PEs become bottlenecks. For a system to be responsive to swings in query patterns and to better utilize all resources, dynamic re-balancing of the workload among the PEs is necessary. This can be achieved by tuning the data placement in the various PEs.

Reorganization of data has been extensively studied in centralized database systems by both researchers and major DBMS providers. [20] investigated how to compact a primary B^+-tree which had become sparse and and [21] described a method for defering secondary index updates. [9] examined the problems of changing from one access method to another, such as from B^+-tree to linear hashing and [10] studied how indexed sequential files can be compacted and clustering organizations described by hypergraphs can be created. [16] detailed methods to increase concurrency during the restoration of clustering indexes in IBM's DB2. [8] described restartable algorithms for online construction of an index.

In parallel database systems, new challenges in online reoganization arise as data and indexes are partitioned across multiple disks, and load imbalance occurs when access patterns change. [14, 15] presented various file striping heuristics for data allocation, data redistribution and load balancing in a shared memory multiprocessing environment. [18] showed how records can be distributed into variable sized fragments and migrated when load imbalance occurs in a shared nothing system. These works involve a significant amount of sophisticated bookkeeping.

Indexes such as B-trees in a multiprocessor environment is typically replicated in all the PEs to provide fast response to queries. However, this has a very serious drawback during reorganization and database updates. Any changes and underflow/overflow in a B-tree has to be propagated to all copies of the B-tree. [4, 5, 6, 7] proposed various techniques aimed at reducing the cost of maintaining replicated search structures and increasing concurrency.

[1] studied two methods to maintain indexes during on-line reorganization: OAT (One-At-a-Time page movement) moves one data page at a time from the source PE to the destination PE and modifies the indexes for records in that page, while BULK (bulk page movement) copies all the data to be moved at the destination PE and then modifies the indexes at the source and destination PEs. In both cases, the conventional B^+-tree insertion algorithm is used to insert the keys into the index in the destination PE. Similarly, the conventional B^+-tree deletion algorithm is used to delete the keys of the migrated data from the index in the source PE. It is important to maintain a good balance between over-heads incurred by data migrations such as communication, concurrency, index maintenance, and improvements in system throughput as a result of the migrations. This calls for efficient index updates and incremental data migration as overheads and heavy data movement may have an adverse effect on system throughput and cause the destination PE to become the next bottleneck.

In this paper, we consider a unique self-tuning approach to data reorganization in parallel database systems. Our work differs from previous research in that we use a two-tier index structure to facilitate fast and efficient data access and migration in a cluster. The novelty of this strategy is four-fold.

1. The amount of data to migrate is obtained from branches of the index at the source PE. This allows the entirety of the branches to be pruned easily without excessive overhead. The granularity of migrated data can be dynamically fine-tuned by using branches at different levels of the index.

2. The migrated data is bulkloaded into a separate rooted tree at the destination PE instead of inserting the migrated data one record at a time. This not only speeds up the insertion time, it also allows the rooted tree to be easily "attached" to the index at the destination PE. Data availability is also maximized.

3. An immediate cost reduction occurs even though the fast detachment and re-attachment of branches only applies to the primary index, and conventional B^+-tree insertions and deletions have to be used for the secondary indexes. This is because index modification is a major overhead in data migration, especially when we have multiple indexes on a relation.

4. Further reduction in migration overheads is achieved when the index structure at all the PEs is of the same height. We introduce an adaptive B^+-tree called the aB^+-tree which maintains the global height-balanced property of indexes in all the PEs by allowing some

indexes to grow "fatter" than normal, while others are kept "lean". Algorithms to search and update the aB^+-tree are also given.

We perform an extensive performance study on the proposed strategy. Our result shows that the proposed strategy is scalable and effective in correcting any workload skews. We also confirm the results by implementing the techniques on the Fujitsu AP3000 machine.

The remainder of this paper is organized as follows. In Section 2, we present our dynamic self-tuning data placement strategy. Section 3 gives the design of the aB^+-tree. Section 4 presents the experimental study and implementation and reports our findings. Finally, we conclude in Section 5.

2. DATA PLACEMENT AND MIGRATION

Data is initially range partitioned across all the PEs. Range partitioning is superior to round-robin and hashing as it can support range queries efficiently in addition to exact match queries. Unfortunately, it can lead to *data skew* where certain values for an attribute occurs more frequently than other values. This causes PEs dealing with large partitions of data to become performance bottlenecks. Similarly, while a shared-nothing system is scalable, *load skew* or load imbalance can occur when access patterns change leading to queries or updates on certain values for an attribute to occur more frequently. This causes PEs with frequently queried or updated data to become "hot" spots. Data skew or load skew can result in disk or processor becoming completely utilized for a small number of PEs, while the disks or processors of the other PEs are only lightly utilized. While data and load skews are inevitable, reducing these skews can increase throughput and reduce response time.

In this section, we present an efficient mechanism for on-line reorganization in a shared nothing context where data is indexed. We employ a two-tier index structure as the basic indexing mechanism. The first tier directs the search to the PE where the data is stored. Since the data is range partitioned, this layer is essentially a partitioning vector with $n-1$ values and n "pointers" for a system of n PEs. We can expect this layer to take up not more than a few pages (even for a system of 1000 PEs), and hence can be easily cached in main memory for fast access. Furthermore, this layer is replicated across all PEs to ensure that there is no central PE through which retrieval and update requests must pass. Otherwise, the PE containing the layer will easily become a bottleneck. Node replication reduces contention but requires a coherence protocol to maintain consistency. However, the maintenance of copies of the layer will hardly be required, if at all, since the layer is often read, but rarely updated. The second tier is a collection of B^+-trees, one at each PE. Each B^+-tree independently indexes the data at its PE. Thus, though the B^+-tree is a balanced structure, the two-tier structure need not be height balanced (since the number of records at the PEs can be different).

2.1 Illustrating Examples

We shall first illustrate with examples the proposed strategy. As data is range partitioned, we can only move data from one PE to its neighbouring PEs. Here, a neighbouring PE refers to the PE with the immediate preceding or succeeding range. So, all but two PEs will have two neighbours; the PE with the starting value, and the PE with the ending value will have only one neighbour. Given this non-overlapping data partitioning and hence non-overlapping indexes, our approach to on-line data reorganization is to migrate the data indexed by a branch of the B$^+$-tree in an overloaded PE and insert it in the destination PE index by bulkloading [12]. Note that the detachment of a branch from the B$^+$-tree in the source PE requires one pointer update. After bulkloading the migrated data into a B$^+$ subtree, the attachment of the subtree to the B$^+$-tree at the destination PE also requires only one pointer update.

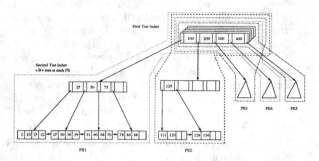

Figure 1: A sample 'global' index structure for illustration.

Consider the example 'global' index structure shown in Figure 1. Suppose the key attribute value ranges from 1 to 500 and we have 5 PEs. Moreover, assume that the records are initially range partitioned on the key attribute across the 5 PEs such that PE i is allocated the range $[(i-1)*100+1, i*100]$. From the figure, we note that there is an obvious data skew in PE 1 while PE 2 is relatively sparsely populated. The data skew in PE 1 also increases the chances of more queries and updates being directed to PE 1 since more records reside there. In order to resolve the data skew, we dynamically move one or more branches from the B$^+$-tree which has more records (the B$^+$-tree in PE 1 in our example) to the neighbouring B$^+$-tree (the B$^+$-tree in PE 2) which has relatively fewer records. Figure 2 shows the index structure after removing the data skew in PE 1. The range of the B$^+$-tree in PE 1 is now narrower with the last key entry *75* replacing the first key entry *100* in the first tier index. The latter now becomes the first key entry in the B$^+$-tree in PE 2.

Next, suppose there are 10000 searches to be performed. Ideally, if there is no data skew or any data skew has been dealt with, then an average of 2000 searches would be directed to each PE. However, we may have an exceptionally large number of searches for records whose keys fall in a certain range, say 0-75. This query skew may cause PE 1 to receive say 3000 queries, which is 50% more than the average load. The B$^+$-tree in PE 1 will be accessed 50% more than the rest of the B$^+$-trees in the index structure and can easily become a bottleneck if the inter-arrival time of the queries is less than the time needed to process a query[1]. In order to resolve load skew, we again dynamically move one or more branches from the B$^+$-tree which is more heavily accessed (the B$^+$-tree in PE 1 in our example) to the B$^+$-tree in the

---

[1]Note that when the inter-arrival time of the queries are far apart, it may be argued that there is no need to "balance" the load, since the response time would be the same anyway. However, this is not true when the system serves multiple users and multiple applications. If a single application accesses some PE more often than others, then this may lead to a load imbalance in the overall system.

neighbouring PE (the B$^+$-tree in PE 2) which has relatively fewer queries (Figure 3). The ranges in the two B$^+$-trees are again adjusted accordingly. We observe that the B$^+$-tree in PE 1 is now "slimmer" while the B$^+$-tree in PE 2 is now "fatter". Note that what we want to achieve is to be able to "take away" one branch from the B$^+$-tree in PE 1, and "pluck it" into the B$^+$-tree in PE 2 without much complexity. In addition, there is minimal disruption as the B$^+$-trees in PE 1 and PE 2 continue to process queries during the migration period.

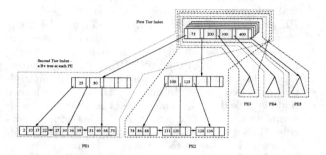

Figure 2: Resultant index structure after migration of data from Node 1 to Node 2 to remove data skew in Node 1.

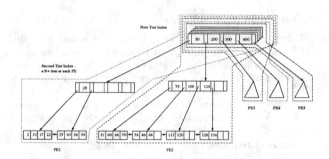

Figure 3: Resultant index structure after migration of data from Node 1 to Node 2 to remove load skew in Node 1.

The migration of branches in the B$^+$-trees also requires that the index entries in the first tier node copies to be updated. While the tier 1 entries at the source and destination PEs are updated in the process of the migration, the other copies at other PEs are updated in a lazy manner by piggy-backing update messages onto messages used for other purposes (such as during migration). The 2-tier index structure remains usable even when some copies of tier 1 have not been updated. Using our example, suppose PE 4 receives a request to retrieve the record with key value 60 after the rightmost branch in PE 1's B$^+$-tree has been moved to the B$^+$-tree in PE 2. Suppose the tier 1 copies at PEs 1 and 2 are updated while that for PEs 3, 4 and 5 have not been updated. Therefore, the search will be directed to PE 1. But, at PE 1, the system will automatically re-direct the search to continue in the B$^+$-tree in its right neighbour (PE 2) since its tier 1 entries indicates that the record can be found in PE 2.

2.2 Tuning Strategies

Several issues need to be addressed when supporting data migration in response to changing access patterns in shared nothing systems. Among these are the initiation of reorganization when load imbalance occurs, determination of the amount of data to be migrated from the overloaded PE, and efficient integration of the migrated data in the destination PE. We present our solutions to these issues here.

1. Initiation of Data Migration:

We can choose to initiate data migration when the load, or response time, or the number of jobs in the queue of a PE exceed a certain threshold. In a centralized approach, a control PE periodically polls every PE for their workload statistics. The control PE will then determine if there is any imbalance in the load or response time among the PEs and trigger the migration of data from the "hot" PE to its neighbouring PEs. This approach has better control when multiple nodes are overloaded. In this case, the most overloaded node is picked for data migration first. Only upon its completion then will the next overloaded node be considered (if it is still overloaded then). A more scalable approach, however, is to use distributed data balancing where a PE determines that it is overloaded and checks its left and right neighbours' loads. For simplicity, we have adopted a centralized approach for the initiation of data migration.

2. Determination of Amount of Data to Migrate:

When reorganization is initiated, it is necessary to determine the amount of data to migrate from the overloaded node. One key factor we have in mind is that of efficiency: the amount of the data should be determined quickly, and should facilitate efficient update to the index structure. Thus, we propose that the amount of data be obtained from subtrees in the index structure. This is efficient as removing the subtrees to be migrated requires only a simple pointer update.

Our approach is a top-down adaptive strategy: at the root, we determine the number of subtrees to be migrated; if a certain subtree's accesses are too large, we can move down to the next level, and repeat the process there. In order to achieve this, we need to maintain statistics on the access pattern. In this paper, we employ a straightforward and practical way to keep only the number of accesses to each PE. Given this minimal information, we adopt the assumption that the accesses are evenly distributed across all subtrees of the root node at the PE. This assumption is recursively applied to the subtrees at each node, i.e., at any node, all accesses are assumed to be directed evenly at its subtrees. We note that to maintain the property of B$^+$-tree that each node be at 50% utilized, if the amount of data obtained leads to a node falling below the utilization, then the entirety of the node will be transmitted.

However, keeping minimal information may not be sufficient for workloads that are skewed towards some subtrees. This may call for detailed statistics to be maintained on the accesses for every level of the B$^+$-tree (or even nodes or individual records). One can then obtain a fairly exact amount to migrate, but the overhead of maintaining the statistics and updating them can be very costly.

3. Integration of Migrated Data:

Without loss of generality, assume that we are moving data from PE p to PE q. Let us refer to the B$^+$-trees at the two PEs as pB$^+$-tree and qB$^+$-tree. Traditionally, the migrated data are inserted one at a time into qB$^+$-tree. This can be inefficient especially if the number of records moved is large. To speed up the process, we exploit the concept of bulkloading. We bulkload the migrated data into a newly created B$^+$-tree at q. We shall refer to this as the newB$^+$-tree. The idea is to try to build newB$^+$-tree such that its height is the same as that at certain level of qB$^+$-tree. The newB$^+$-tree can then be easily integrated into the qB$^+$-tree since the range of key values in the newB$^+$-tree is always smaller (or larger) than the range of key values in qB$^+$-tree. During this migration period, the pB$^+$-tree remains usable as the newB$^+$-tree is being built in PE q. Like the detachment process, the attachment of the newB$^+$-tree to the qB$^+$-tree is essentially a pointer update.

To realize the proposed mechanism, we need to determine a suitable height for newB$^+$-tree. We present our approach here. Let the height of a branch in pB$^+$-tree that has been picked for migration be pH, and the height of qB$^+$-tree be qH. There are two cases to consider:

- pH $\leq$ qH. In this case, for the migrated branch of pB$^+$-tree, the corresponding newB$^+$-tree will be constructed to be of the same height.

- pH $>$ qH. For a B$^+$-tree of order d (and maximum of $2d$ entries), the minimum and maximum number of records to construct a tree of height qH are $2d^{qH-1}$ and $(2d)^{qH}$ respectively. Let the number of records moved to q be N. We adopt the following heuristics: we will construct k branches of height qH with minimum number of records (k $\geq$ 1), and the remaining records are evenly allocated to these k branches, i.e., each of the k branches have such number of records as given by the expression

$$2d^{qH-1} + \frac{N - k \cdot 2d^{qH-1}}{k}$$

Figures 4 and 5 give the algorithms for a branch migration between the source and destination PEs initiated by load imbalance. For simplicity, we only show the case when pH = qH and when the migration involves one branch of the tree. In Figure 4, the algorithm determines the source and destination PEs for the migration (if the load exceeds a certain threshold at the source PE, say 10-20% above the average load of the PEs in the system). The required data (and keys) are then extracted (using routine *extract_keys*), and transmitted to the destination PE (using routine *transmit*). The data and the corresponding branch can then be pruned (using routine *delete_branch*). In Figure 5, the migrated data is first bulkloaded to a tree of the appropriate height (routine *bulkload*). The tree can then be integrated into the existing index structure, and the corresponding separators updated accordingly.

Before we leave this section, we note that migration can wrap around the PEs by allowing the first PE to contain two ranges. Suppose we have 5 PEs with the following key ranges: PE 1 is assigned 1-20, PE 2 21-40, PE 3 41-60, PE 4 61-80 and PE 5 81-100. If both PEs 4 and 5 are both overloaded, then we have the flexibility to migrate data with keys say, ranging from 91 to 100 to PE 1. In this case, PE 1 will have two key ranges, 91-100 and 1-20. At the same time, we can also achieve a smoother load distribution among the PEs by cascading the migration from the most heavily loaded node to the least loaded node which can be several nodes away (*Ripple* migration strategy). For example, PE 4 transfers a branch to PE 3, which in turn transfers a branch to PE 2, which in turn transfers a branch to PE 1. In this way, we can also get a better spread of the load across the PEs. Note that we can schedule the migrations to minimize network congestion.

Algorithm remove_branch()
```
/* Find the PE with the heaviest load */
PE: an array that records load and index information in each PE;
source = 0;
/* Determine the source PE with heaviest load */
for (i=1; i < NUM_PE; i++)
    if (PE[i].Load > PE[source].Load)
        source = i;
if (PE[source].Load > THRESHOLD) {
/* Determine the destination PE */
    if (source == NUM_PE - 1) destination = source -1;
    else if (destination == 0) source = 1;
        else if (PE[source+1].Load > PE[source-1].Load)
                destination = source - 1;
                else destination = source + 1;

    if (destination > source) {
    /* Extract all the keys indexed by the rightmost pointer P_m in the */
    /* B+-tree of the overloaded PE (source) and transmit them to the PE */
    /* on the right (destination). The branch pointed to by P_m is deleted. */
        Keys = extract_keys (PE[source].Root→ P_m);
        transmit (destination, add_branch(Keys, 1));
        delete_branch (PE[source].Root→ P_m);
    }
    else {
    /* Similarly, extract the keys indexed by the leftmost pointer P_0 and */
    /* transmit them to the PE on the left. The index entries are shifted */
    /* one place to the left after deleting the branch pointed to by P_0. */
        Keys = extract_keys (PE[source].Root→ P_0);
        transmit (destination, add_branch(Keys, 0));
        delete_branch (PE[source].Root→ P_0);
        for (i=0; i≤m; i++) {
            PE[source].Root→ P_i = PE[source].Root→ P_{i+1};
            PE[source].Root→ K_i = PE[source].Root→ K_{i+1};
        }
        PE[source].Root→ P_{m-1} = PE[source].Root→ P_m
    }
}
end
```

Figure 4: Algorithm for initiating data migration by detaching a branch from the B+-tree in the source PE

3. AB+-TREE: THE ADAPTIVE B+-TREE

From the last section, we observe that when the heights of the B+-trees at the source and destination PEs are the same,

Algorithm add_branch (Keys, Right)
```
/* Given a set of keys, construct a B+-tree by bulkloading and attach it */
/* to the B+-tree in the destination PE. This requires finding the */
/* separator to be inserted in the root node of the destination index. */
P_new = bulk_load (Keys);
Let n be the number of index entries in the root node of the
B+-tree at destination;
if (Right) {
    PE[destination].Root→ P_{n+1} = PE[destination].Root→ P_n;
    for (i=n-1; i≥0; i- -) {
        PE[destination].Root→ P_{i+1} = PE[destination].Root→ P_i;
        PE[destination].Root→ K_{i+1} = PE[destination].Root→ K_i;
    }
    PE[destination].Root→ P_0 = P_new;
    PE[destination].Root→ K_0 = find_separator();
}
else {
    PE[destination].Root→ K_n = find_separator();
    PE[destination].Root→ P_{n+1} = P_new;
}
end
```

Figure 5: Algorithm for attaching a branch to the B+-tree in the destination PE

migrating a branch from the source PE to the destination PE is an easy task: the migrated branch is reconstructed to be of the same height, and attached to the destination PE. The adaptive B+-tree (aB+-tree) index structure is another two-tier index structure designed to take advantage of this. The structure has two nice properties. First, it is globally height balanced without requiring the PEs to contain approximately the same number of records. Second, the tree is able to exploit the bulkloading mechanism discussed in the previous section without the cost of maintaining additional statistics.

The first tier of the aB+-tree is the same as that of the basic 2-tier structure discussed in the previous section. In the second tier, each PE has a variation of B+-tree that indexes the data at the PE. In our variant B+-tree, the root node can be a "fat" node, i.e., for a B+-tree of order d (and maximum of $2d$ entries), the root node can contain more than $2d$ entries[2]. Furthermore, all the B+-trees across all PEs are of the same height. To ensure this, the height is essentially determined by the PE with the fewest number of records. For PEs with more records, the root of the B+-trees may therefore contain more than $2d$ entries in order to keep the height the same across all PEs.

3.1 Insert Algorithm

Inserting a new record into the aB+-tree involves determining the PE to store the record (by searching the first tier), and inserting the record into the corresponding B+-tree. The algorithm is similar to that of B+-tree conventional insertion algorithm except that we have to determine when the tree grows (since all the B+-trees in the PE must be of the same height). To preserve height balancing, all the B+-trees in the system will grow together. This is done using the following mechanism. When a PE's B+-tree root node

---

[2]Another way of looking at this is that each PE contains multiple B+-trees of the same height.

(recall that root node is a fat node) is full, it will check to see whether all the B$^+$-trees root nodes at other PE contain more than $2d$ entries. Note that this can be achieved by maintaining statistics at each PE, rather than communicating with every PE during runtime. If some PEs' B$^+$-tree root node contains fewer than $2d$ entries, it means that aB$^+$-tree is not ready to grow, and an additional page is assigned as part of the fat node. On the other hand, when all the PEs' root nodes contain more than $2d$ entries, each of them will be split and a new root node will be allocated. The height of each tree will increase by one at the same time. Note that the first tier is unaffected by the growth.

We observe that it is possible that some PEs contain a lot more records than others. Thus, the roots of the B$^+$-trees in these PEs are "fat" and contain many pages while others may contain only one page. This is not a critical issue for two reasons. First, such extreme case is not expected to be common in practice. Second, since the fat root node is the root of the B$^+$-tree, it is not expected to be very large, i.e., the fat root node can be kept memory resident.

3.2 Search Algorithm

Given an exact match query at any PE, the first tier of the aB$^+$-tree is accessed to determine which PE, say p_i, to go to next. The query is passed to the p_i and the B$^+$-tree there is traversed to retrieve the required record. Many such queries can be processed by the processors concurrently as different B$^+$-trees are traversed. Figure 6 gives the details of the search algorithm for exact match queries.

For a range query issued at a PE, we can determine the set of PEs whose dataset satisfy the query. This can be done easily by examining the first tier of the aB$^+$-tree. The query can then be channelled to all the candidate PEs to return the portion of data that is stored there. Figure 7 shows how our range search is conducted.

```
Algorithm search(K)
K : search key value;
/* Given a search key value, search the first tier of the aB+-tree */
/* to find the PE that contains the record. */
/* Search will be subsequently continued in that node. */
i = get_PE (K);
if i < 0 then   abort
/* search_tree is a conventional B+-tree search routine */
transmit (i, search_tree(K));
/* Receive the result from PE i */
receive (i, Record);
return Record;
end
```

Figure 6: Algorithm for exact match query

3.3 Deletion Algorithm

Deleting a record involves searching for the record (using the search algorithm), and then deleting the record as in the traditional B$^+$-tree. However, it is possible that the deleted record causes an underflow that results in the B$^+$-tree shrinking in height. We address this problem as follows. We will first try to initiate data migration in its neighbouring PE to "donate" some branches to it. This minimizes the need to "shrink" the trees. In the event that this is not possible (because the neighbours will underflow and shrink

```
Algorithm range_search(K₁, K₂)
K₁, K₂: the range values of the range query;
Result : list of records returned to the calling routine;
/* Find all the PE that may contain records falling in the range [K₁, K₂] . */
Result = ∅;
for  (i=0; i < NUM_PE; i++)
     if (range of data at PE[i] intersects range [K₁, K₂])  then
     /* Btree_range_search is a conventional B+-tree rangesearch routine */
          transmit(i, Btree_range_search(K₁, K₂);
          receive (i, List);
          Result = Result ∪ List;
return Result;
end
```

Figure 7: Algorithm for range query

too if data is taken from them), then we will proceed with a global shrinking process in order to maintain global height-balance. In other words, when a tree shrink, all trees will also shrink. As a result of the shrinking, some B$^+$-trees will become fat. The algorithm is essentially similar to the traditional B$^+$-tree deletion, where entries from all nodes are concatenated, together with the separators at the parent node being pulled down.

4. PERFORMANCE STUDIES

In this section, we describe our experiments to study the performance of our self-tuning data placement strategy using the proposed aB$^+$-tree. Our performance evaluation consists of both simulation (with an actual implementation of aB+-tree) and implementation on the Fujitsu AP3000 machine. The simulation study allows us to perform sensitivity analysis which we are unable to do on the Fujitsu AP3000 machine (because of the limited number of processors and disk space allocated for our experiments).

For the simulation study, the metrics used are the impact on the response time of the transactions and the load directed to the PEs. We examine the costs of our reorganization strategy in terms of the number of pages accessed. We note that the number of messages generated to update copies of the first tier index will definitely be fewer than existing replicated index structures. As such, we do not study this metric in our experiments. We use a shared nothing parallel database architecture where each PE consists of a processor with its own disk(s) and memory. The PEs in the system communicate with each other by exchanging messages across the interconnection network, set at 200 Mbyte/s. Table 1 summarizes the parameters and their values used in our experiments.

The simulation experiments comprise two phases:

1. Phase 1.
   We first create an initial aB$^+$-tree with the tuple key values generated using a uniform random distribution. The B$^+$-trees in the second tier are distributed to the PEs. Then we generate 10000 queries using a zipf distribution which concentrates the queries in a narrow key range. Therefore, we have about 40% of the queries directed to a "hot" PE. This load skew will initiate the migration of branches in the "hot" PE to its neighbouring PEs. Creating an actual aB$^+$-tree given the number of PEs and relation size allows us

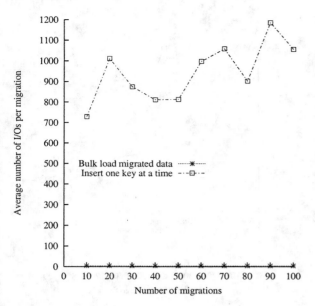

(a) A 16-PE cluster

(b) Effect of varying the number of PEs.

Figure 8: Cost of migration

Parameter	Default	Variations
System Parameters		
index node size	4K	
number of PEs in the cluster	16	8, 32, 64
network bandwidth (in Mbyte/s)	200	
Database Parameters		
number of records (in million)	1	0.5, 2.5, 5
size of key	4 bytes	
time to read or write a page	15 ms	
interarrival time is exponential	10	5, 15, 20
with mean $1/\lambda$		25, 30, 40
Query Parameters		
number of queries	10000	
distribution of queries using	0.1	
zipf distribution, zipf factor		

Table 1: Parameters and their values.

to know the actual number of keys migrated and their key range values when a branch is detached from the B^+-tree in the source PE and attached to the B^+-tree in the destination PE. This information is captured at each migration and used in the second phase.

2. Phase 2.
Here, we implemented a simulation model in CSIM [19], which allows us to measure the response time of the queries and the number of queries waiting in the queue. We model each of the PEs as a resource and the queries as entities. We use the same 10000 queries generated using the zipf distribution. The migration of a branch in a "hot" PE to its neighbouring PE is simulated by adjusting the range of key values indexed by the B^+-trees in the source and destination PEs. This is possible with the trace obtained in the first

phase of our study.

4.1 Cost of Migration

In this section, we first evaluate the cost of migration using our reorganization technique. As reference, we compare our technique with the traditional technique of inserting the keys of the migrated data one at a time. Here, we consider the number of page accesses when data is migrated. This metric tracks the number of index pages accessed when the B^+-trees in the source and destination PEs have to be modified due to data migration. The results are shown in Figure 8. The average number of IOs per migration for the "Insert one key at time" approach fluctuates with the amount of data indexed by the branch to be migrated. It is clear that the traditional method of deleting the keys of the migrated data from the source PE index and inserting these keys to the destination PE index is very expensive because each key requires us to start from the root and go down to the appropriate leaf page. For this experiment, we did not use any buffer replacement strategy because we want to study the effect of limited buffers and to get the true costs of these techniques. We expect the costs of the two methods to be comparable if sufficient buffers are available because the index nodes are likely to stay in the buffer pool between successive insertions and deletions. In contrast, the number of page accesses required for the proposed method is low and relatively constant even when buffering is minimal. Only the root nodes of the indexes in the source and destination PEs are accessed to update the pointers when the data indexed by a branch of the B^+-tree is migrated.

4.2 Impact of Migration on Maximum Load

In this set of experiments, we study the effect of data migration on the maximum load among the PEs. This metric tracks the maximum number of queries directed to a PE. Using this metric, we identify the PEs which are potential bottlenecks and correct the problem by initiating data migration to spread the load of the "hot" PE to its neighbouring PEs. This set of experiments is conducted in the first phase using the actual aB^+-tree constructed. No data migration occurs if the loads of all the PEs are within 15% of the average load[3]. Otherwise, data migration is initiated and a branch at the root level of the overloaded PE's B^+-tree is transferred to its neighbouring PE. Note that the load threshold can be adjusted depending on how close we want the loads of the PEs to be near the ideal.

We observe that our adaptive approach requires us to migrate subtrees from multiple levels. A simple strategy would be to migrate a predetermined number of subtrees from a fixed level only (static approach). To assess the benefits of the adaptive approach, we compare it with the static strategy under two different granularities: *static-coarse* where only branches at the root level can be migrated, and *static-fine* where branches at one level below the root of the B^+-trees can be migrated. For this experiment, we wanted the B^+-trees in the PEs to have at least three levels of index nodes. Therefore, we used a page size of 1024 bytes and 2 million records to build the initial B^+-tree and distributed the second tier B^+-trees to 8 PEs. Figure 9 shows the result of this experiment. All the three strategies show performance gain as data is moved away from the "hot" PE. The performance gain is more gradual for static-fine compared to static-coarse because the amount of data migrated is limited to those indexed by branches of the B^+-tree. The static-fine strategy is important when workloads are extremely skewed towards a particular subtree. If this subtree is to be migrated entirely to the next processor, it will cause an undesirable sharp increase in the destination processor's workload, causing it to be the next bottleneck. In this situation, it will be better to migrate subtrees at the next lower level. Figure 9 shows that our adaptive approach gives superior performance as it is able to determine the right amount of data to migrate.

Since the adaptive approach performs best, we shall not discuss the static approaches further in subsequent experiments. In the next experiment, we study the maximum load and load variation among 16 PEs after 10000 queries. The result is shown in Figure 10. PE 16 is overwhelmingly overloaded while PEs 1-15 are lightly loaded. Migrating data indexed by branches at the root level of the B^+-trees is able to reduce the maximum load in the "hot" PE by 40%.

Finally, we investigate scalability and sensitivity of data migration on maximum load when we vary the number of PEs in the system and the size of the dataset. We observe that the maximum load drops when we increase the number of PEs in the system. This is expected because the dataset is now distributed over more PEs which in turns distribute the load. In addition, the set of queries used is generated using the zipf distribution over 16 buckets to create load skew in our default system of 16 PEs. When we use a highly skewed set of queries generated using the zipf distribution over 64 buckets, there is hardly any reduction in the maximum load. Instead, the bulk of the load is still directed to the "hot" PE in the system which is gradually corrected by data migration. Figure 11 shows the results of these experiments. Figure 12 shows that maximum load in the system of 16 PEs when we vary the size of the dataset. We observe that the maximum load does not change much as the zipf distribution

[3]Average load is the total number of queries divided by the number of PEs in the system

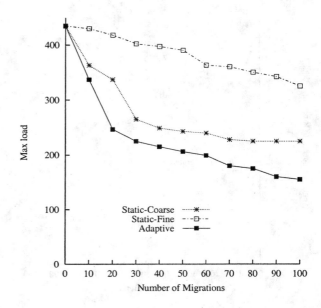

Figure 9: Effect of granularity of migrated data on maximum load

dictates the proportion of queries being directed to each PE. In all cases, we see that the maximum load has been reduced by 50% after migration of data from the overloaded PE.

4.3 Impact of Migration on Response Time

In this set of experiments, we examine the effect of data migration on response time of a query. No data migration occurs if the job queues of all the PEs have fewer than 5 queries waiting to be processed. Otherwise, data migration is initiated by picking the PE with the most number of queries waiting in the queue as the source PE. Figure 13 shows the average response time of a PE and the response time of a query for the most heavily loaded PE in a system of 16 PEs. Our results affirm the effectiveness of distributing some index branches (and hence data pages) in the overloaded PE to its neighbouring PE to reduce the average response time, thus increasing the throughput of the system. In fact, the response time of a query in the "hot" PE differs greatly from the average response time of 30 ms [4] in the lightly loaded PE. Given the extreme skews in the queries, the "hot" PE received a disproportionate number of queries. This extreme response time variation is narrowed with data migration.

Experiments to study the scalability and sensitivity of data migration on the average response time of a query includes varying the mean interarrival time of the queries, the number of PEs in the system and the size of the tuples in the dataset. The results are shown in Figures 14 and 15. We note that the average response time increases exponentially when the mean interarrival time is less than 15 ms. This also occurs when the number of PEs in the system is less than 32. The average response time of the system remains quite the same at about 480 ms when the size of the dataset is less than 2.5 million tuples. There is a sharp increase when the

[4]With 1 million records distributed over 16 PEs, the average height of the B^+-trees in the PEs is 1. Hence, an average of 2 page accesses is needed to retrieve a required tuple.

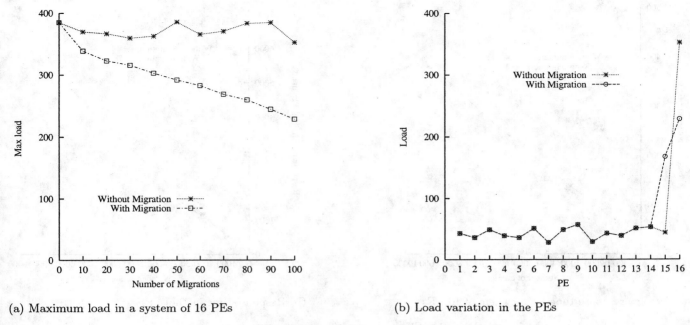

(a) Maximum load in a system of 16 PEs

(b) Load variation in the PEs

Figure 10: Effect of migration on maximum load

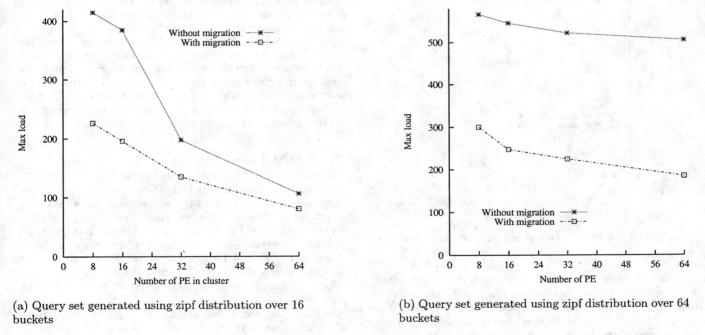

(a) Query set generated using zipf distribution over 16 buckets

(b) Query set generated using zipf distribution over 64 buckets

Figure 11: Effect of number of PEs on maximum load

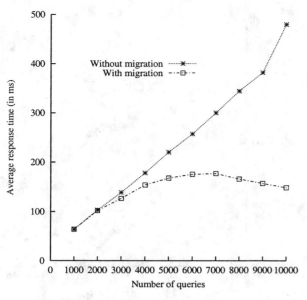

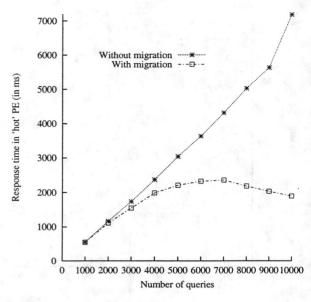

(a) Average response time for a system of 16 PEs

(b) Response time in "hot" PE

Figure 13: Effect of migration on response time

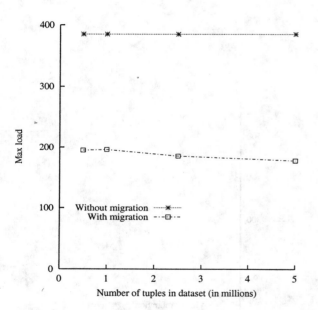

Figure 12: Effect of dataset size on maximum load

dataset is 5 million due to the increase in the height of the B^+ trees in the PEs. In all these cases, data migration is able to improve the average response time by at least 60%. We see that our data migration strategy is able to correct performance degradation of the system effectively.

4.4 Empirical Results on Fujitsu AP3000

We also implemented our reorganization techniques on the Fujitsu AP3000 machine. The Fujitsu AP3000 machine is a massively parallel processor system based on 32 Sun Ultra-Sparc workstations connected by Fujitsu's proprietary high speed switch (200 Mbyte/s), the APnet. Given the high bandwidth of the network, it is hardly a bottleneck during reorganization. We investigate how our techniques perform in a real multi-user environment with competing processes. We run experiments on AP3000 to study the impact of migration on the response time and load directed to the processors. Figure 16 shows the response time in the overloaded processor in a 16 node cluster and the average response time when the number of processors in the cluster varies. Although we could only use up to 16 processors, the empirical results obtained confirm the results from the simulation experiments. In general, while the experimental curves are roughly the same, the actual response time obtained on AP3000 is higher than the simulation results due to competing processes in a multi-user environment.

5. CONCLUSION

To the best of our knowledge, this is the first paper to propose an index-based tuning technique which enables fast determination of the amount of data to be migrated from an overloaded PE and efficient bulkloading of the migrated data in the destination PE. The granularity of the data to be migrated can be suitably varied by using branches at different levels of the index. This adaptive and incremental tuning strategy allows the system to respond sensitively to access changes, minimizing heavy data movement and costly index updates.

We have designed a two-tier index structure to facilitate data access and data migration in clusters. The first tier is a partitioning vector to direct the search in the PE where the data is stored while the second tier is a collection of non-overlapping B^+-trees, one at each PE. The first layer is replicated in all the PEs to ensure that there is no central PE through which retrievals and updates must pass. This design also eases maintenance as updates to copies of this layer during migration is done lazily by piggybacking

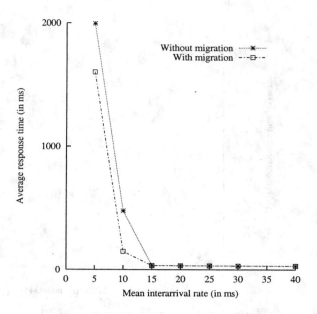

Figure 14: Effect of mean interarrival rate on response time

them on messages used for other purposes. We see further reduction in data migration overheads when the two tier index structure is globally height-balanced as in our adaptive B^+-tree (aB^+-tree).

We have demonstrated how a seemingly simple strategy can be yet scalable and effective in correcting any degradation in system performance when access patterns changes dynamically. We are currently extending this research to indexes for advanced applications [3]. In particular, we believe the approach can be readily adopted for transformation-based indexing schemes for high-dimensional data [11].

REFERENCES

[1] K.J. Achyutuni, E. Omiecinski, and S.B. Navathe. Two techniques for on-line index modification in shared nothing parallel databases. In *Proc. ACM SIGMOD International Conference on Management of Data*, 1996.

[2] T.E. Anderson, D.E. Culler, and D.A. Paterson. A case for now (network of workstations). *IEEE Micro*, 15(1):54–64, 1995.

[3] E. Bertino, B.C. Ooi, R. Sacks-Davis, K.L. Tan, J. Zobel, B. Shilovsky, and B. Catania. *Indexing Techniques for Advanced Database Systems*. Kluwer Academic Publishers, August 1997.

[4] T. Johnson and P. Krishna. Lazy updates for distributed search structure. In *Proc. ACM SIGMOD International Conference on Management of Data*, pages 337–346, 1993.

[5] P. Krishna and T. Johnson. Implementing distributed search structures. Technical report available at *cis.ulf.edu:cis/tech-reports/tr92/tr92-032.ps.Z*, 1992.

[6] B. Kroll and P. Widmayer. Distributing a search tree among a growing number of processors. In *Proc. ACM SIGMOD International Conference on Management of Data*, pages 265–276, 1994.

[7] D. Lomet. Replicated indexes for distributed data. In *Proc. of Conference on Parallel and Distributed Information Systems*, pages 108–119, 1996.

[8] C. Mohan and I. Narang. Algorithms for creating indexes for very large tables without quiescing updates. *SIGMOD Record*, 21(2):361–370, 1992.

[9] E. Omiecinski. Concurrent storage structure conversion: From b^+-tree to linear hash file. In *Proc. of 4th International Conference on Data Engineering*, pages 589–596, 1988.

[10] E. Omiecinski, L. Lee, and P. Scheuermann. Concurrent file reorganization for record clustering: A performance study. In *Proc. of 8th International Conference on Data Engineering*, pages 265–272, 1992.

[11] B.C. Ooi, K.L. Tan, C. Yu, and S. Bressan. Indexing the edges - a simple and yet efficient approach to high-dimensional indexing. In *Proceedings of the 19th ACM SIGMOD-SIGACT-SIGART Symposium on Principles of Database Systems*, May 2000.

[12] R. Ramakrishnan. Database management systems. McGraw-Hill, 1997.

[13] D. Ridge, D. Becker, P. Merkey, and T. Sterling. Beowulf: Harnessing the power of parallelism in a pile of pcs. In *Proc. of IEEE Aerospace*, 1997.

[14] P. Scheuermann, G. Weikum, and P. Zabback. Disk cooling in parallel disk systems. *IEEE Bulletin of the Technical Committee on Data Engineering*, 17(3):29–40, 1994.

[15] P. Scheuermann, G. Weikum, and P. Zabback. Data partitioning and load balancing in parallel disk systems. *VLDB Journal*, 7(1), 1998.

[16] G.H. Sockut and B.R. Iyer. A survey of online reorganization in ibm products and research. *IEEE Bulletin of the Technical Committee on Data Engineering*, 19(2):4–11, 1996.

[17] T. Tamura, M. Oguchi, and M. Kitsuregawa. Parallel database processing on a 100 node pc cluster: Cases for decision support query processing and data mining. In *Proc. of SC97: High Performance Networking and Computing*, 1997.

[18] R. Vingralek, Y. Breitbart, and G. Weikum. Snowball: Scalable storage on networks of workstations. *Distributed and Parallel Databases*, 6(2), 1998.

[19] K. Watkins. Discrete event simulation in c. McGraw-Hill, 1993.

[20] C. Zou and B. Salzberg. On-line reorganization of sparsely-populated b+ trees. In *Proc. ACM SIGMOD International Conference on Management of Data*, pages 115–124, 1996.

[21] C. Zou and B. Salzberg. Safely and efficiently updating references during on-line reorganization. In *Proc. VLDB*, 1998.

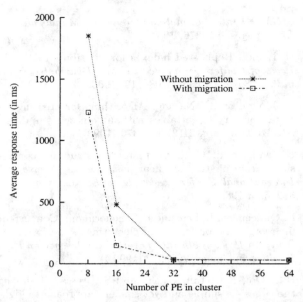

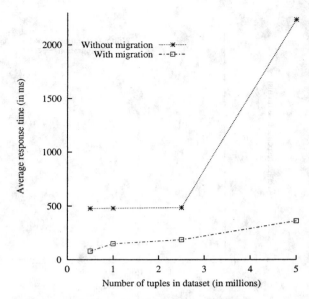

(a) Vary number of PEs in system with 1 million tuples

(b) Vary size of dataset in a system of 16 PEs

Figure 15: Comparison of response time

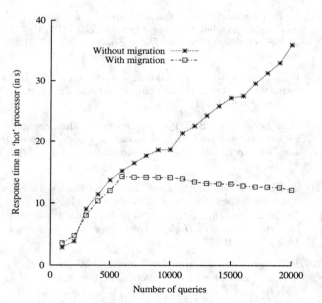

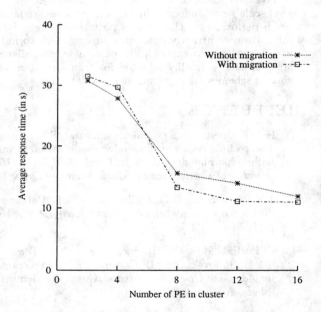

(a) Response time in "hot" PE (16 node cluster)

(b) Average response time when number of PE in cluster vary

Figure 16: Experiments on response time in AP3000

LH*_{RS}: A High-Availability Scalable Distributed Data Structure using Reed Solomon Codes

Witold Litwin
Université Paris 9 (Dauphine),
Pl. du Mal de Lattre, Paris 75016, France,
Witold.Litwin@dauphine.fr

Thomas Schwarz, S.J.
Jesuit School of Theology
1756 Leroy Avenue, Berkeley, CA 94709, USA,
schwarz@scudc.scu.edu

ABSTRACT

LH*RS is a new high-availability Scalable Distributed Data Structure (SDDS). The data storage scheme and the search performance of LH*RS are basically these of LH*. LH*RS manages in addition the parity information to tolerate the unavailability of $k \geq 1$ server sites. The value of k scales with the file, to prevent the reliability decline. The parity calculus uses the Reed-Solomon Codes. The storage and access performance overheads provide the high-availability are about the smallest possible to. The scheme should prove attractive to data-intensive applications.

Keywords

SDDS, scalable, high-availability, Reed-Solomon Codes

1 INTRODUCTION

Multicomputers (collections of computers connected by a high-speed network) are claimed to be the industry choice for the next millennium [M97], [P98]. They combine affordability and high performance, but also demand new data structures and algorithms, [CACM97]. Specifically, the need for scalability led to the proposal of Scalable Distributed Data Structures (SDDS) [LNS96]. SDDSs allow for files whose records reside in buckets at different server sites. The files support key-based searches and parallel/distributed scans with function (query) shipping. They can be hash-partitioned, or ordered with respect to the primary key or support multikey access. Among the SDDS studied [SDDS], probably the best known is the distributed version of Linear Hashing [L80], called LH*, [LNS96], [KLR96], [B99a], [K98], [R98], [SDDS].

An SDDS file is manipulated by the SDDS client sites. Each client has its own addressing schema called image that it uses to access the correct server where the record should be. As the existing buckets fill up, the SDDS splits them into new buckets. The clients are not made aware synchronously of the splits. A client may have an outdated image and address an incorrect server. An SDDS server has the built-in capability to forward incorrect queries. The correct server sends finally the Image Adjustment Message (IAM) to the client. The information in an IAM avoids at least repeating the same error twice. It does not

necessarily make the image totally accurate.

These principles avoid the centralized address calculus that could become a hot spot. They allow SDDS files to scale to thousands sites. The scaling makes however a bucket unavailability (failure) increasingly likely. A high availability scheme retains the accessibility of all records to the application despite failures. A k-availability scheme preserves the availability of all records despite up to k bucket failures. A 0-availability scheme does not tolerate any unavailability. The LH* and the traditional data structures are 0-available by this measure.

Higher values of k enhance the reliability of the file, i.e., the probability that all stored data are available to the application, [LMR98]. Modern databases run the 24/7 regime under web access and exemplify the need for high availability schemes as well as the cost of data unavailability. The well-known crash of eBay in June 1999 resulted in the loss of $4B of market value and of $25M in operations [B99]. The failure of a typical financial database costs $10K-$27K per minute.

The first 1-available SDDS scheme was a variant of LH* called LH*_M, using record mirroring [LN96]. The scalable and distributed generalizations of B+-trees, [BV98] and [VBW98], also use the replication. In both cases, the doubling of the storage cost may be prohibitive. High-availability variants of LH* with lower storage overhead have therefore been developed. The 1-availability scheme LH*_S stripes every data record into m stripes, then places each stripe into a different bucket and stores the bitwise parity of the stripes in parity records in additional parity buckets, [L&al97]. The storage overhead for the high-availability is only about 1/m for m stripes per record.

Striping produces typically meaningless record fragments, and usually impairs the parallel scans requiring entire records at each site. Efficient scans are decisive for many applications of web servers or parallel databases, [R98]. Another 1-availability variant of LH* termed LH*_g addressed this concern [LR97], [L97], [LMRS99]. The application records, called *data records*, remain entire in LH*_g. For the high-availability, they form *m*-member *record groups* provided each with the bitwise parity record. The storage overhead is about 1/*m*, as for the striping. The speed of searches and of parallel scans without failures is that of generic (0-available) LH*. It is unaffected by the additional structure for the high-availability.

The 1-availability or even *k*-availability for any static *k* cannot prevent the reliability decrease in a scaling file. The *scalable availability scheme* LH*_{SA} was therefore designed to dynamically increase k, [LMR98]. It uses an elaborated record grouping, where each data record c is a member of k or k+1 groups that intersect only in c and are 1-available. For each k, the LH*_{SA} file is k-available. The storage overhead may vary substantially while the file scales. It can be close to k/m, the known minimum for k-availability, [H&al94]. But, it can also reach over 50 %.

Below, we present an alternative scalable availability scheme termed LH*$_{RS}$. Through record grouping, it retains the LH* generic efficiency of searches and scans. The k-availability results from k or $k+1$ (generalized) parity records per record group. The parity calculus uses the Reed Solomon (RS) Codes. This mathematically complex tool proves simple and efficient in practice. The advantages of LH*$_{RS}$ are "smoother" storage overhead, always close to the minimal possible, and faster recovery algorithm. The capabilities of LH*$_{RS}$ make the scheme attractive. The other high-availability LH* scheme retain nevertheless some advantages. The diversity should prove attractive to implementers.

Section 2 introduces the LH*$_{RS}$ scheme, focusing on its use of RS calculus. Section 3 presents the actual parity computations in an LH*$_{RS}$ file. We explain the file manipulation in Section 4. Section 5 discusses file performance and Section 6 addresses variants to the scheme. Section 7 presents related work, and Section 8 concludes the article. The Appendix provides some mathematical background of RS-codes and pseudo-code for some algorithms.

2 HIGH-AVAILABILITY OF LH*$_{RS}$ SCHEMA

2.1 Record Grouping

We assume the basic familiarity with LH*. A LH*$_{RS}$ file consists of an LH*-file called *data file* with the *data records* generated by the application in *data* buckets 0,1,...,M-1. The LH* data file is augmented for the high-availability with *parity* buckets to store the parity records at separate servers. A data record is identified by its key c and has also some non-key part. As for the generic LH*, the correct bucket a for data record c in an LH*$_{RS}$ file is given by the *linear hashing* function $h_{j,n}$; $a = h_{j,n}(c)$. The parameters (j,n) called *file state* evolve dynamically. The client image consists also from h, but perhaps with outdated state. Details of the address computations are not important here.

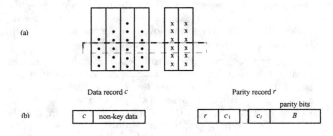

Figure 1. LH*$_{RS}$ file: (a) 2-available bucket group, (b) Data and parity records.

We group successively created data buckets in *bucket groups*. All but perhaps the last bucket group have the same size $m = 2^f$ for some $f > 1$. Bucket a belongs to the group numbered $g = a$ **div** m, where **div** denotes integer division. The last bucket group can contain less than m buckets. For the parity calculus, we formally complement it with dummy (not really existing) buckets with dummy (zero) records. Every bucket group is provided with $k \geq 1$ parity buckets where the parity records for the group are stored. Figure 1a shows a bucket group with four data buckets and their data records (•) and two parity buckets and their parity records (x). Each data record has a *rank* 1,2... that reflects the position of

the record in its data bucket. A *record group* contains all the data records with the same rank r in the same bucket group. The record group with $r = 3$ is enclosed for example in Figure 1a. The k parity buckets contain parity records for each record group. A parity record consists first of the rank r of the record group, then of the primary keys $c_1, c_2, \ldots c_l$ of all the (non-dummy) data records in the record group, and finally of the (generalized) *parity data* calculated from the data records and the number of the parity bucket. The parity data, denoted by B in Figure 1b, differ among the parity records. We call the ensemble of the data records in a record group and its parity records a *record segment* and likewise, the bucket group with its parity buckets a *bucket segment*.

2.2 Scalable Availability

Figure 2 illustrates the expansion of an LH*$_{RS}$ file. Parity buckets are represented shaded and above the data file, right to the last, actual or dummy, bucket of the group they serve. For the sake of the example, we choose $m = 4$. Dummy buckets are delimited with dotted lines. The file is created with data bucket 0 and one parity bucket, Figure 2a. The first insert creates the first parity record, calculated from the data record and from m-1 dummy records. The data record and the parity record receive rank 1. The file is 1-available.

When new records are inserted into data bucket 0, new parity records are generated. Each new data and parity record gets the next rank. When data bucket 0 reaches its capacity of b records, $b \gg 1$, it splits. Usually half of its records move into data bucket 1. During the split, both the remaining and the relocated records receive new consecutive ranks starting with $r = 1$. Since there are now (non-dummy) records with the same rank in both buckets, the parity records are recalculated, Figure 2b.

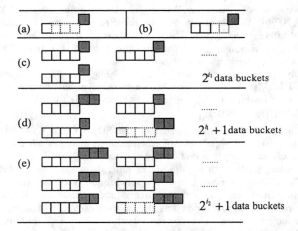

Figure 2. Scalable availability of LH*$_{RS}$ file. (a) initial file, (b) first split, (c) max. 1-available file, (d) beginning 2-availability and (e) 3-availability.

The continuing growth of the file through inserts formally replaces the dummy records in the data buckets with actual records. The splits append new data buckets 2,3… Eventually, a split creates data bucket $m+1$. This starts the second bucket group and its first parity bucket.

While the file continues to scale, the probability of double failure increases. To offset the decline in reliability, the file availability increases gracefully to two parity buckets per group. This process

238

starts, Figure 2c and Figure 2d, when the file reaches some size $M = 2^{i_1}$. Next bucket split is then bucket 0. We recall that LH* scheme splits the buckets in the deterministic order $0,0,1 \ldots 2^i - 1,0 \ldots$ On the one hand, each new bucket group is from now on formed with two parity buckets. On the other hand, a second parity bucket is appended to each existing bucket group during the split of its 1st member. When M reaches $M = 2^{i_1+1}$, i.e., when the file has doubled in size, all groups have two parity buckets. At this point, the file is 2-available and can survive failure of any two buckets.

Further scaling makes a triple failure increasingly likely. To offset the reliability decline, one has to further increase the availability level. This starts again when the file reaches some size $M = 2^{i_2}$; $i_2 > i_1$ so that next bucket to split is again bucket 0, Figure 2e. Each split, starting from that of bucket 0 again, creates then three parity buckets for the newly appended data bucket, and adds a third parity bucket to the two already present for the splitting data bucket. Once data bucket $M = 2^{i_2}$ splits in this way, all bucket groups are 3-available, and the file has reached 3-availability. This process can continue towards 4-availability, etc., making LH*$_{RS}$ a *scalable availability* schema.

The values of i_1, i_2 etc. which determine when the availability level starts to increase, are controlled by the LH*$_{RS}$-*coordinator*. Essentially, the LH*$_{RS}$ coordinator is the LH* coordinator provided with additional capabilities for the high-availability. We recall that the LH* coordinator handles the file state parameters which it uses to calculate next bucket to split when some, usually another, bucket reports an insert creating an overload. In addition, the LH*$_{RS}$ coordinator initiates the creation of parity buckets for new groups and the scaling up of the availability. It also manages the record and bucket recovery.

The scheme allows for a variety of strategies in the management of availability. The basic strategy starts increasing the k-availability towards $(k + 1)$-availability whenever the files reaches m^k buckets. In the notation from above, this variant chooses $2^{i_1} = m$, $2^{i_2} = m^2$ etc. We call this strategy, as any other using predefined values of i, *uncontrolled reliability*. We implement the *reliability control* strategy by dynamically choosing i based on the file reliability as monitored by the coordinator. Whenever bucket 0 is next in line for a split, the scheme decides whether the reliability level would drop under some threshold P_{min} before bucket 0 is again about to be split, and starts to create $(k + 1)$ parity buckets if necessary. The basic P_{min} is the reliability of a single bucket. Section 5.4 discusses the reliability control more in depth.

2.3   Parity Coding

LH*$_{RS}$ parity calculus uses the linear RS codes. These are originally error correcting codes, among most efficient, since they are maximal distance separating (MDS) codes. We use them as *erasure correcting* codes recovering unknown data values. We first recall the theory of Galois Fields, at the basis of the RS codes. We use terms from [MS97].

2.3.1   Galois Fields

A Galois Field $GF(N)$ is a set with N elements and the arithmetic operations of addition, subtraction, multiplication, and division. There are two distinguished elements, a zero element, written 0, and a one element, written 1. The operations over $GF(N)$ possess the usual properties of their analogues in the real numbers including the properties of 0 and 1.

For LH*$_{RS}$, we only use $GF(2^f)$ for some $f > 0$. We represents the elements of the field as f-bit strings. The byte based structure of modern computers suggests $f = 4$ or $f = 8$. Generally, the implementation of multiplication consumes more resources for larger values for f, whereas a smaller value of f limits too much the number of parity records in a record group.

For every f, the bit representation of zero is $0 = 00\ldots0$ and of one is $1 = 0\ldots01$. For bytes, one thus has $0 = 0000\ 0000$ and $1 = 0000\ 0001$. The addition and the subtraction of two elements are the same and equal to their Exclusive-Or (XOR). The definition of multiplication and division is more cumbersome. Mathematically most convenient is the definition of the multiplication based on representing the elements of $GF(2^f)$ as polynomials of degree f over the field $GF(2) = \{0,1\}$. The multiplication is then the multiplication of polynomials and the product is reduced modulo a certain generator polynomial. These generator polynomials are irreducible polynomials of the appropriate degree. The mathematical tables with generator polynomials for interesting field sizes are in [MS97].

String	int	hex	log
0000	0	0	$-\infty$
0001	1	1	0
0010	2	2	1
0011	3	3	4
0100	4	4	2
0101	5	5	8
0110	6	6	5
0111	7	7	10
1000	8	8	3
1001	9	9	14
1010	10	A	9
1011	11	B	7
1100	12	C	6
1101	13	D	13
1110	14	E	11
1111	15	F	12

Table 1. Log table for the multiplication in $GF(16)$.

GF multiplication via polynomial multiplication is hardly efficient. Rather, one uses table look-up. Two methods are attractive: (1) a complete multiplication table supplemented by a table of multiplicative inverses, and (2) the logarithm and the antilogarithm tables. Method (1) is conceptually the easiest. Its drawback is the size of the multiplication table. For bytes, the multiplication table would contain $2^8 \cdot 2^8 = 2^{16}$ entries or 64KB. In addition, the table is two-dimensional and calculating the address of an entry introduces additional overhead.

Method (2) is based on the existence of the *primitive* elements in any GF. The property of each primitive element p is that every non-zero field element is a power of p. We choose p and determine for each element g in the GF the power i such that $p^i = g$. We call i the *logarithm* of g and write $i = log_p(g)$. Inversely, we call g the *anti-logarithm* of i and write $g = antilog_p(i)$. We tabulate logarithms and antilogarithms in two tables, each of the size of the field. We thus have 2^{f+1} entries in total, many times less than method (1) requires for a larger field, e.g. only 512 entries for $GF(256)$. We implement multiplication and division of Galois field elements using these tables. For every two elements g and $h \in GF(2^f)$:

$$g \cdot h = antilog_p (log_p(g) + log_p(h))$$
$$g/h = antilog_p (log_p(g) - log_p(h)).$$

The addition or subtraction is here modulo $2^f - 1$ which is the number of non-zero elements in GF.

2.3.2   Example

Consider $GF(16)$ so $f = 4$ and there are 15 non-zero elements. There are different implementations of this field, one is in Table 1. Each field element can be represented as a bit string, an integer, and as a hexadecimal digit. The primitive element is 2, the zero element is 0, and the one element is 1.

Addition remains the XOR operation as given by the $^\wedge$ operator in C, C++, and Java. As an example of arithmetic, we calculate the sum, product, and quotient of the two field elements $A = 10$ and $B = 11$ in the integer notation. For the sum, we calculate $A+B = 1010 \wedge 1011 = 0001 = 1$. For the product, we take the logarithms 9 and 7, add them up modulo 15, to obtain 1. The number with logarithm 1 is 2, hence $A*B = 2$. To calculate A/B, we subtract the two logarithms, by taking the remainder modulo 15 we change the difference to a number between 0 and 15, and then we take the antilogarithm. Since $log(A) - log(B) = -2 \equiv 13$, and since $antilog(13) = D$, we have $A/B = D$. In the faster version of method (2), we use the offset -2 into the extended anti-logarithm table.

2.3.3   Parity Encoding

We use n for the maximal segment size, m for the record group size, and k for the number of parity buckets. Thus, $n = m + k$, and the group is k-available.

For the parity calculus, we identify the data record with its non-key field and the parity record with its parity field B. Since the data record key is replicated in the parity records, it becomes part of the parity calculus. We assume that data records in a record group are of the same length. Otherwise we pad the shorter records with 0 bits to obtain the same length. We treat any record as a bit string. We break each string into *symbols* of length f. If f does not divide the length of the string, we again pad with 0 bits. If we choose $f = 4, 8$, this padding should not be necessary. We identify the set of all possible symbols with the elements in $GF(2^f)$.

We generate each parity record for the record group from the data records one symbol at a time. For the sake of presentation, we assume that all parity records are generated at the same time. Similarly, we assume that all data records in the record group are inserted into the file simultaneously. We show the actual operations in Section 3. Finally, we assume the coding calculus to be centralized, while – as we will see - it is distributed in the LH*$_{RS}$ scheme.

We are thus given m data records, each of which is a string of symbols. We calculate now the first symbol in all the parity records simultaneously. Subsequent symbols are calculated in precisely the same manner. First, we form the vector $\mathbf{a} = (a_1, a_2, a_3, ..., a_m)$ where a_i is the symbol from the ith record in the group. We collect the first symbol in all records (data and parity) in the vector $\mathbf{u} = (a_1, a_2, ..., a_m, a_{m+1}, ..., a_n)$, to which we refer as a *code word*. The first m coordinates of $\mathbf{u}$ are the coordinates of $\mathbf{a}$. The remaining k coordinates of $\mathbf{u}$ are the newly generated parity bucket symbols.

We obtain $\mathbf{u}$ from $\mathbf{a}$ by multiplying $\mathbf{a}$ from the right with a *generator matrix* $\mathbf{G}$ of the linear (systematic) RS-code; namely $\mathbf{u} = \mathbf{a} \, \mathbf{G}$. $\mathbf{G}$ has m rows and n columns. $\mathbf{G}$ is *systematic*, that is, $\mathbf{G}$ consists of two concatenated sub matrices; namely $\mathbf{G} = \mathbf{I} | \mathbf{P}$. Matrix $\mathbf{I}$ is a $m \times m$ identity matrix, hence $\mathbf{a} \, \mathbf{I} = \mathbf{a}$. That is why first m coordinates of $\mathbf{u}$ form $\mathbf{a}$. Only the columns of the *parity* matrix $\mathbf{P}$ operationally contribute to the k parity symbols. Each parity symbol within i^{th} parity record is produced by the vector multiplication of $\mathbf{a}$ by the ith column of $\mathbf{P}$. The entire record corresponds to the iteration of this multiplication over all the data symbols.

Matrix $\mathbf{G}$ is generated algorithmically through appropriate elementary row transformations from $m \times n$ matrix $\mathbf{V}$ that is a Vandermonde matrix (either simple or extended) [MS97]. The algorithm is in Appendix A. Different values of k lead to different elements in $\mathbf{P}$, despite same n. In practice, there are only the k columns $\mathbf{p}$ of $\mathbf{P}$ present in the file. Each parity bucket contains only one $\mathbf{p}$. This suffices as the parity symbol is the result of the product of $\mathbf{u}$ with the column $\mathbf{p}$.

The maximum number of columns of $\mathbf{G}$ is $2^f + 1$, e.g. 257 for byte sized symbols. The number of parity records for a record group is limited by this bound, which however appears to be sufficient for byte sized symbols. We know a way to overcome this bound dynamically, but this method is beyond our scope here.

2.3.4   Example

For the sake of simplicity, we continue with $GF(16)$. The maximal segment size supported by $GF(16)$ is $n = 17$. We set the bucket group size to $m = 4$. Our file availability level can scale to 13-availability. There is a way to allow even higher availability through dynamic switch to the field $GF(256)$, although we will not present it. We calculate a generator matrix $\mathbf{G}$ as in Appendix A to be

$$\mathbf{G} = \begin{pmatrix} 1 & 0 & 0 & 0 & 8 & F & 1 & 7 & 7 & 9 & 3 & C & 2 & A & E & 7 & 7 \\ 0 & 1 & 0 & 0 & F & 8 & 7 & 1 & 9 & 7 & C & 3 & A & 2 & 7 & E & 7 \\ 0 & 0 & 1 & 0 & 1 & 7 & 8 & F & 3 & C & 7 & 9 & E & 7 & 2 & A & 7 \\ 0 & 0 & 0 & 1 & 7 & 1 & F & 8 & C & 3 & 9 & 7 & 7 & E & A & 2 & 7 \end{pmatrix}$$

The left four columns of $\mathbf{G}$ form the identity matrix. Any four different columns of $\mathbf{G}$ form an invertible matrix. The multiplication of four-dimensional vector $\mathbf{a}$ by $\mathbf{G}$ leads to 17-dimensional vector. Because of the 4 x 4 identity submatrix of $\mathbf{G}$, the first four coordinates of the vector replicate $\mathbf{a}$. The other 13 coordinates are symbols for successive parity records.

Assume the following four data records: "En arche ...", "Dans le ...", "Am Anfang ...", "In the beginning...". The bit strings in GF corresponding to the ASCII encoding for our four records are (in hexadecimal notation): "45 6E 20 41 72 ...", "41 6D 20 41 6E ...", "44 61 6E 73 20 ...", "49 6E 20 70 74...". To calculate the first symbols in each parity record we form the vector $\mathbf{a} = (4,4,4,4)$ and multiply it by $\mathbf{G}$. The product is vector $\mathbf{u} = (4,4,4,4,4,4,4,4,4,4,4,4, 4,4,4,4,0)$. For the second symbol in each parity bucket, we form the vector $\mathbf{a} = (5,1,4,9)$ and multiply by $\mathbf{G}$ to obtain code word $\mathbf{u} = (5,1,4,9,F,8,A,4,B,1,1,2,7,E,9,9,A)$. Notice that the first four coordinates of $\mathbf{u}$ always replicate the coordinates of $\mathbf{a}$. We do not have to calculate all coordinates of $\mathbf{u}$ at once, but can calculate them individually instead. For example, to calculate the fifth coordinate of 2nd $\mathbf{u}$, we multiply vector $\mathbf{a}$ with the fifth column of $\mathbf{G}$. Expressing this more conveniently using the dot product, we calculate (using GF instead of integer operations):

$\mathbf{a} \cdot (8,F,1,7) = (5,1,4,9) \cdot (8,1,F,7) = 5 \cdot 8 + 1 \cdot F + 4 \cdot 1 + 9 \cdot 7 =$
$= E + F + 4 + A = F.$

The matrix notation merely combines all 17 dot product calculations. In this manner, we obtain "4F 63 6E E4 …" for the first parity record, "48 6E DC EE …" for the second parity record, and "4A 66 49 DD …" for the third.

2.3.5 Record Recovery

Assume that LH*$_{RS}$ finds at most k data or parity records of a record segment to be unavailable. Collect any m available records of the segment. Also, concatenate the corresponding columns of **G** into the $m \times m$ matrix **H**. By virtue of the Vandermonde matrix, any $m \times m$ submatrix of **G** is invertible. Using for example Gaussian elimination, we compute $\mathbf{H}^{-1}$. Collect the symbols with the same offset from the m records into a vector **b**. By definition, $\mathbf{a} \cdot \mathbf{H} = \mathbf{b}$ implying $\mathbf{b} \cdot \mathbf{H}^{-1} = \mathbf{a}$. Hence, multiply **b** by $\mathbf{H}^{-1}$ to recover the missing symbols with the same offset. Using the same $\mathbf{H}^{-1}$, iterate through the entire available records, to produce all missing records.

2.3.6 Example

Consider that first three data records above became unavailable, i.e., only the fourth data record and the first, second and third parity records are available. We form **H** from the columns 3 to 6:

$$\mathbf{H} = \begin{pmatrix} 0 & 8 & F & 1 \\ 0 & F & 8 & 7 \\ 0 & 1 & 7 & 8 \\ 1 & 7 & 1 & F \end{pmatrix}$$

Inversion of **H** yields:

$$\mathbf{H}^{-1} = \begin{pmatrix} B & F & A & 1 \\ C & 4 & 2 & 0 \\ 4 & 7 & D & 0 \\ 2 & D & 4 & 0 \end{pmatrix}$$

The first vector **b** formed from the first symbols of the three remaining records is $\mathbf{b} = (4,4,4,4)$. Hence, $\mathbf{b} \cdot \mathbf{H}^{-1} = (4,4,4,4)$. The next symbols lead to $\mathbf{b} = (9,F,8,A)$ and $\mathbf{b} \cdot \mathbf{H}^{-1} = (5,1,4,9)$ etc. The first coordinates of **b** vectors provide the first missing data record "45...", the second coordinates the second data record "41...", the third coordinates the third data record "44...", and the fourth coordinates merely reproduce the fourth data record "49..."

3 ACTUAL PARITY CODING

The basic operations on a data record are that of insertion, deletion, or update. For the parity calculus, the update is the generic operation, the inserts and deletes are seen as special cases. An update basically changes only the non-key data, and related parity records. An update to the key is dealt with as a deletion followed by an insert into usually a new location. An insert is formally an update of a dummy record into the actual one. Vice versa, a deletion is an update into the dummy record.

3.1 Updates

We consider an update to the ith data record in its group. Let **a** be the vector with symbols with the same offset of the data records in the record group before the update and **a'** the vector formed similarly after the update. Vectors a' and a differ in the ith position only. Le **u** and **u'** be the resulting code words.

Thus $\mathbf{u} = \mathbf{a}\,\mathbf{G}$, $\mathbf{u'} = \mathbf{a'}\,\mathbf{G}$ and their difference is $\mathbf{\Delta} = \mathbf{u} - \mathbf{u'} = (\mathbf{a} - \mathbf{a'})\,\mathbf{G}$. We have $a - a' = (0,...,0,\Delta_i,0,...,0)$ where Δ_i is the difference between the same offset symbols in the old and in the new record. We recall that, in a *GF*, both the addition and the subtraction are equal to the XOR operation. To calculate $\mathbf{\Delta}$, we only need the ith row of **G**. Since $\mathbf{u'} = \mathbf{u} + \mathbf{\Delta}$, one can calculate the new parity values by calculating $\mathbf{\Delta}$ first and then XOR this to the current **u** value that is the content of B field of each parity record. In other words, with $\mathbf{G}_i$ being the ith row of **G**:

$$\mathbf{u'} = \mathbf{a'} \cdot \mathbf{G} = (\mathbf{a} + (\mathbf{a'} - \mathbf{a}))\,\mathbf{G} = \mathbf{a}\,\mathbf{G} + (\mathbf{a} - \mathbf{a'})\,\mathbf{G} = \mathbf{u} + \Delta_i\,\mathbf{G}_i.$$

In particular, the new symbol u'_j in bucket j is calculated from the old symbol u_j, the difference Δ_i between the new and the old symbol in the updated record, and the coefficient of **G** located in the ith row and j^{th} column as

$$u'_j = u_j + \Delta_i\,g_{i,j}.$$

We call $\mathbf{\Delta}$-record the string obtained as the XOR of the new and the old symbols with the same offset within the updated record.

To implement an update operation without key change, LH*$_{RS}$ sends the $\mathbf{\Delta}$-record together with the bucket number i and the rank r (to identify the record group) to all parity sites. Each parity site calculates the B field (or parity record proper) according to equation (3.1). Coefficient g_{ij} is stored with the parity bucket as part of the jth column of **G**.

3.2 Inserts and deletions

An insert formally replaces a dummy record with an actual data record. At the data bucket, the key field c and the non-key data field are updated. Through the insertion, the new record obtains a rank r. The data bucket then sends the rank r, the key c, the bucket number i, and the non-key data as the $\mathbf{\Delta}$-record to all parity buckets. The rank identifies the parity record in need of change. If the parity record with this rank does not yet exist, we create it. The field c_i of this parity record changes to c. We calculate field B in the parity record by XORing the $\mathbf{\Delta}$-record with the current contents of B, just as for an update. The justification lies in the fact that the implicit dummy record has been changed to the new record.

Likewise, a data record deletion is an update to a dummy record. The operation proceeds by first finding the data record and removing it from the data bucket. Rank r, bucket number i, and the record itself as $\mathbf{\Delta}$-record are send to all the parity buckets. Rank r identifies the parity record, the field c_i is set to zero, and field B is XORed with the $\mathbf{\Delta}$-record. If the data record was the last in the group, then all key fields c_j in the parity record are now zero. The field B is zero as well. We can then delete the parity record as well.

3.3 Example

Continuing with the running example, assume that we have four data buckets 0..3 with two parity buckets for this group, all buckets being empty. We insert, and update records into successive buckets and at the same rank, disregarding, for the sake of the example, the actual LH* addressing rules. First, we insert record "En arche ..." into data bucket 0. This becomes the $\mathbf{\Delta}$-record, since the previous content is a dummy record, so XORing the symbols in the string "En arche ..." with the zero symbols yields of course the string "En arche ...". The $\mathbf{\Delta}$-record is then sent to the parity buckets, together with its bucket number 0 and rank 1. In hexadecimal notation, the $\mathbf{\Delta}$-record is "45 6E 20 41 72 ...". The first parity bucket is bucket 4, hence it carries $\mathbf{G}_4$. There, the symbols of the $\mathbf{\Delta}$-record get multiplied by 8, the first row coefficient in $\mathbf{G}_4$. The result is the string "6E 59 30 68 ..." which becomes the field B of the first parity record with rank 1.

Formally, the string resulting the multiplication is XORed to the old content of B to become the actual B. As the old B happens to contain only zero symbols, there is no need to actually perform the XOR. Similarly, the second parity bucket multiplies the Δ-record with F, the coefficient in the first row of G_5, yielding "96 45 D0 9F ..." in the parity field B.

Now, we insert the second record "Dans le ..." or "41 6D 20 41 6E ..." into bucket 1. This string is sent to both parity buckets as the Δ-record. It multiplies there respectively F and 8, which are the coefficient in the second rows of G_4 and G_5. The results are "9F 47 D0 9F ..." and "68 53 30 68 ..." respectively. These are XORed to the strings in each B that are the above "6E 59 30 68 ..." and "96 45 DO 9F ...". This yields to "F1 1E E0 F7..." and "FE 17 E0 F7 ..." as the contents of the B-fields in buckets 4 and 5.

We insert the other two data records in the same manner. The final parity record fields B become "4F 63 6E E4 ..." and "48 6E DC EE ...". Assume now that one changes the 1st data record from "En arche ..." to "In initio ...". In hexadecimal notation, the change is from "45 6E 20 41 72 ..." to "49 6E 20 69 ...". We XOR these two strings obtaining the Δ-record "0C 00 00 28...", shipped to the parity buckets. This Δ-record is shipped from bucket 0 to both parity buckets. At the first parity bucket, we first multiply it by the coefficient in the first row of G_4. We obtain "0A 00 00 3C ..." We form the XOR with the existing B that is "4F 63 6E E4...". The result is "45 63 6E D8 ...". The calculation at the second parity bucket proceeds in the same manner, except that we use of the coefficient in the first row of G_5, namely F. The multiplication of the Δ-record by F yields "08 00 00 D1 ...". The final XOR to the old content of B gives "45 63 6E D8 ..." as the new value.

4   FILE MANIPULATION

To create an LH*$_{RS}$ file, the application provides the group size m. The $GF(4)$ or $GF(8)$ are chosen accordingly, and the coordinator computes the generator matrix G. It also initializes bucket 0 and the first parity bucket, where it stores the first column of parity matrix P. All other file creation operations are as for the generic LH*.

Further manipulation is in *normal* mode if it executes as generic LH* operations, except perhaps for additional operations on the parity buckets, assumed all accessible. An operation enters the *degraded* mode if it cannot access a record in normal mode. This happens for an unavailable or *displaced* bucket. The displaced bucket case occurs when a query is sent to the bucket that in the meantime was recovered. Hence, it is elsewhere at the server that was originally a spare. The originator of the query may be unaware of new location. It gets then the correct address if the query terminates successfully in a dedicated IAM. The address is not necessarily of that spare that could itself become unavailable in the meantime.

The operations in degraded mode are handed to the coordinator. From the file state, it may locate the displaced buckets. If a recovery should occur, the coordinator attempts to recover the entire bucket at a spare, or only the searched record. If there are less than m available records for a group, which makes the recovery calculus as defined above impossible, the coordinator enters the *catastrophic mode*. Case specific algorithms are then used. Some records may be unrecoverable, but there may be good

cases. We will not discuss this mode in depth. An example of a good case is at the end of Section 7.

We now overview the LH*$_{RS}$ file manipulations focusing on differences to generic LH*. We start with record and bucket recovery. Recall that the number of data buckets in a bucket group is m and call the number of parity buckets in a given bucket group k'. The number of buckets in a segment of a k-available file is $n = m + k'$, where $k'=k$ or $k'=k+1$.

4.1   Record Recovery

To recover a record with key c, the coordinator probes the k' parity buckets in some order, sending an unicast message with key c, the unavailable data bucket address a, and the address of the client. If no parity bucket is available, then the failure is catastrophic. Otherwise, the first parity bucket p that replies takes the control of the recovery, to avoid turning the coordinator into a bottleneck for recovery. Bucket p searches for the parity record with c among its keys. The rank r of the record cannot be determined from c, hence one uses a sequential scan, or the parity bucket maintains a hash table with entries of the form (c,r). If c is not found, then the search for the key c is unsuccessful, i.e., the record with key c was not in the file. Notice that this constitutes also a successful recovery.

Otherwise, the parity record r found contains key c only or with $x \leq (k'-1)$ other keys. If record r contains only c, then all the other records in its record group are dummy. One trivially computes offset i of c within its group using a and creates H from all columns of I, but column i, and from its column of P. Afterwards, one performs the recovery calculus using the RS-decoding, as described.

If record r contains several keys, the bucket searches for every data record with key $c' \neq c$ in record r. If all are found, and $x = (k'-1)$, then the bucket orders them along their offsets, produces H from all columns of I but i and from its own parity column and performs the recovery calculus. If $x < k'$, but all the records are found, then the records at the other offsets are assumed dummy.

If however $l > 0$ records among x reveal unavailable, and $l < k'$, then bucket p probes other parity buckets. Each probe requests parity record r and column of P stored at the bucket. If $l \geq k'$, then the failure is again catastrophic. *Idem*, if less than l parity buckets respond to the probe. Otherwise, bucket p produces the columns of H from I according to the offsets of the $k' - l$ data records found, completes with the columns of P received and performs the RS-decoding.

Bucket p sends to the client the recovered record c or the information that key c is not in the file. It alerts the coordinator otherwise.

4.2   Bucket Recovery

Both data and parity buckets can be recovered using RS-decoding, as long as there are m buckets in the segment. Parity records can be also recovered from the data buckets through RS-encoding. Record recovery can be performed concurrently with bucket recovery, as the latter is a more involved operation.

Unavailable buckets are recovered at spare servers. To start, the coordinator probes the segment with the bucket to recover for the availability of the other buckets. If m or more reply, then recovery proceeds, otherwise the case is catastrophic. The coordinator passes their addresses and further control of the operation to one of the spare servers. If there are data records to recover, the spare collects columns of parity matrix **P** at the parity buckets, and forms and inverts matrix **H**. It then calculate the missing data records consecutively, stores them or sends to the spares where they should be. The key fields are from the parity records. The non-key fields are calculated from H^{-1}, from the non-key fields of other data records in the group, and from the B-fields of the parity records.

Once data records are recovered, the remaining parity buckets to recover, if any, are produced in turn, using matrix **G**. If only parity buckets should be recovered, then one skips the reconstruction of data buckets. In a final step, the spare notifies perhaps the originator of the query of new locations through IAMs.

4.3 Key search

Normally, the LH^*_{RS} key search for key c is the LH* key search. The degraded mode is triggered by the client or the forwarding server. The coordinator uses the LH* file state parameters to calculate the address of the correct bucket. If this address is not the one of the unavailable or displaced bucket, it forwards c to the correct bucket. If that bucket is available, it replies to the LH^*_{RS} client, including the IAM. If the coordinator finds the correct bucket unavailable, it attempts the record recovery. Likewise, it initiates the recovery of any unavailable forwarding bucket.

4.4 Scan

In the normal mode the scan proceeds as a LH* scan. We recall, that the client starts with a series of unicast messages or a multicast message. The request specifies whether the scan has deterministic or probabilistic termination. In both cases, buckets that have relevant records send them to the client. For the probabilistic termination, then only these buckets reply. Otherwise, every bucket in the file replies at least with the bucket number. The LH* deterministic termination protocol detects whether every bucket has replied, even if the client image was outdated.

The degraded mode occurs only if unicast messages are used to deliver the request or if the deterministic termination is requested. The coordinator attempts the corresponding bucket recovery and the successful termination of the scan.

4.5   Insert

In normal mode, a LH^*_{RS} client performs the insert like a LH* client. The correct data bucket resends the record as **Δ**-record to all the parity buckets of the group. Their addresses are in its header.

The degraded mode is triggered by the client or the forwarding server or the correct data bucket that finds an unavailable or displaced bucket. The finder sends the record to the coordinator. For the client, the operation is then successfully terminated. The coordinator determines the correct bucket for the insertion. If it is unavailable, then it attempts the bucket recovery with the record to be inserted. As for the key search, it also recovers any unavailable forwarding bucket.

4.6 Split

As in the generic LH*, an insert to an overflowing bucket is reported to the coordinator. This usually triggers a split of the bucket pointed out by the *split pointer n* which is one of the file state parameters. Bucket n is typically different from that

receiving the insert. After the split, $n := n + 1 \bmod 2^j$ and, if $n := 0$, then $j = j+1$. Initially, $n = j = 0$.

In normal mode, the coordinator assigns new ranks to all the records, whether they remain in the parent bucket or end up in the new bucket. The move of a record either within the parent bucket (unless by chance the new and the old rank coincide) or to new bucket is formally a deletion followed by an insert. Existing parity buckets are updated accordingly. In practice, it should be more efficient to recreate them.

If a new bucket starts a group, then the coordinator creates new parity buckets and their records. If the number of parity buckets per segment is being upgraded, the split operation appends in addition a new bucket to the group of the parent bucket.

The degraded mode consists basically of the recovery of the bucket, combined in the implementation dependent way with its split.

4.7   Update

In the normal mode, the client performs the update as for LH*. At the correct bucket, the update does not change the rank r of the record, unless a split occurs between the time the client reads the record and the time of the return of the update. In the former case, the bucket calculates the **Δ**-record and sends it with its rank r to the parity buckets. These buckets recalculate their parity records r. In the latter case, the parent bucket gets the updated record anyhow and computes whether it should migrate or stay. In both case the rank r typically changes. The update by definition concerns only non-key data otherwise it is a record deletions and the insert to, usually, different location. If the updated record moves, there is no more parity records concerning it in its parent segment. It suffices thus that whether the record moves or not, only the bucket that finally stores it computes the **Δ**-record and sends it out.

The degraded mode may start during the search for the record to update or when the client sends back the update or when the servers sends out **Δ**-record. If the correct bucket is available, the coordinator resends the record there. Otherwise, the coordinator updates the record in the recovered bucket. If the forwarding bucket was unavailable, the coordinator initiates the recovery of this bucket. The originator of the degraded mode gets the address of the recovered or displaced bucket in the IAM.

4.8   Deletion

In the normal mode, the client performs the deletion of record c as for LH*. The correct bucket in addition sends its address and record c with its rank r, to the parity buckets. Each bucket removes key c from its parity record r. If c is the last key, record r is deleted. Otherwise, its parity field B is adjusted.

In the degraded mode, if the data bucket is unavailable or displaced, the coordinator localizes the correct data bucket. It recovers it without the record to be deleted, as well as, perhaps, the unavailable forwarding or parity buckets.

4.9   Merge

Deletions may trigger a *bucket merge* that is the inverse to a split. In the normal mode, it moves the records of the last data bucket back into its parent bucket and removes the last bucket. The moved records receive new ranks in the parent bucket. The parity buckets of both groups are updated accordingly. If the removed bucket was the only one in its group, then the parity buckets for this group are deleted. The number of parity buckets in the segment might also decrease. In the degraded mode, first all unavailable buckets are recovered.

5 PERFORMANCE

Detailed performance analysis is lengthy [LS99]. Table 2 summarizes basic values, intended as guidelines for the file design. The actual costs may be larger, or noticeably smaller.

5.1 Access

As usual, we measure access performance with the number of messages, as the metric independent of network speed and topology. A message contains at most one record. Table 2 shows the typical and the worst costs of various operations. For convenience, we explicitly show also the typical overhead of high-availability. The worst case of an operation accessing parity records is computed for a $(k+1)$ available group in a k-available file. The worst cost beyond the practical sense is omitted (n/a). For instance, very unlucky hashing could skyrocket the split or merge cost. The typical file has bucket capacity $b >> 1$, size $M >> m$, i.e. has several groups, and the load factor of data buckets of 0.7. It uses unicast messages, except for starting the parallel scans.

Mode	Normal			Degraded
	typical	max	overhd	
Succ. key search	2	4	0	$1+R$
Unsucc key search	2	4	0	4
Scan (det term)	$1+M$	n/a	0	$1+M+yB$
Insert	$1+k$	$3+k+1$	k	$1+R$
Update	$2+k$	$6+k+1$	k	$1+R+B$
Delete	$1+k$	$3+k+1$	k	$1+k+B$
Split	$0.35b+$ $+0.7bk$	n/a	$0/7bk$	$0.35b+0.7bk+$ $+B$
Merge	$\beta b+2\beta+$ $+bk$	n/a	$2\beta bk$	$\beta b+2\beta bk+B$

Mode	Typical	Max
Exist. record recovery (R)	$1+2m$	$2+2m+k$
Bucket recovery (B)	$0.7b(m+x-1)$	n/a
Storage Overhead	k/m	$(k+1)/m$

Table 2 LH*$_{RS}$ data access and high-availability performance.

The performance of key search in normal mode is that of LH*. It is independent of M and does not carry any high-availability overhead. The degraded mode cost includes the record recovery cost R. The successful search cost typically depends on m, but, perhaps surprisingly, not the unsuccessful one. The degraded mode increases the successful search time typically $(m+1)$ times. Notice that this performance is also independent of M and about best possible.

The scan also performs as for LH* and does not carry the high-availability overhead. The degraded mode carries the bucket recovery cost B, times the number y of unavailable buckets encountered in different groups.

An insert, update or delete in normal mode carries the overhead of typically k messages to parity buckets. This is the theoretical minimum for any k-available schema. The actual overhead may be also $k+1$ when the availability starts to scale. This is also the minimal price for the scalable availability. The costs of degraded mode includes B at least.

The split and merge costs in Table 2 are easy to derive. Factor β denotes the data buckets load factor low enough to trigger merges.

Record recovery cost R in Table 2 results directly from the algorithm. The recovery starts with 1 message to the coordinator. Then, there is typically one message to a parity bucket of the failed bucket. If the searched key is not found at this bucket, there is only 1 more message to the client. Otherwise the bucket sends out typically m-1 messages to data buckets. Finally the recovered record is sent to the client.

The worst case corresponds to $k+1$ unavailable buckets probed in vain. Notice from the algorithm that there are also other cases. A group may be incomplete, with $l < m$ actual data records, hence the degraded successful search cost can be substantially under the typical one, reaching even only 4 messages. More precise estimates of R taking to the account the likelihood of each case, and of x-bucket unavailability remains to be done.

The bucket recovery cost B estimates in Table 2 result directly from the algorithm. It considers the typical bucket load of $0.7b$ records, and presence of $x \geq 1$ failures. Notice the efficiency for $x > 1$ due to the simultaneous recovery of <u>all</u> the unavailable buckets. The worst case analysis obviously does not apply here, as the worst bucket load could be assumed arbitrarily high.

Finer estimates remain to be determined. The presence of incomplete groups, likely for groups towards tops of the buckets, decreases the cost. In contrast, a parity bucket to recover should often have more records than a typical data bucket, hence a higher recovery cost. It has indeed as many records as the most loaded data bucket in the group. The deviation should obviously increase with m. It becomes more likely that some data bucket in the group has more records than the average load. The LH* file with 70% load is however known to have only a few overflow records. Hence, regardless of m, a parity bucket with more than b records in such file is unlikely as well.

Notice finally that Table 2 proves globally an excellent scalability of the LH*$_{RS}$ file manipulations. The costs are either independent of the file size M, or typically increase about as little as possible, basically through the necessary increase to k. We recall from Section 2.2 that to scale k with M is mandatory for the reliability. Section 5.4 analyzes this issue more in depth.

5.2 Storage

Each bucket group carries typically k or sometimes $k+1$ parity buckets and bucket is the storage allocation unit for both data and parity records. The file storage overhead, is thus typically k/m. This is the minimal overhead for any k-available file, regardless of the parity calculus method used [H&a94]. The additional overhead of up to $1/m$ constitutes the price for the scalable availability. This is also the minimal cost of this capability.

The overhead storage at each parity bucket server for RS calculus specific data is in practice negligible. One needs stable storage basically only for the m-element single column of **P**, and for the 2^f or $3*2^f$ elements of the log multiplication table. The inversion of the matrix **H** requires only $2m^2$ elements of temporary storage.

5.3 Parity Calculus Time

Parity encoding and decoding speed depend on the network and CPU performance. The decoding also strongly depend on the choice of the group size m whose larger values benefit the storage overhead but make the recovery costs higher in turn. Easy but lengthy evaluations that we skip here show that on a rather typical site with 400 MHZ CPU, and 100 Mb/s network the resulting times should remain acceptable. For quite large $m = 32$, the record recovery time of 1KB records stored in RAM buckets is in the order of milliseconds. Assuming for instance the data bucket capacity of $b = 3000$ records, the bucket recovery should take less than a minute. For similar disk buckets, the time for record recovery is about a second and bucket recovery takes a few minutes.

5.4 Reliability

The *reliability* is the probability that all the data are available, i.e., that there is no catastrophic failure. It depends on b, m, k, M and the probability p that a single bucket is unavailable. One can estimate the reliability of an LH*$_{RS}$ file through formulae using these parameters developed for LH*$_{SA}$, [LMR98]. Both schemes use record grouping. Their differences influence the storage overhead and other performance factors but not the basic calculation of reliability. Same parameters lead to the same estimate.

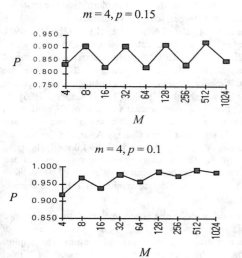

Figure 3 Uncontrolled reliability of an LH*$_{RS}$ file

Figure 3 shows two simulated curves of the reliability P for an LH*$_{RS}$ file with uncontrolled reliability obtained in this way. The values of p chosen seem conservatively realistic [S99]. They mean that a site is unavailable on the average for 3-5 days per month. Each minimum of P is at the size m^i that starts next scaling up of k for the $(k+1)$-availability. Each maximum is at the size $2m^i$ when the (entire) file becomes $(k+1)$-available and $k := k+1$. The files scale to $M=1024$ buckets, i.e., somewhere between $1 \div 100$ Tbyte. In both cases, without the scalable availability, P would start continuously decreasing from $M = 8$, instead of remaining above the value close to the reliability of a single bucket, respectively, above 92% and 82%. For $p = 0.15$ the successive minima of P have the tendency to remain about the same, while for $p = 0.1$ they increase progressively. This tendency would be even stronger for lower p. One may then delay the increase of the availability level k with respect to the basic schema, through the reliability control. The threshold P_{min} on P value could be $P_{min} = 0.9$, i.e., the

reliability $1-p$ of a single bucket. Alternatively, one may choose larger group size m.

The curve for $p = 0.15$ shows in contrast that the reliability evolution is close to optimal. The minimal value of P stays automatically about 0.85. For even higher p, and same m, the uncontrolled reliability would not suffice and the curve would decrease.

Both curves show that, the reliability control is useful for a multicomputer with sites characterized by $p \leq 0.1$. For less reliable sites with $p > 0.15$, it appears necessary in practice, as $m < 4$ seems the smallest useful choice. Detailed analysis in [LMR98] confirms this behavior. While not only higher p but also a larger m may make the reliability control necessary, these results show nevertheless that for $p << 0.1$, the uncontrolled reliability may suffice for a quite large m. For instance for $p = 0.01$, one may choose $m = 16$ and for $p = 0.005$, even $m = 32$ suffices to keep $P \geq 99\%$ up to $M = 32K$.

6 VARIANTS

An application may benefit from selected performance tuning. Specific variants of the basic schema may be designed to address this concern. First, there are numerous variants of LH* schema known, their choice impacts the performance of the LH*$_{RS}$ data file. They differ by the internal structure of buckets, the split algorithm, the strategy for the load factor control... Some variants do not even have the coordinator.

There are also issues specific to the parity management. The implementation choices for GF multiplication, including the data structures for the tables, impact the calculus speed. For instance, we can avoid the calculus modulo 2^f-1 as in Section 2.3.1, and thus increase the speed of the method. These additions or subtractions find an entry in the anti-logarithm table. If one replicates the anti-logarithm table once above and once below the table used in contiguous memory location, then the non-modulo operations suffice. The trade-off is thus to double the table size. The resulting tables have $4*2^f$ entries. In particular, $GF(2^8)$ requires then 1 KB instead of only 512 B.

Furthermore, other algorithms are known for matrix inversion and to generate matrix **G**. The internal structure of a parity bucket obviously influences its access and storage performance. The bucket recovery calculus can be made parallel between the participated buckets. The algorithms recovering from specific catastrophic failures can be added. Finally, the Reed Solomon Codes used are not the only possibility. Some other codes are potentially attractive as well, [ABC97], [H&a94], [BFT98].

The storage of parity buckets allows for interesting optimizations. The basic scheme stores parity buckets at a dedicated servers. This overhead to the number of servers may itself bother an application. Next, while the searches in normal mode do not concern the parity servers, a parity bucket is involved in every update of a data bucket in the group. The processing load from data modification at a parity server is hence about m times larger than at a data server. An application with a large amount of data modifications could see the parity servers becoming bottlenecks.

The correctness of the parity calculus does not depend on parity buckets being stored at separate servers. It merely requires that no server contains two buckets in the same segment. To better balance the load, one may replace then a single parity bucket with m buckets storing b/m records each, stored the different pieces at different servers. The m buckets can form a simple hash subfile.

This variant equalizes the load from of the data modifications. On the negative side, it requires more parity servers and sees more messaging during splits and reconstructions.

To decrease the number of parity servers, one may share a server between a data and a parity bucket. One simple rule locates the ith parity bucket of group j with the ith data bucket of group $j+1$. Figure 2 may be seen as illustrating this rule. It guarantees that all buckets in a segment are stored at different server. It can be easily extended to the above discussed parity subfiles. In this scheme, every server carries at most one data bucket and zero, or some parity buckets. The servers carrying data for the first group will never have parity data. In turn, some servers to serve the data buckets of the next group to be generated carry only parity buckets, but not yet data buckets. The "dark size of the Moon" is obviously increased storage use at each server and processing load.

Finally, one can have the servers for data of group 0 temporarily carrying the parity buckets for the last existing group. If the file expands further, these buckets move to the adequate locations, being replaced by new last buckets. This simple loop-back strategy eliminates the additional parity servers entirely. It minimizes the number of servers for the file to M, required anyway for the data buckets. Notice the potential interest of this variant to the users of the current parallel DBMSs. Their currently 0-available hash or even range-partitioning methods, could be enhanced to the high-availability at no additional hardware cost.

7 RELATED WORK

There were countless high-availability schemes for a single site, usually 1-available and using some RAID-like striping. A few schemes appeared for the (static) $k > 1$ k-availability in this context, [BM93], [BBM93], [H&a94], and [ABC97] recently. There were also studies for the distributed environment, e.g. [SG90] showing the inefficiency of any trivial striping. Deeper discussion of all these schemes, including SDDS schemes with mirroring or replication mentioned in the Introduction, is in [LMR98]. However, besides the LH*$_{RS}$, the only schemes known to satisfy all our goals, including the moderate storage overhead for the high-availability, are the other LH* schemes using the record grouping mentioned in the Introduction. Their mutual comparison appears as follows [LS99].

LH*$_{RS}$ may offer substantially lower overhead than LH*$_{SA}$. The reason is that the number k of parity records to make a group k-available is always exactly the theoretical minimum k/m. This is a remote consequence of the MDS property of RS-codes, [MS97].

LH*$_{RS}$ record recovery cost should typically be lower than that of LH*$_{g}$. It may be higher or lower than that of LH*$_{SA}$. This is due to more complex parity calculus of LH*$_{RS}$ on the one hand, or to possibly more messages for LH*$_{SA}$ to explore multiple groups, on the other hand.

Variants minimizing the number of the file servers through sharing of data and parity buckets are known only for LH*$_{RS}$. Such variant seem at best more difficult to design for the two other schemes.

If 1-availability suffices, then LH*$_{g}$ has the smallest split cost. Its record groups are location independent and there is no need to recalculate the parity data during splits. Generalizing the parity calculus to RS-codes allows perhaps for a k-available variant of LH*$_{g}$ retaining that property [LMRS99].

Finally, LH*$_{SA}$ may often recover from l-bucket failure where $l > k$ which would be catastrophic for LH*$_{RS}$. The difference may be quite substantial. For instance, a 2available LH*$_{SA}$ file may recover records from any $l >> 2$ unavailable buckets in the same group. LH*$_{RS}$ can accommodate at most 3 unavailable buckets per group in a 2-available file, and only, provided it started to build the 3-availability. Notice that LH*$_{RS}$ also has good cases, although the overall balance seems in favor of LH*$_{SA}$. For instance, in our example file with record group size $m = 4$, made 2-available, we can recover from the unavailability of buckets 0,1,4, and 5. This failure is unrecoverable in a 2-available LH*$_{SA}$ file with the same groups.

8 CONCLUSION

LH*$_{RS}$ schema uses the concept of record grouping and the Reed Salomon codes to provide scalable, distributed and high-availability files, badly needed by modern applications. Its interesting properties, including the scalable availability, near-optimal access performance and storage use efficiency, should prove attractive. The schema offers distinct advantages over the other high-availability schemes known.

Among potential applications, there are modern database systems, that need continuously larger scalable databases, and for which the parallel access is already a must [FBW97], [B&al95], [IBM99]. Many of the existing databases or warehouses grow very rapidly. The well-known UPS multidatabase passed from 4 to 13 TB between 97 and 98, and many other similar examples are known. The multimedia servers also start using multicomputers and the success may make them scaling big [B&al95], [H96]. In the Web arena, more and more systems maintain TB of data on large multicomputers. This is the case of the 166–site multicomputer of Inktomi at Santa Clara, CA, and of the 100-site of Yahoo in Vienna, VA, which is also built by Inktomi, [I98]. An implementation of SDDSs is under study for such applications [G99]. For all these needs, both scalability and 24/7 availability are critical. The already mentioned mishap of E-Bay is here to stay as the reminder.

Future work should include the prototype implementation and deeper analysis of various design issues, as well as of performance factors discussed in the related sections. This applies also to the variants. These goals start to be addressed for Wintel multicomputers, [L00]. The prototype described confirms the feasibility of the schema for that environment, and seems to perform as expected in Section 5.

On the other hand, one should port the RS parity schema to other known 0-availaible SDDS schemes. This should especially concern the RP*schema. Finally, one should study the other erasure correcting codes referred to in Section 6.

9 ACKNOWLEDGEMENTS

This research was partly sponsored by a Grant of IBM Almaden Res. Cntr., Storage Systems Div., and by a Grant of Microsoft Research. We also thank Mario Blum, Walter Burkhard, Jim Gray, Mattias Ljungström, Jai Menon, and Tore Risch for helpful discussions.

APPENDIX A

Let n be the maximal segment size and m the maximal group size. We recall that the generator matrix $\mathbf{G}$ of an RS-code has m rows and n columns. The left $m \times m$ submatrix of $\mathbf{G}$ is the identity matrix $\mathbf{I}$, since we use a *systematic* RS code. Any square submatrix formed from any m different columns of **G** is invertible.

We derive matrix **G** from a Vandermonde matrix **V**. **V** has m rows and n columns, these we index by the n elements $g_j \in GF(n)$, $j = 0, ..., n-1$. We number the columns and rows from 0 and order the field elements so that $g_0 = 0$ and $g_1 = 1$. Coefficient $v_{i,j}$ located in the ith row and the jth column of **V** is then defined to be the jth element of the Galois Field raised to the ith power that is:

$$v_{i,j} = g_j^i.$$

Thus,

$$\mathbf{V} = \begin{pmatrix} 1 & 1 & 1 & 1 & \cdots \\ g_0 & g_1 & g_2 & g_3 & \\ g_0^2 & g_1^2 & g_2^2 & g_3^2 & \\ g_0^3 & g_1^3 & g_2^3 & g_3^3 & \\ \vdots & & & & \ddots \end{pmatrix}$$

Row 0 contains only ones since for every j, $g_j^0 = 1$. Since $g_0 = 0$, the first column contains otherwise zeroes. Since $g_1 = 1$, the 2nd column contains only 1's. Vandermonde showed the determinant of any square submatrix of **V** consisting of m columns generated by elements g_i to be

$$\det \mathbf{V} = \prod_{i<j} g_j - g_i \neq 0.$$

It follows that any square m by m submatrix of **V** is invertible. This property holds also for the *extended* V with last column 0, 0, ... 0, 1 that we used to generate our example **G** in Section 2.3.4. We now give the details of our transformation of **V** into **G** = **I**|**P** where **I** is the identity matrix. We denote **m**[i,j], $i,j \geq 0$, the coefficient of matrix **m** in row i and column j. We denote the jth row of the current matrix with $\mathbf{m}_j$. We use *elementary row transformation* [MM92]. These are multiplying a row by a scalar, exchanging two rows, and adding a multiple of one row to another. We denote these transformations by $\mathbf{m}_j \Leftarrow a\mathbf{m}_j$, $\mathbf{m}_j \Leftrightarrow \mathbf{m}_i$, $\mathbf{m}_j \Leftarrow \mathbf{m}_j + a\mathbf{m}_i$, $a \in GF(2^f)$ respectively. Our algorithm uses up to m row transformations to transform a column into a unit vector. The first column is already the first unit vector. The second column has already the one in position [1,1], and we add the second row to all the other rows resulting in the second unit vector for the second column. This operation retains the form of the first column. We now change the third column into the unit vector. The diagonal element **m**[2,2] there is obviously non-zero. We multiply the third row with the inverse of this element, so that the coefficient **m**[2,2] is now 1. Then we generate zeroes in the third column by adding **m**[$i,2$]$\mathbf{m}_2$ to all other rows $\mathbf{m}_i$. This operation does not change the first and second column. Continuing in this manner, we transform m left columns of **V** into unit vectors, i.e. the **I** submatrix. We give pseudo-code, à la [PTVF92], in Figure 4:

```
    Initialize m = V;
for all columns i = 0, ..., m-1 do
        {
(4)     mi ⇐ m[i,i]-1mi;
        for all rows j = 0, ..., m-1, but j≠i, do
                mj ⇐ mj – m[j,i] mi;
        }
```

Figure 4 Pseudo-code to transform V **into generator matrix G.**

Our inversion algorithm proceeds similarly. We form the $m \times 2m$ matrix **H**|**I** from the $m \times m$ invertible matrix **H**. We transform **H**|**I** into **I**|$\mathbf{H}^{-1}$ using the algorithm in Figure 4, with one exception. As the diagonal element **m**[i,i] in line (4) may be zero, we replace line (4) with :

(4a)　　　if **m**[i,i] = = 0 do
(4b)　　　{
(4c)　　　　find a j > i such that **m**[j,i] $\neq$ 0;
(4d)　　　　$\mathbf{m}_j \Leftrightarrow \mathbf{m}_i$;
(4e)　　　}
(4f)　　　$\mathbf{m}_i \Leftarrow \mathbf{m}[i,i]^{-1}\mathbf{m}_i$;

REFERENCES

[ABC97]　　Alvarez, G., Burkhard, W., Cristian, F. Tolerating Multiple-Failures in RAID Architecture with Optimal Storage and Uniform Declustering. Intl. Symp. On Comp. Arch., ISCA-97, 1997.

[B&al95]　　Baru, W., C., & al. DB2 Parallel Edition. IBM Syst. Journal, 34, 2, 1995. 292-322.

[B99]　　Bartalos, G. Internet: D-Day at eBay. Yahoo INDIVIDUAL INVESTOR ONLINE, (Jul 19, 1999).

[B99a]　　Bertino & al. Indexing Techn. for Advanced Database Systems. Kluver, 1999.

[BBM93]　　Blaum, M., Bruck, J., Menon, J. EVENODD: An Efficient Scheme for Tolerating Double Disk Failures in RAID Architectures.　IEEE Trans. on Computers, Vol. C-44, No. 2, pp. 192-202, February 1995.

[BFT98] Blaum, M & al. Array Codes, Handbook of Coding Theory. V.S. Pless and W.C. Huffman, (ed.), Elsevier Science B.V., 1998.

[BV98] Breitbart, Y. Vingralek, R. Distributed and Scalable B+ tree Data Structures. Workshop on Distr. Data and Struct., 1998, Carleton Scientific (publ.)

[BM93]　　W. A. Burkhard, J. Menon: Disk Array Storage System Reliability. 22rd Intl. Symp. on Fault Tolerant Computing, Toulouse, June 1993, 432-441.

[CACM97]　　Special Issue on High-Performance Computing. Comm. Of ACM. (Oct. 1997).

[G99] Gribble, S. Cluster-Based Internet Services with SDDS. Master Th. UC Berkeley, 1999.

[H96] Haskin, R. Schmuck, F. The Tiger Shark File System. COMPCON-96, 1996.

[H&a94] Hellerstein, L, Gibson, G., Karp, R., Katz, R. Patterson, D. Coding Techniques for Handling Failures in Large Disk Arrays. Algorithmica, 1994, 12, 182-208.

[I98] Inktomi Corporation. http://www.inktomi.com/.

[IBM99] Breaking the Scalability Barrier on Windows NT. http://www.software.ibm.com/data/pubs/papers/nt-scale/

[K98] Knuth, D. THE ART OF COMPUTER PROGRAMMING. Vol. 3 Sorting and Searching. 2nd Ed. Addison-Wesley, 1998, 780.

[KLR96] J. Karlson, W. Litwin, T. Risch. LH*LH: A Scalable High Performance Data Structure for Switched Multicomputers. Extending Database Technology, EDBT96, Springer Verlag.

[L80] W. Litwin. Linear Hashing: A New Tool for File and Table Addressing. Reprint from VLDB80 in Readings in Databases, M. Stonebraker, 2nd Edition, Morgan Kaufmann Publishers, 1994.

[L97] Lindberg., R. A Java Implementation of a Highly Available Scalable and Distributed Data Structure LH*g. Master Th. LiTH-IDA-Ex-97/65. U. Linkoping, 1997, 62.

[L&al97] Litwin, W., Neimat, M.-A. Levy, G., Ndiaye, S., Seck, T. LH*$_S$: a high-availability and high-security Scalable Distributed Data Structure. IEEE-Res. Issues in Data Eng. (RIDE-97), 1997.

[L00] Ljungström, M. Implementing LH*$_{RS}$: A Scalable Distributed High-Availability Data Structure. Master Th. (Feb. 2000), CS Dep., U. Linkoping, Suede.

[LMR98] Litwin, W., Menon J., Risch, T..LH* with Scalable Availability. IBM Almaden Res. Rep. RJ 10121 (91937), (May 1998), (subm.).

[LMRS99] Litwin, W., Menon, J.Risch, T., Schwarz, Th. Design Issues For Scalable Availability LH* Schemes with Record Grouping. DIMACS Workshop on Distributed Data and Structures. Carleton Scientific, 1999.

[LNS93] Litwin, W., Neimat, M.-A., Schneider, D. LH* : Linear Hashing for Distributed Files. ACM-SIGMOD Intl. Conf. on Management of Data, 1993.

[LNS96] Litwin, W., Neimat, M.-A., Schneider, D. LH* - A Scalable Distributed Data Structure. ACM Trans. on Database Systems, Dec. 1996.

[LN96] W. Litwin, M.-A. Neimat: "High-Availability LH* Schemes with Mirroring", Intl. Conf. on Coop. Inf. Systems, (COOPIS). IEEE Press 1996.

[LR97] Litwin W., Risch, T. LH*g: a High-Availability Scalable Distributed Data Structure through Record Grouping. Res. Rep. CERIA, U. Dauphine & U. Linkoping (May. 1997).

[LS99] Litwin, W., Schwarz, Th. LH*$_{RS}$: A High-Availability Scalable Distributed Data Structure using Reed Solomon Codes. Res. Rep. CERIA, U. Dauphine (Sept. 1999).

[M97] Gates, B. The Microsoft Scalability Day http://204.203.124.10/backoffice/scalability/coverage.htm

[MM92] Marcus, M., Minc, H. A Survey of Matrix Theory and Matrix Inequalities, Dover, New York, 1992.

[P98] President's Inf. Techn. Advisory Comm. Interim Rep. To the Pres. Of the United States. August 1998.

[MS97] MacWilliams, F. J., Sloane, N. J. A. The Theory of Error Correcting Codes, Elsevier / North Holland, Amsterdam, 1997.

[PTVF92] Press, W. H., Teukolsky, S. A., Vetterling W. T., Flannery, B. P. Numerical Recipes in C: The Art of Scientific Computation, 2nd ed., Cambridge University Press, 1992.

[R98] Ramakrishnan, K. Database Management Systems. McGraw Hill, 1998.

[S99] Smith, D. The Cost of Lost Data. Res. Rep. School of Business and Management, Pepperdine University, 1999.

[SDDS] SDDS-bibliography. http://ceria.dauphine.fr/SDDS-bibliograhie.html

[SG90] M. Stonebraker, G. Schloss: "Distributed RAID – A New Multiple Copy Algorithm", 6th Intl. IEEE Conf. on Data Engineering, 1990, IEEE Press, pp. 430-437.

[VBW94] Vingralek R., Breitbart Y., G. Weikum. Distributed File Organization with Scalable Cost/Performance. ACM-SIGMOD Intl. Conf. on Management of Data, 1994, 253-264.

[VBW98] Vingralek R., Breitbart Y., Weikum G. SNOWBALL: Scalable Storage on Networks of Workstations with Balanced Load. Distr. and Par. Databases, 6, 2, 1998.

Efficient and Extensible Algorithms for Multi Query Optimization

Prasan Roy
I.I.T. Bombay

S. Seshadri
Bell Labs.

S. Sudarshan
I.I.T. Bombay

Siddhesh Bhobe
PSPL Ltd. Pune

{prasan,sudarsha}@cse.iitb.ernet.in
seshadri@research.bell-labs.com, siddhesh@pspl.co.in

Abstract

Complex queries are becoming commonplace, with the growing use of decision support systems. These complex queries often have a lot of common sub-expressions, either within a single query, or across multiple such queries run as a batch. Multi-query optimization aims at exploiting common sub-expressions to reduce evaluation cost. Multi-query optimization has hither-to been viewed as impractical, since earlier algorithms were exhaustive, and explore a doubly exponential search space.

In this paper we demonstrate that multi-query optimization using heuristics is practical, and provides significant benefits. We propose three cost-based heuristic algorithms: Volcano-SH and Volcano-RU, which are based on simple modifications to the Volcano search strategy, and a greedy heuristic. Our greedy heuristic incorporates novel optimizations that improve efficiency greatly. Our algorithms are designed to be easily added to existing optimizers. We present a performance study comparing the algorithms, using workloads consisting of queries from the TPC-D benchmark. The study shows that our algorithms provide significant benefits over traditional optimization, at a very acceptable overhead in optimization time.

1 Introduction

Complex queries are becoming commonplace, especially due to the advent of automatic tools that help analyze information from large data warehouses. These complex queries often have a lot of common sub-expressions since i) they make extensive use of views which are referred to multiple times in the query and ii) many of them are correlated nested queries in which parts of the inner subquery may not depend on the outer query variables, thus forming a common sub-expression for repeated invocations of the inner query.

The scope for finding common sub-expressions increases greatly if we consider a set of queries executed as a batch. For example, SQL-3 stored procedures may invoke

several queries, which can be executed as a batch. Data analysis/reporting often requires a batch of queries to be executed. The work of [SHT$^+$99] on using relational databases for storing XML data, has found that queries on XML data, written in a language such as XML-QL, need to be translated into a sequence of relational queries. The task of updating a set of related materialized views also generates related queries with common sub-expressions [RSS96].

In this paper, we address the problem of optimizing sets of queries which may have common sub-expressions; this problem is referred to as *multi-query optimization*. We note here that common subexpressions are possible even *within* a single query; the techniques we develop deal with such intra-query common subexpressions as well.

Traditional query optimizers are not appropriate for optimizing queries with common sub expressions, since they make locally optimal choices, and may miss globally optimal plans as the following example demonstrates.

Example 1.1 Let Q_1 and Q_2 be two queries whose locally optimal plans (i.e., individual best plans) are $(R \bowtie S) \bowtie P$ and $(R \bowtie T) \bowtie S$ respectively. The best plans for Q_1 and Q_2 do not have any common sub-expressions. However, if we choose the alternative plan $(R \bowtie S) \bowtie T$ (which may not be locally optimal) for Q_2, then, it is clear that $R \bowtie S$ is a common sub-expression and can be computed once and used in both queries. This alternative with sharing of $R \bowtie S$ may be the globally optimal choice.

On the other hand, blindly using a common sub-expression may not always lead to a globally optimal strategy. For example, there may be cases where the cost of joining the expression $R \bowtie S$ with T is very large compared to the cost of the plan $(R \bowtie T) \bowtie S$; in such cases it may make no sense to reuse $R \bowtie S$ even if it were available. □

Example 1.1 illustrates that the job of multi-query optimization, over and above that of ordinary query optimization, is to (i) *recognize the possibilities of shared computation*, and (ii) *modify the optimizer search strategy to explicitly account for shared computation and find a globally optimal plan*.

While there has been work on multi-query optimization in the past ([Sel88, SSN94, PS88]), prior work has concentrated primarily on exhaustive algorithms. Other work has concentrated on finding common subexpressions as a post-phase to query optimization [Fin82, SV98], but this gives limited scope for cost improvement, or has considered only the limited class of OLAP queries [ZDNS98]. (We discuss related work in detail in Section 7.) The search space for multi-query optimization is doubly exponential in the size of the queries, and exhaustive strategies are therefore impractical; as a result, multi-query optimization was hitherto considered too expensive to be useful.

In this paper we show how to make multi-query optimization *practical*, by developing novel heuristic algorithms, and presenting a performance study that demonstrates their practical benefits.

Our algorithms are based on an AND-OR DAG representation [Rou82, GM93] to compactly represents alternative query plans. The DAG representation ensures that they are *extensible*, in that they can easily handle new operations and transformation rules. The DAG can be constructed as in [GM93], with some extensions to ensure that all common sub-expressions are detected and unified. The DAG construction also takes into account sharing of computation based on "subsumption" – examples of such sharing include computing $\sigma_{A<5}(E)$ from the result of $\sigma_{A<10}(E)$.

The task of the heuristic optimization algorithms is then to decide what subexpressions should be materialized and shared. Two of the heuristics we present, Volcano-SH and Volcano-RU are lightweight modifications of the Volcano optimization algorithm. The third heuristic is a greedy strategy which iteratively picks the subexpression that gives the maximum benefit (reduction in cost) if it is materialized and reused. One of our important contributions here lies in three novel optimizations of the greedy algorithm implementation, that make it very efficient. Our performance studies show that each of these optimizations leads to a great improvement in the performance of the greedy algorithm.

In addition to choosing what intermediate expression results to materialize and reuse, our optimization framework also chooses physical properties, such as sort order, for the materialized results. Our algorithms also handle the choice of what (temporary) indices to create on materialized results/database relations.

Our algorithms can be easily extended to perform multi-query optimization on nested queries as well as multiple invocations of parameterized queries (with different parameter values). The AND-OR DAG framework we exploit is used in least two commercial database systems, from Microsoft and Tandem. Our algorithms can, however, be extended to work with System R style bottom-up optimizers.

We conducted a performance study of our multi-query optimization algorithms, using queries from the TPC-D benchmark as well as other queries based on the TPC-D schema. Our study demonstrates not only savings based on estimated cost, but also significant improvements in actual run times on a commercial database.

Our performance results show that our multi-query optimization algorithms give significant benefits over single query optimization, at an acceptable extra optimization time cost. The extra optimization time is more than compensated by the execution time savings. All three heuristics beat the basic Volcano algorithm, but in general greedy produced the best plans, followed by Volcano-RU and Volcano-SH.

We believe that in addition to our technical contributions, another of our contributions lies in showing how to engineer a practical multi-query optimization system — one which can smoothly integrate extensions, such as indexes and nested queries, allowing them to work together seamlessly. In summer '99, our algorithms were partially prototyped on the Microsoft SQL Server optimizer, and multi-query optimization is currently being evaluated by Microsoft for possible inclusion in SQL Server.

2 Setting Up The Search Space For Multi-Query Optimization

As we mentioned in Section 1, the job of a multi-query optimizer is to (i) recognize possibilities of shared computation (thus essentially setting up the search space by identifying common sub-expressions) and (ii) modify the optimizer search strategy to explicitly account for shared computation and find a globally optimal plan. Both of the above tasks are important and crucial for a multi-query optimizer but are *orthogonal*. In other words, the details of the search strategy do not depend on how aggressively we identify common sub-expressions (of course, the efficacy of the strategy does). We have explored both the above tasks in detail, but choose to emphasize the search strategy component of our work in this paper, for lack of space. However, we outline the high level ideas and the intuition behind our algorithms for identifying common sub-expresions in this section and refer to the full version of the paper [RSSB98] for details at the appropriate locations in this section.

Before we describe our algorithms for identifying common-sub expressions, we describe the AND-OR DAG representation of queries. An AND–OR DAG is a directed acyclic graph whose nodes can be divided into AND-nodes and OR-nodes; the AND-nodes have only OR-nodes as children and OR-nodes have only AND-nodes as children.

An AND-node in the AND-OR DAG corresponds to an algebraic operation, such as the join operation ($\bowtie$) or a select operation (σ). It represents the expression defined by the operation and its inputs. Hereafter, we refer to the AND-nodes as *operation nodes*. An OR-node in the AND-OR DAG represents a set of logical expressions that generate the same result set; the set of such expressions is defined by the children AND nodes of the OR node, and their inputs. We shall refer to the OR-nodes as *equivalence nodes* henceforth.

The given query tree is initially represented directly in the AND-OR DAG formulation. For example, the query tree of Figure 1(a) is initially represented in the AND-OR DAG

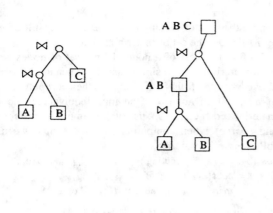

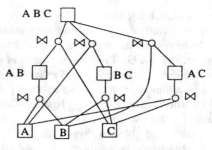

(Commutativity not shown - every join node has
another join node with inputs exchanged, below
the same equivalence node)

(a) Initial Query   (b) DAG representation of query   (c) Expanded DAG after transformations

Figure 1: Initial Query and DAG Representations

formulation, as shown in Figure 1(b). Equivalence nodes (OR-nodes) are shown as boxes, while operation nodes (AND-nodes) are shown as circles.

The initial AND-OR DAG is then expanded by applying all possible transformations on every node of the initial query DAG representing the given set of queries. Suppose the only transformations possible are join associativity and commutativity. Then the plans $A \bowtie (B \bowtie C)$ and $(A \bowtie C) \bowtie B$, as well as several plans equivalent to these modulo commutativity can be obtained by transformations on the initial AND-OR-DAG of Figure 1(b). These are represented in the DAG shown in Figure 1(c). We shall refer to the DAG after all transformations have been applied as the *expanded DAG*. Note that the expanded DAG has exactly one equivalence node for every subset of $\{A, B, C\}$; the node represents all ways of computing the joins of the relations in that subset. For lack of space we omit details of the expanded DAG generation algorithm; details may be found in [RSSB98].

2.1 Extensions to DAG Generation For Multi-Query Optimization

To apply multi-query optimization to a batch of queries, the queries are represented together in a single DAG, sharing subexpressions. To make the DAG rooted, a pseudo operation node is created, which does nothing, but has the root equivalence nodes of all the queries as its inputs.

We now outline two extensions to the DAG generation algorithm to aid multi-query optimization.

The first extension deals with identification of common subexpressions. If a query contains two subexpressions that are logically equivalent, but syntactically different, (e.g., $(A \bowtie B) \bowtie C$, and $A \bowtie (B \bowtie C)$) the initial query DAG would contain two different equivalence nodes representing the two subexpressions. We modify the Volcano DAG generation algorithm so that whenever it finds nodes to be equivalent (after applying join associativity) it *unifies* the nodes, replacing them by a single equivalence node.

The Volcano algorithm uses a hashing scheme to detect repeated derivations, and avoids creating duplicate equivalence nodes due to cyclic derivations (e.g., expression $e1$ is transformed to $e2$, which is then transformed back to $e1$). Our modification additionally uses the hashing scheme to detect and unify duplicate equivalence nodes that were either pre-existing or got created by transformations from different expressions. Details of unification may be found in [RSSB98].

The second extension is to detect and handle *subsumption*. For example, suppose two subexpressions $e1$: $\sigma_{A<5}(E)$ and $e2$: $\sigma_{A<10}(E)$ appear in the query. The result of $e1$ can be obtained from the result of $e2$ by an additional selection, i.e., $\sigma_{A<5}(E) \equiv \sigma_{A<5}(\sigma_{A<10}(E))$. To represent this possibility we add an extra operation node $\sigma_{A<5}$ in the DAG, between $e1$ and $e2$. Similarly, given $e3$: $\sigma_{A=5}(E)$ and $e4$: $\sigma_{A=10}(E)$, we can introduce a new equivalence node $e5$: $\sigma_{A=5 \vee A=10}(E)$ and add new derivations of $e3$ and $e4$ from $e5$. The new node represents the sharing of accesses between the two selection. In general, given a number of selections on an expression E, we create a single new node representing the disjunction of all the selection conditions. Similar derivations also help with aggregations. For example, if we have $e6$: $_{dno}\mathcal{G}_{sum(Sal)}(E)$ and $e7$: $_{age}\mathcal{G}_{sum(Sal)}(E)$, we can introduce a new equivalence node $e8$: $_{dno,age}\mathcal{G}_{sum(Sal)}(E)$ and add derivations of $e6$ and $e7$ from equivalence node $e8$ by further groupbys on dno and age.

The idea of applying an operation (such as $\sigma_{A<5}$ on one subexpression to generate another has been proposed earlier [Rou82, Sel88, SV98]. Integrating such options into the AND-OR DAG, as we do, clearly separates the space of alternative plans (represented by the DAG) from the optimization algorithms. Thereby, it simplifies our optimization algorithms, allowing them to avoid dealing explicitly with such derivations.

2.2 Physical AND-OR DAG

Properties of the results of an expression, such as sort order, that do not form part of the logical data model are called *physical properties* [GM93]. Physical properties of intermediate results are important, since e.g. if an intermediate result is sorted on a join attribute, the join cost can potentially be reduced by using a merge join. It is straightforward to refine the above AND-OR DAG representation to represent physical properties and obtain a physical AND-OR DAG. [1] Our search algorithms can be easily understood on the above AND-OR DAG representation (without physical properties), although they actually work on physical DAGs. Therefore, for brevity, we do not explicitly consider physical properties further; for details see [RSSB98]. Our implementation indeed handles physical properties.

3 Reuse Based Multi-Query Optimization Algorithms

In this section we study a class of multi-query optimization algorithms based on reusing results computed for other parts of the query. We present these as extensions of the Volcano optimization algorithm. Before we describe the extensions, in Section 3.1, we very briefly outline the basic Volcano optimization algorithm, and how to extend it to find best plans given some nodes in the DAG are materialized. Sections 3.2 and 3.3 then present two of our heuristic algorithms, Volcano-SH and Volcano-RU.

3.1 Volcano Optimization Algorithm and Materialized Views

The Volcano optimization algorithm operates on the expanded DAG generated earlier. It finds the best plan for each node by performing a depth first traversal of the DAG starting from that node as follows. Costs are defined for operation and equivalence nodes. The cost of an operation node o is defined as follows:

$cost(o) = $ cost of executing $(o) + \Sigma_{e_i \in children(o)} cost(e_i)$

The children of o (if any) are equivalence nodes.[2] The cost of an equivalence node e is given as

$cost(e) = min\{cost(o_i) | o_i \in children(e)\}$

0 if the node has no children (i.e., it is a base relation).

Volcano also caches the best plan it finds for each equivalence node, in case the node is re-visited during the depth first search of the DAG. A branch and bound pruning is also performed by carrying around a cost limit; for simplicity, we disregard pruning in this paper. For lack of space we omit details, but refer readers to [GM93].

Now we consider how to extend Volcano to find best plans, given that (expressions corresponding to) some equivalence nodes in the DAG are materialized. Let $reusecost(m)$

---

denote the cost of reusing the materialized result of m, and let M denote the set of materialized nodes.

To find the cost of a node given a set of nodes M have been materialized, we simply use the Volcano cost formulae above, with the following change. When computing the cost of a operation node o, if an input equivalence node e is materialized (i.e., in M), use the minimum of $reusecost(e)$ and $cost(e)$ when computing $cost(o)$. Thus, we use the following expression instead:

$cost(o) = $ cost of executing $(o) + \Sigma_{e_i \in children(o)} C(e_i)$
$C(e_i) = cost(e_i)$ if $e_i \notin M$;
$\qquad min(cost(e_i), reusecost(e_i))$ if $e_i \in M$.

3.2 The Volcano-SH Algorithm

In our first strategy, which we call Volcano-SH, the expanded DAG is first optimized using the basic Volcano optimization algorithm. The best plan computed for the virtual root is the combination of the Volcano best plans for each individual query.

The best plans produced by the Volcano optimization algorithm may have common subexpressions; thus nodes in the DAG may occur in the best plans of more than one query. The results of such shared nodes can be materialized when they are first computed, and reused later. Since materialization of a node involves storing the result to the disk, and we assume pipelined execution of operators, it may be possible for recomputation of a node to be cheaper than the cost of materializing and reusing the node.

The Volcano-SH algorithm therefore decides in a cost based manner which of the nodes to materialize and share, as outlined below.

Let us consider first a naive (and incomplete) solution. Consider an equivalence node e. Let $cost(e)$ denote the computation cost of node e. Let $numuses(e)$ denote the number of times node e is used in course of execution of the plan. Let $matcost(e)$ denote the cost of materializing node e. As before, $reusecost(e)$ denote the cost of reusing the materialized result of e. Then, we decide to materialize e if $cost(e) + matcost(e) + reusecost(e) \times (numuses(e) - 1) < numuses(e) \times cost(e)$. The left hand side of this inequality gives the cost of materializing the result when first computed, and using the materialized result thereafter; the right hand side gives the cost of the alternative wherein the result is not materialized but recomputed on every use. The above test can be simplified to

$matcost(e)/(numuses(e) - 1) + reusecost(e) < cost(e)$ (1)

The problem with the above solution is that $numuses(e)$ and $cost(e)$ both depend on what other nodes have been materialized, For instance, suppose node e_1 is used twice in computing node e_2, and node e_2 is used twice in computing node e_3. Now, if no node is materialized, e_1 is used four times in computing e_3. If e_2 is materialized, e_1 gets used twice in computing e_2, and e_2 gets computed only once. Thus, materializing e_2 can reduce both $numuses(e_1)$ and $cost(e_3)$.

The Volcano-SH algorithm resolves this problem heuristically by traversing the tree bottom-up. As each equivalence

---

[1] For example, an equivalence node is refined to multiple physical equivalence nodes, one per required physical property, in the physical AND-OR DAG.

[2] The cost of executing an operation o also takes into account the cost of reading the inputs, if they are not pipelined.

node e is encountered in the traversal, Volcano-SH decides whether or not to materialize e. When making a materialization decision for a node, the materialization decisions for all descendants are already known. Based on this, we can compute $cost(e)$ for a node e, as described in Section 3.1.

To make a materialization decision for a node e, we also need to know $numuses(e)$. Since $numuses(e)$ depends on the materialization status of its ancestors (which is not fixed yet), Volcano-SH uses an underestimate $numuses^-(e)$ of number of uses of e, obtained by simply counting the number of parents of e in the Volcano best plan. We use $numuses^-(e)$ instead of $numuses(e)$ in equation (1) to make a conservative decision on materialization.[3]

Let us now return to the first step of Volcano-SH. Note that the basic Volcano optimization algorithm will not exploit subsumption derivations, such as deriving $\sigma_{A<5}(E)$ by using $\sigma_{A<5}(\sigma_{A<10}(E))$, since the cost of the latter will be more than the former, and thus will not be locally optimal.

To consider such plans, we perform a pre-pass, checking for subsumption amongst nodes in the plan produced by the basic Volcano optimization algorithm. If a subsumption derivation is applicable, we replace the original derivation by the subsumption derivation. At the end of Volcano-SH, if the shared subexpression is not chosen to be materialized, we replace the derivation by the original expressions. In the above example, in the prepass we replace $\sigma_{A<5}(E)$ by $\sigma_{A<5}(\sigma_{A<10}(E))$. If $\sigma_{A<10}(E)$ is not materialized at the end, we replace $\sigma_{A<5}(\sigma_{A<10}(E))$ by $\sigma_{A<5}(E)$.

The algorithm of [SV98] also finds best plans and then chooses which shared subexpressions to materialize. Unlike Volcano-SH, it does not factor earlier materialization choices into the cost of computation.

3.3 The Volcano-RU Algorithm

Consider Q_1 and Q_2 from Example 1.1. With the best plans as shown in the example, namely $(R \bowtie S) \bowtie P$ and $(R \bowtie T) \bowtie S$, no sharing is possible with Volcano-SH. However, when optimizing Q_2, if we realize that $R \bowtie S$ is already used in the best plan for Q_1 and can be shared, the choice of plan $(R \bowtie S) \bowtie T$ may be found to be the best for Q_2.

The intuition behind the Volcano-RU algorithm is therefore as follows. Given a batch of queries, Volcano-RU optimizes them in sequence, keeping track of what plans have already been chosen for earlier queries, and considering the possibility of reusing parts of the plans. The resultant plan depends on the ordering chosen for the queries; we return to this issue after discussing the Volcano-RU algorithm.

Let $Q_1, \ldots, Q_n$ be the queries to be optimized together (and thus under the same pseudo-root of the DAG). The Volcano-RU algorithm optimizes them in the sequence $Q_1, \ldots, Q_n$. After optimizing Q_i, we note equivalence nodes in the DAG that are part of the best plan P_i for Q_i

as candidates for potential reuse later. We also check if each node is worth materializing, if it is used one more time. If so, when optimizing the next query, we will assume it to be available materialized.

After optimizing all the individual queries, the second phase of Volcano-RU executes Volcano-SH on the overall best plan found as above to further detect and exploit common subexpressions. This step is essential since the earlier phase of Volcano-RU does not consider the possibility of sharing common subexpressions within a single query Instead Volcano-SH makes the final decision on what nodes to materialize. The difference from directly applying Volcano-SH to the result of Volcano optimization is that the plan P that is given to Volcano-SH has been chosen taking sharing of parts of earlier queries into account, unlike the Volcano plan.

Note that the result of Volcano-RU depends on the order in which queries are considered. In our implementation we consider the queries in the order in which they are given, as well as in the reverse of that order, and pick the cheaper one of the two resultant plans. Note that the DAG is still constructed only once, so the extra cost of considering the two orders is relatively quite small. Considering further (possibly random) orderings is possible, but the optimization time would increase further.

4 The Greedy Algorithm

In this section, we present the greedy algorithm, which provides an alternative approach to the algorithms of the previous section. Our major contribution here lies in how to *efficiently implement* the greedy algorithm, and we shall concentrate on this aspect.

In this section, we present an algorithm with a different optimization philosophy. The algorithm picks a set of nodes S to be materialized and then finds the optimal plan given that nodes in S are materialized. This is then repeated on different sets of nodes S to find the best (or a good) set of nodes to be materialized.

As before, we shall assume there is a virtual root node for the DAG; this node has as input a "no-op" logical operator whose inputs are the queries $Q_1 \ldots Q_k$. Let Q denote this virtual root node.

For a set of nodes S, let $bestcost(Q, S)$ denote the cost of the optimal plan for Q given that nodes in S are to be materialized (this cost includes the cost of computing and materializing nodes in S). As described in the Volcano-SH algorithm, the basic Volcano optimization algorithm with an appropriate definition of the cost for nodes in S can be used to find $bestcost(Q, S)$.

To motivate our greedy heuristic, we first describe a simple exhaustive algorithm. The exhaustive algorithm, iterates over each subset S of the set of nodes in the DAG, and chooses the subset S_{opt} with the minimum value for $bestcost(Q, S)$. Therefore, $bestcost(Q, S_{opt})$ is the cost of the globally optimal plan for Q.

Procedure GREEDY
Input: Expanded DAG for the consolidated input query Q
Output: Set of nodes to materialize and the corresp. best plan

$$X = \phi$$
$$Y = \text{set of equivalence nodes in the DAG}$$
$$\text{while } (Y \neq \phi)$$
L1:   Pick $x \in Y$ which minimizes $bestcost(Q, \{x\} \cup X)$
       if $(bestcost(Q, \{x\} \cup X) < bestcost(Q, X))$
          $Y = Y - x; \quad X = X \cup \{x\}$
       else $Y = \phi$
    return X

Figure 2: The Greedy Algorithm

It is easy to see that the exhaustive algorithm is doubly exponential in the size of the initial query DAG and is therefore impractical.

In Figure 2 we outline a greedy heuristic that attempts to approximate S_{opt} by constructing it one node at a time. The algorithm iteratively picks nodes to materialize. At each iteration, the node x that gives the maximum reduction in the cost if it is materialized is chosen to be added to X.

The greedy algorithm as described above can be very expensive due to the large number of nodes in the set Y and the large number of times the function *bestcost* is called. We now present three important and novel optimizations to the greedy algorithm which make it efficient and practical.

1. The first optimization is based on the observation that the nodes materialized in the globally optimal plan are obviously a subset of the ones that are shared in some plan for the query. Therefore, it is sufficient to initialize Y in Figure 2, with nodes that are shared in some plan for the query. We call such nodes *sharable nodes*. For instance, in the expanded DAG for Q_1 and Q_2 corresponding to Example 1.1, $R \bowtie S$ is sharable while $R \bowtie T$ is not. We present an efficient algorithm for finding sharable nodes in Section 4.1.

2. The second optimization is based on the observation that there are many calls to *bestcost* at line L1 of Figure 2, with different parameters. A simple option is to process each call to *bestcost* independent of other calls. However, it makes sense for a call to leverage the work done by a previous call. We describe a novel incremental cost update algorithm, in Section 4.2, that maintains the state of the optimization across calls to *bestcost*, and incrementally computes a new state from the old state.

3. The third optimization, which we call the monotonicity heuristic, avoids having to invoke $bestcost(Q, \{x\} \cup X)$, for every $x \in Y$, in line L1 of Figure 2. We describe this optimization in detail in Section 4.3.

4.1 Sharability

In this subsection, we outline how to detect whether an equivalence node can be shared in some plan.

A sub–DAG of a node x consists of the nodes below x along with the edges between these nodes that are in the original DAG. For each node x of the DAG, and every equivalence node z in the sub-DAG rooted at x, we define the *degree of sharing of z in the sub-DAG rooted at x*, $E[x][z]$, as follows. For all equivalence nodes x, $E[x][x]$ is 1. For a given node x, all other $E[x][\_]$ values are computed from the values $E[y][\_]$ for all children y of x as follows.

If x is an operation node
$$E[x][z] = Sum\{E[y][z] \mid y \in children(x)\}$$
and if x is an equivalence node,
$$E[x][z] = Max\{E[y][z] \mid y \in children(x)\}$$

We define the *degree of sharing of an equivalence node z in the full DAG* as $E[r][z]$, where r is the root of the DAG. We can show that this number represents the maximum number of occurrences of z in any plan. Thus, if a node z has degree of sharing in the full DAG as 1, it cannot more than once in any plan. Nodes with degree of sharing > 1 are called *sharable nodes*.

In a reasonable implementation of the above algorithm, the time complexity of computing the row $E[x]$ is proportional to the number of non-zero entries in $E[x]$ (say n_x) times the number of children of x. However, typically, E is fairly sparse since the DAG is typically "short and fat" – as the number of queries grows, the height of the DAG may not increase, but it becomes wider. Thus, n_x is a small fraction of the total number of nodes for most x, making this sharability computation algorithm fairly efficient in practice. In fact, for the queries we considered in our performance study (Section 6), the computation took at most a few tens of milliseconds.

4.2 Incremental Cost Update

The sets with which *bestcost* is called successively at line L1 of Figure 2 are closely related. with their (symmetric) difference being very small. For, line L1 finds the node x with the maximum benefit, which is implemented by calling $bestcost(Q, \{x\} \cup X)$, for different values of x. Thus the second parameter to *bestcost* changes by dropping one node x_i and adding another x_{i+1}. We now present an incremental cost update algorithm that exploits the results of earlier cost computations to incrementally compute the new plan.

Let S be the set of nodes shared at a given point of time, i.e., the previous call to *bestcost* was with S as the parameter. The incremental cost update algorithm maintains the cost of computing every equivalence node, given that all nodes in S are shared, and no other node is shared. Let S' be the new set of nodes that are shared, i.e., the next call to *bestcost* has S' as the parameter. The incremental cost update algorithm starts from the nodes that have changed in going from S to S' (i.e., nodes in $S' - S$ and $S - S'$) and propagates the change in cost for the nodes upwards to all their parents; these in turn propagate any changes in cost to their parents if their cost changed, and so on, until there is no change in cost. Finally, to get the total cost we add the cost of computing and materializing all the nodes in S'.

If we perform this propagation in an arbitrary order then in the worst case we could propagate the change in cost through a node x multiple times (for example, once from a node y which is an ancestor of another node z and then from z). A simple mechanism for avoiding repeated propagation uses topological numbers for nodes of the DAG. During DAG generation the DAG is sorted topologically such that a descendant always comes before an ancestor in the sort order, and nodes are numbered in this order. The cost propagation is then performed according to the topological number ordering using a heap to efficiently find the node with the minimum topological sort number at each step.

In our implementation, we additionally take care of physical property subsumption. Details of how to perform incremental cost update on physical DAGs with physical property subsumption are given in [RSSB98].

4.3 The Monotonicity Heuristic

In Figure 2, the function *bestcost* will be called once for each node in Y, under normal circumstances. We now outline how to determine the node with the smallest value of *bestcost* much more efficiently, using the monotonicity heuristic.

Define $benefit(x, X)$ as

$$bestcost(Q, X) - bestcost(Q, \{x\} \cup X).$$

Notice that, minimizing *bestcost* in line $L1$ corresponds to maximizing benefit as defined here. Suppose the benefit is *monotonic*. Intuitively, the benefit of a node is monotonic if it never increases as more nodes get materialized; more formally *benefit* is monotonic if $\forall X \supseteq Y$, $benefit(x, X) \leq benefit(x, Y)$.

We associate an upper bound on the benefit of a node in Y and maintain a heap C of nodes ordered on these upper bounds.[4] An initial upper bound on the benefit of a node in Y is computed by multiplying the cost of evaluating the node (without any materializations) times the degree of sharing of the node Y in the full DAG (which we defined earlier). The heap C is now used to efficiently find the node $x \in Y$ with the maximum $benefit(x, X)$ as follows: Iteratively, the node n at the top C is chosen, its current benefit is recomputed, and the heap C is reordered. If n remains at the top, it is deleted from the C heap and chosen to be materialized and added to X. Assuming the monotonicity property holds, the other values in the heap are upper bounds, and therefore, the node n added to X above, is indeed the node with the maximum real benefit.

If the monotonicity property does not hold, the node with maximum current benefit may not be at the top of the heap C, but we still use the above procedure as a heuristic for finding the node with the greatest benefit. Our experiments in Section 6 demonstrate that the above procedure greatly speeds up the greedy algorithm. Further, for all queries we experimented with, the results were exactly the same even if the monotonicity heuristic was not used.

---

[4]This cost heap is not to be confused with the heap on topological numbering used earlier.

5 Extensions

In this section, we briefly outline extensions to i) incorporate creation and use of temporary indices, ii) optimize nested queries to exploit common sub-expressions and iii) optimize multiple invocations of parameterized queries.

Costs may be substantially reduced by creating (temporary) indices on database relations or materialized intermediate results. To incorporate index selection, we model the presence of an index as a physical property, similar to sort order. Since our algorithms are actually executed on the physical DAG, they choose not only what results to materialize but also what physical properties they should have. Index selection then falls out as simply a special case of choosing physical properties, with absolutely no changes to our algorithms.

Next we consider nested queries. One approach to handling nested queries is to use decorrelation techniques (see, e.g. [SPL96]). The use of such decorrelation techniques results in the query being transformed to a set of queries, with temporary relations being created. Now, the queries generated by decorrelation have several subexpressions in common, and are therefore excellent candidates for multi-query optimization. One of the queries in our performance evaluation brings out this point.

Correlated evaluation is used in other cases, either because it may be more efficient on the query, or because it may not be possible to get an efficient decorrelated query using standard relational operations [RR98]. In correlated evaluation, the nested query is repeatedly invoked with different values for correlation variables. Consider the following query.

```
select * from a, b, c
where a.x = b.x and b.y = c.y and
a.cost =
   (select min(a1.cost) from a a1, b b1
    where a1.x = b1.x and b1.y = c.y)
```

One option for optimizing correlated evaluation of this query is to materialize $a \bowtie b$, and share it with the outer level query and across nested query invocations. An index on $a \bowtie b$, on attribute $b.y$ is required for efficient access to it in the nested query, since there is a selection on $b.y$ from the correlation variable. If the best plan for the outer level query uses the join order $(a \bowtie b) \bowtie c$, materializing and sharing $a \bowtie b$ may provide the best plan.

In general, parts of the nested query that do not depend on the value of correlation variables can potentially be shared across invocations [RR98]. We can extend our algorithms to consider such reuse across multiple invocations of a nested query. The key intuition is that when a nested query is invoked many times, benefits due to materialization must be multiplied by the number of times it is invoked; results that depend on correlation variables, however, must not be considered for materialization. The nested query invariant optimization techniques of [RR98] then fall out as a special case of ours.

Our algorithms can also be extended to optimize multiple invocations of parameterized queries. Parameterized queries are queries that take parameter values, which are used in selection predicates; stored procedures are a common example. Parts of the query may be invariant, just as in nested queries, and these can be exploited by multi-query optimization.

These extensions have been implemented in our system; details may be found in [RSSB98]. Our algorithms can also be used with System-R style bottom-up optimizers, which use a DAG representation implicitly although not explicitly.

6   Performance Study

Our algorithms were implemented by extending and modifying a Volcano-based query optimizer we had developed earlier. All coding was done in C++, with the basic optimizer taking approx. 17,000 lines, common MQO code took 1000 lines, Volcano-SH and Volcano-RU took around 500 lines each, and Greedy took about 1,500 lines.

The optimizer rule set consisted of select push down, join commutativity and associativity (to generate bushy join trees), and select and aggregate subsumption.

Implementation algorithms included sort-based aggregation, merge join, nested loops join, indexed join, indexed select and relation scan. Our implementation incorporates all the techniques discussed in this paper, including handling physical properties (sort order and presence of indices) on base and intermediate relations, unification and subsumption during DAG generation, and the sharability algorithm for the greedy heuristic.

The block size was taken as 4KB and our cost functions assume 6MB is available to each operator during execution (we also conducted experiments with larger memory sizes up to 128 MB, with similar results). Standard techniques were used for estimating costs, using statistics about relations. The cost estimates contain an I/O component and a CPU component, with seek time as 10 msec, transfer time of 2 msec/block for read and 4 msec/block for write, and CPU cost of 0.2 msec/block of data processed.   We assume that intermediate results are pipelined to the next input, using an iterator model as in Volcano; they are saved to disk only if the result is to be materialized for sharing. The materialization cost is the cost of writing out the result sequentially.

The tests were performed on a single processor 233 Mhz Pentium-II machine with 64 MB memory, running Linux.   Optimization times are measured as CPU time (user+system).

6.1   Basic Experiments

The goal of the basic experiments was to quantify the benefits and cost of the three heuristics for multi-query optimization, Volcano-SH, Volcano-RU and Greedy, with plain Volcano-style optimization as the base case. We used the version of Volcano-RU which considers the forward and reverse orderings of queries to find sharing possibilities, and chooses the minimum cost plan amongst the two.

Experiment 1 (Stand-Alone TPCD):

The workload for the first experiment consisted of four queries based on the TPCD benchmark. We used the TPCD database at scale of 1 (i.e., 1 GB total size), with a clustered index on the primary keys for all the base relations. The results are discussed below and plotted in Figure 3.

TPCD query Q2 has a large nested query, and repeated invocations of the nested query in a correlated evaluation could benefit from reusing some of the intermediate results. For this query, though Volcano-SH and Volcano-RU do not lead to any improvement over the plan of estimated cost 126 secs. returned by Volcano, Greedy results in a plan of with significantly reduced cost estimate of 79 secs. Decorrelation is an alternative to correlated evaluation, and Q2-D is a (manually) decorrelated version of Q2 (due to decorrelation, Q2-D is actually a batch of queries). Multi-query optimization also gives substantial gains on the decorrelated query Q2-D, resulting in a plan with estimated costs of 46 secs., since decorrelation results in common subexpressions. Clearly the best plan here is multi-query optimization coupled with decorrelation.

Observe also that the cost of Q2 (without decorrelation) with Greedy is much less than with Volcano, and is less than even the cost of Q2-D with plain Volcano — this results indicates that multi-query optimization can be very useful in other queries where decorrelation is not possible. To test this, we ran our optimizer on a variant of Q2 where the in clause is changed to not in clause, which prevents decorrelation from being introduced without introducing new internal operators such as anti-semijoin [RR98]. We also replaced the correlated predicate $PS\_PARTKEY = P\_PARTKEY$ by $PS\_PARTKEY \neq P\_PARTKEY$. For this modified query, Volcano gave a plan with estimated cost of 62927 secs., while Greedy was able to arrive at a plan with estimated cost 7331, an improvement by almost a factor of 9.

We next considered the TPCD queries Q11 and Q15, both of which have common subexpressions, and hence make a case for multi-query For Q11, each of our three algorithms lead to a plan of approximately half the cost as that returned by Volcano. Greedy arrives at similar improvements for Q15 also, but Volcano-SH and Volcano-RU do not lead to any appreciable benefit for this query.

Overall, Volcano-SH and Volcano-RU take the same time and space as Volcano. Greedy takes more time than the others for all the queries, but the maximum time taken by greedy over the four queries was just under 2 seconds, versus 0.33 seconds taken by Volcano for the same query. The extra overhead of greedy is negligible compared to its benefits. The total space required by Greedy ranged from 1.5 to 2.5 times that of the other algorithms, and again the absolute values were quite small (up to just over 130KB).

Results on Microsoft SQL-Server 6.5:

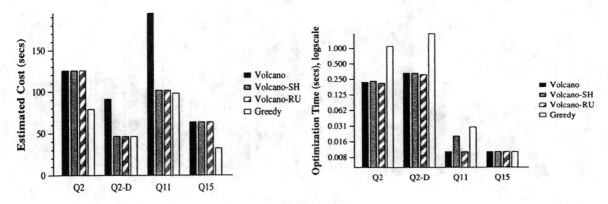

Figure 3: Optimization of Stand-alone TPCD Queries

To study the benefits of multi-query optimization on a real database, we tested its effect on the queries mentioned above, executed on Microsoft SQL Server 6.5, running on Windows NT, on a 333 Mhz Pentium-II machine with 64MB memory. We used the TPCD database at scale 1 for the tests. To do so, we encoded the plans generated by Greedy into SQL. We modeled sharing decisions by creating temporary relations, populating, using and deleting them. If so indicated by Greedy, we created indexes on these temporary relations. We could not encode the exact evaluation plan in SQL since SQL-Server does its own optimization. We measured the total elapsed time for executing all these steps.

The results are shown in Figure 4. For query Q2, the time taken reduced from 513 secs. to 415 secs. Here, SQL-Server performed decorrelation on the original Q2 as well as on the result of multi-query optimization. Thus, the numbers do not match our cost estimates, but clearly multi-query optimization was useful here. The reduction for the decorrelated version Q2-D was from 345 secs. to 262 secs; thus the best plan for Q2 overall, even on SQL-Server, was using multi-query optimization as per Greedy on a decorrelated query. The query Q11 speeded up by just under 50%, from 808 secs. to 424 secs. and Q15 from 63 secs. to 42 secs. using plans with sharing generated by Greedy.

The results indicate that multi-query optimization gives significant time improvements on a real system. It is important to note that the measured benefits are underestimates of potential benefits, for the following reasons. (a) Due to encoding of sharing in SQL, temporary relations had to be stored and re-read even for the first use. (b) The operator set for SQL-Server 6.5 does not support sort-merge join. Our optimizer at times indicated that it was worthwhile to materialize the relation in a sorted order so that it could be cheaply used by a merge-join or aggregation over it, which we could not encode in SQL/SQL-Server. If multi-query optimization were properly integrated into the system, the benefits are likely to be significantly larger, and more consistent with our estimates.

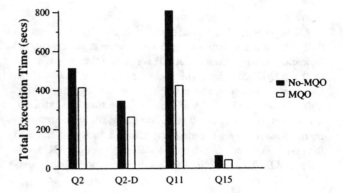

Figure 4: Execution of Stand-alone TPCD Queries on MS SQL Server

Experiment 2 (Batched TPCD Queries):

In the second experiment, the workload models a system where several TPCD queries are executed as a batch. The workload consists of subsequences of the queries Q3, Q5, Q7, Q9 and Q10 from TPCD; none of these queries has any common subexpressions within itself. Each query was repeated twice with different selection constants. Composite query BQi consists of the first i of the above queries, and we used composite queries BQ1 to BQ5 in our experiments. Like in Experiment 1, we used the TPCD database at scale of 1 and assumed that there are clustered indices on the primary keys of the database relations.

Note that although a query is repeated with two different values for a selection constant, we found that the selection operation generally lands up at the bottom of the best Volcano plan tree, and the two best plan trees may not have common subexpressions.

The results on the above workload are shown in Figure 5. Across the workload, Volcano-SH and Volcano-RU achieve up to only about 14% improvement over Volcano with respect to the cost of the returned plan, while incurring negligible overheads. Greedy performs better, achieving up to 56% improvement over Volcano, and is uniformly better

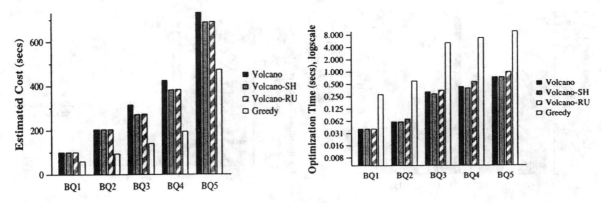

Figure 5: Optimization of Batched TPCD Queries

than the other two algorithms.

As expected, Volcano-SH and Volcano-RU have essentially the same execution time and space requirements as Volcano. Greedy takes about 10 seconds on the largest query in the set, BQ5, while Volcano takes about 0.7 second on the same. However, the estimated cost savings on BQ5 is 260 seconds, which is clearly much more than the extra optimization time cost of 10 secs. Similarly, the space requirements for Greedy were more by about a factor of three to four over Volcano, but the absolute difference for BQ5 was only 60KB. The benefits of Greedy, therefore, clearly outweigh the cost.

6.2 Scaleup Analysis

To see how well our algorithms scale up with increasing numbers of queries, we defined a new set of 22 relations PSP_1 to PSP_{22} with an identical schema (P, SP, NUM) denoting part id, subpart id and number. Over these relations, we defined a sequence of 18 component queries SQ_1 to SQ_{18}: component query SQ_i was a pair of chain queries on five consecutive relations PSP_i to PSP_{i+4}, with the join condition being $PSP_j.SP = PSP_{j+1}.P$, for $j = i..i + 3$. One of the queries in the pair SQ_i had a selection $PSP_i.NUM \geq a_i$ while the other had a selection $PSP_i.NUM \geq b_i$ where a_i and b_i are arbitrary values with $a_i \neq b_i$.

To measure scaleup, we use the composite queries CQ_1 to CQ_5, where CQ_i is consists of queries SQ_1 to SQ_{4i-2}. Thus, CQ_i uses $4i + 2$ relations PSP_1 to PSP_{4i+2}, and has $32i - 16$ join predicates and $8i - 4$ selection predicates. Query CQ5, in particular, is on 22 relations and has 144 join predicates and 36 select predicates. The size of the 22 base relations $PSP_1, \ldots, PSP_{22}$ varied from 20000 to 40000 tuples (assigned randomly) with 25 tuples per block. No index was assumed on the base relations.

The cost of the plan and optimization time for the above workload is shown in Figure 6. The relative benefits of the algorithms remains similar to that in the earlier workloads, except that Volcano-RU now gives somewhat better plans than Volcano-SH. Greedy continues to be

the best, although it is relatively more expensive. The optimization time for Volcano, Volcano-SH and Volcano-RU increases linearly. The increase in optimization time for Greedy is also practically linear, although it has a very small super-linear component. But even for the largest query, CQ5 (with 22 relations, 144 join predicates and 36 select predicates) the time taken was only 30 seconds. The size of the DAG increases linearly for this sequence of queries. From the above, we can conclude that Greedy is scalable to quite large query batch sizes.

We also ran Greedy on queries with larger numbers of relations to test its scale up with query size. Each experiment was run on a batch consisting of a query repeated twice, to make every subexpression of the query shared. We found that the optimization time increased slightly super-linearly with the size of the DAG. For a query of 10 relations and 9 join predicates, the optimization time ranged from 25 to 50 seconds, depending on the predicate pattern. (The predicate pattern affects the size of the DAG, since the transformation rules do not generate cross products.) Greedy should therefore be used with care on queries with a large number of relations.

6.3 Effect of Optimizations

In this series of experiments, we focus on the effect of individual optimizations on the optimization of the scaleup queries. We first consider the effect of the monotonicity heuristic addition to Greedy. Without the monotonicity heuristic, before a node is materialized the benefits would be recomputed for all the sharable nodes not yet materialized. With the monotonicity heuristic addition, we found that on an average only about 45 benefits were recomputed each time, across the range of CQ1 to CQ5. In contrast, without the monotonicity heuristic, even at CQ2 there were about 1558 benefit recomputations each time, leading to an optimization time of 77 seconds for the query, as against 7 seconds with monotonicity. Scaleup is also much worse without monotonicity. Best of all, the plans produced with and without the monotonicity heuristic assumption had virtually the same cost on the queries we ran. Thus, the

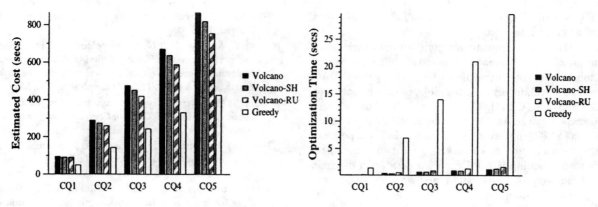

Figure 6: Optimization of Scaleup Queries

monotonicity heuristic provides very large time benefits, without affecting the quality of the plans generated.

To find the benefit of the sharability computation, we measured the cost of Greedy with the sharability computation turned off; every node is assumed to be potentially sharable. Across the range of scaleup queries, we found that the optimization time increased significantly. For CQ2, the optimization time increased from 30 secs. to 46 secs. Thus, sharability computation is also a very useful optimization.

In summary, our optimizations of the implementation of the greedy heuristic result in an order of magnitude improvement in its performance, and are critical for it to be of practical use.

6.4 Discussion

To check the effect of memory size on our results, we ran all the above experiments increasing the memory available to the operators from 6MB to 32MB and further to 128MB. We found that the cost estimates for the plans decreased slightly, but the relative gains (i.e., cost ratio with respect to Volcano) essentially remained the same throughout for the different heuristics.

We stress that while the cost of optimization is independent of the database size, the execution cost of a query, and hence the benefit due to optimization, depends upon the size of the underlying data. Correspondingly, the benefit to cost ratio for our algorithms increase markedly with the size of the data. To illustrate this fact, we ran the batched TPCD query BQ5 (considered in Experiment 2) on TPCD database with scale of 100 (total size 100GB). Volcano returned a plan with estimated cost of 106897 seconds while Greedy obtains a plan with cost estimate 73143 seconds, an improvement of 33754 seconds. The extra time spent during optimization is 10 seconds, as before, which is negligible relative to the gain.

While the benefits of using MQO show up on query workloads with common subexpressions, a relevant issue is the performance on workloads with rare or nonexistent overlaps. To study the overheads of Greedy in a case with no sharing, we took a batch containing TPCD queries Q3, Q5,

Q7, Q9 and Q10, and renamed the relations to remove all overlaps between queries. Basic Volcano optimization took 650 msec, while the Greedy algorithm took 820 msec. Thus the overhead was around 25%, but note that the absolute numbers are very small. The overheads are due to full DAG expansion and sharability detection.

To summarize, for very low cost queries, which take only a few seconds, one may want to use Volcano-RU, which does a "quick-and-dirty" job; especially so if the query is also syntactically complex. For more expensive queries, as well as "canned" queries that are optimized rarely but executed frequently over large databases, it clearly makes sense to use Greedy.

7 Related Work

The multi-query optimization problem has been addressed in [Fin82, Sel88, SSN94, PS88, ZDNS98, SV98]. The work in [Sel88, SSN94, PS88] describe exhaustive algorithms. They also do not exploit the hierarchical nature of query optimization problems, where expressions have subexpressions.

The work in [SV98] considers sharing only amongst the best plans of each query – this is similar to Volcano-SH, and as we have seen, this often does not yield the best sharing. For the special case of OLAP queries (aggregation on a join of fact table with dimension tables) Zhao et al. [ZDNS98] consider multiquery optimization to share scans and subexpressions. They do not consider materialization of shared results, which is required to handle the more general class of SQL queries, which we consider. Their Local Greedy algorithm is similar in spirit to Volcano-RU, while Global Greedy is an extension that allows plans for queries considered earlier to be changed.

The problem of materialized view/index selection is related to multi-query optmization, but needs to consider updates and view maintenance costs (see, e.g., [Rou82, RSS96, Gup97], and in the context of data cubes, [GHRU97]). Several of the algorithms proposed for this problem use a greedy heuristic, but do not discuss efficient implementation, and tight integration with the query optimizer. We are currently working on extending our techniques to handle view/index selection and maintenance.

Our multi-query optimization algorithms implement query optimization in the presence of materialized/cached views, as a subroutine. By virtue of working on a general DAG structure, our techniques are extensible, unlike the solutions of [CKPS95] and [CR94]. The problem of detecting whether an expression can be used to compute another has also been studied in [YL87]; however, they do not address the problem of query optimization or of choosing what to materialize. Query result caching [CR94] can be viewed as a dynamic form of multi-query optimization, and we are currently extending our algorithms to provide better selection of intermediate results to cache.

Rao and Ross [RR98] consider the problem of exploiting invariant parts of a nested subquery. Multi-query optimization on nested queries achieves the same effect, thus our techniques are more general.

8   Conclusions

We have described three novel heuristic search algorithms, Volcano-SH, Volcano-RU and Greedy, for multi-query optimization. We presented a a number of techniques to greatly speed up the greedy algorithm. Our algorithms are based on the AND-OR DAG representation of queries, and are thereby can be easily extended to handle new operators. Our algorithms also handle index selection and nested queries, in a very natural manner. We also developed extensions to the DAG generation algorithm to detect all common sub expressions and include subsumption derivations.

Our implementation demonstrated that the algorithms can be added to an existing optimizer with a reasonably small amount of effort. Our performance study, using queries based on the TPC-D benchmark, demonstrates that multi-query optimization is practical and gives significant benefits at a reasonable cost. The benefits of multi-query optimization were also demonstrated on a real database system.

In conclusion, we believe we have laid the groundwork for practical use of multi-query optimization, and *multi-query optimization will form a critical part of all query optimizers in the future*.

Acknowledgments: This work was supported in part by a grant from Engage Technologies/Redbrick Systems. Part of the work of Prasan Roy was supported by an IBM Fellowship. We wish to thank K. Sriravi, for help with coding, Dan Jaye and Ashok Sawe, for motivating this work through the Engage.Fusion project, Krithi Ramamritham and Sridhar Ramaswamy, for feedback on the paper, and Paul Larson both for feedback on the paper, and for inviting Prasan Roy to participate in prototyping our algorithms on SQL Server at Microsoft.

References

[CKPS95] Surajit Chaudhuri, Ravi Krishnamurthy, Spyros Potamianos, and Kyuseok Shim. Optimizing queries with ma-

terialized views. In *Intl. Conf. on Data Engineering*, Taipei, Taiwan, 1995.

[CR94] C. M. Chen and N. Roussopolous. The implementation and performance evaluation of the ADMS query optimizer: Integrating query result caching and matching. In *Extending Database Technology (EDBT)*, Cambridge, UK, March 1994.

[Fin82] S. Finkelstein. Common expression analysis in database applications. In *SIGMOD Intl. Conf. on Management of Data*, pages 235–245, Orlando,FL, 1982.

[GHRU97] H. Gupta, V. Harinarayan, A. Rajaraman, and J. Ullman. Index selection for olap. In *Intl. Conf. on Data Engineering*, Binghampton, UK, April 1997.

[GM93] Goetz Graefe and William J. McKenna. Extensibility and Search Efficiency in the Volcano Optimizer Generator. In *Intl. Conf. on Data Engineering*, 1993.

[Gup97] H. Gupta. Selection of views to materialize in a data warehouse. In *Intl. Conf. on Database Theory*, 1997.

[PS88] Jooseok Park and Arie Segev. Using common subexpressions to optimize multiple queries. In *Intl. Conf. on Data Engineering*, 1988.

[Rou82] N. Roussopolous. View indexing in relational databases. *ACM Trans. on Database Systems*, 7(2):258–290, 1982.

[RR98] Jun Rao and Ken Ross. Reusing invariants: A new strategy for correlated queries. In *SIGMOD Intl. Conf. on Management of Data*, Seattle, WA, 1998.

[RSS96] Kenneth Ross, Divesh Srivastava, and S. Sudarshan. Materialized view maintenance and integrity constraint checking: Trading space for time. In *SIGMOD Intl. Conf. on Management of Data*, May 1996.

[RSSB98] Prasan Roy, S. Seshadri, S. Sudarshan, and Siddhesh Bhobe. Efficient and extensible algorithms for multi query optimization. Technical report, Indian Institute of Technology, Bombay, October Nov 1998.

[Sel88] Timos K. Sellis. Multiple query optimization. *ACM Transactions on Database Systems*, 13(1):23–52, March 1988.

[SHT+99] J. Shanmugasundaram, G. He, K. Tufte, C. Zhang, D. DeWitt, and J. Naughton. Relational databases for querying XML documents: Limitations and opportunities. In *Intl. Conf. Very Large Databases*, 1999.

[SPL96] Praveen Seshadri, Hamid Pirahesh, and T. Y. Cliff Leung. Complex query decorrelation. In *Intl. Conf. on Data Engineering*, 1996.

[SSN94] Kyuseok Shim, Timos Sellis, and Dana Nau. Improvements on a heuristic algorithm for multiple-query optimization. *Data and Knowledge Engineering*, 12:197–222, 1994.

[SV98] Subbu N. Subramanian and Shivakumar Venkataraman. Cost based optimization of decision support queries using transient views. In *SIGMOD Intl. Conf. on Management of Data*, Seattle, WA, 1998.

[YL87] H. Z. Yang and P. A. Larson. Query transformation for PSJ queries. In *Intl. Conf. Very Large Databases*, pages 245–254, Brighton, August 1987.

[ZDNS98] Y. Zhao, Prasad Deshpande, Jeffrey F. Naughton, and Amit Shukla. Simultaneous optimization and evaluation of multiple dimensional queries. In *SIGMOD Intl. Conf. on Management of Data*, Seattle, WA, 1998.

Eddies: Continuously Adaptive Query Processing

Ron Avnur   Joseph M. Hellerstein

University of California, Berkeley

avnur@cohera.com, jmh@cs.berkeley.edu

Abstract

In large federated and shared-nothing databases, resources can exhibit widely fluctuating characteristics. Assumptions made at the time a query is submitted will rarely hold throughout the duration of query processing. As a result, traditional static query optimization and execution techniques are ineffective in these environments.

In this paper we introduce a query processing mechanism called an *eddy*, which continuously reorders operators in a query plan as it runs. We characterize the *moments of symmetry* during which pipelined joins can be easily reordered, and the *synchronization barriers* that require inputs from different sources to be coordinated. By combining eddies with appropriate join algorithms, we merge the optimization and execution phases of query processing, allowing each tuple to have a flexible ordering of the query operators. This flexibility is controlled by a combination of fluid dynamics and a simple learning algorithm. Our initial implementation demonstrates promising results, with eddies performing nearly as well as a static optimizer/executor in static scenarios, and providing dramatic improvements in dynamic execution environments.

1   Introduction

There is increasing interest in query engines that run at unprecedented scale, both for widely-distributed information resources, and for massively parallel database systems. We are building a system called Telegraph, which is intended to run queries over all the data available on line. A key requirement of a large-scale system like Telegraph is that it function robustly in an unpredictable and constantly fluctuating environment. This unpredictability is endemic in large-scale systems, because of increased complexity in a number of dimensions:

Hardware and Workload Complexity: In wide-area environments, variabilities are commonly observable in the bursty performance of servers and networks [UFA98]. These systems often serve large communities of users whose aggregate behavior can be hard to predict, and the hardware mix in the wide area is quite heterogeneous. Large clusters of computers can exhibit similar performance variations, due to a mix of user requests and heterogeneous hardware evolution. Even in totally homogeneous environments, hardware performance can be unpredictable: for example, the outer tracks of a disk can exhibit almost twice the bandwidth of inner tracks [Met97].

Data Complexity: Selectivity estimation for static alphanu-

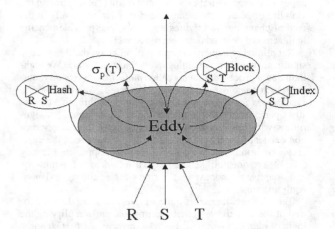

Figure 1: An eddy in a pipeline. Data flows into the eddy from input relations R, S and T. The eddy routes tuples to operators; the operators run as independent threads, returning tuples to the eddy. The eddy sends a tuple to the output only when it has been handled by all the operators. The eddy adaptively chooses an order to route each tuple through the operators.

meric data sets is fairly well understood, and there has been initial work on estimating statistical properties of static sets of data with complex types [Aok99] and methods [BO99]. But federated data often comes without any statistical summaries, and complex non-alphanumeric data types are now widely in use both in object-relational databases and on the web. In these scenarios – and even in traditional static relational databases – selectivity estimates are often quite inaccurate.

User Interface Complexity: In large-scale systems, many queries can run for a very long time. As a result, there is interest in Online Aggregation and other techniques that allow users to "Control" properties of queries while they execute, based on refining approximate results [HAC+99].

For all of these reasons, we expect query processing parameters to change significantly over time in Telegraph, typically many times during a single query. As a result, it is not appropriate to use the traditional architecture of optimizing a query and then executing a static query plan: this approach does not adapt to intra-query fluctuations. Instead, for these environments we want query execution plans to be reoptimized regularly during the course of query processing, allowing the system to adapt dynamically to fluctuations in computing resources, data characteristics, and user preferences.

In this paper we present a query processing operator called an *eddy*, which continuously reorders the application of pipelined operators in a query plan, on a tuple-by-tuple basis. An eddy is an n-ary tuple router interposed between n data sources and a set of query processing operators; the eddy encapsulates the ordering of the operators by routing tuples through them dynamically (Figure 1). Because the eddy observes tuples entering and exiting the pipelined operators, it can adaptively change its routing to effect different operator orderings. In this paper we present initial experimental results demonstrating the viability of eddies: they can indeed reorder effectively in the face of changing selectivities and costs, and provide benefits in the case of delayed data sources as well.

Reoptimizing a query execution pipeline on the fly requires significant care in maintaining query execution state. We highlight query processing stages called *moments of symmetry*, during which operators can be easily reordered. We also describe *synchronization barriers* in certain join algorithms that can restrict performance to the rate of the slower input. Join algorithms with frequent moments of symmetry and adaptive or non-existent barriers are thus especially attractive in the Telegraph environment. We observe that the Ripple Join family [HH99] provides efficiency, frequent moments of symmetry, and adaptive or nonexistent barriers for equijoins and non-equijoins alike.

The eddy architecture is quite simple, obviating the need for traditional cost and selectivity estimation, and simplifying the logic of plan enumeration. Eddies represent our first step in a larger attempt to do away with traditional optimizers entirely, in the hope of providing both run-time adaptivity and a reduction in code complexity. In this paper we focus on continuous operator reordering in a single-site query processor; we leave other optimization issues to our discussion of future work.

1.1 Run-Time Fluctuations

Three properties can vary during query processing: the costs of operators, their selectivities, and the rates at which tuples arrive from the inputs. The first and third issues commonly occur in wide area environments, as discussed in the literature [AFTU96, UFA98, IFF+99]. These issues may become more common in cluster (shared-nothing) systems as they "scale out" to thousands of nodes or more [Bar99].

Run-time variations in selectivity have not been widely discussed before, but occur quite naturally. They commonly arise due to correlations between predicates and the order of tuple delivery. For example, consider an employee table clustered by ascending age, and a selection `salary > 100000`; age and salary are often strongly correlated. Initially the selection will filter out most tuples delivered, but that selectivity rate will change as ever-older employees are scanned. Selectivity over time can also depend on performance fluctuations: e.g., in a parallel DBMS clustered relations are often horizontally partitioned across disks, and the rate of production from various partitions may change over time depending on performance characteristics and utilization of the different disks. Finally, Online Aggregation systems explicitly allow users to control the order in which tuples are delivered based on data preferences [RRH99], resulting in similar effects.

1.2 Architectural Assumptions

Telegraph is intended to efficiently and flexibly provide both distributed query processing across sites in the wide area, and parallel query processing in a large shared-nothing cluster. In this paper we narrow our focus somewhat to concentrate on the initial, already difficult problem of run-time operator reordering in a single-site query executor; that is, changing the effective order or "shape" of a pipelined query plan tree in the face of changes in performance.

In our discussion we will assume that some initial query plan tree will be constructed during parsing by a naive *pre-optimizer*. This optimizer need not exercise much judgement since we will be reordering the plan tree on the fly. However by constructing a query plan it must choose a spanning tree of the query graph (i.e. a set of table-pairs to join) [KBZ86], and algorithms for each of the joins. We will return to the choice of join algorithms in Section 2, and defer to Section 6 the discussion of changing the spanning tree and join algorithms during processing.

We study a standard single-node object-relational query processing system, with the added capability of opening scans and indexes from external data sets. This is becoming a very common base architecture, available in many of the commercial object-relational systems (e.g., IBM DB2 UDB [RPK+99], Informix Dynamic Server UDO [SBH98]) and in federated database systems (e.g., Cohera [HSC99]). We will refer to these non-resident tables as *external tables*. We make no assumptions limiting the scale of external sources, which may be arbitrarily large. External tables present many of the dynamic challenges described above: they can reside over a wide-area network, face bursty utilization, and offer very minimal information on costs and statistical properties.

1.3 Overview

Before introducing eddies, in Section 2 we discuss the properties of query processing algorithms that allow (or disallow) them to be frequently reordered. We then present the eddy architecture, and describe how it allows for extreme flexibility in operator ordering (Section 3). Section 4 discusses policies for controlling tuple flow in an eddy. A variety of experiments in Section 4 illustrate the robustness of eddies in both static and dynamic environments, and raise some questions for future work. We survey related work in Section 5, and in Section 6 lay out a research program to carry this work forward.

2 Reorderability of Plans

A basic challenge of run-time reoptimization is to reorder pipelined query processing operators while they are in flight. To change a query plan on the fly, a great deal of state in the various operators has to be considered, and arbitrary changes can require significant processing and code complexity to guarantee correct results. For example, the state maintained by an operator like hybrid hash join [DKO+84] can grow as large as the size of an input relation, and require modification or recomputation if the plan is reordered while the state is being constructed.

By constraining the scenarios in which we reorder operators, we can keep this work to a minimum. Before describing eddies, we study the state management of various join algorithms; this discussion motivates the eddy design, and forms the basis of our approach for reoptimizing cheaply and continuously. As a philosophy, *we favor adaptivity over best-case performance*. In a highly variable environment, the best-case scenario rarely exists for a significant length of time. So we will sacrifice marginal improvements in idealized query processing algorithms when they prevent frequent, efficient reoptimization.

2.1 Synchronization Barriers

Binary operators like joins often capture significant state. A particular form of state used in such operators relates to the interleaving of requests for tuples from different inputs.

As an example, consider the case of a merge join on two sorted, duplicate-free inputs. During processing, the next tuple is always consumed from the relation whose last tuple had the lower value. This significantly constrains the order in which tuples can be consumed: as an extreme example, consider the case of a slowly-delivered external relation slowlow with many low values in its join column, and a high-bandwidth but large local relation fasthi with only high values in its join column – the processing of fasthi is postponed for a long time while consuming many tuples from slowlow. Using terminology from parallel programming, we describe this phenomenon as a *synchronization barrier*: one table-scan waits until the other table-scan produces a value larger than any seen before.

In general, barriers limit concurrency – and hence performance – when two tasks take different amounts of time to complete (i.e., to "arrive" at the barrier). Recall that concurrency arises even in single-site query engines, which can simultaneously carry out network I/O, disk I/O, and computation. Thus it is desirable to minimize the overhead of synchronization barriers in a dynamic (or even static but heterogeneous) performance environment. Two issues affect the overhead of barriers in a plan: the frequency of barriers, and the gap between arrival times of the two inputs at the barrier. We will see in upcoming discussion that barriers can often be avoided or tuned by using appropriate join algorithms.

2.2 Moments of Symmetry

Note that the synchronization barrier in merge join is stated in an order-independent manner: it does not distinguish between the inputs based on any property other than the data they deliver. Thus merge join is often described as a symmetric operator, since its two inputs are treated uniformly[1]. This is not the case for many other join algorithms. Consider the traditional nested-loops join, for example. The "outer" relation in a nested-loops join is synchronized with the "inner" relation, but not vice versa: after each tuple (or block of tuples) is consumed from the outer relation, a barrier is set until a full scan of the inner is completed. For asymmetric operators like nested-loops join, performance benefits can often be obtained by reordering the inputs.

When a join algorithm reaches a barrier, it has declared the end of a scheduling dependency between its two input relations. In such cases, the order of the inputs to the join can often be changed without modifying any state in the join; when this is true, we refer to the barrier as a *moment of symmetry*. Let us return to the example of a nested-loops join, with outer relation R and inner relation S. At a barrier, the join has completed a full inner loop, having joined each tuple in a subset of R with every tuple in S. Reordering the inputs at this point can be done without affecting the join algorithm, as long as

---

[1]If there are duplicates in a merge join, the duplicates are handled by an asymmetric but usually small nested loop. For purposes of exposition, we can ignore this detail here.

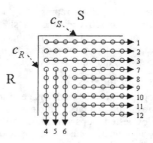

Figure 2: Tuples generated by a nested-loops join, reordered at two moments of symmetry. Each axis represents the tuples of the corresponding relation, in the order they are delivered by an access method. The dots represent tuples generated by the join, some of which may be eliminated by the join predicate. The numbers correspond to the barriers reached, in order. c_R and c_S are the cursor positions maintained by the corresponding inputs at the time of the reorderings.

the iterator producing R notes its current cursor position c_R. In that case, the new "outer" loop on S begins rescanning by fetching the first tuple of S, and R is scanned from c_R to the end. This can be repeated indefinitely, joining S tuples with all tuples in R from position c_R to the end. Alternatively, at the end of some loop over R (i.e. at a moment of symmetry), the order of inputs can be swapped again by remembering the current position of S, and repeatedly joining the next tuple in R (starting at c_R) with tuples from S between c_S and the end. Figure 2 depicts this scenario, with two changes of ordering. Some operators like the pipelined hash join of [WA91] have no barriers whatsoever. These operators are in constant symmetry, since the processing of the two inputs is totally decoupled.

Moments of symmetry allow reordering of the inputs to a single binary operator. But we can generalize this, by noting that since joins commute, a tree of $n - 1$ binary joins can be viewed as a single n-ary join. One could easily implement a doubly-nested-loops join operator over relations R, S and T, and it would have moments of complete symmetry at the end of each loop of S. At that point, all three inputs could be reordered (say to T then R then S) with a straightforward extension to the discussion above: a cursor would be recorded for each input, and each loop would go from the recorded cursor position to the end of the input.

The same effect can be obtained in a binary implementation with two operators, by swapping the positions of binary operators: effectively the plan tree transformation would go in steps, from $(R \bowtie_1 S) \bowtie_2 T$ to $(R \bowtie_2 T) \bowtie_1 S$ and then to $(T \bowtie_2 R) \bowtie_1 S$. This approach treats an operator and its right-hand input as a unit (e.g., the unit $[\bowtie_2 T]$), and swaps units; the idea has been used previously in static query optimization schemes [IK84, KBZ86, Hel98]. Viewing the situation in this manner, we can naturally consider reordering multiple joins and their inputs, even if the join algorithms are different. In our query $(R \bowtie_1 S) \bowtie_2 T$, we need $[\bowtie_1 S]$ and $[\bowtie_2 T]$ to be mutually commutative, but do not require them to be the same join algorithm. We discuss the commutativity of join algorithms further in Section 2.2.2.

Note that the combination of commutativity and moments of symmetry allows for very aggressive reordering of a plan

263

tree. A single n-ary operator representing a reorderable plan tree is therefore an attractive abstraction, since it encapsulates any ordering that may be subject to change. We will exploit this abstraction directly, by interposing an n-ary tuple router (an "eddy") between the input tables and the join operators.

2.2.1 Joins and Indexes

Nested-loops joins can take advantage of indexes on the inner relation, resulting in a fairly efficient pipelining join algorithm. An index nested-loops join (henceforth an "index join") is inherently asymmetric, since one input relation has been pre-indexed. Even when indexes exist on both inputs, changing the choice of inner and outer relation "on the fly" is problematic[2]. Hence for the purposes of reordering, it is simpler to think of an index join as a kind of unary selection operator on the unindexed input (as in the join of S and U in Figure 1). The only distinction between an index join and a selection is that – with respect to the unindexed relation – the selectivity of the join node may be greater than 1. Although one cannot swap the inputs to a single index join, one can reorder an index join and its indexed relation as a unit among other operators in a plan tree. Note that the logic for indexes can be applied to external tables that require bindings to be passed; such tables may be gateways to, e.g., web pages with forms, GIS index systems, LDAP servers and so on [HKWY97, FMLS99].

2.2.2 Physical Properties, Predicates, Commutativity

Clearly, a pre-optimizer's choice of an index join algorithm constrains the possible join orderings. In the n-ary join view, an ordering constraint must be imposed so that the unindexed join input is ordered before (but not necessarily directly before) the indexed input. This constraint arises because of a *physical property* of an input relation: indexes can be probed but not scanned, and hence cannot appear before their corresponding probing tables. Similar but more complex constraints can arise in preserving the ordered inputs to a merge join (i.e., preserving "interesting orders").

The applicability of certain join algorithms raises additional constraints. Many join algorithms work only for equijoins, and will not work on other joins like Cartesian products. Such algorithms constrain reorderings on the plan tree as well, since they always require all relations mentioned in their equijoin predicates to be handled before them. In this paper, we consider ordering constraints to be an inviolable aspect of a plan tree, and we ensure that they always hold. In Section 6 we sketch initial ideas on relaxing this requirement, by considering multiple join algorithms and query graph spanning trees.

2.2.3 Join Algorithms and Reordering

In order for an eddy to be most effective, we favor join algorithms with frequent moments of symmetry, adaptive or non-existent barriers, and minimal ordering constraints: these algorithms offer the most opportunities for reoptimization. In [AH99] we summarize the salient properties of a variety of join algorithms. Our desire to avoid blocking rules out the use of hybrid hash join, and our desire to minimize ordering constraints and barriers excludes merge joins. Nested loops joins

---

[2] In unclustered indexes, the index ordering is not the same as the scan ordering. Thus after a reordering of the inputs it is difficult to ensure that – using the terminology of Section 2.2 – lookups on the index of the new "inner" relation R produce only tuples between c_R and the end of R.

have infrequent moments of symmetry and imbalanced barriers, making them undesirable as well.

The other algorithms we consider are based on frequently-symmetric versions of traditional iteration, hashing and indexing schemes, i.e., the Ripple Joins [HH99]. Note that the original pipelined hash join of [WA91] is a constrained version of the hash ripple join. The external hashing extensions of [UF99, IFF+99] are directly applicable to the hash ripple join, and [HH99] treats index joins as a special case as well. For non-equijoins, the block ripple join algorithm is effective, having frequent moments of symmetry, particularly at the beginning of processing [HH99]. Figure 3 illustrates block, index and hash ripple joins; the reader is referred to [HH99, IFF+99, UF99] for detailed discussions of these algorithms and their variants. These algorithms are adaptive without sacrificing much performance: [UF99] and [IFF+99] demonstrate scalable versions of hash ripple join that perform competitively with hybrid hash join in the static case; [HH99] shows that while block ripple join can be less efficient than nested-loops join, it arrives at moments of symmetry much more frequently than nested-loops joins, especially in early stages of processing. In [AH99] we discuss the memory overheads of these adaptive algorithms, which can be larger than standard join algorithms.

Ripple joins have moments of symmetry at each "corner" of a rectangular ripple in Figure 3, i.e., whenever a prefix of the input stream R has been joined with all tuples in a prefix of input stream S and vice versa. For hash ripple joins and index joins, this scenario occurs between each consecutive tuple consumed from a scanned input. Thus ripple joins offer very frequent moments of symmetry.

Ripple joins are attractive with respect to barriers as well. Ripple joins were designed to allow changing rates for each input; this was originally used to *proactively* expend more processing on the input relation with more statistical influence on intermediate results. However, the same mechanism allows *reactive* adaptivity in the wide-area scenario: a barrier is reached at each corner, and the next corner can adaptively reflect the relative rates of the two inputs. For the block ripple join, the next corner is chosen upon reaching the previous corner; this can be done adaptively to reflect the relative rates of the two inputs over time.

The ripple join family offers attractive adaptivity features at a modest overhead in performance and memory footprint. Hence they fit well with our philosophy of sacrificing marginal speed for adaptability, and we focus on these algorithms in Telegraph.

3 Rivers and Eddies

The above discussion allows us to consider easily reordering query plans at moments of symmetry. In this section we proceed to describe the eddy mechanism for implementing reordering in a natural manner during query processing. The techniques we describe can be used with any operators, but algorithms with frequent moments of symmetry allow for more frequent reoptimization. Before discussing eddies, we first introduce our basic query processing environment.

3.1 River

We implemented eddies in the context of River [AAT+99], a shared-nothing parallel query processing framework that dy-

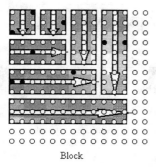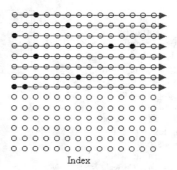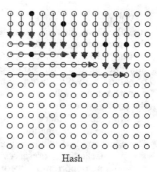

| Block | Index | Hash |

Figure 3: Tuples generated by block, index, and hash ripple join. In block ripple, all tuples are generated by the join, but some may be eliminated by the join predicate. The arrows for index and hash ripple join represent the *logical* portion of the cross-product space checked so far; these joins only expend work on tuples satisfying the join predicate (black dots). In the hash ripple diagram, one relation arrives $3\times$ faster than the other.

namically adapts to fluctuations in performance and workload. River has been used to robustly produce near-record performance on I/O-intensive benchmarks like parallel sorting and hash joins, despite heterogeneities and dynamic variability in hardware and workloads across machines in a cluster. For more details on River's adaptivity and parallelism features, the interested reader is referred to the original paper on the topic [AAT+99]. In Telegraph, we intend to leverage the adaptability of River to allow for dynamic shifting of load (both query processing and data delivery) in a shared-nothing parallel environment. But in this paper we restrict ourselves to basic (single-site) features of eddies; discussions of eddies in parallel rivers are deferred to Section 6.

Since we do not discuss parallelism here, a very simple overview of the River framework suffices. River is a dataflow query engine, analogous in many ways to Gamma [DGS+90], Volcano [Gra90] and commercial parallel database engines, in which "iterator"-style *modules* (query operators) communicate via a fixed dataflow graph (a query plan). Each module runs as an independent thread, and the edges in the graph correspond to finite message queues. When a producer and consumer run at differing rates, the faster thread may block on the queue waiting for the slower thread to catch up. As in [UFA98], River is multi-threaded and can exploit barrier-free algorithms by reading from various inputs at independent rates. The River implementation we used derives from the work on Now-Sort [AAC+97], and features efficient I/O mechanisms including pre-fetching scans, avoidance of operating system buffering, and high-performance user-level networking.

3.1.1 Pre-Optimization

Although we will use eddies to reorder tables among joins, a heuristic pre-optimizer must choose how to initially pair off relations into joins, with the constraint that each relation participates in only one join. This corresponds to choosing a spanning tree of a query graph, in which nodes represent relations and edges represent binary joins [KBZ86]. One reasonable heuristic for picking a spanning tree forms a chain of cartesian products across any tables known to be very small (to handle "star schemas" when base-table cardinality statistics are available); it then picks arbitrary equijoin edges (on the assumption

that they are relatively low selectivity), followed by as many arbitrary non-equijoin edges as required to complete a spanning tree.

Given a spanning tree of the query graph, the pre-optimizer needs to choose join algorithms for each edge. Along each equijoin edge it can use either an index join if an index is available, or a hash ripple join. Along each non-equijoin edge it can use a block ripple join.

These are simple heuristics that we use to allow us to focus on our initial eddy design; in Section 6 we present initial ideas on making spanning tree and algorithm decisions adaptively.

3.2 An Eddy in the River

An eddy is implemented via a module in a river containing an arbitrary number of input relations, a number of participating unary and binary modules, and a single output relation (Figure 1)[3]. An eddy encapsulates the scheduling of its participating operators; tuples entering the eddy can flow through its operators in a variety of orders.

In essence, an eddy explicitly merges multiple unary and binary operators into a single n-ary operator within a query plan, based on the intuition from Section 2.2 that symmetries can be easily captured in an n-ary operator. An eddy module maintains a fixed-sized buffer of tuples that are to be processed by one or more operators. Each operator participating in the eddy has one or two inputs that are fed tuples by the eddy, and an output stream that returns tuples to the eddy. Eddies are so named because of this circular data flow within a river.

A tuple entering an eddy is associated with a tuple descriptor containing a vector of *Ready* bits and *Done* bits, which indicate respectively those operators that are elgible to process the tuple, and those that have already processed the tuple. The eddy module ships a tuple only to operators for which the corresponding Ready bit turned on. After processing the tuple, the operator returns it to the eddy, and the corresponding Done bit is turned on. If all the Done bits are on, the tuple is sent to the eddy's output; otherwise it is sent to another eligible operator for continued processing.

---

[3]Nothing prevents the use of n-ary operators with $n > 2$ in an eddy, but since implementations of these are atypical in database query processing we do not discuss them here.

When an eddy receives a tuple from one of its inputs, it ze-roes the Done bits, and sets the Ready bits appropriately. In the simple case, the eddy sets all Ready bits on, signifying that any ordering of the operators is acceptable. When there are ordering constraints on the operators, the eddy turns on only the Ready bits corresponding to operators that can be ex-ecuted initially. When an operator returns a tuple to the eddy, the eddy turns on the Ready bit of any operator eligible to pro-cess the tuple. Binary operators generate output tuples that correspond to combinations of input tuples; in these cases, the Done bits and Ready bits of the two input tuples are ORed. In this manner an eddy preserves the ordering constraints while maximizing opportunities for tuples to follow different possi-ble orderings of the operators.

Two properties of eddies merit comment. First, note that ed-dies represent the full class of bushy trees corresponding to the set of join nodes – it is possible, for instance, that two pairs of tuples are combined independently by two different join mod-ules, and then routed to a third join to perform the 4-way con-catenation of the two binary records. Second, note that eddies do not constrain reordering to moments of symmetry across the eddy as a whole. A given operator must carefully refrain from fetching tuples from certain inputs until its next moment of symmetry – e.g., a nested-loops join would not fetch a new tuple from the current outer relation until it finished rescan-ning the inner. But there is no requirement that *all* operators in the eddy be at a moment of symmetry when this occurs; just the operator that is fetching a new tuple. Thus eddies are quite flexible both in the shapes of trees they can generate, and in the scenarios in which they can logically reorder operators.

4 Routing Tuples in Eddies

An eddy module directs the flow of tuples from the inputs through the various operators to the output, providing the flex-ibility to allow each tuple to be routed individually through the operators. The routing policy used in the eddy determines the efficiency of the system. In this section we study some promising initial policies; we believe that this is a rich area for future work. We outline some of the remaining questions in Section 6.

An eddy's tuple buffer is implemented as a priority queue with a flexible prioritization scheme. An operator is always given the highest-priority tuple in the buffer that has the corre-sponding Ready bit set. For simplicity, we start by considering a very simple priority scheme: tuples enter the eddy with low priority, and when they are returned to the eddy from an oper-ator they are given high priority. This simple priority scheme ensures that tuples flow completely through the eddy before new tuples are consumed from the inputs, ensuring that the eddy does not become "clogged" with new tuples.

4.1 Experimental Setup

In order to illustrate how eddies work, we present some initial experiments in this section; we pause briefly here to describe our experimental setup. All our experiments were run on a single-processor Sun Ultra-1 workstation running Solaris 2.6, with 160 MB of RAM. We used the Euphrates implementation of River [AAT+99]. We synthetically generated relations as in Table 1, with 100 byte tuples in each relation.

To allow us to experiment with costs and selectivities of se-lections, our selection modules are (artificially) implemented

Table	Cardinality	values in column a
R	10,000	500 - 5500
S	80,000	0 - 5000
T	10,000	N/A
U	50,000	N/A

Table 1: Cardinalities of tables; values are uniformly dis-tributed.

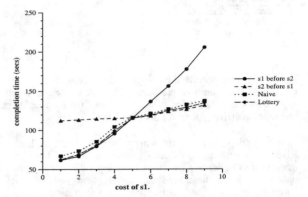

Figure 4: Performance of two 50% selections, $s2$ has cost 5, $s1$ varies across runs.

as spin loops corresponding to their relative costs, followed by a randomized selection decision with the appropriate selec-tivity. We describe the relative costs of selections in terms of abstract "delay units"; for studying optimization, the absolute number of cycles through a spin loop are irrelevant. We imple-mented the simplest version of hash ripple join, identical to the original pipelining hash join [WA91]; our implementation here does not exert any statistically-motivated control over disk re-source consumption (as in [HH99]). We simulated index joins by doing random I/Os within a file, returning on average the number of matches corresponding to a pre-programmed selec-tivity. The filesystem cache was allowed to absorb some of the index I/Os after warming up. In order to fairly compare eddies to static plans, we simulate static plans via eddies that enforce a static ordering on tuples (setting Ready bits in the correct order).

4.2 Naive Eddy: Fluid Dynamics and Operator Costs

To illustrate how an eddy works, we consider a very simple single-table query with two expensive selection predicates, un-der the traditional assumption that no performance or selec-tivity properties change during execution. Our SQL query is simply the following:

```
SELECT    *
  FROM    U
 WHERE    s1() AND s2();
```

In our first experiment, we wish to see how well a "naive" eddy can account for differences in costs among operators. We run the query multiple times, always setting the cost of $s2$ to 5 delay units, and the selectivities of both selections to 50%. In each run we use a different cost for $s1$, varying it between 1 and 9 delay units across runs. We compare a naive eddy of the two selections against both possible static orderings of

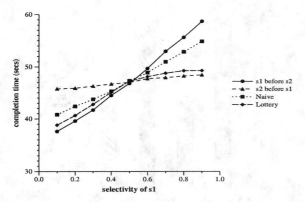 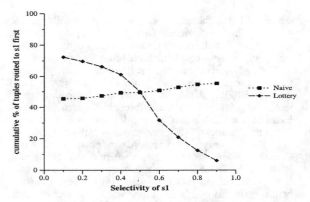

Figure 5: Performance of two selections of cost 5, $s2$ has 50% selectivity, $s1$ varies across runs.

Figure 6: Tuple flow with lottery scheme for the variable-selectivity experiment(Figure 5).

the two selections (and against a "lottery"-based eddy, about which we will say more in Section 4.3.) One might imagine that the flexible routing in the naive eddy would deliver tuples to the two selections equally: half the tuples would flow to $s1$ before $s2$, and half to $s2$ before $s1$, resulting in middling performance over all. Figure 4 shows that this is not the case: the naive eddy nearly matches the better of the two orderings in all cases, without any explicit information about the operators' relative costs.

The naive eddy's effectiveness in this scenario is due to simple fluid dynamics, arising from the different rates of consumption by $s1$ and $s2$. Recall that edges in a River dataflow graph correspond to fixed-size queues. This limitation has the same effect as *back-pressure* in a fluid flow: production along the input to any edge is limited by the rate of consumption at the output. The lower-cost selection (e.g., $s1$ at the left of Figure 4) can consume tuples more quickly, since it spends less time per tuple; as a result the lower-cost operator exerts less back-pressure on the input table. At the same time, the high-cost operator *produces* tuples relatively slowly, so the low-cost operator will rarely be required to consume a high-priority, previously-seen tuple. Thus most tuples are routed to the low-cost operator first, even though the costs are not explicitly exposed or tracked in any way.

4.3 Fast Eddy: Learning Selectivities

The naive eddy works well for handling operators with different costs but equal selectivity. But we have not yet considered differences in selectivity. In our second experiment we keep the costs of the operators constant and equal (5 units), keep the selectivity of $s2$ fixed at 50%, and vary the selectivity of $s1$ across runs. The results in Figure 5 are less encouraging, showing the naive eddy performing as we originally expected, about half-way between the best and worst plans. Clearly our naive priority scheme and the resulting back-pressure are insufficient to capture differences in selectivity.

To resolve this dilemma, we would like our priority scheme to favor operators based on both their consumption and production rate. Note that the consumption (input) rate of an operator is determined by cost alone, while the production (output) rate is determined by a product of cost and selectivity. Since an operator's back-pressure on its input depends largely on its consumption rate, it is not surprising that our naive scheme

does not capture differing selectivities.

To track both consumption and production over time, we enhance our priority scheme with a simple learning algorithm implemented via *Lottery Scheduling* [WW94]. Each time the eddy gives a tuple to an operator, it credits the operator one "ticket". Each time the operator returns a tuple to the eddy, one ticket is debited from the eddy's running count for that operator. When an eddy is ready to send a tuple to be processed, it "holds a lottery" among the operators eligible for receiving the tuple. (The interested reader is referred to [WW94] for a simple and efficient implementation of lottery scheduling.) An operator's chance of "winning the lottery" and receiving the tuple corresponds to the count of tickets for that operator, which in turn tracks the relative efficiency of the operator at draining tuples from the system. By routing tuples using this lottery scheme, the eddy tracks ("learns") an ordering of the operators that gives good overall efficiency.

The "lottery" curve in Figures 4 and 5 show the more intelligent lottery-based routing scheme compared to the naive back-pressure scheme and the two static orderings. The lottery scheme handles both scenarios effectively, slightly improving the eddy in the changing-cost experiment, and performing much better than naive in the changing-selectivity experiment.

To explain this a bit further, in Figure 6 we display the percent of tuples that followed the order $s1, s2$ (as opposed to $s2, s1$) in the two eddy schemes; this roughly represents the average ratio of lottery tickets possessed by $s1$ and $s2$ over time. Note that the naive back-pressure policy is barely sensitive to changes in selectivity, and in fact drifts slightly in the wrong direction as the selectivity of $s1$ is increased. By contrast, the lottery-based scheme adapts quite nicely as the selectivity is varied.

In both graphs one can see that when the costs and selectivities are close to equal ($s1 = s2 = 50\%$), the percentage of tuples following the cheaper order is close to 50%. This observation is intuitive, but quite significant. The lottery-based eddy approaches the *cost* of an optimal ordering, but does not concern itself about strictly observing the optimal ordering. Contrast this to earlier work on runtime reoptimization [KD98, UFA98, IFF$^+$99], where a traditional query optimizer runs during processing to determine the optimal plan remnant. By focusing on overall cost rather than on finding the optimal plan, the lottery scheme probabilistically provides nearly optimal performance with much less effort, allowing re-optimization to be done with an extremely lightweight technique that can be executed multiple times for every tuple.

A related observation is that the lottery algorithm gets closer to perfect routing ($y = 0\%$) on the right of Figure 6 than it does ($y = 100\%$) on the left. Yet in the corresponding performance graph (Figure 5), the differences between the lottery-based eddy and the optimal static ordering do not change much in the two settings. This phenomenon is explained by examining the "jeopardy" of making ordering errors in either case. Consider the left side of the graph, where the selectivity of $s1$ is 10%, $s2$ is 50%, and the costs of each are $c = 5$ delay units. Let e be the rate at which tuples are routed erroneously (to $s2$ before $s1$ in this case). Then the expected cost of the query is $(1 - e) \cdot 1.1c + e \cdot 1.5c = .4ec + 1.1c$. By contrast, in the second case where the selectivity of $s1$ is changed to 90%, the expected cost is $(1 - e) \cdot 1.5c + e \cdot 1.9c = .4ec + 1.5c$. Since the jeopardy is higher at 90% selectivity than at 10%, the lottery more aggressively favors the optimal ordering at 90% selectivity than at 10%.

4.4 Joins

We have discussed selections up to this point for ease of exposition, but of course joins are the more common expensive operator in query processing. In this section we study how eddies interact with the pipelining ripple join algorithms. For the moment, we continue to study a static performance environment, validating the ability of eddies to do well even in scenarios where static techniques are most effective.

We begin with a simple 3-table query:

```
SELECT    *
FROM      R, S, T
WHERE     R.a = S.a
AND       S.b = T.b
```

In our experiment, we constructed a preoptimized plan with a hash ripple join between R and S, and an index join between S and T. Since our data is uniformly distributed, Table 1 indicates that the selectivity of the RS join is 1.8×10^{-4}; its selectivity *with respect to* S is 180% – i.e., each S tuple entering the join finds 1.8 matching R tuples on average [Hel98]. We artificially set the selectivity of the index join w.r.t. S to be 10% (overall selectivity 1×10^{-5}). Figure 7 shows the relative performance of our two eddy schemes and the two static join orderings. The results echo our results for selections, showing the lottery-based eddy performing nearly optimally, and the naive eddy performing in between the best and worst static plans.

As noted in Section 2.2.1, index joins are very analogous to selections. Hash joins have more complicated and symmetric behavior, and hence merit additional study. Figure 8 presents performance of two hash-ripple-only versions of this query. Our in-memory pipelined hash joins all have the same cost. We change the data in R, S and T so that the selectivity of the ST join w.r.t. S is 20% in one version, and 180% in the other. In all runs, the selectivity of the RS join predicate w.r.t. S is fixed at 100%. As the figure shows, the lottery-based eddy continues to perform nearly optimally.

Figure 9 shows the percent of tuples in the eddy that follow one order or the other in all four join experiments. While the eddy is not strict about following the optimal ordering, it is

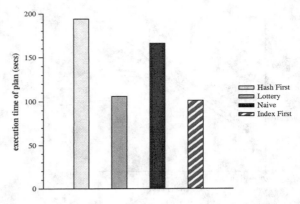

Figure 7: Performance of two joins: a selective Index Join and a Hash Join

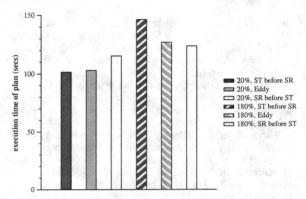

Figure 8: Performance of hash joins $R \bowtie S$ and $S \bowtie T$. $R \bowtie S$ has selectivity 100% w.r.t. S, the selectivity of $S \bowtie T$ w.r.t. S varies between 20% and 180% in the two runs.

quite close in the case of the experiment where the hash join should precede the index join. In this case, the relative cost of index join is so high that the jeopardy of choosing it first drives the hash join to nearly always win the lottery.

4.5 Responding to Dynamic Fluctuations

Eddies should adaptively react over time to the changes in performance and data characteristics described in Section 1.1. The routing schemes described up to this point have not considered how to achieve this. In particular, our lottery scheme weighs all experiences equally: observations from the distant past affect the lottery as much as recent observations. As a result, an operator that earns many tickets early in a query may become so wealthy that it will take a great deal of time for it to lose ground to the top achievers in recent history.

To avoid this, we need to modify our point scheme to forget history to some extent. One simple way to do this is to use a *window* scheme, in which time is partitioned into windows, and the eddy keeps track of two counts for each operator: a number of *banked* tickets, and a number of *escrow* tickets. Banked tickets are used when running a lottery. Escrow tickets are used to measure efficiency during the window. At the beginning of the window, the value of the es-

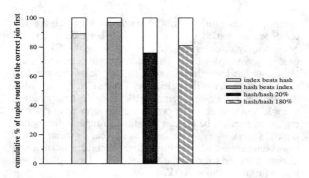

Figure 9: Percent of tuples routed in the optimal order in all of the join experiments.

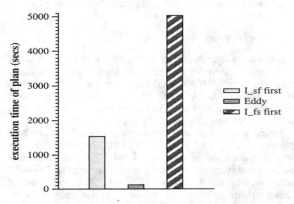

Figure 10: Adapting to changing join costs: performance.

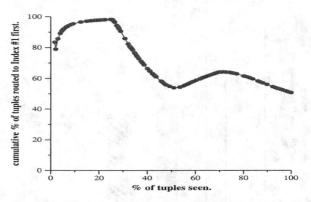

Figure 11: Adapting to changing join costs: tuple movement.

crow account replaces the value of the banked account (i.e., `banked = escrow`), and the escrow account is reset (`escrow = 0`). This scheme ensures that operators "re-prove themselves" each window.

We consider a scenario of a 3-table equijoin query, where two of the tables are external and used as "inner" relations by index joins. Our third relation has 30,000 tuples. Since we assume that the index servers are remote, we implement the "cost" in our index module as a time delay (i.e., `while (gettimeofday() < x) ;`) rather than a spin loop; this better models the behavior of waiting on an external event like a network response. We have two phases in the experiment: initially, one index (call it I_{fs}) is fast (no time delay) and the other (I_{sf}) is slow (5 seconds per lookup). After 30 seconds we begin the second phase, in which the two indexes swap speeds: the I_{fs} index becomes slow, and I_{sf} becomes fast. Both indexes return a single matching tuple 1% of the time.

Figure 10 shows the performance of both possible static plans, compared with an eddy using a lottery with a window scheme. As we would hope, the eddy is much faster than either static plan. In the first static plan (I_{sf} before I_{fs}), the initial index join in the plan is slow in the first phase, processing only 6 tuples and discarding all of them. In the remainder of the run, the plan quickly discards 99% of the tuples, passing 300 to the (now) expensive second join. In the second static

plan (I_{fs} before I_{sf}), the initial join begins fast, processing about 29,000 tuples, and passing about 290 of those to the second (slower) join. After 30 seconds, the second join becomes fast and handles the remainder of the 290 tuples quickly, while the first join slowly processes the remaining 1,000 tuples at 5 seconds per tuple. The eddy outdoes both static plans: in the first phase it behaves identically to the second static plan, consuming 29,000 tuples and queueing 290 for the eddy to pass to I_{sf}. Just after phase 2 begins, the eddy adapts its ordering and passes tuples to I_{sf} – the new fast join – first. As a result, the eddy spends 30 seconds in phase one, and in phase two it has less then 290 tuples queued at I_{sf} (now fast), and only 1,000 tuples to process, only about 10 of which are passed to I_{fs} (now slow).

A similar, more controlled experiment illustrates the eddy's adaptability more clearly. Again, we run a three-table join, with two external indexes that return a match 10% of the time. We read 4,000 tuples from the scanned table, and toggle costs between 1 and 100 cost units every 1000 tuples – i.e., three times during the experiment. Figure 11 shows that the eddy adapts correctly, switching orders when the operator costs switch. Since the cost differential is less dramatic here, the jeopardy is lower and the eddy takes a bit longer to adapt. Despite the learning time, the trends are clear – the eddy sends most of the first 1000 tuples to index #1 first, which starts off cheap. It sends most of the second 1000 tuples to index #2 first, causing the overall percentage of tuples to reach about 50%, as reflected by the near-linear drift toward 50% in the second quarter of the graph. This pattern repeats in the third and fourth quarters, with the eddy eventually displaying an even use of the two orderings over time – always favoring the best ordering.

For brevity, we omit here a similar experiment in which we fixed costs and modified selectivity over time. The results were similar, except that changing only the selectivity of two operators results in less dramatic benefits for an adaptive scheme. This can be seen analytically, for two operators of cost c whose selectivites are swapped from low to hi in a manner analogous to our previous experiment. To lower-bound the performance of either static ordering, selectivities should be toggled to their extremes (100% and 0%) for equal amounts of time – so that half the n tuples go through both operators. Either static plan thus takes $nc + 1/2nc$ time, whereas an optimal

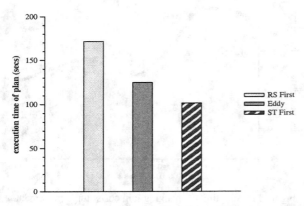

Figure 12: Adapting to an initial delay on R: performance

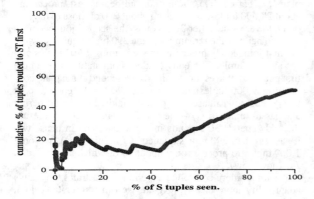

Figure 13: Adapting to an initial delay on R: tuple movement.

dynamic plan takes nc time, a ratio of only 3/2. With more operators, adaptivity to changes in selectivity can become more significant, however.

4.5.1 Delayed Delivery

As a final experiment, we study the case where an input relation suffers from an initial delay, as in [AFTU96, UFA98]. We return to the 3-table query shown in the left of Figure 8, with the RS selectivity at 100%, and the ST selectivity at 20%. We delay the delivery of R by 10 seconds; the results are shown in Figure 12. Unfortunately, we see here that our eddy – even with a lottery and a window-based forgetting scheme – does not adapt to initial delays of R as well as it could. Figure 13 tells some of the story: in the early part of processing, the eddy incorrectly favors the RS join, even though no R tuples are streaming in, and even though the RS join should appear second in a normal execution (Figure 8). The eddy does this because it observes that the RS join does not produce any output tuples when given S tuples. So the eddy awards most S tuples to the RS join initially, which places them in an internal hash table to be subsequently joined with R tuples when they arrive. The ST join is left to fetch and hash T tuples. This wastes resources that could have been spent joining S tuples with T tuples during the delay, and "primes" the RS join to produce a large number of tuples once the Rs begin appearing.

Note that the eddy does far better than pessimally: when R

begins producing tuples (at 43.5 on the x axis of Figure 13), the S values bottled up in the RS join burst forth, and the eddy quickly throttles the RS join, allowing the ST join to process most tuples first. This scenario indicates two problems with our implementation. First, our ticket scheme does not capture the growing selectivity inherent in a join with a delayed input. Second, storing tuples inside the hash tables of a single join unnecessarily prevents other joins from processing them; it might be conceivable to hash input tuples within multiple joins, if care were taken to prevent duplicate results from being generated. A solution to the second problem might obviate the need to solve the first; we intend to explore these issues further in future work.

For brevity, we omit here a variation of this experiment, in which we delayed the delivery of S by 10 seconds instead of R. In this case, the delay of S affects both joins identically, and simply slows down the completion time of all plans by about 10 seconds.

5 Related Work

To our knowledge, this paper represents the first general query processing scheme for reordering in-flight operators within a pipeline, though [NWMN99] considers the special case of unary operators. Our characterization of barriers and moments of symmetry also appears to be new, arising as it does from our interest in reoptimizing general pipelines.

Recent papers consider reoptimizing queries at the ends of pipelines [UFA98, KD98, IFF+99], reordering operators only after temporary results are materialized. [IFF+99] observantly notes that this approach dates back to the original INGRES query decomposition scheme [SWK76]. These inter-pipeline techniques are not adaptive in the sense used in traditional control theory (e.g., [Son98]) or machine learning (e.g., [Mit97]); they make decisions without any ongoing feedback from the operations they are to optimize, instead performing static optimizations at coarse-grained intervals in the query plan. One can view these efforts as complementary to our work: eddies can be used to do tuple scheduling within pipelines, and techniques like those of [UFA98, KD98, IFF+99] can be used to reoptimize across pipelines. Of course such a marriage sacrifices the simplicity of eddies, requiring both the traditional complexity of cost estimation and plan enumeration along with the ideas of this paper. There are also significant questions on how best to combine these techniques – e.g., how many materialization operators to put in a plan, which operators to put in which eddy pipelines, etc.

DEC Rdb (subsequently Oracle Rdb) used competition to choose among different access methods [AZ96]. Rdb briefly observed the performance of alternative access methods at run-time, and then fixed a "winner" for the remainder of query execution. This bears a resemblance to sampling for cost estimation (see [BDF+97] for a survey). More distantly related is the work on "parameterized" or "dynamic" query plans, which postpone some optimization decisions until the beginning of query execution [INSS97, GC94].

The initial work on Query Scrambling [AFTU96] studied network unpredictabilities in processing queries over wide-area sources. This work materialized remote data while processing was blocked waiting for other sources, an idea that can be used in concert with eddies. Note that local materialization ameliorates but does not remove barriers: work to be done locally after a barrier can still be quite significant. Later work focused on rescheduling runnable sub-plans during initial delays in delivery [UFA98], but did not attempt to reorder in-flight operators as we do here.

Two out-of-core versions of the pipelined hash join have been proposed recently [IFF+99, UF99]. The X-Join [UF99] enhances the pipelined hash join not only by handling the out-of-core case, but also by exploiting delay time to aggressively match previously-received (and spilled) tuples. We intend to experiment with X-Joins and eddies in future work.

The Control project [HAC+99] studies interactive analysis of massive data sets, using techniques like online aggregation, online reordering and ripple joins. There is a natural synergy between interactive and adaptive query processing; online techniques to pipeline best-effort answers are naturally adaptive to changing performance scenarios. The need for optimizing pipelines in the Control project initially motivated our work on eddies. The Control project [HAC+99] is not explicitly related to the field of control theory [Son98], though eddies appears to link the two in some regards.

The River project [AAT+99] was another main inspiration of this work. River allows modules to work as fast as they can, naturally balancing flow to whichever modules are faster. We carried the River philosophy into the intial back-pressure design of eddies, and intend to return to the parallel load-balancing aspects of the optimization problem in future work.

In addition to commercial projects like those in Section 1.2, there have been numerous research systems for heterogeneous data integration, e.g. [GMPQ+97, HKWY97, IFF+99], etc.

6   Conclusions and Future Work

Query optimization has traditionally been viewed as a coarse-grained, static problem. Eddies are a query processing mechanism that allow fine-grained, adaptive, online optimization. Eddies are particularly beneficial in the unpredictable query processing environments prevalent in massive-scale systems, and in interactive online query processing. They fit naturally with algorithms from the Ripple Join family, which have frequent moments of symmetry and adaptive or non-existent synchronization barriers. Eddies can be used as the sole optimization mechanism in a query processing system, obviating the need for much of the complex code required in a traditional query optimizer. Alternatively, eddies can be used in concert with traditional optimizers to improve adaptability within pipelines. Our initial results indicate that eddies perform well under a variety of circumstances, though some questions remain in improving reaction time and in adaptively choosing join orders with delayed sources. We are sufficiently encouraged by these early results that we are using eddies and rivers as the basis for query processing in the Telegraph system.

In order to focus our energies in this initial work, we have explicitly postponed a number of questions in understanding, tuning, and extending these results. One main challenge is to develop eddy "ticket" policies that can be formally proved to converge quickly to a near-optimal execution in static scenarios, and that adaptively converge when conditions change. This challenge is complicated by considering both selections and joins, including hash joins that "absorb" tuples into their hash tables as in Section 4.5.1. We intend to focus on multiple performance metrics, including time to completion, the rate of output from a plan, and the rate of refinement for online aggregation estimators. We have also begun studying schemes to allow eddies to effectively order dependent predicates, based on reinforcement learning [SB98]. In a related vein, we would like to automatically tune the aggressiveness with which we forget past observations, so that we avoid introducing a tuning knob to adjust window-length or some analogous constant (e.g., a hysteresis factor).

Another main goal is to attack the remaining static aspects of our scheme: the "pre-optimization" choices of spanning tree, join algorithms, and access methods. Following [AZ96], we believe that competition is key here: one can run multiple redundant joins, join algorithms, and access methods, and track their behavior in an eddy, adaptively choosing among them over time. The implementation challenge in that scenario relates to preventing duplicates from being generated, while the efficiency challenge comes in not wasting too many computing resources on unpromising alternatives.

A third major challenge is to harness the parallelism and adaptivity available to us in rivers. Massively parallel systems are reaching their limit of manageability, even as data sizes continue to grow very quickly. Adaptive techniques like eddies and rivers can significantly aid in the manageability of a new generation of massively parallel query processors. Rivers have been shown to adapt gracefully to performance changes in large clusters, spreading query processing load across nodes and spreading data delivery across data sources. Eddies face additional challenges to meet the promise of rivers: in particular, reoptimizing queries with intra-operator parallelism entails repartitioning data, which adds an expense to reordering that was not present in our single-site eddies. An additional complication arises when trying to adaptively adjust the degree of partitioning for each operator in a plan. On a similar note, we would like to explore enhancing eddies and rivers to tolerate failures of sources or of participants in parallel execution.

Finally, we are exploring the application of eddies and rivers to the generic space of dataflow programming, including applications such as multimedia analysis and transcoding, and the composition of scalable, reliable internet services [GWBC99]. Our intent is for rivers to serve as a generic parallel dataflow engine, and for eddies to be the main scheduling mechanism in that environment.

Acknowledgments

Vijayshankar Raman provided much assistance in the course of this work. Remzi Arpaci-Dusseau, Eric Anderson and Noah Treuhaft implemented Euphrates, and helped implement eddies. Mike Franklin asked hard questions and suggested directions for future work. Stuart Russell, Christos Papadimitriou, Alistair Sinclair, Kris Hildrum and Lakshminarayanan Subramanian all helped us focus on formal issues. Thanks to Navin Kabra and Mitch Cherniack for initial discussions on run-time reoptimization, and to the database group at Berkeley for feedback. Stuart Russell suggested the term "eddy".

This work was done while both authors were at UC Berkeley, supported by a grant from IBM Corporation, NSF grant IIS-9802051, and a Sloan Foundation Fellowship. Computing and network resources for this research were provided through NSF RI grant CDA-9401156.

References

[AAC+97]   A. C. Arpaci-Dusseau, R. H. Arpaci-Dusseau, D. E. Culler, J. M. Hellerstein, and D. A. Patterson. High-Performance Sorting on Networks of Workstations. In *Proc. ACM-SIGMOD International Conference on Management of Data*, Tucson, May 1997.

[AAT+99]   R. H. Arpaci-Dusseau, E. Anderson, N. Treuhaft, D. E. Culler, J. M. Hellerstein, D. A. Patterson, and K. Yelick. Cluster I/O with River: Making the Fast Case Common. In *Sixth Workshop on I/O in Parallel and Distributed Systems (IOPADS '99)*, pages 10–22, Atlanta, May 1999.

[AFTU96]   L. Amsaleg, M. J. Franklin, A. Tomasic, and T. Urhan. Scrambling Query Plans to Cope With Unexpected Delays. In *4th International Conference on Parallel and Distributed Information Systems (PDIS)*, Miami Beach, December 1996.

[AH99]   R. Avnur and J. M. Hellerstein. Continuous query optimization. Technical Report CSD-99-1078, University of California, Berkeley, November 1999.

[Aok99]   P. M. Aoki. How to Avoid Building DataBlades That Know the Value of Everything and the Cost of Nothing. In *11th International Conference on Scientific and Statistical Database Management*, Cleveland, July 1999.

[AZ96]   G. Antoshenkov and M. Ziauddin. Query Processing and Optimization in Oracle Rdb. *VLDB Journal*, 5(4):229–237, 1996.

[Bar99]   R. Barnes. Scale Out. In *High Performance Transaction Processing Workshop (HPTS '99)*, Asilomar, September 1999.

[BDF+97]   D. Barbara, W. DuMouchel, C. Faloutsos, P. J. Haas, J. M. Hellerstein, Y. E. Ioannidis, H. V. Jagadish, T. Johnson, R. T. Ng, V. Poosala, K. A. Ross, and K. C. Sevcik. The New Jersey Data Reduction Report. *IEEE Data Engineering Bulletin*, 20(4), December 1997.

[BO99]   J. Boulos and K. Ono. Cost Estimation of User-Defined Methods in Object-Relational Database Systems. *SIGMOD Record*, 28(3):22–28, September 1999.

[DGS+90]   D. J. DeWitt, S. Ghandeharizadeh, D. Schneider, A. Bricker, H.-I Hsiao, and R. Rasmussen. The Gamma database machine project. *IEEE Transactions on Knowledge and Data Engineering*, 2(1):44–62, Mar 1990.

[DKO+84]   D. J. DeWitt, R. H. Katz, F. Olken, L. D. Shapiro, M. R. Stonebraker, and D. Wood. Implementation Techniques for Main Memory Database Systems. In *Proc. ACM-SIGMOD International Conference on Management of Data*, pages 1–8, Boston, June 1984.

[FMLS99]   D. Florescu, I. Manolescu, A. Levy, and D. Suciu. Query Optimization in the Presence of Limited Access Patterns. In *Proc. ACM-SIGMOD International Conference on Management of Data*, Phildelphia, June 1999.

[GC94]   G. Graefe and R. Cole. Optimization of Dynamic Query Evaluation Plans. In *Proc. ACM-SIGMOD International Conference on Management of Data*, Minneapolis, 1994.

[GMPQ+97]   H. Garcia-Molina, Y. Papakonstantinou, D. Quass, A Rajaraman, Y. Sagiv, J. Ullman, and J. Widom. The TSIMMIS Project: Integration of Heterogeneous Information Sources. *Journal of Intelligent Information Systems*, 8(2):117–132, March 1997.

[Gra90]   G. Graefe. Encapsulation of Parallelism in the Volcano Query Processing System. In *Proc. ACM-SIGMOD International Conference on Management of Data*, pages 102–111, Atlantic City, May 1990.

[GWBC99]   S. D. Gribble, M. Welsh, E. A. Brewer, and D. Culler. The MultiSpace: an Evolutionary Platform for Infrastructural Services. In *Proceedings of the 1999 Usenix Annual Technical Conference*, Monterey, June 1999.

[HAC+99]   J. M. Hellerstein, R. Avnur, A. Chou, C. Hidber, C. Olston, V. Raman, T. Roth, and P. J. Haas. Interactive Data Analysis: The Control Project. *IEEE Computer*, 32(8):51–59, August 1999.

[Hel98]   J. M. Hellerstein. Optimization Techniques for Queries with Expensive Methods. *ACM Transactions on Database Systems*, 23(2):113–157, 1998.

[HH99]   P. J. Haas and J. M. Hellerstein. Ripple Joins for Online Aggregation. In *Proc. ACM-SIGMOD International Conference on Management of Data*, pages 287–298, Philadelphia, 1999.

[HKWY97]   L. Haas, D. Kossmann, E. Wimmers, and J. Yang. Optimizing Queries Across Diverse Data Sources. In *Proc. 23rd International Conference on Very Large Data Bases (VLDB)*, Athens, 1997.

[HSC99]   J. M. Hellerstein, M. Stonebraker, and R. Caccia. Open, Independent Enterprise Data Integration. *IEEE Data Engineering Bulletin*, 22(1), March 1999. http://www.cohera.com.

[IFF+99]   Z. G. Ives, D. Florescu, M. Friedman, A. Levy, and D. S. Weld. An Adaptive Query Execution System for Data Integration. In *Proc. ACM-SIGMOD International Conference on Management of Data*, Philadelphia, 1999.

[IK84]   T. Ibaraki and T. Kameda. Optimal Nesting for Computing N-relational Joins. *ACM Transactions on Database Systems*, 9(3):482–502, October 1984.

[INSS97]   Y. E. Ioannidis, R. T. Ng, K. Shim, and T. K. Sellis. Parametric Query Optimization. *VLDB Journal*, 6(2):132–151, 1997.

[KBZ86]   R. Krishnamurthy, H. Boral, and C. Zaniolo. Optimization of Nonrecursive Queries. In *Proc. 12th International Conference on Very Large Databases (VLDB)*, pages 128–137, August 1986.

[KD98]   N. Kabra and D. J. DeWitt. Efficient Mid-Query Reoptimization of Sub-Optimal Query Execution Plans. In *Proc. ACM-SIGMOD International Conference on Management of Data*, pages 106–117, Seattle, 1998.

[Met97]   R. Van Meter. Observing the Effects of Multi-Zone Disks. In *Proceedings of the Usenix 1997 Technical Conference*, Anaheim, January 1997.

[Mit97]   T. Mitchell. *Machine Learning*. McGraw Hill, 1997.

[NWMN99]   K. W. Ng, Z. Wang, R. R. Muntz, and S. Nittel. Dynamic Query Re-Optimization. In *11th International Conference on Scientific and Statistical Database Management*, Cleveland, July 1999.

[RPK+99]   B. Reinwald, H. Pirahesh, G. Krishnamoorthy, G. Lapis, B. Tran, and S. Vora. Heterogeneous Query Processing Through SQL Table Functions. In *15th International Conference on Data Engineering*, pages 366–373, Sydney, March 1999.

[RRH99]   V. Raman, B. Raman, and J. M. Hellerstein. Online Dynamic Reordering for Interactive Data Processing. In *Proc. 25th International Conference on Very Large Data Bases (VLDB)*, pages 709–720, Edinburgh, 1999.

[SB98]   R. S. Sutton and A. G. Bartow. *Reinforcement Learning*. MIT Press, Cambridge, MA, 1998.

[SBH98]   M. Stonebraker, P. Brown, and M. Herbach. Interoperability, Distributed Applications, and Distributed Databases: The Virtual Table Interface. *IEEE Data Engineering Bulletin*, 21(3):25–34, September 1998.

[Son98]   E. D. Sontag. *Mathematical Control Theory: Deterministic Finite-Dimensional Systems, Second Edition*. Number 6 in Texts in Applied Mathematics. Springer-Verlag, New York, 1998.

[SWK76]   M. R. Stonebraker, E. Wong, and P. Kreps. The Design and Implementation of INGRES. *ACM Transactions on Database Systems*, 1(3):189–222, September 1976.

[UF99]   T. Urhan and M. Franklin. XJoin: Getting Fast Answers From Slow and Bursty Networks. Technical Report CS-TR-3994, University of Maryland, February 1999.

[UFA98]   T. Urhan, M. Franklin, and L. Amsaleg. Cost-Based Query Scrambling for Initial Delays. In *Proc. ACM-SIGMOD International Conference on Management of Data*, Seattle, June 1998.

[WA91]   A. N. Wilschut and P. M. G. Apers. Dataflow Query Execution in a Parallel Main-Memory Environment. In *Proc. First International Conference on Parallel and Distributed Info. Sys. (PDIS)*, pages 68–77, 1991.

[WW94]   C. A. Waldspurger and W. E. Weihl. Lottery scheduling: Flexible proportional-share resource management. In *Proc. of the First Symposium on Operating Systems Design and Implementation (OSDI '94)*, pages 1–11, Monterey, CA, November 1994. USENIX Assoc.

A Chase Too Far?

Lucian Popa*   **Alin Deutsch**   **Arnaud Sahuguet**   **Val Tannen**

University of Pennsylvania

Abstract

In a previous paper we proposed a novel method for generating alternative query plans that uses chasing (and back-chasing) with logical constraints. The method brings together use of indexes, use of materialized views, semantic optimization and join elimination (minimization). Each of these techniques is known separately to be beneficial to query optimization. The novelty of our approach is in allowing these techniques to interact systematically, eg. non-trivial use of indexes and materialized views may be enabled only by semantic constraints.

We have implemented our method for a variety of schemas and queries. We examine how far we can push the method in term of complexity of both schemas and queries. We propose a technique for reducing the size of the search space by "stratifying" the sets of constraints used in the (back)chase. The experimental results demonstrate that our method is practical (i.e., feasible *and* worthwhile).

1 Introduction

In [9] we proposed a new optimization technique aimed at several heretofore (apparently) disparate targets. The technique captures and extends many aspects of semantic optimizations, physical data independence (use of primary and secondary indexes, join indexes, access support relations and gmaps), use of materialized views and cached queries, as well as generalized tableau-like minimization. Moreover, and most importantly, using a uniform representation with *constraints* the technique makes these disparate optimization principles *cooperate* easily. This presents a new class of optimization opportunities, such as the non-trivial use of indexes and materialized views enabled only by the presence of certain integrity constraints. In section 2 we motivate the

technique and some of the experimental configurations we use with two such examples.

We will call this technique the **C&B technique** from *chase* and *backchase*, the two principal phases of the optimization algorithm. The optimization is completely specified by a set of constraints, namely schema integrity constraints together with constraints that capture physical access structures and materialized views. In the first phase, the original query is chased using applicable constraints into a *universal* plan that gathers all the pathways and structures that are relevant for the original query and the constraints used in the chase. The search space for optimal plans consists of subqueries of this universal plan. In the second phase, navigating through these subqueries is done by chasing *backwards* trying to eliminate joins and scans. Each backchase step needs a constraint to hold and the algorithm checks if it follows from the existing ones. Thus, everything we do is captured by constraints, and only two (one, really!) generic rules.

The chase transformation was originally defined for conjunctive (tableau) queries and embedded implicational dependencies. We are using a significant extension of the chase to *path-conjunctive* queries and dependencies [19] that allows us to capture object-oriented queries, as well as queries against Web-like interfaces described by dictionary (finite function) operations. Dictionaries also describe many physical access structures giving us succinct declarative descriptions of query plans, in the same language as queries.

While sound and *complete* for the important case of path-conjunctive materialized views [9, 16], the **C&B** technique is sound for a larger class of queries, physical structures and constraints. We describe here the performance of a first prototype that uses path-conjunctive query graphs internally. The optimizations on which we concentrate here are increasingly relevant as more queries are generated automatically by mediator tools in heterogenous applications, while materialized views are increasingly used in dealing with source capabilities, security, encapsulation and multiple layers of logical/physical separation.

---

*Contact author. Email: lpopa@gradient.cis.upenn.edu

Contributions Our previous paper was promising on the potential of the C&B technique but raised the natural question: is this technique *practical*? This means two sets of issues:

1. Are there *feasible* implementations of the technique? In particular:

   (a) Is the chase phase feasible, given that even determining if a constraint is applicable requires searching among exponentially many variable mappings?

   (b) Is the backchase feasible, given that even if each chase or backchase step is feasible, the backchase phase may visit exponentially many subqueries?

2. Is the technique *worthwhile*? That is, when you add the significant cost of C&B optimization, is the cost of an alternative plan that only the C&B technique would find still better than the cost of the plan you had without C&B?

In this paper we show the following:

1. The technique is definitely feasible, for practical schemas and queries, as follows:

   (a) By using congruence closure and a homomorphism pruning technique, we can implement the chase very efficiently in practice.

   (b) The backchase quickly becomes impractical if we increase both query complexity and the size of the constraint set. But we have designed several *stratification* strategies that reduce the size of either the query or the constraint set by partitioning them into subparts that can be dealt with independently, in a dynamic programming style. Both strategies work well in common situations and one of them is *complete* for the case of path-conjunctive materialized views [9, 16].

2. We find the technique very valuable when only the presence of semantic integrity constraints enables the use of physical access structures or materialized views. This situation clearly justifies the original intuition for this research direction [9, 19].

Experiments We have built a prototype implementation of the C&B technique for path-conjunctive queries and constraints. With this implementation, we have used three experimental configurations to answer the above questions, repeating the experiments on families of queries and schemas of similar structure but of increasing complexity. This allows us to find out *how far* (as the title of the paper asks) the technique can take us and to show that the applicability range of the implementation likely includes many practical queries. For one of the configurations where we can use a conventional execution engine, we have also measured the global benefit of the C&B technique by measuring the

reduction in total processing (optimization + execution) time, as a function of the complexity of the queries and the schema.

Overview of the paper Section 2 presents two motivating examples that support the goals of the C&B technique. Section 3 describes the implementation techniques we have designed to make C&B feasible and worthwhile. The architecture of our prototype is shown in section 4. Section 5 describes our experimental configurations and results. We survey related work in section 6. Section 7 discusses some possible improvements and extensions.

The rest of this paper requires familiarity with some concepts in [9], such as dictionaries, constraints, chase, universal plan, backchase, minimal plans.

2   Motivating Examples

In this section, we illustrate with two examples certain optimizations that one would like to see performed automatically in a database system.

Example 2.1 This is a very simple and common relational scenario adapted from [1], showing the benefits of exploiting referential integrity constraints. Consider a relation $R(A, B, C, E)$ and a query that selects all tuples in R with given values for attributes B and C:

(Q) <u>select</u>   <u>struct</u> $(A = r.A,\ E = r.E)$ <u>from</u> R r
        <u>where</u> $r.B = b$ <u>and</u> $r.C = c$

The relation is very large, but the number of tuples that meet the <u>where</u> clause criteria is very small. However, the SQL engine is taking a long time in returning an answer. Why isn't the system using an index on R ? Simply because there is no index on the attributes B and C. The only index on R that includes B and C is an index on ABC. There is no index with B and/or C in the high-order position(s), and the SQL optimizer chooses to do a table scan of R. The only way of forcing the SQL optimizer to use the index on ABC is to rewrite Q into an equivalent query that does a join of R with a small table S on attribute A knowing that there is a foreign key constraint from R into S on A:

(Q') <u>select</u>   <u>struct</u> $(A = r.A,\ E = r.E)$ <u>from</u> R r, S s
        <u>where</u> $r.B = b$ <u>and</u> $r.C = c$ <u>and</u> $r.A = s.A$

Although we have not selected any attributes from S, the join with S is of a great benefit. The SQL optimizer chooses (only now!) to use S as the outer table in the join and while scanning S, as each value a for A is retrieved, the index is used to lookup the tuples corresponding to a, b, c.

Example 2.2 Integrity constraints also create opportunities for rewriting queries using materialized views. Consider the query Q given below, which joins relations $R_1(K, A_1, A_2, F, \ldots)$, $R_2(K, A_1, A_2, \ldots)$ with $S_{ij}(A_i, B, \ldots)$ $(1 \leq i \leq 2, 1 \leq j \leq 2)$. Figure 1 depicts Q's join graph, in which the nodes represent the query variables and the edges represent equijoins between them.

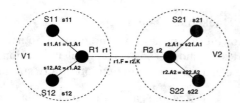

Figure 1: Query graph of Q

One can think of R_1, S_{11} and S_{12} as storing together one large conceptual relation U_1 that has been normalized for storage efficiency. Thus, the attributes A_1 and A_2 of R_1 are foreign keys into S_{11} and, respectively, S_{12}. The attribute K of R_1 is the key of U_1 and therefore of R_1. Similarly, R_2, S_{21} are S_{22} are the result of normalizing another large conceptual relation U_2. For simplicity, we used the same name for attributes A_1, A_2 and K of U_1 and U_2 but they can store different kind of information. In addition, the conceptual relation U_1 has a foreign key attribute F into U_2 and this attribute is stored in R_1. We want to perform the foreign key join of U_1 and U_2, which translates to a complex join across the entire database. The query returns the values of the attribute B from each of the "corner" relations $S_{11}, S_{12}, S_{21}, S_{22}$. (Again for simplicity we use the same name B here, but each relation may store different kind of information).

(Q) <u>select</u>   <u>struct</u>$(B_{11} : s_{11}.B, B_{12} : s_{12}.B,$
                               $B_{21} : s_{21}.B, B_{22} : s_{22}.B)$
        <u>from</u> R_1 r_1, S_{1r} s_{11}, S_{12} s_{12},
                  R_2 r_2, S_{21} s_{21}, S_{22} s_{22}
        <u>where</u> $r_1.F = r_2.K$ <u>and</u>
                  $r_1.A_1 = s_{11}.A_1$ <u>and</u> $r_1.A_2 = s_{12}.A_2$ <u>and</u>
                  $r_2.A_1 = s_{21}.A_1$ <u>and</u> $r_2.A_2 = s_{22}.A_2$

Suppose now that the attributes B of the "corner" relations have few distinct values, therefore the size of the result is relatively small compared to the size of the database. However, in the absence of any indexes on the attributes B of the "corner" relations, the execution time of the query is very long. Instead of indexes, we assume the existence of materialized *views* $V_i(K, B_1, B_2)$ $(1 \leq i \leq 2)$, where each V_i joins R_i with S_{i1} and S_{i2} and retrieves the B attributes from S_{i1} and S_{i2} together with the key K of R_i :

(V_i) <u>select</u>   <u>struct</u>$(K : r.K, B_1 : s_1.B, B_2 : s_2.B)$
        <u>from</u> R_i r, S_{i1} s_1, S_{i2} s_2
        <u>where</u> $r.A_1 = s_l.A_1$ <u>and</u> $r.A_2 = s_2.A_2$

It is easy to see that the join of R_2, S_{21}, and S_{22} can now be replaced by a scan over V_2:

(Q') <u>select</u>   <u>struct</u>$(B_{11} : s_{11}.B, B_{12} : s_{12}.B,$
                               $B_{21} : v_2.B_1, B_{22} : v_2.B_2)$
        <u>from</u> R_1 r_1, S_{11} s_{11}, S_{12} s_{12}, V_2 v_2
        <u>where</u> $r_1.F = v_2.K$ <u>and</u>
                  $r_1.A_1 = s_{11}.A_1$ <u>and</u> $r_1.A_2 = s_{12}.A_2$

However, the join of R_1, S_{11}, and S_{12} cannot be replaced by a scan over V_1. Q'', the obvious candidate for a rewriting of Q using both V_1 and V_2 is *not* equivalent to Q in the absence of additional semantic information.

(Q'') <u>select</u>   <u>struct</u>$(B_{11} : v_1.B_1, B_{12} : v_1.B_2,$
                               $B_{21} : v_2.B_1, B_{22} : v_2.B_2)$
        <u>from</u> R_1 r_1, V_1 v_1, V_2 v_2
        <u>where</u> $r_1.K = v_1.K$ <u>and</u> $r_1.F = v_2.K$

The reason is that V_1 does not contain the F attribute of R_1, and there is no guarantee that joining the latter with V_1 will recover the *correct* values of F. On the other hand, if we know that K is a key in R_1 then Q'' is guaranteed to be equivalent to Q, being therefore an additional (and likely better) plan.

The C&B technique covers and amply generalizes the two examples shown in this section.

3   Practical Solutions

In this section we describe the implementation techniques used to make C&B feasible and worthwhile and we point to some of the experiments that show that this goal can be achieved. In particular, we discuss:

Feasibility of the chase (section 3.1)
This is critical because the chase is heavily used: both to build the universal plan and in order to check the validity of a constraint used in a backchase step. In section 5.2 we measure for all our experimental configurations the time to obtain the universal plan as a function of the size of the query and the number of constraints. The results prove that the cost of the (efficiently implemented) chase is negligible.

Feasibility of the backchase (section 3.2)
A *full implementation of the backchase* (FB) consists of backchasing with all available constraints starting from the universal plan obtained by chasing also with all constraints. This implementation exposes the bottleneck of the approach: the exponential (in the size of the universal plan) number of subqueries explored in the back chase phase. A general analysis suggests using *stratification* heuristics: dividing the constraints in smaller groups and chasing/backchasing with each group successively.

We examine two approaches to this: (1) fragmenting the query and stratifying the constraints by relevance to each fragment (*On-line Query Fragmentation (OQF)*, section 3.2.1); and (2) splitting the constraints independently of the query (*Off-line Constraint Stratification (OCS)*, section 3.2.2). In the important case of materialized views [16], OQF can be used without losing any plan that might have been found by the full implementation (theorem 3.3). To evaluate and compare FB, OCS and OQF strategies, we measure in section 5.3: (1) number of plans generated, (2) the time spent per generated plan and (3) the effect of fragment granularity.

3.1   Chase Feasibility

Each chase step includes searching for homomorphisms mapping a constraint into the query. A **homomorphism** from a constraint $c = \forall(\vec{u} \in \vec{U})$ $B_1(\vec{u}) \Rightarrow \exists(\vec{e} \in$

$\vec{E}$) $B_2(\vec{u},\vec{e})$ into a query Q is a mapping from the universally quantified variables of c into the variables of Q such that, when extended in the natural way to paths, it obeys the following conditions:

1) any universal quantification $u \in U$ of c corresponds to a binding $P\ h(u)$ of Q such that either $h(U)$ and P are the same expression or $h(U) = P$ follows from the <u>where</u> clause of Q.

2) for every equality $P_1 = P_2$ that occurs in B_1 either $h(P_1)$ and $h(P_2)$ are the same expression or $h(P_1) = h(P_2)$ follows from the <u>where</u> clause of Q.

Finding a homomorphism is NP-complete, but only in the size of the constraint (always small in practice). However, the basis of the exponent is the size of the query being chased which can become large during the chase. Since our language is more complicated than a relational one because of dictionaries and set nesting, homomorphisms are more complicated than just simple mappings between goals of conjunctive queries, and checking that a mapping from a constraint into a query is indeed a homomorphism is not straightforward.

We list below some techniques that we use to avoid unnecessary checks for homomorphisms, and to speed up the chase:

- Use of congruence closure, a variation of [17], for fast checking if an equality is a consequence of the <u>where</u> clause of the query.
- Pruning variable mappings that cannot become homomorphisms by reasoning early about equality. Instead of building the entire mapping and checking in one big step whether it is a homomorphism, this is done incrementally. For example, if h is a mapping that is defined on x and y and $x.\mathtt{A} = y.\mathtt{A}$ occurs in the constraint then we check whether $h(x).\mathtt{A} = h(y).\mathtt{A}$ is implied by the <u>where</u> clause of the query. This works well in practice because the "good" homomorphisms are typically just a few among all possible mappings.
- Implementation of the chase as an inflationary procedure that evaluates the input constraints on the internal representation of the input query. The evaluation looks for homomorphisms from the universal part of constraints into the query, and "adds" to the internal query representation (if not there already[1]) the result of each homomorphism applied to the existential part of the constraint. The analogy with query evaluation on a small database is another explanation of why the chase is fast.

The experimental results about the chase shown in section 5.2 are very positive and show that even chasing queries consisting of more than 15 joins with more than 15 constraints is quite practical.

---

[1]This is translated as a check for trivial equivalence.

3.2 Backchase Feasibility

The following analysis of a simple but important case (just indexes) shows that a full implementation of the backchase can unnecessarily explore many subqueries.

Example 3.1 Assume a chain query that joins n relations $\mathtt{R}_1(\mathtt{A},\mathtt{B}), \ldots, \mathtt{R}_n(\mathtt{A},\mathtt{B})$:

(Q) <u>select</u> $\mathtt{struct}(\mathtt{A} = r_1.\mathtt{A},\ \mathtt{B} = r_n.\mathtt{B})$
       <u>from</u> $\mathtt{R}_1\ r_1, \ldots,\ \mathtt{R}_n\ r_n$
       <u>where</u> $r_1.\mathtt{B} = r_2.\mathtt{A}$ <u>and</u> $\ldots$ <u>and</u> $r_{n-1}.\mathtt{B} = r_n.\mathtt{A}$

and suppose that each of the relations has a primary index $\mathtt{I}_i$ on $\mathtt{A}$. Let $D = \{d_1, d_1^-, \ldots, d_n, d_n^-\}$ be all the constraints defining the indexes (here d_i and d_i^- are the constraints for $\mathtt{I}_i$).

In principle, any of the 2^n plans obtained by either choosing the index $\mathtt{I}_i$ or scanning $\mathtt{R}_i$, for each i, is plausible. One direct way to obtain all of them is to chase Q with the entire set of constraints D, obtain the universal plan U (of size $2n$), and then backchase it with D. The backchase inspects top-down all subqueries of U, from size $2n - 1$ to size n (any subquery with less than n loops cannot be equivalent to U), for a total of: $C_{2n}^{2n-1} + \ldots + C_{2n}^n = 2^{2n-1} + \frac{1}{2}C_{2n}^n - 1$.

The same 2^n plans can be obtained with a different strategy, much closer to the one implemented by standard optimizers. For each i, handle the ith loop of Q independently: chase then backchase the query fragment Q_i of Q that contains only $\mathtt{R}_i$ with $\{d_i, d_i^-\}$ to obtain two plans for Q_i, one using $\mathtt{R}_i$ the other using the index $\mathtt{I}_i$. At the end, assemble all plans generated for each fragment Q_i in all possible combinations to produce the 2^n plans for Q.

The number of plans inspected by this "stratified" approach can be computed as follows. For each stage i the universal plan for fragment Q_i has only 2 loops (over $\mathtt{R}_i$ and $\mathtt{I}_i$) and therefore the number of plans explored by the subsequent backchase is 2. Thus the work to produce all the plans for all fragments is $2n$. The total work, including assembling the plans, is then $2n + 2^n$. This analysis suggests that detecting classes of constraints that do not "interact", grouping them accordingly and then stratifying the chase/backchase algorithm, such that only one group is considered at a time, can *decrease exponentially* the size of the search space explored.

The crucial intuition that explains the difference in efficiencies of the two approaches is the following. In the first strategy, for a given i, the universal plan contains at the beginning of the backchase both $\mathtt{R}_i$ and $\mathtt{I}_i$. At some point during the backchase, since a plan containing both is not minimal, there will be a backchase step that eliminates R_i and another backchase step, at the same level, that eliminates I_i (see figure 2). The minimization work that follows is exactly the same in both cases because it operates only on the rest of the relations. This duplication of work is avoided in the second strategy because each loop of Q is handled exactly once. A solution that naturally comes to mind to avoid such situations is to use dynamic programming. Unfortunately, there is no direct way to do this in general (we discuss this more in section 7). Instead, the next section gives a stratification algorithm that solves the problem for a restricted but common case.

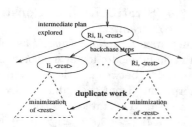

Figure 2: Duplication of work during minimization

3.2.1 On-line Query Fragmentation (OQF)

The main idea behind the OQF strategy is illustrated on the following example.

Example 3.2 Consider a slightly more complicated version of example 2.2 shown in figure 3. The query graph is shaped like a chain of 2 stars, star i having R_i for its hub and S_{ij} for its corners ($1 \leq i \leq 2$, $1 \leq j \leq 3$). The attributes selected in the output are the B attributes of all corners S_{ij}. Assume the existence of materialized views $V_{il}(K, B_1, B_2)$ ($1 \leq i \leq 2, 1 \leq l \leq 2$), where each V_{il} joins the hub of star i (R_i) with two of its corners (S_{il} and $S_{i(l+1)}$). Each V_{il} selects the B attributes of the corner relations it joins, as well as the K attribute of R_i.

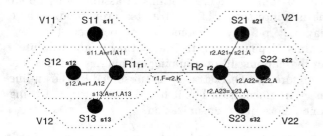

Figure 3: Chain-of-stars query Q with views

If we apply the FB algorithm with all the constraints describing the views we obtain all possible plans in which views replace some parts of the original query. However V_{11} or V_{12} can only replace relations from the first star, thus not affecting any of the relations in the second star. If a plan P using V_{11} and/or V_{12} is obtained for the first star, such that it "recovers" the B attributes needed in the result of Q, as well as the F attribute of R_1 needed in the join with R_2, then P can be joined back with the rest of the query to obtain a query equivalent

to Q. We say that V_{11} overlaps with neither V_{21} nor V_{22}. On the other hand this does not apply to V_{11} and V_{12}, because the parts of the query that they cover overlap (and any further decomposition will lose the plan that uses both V_{11} and V_{12}). Q can thus be decomposed into precisely two query fragments, one for each star, that can be optimized independently.

Before we give the full details of the OQF algorithm, we need to formalize the ideas introduced in the previous example.

Query Fragments. We define the *closure* Q^* of query Q as a query with the same <u>select</u> and <u>from</u> clauses as Q while the <u>where</u> clause consists of all the equalities occuring in or implied by Q's <u>where</u> clause. Q^* is computable from Q in PTIME and is equivalent to Q ([18] shows a congruence closure algorithm for this construction).

Given a query Q and a subset S of its <u>from</u> clause bindings we define a *query fragment Q' of Q induced by S* as follows: 1) The <u>from</u> clause consists of exactly the bindings in S; 2) The <u>where</u> clause consists of all the conditions in the <u>where</u> clause of Q^* which mention only variables bound in S; 3) The <u>select</u> clause consists of all the paths P over S that occur in the <u>select</u> clause of Q or in an equality $P = P'$ of Q^*'s <u>where</u> clause where P' depends on at least one binding that is not in S. In the latter case, we call such P a *link path* of the fragment.

Skeletons. While in general the chase/backchase algorithm can mix semantic with physical cosntraints, in the remainder of this section we describe a stratification algorithm that can be applied to a particular class of constraints which we call *skeletons*. This class is sufficiently general to cover the usual physical access structures: indexes, materialized views, ASRs, GMAPs. Each of these can be described by a pair of complementary inclusion constraints. We define a *skeleton* as a pair of complementary constraints:

$$d = \forall(\vec{x} \in \vec{R}) \, [\, B_1(\vec{x}) \, \Rightarrow \, \exists(\vec{v} \in \vec{V}) \, B_2(\vec{x}, \vec{v}) \,]$$
$$d^- = \forall(\vec{v} \in \vec{V}) \, \exists(\vec{x} \in \vec{R}) \, B_1(\vec{x}) \, \underline{and} \, B_2(\vec{x}, \vec{v})$$

such that all schema names occuring among $\vec{V}$ belong to the physical schema, while all schema names occuring among $\vec{R}$ belong to the logical schema.

Algorithm 3.1 (Decomposition into Fragments.) Given a query Q and a set of skeletons $\mathcal{V}$:
1. Construct an *interaction graph G* as follows: 1) there is a node labeled (V, h) for every skeleton $V = (d, d^-)$ in $\mathcal{V}$ and homomorphism h from d to Q; 2) there is an edge between (V_1, h_1) and (V_2, h_2) iff the intersection between the bindings of $h(d_1)$ and $h(d_2)$ is nonempty.
2. Compute the connected components $\{C_1, \ldots, C_k\}$ of G.
3. For each $C_m = \{(V_1, h_1), \ldots, (V_n, h_n)\}$ ($1 \leq m \leq k$) let S be the union of the sets of bindings in $h_i(d_i)$ for all $1 \leq i \leq n$ and compute F_m as the fragment of Q induced by S.

4. The decomposition of Q into fragments consists of $F_1, \ldots, F_k$ together with the fragment F_{k+1} induced by the set of bindings that are not covered by $F_1, \ldots, F_k$.

The resulting fragments are disjoint, and Q can be reconstructed by joining them on the link paths.

Now we are ready to define the on-line query fragmentation strategy:

Algorithm 3.2 (OQF) Given a query Q and a set $\mathcal{V}$ of skeletons:

1. Decompose Q into query fragments $\{F_1, \ldots, F_n\}$ based on $\mathcal{V}$ using Algorithm 3.1.

2. For each fragment F_i find the set of all minimal plans by using the chase/backchase algorithm

3. A plan for Q is the "cartesian product" of sets of plans for fragments (cost-based refinement: the best plan for Q is the join of the best plans for each individual fragment)

Theorem 3.3 *For a skeleton schema, OQF produces the same plans as the full backchase (FB) algorithm.*

In the limit case when the physical schema contains skeletons involving only one logical schema name (such as primary/secondary indexes), OQF degenerates smoothly into a backchase algorithm that operates individually on each loop of the query to find the access method for that loop. One of the purposes of the experimental configuration **EC1** is to demonstrate that OQF performs well in a typical relational setting. However, OQF can be used in more complex situations, such as rewriting queries with materialized views. While in the worst case when the views are strongly overlapping, the fragmentation algorithm may result in one fragment (the query itself), in practice we expect to achieve reasonably good decompositions in fragments. Scalability of OQF in a setting that exhibits a reasonable amount of non-interaction between views is demonstrated by using the experimental configuration **EC2**.

3.2.2 Off-line Constraint Stratification

One disadvantage of OQF is that it needs to find the fragments of a query Q. While this has about the same complexity as chasing Q [2] (and we have argued that chase itself is not a problem) in practice there may be situations in which interaction between constraints can be estimated in a pre-processing phase that examines only the constraints in the schema. The result of this phase is a partitioning of constraints into disjoint sets (*strata*) such that only the constraints in one set are used at one time by the algorithm.

As opposed to OQF this method tries to isolate the independent optimizations that may affect a query

---

[2]The chase also needs to find all homomorphisms between constraints and the query.

by stratifying the constraints without fragmenting the query. During the optimization the entire query is pipelined through stages in which the chase/backchase algorithm uses only the constraints in one set. At each stage different parts of the query are affected.

We first give the algorithm that computes the stratification of the constraints.

Algorithm 3.4 (Stratification of Constraints.) Given a schema with constraints, do:

1. Construct an *interaction graph* G as follows:
a) there is a node labeled c for every constraint c.
b) there is an edge between nodes c_1 and c_2 if there is a homomorphism[3] from the tableau of c_1 into that of c_2, or viceversa. The tableau $T(c)$ of a constraint $c = \forall(\vec{u} \in \vec{U})\ B_1(\vec{u}) \Rightarrow \exists(\vec{e} \in \vec{E})\ B_2(\vec{u}, \vec{e})$ is obtained by putting together both universally and existentially quantified variables and by taking the conjunction of all conditions: $T(c) = \forall(\vec{u} \in \vec{U})\ \forall(\vec{e} \in \vec{E})\ B_1(\vec{u}) \wedge B_2(\vec{u}, \vec{e})$.

2. Compute the connected components $\{C_1, \ldots, C_k\}$ of G. Each C_i is a stratum.

Using algorithm 3.4, we define the following refinement of the C&B strategy, the *off-line constraint stratification* (OCS) algorithm:

Algorithm 3.5 (OCS) Given a query Q and a set of constraints $\mathcal{C}$:

1. Partition $\mathcal{C}$ into disjoint sets of constraints $\{S_i\}_{1 \le i \le k}$ by using algorithm 3.4.

2. Let $P_0 = \{Q\}$. For every $1 \le i \le k$, let P_i be the union of the sets of queries obtained by chase/backchase each element of P_{i-1} with the constraints in S_i.

3. Output P_k as the set of plans.

Algorithm 3.4 makes optimistic assumptions about the non-interaction of constraints: even though there may not be any homomorphism between the constraints, depending on the query they might still interact by mapping to overlapping subqueries at run time. Therefore, the OCS strategy is subsumed by the on-line query fragmentation but it has the advantage of being done before query optimization.

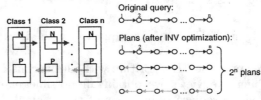

Figure 4: Inverse Relationships

Example 3.3 Consider 3 classes (see figure 4 with $n = 3$) described by dictionaries M_1, M_2, M_3. Each M_i includes a set-valued attributed N ("next") and a set-valued attribute P ("previous"). For each $i = 1, 2$, there

---

[3]Similar to those defined in section 3.1.

exists a many-many inverse relationship between M_i and M_{i+1} that goes from M_i into M_{i+1} by following the N references and comes back from M_{i+1} into M_i by following the P references. The inverse relationship is described by two constraints, INV_{iN} and INV_{iP}, of which we show below the first:

$$\forall(k \in \underline{\text{dom}}\, M_i)\forall(o \in M_i[k].\text{N})$$
$$\exists(k' \in \underline{\text{dom}}\, M_{i+1})\exists(o' \in M_{i+1}[k'].\text{P})\ k' = o\ \underline{\text{and}}\ o' = k$$

By running algorithm 3.4 we obtain the following stratification of constraints into two strata: $\{\text{INV}_{1N}, \text{INV}_{1P}\}$ and $\{\text{INV}_{2N}, \text{INV}_{2P}\}$. Suppose now that the incoming query Q is a typical navigation, following the N references from class M_1 to class M_2 and from there to M_3:

select	struct(F = k_1, L = o_2)
from	$\underline{\text{dom}}\, M_1\ k_1$, $M_1[k_1].\text{N}\ o_1$, $\underline{\text{dom}}\, M_2\ k_2$, $M_2[k_2].\text{N}\ o_2$
where	$o_1 = k_2$

By chase/backchasing Q with the constraints of the first stratum, $\{\text{INV}_{1N}, \text{INV}_{1P}\}$, we obtain, in addition to Q, query Q_1 in which the sense of navigation from M_1 to M_2 following the N attribute is "flipped" to a navigation in the opposite sense: from M_2 to M_1 along the P attribute.

(Q_1)	select	struct(F = o_1, L = o_2)
	from	$\underline{\text{dom}}\, M_2\ k_2$, $M_2[k_2].\text{P}\ o_1$, $M_2[k_2].\text{N}\ o_2$

In the stage corresponding to stratum 2, we chase and backchase $\{Q, Q_1\}$ with $\{\text{INV}_{2N}, \text{INV}_{2P}\}$, this time flipping in each query the sense of navigation from M_2 to M_3 via N to a navigation from M_3 to M_2 via P. The result of this stage consists of four queries: the original Q and Q_1 (obtained by chasing and then backchasing with the same constraint), plus two additional queries. One of them, obtained from Q_1, is shown below:

select	struct(F = o_1, L = k_3)
from	$\underline{\text{dom}}\, M_3\ k_3$, $M_3[k_3].\text{P}\ o_3$, $\underline{\text{dom}}\, M_2\ k_2$, $M_2[k_2].\text{P}\ o_1$
where	$o_3 = k_2$

The OCS strategy does not miss any plans for this example (see also the experimental results for OCS with **EC2**), but in general it is just a heuristic. Our algorithm 3.4 makes optimistic assumptions about the non-interaction of constraints, which depending on the input query, may turn out to be false, therefore it is not complete. **EC2** is an example of such a case and we leave open the problem of finding a more general algorithm for stratification of constraints.

4 The Architecture of the Prototype

The architecture of the system that implements the C&B technique (about $25,000$ lines of Java code), is shown in figure 5. The arrowed lines show the main flow of a query being optimized, constraints from the schema, and resulting plans. The thick lines show the interaction between modules. The main module is the *plan generator* which performs the two basic phases of the C&B : chase and backchase. The backchase is implemented top-down by removing one binding at a time and minimizing recursively the

subqueries obtained (if they are equivalent). Checking for equivalence is performed by verifying that the dependency equivalent to one of the containments is implied by the input constraints[4]. The module that does the check, *dependency implication* shown in the figure as $D \Rightarrow d$, uses the chase. The most salient features of the implementation are summarized below:

- queries and constraints are compiled into a (same!) internal congruence closure based canonical database representation (shown in the figure as $DB(Q)$ for a query Q, respectively $DB(d)$ for a constraint D) that allows for fast reasoning about equality.
- compiling a query Q into the canonical database is implemented itself as a chase step on an empty canonical database with one constraint having no universal but one existential part isomorphic to Q's <u>from</u> and <u>where</u> clauses put together. Hence, the query compiler, constraint compiler and the chase modules are basically one module.
- a language for queries and constraints that is in the spirit of OQL.
- a script language that can control the constraints that are fed into the chase/backchase modules. This is how we implemented the off-line stratification strategy and various other heuristics.

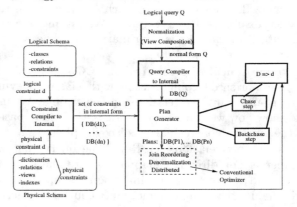

Figure 5: C&B Optimizer Architecture

5 Experiments

In this section we present our experimental configuration and report the results for the chase and the backchase. Finallly, we address in section 5.4 the question whether the time spent in optimization is gained back at execution time.

5.1 Experimental configurations

We consider for our experiments three different settings that exhibit the mix of physical structures and semantic

---

[4]The other containment is always true.

constraints that we want to take advantage of in our optimization approach. We believe that the scenarios that we consider are relevant for many practical situations.

Experimental Configuration EC1: The first setting is used to demonstrate the use of our optimizer in a relational setting with indexes. This is a simple but frequent practical case and therefore we consider it as a baseline.

The schema includes n relations, each relation R_i with a key attribute K on which there is a primary index PI_i, a foreign key attribute N, and additional attributes. The first j of the relations have secondary indexes SI_i on N, thus the total number of indexes in the physical schema is $m = n + j$. As in Example 3.1 we consider chain queries, of size n, in which there is a foreign key join (equating attributes N and K) between each R_i and R_{i+1}. The scaling parameters for **EC1** are n and m.

Experimental Configuration EC2: The second setting is designed to illustrate experimental results in the presence of materialized views and key constraints. We consider a generalization of the chain of stars query of examples 2.2 and 3.2 in which we have i stars with j corner relations, $S_{i1}, \ldots, S_{ij}$, that are joined with the hub of the star R_i. The query returns all the B attributes of the corner relations. For each we assume $v \leq j - 1$ materialized views $V_{i1}, \ldots, V_{iv}$ each covering, as in the previous examples, three relations. We assume that the attribute K of each R_i is a primary key. The scaling parameters are i, j and v.

Experimental Configuration EC3: This is an object-oriented configuration with classes obeying many-to-many inverse relationship constraints. We use it to show how we can mix semantic optimization based on the inverse constraints to discover plans that use access support relations (ASRs). The query that we consider is not directly "mappable" into the existing ASRs, and the semantic optimization "component" of C&B enables rewriting the query into equivalent queries that *can* map into the ASRs.

We generalize here the scenario of example 3.3 by considering n classes with inverse relationships. The queries Q (see figure 4) that we consider are long navigation queries across the entire database following the N references from class M_1 to class M_n. In addition we have, as part of the physical schema, access support relations (ASRs) that are materialized navigation joins across three classes going in the backwards direction (i.e. following two P references). Each ASR is a binary table storing oids from the beginning and from the end of the navigation path. Plans obtained after the inverse optimization phase are rewritten in the second phase into plans that replace a navigation chain of size 2 with one navigation chain of size 1 that uses an ASR (thus being likely better plans). The parameter of the

configuration is the number of classes n. There are $\frac{n-1}{2}$ non-overlapping ASRs that cover the entire navigation chain.

Experimental settings. All the experiments have been realized on a dedicated commodity workstation (Pentium III, Linux RH-6.0, 128MB of RAM). The optimization algorithm is run using IBM JRE-1.1.8. The database management system used to execute queries is IBM DB2 version 6.1.0 (out-of-the-box configuration). For **EC2**, materialized views have been produced by creating and populating tables. All times measured are *elapsed times*, obtained using the Unix shell `time` command. In all the graphs shown in this section, whenever values are missing, it means that the time to obtain them was longer than the timeout used (2 mins).

5.2 Chase Feasibility: Experiments

We measured the complexity of the chase in all our experimental configurations varying both the size of the input query and the number of constraints.

In **EC1** (figure 6, left) the constraints used in the chase are the ones describing the primary (2 constraints/index) and/or secondary (3 constraints/index) indexes. For example, chasing with 10 indexes, therefore 20+ constraints, takes under 1s. For **EC2** (figure 6, middle) the variable is the number of relations in the <u>from</u> clause, giving a measure of the query size. The number of constraints comes from the number of views (2 constraints/view) and the number of key constraints (1 constraint/star hub). For **EC3** (figure 6, right) the variable is the number of classes n (measuring both the size of the schema and that of the queries we use). The chase is done with the inverse relationship constraints and with the ASR constraints. Chasing with 8 classes (20 constraints) takes 3s. Overall, we conclude that the normalized chase time grows significantly with the size of the query and the number of constraints. In comparison, numbers for the chase time are much smaller than those of the backchase.

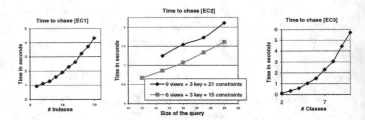

Figure 6: Chase time

5.3 Backchase Feasibility: Experiments

To evaluate and compare the two stratification strategies (OQF and OCS) and the full approach (FB) we measure the following:

- **The number of plans generated** measures the completeness with respect to FB. We found that OQF was complete for all experimental configurations considered, beyond what theorem 3.3 guarantees, while OCS is not complete for **EC2**.
- **The time spent per generated plan** allows for a fair comparison between all three strategies. We measured the time per plan as a function of the query size and number of constraints. Moreover, we studied the scale-up for each strategy by pushing the values of the parameters to the point at which the strategy became ineffective. We found that OQF performed much better than OCS which in turn outperformed FB.
- **The effect of fragment granularity on optimization time** is measured by keeping the query size constant and varying the number of strata in which the constraints are divided. This evaluates the benefits of finding a decomposition of the query into minimal fragments. The OQF strategy performs best by achieving the minimal decomposition that doesn't lose plans. The results also show that OCS is a trade-off giving up completeness for optimization time.

Number of generated plans. This experiment compares *for completeness* the full backchase algorithm with our two refinements: OQF (section 3.2.1) and OCS (section 3.2.2). We measured the number of generated plans, as a function of the size of the query and the number of constraints. The three strategies yielded the same number of generated plans in configurations **EC1** and **EC3**. The table below shows some results for configuration **EC2** in which OCS cannot produce all plans. However, the time spent for generating the plans differs spectacularly among the three techniques, as shown by the next experiment.

s	c	v	FB	OQF	OCS
1	5	1	2	2	2
1	5	2	4	4	3
1	5	3	7	7	5
1	5	4	13	13	8
2	5	1	4	4	4

Time per plan. This experiment compares the three backchase strategies by *optimization time*. Because not all strategies are complete and hence output different numbers of plans, we ensured fairness of the comparison by normalizing the optimization time which was divided by the number of generated plans. This normalized measure is called *time per plan* and was measured as a function of the size of the query and the number of constraints. The results are shown in figures 7 and 8.

By running the experiment in configuration **EC1** we showed that for the trivial yet common case of index introduction, our algorithm's performance is comparable to that of standard relational optimizers.

Figure 7 shows the results obtained for three query sizes: 3, 4 and 5. By varying the number of secondary indexes for each query size, we observed an exponential behavior of the time per plan for the FB strategy, but a negligible time per plan for both OQF and OCS.

For configuration **EC3**, OQF degenerates into FB because the images of the inverse constraints overlap. We show a comparison of FB(=OQF) and OCS. OCS outperforms the other two strategies on this example because each pair of inverse constraints ends up in its own stratum. This stratification results in a *linear* time per plan (each stratum flips one join direction).

The most challenging configuration is **EC2**, dealing with large queries and numerous constraints: the point [2,3,5] of figure 8 corresponds to a query with 17 joins, 6 views (12 constraints), and 3 key constraints. Figure 8 divides the points into 3 groups, each corresponding to the same number of views per star. This value determines the size of the query fragments for OQF and is the most important factor influencing its time per plan[5]. While all strategies exhibit exponential time per plan, OCS is fastest, while FB cannot keep pace with the other two strategies [6].

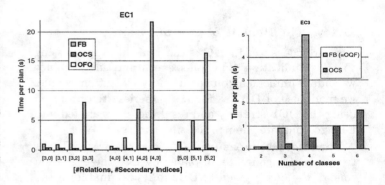

Figure 7: Comparison of FB, OQF, OCS for EC1, EC3

The effect of stratification. This experiment was run in configurations **EC2** and **EC3** by keeping the query size constant and varying the number of strata in which the constraints are divided[7]. For **EC3**, we considered two queries: one navigating over 5 classes and one over 6 classes, with 8, respectively 10 applicable constraints. The query considered in **EC2** joins three stars of 3 corners each, with one view applicable per star (for a total of 9 constraints). The results are shown in figure 9 and exhibit the exponential reduction inferred in example 3.1.

---

[5]OCS achieves a finer stratification than OQF, but misses the best plan, which uses all the views.

[6]We only measure time per plan here, not the quality of the plans. We compare the two in 5.4.

[7]Stratum size 1 corresponds for **EC3** to OCS.

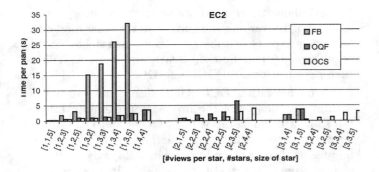

Figure 8: Comparison of FB, OQF, OCS for EC2

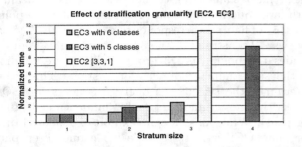

Figure 9: Stratification vs. optimization time

5.4   The Benefit of Optimization

Next we measure, in **EC2**, the real query processing time (optimization time plus execution time). Since we didn't implement our own query execution engine, we made use of DB2 as follows. Queries are optimized using the OQF strategy and resulting plans are fed into DB2 to compare their processing times.

Parameters measured We denote by OptT the time taken to generate all plans; by ExT the execution time of the query given to DB2 in its original form (no C&B optimizaton); and by ExTBest, the DB2 execution time of the best plan generated by the C&B. We assume that the cost of picking the best plan among those generated by the algorithm is negligible. Figure 10 gives the details of the plans generated and their ExT values for a setting with 3 stars, each with 2 corners and 1 view. OptT is 8s; plan 8 is the original query. For each plan, we present the views and corner relations used (in addition to the star hubs which appear in all plans).

Plan	ExT	Views	Corner relations
1	5.54s	V_{11},V_{21},V_{31}	
2	66.39s	V_{11},V_{21}	S_{31},S_{32}
3	33.13s	V_{11},V_{31}	S_{21},S_{22}
4	143.75s	V_{11}	$S_{21},S_{22},S_{31},S_{32}$
5	105.82s	V_{21},V_{31}	S_{11},S_{12}
6	61.45s	V_{21}	$S_{11},S_{12},S_{31},S_{32}$
7	43.54s	V_{31}	$S_{11},S_{12},S_{31},S_{32}$
8	132.90s		$S_{11},S_{12},S_{21},S_{22},S_{31},S_{32}$

Figure 10: Generated plans.

Performance indices We define and display in figure 11, for increasing complexity of the experimental parameters, the following performance indices:

$$\text{Redux} \quad = \quad \frac{\text{ExT}-(\text{ExTBest}+\text{OptT})}{\text{ExT}}$$

$$\text{ReduxFirst} \quad = \quad \frac{\text{ExT}-(\text{ExTBest}+(\text{OptT}/\#plans))}{\text{ExT}}$$

Redux represents the time reduction resulting from our optimization with respect to ExT assuming that no heuristic is used to stop the optimization as soon as reasonable. ReduxFirst represents the time reduction resulting from our optimization with respect to ExT assuming that a heuristic is used to return the best plan first and stop the optimization. Our current implementation of OQF (similar for OCS) is able to return the best plan first for all the experiments presented in this paper (see section 7 for a discussion).

Dataset used These performance indices correspond to experiments conducted on a small size database with the following characteristics[8]:

$|R_i|$	$|S_{i,j}|$	$\sigma(R_i \bowtie S_{i,j})$	$\sigma(R_i \bowtie R_{i+1})$
5000 tup.	5000 tup.	4%	2%

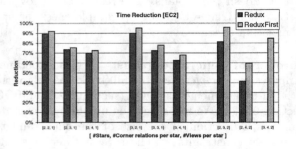

Figure 11: Time reduction (negative Redux not shown).

Our current implementation is not tuned for maximum performance, thus skewing the results against us. Using C or C++ and embedding the C&B as a built-in optimization (e.g. inside DB2) would lead to even better performance. We obtain excellent results nevertheless, proving that the time spent in optimization is well worth the gained execution time.

Even without the heuristic of stopping the optimization after the first plan, the C&B posts significant time reductions (40% to 90%), up to optimizing chain of stars queries with 9 joins, using 4 views ([2,4,2] in figure 11). The practicality range is extended even further when using the *"best plan first"* heuristic, with reductions of 60% to 95%, up to optimizing queries with 14 joins, using 6 views ([3,4,2] in figure 11).

6   Related work

There are many papers that discuss semantic query optimization for relational systems([6, 13, 4] and the

---

[8]On a larger database, the benefits of C&B should be even more important.

references therein). The techniques most frequently used are [6] *index introduction, join elimination, scan reduction, join introduction, predicate elimination* and detection of *empty answers*. Of these, scan reduction, predicate elimination and empty answers use boolean and numeric bounds reasoning of a kind that we have left out of our optimizer for now. We have shown examples of index and join introduction in section 2 and [13] contains a nice example of join introduction. The C&B technique covers index and join introduction and in fact extends them by trying to introduce any relevant physical access structure. The experiments with **EC2** and **EC3** are already more complex than the examples in section 2 and [13]. It also covers join elimination (at the same time as tableau-like minimization) as part of subquery minimization during the backchase. The work that comes closest to ours in its theoretical underpinnings is [14] where chasing with functional dependencies, tableau minimization and join elimination with referential integrity constraints are used. Surprisingly, very few experimental results are actually reported in these papers. [6] reports on join elimination in star queries that are less complex than our experiments with **EC2**. Examples of SQO for OO systems appear in [8, 2, 10, 13, 7]. A general framework for SQO using rewrite rules expressed using OQL appears in [12, 11].

Techniques for using materialized views in query optimization are discussed in [5, 11, 12, 20, 3]. A survey of the area appears in [16]. From our perspective, the work on join indexes [21] and precomputed access support relations [15] belongs here too. The general problem is forced by data independence: how to reformulate a query written against a "user"-level schema into a plan that also/only uses physical access structures and materialized views efficiently. The GMAP approach [20] works with a special case of conjunctive queries (PSJ queries). The core algorithm is exponential but the restriction to PSJ is used to provide polynomial algorithms for the steps of checking relevance of views and checking a restricted form of query equivalence. However, the results we report here on using the chase show that there is no measurable practical benefit from all these restrictions. In the end, the exponential behavior of the GMAP algorithm and the difficulties we had to resolve for the backchase phase are closely related.

Our experiments include schemas, views and queries of significantly bigger complexity than those reported in [22, 20, 5]. Their experiments show that using views can be done and in the case of [20] that it can produce faster plans. But [22] measures only optimization time and [20] does not separate the cost of the optimization itself, so they do not offer any numbers that we can compare with our time reduction figures (section 5.4).

[5] shows a very good behavior of the optimization time as a function of plans produced, but cannot be compared with our figures because the bag semantics they use restricts variable mappings to isomorphisms thus greatly reducing the search space.

7 Discussion and Extensions

Dynamic programming and cost-based pruning. Dynamic programming can only be applied when a problem is decomposable into independent subproblems, where common subproblems are solved only once and the results reused. Unfortunately, the minimization problem lacks common subproblems of big enough granularity: one cannot minimize in general a subpart of a subquery independently of how the subpart interacts with the rest of the query. In general, each subset of the bindings of the original query explored by the backchase must be considered as a different subproblem.

The non-applicability of dynamic programming is in general a problem for rewriting queries using views. What [20, 5] mean by incorporate optimization with views/GMAPs into standard System R-style optimizer is actually the blending of the usual cost-based dynamic programming algorithm with a brute-force exponential search of all possible covers. The algorithms remain exponential but cost-based pruning can be done earlier in the process.

Our optimizer can be easily extended in the same way. We have not yet done this, nor have we added any cost-based pruning to our system/experiments because we considered valuable as a first step to measure the effect of the C&B-specific issues in isolation. On the other hand, OQF already incorporates the principle of dynamic programming in the sense that it identifies query fragments that can be minimized independently.

Top-down vs bottom-up. In the top-down, full approach, the backchase explores only *equivalent* subqueries (call them *candidates*), and tries to remove one <u>from</u> binding at a time until a candidate cannot be minimized anymore (all of its subqueries are not equivalent). The main advantage of this approach is that through depth-first search it finds a first plan fast while the main disadvantage is that the cost of a subquery explored cannot be used [9] for cost-based pruning because a backchase step further might improve the cost. In the bottom-up approach the backchase would explore *non-equivalent* candidates. It would assemble subqueries of the universal plan by considering first candidates of size 1 then of size 2 and so on, until an equivalent candidate is reached. Then cost-based pruning is possible because a step of the algorithm can only increase the cost. A best-first strategy can

---

[9]We are ignoring here heuristics that need preliminary cost estimates.

be easily implemented by sorting the fragments being explored based on cost. The main disadvantage of this strategy is that it involves breadth-first search and the time for finding the first plan can be long.

In practice one could combine the two approaches: start top-down, find the first plan, then switch to bottom-up (combined with cost-based pruning) using the cost of the first plan as the cost of the best plan. While our FB implementation is a top-down approach now, we plan to extend it to include both strategies.

Other extensions. The two stratification strategies (OQF and OCS) introduced here are a first promising step in the direction of a deeper understanding of how the interference of constraints affects the chase/backchase rewrites. This is an attractive theoretical problem which we believe to be more tractable than the study of interference of rules in arbitrary rule-based optimizers. We intend to explore backchase strategies that are complete for query reformulation with other commonly used physical structures and integrity constraints.

Conclusion. In this work, we report on the implementation and evaluation of the uniform approach to semantic optimization and physical independence proposed in [9]. We developed and evaluated two refinements of the full C&B algorithm: OQF, a strategy preserving completeness in restricted but common scenarios, and OCS, a heuristic which achieves the best running times. Our experiments show that the strategies are practical and that OQF scales reasonably well, while OCS scales even better.

Finally, we remark that our comprehensive approach to optimization tries to exploit more optimization opportunities than common systems, thus trading optimization time for quality of generated plans. The experiments clearly show the benefits of this trade-off, even though we used a prototype rather than an implementation tuned for performance.

References

[1] Bonnie Baker. Responsible SQL: Creative Solutions for Performance Problems in DB2 for OS/390. *DB2 Magazine*, 4(2):54–55, Summer 1999. Available at http://www.db2mag.com/summer99/99sp_prog.shtml.

[2] Catriel Beeri and Yoram Kornatzky. Algebraic optimisation of object oriented query languages. *Theoretical Computer Science*, 116(1):59–94, August 1993.

[3] R. Bello and al. Materialized Views in Oracle. In *Proc. of 24th VLDB Conference*, pages 659–664, 1998.

[4] U. Chakravarthy, J. Grant, and J. Minker. Logic-based approach to semantic query optimization. *ACM Transactions on Database Systems*, 15(2):162–207, 1990.

[5] S. Chaudhuri, R. Krishnamurty, S. Potamianos, and K. Shim. Optimizing queries with materialized views. In *Proceedings of ICDE*, Taipei, Taiwan, March 1995.

[6] Qi Cheng, Jarek Gryz, Fred Koo, T. Y. Cliff Leung, Linqi Liu, Xiaoyan Qian, and Berni Schiefer. Implementation of Two Semantic Query Optimization Techniques in DB2 Universal Database. In *Proc. of VLDB*, pages 687–698, September 1999.

[7] M. Cherniack and S. B. Zdonik. Inferring Function Semantics to Optimize Queries. In *Proc. of 24th VLDB Conference*, pages 239–250, 1998.

[8] Sophie Cluet and Claude Delobel. A general framework for the optimization of object oriented queries. In M. Stonebraker, editor, *Proceedings ACM-SIGMOD International Conference on Management of Data*, pages 383–392, San Diego, California, June 1992.

[9] Alin Deutsch, Lucian Popa, and Val Tannen. Physical Data Independence, Constraints and Optimization with Universal Plans. In *VLDB*, September 1999.

[10] L. Fegaras and D. Maier. An algebraic framework for physical oodb design. In *Proc. of the 5th Int'l Workshop on Database Programming Languages (DBPL95)*, Umbria, Italy, August 1995.

[11] D. Florescu. *Design and Implementation of the Flora Object Oriented Query Optimizer*. PhD thesis, Universite of Paris 6, 1996.

[12] D. Florescu, L. Rashid, and P. Valduriez. A methodology for query reformulation in cis using semantic knowledge. *International Journal of Cooperative Information Systems*, 5(4), 1996.

[13] J. Grant, J. Gryz, J. Minker, and L. Raschid. Semantic query optimization for object databases. In *Proc. of ICDE*, April 1997.

[14] M. Jarke, J. Clifford, and Y. Vassiliou. An optimizing prolog front-end to a relational query system. In *Proceedings of ACM-SIGMOD*, pages 316–325, 1984.

[15] A. Kemper and G. Moerkotte. Access support relations in object bases. In *Proceedings of ACM-SIGMOD International Conference on Management of Data*, pages 364–374, 1990.

[16] A. Levy. Answering Queries Using Views: A Survey. Forthcoming.

[17] Greg Nelson and Derek C. Oppen. Fast decision algorithms based on union and find. In *FOCS*, pages 114–119.

[18] Lucian Popa and Val Tannen. Chase and axioms for PC queries and dependencies. Technical Report MS-CIS-98-34, University of Pennsylvania, 1998. Available online at http://www.cis.upenn.edu/~techreports/.

[19] Lucian Popa and Val Tannen. An equational chase for path-conjunctive queries, constraints, and views. In *Proceedings of ICDT*, Jerusalem, Israel, January 1999.

[20] O. Tsatalos, M. Solomon, and Y. Ioannidis. The GMAP: A Versatile Tool for Physical Data Independence. *VLDB Journal*, 5(2):101–118, 1996.

[21] P. Valduriez. Join indices. *ACM Trans. Database Systems*, 12(2):218–452, June 1987.

[22] H.Z. Yang and P.A. Larson. Query transformation for psj queries. In *Proceedings of the 13th International VLDB Conference*, pages 245–254, 1987.

WSQ/DSQ: A Practical Approach for Combined Querying of Databases and the Web*

Roy Goldman, Jennifer Widom

Stanford University

{royg,widom}@cs.stanford.edu, http://www-db.stanford.edu

Abstract

We present WSQ/DSQ (pronounced "wisk-disk"), a new approach for combining the query facilities of traditional databases with existing search engines on the Web. WSQ, for *Web-Supported (Database) Queries*, leverages results from Web searches to enhance SQL queries over a relational database. DSQ, for *Database-Supported (Web) Queries*, uses information stored in the database to enhance and explain Web searches. This paper focuses primarily on WSQ, describing a simple, low-overhead way to support WSQ in a relational DBMS, and demonstrating the utility of WSQ with a number of interesting queries and results. The queries supported by WSQ are enabled by two *virtual tables*, whose tuples represent Web search results generated dynamically during query execution. WSQ query execution may involve many high-latency calls to one or more search engines, during which the query processor is idle. We present a lightweight technique called *asynchronous iteration* that can be integrated easily into a standard sequential query processor to enable concurrency between query processing and multiple Web search requests. Asynchronous iteration has broader applications than WSQ alone, and it opens up many interesting query optimization issues. We have developed a prototype implementation of WSQ by extending a DBMS with virtual tables and asynchronous iteration; performance results are reported.

1   Introduction

Information today is decidedly split between structured data stored in traditional databases and the huge amount of unstructured information available over the World-Wide Web. Traditional relational, object-oriented, and object-relational databases operate over well-structured, typed data, and languages such as SQL and OQL enable expressive ad-hoc queries. On the Web, millions of hand-written and automatically-generated HTML pages form a vast but unstructured amalgamation of information. Much of the Web data is indexed by search engines, but search engines support only fairly simple keyword-based queries.

---

*This work was supported by the National Science Foundation under grant IIS-9811947 and by NASA Ames under grant NCC2-5278.

In this paper we propose a new approach that combines the existing strengths of traditional databases and Web searches into a single query system. *WSQ/DSQ* (pronounced "wisk-disk") stands for *Web-Supported (Database) Queries/Database-Supported (Web) Queries*. WSQ/DSQ is not a new query language. Rather, it is a practical way to exploit existing search engines to augment SQL queries over a relational database (WSQ), and for using a database to enhance and explain Web searches (DSQ). The basic architecture is shown in Figure 1. Each WSQ/DSQ instance queries one or more traditional databases via SQL, and keyword-based Web searches are routed to existing search engines. Users interacting with WSQ/DSQ can pose queries that seamlessly combine Web searches with traditional database queries.

As an example of WSQ (Web-Supported Database Queries), suppose our local database has information about all of the U.S. states, including each state's population and capital. WSQ can enhance SQL queries over this database using Web search engines to pose the following interesting WSQ queries (fully specified in Section 3.1):

- Rank all states by how often they are mentioned by name on the Web.
- Rank states by how often they appear, normalized by state population.
- Rank states by how often they appear on the Web near the phrase "four corners".
- Which state capitals appear on the Web more often than the state itself?
- Get the top two URLs for each state.
- If Google and AltaVista both agree that a URL is among the top 5 URLs for a state, return the state and the URL.

WSQ does not perform any "magic" interpretation, cleaning, or filtering of data on the Web. WSQ enables users to write intuitive SQL queries that automatically execute Web searches relevant to the query and combine the search results with the structured data in the database. With WSQ, we can easily write interesting queries that would otherwise require a significant amount of programming or manual searching.

DSQ (Database-Supported Web Queries) takes the converse approach, enhancing Web keyword searches with information in the database. For example, suppose our database contains information about movies, in addition to information about U.S. states. When a DSQ user searches for the keyword phrase "scuba diving", DSQ uses the Web to correlate that phrase with terms in the known database. For example, DSQ could identify the states and the movies that appear on the Web most often near the phrase "scuba diving", and might even find state/movie/scuba-diving triples

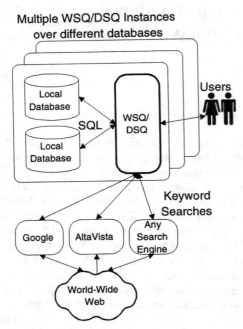

Figure 1: Basic WSQ/DSQ architecture

- The latency for a single request is very high.
- Unless it explicitly supports parallelism, the query processor is idle during the request.
- Search engines (and the Web in general) can handle many concurrent requests.

Thus, for maximum efficiency, a query processor must be able to issue many Web requests concurrently while processing a single query. As we will discuss in Section 4, traditional (non-parallel) query processors are not designed to handle this requirement. We might be able to configure or modify a parallel query processor to help us achieve this concurrency. However, parallel query processors tend to be high-overhead systems designed for multiprocessor computers, geared towards large data sets and/or complex queries. In contrast, the basic problem of issuing many concurrent Web requests within a query has a more limited scope that does not require traditional parallelism for a satisfactory solution. To support our WSQ framework, we introduce a query execution technique called *asynchronous iteration* that provides low-overhead concurrency for external virtual table accesses and can be integrated easily into conventional relational database systems.

The main contributions of this paper are:

- Definitions of the WebPages and WebCount virtual tables and their integration into SQL, with several examples illustrating the powerful WSQ queries enabled by this approach, and a discussion of support for such virtual tables in existing systems (Section 3).
- *Asynchronous iteration*, a technique that enables non-parallel relational query processors to execute multiple concurrent Web searches within a single query (Section 4). Although we discuss asynchronous iteration in the context of WSQ, it is a general query processing technique applicable to other scenarios as well, and it opens up interesting new query optimization issues.
- Experimental results from our WSQ prototype (Section 5), showing that asynchronous iteration can speed up WSQ queries by a factor of 10 or more.

2 Related Work

Several approaches have been proposed for bridging the divide between structured databases and the unstructured Web. *Wrappers* are used in many systems to make information in Web pages act logically as database elements, e.g., [PGGMU95]. Wrappers are a useful means of enabling expressive queries over data that was not necessarily designed for querying, and wrappers also facilitate the integration of data from multiple, possibly heterogeneous sources, e.g., [CGMH+94, RS97]. Unfortunately, wrappers over Web data tend to be labor-intensive and brittle, often requiring "screen-scraping" to parse HTML into meaningful structures. *Semistructured* data models [Abi97], in particular *XML* [XML97], provide some hope for introducing structure into Web data and queries [DFF+99, GMW99]. However, we believe that vast amounts of information will remain in HTML, and will continue to be queried through search engines such as AltaVista, Google, and others. New query languages have been proposed for dynamically navigating and

(e.g., an underwater thriller filmed in Florida). DSQ can be supported using the system and techniques we present in this paper, but we focus primarily on Web-supported queries (WSQ), leaving detailed exploration of DSQ for future work.

WSQ is based on introducing two *virtual tables*, WebPages and WebCount, to any relational database. A virtual table is a program that "looks" like a table to a query processor, but returns dynamically-generated tuples rather than tuples stored in the database. We will define explicitly our virtual tables in Section 3, but for now it suffices to think of WebPages as an infinite table that contains, for each possible Web search expression, all of the URLs returned by a search engine for that expression. WebCount can be thought of as an aggregate view over WebPages: for each possible Web search expression, it contains the total number of URLs returned by a search engine for that expression. We use WebPages_AV and WebCount_AV to denote the virtual tables corresponding to the AltaVista search engine, and we can have similar virtual tables for Google or any other search engine. By referencing these virtual tables in a SQL query, and assuring that the virtual columns defining the search expression are always bound during processing, we can answer the example queries above, and many more, with SQL alone.

While the details of WSQ query execution will be given later, it should be clear that many calls to a search engine may be required by one query, and it is not obvious how to execute such queries efficiently given typical search engine latency. One possibility is to modify search engines to accept specialized calls from WSQ database systems, but in this paper we instead show how small modifications to a conventional database query processor can exploit properties of existing search engines.

When query processing involves many search engine requests, the key observations are:

extracting data from the Web, e.g., [KS95, MMM97]. Our work differs in that we do not invent a new query language, and our queries combine results from Web searches with traditional structured data.

The techniques we know of that most closely relate to WSQ/DSQ are reported in [CDY95] and [DM97]. Written before the explosion of the World-Wide Web, [CDY95] focuses on execution and optimization techniques for SQL queries integrated with keyword-based external text sources. There are three main differences between [CDY95] and our work. First, they aim to minimize the number of external calls, rather than providing a mechanism to launch the calls concurrently. Nevertheless, some of techniques they propose are complementary to our framework and could be incorporated. Second, they assume that external text sources return search results as unordered sets, which enables optimizations that are not always possible when integrating SQL with (ranked) Web search results. Third, some of their optimizations are geared towards external text searches that return small (or empty) results, which we believe will be less common in WSQ given the breadth of the World-Wide Web. [DM97] discusses approaches for coupling a search engine with SQL, again without focusing on the World-Wide Web. A query rewrite scheme is proposed for automatically translating queries that call a search engine via a user-defined predicate into more efficient queries that integrate a search engine as a virtual table. While we also use a virtual table abstraction for search engines, [DM97] does not address the issue of high-latency external sources, which forms the core of much of this paper.

The integration of external relations into a cost-based optimizer for LDL is discussed in [CGK89]. The related, more general problem of creating and optimizing query plans over external sources with limited access patterns and varying query processing capabilities has been considered in work on data integration, e.g., [HKWY97, LRO96, RSU95]. In contrast, we focus on a specific scenario of one type of external source (a Web search engine) with known query capabilities. [BT98] addresses the situation where an external source may be unavailable at a particular time: a query over multiple external sources is rewritten into a sequence of incremental queries over subsets of sources, such that the query results can be combined over time to form the final result. Although the asynchronous iteration technique we introduce shares the general spirit of computing portions of a query and filling in remaining values later, our technique operates at a much finer (tuple-level) granularity, it does not involve query rewriting, and the goal is to enable concurrent processing of external requests rather than handling unavailable sources.

As will be seen in Section 4, we rely on *dependent joins* to supply bindings to our virtual tables when we integrate Web searches into a SQL query. Hence, previous work on optimizing and efficiently executing queries involving dependent joins is highly applicable. A general-purpose query optimization algorithm in the presence of dependent joins is provided in [FLMS99]. A caching technique that can be applied to improve the implementation of dependent

joins is discussed in [HN96].

Much of the research discussed in this section is either preliminary or complementary to WSQ/DSQ. To the best of our knowledge, no previous work has taken our approach of enabling a non-parallel database engine to support many concurrent calls to external sources during the execution of a single query.

3   Virtual Tables in WSQ

For the purpose of integrating Web searches with SQL, we can can abstract a Web search engine through a virtual WebPages table:

WebPages(SearchExp, T1, T2, ..., Tn, URL, Rank, Date)

where SearchExp is a parameterized string representing a Web search expression. SearchExp uses "%1", "%2", and so on to refer to the values that are bound during query processing to attributes T1, T2, ..., Tn, in the Unix printf or scanf style. For example, if SearchExp is "%1 near %2", T1 is bound to "Colorado" and T2 is bound to "Denver", then the corresponding Web search is "Colorado near Denver". For a given SearchExp and given bindings for T1, T2, ... Tn, WebPages contains 0 or more (virtual) tuples, where attributes URL, Rank, and Date are the values returned by the search engine for the search expression. The first URL returned by the search engine has Rank = 1, the second has Rank = 2, and so on. It is only practical to use WebPages in a query where SearchExp, T1, T2, ..., Tn are all bound, either by default (discussed below), through equality with a constant in the Where clause, or through an equi-join. In other words, these attributes can be thought of as "inputs" to the search engine. Furthermore, because retrieving all URLs for a given search expression could be extremely expensive (requiring many additional network requests beyond the initial search), it is prudent to restrict Rank to be less than some constant (e.g., Rank < 20), and this constant also can be thought of as an input to the search engine.

A simple but very useful view over WebPages is:

WebCount(SearchExp, T1, T2, ..., Tn, Count)

where Count is the total number of pages returned for the search expression. Many Web search engines can return a total number of pages immediately, without delivering the actual URLs. As we will see, WebCount is all we need for many interesting queries.

Note that for both tables, not only are tuples generated dynamically during query processing, but the number of columns is also a function of the given query. That is, a query might bind only column T1 for a simple keyword search, or it might bind T1, T2, ..., T5 for a more complicated search. Thus, we really have an infinite family of infinitely large virtual tables. For convenience in queries, SearchExp in both tables has a default value of "%1 near %2 near %3 near ... near %n".[1] For WebPages, if no restriction on Rank is included in the query, currently we assume a default selection predicate Rank < 20 to prevent "runaway" queries.

---

[1] For search engines such as Google that do not explicitly support the "near" operator, we use "%1 %2 ... %n" as the default.

Such defaults serve to keep the queries simple; in Section 3.1 we will see several queries that override the query defaults.

Note also that virtual table WebCount could be viewed instead as a scalar function, with input parameters Search-Exp, T1, T2, ..., Tn, and output value Count. However, since WebPages and other virtual tables can be more general than scalar functions—they can "return" any number of columns and any number of rows—our focus in this paper is on supporting the general case.

3.1 Examples

In this section we use WebPages and WebCount to write SQL queries for the examples presented informally in Section 1. In addition to the two virtual tables, our database contains one regular stored table:

States(Name, Population, Capital)

For each query, we restate it in English, write it in SQL, and show a small fraction of the actual result. The population values used for Query 2 are 1998 estimates from the U.S. Census Bureau [Uni98]. Queries 1–5 were issued to AltaVista (altavista.com), and Query 6 integrates results from both AltaVista and Google (google.com). All searches were performed in October 1999.[2]

Query 1: Rank states by how often they appear on the Web.

```
Select Name, Count
From States, WebCount
Where Name = T1
Order By Count Desc
```

Note that we are relying on the default value of "%1" for WebCount.SearchExp. The first five results are:

<California, 4995016><Washington, 4167056><New York, 3764513><Texas, 2724285><Michigan, 1621754>

Readers might be unaware that Texas and Michigan are the 2nd and 8th most populous U.S. states, respectively. Washington ranks highly because it is both a state and the U.S. capital; a revised query could exploit search engine features to avoid some false hits of this nature, but remember that our current goal is not one of "cleansing" or otherwise improving accuracy of Web searches.

Query 2: Rank states by how often they appear, normalized by state population.

```
Select Name, Count/Population As C
From States, WebCount
Where Name = T1
Order By C Desc
```

Now, the first five results are:

<Alaska, 1149><Washington, 733>
<Delaware, 690><Hawaii, 635><Wyoming, 603> ...

Query 3: Rank states by how often they appear on the Web near the phrase "four corners".

```
Select Name, Count
From States, WebCount
Where Name = T1 and T2 = 'four corners'
Order By Count Desc
```

---
[2]It turns out that repeated identical Web searches may return slightly different results, so your results could exhibit minor differences.

Recall that "%1 near %2" is the default value for Web-Count.SearchExp when T1 and T2 are bound. There is only one location in the United States where a person can be in four states at once: the "four corners" refers to the point bordering Colorado, New Mexico, Arizona, and Utah. Note the dramatic dropoff in Count between the first four results and the fifth:

<Colorado, 1745><New Mexico, 1249><Arizona, 1095>
<Utah, 994><California, 215> ...

Query 4: Which state capitals appear on the Web more often than the state itself?

```
Select Capital, C.Count, Name, S.Count
From States, WebCount C, WebCount S
Where Capital=C.T1 and Name=S.T1 and C.Count>S.Count
```

In the following (complete) results, we again see some limitations of text searches on the Web—more than half of the results are due to capitals that are very common in other contexts, such as "Columbia" and "Lincoln":

<Atlanta, 1053868, Georgia, 958280><Lincoln, 669059, Nebraska, 385991><Boston, 1409828, Massachusetts, 1006946> <Jackson, 1120655, Mississippi, 662145> <Pierre, 663310, South Dakota, 283821><Columbia, 1668270, South Carolina, 540618>

Query 5: Get the top two URLs for each state. We omit query results since they are not particularly compelling.

```
Select Name, URL, Rank
From States, WebPages
Where Name = T1 and Rank <= 2
Order By Name, Rank
```

Query 6: If Google and AltaVista both agree that a URL is among the top 5 URLs for a state, return the state and the URL.

```
Select Name, AV.URL
From States, WebPages_AV AV, WebPages_Google G
Where Name = AV.T1 and Name = G.T1 and
    AV.Rank <= 5 and G.Rank <= 5 and AV.URL = G.URL
```

Surprisingly, Google and AltaVista only agreed on the relevance of 4 URLs:

<Indiana, www.indiana.edu/copyright.html>
<Louisiana, www.usl.edu><Minnesota, www.lib.umn.edu>
<Wyoming, www.state.wy.us/state/welcome.html>

3.2 Support for virtual tables in existing systems

Both IBM DB2 and Informix currently support virtual tables in some form. We give a quick overview of the support options in each of these products, summarizing how we can modify our abstract virtual table definitions to work on such systems. (We understand that Oracle also expects to support virtual tables in a future release.) See [RP98] for more information about support for virtual tables in database products.

In DB2, virtual tables are supported through *table functions*, which can be written in Java or C [IBM]. A table function must export the number and names of its columns. Hence, DB2 cannot support a variable number of columns, so we would need to introduce a family of table functions

WebPages1, WebPages2, etc. to handle the different possible number of arguments, up to some predetermined maximum; similarly for WebCount. To the query processor, a table function is an iterator supporting methods *Open*, *GetNext*, and *Close*. Currently, DB2 provides no "hooks" into the query processor for pushing selection predicates into a table function. At first glance, this omission apparently prevents us from implementing WebPages or WebCount, since both tables logically contain an infinite number of tuples and require selection conditions to become finite. However, DB2 table functions support parameters that can be correlated to the columns of other tables in a From clause. For example, consider:

Select R.c1, S.c3
From R, Table(S(R.c2))

In this query, S is a table function that takes a single parameter. DB2 will create a new table function iterator for each tuple in R, passing the value of c2 in that tuple to the *Open* method of S. (DB2 requires that references to S come after R in the From clause.) With this feature, we can implement WebPages and WebCount by requiring that SearchExp and the n search terms are supplied as table function parameters, either as constants or using the From clause join syntax shown in the example query above. In the case of WebPages, we must pass the restriction on Rank as a parameter to the table function as well.

Informix supports virtual tables through its *virtual table interface* [SBH98]. Unlike DB2, Informix provides hooks for a large number of functions that the DBMS uses to create, query, and modify tables. For example, in Informix a virtual table scan can access the associated Where conditions, and therefore can process selection conditions. However, the Informix query processor gives no guarantees about join ordering, even when virtual tables are involved, so we cannot be sure that the columns used to generate the search expression are bound by the time the query processor tries to scan WebPages or WebCount. Thus, Informix currently cannot be used to implement WebPages or WebCount (although, as mentioned earlier, WebCount could be implemented as a user-defined scalar function, which is supported in Informix).

4   WSQ Query Processing

Even with an ideal virtual table interface, traditional execution of queries involving WebCount or WebPages would be extremely slow due to many high-latency calls to one or more Web search engines. As mentioned in Section 2, [CDY95] proposes optimizations that can reduce the number of external calls, and caching techniques [HN96] are important for avoiding repeated external calls. But these approaches can only go so far—even after extensive optimization, a query involving WebCount or WebPages must issue some number of search engine calls.

In many situations, the high latency of the search engine will dominate the entire execution time of the WSQ query. Any traditional non-parallel query plan involving WebCount or WebPages will be forced to issue Web searches sequen-

tially, each of which could take one or more seconds, and the query processor is idle during each request. Since Web search engines are built to support many concurrent requests, a traditional query processor is making poor use of available resources.

Thus, we want to find a way to issue as many concurrent Web searches as possible during query processing. While a parallel query processor (such as Oracle, Informix, Gamma [DGS+90], or Volcano [Gra90]) is a logical option to evaluate, it is also a heavyweight approach for our problem. For example, suppose a query requires 50 independent Web searches (for 50 U.S. states, say). To perform all 50 searches concurrently, a parallel query processor must not only dynamically partition the problem in the correct way, it must then launch 50 query threads or processes. Supporting concurrent Web searches during query processing is a problem of restricted scope that does not require a full parallel DBMS.

In the remainder of this section we describe *asynchronous iteration*, a new query processing technique that can be integrated easily into a traditional non-parallel query processor to achieve a high number of concurrent Web searches with low overhead. As we will discuss briefly in Section 4.2, asynchronous iteration is in fact a general query processing technique that can be used to handle a high number of concurrent calls to any external sources. (In future work, we plan to compare asynchronous iteration against the performance of a parallel query processor over a range of queries involving many calls to external sources.) As described in the following subsections, asynchronous iteration also opens up interesting new query optimization problems.

4.1   Asynchronous Iteration

Let us start with an example. Suppose in our relational database we have a simple table Sigs(Name), identifying the different ACM Special Interest Groups, called "Sigs"—e.g., SIGMOD, SIGOPS, etc. Now we want to use WebCount to rank the Sigs by how often they appear on the Web near the keyword "Knuth":[3]

Select *
From Sigs, WebCount
Where Name = T1 and T2 = 'Knuth'
Order By Count Desc

Figure 2 shows a possible query plan for this query. For this plan, and for all other plans in this paper, we assume an iterator-based execution model [Gra93] where each operator in the plan tree supports *Open*, *GetNext*, and *Close* operations. The *Dependent Join* operator requires each *GetNext* call to its right child to include a binding from its left child, thus limiting the physical join techniques that can be used to those of the nested-loop variety (although work in [HN96] describes hashing and caching techniques that can improve performance of a dependent join). The *EVScan* operator is an external virtual table scan. We assume that we are working with a query processor that can produce

---

[3]Incidentally, the results (in order) from AltaVista are: SIGACT, SIGPLAN, SIGGRAPH, SIGMOD, SIGCOMM, SIGSAM. For all other Sigs, Count is 0.

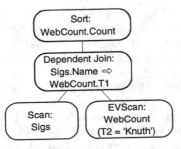

Figure 2: Query plan for Sigs ⋈ WebCount

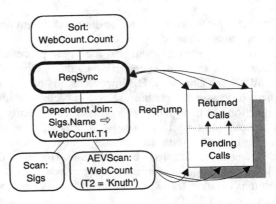

Figure 3: Asynchronous iteration

plans of this sort—with dependent joins and scans of virtual tables—such as IBM DB2 (recall Section 3.2).

Without parallelism, EVScan performs a sequence of Web searches during execution of this query plan (one for each *GetNext* call), and the query processor may be idle for a second or more each time. Intuitively, we would like the query processor to issue many Web searches simultaneously, without the overhead of a parallel query processor. For this small data set—37 tuples for the 37 ACM Sigs—we would like to issue all 37 requests at once. To achieve this behavior we propose asynchronous iteration, a technique involving three components:

1. A modified, asynchronous version of EVScan that we call *AEVScan*.
2. A new physical query operator called *ReqSync* (for "Request Synchronizer"), which waits for asynchronously launched calls to complete.
3. A global software module called *ReqPump* (for "Request Pump"), for managing all asynchronous external calls.

The general idea is that we modify a query plan to incorporate asynchronous iteration by replacing EVScans with AEVScans and inserting one or more ReqSync operators appropriately within the plan. AEVScan and ReqSync operators both communicate with the global ReqPump module. No other query plan operators need to be modified to support asynchronous iteration.

Now we walk through the actual behavior of asynchronous iteration using our example. Consider the query plan in Figure 3. In comparison to Figure 2, the EVScan has been replaced by an AEVScan, the ReqSync operator has been added, and the global ReqPump is used. When tuples are constructed during query processing, we allow any attribute value to be marked with a special *placeholder* that serves two roles:

1. The placeholder indicates that the attribute value (and thus the tuple it's a part of) is incomplete.
2. The placeholder identifies a pending ReqPump call associated with the missing value—that is, the pending call that will supply the true attribute value when the call finishes.

Recall that all of our operators, including AEVScan and ReqSync, obey a standard iterator interface, including *Open*, *GetNext*, and *Close* methods. We now discuss in turn how the operators in our example query plan work.

The Scan and Sort operators are oblivious to asynchronous iteration. The Dependent Join (hereafter DJ) is a standard nested-loop operator that also knows nothing about asynchronous iteration. Now consider the AEVScan. When DJ gets a new tuple from Sigs, it calls *Open* on AEVScan and then calls *GetNext* with Sigs.Name. AEVScan in turn contacts ReqPump and registers an external call C with T1 = Sigs.Name and T2 = 'Knuth'. (C is a unique identifier for the call.) ReqPump is a module that issues asynchronous network requests and stores the responses to each request as they return. In the case of call C, the returned data is simply a value for Count; ReqPump stores this value in a hash table *ReqPumpHash*, keyed on C. To achieve concurrency, as soon as AEVScan registers its call with ReqPump, it returns to DJ (as the result of *GetNext*) one WebCount tuple T where the Count attribute contains as a placeholder the call identifier C. DJ combines T with Sigs.Name and returns the new tuple to its parent (ReqSync).

Now let us consider the behavior of ReqSync. When its *Open* method is called from above by Sort, ReqSync calls *Open* on DJ below and then calls *GetNext* on DJ until exhaustion, buffering all returned (incomplete) tuples inside ReqSync. We choose this full-buffering implementation for the sake of simplicity, and we will revisit this decision momentarily. ReqSync needs to coordinate with ReqPump to fill in placeholders before returning tuples to its parent. The problem is a variation of the standard "producer/consumer" synchronization problem. Each ReqPump call is a producer: when a call C' completes (and its data is stored in ReqPumpHash), ReqPump signals to the consumer (ReqSync) that the data for C' is available. When signaled by ReqPump, ReqSync locates the incomplete tuple containing C' as a placeholder (using its own local hash table), and replaces C' with the Count value retrieved from ReqPumpHash. When ReqSync's *GetNext* method is called from above, if ReqSync has no completed tuples then it must wait for the next signal from ReqPump before it can return a tuple to its parent. Note that in the general case, tuples that do not depend on pending ReqPump calls may pass directly through a ReqSync operator.

In our simple implementation of ReqSync's *Open* method, all (incomplete) tuples generated by DJ are buffered inside ReqSync before ReqSync can return any (completed) tuples to its parent. In the case of very large joins it might make sense for ReqSync to make completed tuples available to its parent before exhausting execution of its child subplan. As with query execution in general, the question of materializing temporary results versus returning tuples as they become available is an optimization issue [GMUW00].

As we will show in Section 5, asynchronous iteration can improve WSQ query performance by a factor of 10 or more over a standard sequential query plan. However, there are still three important lingering issues that we will discuss in Sections 4.3, 4.4, and 4.5, respectively:

1. As seen in our example, an external call for WebCount always generates exactly one result tuple. But a call for WebPages may produce any number of tuples, including none, and the number of generated tuples is not known until the call is complete.

2. When a query plan involves more than one AEVScan, we must account for the possibility that an incomplete tuple buffered in ReqSync could contain placeholders for two or more different pending ReqPump calls.

3. We need to properly place ReqSync operators in relation to other query plan operators, both to guarantee correctness and maximize concurrency.

Monitoring and controlling resource usage is also an important issue when we use asynchronous iteration. So far we have assumed that during query execution we can safely issue an unbounded number of concurrent search requests. Realistically, we need to regulate the amount of concurrency to prevent a search engine from being inundated with an "unwelcome" number of simultaneous requests. Similarly, we may want to limit the total number of concurrent outgoing requests to prevent WSQ from exhausting its own local resources, such as network bandwidth. It is quite simple to modify ReqPump to handle such limits: we need only add one counter to monitor the total number of active requests, and one counter for each external destination. An administrator can configure each counter as desired. When a call is registered with ReqPump but cannot be executed because of resource limits, the call is placed on a queue. As resources free up, queued calls are executed.

4.2 Applicability of asynchronous iteration

Before delving into details of the three remaining technical issues outlined in the previous subsection, let us briefly consider the broader applicability of asynchronous iteration. Although this paper describes asynchronous iteration in the specific context of WSQ, the technique is actually quite general and applies to most situations where queries depend on values provided by high-latency, external sources. More specifically, if an external source can handle many concurrent requests, or if a query issues independent calls to many different external sources, then asynchronous iteration is appropriate. Our WSQ examples primarily illustrate the first case (many concurrent requests to one or two search engines). As an example of the second case, asynchronous iteration could be used to implement a Web crawler: given a table of thousands of URLs, a query over that table could be used to fetch the HTML for each URL (for indexing and to find the next round of URLs). In this scenario, WSQ

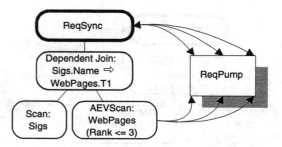

Figure 4: Query plan for Sigs ⋈ WebPages

can exploit all available resources without burdening any external sources.

As mentioned earlier, if we try to use a parallel query processor to achieve the high level of concurrency offered by asynchronous iteration, then we would need to partition tables dynamically into many small fragments and spawn many query threads or processes. Issuing many threads can be expensive. For example, the highest performance Web servers do not use one thread per HTTP request; rather, many network requests are handled asynchronously by an event-driven loop within a single process [PDZ99]. By implementing the ReqPump module of asynchronous iteration in a similar manner, we can enable many simultaneous calls with low overhead. Nonetheless, as future work we plan to conduct experiments comparing the performance of asynchronous iteration against a parallel DBMS for managing concurrent calls to external sources.

4.3 ReqSync tuple generation or cancellation

The previous example (Figure 3) was centered on a dependent join with WebCount, which always yields exactly one matching tuple. But WebPages, and any other virtual table in general, may return any number of tuples for given bindings—including none. Because we want AEVScan to return from a *GetNext* call without waiting for the actual results, we always begin by assuming that exactly one tuple joins, then "patch" our results in ReqSync.

Consider the following query, which retrieves the top 3 URLs for each Sig.

Select *
From Sigs, WebPages
Where Name = T1 and Rank <= 3

For each Sig, joining with WebPages may generate 0, 1, 2, or 3 tuples. Assume a simple query plan as shown in Figure 4. As in our previous example, AEVScan will use ReqPump to generate 37 search engine calls, and ReqSync will initially buffer 37 tuples. Now consider what happens for a tuple T, waiting in a ReqSync buffer for a call C to complete. When C returns, there are three possibilities:

1. If C returns no rows, then ReqSync deletes T from its buffer.

2. If C returns 1 row, then ReqSync fills in the attribute values for T as generated by C.

3. If C returns n rows, where $n > 1$, then ReqSync dynamically creates $n - 1$ additional copies of T, and fills in the attribute values accordingly.

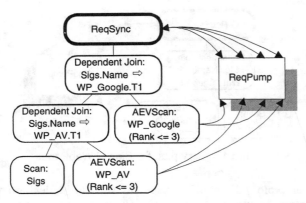

Figure 5: Query plan for Sigs ⋈ WebPages_AV ⋈ Web-Pages_Google

In our example, since all Sigs are mentioned on at least 3 Web pages, 111 tuples are ultimately produced by ReqSync.

4.4 Handling multiple AEVScans

Now let us consider query plans involving multiple AEVS-cans. For example, the following query finds the top 3 URLs for each Sig from two different search engines.[4]

Select *
From Sigs, WebPages_AV AV, WebPages_Google G,
Where Name = AV.T1 and Name = G.T1 and
AV.Rank <= 3 and G.Rank <= 3

Figure 5 shows a query plan that maximizes concurrent requests. Note that there is only one ReqSync operator, not one for each AEVScan. The placement and merging of ReqSync operators is discussed in Section 4.5. In this plan, the bottom Dependent Join will generate 37 tuples, each with placeholders identifying a ReqPump call for WebPages_AV. The upper join will augment each of these tuples with additional placeholders corresponding to a ReqPump call for WebPages_Google. Hence, ReqSync will buffer 37 incomplete tuples, each one with placeholders for two different ReqPump calls.

The algorithm for tuple cancellation, completion, and generation at the end of Section 4.3 applies in this case as well, with a slight nuance: dynamically copied tuples (case 3 in the algorithm) may proliferate references to pending calls. For example, suppose one of the incomplete tuples T in the ReqSync buffer is waiting for the completion of two calls, indicated by two different placeholders: one for call C_A to AltaVista and the other for call C_G to Google. If C_A returns first, with 3 tuples, then ReqSync will make two additional copies of T. When copying T, references to pending call C_G are also copied. Once C_G returns, all tuples referencing C_G must be updated.

4.5 Query plan generation

Recall that converting a query plan to use asynchronous iteration has two parts: (1) EVScan operators are converted

---

[4]The query actually finds all combinations of the top 3 URLs from each search engine, but it nonetheless serves to illustrate the point of this section.

to AEVScans, and (2) ReqSync operators are added to the plan. In this section we describe an algorithm for placing ReqSync operators within plans. Our primary goal is to introduce a correct and relatively simple algorithm that: (1) attempts to maximize the number of concurrent Web searches; (2) attempts to maximize the amount of query processing work that can be performed while waiting for Web requests to be processed; and (3) is easy to integrate into existing query compilers. ReqSync operators can significantly alter the cost of a query plan, and the effects on query execution time will often depend on the specific database instance being queried, as well as the results returned by search engines. Fully addressing cost-based query optimization in the presence of asynchronous iteration is an important, interesting, and broad problem that is beyond the scope of this paper. We intend to focus on optimization in future work.

We assume that the optimizer can generate plans with dependent joins [FLMS99] and EVScans, but knows nothing about asynchronous iteration; a plan produced by the optimizer is the input to our algorithm. We continue to assume an iterator model for all plan operators. We now describe the three steps in our placement of ReqSync operators: *Insertion*, *Percolation*, and *Consolidation*.

4.5.1 ReqSync Insertion

Recall that we first convert each EVScan operator in our input plan P to an asynchronous AEVScan. Next, a ReqSync operator is inserted directly above each AEVScan. More formally, for each AEVScan$_i$ in P, we insert ReqSync$_i$ into P as the parent of AEVScan$_i$. The previous parent of AEVScan$_i$ becomes the parent of ReqSync$_i$. This transformation is obviously correct since no operations occur between each asynchronous call and the blocking operator that waits for its completion.

4.5.2 ReqSync Percolation

Next, we try to move ReqSync operators up the query plan. Intuitively, each time we pull up a ReqSync operator we are increasing the amount of query processing work that can be done before blocking to wait for external calls to complete. Sometimes we can rewrite the query plan slightly to enable ReqSync pull-up. For example, if the parent of a ReqSync is a selection predicate that depends on attribute values filled in by ReqSync, we can pull ReqSync higher by pulling the selection predicate up first. Similarly, if a join depends on values filled in by ReqSync, we can rewrite the join as a selection over a cross-product and move the ReqSync above the cross-product.

Our actual algorithm is based on the notion of an operator O *clashing* with a ReqSync operator, in which case we cannot pull ReqSync above O. Let ReqSync$_i$.A denote the set of attributes whose values are filled in by the ReqSync$_i$ operator as ReqPump calls complete, i.e., the attributes whose values are substituted with placeholders by AEVScan$_i$. We say that O *clashes* with ReqSync$_i$ iff:

1. O depends on the value of an attribute in ReqSync$_i$.A, or
2. O removes an attribute in ReqSync$_i$.A via projection, or

3. O is an aggregation or existential operator

Case 1 is clear: an operator clashes if it needs the attributes filled in by $ReqSync_i$ to continue processing. Case 2 is a bit more subtle. If we project away placeholders before the corresponding calls are complete, then tuple cancellation or generation (Section 4.3) cannot take place properly, and extra tuples or incorrect numbers of duplicates may be returned. Case 3 is similar to case 2: aggregation (e.g., Count) and existential quantification require an accurate tally of incoming tuples.

For each $ReqSync_i$ in the plan, we repeatedly pull $ReqSync_i$ above any non-clashing operators. If an operator O does clash, we check to see if O is a projection or selection; if so, we can pull O above its parent first. Otherwise, if O is a clashing join, we rewrite it as a selection over a cross-product. Other similar rewrites are possible. For example, a set union operator must examine each complete tuple to perform duplicate elimination; we can rewrite this clashing operator as a "Select Distinct" over a non-clashing bag union operator. Our percolation algorithm clearly terminates since operators are only pulled up the plan. Also, the order in which we percolate ReqSync operators does not matter—the only potential effect is a different final ordering between adjacent ReqSync operators, something that is made irrelevant by ReqSync Consolidation, which we discuss next. We will illustrate the percolation algorithm through examples momentarily.

4.5.3 ReqSync Consolidation

After percolation, we may find that two or more ReqSync operators are now adjacent in the plan. At this point we can merge adjacent ReqSync operators since they perform the same overall function, and a single ReqSync operator can manage multiple placeholder values in tuples as discussed in Section 4.4. When merging $ReqSync_i$ with $ReqSync_j$, $ReqSync_i.A \cup ReqSync_j.A$ is the set of attributes that must be filled in by the new ReqSync operator.

4.5.4 Plan generation examples

We now show three examples demonstrating our ReqSync placement algorithm. We point out the performance gains asynchronous iteration can provide, along with some potential pitfalls of our current algorithm.

Example 1: Figure 6 shows how our ReqSync placement algorithm generates the query plan we saw earlier in Figure 5 for the Sigs ⋈ WebPages_AV ⋈ WebPages_Google query. We omit ReqPump from these (and all remaining) query plans. Figure 6(a) shows the input to the algorithm, a simple left-deep query plan without asynchronous iteration. Figure 6(b) shows the plan after ReqSync Insertion: the EVScans are converted to AEVScans and a ReqSync operator is inserted directly above each EVScan. Figure 6(c) shows the plan after ReqSync Percolation. We first move $ReqSync_1$ above both dependent joins, since neither join depends on any values returned by WebPages_AV (i.e., URL, Date, Rank). $ReqSync_2$ is then pulled above its parent dependent join. The final plan after ReqSync Consolidation is shown in Figure 6(d). With this plan, the query processor

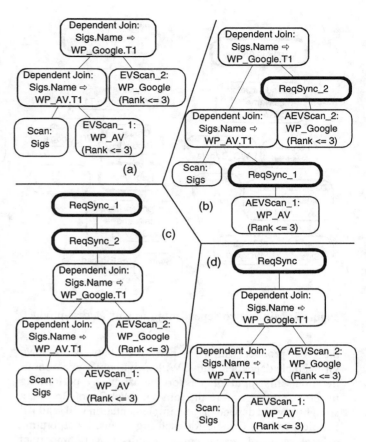

Figure 6: Generating the query plan for Sigs ⋈ Web-Pages_AV ⋈ WebPages_Google in Figure 5

can process all 74 external calls (37 Sigs per join) concurrently.

This example demonstrates some interesting advantages of asynchronous iteration over possible alternatives. First, one might consider simply modifying the dependent join operator to work in parallel: change the dependent join to launch many threads, each one for joining one left-hand input tuple with the right-hand EVScan. While this approach will provide maximal concurrency for many simple queries, it prevents concurrency among requests from multiple dependent joins: the query processor will block until the first join completes. Another approach, as discussed in Section 4.2, is to use a (modified) parallel query processor for this query. However, performing both dependent joins in parallel requires a nontrivial rewrite to transform our 2-join plan into a 3-join plan where both dependent joins are children of a final "merging" join. □

Example 2: Consider the following query, where a cross-product with a meaningless table R is introduced for illustrative purposes:

```
Select *
From Sigs, WebCount_AV AV, R, WebCount_Google G
Where Name = AV.T1 and Name = G.T1
```

Figure 7(a) shows the result of running our ReqSync placement algorithm over a left-deep input plan in which

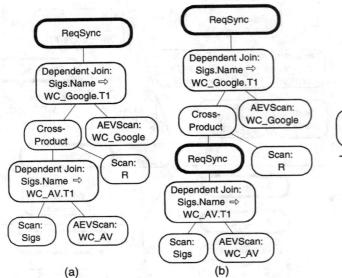

Figure 7: Mixing two dependent joins with a cross-product

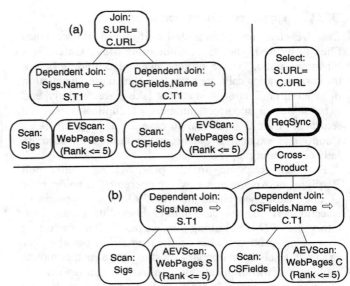

Figure 8: Plans for query over Sigs and CSFields

the cross-product with R is performed between the two virtual table dependent joins. With or without asynchronous iteration, this input plan is problematic: by performing the cross-product before the join with WebCount_Google, a straightforward dependent join implementation will send |R| identical calls to Google for each Sig. Thus, incorporating a local cache of search engine results is very important for such a plan. Furthermore, when using asynchronous iteration with the plan in Figure 7(a), the cross-product with table $\bar{R}$ will generate |R| copies of the incomplete tuples from WebCount_AV that must be buffered and then patched by ReqSync. Depending on the data, it may be preferable to use two ReqSync operators as shown in Figure 7(b). By doing so, we reduce the total number of attribute values to be patched by $|Sigs| \cdot (|R| - 1)$, or roughly a factor of 2 for reasonably large |R|. On the down side, we will block after the first join, preventing us from concurrently issuing the Web requests for WebCount_Google. Had the cross-product with R been placed last in the original input plan, another alternative would be to place a single ReqSync operator above the dependent joins but below the cross-product.

This contrived example serves to illustrate the challenging query optimization problems that arise when we introduce AEVScan and ReqSync operators. Still, in many cases our simple ReqSync placement algorithm does perform well, as we will see in Section 5. □

Example 3: Finally, suppose that we also have a table CSFields(Name) containing computer science fields (e.g., "databases", "operating systems", "artificial intelligence", etc.). Consider the following query, which finds URLs that are among the top 5 URLs for both a Sig and a CSField.

Select S.URL
From Sigs, WebPages S, CSFields, WebPages C
Where Sigs.Name = S.T1 and CSFields.Name = C.T1
  and S.Rank <= 5 and C.Rank <= 5 and S.URL = C.URL

An input query plan is shown in Figure 8(a). Note that the input plan is bushy, and the join at the root of the plan may well be implemented as a sort-merge or hash join. After inserting the two ReqSync operators, we first pull them above the dependent joins. To pull the ReqSyncs above the upper join, we rewrite the join into a selection over a cross-product, as described in Section 4.5.2. (Because the join depends on attributes supplied by WebPages, we can't pull the ReqSync above it without the rewrite.) Figure 8(b) shows the final plan.

In this query, given that the Sigs and CSFields tables are tiny, rewriting the join as a cross-product is a big performance win: it enables the query processor to execute all external calls (from both the left and right subplans) concurrently. However, in other situations, such as if the cross-product is huge, this rewrite could be a mistake.

This example illustrates one more important issue. Suppose that a Sig does not have any URLs on a given search engine. Indeed, assume for the moment that all Sigs have no URLs, so all Sig tuples generated will ultimately be canceled. In that case, pulling the ReqSync operator up as in Figure 8(b) results in an unnecessary cross-product between placeholder tuples for CSFields and WebPages, since ultimately the cross-product (and therefore the join) will be empty. In the general case, because AEVScan always returns exactly one matching tuple before the final result is known, a plan could perform unnecessary work—work that would not be done if the query processor waited for the true Web search result before continuing. □

To summarize, the above examples demonstrate how our ReqSync placement algorithm focuses on maximizing the number of concurrent external calls for any given query plan. If external calls dominate query execution time, then asynchronous iteration can provide dramatic performance improvements, as we demonstrate in Section 5.

5 Implementation and Experiments

We have integrated the two WSQ virtual tables and our asynchronous iteration technique into a homegrown relational database management system called *Redbase*. (Redbase is constructed by students at Stanford in a course on DBMS implementation.) Redbase supports a subset of SQL for select-project-join queries, and it includes a page-level buffer and iterator-based query execution. However, it was not designed to be a high-performance system: the only available join technique is nested-loop join, and there is no query optimizer although users can specify a join ordering manually. Nevertheless, Redbase is stable and sophisticated enough to support the experiments in this section, which demonstrate the potential of asynchronous iteration. Our experiments show the considerable performance improvement of running WSQ queries with asynchronous iteration as opposed to conventional sequential iteration.

Measuring the performance of WSQ queries has some inherent difficulties. First, performance of a search engine such as AltaVista can fluctuate considerably depending on load and network delays beyond our control. Second, because of caching behavior beyond our control, repeated searches with identical keyword expressions may run far faster the second (and subsequent) times. To mitigate these issues, we waited at least two hours between queries that issue identical searches, which we verified empirically is long enough to eliminate caching behavior. Also, we performed our experiments late at night when the load on search engines is low and, more importantly, consistent.

In order to run many experiments without waiting hours between each one, we use *template* queries and instantiate multiple versions of them that are structurally similar but result in slightly different searches being issued. Consider the following template.

Template 1:

    Select Name, Count
    From States, WebCount
    Where Name = T1 and WebCount.T2 = V1

$V1$ represents a constant that is chosen from a pool of different common constants, such as "computer", "beaches", "crime", "politics", "frogs", etc. For our experiments, we created 8 instances of the template by choosing 8 different constants from the pool. After timing all queries using asynchronous iteration, we waited two hours and then timed all queries using the standard query processor. For corroboration, we repeated the test with 8 new query instances.

The results for this template (and the two below) are shown in Table 1. For each template, we list the results of two runs. The times listed are the average execution time in seconds for the 8 queries, with and without asynchronous iteration. AltaVista is used for the first two templates; the third uses both AltaVista and Google. Experiments were conducted on a Sun Sparc Ultra-2 (2 x 200Mhz) 256MB RAM machine running SunOS 5.6. The computer is connected to the Internet via Stanford University's network.

	Synch (secs)	Asynch (secs)	Speedup
Template 1			
Run 1 (8 queries)	23.13	3.88	6.0x
Run 2 (8 others)	32.8	3.5	9.4x
Template 2			
Run 1 (8 queries)	70.75	5.25	13.5x
Run 2 (8 others)	64.25	5.13	12.5x
Template 3			
Run 1 (8 queries)	122.5	6.25	19.6x
Run 2 (8 others)	76.13	4.63	16.4x

Table 1: Experimental results

Template 2:

    Select Name, Count, URL, Rank
    From States, WebCount, WebPages
    Where Name = WebCount.T1 and WebCount.T2 = V1 and
        Name = WebPages.T1 and WebPages.T2 = V2 and
        WebPages.Rank <= 2

In this query template, we issue two searches for each tuple in States, one for WebCount and one for WebPages. When instantiating the template we wanted to ensure that $V1 \neq V2$, so we selected 16 distinct constants to create 8 query instances. In our prototype system, the join order is always specified by the order of tables in the From clause, so for this query we joined States with WebCount, then joined the result with WebPages. Results are shown in Table 1.

Template 3: The following template is similar to the example in Section 4.4 (Figure 5), with the added constant $V1$. Again, we created 8 queries by instantiating $V1$ with constants, and results are shown in Table 1.

    Select Name, AV.URL, G.URL
    From Sigs, WebPages_AV AV, WebPages_Google G,
    Where Name = AV.T1 and Name = G.T1 and
        AV.Rank <= 3 and G.Rank <= 3 and AV.T2 = V1 and
        G.T2 = V1

Our results show clearly that asynchronous iteration can improve the performance of WSQ queries by a factor of 10 or more. Of course, all of the example queries here are over very small local tables, so network costs dominate. These results in effect illustrate the best-case improvement offered by asynchronous iteration. For queries involving more complex local query processing over much larger relations, the speedup may be less dramatic, and the results of any such experiment would be highly dependent on the sophistication of the database query processor (independent of asynchronous iteration). Further, as illustrated in Section 4, complex queries may introduce optimization decisions that could have a significant impact on performance. In future work we plan a comprehensive study of query optimization incorporating asynchronous iteration, including additional experiments and performance comparisons to alternate approaches such as parallel query processing.

We have created a simple interface that allows users to pose limited queries over our WSQ implementation. Please visit http://www-db.stanford.edu/wsq.

Acknowledgments

We thank Serge Abiteboul for his contributions to early WSQ/DSQ discussions, and Jason McHugh for helpful comments on an initial draft of this paper. We also thank Berthold Reinwald and Paul Brown for information about IBM DB2 and Informix, respectively.

References

[Abi97] S. Abiteboul. Querying semistructured data. In *Proc. of the Intl. Conference on Database Theory*, Delphi, Greece, January 1997.

[BT98] P. Bonnet and A. Tomasic. Partial answers for unavailable data sources. In *Proc. of the Third Intl. Conference on Flexible Query Answering Systems (FQAS)*, pages 43–54, Roskilde, Denmark, May 1998.

[CDY95] S. Chaudhuri, U. Dayal, and T. Yan. Join queries with external text sources: Execution and optimization techniques. In *Proc. of the ACM SIGMOD Intl. Conference on Management of Data*, pages 410–422, San Jose, California, 1995.

[CGK89] D. Chimenti, R. Gamboa, and R. Krishnamurthy. Towards an open architecture for LDL. In *Proc. of the Fifteenth Intl. Conference on Very Large Data Bases*, pages 195–203, Amsterdam, The Netherlands, August 1989.

[CGMH+94] S. Chawathe, H. Garcia-Molina, J. Hammer, K. Ireland, Y. Papakonstantinou, J. Ullman, and J. Widom. The Tsimmis project: Integration of heterogeneous information sources. In *Proc. of 100th Anniversary Meeting of the Information Processing Society of Japan*, pages 7–18, Tokyo, Japan, October 1994.

[DFF+99] A. Deutsch, M. Fernandez, D. Florescu, A. Levy, and D. Suciu. A query language for XML. In *Proc. of the Eighth Intl. World Wide Web Conference (WWW8)*, Toronto, Canada, 1999.

[DGS+90] D.J. DeWitt, S. Ghandeharizadeh, D.A. Schneider, A. Bricker, H.I. Hsiao, and R. Rasmussen. The Gamma database machine project. *IEEE Transactions on Knowledge and Data Engineering*, 2(1):44–62, 1990.

[DM97] S. Dessloch and N. Mattos. Integrating SQL databases with content-specific search engines. In *Proc. of the Twenty-Third Internatial Conference on Very Large Databases*, pages 276–285, Athens, Greece, August 1997.

[FLMS99] D. Florescu, A. Levy, I. Manolescu, and D. Suciu. Query optimization in the presence of limited access patterns. In *Proc. of the ACM SIGMOD Intl. Conference on Management of Data*, pages 311–322, Philadelphia, Pennsylvania, June 1999.

[GMUW00] H. Garcia-Molina, J.D. Ullman, and J. Widom. *Database System Implementation*. Prentice Hall, Upper Saddle River, New Jersey, 2000.

[GMW99] R. Goldman, J. McHugh, and J. Widom. From semistructured data to XML: Migrating the Lore data model and query language. In *Proc. of the 2nd Intl. Workshop on the Web and Databases (WebDB '99)*, pages 25–30, Philadelphia, Pennsylvania, June 1999.

[Gra90] G. Graefe. Encapsulation of parallelism in the Volcano query processing system. In *Proc. of the ACM SIGMOD Intl. Conference on Management of Data*, pages 102–111, Atlantic City, New Jersey, May 1990.

[Gra93] G. Graefe. Query evaluation techniques for large databases. *ACM Computing Surveys*, 25(2):73–170, 1993.

[HKWY97] L. Haas, D. Kossmann, E. Wimmers, and J. Yang. Optimizing queries across diverse data sources. In *Proc. of the Twenty-Third Internatial Conference on Very Large Databases*, pages 276–285, Athens, Greece, August 1997.

[HN96] J.M. Hellerstein and J.F. Naughton. Query execution techniques for caching expensive methods. In *Proc. of the ACM SIGMOD Intl. Conference on Management of Data*, pages 423–434, Montreal, Canada, June 1996.

[IBM] IBM DB2 Universal Database SQL Reference Version 6. ftp://ftp.software.ibm.com/ps/products/db2/ info/vr6/pdf/letter/db2s0e60.pdf.

[KS95] D. Konopnicki and O. Shmueli. W3QS: A query system for the World Wide Web. In *Proc. of the Twenty-First Intl. Conference on Very Large Data Bases*, pages 54–65, Zurich, Switzerland, September 1995.

[LRO96] A. Levy, A. Rajaraman, and J. Ordille. Querying heterogeneous information sources using source descriptions. In *Proc. of the Twenty-Second Intl. Conference on Very Large Databases*, pages 251–262, Bombay, India, September 1996.

[MMM97] A.O. Mendelzon, G. Mihaila, and T. Milo. Querying the World Wide Web. *Intl. Journal on Digital Libraries*, 1(1):54–67, April 1997.

[PDZ99] V. Pai, P. Druschel, and W. Zwaenepoel. Flash: An efficient and portable web server. In *Proc. of the USENIX 1999 Annual Technical Conference*, Monterey, CA, June 1999.

[PGGMU95] Y. Papakonstantinou, A. Gupta, H. Garcia-Molina, and J. Ullman. A query translation scheme for rapid implementation of wrappers. In *Proc. of the Fourth Intl. Conference on Deductive and Object-Oriented Databases*, pages 161–186, Singapore, December 1995.

[RP98] B. Reinwald and H. Pirahesh. SQL open heterogenous data access. In *Proc. of the ACM SIGMOD Intl. Conference on Management of Data*, pages 506–507, Seattle, Washington, June 1998.

[RS97] M.T. Roth and P.M. Schwarz. Don't scrap it, wrap it! A wrapper architecture for legacy data sources. In *Proc. of the Twenty-Third Internatial Conference on Very Large Databases*, pages 266–275, Athens, Greece, August 1997.

[RSU95] A. Rajaraman, Y. Sagiv, and J.D. Ullman. Answering queries using templates with binding patterns. In *Proc. of the Fourteenth ACM SIGACT-SIGMOD-SIGART Symposium on Principles of Database Systems*, pages 105–112, San Jose, California, May 1995.

[SBH98] M. Stonebraker, P. Brown, and M. Herbach. Interoperability, distributed applications and distributed databases: The virtual table interface. *Data Engineering Bulletin*, 21(3):25–33, 1998.

[Uni98] United States Bureau of the Census. State population estimates and demographic components of population change: July 1, 1997 to July 1, 1998. http://www.census.gov/ population/estimates/state/st-98-1.txt, December 1998.

[XML97] World Wide Web Consortium. Extensible markup language (XML). http://www.w3.org/ TR/WD-xml-lang-970331.html, December 1997.

A Framework for Expressing and Combining Preferences

Rakesh Agrawal   *Edward L. Wimmers*

IBM Almaden Research Center
San Jose, CA 95120

Abstract

The advent of the World Wide Web has created an explosion in the available on-line information. As the range of potential choices expand, the time and effort required to sort through them also expands. We propose a formal framework for expressing and combining user preferences to address this problem. Preferences can be used to focus search queries and to order the search results. A preference is expressed by the user for an entity which is described by a set of named fields; each field can take on values from a certain type. The * symbol may be used to match any element of that type. A set of preferences can be combined using a generic combine operator which is instantiated with a value function, thus providing a great deal of flexibility. Same preferences can be combined in more than one way and a combination of preferences yields another preference thus providing the closure property. We demonstrate the power of our framework by illustrating how a currently popular personalization system and a real-life application can be realized as special cases of our framework. We also discuss implementation of the framework in a relational setting.

1   Introduction

The World Wide Web is suffering from abundance. The publicly indexable web contains an estimated 800 million pages [LG99]. The number of pages is anticipated to expand 1000% over the next few years [BP96]. The current on-line catalog of Amazon.com contains more than 3 million books, 225,000 CDs, 60,000 Videos, and other merchandise. The auctioning site eBay has on-line information on more than 3 million items on sale at any time. The emergence of industry-specific exchanges such as Sciquest, Chemdex, Chipcenter, etc. will cause the amount of on-line information about product and services to further explode.

As the range of potential choices expand, the time and effort required to sort through them also expands. These problems are difficult enough when a person is actively searching for a product to meet a specific need. The problem becomes even more severe when people are browsing. The effort required to browse through thousands, if not millions, of product variants within specific categories becomes like searching for the proverbial needle in a haystack [HS99]. The importance and potential commercial impact of managing this data so that users can quickly and flexibly state their preferences represents an important new potential direction for database technology.

We propose a framework for expressing and combining user preferences to address the above problem. Preferences can be used to focus search queries and to order the search results. While the Web applications motivated our work, the framework is more generally applicable.

The salient features of our framework are:

- A user expresses preference for an entity by providing a numeric score between 0 and 1[1], or vetoing it, or explicitly stating indifference. By default, indifference is assumed. Thus, a user states preference for only those entities that the user cares about.

- An entity is described by a set of named fields; each field can take on values from a certain type. The * symbol may be used to match any element of that type. For example, (painting, cubist, *) refers to any cubist painting, (painting, *, Picasso) refers to paintings of Picasso, and (*, *, Picasso) refers to any artwork of Picasso.

- Preferences can be combined. There is one generic combine operation for this purpose. This operator is instantiated by value functions to yield specific instances of the combine operation. Having a single

---

[1] Extension to the case where the scores are discretized and assigned symbolic labels is straightforward.

generic combine operation makes for a lean and easy to understand and implement system. Allowing value functions provides a great deal of flexibility.

- Specification of preferences is decoupled from how they are combined. The same preferences may be combined in different ways depending upon the application.

- Autonomy of various preferences is preserved. Preference for an entity can be changed without affecting any score of an unrelated entity.

- The combining operation has the closure property so that the result of combining two preferences may be further combined with another preference.

To illustrate the flexibility of our framework, we take a current popular personalization system and a real-life application and show how they can be modeled within our framework. We also sketch how to implement our framework in a relational setting.

Related Work The problem of expressing and combining preferences arises in several applications. Customization by selecting from a menu of choices (e.g. ticker symbols for tracking stocks, city names for weather forecast) can be thought of as a simple expression of preferences. Term expressions used for filtering documents (e.g. myexcite) can also be viewed as simple form of preferences. The recommendation systems based on collaborative filtering [RV97] ask users to rank items and combine preferences of similar users to make recommendations. The need for combining rankings of different models has arisen in meta-search problems [EHJ+96] [FISS98], multi-media systems [Fag98], and information retrieval [SM83]. Perhaps the most famous theorem related to combining preferences is the Arrow Impossibility Theorem in Economics [Arr50]. The theorem says that it is impossible to construct a "social preference function" (ranking the desirability of various social arrangements) out of individual preferences while retaining a particular set of features.

While related, the main thrust of our work is quite orthogonal to the above literature. Our main concern is to develop a flexible framework for expressing and combining preferences that has certain desirable properties. The specific function used in combining some preferences is a parameter in our framework; we only require that this function obey certain constraints. (Arrow's social preference function does not obey these constraints.)

Paper Organization The rest of the paper is structured as follows. In Section 2, we present our preference framework. We formally define preference functions and how they are combined. We introduce modular combining forms that have the desirable properties of efficiency and conservation of the autonomy of various preferences. Modular combining forms are closed under composition. We show that all the preference combining forms defined using our framework are indeed modular.

In Section 3, we model the Personalogic system (http://www.personalogic.com) using our framework. In this case study, we combine several preference functions from the same person that cover different aspects of a total picture. We also model a real-life design application in which a company's preferences are combined with an engineer's preferences into a single preference function. We then present a completeness result that explains the power of our framework.

In Section 4, we sketch how our preference system can be implemented on a relational database system. We conclude with a summary in Section 5.

In this paper, we assume that the user explicitly provides preferences. It is easy to extrapolate how such a system can be used in conjunction with a data mining system that observes a user's past interactions and offers suggestions for preferences.

2 The Framework

2.1 Preference Functions

In this section, we formalize the notion of a preference function.

We start with a set of (base) types which typically include ints, strings, floats, booleans, etc.

We introduce a data type called *score* that represents a user preference. Formally, this is $[0,1] \cup \{ \natural, \perp \}$. A score of 1 indicates the highest level of user preference. A score of 0 indicates the lowest level of user preference. The "$\natural$" score represents a veto. The "$\perp$" score represents that no user preference has been indicated.

We also make use of record types. Since it is an important building block of preference functions, it is worth briefly reviewing. A *record type* is a set of pairs { name_1:type_1, ..., name_n:type_n } in which all n names (a name is simply a non-empty string) are different (although the types are allowed to be the same). In this case, name_i is the name of a field in the record and type_i is the type of that field. A record is where each field takes on a value in the type of that field. More formally, a record is a function r whose domain is { name_1 , ..., name_n } such that $r(\text{name\_i})$ is an element of type_i. Usually, $r(\text{name\_i})$ is written as $r.\text{name\_i}$.

A type is called *wild* iff it contains "*". The "*" symbol is used to indicate a wild card that "matches" any value.

Definition 2.1 *A preference function is a function that maps records of a given record type to a score. If p* *is a preference function, we use dom(p) to refer to the given record type that is the domain of p.*

Since we sometimes wish to apply a preference function to a record with more fields than are present in the domain of the preference function, we introduce a projection operator to eliminate the extra fields. This is formalized in Definition 2.2.

Definition 2.2 *Let rt be the record type $\{n_1 : t_1, \ldots, n_k : t_k\}$. Let r be a record of type $\{n_1 : t_1, \ldots, n_k : t_k, n_{k+1} : t_{k+1}, \ldots n_l : t_l\}$ where $k \leq l$. Then $\pi_{rt}(r)$ is the record of type rt where $\pi_{rt}(r).n_i = r.n_i$ for $i \leq k$.*

While a preference function does not require that the types of fields in the record type that is the domain of a preference function be wild, most of the time these fields will be wild so as to allow the user a convenient method for specifying a whole class of preferences.

Definition 2.3 *Given two records r_1, r_2 of type $rt = \{n_1 : t_1, \ldots, n_k : t_k\}$, we say r_2 generalizes r_1 (which is written as $r_2 \triangleright r_1$) iff for all $i \leq k$, either $r_2.n_i = r_1.n_i$ or $r_2.n_i = *$.*

It is clear that the $\triangleright$ relation is reflexive and transitive. Note that for any record r there are 2^j records that generalize r where j is the number of fields that have a wild type and for which the value of the field in r is not "*"

2.2 Combining Preference Functions

It is frequently desirable to combine preference functions to form a new preference function. We define a preference function meta-combining form called *combine* which takes a "value function" that says how to compute a new score based on the original scores and produces a preference function combining form (which takes a finite list of preference functions and produces the new preference function). Imagine two roommates, Alice (who never cooks but likes to decorate) and Betty (who does all the cooking) are purchasing a refrigerator. Alice has a preference function (called A_0) whose domain is $\{model : int, color : string \cup \{*\}\}$; Betty has a preference function (called B_0) whose domain is $\{model : int, quality : int\}$. The *model* field indicates the model number, the *color* field is a string describing the color, and *quality* is an integer between 1 and 4 indicating the quality of the refrigerator. Notice that *color* is the only field with a wild type. The two roommates agree that the combined preference function should be what Betty wants (since she does all the cooking) but that Alice should have veto power over any refrigerator they buy. In this subsection, we define a preference function combining form and show how this roommate example can be expressed using this preference function combining form.

We assume the existence of a special character "!" that is reserved for system use and is not allowed to appear in the name of any (user) record field.

Definition 2.4 *Given a record type, $rt = \{n_1 : t_1, \ldots, n_k : t_k\}$, define $ScoreBoard(rt) = \{n'_1! \ldots !n'_k : score | (t_i \text{ is wild} \land n'_i = "star!'') \lor n'_i = n_i\}$.*

Notice that we are using the special character "!" both as a separator character as well as at the end of the "star!" string to avoid conflict with the name of a user field (which is not allowed to contain the "!" character). Thus, $ScoreBoard(rt)$ has 2^j fields where j is the number of t_i types that are wild. The careful reader will note that the record type is a set which is unordered whereas the new field names have an order (namely n'_1 occurs before n'_2, etc.). This gap is easy to remedy by simply taking the names in the new record field to be listed in alphabetical order. In the roommate example, $ScoreBoard(dom(A_0)) = \{color!model : score, star!!model : score\}$ and $ScoreBoard(dom(B_0)) = \{model!quality : score\}$.

Definition 2.5 *Given a record type $rt = \{n_1 : t_1, \ldots, n_k : t_k\}$ and the name of a field $n'_1! \ldots !n'_k$ in record type $ScoreBoard(rt)$, and a record r of type rt, define $RecordOf_{rt}(r, n'_1! \ldots !n'_k)$ to be a record of type rt such that, for each field name n_j in rt,*

$$RecordOf_{rt}(r, n'_1! \ldots !n'_k).n_j = \begin{cases} r.n_j & \text{if } n'_j = n_j \\ * & \text{if } n'_j = star! \end{cases}$$

Notice that $RecordOf_{rt}$ completely specifies the record since a value is supplied for every field in the record of type rt. Also note that n'_j can be "star!" only if t_j is wild so that the n_j field in the record $RecordOf_{rt}$ is always a valid member of type t_j. For example, in the roommate example, $RecordOf_{dom(A_0)}(r, star!!model) = \{color = *, model = r.model\}$. (Note that we use the $=$ sign (rather than :) when giving a specific instance of a record.) It is clear that, when applied to a record of type rt, $RecordOf_{rt}$ produces a generalization of that record.

Definition 2.6 *Given a preference function p whose domain is the record type $rt = \{n_1 : t_1, \ldots, n_k : t_k\}$, and a record r of type rt, define $Scores(p, r)$ to be a record of type $ScoreBoard(rt)$ such that $Scores(p, r).n'_1! \ldots !n'_k = p(RecordOf_{rt}(r, n'_1! \ldots !n'_k))$.*

The basic idea is that $Scores(p, r)$ provides the value of $p(r')$ for all the generalizations r' of r when the type of r is $dom(p)$. Clearly, $Scores(p, r) : ScoreBoard(dom(p))$ provided r is of type $dom(p)$. In the roommate example, $Scores(A_0, r) =$

$\{star!!model = A_0(\{color = *, model = r.model\}),$
$color!model = A_0(\{color = r.color, model = r.model\})\}.$
In the case that $n_i' = n_i$ for each i (i.e., none of the n_i' are "star!"), note that
$Scores(A_0, r).n_1!\ldots!n_k = A_0(r).$

Definition 2.7 *A finite set of record types* $\{rt_1, \ldots, rt_n\}$ *is* compatible *iff whenever* rt_i *and* rt_j *share a field with the same name, then those two fields have the same type.*

If $\{rt_1, \ldots, rt_n\}$ *is compatible, define* $merge(rt_1, \ldots, rt_n)$ *to be the record type that has a field* $n : t$ *iff at least one of the record types has the field* $n : t$.

Note that, by compatibility, each field in the merged record type will have a uniquely determined type. In other words, $merge(rt_1, \ldots, rt_n)$ is the "smallest" record type that "contains" all of the record types $rt_1, \ldots, rt_n$. Also note that the order of the arguments to $merge$ is irrelevant. In the roommate example, $dom(A_0)$ and $dom(B_0)$ are compatible types and $merge(dom(A_0), dom(B_0)) = \{model : int, color : string \cup \{*\}, quality : int\}$.

Definition 2.8 *For every set* $\{rt_1, \ldots, rt_n\}$ *of compatible record types,* C *is called a* preference combining form based on $(rt_1, \ldots, rt_n)$ *iff* C *maps* n *preference functions* $p_1, \ldots, p_n$ *with* $dom(p_i) = rt_i$ *into a new preference function with domain* $merge(rt_1, \ldots, rt_n)$. *This new preference function is denoted by* $C(p_1, \ldots, p_n)$.

Definition 2.9 *Let* $\{rt_1, \ldots, rt_n\}$ *be a set of compatible record types. A function* f *is called a* value function *based on* $(rt_1, \ldots, rt_n)$ *iff* $f : ScoreBoard(rt_1) \times \ldots \times ScoreBoard(rt_n) \times merge(rt_1, \ldots, rt_n) \to score$.

We are now ready to define the meta-combining form *combine* which is at the heart of the combining preference functions.

Definition 2.10 *Let* $\{rt_1, \ldots, rt_n\}$ *be a set of compatible types. Let* f *be a value function based on* $(rt_1, \ldots, rt_n)$. *Then* $combine(f)$ *is preference combining form based on* $(rt_1, \ldots, rt_n)$ *defined by*
$combine(f)(p_1, \ldots, p_n)(r)$
$= f(Scores(p_1, \pi_{rt_1}(r)), \ldots, Scores(p_n, \pi_{rt_n}(r)), r)$
for all records r *of type* $merge(rt_1, \ldots, rt_n)$
and all preference functions with $dom(p_i) = rt_i$ *for all* $i \le n$.

The idea behind this notion of combining preference functions is that only the "relevant" scores are examined. The relevant scores are the scores associated with a record as well as any generalizations of that record. All the other values are irrelevant.

Notice that a value function is based on a list (rather than a set) of record types since the order of the arguments to a value function might make a difference.

In the roommate example, the computation that gives Alice veto power would be the function FirstVeto defined as follows:
FirstVeto(a : ScoreBoard(dom(A_0)) ,
        b : ScoreBoard(domB_0),
        c : merge(dom(A_0),dom(B_0))) returns score
{
    if a.color!model = $\natural$ then return $\natural$;
    else if a.star!!model = $\natural$ then return $\natural$;
    else return b.model!quality;
}

The preference function $combine(FirstVeto)(A_0, B_0)$ would be the desired combined preference function. If Alice can't stand a particular refrigerator, then she would veto it and the result would be a veto. If Alice chooses not to veto a particular refrigerator, then Betty's preference would be the one that is returned.

For example, assume Alice hated all the model 123 refrigerators and the green refrigerator in model 234; if she had no preference among the other refrigerators, then her preference function A_0 would be:
$$A_0(\{color = *, model = 123\}) = \natural$$
$$A_0(\{color = green, model = 234\}) = \natural$$
$$A_0(r) = \bot \text{ for all other records } r.$$

Let's look at a particular example in which Alice's veto prevails. Let $r_1 = \{color = purple, model = 123, quality = 2\}$.
$$combine(FirstVeto)(A_0, B_0)(r_1)$$
$$= FirstVeto(Scores(A_0, r_1), Scores(B_0, r_1), r_1)$$
$$= FirstVeto(\{color!model = \bot, star!!model = \natural\},$$
$$\{model!quality = B_0(r_1)\}, r_1)$$
$$= \natural$$

Let's look at a particular example in which Betty's preference prevails. Let $r_2 = \{color = purple, model = 234, quality = 2\}$.
$$combine(FirstVeto)(A_0, B_0)(r_2)$$
$$= FirstVeto(Scores(A_0, r_2), Scores(B_0, r_2), r_2)$$
$$= FirstVeto(\{color!model = \bot, star!!model = \bot\},$$
$$\{model!quality = B_0(r_2)\}, r_2)$$
$$= B_0(r_2)$$

In the roommate example, note that the final argument to *FirstVeto* is ignored. A variation on the example would be that Alice can not veto a refrigerator with a quality rating of at least 3. In this case, the definition of *FirstVeto* would change to:
FirstVetoSometimes(a : ScoreBoard(dom(A_0)) ,
        b : ScoreBoard(domB_0),
        c : merge(dom(A_0),dom(B_0))) returns score
{
    if c.quality $\ge$ 3 then return b.model!quality;
    else if a.color!model = $\natural$ then return $\natural$;
    else if a.star!!model = $\natural$ then return $\natural$;
    else return b.model!quality;
}

2.3 Modular Combining Forms

In this section, we formalize and study the notion of the modular combining forms (see Definition 2.12). Having modular combining forms has two desirable results. The first desirable result is that autonomy of various preferences is conserved. If a preference function is created using only modular combining forms, then a user may change a preference for a particular record (in one of the original preference functions) without affecting any preference (in the final preference function) for any unrelated records. For example, if Alice changes her perference towards yellow refrigerators in model 123, this will have no affect on the final preference for green refrigerators in model 123. The second desirable result is that an implementation need only provide first order value functions. The value functions do not need to take entire preference functions as arguments. Instead, they only require the finite amount of information that is contained in a scoreboard.

Next we say when two preference functions are equivalent with respect to a record in their domain. The idea is that they agree on all the information that is relevant to a record.

Definition 2.11 *Let p and p' be preference functions with the same domain. Let r be a record of type $dom(p)$. We say p and p' are* equivalent with respect to r *iff $p(\bar{r}) = p'(\bar{r})$ for all $\bar{r} \triangleright r$*

We are now ready to define the modular combining forms.

Definition 2.12 *A combining form C based on $(rt_1, \ldots, rt_n)$ is* modular *iff $C(p_1, \ldots, p_n)(r) = C(p'_1, \ldots, p'_n)(r)$ provided that for all $i \leq n$, p_i and p'_i are equivalent with respect to $\pi_{rt_i}(r)$.*

It is clear this definition captures the desired notion of relevance. If a user changes their preference on a given record r (thereby changin their preference function from p to p'), it is clear that p and p' are equivalent with respect to any record which is not generalized by r. The result of the new combined preference function will agree with the old combined preference function on all the records that are not generalized by r.

Modular combining forms enjoy the property of being closed under composition. This is formalized in Proposition 2.13 which, to enhance readability, is stated only for binary combining forms.

Proposition 2.13
Let $\{rt_1, rt_2, rt_3, rt_4\}$ be a compatible set of record types. Let C_1, C_2, and C_3 be modular preference combining forms based on (rt_1, rt_2), (rt_3, rt_4), and $(merge(rt_1, rt_2), merge(rt_3, rt_4))$ respectively. Then the combining form C_0 based on (rt_1, rt_2, rt_3, rt_4) defined by $C_0(p_1, p_2, p_3, p_4) = C_3(C_1(p_1, p_2), C_2(p_3, p_4))$ is a modular combining form.

Proof: This is proven as Proposition 6.1 in Appendix A (Section 6). □

Now that we have seen that modular combining forms are desirable to have around, Theorem 2.14 is important because it guarentees that all the preference combining forms defined using *combine* are modular.

Theorem 2.14
If f is a value function based on $(rt_1, \ldots, rt_n)$, then combine(f) is a modular combining form based on $(rt_1, \ldots, rt_n)$.

Proof: This is proven as Theorem 6.2 in Appendix A (Section 6). □

2.4 Preference System

Definition 2.15 *A* basic preference system *is a collection of record types, and for each record type, a collection of preference functions with that domain (called the* available *preference functions), and a collection of value functions (called the* available *value functions) each of which is based on a finite collection of those record types.*

A basic preference system is closed *iff combine$(f)(p_1, \ldots, p_n)$ is an available preference function provided $p_1, \ldots, p_n$ are available preference functions and f is an available value function that is based on $\{dom(p_1), \ldots, dom(p_n)\}$.*

It is important to note that a basic preference system need not make available all possible preference functions. We expect that it will be the case that most basic preference systems will be closed but to increase flexibility, we do not require this. For example, a system designer might put a sematic condition that a score for any record be within ten percent of the score of any of its generalizations. Since this might be a difficult condition to enforce within the value functions, all the possible value functions might be available even though the combined preference function might not be available. This system would, therefore, not be closed.

3 Flexibility

In this section, we discuss how flexible basic preference systems are. We first model a single person system in which several preference functions from the same person that cover different aspects of a total picture are combined. We use the popular Personalogic system for this purpose. We then consider a multiple person system in which preferences of two (or more) individuals are combined into a single preference function. We have already seen an instance of this in the roommate example; we now model a real-life design application. Finally, we present a completeness results that explains the power of our framework.

3.1 Modeling Personalogic

The Personalogic system[2] is a popular system for making selections and ordering results based on user provided preferences. We sketch below how the functionality provided by Personalogic can be realized as a special case of our framework. We will use Personalogic's decision guide for selecting a dog for illustration.

The dog decision guide allows users to express preferences for various attributes of different breeds of dogs through a series of questions. These attributes include size, indoor energy, exercise time, trainability, barking, history of inflicting injuries, dog group, and coat characteristics such as length, shedding, and hypoallerginicity. The user can also specify the importance of indoor energy, exercise time, trainability, and barking. The values not selected for some of the attributes (size, dog group, coat length) act as vetoes. For other attributes, the user may indicate preference or no opinion. For the history of inflicting injuries and hypoallerginicity attributes, the user may also specify must not have values. The system computes a combined score for each dog in the database based on the weightings of all the individual preferences, provided that all the predicates are satisfied, and returns results ordered by score.

The reader can immediately note that this system is easy to model in our basic preference system. The choices on individual attributes would be a preference function on that attribute. A predicate could be treated as a veto if the predicate is not satisfied. The user controlled weighting could be modeled as a value function.

The reader can also note that a system built on the basic preference system would provide more flexibility in allowing users to express preferences. For instance, the user does not have the option of specifying preference values for a combination of attributes in the Personalogic system. This can be important for a user who wants to veto a combination of some specific values for different attributes while admitting those values in other combinations.

3.2 Design Application

Design houses typically have component engineering departments that are responsible for approving and rating parts that are allowed to be used by design engineers in the company products. Within the guidelines provided by the component engineering, design engineers have considerable flexibility in exercising their preferences. We illustrate below how to model this common situation in our basic preference system so that searches over

[2]http://www.personalogic.com. Personalogic is now owned by America Online (AOL) and their customers include National Geographic, American Express, and E-Trade.

part databases become cognizant of individual preferences.

A design house deals with three major product categories: inductors, capacitors, and resistors; these are represented by a field called "Product". For each of these categories, there are further subcategories; these are represented by a field called "Subcatory". Manufacturers X, Y, and Z supply all the three categories; these are represented by a field call "Manufacturer". The component engineering has forbidden the use of all parts from Z. It has rated inductors from X as superior (score $= 0.8$) and capacitors as good (score $= 0.6$). On the other hand, the ratings for inductors and capacitors from Y are good and superior respectively. Component engineering has not yet rated resistors. To save writing, we present the records as a (Manufacturer,Product,Subcategory) list. The component engineering expresses these preferences as follows:

$$C_0(Z, *, *) = \natural$$
$$C_0(X, \text{inductors}, *) = 0.8$$
$$C_0(X, \text{capacitors}, *) = 0.6$$
$$C_0(Y, \text{inductors}, *) = 0.6$$
$$C_0(Y, \text{capacitors}, *) = 0.8$$

Engineer Elizabeth generally likes products from Y better than products from X, except that she really likes ceramic resistors built by X. She also thinks highly of resistors made by Z. She expresses her preferences as follows:

$$E_0(Y, *, *) = 0.8$$
$$E_0(X, *, *) = 0.7$$
$$E_0(X, \text{capacitors}, \text{ceramic}) = 1.0$$
$$E_0(Z, \text{resistors}, *) = 0.9$$

By providing different combining forms, it is possible to implement different policies that affect search results in different ways. Note that neither component engineering nor Elizabeth has to restate any of their preferences. Example of policies include:

- *Component engineering has priority.* Elizabeth's searches for inductors will resolve in favor of X, searches for capacitors will resolve in favor of Y, and searches for resistors will resolve in favor of Y. The interesting case is the resistor case. Elizabeth's preference for Z for resistor is vetoed because of blanket ban on Z. However, since component engineering has no preference between X and Y for resistors, Elizabeth's general preference for Y over X prevails.

- *Engineer's preferences have priority unless vetoed by component engineering.* All of Elizabeth's searches now resolve in favor of Y since she prefers Y over X, except for ceramic capacitors for which she has explicit higher preference for X. Her preference for Z for resistors has been vetoed by the component engineering's veto on Z.

As the time goes by, Elizabeth was able to convince component engineering to loosen its ban on Z for resistors. However, component engineering still rates resistors from Z below than those from X. It can simply add the following preferences:

$$C_0(X, \text{resistors}, *) = 0.8$$
$$C_0(Z, \text{resistors}, *) = 0.6$$

No change is required in the combining forms. The reader can easily verify that these additions do not affect the results of searches for inductors or capacitors. Elizabeth's search for resistors now resolve in favor of X under the first policy and in favor of Z under the second.

3.3 Completeness of Combine Operator

We have seen the tremendous flexibility of a basic preference system. In fact, there is good reason for this. The *combine* meta-combining form (Definition 2.10) is complete in that all modular combining forms are definable using *combine*!!!

This is formalized in Theorem 3.1.

Theorem 3.1
Let C be a modular combing form based on $(rt_1, \ldots, rt_n)$. Then there is a value function f based on $(rt_1, \ldots, rt_n)$ such that $C = combine(f)$

Proof: This is proven as Theorem 6.3 in Appendix A (Section 6). □

Putting this result together with the fact that $combine(f)$ is always modular gives us the following complete characterization of the modular combining forms.

Theorem 3.2 *C is a modular combining form based on $(rt_1, \ldots, rt_n)$ iff there exists a value function f based on $(rt_1, \ldots, rt_n)$ such that $C = combine(f)$.*

Proof: Follows from Theorems 2.14 and 3.1. □

4 Implementation on a Relational Database System

Let us consider the roommate example and see how it might be represented using a relational database system. The purpose of this example is to show how a relational database system could be used to implement a basic preference system. There are many other possible ways to implement a basic preference system and we think there is a good bit of interesting research to be done to take full advantage of a database system.

In one such implementation, Alice and Betty's preference functions can be stored in separate tables. Records with score of $\perp$ are not represented.

Alice's preference function:

Color	Model	Score
Red	123	0.4
*	123	♮
Green	234	♮
White	456	0.8
White	234	0.6

Betty's preference function:

Model	Quality	Score
123	3	0.7
123	4	0.9
234	4	0.5
345	3	0.3
345	4	0.5

Here is how a system would compute the combined preference function defined by $combine(FirstVeto)(A_0, B_0)$. Given a record r, the system would perform the following steps:

1. Form the ScoreBoard called sb_a for A_0 as follows:

   (a) Issue the query: SELECT Score FROM Alice WHERE Color = r.color AND Model = r.model Store the unique answer in sb_a.color!model (and let this value be $\perp$ if the query returns an empty answer).

   (b) Issue the query: SELECT Score FROM Alice WHERE Color = * AND Model = r.model Store the unique answer in sb_a.star!!model (and let this value be $\perp$ if the query returns an empty answer).

2. Form the ScoreBoard called sb_b for B_0 as follows:

   (a) Issue the query: SELECT Score FROM Betty WHERE Model = r.model AND Quality = r.quality Store the unique answer in sb_b.model!quality (and let this value be $\perp$ if the query returns an empty answer).

3. Return the value obtained from the user-defined function $FirstVeto(sb_a, sb_b, r)$

The implementor might choose to materialize this new preference function for retrieval efficiency. In this example, we assume that there are four colors: Red, Green, White, and Purple; we assume four models: 123, 234, 345, and 456; and we assume that there are four quality levels: 1, 2, 3, and 4. Under these assumptions, the combined preference function would look like the following:

Color	Model	Quality	Score
Red	123	1	♮
Green	123	1	♮
Purple	123	1	♮
White	123	1	♮
*	123	1	♮
Red	123	2	♮
Green	123	2	♮
Purple	123	2	♮
White	123	2	♮
*	123	2	♮
Red	123	3	♮
Green	123	3	♮
Purple	123	3	♮
White	123	3	♮
*	123	3	♮
Red	123	4	♮
Green	123	4	♮
Purple	123	4	♮
White	123	4	♮
*	123	4	♮

Color	Model	Quality	Score
Red	234	4	0.5
Green	234	1	♮
Green	234	2	♮
Green	234	3	♮
Green	234	4	♮
Purple	234	4	0.5
White	234	4	0.5
*	234	4	0.5
Red	345	3	0.3
Green	345	3	0.3
Purple	345	3	0.3
White	345	3	0.3
*	345	3	0.3
Red	345	4	0.5
Green	345	4	0.5
Purple	345	4	0.5
White	345	4	0.5
*	345	4	0.5

Of course, there is a lot of redundancy in the above table. There are many interesting research questions that merit further investigation such as: when to materialize; how to have more compact representations of the preference functions; what restrictions to put on the available preference functions and available value functions to permit an efficient implementation; etc.

5 Summary

We have presented a framework for expressing and combining user preferences. The system is very lean in that it only has two basic notions:

1. A preference function (Definition 2.1) that specifies user preferences.

2. A single meta combining form *combine* (Definition 2.10) that is based on value functions (Definition 2.9).

Yet, in spite of its very lean nature, the framework is very powerful. The single combine meta-function is able (in conjunction with the value functions) to express all modular preference combining forms (Theorem 3.1).

In addition to being quite powerful, the basic preference system is quite flexible since it does not require the system to provide every possible preference function or every possible value function. Limits might be placed to facilitate user interaction, impose semantic conditions, or enable an efficient implementation. Furthermore, there is flexibility in that the system does not arbitrarily limit the possible value functions.

Future Work Since this paper presents a framework, there is a lot of work that can be done realizing this framework. There is considerable room for system implementors to address efficiency issues and experiment with user interfaces. In fact, a generic user interface could be built for a basic preference system that would work with any preference system. Different representations of preference functions are possible. Another important issue concerns value functions. We expect the system to have a library of canned value functions that should meet the needs of a large number of users. But should value functions be definable by end users and what would be a good interface?

References

[Arr50] K.J. Arrow. A difficulty in the concept of social welfare. *J. of Political Economy*, 58:328–346, 1950.

[BP96] John M. Berrie and David E. Presti. The word wide web as an instructional tool. *Science*, 274:371–372, 1996.

[EHJ$^+$96] O. Etzioni, S. Hanks, T. Jiang, R.M. Karp, O. Madani, and O. Waarts. Efficient information gathering on the internet. In *37th Annual Symp. Foundations of Computer Science*, 1996.

[Fag98] Ronald Fagin. Fuzzy queries in multimedia database systems. In *17th ACM Symp. Principles of Database Systems*, June 1998.

[FISS98] Yoav Freund, Raj Iyer, Robert E. Schapire, and Yoram Singer. An efficient boosting algorithm for combining preferences. In *Machine Learning: 15th Int. Conf*, 1998.

[HS99]   John Hagel and Marc Singer. *Net Worth.* Harvard Business School Press, 1999.

[LG99]   Steve Lawrence and C. Lee Giles. Accessibility of information on the web. *Nature*, 400:107–109, 1999.

[RV97]   P. Resnick and H. Varian. Recommender systems. *Communications of the ACM*, 40(3), 1997.

[SM83]   G. Salton and M. McGill. *Introduction to Modern Information Retrieval.* McGraw-Hill, New York, 1983.

6   Appendix A: Modular Combining Form Proofs

Proposition 6.1 (Restatement of Proposition 2.13)
Let $\{rt_1, rt_2, rt_3, rt_4\}$ be a compatible set of record types. Let C_1, C_2, and C_3 be modular preference combining forms based on (rt_1, rt_2), (rt_3, rt_4), and $(merge(rt_1, rt_2), merge(rt_3, rt_4))$ respectively. Then the combining form C_0 based on (rt_1, rt_2, rt_3, rt_4) defined by $C_0(p_1, p_2, p_3, p_4) = C_3(C_1(p_1, p_2), C_2(p_3, p_4))$ is a modular combining form.

Proof: First note that it is clear that C_0 is based on (rt_1, rt_2, rt_3, rt_4). Let r be a record of type $merge(rt_1, rt_2, rt_3, rt_4)$. Assume that p_i and p_i' are equivalent with respect to $\pi_{rt_i}(r)$ for $i = 1, 2, 3, 4$ with the goal of showing that $C_0(p_1, p_2, p_3, p_4)(r) = C_0(p_1', p_2', p_3', p_4')(r)$.

First we show that $C_1(p_1, p_2)$ and $C_1(p_1', p_2')$ are equivalent with respect to $\pi_{merge(rt_1, rt_2)}(r)$. Let $r' \triangleright \pi_{merge(rt_1, rt_2)}(r)$. Let $r'' \triangleright r'$. Then $\pi_{rt_1}(r'') \triangleright \pi_{rt_1}(r') \triangleright \pi_{rt_1}(\pi_{merge(rt_1, rt_2)}(r)) = \pi_{rt_1}(r)$. Thus, $p_1(\pi_{rt_1}(r'')) = p_1'(\pi_{rt_1}(r''))$ since p_1 and p_1' are equivalent with respect to $\pi_{rt_1}(r)$. Thus, p_1 and p_1' are equivalent with respect to r'. Similarly, p_2 and p_2' are equivalent with respect to r'. Since, C_1 is modular, it follows that $C_1(p_1, p_2)(r') = C_1(p_1', p_2')(r')$. This proves that $C_1(p_1, p_2)$ and $C_1(p_1', p_2')$ are equivalent with respect to $\pi_{merge(rt_1, rt_2)}(r)$. Similarly, $C_2(p_3, p_4)$ and $C_2(p_3', p_4')$ are equivalent with respect to $\pi_{merge(rt_3, rt_4)}(r)$. Since C_3 is a modular combining form based on $(merge(rt_1, rt_2), merge(rt_3, rt_4))$, it follows that $C_3(C_1(p_1, p_2), C_2(p_3, p_4))(r) = C_3(C_1(p_1', p_2'), C_2(p_3', p_4'))(r)$. This proves that $C_0(p_1, p_2, p_3, p_4)(r) = C_0(p_1', p_2', p_3', p_4')(r)$ as desired. □

Next we show that every combining form defined using the *combine* operator is modular. This is formalized in Theorem 2.14.

Theorem 6.2 (Restatement of Theorem 2.14)
If f is a value function based on $(rt_1, \ldots, rt_n)$, then $combine(f)$ *is a modular combining form based on* $(rt_1, \ldots, rt_n)$.

Proof: Let $p_1, \ldots, p_k$ and $p_1', \ldots, p_n'$ be preference functions such that $dom(p_i) = rt_i = dom(p_i')$ for all $i \leq n$. Let r be a record of type $RT = merge(rt_1, \ldots, rt_n)$. Let f be a value function based on $(rt_1, \ldots, rt_n)$. Assume that p_i and p_i' are equivalent with respect to rt_i for all $i \leq n$. The goal is to show that $combine(f)(p_1, \ldots, p_k)(r) = combine(f)(p_1', \ldots, p_k')(r)$.

Let n_0 be an arbitrary name of a field in $ScoreBoard(rt_i)$.

$$
\begin{aligned}
& Scores(p_i, \pi_{rt_i}(r)).n_0 \\
= {} & p_i(RecordOf_{rt_i}(\pi_{rt_i}(r), n_0)) \\
= {} & p_i'(RecordOf_{rt_i}(\pi_{rt_i}(r), n_0)) \\
& \text{since } RecordOf_{rt_i}(\pi_{rt_i}(r), n_0)) \triangleright \pi_{rt_i}(r) \\
= {} & Scores(p_i', \pi_{rt_i}(r)).n_0
\end{aligned}
$$

Since the choice of n_0 was an arbitrary name in $ScoreBoard(rt_i)$, it follows that $Scores(p_i, \pi_{rt_i}(r)) = Scores(p_i', \pi_{rt_i}(r))$ for all $i \leq n$. We can compute as follows:

$$
\begin{aligned}
& combine(f)(p_1, \ldots, p_k)(r) \\
= {} & f(Scores(p_1, \pi_{rt_1}(r)), \ldots, Scores(p_k, \pi_{rt_k}(r)), r) \\
= {} & f(Scores(p_1', \pi_{rt_1}(r)), \ldots, Scores(p_k', \pi_{rt_k}(r)), r) \\
= {} & combine(f)(p_1', \ldots, p_k')(r)
\end{aligned}
$$

as desired. □

Now that we know that every combining form $combine(f)$ is modular, the next question to address is are there any other modular combining forms other than the ones definable by *combine*. It turns out the answer is no. This means that *every* modular combining form can be expressed using the *combine* operator. This is formalized in Theorem 3.1.

Theorem 6.3 (Restatement of Theorem 3.1)
Let C be a modular combing form based on $(rt_1, \ldots, rt_n)$. Then there is a value function f based on $(rt_1, \ldots, rt_n)$ such that $C = combine(f)$.

Proof: It is helpful to have a function $NameOf$ that takes a record of type rt for any type rt with field names $n_1, \ldots, n_k$ and produces a name of a field in $ScoreBoard(rt)$ as follows: $NameOf(r_0) = n_1'!\ldots!n_k'$ where $n_i' = n_i$ if $r_0.n_i \neq *$ and $n_i' = star!$ if $r_0.n_i = *$. It is clear that if $r_0 \triangleright r$, then $RecordOf_{rt_i}(r, NameOf(r_0)) = r_0$.

First defined a set valued function
$$S : ScoreBoard(rt_1) \times \ldots \times ScoreBoard(rt_n)$$
$$\times merge(rt_1, \ldots, rt_n) \rightarrow \mathcal{P}(score).$$
Recall that $\mathcal{P}$ represents the power set operation so that $\mathcal{P}(score)$ is the set of all subsets of $score$. The definition of S is as follows: Define $s_0 \in S(sb_1, \ldots, sb_n, r)$ iff there exist preference functions $p_1, \ldots, p_n$ such that $C(p_1, \ldots, p_n)(r) = s_0$ and $\forall i \leq n(dom(p_i) = rt_i \& Scores(p_i, \pi_{rt_i}(r)) = sb_i)$. It is clear that
$$C(p_1, \ldots, p_n)(r) \in$$
$$S(Scores(p_1, \pi_{rt_1}(r)), \ldots, Scores(p_n, \pi_{rt_n}(r)), r).$$

Assume that s_0 and s_0' are elements of $S(sb_1, \ldots, sb_n, r)$. Hence, it follows that $s_0 = C(p_1, \ldots, p_n)(r)$, $s_0' = C(p_1', \ldots, p_n')(r)$, and $\forall i \leq n(Scores(p_i, \pi_{rt_i}(r)) = sb_i = Scores(p_i, \pi_{rt_i}(r))$. Let $r_i \rhd \pi_{rt_i}(r)$.

$$
\begin{aligned}
& p_i(r_i) \\
= \; & p_i(RecordOf_{rt_i}(\pi_{rt_i}(r), NameOf(r_i))) \\
= \; & Scores(p_i, \pi_{rt_i}(r)).NameOf(r_i) \\
= \; & Scores(p_i', \pi_{rt_i}(r)).NameOf(r_i) \\
& \text{since } Scores(p_i, \pi_{rt_i}(r)) = \\
& \qquad Scores(p_i', \pi_{rt_i}(r)) \\
= \; & p_i'(RecordOf_{rt_i}(\pi_{rt_i}(r), NameOf(r_i))) \\
= \; & p_i'(r_i)
\end{aligned}
$$

Hence, it follows that p_i and p_i' are equivalent with respect to $\pi_{rt_i}(r)$ for all $i \leq n$. Since C is a modular combining form, it follows that
$$s_0 = C(p_1, \ldots, p_n)(r) = C(p_1', \ldots, p_n')(r) = s_0'.$$
This proves that $S(sb_1, \ldots, sb_n, r)$ has at most one element.

If $S(sb_1, \ldots, sb_n, r)$ is empty, then define
$$f(sb_1, \ldots, sb_n, r) = \bot;$$
otherwise, define $f(sb_1, \ldots, sb_n, r)$ to be the unique member of $S(sb_1, \ldots, sb_n, r)$.
Since $C(p_1, \ldots, p_n)(r) \in$
$$S(Scores(p_1, \pi_{rt_i}(r)), \ldots, Scores(p_n, \pi_{rt_i}(r)), r),$$
it follows that $C(p_1, \ldots, p_n)(r)$
$$= f(Scores(p_1, \pi_{rt_i}(r)), \ldots, Scores(p_n, \pi_{rt_i}(r)), r).$$
By Definition 2.8, it follows that
$$C(p_1, \ldots, p_n)(r) = combine(f)(p_1, \ldots, p_n)(r)$$
as desired. $\square$

Microsoft TerraServer: A Spatial Data Warehouse

Tom Barclay
Microsoft Research
301 Howard St., Suite 830
San Francisco, CA 94105
415 778 8223

tbarclay@microsoft.com

Jim Gray
Microsoft Research
301 Howard St., Suite 830
San Francisco, CA 94105
415 778 8222

gray@microsoft.com

Don Slutz
Microsoft Research
301 Howard St., Suite 830
San Francisco, CA 94105
415 778 8226

dslutz@microsoft.com

ABSTRACT

Microsoft® TerraServer stores aerial, satellite, and topographic images of the earth in a SQL database available via the Internet. It is the world's largest online atlas, combining eight terabytes of image data from the United States Geological Survey (USGS) and SPIN-2. Internet browsers provide intuitive spatial and text interfaces to the data. Users need no special hardware, software, or knowledge to locate and browse imagery. This paper describes how terabytes of "Internet unfriendly" geo-spatial images were scrubbed and edited into hundreds of millions of "Internet friendly" image tiles and loaded into a SQL data warehouse. All meta-data and imagery are stored in the SQL database. TerraServer demonstrates that general-purpose relational database technology can manage large scale image repositories, and shows that web browsers can be a good geo-spatial image presentation system.

Keywords

Geo-spatial, VLDB, image databases, internet.

1. Overview

The TerraServer is the world's largest public repository of high-resolution aerial, satellite, and topographic data. It is designed to be accessed by thousands of simultaneous users using Internet protocols via standard web browsers. TerraServer is an image "tile" server that delivers a set of raster images based on a users search criteria. Once an image of interest is located, users can pan, zoom in, zoom out, or display meta-data about the image they are viewing.

The TerraServer is a multi-media data warehouse. It differs from a traditional data warehouse in several ways: (1) it is accessed by millions of users, (2) the users extract relatively few records (thousands) in a particular session and, (3) the records are relatively large (10 kilobytes). By contrast, classic data warehouses are (1) accessed by a few hundred users via proprietary interfaces, (2) queries examine millions of records, to discover trends or anomalies, (3) the records themselves are generally less than a kilobyte. In addition, classic data warehouse queries may run for days before delivering results. Initial results typically cause users to modify and re-run queries to further refine results.

One thing the TerraServer has in common with classic data warehouses is that both manage huge databases: several terabytes of data. TerraServer's topographic maps cover all of the United States at 2 meter resolution 10 million square kilometers), the aerial photos cover 40% of the United States today (3 million square kilometers) at one-meter resolution, and 1% of the urban areas outside the United States (1 million square kilometers) at 2 meter resolution.

This report describes the design of the TerraServer and its operation over the last 18 months. It also summarizes what we have learned from building and operating the TerraServer.

Our research group explores scaleable servers. We wanted first-hand experience building and operating a large Internet server with a large database and heavy web traffic. To generate the traffic we needed to build an application that would be interesting to millions of web users.

Based on our exposure to the EOS/DIS project [2], we settled on building a web site that serves aerial, satellite, and topographic imagery. We picked this application for four reasons:

1. The web is inherently a graphical environment, and these images of neighborhoods are recognizable and interesting throughout the world.

2. We believed this application would generate the billions of web hits needed to test our scalability ideas.

3. The data was available. The USGS was cooperative, an since the cold war had ended, other agencies were more able to share satellite image data. The thaw relaxed regulations that had previously limited the access to high-resolution imagery on a global basis.

4. The solution as we defined it – a wide-area, client/server imagery database application stored in a commercially available SQL database system – had not been attempted before. Indeed, many people felt it was impossible without using an object-oriented or object-relational system.

This paper describes the application design, database design, hardware architecture, and operational experience of the TerraServer. The TerraServer has been operating for eighteen months now. We have deployed the third redesign of the database, user interface, and process of adding new images to the database.

2. Application Design

TerraServer is accessed via the Internet through any graphical web browser. Users can zoom and pan across a mosaic of tiles within a TerraServer scene. The user interface is designed to function adequately over low-speed (28.8kbps) connections. Any modern PC, MAC, or UNIX workstation can access the TerraServer using a standard web browser – Internet Explorer 3.0 or later, or Netscape Navigator 3.0 or later. If you have never used it, look at the TerraServer web site at http://terraserver.microsoft.com/.

There are four methods by which a user locates an image:

(1) **Coverage Map:** clicking on low resolution map of the world shaded to show where coverage exists,

(2) **Place Query:** entering a place name, e.g. San Francisco,

(3) **Coordinate Query:** entering the longitude and latitude of interest, or

(4) **Famous Place:** selecting a location from a pre-compiled list of places.

A successful search presents the user with a web page containing an HTML table of image tiles fetched from a SQL database. GIF images surrounding the image tile table provide the user with the following basic controls:

- Pan and zoom
- Display image meta data
- Download an image copy
- Control the size of the image table. There are three fixed sizes – Small (400 x 200 pixels), Medium (600 x 400 pixels), and Large (800 x 600 pixels).
- Choose the image "style" or theme. TerraServer stores three image styles -- imagery stored in TerraServer – shaded relief, topographic map, and photograph (aerial or satellite).

We expect and support the use of TerraServer image tiles on remote web sites. Most data on TerraServer is public domain data. Therefore, we deliberately chose simple graphics and storage methods so that users could craft their own web pages that display TerraServer image tiles.

Imagery is categorized into "themes" by data source, projection system, and image "style". Currently, there are four data themes:

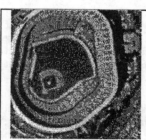

Figure 1. A USGS DOQ Image of 3Com Park near San Francisco

USGS Digital Ortho-Quadrangles (DOQ) are gray-scale or color infrared, 1-meter resolution aerial photos. Cars can be seen, but 1-meter resolution is too coarse to show people. Imagery is ortho-rectified to 1-meter square pixels. Approximately 50% of the U.S. has been digitized. The conterminous U.S. is expected to be completed by the end of 2001. Some locations have more than one DOQQ image available varying by image source date or color mode. TerraServer stores the latest grayscale

image. If only a color infrared image is available, they it is converted to grayscale before tiling and storing in the database.

USGS Digital Raster Graphics (DRG) DRGs are the digitized versions of the popular USGS topographic maps. The complete set of USGS topographic maps have been scanned for the conterminous United States and Hawaii. The original images are available in three map scales – 24,000:1 (2.4 meters/pixel), 100,000:1 (10 meters per pixel) and 250,000 meters per pixel. The raster images are re-sampled to nearest power of 2 meters per pixel.

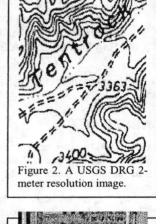

Figure 2. A USGS DRG 2-meter resolution image.

Aerial Images SPIN-2™ are grayscale 1.56-meter resolution de-classified Russian military satellite images. The images are re-sampled to 2-meter resolution. Terra-Server contains SPIN-2 images of Western Europe, the United States, and the Far East. Unfortunately, there is little coverage of Canada, South America, Africa, and Southeast Asia. The SPIN-2 imagery is rectified, i.e. rotated so north is up, but is not ortho-rectified. That is, the image is not "rubber sheeted" so that each pixel covers a consistent square number of square meters. However, given the height of the satellite, the difference in ground area between individual pixels is small.

Figure 3. a SPIN-2: 1.56-meter image of Atlanta's Fulton County Stadium.

Encarta Shaded Relief is natural color, shaded relief map of the globe. The full resolution image detail is approximately 1 kilometer per pixel. The image is a seamless image of the globe between latitude +80° and -80°. The Microsoft Geography Business Unit assembled the image from a public domain combination of weather satellite data and elevation data. The image appears in the Encarta Virtual Globe add-on product to the Encarta Encyclopedia CD title.

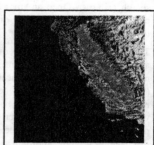

Figure 4: Encarta Virtual Globe shaded relief image of California, 8km / pixel.

2.1 System Architecture

TerraServer is a "thin-client / fat-server" design. The TerraServer has a 3-tier architecture:

Tier 1: *The Client* is a graphical web browser or other hardware/software system that supports HTTP 1.1 protocols and HTML 3.2 document structure. TerraServer is built and tested with Netscape Navigator and Internet Explorer on Windows, MacOS, and UNIX.

Tier 2: *The Application Logic* is a web server application that responds to HTTP requests submitted by clients by interacting with the Tier 3 database system and applying logic to the results returned.

Tier 3: *The Database System* is a SQL Server 7.0 Relational DBMS containing **all image** and meta-data required by the Application Logic tier.

Most web pages are dynamically formed and contain standard HTML 3.2 tags. All imagery is stored within SQL Server "blob fields" and compressed in Jpeg or Gif format. There is one row per image tile. The row contains the meta-data describing the tile's geographic attributes and one blob field containing the image data. Imagery is presented via <IMG SRC=...> tags without the aid of java applets, or other specialized client side controls. The SRC URL references a script executed on the web server that is fetched from the database and sent back to the browser prefixed with the appropriate mime type. TerraServer supports Netscape Navigator and Internet Explorer V3.0 or later browsers.

"Zoomed out" or sub-sampled imagery is also stored in the database, one-row per tile. Four higher resolution tiles are sub-sampled into one lower resolution tile. The process is repeated for the number of levels in the image hierarchy. We found, and our graphics colleagues have confirmed, that a 7 level image pyramid is the maximum for grayscale imagery. All levels of the image pyramid are pre-computed and stored in the database for the following reasons:

1. We wanted to build the largest physical database that we could.

2. A 7 level image pyramid would require 25,600 tiles to be sub-sampled to create one single 64:1 resolution tile. We do not believe users are willing to wait for this operation to be completed "on-the-fly".

3. We did not have the resources to develop and support a high performance, server-side sub-sampling and dynamic image generation application.[1]

4. We wanted users to reference TerraServer imagery on their own web pages with a simple <IMG SRC...> tag and not require a client-side control to display and sub-sample the imagery.

The web site is a cluster of machines. A set of servers executes Microsoft Internet Information Server (IIS) web server software that interfaces with the SQL Server databases. The site is designed to support a variable number of web servers for performance (more net cards for increased bandwidth) and reliability reasons (a failed web server does not take down the whole web site). Increasing the throughput of the web site is as simple as adding another web server until the network web and database servers saturate.

The web servers connect to the database servers that host the SQL Server database via a separate internal network. This protects the SQL Servers provides an extra level of security from hackers and a separate private network that does not compete with Internet or other network traffic. Currently, there are two database servers – one for aerial and satellite imagery, and a second for the topographic maps. There are also two 100mbit subnets between the database and web servers.

The number and size of database servers is determined by the popularity of the data and convenience. The bandwidth between database servers and web servers drives the hardware configuration. Topo maps are expected to be popular, so we decided to host them on a separate machine where queries for aerial photography data do not have to compete for bandwidth with queries for topo data. The shaded relief data is small and replicated on both the topo and aerial photography server.

Web pages containing imagery have a consistent layout. Users can control the number of image tiles that appear on a single page. The user's monitor size and Internet connection speed dictate their choice. Web pages are dynamically created on the web servers due to the millions of combinations of possible web pages.

There are a wide number of choices for dynamic web page construction on Internet Information Server based web servers – ISAPI, Active Server Pages, CGI/Perl, Cold Fusion, etc. We chose Active Server Pages (ASP) for a number of reasons:

- Fast and easy development – ASP host Visual Basic or JavaScript engines. An ASP document can be written and debugged without requiring a compiler or other elaborate development tools.

- The execution time of our ASP scripts was dominated by the SQL execution time and the data transfer time between database and web server. There was little or no performance gain in using a compiled language.[2]

We chose Visual Basic as the scripting language because it had better support for error handling. The Active Data Object (ADO), an OLEDB object, is used to access the SQL Server database engine. The Visual Basic error object could trap the errors raised by the ADO object. Our Visual Basic scripts process URL query strings, access the Imagery SQL database, and dynamically generate HTML pages. One ASP page, Tile.asp, is responsible for retrieving Jpeg or GIF formatted blobs from the database and sending it back to the client. A second ASP page, image.asp, is responsible for executing SQL queries to fetch the meta data necessary to dynamically produce the HTML tags which format an image page. These two web scripts are called 85% of the time.

The Cmap.asp (coverage map), Place.asp, Geo.asp, and Famous.asp implement the four search methods described

---

[1] The entire TerraServer web and database application was developed by one person.

[2] Originally we built the web application in C and accessed the web server via the ISAPI interface. We abandoned this approach after determining there was no performance gain in our case and a substantial increase in development cost.

previously. Each major function, e.g. Download, Image Information, the Home Page, etc., is implemented by a separate ASP page.

All TerraServer ASP scripts have a common structure. Database access is performed by calling a single SQL Server stored procedure function. The SQL stored procedure returns one or more record sets. The ASP script calls ADO methods to connect to the database server, call one stored procedure, iterate through the returned result set(s), and disconnect. This design achieves the highest performance as we learned during the first few weeks of service.

2.2 Tuning the Application

TerraServer was our group's very first web site. While we had some professional graphics design assistance, we developed the web application by the classic seat-of-the-pants method. Also like most software projects, particularly Internet projects, we were under marketing pressure to release to the web quickly. We learned a lot about our design and products we chose during an all too brief beta period and during the first month of live service.

We initially estimated the application was interesting enough to generate 1 million hits or 250,000 page views a day. Later we increased our estimate to 5 million hits and 1 million page views a day. We configured 4 web servers to support the 5 million hits and 1 million page views per day estimate. Officially, TerraServer went live on June 24, 1998. However, there was an article published on the front of the USA Today Business page on June 22, 1998. The article proved we grossly underestimated the popularity of the web site.

Starting on June 22, our four web servers managed to deliver 35 million web hits and 8 million page views. Millions more were rejected. We quickly grew our site to 10 web servers by the weekend and learned the following:

1. Web server software is really a TP Monitor. Once we realized this point, we used the tuning skills we learned back in the late 70s and 80s to good use. We treated the database server as a scarce resource and used the web server configuration tools to optimally schedule requests to the back end. Prior to this discovery, we unleashed requests from the web servers to the backend via a "fire hose" and were genuinely surprised when the database server ground to a halt.

2. Round trips to the database server are costly. Therefore, do as much as possible in one trip.

3. People look at imagery of where they live. While spending many a sleepless night the first week, we noticed that there was the interesting "sine wave" of Internet connection and disk activity. In highly populated and covered areas, we would notice a precipitous rise in user connections at the start of that time zone's day. Between 5 am and 6am PST or 8 am and 9am EST, the number of user connections would rise steeply. About one hour later, the number of connections continued to rise, but the disk activity began to drop and reach a steady state. Over time, we realized that separate users were requesting the same data as their neighbors. We had 2 GB of physical memory on the database server, about 1.8 GB was SQL Server's memory cache. Thus many of the queries were

resolved out of the database cache.

Over time, we realized the TerraServer web site is busiest in the mornings where we have coverage. Thus our web site is very active from 11pm to 3 am (Europe) and from 5 am to 3 or 4 pm. But it is not very busy around 5 pm because we have very little coverage in the Pacific Rim and East Asia.

4. Our Microsoft.com and msn.com colleagues confirmed some other web usage facts. The internet is busiest on Mondays and Tuesdays. Saturday and Sunday is half the volume of Monday and Tuesday. A steady slide occurs from Wednesday thru Friday. Thus, we do on-line database maintenance on the weekends – on-line backups, table reconfigurations, etc.

2.3 Scenes and Projection Systems

TerraServer is map and image data tiling system. Unlike online mapping web sites, e.g. MapQuest, TerraServer does not re-project the data to match the user's request. Instead, TerraServer displays the image or topographical map data in the projection chosen by the data provider.

TerraServer allows a user to navigate the length and width of an entire scene. A web page contains tiles from only one scene. Lists of links to scenes that overlap the viewed scene are offered to the user. Thus TerraServer really is a collection of seamless scenes and not a single seamless view of earth.

The reason for this is geometry and geography. The earth is a bumpy ellipsoid. Maps and computer monitors are flat. It is impossible to accurately present a spherical object on a flat surface.

Cartographers have addressed this issue by developing projections of the geoid onto flat surfaces [5]. There are many projection systems, each suited to present certain regions or properties. Multiple images in a projection system can often be joined together to form a seamless mosaic within certain boundary conditions. These mosaics either have extreme distortion as they scale out, or they introduce seams.

DOQ and DRG data are projected by the USGS into Universal Transverse Mercator (UTM) projection using the North American Datum (NAD) ellipsoid created in 1983 [7]. UTM is a projection system that divides the earth into 60 wedge shaped *zones* numbered 1 thru 60 beginning at the International Date Line. Each zone is 6 degrees wide and goes from the equator to the poles. UTM grid coordinates are specified as zone number, then meters from the equator and from the zone meridian[3].

The conterminous United States is divided into 10 zones (see Figure 5). Each of these UTM zones is a *scene*. The TerraServer mosaics each scene, but two adjacent scenes are not mosaiced together. Users can pan and zoom within a scene, and can jump from one scene to another.

---

[3] Actually, UTM grid units can be in inches, feet, meters, or kilometers. The USGS chose meters for most of their assets in the UTM projection. UTM is not used above 80N or 70S [5].

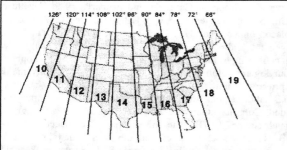

Figure 5: The ten UTM zones in the continental United States.

The SPIN-2 imagery is digitized from Russian satellite photographs. The Russian satellite captures 160km wide by 40km high areas in a single image. The satellite takes one image and then begins the adjacent image, overlapping the last image. The overlap is variable, and when digitized does not line up on a pixel boundary.

To create a seamless mosaic of SPIN-2 imagery, all SPIN-2 imagery would have to be ortho-rectified. This requires precise geo-location of each image, which was not available due to security concerns. Without rectification, if tiles extracted from separate SPIN-2 satellite images are mosaiced, the tile edges are misaligned. Roads, rivers, and other geographic features do not line up. While this may be understandable to GIS experts, it is disorienting and unacceptable to novice users.

Consequently, the TerraServer treats each 160km x 40km SPIN2 image as a separate scene. These scenes are not mosaiced together. Users can pan and zoom within a scene, and can jump from one scene to another.

2.4 TerraServer Grid System

Users can zoom and pan across a mosaic of tiles within a TerraServer scene. The tiles are organized in the database by theme, resolution, scene, and location within a scene in the TerraServer grid system.

TerraServer supports a fixed number of resolutions in powers of 2 from 1/1024 meters per pixel (scale 0) through 16384 meter per pixel (scale 24). One-meter per pixel is scale 10.

For UTM projection data sets, the SceneID is the UTM zone assigned to the original image a tile's pixels were extracted from. For SPIN2 data sets, a unique SceneID is assigned for each scene loaded per theme.

Each TerraServer scene is planar. A tile can be identified by its position in the scene. The tile loading program assigns a relative X and Y tile identifier to each tile as it is loaded.

For UTM projected data, the X and Y tile address is the UTM coordinate of the top-left most pixel in the tile divided by the tile image size in UTM units in meters. The following are the formulas:

$$X = TopLeftUTM\_X / (TilePixWidth \cdot Resolution)$$
$$Y = TopLeftUTM\_Y / (TilePixHeight \cdot Resolution)$$

For SPIN2 scenes, the X and Y tile addresses are relative to the upper left corner of the scene.

The six fields – Resolution, Theme, SceneID, Scale, X, and, Y - form the unique key by which any TerraServer image tile can be directly addressed. Each TerraServer web page contains image tiles from a single Theme, Scale, and SceneID combination. For example, our office building in USGS DOQ theme (T=1), has scene UTM zone 10 (S=10), at scale 1 meter (Z=10) with X=2766 and Y=20913. The URL is:
http://terraserver.microsoft.com/tile.asp?S=10&T=1&Z=10&X=2766&Y=20913.

The TerraServer search system performs the conversion from geographic coordinate systems to the TerraServer coordinate system. The TerraServer image display system uses TerraServer grid system coordinates to pan and zoom between tiles and resolutions of the same theme and scene.

2.5 Imagery Database Schema

Each theme has an Source Meta-data table. This table has a row for each image that is tiled and loaded into the TerraServer database. The *OrigMetaTag* field is the primary key. The meta-fields vary widely from theme to theme. Some of the meta fields are displayed by the Image Info Active Server Page (for example http://terraserver.microsoft.com/imageinfo.asp?S=17&T=2&X=17&Y=122&Z=17&W=1&O=c28080a1&P=28+km+SW+of+Orlando%2C+Florida%2C+United+States

All the image tiles and their metadata are stored in an SQL database. One table is maintained for each (theme, resolution) pair so that tiles are clustered together for better locality. USGS DOQ supports resolutions from 1-meter resolution through 64-meter resolution. USGS DRG data supports 2-meter resolution through 128-meter resolution. SPIN supports resolutions from 1-meter to 64-meter.

Each theme table has the same five-part primary key:

- *SceneID* –individual scene identifier
- *X* – tile's relative position on the X-axis
- *Y* – tile's relative position on the Y-axis
- *DisplayStatus* – Controls display of an image tile
- *OrigMetaTag* – image the tile was extracted from

There are 28 other fields that describe the geo-spatial coordinates for the image and other properties. One field is a "blob type" that contains the compressed image.

These tile blobs are chosen to be about ten kilobytes so that they can be quickly downloaded via a standard modem (within three seconds via a 28.8 modem).

2.6 Gazetteer Database Schema

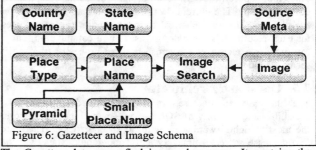

Figure 6: Gazetteer and Image Schema

The Gazetteer lets users find images by name. It contains the names for about 1.5 million places, with many alternate spellings. It is a simplified version of the Gazetteer found in the Encarta Virtual Globe™ and Microsoft Streets™ products.

The Gazetteer Schema is a snowflake database design. *PlaceName* is the center table. It contains the formal name for unique location on earth and maps a unique named location to the TerraServer Grid System. The *AltPlace* table contains all the synonyms of a unique place. The *StateName* and *CountryName* parent tables identify a place's state/province and country. The *AltState* and *AltCountry* tables contain the state/province and country synonyms.

Lookup by place name is surprisingly common (40%). So the user interface was modified to make it even easier. The top of each web page has a simple name lookup field where the user can enter city, state/province, or country separated by commas. The home page has an additional link that takes the user to an "advanced" name lookup web page.

The *find a place* input field allows the user to enter a subset of *PlaceName*, *StateName*, and *CountryName*. The supporting database stored procedure builds a cursor that searches for the name by performing a join on the appropriate tables depending on which fields the user specified. Name searches are performed on the "Alt" tables, which have synonyms and abbreviations for places (USA for example). Formal names matching the search criteria are returned from the *PlaceName, StateName,* and *CountryName* tables.

The *ImageSearch* table forms the association between a named place and a visible image. The *ImageSearch* table identifies the Theme, *SceneID, Scale, X, Y,* and *ImageDate* of a visible image tiles that cover the associated kilometer square cell. The load program inserts rows into the *ImageSearch* table when it has completed the image pyramid for a certain area. The *ImageSearch* table serves as a one-level quad-tree index of the image data [6].

The image display Active Server Page scripts use an additional table, the *Pyramid* table, to display the name and distance to the location closest to the center tile on an image display web page. This table is a two-level quad-tree is used to find population-weighted nearest neighbors of a given latitude and longitude. The SQL stored procedure scans a rectangle of the quad-tree to determine the closest city to latitude-longitude in the center of the web page image. The quad tree is implemented atop a B-tree by giving each quadrangle a name that is a prefix of the key for records in that quadrangle.

In total, the Gazetteer contains about 4 million rows and consumes 3.3 GB of space. Our first design used a fine-granularity (quarter kilometer) quad-tree and so used a hundred times more space (400GB). That design needed no computation during lookup. The current design must examine 50 records on average and do some spherical trigonometry on the coordinates for each record. The new design uses more computation, but it can process a record in 3 microseconds of processor time, so it seems a good tradeoff.

2.7 Database Architecture

The database architecture was chosen to demonstrate the scalability and usability of SQL Server—everything was done in the most straightforward way, with no special tricks. There are two database servers – Imagery and Topographic Map. On the Imagery database server, a single SQL server database was created

with two File Groups – Gazetteer and Primary.[4] The Gazetteer File Group is comprised of one, 5 GB file named t2b2gaz0.ndf and placed on volume "G:". The Imagery, Image Search, Load Management, and all other tables are stored in the Primary File Group consisting of many NTFS files. Each file resided on one of the four logical volumes and was 20GB, which is a convenient backup/recovery unit. Initially, 53 files were created to achieve the 1TB database goal. Additional files are added as new imagery is loaded. Currently, there are 71 20GB files. Plans are to grow the database to 2.0 TB. The initial files were placed on two 595GB NT stripe-set volumes and the files added later were placed on two other similar volumes. SQL Server makes all allocation and placement decisions within and among the files.

The Topographical Map database is similarly configured. There are two File Groups – Gazetteer and Primary. The Gazetteer data is replicated from the Imagery database server. There are 42 20 GB files spread over two 559 GB NTFS volumes.

The TerraServer database was created using default settings with two exceptions. A *bulk copy* option was set to improve load times by reducing logging. Also, a *truncate log on checkpoint* option was set. These options preclude media recovery using the log. Instead, Terraserver would restore from an online database backup and reload any data that had been added since that backup.

All tables are clustered on their primary key and a few secondary indexes, mostly in the Gazetteer, were added to support searching for different name combinations and for on-line loading. Retrieving one image tile requires the simplest of SQL statements:

Select * from Image where PrimaryKey='value'

One set of Gazetteer tables and one *ImageSearch* table serve to locate images by name in all themes. The *Loadjob, Scalejob,* and *SearchJob* tables are used to manage the online loading of images. They hold the state of load jobs and are used for monitoring and restart.

2.8 Hardware Architecture

The web site is configured to minimize single points of failure, protect the database from hackers, and scale to support additional users or data over time.

The Tier 2 and Tier 3 software runs on separate computer systems. There is an HTTP firewall in front of the web servers and a packet filter firewall between the web servers and the database server. Having the database server inside the corporate firewall allows us to load data to the TerraServer from within the Microsoft corporate network.

The web site has eight Windows NT servers – 6 web servers and 2 database servers. The USGS aerial imagery is maintained on a Compaq AlphaServer™ 8400 containing 8 440 Mhz Alpha processors and 10 GB of RAM. The processor is attached to 7 StorageWorks™ Enterprise Storage Array 10000 (ESA-10000) cabinets. The disk arrays are based on UltraSCSI technology.

Each ESA-10000 contains 48 9 GB disk drives and 2 HSZ70 dual-redundant RAID-5 controllers. 4 sets of 11 disks each are

---

[4] SQL Server 7.0 supports a new concept called "File Groups", which replace the previous "Database Device" concept. A File Group is a named entity which lists the physical files that store a specific list of tables in a database.

configured into a single RAID-5 stripe-set and managed as a single logical disk by the HSZ70 controller. 2 drives per cabinet are available as hot spares. Should a disk fail, the HSZ70 controllers automatically swap a spare drive into a RAID set.

Windows NT Server sees each large (85 GB each) disk created by the RAID controllers of each of the seven disk cabinets. It stripes these into 4 large (595 GB) volumes which are then each formatted and managed by the Windows NT file system (NTFS). Each 595 GB volume contains about thirty 20GB files. SQL Server stores its databases in these large files. We chose this 20GB file size since it fits conveniently on one DLT magnetic tape cartridge.

Connected to the AlphaServer 8400 is a StorageTek 9710 automated tape robot. The tape robot contains 10 Quantum DLT7000 tape drives. Legato Networker backup software can backup the entire 1.5 TB TerraServer SQL database to the StorageTek tape robot in 7 hours and 15 minutes – or 17 GB/hour.

The USGS topographic maps are maintained on a Compaq ProLiant 8500 containing 8 550 mhz Pentium III processors and 4 GB of RAM. Two racks contain 140 9GB hard drives. A row of 10 drives is configured into a RAID-5 disk volume by the Compaq SmartArray hardware controller. The RAID-5 sets are connected to the processor via Fiber Channel.

For reliability and performance, the database servers contain three 100 Mbit Ethernet cards and is connected to three separate local area networks. One network card connects the database server to three of the Compaq ProLiant 5500 web servers. A second network card connects the database server to three other Compaq ProLiant 5500 web servers. The third network card connects the database server to the TerraServer image-processing center which is inside the Microsoft corporate network.

The TerraServer web site is housed at the Microsoft Internet Data Center – a well-managed and secure facility with excellent environmental protection (emergency power, good physical security,...), and with high bandwidth to the Internet (about 3.6 Tbps at present).

2.9 Hardware Capacity Planning

It is difficult to size an Internet application in advance. We originally planned for one-million web hits per day, which is far beyond what we actually expected. At the time, other groups were reporting small numbers (e.g. 17 million hits per week for the 1997 winter Olympics.) But, publicity and interest in the site was very high. During the first week, demand was in excess of 30 million web hits per day. Ten times what we expected. This was not a pleasant experience for us or for our users.

Now that the novelty has worn off, demand averages 7 million hits per day with peaks of 15. The web site is configured to support a maximum of 6,000 simultaneous web browser connections (see Table 1). Additional Tier 2 Web Servers could increase this number.

Table 1. TerraServer hardware configuration parameters	
Max hits per day	40 million/day
Max SQL queries per day	37 million/day
Max image downloads / day	35 million/day
Bandwidth to Internet	200 Mbps = 2 Terabytes/day
Concurrent connections	6,000 connections
Web front ends	6 4-way 200 Mhz Compaq Proliant 5500, .5GB ram
Database back-end	1 8-way 440Mhz Compaq AlphaServer 8400 10GB ram, 3.2 TB raid5 324 9GB Ultra SCSI disks 1 8-way 550 mhz Compaq ProLiant 8500, 4GB ram, 1.2 TB Raid-5 (140 9GB Fiber Channel disks

3. TerraServer Data Load Process

As with other data warehouses, most of the labor of building the TerraServer consists of data scrubbing and data loading. The TerraServer database is organized to simplify the TerraServer web application that presents image and meta data to end users. The TerraServer design avoids dynamic projection, rotation, and other sophisticated features found in commercial GIS systems. The data loading programs pre-compute the GIS details and present each scene as a seamless mosaic of 200 by 200 pixel tiles. All knowledge of projection systems, re-sampling pixels, edge alignment, merging pixels from multiple images, etc., is implemented in the load programs.

There are two image load programs in the TerraServer system – TerraCutter and TerraScale. *TerraCutter* re-formats imagery received from data sources, tiles it into formats acceptable to the TerraServer web application, and inserts the tiles and metadata into the database. *TerraScale* computes the lower resolution image-pyramid tiles for a theme by sub-sampling the tiles created by TerraCutter.

We implemented a simple job-scheduler system to manage and track the data loading process. Each processing program leaves a "popcorn trail" in the Load Management database so administrators can monitor progress on loading new data.

New imagery is inserted into the TerraServer database on-line while web users browse imagery. The table design and load program insertion order ensures that all the required metadata and imagery is place before the image is made visible to the web application.

3.1 Data Flow

USGS DOQ data is shipped DLT media written in the "tar" format. DOQ files are in a custom USGS format. Meta-data and image pixels are contained in one file. Data is 8-bit grayscale or 24-bit, RGB color infrared. TerraCutter converts color infrared to 8-bit grayscale. DOQ files cover a USGS "standard quarter-quadrangle", which is a 3.75-minute by 3.75-minute square area.

The order of DOQ files on tape is random. Adjacent DOQ files can arrive in any order.

USGS DRG data is shipped on CDROM media. All 1:24,000, 1:100,000, and 1:250,000 scale maps for a square degree are contained on one CDROM. Images are in the GeoTiff format and have a fixed color map of 13 colors. Meta-data and image pixels are separate files. Files for a single square degree are grouped onto one CDROM.

SPIN-2 data is shipped on DLT media written in "NT Backup" format. SPIN-2 files are in a custom "Kodak/Microsoft/Aerial Images" format. Meta-data and image pixels are in separate files. Data is 8-bit grayscale.

TerraServer System Administrators use the appropriate "off-the-shelf" program to download a tape or CDROM to a directory on an image editing system. The current image editing system is a Compaq ProLiant 8500 with 8 550 mhz processors, 4 GB of RAM, and 450 GB of disk.

The TerraServer System Administrators launch the TerraCutter image-editing program against a directory containing the image and meta files downloaded from tape or CDROM. TerraCutter uses the Load Management schema tables to make sure the job has not been processed previously. Or, if a previous run had aborted, TerraCutter will pick up where it had left off. TerraCutter uses the Load Management schema to catch duplicate files sent on previously processed tapes or CDROMs. When a directory has been successfully processed, the download directory is deleted; the tape is physically marked as "processed" and shelved. All further processing – sub-sampling to create lower resolution scales, correlating tiles with named locations, merging pixels between tiles, etc. – occurs within the memory of a custom program or T-SQL database statements.

3.2 Load Management Schema

The TerraServer load system maintains a set of tables in the TerraServer database. These tables are not visible to end users on the Internet. A set of Active Server Page scripts allow the TerraServer System Administrators to schedule and monitor the TerraServer database load process.

A *LoadJob* row is created when a load program is instructed to process a directory or a specific list of imagery received from a data source. The *LoadJob* row describes the on-disk location of the input data, the source tape/CD, the computer system the load program ran on, the load program version, the date the job started, and the job's current status.

Load programs update the *LoadJob* record each time they complete an input file found in the source path and insert a row into the *ScaleJob* table. This is the signal to the TerraScale program that a block of image tiles is ready to have its image pyramid created.

The TerraScale program updates the *ScaleJob* table with its progress information. There is a set of administrative Active Server Pages that TerraServer Administrators use to monitor the progress of image pyramid creation.

3.3 TerraCutter

TerraCutter is a fairly complicated C program. The simple part is formatting tiles suitable for the TerraServer web application and inserting them into the database.

The ground size covered by a pixel must also be fixed to multiples of 1-meter resolution –¼, ½, 1, 2, 4, 8, 16, etc. If necessary, TerraCutter re-samples the input image to the appropriate resolution as the image is read in. As tiles are produced, TerraCutter saves the tile image into a temporary file, computes the Image table metadata fields, and inserts the new tile into the database using ODBC API calls. A single image tile is inserted in the scope of one transaction.

The challenging aspect to the TerraCutter program is handling the image overlap that generally exists within original imagery. For example, USGS DOQ images cover a 3.75 minutes by 3.75 minutes. Generally, there is a 200 to 300 meter / pixel collar surrounding the 3.75 x 3.75 minute rectangle. Thus adjacent DOQ images contain a certain number of duplicate pixels along an edge.

TerraCutter combines pixels from multiple input images into one tile. The merge must ensure geographic alignment so that roads, buildings and other structures that cross tile boundaries do not

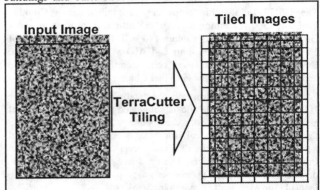

Figure 7: The TerraCutter breaks a large image up into tiles that then can be mosaiced into a scene.

appear interrupted. TerraCutter does this by carefully computing the starting point - location 0,0 in the image tile. For UTM based data-sets (USGS DOQ and DRG), TerraCutter looks for the first pixel in the input image that has a UTM X and Y address that is evenly divisible by width and height of an image tile. For example, USGS DOQ images are 1-meter resolution, so DOQ tiles start at 200-meter boundaries. DRG images are 2-meter resolution, so DRG tiles start at 400-meter boundaries.

Rounding the starting UTM X and Y coordinate up to width and height of the image tile simplifies aligning layered maps containing multiple TerraServer data-sets. The UTM address for pixel 0,0 in a DOQ Image Tile at 2-meter resolution is the same UTM address for pixel 0,0 in a DRG tile with the same X, Y, zone address.

Input image files of projected data-sets, like USGS DOQ and DRG, will overlap other image files along the edges. TerraCutter must choose which input image to take a duplicate pixel from. The amount of overlap varies from file to file in each data-set. Figure 8 depicts how input imagery files, numbered and outlined with solid thick lines, overlap each other within the UTM coordinate system. The tiles, outlined with light dashed lines within the numbered rectangles, depict the challenge in edge matching.

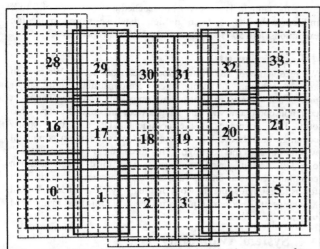

Figure 8. Tiling overlapping UTM images into a seamless mosaic. The dotted lines represent the mosaic grid. Up to four files can contribute pixels to a tile.

DOQ image files typically overlap each other by 100 to 300 pixels. DRG image files can overlap each other by 50 to 1500 pixels. However, only one file will contain "map data" while the others will contain map notes and tick marks found along the border of USGS topographical maps [4].

Conceptually, it is possible for up to four input images to contribute to a single TerraServer tile. To complete all the tiles for a single input image, a total of nine input images are needed – the center image and eight surrounding images. Unfortunately, the projected data sets are not delivered in sorted order. Finding all the adjacent input images would be a tape-shuffling nightmare. Hence, TerraCutter uses an incremental load algorithm.

TerraCutter tiles each input image independently. White space is added around the input image edge to align to the TerraServer grid system and the input data is re-sampled to the appropriate TerraServer resolution. Tiles are then cut and held in memory uncompressed.

After compressing each tile, TerraCutter looks for a tile with the matching Theme, Scale, X, Y, and SceneID properties in the appropriate TerraServer database imagery table. If there is not an existing tile, then TerraCutter inserts the image into the table and sets a "visibility flag" to "visible".

If a tile does exist in the database, TerraCutter compares the "blankness" of the newly cut tile with the "blankness" of the tile in the database. The following table contains the TerraCutter decision tree for handling image overlap:

New Tile Blankness	Db Tile Blankness	Action
0 %	0% – 99%	Discard Db Tile, Insert New Tile
1% – 99%	1% – 99%	Merge pixels from New & Db Tile
1% – 99%	0%	Discard New Tile, Keep Db tile

TerraCutter performs the following steps in one transaction –

(1) check for an existing image,

(2) fetch the image and merge pixels with the in memory copy,

(3) compress the new or merged tile,

(4) insert new tile row,

(5) and delete old tile if necessary.

Using the SQL Server concurrency control, other executing TerraCutters are automatically blocked from modifying the same tile, but can be updating other tiles in the same table. The TerraServer web application performs "dirty reads" of the imagery tables and is not blocked from reading the currently visible row. Thus, we are careful to delete the old tile as the last step so that the web application can get to a valid, but soon to be replaced tile, when TerraCutter is at step 2 or 3.

The program proceeds on to the next tile and repeats the process. When all tiles are cut from an input image file, TerraCutter updates the production status field in the Theme's Original Meta row to indicate that the input image has been completely tiled. TerraServer Administrators monitor the progress of the TerraCutter program through database queries against the Theme Original Meta table.

3.4 TerraScale

TerraScale re-samples the tiles created by TerraCutter to create the lower resolution tiles in the theme's image pyramid. To create a lower resolution tile, TerraScale takes four tiles from the next higher resolution and averages four pixel values into one pixel value. TerraScale repeats this process at every resolution level until it tiles the lowest resolution tile for a given theme

Figure 9 depicts how the highest resolution tiles loaded by TerraCutter contribute to the pixels at lower resolution. We refer to the tiles loaded by the TerraCutter program as the "base scale" or "base tiles".

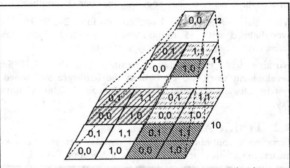

Figure 9: The TerraScale program computes the image pyramid by using averaging or using nearest neighbor algorithms on the four lower-level pixels.

The number of lower resolution tile levels created by the TerraScale program is theme dependent. The USGS DOQ and SPIN-2 data base scale is 1-meter resolution. TerraScale creates 2-meter resolution through 64-meter resolution – a total of seven levels.

The TerraScale program continuously scans the *ScaleJob* table for new work to do. If it finds a row with a "job queued", then it reads the job characteristics and updates the *ScaleJob* row to indicate that the TerraScale program is handling the job. This lets multiple TerraScale programs consume jobs on the same queue.

A *ScaleJob* row describes one complete image pyramid. The TerraCutter inserts or modifies a *ScaleJob* row when it inserts or updates a tile in the bounds defined by the top level of the Theme's image pyramid. In the USGS DOQ case, a single top-level 64m-resolution tile has a 64 by 64 tile 1m resolution base. Several *ScaleJob* rows will be inserted for each DOQ processed by the TerraCutter since a single USGS DOQ does not line up on an image pyramid boundary.

TerraScale begins a loop to create the tiles at the lowest resolution. This is the top of the image pyramid. It recurses down the image pyramid (higher resolution levels) until it fetches the four base tiles in one corner. The four tiles are averaged into one tile and inserted into the database. If the low-resolution tile had been sub-sampled previously, then the old tile is deleted.

The TerraScale program continues to walk up-and-down the image pyramid underneath the lowest resolution tile it is generating. When the top tile is sub-sampled, the ScaleJob is marked as completed and the program moves on to another job.

TerraScale is told which resolution levels are to represent the image pyramid in the search system. As a last step in building an image pyramid for a particular low resolution X,Y value, TerraScale inserts the appropriate rows into the *ImageSearch* tables. A tile is not visible in the TerraServer application until a row is inserted into the *ImageSearch table*.

4. What We Learned

4.1 Initial Results

The TerraServer project began in late 1996. A prototype was demonstrated in May 1997. Aerial Images went live with a demonstration web site in January 1998. The full site went live in June 1998. It has now been operating for over 18 months.

When the web site was launched on June 24, 1998, it was overwhelmed with 35 million "hits". We had clearly under-estimated the popularity of this type of data.

Working with the hardware partners and the SQL Server development team, we configured the hardware and tuned the system software to handle 40 million hits and 300,000 visitors per day.

4.2 Traffic Analysis

TerraServer continues to be a very popular web site. Below are the usage statistics for TerraServer's first year on the web:

Table 2: TerraServer traffic summary July 1998 to July 1999.

Summary	Total	Average	Max
Users	23,104,798	63,128	149,615
Sessions	31,011,284	84,730	172,545
Hits	2,287,259,402	6,624,607	29,265,400
Page Views	367,528,901	1,004,177	6,626,921
DB Querys	2,015,132,166	5,505,826	17,799,309
Image Xfers	1,731,338,052	4,704,723	14,984,365

Since the launch, TerraServer has reached a steady state of 5 to 8 million web hits, 5 to 6 million database stored procedure executions, and 50 GB of image tile downloads per day.

4.3 User Input

We received over 18,000 mail messages from users. We tried to answer each one. Most messages were constructive criticism or praise, but there were substantial complaints as well. The most common complaint was that images were missing. The server has only 30% coverage of the continental US and very spotty coverage outside the US. The second most common complaint was that images did not align. This forced us to go to the "scene" oriented design described here. The third most common complaint centered on the Java applet we wrote: it was difficult for us to get that applet to work on the many different Java Virtual Machines of the common platforms (each platform has many JVM variants).

4.4 System Availability

The Compaq database server and SQL Server 7.0 database management system containing aerial imagery have been extremely reliable. Table 3 summarizes the availability statistics for the period through 1 July 1998 through 1 July 1999. The system went out of service for 3 hours for software upgrades, 2.5 hours to move the server within the data center, and 33 minutes due to a software bug.

Table 3: Availability statistics for TerraServer SQL Server.

	Hours	%
Elapsed Time	8760	100.00 %
Availability	8754	99.93 %
Scheduled Availability	8757	99.97 %

The topographical map database server went into service in December 1999. Except for a 30 minute period for a software upgrade, the new server has not be out of service at all.

4.5 Database Size

Table 4 summarizes the database size as of February 2000.

Table 4: TerraServer Databases

	Aerial Imagery Db	Topo Map Db
Db Allocation	1.5 TB	1.0 TB
User Data Rows	170.7 million	104.4 million
User Data Bytes	1.1 TB	.75 TB
Log Size	75 GB	25 GB

The database is backed up regularly to the StorageTek 9710 TimberWolf tape robot using SQL Backup integrated with Legato Networker. In on-line mode, the backup consumes approximately 20% of the CPU resources and takes approximately 8.5 hours to complete including tape changes.

Table 5 summarizes the number of uncompressed images received from each organization and compression results:

Table 5: Image Counts

	Comp. Ratio	Input Images	Input Size (GB)	Tiles (M)	Tile Size (GB)
Aerial	5	97,500	5,864	133.6	1,136
Topo	5.4	4,335	2,006	39.6	762

4.6 Application Size and Complexity

Table 6 summarizes the size of the TerraServer application source code:

Table 6: Application Source Code.

Item	Modules	Files	Lines
T-SQL Stored Procedures	20	20	5468
Active Server Pages (Tier 2 Web App)	33	41	5727
Load Programs	3	70	39301

One full-time developer and 4 part-time developers built TerraServer. 1 full-time system administrator and 1 full-time data-load specialist maintain the web site.

4.7 New Satellite Imagery Users

Remote sensing and aerial photography have been a niche application due to the high complexity and expense of tools that can view it. TerraServer dramatically reduced the access complexity and cost for simple applications. The application is so simple to use that, high-resolution imagery is now available to the entire Internet population. We and others have been astonished at the wide interest in the data: tens of thousands of people visit the site each day (see Table 2).

4.8 Relational Databases as Image Repositories

Using relational databases to store image pyramids of common graphics file formats, e.g. Jpeg and GIF, forces the separation of storage management from image presentation. The tiled design allows rapid pan and zoom to any part of the image database. It also supports background loading of new images while the current data is being viewed. The database system is able to handle much larger image bases than a file-per-image design used by earlier efforts. Storing tiles individually also allows for easy on-line editing of any portion of an image. Choosing a ubiquitous medium like the Internet and the common web browser as the presentation tool enabled the rapid dissemination of high-resolution imagery to new users and applications.

4.9 The Value of Cooperative Joint Research

Because the project had to use real data, and that data was expensive, it forced us to enlarge the project team beyond database and systems researchers. By including additional companies and organizations, the project goals and requirements expanded. This brought additional skills to the table – geographers, graphics researchers, high-resolution image interpreters (a.k.a. spies), and GIS experts. We were able to blend the knowledge and skills of diverse partners to build a powerful spatial data warehouse and produce a more complete result by solving a wider set of problems than just a database or operating system problem.

4.10 Integration With Encarta Online

TerraServer became part of the Encarta Online web site in May 1999. The Microsoft Encarta product team cross-referenced Encarta Encyclopedia articles with the TerraServer imagery. As users navigate the imagery, hypertext links appear to related Encarta Encyclopedia articles. This vastly improves the richness of the user interface.

5. Future Work

5.1 Layered Maps

We are collaborating with UC Berkeley Digital Library Project, http://elib.cs.berkeley.edu/, on layered maps. The USGS DOQ and DRG data sets are in a common projection system. The TerraServer tiling algorithm cuts tiles so that client applications can identify overlapping tiles from separate themes. We plan to work with the UCB Digital Library team to build a client application which will display TerraServer projected data-sets that are in the same projection as a layered map set. The layered map user interfaces has the same ease-of-use goals as our traditional single-layer HTML interface

5.2 Dense vs. Sparse Coverage

The feedback from users has encouraged us to acquire complete coverage of smaller geographic areas. Thus, in the last 9 months, we have concentrated on adding the USGS DRG topographical map theme. The USGS DRG data-set completely covers the conterminous United States and Hawaii. Thus any U.S. user is guaranteed to find some information about where they live.

We have focused the corpus of the TerraServer image on the United States instead of attempting to load a sparse set of scenes from around the world.

5.3 Distributed Web Sites

The popularity of the web site has encouraged other data providers to offer interesting data sets. These firms generally have a commercial interest in advertising, selling, and distributing their data. They often have data volume, security, and user interface requirements beyond the scope of our research project.

The present TerraServer design allows multiple database servers and multiple web sites to be configured into a single TerraServer web service. Currently, we are experimenting with off-loading the SPIN-2 data to Aerial Images, Inc. located in Raleigh, NC. The Microsoft TerraServer site, http://terraserver.microsoft.com, and Aerial Images site, http://terraserver.com, gazetteers cross reference each other.

The multi-web site service design allows us to locate web sites near the users with the most interest in the data. It also allows individual data providers to tailor the TerraServer web application to their specific requirements and taste. We hope to add other data providers in the future preferably at least one per continent.

6. References

[1] Barclay, T., et. al., The Microsoft TerraServer, Microsoft Technical Report MS TR 98 17, Microsoft Corp, Redmond, WA. http://research.microsoft.com/scripts/pubDB/pubsasp.asp?RecordID=155

[2] F. Davis, W. Farrell, Jim Gray, R. Mechoso, R. Moore, S. Sides, M. Stonebraker., "EOSDIS Alternative Architecture Final Report," Sept., 1994, http://research.microsoft.com/~gray/EOS_DIS/

[3] B. Kobler, J. Berbert, P. Caulk, P. C. Hariharan: "Architecture and Design of Storage and Data Management for the NASA Earth Observing System Data and Information System (EOSDIS)". IEEE Symposium on Mass Storage Systems 1995: 65-76

[4] Laurence Moore, "Transverse Mercator Projections and U.S. Geological Survey Digital Products", U.S. Geological Survey, Professional Paper.

[5] Arther H. Robinson, Joel L. Morrison, Phillip C. Muehrcke, A. Jon Kimerling, Stehen C. Guptill, *Elements of Cartography, Sixth Edition*, John Wiley & Sons, Inc., U.S.A. 1995, ISBN 0-471-55579-7.

[6] H. Samet, *The Design and Analysis of Spatial Data Structures*, Addison-Wesley, Reading, MA, 1990. ISBN 0-201-50255-0.

[7] Snyder, J.P., "An Album of Map Projections", U.S. Geological Survey, Professional Paper, 1453, (1989).

[8] Microsoft SQL Server 7.0 http://microsoft.com/SQL/

A Data Model and Data Structures
for Moving Objects Databases*

Luca Forlizzi[†], Ralf Hartmut Güting[‡],

Enrico Nardelli[†], and Markus Schneider[‡]

Abstract

We consider spatio-temporal databases supporting spatial
objects with continuously changing position and extent,
termed *moving objects databases*. We formally define a data
model for such databases that includes complex evolving
spatial structures such as line networks or multi-component
regions with holes. The data model is given as a collection of
data types and operations which can be plugged as attribute
types into any DBMS data model (e.g. relational, or object-
oriented) to obtain a complete model and query language.
A particular novel concept is the *sliced representation* which
represents a temporal development as a set of *units*, where
unit types for spatial and other data types represent certain
"simple" functions of time. We also show how the model
can be mapped into concrete physical data structures in a
DBMS environment.

1   Introduction

A wide and increasing range of database applications has
to deal with spatial objects whose position and/or extent
changes over time. This applies on the one hand to objects
usually represented in maps such as countries, rivers, roads,
pollution areas, land parcels and so forth. On the other hand
it includes physical objects moving around such as taxis, air
planes, oil tankers, criminals, polar bears, hurricanes, or
flood areas, to name but a few examples. The management
of the first class of objects is the more traditional task
of spatio-temporal databases. The goal of our research
is to support representation and querying not only of the
first, but in particular of the more dynamic second class
of objects; to emphasize this we speak of *moving objects
databases*.

In previous work, we have proposed a *data type oriented*

approach for modeling and querying such data [EGSV99,
EGSV98]. The idea is to represent the temporal development of spatial entities in certain data types such as *moving
point* or *moving region*. Values of such types are functions
that associate with each instant in time a point or a region value. Suitable operations are provided on these types
to support querying. Such data types can be embedded as
attribute types into object-relational or other data models;
they can be implemented and provided as extension packages (e.g. data blades) for suitable extensible DBMS environments.

Following this approach, two questions arise. First,
exactly which types and operations should be offered?
Second, at what level of abstraction should these types and
operations be described?

By "level of abstraction" we mean the following. A
moving point can be defined either as a continuous function
from time into the 2D plane, or as a polyline in the three-
dimensional (2D + time) space. A region can be defined as
a connected subset of the plane with non-empty interior, or
as a polygon with polygonal holes. The essential difference
is that in the first case we define the domains of data types
just in terms of infinite sets, whereas in the second case we
describe certain finite representations for the types.

In [EGSV98] we have discussed the issue at some depth
and introduced the terms *abstract model* for the first and
discrete model for the second level of abstraction. Both
levels have their respective advantages. An abstract model
is relatively clean and simple; it allows one to focus
on the essential concepts and not get bogged down by
representation details. However, it has no straightforward
implementation. A discrete model fixes representations and
is generally far more complex. It makes particular choices
and thereby restricts the range of values of the abstract
model that can be represented. For example, a moving
point could be represented not only by a 3D polyline but
also by higher order polynomial splines. Both cases (and
many more) are included within the abstract model. On
the other hand, once such a finite representation has been
selected, it can be translated directly to data structures.

In [EGSV98] we came to the conclusion that both levels
of modeling are needed and that one should first design
an abstract model of spatio-temporal data types and then
continue by defining a corresponding discrete model. Such
an abstract model has been developed in [GBE[+]00]. The
main concerns in that design have been orthogonality in the
type system, genericity and consistency of operations, and
closure and consistency between structure and operations of
related non-temporal and temporal types. Semantics of all
types and operations have been defined formally.

* This work was partially supported by the CHOROCHRO-
NOS project, funded by the EU under the Training and Mobility
of Researchers Programme, Contract No. ERB FMRX-CT96-0056.

† Dipartimento di Matematica Pura ed Applicata, Universita
Degli Studi di L'Aquila, L'Aquila, Italy, {forlizzi, nardelli}@univaq.it

‡ Praktische Informatik IV, FernUniversität Hagen, D-58084
Hagen, Germany, {gueting, markus.schneider}@fernuni-hagen.de

The purpose of this paper is to continue this work by defining a discrete data model implementing the abstract model of [GBE⁺00]. This means that for all data types of the abstract model we introduce corresponding "discrete" types whose domains are defined in terms of finite representations. We define precisely which constraints apply so that a finite representation does indeed describe a value of the abstract model. For example, a region will be described by a set of line segments, but not every set of line segments describes a valid region value.

The discrete model is a high-level specification of data structures for a spatio-temporal DBMS. In the last part of the paper we show how the discrete model can be mapped to real data structures that can be used to implement attribute data types in a DBMS. Hence the paper offers a good basis for the implementation of a "moving objects data blade."

Earlier work on spatio-temporal databases has generally been restricted to accommodate discrete changes of spatial values. Worboys [Wor94] has proposed such a model which represents spatio-temporal entities as the cross-product of a spatial and a temporal description, using simplicial complexes for the spatial part and sets of rectangles (for two time dimensions) for the temporal part. Other such models are [CG94] or [PD95].

More recently, research has addressed the more dynamic applications that we (and others) call "moving objects databases". Wolfson and colleagues [Wol98, WCD⁺98] consider the management of collections of moving points in the plane. However, their model describes only the current and the expected position of a point in the near future, as represented by a motion vector. The main issue is to determine how often updates of motion vectors are needed to balance the cost of updates against imprecision in the knowledge of positions. Their model does not describe complete trajectories of moving objects, and it also does not address more complex spatial structures such as regions. Chomicki and Revesz [CR99] study a framework where spatio-temporal objects can be described as collections of *atomic geometric objects*, and each such atomic object is essentially given as a spatial object of some dimension d together with a continuous function describing the development of the spatial object over time. For the continuous functions, affine mappings (allowing translation, rotation, and scaling) and subclasses thereof are considered. They establish some basic results, e.g., rectangles with linear translation and scaling are closed under set operations whereas polygons with linear translation and scaling are only closed under union.

The CHOROCHRONOS project, in which we participate, has addressed some issues related to moving objects databases. Conceptual modeling is discussed in [TH97], indexing in [TSPM98]. Reference [PJ99] addresses the uncertainty in capturing moving point trajectories.

The constraint database approach can also be used to describe spatial as well as spatio-temporal data. Papers that explicitly address spatio-temporal examples and models are [GRS98, CR97].

However, except for [GBE⁺00] to our knowledge there does not exist in the literature a comprehensive design of spatio-temporal types and operations, let alone a corresponding discrete data model as it is given in this paper. Our own earlier work [EGSV99, EGSV98] discusses the idea and some basic issues related to spatio-temporal data types, but does not yet define a discrete data model.

The paper is structured as follows. In Section 2 the abstract model as the basis for our design is briefly reviewed. Section 3 defines the discrete data types, first for non-temporal, and then for temporal types. Section 4 describes data structures for the discrete types. Two example algorithms illustrating the use of the model and the data structures are given in Section 5. Section 6 offers conclusions.

2   Review of the Abstract Model

The abstract model of [GBE⁺00] offers the data types, or actually the *type system* shown in Table 1.

	→ BASE	*int*, *real*, *string*, *bool*
	→ SPATIAL	*point*, *points*, *line*, *region*
	→ TIME	*instant*
BASE ∪ TIME	→ RANGE	*range*
BASE ∪ SPATIAL	→ TEMPORAL	*intime*, *moving*

Table 1: Signature describing the abstract type system

The type system is described by a signature. A signature in general has *sorts* and *operators* and defines a set of terms. In this case the sorts are called *kinds* and the operators are *type constructors*.[1] The terms generated by the signature are the available *data types*. Some data types defined by this signature are *int*, *region*, *range(instant)*, or *moving(point)*.

The meaning of the data types, informally, is the following. The constant types *int*, *real*, *string*, *bool* are as usual, except that the domains are extended by a special value "undefined". A value of type *point* is a point in the real (2D) plane, a *points* value a finite set of points. A *line* value is a finite set of continuous curves in the plane. A *region* value is a finite set of disjoint *faces* where each face is a connected subset of the plane with non-empty interior. Faces may have holes and lie within holes of other faces. Types *line* and *region* are illustrated in Figures 2 and 3, respectively.

Type *instant* offers a time domain isomorphic to the real numbers. The *range* type constructor produces types whose values are finite sets of pairwise disjoint intervals over the argument domain. The *intime* constructor yields types associating a time instant with a value of the argument domain.

The most important type constructor is *moving*. Given an argument type α in BASE or SPATIAL, it constructs a type whose values are functions from time (the domain of *instant*) into the domain of α. Functions may be partial and must consist of only a finite number of continuous components (which is made precise in [GBE⁺00]). For example, a *moving(region)* value is a function from time into *region* values.

Over the types so defined, the abstract model offers a large set of operations. It defines first generic operations over the non-temporal types (all types except those constructed by *moving* or *intime*). These operations include predicates (e.g. **inside** or ≤), set operations (e.g. **union**), aggregate operations, operations with numeric result (e.g. **size** of a region), and distance and direction operations.

In a second step, by a mechanism called temporal *lifting*, all operations defined in the first step over non-temporal

---

[1] We write signatures by giving first the argument and result sorts, and then the operators with this functionality. Kinds are denoted by capitals and type constructors in italic underlined. Operations on data types are written in bold face.

types are uniformly and consistently made applicable to the corresponding temporal ("moving") types. For example, the operation **inside**, applicable e.g. to a *point* and a *region* argument and returning *bool*, is by lifting also applicable to a *moving(point)* vs. a *region*, or a *point* vs. a *moving(region)*, or a *moving(point)* vs. a *moving(region)*; in all these cases it returns a *moving(bool)*.

Third, special operations are offered for temporal types *moving(α)* whose values are functions. They can all be projected into domain (time) and range. Their intersection with values or sets of values from domain or range can be formed (e.g. **atinstant** restricts the function to a certain time instant). The rate of change (**derivative**, **speed**) can also be observed.

An example now shall briefly demonstrate how these data types can be embedded into any DBMS data model as attribute types and how pertaining operations can be used in queries. For example, we can integrate them into the relational model and have a relation

```
planes (airline: string, id: string, flight: mpoint)
```

where *mpoint* is used as a synonym for *moving(point)* and included into the relation schema as an *abstract data type*. The term flight denotes a spatio-temporal attribute whose values record the locations of planes over time.

For posing queries we introduce the signatures of some operations. We only formulate special instances of them as far as they are needed for our examples. Corresponding generic signature specifications can be found in [GBE+00].

Operation	Signature	
trajectory	*moving(point)*	$\rightarrow$ *line*
length	*line*	$\rightarrow$ *real*
distance	*moving(point)* $\times$ *moving(point)*	$\rightarrow$ *moving(real)*
atmin	*moving(real)*	$\rightarrow$ *moving(real)*
initial	*moving(real)*	$\rightarrow$ *intime(real)*
val	*intime(real)*	$\rightarrow$ *real*

The projection of moving points into the plane may consist of points and lines. The operation **trajectory** computes the line parts of such a projection. The operation **length** determines the length of a *line* value. The distance between two moving points is calculated by **distance**. Operation **atmin** here restricts a moving real to all times with the same minimal *real* value. The first (*instant*, *real*) pair of a moving real is returned by the operation **initial**. Operation **val** is here applied to a (*instant*, *real*) pair and projects onto the second component.

We can now ask a query "Give me all flights of Lufthansa longer than 5000 kms":

```
SELECT airline, id
FROM planes
WHERE airline = ''Lufthansa''
  AND length(trajectory(flight)) > 5000
```

This query just employs projection into space. An example of a genuine spatio-temporal query, which cannot be answered with the aid of projections, is: "Find all pairs of planes that during their flight came closer to each other than 500 meters!":

```
SELECT p.airline, p.id, q.airline, q.id
FROM planes p, planes q
WHERE val(initial(atmin(
  distance(p.flight, q.flight)))) < 0.5
```

This query represents an instance of a *spatio-temporal join*. Note that the **distance** operation is here used in its temporally lifted version.

Many further illustrating query examples from different application scenarios (e.g., multimedia presentations, forest fire control management) can be found in [GBE+00]. These applications demonstrate that a very flexible and powerful query language results from this design.

In the following development of a discrete model, we focus on defining finitely and efficiently representable domains for the data types. Of course, the discrete model also includes operations. Almost all operations of the abstract model will also be available in the discrete model.[2] The next step is to develop algorithms for implementing these operations on the discrete representations. Two examples for this are shown in Section 5.

3 Data Types

3.1 Overview

In Section 3 we define data types that can represent values of corresponding types of the abstract model. Of course, the discrete types can in general only represent a subset of the values of the corresponding abstract type.

All type constructors of the abstract model will have direct counterparts in the discrete model except for the *moving* constructor. This is, because it is impossible to introduce at the discrete level a type constructor that automatically transforms types into corresponding temporal types. The type system for the discrete model therefore looks quite the same as the abstract type system up to the *intime* constructor, but then introduces a number of new type constructors to implement the *moving* constructor, as shown in Table 2.

	$\rightarrow$ BASE	*int*, *real*, *string*, *bool*
	$\rightarrow$ SPATIAL	*point*, *points*, *line*, *region*
	$\rightarrow$ TIME	*instant*
BASE $\cup$ TIME	$\rightarrow$ RANGE	*range*
BASE $\cup$ SPATIAL	$\rightarrow$ TEMPORAL	*intime*
BASE $\cup$ SPATIAL	$\rightarrow$ UNIT	*const*
	$\rightarrow$ UNIT	*ureal*, *upoint*, *upoints*, *uline*, *uregion*
UNIT	$\rightarrow$ MAPPING	*mapping*

Table 2: Signature describing the discrete type system

Let us give a brief overview of the meaning of the discrete type constructors. The base types *int*, *real*, *string*, *bool* can be implemented directly in terms of corresponding programming language types. The spatial types *point* and *points* also have direct discrete representations whereas for the types *line* and *region* linear approximations (i.e., polylines and polygons) are introduced. Type *instant* is also represented directly in terms of programming language real numbers. The *range* and *intime* types represent sets of intervals, or pairs of time instants and values, respectively. These representations are also straightforward.

The interesting part of the model is how temporal ("moving") types are represented. In this paper we describe the *sliced representation*. The basic idea is to decompose the temporal development of a value into fragments called "slices" such that within the slice this development can

---

[2]A few operations, especially **derivative**, cannot be transferred, as they are not closed in the chosen discrete representation.

be described by some kind of "simple" function. This is illustrated in Figure 1.

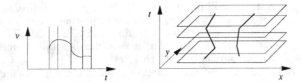

Figure 1: Sliced representation of moving *real* and moving *points* value

The sliced representation is built by a type constructor *mapping* parameterized by the type describing a single slice which we call a *unit* type. A value of a unit type is a pair (i, v) where i is a time interval and v is some representation of a simple function defined within that time interval. We define unit types *ureal*, *upoint*, *upoints*, *uline*, and *uregion*. For values that can only change discretely, there is a trivial "simple" function, namely the constant function. It is provided by a *const* type constructor which produces units whose second component is just a constant of the argument type. This is in particular needed to represent moving *int*, *string*, and *bool* values. The *mapping* data structure basically just assembles a set of units and makes sure that their time intervals are disjoint.

In summary, we obtain the correspondence between abstract and discrete temporal types shown in Table 3.

In Table 3 we have omitted the representations *mapping*(*const*(*real*)), etc. which can be used to represent discretely changing real values and so forth, but are not so interesting for us.

In the remainder of Section 3 we formally define the data types of the discrete model. That means, for each type we define its *domain* of values in terms of some finite representation. From an algebraic point of view, we define for each *sort* (type) a *carrier set*. For a type α we denote its carrier set as D_α.

Of course, each value in D_α is supposed to represent some value of the corresponding abstract domain, that is, the carrier set of the corresponding abstract type. For a type α of the abstract model, let A_α denote its carrier set. We can view the value $a \in A_\alpha$ that is represented by $d \in D_\alpha$ as the *semantics* of d. We will always make clear which value from A_α is meant by a value from D_α. Often this is obvious, or an informal description is sufficient. Otherwise we provide a definition of the form $\sigma(d) = a$ where σ denotes the "semantics" function.

The following Section 3.2 contains definitions for all non-temporal types and for the temporal types in the sliced representation. For the spatial temporal data types *moving*(*points*), *moving*(*line*), and *moving*(*region*) one can also define direct three-dimensional representations in terms of polyhedra etc.; these representations will be treated elsewhere.

3.2 Definition of Discrete Data Types

3.2.1 Base Types and Time Type

The carrier sets of the *discrete base types* and the type for time rest on available programming language types. Let $Instant = \texttt{real}$.

$$D_{int} = \texttt{int} \cup \{\bot\} \qquad D_{real} = \texttt{real} \cup \{\bot\}$$
$$D_{string} = \texttt{string} \cup \{\bot\} \qquad D_{bool} = \texttt{bool} \cup \{\bot\}$$
$$D_{instant} = Instant \cup \{\bot\}$$

Abstract Type	Discrete Type
moving(*int*)	*mapping*(*const*(*int*))
moving(*string*)	*mapping*(*const*(*string*))
moving(*bool*)	*mapping*(*const*(*bool*))
moving(*real*)	*mapping*(*ureal*)
moving(*point*)	*mapping*(*upoint*)
moving(*points*)	*mapping*(*upoints*)
moving(*line*)	*mapping*(*uline*)
moving(*region*)	*mapping*(*uregion*)

Table 3: Correspondence between abstract and discrete temporal types

The only special thing about these types is that they always include the undefined value $\bot$ as required by the abstract model. Since we are interested in continuous evolutions of values, type *instant* is defined in terms of the programming language type `real`.

We sometimes need to speak about only the defined values of some carrier set and therefore introduce a notation for it: Let $D'_\alpha = D_\alpha \setminus \{\bot\}$. We will later introduce carrier sets whose elements are sets themselves; for them we extend this notation to mean $D'_\alpha = D_\alpha \setminus \{\emptyset\}$.

3.2.2 Spatial Data Types

Next, we define finite representations for single points, point collections, lines, and regions in two-dimensional (2D) Euclidean space. A point is, as usual, given by a pair (x, y) of coordinates. Let $Point = \texttt{real} \times \texttt{real}$ and

$$D_{point} = Point \cup \{\bot\}$$

The semantics of an element of D_{point} is obviously an element of A_{point}. We assume lexicographical order on points, that is, given any two points $p, q \in Point$, we define: $p < q \Leftrightarrow (p.x < q.x) \vee (p.x = q.x \wedge p.y < q.y)$.

A value of type *points* is simply a set of points.

$$D_{points} = 2^{Point}$$

Again it is clear that a value of D_{points} represents a value of the abstract domain A_{points}.

The definition of discrete representations for the types *line* and *region* is based on linear approximations. A value of type *line* is essentially just a finite set of line segments in the plane. Figure 2 shows the correspondence between

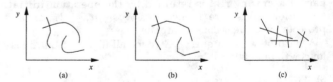

Figure 2: (a) *line* value of the abstract model (b) *line* value of the discrete model (c) any set of line segments is also a *line* value

the abstract type for *line* and the discrete type. The abstract type is a set of curves in the plane which was viewed in [GBE+00] as a planar graph whose nodes are intersections of curves and whose edges are intersection-free pieces of curves. The discrete *line* type represents curves by polylines. However, one can assume a less structured view and consider the same shape to be just a collection of line segments. At the same time, any collection of line segments in the plane defines a valid collection of curves (or planar graph) of the abstract model (see Figure 2 (c)).

Hence, modeling *line* as a set of line segments is no less expressive than the polyline view. It has the advantage that computing the projection of a (discrete representation) moving point into the plane can be done very efficiently as it is not necessary to compute the polyline or graph structure. Hence we prefer to use this unstructured view. Let

$$Seg = \{(u,v) \mid u,v \in Point, u < v\}$$

be the set of all line segments.

$$D_{\underline{line}} = \{S \subset Seg \mid \forall s,t \in Seg :$$
$$s \neq t \wedge collinear(s,t) \Rightarrow disjoint(s,t)\}$$

The predicate *collinear* means that two line segments lie on the same infinite line in 2D space. Hence for a set of line segments to be a *line* value we only require that there are no collinear, overlapping segments. This condition ensures unique representation, as collinear overlapping segments could be merged into a single segment. The semantics of a *line* value is, of course, the union of the points on all of its segments.

A *region* value at the discrete level is essentially a collection of polygons with polygonal holes (Figure 3). Formal definitions are based on the notions of *cycles* and

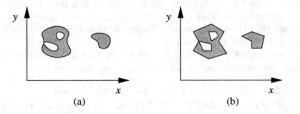

Figure 3: (a) *region* value of the abstract model (b) *region* value of the discrete model

faces. These definitions are similar to those of the ROSE algebra [GS95]. We need to reconsider such definitions here for two reasons: (i) They have to be modified a bit because here we have no "realm-based" [GS95] environment any more, and (ii) we are going to extend them to the "moving" case in the following sections.

A *cycle* is a simple polygon, defined as follows:

$$Cycle = \{S \subset Seg \mid |S| = n, n \geq 3, \text{ such that}$$
- (i) $\forall s,t \in S : s \neq t \Rightarrow \neg p\text{-}intersect(s,t)$
       $\wedge \neg touch(s,t)$
- (ii) $\forall p \in points(S) : card(p,S) = 2$
- (iii) $\exists \langle s_0,\ldots,s_{n-1}\rangle : \{s_0,\ldots,s_{n-1}\} = S \wedge$
       $(\forall i \in \{0,\ldots,n-1\} : meet(s_i, s_{(i+1) \bmod n}))\}$

Two segments *p-intersect* ("properly intersect") if they intersect in their interior (a point other than an end point); they *touch* if one end point lies in the interior of the other segment. Two segments *meet* if they have a common end point. The set $points(S)$ contains all end points of segments, hence is $points(S) = \{p \in Point \mid \exists s \in S : s = (p,q) \vee s = (q,p)\}$. The function $card(p,S)$ tells how often point p occurs in S and is defined as $card(p,S) = |\{s \in S \mid s = (p,q) \vee s = (q,p)\}|$. Hence a collection of segments is a cycle, if (i) no segments intersect properly, (ii) each end point occurs in exactly two segments, and (iii) segments can be arranged into a single cycle rather than several disjoint ones (the notation $\langle s_0,\ldots,s_{n-1}\rangle$ refers to an ordered list of segments).

A *face* is a pair consisting of an outer cycle and a possibly empty set of hole cycles.

$$Face = \{(c,H) \mid c \in Cycle, H \subset Cycle, \text{ such that}$$
- (i) $\forall h \in H : edge\text{-}inside(h,c)$
- (ii) $\forall h_1, h_2 \in H : h_1 \neq h_2 \Rightarrow edge\text{-}disjoint(h_1,h_2)$
- (iii) any cycle that can be formed from the segments of c or H is either c or one of the cycles of H

A cycle c is *edge-inside* another cycle d if its interior is a subset of the interior of d and no edges of c and d overlap. They are *edge-disjoint* if their interiors are disjoint and none of their edges overlap. Note that it is allowed that a segment of one cycle *touches* a segment of another cycle. Overlapping segments are not allowed, since then one could remove the overlapping parts entirely (e.g. two hole cycles could be merged into one hole). The last condition (iii) ensures unique representation, that is, there are no two different interpretations of a set of segments as sets of faces. This implies that a face cannot be decomposed into two or more edge-disjoint faces.

A *region* is then basically a set of disjoint faces.

$$D_{\underline{region}} = \{F \subset Face \mid f_1, f_2 \in F \wedge$$
$$f_1 \neq f_2 \Rightarrow edge\text{-}disjoint(f_1,f_2)\}$$

More precisely, faces have to be *edge-disjoint*. Two faces (c_1, H_1) and (c_2, H_2) are *edge-disjoint* if either their outer cycles c_1 and c_2 are edge-disjoint, or one of the outer cycles, e.g. c_1, is *edge-inside* one of the holes of the other face (some $h \in H_2$). Hence faces may also touch each other in an isolated point, but must not have overlapping boundary segments.

The semantics of a region value should be clear: A cycle c represents all points of the plane enclosed by it as well as the points on the boundary. Given $\sigma(c)$, we have for a face $\sigma((c,H)) = closure(\sigma(c) \setminus \bigcup_{h \in H} \sigma(h))$, that is, hole areas are subtracted from the outer cycle area, but then the resulting point set is closed again in the abstract domain. The area of a region is then obviously the union of the area of its faces.

3.2.3   Sets of Intervals

In this subsection, we introduce the *non-constant range* type constructor which converts a given type $\alpha \in$ BASE $\cup$ TIME into a type whose values are finite sets of intervals over α. Note that on all such types α a total order exists. Range types are needed, for example, to represent collections of time intervals, or the values taken by a moving real.

Let $(S, <)$ be a set with a total order. The representation of an interval over S is given by the following definition.

$$Interval(S) = \{(s,e,lc,rc) \mid s,e \in S, lc, rc \in \text{bool},$$
$$s \leq e, (s = e) \Rightarrow (lc = rc = true)\}.$$

Hence an interval is represented by its end points s and e and two flags lc and rc indicating whether it is left-closed and/or right-closed. The meaning of an interval representation (s,e,lc,rc) is

$$\sigma((s,e,lc,rc)) = \{u \in S \mid s < u < e\} \cup LC \cup RC$$

where the two sets LC and RC are defined as

$$LC = \begin{cases} \{s\} & \text{if } lc \\ \emptyset & \text{otherwise} \end{cases} \qquad RC = \begin{cases} \{e\} & \text{if } rc \\ \emptyset & \text{otherwise} \end{cases}$$

Given an interval i, we denote with $\sigma'(i)$ the semantics expressed by $\sigma(i)$ restricted to the open part of the interval.

Whether two intervals $u = (s_u, e_u, lc_u, rc_u)$ and $v = (s_v, e_v, lc_v, rc_v) \in Interval(S)$ are *disjoint* or *adjacent* is defined as follows:

$$
\begin{aligned}
r\text{-}disjoint(u, v) &\Leftrightarrow e_u < s_v \lor (e_u = s_v \land \neg(rc_u \land lc_v)) \\
disjoint(u, v) &\Leftrightarrow r\text{-}disjoint(u, v) \lor r\text{-}disjoint(v, u) \\
r\text{-}adjacent(u, v) &\Leftrightarrow disjoint(u, v) \\
&\quad \land (e_u = s_v \land (rc_u \lor lc_v)) \lor \\
&\quad ((e_u < s_v \land rc_u \land lc_v) \land \\
&\quad \neg(\exists w \in S \mid e_u < w < s_v)) \\
adjacent(u, v) &\Leftrightarrow r\text{-}adjacent(u, v) \lor r\text{-}adjacent(v, u)
\end{aligned}
$$

The last condition for *r-adjacent* is important for discrete domains such as *int*. Representations of finite sets of intervals over S can now be defined as

$$IntervalSet(S) = \{V \subseteq Interval(S) \mid$$
$$(u, v \in S \land u \neq v) \Rightarrow disjoint(u, v) \land \neg adjacent(u, v)\}$$

The conditions ensure that a set of intervals has a unique and minimal representation. The *range* type constructor can then be defined as:

$$D_{range(\alpha)} = IntervalSet(D'_\alpha) \quad \forall \alpha \in \text{BASE} \cup \text{TIME}$$

We also define the *intime* type constructor in this subsection which yields types whose values consist of a time instant and a value, as in the abstract model.

$$D_{intime(\alpha)} = D_{instant} \times D_\alpha \quad \forall \alpha \in \text{BASE} \cup \text{SPATIAL}$$

3.2.4 Sliced Representation for Moving Objects

In this subsection we introduce and formalize the *sliced representation* for moving objects. The sliced representation is provided by the *mapping* type constructor which represents a moving object as a set of so-called *temporal units* (*slices*). Informally speaking, a temporal unit for a moving data type α is a maximal interval of time where values taken by an instance of α can be described by a "simple" function. A temporal unit therefore records the evolution of a value v of some type α in a given time interval i, while ensuring the maintenance of type-specific constraints during such an evolution.

For a set of temporal units representing a moving object their time intervals are mutually disjoint, and if they are adjacent, their values are distinct. These requirements ensure unique and minimal representations.

Temporal units are described as a generic concept in this subsection. Their specialization to various data types is given in the next two subsections. Let S be a set. The concept of temporal unit is defined by:

$$Unit(S) = Interval(Instant) \times S$$

A pair (i, v) of $Unit(S)$ is called a *temporal unit* or simply a *unit*. Its first component is called the *unit interval*, its second component the *unit function*.

The *mapping* type constructor allows one to build sets of units with the required constraints. Let

$$Mapping(S) = \{U \subseteq Unit(S) \mid \forall (i_1, v_1) \in U, \forall (i_2, v_2) \in U :$$
$$(i) \quad i_1 = i_2 \Rightarrow v_1 = v_2$$
$$(ii) \quad i_1 \neq i_2 \Rightarrow (disjoint(i_1, i_2) \land (adjacent(i_1, i_2) \Rightarrow$$
$$v_1 \neq v_2))\}$$

The *mapping* type constructor is defined for any type $\alpha \in UNIT$ as:

$$D_{mapping(\alpha)} = Mapping(D_\alpha) \quad \forall \alpha \in UNIT.$$

In the next subsections we will define the types *ureal*, *upoint*, *upoints*, *uline*, and *uregion*. Since all of them will have the structure of a unit, the just introduced type constructor *mapping*(α) can be applied to all of them.

Units describe certain simple functions of time. We will define a generic function ι on units which evaluates the unit function at a given time instant. More precisely, let α be a non-temporal type (e.g. *real*) and u_α the corresponding unit type (e.g. *ureal*) with $D_{u_\alpha} = Interval(Instant) \times S_\alpha$, where S_α is a suitably defined set. Then ι_α is a function

$$\iota_\alpha : S_\alpha \times Instant \to D_\alpha$$

Usually we will omit the index α and just denote the function by ι. Hence, ι maps a discrete representation of a unit function for a given instant of time into a discrete representation of the function value at that time. The ι function serves three purposes: (i) It allows us to express constraints on the structure of a unit in terms of constraints on the structure of the corresponding non-temporal value. (ii) It allows us to express the semantics of a unit by reusing the semantics definition of the corresponding non-temporal value. (iii) It can serve as a basis for the implementation of the **atinstant** operation on the unit.

The use of ι will become clear in the next subsections when we instantiate it for the different unit types.

3.2.5 Temporal Units for Base Types

For a type $\alpha \in \text{BASE} \cup \text{SPATIAL}$, we introduce the type constructor *const* that produces a temporal unit for α. Its carrier set is defined as:

$$D_{const(\alpha)} = Interval(Instant) \times D'_\alpha$$

Recall that the notation D'_α refers to the carrier set of α without undefined elements or empty sets. A unit containing an undefined or empty value makes no sense as for such time intervals we can simply let no unit exist (within a *mapping*).

Note that, even if we introduce the type constructor *const* with the explicit purpose of defining temporal units for *int*, *string*, and *bool*, it can nevertheless be applied also to other types. This may be useful for applications where values of such types change only in discrete steps.

The trivial temporal function described by such a unit can be defined as $\iota(v, t) = v$. Note that in defining ι for a specific unit type we automatically define the semantics of the unit which should be a temporal function in the abstract model. For example, for a value u of a unit type *const(int)* the semantics $\sigma(u)$ should be a partial function $f : A'_{instant} \to A'_{int}$. This is covered by a generic definition of the semantics of unit types: Let $u = (i, v)$ be a value of a unit type u_α. Then

$$
\begin{aligned}
\sigma(u) &= f_u : A'_{instant} \cap \sigma(i) \to A'_\alpha \quad \text{where} \\
f_u(t) &= \sigma(\iota(v, t)) \quad \forall t \in \sigma(i)
\end{aligned}
$$

Hence we reuse the semantics defined for the discrete value $\iota(v, t) \in D'_\alpha$.

This semantics definition will in most cases be sufficient. However, for some unit types (namely *uline* and *uregion*) the discrete value obtained in the end points of the time interval by ι may be an incorrect one due to degeneracies: in

324

such a case it has to be "cleaned up." We will below slightly extend the generic semantics definition to accommodate this. For all other units, this semantics definition suffices so that we will only define the ι function in each case.

For the representation of moving reals we introduce a unit type <u>ureal</u>. The "simple" function we use for the sliced representation of moving reals is either a polynomial of degree not higher than two or a square root of such a polynomial. The motivation for this choice is a trade-off between richness of the representation (e.g. square roots of degree two polynomials are needed to express time-dependent distance functions in the Euclidean metric) and simplicity of the representation of the discrete type and of its operations. With this particular choice one can implement (i.e., the discrete model is closed under) the lifted versions of **size**, **perimeter**, and **distance** operations; one cannot implement the **derivative** operation of the abstract model. The carrier set for type <u>ureal</u> is

$$D_{\underline{ureal}} = Interval(Instant)$$
$$\times \{(a, b, c, r) \,|\, a, b, c \in \texttt{real}, r \in \texttt{bool}\}$$

and evaluation at time t is defined by:

$$\iota((a, b, c, r), t) = \begin{cases} at^2 + bt + c & \text{if } \neg r \\ \sqrt{at^2 + bt + c} & \text{if } r \end{cases}$$

3.2.6 Temporal Units for Spatial Data Types

In this subsection we specialize the concept of unit to moving instances of spatial data types.

Similar to moving reals, the temporal evolution of moving spatial objects is characterized by continuity and smoothness and can be approximated in various ways. Again we have to find the balance between richness and simplicity of representation. As indicated before, in this paper we make the design decision to base our approximations of the temporal behavior of moving spatial objects on linear functions. Linear approximations ensure simple and efficient representations for the data types and a manageable complexity of the algorithms. Nevertheless, more complex functions like polynomials of a degree higher than one are conceivable as the basis of representation but are not considered in this paper.

Due to the concept of sliced representation, also for moving spatial objects we have to specify constraints in order to describe the permitted behavior of a value of such a type within a temporal unit. Since the end points of a time interval mark a change in the description of the data type, we require that constraints are satisfied only for the respective open interval. In the end points of the time interval a collapse of components of the moving object can happen. This is completely acceptable, since one of the reasons to introduce the sliced representation is exactly to have "simple" and "continuous" description of the moving value within each time interval and to limit "discontinuities" in the description to a finite set of instants.

Moving Points and Point Sets. The structurally simplest spatial object that can move is a single point. Hence, we start with the definition of the spatial unit type <u>upoint</u>. First we introduce a set *MPoint* which defines 3D lines that describe unlimited temporal evolution of 2D points.

$$MPoint = \{(x_0, x_1, y_0, y_1) \,|\, x_0, x_1, y_0, y_1 \in \texttt{real}\}$$

This describes a linearly moving point for which evaluation at time t is given by:

$$\iota((x_0, x_1, y_0, y_1), t) = (x_0 + x_1 \cdot t, y_0 + y_1 \cdot t) \quad \forall t \in Instant$$

The carrier set of <u>upoint</u> can then be very simply defined as:

$$D_{\underline{upoint}} = Interval(Instant) \times MPoint$$

We pass now to describe a set of moving points. The carrier set of <u>upoints</u> can be defined as:

$$D_{\underline{upoints}} = \{(i, M) \,|\, i \in Interval(Instant),$$
$$M \subset MPoint, |M| \geq 1, \text{ and}$$
$$(i) \quad \forall t \in \sigma'(i), \forall l, k \in M : l \neq k \Rightarrow \iota(l, t) \neq \iota(k, t)$$
$$(ii) \quad i = (s, e, lc, rc) \wedge s = e \Rightarrow$$
$$(\forall l, k \in M : l \neq k \Rightarrow \iota(l, s) \neq \iota(k, s))\}$$

Here we encounter for the first time a constraint valid during the open time interval of the unit (condition (i)). Namely, a <u>upoints</u> unit is a collection of linearly moving points that do not intersect within the open unit interval. Condition (ii) concerns units defined only in a single time instant; for them all points have to be distinct at that instant.

For $(i, M) \in D_{\underline{upoints}}$, evaluation at time t is given by

$$\iota(M, t) = \bigcup_{m \in M} \{\iota(m)\} \quad \forall t \in \sigma(i)$$

which is clearly a set of points in $D'_{\underline{points}}$. We will generally assume that ι distributes through sets and tuples so that $\iota(M, t)$ is defined for any set M as above, and for a tuple $r = (r_1, \ldots, r_n)$, we have $\iota(r, t) = (\iota(r_1), \ldots, \iota(r_n))$.

Moving Lines. We now introduce the unit type for <u>line</u> called <u>uline</u>. Here we restrict movements of segments so that in the time interval associated to a value of <u>uline</u> each segment maintains its direction in the 2-dimensional space. That is, segments which rotate during their movement are not admitted. See in Figure 4 an example of a valid <u>uline</u> value. This constraint derives from the need of keeping a

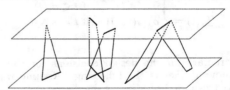

Figure 4: An instance of <u>uline</u>

balance between ease of representation and manipulation of the data type and its expressive power. Rotating segments define curved surfaces in the 3D space that, even if they constitute a more accurate description, can always be approximated by a sequence of plane surfaces.

The carrier set of <u>uline</u> is therefore based on a set of moving segments with the above restriction and which never overlaps at any instant internal to the associated open time interval. Overlapping has a meaning equivalent to the one used for <u>line</u> values: to be collinear and to have a non-empty intersection.

To prepare the definition of <u>uline</u> we introduce the set of all pairs of lines in a 3D space that are coplanar, which will be used to represent moving segments:

$$MSeg = \{(s, e) \,|\, s, e \in MPoint, s \neq e, s \text{ is coplanar with } e\}$$

The carrier set for _uline_ can now be defined as:

$$D_{\underline{uline}} = \{(i, M) \mid i \in Interval(Instant), M \subset MSeg,$$
$$|M| \geq 1, \text{ such that}$$
$$(i) \quad \forall t \in \sigma'(i) : \iota(M, t) \in D'_{\underline{line}}$$
$$(ii) \quad i = (s, e, lc, rc) \wedge s = e \Rightarrow \iota(M, s) \in D'_{\underline{line}}\}$$

Here again the first condition defines constraints for the open time interval and the second treats the case of units defined only at a single instant. Note that $\iota(M, t)$ is defined due to the fact that ι distributes through sets and tuples. A _uline_ value therefore inherits the structural conditions on _line_ values and segments. For example, condition (i) requires that

$$(s, e) \in M \Rightarrow (\iota(s, t), \iota(e, t)) \in Seg \quad \forall t \in \sigma'(i)$$

and therefore $\iota(s, t) < \iota(e, t) \quad \forall t \in \sigma'(i)$.

The semantics defined for _uline_ via ι according to the generic definition given earlier needs to be slightly changed to cope with degeneracies in the end points of a unit time interval, as we anticipated. In these points, in fact, moving segments can degenerate into points and different moving segments can overlap. We accommodate this by defining separate ι functions for the start time and the end time of the time interval, called ι_s and ι_e, respectively. Let $((s, e, lc, rc), M) \in D_{\underline{uline}}$. Then

$$\iota_s(M, t) = \iota_e(M, t) = merge\text{-}segs(\{(p, q) \in \iota(M, t) \mid p < q\})$$

This definition removes pairs of points returned by $\iota(M, t)$ that are not segments (i.e., segments degenerated into a single point); it also merges overlapping segments into maximal ones (this is the meaning of the _merge-segs_ function). The generic semantics definition is then extended as follows:

$$\sigma(u) = f_u : A'_{instant} \cap \sigma(i) \to A'_\alpha$$

where for $u = (i, v)$ and $i = (s, e, lc, rc)$

$$f_u(t) = \begin{cases} \sigma(\iota(v, t)) & \text{if } t \in \sigma'(i) \\ \sigma(\iota_s(v, t)) & \text{if } t = s \wedge lc \\ \sigma(\iota_e(v, t)) & \text{if } t = e \wedge rc \end{cases}$$

A final remark on the design decisions for the discrete type for moving lines is the following. Assume we choose instance u_1 (resp., u_2) of _uline_ as the discrete representation at the initial (resp., final) time t_1 (t_2) of a unit for the (continuously) moving line l. Then the constraint that segments making up the discrete representation of l cannot rotate during the unit does not restrict too much the fidelity of the discrete representation. Indeed, since members of _MSeg_ in a unit can be triangles, this leaves the possibility of choosing among many possible mappings between endpoints of their segments in t_1 and those in t_2, as long as the non-rotation constraint is satisfied. In Figure 5 an example of a discrete representation of a continuously moving line by means of an instance of _uline_ is shown.

If this approach causes a too rough approximation internally to the time unit, then possibly an additional instant, internal to the unit, has to be chosen and an additional discrete representation of l at that instant has to be introduced so that a better approximation is obtained. It can be easily seen that in the limit this sequence of discrete representations can reach an arbitrary precision in representing l.

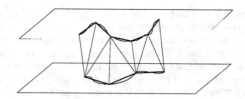

Figure 5: A discrete representation of a moving line

Moving Regions. We now introduce the moving counterpart for _region_, namely the _uregion_ data type. We adopt the same restriction used for moving lines, i.e., that rotation of segments in the 3-dimensional space is not admitted. We therefore base the definition of _uregion_ on the same set of all pairs of lines in a 3D space that are coplanar, namely _MSeg_, with additional constraints ensuring that throughout the whole unit we always obtain a valid instance of the _region_ data type. Figure 6 shows an example of a valid _uregion_ value. (It also shows the degeneracies that can occur in the end points of a unit interval.)

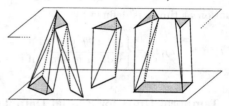

Figure 6: An instance of _uregion_.

As for a _region_ value, we can have moving regions with (moving) holes, hence the basic building blocks are given by the concepts of _cycle_ and _face_ already introduced in the definition of _region_.

The carrier set of _uregion_ is therefore based, informally speaking, on a set of (possibly nested) faces which never intersect at any instant internal to the associated time interval. For the formal definition of _uregion_, we first introduce a set intended to describe the moving version of a cycle, without restriction on time:

$$MCycle = \{\{s_0, \ldots, s_{n-1}\} \mid n \geq 3,$$
$$\forall i \in \{0, \ldots, n-1\} : s_i \in MSeg\}$$

We then introduce a set for the description of the moving version of a face, without restriction on time:

$$MFace = \{(c, H) \mid c \in MCycle, H \subset MCycle\}.$$

Note that in the definitions of _MCycle_ and _MFace_ we have not given the constraints to impose on the sets the semantics of cycles and faces because this will be done directly in the moving region definition. The carrier set for _uregion_ is now defined as

$$D_{\underline{uregion}} = \{(i, F) \mid i \in Interval(Instant),$$
$$F \subset MFace, \text{ such that}$$
$$(i) \quad \forall t \in \sigma'(i) : \iota(F, t) \in D'_{\underline{region}}$$
$$(ii) \quad i = (s, e, lc, rc) \wedge s = e \Rightarrow \iota(F, s) \in D'_{\underline{region}}\}$$

For the end points of the time interval again we have to provide separate functions ι_s and ι_e. Essentially these work as follows. From the pairs of points (p, q) (segments) obtained by evaluating $\iota(F, s)$ or $\iota(F, e)$, remove all pairs that are no proper segments (as for *uline*). Next, for all collections of overlapping segments on a single line, partition the line into fragments belonging to the same set of segments (e.g. if segment (p, q) overlaps (r, s) such that points are ordered on the line as $\langle p, r, q, s \rangle$ then there are fragments $(p, r), (r, q)$, and (q, s)). For each fragment, count the number of segments containing it. If this number is even, remove the fragment; if it is odd, put the fragment as a new segment into the result. A complete formalization of this is lengthy and omitted.

4   Data Structures

The discrete model developed in Section 3 offers a precise basis for the implementation of data structures for a spatio-temporal database system; it is in fact a high-level specification of such data structures. In this section we can therefore, relatively briefly, explain how these definitions translate into data structures. Two general issues need to be considered in that step.

First, some requirements arise from the fact that the data structures implementing the data types are to be used within a database system, and in particular to represent attribute data types within some given data model implementation. This means that values are placed under control of the DBMS into memory which in turn implies that (i) one should not use pointers, and (ii) representations should consist of a small number of memory blocks that can be moved efficiently between secondary and main memory.

One way to fulfill these requirements is to implement each data type by a fixed number of records and arrays; arrays are used to represent the varying size components of a data type value and are allocated to the required size. All pointers are expressed as array indices.

The Secondo extensible DBMS [DG99, GDF+99], under which we are implementing this model, offers a specific concept for the implementation of attribute data types. Such a type has to be represented by a record (called the "root record") which may have one or more components that are (references to) so-called "database arrays". Database arrays are basically arrays with any desired field size and number of fields; additionally they are automatically either represented "inline" in a tuple representation, or outside in a separate list of pages, depending on their size [DG98]. The root record is always represented within the tuple. In our subsequent design of data structures we will apply this concept. Hence each data type will be represented by a record and possibly some (database) arrays. In other DBMS environments one can store the arrays using the facilities offered there for large object management.

Second, many of the data types of Section 3 are set-valued. Sets will be represented in arrays. We always define a unique order on the set domains and store elements in the array in that order. In this way we can enforce that two set values are equal iff their array representations are equal, which makes efficient comparisons possible.

4.1   Non-Temporal Data Types

For the simple types of Section 3.2.1, the implementation is straightforward: they are represented as a record consisting of the given programming language value[3] plus a boolean flag indicating whether the value is defined. Type *point* is represented similarly by a record with two reals and a flag.

A *points* value is represented as an array containing records with two **real** fields, representing points. Points are in lexicographic order. The root record contains the number of points and the (database) array.

The data structures for *line* and *region* values are designed somewhat similar to [GdRS95]. A *line* value is a set of line segments. This is represented as a list of *halfsegments*. The idea of halfsegments is to store each segment twice: once for the left (i.e., smaller) end point and once for the right end point. These are called the left and right halfsegment, respectively, and the relevant point in the halfsegment is called the *dominating* point. The purpose is to support plane-sweep algorithms which traverse a set of segments from left to right and have to perform an action (e.g. insertion into a sweep status structure) on encountering the left and another action on meeting the right end point of a segment. A total order is defined on halfsegments which is lexicographic order extended to treat halfsegments with the same dominating point (see [GdRS95] for a definition).

Hence the *line* value is represented as an array containing a sequence of records each of which represents a halfsegment (four reals plus a flag to indicate the dominating point); these are ordered according to the order just mentioned. The root record manages the array plus some auxiliary information such as the number of segments, total length of segments, bounding box, etc.

A *region* value can be viewed as a set of line segments with some additional structure. This set of line segments is represented by an array *halfsegments* containing the ordered sequence of halfsegment records, as for *line*. In addition, all halfsegments belonging to a cycle, and to a face, are linked together (via extra fields such as *next-in-cycle* within halfsegment records). Two more arrays *cycles* and *faces* represent the structure. The array *cycles* contains records representing cycles by a pointer[4] to the first halfsegment of the cycle and a pointer to the next cycle of the face. The latter is used to link together all cycles belonging to one face. Array *faces* contains for each face a pointer into the *cycles* array to the first cycle of the face. Some unique order is defined on cycles and faces which need not be detailed here.

The root record for *region* manages the three arrays and has additional information such as bounding box, number of faces, number of cycles, total area, perimeter, etc. Algorithms constructing region values generally compute the list of halfsegments and then call a *close* operation offered by the *region* data type, which determines the structure of faces and cycles and represents it by setting pointers.

More details on the representation strategy can be found in [GdRS95] although some details are different here.

Intervals (s, e, lc, rc) are represented by corresponding records. A value of type $\underline{range}(\alpha)$ is represented as an array of interval records ordered by value (all intervals are disjoint, hence there exists a total order). A value of type $\underline{intime}(\alpha)$ is represented by a corresponding record.

4.2   Unit Types

We have to distinguish units that can be represented in a fixed amount of space, called *fixed size units*, and *variable size units*. Fixed size units are $\underline{const}(\underline{int})$, $\underline{const}(\underline{string})$, $\underline{const}(\underline{bool})$[5], $\underline{ureal}$, and $\underline{upoint}$. Variable size units are

---

[3]For *string* we assume an implementation as a fixed length array of characters.

[4]From now on, when we say "pointer" we always mean integer indices referring to a field of some array.

[5]We do not consider the other $\underline{const}(\alpha)$ types here, as they are not so relevant in this paper.

upoints, *uline*, and *uregion*.

Fixed size units can be represented simply in a record that has two component records to represent the time interval and the unit function, respectively. For example, for *ureal* the second record represents the quadruple (a, b, c, r).

For the representation of variable size units, we introduce *subarrays*. Conceptually, a subarray is just an array. Technically it consists of a reference to a (database) array together with two indices identifying a subrange within that array. The idea is that all units within a *mapping* (i.e., a sliced representation) share the same database arrays.

Variable sized units are also all represented by a record whose first component is a time interval record. In the sequel we only describe the second component.

A *upoints* unit function is stored in a subarray containing a sequence of records representing *MPoint* quadruples, in lexicographic order on the quadruples. The *upoints* unit is represented in a record whose second component record contains a subarray reference and a bounding cube[6] (the number of points can be inferred from the subarray indices).

A *uline* unit function is stored similarly in a subarray containing a sequence of records representing *MSeg* pairs which in turn are *MPoint* quadruples. Pairs are ordered lexicographically by their two component quadruples on which again lexicographic order applies. Again the *uline* unit is represented in a record whose second component consists of a subarray reference and a bounding cube.

A *uregion* unit function is basically a set of *MSeg* values (moving segments, trapeziums in 3D) with some additional constraints. We store these *MSeg* records in the same way and order in a subarray *msegments* as for *uline*. In addition, each record has two extra fields that allow for linking together all moving segments within a cycle and within a face. Furthermore, *uregion* has two additional subarrays *mcycles* and *mfaces* identifying cycles and faces, as in the *region* representation. The second component record of a *uregion* unit contains the three subarrays and a bounding cube for the unit.

For both *uline* and *uregion* one might add further summary information in the second component record, such as the (a, b, c, r) quadruples for the time-dependent length (for *uline*) or for perimeter and size (for *uregion*).

4.3 Sliced Representation

The data structure associated with the *mapping* type constructor organizes a collections of units (slices) as a whole. Obviously this data structure is parameterized by the unit data structures. We observe that all unit data structures are records whose first component represents a time interval, and whose second component may contain one or more subarrays. It is basically a (database) array *units*

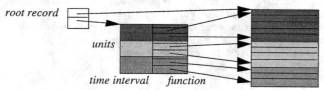

Figure 7: A *mapping* data structure containing three units, for a unit type with one subarray, such as *upoints*.

containing the unit records ordered by their time intervals. If the unit type uses k subarrays, then the *mapping* data

[6]This is a bounding box in 3D.

structure has k additional database arrays. Obviously, the database arrays mentioned in the unit subarray references will be the database arrays provided in the mapping data structure. The main array *units* as well as the k additional arrays are referenced from a single root record for the *mapping* data structure. Note that the structure has the general form required for attribute data types.

5 Two Example Algorithms

In this section we briefly show two algorithms in order to illustrate the use of the data model and data structures defined in the previous sections. The first one implements the **atinstant** operation on a moving region, i.e., it determines the region value at a given instant of time. The second one implements the **inside** operation on a moving point and a moving region, hence it returns a moving boolean describing when the point was inside the region.

5.1 Algorithm *atinstant*

The moving region is represented as a value of type *mapping*(*uregion*). The idea of the algorithm is to perform binary search on the array containing the region units to determine the unit u containing the argument time instant t. Then a subalgorithm is called which evaluates each moving segment within the region unit at time t resulting in a line segment in two dimensions. These are composed to obtain the region value returned as a result.

> **algorithm** *atinstant* (mr, t)
> **input:** a moving region mr as a value of type
>   *mapping*(*uregion*), and an instant t
> **output:** a region r representing mr at instant t
> **method:**
>   determine $u \in mr$ such that its time interval
>   contains t;
>   **if** u exists **then return** *uregion_atinstant*(u, t)
>   **else return** $\emptyset$ **endif**
> **end** *atinstant*.

> **algorithm** *uregion_atinstant*(u, t)
> **input:** a moving region unit ur (of type *uregion*)
>   and an *instant* t
> **output:** a *region* r, the function value of ur at
>   instant t
> **method:**
>   let $ur = (i, F)$; $r := \emptyset$;
>   **for each** mface $(c, H) \in F$ **do**
> $c' := \{\iota(s, t) | s \in c\}$; $H' := \emptyset$;
>   **for each** $h \in H$ **do**
> $h' := \{\iota(s, t) | s \in h\}$; $H' := H' \cup \{h'\}$
>   **endfor**;
> $r := r \cup \{(c', H')\}$
>   **endfor**;
>   **return** r
> **end** *uregion_atinstant*.

In the second algorithm the ι function defined in Section 3 is used to evaluate a moving segment at an instant of time to get a line segment.

The time complexity of this algorithm is basically $O(\log n + r)$ where n is the number of units in mr, and r is the size of the region returned (the number of segments). This is because in the first step of *atinstant* the unit can be found by binary search in $O(\log n)$ time, and the traversal of the unit data structure takes linear time. However, to construct a proper region data structure as described in Section 4.1, one has to produce the list of halfsegments in lexicographic order, and hence needs to sort the r result segments, which results in a time complexity of $O(\log n + r \log r)$. Note that if the region value is just needed for output (e.g. for display on a graphics screen) then $O(\log n + r)$ is indeed sufficient.

The above algorithm works correctly if instant t is internal to the unit time interval. For simplicity, we have ignored in this description the problem of possibly degenerated region values in the end points of the unit time interval, which requires a more complex cleanup after finding the line segments, as sketched at the end of Section 3. This problem can be avoided altogether, by the way, if we spend a little more storage space, and represent a unit with a degenerated region at one end instead by two units, one with an open time interval, and the other with a correct region representation for the single instant at the end.

Analogous implementations of the *atinstant* operation can be obtained for all other moving data types. The first algorithm *atinstant* is in fact generic; one only needs to plug in subalgorithms for other data types.

5.2 Algorithm *inside*

Here the arguments are two lists (arrays) of units, one representing a moving point, the other a moving region. The idea is to traverse the two lists in parallel, computing the refinement partition of the time axis on the way (Figure 1).

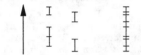

Figure 8: Two sets of time intervals on the left, their refinement partion on the right

For each time interval i in the refinement partition, an *inside* algorithm is performed on the point and region units valid at that time interval. It produces a set of boolean units representing when the point was inside the region. Note that even a linearly moving point within a single *upoint* unit can enter and leave the region of the region unit several times.

algorithm *inside* (mp, mr)
input: a moving point mp (as a *mapping(upoint)*),
 and a moving region mr (*mapping(uregion)*)
output: a moving boolean mb, as a value of type
 mapping(const(bool)), representing when mp was
 inside mr
method:
 let $mp = \{up_1, \dots, up_n\}$ such that the list
 $\langle up_1, \dots, up_n \rangle$ is ordered by time intervals;
 let $mr = \{ur_1, \dots, ur_m\}$ such that the list
 $\langle ur_1, \dots, ur_m \rangle$ is ordered by time intervals;
 $mb := \emptyset$;
 scan the two lists $\langle up_1, \dots, up_n \rangle$ and $\langle ur_1, \dots, ur_m \rangle$ in parallel, determining in each step a new
 refinement time interval i and from each of the
 two lists either a unit up or ur, respectively, whose
 time interval contains i, or *undefined*, if there is
 no unit in the respective list overlapping i:
 for each refinement interval i **do**
  if both up and ur exist **then**
   $ub := upoint\_uregion\_inside(up, ur)$;
   $mb := concat(mb, ub)$
  endif
 endfor;
 return mb
end *inside*.

The operation *concat* on two sets of units is essentially the union, but merges adjacent intervals with the same unit value into a single unit. On the array or list representations, as given in the mapping data structure, this can be done in constant time (comparing the last unit of mb with the first unit of ub).

algorithm *upoint_uregion_inside*(up, ur)
input: a *upoint* unit up, and a *uregion* unit ur
output: a set of moving boolean units, as a value
 of type *mapping(const(bool))*, representing when
 the point of up was inside the region of ur during
 their intersection time interval
method:
 let $up = (i', mpo)$ and $ur = (i'', F)$ and let
 $i = (s, e, lc, rc)$ be the intersection time interval
 of i' and i'';[7]
 if the 3d bounding boxes of mpo and F do not
 intersect
 then return $\emptyset$
 else
  determine all intersections between mpo and
  msegments occurring in (the cycles of faces of)
  F. Each intersection is represented as a pair
  $(t, action)$ where t is the time instant of the
  intersection, and $action \in \{enter, leave\}$;[8]
  sort intersections by time, resulting in a list
  $\langle (t_1, a_1), \dots, (t_k, a_k) \rangle$ if there are k intersections. Note that actions in the list must be
  alternating, i.e., $a_i \neq a_{i+1}$;
  let $t_0 = s$ and $t_{k+1} = e$;
  if $k = 0$ **then**
   if mpo is inside F (both taken at instant s)
   then return $\{((s, e, true, true), true)\}$
   else return $\{((s, e, true, true), false)\}$
   endif
  else
   if $a_1 = leave$ **then**
    return $\{((t_i, t_{i+1}, true, true), true)|$
    $i \in \{0, \dots, k\}, i$ is even$\}$
    $\cup \{((t_i, t_{i+1}, false, false), false)|$
    $i \in \{0, \dots, k\}, i$ is odd$\}$
   else
    return $\{((t_i, t_{i+1}, true, true), true)|$
    $i \in \{0, \dots, k\}, i$ is odd$\}$
    $\cup \{((t_i, t_{i+1}, false, false), false)|$
    $i \in \{0, \dots, k\}, i$ is even$\}$
   endif
  endif
 endif
end *upoint_uregion_inside*.

Here the moving point mpo is a line segment in 3D that may stab some of the moving segments of F, which are trapeziums in 3D. In the order of time, with each intersection the moving point alternates between entering and leaving the moving region represented in the region unit. Hence a list of boolean units is produced that alternates between *true* and *false*. In case no intersections are found $(k = 0)$, one needs to check whether at the start time of

---

[7]For simplicity, the remainder of the algorithm assumes the intersection interval is closed. It is straightforward, but a bit lengthy, to treat the other cases.

[8]The *action* can be determined if we store with each msegment (trapezium or triangle in 3D) a face normal vector indicating on which side is the interior of the region.

the time interval considered the point was inside the region. This can be implemented by a well-known technique in computational geometry, the "plumbline" algorithm which counts how many segments in 2D are above the point in 2D.

For the following analysis we assume that the numbers of point and region units are "balanced" in the sense that each point unit overlaps in time only a constant number of region units and vice-versa.

The first algorithm *inside* requires time $O(n + m)$, where n and m are the numbers of units in the two arguments, except for the calls to algorithm *upoint_uregion_inside*.

This second algorithm, applied to a single pair of units, requires $O(s)$ time for finding all intersections, with s the number of msegments in F. Furthermore, $O(k \log k)$ time is needed to sort the k intersections, and to return the $k + 1$ boolean units. If no intersections are found, the check whether *mpo* is inside F at the start time s requires $O(s)$ time.

The total time for all calls to *upoint_uregion_inside* is $O(S + K \log k')$ where S is the total number of msegments in all units, K is the total number of intersections between the moving point and faces of the moving region, and k' is the largest number of intersections occurring in a single pair of units. In practical cases, k' is likely to be a small constant, and $K \log k'$ will be dominated by S, hence the total running time will be $O(n + m + S)$. If the moving point and the moving region are sufficiently far apart, so that not even the bounding boxes intersect, then the running time is $O(n + m)$.

This algorithm illustrates nicely how algorithms for binary operations on moving objects can generally be reduced to simpler algorithms on pairs of units. Again, the first algorithm is generic; one only needs to plug in algorithms for specific operations on pairs of units.

6 Conclusions

We have presented and formally defined a discrete data model that implements the data types defined in the abstract model of [GBE+00]. We have also demonstrated how the discrete representations can be mapped into data structures that can be realistically used in a DBMS environment, and how algorithms can use these data structures. Hence the paper offers a precise basis for the implementation of a "spatio-temporal extension package" to be added to a suitable extensible architecture (e.g. as a data blade to Informix Universal Server).

The next step is to design (more) algorithms for the operations of [GBE+00] and to implement them on these data structures. We are currently building such an extension package and plan to integrate it into the Secondo system as well as make it a data blade for Informix.

References

[CG94]   T.S. Cheng and S.K. Gadia. A Pattern Matching Language for Spatio-Temporal Databases. In *Proc. ACM Conf. on Information and Knowledge Management*, pages 288–295, November 1994.

[CR97]   J. Chomicki and P. Revesz. Constraint-Based Interoperability of Spatio-Temporal Databases. In *Proc. 5th Intl. Symp. on Large Spatial Databases*, pages 142–161, Berlin, Germany, 1997.

[CR99]   J. Chomicki and P. Revesz. A Geometric Framework for Specifying Spatiotemporal Objects. In *Proc. 6th Intl. Workshop on Temporal Representation and Reasoning (TIME)*, pages 41–46, 1999.

[DG98]   S. Dieker and R.H. Güting. Efficient Handling of Tuples with Embedded Large Objects. Technical Report Informatik 236, FernUniversität Hagen, 1998. To appear in *Data and Knowledge Engineering*.

[DG99]   S. Dieker and R.H. Güting. Plug and Play with Query Algebras: Secondo. A Generic DBMS Development Environment. Technical Report Informatik 249, FernUniversität Hagen, 1999.

[EGSV98]   M. Erwig, R.H. Güting, M. Schneider, and M. Vazirgiannis. Abstract and Discrete Modeling of Spatio-Temporal Data Types. In *Proc. 6th ACM Symp. on Geographic Information Systems*, pages 131–136, Washington, D.C., November 1998.

[EGSV99]   M. Erwig, R.H. Güting, M. Schneider, and M. Vazirgiannis. Spatio-Temporal Data Types: An Approach to Modeling and Querying Moving Objects in Databases. *GeoInformatica*, 3(3):265–291, 1999.

[GBE+00]   R.H. Güting, M.H. Böhlen, M. Erwig, C.S. Jensen, N.A. Lorentzos, M. Schneider, and M.Vazirgiannis. A Foundation for Representing and Querying Moving Objects. *ACM Transactions on Database Systems*, 25(1), 2000. To appear.

[GDF+99]   R.H. Güting, S. Dieker, C. Freundorfer, L. Becker, and H. Schenk. SECONDO/QP: Implementation of a Generic Query Processor. In *Proc. 10th Intl. Conf. on Database and Expert Systems Applications*, pages 66–87, Florence, Italy, September 1999.

[GdRS95]   R.H. Güting, T. de Ridder, and M. Schneider. Implementation of the ROSE Algebra: Efficient Algorithms for Realm-Based Spatial Data Types. In *Proc. 4th Intl. Symp. on Large Spatial Databases*, pages 216–239, Portland, Maine, August 1995.

[GRS98]   S. Grumbach, P. Rigaux, and L. Segoufin. The Dedale System for Complex Spatial Queries. In *Proc. ACM SIGMOD Intl. Conf. on Management of Data*, pages 213–224, 1998.

[GS95]   R.H. Güting and M. Schneider. Realm-Based Spatial Data Types: The ROSE Algebra. *VLDB Journal*, 4(2):100–143, 1995.

[PD95]   D.J. Peuquet and N. Duan. An Event-Based Spatiotemporal Data Model (ESTDM) for Temporal Analysis of Geographical Data. *Intl. Journal of Geographical Information Systems*, 9(1):7–24, 1995.

[PJ99]   D. Pfoser and C.S. Jensen. Capturing the Uncertainty of Moving-Object Representations. In *Proc. 6th Intl. Symp. on Spatial Databases*, pages 111–131, Hong Kong, China, 1999.

[TH97]   N. Tryfona and T. Hadzilacos. Logical Data Modeling of Spatio-Temporal Applications: Definitions and a Model. In *Proc. Intl. Database Engineering and Applications Symposium*, 1997.

[TSPM98]   Y. Theodoridis, T. Sellis, A. Papadopoulos, and Y. Manolopoulos. Specifications for Efficient Indexing in Spatiotemporal Databases. In *Proc. 10th Intl. Conf. on Scientific and Statistical Database Management*, Capri, Italy, 1998.

[WCD+98]   O. Wolfson, S. Chamberlain, S. Dao, L. Jiang, and G. Mendez. Cost and Imprecision in Modeling the Position of Moving Objects. In *Proc. 14th Intl. Conf. on Data Engineering*, pages 588–596, Orlando, Florida, 1998.

[Wol98]   O. Wolfson. Moving Objects Databases: Issues and Solutions. In *Proc. 10th Intl. Conf. on Scientific and Statistical Database Management*, Capri, Italy, 1998.

[Wor94]   M.F. Worboys. A Unified Model for Spatial and Temporal Information. *The Computer Journal*, 37(1):25–34, 1994.

Indexing the Positions of Continuously Moving Objects

Simonas Šaltenis†   Christian S. Jensen†   Scott T. Leutenegger‡   Mario A. Lopez‡

† Department of Computer Science, Aalborg University, Denmark

‡ Department of Mathematics and Computer Science, University of Denver, Colorado, USA

Abstract

The coming years will witness dramatic advances in wireless communications as well as positioning technologies. As a result, tracking the changing positions of objects capable of continuous movement is becoming increasingly feasible and necessary. The present paper proposes a novel, R*-tree based indexing technique that supports the efficient querying of the current and projected future positions of such moving objects. The technique is capable of indexing objects moving in one-, two-, and three-dimensional space. Update algorithms enable the index to accommodate a dynamic data set, where objects may appear and disappear, and where changes occur in the anticipated positions of existing objects. A comprehensive performance study is reported.

1   Introduction

The rapid and continued advances in positioning systems, e.g., GPS, wireless communication technologies, and electronics in general promise to render it increasingly feasible to track and record the changing positions of objects capable of continuous movement.

In a recent interview with Danish newspaper Børsen, Michael Hawley from MIT's Media Lab described how he was online when he ran the Boston Marathon this year [19]. Prior to the race, he swallowed several capsules, which in conjunction with other hardware enabled the monitoring of his position, body temperature, and pulse during the race. This scenario demonstrates the potential for putting bodies, and, more generally, objects that move, online. Achieving this may enable a multitude of applications. It becomes possible to detect the signs of an impending medical emergency in a person early and warn the person or alert a medical service. It becomes possible to have equipment recognize its user; and the equipment may alert its owner in the case of unauthorized use or theft.

Industry leaders in the mobile phone market expect

more than 500 million mobile phone users by year 2002 (compared to 300 million Internet users) and 1 billion by year 2004, and they expect mobile phones to evolve into wireless Internet terminals [14, 25]. Rendering such terminals location aware may substantially improve the quality of the services offered to them [12, 25]. In addition, the cost of providing location awareness is expected to be relatively low. These factors combine to promise the presence of substantial numbers of location aware, on-line objects capable of continuous movement.

Applications such as process monitoring do not depend on positioning technologies. In these, the position of a moving point object could for example be a pair of temperature and pressure values. Yet other applications include vehicle navigation, tracking, and monitoring, where the positions of air, sea, or land-based equipment such as airplanes, fishing boats and freighters, and cars and trucks are of interest. It is diverse applications such as these that warrant the study of the indexing of objects that move.

Continuous movement poses new challenges to database technology. In conventional databases, data is assumed to remain constant unless it is explicitly modified. Capturing continuous movement with this assumption would entail either performing very frequent updates or recording outdated, inaccurate data, neither of which are attractive alternatives.

A different tack must be adopted. The continuous movement should be captured directly, so that the mere advance of time does not necessitate explicit updates [27]. Put differently, rather than storing simple positions, functions of time that express the objects' positions should be stored. Then updates are necessary only when the parameters of the functions change. We use one linear function per object, with the parameters of a function being the position and velocity vector of the object at the time the function is reported to the database.

Two different, although related, indexing problems must be solved in order to support applications involving continuous movement. One problem is the indexing of the current and anticipated future positions of moving objects. The other problem is the indexing of the histories, or trajectories, of the positions of moving objects. We focus on the former problem. One approach to solving the latter problem (while simultaneously solving the first) is to render the solution to the first problem partially persistent [6, 15].

We propose an indexing technique, the time-parameterized R-tree (the TPR-tree, for short), which efficiently indexes the current and anticipated future positions of moving point objects (or "moving points," for short). The technique naturally extends the R*-tree [5].

Several distinctions may be made among the possible approaches to the indexing of the future linear trajectories of moving points. First, approaches may differ according to the space that they index. Assuming the objects move in d-dimensional space ($d = 1, 2, 3$), their future trajectories may be indexed as lines in $(d + 1)$-dimensional space [26]. As an alternative, one may map the trajectories to points in a higher-dimensional space which are then indexed [13]. Queries must subsequently also be transformed to counter the data transformation. Yet another alternative is to index data in its native, d-dimensional space, which is possible by parameterizing the index structure using velocity vectors and thus enabling the index to be "viewed" as of any future time. The TPR-tree adopts this latter alternative. This absence of transformations yields a quite intuitive indexing technique.

A second distinction is whether the index partitions the data (e.g., as do R-trees) or the embedding space (e.g., as do Quadtrees). When indexing the data in its native space, an index based on data partitioning seems to be more suitable. On the other hand, if trajectories are indexed as lines in $(d + 1)$-dimensional space, a data partitioning access method that does not employ clipping may introduce substantial overlap.

Third, indices may differ in the degrees of data replication they entail. Replication may improve query performance, but may also adversely affect update performance. The TPR-tree does not employ replication.

Fourth, we may distinguish approaches according to whether or not they require periodic index rebuilding. Some approaches (e.g., [26]) employ individual indices that are only functional for a certain time period. In these approaches, a new index must be provided before its predecessor is no longer functional. Other approaches may employ an index that in principle remains functional indefinitely [13], but which may be optimized for some specific time horizon and perhaps deteriorates as time progresses. The TPR-tree belongs to this latter category.

In the TPR-tree, the bounding rectangles in the tree are functions of time, as are the moving points being indexed. Intuitively, the bounding rectangles are capable of continuously following the enclosed data points or other rectangles as these move. Like the R-trees, the new index is capable of indexing points in one-, two-, and three-dimensional space. In addition, the principles at play in the new index are extendible to non-point objects.

The next section presents the problem being addressed, by describing the data to be indexed, the queries to be supported, and problem parameters. In addition, related re-

search is covered. Section 3 describes the tree structure and algorithms. It is assumed that the reader has some familiarity with the R*-tree. To ease the exposition, one-dimensional data is generally assumed, and the general n-dimensional case is only considered when the inclusion of additional dimensions introduces new issues. Section 4 reports on performance experiments, and Section 5 summarizes and offers research directions.

2 Problem Statement and Related Work

We describe the data being indexed, the queries being supported, the problem parameters, and related work in turn.

2.1 Problem Setting

An object's position at some time t is given by $\bar{x}(t) = (x_1(t), x_2(t), \ldots, x_d(t))$, where it is assumed that the times t are not before the current time. This position is modeled as a linear function of time, which is specified by two parameters. The first is a position for the object at some specified time t_{ref}, $\bar{x}(t_{ref})$, which we term the reference position. The second parameter is a velocity vector for the object, $\bar{v} = (v_1, v_2, \ldots, v_d)$. Thus, $\bar{x}(t) = \bar{x}(t_{ref}) + \bar{v}(t - t_{ref})$. An object's movement is observed at some time, t_{obs}. The first parameter, $\bar{x}(t_{ref})$, may be the object's position at this time, or it may be the position that the object would have at some other, chosen reference time, given the velocity vector $\bar{v}$ observed at t_{obs} and the position $\bar{x}(t_{obs})$ observed at t_{obs}.

Modeling the positions of moving objects as functions of time not only enables us to make tentative future predictions, but also solves the problem of the frequent updates that would otherwise be required to approximate continuous movement in a traditional setting. For example, objects may report their positions and velocity vectors when their actual positions deviate from what they have previously reported by some threshold. The choice of the update frequency then depends on the type of movement, the desired accuracy, and the technical limitations [28, 20, 17].

As will be illustrated in the following and explained in Section 3, the reference position and the velocity are used not only when recording the future trajectories of moving points, but also for representing the coordinates of the bounding rectangles in the index as functions of time.

As an example, consider Figure 1. The top left diagram shows the positions and velocity vectors of 7 point objects at time 0.

Assume we create an R-tree at time 0. The top right diagram shows one possible assignment of the objects to minimum bounding rectangles (MBRs) assuming a maximum of three objects per node. Previous work has shown that attempting to minimize the quantities known as overlap, dead space, and perimeter leads to an index with good query performance [11, 18], and so the chosen assignment appears to be well chosen. However, although it is good for queries at

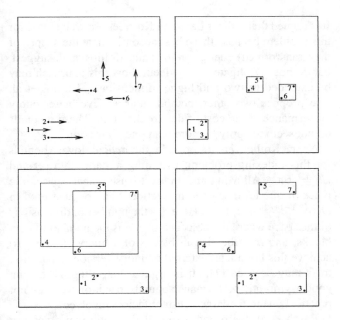

Figure 1: Moving Points and Resulting Leaf-Level MBRs

Let R, R_1, and R_2 be three d-dimensional rectangles and t, $t^\vdash < t^\dashv$, three time values that are not less than the current time.

Type 1 timeslice query: $Q = (R, t)$ specifies a hyper-rectangle R located at time point t.

Type 2 window query: $Q = (R, t^\vdash, t^\dashv)$ specifies a hyper-rectangle R that covers the interval $[t^\vdash, t^\dashv]$. Stated differently, this query retrieves points with trajectories in $(\bar{x}, t)$-space crossing the $(d+1)$-dimensional hyper-rectangle $([a_1^\vdash, a_1^\dashv], [a_2^\vdash, a_2^\dashv], \ldots, [a_d^\vdash, a_d^\dashv], [t^\vdash, t^\dashv])$.

Type 3 moving query: $Q = (R_1, R_2, t^\vdash, t^\dashv)$ specifies the $(d+1)$-dimensional trapezoid obtained by connecting R_1 at time $t^\vdash$ to R_2 at time $t^\dashv$.

The second type of query generalizes the first, and is itself a special case of the third type. To illustrate the query types, consider the one-dimensional data set in Figure 2, which represents temperatures measured at different locations. Here, queries $Q0$ and $Q1$ are timeslice queries, $Q2$ is a

the present time, the movement of the objects may adversely affect this assignment.

The bottom left diagram shows the locations of the objects and the MBRs at time 3, assuming that MBRs grow to stay valid. The grown MBRs adversely affect query performance; and as time increases, the MBRs will continue to grow, leading to further deterioration. Even though the objects belonging to the same MBR (e.g., objects 4 and 5) were originally close, the different directions of their movement cause their positions to diverge rapidly and hence the MBRs to grow.

From the perspective of queries at time 3, it would have been better to assign objects to MBRs as illustrated by the bottom right diagram. Note that at time 0, this assignment will yield worse query performance than the original assignment. Thus, the assignment of objects to MBRs must take into consideration when most queries will arrive.

The MBRs in this example illustrate the kind of time-parameterized bounding rectangles supported by the TPR-tree. The algorithms presented in Section 3, which are responsible for the assignment of objects to bounding rectangles and thus control the structure and quality of the index, attempt to take observations such as those illustrated by this example into consideration.

2.2 Query Types

The queries supported by the index retrieve all points with positions within specified regions. We distinguish between three kinds, based on the regions they specify. In the sequel, a d-dimensional rectangle R is specified by its d projections $[a_1^\vdash, a_1^\dashv], \ldots [a_d^\vdash, a_d^\dashv]$, $a_j^\vdash \leq a_j^\dashv$, into the d coordinate axes.

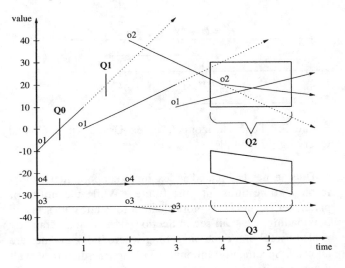

Figure 2: Query Examples for One-Dimensional Data

window query, and $Q3$ is a moving query.

Let $iss(Q)$ denote the time when a query Q is issued. The two parameters, reference position and velocity vector, of an object as seen by a query Q depend on $iss(Q)$, because objects update their parameters as time goes. Consider object $o1$: its movement is described by one trajectory for queries with $iss(Q) < 1$, another trajectory for queries with $1 \leq iss(Q) < 3$, and a third trajectory for queries with $3 \leq iss(Q)$. For example, the answer to query $Q1$ is $o1$, if $iss(Q1) < 1$, and no object qualifies for this query if $iss(Q1) \geq 1$.

This example illustrates that queries far in the future are likely to be of little value, because the positions as predicted at query time become less and less accurate as queries move into the future, and because updates not known at query time may occur. Therefore, real-world applications may be expected to issue queries that are concentrated in some limited time window extending from the current time.

2.3 Problem Parameters

The values of three problem parameters affect the indexing problem and the qualities of a TPR-tree. Figure 3 illustrates these parameters, which will be used throughout the paper.

- *Querying window* (W): how far queries can "look" into the future. Thus, $iss(Q) \leq t \leq iss(Q) + W$, for Type 1 queries, and $iss(Q) \leq t^{\vdash} \leq t^{\dashv} \leq iss(Q) + W$ for queries of Types 2 and 3.

- *Index usage time* (U): the time interval during which an index will be used for querying. Thus, $t_l \leq iss(Q) \leq t_l + U$, where t_l is the time when index is created/loaded.

- *Time horizon* (H): the length of the time interval from which the times t, $t^{\vdash}$, and $t^{\dashv}$ specified in queries are drawn. The time horizon for an index is the index usage time plus the querying window.

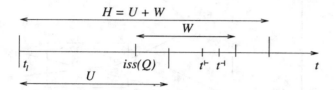

Figure 3: Time Horizon H, Index Usage Time U, and Querying Window W

Thus, a newly created index must support queries that reach H time units into the future. While the utility of parameter U (and H) is more clearcut for static data sets and bulkloading, we shall see in Section 3.4 that this parameter is also useful in a dynamic setting where index updates are allowed. Specifically, although a TPR-tree is functional at all times after its creation, using different values for parameter U during insertions affects the search properties of the tree.

2.4 Previous Work

Related work on the indexing of the current and future positions of moving objects has concentrated mostly on points moving in one-dimensional space.

Tayeb et al. [26] use PMR-Quadtrees [22] for indexing the future linear trajectories of one-dimensional moving point objects as line segments in (x, t)-space. The segments span the time interval that starts at the current time and extends H time units into the future. A tree expires after U time units, and a new tree must be made available for querying. This approach introduces substantial data replication in the index—a line segment is usually stored in several nodes.

Kollios et al. [13] employ the dual data transformation where a line $x = x(t_{ref}) + v(t - t_{ref})$ is transformed to the point $(x(t_{ref}), v)$, enabling the use of regular spatial indices.

It is argued that indices based on Kd-trees are well suited for this problem because these best accommodate the shapes of the (transformed) queries on the data. Kollios et al. suggest, but do not investigate in any detail, how this approach may be extended to two and higher dimensions. Kollios et al. also propose two other methods that achieve better query performance at the cost of data replication. These methods do not seem to apply to more than one dimension.

Next, Kollios et al. provide theoretical lower bounds for this indexing problem, assuming a static data set and $H = \infty$. Allowing the index to use linear space, the types of queries discussed in Section 2 can be answered in $O(n^{(2d-1)/2d} + k)$ time. Here d is the number of dimensions of the space where the objects move, n is the number of data blocks, and k is the size in blocks of a query answer. To achieve this bound, an external memory version of partition trees may be used [1]. It is argued that, although having good asymptotic performance bounds, partition trees are not practical due to the large constant factors involved.

Basch et al. [4] propose so-called kinetic main-memory data structures for mobile objects. The idea is to schedule future events that update a data structure so that necessary invariants hold. Agarwal et al. [2] apply these ideas to external range trees [3]. Their approach may possibly be applicable to R-trees or time-parameterized R-trees where events would fix MBRs, although it is unclear how to contend with future queries that arrive in non-chronological order. Agarwal et al. address non-chronological queries using partial persistence techniques and also show how to combine kinetic range trees with partition trees to achieve a trade-off between the number of kinetic events and query performance.

The problem of indexing moving points is related to the problem of indexing now-relative temporal data. The GR-tree [7] is an R-tree based index for now-relative bitemporal data. Combined valid and transaction time intervals with end-times related to the continuously progressing current time result in regions that grow, albeit in a restricted way. The idea in this index is to accommodate growing data regions by introducing bounding regions that also grow. Specifically, bounding regions are time-parameterized, and their extents are computed each time a query is asked.

The R^{ST}-tree [24] is the spatiotemporal index that indexes the histories of the positions of objects. Positions are assumed to remain constant in-between explicit index updates, and their histories are captured by associating valid and transaction time intervals, which may be now-relative, with them. The continuity thus stems from the temporal aspects rather than the spatial, and the techniques employed in this index are more akin to those employed in the GR-tree than those employed here.

Finally, Pfoser et al. [21] consider the separate, but related problem of indexing the past trajectories of moving points, which are represented as polylines (connected line segments).

3 Structure and Algorithms

This section presents the structure and algorithms of the TPR-tree. The notion of a time-parameterized bounding rectangle is defined. It is shown how the tree is queried, and dynamic update algorithms are presented that tailor the tree to a specific time horizon H. In the following, we use the term bounding interval for a one-dimensional bounding rectangle and the term bounding rectangle for any d-dimensional hyper-rectangle.

3.1 Index Structure

The TPR-tree is a balanced, multi-way tree with the structure of an R-tree. Entries in leaf nodes are pairs of the position of a moving point and a pointer to the moving point, and entries in internal nodes are pairs of a pointer to a subtree and a rectangle that bounds the positions of all moving points or other bounding rectangles in that subtree.

As suggested in Section 2, the position of a moving point is represented by a reference position and a corresponding velocity vector—(x, v) in the one-dimensional case, where $x = x(t_{ref})$. We let t_{ref} be equal to the index creation time, t_l. Other possibilities include setting t_{ref} to some constant value, e.g., 0, or using different t_{ref} values in different nodes.

To bound a group of d-dimensional moving points, d-dimensional bounding rectangles are used that are also time-parameterized, i.e., their coordinates are functions of time. A time-parameterized bounding rectangle bounds all enclosed points or rectangles at all times not earlier than the current time.

A tradeoff exists between how tightly a bounding rectangle bounds the enclosed moving points or rectangles across time and the storage needed to capture the bounding rectangle. It would be ideal to employ time-parameterized bounding rectangles that are *always minimum*, but the storage cost appears to be excessive. In the general case, doing so deteriorates to enumerating all the enclosed moving points or rectangles. This is exemplified by Figure 4, where a node consists of two one-dimensional points A and B moving towards each other. Each of these points plays the role of lower (resp. upper) bound of the minimum bounding interval at some time. Examples with this property may be constructed for any number of points.

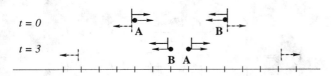

Figure 4: Conservative (Dashed) Versus Always Minimum (Solid) Bounding Intervals

Instead of using true, always minimum bounding rectangles, the TPR-tree employs what we term *conservative*

bounding rectangles, which are minimum at some time point, but possibly (and most likely!) not at later times. In the one-dimensional case, the lower bound of a conservative interval is set to move with the minimum speed of the enclosed points, while the upper bound is set to move with the maximum speed of the enclosed points (speeds are negative or positive, depending on the direction). This ensures that conservative bounding intervals are indeed bounding for all times considered.

Figure 4 illustrates conservative bounding intervals. The left hand side of the conservative interval in the figure starts at the position of object A at time 0 and moves left at the speed of object B, and the right hand side of the interval starts at object B at time 0 and moves right at the speed of object A. Conservative bounding intervals never shrink. At best, when all of the enclosed points have the same velocity vector, a conservative bounding interval has constant size, although it may move.

Following the representation of moving points, we let $t_{ref} = t_l$ and capture a one-dimensional time-parameterized bounding interval $[x^\vdash(t), x^\dashv(t)] = [x^\vdash(t_l) + v^\vdash(t - t_l), x^\dashv(t_l) + v^\dashv(t - t_l)]$ as $(x^\vdash, x^\dashv, v^\vdash, v^\dashv)$, where

$$
\begin{aligned}
x^\vdash &= x^\vdash(t_l) = \min_i\{o_i.x^\vdash(t_l)\} \\
x^\dashv &= x^\dashv(t_l) = \max_i\{(o_i.x^\dashv(t_l)\} \\
v^\vdash &= \min_i\{o_i.v^\vdash\} \\
v^\dashv &= \max_i\{o_i.v^\dashv\}
\end{aligned}
$$

Here, the o_i range over the bounding intervals to be enclosed. If instead the bounding interval being defined is to bound moving points, the o_i range over these points, $o_i.x^\vdash(t_l)$ and $o_i.x^\dashv(t_l)$ are replaced by $o_i.x(t_l)$, and $o_i.v^\vdash$ and $o_i.v^\dashv$ are replaced by $o_i.v$.

The rectangles defined above are termed load-time bounding rectangles and are bounding for all times not before t_l. Because the rectangles never shrink, but may actually grow too much, it is desirable to be able to adjust them occasionally. Specifically, as the index is only queried for times greater or equal to the current time, it is possible and probably attractive to adjust the bounding rectangles every time any of the moving points or rectangles that they bound are updated. The following formulas specify the adjustments to the bounding rectangles that may be made during updates.

$$
\begin{aligned}
x^\vdash &= \min_i\{o_i.x^\vdash(t_{upd})\} - v^\vdash(t_{upd} - t_l) \\
x^\dashv &= \max_i\{o_i.x^\dashv(t_{upd})\} - v^\dashv(t_{upd} - t_l)
\end{aligned}
$$

Here, t_{upd} is the time of the update, and the formulas may be restricted to apply to the bounding of points rather than intervals, as before. Each formula involves five terms, which may differ by orders of magnitude. Special care must be taken to manage the rounding errors that may occur in the finite-precision floating-point arithmetic (e.g., IEEE standard 754) used for implementing the formulas [8].

We call these rectangles update-time bounding rectangles. The two types of bounding rectangles are shown in Figure 5.

The bold top and bottom lines capture the load-time, time-parameterized bounding interval for the four moving objects represented by the four lines. At time t_{upd}, a more narrow and thus better update-time bounding interval is introduced that is bounding from t_{upd} and onwards.

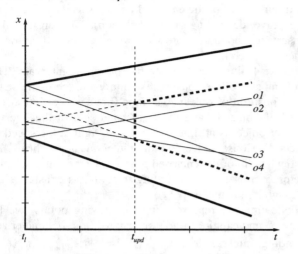

Figure 5: Load-Time (Bold) and Update-Time (Dashed) Bounding Intervals for Four Moving Points

It is worth noticing that the sole use of load-time bounding rectangles corresponds to simply bounding the $2d$-dimensional points that result from the dual transformation of the linear trajectories, as proposed by Kollios et al. [13]. Update-time bounding rectangles go beyond this approach.

3.2 Querying

With the definition of bounding rectangles in place, we show how the three types of queries presented in Section 2 are answered using the TPR-tree.

Answering a timeslice query proceeds as for the regular R-tree, the only difference being that all bounding rectangles are computed for the time t^q specified in the query before intersection is checked. Thus, a bounding interval specified by $(x^\vdash, x^\dashv, v^\vdash, v^\dashv)$ satisfies a query $(([a^\vdash, a^\dashv]), t^q)$ if and only if $a^\vdash \leq x^\dashv + v^\dashv(t^q - t_l) \wedge a^\dashv \geq x^\vdash + v^\vdash(t^q - t_l)$.

To answer window queries and moving queries, we need to be able to check if, in $(\bar{x}, t)$-space, the trapezoid of a query (cf. Figure 6) intersects with the trapezoid formed by the part of the trajectory of a bounding rectangle that is between the start and end times of the query. With one spatial dimension, this is relatively simple. For more dimensions, generic polyhedron-polyhedron intersection tests may be used [9], but due to the restricted nature of this problem, a simpler and more efficient algorithm may be devised.

Specifically, we provide an algorithm for checking if a d-dimensional time-parameterized bounding rectangle R given by parameters $(x_1^\vdash, x_1^\dashv, x_2^\vdash, x_2^\dashv, \ldots, x_d^\vdash, x_d^\dashv, v_1^\vdash, v_1^\dashv, v_2^\vdash, v_2^\dashv, \ldots, v_d^\vdash, v_d^\dashv)$ intersects a moving query $Q = (([a_1^\vdash, a_1^\dashv], [a_2^\vdash, a_2^\dashv], \ldots, [a_d^\vdash, a_d^\dashv], [w_1^\vdash, w_1^\dashv], [w_2^\vdash, w_2^\dashv], \ldots, [w_d^\vdash, w_d^\dashv]),$

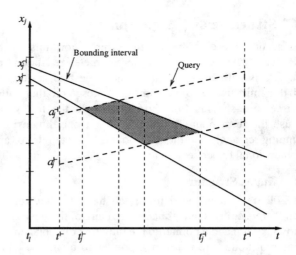

Figure 6: Intersection of a Bounding Interval and a Query

$t^\vdash, t^\dashv)$. This formulation of a moving query as a time-parameterized rectangle with starting and ending times is more convenient than the definition given in Section 2.2. The velocities w are obtained by subtracting R_2 from R_1 in the earlier definition and then normalizing them with the length of interval $[t^\vdash, t^\dashv]$.

The algorithm is based on the observation that for two moving rectangles to intersect, there has to be a time point when their extents intersect in each dimension. Thus, for each dimension j ($j = 1, 2, \ldots, d$), the algorithm computes the time interval $I_j = [t_j^\vdash, t_j^\dashv] \subset [t^\vdash, t^\dashv]$ when the extents of the rectangles intersect in that dimension. If $I = \bigcap_{j=1}^{d} I_j = \emptyset$, the moving rectangles do not intersect and an empty result is returned; otherwise, the algorithm provides the time interval I when the rectangles intersect. The intervals for each dimension are computed according to the following formulas.

$$I_j = \begin{cases} \emptyset & \text{if } a_j^\vdash > x_j^\dashv(t^\vdash) \wedge a_j^\vdash(t^\dashv) > x_j^\dashv(t^\dashv) \vee \\ & \quad a_j^\dashv < x_j^\vdash(t^\vdash) \wedge a_j^\dashv(t^\dashv) < x_j^\vdash(t^\dashv) \\ [t_j^\vdash, t_j^\dashv] & \text{otherwise} \end{cases}$$

The first disjunct in the condition expresses that Q is above R and the second means that Q is below R. Formulas for $t_j^\vdash$ and $t_j^\dashv$ follow.

$$t_j^\vdash = \begin{cases} t^\vdash + \dfrac{x_j^\dashv(t^\vdash) - a_j^\vdash}{w_j^\vdash - v_j^\dashv} & \text{if } a_j^\vdash > x_j^\dashv(t^\vdash) \\ t^\vdash + \dfrac{x_j^\vdash(t^\vdash) - a_j^\dashv}{w_j^\dashv - v_j^\vdash} & \text{if } a_j^\dashv < x_j^\vdash(t^\vdash) \\ t^\vdash & \text{otherwise} \end{cases}$$

Here, the first condition states that Q is above R at $t^\vdash$, and the second states that Q is below R at $t^{\vdash}$.

$$t_j^{\dashv} = \begin{cases} t^{\vdash} + \dfrac{x_j^{\dashv}(t^{\vdash}) - a_j^{\vdash}}{w_j^{\vdash} - v_j^{\dashv}} & \text{if } a_j^{\vdash}(t^{\dashv}) > x_j^{\dashv}(t^{\dashv}) \\[2ex] t^{\vdash} + \dfrac{x_j^{\vdash}(t^{\vdash}) - a_j^{\dashv}}{w_j^{\dashv} - v_j^{\vdash}} & \text{if } a_j^{\dashv}(t^{\dashv}) < x_j^{\vdash}(t^{\dashv}) \\[2ex] t^{\dashv} & \textbf{otherwise} \end{cases}$$

In this formula, the first condition states that Q is above R at $t^{\dashv}$, and the second states that Q is below R at $t^{\dashv}$.

To see how $t_j^{\vdash}$ and $t_j^{\dashv}$ are computed, consider the case where Q is below R at $t^{\dashv}$. Then Q must not be below R at $t^{\vdash}$, as otherwise Q is always below R and there is no intersection (the case of no intersection is already accounted for). This means that the line $a_j^{\dashv} + w_j^{\dashv}(t - t^{\vdash})$ intersects the line $x_j^{\vdash}(t^{\vdash}) + v_j^{\vdash}(t - t^{\vdash})$ within the time interval $[t^{\vdash}, t^{\dashv}]$. Solving for t gives the desired intersection time $(t_j^{\dashv})$.

Figure 6 exemplifies a moving query, a bounding rectangle, and their intersection time interval in one dimension.

3.3 Heuristics for Tree Organization

As a precursor to designing the insertion algorithms for the TPR-tree, we discuss how to group moving objects into nodes so that the tree most efficiently supports timeslice queries when assuming a time horizon H. The objective is to identify principles, or heuristics, that apply to both dynamic insertions and bulkloading, and to any number of dimensions. The goal is to obtain a versatile index.

It is clear that when H is close to zero, the tree may simply use existing R-tree insertion and bulkloading algorithms. The movement of the point objects and the growth of the bounding rectangles become irrelevant—only their initial positions and extents matter. In contrast, when H is large, grouping the moving points according to their velocity vectors is of essence. It is desirable that the bounding rectangles are as small as possible at all times in $[t_l, t_l + H]$, the interval during which the result of the operation (insertion or bulkloading) may be visible to queries (t_l is thus the time of an insertion or the index creation time). An important aspect in achieving this is to keep the growth rates of the bounding rectangles, and thus the values of their "velocity extents," low. (In one-dimensional space, the velocity extent of a bounding interval is equal to $v^{\dashv} - v^{\vdash}$.)

This leads to the following general approach. The insertion and bulkloading algorithms of the R*-tree, which we consider extending to moving points, aim to minimize objective functions such as the areas of the bounding rectangles, their margins (perimeters), and the overlap among the bounding rectangles. In our context, these functions are time dependent, and we should consider their evolution in $[t_l, t_l + H]$. Specifically, given an objective function $A(t)$, the following integral should be minimized.

$$\int_{t_l}^{t_l + H} A(t)\,dt \qquad (1)$$

If $A(t)$ is area, the integral computes the area (volume) of the trapezoid that represents part of the trajectory of a bounding rectangle in $(\bar{x}, t)$-space (see Figure 6).

We use the integral in Formula 1 in the dynamic update algorithms, described next, and in the bulkloading algorithms, described elsewhere [23].

3.4 Insertion and Deletion

The insertion algorithm of the R*-tree employs functions that compute the area of a bounding rectangle, the intersection of two bounding rectangles, the margin of a bounding rectangle (when splitting a node), and the distance between the centers of two bounding rectangles (used when doing forced reinsertions) [5]. The TPR-tree's insertion algorithm is the same as that of the R*-tree, with one exception: instead of the functions mentioned here, integrals as in Formula 1 of those functions are used.

Computing the integrals of the area, margin, and distance are relatively straightforward [23]. The algorithm that computes the integral of the intersection of two time-parameterized rectangles is an extension of the algorithm for checking if such rectangles overlap (see Section 3.2). At each time point when the rectangles intersect, the intersection region is a rectangle and, in each dimensions, the upper (lower) bound of this rectangle is defined by the upper (lower) bound of one of the two intersecting rectangles.

The algorithm thus divides the time interval returned by the overlap-checking algorithm into consecutive time intervals so that, during each of these, the intersection is defined by a time-parameterized rectangle. The intersection area integral is then computed as a sum of area integrals. Figure 6 illustrates the subdivision of the intersection time interval into three smaller intervals for the one-dimensional case. The algorithm is given elsewhere [23].

In Section 2.3, parameter $H = U + W$ was introduced. This parameter is most intuitive in a static setting, and for static data. In a dynamic setting, W remains a component of H, which is the length of the time period where integrals are computed in the insertion algorithm. How large the other component of H should be depends on the update frequency. If this is high, the effect of an insertion on the tree will not persist long and, thus, H should not exceed W by much. The experimental studies in Section 4 aim at determining what is a good range of values for H in terms of the update frequency.

The introduction of the integrals is the most important step in rendering the R*-tree insertion algorithm suitable for the TPR-tree, but one more aspect of the R*-tree algorithm must be revisited. The R*-tree split algorithm selects one distribution of entries between two nodes from a set of candidate distributions, which are generated based on sortings of point positions along each of the coordinate axes. In the TPR-tree split algorithm, moving point (or rectangle) positions at different time points are used when sorting. With load-time bounding rectangles, positions at t_l are used, and with update-time bounding rectangles, positions at the current time are used.

Finally, in addition to sortings along the spatial dimensions, the split algorithm is extended to consider also sortings along the velocity dimensions, i.e., sortings obtained by sorting on the coordinates of the velocity vectors. The rationale is that distributing the moving points based on the velocity dimensions may result in bounding rectangles with smaller "velocity extents" and which consequently grow more slowly.

Deletions in the TPR-tree are performed as in the R*-tree. If a node gets underfull, it is eliminated and its entries are reinserted.

4 Performance Experiments

In this section we report on performance experiments with the TPR-tree. The generation of two- and three-dimensional moving point data and the settings for the experiments are described first, followed by the presentation of the results of the experiments.

4.1 Experimental Setup and Workload Generation

The implementation of the TPR-tree used in the experiments is based on the Generalized Search Tree Package, GiST [10]. The page size (and tree node size) is set to 4k bytes, which results in 204 and 146 entries per leaf-node for two- and three-dimensional data, respectively. A page buffer of 200k bytes, i.e., 50 pages, is used [16], where the root of a tree is pinned and the least-recently-used page replacement policy is employed. The nodes that are modified during an index operation are marked as "dirty" in the buffer and are written to disk at the end of the operation or when they otherwise have to be removed from the buffer.

The performance studies are based on workloads that intermix queries and update operations on the index, thus simulating index usage across a period of time. In addition, each workload initially bulkloads the index. An efficient bulkloading algorithm developed for the TPR-tree is used [23]. This algorithm is based on the heuristic of minimizing area integrals and has H as a parameter. We proceed to describe how the updates, queries, and initial bulkloading data are generated.

Because moving objects with positions and velocities that are uniformly distributed seems to be rather unrealistic, we attempt to generate more realistic (and skewed) two-dimensional data by simulating a scenario where the objects, e.g., cars, move in a network of routes, e.g., roads, connecting a number of destinations, e.g., cities. In addition to simulating cars moving between cities, the scenario is also motivated by the fact that usually, even if there is no underlying infrastructure, moving objects tend to have destinations.

With the exception of one experiment, the simulated objects in the scenario move in a region of space with dimensions 1000×1000 kilometers. A number ND of destinations are distributed uniformly in this space and serve as

the vertices in a fully connected graph of routes. In most of the experiments, $ND = 20$. This corresponds to 380 one-way routes. The number of points is $N = 100,000$ for all but one experiment. No objects disappear, and no new objects appear for the duration of a simulation.

For the generation of the initial data set that is bulkloaded, objects are placed at random positions on routes. The objects are assigned with equal probability to one of three groups of points with maximum speeds of 0.75, 1.5, and 3 km/min (45, 90, and 180 km/h). During the first sixth of a route, objects accelerate from zero speed to their maximum speeds; during the middle two thirds, they travel at their maximum speeds; and during the last one sixth of a route, they decelerate. When an object reaches its destination, a new destination is assigned to it at random.

The workload generation algorithm distributes the updates of an object's movement so that updates are performed during the acceleration and deceleration stretches of a route. The number of updates is chosen so that the total average time interval between two updates is approximately equal to a given parameter UI, which is fixed at 60 in most of the experiments.

In addition to using data from the above-described simulation, some experiments also use workloads with two- and three-dimensional uniform data. In these workloads, the initial positions of objects are uniformly distributed in space. The directions of the velocity vectors are assigned randomly, both initially and on each update. The speeds (lengths of velocity vectors) are uniformly distributed between 0 and 3 km/min. The time interval between successive updates is uniformly distributed between 0 and $2UI$.

To generate workloads, the above-described scenarios are run for 600 time units (minutes). For $UI = 60$, this results in approximately one million update operations.

In addition to updates, workloads include queries. Each time unit, four queries are generated (2400 in total). Timeslice, window, and moving queries are generated with probabilities 0.6, 0.2, and 0.2. The temporal parts of queries are generated randomly in an interval of length W and starting at the current time. The spatial part of each query is a square occupying a fraction QS of the space ($QS = 0.25\%$ in most of the experiments). The spatial parts of timeslice and window queries have random locations. For moving queries, the center of a query follows the trajectory of one of the points currently in the index.

The workload generation parameters that are varied in the experiments are given in Table 1. Standard values, used if a parameter is not varied in an experiment, are given in boldface.

4.2 Investigating the Insertion Algorithm

As mentioned in Section 3.4, the TPR-tree insertion algorithm depends on the parameter H, which is equal to W plus some duration that is dependent on the frequency of updates. How the frequency of updates affects the choice of a value

Parameter	Description	Values Used
ND	Number of destinations [cardinal number]	0, 2, 10, **20**, 40, 160
N	Number of points [cardinal number]	**100,000**, 300,000, 500,000, 700,000, 900,000
UI	Update interval length [time units]	**60**, 120
W	Querying window size [time units]	0, 20, **40**, 80, 160, 320
QS	Query size [% of the data space]	0.1, **0.25**, 0.5, 1, 2

Table 1: Workload Parameters

for H was explored in two sets of experiments, for data with $UI = 60$ and for data with $UI = 120$. Workloads with uniform data were run using the TPR-tree. Different values of H were tried out in each set of experiments.

Figure 7 shows the results for $UI = 60$. Curves are shown for experiments with different querying windows W. The leftmost point of each curve corresponds to a setting of $H = 0$.

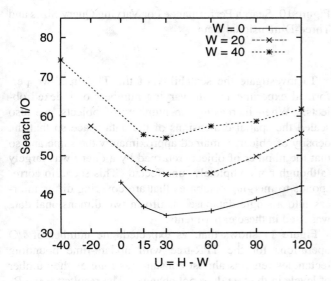

Figure 7: Search Performance For $UI = 60$ and Varying Settings of H

The experiments demonstrate a pattern, namely that the best values of H lie between $UI/2 + W$ and $UI + W$. This is not surprising. In $UI/2$ time units, approximately half of the entries of each leaf node in the tree are updated, and after UI time units, almost all entries are updated. The leaf-node bounding rectangles, the characteristics of which we integrate using H, survive approximately similar time durations. In the subsequent studies, we use $H = UI/2 + W$.

4.3 Comparing the TPR-Tree To Its Alternatives

A set of experiments with varying workloads were performed in order to compare the relative performance of the R-tree, the TPR-tree with load-time bounding rectangles, and the TPR-tree with update-time bounding rectangles.

For the former, the regular R*-tree is used to store

fragments of trajectories of points in $(\bar{x}, t)$-space. For this to work correctly, the inserted trajectory fragment for a moving point should start at the insertion time and should span H time units, where H is at least equal to the maximum possible period between two successive updates of the point. Not meeting this requirement, the R-tree may return incorrect query results because its bounding rectangles "expire" after H time units. In our simulation-generated workloads, the slowest moving points on routes spanning from one side of the data space to the other may not be updated for as much as 600 time units. For the R-tree we, thus, set $H = 600$, which is the duration of the simulation.

Figure 8 shows the average number of I/O operations per query for the three indices when the number of destinations in the simulation is varied. Decreasing the number of destinations adds skew to the distribution of the object positions and their velocity vectors. Thus, uniform data is an extreme case.

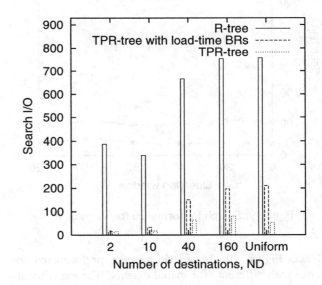

Figure 8: Search Performance For Varying Numbers of Destinations and Uniform Data

As shown, increased skew leads to a decrease in the numbers of I/Os for all three approaches, especially for the TPR-tree. This is expected because when there are more objects with similar velocities, it is easier to pack them into bounding rectangles that have small velocity extents and also are relatively narrow in the spatial dimensions.

The figure demonstrates that the TPR-tree is an order of magnitude better than the R-tree. The utility of update-time bounding rectangles can also be seen, although it should be noted that tightening of bounding rectangles increases the update cost. For example, for a workload with 10 destinations, the use of update-time bounding rectangles decreases the average number of I/Os for searches from 33 to 17, while update cost changes from 1.3 to 1.6 I/Os. For uniform data, the change is from 211 to 54, for searches, and from 2 to 3.5, for updates.

Figure 9 explores the effect of the length of the querying window, W, on querying performance. The relatively constant performance of the TPR-tree may be explained by noting that the data in this experiment is skewed ($ND = 20$), with groups of points having similar velocity vectors. Results would be different for uniform data (cf. Figure 7). The relatively constant performance of the R-tree can be explained by viewing the three-dimensional minimum bounding rectangles used in this tree as two-dimensional bounding rectangles that do not change over time. That is why queries issued at different future times have similar performance.

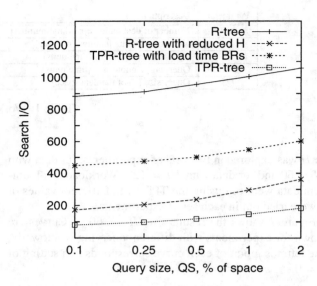

Figure 10: Search Performance For Varying Query Sizes and Three-Dimensional Data

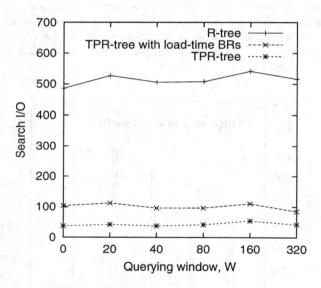

Figure 9: Search Performance for Varying W

Next, Figure 10 shows the average performance for queries with different-size spatial extents. The experiments were performed with three-dimensional data. The relatively high costs of the queries in this figure are indicative of how the increased dimensionality of the data adversely affects performance. An experiment with an R-tree using the shorter H of 120 is also included. Using this value for H is possible because uniform data is generated where no update interval is longer than $2UI$, and $UI = 60$ in our experiments. This significantly improves the performance of the R-tree, but it remains more than a factor of two worse than the TPR-tree.

To investigate the scalability of the TPR-tree, we performed experiments with varying numbers of indexed objects. When increasing the numbers of objects, we also scaled the spatial dimensions of the data space so that the density of objects remained approximately the same and so that the number of objects returned by a query was largely (although not completely) unaffected. This scenario corresponds to merging databases that are covering different areas into a single database. Uniform two-dimensional data was used in these experiments.

Figure 11 shows that, as expected, the number of I/O operations for the TPR-tree with update-time bounding rectangles remains almost constant (as long as the number of levels in the tree does not change). The results for the R-tree are not provided, because of excessively high numbers of I/O operations.

To explore how the search performances of the indices evolve with the passage of time, we compute, after each 60 time units, the average query performance for the previous 60 time units. Figure 12 shows the results. In this experiment (and in other similar experiments), the performance of the TPR-tree after 360 time units becomes more than two times worse than the performance at the beginning of the experiment, but from 360 to 600, no degradation occurs. This behavior is similar to the degradation of the performance of most multidimensional tree structures. When, after bulkloading, dynamic updates are performed, node splits occur, the average fan-out of the tree decreases, and the bounding rectangles created by the bulkloading algorithm change. After some time, the tree stabilizes.

As expected, the TPR-tree with load-time bounding rectangles shows an increasing degradation of performance. The bounding rectangles computed at bulkloading time become

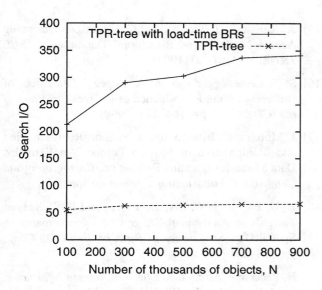

Figure 11: Search Performance for Varying Number of Objects

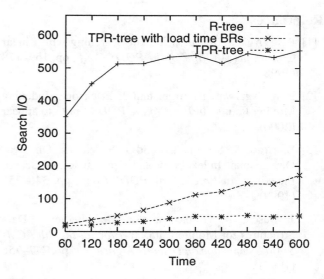

Figure 12: Degradation of Search Performance with Time

unavoidably larger as the more distant future is queried. The insertion algorithms try to counter this by making the velocity extents of bounding rectangles as small as possible. For example, in this experiment the average velocity extent of a rectangle (in one of the two velocity dimensions) is 1.32 after the bulkloading and becomes 0.35 after 600 time units (recall that the extent of the data space in each velocity dimension is 6 in our simulation).

5 Summary and Future Work

Motivated mainly by the rapid advances in positioning systems, wireless communication technologies, and electronics in general, which promise to render it increasingly feasible to track the positions of increasingly large collections of continuously moving objects, this paper proposes a versatile adaptation of the R*-tree that supports the efficient querying of the current and anticipated future locations of moving points in one-, two-, and three-dimensional space.

The new TPR-tree supports timeslice, window, and so-called moving queries. Capturing moving points as linear functions of time, the tree bounds these points using so-called conservative bounding rectangles, which are also time-parameterized and which in turn also bound other such rectangles. The tree is equipped with dynamic update algorithms as well as a bulkloading algorithm. Whereas the R*-tree's algorithms use functions that compute the areas, margins, and overlaps of bounding rectangles, the TPR-tree employs integrals of these functions, thus taking into consideration the values of these functions across the time when the tree is queried. The bounding rectangles of tree nodes that are read during updates are tightened, the objective being to improve query performance without affecting update performance much. When splitting nodes, not only the positions of the moving points are considered,

but also their velocities.

Because no other proposals for indexing two- and three-dimensional moving points exist, the performance study compares the TPR-tree with the TRP-tree without the tightening of bounding rectangles during updates and with a relatively simple adaptation of the R*-tree. The study indicates quite clearly that the TPR-tree indeed is capable of supporting queries on moving objects quite efficiently and that it outperforms its competitors by far. The study also demonstrates that the tree does not degrade severely as time passes. Finally, the study indicates how the tree can be tuned to take advantage of a specific update rate.

This work points to several interesting research directions. Among these, it would be interesting to study the use of more advanced bounding regions as well as different tightening frequencies of these. While the tightening of bounding rectangles increases query performance, it negatively affects the update performance, which is also very important. Next, periodic, partial reloading of the tree appears worthy of further study. It may also be of interest to include support for transaction time, thus enabling the querying of the past positions of the moving objects as well. This may be achieved by making the tree partially persistent, and it will likely increase the data volume to be indexed by several orders of magnitude.

Acknowledgments

This research was supported in part by a grant from the Nykredit Corporation; by the Danish Technical Research Council, grant 9700780; by the US National Science Foundation, grant IRI-9610240; and by the CHOROCHRONOS project, funded by the European Commission, contract no. FMRX-CT96-0056.

References

[1] P. K. Agarwal et al. Efficient Searching with Linear Constraints. In *Proc. of the PODS Conf.*, pp. 169–178 (1998).

[2] P. K. Agarwal, L. Arge, and J. Erickson. Indexing Moving Points. In *Proc. of the PODS Conf.*, to appear (2000).

[3] L. Arge, V. Samoladas, and J. S. Vitter. On Two-Dimensional Indexability and Optimal Range Search Indexing. In *Proc. of the PODS Conf.*, pp. 346–357 (1999).

[4] J. Basch, L. Guibas, and J. Hershberger. Data Structures for Mobile Data. In *Proc. of the 8th ACM-SIAM Symposium on Discrete Algorithms*, pp. 747–756 (1997).

[5] N. Beckmann, H.-P. Kriegel, R. Schneider, and B. Seeger. The R*-tree: An Efficient and Robust Access Method for Points and Rectangles. In *Proc. of the ACM SIGMOD Conf.*, pp. 322–331 (1990).

[6] B. Becker et al. An Asymptotically Optimal Multiversion B-Tree. *The VLDB Journal* 5(4): 264–275 (1996).

[7] R. Bliujūtė, C. S. Jensen, S. Šaltenis, and G. Slivinskas. R-tree Based Indexing of Now-Relative Bitemporal Data. In *the Proc. of the 24th VLDB Conf.*, pp. 345–356 (1998).

[8] J. Goldstein, R. Ramakrishnan, U. Shaft, and J.-B. Yu. Processing Queries By Linear Constraints. In *Proc. of the PODS Conf.*, pp. 257–267 (1997).

[9] O. Günther and E. Wong. A Dual Approach to Detect Polyhedral Intersections in Arbitrary Dimensions. *BIT*, 31(1): 3–14 (1991).

[10] J. M. Hellerstein, J. F. Naughton, and A. Pfeffer. Generalized Search Trees for Database Systems. In *Proc. of the VLDB Conf.*, pp. 562–573 (1995).

[11] I. Kamel and C. Faloutsos. On Packing R-trees. In *Proc. of the CIKM*, pp. 490–499 (1993).

[12] J. Karppinen. Wireless Multimedia Communications: A Nokia View. In *Proc. of the Wireless Information Multimedia Communications Symposium*, Aalborg University, (November 1999).

[13] G. Kollios, D. Gunopulos, and V. J. Tsotras. On Indexing Mobile Objects. In *Proc. of the PODS Conf.*, pp. 261–272 (1999).

[14] W. Konháuser. Wireless Multimedia Communications: A Siemens View. In *Proc. of the Wireless Information Multimedia Communications Symposium*, Aalborg University, (November 1999).

[15] A. Kumar, V. J. Tsotras, and C. Faloutsos. Designing Access Methods for Bitemporal Databases. *IEEE TKDE*, 10(1): 1–20 (1998).

[16] S. T. Leutenegger and M. A. Lopez. The Effect of Buffering on the Performance of R-Trees. In *Proc. of the ICDE Conf.*, pp. 164–171 (1998).

[17] J. Moreira, C. Ribeiro, and J. Saglio. Representation and Manipulation of Moving Points: An Extended Data Model for Location Estimation. *Cartography and Geographical Information Systems*, to appear.

[18] B.-U. Pagel, H.-W. Six, H. Toben, and P. Widmayer. Towards an Analysis of Range Query Performance in Spatial Data Structures. In *Proc. of the PODS Conf.*, pp. 214–221 (1993).

[19] H. Pedersen. Alting bliver on-line. *Børsen Informatik*, p. 14, September 28, 1999. (In Danish)

[20] D. Pfoser and C. S. Jensen. Capturing the Uncertainty of Moving-Object Representations. In *Proc. of the SSDBM Conf.*, pp. 111–132 (1999).

[21] D. Pfoser, Y. Theodoridis, and C. S. Jensen. Indexing Trajectories of Moving Point Objects. Chorochronos Tech. Rep. CH–99–3, June 1999.

[22] H. Samet. *The Design and Analysis of Spatial Data Structures*. Addison-Wesley, Reading, MA, 1990.

[23] S. Šaltenis, C. S. Jensen, S. T. Leutenegger, and M. A. Lopez. Indexing the Positions of Continuously Moving Objects. Technical Report R-99-5009, Department of Computer Science, Aalborg University (1999).

[24] S. Šaltenis and C. S. Jensen. R-Tree Based Indexing of General Spatio-Temporal Data. TimeCenter Tech. Rep. TR-45 (1999).

[25] A. Schieder. Wireless Multimedia Communications: An Ericsson View. In *Proc. of the Wireless Information Multimedia Communications Symposium*, Aalborg University, (November 1999).

[26] J. Tayeb, Ö. Ulusoy, and O. Wolfson. A Quadtree Based Dynamic Attribute Indexing Method. *The Computer Journal*, 41(3): 185–200 (1998).

[27] O. Wolfson, B. Xu, S. Chamberlain, and L. Jiang. Moving Objects Databases: Issues and Solutions. In *Proc. of the SSDBM Conf.*, pp. 111–122 (1998).

[28] O. Wolfson, A. P. Sistla, S. Chamberlain, and Y. Yesha. Updating and Querying Databases that Track Mobile Units. *Distributed and Parallel Databases* 7(3): 257–387 (1999).

Adaptive Multi-Stage Distance Join Processing [*]

Hyoseop Shin[†]
School of Computer Engr
Seoul National University
Seoul, Korea
hsshin@db.snu.ac.kr

Bongki Moon
Dept. of Computer Science
University of Arizona
Tucson, AZ 85721
bkmoon@cs.arizona.edu

Sukho Lee
School of Computer Engr
Seoul National University
Seoul, Korea
shlee@comp.snu.ac.kr

ABSTRACT

A spatial distance join is a relatively new type of operation introduced for spatial and multimedia database applications. Additional requirements for ranking and stopping cardinality are often combined with the spatial distance join in on-line query processing or internet search environments. These requirements pose new challenges as well as opportunities for more efficient processing of spatial distance join queries. In this paper, we first present an efficient k-distance join algorithm that uses spatial indexes such as R-trees. Bidirectional node expansion and plane-sweeping techniques are used for fast pruning of distant pairs, and the plane-sweeping is further optimized by novel strategies for selecting a sweeping axis and direction. Furthermore, we propose adaptive multi-stage algorithms for k-distance join and incremental distance join operations. Our performance study shows that the proposed adaptive multi-stage algorithms outperform previous work by up to an order of magnitude for both k-distance join and incremental distance join queries, under various operational conditions.

1. Introduction

A spatial distance join operation was recently introduced to spatial databases to associate one or more sets of spatial data by distances between them [13]. A distance is usually defined in terms of spatial attributes, but it can be defined in many different ways according to various application specific requirements. In multimedia and image database applications, for example, other metrics such as a *similarity distance function* can be used to measure a distance between two objects in a feature space.

In on-line decision support and internet search environments, it is quite common to pose a query that finds the

---

[*]This work was sponsored in part by National Science Foundation CAREER Award (IIS-9876037) and Research Infrastructure program EIA-9500991. It was also supported by Korea Science and Engineering Foundation under Exchange Student Program. The authors assume all responsibility for the contents of the paper.

[†]This work was done while the author was visiting the University of Arizona.

best k matches or reports the results incrementally in the decreasing order of well-matchedness. This type of operations allow users to interact with database systems more effectively and focus on the "best" answers. Since users can say "It is enough already" at any time after obtaining the best answers [8], the waste of system resources can be reduced and thereby delivering the results to users more quickly.

This ranking requirement is often combined with a spatial distance join query, and the ranking requirement provides a new opportunity of optimization for spatial distance join processing [9, 10]. For example, consider a query that retrieves the top k pairs (*i.e.*, the nearest pairs) of hotels and restaurants:

```
SELECT h.name, r.name
FROM Hotel h, Restaurant r
ORDER BY distance(h.location, r.location)
STOP AFTER k;
```

For a relatively small stopping cardinality k, the processing time can be reduced significantly by sorting only a fraction of intermediate results enough to produce the k nearest pairs, instead of sorting an entire set of intermediate results (*i.e.*, a Cartesian product of hotels and restaurants).

A spatial distance join query with a stopping cardinality can be formulated as follows:

$$\sigma_{dist(r,s) < \mathcal{D}_{max}}(R \bowtie S)$$

where $dist(r, s)$ is a distance between two spatial objects $r \in R$ and $s \in S$, and $\mathcal{D}_{max}$ is a cutoff distance that is determined by a stopping cardinality k and the spatial attribute values of two data sets R and S. It may then be argued that a spatial distance join query can be processed by a spatial join operation [1, 6, 7, 15, 16, 19] followed by a sort operation. Specifically, if a $\mathcal{D}_{max}$ value can be predicted precisely for a given stopping cardinality k, we can use a spatial join algorithm with a `within` predicate instead of an `intersect` predicate to find the k nearest pairs of objects. Then, a sort operation will be performed only on the k pairs of objects.

In practice, however, it is almost impossible to estimate an accurate $\mathcal{D}_{max}$ value for a given stopping cardinality k, and, to the best of our knowledge, no method for estimating such a cutoff value has been reported in the literature. If the $\mathcal{D}_{max}$ value is overestimated, then the results from a spatial join operation may contain too many candidate pairs, which may cause a long delay in a subsequent stage to sort all the candidate pairs. On the other hand, if the $\mathcal{D}_{max}$ value is underestimated, a spatial join operation may not return a sufficient number of object pairs. Then, the spatial join operation should be repeated with a new estimate of

$\mathcal{D}_{max}$, until k or more pairs are returned. This may cause a significant amount of waste in processing time and resources.

There is another reason that makes it impractical to apply a spatial join algorithm to spatial distance join queries. A spatial join query is typically processed in two steps, *filter* and *refinement*, as proposed in [18]. In a filter step, MBR approximations are used to find pairs of potentially intersected spatial objects. Then, in a refinement step, it is guaranteed that all the qualified (*i.e.*, actually intersected) pairs can be produced from the results returned from the filter step.

In contrast, it is completely unreasonable to process a spatial distance join query in two separate filter and refinement steps, because of the fact that a filtering process is based on MBR approximations. A set of object pairs sorted by distances measured by MBR approximations does not reflect a true order based on actual representations. This is because, for any two pairs of spatial objects $\langle r_1, s_1 \rangle$ and $\langle r_2, s_2 \rangle$, the fact that $dist(MBR(r_1), MBR(s_1)) < dist(MBR(r_2), MBR(s_2))$ does not necessarily imply that $dist(r_1, s_1) < dist(r_2, s_2)$. Consequently, any processing done in the filter step will be of no use for finding the k nearest object pairs.

In this paper, we propose new strategies for efficiently processing spatial distance join queries combined with ranking requirements. The main contributions of the proposed solutions are:

- New efficient methods are proposed to process distance join queries using spatial index structures such as R-trees. *Bi-directional node expansion* and *optimized plane-sweep* techniques are used for fast pruning of distant pairs, and the plane-sweep is further optimized by novel strategies for selecting a sweeping axis and direction.

- Adaptive multi-stage algorithms are proposed to process distance join queries in a way that the k nearest pairs are returned *incrementally*. When a stopping cardinality is not known a priori (*e.g.*, in on-line query processing environments or a complex query containing a distance join as a sub-query whose results need to be pipelined to the next stage of the complex query), the adaptive multi-stage algorithms can produce pairs of objects in a stepwise manner.

- We provide a systematic approach for *estimating the maximum distance* for a distance join query with a stopping cardinality. This estimated distance allows the adaptive multi-stage algorithms to avoid a *slow start* problem, which may cause a substantial delay in the query processing. This approach for estimating the maximum distance also allows the size of memory to be parameterized into a queue management scheme, so that data movement between memory and disk can be minimized.

The proposed algorithms achieve up to an order of magnitude performance improvement over previous work for both k-distance join and incremental distance join queries, under various operational conditions.

The rest of this paper is organized as follows. Section 2 surveys the background and related work on processing spatial distance join queries. Major limitations of previous work are also discussed in the section. In Section 3, we present a new improved algorithm based on bi-directional expansion and optimized plane-sweep techniques for k-distance join queries. In Section 4, adaptive multi-stage algorithms are presented for k-distance join and incremental distance

join queries. A queue management scheme parameterized by memory capacity is also presented. Section 5 presents the results of experimental evaluation of the proposed solutions. Finally, Section 6 summarizes the contributions of this paper and gives an outlook to future work.

2. Background and Previous Work

A spatial index structure R-tree and its variants [3, 5, 11] have been widely used to efficiently access multidimensional data – either spatial or point. Like other tree-structured index structures, an R-tree index partitions a multidimensional space by grouping objects in a hierarchical manner. A subspace occupied by a tree node is always contained in the subspace of its parent node. This hierarchy of spatial containment between R-tree nodes is readily used by spatial distance join algorithms as well as spatial join algorithms.

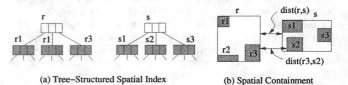

(a) Tree–Structured Spatial Index   (b) Spatial Containment

Figure 1: Hierarchy of Spatial Containment of R-Tree Nodes

Suppose r and s are non-leaf nodes of two R-tree indexes R and S, respectively, as in Figure 1. Then, the minimum distance between r and s is always less than or equal to the minimum distance between one of the child nodes of r and one of the child nodes of s. Likewise, the maximum distance between r and s is always greater than or equal to the maximum distance between one of the child nodes of r and one of the child nodes of s. This observation leads to the following lemma.

LEMMA 1. *For two R-tree indexes R and S, if neither $r \in R$ nor $s \in S$ is a root node, then*

$$dist(r, s) \geq dist(parent(r), parent(s)),$$
$$dist(r, s) \geq dist(r, parent(s)), \qquad (1)$$
$$dist(r, s) \geq dist(parent(r), s).$$

where $dist(r, s)$ is the minimum distance between the MBR representations of r and s.

Proof. From the observation above. $\qquad \square$

Lemma 1 allows us to limit the search space, while R-tree indexes are traversed in a top-down manner to process a spatial distance join query. For example, if a pair of non-leaf nodes $\langle r, s \rangle$ turn out to be too far from each other (or their distance is over a certain threshold), then it is not necessary to traverse further down the tree indexes below the nodes r and s. Thus, this lemma provides the key leverage to processing distance join queries efficiently using R-tree indexes.

2.1 Incremental and k-Distance Joins

During top-down traversals of R-tree indexes, it is desirable to store examined node pairs in a priority queue, where the node pairs are kept in an increasing order of distances. We call it a *main queue* as opposed to a *distance queue* we will describe later. The main queue initially contains a pair of the root nodes of two R-tree indexes. Each time a pair of non-object nodes are retrieved from the main queue, the child nodes of one node are paired up with the child nodes of the other to generate a new set of node pairs, which are then inserted into the main queue. This process that we call *node expansion* is repeated until the main queue becomes empty or until stopped by an interactive user. If an element retrieved from the main queue is a pair of two objects, the pair is returned immediately to the user as a query result. This is how a spatial distance join query is processed *incrementally*. Figure 2 depicts a typical framework of processing an incremental distance join (**IDJ**) query using R-tree indexes.

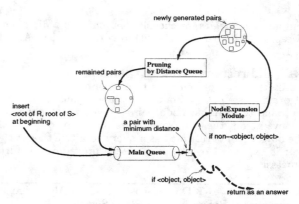

Figure 3: Framework of k-Distance Join (**KDJ**)

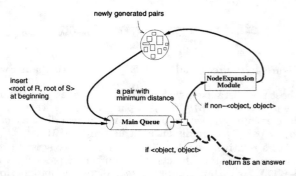

Figure 2: Framework of Incremental Distance Join (**IDJ**)

A distance join query is often given with a stopping cardinality k as in the "stop after" clause of the sample query in Section 1. Since it is known a priori how many object pairs need to be produced for a distance join query, this knowledge can be exploited to improve the performance of the query processing. Suppose a maximum of k nearest pairs of objects are to be retrieved by a query. One plausible approach is to maintain k candidate pairs of objects during the entire course of query processing. As they are the k nearest object pairs known at each stage of query processing, any pair of nodes (and any pair of their child nodes) whose distance is longer than *all* of the k candidate pairs cannot be qualified as a query result. Thus, we can use another priority queue to store the k minimum distances, and use the queue to avoid having to insert unqualified pairs into the main queue during the node expansions. We call the priority queue a *distance queue*. Figure 3 depicts a typical framework of processing a k-distance join (**KDJ**) query using R-tree indexes and both main and distance queues.

Both main and distance queues can be implemented by heap structures. A main queue is normally implemented as a min-heap, because the query results are produced in an increasing order of distances. In contrast, a distance queue should be implemented as a max-heap, as the cutoff distance is determined by the maximum value among the k distances stored in the distance queue at each stage of query processing. Pruning node pairs by the distance queue was shown to be very efficient from our experiments, especially when k was rather small.

2.2 Previous Work

The distance join algorithms proposed in [13] are based on uni-directional node expansions. When a pair of nodes $\langle r, s \rangle$ are retrieved from a main queue, either node r is paired up with the child nodes of s, or node s is paired up with the child nodes of r. None of the pairs are generated from a child node of r and a child node of s. The advantage of the uni-directional expansion is that the number of pairs generated at each expansion step is limited to the fanout of an R-tree index being traversed, and an explosion of the main queue can be avoided. As is acknowledged by the authors

of the algorithms, however, the main disadvantage of this approach is that the uni-directional expansion may lead to each node being accessed from disk more than necessary. And also, the uni-directional expansion requires pairing up node r exhaustively with all the child nodes of node s or vice versa.

For a spatial distance join query with a relatively small stopping cardinality k, the use of a distance queue is an effective means to prevent distant pairs from entering a main queue. For a large k value, however, the distance queue may not work well as an effective pruning tool, because the cutoff value stored in the distance queue may remain too high for a long duration. This may in turn lead to a long delay particularly in the early stage of query processing. For these reasons, the previous algorithms suffer from poor performance for a k-distance join query with a large k and an incremental distance join query, for which k is unknown in advance.

Moreover, there is an important issue that was not fully addressed in [13]. A hybrid memory/disk technique was proposed as a queue management scheme, which partitions a queue based on the distance range. This technique keeps a partition in the shortest distance range in memory, while the rest of partitions are stored on disk. However, no mechanism was provided to determine a boundary distance value between the partition in memory and the rest, which may have a crucial impact on the performance of queue management.

Several closely related studies for nearest neighbor queries have been reported in the literature. Among those are nearest neighbor search algorithms based on Voronoi cells [2, 4] and branch and bound techniques [21], a nearest neighbor search algorithm for ranking requirement [12], and multi-step k-nearest neighbor search algorithms [14, 22].

3. Optimized Plane-Sweep for Fast Pruning

In this section, we propose a new distance join algorithm $\mathcal{B}$-**KDJ** (Bidirectional expanding k-Distance Join) using a *bi-directional* node expansion, in an attempt to avoid redundant accesses to R-tree nodes. As is pointed out in Section 2, distance join algorithms based on an uni-directional expansion require accessing an R-tree node more than those based on bi-directional expansions. Under the bidirectional node expansion, for a pair $\langle r, s \rangle$, each of the child nodes of r is paired up with each of the child nodes of s. This is essentially a Cartesian product, which may generate more redundant pairs than the uni-directional expansion does. Nonetheless, we will show $\mathcal{B}$-**KDJ** algorithm can effectively avoid generating redundant pairs by a plane sweeping technique [20] and novel strategies for choosing an axis and a direction for sweeping. The $\mathcal{B}$-**KDJ** algorithm is described in Algorithm 1.

3.1 Bidirectional Node Expansion

Like the distance join algorithms proposed in [13], $\mathcal{B}$-**KDJ** algorithm uses $q\mathcal{D}_{max}$ from the distance queue $\mathcal{Q}_D$ as a cut-off value to examine node pairs. If a pair of nodes $\langle r, s \rangle$ removed from the main queue are a pair of objects, then the object pair is returned as a query result. Otherwise, the pair is expanded by the *PlaneSweep* procedure for further processing.

Algorithm 1: $\mathcal{B}$-**KDJ**: K-Distance Join Algorithm with Bi-directional Expansion and Plane Sweep

---

1: set $AnswerSet \leftarrow$ an empty set;
2: set $\mathcal{Q}_M$, $\mathcal{Q}_D \leftarrow$ empty main and distance queues;
3: insert a pair $\langle R.root, S.root \rangle$ into the main queue $\mathcal{Q}_M$;
4: **while** $|AnswerSet| < k$ and $\mathcal{Q}_M \neq \emptyset$ **do**
5:     set $c \leftarrow$ dequeue($\mathcal{Q}_M$);
6:     **if** c *is an* $\langle object, object \rangle$ **then**
            $AnswerSet \leftarrow \{c\} \cup AnswerSet$;
7:     **else** $PlaneSweep(c)$;
   end

   procedure PlaneSweep($\langle l, r \rangle$)
8: set L $\leftarrow$ sort_axis({child nodes of l}); // by axis values.
9: set R $\leftarrow$ sort_axis({child nodes of r}); // by axis values.
10: **while** $L \neq \emptyset$ and $R \neq \emptyset$ **do**
11:     $n \leftarrow$ an anchor node with the min axis value $\in L \cup R$;
12:     **if** $n \in L$ **then**
13:         $L \leftarrow L - \{n\}$; $SweepPruning(n, R)$;
        else
14:         $R \leftarrow R - \{n\}$; $SweepPruning(n, L)$;
        end
   end

   procedure SweepPruning($n, List$)
15: **for** *each* $m \in List$ *in an incr. order of axis value* **do**
16:     **if** $axis\_distance(n, m) > q\mathcal{D}_{max}$ **then** return;
17:     **if** $real\_distance(n, m) \leq q\mathcal{D}_{max}$ **then**
18:         insert $\langle n, m \rangle$ into $\mathcal{Q}_M$;
19:         **if** $\langle n, m \rangle$ is an $\langle object, object \rangle$ **then**
                insert $real\_distance(n, m)$ into $\mathcal{Q}_D$;
                // $q\mathcal{D}_{max}$ is modified.
        end
   end

Assume that a sweeping axis (*i.e.*, x or y dimensional axis) and a sweeping direction (*i.e.*, forward or backward) are determined, as we will describe in Sections 3.2 and 3.3. Then, the child nodes of r and s are sorted by x or y coordinates of one of the corners of their MBRs in an increasing or decreasing order, depending on the choice of sweeping axis and sweeping direction. Each node encountered during a plane sweep is selected as an *anchor*, and it is paired up with child nodes in the other group. For example, in Figure 4, a child node r_1 of r is selected as an anchor, and the child nodes s_1, s_2, s_3 and s_4 of s are examined for pairing, as they are within $q\mathcal{D}_{max}$ distance from r_1 along the sweeping axis (lines 11-14 and line 16).

Since an axis distance between any pair $\langle r, s \rangle$ is always smaller than or equal to their real distance (*i.e.*, $axis\_distance(r, s) \leq real\_distance(r, s)$), real distances are computed only for nodes whose axis distances from the anchor are within the current $q\mathcal{D}_{max}$ value (line 17). Given that a real distance is more expensive to compute than an axis distance, it may yield non-trivial performance gain. Then, each pair

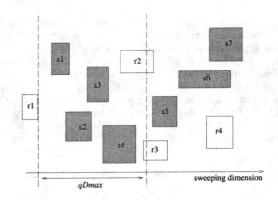

Figure 4: Bidirectional Node Expansion with Plane Sweep

whose real distance is within $q\mathcal{D}_{max}$ is inserted into the main queue $\mathcal{Q}_M$ (line 18). If it is a pair of objects, then update the current $q\mathcal{D}_{max}$ value by inserting the real distance of the object pair into the distance queue $\mathcal{Q}_D$ (line 19). [1]

For a relatively small $q\mathcal{D}_{max}$ value and two sets of evenly distributed spatial objects, the number of pairs for which $\mathcal{B}$-**KDJ** algorithm computes real distances and performs queue management operations is expected to be $\mathcal{O}(|r|+|s|)$ roughly. This justifies the additional cost of sorting child nodes for plane-sweeping, because the overall cost of $\mathcal{B}$-**KDJ** algorithm would otherwise be $\mathcal{O}(|r| \times |s|)$ by Cartesian products.

3.2 Sweeping Axis

We can improve $\mathcal{B}$-**KDJ** algorithm one step further by deciding the sweeping axis and direction on an individual pair basis. Intuitively, if child nodes (or data objects) are spread more widely along one dimension (say, x) than the other dimensions, then the bi-directional node expansion is likely to generate a smaller number of node pairs to compute the real distances for by plane-sweeping along the dimension x. This is because, when the nodes are more widely spread along a sweeping axis, the chance that a pair of nodes are within a $q\mathcal{D}_{max}$ distance along the sweeping axis is lower.

For a pair of parent nodes shown in Figure 5, as an example, it would be better to choose y-axis as a sweeping axis, as the child nodes are more widely spread along the y-dimension. On the other hand, if x-axis is chosen as a sweeping axis, no pair of the child nodes will be pruned by x-axis distance comparison with $q\mathcal{D}_{max}$, because the x-axis distance between any pair of the child nodes is shorter than the $q\mathcal{D}_{max}$ value.

Formally, we define a new metric **sweeping index** as follows, and we use the metric to determine which axis a plane-sweep will be performed on. For a given pair $\langle r, s \rangle$ of R-tree nodes and a given $q\mathcal{D}_{max}$ value, we can compute a sweeping index for each dimension. Conceptually, a sweeping index is a normalized estimation of the number of node

---

[1] There are alternatives as to what pairs are to be inserted into a distance queue: (1) any pairs encountered during node expansions, or (2) pairs of objects only. If a pair of non-object R-tree nodes is inserted into a distance queue, its maximum distance should be inserted as well [13]. Since the maximum distance tends to be larger than those of pairs of objects, most of non-object pairs are inserted into a distance queue only to be removed from the distance queue without reducing $q\mathcal{D}_{max}$ value. Thus, we decide to follow the second option.

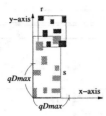

Figure 5: Effect of Right Selection of the Sweeping Axis

pairs that we need to compute the real distances for.[2]

$$\text{Sweeping Index}_x = \int_0^{|r|_x} \frac{Overlap(q\mathcal{D}_{max}, r, t)}{|s|_x} dt$$

$$+ \int_0^{|s|_x} \frac{Overlap(q\mathcal{D}_{max}, s, t)}{|r|_x} dt \qquad (2)$$

In the first integral term of the equation above, $|r|_x$ is the side length of node r along the dimension x. The function $Overlap(q\mathcal{D}_{max}, r, t)$ is a portion of the side length of s along the dimension x, overlapped with a window of length $q\mathcal{D}_{max}$ whose left end point is located at a point t within $|r|_x$ (i.e., $0 \le t \le |r|_x$). (See the left diagram in Figure 6.) Thus, $Overlap(q\mathcal{D}_{max}, r, t)/|s|_x$ represents a fraction of s's child nodes intersected with a window $[t, t + q\mathcal{D}_{max}]$. The value of the function varies as the window moves along the dimension x from $[0, q\mathcal{D}_{max}]$ to $[|r|_x, |r|_x + q\mathcal{D}_{max}]$. Therefore, the first integral term represents a relative estimation of the number of s's child nodes encountered during the plane-sweeps performed for all the child nodes of r. The second integral term is symmetric with the first integral, and an identical description can be offered by exchanging r and s.

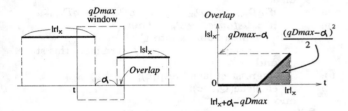

Figure 6: Sweeping Index

A smaller sweeping index indicates that the bi-directional expansion needs to compute real distances for a smaller number of nodes pairs. For the reason, $\mathcal{B}$-**KDJ** algorithm chooses a dimension with the minimum sweeping index as a sweeping axis.

One thing we may be concerned about is the cost of computing a sweeping index for each dimension. The sweeping index may appear expensive to compute, as it includes two integral terms. For given $q\mathcal{D}_{max}$, $|r|_x$ and $|s|_x$ values, however, the sweeping index is reduced to a formula that involves only a few simple arithmetic operations. Suppose nodes r and s are not intersected along a dimension x, the

---

[2] An actual number of node pairs for which we need to compute the real distances would be computed by counting the number of s's child nodes within $q\mathcal{D}_{max}$ axis distance from each child node of r, counting the number of r's child nodes within $q\mathcal{D}_{max}$ axis distance from each child node of s, and then adding all the counts and dividing the count sum by two. However, this process will be very expensive.

minimum x-axis distance between them is α, and node r appears before node s in the plane-sweep direction along x-axis. (Again, see the left diagram in Figure 6.) Then, the second integral term of Equation (2) become zero, because all the child nodes of r have already been swept when the first child node of s is encountered. The first integral term varies depending on the conditions among $q\mathcal{D}_{max}$, $|r|_x$ and $|s|_x$ values and the proximity (i.e., α) of nodes r and s along a chosen dimension. Table 1 summaries the formulae of the sweeping index for non-overlapping nodes r and s. The right diagram in Figure 6 illustrates how we can compute the first integral term and obtain a simple expression when $|s|_x + \alpha \le q\mathcal{D}_{max} \le |r|_x + \alpha$ is satisfied.

If nodes r and s are intersected, both the integral terms of Equation 2 become non-zero. By a similar reasoning, each integral term is also transformed into a formula with only a few simple arithmetic operations. Considering that each R-tree node may contain hundreds of child nodes, it will be a trivial cost to compute a sweeping index for each dimension, while the performance gain by the sweeping axis selection is expected to be significant. This is empirically corroborated by our experiments in Section 5.

3.3 Sweeping Direction

Once a sweeping axis is determined, a sweeping direction can be chosen to be either a *forward* sweep or a *backward* sweep. For a pair of nodes r and s, we can define the forward and backward sweeps as follows.

- A forward plane-sweep scans the child nodes of r and s in an increasing order of coordinates along the chosen sweeping axis.

- A backward plane-sweep scans the child nodes of r and s in a decreasing order of coordinates along the chosen sweeping axis.

Consider nodes r and s projected on a sweeping axis. The projected images generate three consecutive closed intervals on the sweeping axis, unless the projected images are completely overlapped. For example, if nodes r and s are intersected as in Figure 7(a), an interval in the left is projected from r, one in the middle from both r and s, and one in the right from s. The interval in the middle may be projected from none of r and s, if r and s are separate as in Figure 7(b). Both the intervals in the left and right may be projected from the same node, if one node is contained in the other as in Figure 7(c).

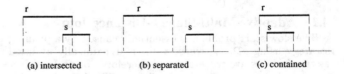

| (a) intersected | (b) separated | (c) contained |

Figure 7: Three intervals projected from two nodes r and s

However, it does not matter which node an interval is projected from, because the a sweeping direction is determined solely on the relative length of the intervals in the left and right. A sweeping direction is determined by comparing the length of the left and right intervals: *if the left projected interval is shorter than the right one, then a forward direction is chosen. Otherwise, a backward direction is chosen.* By this strategy of choosing a sweeping direction, a pair of nodes closer to each other are likely to be examined earlier than those farther to each other. This in turn allows a pair of closer nodes are inserted into the main queue (and the

Condition	The first integral term of Equation (2)
$q\mathcal{D}_{max} \leq \alpha$	0
$\alpha < q\mathcal{D}_{max} \leq |r|_x + \alpha$	$\begin{cases} \frac{(q\mathcal{D}_{max}-\alpha)^2}{2|s|_x} & \text{if } q\mathcal{D}_{max} \geq |s|_x + \alpha, \\ \frac{(q\mathcal{D}_{max}-\alpha)^2}{2|s|_x} - \frac{|s|_x}{2} & \text{otherwise.} \end{cases}$
$q\mathcal{D}_{max} \geq |r|_x + \alpha$	$\begin{cases} \frac{1}{2|s|_x}(|r|_x^2 - (q\mathcal{D}_{max}-|r|_x-\alpha)^2) & \text{if } |r|_x \leq |s|_x, \\ \frac{1}{2|s|_x}(|r|_x^2 - (q\mathcal{D}_{max}-|r|_x-\alpha)^2 - (|r|_x-|s|_x)^2) & \text{if } (q\mathcal{D}_{max}-|r|_x-\alpha) \leq |s|_x < |r|_x, \\ |r|_x & \text{if } |s|_x < (q\mathcal{D}_{max}-|r|_x-\alpha). \end{cases}$

Table 1: Sweeping index for non-overlapping r and s (α is the minimum distance between $\langle r, s \rangle$)

distance queue as well if they are an object pair), and helps reduce the $q\mathcal{D}_{max}$ value more rapidly.

In summary, the sweeping axis selection improves the bi-directional node expansion step by pruning more child node pairs whose axis distances are larger than the $q\mathcal{D}_{max}$, while, the sweeping direction selection does by reducing the $q\mathcal{D}_{max}$ value more rapidly.

4. Adaptive Multi-Stage Distance Join

In $\mathcal{B}$-**KDJ** algorithm, $q\mathcal{D}_{max}$ value is initially set to an infinity and becomes smaller as the algorithm proceeds. The adaptation of the $q\mathcal{D}_{max}$ value has a crucial impact on the performance of $\mathcal{B}$-**KDJ** algorithm, as $q\mathcal{D}_{max}$ is used as a cutoff to prevent pairs of distant nodes from entering the main queue. If the $q\mathcal{D}_{max}$ value approaches to the real $\mathcal{D}_{max}$ value slowly, the early stage of $\mathcal{B}$-**KDJ** algorithm will be delayed considerably for handling too many pairs of distant nodes. Consequently, at the end of the algorithm processing, the main queue may end up with a large number of distant pairs whose insertions to the main queue were not necessary. The performance effect of *slow start* is more pronounced for a larger k, as the main queue and distance queue tend to grow large for a large k, and thereby increasing the $q\mathcal{D}_{max}$ value. From our experiments with k as high as 100,000, we observed that more than 90 percent of execution time of k-distance join algorithms was spent to produce the first one percent (*i.e.*, 1,000 pairs) of final query results.

In this section, we propose new adaptive multi-stage distance join algorithms $\mathcal{AM}$-**KDJ** and $\mathcal{AM}$-**IDJ** that mitigate the slow start problem by *aggressive pruning* and *compensation*.

4.1 Adaptive Multi-Stage k-Distance Join

The slow start problem is essentially caused by a pruning strategy using $q\mathcal{D}_{max}$, whose value is dynamically updated as tree indexes are traversed and therefore not under direct control of the distance join algorithms. To circumvent this problem, we introduce a new pruning measure $e\mathcal{D}_{max}$, which is an estimated $\mathcal{D}_{max}$ value for a given k. The $e\mathcal{D}_{max}$ value is set to an initial estimation at the beginning and adaptively corrected during the algorithm processing. We will discuss techniques for initial estimation and adaptive correction in Section 4.3.

$\mathcal{AM}$-**KDJ** algorithm is similar to $\mathcal{B}$-**KDJ** algorithm in that both the algorithms use a bi-directional node expansion. However, unlike the single-stage $\mathcal{B}$-**KDJ** algorithm, where only $q\mathcal{D}_{max}$ is used for pruning, both $q\mathcal{D}_{max}$ and $e\mathcal{D}_{max}$ are used as cutoff values for pruning distant pairs in $\mathcal{AM}$-**KDJ** algorithm. Specifically, in the *aggressive pruning* stage (described in Algorithm 2),

- $e\mathcal{D}_{max}$ is used for pruning based on *axis distances* for aggressive pruning and thereby limiting the size of main and distance queues (line 22),

- $q\mathcal{D}_{max}$ is used for further pruning on *real distances* for nodes whose axis distances are within $e\mathcal{D}_{max}$, in the same way as $\mathcal{B}$-**KDJ**.

Algorithm 2: $\mathcal{AM}$-**KDJ**: Adaptive Multi-Stage K-Distance Join Algorithm (Aggressive Pruning)

1: set $AnswerSet \leftarrow$ an empty set;
2: set $\mathcal{Q}_M, \mathcal{Q}_D, \mathcal{Q}_C \leftarrow$ empty queues ;
3: set $e\mathcal{D}_{max} \leftarrow$ an initial estimated $\mathcal{D}_{max}$;
4: insert a pair $\langle R.root, S.root \rangle$ to the main queue $\mathcal{Q}_M$;
5: **while** $|AnswerSet| < k$ and $\mathcal{Q}_M \neq \emptyset$ **do**
6:   set c $\leftarrow$ dequeue($\mathcal{Q}_M$);
7:   **if** c *is an* $\langle object, object \rangle$ **then**
    $AnswerSet \leftarrow \{c\} \cup AnswerSet$;
  else
8:     **if** $q\mathcal{D}_{max} \leq e\mathcal{D}_{max}$ **then** $e\mathcal{D}_{max} \leftarrow q\mathcal{D}_{max}$;
9:     **if** c.distance $< e\mathcal{D}_{max}$ **then**
      reinsert c back into $\mathcal{Q}_M$;
      break;   // Terminate this stage.
    end
10:     AggressivePlaneSweep(c);
11:     enqueue($\mathcal{Q}_C$, c);
  end
end
12: **if** $|AnswerSet| < k$ **then** execute Algorithm 3;

  procedure AggressivePlaneSweep($\langle l, r \rangle$)
13: set L $\leftarrow$ sort_axis({child nodes of l}); // by axis values.
14: set R $\leftarrow$ sort_axis({child nodes of r}); // by axis values.
15: **while** $L \neq \emptyset$ and $R \neq \emptyset$ **do**
16:   $n \leftarrow$ an anchor node with the min axis value $\in L \cup R$;
17:   **if** $n \in L$ **then**
18:     $L \leftarrow L - \{n\}$; AggressiveSweepPruning(n, R);
19:     $n.compensate \leftarrow$ a node in R with
    the min axis value and not yet paired with n;
  else
20:     $R \leftarrow R - \{n\}$; AggressiveSweepPruning(n, L);
21:     $n.compensate \leftarrow$ a node in L with
    the min axis value and not yet paired with n;
  end
end

  procedure AggressiveSweepPruning($n, List$)
Same as the SweepPruning procedure in Algorithm 1 except line 16 replaced with the following:
22: **if** $axis\_distance(n, m) > e\mathcal{D}_{max}$ **then** return;

With a properly estimated $e\mathcal{D}_{max}$ value, $\mathcal{AM}$-**KDJ** algorithm can prune a large number of distant pairs in the first stage and avoid a significant portion of delay due to the slow start. However, if $\mathcal{AM}$-**KDJ** algorithm becomes too aggressive by choosing an underestimated $e\mathcal{D}_{max}$ value, even close enough pairs may be discarded incorrectly. To avoid any false dismissals, we introduce another queue called *compensation queue* ($\mathcal{Q}_C$). The compensation queue stores every node pair retrieved from the main queue (line 11), if it is not a pair of objects or all the child nodes of the pair are examined by plane sweeping. It should also be noted that $q\mathcal{D}_{max}$ but not $e\mathcal{D}_{max}$ is used for nodes whose axis distances are within $e\mathcal{D}_{max}$. If $e\mathcal{D}_{max}$ values are used instead, the compensation stage will become very costly in order to keep track of an exhaustive set of pruned pairs and recover qualified pairs from them. Using $q\mathcal{D}_{max}$ values also makes the performance of $\mathcal{AM}$-**KDJ** fairly insensitive to estimated $e\mathcal{D}_{max}$ values.

For example, in Figure 8 (drawn from Figure 4), an anchor node r_1 is paired up with nodes s_1 and s_2 but not with s_3 and s_4 in the aggressive pruning stage, because only s_1 and s_2 are within $e\mathcal{D}_{max}$ from the anchor node r_1. Thus, $\mathcal{AM}$-**KDJ** algorithm inserts only two pairs ($\langle r_1, s_1 \rangle$, $\langle r_1, s_2 \rangle$) into a main queue, instead of all four pairs ($\langle r_1, s_1 \rangle$, $\langle r_1, s_2 \rangle$, $\langle r_1, s_3 \rangle$, $\langle r_1, s_4 \rangle$) that would be enqueued by $\mathcal{B}$-**KDJ** algorithm. Then, the pair $\langle r, s \rangle$ currently being expanded is inserted into a compensation queue.

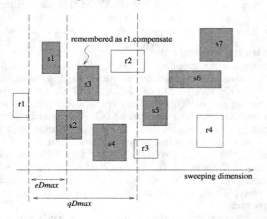

Figure 8: Aggressive pruning with $q\mathcal{D}_{max}$ and $e\mathcal{D}_{max}$

The aggressive pruning stage ends when one of the following conditions is satisfied: (1) the main queue becomes empty (line 5), (2) k or more query results have been returned (line 5), or (3) the distance of a node pair retrieved from the main queue becomes smaller than $e\mathcal{D}_{max}$ (line 9). When the condition (2) is satisfied, obviously it is not necessary to execute the compensation stage of the $\mathcal{AM}$-**KDJ** algorithm. (An overestimated $e\mathcal{D}_{max}$ can also be detected by comparing with $q\mathcal{D}_{max}$ value (line 8). In this case, instead of terminating the first stage, $\mathcal{AM}$-**KDJ** behaves exactly the same as $\mathcal{B}$-**KDJ** algorithm by using $q\mathcal{D}_{max}$ alone as a cutoff value.) When the condition (3) is satisfied, $e\mathcal{D}_{max}$ must have been underestimated and the compensation stage (described in Algorithm 3) begins its processing by inserting all the pairs stored in the compensation queue to the main queue.

In the compensation stage, the pairs in the main queue are processed in a similar way as $\mathcal{B}$-**KDJ** algorithm, but there are two notable differences from $\mathcal{B}$-**KDJ** algorithm. First, the child nodes are not sorted again because they have already been sorted in the first stage. Second, for the pairs already expanded once in the first stage, only child

Algorithm 3: $\mathcal{AM}$-**KDJ**: Adaptive Multi-Stage K-Distance Join Algorithm (Compensation Stage)

23: insert all elements in $\mathcal{Q}_C$ into $\mathcal{Q}_M$;
24: **while** $|AnswerSet| < k$ and $\mathcal{Q}_M \neq \emptyset$ **do**
25:    set c $\leftarrow$ dequeue($\mathcal{Q}_M$);
26:    **if** c *is an* $\langle object, object \rangle$ **then**
          $AnswerSet \leftarrow \{c\} \cup AnswerSet$;
27:    **else** CompensatePlaneSweep(c);
    end

    procedure CompensatePlaneSweep($\langle l, r \rangle$)
28: L $\leftarrow$ {child nodes of l sorted in Stage One};
29: R $\leftarrow$ {child nodes of r sorted in Stage One};
30: **while** $L \neq \emptyset$ and $R \neq \emptyset$ **do**
31:    $n \leftarrow$ an anchor node with the min axis value $\in L \cup R$;
32:    **if** $n \in L$ **then**
33:       $L \leftarrow L - \{n\}$; $R' \leftarrow$ {nodes in R not paired with n in Stage One};
34:       $SweepPruning(n, R')$;
       else
35:       $R \leftarrow R - \{n\}$; $L' \leftarrow$ {nodes in L not paired with n in the Stage One };
36:       $SweepPruning(n, L')$;
    end
end

pairs not examined in the first stage are processed by plane sweeping. This is feasible by bookkeeping done in the first stage (lines 19 and 21). For these reasons, the cost of the compensating stage is not considerable compared with the cost of restarting the algorithm. In summary, $\mathcal{AM}$-**KDJ** algorithm uses $e\mathcal{D}_{max}$ to avoid the slow start problem in the aggressive pruning stage and speeds up the query processing.

4.2 Adaptive Multi-stage Incremental Distance Join

Consider on-line query processing and internet database search environments, where users interact with database systems in a way the number of required matches can be determined interactively or changed at any point of query processing. Consider also a complex query that pipelines the results from a spatial distance join to a filter stage. Under these circumstances, the number of pairs (k) that should be returned from a distance join is not known a priori, and hence a k-distance join algorithm proposed in [13] and $\mathcal{B}$-**KDJ** algorithm presented in Section 3 cannot be used directly.

An important advantage of $\mathcal{AM}$-**KDJ** algorithm proposed in the previous section is that $\mathcal{AM}$-**KDJ** algorithm can be extended to an incremental algorithm (we call $\mathcal{AM}$-**IDJ**) to support the interactive applications described above. The main difference between $\mathcal{AM}$-**KDJ** and $\mathcal{AM}$-**IDJ** algorithms is that $\mathcal{AM}$-**IDJ** does not maintain a distance queue. This is because it is not feasible to keep an unknown number of distances in a distance queue, due to the lack of a priori knowledge about k, Thus, $\mathcal{AM}$-**IDJ** algorithm uses $e\mathcal{D}_{max}$ alone as a cutoff value for pruning distant pairs, because $q\mathcal{D}_{max}$ would be drawn only from a distance queue.

Without $q\mathcal{D}_{max}$, $\mathcal{AM}$-**IDJ** works as a stepwise incremental algorithm. First, $\mathcal{AM}$-**IDJ** starts by determining an initial value k_1 and estimating an initial $e\mathcal{D}_{max1}$ for k_1. Then, it performs the same way as the first stage of $\mathcal{AM}$-**KDJ** algorithm without $q\mathcal{D}_{max}$. However, the first stage may terminates before producing enough object pairs (*i.e.*, less than k_1), because $\mathcal{AM}$-**IDJ** does not use $q\mathcal{D}_{max}$ as a cutoff value. If that happens, $\mathcal{AM}$-**IDJ** algorithm estimates $e\mathcal{D}_{max2}$ value for k_2 ($k_2 > k_1$) and initiates a compensation stage.

Even when a sufficient number of object pairs have been returned from the first stage, users may request more answers. Then, $\mathcal{AM}$-**IDJ** initiates a compensation stage by determining k_2 and estimating a new $e\mathcal{D}_{max2}$ accordingly. As shown in Figure 9 (drawn from Figure 4), the compensation stage can initiate another compensation stage at the end of its processing, by choosing k_3 and $e\mathcal{D}_{max3}$. This process continues until users stop requesting more answers. In this way, $\mathcal{AM}$-**IDJ** algorithm can be used to produce query results incrementally without limiting the maximum number of pairs in advance.

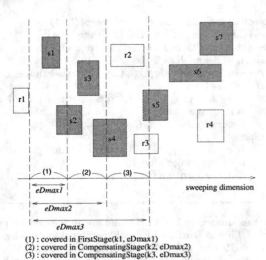

(1) : covered in FirstStage(k1, eDmax1)
(2) : covered in CompensatingStage(k2, eDmax2)
(3) : covered in CompensatingStage(k3, eDmax3)

Figure 9: Adaptive Multi-Stage Incremental Distance Join

4.3 Estimating the Maximum Distance ($e\mathcal{D}_{max}$)

Both $\mathcal{AM}$-**KDJ** and $\mathcal{AM}$-**IDJ** algorithms process a distance join query based on an estimated cutoff value $e\mathcal{D}_{max}$. Thus, there should be a way to obtain an initial estimate and correct the estimate adaptively as the algorithms proceed. Assuming data sets are uniformly distributed, we provide mechanisms to choose an initial estimate of $e\mathcal{D}_{max}$, and to adaptively correct it.

If the distribution of a data set is skewed, then a larger number of close pairs can be found in a smaller dense region of the data space. We expect that the formulae given in this section tend to overestimate $e\mathcal{D}_{max}$ value for non-uniformly distributed data sets, especially when a stopping cardinality k is far smaller than the number of all pairs of objects (i.e., $k \ll |R| \times |S|$). This was corroborated by our experiments as described in Section 5.4.

4.3.1 Initial estimation

Let $|R|$ and $|S|$ be the number of data objects in sets R and S, respectively. Then, the number of data objects in S within a distance d from a data object in R is approximated by $|S| \times \frac{\pi \times d^2}{area(R \cap S)}$. Therefore, the total number of object pairs (k) within a distance d is given by

$$k = |R| \times |S| \times \frac{\pi \times d^2}{area(R \cap S)}.$$

For a given k value as the number of requested query results, an initial estimation of $e\mathcal{D}_{max}$ can be obtained from the above equation as follows:

$$e\mathcal{D}_{max} = \sqrt{k \times \rho} \qquad \text{(where } \rho = \frac{area(R \cap S)}{\pi \times |R| \times |S|}). \qquad (3)$$

4.3.2 Adaptive Correction of Estimated Distance $e\mathcal{D}_{max}$

The performance of $\mathcal{AM}$-**KDJ** and $\mathcal{AM}$-**IDJ** algorithms can be further improved by adaptively adjusting the value of $e\mathcal{D}_{max}$ at runtime. Adaptive correction of $e\mathcal{D}_{max}$ can be done at any point of query processing by estimating a new $e\mathcal{D}_{max}$ from the number of object pairs k_0 ($k_0 < k$) obtained up to the point and the real distance of the k_0-th object pair, $\mathcal{D}_{max(k_0)}$. Specifically, the new estimate $e\mathcal{D}_{max}'$ can be computed from Equation (3) as

$$e\mathcal{D}_{max}' = \sqrt{\mathcal{D}_{max(k_0)}^2 + (k - k_0)\rho} \qquad (4)$$

by arithmetic correction, or as

$$e\mathcal{D}_{max}' = \mathcal{D}_{max(k_0)} \times \sqrt{k/k_0} \qquad (5)$$

by geometric correction if $\mathcal{D}_{max}(k_0) \neq 0$. In practice, we propose computing $e\mathcal{D}_{max}'$ in both ways, and then choose the minimum if the query processing needs to be err on the aggressive side. Otherwise, the maximum is chosen as $e\mathcal{D}_{max}'$.

Note that the new estimate $e\mathcal{D}_{max}'$ can sometimes grow beyond the previous estimate. If this happens, some pairs whose distances are larger than the previous estimate but smaller than the new estimate could have already been pruned and will never be examined in the current processing stage under the new estimate. Thus, to guarantee the correctness of the distance join, the algorithm should initiate a compensation stage, as soon as a pair whose distance is smaller than the smallest $e\mathcal{D}_{max}$ is dequeued from the main queue.

4.4 Queue Management

Efficient queue management is one of the key components of the distance join algorithms proposed in this paper. Each of the $\mathcal{B}$-**KDJ**, $\mathcal{AM}$-**KDJ**, and $\mathcal{AM}$-**IDJ** algorithms relies on the use of one or more priority queues for query processing. In particular, the main queue ($\mathcal{Q}_M$) is heavily used by all of the proposed algorithms, and its performance impact is significant. In the worst case, the main queue can grow as large as the product of all objects of two R-tree indexes. That is, the size of $\mathcal{Q}_M$ is in $\mathcal{O}(|R_{obj}| \times |S_{obj}|)$, where $|R_{obj}|$ and $|S_{obj}|$ are the number of all objects in R and S, respectively. Thus, it is not always feasible to store the main queue in memory.

It was reported in [13] that a simple memory-based implementation might slow down query processing severely, due to excessive virtual memory thrashing. A hybrid memory/disk scheme [13] and a technique based on range partitioning [9] have been proposed to improve queue management and to avoid wasted sorting I/O operations. We adopt a similar scheme for queue management, which partitions a queue by range based on distances of pairs. A partition in the shortest distance range is kept in memory as a heap structure, while the rest of partitions are stored on disk as merely unsorted piles.

When the in-memory heap becomes full, it is *split* into two parts, and then one in the longer distance range is moved to disk as a new segment. When the in-memory heap becomes empty, a disk-resident segment in the shortest distance range or a part of the segment is *swapped in* to memory to fill up the in-memory heap. Each of the split and swap-in operations requires $\mathcal{O}(n \log n)$ computational cost for a heap of n elements as well as I/O cost for reading and writing a segment. Thus, it is important to minimize the required number of those operations, which largely depends on the partition boundary values between the in-memory heap and the first disk-resident segment, and between those consecutive segments. However, as it is impossible to predict an exact $\mathcal{D}_{max}$ value for a given k, so is it difficult to determine optimal distance values as segment boundaries.

To address this issue, we use Equation (3) to determine the boundary distance values. Suppose n is the number of elements that can be stored in an in-memory heap. Then, the boundary value between the in-memory heap and the first disk-resident segment is given by $\sqrt{n \times \rho}$, and the boundary value between the first and second segments is given by $\sqrt{(2 \times n) \times \rho}$, and so on.

In addition to a main queue, multi-stage algorithms $\mathcal{AM}$-**KDJ** and $\mathcal{AM}$-**IDJ** use a compensation queue ($\mathcal{Q}_C$) in the compensation stage. Unlike the main queue, a compensation queue does not store any pair of objects. In other words, a compensation queue can store pairs of non-object R-tree nodes only. Thus, the size of $\mathcal{Q}_C$ is in $\mathcal{O}(|R_{node}| \times |S_{node}|)$, where $|R_{node}|$ and $|S_{node}|$ are the number of nodes (both internal and leaf nodes) in R and S, respectively. This is a significantly lower upper-bound than a main queue has. We also observed from our experiments that compensation queues were several orders of magnitude smaller than main queues. As for a distance queue used by $\mathcal{B}$-**KDJ** and $\mathcal{AM}$-**KDJ** algorithms, its size is always bounded by a given k value. For these reasons, under most circumstances, we assume either a compensation queue and a distance queue fits in memory. If any of these queues outgrows memory, the same partitioning technique used for a main queue will be applied.

5. Performance Evaluation

In this section, we evaluate the proposed algorithms empirically and compare with previous work. In particular, the proposed $\mathcal{B}$-**KDJ**, $\mathcal{AM}$-**KDJ** and $\mathcal{AM}$-**IDJ** algorithms were compared with Hjaltason and Samet's k-distance and incremental distance join algorithms (hereinafter denoted as HS-**KDJ** and HS-**IDJ**, respectively) for k-distance join (**KDJ**) and incremental distance join (**IDJ**) queries. We also include the performance of an R-tree based spatial join algorithm [7] combined with a sort operation (denoted as SJ-**SORT**) in most of the experiments. For each distance join query, a spatial join operation was performed with a real $\mathcal{D}_{max}$ value to generate the k nearest pairs. Then, an external sort operation was performed to return the query results in an increasing order of distances. Note that we made a favorable assumption for SJ-**SORT** that a real $\mathcal{D}_{max}$ value was known a priori.

5.1 Experimental Settings

Experiments were performed on a Sun Ultrasparc-II workstation running on Solaris 2.7. This workstation has 256 MBytes of memory and 9 GBytes of disk storage (Seagate ST39140A) with Ultra 10 EIDE interface. The disk is locally attached to the workstation and used to store databases, queues and any temporary results. We used the direct I/O feature of Solaris for all the experiments to avoid operating system's cache effects, and the average disk access bandwidth was about 0.5 MBytes/sec for random accesses and about 5 MBytes/sec for sequential accesses.

Data sets To evaluate distance join algorithms, we used real-world data sets in TIGER/Line97 from the U.S. Bureau of Census [17]. The particular data sets we used were 633,461 streets and 189,642 hydrographic objects from the Arizona state. Throughout the entire set of experiments, the same page size of 4 KBytes was used for disk I/O and R*-tree [3] nodes.

Metrics We measured the performance of various algorithms based on the following metrics to compare the algorithms in different aspects such as computational cost and I/O cost.

1. *number of distance computations*: The cost of computing distances between pairs of nodes (or objects) constitutes a significant portion of the computational cost of a distance join operation. Thus, the total number of distance computations required by a distance join algorithm provides a direct indication of its computational performance.

2. *number of queue insertions*: The task of managing a main queue is largely I/O intensive as well as CPU intensive. Thus, the total number of insertions to a main queue required by a distance join algorithm provides a reasonable indication of its I/O performance, because insertions are much more frequent than deletions.

3. *response time*: Actual query response times were measured for overall performance of distance join algorithms.

5.2 Evaluation of k-Distance Joins

In this set of experiments, we varied a stopping cardinality k from 10 to 100,000 to compare the performance of HS-**KDJ**, $\mathcal{B}$-**KDJ** and $\mathcal{AM}$-**KDJ** algorithms. The sizes of in-memory portion of a main queue and R-tree buffer were fixed to 512 KBytes. For $\mathcal{AM}$-**KDJ** algorithm, we used Equation (3) to estimate $e\mathcal{D}_{max}$ values, and we observed a tendency for $e\mathcal{D}_{max}$ values to be overestimated with respect to real $\mathcal{D}_{max}$ values. For example, for $k = 100,000$, $e\mathcal{D}_{max}$ was about 2.3 times larger than a real $\mathcal{D}_{max}$.

Figure 10(a) shows that both $\mathcal{B}$-**KDJ** and $\mathcal{AM}$-**KDJ** reduced the number of distance computations significantly. The numbers of distance computations required by the algorithms were smaller than those required by HS-**KDJ** algorithm by up to two orders of magnitude. $\mathcal{AM}$-**KDJ** was almost identical to SJ-**SORT** by this metric. This demonstrates that the optimized plane-sweep method was very effective in pruning distant pairs generated by bi-directional expansions. On the other hand, HS-**KDJ** algorithm examines all possible pairs exhaustively in uni-directional expansions.

In Figure 10(b), Both $\mathcal{B}$-**KDJ** and $\mathcal{AM}$-**KDJ** achieved significant reductions in queue insertions for all k values. $\mathcal{AM}$-**KDJ** was always better than $\mathcal{B}$-**KDJ** particularly for large k values. This result confirms our conjecture that the optimized plane-sweep method can prevent an explosion of a main queue that would be caused by bi-directional node expansions without the optimized plane-sweep.

As Figure 10(c) shows, $\mathcal{B}$-**KDJ** and $\mathcal{AM}$-**KDJ** outperformed HS-**KDJ** by a factor of two to three in response time. For small k values, both $\mathcal{B}$-**KDJ** and $\mathcal{AM}$-**KDJ** were comparable with SJ-**SORT**. For large k values, the response time of $\mathcal{AM}$-**KDJ** was within about 80 percent above that of SJ-**SORT**.

Table 2 compares the number of R-tree nodes fetched from disk by each algorithm. For large k values, the proposed $\mathcal{B}$-**KDJ** and $\mathcal{AM}$-**KDJ** algorithms based on bi-directional node expansions require a far smaller number of R-tree node accesses than HS-**KDJ** algorithm, which is based on uni-directional node expansions. The numbers in parentheses represent the number of R-tree nodes that would be fetched from disk without any buffer pages alloted for R-trees.

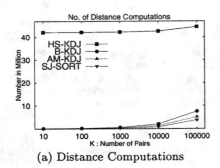

(a) Distance Computations

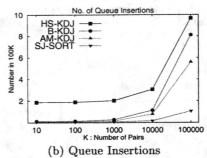

(b) Queue Insertions

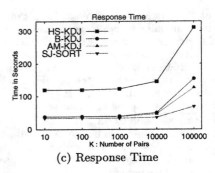

(c) Response Time

Figure 10: Performance k-Distance Joins

KDJ	Stopping cardinality k			
Algorithms	100	1,000	10,000	100,000
HS-**KDJ**	4,039 (186,403)	4,392 (186,801)	5,836 (188,354)	13,958 (197,113)
$\mathcal{B}$-**KDJ**	4,355 (12,660)	4,367 (12,672)	4,381 (12,688)	4,555 (12,916)
$\mathcal{AM}$-**KDJ**	4,355 (12,660)	4,367 (12,672)	4,381 (12,688)	4,555 12,916)
SJ-**SORT**	4,190 (12,660)	4,193 (12,672)	4,197 (12,688)	4,219 (12,916)

Table 2: No. of R-tree Node Accesses for k-Distance Joins

5.3 Impact of Optimized Plane-Sweep

To further analyze the performance impacts of the optimized plane-sweep method proposed in Section 3, we measured the performance of $\mathcal{B}$-**KDJ** with the optimization turned off. Specifically, a sweeping axis and direction were fixed to x-axis and forward direction, for $\mathcal{B}$-**KDJ** with the optimization turned off. As Figure 11 shows, the optimized plane-sweep alone reduced the number of required axis and real distance computations by up to 20 percent.

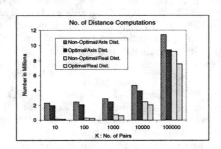

Figure 11: Improvements by Optimized Plane Sweep

5.4 Evaluation of Incremental Distance Joins

As in the previous section, we varied a stopping cardinality k from 10 to 100,000 to compare the performance of incremental distance join algorithms *HS*-**IDJ** and $\mathcal{AM}$-**IDJ**. Like the previous experiments, the sizes of in-memory portion of a main queue and R-tree buffer were fixed to 512 KBytes.

As Figures 12(a) and 12(b) show, 75 to 98 percent of distance computations and queue insertions required by *HS*-**IDJ** algorithm were eliminated by $\mathcal{AM}$-**IDJ** algorithm. The significant improvement in these two metrics in turn led to improvement in response time by an order of magnitude in Figure 12(c). Like $\mathcal{AM}$-**KDJ** algorithm, Equation (3) was used to estimate $e\mathcal{D}_{max}$ values for $\mathcal{AM}$-**IDJ** algorithm.

5.5 Impact of Memory Size

In this set of experiments, we examined the performance impact of memory constraint of queue management and R-tree buffers. The sizes of in-memory portion of a main queue and R-tree buffer were varied from 64 KBytes to 1024 KBytes. We measured the response time of *HS*-**KDJ**, $\mathcal{B}$-**KDJ** and $\mathcal{AM}$-**KDJ** algorithms for a fixed stopping cardinality $k = 100,000$. As Figure 13 shows, the response time of all four algorithms improved as the size of available memory increased. Moreover, the proposed $\mathcal{B}$-**KDJ** and $\mathcal{AM}$-**KDJ** algorithms showed consistently better performance than *HS*-**KDJ** all over the examined range of memory size.

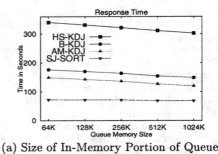

(a) Size of In-Memory Portion of Queue

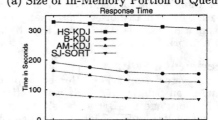

(b) Size of R-tree Buffer

Figure 13: Performance Impact of Memory Size

5.6 Impact of $e\mathcal{D}_{max}$ Estimation on $\mathcal{AM}$-KDJ Performance

We designed a set of experiments to characterize the performance of $\mathcal{AM}$-**KDJ** algorithm with respect to the accuracy of estimated $e\mathcal{D}_{max}$ values. Instead of using Equation (3) to estimate $e\mathcal{D}_{max}$, we varied the $e\mathcal{D}_{max}$ value from $0.1 \times \mathcal{D}_{max}$ to $10 \times \mathcal{D}_{max}$. Recall that $\mathcal{D}_{max}$ is a real distance between the k-th nearest pair of objects. Again, we fixed a stopping cardinality k to 100,000, and the sizes of in-memory portion of a main queue and R-tree buffer were fixed to 512 KBytes.

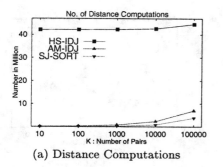
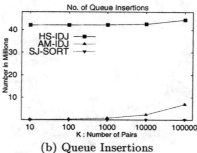
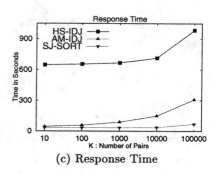

| (a) Distance Computations | (b) Queue Insertions | (c) Response Time |

Figure 12: Performance of Incremental Distance Joins

When $e\mathcal{D}_{max}$ is overestimated ($e\mathcal{D}_{max} > \mathcal{D}_{max}$), the compensation stage of $\mathcal{AM}$-KDJ algorithm is not necessary, because all the k nearest pairs will be produced in the first (aggressive pruning) stage. Even when $e\mathcal{D}_{max}$ is overestimated, $\mathcal{AM}$-KDJ guarantees that $e\mathcal{D}_{max}$ is always smaller than or equal to $q\mathcal{D}_{max}$ (obtained from a distance queue) throughout the first stage. Thus, $\mathcal{AM}$-KDJ always requires no more distance computation and queue insertion operations than $\mathcal{B}$-KDJ algorithm does.

On the other hand, if $e\mathcal{D}_{max}$ is underestimated ($e\mathcal{D}_{max} < \mathcal{D}_{max}$), the node pairs in the compensation queue will be revisited in the compensation stage. Thus, the cost of tree traversals and queue management will increase, but it will be bounded by twice the cost of $\mathcal{B}$-KDJ algorithm. As discussed in Section 4.1, for a pair already expanded once in the first stage, only child pairs not examined in the first stage are paired up in the compensation stage and thereby wasting no time for redundant work. The value of $q\mathcal{D}_{max}$ is likely to become quite close to a real $\mathcal{D}_{max}$ value in the compensation stage. So, $\mathcal{AM}$-KDJ algorithm usually prunes distant pairs much more efficiently in the compensation stage than $\mathcal{B}$-KDJ algorithm would do in a single stage. Therefore, $\mathcal{AM}$-KDJ outperforms the k-distance join algorithms HS-KDJ and $\mathcal{B}$-KDJ, despite the additional cost of compensation stage.

Figure 14 shows that as $e\mathcal{D}_{max}$ approaches to a real $\mathcal{D}_{max}$ value, the performance of $\mathcal{AM}$-KDJ improves consistently in all three metrics. When $e\mathcal{D}_{max}$ increases far beyond the real $\mathcal{D}_{max}$ value, the performance of $\mathcal{AM}$-KDJ converges to that of $\mathcal{B}$-KDJ algorithm. Importantly, however, $\mathcal{AM}$-KDJ always outperformed $\mathcal{B}$-KDJ, not to mention HS-KDJ, with $e\mathcal{D}_{max}$ in a wide spectrum of estimated value range.

We have not measured the cost of compensation queue management. A compensation queue contains pairs of non-object R-tree nodes. During the first (aggressive pruning) stage of $\mathcal{AM}$-KDJ algorithm, The number of pruned pairs is far larger than the number of non-object pairs inserted into a compensation queue. In most of our experiments, the size of a compensation queue was *less than 0.5 percent* of the size of a main queue. Thus, the additional cost required for the compensation queue was almost negligible. This is one of the reasons why $\mathcal{AM}$-KDJ algorithm always outperformed $\mathcal{B}$-KDJ, which does not need a compensation queue.

5.7 Stepwise Incremental Execution of $\mathcal{AM}$-IDJ

Incremental distance join algorithms do not require a preset stopping cardinality k. Thus, in this set of experiments, we simulated a situation where users repeatedly requested a set of 10,000 nearest pairs at a time until a total of 100,000 nearest pairs were generated. Incremental algorithms HS-IDJ and $\mathcal{AM}$-IDJ each were executed once in a single experiment run, until a total of 100,000 nearest pairs were generated. The sizes of in-memory portion of a main queue and R-tree buffer were fixed to 512 KBytes both for HS-IDJ and $\mathcal{AM}$-IDJ.

On the other hand, since SJ-SORT is not an incremental algorithm, we restarted its processing each time $i \times 10,000$ nearest pairs were generated for i ($1 \leq i \leq 9$). Thus, the performance measurements of SJ-SORT presented in Figure 15 are cumulative. For example, the response time of SJ-SORT for $k = 20,000$ includes the times spent on executing SJ-SORT twice, once for $k = 10,000$ and another for $k = 20,000$. For each run of SJ-SORT, we used a real $\mathcal{D}_{max}$ value for each of different stopping cardinalities.

In Figure 15, we measured the response time of $\mathcal{AM}$-IDJ algorithm in two different ways: (1) with $e\mathcal{D}_{max}$ values estimated by Equation (3), and (2) with real $\mathcal{D}_{max}$ values. When estimated $e\mathcal{D}_{max}$ values were provided, $\mathcal{AM}$-IDJ needed compensation processing only after generating 30,000 pairs and 90,000 pairs, due to overestimated $e\mathcal{D}_{max}$ values. In contract, when real $e\mathcal{D}_{max}$ values were provided, $\mathcal{AM}$-IDJ needed to initiate a compensation stage each time the next set of 10,000 pairs of object were requested by users. This overhead slowed down the processing due mainly to redundant R-tree node accesses. Overall, $\mathcal{AM}$-IDJ showed a fairly consistent performance over varying $e\mathcal{D}_{max}$ estimates, as $\mathcal{AM}$-KDJ did in Section 5.6. For all the k values, $\mathcal{AM}$-IDJ with estimated $e\mathcal{D}_{max}$ improved the response time by a factor of two to four, when compared with HS-IDJ.

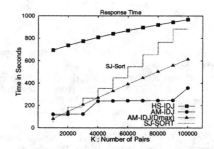

Figure 15: Step-Wise Incremental Execution

6. Conclusions

We have developed new distance join algorithms for spatial databases. The proposed algorithms provide significant performance improvement over previous work. The plane-sweep technique optimized by novel strategies for selecting

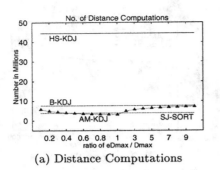

(a) Distance Computations

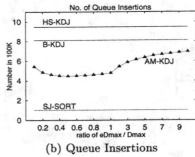

(b) Queue Insertions

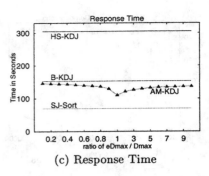

(c) Response Time

Figure 14: Performance Impact of $e\mathcal{D}_{max}$

a sweeping axis and direction minimizes the computational overhead incurred by bi-directional node expansions. We have shown that this optimized plane-sweep technique alone improves processing of a k-distance join query considerably.

The adaptive multi-stage algorithms employ aggressive pruning and compensation methods to further optimize the distance join processing. These algorithms address a slow start problem by using estimated maximum distances as cutoff values for pruning distant pairs. Assuming data objects are uniformly distributed, we have developed strategies to choose an initial estimate and to correct the estimate adaptively during the query processing. Our experimental study shows that the proposed algorithms outperformed previous work significantly and consistently over a wide spectrum of estimated maximum distances. In particular, for a relatively small stopping cardinality, the proposed algorithms achieved up to an order of magnitude improvement over previous work.

When the stopping cardinality of a distance join query is unknown (as in on-line query processing environments or a complex query that contains a distance join as a sub-query), the adaptive multi-stage algorithms process the query in a stepwise manner so that the query results can be returned incrementally. We plan to develop new strategies for estimating the maximum distances and managing queues for non-uniform data sets.

7. References

[1] L. Arge, O. Procopiuc, S. Ramaswamy, T. Suel, and J. S. Vitter. Scalable sweeping-based spatial join. In *Proceedings of the 24th VLDB Conference*, pages 259–270, New York, USA, June 1998.

[2] S. Arya, D. M. Mount, and O. Narayan. Accounting for boundary effects in nearest neighbor searching. In *Proc. 11th Annual Symp. on Computational Geometry*, pages 336–344, Vancouver, Canada, 1995.

[3] Norbert Beckmann, Hans-Peter Kriegel, Ralf Schneider, and Bernhard Seeger. The R^*-tree: An efficient and robust access method for points and rectangles. In *Proceedings of the 1990 ACM-SIGMOD Conference*, pages 322–331, Atlantic City, NJ, May 1990.

[4] S. Berchtold, B. Ertl, D. Keim, H.-P. Kriegel, and T. Seidl. Fast nearest neighbor search in high-dimensional spaces. In *Proceedings of the 14th Intl. Conf. on Data Engineering*, Orlando, Florida, September 1998.

[5] S. Berchtold, D. A. Keim, and H.-P. Kriegel. The X-tree: An index structure for high-dimensional data. In *Proceedings of the 22nd VLDB Conference*, Bombay, India, September 1996.

[6] Thomas Brinkhoff, Hans-Peter Kriegel, Ralf Schneider, and Bernhard Seeger. Multi-step processing of spatial joins. In *Proceedings of the 1994 ACM-SIGMOD Conference*, pages 197–208, Minneapolis, Minnesota, May 1994.

[7] Thomas Brinkhoff, Hans-Peter Kriegel, and Bernhard Seeger. Efficient processing of spatial joins using R-Trees. In *Proceedings of the 1993 ACM-SIGMOD Conference*, pages 237–246, Washington, DC, May 1993.

[8] Michael J. Carey and Donald Kossmann. On saying "enough already!" in SQL. In *Proceedings of the 1997 ACM-SIGMOD Conference*, pages 219–230, Tucson, AZ, May 1997.

[9] Michael J. Carey and Donald Kossmann. Reducing the braking distance of an SQL query engine. In *Proceedings of the 24th VLDB Conference*, pages 158–169, New York, NY, August 1998.

[10] Donko Donjerkovic and Raghu Ramakrishnan. Probabilistic optimization of top N queries. In *Proceedings of the 25th VLDB Conference*, Edinburgh, Scotland, September 1999.

[11] Antonin Guttman. R-Trees: A dynamic index structure for spatial searching. In *Proceedings of the 1984 ACM-SIGMOD Conference*, pages 47–57, Boston, MA, June 1984.

[12] G. R. Hjaltason and H. Samet. Ranking in spatial databases. In *Proc. of 4th Intl. Symposium on Large Spatial Databases(SSD'95)*, pages 83–95, September 1995.

[13] Gisli R. Hjaltason and Hanan Samet. Incremental distance join algorithms for spatial databases. In *Proceedings of the 1998 ACM-SIGMOD Conference*, pages 237–248, Seattle, WA, June 1998.

[14] F. Korn, N. Sidiropoulos, C. Faloutsos, E. Siegel, and Z. Protopapas. Fast nearest neighbor search in medical image databases. In *Proceedings of the 22nd VLDB Conference*, pages 215–226, June 1996.

[15] Ming-Ling Lo and Chinya V. Ravishankar. Spatial joins using seeded trees. In *Proceedings of the 1994 ACM-SIGMOD Conference*, pages 209–220, Minneapolis, Minnesota, May 1994.

[16] Ming-Ling Lo and Chinya V. Ravishankar. Spatial hashjoin. In *Proceedings of the 1996 ACM-SIGMOD Conference*, pages 247–258, Montreal, Canada, June 1996.

[17] Bureau of the Census. *Tiger/Line Precensus Files: 1997 technical documentation*. Washington, DC, 1997.

[18] Jack A. Orenstein. A comparison of spatial query processing techniques for native and parameter spaces. In *Proceedings of the 1990 ACM-SIGMOD Conference*, pages 343–352, Atlantic City, New Jersey, May 1990.

[19] Jignesh M. Patel and David J. DeWitt. Partition based spatial-merge join. In *Proceedings of the 1996 ACM-SIGMOD Conference*, pages 259–270, Montreal, Canada, June 1996.

[20] Franco P. Preparata and Michael Ian Shamos. *Computational Geometry: An Introdution*. Springer-Verlag, New York, NY, 1985.

[21] Nick Roussopoulos, Stephen Kelley, and Frederic Vincent. Nearest neighbor queries. In *Proceedings of the 1995 ACM-SIGMOD Conference*, pages 71–79, San Jose, CA, May 1995.

[22] Thomas Seidl and Hans-Peter Kriegel. Optimal multi-step k-nearest neighbor search. In *Proceedings of the 1998 ACM-SIGMOD Conference*, pages 154–165, Seattle, Washington, June 1998.

Finding replicated web collections

Junghoo Cho   Narayanan Shivakumar   Hector Garcia-Molina
Department of Computer Science
Stanford, CA 94305.
{*cho, shiva, hector*}@*db.stanford.edu*

Abstract

Many web documents (such as JAVA FAQs) are being replicated on the Internet. Often entire document collections (such as hyperlinked Linux manuals) are being replicated many times. In this paper, we make the case for identifying replicated documents and collections to improve web crawlers, archivers, and ranking functions used in search engines. The paper describes how to efficiently identify replicated documents and hyperlinked document collections. The challenge is to identify these replicas from an input data set of several tens of millions of web pages and several hundreds of gigabytes of textual data. We also present two real-life case studies where we used replication information to improve a crawler and a search engine. We report these results for a data set of 25 million web pages (about 150 gigabytes of HTML data) crawled from the web.

1   Introduction

Many documents are replicated across the web. For instance, a document containing JAVA Frequently Asked Questions (FAQs) is replicated at many sites. Furthermore, entire "collections" of hyperlinked pages are often copied across servers for fast local access, higher availability, or "marketing" of a site. We illustrate such replicated collections in Figure 1. The figure shows four actual sites that make available two collections: the JAVA 1.0.2 API documentation, and the Linux Documentation Project (LDP) manual. Other examples of commonly replicated collections include JAVA tutorials, Windows manuals, C++ manuals and even entire web sites such as ESPN's Sportszone and Yahoo. Even the Call For Papers for a database conference such as SIGMOD'00 is replicated in three web sites (`www.seas.smu.edu/sigmod2000/`, `www.dcc. unicamp.br/~mario/sigmod2000`, `www.dbai.tuwien. ac.at/pods`) across three continents. In this case, the collection is small and has a few hyperlinked documents such as the CFP, pages describing the conference com-

mittee, organizing committee and sponsorship information. In general, replicated collections constitute several hundreds or thousands of pages and are *mirrored*[1] in several tens or hundreds of web sites. For instance, the LDP collection is a 25 megabyte collection of several thousand pages, mirrored in around 180 servers across the world.

Our goal in this paper is to study how to automatically identify mirrored "collections" on the web, so that a variety of tasks can be performed more effectively. These tasks include:

- **Crawling:** A crawler fetches web pages for use by search engines and other data mining applications. A crawler can finish its job faster if it skips replicated pages and entire collections that it has visited elsewhere.

- **Ranking:** A page that has many copies, in a sense, is more important than one that does not. Thus, search results may be ranked by replication factor. If a replicated page is a member of a collection, it may also be useful to indicate this in the search result, and perhaps to provide some main entry point to the collection (e.g., its root or home page).

- **Archiving:** An archive stores a subset of the web, for historical purposes [1]. If the archive cannot store the entire web, it may give priority to collections that are known to be replicated, because of their importance and because they may represent coherent units of knowledge.

- **Caching:** A cache holds web pages that are frequently accessed by some organization. Again knowledge about collection replication can be used to save space. Furthermore, caching collections as a whole may help improve hit ratios (e.g., if a user is accessing a few pages in the LDP, chances are he will also access others in the collection).

As we will see in this paper, replication is widespread on the web, so the potential savings are very significant for each of the above tasks. For instance, consider the potential savings to the crawling task. A crawler that

---

[1]The term mirror is often used to denote a replicated collection or web site; often a mirror site has the connotation of being a "secondary copy."

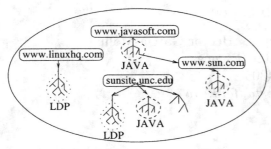

Figure 1: Mirrored document collections.

only visits one of the 180 LDP collections can avoid fetching about 4.5 gigabytes (25 MB * 180) of data. Indeed we will see in Section 5 that the crawler may save significant (over 40%!) bandwidth and time by avoiding major mirrored collections, such as LDP, JAVA API documents and Linux manuals. Recently, Bharat and Broder [2] observed similar results on data crawled by the AltaVista web crawler.

We have intuitively motivated the usefulness of detecting "replicated collections." However, there are important challenges in (1) defining the notion of a replicated collection precisely, (2) developing efficient algorithms that can identify such collections, and (3) effectively exploiting this knowledge of replication. One of the major difficulties in detecting replicated collections is that many replicas may not be strictly identical to each other. The reasons include:

1. **Update frequency:** The primary copy of a collection may often be constantly updated, while mirror copies are updated only daily, weekly, monthly, or by operator control. For instance, the Javasoft corporation maintains the primary JAVA API manuals, and the University of Edinburgh hosts the LDP collection. These primary copies are regularly updated to incorporate the most recent bug fixes and documentation updates. However the mirrors of these collections are usually out of date, depending on how often they are updated.

2. **Mirror partial coverage:** Mirror collections differ in how much they overlap with the primary. In many cases, a collection is replicated entirely. In other cases, only a subset of a collection may be mirrored, and hyperlinks point to uncopied portions in another mirror site, or at the primary.

3. **Different formats:** The documents in a collection may *not* themselves appear as exact replicas in another collection. For instance, one collection may have documents in HTML while another collection may have them in PostScript, Adobe PDF or Microsoft Word. Similarly, the documents in one collection may have additional buttons, links and inlined images that make them slightly different from other versions of the document. Still, for some applications we may wish to consider two collections in different formats to be "similar."

4. **Partial crawls:** In most cases we need to identify

replicated collections from a snapshot of the web that has been crawled or cached at one site, not by examining the original data. Thus, the data we are examining may be incomplete, e.g., because the crawler does not have the resources to fetch all data. So even if two collections are perfect replicas, their snapshots may not overlap fully. Furthermore, if the snapshots were crawled at different times, they may represent different versions, even if the originals were in perfect synchrony.

In such a scenario, it is challenging to even define what is a replicated collection, or even what is the "boundary" of a collection. For example, suppose that one site has a set S_1 of 10 pages, a second site has a set S_2 that is an exact copy of S_1, and a third site has a set S_3 containing only 5 of the S_1 pages. In this case we have at least two choices: we could say that S_1 is a replica of S_2 (ignoring S_3), or we could say that there are two additional replicas of the S_3 collection, each with 5 replicated pages. That is, in the former case we have a 10-page collection at two sites, and in the latter case we have a 5-page collection at 3 sites. If we wish to consider page and link structure similarity, we have even more choices. For instance, suppose that only 8 of the 10 pages in S_2 are identical copies of their S_1 counterparts. The remaining 2 are variants, e.g., they may have slightly different content, or may have missing or extra links. Do we still consider S_1 and S_2 to be replicas, or do we only consider corresponding sub-collections with 8 identical pages to be replicas? In the former case we have a larger collection, but in the latter case we have a more faithful replica. In this paper we study these issues, and propose a mechanism for making such decisions.

The amount of data on the web is staggering, on the order of hundreds of millions of pages and hundreds of gigabytes, and growing rapidly. Thus, whatever techniques we use for identifying replicated pages and collections must scale to very large sizes. Thus, we develop new techniques for analyzing and manipulating our data.

After replicated collections have been identified, a final challenge is how to exploit effectively this information to improve crawling, ranking, archiving, caching and other applications. For instance, should a crawler try to identify replicas as it performs its first crawl, or should it first do a full crawl, then identify replicas, and skip mirrors on subsequent crawls? If replicas are skipped, should the crawler still visit them infrequently to make sure they are still copies? In this paper while we do *not* focus on this category of challenges, we briefly touch on some of the crawling and ranking issues in Section 5, where we present our experimental results.

In summary, the contributions of this paper are the following:

- **Computable similarity measures:** We define a

practical similarity measure for collections of web pages, and study options for defining boundaries of replicated collections. We carefully design these measures so that in addition to being "good" measures, we can efficiently compute them over hundreds of gigabytes of data on disk. Our work is in contrast to recent work in the Information Retrieval domain [10] where the emphasis is on accurately comparing link structures of document collections, when the document collections are small. We then develop efficient heuristic algorithms to identify replicated sets of pages and collections.

- **Improved crawling:** We discuss how we use replication information to improve web crawling by avoiding redundant crawling in the Google system.[2] We report on how our algorithms and similarity measures performed on over 150 gigabytes of textual data crawled from the web (about 25 million web pages).

- **Reduce clutter from search engines:** Finally, we discuss how we used replication information for another task, that of improving how web search engines present search results. We have built an alternative search interface to the Google web search engine. This prototype shows significantly less clutter than in current web search engines, by clustering together replicated pages and collections. Based on informal user testing, we have observed this simple new interface helps the user quickly focus on the key results for a search over web data.

In Section 2 we discuss our similarity measures for pages and collections. Then in Section 3 we present our algorithm for efficiently identifying groups of similar collections. In Section 4 we informally evaluate the quality of our similarity measure, while in Section 5 we report on our experience using our techniques for improving web crawling and result displaying.

2 Similarity of collections

Our goal is to identify collections of web pages that are "approximate replicas" or "similar." As a first step, it is instructive to define the notion of "identical collections." By relaxing that definition, we will then be able to obtain a useful notion of approximate collections.

The following definitions set the stage for our definition of identical collections. Note that when we refer to a web page we refer to its textual (or image) content. The hyperlinks are modeled separately, as arcs between pages.

Definition 1 (Web graph) Given a set of web pages, the web graph $G = (V, E)$ has a node v_i for each web page p_i, and a directed edge from v_i to v_j if there is a hyperlink from page p_i to p_j. □

Definition 2 (Collection) A collection is an induced subgraph of the web graph G. (Recall that an induced subgraph $G' = (V', E')$ of a graph $G = (V, E)$, only has edges between the vertices in the subgraph.) The number of pages in the collection is the *collection size*. Collection C' is a *subcollection* of C, if it is an induced subgraph of C. □

Notice that our graph model does not capture the position or anchor text of web hyperlinks within their pages. For example, our model does not distinguish between two pages with identical text and identical hyperlinks that are located in different places on the page. This is an acceptable simplification since our ultimate goal is to find similar clusters.

Also notice that we have not restricted a collection to reside at a single web site or to be connected. In practice, one may be only interested in collections at a single site (e.g., when improving crawling), but this single-site condition can be enforced later as (or after) collections are identified. Similarly, a collection whose pages are not connected via hyperlinks may be undesirable because it represents a set of unrelated pages. Again, this additional restriction can be enforced as collections are identified.

Definition 3 (Identical[3] collections) Equi-sized collections C_1 and C_2 are identical ($C_1 \equiv C_2$) if there is a one-to-one mapping M that maps all C_1 pages to C_2 pages (and vice-versa) such that:

- **Identical pages:** For each page $p \in C_1$, $p \equiv M(p)$. That is, the corresponding pages have identical content.

- **Identical link structure:** For each link in C_1 from page a to b, we have a link from $M(a)$ to $M(b)$ in C_2. □

As discussed in the Introduction, many replicated collections of interest are not strictly identical. Thus, we need to relax Definition 3 so that "similar" collections can be identified. Since there are many different ways to relax this definition, we need to keep in mind two important objectives: (a) We want a notion of similarity that tracks our intuitive notions. That is, the collections we identify as similar should appear to a human to be "close copies" of each other. (b) It should be possible to efficiently and automatically check for similarity, so it is feasible to search for similar collections over huge number of web pages. In the rest of this section we discuss the relaxations we believe meet these criteria and that lead to our definition of similarity. In Sections 3 and 4 we use our definition to identify similar clusters on the web and to validate our reasoning.

2.1 Similarity of web pages

Definition 3 requires that matching pages in identical collections be identical. One first step in relaxing

---

[2]Google [3] is a search engine developed in our group; it is currently commercially available at www.google.com.

[3]These are sometimes referred to as *label preserving isomorphs* in graph terminology. We use the term *identical* to be consistent with other definitions we introduce.

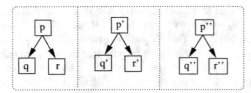

Figure 2: Collections with similar pages.

this definition is to allow the matching pages to be approximate replicas. For example, in Figure 2 we show three collections. Solid, small boxes represent pages, arrows between pages are the hyperlinks, and the dotted boxes encompass collections. We have labeled the top page in each collection as p, p' and p'' to suggest that their contents are similar. We have labeled the other pages analogously. Given that the link structure across these collections is identical, it seems natural to say that this cluster of three collections is similar.

One can determine the similarity of two pages in a variety of ways. For instance, one can use the information retrieval notion of textual similarity [11]. One could also use data mining techniques to cluster pages into groups that share meaningful terms (e.g., [9]), and then define pairs of pages within a cluster to be similar. A third option is to compute textual overlap by counting the number of *chunks* of text (e.g., sentences or paragraphs) that pages share in common [12, 13, 5, 2]. In all schemes, there is a threshold parameter that indicates how close pages have to be (e.g., in terms of number of shared words, n-dimensional distance, number of overlapping chunks) to be considered similar. This parameter needs to be empirically adjusted according to the target application.

We expand on the textual overlap option since it is the one we use in our experiments. To compute text overlap, we first convert each page from its native format (e.g., HTML, PostScript) into simple textual information using standard converters.[4] The resulting page is then chunked into smaller textual units (e.g., lines or sentences). Each textual chunk is then hashed down to a 32-bit *fingerprint*. If two pages share more than some threshold T of chunks with identical fingerprints, then the pages are said to be similar.

In prior work [12, 13], we have shown this definition to be effective in approximating the human notion of pages that share significant content. (We also discuss the choices of textual units and threshold T in these references.) Broder et al. [5, 4, 2] also report similar results. Furthermore, these references also show that checking for similarity has a low cost, so it is feasible to compute page similarity over very large collections. Hence, this is the definition of similarity we use in our experiments. However, it is important to note that any definition of page similarity could be used in

---

[4]Converters such as ps2ascii and html2ascii are not always exact converters and cannot handle non-ASCII objects such as figures and equations in the text. But for our application, we believe this problem is not significant.

our forthcoming definition of similar collections, and that any definition could be used in our algorithm for identifying similar clusters (although performance would suffer if a more expensive definition were used).

Given that we have a function to determine similarity of two pages, we still need to discuss how it is used to compare collections. Returning to our example, suppose that p is similar to p', that p' is similar to p'', but that p and p'' are *not* similar. Do we still wish to consider the three collections shown in Figure 2 similar, or do we wish to consider them pair-wise similar (e.g., the leftmost collection is only similar to the center one)? Our decision here is to consider all three collections similar (transitive similarity), mainly because it significantly reduces the cost of computing similarity. If we wished to compute pair-wise similarities, we would need to consider all possible pairs of all possible collections (in our example we would have to try to match the center collection against the left one and the right one). With transitive similarities, we only need to figure out how to partition our pages into similar collections. (This tradeoff will become more apparent as we describe the cluster identification algorithm.)

In our experience, transitive similarity still identifies groups of pages that are closely related. For example, p' may have been obtained from p (e.g., by extracting the plain text from a postscript file), and then p'' may have been obtained from p' (e.g., by appending some comments to the file). Even though the similarity test fails for p and p'', in most cases a human would still consider all three pages to be approximate copies.

The following definition formalizes the notion of transitive similarity that will be used in our definition of cluster similarity.

Definition 4 (Page similarity) We are given a test, $ST(p_i, p_j)$, for determining if a pair of pages p_i and p_j are pair-wise similar. Based on this test, we say that two pages are (transitively) similar, $p_i \approx p_j$, if there is some sequence of pages $p_1, p_2, \ldots, p_k$ in our web graph, such that $ST(p_i, p_1), ST(p_1, p_2), \ldots, ST(p_k, p_j)$. □

2.2 Similarity of link structure

We also wish to consider collections as similar even if their link structure does not match exactly. The following four examples illustrate the decision that we must make in defining precisely what it means for link structures to match approximately. The examples are shown in Figures 3 (a) – (d). In each example, we refer to the first collection as $[i]$ and the second collection as $[ii]$. If two pages have the same label, then they are similar. For example, $[i].p \approx [ii].p$.

- **Collection sizes:** In Figure 3(a), we show two collections. They are identical except for the additional page $[ii].s$ and the link from $[ii].p$ to $[ii].s$. It seems natural to say that these two collections are similar, since the differences are "relatively small." That is, we can find a function M, analogous to

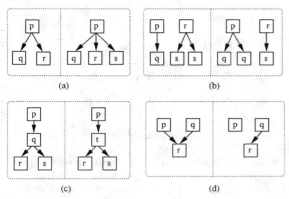

Figure 3: Example pairs of collections.

the one in Definition 3, that maps "almost all" pages in one collection to similar pages in the other collection. However, we will require similar collections to be equi-sized for two reasons. The first is that identifying collections that are similar (and the corresponding mapping functions) is much simpler if we are only looking for collections of equal size. Trying to locate collections of different sizes means we need to compare many more collections. The second reason is that, if desired, one can add a second phase to the search process to identify collections of different sizes. In our example, we would first identify the core similar collections (with pages p, q and r). Then the second phase would search for pages (like s) that could be added to one or the other collection, while still maintaining some notion of similarity. In this paper we only cover the first phase where equi-sized collections are identified.

- **One-to-one:** In Figure 3(b) we show two equi-sized collections that, again, could be considered similar by some. Notice that $[ii].p$ points to two copies of $[ii].q$, while $[i].p$ points to one copy of $[i].q$. Similarly, $[i].r$ and $[ii].r$ point to two copies of $[i].s$ and one copy of $[ii].s$ respectively. In this case, we can easily compute a mapping M from all pages in one collection to some similar page in the other collection. However, this mapping is not one-to-one. In this paper we will restrict our search to one-to-one mappings in order to constrain complexity. Collections like the ones in Figure 3(b) will be deemed dissimilar, but we believe that this is tolerable in practice. The collections that might be missed because they cannot be matched by one-to-one mappings are not common because they contain replicas within the collection, which is unusual.

- **Break points:** In Figure 3(c) we see that the two link structures look similar, with the exception that pages $[i].q$ and $[ii].t$ are different. We could define the two collections to be similar since most of the pages in one collection can be mapped to a similar page in the other collection. For instance, we can compute a mapping M that maps $[i].p$ to $[ii].p$, $[i].r$ to $[ii].r$ and $[i].s$ to $[ii].s$ (and

vice versa). This only omits $[i].q$ and $[ii].t$ from the mapping since they have different content. Thus, when defining collection similarity, we could require that only a "large fraction" of the pages be mapped (by a one-to-one mapping) to similar pages. However, to control complexity, we will again be more conservative and *require that all pages be mapped to similar pages*. The price we pay is that certain collections, like the one in Figure 3(c), will not be identified as similar. Instead, the dissimilar pages (like q and t) will break the collection into smaller collections. In our very simple example, pages $[i].p$ and $[ii].p$ would be identified as similar collections. The r and the s pages would form other collections. We call pages like q and r *break points* because they split similar collections. If break points are a problem, we could introduce a second phase that tries to combine similar collections that are connected via "short" segments. We do not discuss such a second phase further in this paper. In Section 5 we will informally evaluate the occurrance of break points.

- **Link similarity:** Figure 3(d) highlights another issue. We could say the two collections are similar since each similar page shares similar incoming links. For instance, $[ii].r$ has an incoming link from $[ii].q$, and the page that matches with $[ii].r$, i.e., $M([ii].r) = [i].r$, has one from the corresponding page $M([ii].q) = [i].q$. In the reverse direction, $[i].r$ has two incoming links, and at least of one them ($[i].q$ to $[i].r$) has a matching link. Note that the incoming links to the p and q pages match across the collections (no incoming links in either case).

  For our similarity test, we will require that matching pages have *at least one* matching incoming link, unless neither page has any incoming links. Having at least one link ensures that if one collection is a tree, then any similar collection must have the same tree structure. If one collection is a DAG with a single root page from which all pages can be reached, then the property ensures that in a similar collection all pages will be reachable from the node that matches the root.

  One could use a stronger definition requiring more matching incoming links. For instance, if $[i].r$ had 10 incoming links, we could require $[ii].r$ to have not just one analogous link, but say 8 (80%) analogous links. We do not use here such conservative definitions because they lead to more expensive similarity tests, and because most collections of interest have root pages or tree-like structures, and the at-least-one-link test is quite good at identifying what humans consider similar collections. Also note that we could phrase our test in terms of outgoing (as opposed to incoming) links, but we believe that this gives a test of equivalent usefulness.

We have described step by step the considerations that lead us to the following definition for similar

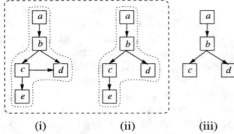

(i)   (ii)   (iii)

Figure 4: One possible similar cluster.

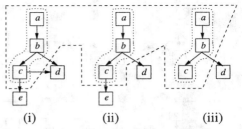

(i)   (ii)   (iii)

Figure 5: Another possible similar cluster.

collections. As we have stated, there are many different ways to define similarity, and our contribution here is to present one that is logically sound, that leads to efficient algorithms, and that identifies many of the collections that humans would call similar. After our definitions, we will present an algorithm for efficiently identifying similar collections, and in Section 5 we will present experimental results to substantiate our claim that our notions of similarity are useful and natural for the web.

Definition 5 (Similar collections) Equisized collections C_1 and C_2 are similar (i.e, $C_1 \cong C_2$) if there is a one-to-one mapping M (and vice-versa) that maps all C_1 pages to all C_2 pages such that:

- **Similar pages:** Each page $p \in C_1$ has a matching page $M(p) \in C_2$, such that $p \approx M(p)$.

- **Similar links:** For each page p in C_1, let $P_1(p)$ be the set of pages in C_1 that have a link to page p. Similarly define $P_2(M(p))$ for pages in C_2. Then we have pages $p_1 \in P_1(p)$ and $p_2 \in P_2(M(p))$ such that $p_1 \approx p_2$ (unless both $P_1(p)$ and $P_2(M(p))$ are empty). That is, two corresponding pages should have at least one parent (in their corresponding collections) that are also similar pages.   □

We will call a group of collections a *cluster*, and if the collections in a cluster are similar, then we will call it a *similar cluster*. The following definitions formalize these notions.

Definition 6 (Cluster) We define a set of equi-sized collections to be a *cluster*. The number of collections in the cluster is the *cluster cardinality*. If s is the collection size of each collection in the cluster, the *cluster size* is s as well.   □

Definition 7 (Identical cluster) Cluster $R = \{C_1, C_2, \ldots, C_n\}$ is an *identical cluster* if $\forall i, j$, $C_i \equiv C_j$. That is, all its collections are identical.   □

Definition 8 (Similar cluster) A cluster $R = \{C_1, C_2, \ldots, C_n\}$ is similar if all of its collections are pairwise similar, i.e., if for $\forall i, j$, $C_i \cong C_j$.   □

3   Computing similar clusters

Our goal is now to identify similar clusters within a given web graph. To illustrate the challenges, consider the graph shown in Figure 4. In this figure we have identified one similar cluster (dashed line), consisting of

two collections (dotted lines). (Again, pages with the same label are similar.) Here the cluster cardinality is 2, while the collection size is 5. Figure 5 shows a different cluster in exactly the same web graph. This cluster has cardinality 3 and its collections have size 3. Our examples show that different types of similar clusters can be found in a web graph, and that there are complex interactions between the number of clusters found, their cardinalities, and the sizes of their collections.

In general, we could postulate an objective function to optimize in our cluster search process. This function would give a value to a particular set of clusters, based on the number of clusters, their cardinalities, and the sizes of the collections. Unfortunately, searching for the optimal clustering would be extremely expensive, since in principle one would have to consider all possible ways to form collections and clusters.

Instead of such a generalized search for the best clustering, we propose here a clustering algorithm that "grows" clusters from smaller sized ones. As we will see, the algorithm favors larger cardinalities over larger collections.

Figure 6 illustrates how the algorithm works. The algorithm first computes *trivial clusters* on the given web graph. These clusters have collections of size one and are found by grouping similar pages. For example, the two pages labeled t are determined to be similar, and form one of the trivial clusters. (This cluster has two collections, each with a single page. We do not show the dotted lines that form the collections to avoid cluttering the figure.) Figure 6(a) shows the trivial clusters found in this example web graph.

Next, the algorithm merges trivial clusters that can lead to similar clusters with larger collections. We detail this process below (Figure 6(b)). The outcome is shown in Figure 6(c), where trivial clusters a, b, c and d have been merged into a larger-size cluster. (Again, clusters are shown with dashed lines, collections with dotted lines. Collections with a single page are not shown to avoid clutter.) The remaining trivial clusters are not merged. For example, the t cluster is not merged with the larger cluster because it would lead the collections to be of different sizes and hence not similar by our definition. Notice that the s and g clusters could form a larger cluster (with a single collection of size 2). However, our algorithm does *not* generate disconnected collections (see Section 2), so s and g are left as separate clusters.

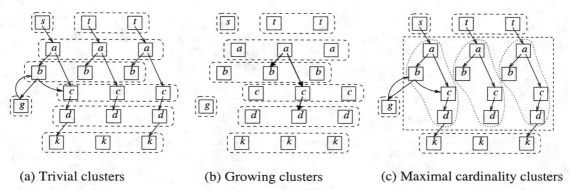

| (a) Trivial clusters | (b) Growing clusters | (c) Maximal cardinality clusters |

Figure 6: Growing similar clusters.

3.1 Growth strategy

We now discuss how to merge clusters. Consider two trivial similar clusters $R_i = \{p_1, p_2, \ldots, p_n\}$ and $R_j = \{q_1, q_2, \ldots, q_m\}$, where p_k and q_k $(1 \leq k \leq n)$ are pages in R_i and R_j. We define:

1. $s_{i,j}$ to be the number of pages in R_i with links *to* at least one page in R_j,
2. $d_{i,j}$ to be the number of pages in R_j with links *from* at least one page in R_i,
3. $|R_i|$ to be the number of pages in R_i, and
4. $|R_j|$ to be the number of pages in R_j.

We say that two trivial clusters R_i and R_j can be joined if they satisfy the *merge condition* $|R_i| = s_{i,j} = d_{i,j} = |R_j|$. This condition implies that each page in R_i has a hyperlink to a unique page in R_j. For example, consider trivial clusters a and b in Figure 6(a). They each have three collections, and each of the three b pages has an incoming link from one of the a pages. Thus, these two trivial clusters satisfy the merge condition, and can form a larger cluster of three collections, where each collection has one of the a pages and the b page it points to. Such a larger cluster clearly meets the conditions of Definition 5.

Continuing with the example, notice that trivial cluster c can be joined with the $\{a, b\}$ cluster we have just formed. This is because the merge condition holds between c and one of the trivial clusters (b) that formed the $\{a, b\}$ cluster. The new cluster can be formed by adding each c page to the collection containing the b page that points to that c page. Similarly, we can merge the d cluster, to obtain the cluster shown in Figure 6(c).

We can see that the resulting cluster (with collections of size 4) satisfies Definition 8, that is, each collection is similar to the others in the cluster. For instance, consider page c in the leftmost collection of Figure 6(c). It has matching pages in the other two collections of the cluster, and at least one of the incoming arcs (the one from a) is found in the other collections. This guaranteed arc is the one that was used to grow trivial cluster c into this larger cluster. Similarly, all pages in the leftmost collection have matching pages in the other collections.

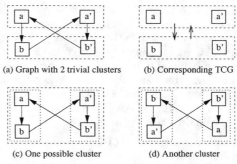

| (a) Graph with 2 trivial clusters | (b) Corresponding TCG |
| (c) One possible cluster | (d) Another cluster |

Figure 7: Impact of start point for merge.

Our clustering algorithm proceeds in this fashion. Conceptually, it consists of the following steps:

1. Find all trivial clusters.
2. Form a trivial cluster graph (TCG) $G = (V, E)$, where each vertex v_i in V corresponds to one of the trivial clusters, and we have an edge from v_i to v_j if v_i, v_j satisfy the merge condition. The TCG for our running example is shown in Figure 6(b).
3. Merge each connected component of the TCG into a similar cluster. The merge process for a connected component can start at any node from which all the others in the component can be reached.

In some cases there can be more than one place to start the merge process for a connected component. Figure 7 shows one example with two trivial clusters a and b. The TCG has a cycle between these two nodes, so we can start the process at either node. If we start at a, we obtain the cluster shown in Figure 7(c), while if we start with b we obtain the cluster in Figure 7(d). In practice, one of these clusters may be better than the other because the collections have a more natural entry point or root. One possible way to identify the more natural starting point is to select the page with the largest number of incoming links *from other web sites*. Thus, if more sites have links to a (either copy) than to b, then a may be a more natural starting point, and the cluster in Figure 7(c) would be preferable.

It can be shown that our clustering algorithm yields similar clusters, using the arguments outlined in our

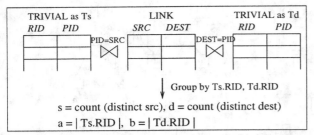

Figure 8: Join-based construction of *LinkSummary* table

Algorithm 0.1   *Cluster growing algorithm*
Inp :   Tables *Trivial* and *Link*,
Out :   The set of similar clusters
Procedure
   [0] $S \leftarrow \{\}$ // S: the set of similar clusters
   [1] Construct *LinkSummary* table with schema
      $\langle Ts.RID, Td.RID, a, b, s, d \rangle$ based on Figure 8
   [2] For each entry in *LinkSummary*
   [3]   If $(a = s = d = b)$
   [4] $S \leftarrow S \cup \{\langle Ts.RID, Td.RID \rangle\}$
        // Coalesce Ts.RID and Td.RID
   [5] Return "UNION-FIND(S)"
      // Find connected components

Figure 9: Cluster growing algorithm.

example. As illustrated by our example, our algorithm only produces clusters with connected collections (e.g., s and g were not merged in Figure 6). We believe this yields more natural results. However, the merge condition can easily be extended to merge collections that have no links between them. Finally, the algorithm gives preference to cardinality over collection size. That is, the algorithm will identify the largest-cardinality similar cluster that may be formed (with connected collections), even if its collections have only one page. From the remaining pages, it will identify the next largest-cardinality cluster, and so on.

3.2   Implementing the cluster growing algorithm

The clustering algorithm we have described can be implemented very efficiently by relying on good database algorithms. Initially we compute all similar page pairs using an iceberg algorithm [7]. These algorithms efficiently find tuples in a table that occur more than some threshold number of times. In our case, the table contains each instance of a shared chunk between two pages, and the threshold is the number of common chunks needed between similar pages (Section 2). The output of the iceberg algorithm is a second table containing the pairs of pages that are directly similar (function ST of Definition 4). We then perform a simple disk-based UNION-FIND [6] algorithm that performs sequential scans over this table and computes trivial similar clusters. The output of this phase is a table TRIVIAL(rid, pid), which contains tuple $\langle R_i, p_j \rangle$ to indicate that page p_j is in trivial cluster R_i. This table materializes all trivial similar clusters as per Definition 8.

Figure 9 shows how to implement the cluster growing algorithm efficiently. It expects as input table TRIVIAL(rid, pid) and a second table, LINK($src, dest$), giving the links in the web graph. (Tuple $\langle p_i, p_j \rangle$ is in LINK if p_i has a hyperlink to p_j.) In Step [1] we preprocess the data, using relational operators, to compute link statistics ($s_{i,j}, d_{i,j}, |R_i|$, and $|R_j|$) for every pair of trivial clusters, R_i and R_j. Well known relational query optimization techniques can be used to execute this step efficiently. In Steps [2] – [4] we compute all pairs of trivial clusters that satisfy the merge condition. Finally, we compute our maximal-cardinality similar clusters in Step [5] using the classical UNION-FIND algorithm [6]. In this step, we are conceptually regaining the collec-

tion structure (i.e., Figure 6(c)) by merging collections based on computing connected components.

4   Quality of similarity measures

In defining our notion of similar clusters we made a number of choices, to arrive at an efficient algorithm for identifying clusters. In this section we describe experiments performed to *informally* evaluate the "quality" of the clusters found by our algorithm. We stress that since there is no single way to identify similar clusters, even if performance were not an issue, there is no definitive quality measure. Instead, we simply provide some examples and statistics to describe the characteristics of the clusters identified by our algorithm and by our definition of similarity.

We chose 25 widely replicated web collections (e.g., Perl, XML, JAVA manuals) from their primary sites (e.g., www.perl.org). We call these collections the *targets* to distinguish them from the potentially different collections that may be identified by our algorithm. The sizes of the targets varied between 50 and 1000 pages. For each target we automatically downloaded between five and ten mirrored versions from the web. The mirrored targets were different versions of the primary version, either older or slightly modified versions (e.g., additional links or inlined images). The total number of web pages so downloaded was approximately 35,000. In addition, we added 15,000 randomly crawled pages to this data set. We assume these pages were unrelated to each other and the targets we had already downloaded.

On this data set we computed similar clusters using our cluster growing algorithm. We then manually examined these clusters to see if they corresponded to the mirrored targets. Our algorithm identified 180 nontrivial collections. Of these, 149 collections formed 25 clusters, corresponding to our 25 targets. Each of these clusters had at least 2 collections.

The remaining 31 collections did not correspond to a target, and hence we call them "problem" collections. Upon examining the problem collections, we discovered that many were caused by what we call *partial mirrors*, as illustrated by Figure 10(a). The figure (left side) shows a collection [ii] that is a partial mirror of the [i] collection. That is, some of the [ii] pages point to

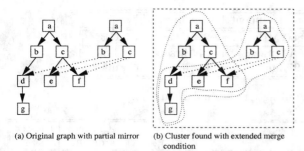

(a) Original graph with partial mirror

(b) Cluster found with extended merge condition

Figure 10: Example of partial mirrors.

the unmirrored portions of the first collection. In this case, our cluster growing algorithm would only identify a cluster with the collections $[i].\{a, b, c\}$ and $[ii].\{a, b, c\}$, leaving the other pages as "problem collections."

In some cases (e.g., for improving crawling), it is more useful if similar collections include the partially mirrored pages. In our example, it may be better to identify the two collections shown in Figure 10(b), where pages d, e, f and g appear in both collections.

Our cluster growing algorithm can be easily extended to identify partially mirrored collections, if so desired. This can be achieved by modifying the merge condition used by the algorithm: We now merge trivial clusters R_i and R_j whenever $|R_i| = s_{i,j} \geq d_{i,j} = |R_j|$. This weaker condition arises when pages in R_j have "virtual" links from pages in R_i, i.e., the R_j pages are not mirrored in as many sites as the R_i pages. We call the clusters produced by our modified merging condition as *extended clusters*.

Returning to our experiment, we ran the extended algorithm on our data set, and observed that only 8 collections were "problem collections." That is, 23 $(31 - 8)$ of the collections found by the original algorithm were caused by partial mirrors, and were now properly clustered by the extended condition. All the remaining collections $(180 - 8)$ correspond to the desired targets.

In summary, our algorithm (especially with the extension we have described) is very good at identifying what a human would call a replicated collection of web pages (i.e., our target collections). However, it is important to note that in this experiment, the target collections were fully crawled. In practice, our algorithm may be run on data that includes partially crawled collections, and clearly it will not be possible to identify the complete target collection, no matter what clustering algorithm is used. In the next section we explore this more realistic scenario, and show that even with partial crawls, our algorithm can still yield significant benefits.

5 Exploiting similar clusters

To demonstrate the usefulness of similar clusters, we explored the use of our cluster growing algorithm in two applications, crawling and searching. Our results also demonstrate that the algorithm is efficient, since we had to identify clusters in hundreds of gigabytes of web data.

For our work we used data crawled by the Stanford Google web crawler [3]. We ran our experiments on a SUN UltraSPARC with dual processors, 256 MBs of RAM and 1.4 GBs of swap space, running SunOS 5.5.1.

5.1 Improving crawling

For the first application, we performed a comprehensive performance analysis of web crawlers to identify how much redundant data they crawl. This allowed us to quantify the resources (such as network bandwidth) crawlers waste in visiting multiple copies of pages and collections. As we will see, our performance analysis helped us significantly improve the performance of the Google crawler.

We used the Google crawler since it was developed within our group and we had direct access to its data. We believe that analogous results could be obtained using the data from other crawlers. Indeed, in some recent work, other researchers report results similar to our own in the context of the AltaVista web crawler [5, 2]. The Google crawler fed us approximately 25 million web pages primarily from domains located in the United States of America. This dataset corresponds to about 150 gigabytes of textual information.

We experimented with three different chunking strategies for identifying similar pages: (1) one fingerprint for the entire document, (2) one fingerprint for every four lines of text, and (3) one fingerprint for every two lines of text. For each scheme we generated a *DocChunks* table, where each tuple gives a URL (represented as a 32-bit integer) and the fingerprint (32 bits) for one chunk in that document. By joining the *DocChunks* table with itself, we can generate the table of shared fingerprints that is the input to the cluster growing algorithm (Section 3.2). To give the reader an idea of the resources utilized, we report in Table 1 the storage cost for table *DocChunks*, as well as the time breakdown in computing the set of trivial similar clusters. The thresholds used were $T = 15$ and $T = 25$ for the "four line" and "two line" fingerprints respectively.

In Figure 11 we report the number of similar pages for each the three chunkings. For instance, let us consider the case when we compute one fingerprint on the entire document. About 64% of the 25 million web pages have no replicas (the left-most darkest bar) except itself: about 18% of pages have an additional exact copy – that is, there are about $\frac{1}{2} * \frac{18}{100} * 25 * 10^6$ distinct pages that have one exact copy among the other $\frac{1}{2} * \frac{18}{100} * 25 * 10^6$ pages in this category. Similarly, about 5% of pages have between 10 and 100 replicas. As expected, the percentage of pages with more than one similar page increases when we relax the notion of similarity from 36% $(100 - 64\%)$ for exact replicas, to about 48% $(100 - 52\%)$ for "two-line" chunks.

From the above experiments, it is clear that the Google crawler wastes significant resources crawling multiple copies of pages. Our next step was to identify the similar clusters, in order to help Google avoid

	Measures / Signatures	Entire document	Four lines	Two lines
Space	Fingerprints	800 MBs	2.4 GBs	4.6 GBs
Time	Compute fingerprints	44 hrs	44 hrs	44 hrs
	Compute trivial similar clusters	97 mins	302 mins	630 mins

Table 1: Storage and time costs for computing trivial similar clusters.

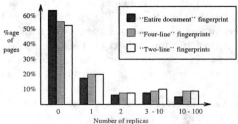

Figure 11: Document replication on 25 million web pages.

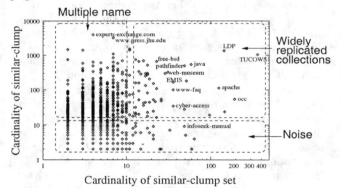

Figure 12: Distribution of maximal clusters.

	Description	Cluster cardinality	Cluster size
1	TUCOWS WinSock utilities `http://www.tucows.com`	360	1052
2	Linux Documentation Project `http://sunsite.unc.edu/LDP`	143	1359
3	Apache Web server `http://www.apache.org`	125	115
4	JAVA 1.0.2 API `http://java.sun.com`	59	552
5	Mars Pathfinder `http://mars.jpl.nasa.gov`	49	498

Table 2: Popular web collections.

crawling similar collections. We ran our extended cluster growing algorithm on the collected web graph, a process that took about 20 hours total. The algorithm was modified to consider only collections at a single web site.

In Figure 12, we visualize each cluster as a point in the graph, based on the cluster cardinality and size. For the reader's convenience, we annotate some of the points that correspond to document collections (we manually labeled these points after automatically computing extended clusters). For instance, the LDP point (near the top right corner) indicates that the LDP collection constitutes 1349 pages and has 143 replicas in our crawled data set. Based on our manual examination of the data, we *roughly* partitioned the clusters into the following categories, which are also shown in Figure 12.

1. **Widely replicated collections:** We found several extended clusters that corresponded to widely replicated collections. We list the five clusters with the largest cardinalities in Table 2. For instance, the TUCOWS WinSock utilities is replicated at 360 web sites across the world, constitutes about 1052 web pages and the principal copy is located at the listed URL.

2. **Multiple name servers:** In many cases, a set of machines in a single domain share content even if the machines have different IP addresses. Web sites such as `www.experts-exchange.com` fall into this category.

3. **Noise:** Most of the identified clusters in the area labeled "Noise" were not significant or very meaningful. For instance, many web sites have HTML versions of PowerPoint slides created by the "Save As HTML" feature in Microsoft PowerPoint. Readers may be aware that PowerPoint saves each slide as an image file (such as in .GIF format) and creates a slide-show of HTML pages. Each such HTML page has the same content and hyperlink structure but points to the inlined GIF rendering of the corresponding slide. Since our system computes page similarity based on textual content and not based on image similarity, PowerPoint slide-shows are placed into the same cluster. In a few cases, small clusters were induced by "break point" pages. Fortunately, the noise clusters can easily be identified by their small size (less than 10 pages in their collections), so it is easy to ignore them when using similar clusters to improve crawling.

Based on the above rough classification, we precoded information about the widely replicated collections and machines with multiple names into the Google web crawler. We then ran the crawler again and the crawler avoided the precoded collections and machines. This time, 35 million web pages corresponding to about 250 gigabytes of textual data were crawled. Notice that this is a larger crawl than the original one (which was for 25 million pages), so it included a significant amount of new data. Of course, since the web is very dynamic, a significant amount of the "old" data had also changed.

Nevertheless, the second crawl avoided many of the replicated collections very successfully. To confirm this, we again computed the set of similar pages as in the earlier experiments. We observed that the number of similar pages had dropped from a staggering 48% in the previous crawl to a more reasonable 13%. Similarly, the number of identical copies also fell to about 8%. The number of similar and exact pages did not drop to zero in the new crawl because new clusters were identified in the new data. These newly identified replicated collections could be added to the list of pages to avoid in future crawls.

In general, the replica avoiding process is a continuous one. Each crawl identifies new replicated collections that can be avoided in the future. In steady state, the number of newly identified replicas should be relatively small at each iteration. In addition, it is important to periodically revisit what are thought to be replicated collections to see if they have changed and need to be removed from the avoid list. We have not yet implemented such a general replica-avoidance scheme into our crawler, but we believe that the results we have shown here clearly illustrate the large potential savings. As the web continues to grow, and crawlers struggle to keep up [8], it will be even more important to avoid replicated pages!

5.2 Improving search engine result presentation

For some applications it makes sense for the crawler to continue gathering multiple copies of a collection. For example, in searching the web, one of the page replicas may be unavailable, so the user may wish to visit another copy. For some data mining, for instance, it may be better to analyze all copies, not just a representative collection. But even if the crawler collects all pages, it may still be very useful to filter out redundancy as information is presented to the user.

To illustrate this point, consider how a web search engine operates today. When we search for concepts such as "object-oriented programming" or "Linux" on the web, search engines return a list of pages ranked using some proprietary ranking function. The resulting display is often distracting for the following two reasons:

- Multiple pages within a hyperlinked collection are displayed. For instance, in Figure 13 we show an example of how the Google search engine displays[5] results for the search for "XML databases." We see that several pages in www.techweb.com satisfy this query and links to all these pages are displayed.
- Links to replicated collections are displayed several times. For instance, in Figure 13, the TechWeb collection that is available at www.techweb.com and techweb.cmp.com (among other sites), is displayed multiple times.

---
[5]The screen shots are for the initial Google prototype, not the newer commercial version.

We have implemented a prototype presentation filter that runs on top of the Google search engine to illustrate how search results can be better organized. The prototype computes similar clusters on the complete data collected by the crawler, and then uses the information to address the two problems identified above. In Figure 14 we show how our prototype displays the results for the user query "XML databases." As we can see, the prototype "rolls up" collections so that it only displays the link of one page in a collection, even if multiple pages within the collection satisfy the query. For example, there is a single page listed from www.techweb.com. Also the prototype automatically "rolls up" replicas of collections as well. In our example, the replica pages for techweb.cmp.com are not listed at all.

Notice that in our prototype display each result has two additional links marked **Collection** and **Replica**. When a user clicks on the **Collection** link, the collection is rolled down and all pages satisfying the user query are displayed. Similarly, when the user clicks on the **Replica** link, the prototype displays all the replicas of the collection. We believe such an interface is useful to a user, since the interface gives the user a "high-level" overview of the results rather than just a long list of URLs.

We evaluated the above search interface informally within our group. In general, users have found this prototype to be valuable especially for queries in technical areas. For instance, when our users tried queries in topics such as Latex, C++, Latex, JAVA, XML and GNU software, traditional search engines typically yield many redundant results. The same queries yielded much better results in our prototype because of the clustering. Hence we believe that by computing similar clusters and rolling up collections and clusters, we can improve current search engines significantly.

6 Conclusion

In this paper we have introduced a new definition for similarity of collections of web pages. We have also proposed a new algorithm for efficiently identifying similar collections that form what we call a similar cluster. In developing our definitions and algorithm, we have made tradeoffs between the generality of the similar cluster concept and the cost of identifying collections that meet the criteria. No definition of similarity will capture precisely what a human would consider a similar cluster (indeed, more than one human would probably not agree either). Nevertheless, by using our definition and cluster growing algorithm to improve crawling and result displaying, we have shown that our definition and algorithm can be very useful on very large web graphs: the work of a crawler can be reduced by 40%, and results can be much better organized when presented to a user.

There are various directions for future research in

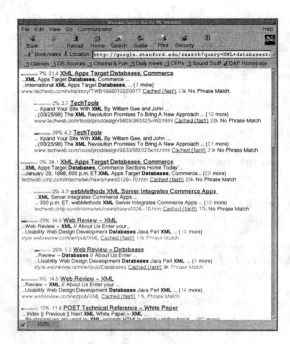

Figure 13: Search results for "XML databases" from Google search engine.

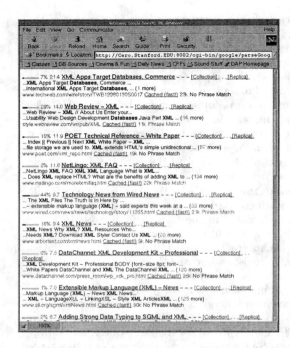

Figure 14: Rolled up search results for "XML databases".

the area of replicated web collections. In particular, as mentioned in Section 2, we believe it is possible to post-process the output of our cluster growing algorithm to (a) join together clusters that are separated by small web segments, and (b) extend clusters by adding "nearby" pages. This would require an extended definition of similarity that would allow (a) some small number of pages in one collection not be be mapped, and (b) collections to be of slightly different sizes. An evaluation would be needed to see if the extra processing cost is worth the more general notion of similarity. Also, the concept of similar clusters may be applicable in other domains beyond the web. For instance, any XML or semi-structured database can be viewed as a graph, and hence may contain similar clusters. A clustering algorithm like ours could be used, say, to identify customers with similar interests or similar purchasing patterns.

References

[1] Alexa Corporation. http://www.alexa.com, 1999.

[2] Krishna Bharat and Andrei Z. Broder. Mirror, Mirror, on the Web: A study of host pairs with replicated content. In *Proceedings of 8th International Conference on World Wide Web (WWW'99)*, May 1999.

[3] Sergey Brin and Lawrence Page. Google search engine. http://www.google.com, 1999.

[4] Andrei Broder. On the resemblance and containment of documents. In *Compression and complexity of Sequences (SEQUENCES'97)*, pages 21 – 29, 1997.

[5] Andrei Broder, Steve C. Glassman, and Mark S. Manasse. Syntactic clustering of the web. In *Sixth International World Wide Web Conference*, pages 391 – 404, April 1997.

[6] Thomas H. Cormen, Charles E. Leiserson, and Ronald L. Rivest. *Introduction to algorithms*. The MIT Press, 1991.

[7] Min Fang, Narayanan Shivakumar, Hector Garcia-Molina, Rajeev Motwani, and Jeffrey D. Ullman. Computing iceberg queries efficiently. In *Proceedings of International Conference on Very Large Databases (VLDB '98)*, pages 299 – 310, August 1998.

[8] Steve Lawrence and C. Lee Giles. Accessibility of information on the web. *Nature*, 400:107–109, 1999.

[9] M. Perkowitz and O. Etzioni. Adaptive web sites: Automatically synthesizing web pages. In *Fifteenth National Conference on Artificial Intelligence*, 1998.

[10] James Pitkow and Peter Pirolli. Life, death, and lawfulness on the electronic frontier. In *International conference on Computer and Human Interaction (CHI'97)*, 1997.

[11] Gerard Salton. *Itroduction to modern information retrieval*. McGraw-Hill, New York, 1983.

[12] Narayanan Shivakumar and Hector Garcia-Molina. SCAM:a copy detection mechanism for digital documents. In *Proceedings of 2nd International Conference in Theory and Practice of Digital Libraries (DL'95)*, Austin, Texas, June 1995.

[13] Narayanan Shivakumar and Hector Garcia-Molina. Building a scalable and accurate copy detection mechanism. In *Proceedings of 1st ACM Conference on Digital Libraries (DL'96)*, Bethesda, Maryland, March 1996.

WebView Materialization*

Alexandros Labrinidis[†]
Department of Computer Science
University of Maryland, College Park
labrinid@cs.umd.edu

Nick Roussopoulos[‡]
Department of Computer Science
University of Maryland, College Park
nick@cs.umd.edu

Abstract

A *WebView* is a web page automatically created from base data typically stored in a DBMS. Given the multi-tiered architecture behind database-backed web servers, we have the option of materializing a WebView inside the DBMS, at the web server, or not at all, always computing it on the fly (virtual). Since WebViews must be up to date, materialized WebViews are immediately refreshed with every update on the base data. In this paper we compare the three materialization policies (materialized inside the DBMS, materialized at the web server and virtual) analytically, through a detailed cost model, and quantitatively, through extensive experiments on an implemented system. Our results indicate that materializing at the web server is a more scalable solution and can facilitate an order of magnitude more users than the virtual and materialized inside the DBMS policies, even under high update workloads.

1 Introduction

There is no doubt that the Web has penetrated our lives. From reading the newspaper and shopping online, to searching for the best prices on books or airplane tickets, the Web is increasingly being used as the means to do everyday tasks. One common denominator for most of these activities, is that the web pages we access are *generated dynamically*, usually due to *personalization* [BBC+98]. Personalized web pages, that are created from base data, are one of the many instances of *WebViews*. In general, we define WebViews as web pages that are automatically generated from base data, which are typically stored in a DBMS.

*Prepared through collaborative participation in the Advanced Telecommunications/Information Distribution Research Program (ATIRP) Consortium sponsored by the U.S. Army Research Laboratory under the Federated Laboratory Program, Cooperative Agreement DAAL01-96-2-0002.

[†] Also with the Institute for Systems Research, University of Maryland.

[‡] Also with the Institute for Advanced Computer Studies, University of Maryland.

Similarly to traditional database views, WebViews can be in two forms: *virtual* or *materialized*. Virtual WebViews are computed dynamically on-demand, whereas materialized WebViews are precomputed. In the virtual case, the cost to compute the WebView increases the time it takes the web server to service the access request, which we will refer to as the *query response time*. On the other hand, in the materialized case, every update to base data leads to an update to the WebView, which increases the server load. Having a WebView materialized can potentially give significantly lower query response times, compared to the virtual approach. However, it may also lead to performance degradation, if the update workload is too high.

The decision whether to materialize a WebView or not, is similar to the problem of selecting which views to materialize in a data warehouse [GM95, Gup97, Rou98], known as the *view selection problem*. There are, however, many substantial differences. First of all, the multi-tiered architecture of typical database-backed web servers raises the question of *where* to materialize a WebView. Secondly, updates are performed *online* at web servers, as opposed to data warehouses which are usually off-line during updates. Thirdly, although both problems aim at decreasing query response times, warehouse views are materialized in order to speed up the execution of a few, long analytical (OLAP) queries, whereas WebViews are materialized to avoid repeated execution of many small OLTP-style queries. Finally, the general case of the WebView materialization problem has no constraints, whereas most view selection algorithms impose some resource constraints (e.g. maximum storage or maintenance window limits [KR99]).

In the next section we briefly describe the architecture of typical database-backed web servers, followed by some motivating examples of WebViews.

1.1 Architecture

When only servicing requests for static pages, the web server simply parses user requests, reads the appropriate files from a disk and sends them to the clients that requested them (Figure 1a). Usually, copies of the requested pages are *cached* in an intermediate node, the *proxy*, or at the client site in anticipation of future requests on the same pages. By

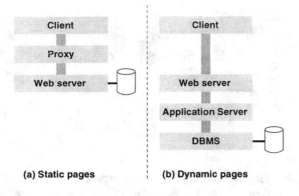

(a) Static pages   **(b) Dynamic pages**

Figure 1: Multi-tier architecture for web servers

replicating pages at the proxy or at the client, *web caching* strives to eliminate unnecessary data transmissions across the network [Mal98].

On the other hand, in order to serve dynamically generated pages (*WebViews*), the web server has to be interfaced to a relational database (Figure 1b). In this case, after parsing the user requests, the web server sends the corresponding query to the DBMS, often times via a middleware layer, the application server [Gre99]. Then, the query results are send back to the web server, which formats them in html and transmits the resulting web page to the client that requested it. Since these web pages are generated dynamically, they are usually marked "non-cacheable" and thus cannot be copied at the proxy or at the client.

Existing database-backed web servers, that publish dynamically generated pages, support either virtual or periodically refreshed WebViews, depending on whether users can tolerate stale results or not. For example, at the online auction site eBay (http://www.ebay.com) we have both types of WebViews. The summary pages for each auction category, which contain a list of all the available items together with the highest bid values, are periodically refreshed every few hours. This means that they can easily become out of date. On the other hand, the WebViews for the individual items are virtual, and are always computed on the fly.

Given the multi-tiered architecture of web servers, there are two more WebView materialization options that can guarantee fresh results and have not yet been used: materializing *inside the DBMS* and materializing *at the web server*. For the former, we can use the DBMS to also store the query results in the form of *materialized views* [GM99], whereas for the latter, we can use the web server's disk to store WebViews as files [LR99]. By materializing inside the DBMS we avoid expensive recomputation, whereas by materializing at the web server, we also eliminate the latency of going to the DBMS every time, which could lead to DBMS overloading [Sin98]. However, in order to guarantee freshness for both cases, the materialized WebViews need to be immediately refreshed with every update on the base data.

1.2   Motivation

There are many examples of WebViews other than personalized web pages. A search at an online bookstore for books by a particular author returns a WebView that is generated dynamically; a query on a cinema server generates a WebView that lists the current playing times for a particular movie; a request for the current sports scores at a newspaper site returns a WebView which is generated on the fly. Except for generating web pages as a result of a specific query, WebViews can also be used to produce multiple versions (*views*) of the same data. An emerging need in this area is for the ability to *support multiple web devices*, especially browsers with limited display or bandwidth capabilities, such as cellular phones or networked PDAs.

Although there are a few web servers that support arbitrary queries on their base data, most web applications "publish" a relatively small set of *predefined* or *parameterized* WebViews, which are to be generated automatically through DBMS queries. A weather web server, for example, would most probably report current weather information and forecast for an area based on a ZIP code, or a city/state combination. Given that weather web pages can be very popular and that the update rate for weather information is not high, materializing such WebViews would most likely improve performance. In general, WebViews that are a result of arbitrary queries, are not expected to be shared, and hence need not be considered for materialization. This category would include, for example, WebViews that were generated as a result of a query on a search engine. On the other hand, predefined or parameterized WebViews can be popular and thus should be considered for materialization in order to improve the web server's performance.

Personalized WebViews can also be considered for materialization, if first they are decomposed into a *hierarchy* of WebViews. Take for example a personalized newspaper. It can have a selection of news categories (only metro, international news), a localized weather forecast and a horoscope page (for Scorpio). Although this particular combination might be unique or unpopular, if we decompose the page into four WebViews, one for metro news, one for international news, one for the weather and one for the horoscope, then these WebViews can be accessed frequently enough to merit materialization.

Stock server example

One motivating example, which we will use throughout the paper, is that of a stock web server. Such a system can have three types of WebViews: summary pages, individual company pages and personalized portfolio pages. Summary pages list companies either by industry group (e.g. consumer goods, financial, transportation, utilities) or by activity (e.g. most active, biggest gainers, biggest losers). Individual company pages have the latest stock price, graphs at various time-scales (from intra-day to multi-year charts) and pointers to news articles about the company. Finally, personalized portfolio pages are expected to have a list of the stocks that one owns, along with calculations for their current value and profits/losses, based on the latest stock prices.

The aforementioned WebViews display a wide variety of access and update patterns. For example, the summary pages based on industry groups are typically less update-intensive than the summary pages based on stock activity (e.g. biggest gainers). Even WebViews of the same category can exhibit substantially different access or update characteristics. For example, individual company WebViews are expected to follow the popularity of the company: heavily traded stocks will correspond to WebViews that are accessed frequently and are also update-intensive.

Existing stock web servers typically generate all of their WebViews on the fly, which results in really poor response times at peak hours. Materialization can improve performance dramatically by precomputing popular WebViews and keeping them up to date in the background, instead of repeating their generation with every request. Although the personalized portfolio WebViews are obviously too specific to be considered for materialization, both the WebViews for individual companies and the summary WebViews are candidates for materialization, even under high update rates. The reason for this is that even if, for example, a stock price is updated 10 times a second, it is beneficial to precompute WebViews that are based on it, if they are accessed more often (e.g. 20 times a second).

1.3 Contributions

In this paper we consider the full spectrum of materialization choices for WebViews in a database-backed web server. We compare them analytically using a detailed cost model that accounts for both the inherent parallelism in multitasking systems and also for the fact that updates on the base data are to be done concurrently with the accesses. We have implemented all flavors of WebView materialization on an industrial strength database-backed web server (WebMat) and ran extensive experiments. We then compared the various materialization choices quantitatively. Our results showed that the policy of materializing at the web server scales substantially better than the other two, and that the virtual policy is better than materializing inside the DBMS, except for a very limited number of cases.

The rest of the paper is organized as follows. In the next section we give an overview of related work. Section 3 presents the three materialization policies and compares them analytically. In Section 4 we discuss the results of our experiments, and in the last section we present our conclusions.

2 Related Work

As we mentioned earlier, although the decision whether to materialize a WebView or not, is similar to the view selection problem in data warehouses, there are a few major differences. The most important ones are the multi-tiered architecture of database-backed web servers, which raises the question of *where* to materialize, and the need to perform updates at the web server *online*, as opposed to data warehouses in which updates are usually off-line. WebView materialization is also different from the traditional web caching techniques, since it is targeted at dynamically generated pages and guarantees that the WebView is always up to date. Finally, WebView materialization is performed at the web *server*, whereas web caching is done at the *clients* or at proxies.

There is some recent work on caching *dynamic web data*. The *Active Cache* scheme [CZB98] supports caching of dynamic web objects at proxies. This is done by allowing servers to supply cache applets to be executed on cache hits at the proxies without contacting the server. In [IC97] the authors present the *DynamicWeb cache* which has the ability to cache dynamic web pages at the server the first time they are created, and in [LISD99] they provide an API which allows application programs to explicitly add, delete and update cached data. Finally, [CID99] describes an algorithm to identify which cached objects are affected by a change to the underlying data. Unfortunately, none of the aforementioned papers deals with the *selection* problem: identifying which dynamic data to cache and which not to cache.

Although there is a lot of recent literature on building and maintaining web sites [CFP99, AMM98, FFK+98, FLM98], there is little work on the performance issues associated with WebViews. [MMM98] provide an algorithm to support client-side materialization of WebViews, and [Sin98, AMR+98] present algorithms to maintain them incrementally. In [LR99], we presented preliminary results that materializing WebViews at the web server is often times better than computing them on the fly. However, we did not consider materialization inside the DBMS, as we do in this paper.

[FLSY99] consider the problem of automatically optimizing the run-time management of declaratively specified web sites. Although they report considerable speedup rates from view materialization, they dismiss it on the grounds of space overhead. We believe that storage overhead is not an issue when it comes to web servers since it refers to disk space and not main memory.

Finally, by materializing WebViews, we allow the web server to scale up well under peak workloads, by serving slightly stale data. This is one way of performing *web content adaptation* to improve server overload behavior. [AB99] propose to resolve the overload problem by adapting delivered content to load conditions.

3 WebView materialization strategies

The WebMat system is our implementation of a database-backed web server that can support all flavors of WebView materialization. It has three software components: the *web*

name	curr	prev	diff	volume
AMZN	76	79	-3	8.06M
AOL	111	115	-4	13.29M
EBAY	138	141	-3	2.16M
IBM	107	107	0	8.81M
IFMX	6	6	0	1.42M
LU	60	61	-1	10.98M
MSFT	88	90	-2	23.49M
ORCL	45	46	-1	9.19M
T	43	44	-1	5.97M
YHOO	171	173	-2	7.10M

name	curr	prev	diff
AOL	111	115	-4
EBAY	138	141	-3
AMZN	76	79	-3

```
<html><head>
<title>Biggest Losers</title>
</head><body>
<h1>Biggest Losers</h1><p>

<table>
<tr><td> name <td> curr <td> diff
<tr><td> AOL  <td>  111 <td> -4
<tr><td> EBAY <td>  141 <td> -3
<tr><td> AMZN <td>   76 <td> -3
</table>

Last update on Oct 15, 13:16:05
</body></html>
```

(a) source   (b) view   (c) WebView

Table 1: Derivation path for the stock server example

server, the *DBMS* and the *updater*. Each of them typically spawns a lot of processes or threads that run in parallel.

The web server services the access requests. Depending on the materialization policy, it may execute a query at the DBMS or read a file from disk. The DBMS computes answers to queries, or applies updates to tables. Finally, the updater runs in the background and services the update stream. It supplies the DBMS with updates to the base tables and may also cause the refresh of derived data inside the DBMS, or write the new version of a WebView to disk, by executing the appropriate query[1] at the DBMS, formatting the results in html, and saving them to a file.

One important property of the WebMat system is *transparency*: clients sending access requests to the web server do not have to know what kind of materialization a WebView has, if any.

3.1   WebView Derivation Path

Before describing the materialization policies in detail, we give an overview of the derivation path for each WebView. First, a set of base tables, the *sources*, is queried, and, then, the query results, the *view*, are formatted into an html page, the *WebView*.

Table 1 illustrates how WebView derivation works for the summary pages from the stock server example. In order, for example, to generate the WebView for the biggest losers, we start from the base table with all the stocks (the source), and issue a query to get the ones with the biggest decrease (the view) and, then, format the query results into html (the WebView).

We will use s_i to denote a source table, and $S_i = \{s_{i_1}, s_{i_2}, \ldots, s_{i_n}\}$ for a set of sources. Similarly, we will use v_i for a view, and $V_i = \{v_{i_1}, v_{i_2}, \ldots, v_{i_n}\}$ for a set of views. Finally, we will use w_i for a WebView, and $W_i = \{w_{i_1}, w_{i_2}, \ldots, w_{i_n}\}$ for a set of WebViews.

Formally, if S_i is the set of sources, we define the *query operator* $\mathcal{Q}$, such that $\mathcal{Q}(S_i) = v_i$, where v_i is the view corresponding to the query results. Moreover, we define the *formatting operator* $\mathcal{F}$, such that $\mathcal{F}(v_i) = w_i$, where w_i is a WebView, the result of formatting view v_i into html. If we want to associate a view v_i with the set of sources that generated it, we use the inverse query operator $\mathcal{Q}^{-1}$: $v_i = \mathcal{Q}^{-1}(S_i)$. Similarly, to associate a WebView with the view it was generated from, we use the inverse formatting operator $\mathcal{F}^{-1}$: $w_i = \mathcal{F}^{-1}(V_i)$. Finally, since there can be a hierarchy of views, we extend $\mathcal{Q}$ to take as argument other views, if necessary. So, for example, in the general case we have $\mathcal{Q}(S_i) = v_i^1$, $\mathcal{Q}(v_i^1) = v_i^2, \ldots, \mathcal{Q}(v_i^{n-1}) = v_i^n$, $w_i = \mathcal{F}(v_i^n)$. If $n = 1$, we have a *flat schema*.

All WebViews have the same derivation path regardless of the materialization policy. The only difference among the three policies is that the materialized strategies choose to cache (and keep consistent) parts of the intermediate results, whereas in the virtual strategy everything is computed from scratch. In the next sections, we describe the three policies in detail.

3.2   Virtual Policy

In the virtual policy, everything is computed on the fly. To produce a WebView w_i we would need to query the DBMS and format the results in html. Therefore, the cost of accessing WebView w_i would be:

$$A_{\text{virt}}(w_i) = \underbrace{C_{query}(S_i)}_{@dbms} + \underbrace{C_{format}(v_i)}_{@web\ server} \qquad (1)$$

where $v_i = \mathcal{F}^{-1}(w_i)$ is the view from which the WebView w_i is generated, $S_i = \mathcal{Q}^{-1}(v_i)$ is the set of sources needed to answer the query, $C_{query}(S_i)$ is the cost to query the sources, and, $C_{format}(v_i)$ is the cost of formatting view v_i into html. We notice that the query part of the access cost is executed at the DBMS, whereas the formatting part is performed at the web server.

---

[1] It should be noted that the query is exactly the same as the one used by the web server to generate virtual WebViews and, as such, we do not need to duplicate any DBMS functionality at the updater.

Since nothing is being cached under the virtual policy, whenever there is an update on the base tables that produce the WebView, we only need to update the base tables. Therefore, the cost of an update to source s_j is:

$$U_{\text{virt}}(s_j) = \underbrace{C_{update}(s_j)}_{@dbms} \qquad (2)$$

where s_j is one of the base tables that are used to produce WebView w_i, or $s_j \in \mathcal{Q}^{-1}(\mathcal{F}^{-1}(w_i))$, and $C_{update}(s_i)$ is the cost to update table s_j.

We realize that the formatting of the query results during accesses can be done *in parallel* with the updating of the sources, as they are done at different processes (the former is being done at the web server, while the latter is done at the DBMS). However, we also realize that there is a possible source of data contention between the query phase during the accesses and the updates, since they both have to be done at the DBMS.

3.3 Materializing inside the DBMS

When materializing inside the DBMS (the `matdb` policy) we save the results of the query that is used to generate the WebView. To produce the WebView, we would need to access the stored results and format them in html. Therefore, the access cost for WebView w_i in this case is:

$$A_{\text{matdb}}(w_i) = \underbrace{C_{access}(v_i)}_{@dbms} + \underbrace{C_{format}(v_i)}_{@web\ server} \qquad (3)$$

where $v_i = \mathcal{F}^{-1}(w_i)$ is the view from which the WebView w_i is generated, and $C_{access}(v_i)$ is the cost of accessing the materialized view v_i. We notice that, similarly to the virtual policy, the first part of the access cost is executed at the DBMS, whereas the formatting part is performed at the web server.

Since we assumed a no staleness requirement, the stored query results need to be kept up to date all the time. This leads to an immediate refresh of the materialized views inside the DBMS with every update to the base tables they are derived from. So the cost of an update to source s_j is:

$$U_{\text{matdb}}(s_j) = \underbrace{C_{update}(s_j) + \sum_{v_k \in V_j} C_{update}(v_k)}_{@dbms} \qquad (4)$$

where $C_{update}(s_j)$ is the cost to update source s_j, V_j is the set of materialized views that are affected by the update to table s_j, or $V_j = \{v_m | s_j \in \mathcal{Q}^{-1}(v_m)\}$, and, $C_{update}(v_k)$ is the cost to update the materialized view v_k. There are two options for updating the materialized view v_k: *incremental refresh* and *recomputation*. For the incremental refresh case, the cost to update v_k is simply:

$$C_{update}(v_k) = C_{refresh}(v_k) \qquad (5)$$

whereas in the recomputation case, the cost to update v_k is:

$$C_{update}(v_k) = C_{query}(S_k) + C_{store}(v_k) \qquad (6)$$

where $S_k = \mathcal{Q}^{-1}(v_k)$ is the set of sources needed to answer the query that corresponds to view v_k, and $C_{store}(v_k)$ is the cost to store the query results inside the DBMS, which includes the cost to delete the previous "version" of v_k. Although the incremental refresh is expected to have the lowest cost, there are classes of views which cannot be updated incrementally and thus must be recomputed every time.

We realize that, like the virtual case, the formatting of the query results during accesses can be done in parallel with the updating of the sources and the materialized views, as they are done at different processes (the former is being done at the web server, while the latter is done at the DBMS). However, there is a possible source of data contention between the queries executed during the servicing of the access requests and the updates of the sources or of the materialized views, since they are all done at the DBMS.

3.4 Materializing at the web server

When we materialize a WebView at the web server (the `matweb` policy) we do not need to query the DBMS or perform any further formatting in order to satisfy user requests. We simply have to read it from disk, which makes the cost of accessing a WebView w_i rather small:

$$A_{\text{matweb}}(w_i) = \underbrace{C_{read}(w_i)}_{@web\ server} \qquad (7)$$

where $C_{read}(w_i)$ is the cost to read w_i which has been saved as a file to disk.

Because of the no staleness requirement, the materialized WebView needs to be kept up to date all the time. This means that on every update to one of the base tables s_j that produce the WebView, we have to regenerate the WebView from scratch and save it as a file for the web server to read. So the cost of an update to source s_j is:

$$U_{\text{matweb}}(s_j) = \underbrace{C_{update}(s_j)}_{@dbms} + \sum_{v_k \in V_j} \underbrace{C_{query}(S_k)}_{@dbms}$$
$$+ \sum_{v_k \in V_j} \underbrace{C_{format}(v_k) + C_{write}(w_k)}_{@updater} \qquad (8)$$

where V_j is the set of views that are affected by the update to table s_j, or $V_j = \{v_m | s_j \in \mathcal{Q}^{-1}(v_m)\}$, $v_k = \mathcal{F}^{-1}(w_k)$ is the view that generates WebView w_k, $S_k = \mathcal{Q}^{-1}(v_k)$ is the set of sources needed to answer the query that corresponds to view v_k, and $C_{write}(w_k)$ is the cost to write the WebView w_k to disk.

We realize that the handling of user requests and the updates can be done entirely in parallel. Moreover, parts of the execution of an update can also be done in parallel, since the work is distributed among the DBMS and the updater

	web server	DBMS	updater
virt	√	√	
matdb	√	√	
matweb	√		

(a) Accesses

	web server	DBMS	updater
virt		√	
matdb		√	
matweb		√	√

(b) Updates

Table 2: Work distribution among processes for each policy

processes. However, there is some data contention, mainly between the $read(w_i)$ and the $write(w_i)$ operations which both involve the web server's disk.

3.5 The selection problem

The choice of materialization policy for each WebView has a big impact on the overall performance. For example, a WebView that is costly to compute and has very few updates, should be materialized to speed up access requests. On the other hand, a WebView that can be computed fast and has much more updates than accesses, should not be materialized, since materialization would mean more work than necessary. We define the WebView selection problem as following:

*For every WebView at the server, select the materialization strategy (virtual, materialized inside the DBMS, materialized at the web server), which **minimizes the average query response time** on the clients. We assume that there is no storage constraint.*

The assumption that there is no storage constraint is not unrealistic, since storage means disk space (and not main memory) for both materialization policies (inside the DBMS or at the web server) and also WebViews are expected to be relatively small. With the average web page at 30KB [AW97], a single 50GB hard disk for example could hold approximately 1.5 million pages. In this paper, we also assume a no staleness requirement, i.e. the WebViews must always be up to date.

3.6 Cost aggregation

In order to solve the WebView selection problem, except for the cost functions presented in Sections 3.2 - 3.4, we will need to aggregate the access and update costs, taking into account the frequencies with which they occur. Unlike traditional materialized view applications, updates in a database-backed web server are *online*, executing in the background while the server is processing access requests. However, since the objective of the WebView selection problem is to minimize the *average query response time*, we expect the aggregate cost formulas to be more sensitive to the access costs than the update costs.

Let $f_a(w_i)$ be the *access frequency* for WebView w_i, and $f_u(s_j)$ be the *frequency of updates* for source s_j, from which w_i is derived. If W is the set of all WebViews at the web server, we want to partition W into three disjoint sets $W_{\mathtt{virt}}$, $W_{\mathtt{matdb}}$ and $W_{\mathtt{matweb}}$, such that the average query response time is minimized. $W_{\mathtt{virt}}$ would contain all the WebViews under the virtual policy, $W_{\mathtt{matdb}}$ would contain all the WebViews materialized inside the DBMS, and, $W_{\mathtt{matweb}}$ would contain all the WebViews materialized at the web server. Finally, let $S_{\mathtt{virt}}$ be the set of sources that have to be queried to generate the WebViews in $W_{\mathtt{virt}}$, or $S_{\mathtt{virt}} = Q^{-1}(\mathcal{F}^{-1}(W_{\mathtt{virt}}))$, and similarly $S_{\mathtt{matdb}}$ the set of sources that have to be queried to generate the WebViews in $W_{\mathtt{matdb}}$, and $S_{\mathtt{matweb}}$ the set of sources needed for generating $W_{\mathtt{matweb}}$.

Since we are minimizing the average query response time, in order to calculate the total cost we simply need to identify for each policy how much the concurrent updates influence the access requests. Table 2 lists which subsystems are involved when servicing (a) access or (b) update operations under each policy. For example, when a WebView is accessed under the $\mathtt{virt}$ policy, both the web server and the DBMS are involved (Table 2a, first line). The same holds for the $\mathtt{matdb}$ policy (second line), whereas for accessing WebViews under the $\mathtt{matweb}$ policy only the web server is required (third line). On the other hand, the DBMS is required for servicing updates under all three policies (Table 2b), whereas the updater processes are involved only under the $\mathtt{matweb}$ policy (Table 2b, third line). We clearly see that the DBMS is used at all times, except for when accessing a WebView which is materialized at the web server. This means that the database server can become the bottleneck of the system, and thus the load on the DBMS is expected to dominate the average query response time.

Let TC be the total cost for servicing access requests, which is the amount that we want to minimize. Obviously, TC will include the access costs for the WebViews in our system, but it must also include the influence to the access costs from the updates that are executed concurrently. As we mentioned earlier, the DBMS is expected to be the bottleneck of the system, so we isolate from the update costs the parts that are executed in the DBMS. Formally, we use $\pi_{dbms}(C)$ to select from cost C the part that is executed in the DBMS. From Eq. 2, we have that $\pi_{dbms}(U_{\mathtt{virt}}) = U_{\mathtt{virt}}$, and from Eq. 4, $\pi_{dbms}(U_{\mathtt{matdb}}) = U_{\mathtt{matdb}}$. To get $\pi_{dbms}(U_{\mathtt{matweb}})$ from Eq. 8 we simply ignore the parts that are executed in the updater processes (third term).

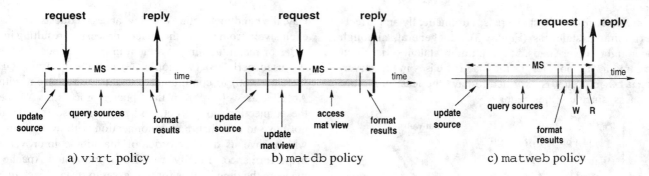

a) `virt` policy　　　　b) `matdb` policy　　　　c) `matweb` policy

Figure 2: Staleness measurement

Putting it all together, we have that the total cost for servicing access requests is:

$$
\begin{aligned}
TC =\ & \sum_{w_k \in W_{\mathtt{matweb}}} f_a(w_k) \times A_{\mathtt{matweb}}(w_k) \\
+\ & \sum_{s_k \in S_{\mathtt{matweb}}} b \times f_u(s_k) \times \pi_{dbms}(U_{\mathtt{matweb}}(s_k)) \\
+\ & \sum_{w_i \in W_{\mathtt{virt}}} f_a(w_i) \times A_{\mathtt{virt}}(w_i) \\
+\ & \sum_{s_i \in S_{\mathtt{virt}}} f_u(s_i) \times U_{\mathtt{virt}}(s_i) \qquad (9) \\
+\ & \sum_{w_j \in W_{\mathtt{matdb}}} f_a(w_j) \times A_{\mathtt{matdb}}(w_j) \\
+\ & \sum_{s_j \in S_{\mathtt{matdb}}} f_u(s_j) \times U_{\mathtt{matdb}}(s_j)
\end{aligned}
$$

where $b = 0$, if $W_{\mathtt{virt}} = W_{\mathtt{matdb}} = \emptyset$, and $b = 1$, otherwise. The meaning of b is that when we only have WebViews materialized at the web server, the cost of updating them in the background using the DBMS does not have a direct impact on the average query response time. However, when we have WebViews that are either virtual or materialized inside the DBMS, the cost of updating the `matweb` WebViews in the background will influence the average query response time of the `virt` and `matdb` WebViews.

3.7　Staleness calculation

Although, at first sight, the virtual policy would seem to provide the most up to date responses, this misconception is quickly cleared away if we consider the basis of our freshness measurement to be the time of the *reply* instead of the request. Using the time of the reply is more meaningful, since that is the time when the users get to access the answer to their query. We call *minimum staleness, MS*, the time it takes for an update to propagate to the user, or, in other words, the time between the reply to a WebView request and the time of the last database update that affected this reply. All points of time refer to the web server in order to avoid network delays, so the time of the reply is actually the time

the web server sends the reply back to the user and not the time the user receives the reply.

Figure 2(a) illustrates the minimum staleness under the virtual policy (`virt`), which is

$$
MS_{\mathtt{virt}} = \underbrace{T_{update}(s_j)}_{\text{before request}} + \underbrace{T_{query}(S_i) + T_{format}(v_i)}_{\text{during request}}
$$

For the materialized inside the DBMS policy (`matdb`), Figure 2(b) gives us

$$
MS_{\mathtt{matdb}} = \underbrace{T_{update}(s_j) + T_{refresh}(v_i)}_{\text{before request}} + \underbrace{T_{access}(v_i) + T_{format}(v_i)}_{\text{during request}}
$$

Finally, Figure 2(c), illustrates that the minimum staleness when materializing a WebView at the web server (`matweb` policy) is

$$
\begin{aligned}
MS_{\mathtt{matweb}} =\ & \underbrace{T_{update}(s_j) + T_{query}(S_i) + T_{format}(v_i)}_{\text{before request}} \\
+\ & \underbrace{T_{write}(w_i)}_{\text{before request}} + \underbrace{T_{read}(w_i)}_{\text{during request}}
\end{aligned}
$$

By comparing the three minimum staleness formulas, we have:

$$
MS_{\mathtt{matdb}} - MS_{\mathtt{virt}} = T_{refresh}(v_i) + T_{access}(v_i) - T_{query}(S_i)
$$
$$
MS_{\mathtt{matweb}} - MS_{\mathtt{virt}} = T_{write}(w_i) + T_{read}(w_i)
$$

Under light load conditions, we expect to have the virtual policy to have slightly lower minimum staleness than the other two policies: $MS_{\mathtt{virt}} \leq MS_{\mathtt{matweb}} \leq MS_{\mathtt{matdb}}$. However, this will not hold when the load at the server increases. As we will see later in the experiments section, all policies do not scale up in the same way. Specifically, the `matweb` policy can support at least 10 times more requests than the other two policies (`virt`, `matdb`), since it allows for more parallelism between the access and update requests. This means that as the load at the system increases, the `virt` and `matdb` policies will reach the heavy load mark much faster than the `matweb` policy. After that point, the time to service access requests increases dramatically and affects the minimum staleness (Figure 3). In general, although under light server loads, the minimum staleness is about the same for all policies, as the load increases in the server, the `matweb` policy is expected to have the least minimum staleness, since it scales better.

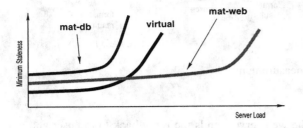

Figure 3: Minimum staleness under heavy loads

3.8 Discussion

As mentioned during the presentation of the materialization strategies, there is a lot of *parallelism* in a database-backed web server. For example, the formatting of the query results at the web server can be done in parallel with the updates at the DBMS. In a single-processor machine, this parallelism means that we are able to recover idle time due to I/O blocking or data contention by performing other useful tasks.

Furthermore, we expect that the virtual and the materialized inside the DBMS policies make the database server the bottleneck, since every request (accesses and updates alike) has to query the DBMS. For accesses, this means that each user request has to go through an extra layer of software, communicating data back and forth. On the other hand, the materialized at the web server policy breaks this bottleneck, by performing a lot of the work in the background (the updater processes) and relying on the web server alone to service user requests. This was verified by our experiments, which we present in the next section.

4 Experiments

As we mentioned earlier, the WebMat system consists of three software components: the web server, the DBMS and the updater. We used the Apache[2] web server, version 1.3.6 and the Informix Dynamic Server with Universal Data Option ver. 9.14. The updater was written in Perl.

Web server extensions In order for the web server to generate pages dynamically, we need to execute scripts that communicate with the DBMS. To avoid the overhead of creating a new Unix process with every access request (which is what happens with cgi-bin), we used the *mod_perl* package ver. 1.19 on top of the Apache web server. This

---

[2]Apache is the most popular web server according to the February 2000 Netcraft Web Server Survey, with a 58% market share. The survey is available online at `http://www.netcraft.com/survey/`

way, the handling of the WebView access requests was done exclusively from within the apache processes, resulting in an order of magnitude improvement in performance [LR00a]. We used perl DBI (version 1.08) and the Informix DBD (version 0.60) to communicate to the DBMS, from within Apache, as well as from the updater processes. We kept the connections to the database *persistent*, so that we did not have to establish a new connection with every request, which gave us another order of magnitude improvement in performance. Finally, we also instrumented Apache to measure the time it takes for the server to service each query request. Note that we made our measurements of query response time at the *server*, thus eliminating any network latency.

Updater We had 10 updater processes running in the background. Informix does not have native support for materialized views, so for the `matdb` policy, we stored the materialized views as tables, and had the updater issue an update SQL statement whenever there was an update on the base data. It should be noted that most DBMS products that support materialized views, also store them as relational tables (e.g. Oracle [BD+98]).

Hardware We used a SUN UltraSparc-5 with 320MB of memory, a 3.6GB Seagate Medalist disk as our server, and, a cluster of 22 SUN Ultra-1 workstations as clients. All of the machines were on the same local area network and were running Solaris 2.6.

Workload Unless noted otherwise, in each experiment we had 1000 WebViews that were defined over 10 source tables (100 per table). The queries corresponding to the WebViews were selections on an indexed attribute, which returned 10 tuples each. The WebView size in html was 3KB. Each experiment was executed for 10 minutes. Finally, the update operations were changing the value of one attribute at the source table.

4.1 Scaling up the access rate

In this group of experiments we increased the access request rate from 10 requests per second up to 100 requests per second and measured the average query response time under the three different materialization policies: virtual (`virt`), materialized inside the DBMS (`matdb`) and materialized at the web server (`matweb`).

A load of 10 access requests per second should correspond to a "moderate" load at the server of about 0.8 million hits per day. On the other hand, 100 requests per second should correspond to a rather "heavy" load at the web server of about 8.6 million hits per day. For comparison, our department's web server (`http://www.cs.umd.edu`) gets about 95,000 requests per day or 1.1 request per second, whereas the widely popular online auction site eBay

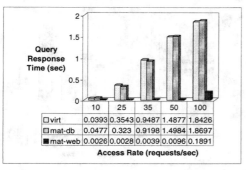
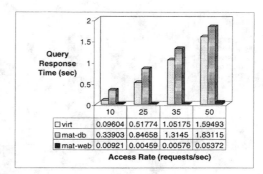

	10	25	35	50	100
□ virt	0.0393	0.3543	0.9487	1.4877	1.8426
▨ mat-db	0.0477	0.323	0.9198	1.4984	1.8697
■ mat-web	0.0026	0.0028	0.0039	0.0096	0.1891

Access Rate (requests/sec)

	10	25	35	50
□ virt	0.09604	0.51774	1.05175	1.59493
▨ mat-db	0.33903	0.84658	1.3145	1.83115
■ mat-web	0.00921	0.00459	0.00576	0.05372

Access Rate (requests/sec)

(a) No updates   (b) 5 updates/sec

Figure 4: Scaling up the access rate

(`http://www.ebay.com`) gets about 50 million hits per day or 580 requests per second on average[3] (October 1999).

We run two sets of experiments: one with no updates, and one with 5 updates/sec. The access and the update requests were distributed uniformly over all 1000 WebViews. Each experiment was scheduled to run for 10 minutes and was repeated three times: in the first one, all WebViews were kept virtual, in the second one all were materialized inside the DBMS and in the last one they were materialized at the web server. We report the average query response times per WebView as they were measured at the web server. At the 95% confidence level, the margin of error was 0.14% - 2.7% for the `virt` policy, 0.17% - 3.16% for the `matdb` policy and 1.3% - 6.5% for the `matweb` policy.

Figure 4a depicts the results of our experiments with no updates and Figure 4b when we have 5 updates/sec. We immediately notice that the `matweb` policy has average query response times that are consistently at least an order of magnitude (10 - 230 times) less than those of the `virt` or `matdb` policies. This was expected, as the `matweb` policy, in order to service a request, simply reads a file from disk (even if the updater process is running in the background, constantly updating this file), whereas under the `virt`, `matdb` policies we have to compute a query at the DBMS for every request (even if the WebView is materialized inside the DBMS, we still have to access it). Furthermore, since the web processes are "lighter" than the processes in the DBMS, the `matweb` policy scales better than the other two.

Figure 4a also shows that the `virt` and the `matdb` policies have similar query response times. This is explained by the fact that although the `matdb` policy had precomputed the query results, the cost of accessing them is about the same as the cost of generating them from scratch, using the `virt` policy. This will also be true for other DBMS

products with native support for materialized views, if they use relational tables to store the materialized views. However, when we also have updates (Figure 4b), except for updating the source tables, the `matdb` policy has to refresh the materialized views as well. This means that the DBMS (which is the bottleneck) will become significantly more loaded, which results in a substantial drop in performance for the `matdb` policy, compared to the `virt` policy. For example at 25 requests/sec, although with no updates the `matdb` policy is 9.69% faster than the `virt` policy, when we have 5 updates/sec, the `virt` policy is 63.53% faster than the `matdb` policy.

4.2 Scaling up the update rate

In this group of experiments we increased the update rate up to 25 updates/sec, while the access rate was constant at 25 requests/sec. Each experiment was scheduled to run for 10 minutes and was repeated three times, one for each policy (`virt`, `matdb` and `matweb`). We report the average query response times per WebView in Figure 5.

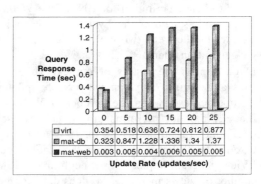

	0	5	10	15	20	25
□ virt	0.354	0.518	0.636	0.724	0.812	0.877
▨ mat-db	0.323	0.847	1.228	1.336	1.34	1.37
■ mat-web	0.003	0.005	0.004	0.006	0.005	0.005

Update Rate (updates/sec)

Figure 5: Scaling up the update rate

Our first observation is that the average query response time remains practically unchanged for the `matweb` policy despite the updates. The reason behind this is that, as predicted by the total cost formula of Eq. 9, the cost of the

---

[3]Of course, eBay does not have just one plain SUN UltraSparc-5 to serve all these hits, but, rather, they rely on many machines. A simple search on the ebay.com domain, lists 478 machines, out of which 35 have the word "cgi" as part of their name and are most probably used to serve dynamically generated web pages.

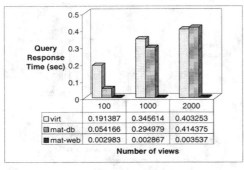

(a) No updates

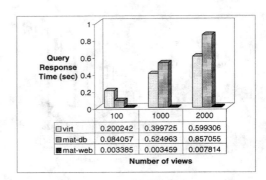

(b) 5 updates/sec

Figure 6: Scaling up the number of WebViews

accesses under the `matweb` policy is not affected by the updates, since they are done at the background by another process, the updater.

The second observation is that the `matdb` policy is performing significantly worse than the `virt` policy in the presence of updates. This is explained by the fact that updates under the `matdb` policy lead to extra work at the DBMS in order for the materialized views to be kept up to date. On the other hand, since the queries are not expensive, the gain from precomputing is negligible. As a result, the `virt` policy gives 56% - 93% faster query response times compared to the `matdb` policy in the presence of updates.

4.3 Scaling up the number of WebViews

In this group of experiments we varied the number of WebViews in the system. We ran one set of experiments with 100 WebViews, a second set with 1000 WebViews and a third set with 2000 WebViews. In all experiments, the aggregate access rate was 25 requests / sec. Each experiment ran for 20 minutes and was repeated three times, one for each policy (`virt`, `matdb` and `matweb`). In all experiments, we modified the view definition for 10% of the WebViews: instead of a simple selection, they were defined as a join on the index attribute between two tables, resulting in a more expensive generation query.

Figure 6a depicts the results of our experiments with no updates and Figure 6b when we have 5 updates/sec. In the no update case, when the number of WebViews is small, the `virt` policy performs substantially worse than the `matdb` policy (3.5 times worse for 100 WebViews, and 21% worse for 1000 WebViews), since the time to compute the WebView generation query is not negligible. However, as the number of views increases, so does data contention. The `matdb` policy will exhibit more data contention than the `virt` policy, because the number of materialized views is much higher than the number of source tables. Eventually (when the number of WebViews is 2000), the performance of the `virt` policy will be better than that of the `matdb` policy, even for expensive queries. If we consider the case

with 5 updates/sec, the crossover point where the `virt` policy outperforms the `matdb` policy is even earlier, at 1000 WebViews, whereas for 2000 WebViews, the `virt` policy gives 43% faster query response times than the `matdb` policy.

4.4 Scaling up the WebView size

The size of a WebView can increase in two ways: (a) by increasing the number of tuples in each view, or (b) by increasing the size of the resulting html page. We investigated both options in this group of experiments.

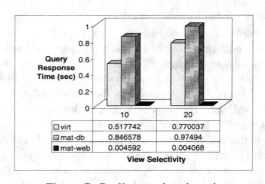

Figure 7: Scaling up the view size

In the first set of experiments, we increased the number of tuples in a WebView from 10 to 20. The access rate was 25 requests/sec, and we also had 5 updates/sec. The experiment run for 10 minutes, and was repeated 3 times, one for each policy. We report the average query response time per WebView in Figure 7. We can see that although the response time increases for the `virt` and `matdb` policies, it does not double: there is a 50% increase for the `virt` policy and a 15% increase for the `matdb` policy. Moreover, the response time for the `matweb` policy remains virtually unaffected, since all the "extra work" generated from the increase in the view size is executed at the updater process and does not have a direct effect on the web server.

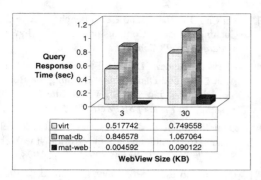

Figure 8: Scaling up the html size

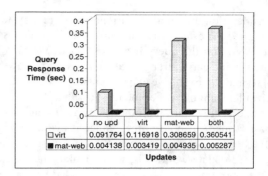

Figure 9: Verifying the cost model

In the second set of experiments, we increased the size of the html page (WebView) from 3KB to 30KB. The access rate was 25 requests/sec, and we also had 5 updates/sec. The experiment run for 10 minutes, and was repeated 3 times, one for each policy. We report the average query response time per WebView in Figure 8. Again we see that the response times for the `virt` and `matdb` policies increase. However, unlike the previous experiment, in this case, the response time for the `matweb` policy increases significantly. This is explained by the fact that a big change in the WebView size (from 3KB to 30KB) is actually affecting the web server, since it will have to spend more time reading the files from disk.

4.5 Zipf vs uniform access distribution

In all of our experiments, we used a uniform distribution for the access rates. We ran two sets of experiments where the access rates followed a Zipf distribution with a theta of 0.7 as suggested in [BCF+99] and compared them against the uniform distribution case (due to lack of space we do not include the graphs, the reader is referred to [LR00b]). We saw that the query response times are significantly lower (11% - 23%) under the Zipf distribution for all policies. This is due to the fact that there is more reference locality in the Zipf workload than in the uniform case. Therefore, by using a uniform distribution in our experiments, we exposed the WebMat system to a "worst case" scenario for the access requests.

4.6 Verifying the cost model

In the final set of experiments we tried to verify the total cost formula from Eq. 9. We had 1000 WebViews (500 of them were kept virtual and 500 were materialized under the `matweb` policy), with an aggregate access rate of 25 requests / sec. We ran four experiments. In the first one, we had no updates. In the second experiment, updates were made only to the 500 `virt` WebViews, at an aggregate rate of 5 updates / sec. In the third experiment, updates were made only to the 500 `matweb` WebViews, at a rate of 5 updates / sec. Finally, in the last experiment, both types of WebViews had updates, with an aggregate rate of 5 upd / sec.

Figure 9 depicts the results of our experiments. For each experiment, we report the average query response time of WebViews under the `virt` policy (left, light-colored column) and the average query response time for `matweb` WebViews (right, dark-colored column). As we showed in section 4.2, the average query response time for WebViews under the `matweb` policy changes very little with increases in the update workload, which agrees with the total cost formula and the results from this experiment. For `virt` WebViews however, there is a significant increase in the average query response time when there are updates, which also agrees with our formula. The case of updates on `virt` WebViews (second pair of columns) has 27% higher average query response times compared to the no updates case. When the updates are on `matweb` WebViews (third pair of columns) the increase in average query response time is even higher: 236% compared to the no updates case. The reason for this is that the updates on the `matweb` WebViews are using the DBMS, which has adverse effects on the performance of `virt` access queries. This was clearly predicted by the total cost formula, since we included the cost of updates on `matweb` WebViews in the case where there are other types of WebViews in the system (second line of Eq. 9, $b = 1$). The reason for such a big difference in our case is that except for putting more load on the DBMS, updates on `matweb` WebViews also compete against `virt` queries for resources inside the DBMS. In the case of `virt` updates, this did not happen, because both the queries and the updates were referring to the same tables.

5 Conclusions

WebView materialization can speed up the query response times of database-backed web servers significantly. However, the multi-tiered architecture of typical web servers and the need for online updates raise new issues, when compared to the view selection problem in data warehouses. In this paper, we compared three materialization policies: virtual (`virt`), materialized inside the DBMS (`matdb`) and materialized at the web server (`matweb`), both analytically and quantitatively. We developed a detailed cost model that takes into consideration the parallelism inherent in real systems, and examined the effects of each policy on the staleness of WebViews and on the query response times. We also implemented an industrial strength database-backed web server (WebMat) and run extensive experiments.

The results from our experiments show that the `matweb` policy scales better than the other two, giving at least 10 times faster query response times, since it avoids going to the DBMS on every access request. This is true even under high access / update workloads, which makes the `matweb` policy the preferred choice on heavily loaded servers. On the other hand, the `matdb` policy was better than the `virt` policy only for a very limited number of cases: when the number of WebViews was small (100) or when the update rates were low (<5 updates/sec). Even for cases where the queries are expensive, precomputing them using the `matdb` policy usually leads to a decrease in performance (compared to the `virt` case) except for when the number of WebViews is small, or when there are no updates.

Acknowledgements We would like to thank Manuel Rodriguez, Damianos Karakos and Yannis Kotidis for their suggestions, and the reviewers for their useful comments.

References

[AB99] Tarek F. Abdelzaher and Nina Bhatti. "Web Content Adaptation to Improve Server Overload Behavior". In *Proc. of WWW8 Conference*, May 1999.

[AMM98] Paolo Atzeni, Giansalvatore Mecca, and Paolo Merialdo. "Design and Maintenance of Data-Intensive Web Sites". In *Proc. of EDBT'98*, March 1998.

[AMR+98] Serge Abiteboul, Jason McHugh, Michael Rys, Vasilis Vassalos, and Janet L. Wiener. "Incremental Maintenance for Materialized Views over Semistructured Data". In *Proc. of VLDB'98*, August 1998.

[AW97] Martin F. Arlitt and Carey Williamson. "Internet Web Servers: Workload Characterization and Performance Implications". *IEEE/ACM Transactions on Networking*, 5(5), October 1997.

[BBC+98] Phil Bernstein, Michael Brodie, Stefano Ceri, et al. "The Asilomar Report on Database Research". *SIGMOD Record*, 27(4), December 1998.

[BCF+99] Lee Breslau, Pei Cao, Li Fan, Graham Phillips, and Scott Shenker. "Web Caching and Zipf-like Distributions: Evidence and Implications". In *Proc. of INFOCOM'99*, March 1999.

[BD+98] Randall G. Bello, Karl Dias, et al. "Materialized Views in Oracle". In *Proc. of VLDB'98*, August 1998.

[CFP99] Stefano Ceri, Piero Fraternali, and Stefano Paraboschi. "Data-Driven, One-To-One Web Site Generation for Data-Intensive Applications". In *Proc. of VLDB'99*, September 1999.

[CID99] Jim Challenger, Arun Iyengar, and Paul Dantzig. "A Scalable System for Consistently Caching Dynamic Web Data". In *Proc. of INFOCOM'99*, March 1999.

[CZB98] Pei Cao, Jin Zhang, and Kevin Beach. "Active Cache: Caching Dynamic Contents on the Web". In *Proc. of Middleware '98 Conference*, 1998.

[FFK+98] Mary Fernandez, Daniela Florescu, Jaewoo Kang, Alon Levy, and Dan Suciu. "Catching the Boat with Strudel: Experiences with a Web-Site Management System". In *Proc. of SIGMOD'98*, June 1998.

[FLM98] Daniela Florescu, Alon Levy, and Alberto Mendelzon. "Database Techniques for the World-Wide Web: A Survey". *SIGMOD Record*, 27(3), Sep. 1998.

[FLSY99] Daniela Florescu, Alon Levy, Dan Suciu, and Khaled Yagoub. "Optimization of Run-time Management of Data Intensive Web-sites". In *Proc. of VLDB'99*, September 1999.

[GM95] Ashish Gupta and Inderpal Singh Mumick. "Maintenance of Materialized Views: Problems, Techniques, and Applications". *Data Engineering Bulletin*, 18(2), June 1995.

[GM99] Ashish Gupta and Inderpal Singh Mumick, editors. *"Materialized Views: Techniques, Implementations, and Applications"*. MIT Press, June 1999.

[Gre99] Philip Greenspun. *"Philip and Alex's Guide to Web Publishing"*. Morgan Kaufmann, June 1999.

[Gup97] Himanshu Gupta. "Selection of Views to Materialize in a Data Warehouse". In *Proc. of ICDT'97*, Jan. 1997.

[IC97] Arun Iyengar and Jim Challenger. "Improving Web Server Performance by Caching Dynamic Data". In *Proc. of USITS '97*, Monterey, CA, December 1997.

[KR99] Yannis Kotidis and Nick Roussopoulos. "DynaMat: A Dynamic View Management System for Data Warehouses". In *Proc. of SIGMOD'99*, June 1999.

[LISD99] Eric Levy, Arun Iyengar, Junehwa Song, and Daniel Dias. "Design and Performance of a Web Server Accelerator". In *Proc. of INFOCOM'99*, March 1999.

[LR99] Alexandros Labrinidis and Nick Roussopoulos. "On the Materialization of WebViews". In *Proc. of WebDB'99*, June 1999.

[LR00a] Alexandros Labrinidis and Nick Roussopoulos. "Generating dynamic content at database-backed web servers: cgi-bin vs mod_perl". *SIGMOD Record*, 29(1), March 2000.

[LR00b] Alexandros Labrinidis and Nick Roussopoulos. "WebView Materialization". Technical report, Institute for Systems Research, University of Maryland, March 2000.

[Mal98] Susan Malaika. "Resistance is Futile: The Web Will Assimilate Your Database". *Data Engineering Bulletin*, 21(2), June 1998.

[MMM98] Giansalvatore Mecca, Alberto Mendelzon, and Paolo Merialdo. "Efficient Queries over Web Views". In *Proc. of EDBT'98*, March 1998.

[Rou98] Nick Roussopoulos. "Materialized Views and Data Warehouses". *SIGMOD Record*, 27(1), March 1998.

[Sin98] Giuseppe Sindoni. "Incremental Maintenance of Hypertext Views". In *Proc. of WebDB'98*, Mar. 1998.

NiagaraCQ: A Scalable Continuous Query System for Internet Databases

Jianjun Chen   David J. DeWitt   Feng Tian   Yuan Wang
Computer Sciences Department
University of Wisconsin-Madison

{jchen, dewitt, ftian, yuanwang}@cs.wisc.edu

ABSTRACT

Continuous queries are persistent queries that allow users to receive new results when they become available. While continuous query systems can transform a passive web into an active environment, they need to be able to support millions of queries due to the scale of the Internet. No existing systems have achieved this level of scalability. NiagaraCQ addresses this problem by grouping continuous queries based on the observation that many web queries share similar structures. Grouped queries can share the common computation, tend to fit in memory and can reduce the I/O cost significantly. Furthermore, grouping on selection predicates can eliminate a large number of unnecessary query invocations. Our grouping technique is distinguished from previous group optimization approaches in the following ways. First, we use an incremental group optimization strategy with dynamic re-grouping. New queries are added to existing query groups, without having to regroup already installed queries. Second, we use a query-split scheme that requires minimal changes to a general-purpose query engine. Third, NiagaraCQ groups both change-based and timer-based queries in a uniform way. To insure that NiagaraCQ is scalable, we have also employed other techniques including incremental evaluation of continuous queries, use of both pull and push models for detecting heterogeneous data source changes, and memory caching. This paper presents the design of NiagaraCQ system and gives some experimental results on the system's performance and scalability.

1. INTRODUCTION

Continuous queries [TGNO92][LPT99][LPBZ96] allow users to obtain new results from a database without having to issue the same query repeatedly. Continuous queries are especially useful in an environment like the Internet comprised of large amounts of frequently changing information. For example, users might want to issue continuous queries of the form:

> *Notify me whenever the price of Dell or Micron stock drops by more than 5% and the price of Intel stock remains unchanged over next three month.*

In order to handle a large number of users with diverse interests, a continuous query system must be capable of supporting a large number of triggers expressed as complex queries against web-resident data sets.

The goal of the Niagara project is to develop a distributed database system for querying distributed XML data sets using a query language like XML-QL [DFF+98]. As part of this effort, our goal is to allow a very large number of users to be able to register continuous queries in a high-level query language such as XML-QL. We hypothesize that many queries will tend to be similar to one another and hope to be able to handle millions of continuous queries by grouping similar queries together. Group optimization has the following benefits. First, grouped queries can share computation. Second, the common execution plans of grouped queries can reside in memory, significantly saving on I/O costs compared to executing each query separately. Third, grouping makes it possible to test the "firing" conditions of many continuous queries together, avoiding unnecessary invocations.

Previous group optimization efforts [CM86] [RC88] [Sel86] have focused on finding an optimal plan for a small number of similar queries. This approach is not applicable to a continuous query system for the following reasons. First, it is computationally too expensive to handle a large number of queries. Second, it was not designed for an environment like the web, in which continuous queries are dynamically added and removed. Our approach uses a novel incremental group optimization approach in which queries are grouped according to their signatures. When a new query arrives, the existing groups are considered as possible optimization choices instead of re-grouping all the queries in the system. The new query is merged into existing groups whose signatures match that of the query.

Our incremental group optimization scheme employs a query-split scheme. After the signature of a new query is matched, the sub-plan corresponding to the signature is replaced with a scan of the output file produced by the matching group. This optimization process then continues with the remainder of the query tree in a bottom-up fashion until the entire query has been analyzed. In the case that no group "matches" a signature of the new query, a new query group for this signature is created in the system. Thus, each continuous query is split into several smaller queries such that inputs of each of these queries are monitored using the same techniques that are used for the inputs of user-defined continuous queries. The main advantage of this approach is that it can be implemented using a general query engine with only minor modifications. Another advantage is that the approach is easy to implement and, as we will demonstrate in Section 4, very scalable.

Since queries are continuously being added and removed from groups, over time the quality of the group can deteriorate, leading to a reduction in the overall performance of the system. In this case, one or more groups may require "dynamic re-grouping" to re-establish their effectiveness.

Continuous queries can be classified into two categories depending on the criteria used to trigger their execution. *Change-based* continuous queries are fired as soon as new relevant data becomes available. *Timer-based* continuous queries are executed only at time intervals specified by the submitting user. In our previous example, day traders would probably want to know the desired price information immediately, while longer-term investors may be satisfied being notified every hour. Although change-based continuous queries obviously provide better response time, they waste system resources when instantaneous answers are not really required. Since timer-based continuous queries can be supported more efficiently, query systems that support timer-based continuous queries should be much more scalable. However, since users can specify various overlapping time intervals for their continuous queries, grouping timer-based queries is much more difficult than grouping purely change-based queries. Our approach handles both types of queries uniformly.

NiagaraCQ is the continuous query sub-system of the Niagara project, which is a net data management system being developed at University of Wisconsin and Oregon Graduate Institute. NiagaraCQ supports scalable continuous query processing over multiple, distributed XML files by deploying the incremental group optimization ideas introduced above. A number of other techniques are used to make NiagaraCQ scalable and efficient. 1) NiagaraCQ supports the incremental evaluation of continuous queries by considering only the changed portion of each updated XML file and not the entire file. Since frequently only a small portion of each file gets updated, this strategy can save significant amounts of computation. Another advantage of incremental evaluation is that repetitive evaluation is avoided and only new results are returned to users. 2) NiagaraCQ can monitor and detect data source changes using both push and poll models on heterogeneous sources. 3) Due to the scale of the system, all the information of the continuous queries and temporary results cannot be held in memory. A caching mechanism is used to obtain good performance with limited amounts of memory.

The rest of the paper is organized as follows. In Section 2 the NiagaraCQ command language is briefly described. Our new group optimization approach is presented in Section 3 and its implementation is described in Section 4. Section 5 examines the performance of the incremental continuous query optimization scheme. Related work is described in Section 6. We conclude our paper in Section 7.

2. NIAGARACQ COMMAND LANGUAGE

NiagaraCQ defines a simple command language for creating and dropping continuous queries. The command to create a continuous query has the following form:

> **CREATE** *CQ_name*
> *XML-QL query*
> **DO** *action*
> {**START** *start_time*} {**EVERY** *time_interval*} {**EXPIRE** *expiration_time*}

To delete a continuous query, the following command is used:

> **Delete** *CQ_name*

Users can write continuous queries in NiagaraCQ by combining an ordinary XML-QL query with additional time information. The query will become effective at the *start_time*. The *Time_interval* indicates how often the query is to be executed. A query is timer-based if its *time_interval* is not zero; otherwise, it is change-based. Continuous queries will be deleted from the system automatically after their *expiration_time*. If not provided, default values for the time are used. (These values can be set by the database administrator.) *Action* is performed upon the XML-QL query results. For example, it could be ``MailTo dewitt@cs.wisc.edu'' or a complex stored procedure to further processing the results of the query. Users can delete installed queries explicitly using the delete command.

3. OUR INCREMENTAL GROUP OPTIMIZATION APPROACH

In Section 3.1, we present a novel incremental group optimization strategy that scales to a large number of queries. This strategy can be applied to a wide range of group optimization methods. A specific group optimization method based on this approach is described in Section 3.2. Section 3.3 introduces our query-split scheme that requires minimal changes to a general-purpose query engine. Section 3.4 and 3.5 apply our group optimization method to selection and join operators. We discuss how our system supports timer-based queries in Section 3.6. Section 3.7 contains a brief discussion of the caching mechanisms in NiagaraCQ to make the system more scalable.

3.1 General Strategy of Incremental Group Optimization

Previous group optimization strategies [CM86] [RC88] [Sel86] focused on finding an optimal global plan for a small number of queries. These techniques are useful in a query environment where a small number of similar queries either enter the system within a short time interval or are given in advance. A naive approach for grouping continuous queries would be to apply these methods directly by reoptimizing all queries whenever a new query is added. We contend that such an approach is not acceptable for large dynamic environments because of the associated performance overhead.

We propose an incremental group optimization strategy for continuous queries in this paper. Groups are created for existing queries according to their signatures, which represent similar structures among the queries. Groups allow the common parts of two or more queries to be shared. Each individual query in a query group shares the results from the execution of the group plan. When a new query is submitted, the group optimizer considers existing groups as potential optimization choices. The new query is merged into those existing groups that match its signatures. Existing queries are not, however, re-grouped in our approach. While this strategy is likely to result in sub-optimal groups, it reduces the cost of group optimization significantly. More importantly it is very scalable in a dynamic environment. Since continuous queries are frequently added and removed, it is possible that current groups may become inefficient. "Dynamic re-grouping" would be helpful to re-group part or all of the queries either periodically or when the system performance degrades below some threshold. This is left as future work.

3.2 Incremental Group Optimization using Expression Signature

Based on our incremental grouping strategy, we designed a scalable group optimization method using expression signatures. Expression signatures [HCH+99] represent the same syntax structure, but possibly different constant values, in different queries. It is a specific implementation of the signature concept.

3.2.1 Expression Signature

For purposes of illustration, we use XML-QL queries on a database of stock quotes.

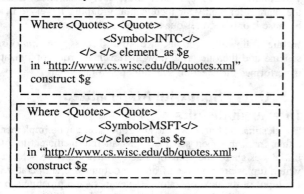

Figure 3.1 XML-QL query examples

The two XML-QL queries in Figure 3.1 retrieve stock information on either Intel (symbol INTC) or Microsoft (symbol MSFT). Many users are likely to submit similar queries for different stock symbols. An expression signature is created for the selection predicates by replacing the constants appearing in the predicates with a placeholder. The expression signature for the two queries in Figure 3.1 is shown in Figure 3.2.

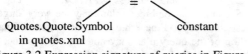

Figure 3.2 Expression signature of queries in Figure 3.1

A query plan is generated by Niagara query parser. Figure 3.3 shows the query plans of the queries in Figure 3.1. The lower part in each query plan corresponds to the expression signature of the queries. A new operator TriggerAction is added on the top

of the XML-QL query plan after the query is parsed. Expression signatures allow queries with the same syntactic structure to be grouped together to share computation [HCH+99]. Expression signatures for different queries will be discussed later. Note, in NiagaraCQ, users can specify an XML-QL query without specifying the destination data sources by using a "*" in the file name position and giving a DTD name. This allows users to specify continuous queries without naming the data sources. Our group query optimizer is easily extended to support this capability by using a mapping mechanism offered by the Niagara Search Engine. Without losing generality for our incremental grouping algorithm, we assume continuous queries are defined on a specific data source in this paper.

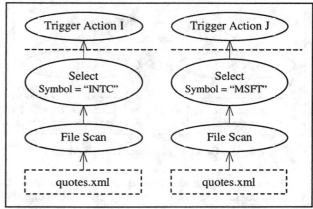

Figure 3.3 Query plans of queries in Figure 3.1

3.2.2 Group

Groups are created for queries based on their expression signatures. For example, a group is generated for the queries in Figure 3.1 because they have same expression signature. We use this group in following discussion. A group consists of three parts.

1. Group signature

The *group signature* is the common expression signature of all queries in the group. For the example above, the expression signature is given in Figure 3.2.

Constant_value	Destination_buffer
....	....
INTC	Dest. i
MSFT	Dest. j
....	....

Figure 3.4 an example of group constant table

2. Group constant table

The *group constant table* contains the signature constants of all queries in the group. The constant table is stored as an XML file. For the example above, "INTC" and "MFST" are stored in this table (Figure 3.4). Since the tuples produced by the shared computation need to be directed to the correct individual query for further processing, the destination information is also stored with the constant.

381

3. Group plan

The *group plan* is the query plan shared by all queries in the group. It is derived from the common part of all single query plans in the group. Figure 3.5 shows the group plan for the queries in Figure 3.1.

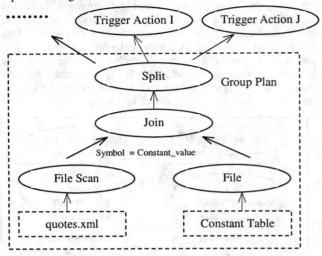

Figure 3.5 Group plan for queries in Figure 3.1

An expression signature allows queries in a group to have different constants. Since the result of the shared computation contains results for all the queries in the group, the results must be filtered and sent to the correct destination operator for further processing. NiagaraCQ performs filtering by combining a special *Split* operator with a Join operator based on the constant values stored in the constant table. Tuples from the data source (e.g. Quotes.xml) are joined with the constant table. The *Split* operator distributes each result tuple of the Join operator to its correct destination based on the destination buffer name in the tuple (obtained from the Constant Table). The *Split* operator removes the name of the destination buffer from the tuple before it is put into the output stream, so that subsequent operators in the query do not need to be modified. In addition, queries with the same constant value also share the same output stream. This feature can significantly reduce the number of output buffers.

Since generally the number of active groups is likely to be on the order of thousands or ten of thousands, group plans can be stored in a memory-resident hash table (termed a *group table*) with the group signature as the hash key. Group constant tables are likely to be large and are stored on disk.

3.2.3 Incremental Grouping Algorithm

In this section we briefly describe how the NiagaraCQ group optimizer performs incremental group optimization.

When a new query (Figure 3.6) is submitted, the group optimizer traverses its query plan bottom up and tries to match its expression signature with the signatures of existing groups. The expression signature of the new query, which is the same as the signature in Figure 3.2, matches the signature of the group in Figure 3.5. The group optimizer breaks the query plan (Figure 3.7) into two parts. The lower part of the query is removed. The upper part of the query is added onto the group plan. If the

constant table does not have an entry "AOL", it will be added and a new destination buffer allocated.

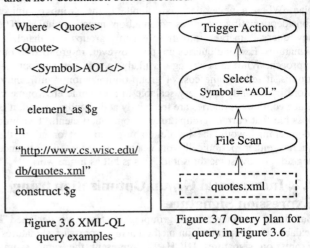

Figure 3.6 XML-QL query examples

Figure 3.7 Query plan for query in Figure 3.6

In the case that the signature of the query does not match any group signature, a new group will be generated for this signature and added to the group table.

In general, a query may have several signatures and may be merged into several groups in the system. This matching process will continue on the remainder of the query plan until the top of the plan is reached. Our incremental grouping is very efficient because it only requires one traversal of the query plan.

In the following sections, we first discuss our *query-split* scheme and then describe how incremental group optimization is performed on selection and join operators.

3.3 Query Split with Materialized Intermediate Files

The destination buffer for the split operator can be implemented either in a pipelined scheme or as an intermediate file. Our initial design of the split operator used a pipeline scheme in which tuples are pipelined from the output of one operator into the input of the next operator. However, such a pipeline scheme does not work for grouping timer-based continuous queries. Since timer-based queries will only be fired at specified time, output tuples must be retained until the next firing time. It is difficult for a split operator to determine which tuples should be stored and how long they should be stored for.

In addition, in the pipelined approach, the ungrouped parts of all query plans in a group are combined with the group plan, resulting in a single execution plan for all queries in the group. This single plan has several disadvantages. First, its structure is a directed graph, and not a tree. Thus, the plan may be too complicated for a general-purpose XML-QL query engine to execute. Second, the combined plan may be very large and require resources beyond the limits of some systems. Finally, a large portion of the query plan may not need to be executed at each query invocation. For example, in Figure 3.5, suppose only the price of Intel stock changes. Although the destination buffer for Microsoft is empty, the upper part of the Microsoft query (Trigger Action J) is also executed. This problem can be avoided only if the execution engine has the ability to selectively load part of a query plan in a bottom-up manner. Such a capability would require a special implementation of the XML-QL query engine.

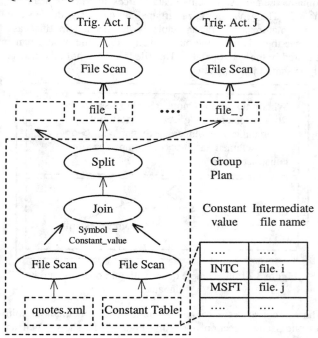

Figure 3.8 query-split scheme using intermediate files

Since a split operator has one input stream and multiple (possibly tens of thousands) output streams, split operators may become a bottleneck when the ungrouped parts of queries consume output tuples from the split stream at widely varying rates. For example, suppose 100 queries are grouped together, 99 of which are very simple selection queries, and one is a very expensive query involving multiple joins. Since this expensive query may process the input from the split operator very slowly, it may block all the other simple queries.

The pipeline scheme can be used in systems that support only a small number of change-based continuous queries. Since our goal is to support millions of both change-based and timer-based continuous queries, we adopt an approach that is more scalable and easier to implement. We also try to use a general query engine to the maximal extent possible.

In our new design (Figure 3.8), the split operator writes each output stream into an intermediate file. A query plan is cut into two parts at the split operator and a file scan operator is added to the upper part of plan to read the intermediate file. NiagaraCQ treats the two new queries like normal user queries. In particular, changes to the intermediate files are monitored in the same way as those to ordinary data sources! Since a new continuous query may overlap with multiple query groups, one query may be split into several queries. However, the total number of queries in the system will not exceed the number of groups plus the number of original user queries. Since we assume that no more than thousands of groups will be generated for millions of user queries, the overall number of queries in the system will increase only slightly. Intermediate file names are stored in the constant table and grouped continuous queries with the same constant share the same intermediate file.

The advantages of this new design include:

1.   Each query is scheduled independently, thus only the necessary queries are executed. For example, in Figure 3.8, if only the price of Intel stock changes, queries on intermediate files other than "file_i" will not be scheduled. Since usually only a small amount of data is changed, only a few of the installed continuous queries will be fired. Thus, computation time and system resource usage is significantly reduced.

2.   Queries after a split operator will be in a standard, tree-structured query format and thus can be scheduled and executed by a general query engine.

3.   Each query in the system is about the size of a common user query, so that it can be executed without consuming an unusual amount of system resources.

4.   This approach handles intermediate files and original data source files uniformly. Changes to materialized intermediate files will be processed and monitored just like changes to the original data files.

5.   The potential bottleneck problem of the pipelined approach is avoided.

There are some potential disadvantages. First, the split operator becomes a blocking operator since the execution of the upper part of the query must wait for the intermediate files to be completely materialized. Since continuous queries run over data changes that are usually not very large, we do not believe that the impact of this blocking will be significant. Second, reading and writing the intermediate files incurs extra disk I/Os. Since most data changes will be relatively small, we anticipate that they will be buffered in memory before the upper part queries consume them. There will be disk I/Os in the case of timer-based queries that have long time intervals because data changes may be accumulated. In this situation, data changes need to be written to disk no matter what strategy is used. As discussed in Section 3.7, NiagaraCQ uses special caching mechanisms to reduce this cost.

3.4   Incremental Grouping of General Selection Predicates

Our primary focus is on predicates that are in the format of "*Attribute op Constant.*" *Attribute* is a path expression without wildcards in it. Op includes "=", "<", ">". Such formats dominate in selection queries. Other predicate formats could also be handled in our approach, but we do not discuss them further in this paper.

Figure 3.9 shows an example of a range selection query that returns every stock whose price has risen more than 5%. Figure 3.9 also gives its expression signature. The group plan for queries with this signature is the same in Figure 3.5, except the join condition is *Change_Ratio > constant.*

A general range-query has both lower_bound and upper_bound values. Two columns are needed to represent both bounds in the constant table. Thus each entry of the constant table will be [lower_bound, upper_bound, intermediate_file_name]. The join condition is *Change_Ratio < upper_bound and Change_Ratio > lower_bound.* A special index would be helpful to evaluate this predicate. For example, an interval skip list [HJ94] could be used for this purpose when all the intervals fit in memory. We are considering developing a new index method that handles this case more efficiently.

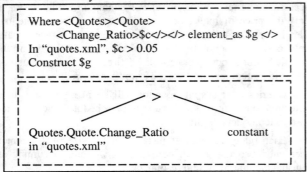

Figure 3.9 Range selection query example and its expression signature

One potential problem for range-query groups is that the intermediate files may contain a large number of duplicate tuples because range predicates of the different queries might overlap. "Virtual intermediate files" are used to handle this case. Each virtual intermediate file stores a value range instead of actual result tuples. All outputs from the split operator are stored in one real intermediate file, which has a clustered index on the range attribute. Modification on virtual intermediate files can trigger upper-level queries in the same way as ordinary intermediate files. The value range of a virtual intermediate file is used to retrieve data from the real intermediate file. Our query-split scheme need not be changed to handle virtual intermediate files.

In general, a query may have multiple selection predicates, i.e. multiple expression signatures. Predicates on the same data source can be represented in conjunctive normal form. The group optimizer chooses the most selective conjunct, which does not contain "or", to do incremental grouping. Other predicates are evaluated in the upper levels of the continuous query after the split operator.

```
Where <Quotes><Quote><Symbol>"INTC"</>
        <Current_Price>$p</></>  element_as $g </>
in "quotes.xml", $p < 100
Construct $g
```

Figure 3.10 an example query with two selection predicates

Figure 3.10 shows a query with two selection predicates, which retrieves Intel stock whenever its price falls below $100. This query has two expression signatures, one is an equal selection predicate on *Symbol* and the other is a range selection predicate on *Current_price*. The expression signature on the equal selection predicate (i.e. on *Symbol*) is used for grouping because it is more selective. In addition, a new select operator with the second selection predicate (i.e. the range select on *Current_price*) will be added above the file scan operator.

3.5   Incremental Grouping of Join Operators

Since join operators are usually expensive, sharing common join operations can significantly reduce the amount of computation. Figure 3.11 shows a query with a join operator that, for each company, retrieves the price of its stock and the company's

profile.   The signature for the join operation is shown on the right side of the figure. A join signature in our approach contains the names of the two data sources and the predicate for the join. The group optimizer groups join queries with the same join signatures. A constant table is not needed in this case because there is only one output intermediate file, whose name is stored in the split operator. This file is used to hold the results of the shared join operation.

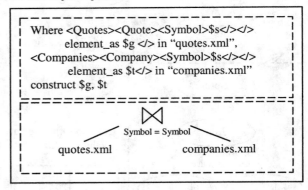

Figure 3.11 an example query with join operator and its signature

There are two ways to group queries that contain both join operators and selection operators. Figure 3.12 shows such an example, which retrieves all stocks in the computer service industry and the related company profiles. The group optimizer can place the selection either below or above the join, so that two different grouping sequences can be used during incremental group optimization process. The group optimizer chooses the better one based on a cost model. We discuss these alternatives below using the query example in Figure 3.12.

```
Where <Quotes><Quote><Symbol>$s</>
        <Industry>"Computer Service"</></>
            element_as $g </> in "quotes.xml",
    <Companies><Company><Symbol>$s</></>
            element_as $t</> in "companies.xml"
construct $g, $t
```

Figure 3.12 an example query with both join and selection operators

If the selection operator (e.g., on *Industry*) is pulled above the join operator, the group optimizer first groups the query by the join signature. The selection signature, which contains the intermediate file, is grouped next. The advantage of this method is that it allows the same join operator to be shared by queries with different selection operators. The disadvantage is that the join, which will be performed before the selection, may be very expensive and may generate a large intermediate file. If there are only a small number of queries in the join group and each of them has a highly selective selection predicate, then this grouping method may be even more expensive than evaluating the queries individually.

Alternatively, the group optimizer can push down the selection operator (e.g., on *Industry*) to avoid computing an expensive join. First, the signature for the selection operator is matched with an existing group. Then a file scan operator on the intermediate file produced by the selection group is added and the join operator is rewritten to use the intermediate file as one of its inputs. Finally, the group optimizer incrementally groups the join operation using its signature. Compared to the first approach, this approach may create many join groups with significant overlap between them. Note, however, that this same overlap exists in the non-grouping approach. Thus, in general, this method always outperforms than non-grouping approach.

The group optimizer will select one of these two strategies based on a cost model. To date we have implemented the second approach in NiagaraCQ. In the future we plan on implementing the first strategy and compare the performance of the two approaches.

3.6 Grouping Timer-based Continuous Queries

Since timer-based queries are only periodically executed their use can significantly reduce computation time and make the system more scalable. Timer-based queries are grouped in the same way as change-based queries except that the time information needs to be recorded at installation time. Grouping large number of timer-based queries poses two significant challenges. First, it is hard to monitor the timer events of those queries. Second, sharing the common computation becomes difficult due to the various time intervals. For example, two users may both request the query in Figure 3.1 with different time intervals, e.g. weekly and monthly. The query with the monthly interval should not repeat the weekly query's work. In general, queries with various time intervals should be able to share the results that have already been produced.

3.6.1 Event Detection

Two types of events in NiagaraCQ can trigger continuous queries. They are data-source change events and timer events. Data sources can be classified into push-based and pull-based. Push-based data sources will inform NiagaraCQ whenever interesting data is changed. On the other hand, changes on pull-based data sources must be checked periodically by NiagaraCQ.

Timer-based continuous queries are fired only at specified times. However, queries will not be executed if the corresponding input files have not been modified. Timer events are stored in an event list, which is sorted in time order. Each entry in the list corresponds to a time instant where there exists a continuous query to be scheduled. Each query in NiagaraCQ has a unique id. Those query ids are also stored in the entry. Whenever a timer event occurs, all related files will be checked. Each query in the entry will be fired if its data source has been modified since its last firing time. The next firing times for all queries in the entry are calculated and the queries are added into the corresponding entries on the list.

3.6.2 Incremental Evaluation

Incremental evaluation allows queries to be invoked only on the changed data. It reduces the amount of computation significantly because typically the amount of changed data is smaller than the original data file. For each file, on which continuous queries are defined, NiagaraCQ keeps a "delta file" that contains recent changes. Queries are run over the delta files whenever possible instead of their original files. However, in some cases the complete data files must be used, e.g., incremental evaluation of join operators. NiagaraCQ uses different techniques for handling delta files of ordinary data sources and those of

intermediate files used to store the output of the split operator. NiagaraCQ calculates the changes to a source XML file and merges the changes into its delta file. For intermediate files, outputs from the split operators are directly appended to the delta file.

In order to support timer-based queries, a time stamp is added to each tuple in the delta file. Since timer-based queries with different firing times can be defined on one file, the delta file must keep data for the longest time interval among those queries that use the file as an input. At query execution time, NiagaraCQ fetches only tuples that were added to the delta file since the query's last firing time.

Whenever a grouped plan is invoked, the results of its execution are stored in an intermediate file regardless of whether or not queries defined on these intermediate files should be fired immediately. Subsequent invocations of this group query do not need to repeat previous computation. Upper level queries defined on intermediate files will still be fired at their scheduled execution time. Thus, the shared computation is totally transparent to these subsequent operators.

3.7 Memory Caching

Due to the desired scale of the system, we do not assume that all the information required by the continuous queries and intermediate results will fit in memory. Caching is used to obtain good performance with a limited amount of memory. NiagaraCQ caches query plans, system data structures, and data files for better performance.

1. Grouped query plans tend to be memory resident since we assume that the number of query groups is relatively small. Non-grouped change-based queries may be cached using an LRU policy that favors frequently fired queries. Timer-based queries with shorter firing intervals will have priority over those with longer intervals.

2. NiagaraCQ caches recently accessed files. Small delta files generated by split operators tend to be consumed and discarded. A caching policy that favors these small files saves lots of disk I/Os.

3. The event list for monitoring the timer-based events can be large if there are millions of timer-based continuous queries. To avoid maintaining the whole list in memory, we keep only a "time window" of this list. The window contains the front part of the list that should be kept in memory, e.g. within 24 hours.

4. IMPLEMENTATION

NiagaraCQ is being developed as a sub-system of Niagara project. The initial version of the system was implemented in Java (JDK1.2). A validating XML parser (IBM XML4J) from IBM is used to parse XML documents. We describe the system architecture of NiagaraCQ in Section 4.1 and how continuous queries are processed in Section 4.2.

4.1 System Architecture

Figure 4.1 shows the architecture of Niagara system. NiagaraCQ is a sub-system of Niagara that handles continuous queries. NiagaraCQ consists of

1. A continuous query manager, which is the core module of NiagaraCQ system. It provides a continuous query interface to

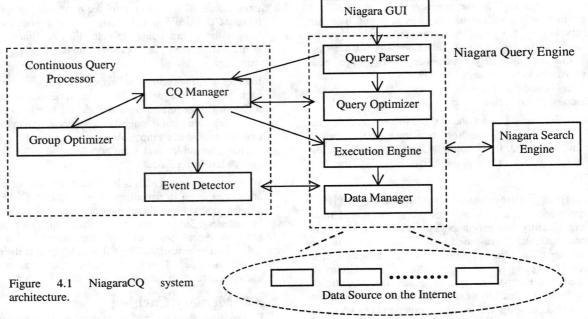

Figure 4.1 NiagaraCQ system architecture.

users and invokes the Niagara query engine to execute fired queries.

2. A group optimizer that performs incremental group optimization.

3. An event detector that detects timer events and changes of data sources.

In addition, the Niagara data manager was enhanced to support the incremental evaluation of continuous queries.

4.2 Processing Continuous Queries

Figure 4.2 shows the interactions among the Continuous Query Manager, the Event Detector and the Data Manager as continuous queries are installed, detected, and executed. Continuous query processing is discussed in following sections.

4.2.1 Continuous Query Installation

When a new continuous query enters the system, the query is parsed and the query plan is fed into the group optimizer for incremental grouping. The group optimizer may split this query into several queries using the query-split scheme described in Section 3. The continuous query manager then invokes the Niagara query optimizer to perform common query optimization for these queries and the optimized plans are stored for future execution. Timer information and data source names of these queries are given to the Event Detector (Step 1 in Figure 4.2). The Event Detector then asks the Data Manager to monitor the related source files and intermediate files (Step 2 in Figure 4.2), which in turn caches a local copy of each source file. This step is necessary in order to detect subsequent changes to the file.

The Event Detector monitors two types of events: *timer events* and *file-modification* events. Whenever such events occur, the Event Detector notifies the Continuous Query Manager about which queries need to be fired and on which data sources.

The Data Manager in Niagara monitors web XML sources and intermediate files on its local disk. It handles the disk I/O for both ordinary queries and continuous queries and supports both push-based and pull-based data sources. For push-based data sources, the Data Manager is informed of a file change and notifies Event Detector actively. Otherwise, the Event Detector periodically asks the Data Manager to check the last modified time.

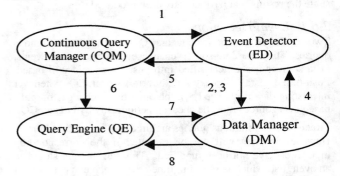

1. CQM adds continuous queries with file and timer information to enable ED to monitor the events.
2. ED asks DM to monitor changes to files.
3. When a timer event happens, ED asks DM the last modified time of files.
4. DM informs ED of changes to push-based data sources.
5. If file changes and timer events are satisfied, ED provides CQM with a list of firing CQs.
6. CQM invokes QE to execute firing CQs.
7. File scan operator calls DM to retrieve selected documents.
8. DM only returns data changes between last fire time and current fire time.

Figure 4.2 Continuous Query processing in NiagaraCQ

4.2.2 Continuous Query Deletion

A system unique name is generated for every user-defined continuous query. A user can use this name to retrieve the query status or to delete the query. Queries are automatically removed from the system when they expire.

4.2.3 Execution of Continuous Queries

The invocation of a continuous query requires a series of interactions among the Continuous Query Manager, Event Detector and Data Manager.

When a timer event happens, the Event Detector first asks the Data Manager if any of the relevant data sources have been modified (Step 3 in Figure 4.2). The Data Manager returns a list of names of modified source files. The Data Manager also notifies the Event Detector when push-based data sources have been changed (Step 4 in Figure 4.2). If a continuous query needs to be executed, its query id and the names of the modified files are sent to the Continuous Query Manager (Step 5 in Figure 4.2). The Continuous Query Manager invokes the Niagara query engine to execute the triggered queries (Step 6 in Figure 4.2). At execution time, the Query Engine requests data from the Data Manager (Step 7. in Figure 4.2). The Data Manager recognizes that it is a request for a continuous query and returns only the delta file (Step 8 in Figure 4.2). Delta files for source files are computed by performing an XML-specific "diff" operation using the original file and the new version of the file.

5. EXPERIMENTAL RESULTS

We expect that for a continuous query system over the Internet, incremental group optimization will provide substantial improvement to system performance and scalability. In the following experiments, we compare our incremental grouping approach with a non-grouping approach to show benefits from sharing computation and avoiding unnecessary query invocations.

5.1 Experiment Setting

The following experiments were conducted on a Sun Ultra 6000 with 1GB of RAM, running JDK1.2 on Solaris 2.6.

```
<!ELEMENT Quotes ( Quote )*>
<!ELEMENT Quote ( Symbol, Sector, Industry,
Current_Price, Open, PrevCls, Volume, Day's_range,
52_week_range?, Change_Ratio>
<!ELEMENT Day's_range (low, high)>
<!ELEMENT 52_week_change (low, high)>
```

Figure 5.1 DTD of quotes.xml

```
<!ELEMENT Companies ( Company )*>
<!ELEMENT Company ( Symbol, Name, Sector, Industry,
Company_profiles?>
<!ELEMENT Company_profiles (Capital, Employees,
Address, Description)>
<!ELEMENT Address (City, State)>
```

Figure 5.2 DTD of companies.xml

Data Sets

Our experiments were run against a database of stock information consisting of two XML files, "quotes.xml" and "companies.xml". "Quotes.xml" contains stock information on about 5000 NASDAQ companies. The size of "quotes.xml" is about 2 MB. Related company information is stored in "companies.xml", whose size is about 1MB. The DTDs of these two XML files are given in Figure 5.1 and 5.2, respectively.

Data changes on "quotes.xml" are generated artificially to simulate the real stock market and continuous queries are triggered by these changes. The "companies.xml" file was not changed during our experiments.

We give a brief description of the assumptions that we made to generate "quotes.xml". Each stock has a unique *Symbol* value. The *Industry* attribute takes a value randomly from a set with about 100 values. The *Change_Ratio* represents the change percentage of the current price to the closing price for the previous session. It follows a normal distribution with a mean value of 0 and standard deviation of 1.0.

Since time spent calculating changes in source files is the same for both the grouped and non-grouped approaches, we run our experiments directly against the data changes. Unless specified, the number of "tuples" modified is 1000, which is about 400K bytes.

Queries

Although users may submit many different queries, we hypothesize that many queries will contain similar expression signatures. In our experiments, we use four types of queries to represent the effect of grouping queries in a stock environment by their expression signatures.

```
Where <Quotes><Quote><Symbol>"INTC"</></>
element_as $g </> in "quotes.xml", construct $g
```

Query Type-1 Example: Notify me when Intel stocks change.

```
Where <Quotes><Quote><Change_Ratio>$c</></>
element_as $g </> in "quotes.xml", $c > 0.05
construct $g
```

Query Type-2 Example: Notify me of all stocks whose prices rise more than 5 percent.

```
Where <Quotes><Quote><Symbol>"INTC"</>
<Current_Price>$p</></> element_as $g </>
in "quotes.xml", $p < 100,   construct $g
```

Query Type-3 Example: Notify me when Intel stock trades below 100 dollars.

```
Where <Quotes><Quote><Symbol>$s</></><Industry>
"Computer Service"</></> element_as $g </>
in "quotes.xml",
<Companies><Company><Symbol>$s</></></>
element_as $t</> in "companies.xml"
construct $g, $t
```

Query Type-4 Example: Notify me all of changes to stocks in the computer service industry and related company information.

- Type-1 queries have the same expression signature on the equal selection predicate on *Symbol*.

- Type-2 queries have the same expression signature on the range selection predicate on *Change_ratio*.

- Type-3 queries have two common expression signatures, one is on the equal selection predicate on *Symbol*, and the other is on the range selection predicate on *Current_price*. The expression signature of the equal selection predicate is used for grouping Type-3 queries because it is more selective than that of the range predicate.

- Type-4 queries contain expression signatures for both selection and join operators. Selection operators are pushed down under join operators. The incremental group optimizer first groups selection signatures and then join signatures.

Queries of Type-3 are generated following a normal distribution with a mean value of 3 and a standard deviation of 1.0. Queries of the other types are generated using different constants following a uniform distribution on the range of values in the data unless specified.

5.2 Interpretation of Experimental Result

The parameters in our experiments are:

1. N, the number of installed queries, is an important measure of system scalability.

2. F, the number of fired queries in the grouping case. The number of fired queries may vary depending on triggering conditions in the grouping case. For example, in a Tye-1 query, if Intel stock does not change, queries defined on "INTC" are not scheduled for execution after the common computation of the group. This parameter does not affect non-grouping queries.

3. C, the number of tuples modified.

In our grouping approach, a user-defined query consists of grouped part and non-grouped part. T_g and T_{ng} represent the execution time of each part. The execution time T for evaluating N queries is the sum of T_g and T_{ng} of each of F fired queries,

$$T = T_g + \sum_F T_{ng}$$

, because the grouped portion is executed only once.

Since the non-grouping strategy needs to scan each XML data source file multiple times, we cache parsed XML files in memory so that both approaches scan and parse XML files only once. This ensures that the comparison between the two approaches is fair. However, in a production system, parsed XML files probably could not be retained in memory for long periods of time. Thus, many non-grouped queries may each have to scan and parse the same XML files multiple times.

5.2.1 Experimental results on single type queries
We studied how effectively incremental group optimization works for each type of query. We measured and compared execution time for queries of each type for both the grouping and non-grouping approaches.

Experiment results on type-1 queries

Experiment 1. (Figure 5.3) C =1000 tuples.

- **Case 1**: F = N, i.e. all queries are fired in both approaches.

The execution time of the non-grouping approach grows dramatically as N increases. It cannot be applied to a highly loaded system. On the other hand, the grouping approach consumes significantly less execution time by sharing the computation of the selection operator. It also grows more slowly because in a single Type-1 query T_{ng} is much smaller than T_g.

- **Case 2**: F = 100, i.e., 100 queries are invoked in the grouping approach.

In the grouping approach, the execution time of Case 2 is almost constant when F is fixed. The execution time of the grouping approach depends on number of fired queries F, not on the total number of installed queries N. The reason is that, although T_g increases as N grows, this shared computation is executed only once and is a very small portion of total execution time. The execution time for the upper queries, which is proportional to the number of fired queries F, dominates the total execution time. On the other hand, the execution time for the non-grouping approach is proportional to N because all queries are scheduled for execution.

Experiment 2. (Figure 5.4) F = N = 2000 queries

In this experiment we explore the impact of C, the number of modified tuples, on the performance of the two approaches. C is varied from 100 tuples (about 40K bytes) to 2000 tuples (about 800K bytes). Increasing C will increase the query execution time. For the non-grouping approach, the total execution time is proportional to C because the selection operator of every installed query needs to be executed. For the grouping approach, the execution time is not sensitive to the change of C because the increase of T_g only counts for a small percentage of the total execution time and the sum of T_{ng} of all fired queries does not change because of the predicate's selectivity.

Experiment results for Type-2, 3, 4 queries (Figure 5.5, 5.6, 5.7) C =1000 tuples, F = N

We discuss the influence of different expression signatures in this set of experiments.

Figure 5.5 and Figure 5.6 show that our group optimization works well for various selection predicates. Type-2 queries are grouped according to their range selection signature. Type-3 queries have two signatures. The group optimizer chooses an equal predicate to group queries since it is more selective.

Figure 5.7 shows the results for Type-4 queries. Type-4 queries have one selection signature and one join signature. The selection operator is pushed below the join operator. Queries are first grouped by their selection signature. There are 100 different industries in our test data set. The output of the selection group is written to 100 intermediate files and one hundred join groups are created. Each join group consumes one of the intermediate files as its input. The difference between the execution time with and without grouping is much larger than in the previous experiments because a join operator is more expensive than a selection operator.

5.2.2 Experiment results on mixed queries of Type-1 and type-3 (Figure 5.8) C =1000 tuples, F = N (N/2 Type-1 queries and N/2 Type-3 queries)

Previous experiments studied each type of query separately for the purpose of showing the effectiveness of different kinds of expression signatures. Our incremental group optimizer is not limited to group only one type of queries. Different types of queries can also be grouped together if they have common

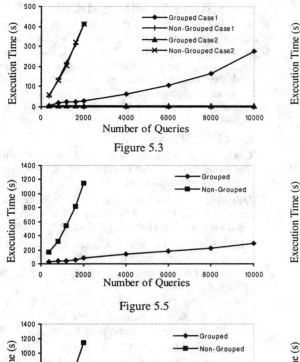

Figure 5.3

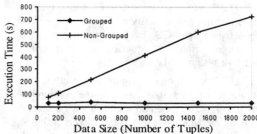
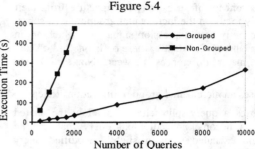

Figure 5.4

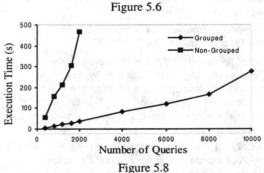

Figure 5.5

Figure 5.6

Figure 5.7

Figure 5.8

signatures. In this experiment, Type-1 queries and Type-3 queries are grouped together because they have the same selection signature. Figure 5.8 shows the performance difference between the grouped and non-grouped cases.

5.3 System Status and Future Work

A prototype version of NaigraCQ has been developed, which includes a Group Optimizer, Continuous Query Manager, Event Detector, and Data Manager. As the core of our incremental group optimization, the Group Optimizer currently can incrementally group selection and join operators. Our incremental group optimizer is still at a preliminary stage. However, incremental group optimization has been shown to be a promising way to achieve good performance and scalability. We intend to extend incremental group optimization to queries containing operators other than selection and join. For example, sharing computation for expensive operators, such as aggregation, may be very effective. "Dynamic regrouping" is another interesting future direction that we intend to explore.

6. RELATED WORK AND DISCUSSION

Terry et al. first proposed the notion of "continuous queries" [TGNO92] as queries that are issued once and run continuously. He used an incremental evaluation approach to avoid repetitive computation and return only new results to users. Their approach was restricted to append-only systems, which is not suitable for our target environment. NiagaraCQ uses an incremental query evaluation method but is not limited to append-only data sources. We also include action and timer events in Niagara continuous queries.

Continuous queries are similar to triggers in traditional database systems. Triggers have been widely studied and implemented [WF89][MD89][SJGP90][SPAM91][SK95]. Most trigger systems use an Event-Condition-Action (ECA) model [MD89]. General issues of implementing triggers can be found in [WF89].

NiagaraCQ is different from traditional trigger systems in the following ways.

1. The main purpose of the NiagaraCQ is to support continuous query processing rather than to maintain data integrity.

2. NiagaraCQ is intended to support millions of continuous queries defined on large number of data sources. In a traditional DBMS, a very limited number of triggers can be installed on each table and a trigger can usually only be defined on a single table.

3. NiagaraCQ needs to monitor autonomous and heterogeneous data sources over the Internet. Traditional trigger systems only handle local tables.

4. Timer-based events are supported in NiagaraCQ.

389

Open-CQ [LPT99] [LPBZ96] also supports continuous queries on web data sources and has functionality similar to NiagaraCQ. NiagaraCQ differs from Open-CQ in that we explore the similarity among large number of queries and use group optimization to achieve system scalability.

The TriggerMan [HCH+99] project proposes a method for implementing a scalable trigger system based on the assumption that many triggers may have common structure. It uses a special selection predicate index and an in-memory trigger cache to achieve scalability. We share the same assumption in our work and borrow the concept of an expression signature from their work. We mainly focus on the incremental grouping of a subset of the most frequently used expression signatures, which are in the format "Attribute op Constant", where op is one of "<", "=" and ">". The major differences between NiagaraCQ and TriggerMan are:

1. NiagaraCQ uses an incremental group optimization strategy.

2. NiagaraCQ uses a query-split scheme to allow the shared computation to become an individual query that can be monitored and executed using a slightly modified query engine. TriggerMan uses a special in-memory predicate index to evaluate the expression signature.

3. NiagaraCQ supports grouping of timer-based queries, a capability not considered in [HCH+99].

Sellis's work [Sel86] focused on finding an optimal plan for a small group of queries (usually lower than ten) by recognizing a containment relationship among the selection predicates of queries with both selection and join operators. This approach for group optimization was very expensive and not extendable to a large number of queries.

Recent work [ZDNS98] on group optimization mainly focuses on applying group optimization to solve a specific problem. Our approach also falls into this category. Alert [SPAM91] was among the earliest active database systems. It tried to reuse most parts of a passive DBMS to implement an active database.

7. CONCLUSION

Our goal is to develop an Internet-scale continuous query system using group optimization based on the assumption that many continuous queries on the Internet will have some similarities. Previous group optimization approaches consider grouping only a small number of queries at the same time and are not scalable to millions of queries. We propose a new "incremental grouping" methodology that makes group optimization more scalable than the previous approaches. This idea can be applied to very general group optimization methods. We also propose a grouping method using a query-split scheme that requires minimal changes to a general purposed query engine. In our system, both timer-based and change-based continuous queries can be grouped together for event detection and group execution, a capability not found in other systems. Other techniques to make our system scalable include incremental evaluation of continuous queries, use of both pull and push models for detecting heterogeneous data source changes and a caching mechanism. Preliminary experiments demonstrate that our incremental group optimization significantly improves the execution time comparing to non-grouping approach. The results of experiments also show that the system can be scaled to support very large number of queries.

8. ACKNOWLEDGEMENT
We thank Zhichen Xu for his discussion with the first author during initial writing of the paper. We are particularly grateful to Ashraf Aboulnaga, Navin Kabra and David Maier for their careful review and helpful comments on the paper. We also thank the anonymous referees for their comments. Funding for this work was provided by DARPA through NAVY/SPAWAR Contract No. N66001-99-1-8908 and NSF award CDA-9623632.

9. REFERENCES
[CM86] U..S. Chakravarthy and J. Minker. Multiple Query Processing in Deductive Databases using Query Graphs. VLDB Conference 1986: 384-391.

[DFF+98] A. Deutsch, M. Fernandez, D. Florescu, A. Levy, D. Suciu. XML-QL: A Query Langaage for XML. http://www.w3.org/TR/NOTE-xml-ql.

[HCH+99] E. N. Hanson, C. Carnes, L. Huang, M. Konyala, L. Noronha, S. Parthasarathy, J.B.Park and A. Vernon. Scalable Trigger Processing. In proceeding of 15th ICDE, page 266-275, Sydney, Australia, 1999.

[HJ94] E. N. Hanson and T. Johnson. Selection Predicate Indexing for Active Databases Using Interval Skip List. TR94-017. CIS department, University of Florida, 1994.

[LPBZ96] L. Liu, C. Pu, R. Barga, T. Zhou. Differential Evaluation of Continual Queries. ICDCS 1996: 458-465.

[LPT99] L. Liu, C. Pu, W. Tang. Continual Queries for Internet Scale Event-Driven Information Delivery. TKDE 11(4): 610-628 (1999).

[MD89] D. McCarthy and U. Dayal. The architecture of an active database management system. SIGMOD 1989: 215-224.

[RC88] A. Rosenthal and U. S. Chakravarthy. Anatomy of a Modular Multiple Query Optimizer. VLDB 1988: 230-239.

[Sel86] T. Sellis. Multiple query optimization. ACM Transactions on Database Systems, 10(3), 1986.

[SJGP90]M. Stonebraker, A. Jhingran, J. Goh and S. Potamianos. On Rules, Procedures, Caching and Views in Data Base Systems. SIGMOD Conference 1990: 281-290.

[SK95] E. Simon, A. Kotz-Dittrich. Promises and Realities of Active Database Systems. VLDB 1995: 642-653.

[SPAM91] U. Schreier, H. Pirahesh, R. Agrawal, and C. Mohan. Alert: An architecture for transforming a passive dbms into an active dbms. VLDB 1991: 469-478.

[TGNO92] D. Terry, D. Goldberg, D. Nichols, and B. Oki. Continuous Queries over Append-Only Databases. SIGMOD 1992: 321-330.

[WF89] J. Widom and S.J. Finklestein. Set-Oriented Production Rules in Relational Database Systems. SIGMOD Conference 1990: 259-270.

[ZDNS98] Y. Zhao, P. Deshpande, J. F. Naughton, A. Shukla. Simultaneous Optimization and Evaluation of Multiple Dimensional Queries. SIGMOD 1998: 271-282.

The Onion Technique: Indexing for Linear Optimization Queries

Yuan-Chi Chang, Lawrence Bergman, Vittorio Castelli,
Chung-Sheng Li, Ming-Ling Lo, and John R. Smith

Data Management, IBM T. J. Watson Research Center, P. O. Box, 704, Yorktown Heights, NY 10598

Abstract

This paper describes the Onion technique, a special indexing structure for linear optimization queries. Linear optimization queries ask for top-N records subject to the maximization or minimization of linearly weighted sum of record attribute values. Such query appears in many applications employing linear models and is an effective way to summarize representative cases, such as the top-50 ranked colleges. The Onion indexing is based on a geometric property of convex hull, which guarantees that the optimal value can always be found at one or more of its vertices. The Onion indexing makes use of this property to construct convex hulls in layers with outer layers enclosing inner layers geometrically. A data record is indexed by its layer number or equivalently its depth in the layered convex hull. Queries with linear weightings issued at run time are evaluated from the outmost layer inwards. We show experimentally that the Onion indexing achieves orders of magnitude speedup against sequential linear scan when N is small compared to the cardinality of the set. The Onion technique also enables progressive retrieval, which processes and returns ranked results in a progressive manner. Furthermore, the proposed indexing can be extended into a hierarchical organization of data to accommodate both global and local queries.

Keywords: database indexing, linear optimization

1   Introduction

Linear optimization queries return database records whose linearly weighted sums of numerical attributes are ranked *top-N* maximally or minimally in the database. In recent years, *top-N* queries are often referred in the context of nearest neighbor (NN) search. The research problem we addressed and reported in this paper differs from NN search. We named it *top-N model-based query* for distinction. In top-N model-based queries, the types of models (e.g. linear,

quadratic, lognormal) are given ahead of the query but short of the exact model parameters, which are issued at run time. Under such circumstances, the indexing structure must take advantage of features of the given model type to avoid expensive linear scan. We began our research at the commonly used linear model, in which the sum of linearly weighted attribute values is calculated as the ranking criterion. We assume weights assigned to those attributes are unknown at the time when the index is constructed.

Model-based optimization queries play an important role in information retrieval and analysis, because limiting the number of query results effectively summarizes the most relevant and crucial information through representative cases. In many knowledge domains, linear models are widely used for their simple mathematical properties. Depending on application scenarios, weights of the linear criterion may be known in advance, in which cases results may be pre-ranked for future queries. In other cases, weights are dynamic and thus may not be feasible to pre-compute all possible combinations. The indexing structure proposed in this paper mainly addresses the dynamic scenario.

A prominent example of a linear optimization query is college ranking. Each year *US News and World Report* conducts studies of college education and ranks school performance by a linear weighting of quality factors such as academic reputation, faculty resources, retention rate, and so on. One such sorted table for the 1998 college ranking is shown in Figure 1. Similar examples may be found in news media and scientific studies like ranking of the most costly cities and ranking of areas with densely populated Lyme disease vectors [6].

While the above college ranking example is based on static weights determined by magazine editors, weights can be dynamically adjusted through a web interface, which allows perspective students to generate their own ranking. If the top-N query were implemented as a SQL query like the select statement below, the whole college database would be scanned linearly. Linear scan is necessary for the full ranking. However, if only top-ten ranked schools are asked for, the fully ranked approach is undesirable. In several scientific data retrieval scenarios we investigated, the cardinality of the database is on the order of hundreds of millions of records. Pre-processing the data to speed up run time performance becomes necessary because of its large

Rank	School (State)	Overall score	Reputation score	Graduation rank	Retention rate	1997 predicted graduation rate	1997 actual graduation rate	'97 over perf. (+) (-)	Fac. resources rank	% classes under 20	% with 50 or more	Student/fac. ratio	% of full-time faculty	Selectivity rank	SAT/ACT 25th-75th percentile	Top 10% of class	Accept rate	Fin. resources rank	Alumni giving rate
1	Harvard University (MA)	100.0	4.9	1	96%	97%	97%	None	2	59%	11%	6/1	90%	1	1390-1580	90%	13%	8	6	46%
1	Princeton University (NJ)	100.0	4.9	2	98%	95%	96%	+1	3	68%	12%	6/1	91%	2	1350-1530	93%	13%	15	1	56%
1	Yale University (CT)	100.0	4.9	2	98%	97%	96%	-1	6	77%	8%	7/1	92%	2	1350-1530	95%	18%	6	3	50%
4	Massachusetts Inst. of Technology	98.0	4.9	14	97%	97%	89%	-8	3	69%	6%	5/1	90%	5	1390-1560	93%	25%	4	8	44%
4	Stanford University (CA)	96.0	4.9	4	97%	96%	92%	-4	12	70%	12%	15/1	83%	5	1340-1540	87%	15%	5	13	34%
6	Cornell University (NY)	97.0	4.7	10	95%	88%	90%	+2	9	74%	10%	9/1	97%	16	1250-1440	82%	34%	17	16	35%
6	Duke University (NC)	97.0	4.6	4	97%	92%	92%	None	8	59%	7%	11/1	100%	13	1300-1460	87%	30%	13	15	37%

Figure 1: Linearly weighted rankings such as the college survey shown from *US News and World Report*(c) are widely applied as a way of information summarization

volume.

```
SELECT COLLEGE, 0.4*REPUTATION+0.3*RESOURCE+...
+0.3*SELECTIVITY AS SCORE
FROM COLLEGE_DATABASE
ORDER BY SCORE DESC
```

Recognizing the need of efficient processing of *top-N linear model-based queries*, we propose the Onion technique as a special indexing for such queries. The Onion indexing is based on a geometric property of convex hull, which guarantees that the optimal value of a linearly weighted sum can always be found at one or more of its vertices. A convex hull is the boundary of the smallest convex region of a group of points in space. The subset of points on the boundary are the vertices. The basic idea of the Onion technique is to extend this property to construct convex hulls in layers, with outer layers enclosing inner layers geometrically. Records, along with the ID and attribute values, are indexed and grouped on disk files by the layers to which they belong.

When a new query is issued with weighted numbers of record attributes, the query processing always starts from the outmost layer and evaluates records progressively inwards, much like peeling off an onion. We show experimentally that the Onion technique achieves orders of magnitude speedup against linear scan when N is small compared to the cardinality of the set. The indexing structure has almost no overhead since we group records by their layer number and store them sequentially on disk. Furthermore, the Onion technique enables progressive retrieval which promises results returned earlier are always better than results returned later. Instead of packing the top-100, say, records together and returning them simultaneously, the Onion query processing can return the first and best 50, while it continue on to locate the next best 50. Since the processing sequence guarantees the accuracy of ordered retrievals, this technique is most suitable to

occasions where short response time is desired.

Although the Onion technique performs well on linear model-based queries with queries against the whole indexed set, it is much less effective to process queries with additional constraints to confine the search space. The additional constraints may be as simple as bounded ranges on one or more numerical attributes or selected categorical attributes. For example, one used the Onion technique to index one million records but extra constraints from a query confine the search to one thousand records. As a result, top-N records from the one-million index may not satisfy the additional constraints at all. Using the Onion technique, the query processor will then expand the search to top-M, with M greater than N. The local versus global query dilemma is not unique to the Onion technique but applies to most nearest-neighbor indexing as well.

We thus extend the Onion technique to address the local vs. global query dilemma by a hierarchical index. The hierarchy may be constructed by observing local queries to determine how to partition spatial data set or categorical attribute values. We call each partition a cluster and *local* queries are directed to the cluster level. Each cluster is still indexed by the aforementioned layered convex hull to achieve high performance. To keep the overhead in storage space small, the hierarchy only takes the outmost layer of each cluster to form a new convex hull at the upper level to address *global* queries. An alternative which doubles the storage space requirement is to construct this new convex hull with all the records from all the clusters, which we believe is a less scalable solution.

The rest of the paper is organized as follows. In Section 2, we gave an overview of related work that may be used to process linear optimization queries. To the best of our knowledge, the Onion technique is the first special indexing structure for top-N linear model-based queries. Therefore, we do not really have a reference point for comparison. Section 3 details the procedures of constructing and maintaining Onion indices as well as the query processing algorithm. Section 4 discusses how to build a hierarchical index, which addresses the issues of local and global queries. Section 5 presents our experimental evaluations with regard to the impact of dimension, distribution, and query size on the performance of the Onion. We conclude the paper by summarizing its benefits and weaknesses.

2   Related Work

The task of finding top-N records may be posed with the maximization or minimization criterion. Since queries asking for minimal values can be conveniently turned into maximization queries by simply switching the signs of weights (coefficients), in the rest of the paper we assume maximization queries are issued. The *top-N linear model-based query* problem we wanted to solve can be written as follows. Given a set of records with m numerical attributes, find the top N that maximizes the following linear equation.

$$\max_{topN}\{a_1 * x_1^i + a_2 * x_2^i + \ldots + a_{m-1} * x_{m-1}^i + a_m * x_m^i\}$$
(1)

where $(x_1^i, x_2^i, \ldots, x_{m-1}^i, x_m^i)$ is the attribute value vector of the ith record and $(a_1, a_2, \ldots, a_{m-1}, a_m)$ is the weighting vector. One or more of a_i's may be set to zero. When all but one dimensions are degenerated, the problem may be solved by sorting the records along the dimension with nonzero weight.

One area closely related to our problem is the discipline of linear programming. In earlier works, however, linear optimization queries were referred as the problem of finding a *single* point or hyperplane in space which optimizes the linear criterion [7]. The search region is constrained to the intersection of half spaces specified by a set of linear inequalities. The processing of such a query is equivalent to solving a linear programming problem, which can be approached by techniques such as the simplex method and the ellipsoid method. Later discoveries in randomized algorithms suggested possible ways to reduce expected query response time. Seidel reported the expected time is proportional to the number of half-space constraints [13]. Matousek reported a data structure that is based on a simplicial partition tree, which is pruned by parametric search to narrow the search space [11]. Chan applied the same data structure with randomized algorithms used in tree pruning [4] to further reduce expected query processing. While linear programming sets the cornerstone of our proposed Onion technique, none of the above works, however, suggested direct extensions to answer top-N linear optimization queries.

Besides the linear programming approach, it is also possible to apply linear constraint queries to spatial data indexing and then post-process the outputs. Instead of seeking for the top-N records directly, the query is processed by retrieving all the records that are greater than some threshold. Retrieved records are then evaluated and sorted to find the top-N answers. Most studies in linear constraint queries apply spatial data structures such as R-tree and k-d-B tree. Algorithms are developed to prune the

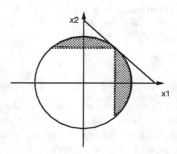

Figure 2: Based on Fagin's algorithm [8], records falling in shaded area are retrieved to find the maximum of $x_1 + x_2$

spatial partition tree to improve response speed. Recent publications can be found in [10]. The main difficulty of taking this two-step approach (thresholding and sorting) lies in determining the threshold which bounds the search space, especially when the spatial distribution of data is hard to estimate. A poorly chosen threshold may lead to too many or too few returns. It is also impossible to perform progressive retrieval, which allows records to be returned successively in ranking order.

Another important related work is an algorithm proposed by Fagin for processing fuzzy joins [8]. He showed the applicability of the algorithm to any "upward closed" functions, which include linear weighted sum of record attributes. The algorithm was originally proposed for processing fuzzy join of multi-attribute multimedia objects in the IBM Garlic project. The query is to find objects with maximal fuzzy combinations of attributes measured in similarity (e.g. color, shape, texture). One important distinction between Fagin's and other aforementioned works is that Fagin's algorithm does not exploit attribute correlation. Each attribute is treated independently. While this property is applicable in similarity search where attribute correlation depends on query examples, it penalizes query performance of linear optimization. An example of showing such inefficiency is illustrated in Figure 2, where all records have two attributes, x_1 and x_2. The records are distributed in a circle shown in the figure. When an optimization query is issued to find the maximum (top-1) of the sum of the two attributes with equal weights, records falling in the shaded area marked in the circle will be retrieved and evaluated, according to the algorithm [8]. This example can be solved more efficiently through the Onion technique. We believe while Fagin's algorithm is most applicable for applications where pre-processing is not allowed, one should take advantage of pre-processing where possible to exploit attribute correlations.

3   The Onion Technique

The basic idea of the Onion technique is to partition the collection of d-dimensional data points, which correspond to records with d numerical attributes, into sets that are *optimally linearly ordered*.

Definition 1 Optimally Linearly Ordered Sets: *A collection of sets $\{\mathcal{S}_1, \mathcal{S}_2, \ldots, \mathcal{S}_n\}$ are optimally linearly ordered iff given any d-dimensional vector $\underline{a}$,*

$$\exists \underline{x} \in \mathcal{S}_i \ s.t.$$

$$\forall \underline{y} \in \mathcal{S}_{i+j} \ and \ j > 0, \quad \underline{a}^t \underline{x} > \underline{a}^t \underline{y}$$

where $\underline{a}^t\underline{x}$ represents the inner product of the two vectors.

By this definition, sets with lower indices always have one or more vectors whose linearly weighted sums are strictly greater than sets with higher indices.

Optimally linearly ordered sets only require the existence of a d-dim vector from set $\mathcal{S}_i$ to have a greater linearly weighted sum than any other vector from the sets ordered after $\mathcal{S}_i$, e.g. $\mathcal{S}_{i+1}$, $\mathcal{S}_{i+2}$, etc. This property does not guarantee the sets are nonredundant, i.e. each $\mathcal{S}_i$ has the minimal number of vectors needed. Nevertheless, one can see any partition that generates optimally linearly ordered sets provides a valid indexing structure which prunes the search space of linear optimization queries. It is not difficult to show that, for a *top-N* linear model-based query, at most $\sum_{i=1}^{N} |\mathcal{S}_i|$ records have to be evaluated. $|\mathcal{S}_i|$ is the size of set $\mathcal{S}_i$.

Partitioning a set of data points into optimally linearly ordered sets may seem difficult at first sight. Fortunately, a theorem exists in the linear programming literature which indicates how one may perform the set partitioning.

Theorem 1 *Given a set of records $\mathcal{R}$ mapped to a d-dimensional space, and a linear maximization (minimization) criterion, the maximum (minimum) objective value is achieved at one or more vertices of the convex hull of $\mathcal{R}$.*

The proof of this theorem can be found in [7] and other linear programming textbooks. The convex hull of a set $\mathcal{R}$ of d-dimensional vectors is defined as the boundary of the smallest convex region containing $\mathcal{R}$. The subset of vectors at the convex hull are referred as *vertices* or *extreme points*. In two dimensions, the shape of a convex hull is a polygon. In higher dimensions, its shape is a polyhedron.

To see how Theorem 1 may be applied to generate optimally linearly ordered sets, one may consider the extreme case in which we only partition the set $\mathcal{R}$ into two subsets $\mathcal{S}_1$ and $\mathcal{S}_2$. We compute the convex hull of $\mathcal{R}$ and put the vertex points into set $\mathcal{S}_1$ and non-vertical points into set $\mathcal{S}_2$. By Theorem 1, $\{\mathcal{S}_1, \mathcal{S}_2\}$ forms optimally linearly ordered sets. This simple partition is sufficient to prune the search space for any top-1 queries. If N is more than one, both $\mathcal{S}_1$ and $\mathcal{S}_2$ will be searched and there is no performance advantage over linear scan.

Although we will not provide a proof here, it can be shown that the set $\mathcal{S}_1$ is nonredundant and it contains no more vectors than necessary to satisfy the optimally linearly ordered property. The non-redundancy is desirable because this enables a partition scheme to generate the most number of subsets possible. The worst case bound $\sum_{i=1}^{N} |\mathcal{S}_i|$ will be smaller.

The Onion technique is based on an iteration of the convex hull partitioning. The iteration continues until the last subset can not be partitioned further without violating the linearly ordered property. We name each subset a layer and number them geometrically from outside inwards starting at one. The set of layers $\{\mathcal{L}_1, \mathcal{L}_2, \ldots, \mathcal{L}_m\}$ are optimally linearly ordered. These layers constitute the index of the Onion technique. In the following subsections, we present the procedures of creating and maintaining the Onion indexing as well as the query processing steps.

3.1 Index Creation and Storage

The Onion technique partitions the input data set into layers, each of which is a set of data vectors. The relation between layers is best depicted geometrically using an example. Figure 3 illustrates a data set after the partition. In this figure, data records of two attributes x_1 and x_2 are represented as black dots scattered on the 2D plane. Three layers are formed and labeled from the outmost layer inwards, starting at Layer 1 assigned to the outmost layer. Each layer contains a variable number of records, which may be as little as one. The set of points in layer i are vertices of the convex hull of the union of all the layers below it, including itself.

The Onion index is created iteratively using the convex hull construction algorithm. The procedure is described below in pseudocode.

```
The procedure of index creation
        Input: the set R of data records
1       k = 1;
2       while (sizeof(R) > 0)
                {
3               construct a convex hull of set R;
4               store records of the hull vertices in set V;
5               assign records in set V to layer k;
6               R = R - V;
7               k = k + 1;
                }
```

At each iteration, a convex hull of a set of data records is first constructed using algorithms such as the gift-wrapping method and the beneath-beyond method [12]. Fast convex hull construction algorithms are not discussed in this paper and left for future topics. Records appeared as convex hull vertices are assigned to the new layer and removed from the input set. Therefore the size of the input set decreases as the iterations continue. The iteration stops when the input set becomes empty.

Geometrically the partitioned structure looks like an onion, with layers corresponding to peels. Inner layers, with outer layers being vertices of their convex hulls, are wrapped spatially. This onion structure is later referred as *layered convex hull*.

We store the data points in each layer in a number of consecutive disk pages and record the pointers to the starting and ending pages. For simplicity, each set of such pages is called a *flat file*. Similar to the assumption made in [3], attribute values and IDs of the data records are stored together in flat files. It is possible to add auxiliary indexing structures to further accelerate access to the flat file. This, however, is not the focus of this paper and left for future work. This storage arrangement in effect clusters the input records belonging to the same Onion layer close together on disks.

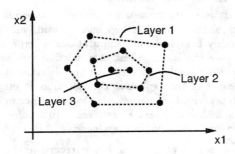

Figure 3: A three-layered convex hull in two-dimensional space

This storage structure for the Onion index has almost no overhead. After the flat files are created, the only information that needs to be kept in the Onion index for later query processing is the beginning and ending page locations for each layer. As our experiments demonstrated, each layer typically contains several hundred or more data points, which makes the storage overhead negligible.

While the Onion index has negligible storage overhead, the computation cost at the creation time is very high. All known algorithms of constructing convex hulls have computational complexity in the order of $O(N^{d/2})$, where N is the size of the input data set. We acknowledge that the exponential growth in complexity as the number of dimensions increases is a serious obstacle to the Onion's applicability to high dimensional data. We leave the study of this subject to future work.

3.2 Query Evaluation

Similar to index creation, the processing of a linear optimization query also starts from the outmost layer and progresses inwards. This procedure is described as follows.

The procedure of evaluating a query
Input: the number of top records to return N;
coefficients of the linear criterion
1 candidate set $\mathcal{C} = \emptyset$;
2 result set $\mathcal{O} = \emptyset$;
3 $k = 1$;
4 while ($N > 0$)
   {
5   retrieve records in layer k and put them in a set $\mathcal{L}_k$;
6   evaluate records in $\mathcal{L}_k$ with the given coefficients;
7   select the top N records from $\mathcal{L}_k$ and put them in a set $\mathcal{T}$;
8   if ($k = 1$) {
9          $\mathcal{C} = \mathcal{T}$;
10   add the record with the maximum value in $\mathcal{C}$ to the result set $\mathcal{O}$;
11   remove the record from $\mathcal{C}$;
12         $N = N - 1$;
       }
13   else   {

14         $maxT = \max\{\mathcal{T}\}$;
15   foreach $c \in \mathcal{C}$ {
16   if (value of $c > maxT$)
17   move c from $\mathcal{C}$ to the result set $\mathcal{O}$;
18                 $N = N - 1$;
19   if ($N = 0$)
20   stop and return the result set $\mathcal{O}$;
           }
21   move the maximal record from $\mathcal{T}$ to $\mathcal{O}$;
22         $\mathcal{C} = \mathcal{C} \cup \mathcal{T}$;
23         $N = N - 1$;
       }
24     $k = k + 1$;
   }
25 return the result set $\mathcal{O}$;

In this procedure, we created a candidate set, which is a container for hopeful top-N records, and a result set, which stores the records made to top N. Every time new records are added to the result set, N is decremented accordingly. In the first iteration beginning at line number 4, the candidate set is empty and this condition is treated separately. Records at Layer 1 (the outmost layer) are retrieved and evaluated. The record with the maximum value is added to the result set. The top-2 to top-N records at Layer 1 are stored in the candidate set.

Starting at Layer 2, iteration steps are identical and the iteration continues until N is decremented to zero. Without loss of generality, assume the iteration proceeds to Layer k. First, records in Layer k are read from the disk and evaluated. The best N records are kept in a set $\mathcal{T}$ (line 7). Next, find the maximum value, $maxT$, of the set $\mathcal{T}$ (line 14). We describe line 7 and 14 separately for clarity while they can be implemented together. Any record in in the candidate set $\mathcal{C}$ that has a greater value than $maxT$ is returned as a result. Finally, return the maximum record of Layer k and merge what remains in $\mathcal{T}$ into the candidate set (line 22). At any point of the process, if N becomes zero, query processing stops and the result set is returned to the client.

Proof of correctness: From Theorem 1 we know the optimal record value at each layer is always greater than any record value from its inner layers. However, records in the candidate set, which come from outer layers, may still be greater than the optimal value of the next layer. The FOR loop from line 15 to 21 makes sure that those which have greater values are returned first. Since top-N records from each layer are always added to the candidate set, one would have returned all in the candidate set, should they be greater than the maximum of the current layer. Correctness of the top-N results is thus guaranteed.

Example: We use the three-layered convex hull from Figure 3 as an example to illustrate the query processing procedure. As shown in Figure 4(a), records in layer-1 are marked as *1a, 1b, 1c, 1d,* and *1e.* The linear optimization criterion is shown as a line which moves in its orthonormal direction. In this example, we assume the objective is to maximize the criterion and therefore, the farther away a point from the origin in the line direction, the greater its value. N is set to three. In this example, point $1a$ has the largest value and is returned first. Points $1b$ and $1e$ are put into the candidate set. Next in Figure 4(b), records in layer-2 are evaluated and $2a$ is returned since both $1b$ and $1e$ are smaller than $2a$. At this iteration, $2e$ is added to the candidate set. Finally, records in layer-3 are evaluated. At this iteration, $2e$ from the candidate set is greater than the largest value of layer-3, $3a$. Therefore, $2e$ is returned.

The disk I/O cost of the query processing is contributed by two factors: the random access to move the disk head to the beginning disk page of a layer and the sequential access of reading pages into main memory. We assume the main memory is large enough to hold all the records in a layer. If the main memory does not have sufficient space, the sequential access may be divided into several reads. Since the query processing only requires top-N records of each layer to be kept in main memory and N is usually small, multiple disk reading operations do not increase the complexity of the processing. In the following, we prove the disk I/O cost is bounded in the worst case.

Theorem 2 *The disk I/O cost of evaluating a top-N linear optimization query is bounded in the worst case by N random accesses and $\sum_{k=1}^{N} |\mathcal{L}_k|/B$ sequential accesses, where $|\mathcal{L}_k|$ is the number of records stored in the kth layer and B is the number of records per disk page.*

Proof: By Theorem 1, each layer of the Onion index is guaranteed to provide at least one "optimal" record. When a query is issued for top-N records, at most N layers need to be accessed. Since there is one random access per layer, in the worst case there would be N random I/O's. For the rest of record retrievals, there are sequential I/O's. The cost associated with sequential I/O's is thus $\sum_{k=1}^{N} |\mathcal{L}_k|/B$.

3.3 Progressive Retrieval

One important feature enabled by the Onion indexing structure is progressive retrieval. This feature is uncommon to most indexing techniques used in ranking results. We thus wish to emphasize this feature. In many other techniques, all the records in the pruned search space are evaluated before the ranked ordering can be determined. This is not necessary using the Onion technique. As we have shown in the descriptions of query processing, the Onion technique guarantees the following property.

Corollary 1 *Given a linear maximization (minimization) criterion and a layered convex hull constructed using the stated procedure, the maximum (minimum) objective value achieved at layer k is strictly greater (less) than the maximum (minimum) value achieved at layer $k + 1$.*

Proof: The corollary can be easily proved by Theorem 1 and the construction procedure of the Onion index.

By Corollary 1, top-N results can be progressively delivered to the client since the record ranked M is always retrieved earlier than the one ranked $M + m$ with positive m. From the user's view point, the database thus appears to be faster since the response time to get the first record is shortened.

3.4 Index Maintenance

In contrast to query processing, index maintenance operations such as inserting, deleting, and updating an Onion index are fairly complex and computationally expensive. An update operation is equivalent to a deletion followed by an insertion. We thus discuss insertion and deletion in this section. Because of the expensive computation, it may be advisable in practice to perform index maintenance in batches.

The algorithm to insert a new record to an already built index is described below in pseudocode.

```
The procedure of inserting a new record to the index
        Input: the new record, r
1       locate layer k such that the new record is
        inside the convex hull of layer k − 1 and outside
        the hull of layer k; (this step may be done by
        binary search or other methods)
2       let the set S = {r};
3       while (sizeof(S) > 0) {
4           L_k,merge = S ∪ L_k;
5           construct a convex hull of L_k,merge;
6           store the hull vertices in set L_k,new;
7           L_k = L_k,new;
8           S = L_k,merge − L_k;
9           k = k + 1;
        }
```

The key concept is that vertices of a convex hull are not affected by adding or deleting points inside of the hull. As illustrated in Figure 5(a), the new record represented by the white dot is inside the hull of Layer-1. Data points in Layer-1 do not change by this insertion operation. In contrast, the white dot is outside of Layer-2. Hence points stored from Layer-2 and inner layers may have to be shifted down. The first step of processing an insertion is to locate the neighboring layers where the new record falls in between. Once they are found, the iterations start to insert the new point and relocate existing data (line 3 to 9). Inserting a new record to a layer may cause one or more points in that layer to be expelled, as illustrated in Figure 5(b). The expelled records are inserted to the next inner layer and the operations may again expel some records from the next layer. The iteration continues when no more records are expelled or it reaches the inner-most layer. Figure 5(c) depicts such an ending.

Similar to the record insertion operation, record deletions do not affect records in outer layers. If a record in Layer-k is deleted, one or more records in Layer-$(k + 1)$ will be moved up to Layer-k. The moved records can be thought as deletions made to Layer-$(k + 1)$, which again solicit records from the immediately inner layer. The procedure is described below in pseudocode. Because the basic concept of the deletion operation is similar to that of insertion, we believe the pseudocode is self-descriptive and do not provide further explanations.

```
The procedure of deleting a record
        Input: the record to be deleted, r
1       locate layer k where r belongs to; (this step
        may be implemented by a binary search since r is
        inside of some layers and outside of other layers)
```

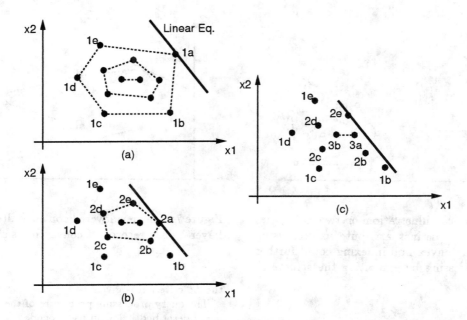

Figure 4: An illustration of retrieving and evaluating layers from the outmost inwards

4 Hierarchical Indexing of Onions

Although the Onion technique performs well on linear model-based queries with queries against the whole indexed set, it is much less effective in dealing with *local* queries, which have additional constraints to confine search space. The additional constraints may be as simple as bounded attribute ranges or selected categorical attributes. Using the college ranking as an example, we found an Onion index built for colleges in the whole nation does not respond well to queries such as "top-10 colleges in the northwestern region" or "top-10 colleges with tuition below $15,000". The Onion technique does not perform well for two reasons. First, an Onion index accounts for numerical attributes of data records only, not their categorical attributes. Second, range constraints on numerical attributes effectively restrict the search to a subset of records that may be ranked behind globally, say starting at the 200th best. An Onion index can quickly rank and order records globally but has no way to jump directly to the 200th record. The global vs. local query dilemma does not occur to the Onion technique only. Additional constraints on most proposed indexing techniques for nearest neighbor search cause similar inefficiency. Fortunately, for the Onion technique, we have a partial solution to the dilemma.

Recognizing the global vs. local query dilemma, we extend the Onion indexing into a hierarchy with popular local queries clustered at the bottom of the hierarchy. Clusters are then selectively grouped together to form new indices at the top of the hierarchy. The grouping of clusters depends on the usage distribution of local queries as well as problem domains. In the college ranking example, it may be natural to group schools into clusters based on geological locations such as northwestern and southeastern regions. A separate Onion index is constructed for each

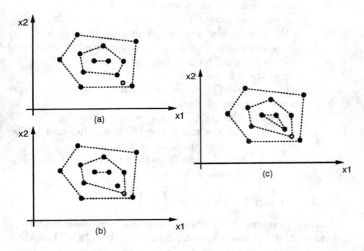

Figure 5: An illustration of inserting a new record into an Onion index; the white dot represents the new record

```
2    let the set S = L_k − {r};
3    while (sizeof(S) > 0) {
4        L_{k,merge} = S ∪ L_{k+1};
5        construct a convex hull of L_{k,merge};
6        store the hull vertices in set L_{k,new};
7        L_k = L_{k,new};
8        S = L_{k,merge} − L_k;
9        k = k + 1;
        }
```

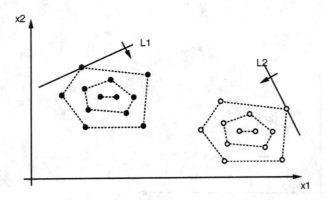

Figure 6: A graphical illustration of two categories of data records with distinct attribute values; using hierarchical layered convex hull indexing could further improve query processing by exploiting the structural differences

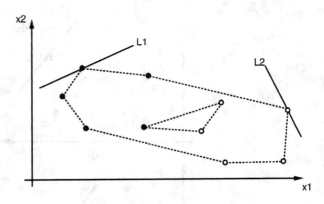

Figure 7: The new layered convex hull constructed from Layer-1 data records of convex hulls shown in Fig. 6

cluster to facilitate local queries. For global queries against schools nationwide, one can choose to construct a separate index to include all records. This will double the storage space requirement. Our proposed solution for hierarchical indexing is to build a global index by relying on existing local indeces.

To keep the overhead in the storage space to the minimum, the global index takes the outmost layer of each cluster's index to form a new Onion. If we assume the size and location of the outmost layer approximately reflect the size and location of its cluster, the new Onion will then direct the processing to clusters which are likely to answer the query. The basic idea is best illustrated in Figures 6 and 7. In Figure 6, there are two clusters of data points expressed in black and white dots. We assume data clustering is provided by query analysis methods beyond the scope of this paper. As shown in the figure, a layered convex hull is built for each cluster to facilitate efficient local queries. The two straight lines represent two different linear optimization criterion. Due to the distinct distributions of black and white points, a linear query may be processed by one cluster only. For example, a linear query shown as a line $L1$ is likely to be answered by the black cluster at the left. Similarly, line $L2$ is likely to be answered by the white cluster. The purpose of this example is to show the possibility of pruning the search space by identifying the most relevant Onions to a given query.

Figure 7 plots the new Onion index built from the outmost layers of the two Onions in Figure 6. The new index has five records from the black cluster and five from the white cluster. From the ten records, the new Onion forms two layers. We refer the new Onion as the parent of the white and black Onion. With a small overhead of replicating Layer-1 records, this parent index serves the purpose of pruning search space. Using this parent Onion, the query processing then knows to process the black cluster first if the $L1$ criterion is given and to process the white cluster first if

the $L2$ criterion is given.

The query processing procedure of the hierarchical indexing is described below in pseudocode.

The procedure of evaluating a query in the hierarchical indexing

    Input: the number of top records to return N; coefficients of the linear criterion

1   locate the parent Onion $\mathcal{P}$ corresponding to the constrained search space;

2   use the single Onion processing procedure described in Section 3.2 to find the top-N records in $\mathcal{P}$; put them in set $\mathcal{T}$;

3   locate child Onions from which the top-N records were originated from;

4   foreach (the child Onions located above) {

5   find the top-N records from the child Onion and put them in set $\mathcal{C}$;

6   find the top-N records from sets $\mathcal{T}$ and $\mathcal{C}$;

7   update $\mathcal{T}$;
        }

8   return $\mathcal{T}$;

Query evaluation starts at locating the parent Onion whose child Onions meet the query constraints. Then the top-N records of the parent Onion are retrieved. At this step, these records are almost always not the top-N records we wanted since they all came from the outmost layers of child Onions. However, the child Onions where they were originated hold the true top-N records. These child Onions are accessed and combined to obtain final results. We acknowledge that there exists better procedures that do not require each selected child Onion to generate its own top-N records. These procedures will be reported separately.

5   Experimental Evaluation

We evaluated the query processing performance of Onion indexing against simple sequential scan, which we believe serves as a good reference point since there are no other techniques addressing model-based queries. We examined the performance impact by changing the spatial distribution of the data, its dimensionality, and the target number, N. Our evaluations comprised both real and synthetic data sets. The real data sets came from an environmental epidemiology study. Since experimental results from both sets behave similarly and the real data sets are not freely available for verification, we focus our reports on the evaluation of synthetic data sets.

Our synthetic data sets comprised of four test sets, each of which contains 1,000,000 data points. In the first and second test sets, attribute values are Gaussian distributed with mean equal to zero and variance equal to one. Points in the first set are in a 3-dimensional space while those in the second set have 4 dimensions. The third and fourth test sets have attribute values uniformly distributed between -0.5 and 0.5. They are in 3 and 4 dimensional space, respectively. Attributes are independent of each other.

Our first measurement characterizes the spread of data points across layers in an Onion index. Figure 8 plots the density distributions of points in each layer. For both uniform and Gaussian distributions, the number of layers in an Onion significantly decreases when the dimension increases. Less data spreading implies that query processing will be less efficient since the partition granularity of the search space decreases.

In Figure 8 we also observed an Onion of Gaussian distributed data has a larger spread than one of uniformly distributed data. This is expected since the tail of the Gaussian distribution extends to infinity, while uniformly distributed data is confined in a data cube. The rate of decay of the probability density function affects data spread. Distributions with slower decay rate than Gaussian, such as exponential and Gamma, will generate even more layers.

We next examine the query performance by varying N from one to one thousand. Coefficients used in the linear criterion were randomly generated. For each test set, we ran 1,000 queries and asked for top-1,000 records. Numbers reported in Table 1 and Figure 9 are averaged over the 1,000 trials. Both in the table and the figure, the number of records evaluated and the number of layers accessed are reported.

From Table 1 and Figure 9, we noticed the extent of data spreads does have a significant effect on the numbers of records and layers. In both 3 and 4 dimensional data sets, an Onion of uniform distribution requires two to three times more access than an Onion of Gaussian distribution. In higher dimensions, since more points are concentrated at the first several layers, there are less number of layers accessed overall. However, since there are more points in each layer, high dimensional indices still require more computation.

In terms of performance gain in computation, the Onion technique performed very well, especially when N is small. Table 2 lists the speedup against sequential scan in multiples. The numbers are generated by taking values in Table 1 and compute their ratio to 1,000,000. Orders of magnitude speedup is achievable at low N. The gain can even be higher as the size of the data set increases. In our evaluation with the real data set, we found the rate of increase in the number of evaluated records is *less* than the rate of increase in the

Table 2: The speedup multiple measured in computational complexity; G: Gaussian distribution, U: Uniform distribution

N	3D G	4D G	3D U	4D U
1	13,333	3,717	3,584	775
10	1,427	492	464	137
100	280	93	98	32
1000	41	18	18	7

Table 3: The speedup multiple measured in disk I/O cost; G: Gaussian distribution, U: Uniform distribution

N	3D G	4D G	3D U	4D U
1	930	935	781	478
10	208	217	162	104
100	68	59	47	27
1000	16	14	11	6

size of the set. The more points an Onion has, the better it performs.

Lastly, the performance gain measured in disk I/O is evaluated. We assume there is sufficient main memory to hold records from a single layer. Since data records in a layer are stored in a *flat file*, sequential I/O best characterizes their access cost. One random I/O is required for loading a layer into the main memory, which requires a disk seek. Attribute values are stored in double precision. We assume a three dimensional record needs 32 bytes for storage and a four dimensional one needs 40 bytes. Each disk page holds 4K bytes. We conservatively assume the cost of one random I/O is equal to 8 times the cost of a single sequential I/O. The performance of the Onion technique will further improve if the cost of random I/O is cheaper. The formula used to compute disk I/O cost is shown in Eq. 2.

Figure 10 plotted the estimated I/O cost of the four test sets. We further assume there is no random I/O cost associated with sequential linear scan. This assumption favors linear scan since it is unlikely that the main memory is always large enough. The I/O cost of scanning 1,000,000 records is fixed at 8,000 sequential access for the 3D data and 10,000 access for the 4D data. Performance speedups of sampled values of N are tabulated in Table 3.

6 Conclusions

We conclude this paper by summarizing the benefits of the Onion technique and pointing out its weaknesses and future research directions. The most appealing feature of Onion is its query processing performance, as shown in the experimental evaluations. It has almost no storage overhead, which makes it a good alternative to unstructured linear storage. Furthermore, the technique enables progressive retrieval which returns the first record to the client at very little latency. In addition, the geometric property of convex hull which the Onion technique is based upon allows one to scale, rotate, and shift the spatial structure without changing its property. This implies the applicability of the

Table 1: The average number of records evaluated and layers accessed to retrieve top-N results from 1,000,000 points

N	3D Gaussian Records	Layers	4D Gaussian Records	Layers	3D Uniform Records	Layers	4D Uniform Records	Layers
1	75.0	1.0	269.0	1.0	279.0	1.0	1,289.0	1.0
10	695.5	4.1	2,030.2	3.2	2,151.0	4.0	7,271.3	2.9
50	2,053.7	8.0	6,345.9	5.9	6,342.7	8.0	21,791.1	5.6
100	3,566.0	11.1	10,641.2	7.8	10,120.6	10.8	30,743.4	6.9
500	13,773.0	25.0	33,450.0	14.4	33,173.7	23.7	90,837.0	13.4
1000	24,308.5	35.2	54,820.2	18.8	54,103.80	33.0	132,220.4	17.1

$$I/O\ cost = 8 * accessed\ layers + 1 * \frac{records\ evaluated * \left\{ \begin{array}{ll} 32 & if\ d = 3 \\ 40 & if\ d = 4 \end{array} \right\}}{4000} \qquad (2)$$

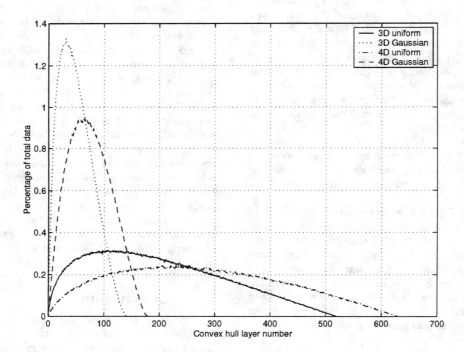

Figure 8: The density distributions of data points spread across layers in the four test sets

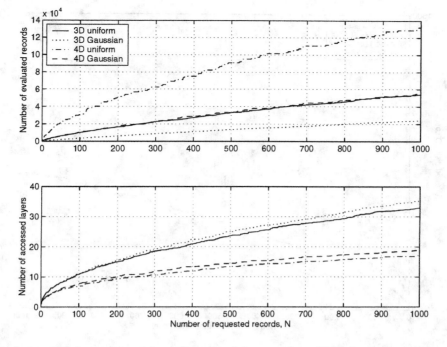

Figure 9: Numbers of evaluated records and accessed layers when N varies from one to one thousand

Onion index to a much broader category of models, not just linear weighted sums.

There are a few weaknesses we have identified in the paper. The most prominent one is the computational complexity at the index construction time. The convex hull algorithm does not scale well into high dimensions. The dimensionality curse not only increases computational complexity but also decreases the number of layers available. Less number of layers implies lower efficiency in pruning the search space. This is the same phenomenon that plagues spatial indexing for similarity queries, which was offered an explanation in [2]. Another potential weakness is its compatibility to other indexing techniques. The Onion technique is really not compatible with other spatial indexing structures like R-tree and is not effective in processing data cube queries. As a part of our future work, we will investigate a hybrid form of indexing structures, which hopefully will answer both top-N model-based and range queries equally well.

Lastly, in our current implementation, records in a layer are flatly laid out on disk. Evaluating all the records in a layer will not only obtain the maximum but also the minimum, one of which is not needed. In the future, we plan to add an auxiliary structure to organize data in a layer to avoid the inefficiency. One simple solution is to map the Onion layers to spherical shells, which is illustrated in Figure 11. Spherical shells express layered convex hulls in concentric shells, each of which contains a layer. This figure illustrates the equivalent spherical shells of a three-layer convex hull in two dimensions. The polar coordinate of a data record is computed and only its angle is used to

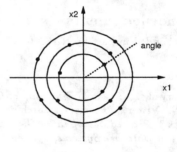

Figure 11: A graphical illustration of introducing an auxiliary structure in a layer by the angle of a data vector

order the record. The radius of a record is not used in a spherical shell and thus all data records in the same layer are shown equally distant from the origin. The query processing procedure is modified as follows. The linear weights of the query are first expressed in polar coordinates, say $(R, \theta_1, \theta_2, \theta_3, ..., \theta_{d-1})$. Instead of evaluating all data records in a layer, only those records are evaluated with angles in the range of $(\theta_1 \pm \pi/2, \theta_2 \pm \pi/2, , ..., \theta_{d-1} \pm \pi/2)$. It is not hard to see that when data records are uniformly distributed, the spherical shell representation further decreases the number of evaluated records by half.

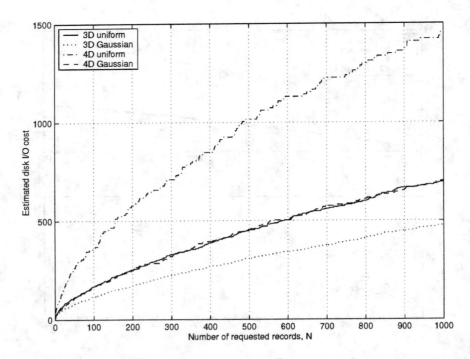

Figure 10: Estimated disk I/O cost of the query evaluation; for linear scan, the I/O cost is fixed at 8,000 sequential page access for the 3D data and 10,000 page access for the 4D data.

7   Acknowledgments

This work was funded in part by NASA/CAN NCC5-305.

References

[1] P. K. Agarwal, L. Arge, J. Erickson, P. G. Franciosa, and J. S. Vitter, "Efficient searching with linear constraints," *Proceedings of the ACM Symposium on Principles of Database Systems*, pp. 169-177, 1998.

[2] K. S. Beyer, J. Goldstein, R. Ramakrishnan, U. Shaft, "When is nearest neighbor meaningful," *Proceedings of International Conference on Database Theory*, pp. 217-235, 1999.

[3] S. Berchtold, C. Bohm, and H. P. Kriegel, "The Pyramid-technique: towards breaking the curse of dimensionality," *Proceedings of the ACM Symposium on Management of Data*, pp. 142-153, 1998.

[4] T. M. Chan, "Fixed-dimensional linear programming queries made easy," *Proceedings of the ACM Symposium on Computational Geometry*, pp. 284-290, 1996.

[5] Y. C. Chang, L. Bergman, J. R. Smith, and C. S. Li, "Efficient multidimensional indexing structure for linear maximization queries," *Proceedings of Multimedia Storage and Archiving Systems*, Boston, MA 1999.

[6] A. Das, S. R. Lele, G. E. Glass, T. Shields, and J. A. Patz, "Spatial modeling of vector abundance using generalized linear mixed models: application to Lyme disease," submitted to *Biometrics* for publication.

[7] G. B. Dantzig, *Linear programming and extensions*, Princeton University Press, Princeton, NJ, 1963.

[8] R. Fagin, "Fuzzy queries in multimedia database systems, " *Proceedings of the ACM Symposium on Principles of Database Systems*, pp. 1-10, 1998.

[9] S. C. Fang and S. Puthenpura, *Linear optimization and extentions*, Prentice-Hall, Inc., Englewood Cliffs, NJ, 1993.

[10] J. Goldstein, R. Ramakrishnan, U. Shaft, and J. Yu, "Processing queries by linear constraints," *Proceedings of the ACM Symposium on Principles of Database Systems*, pp. 257-267, 1997.

[11] J. Matousek and O. Schwarzkopf, "Linear optimization queries," *Proceedings of the ACM Symposium on Computational Geometry*, pp. 16-25, 1992.

[12] F. P. Preparata and M. I. Shamos, *Computational geometry: an introduction*, Springer Verlag, 1991.

[13] R. Seidel, "Linear programming and convex hulls made easy," *Proceedings of the ACM Symposium on Computational Geometry*, pp. 211-215, 1990.

On Effective Multi-Dimensional Indexing for Strings

H. V. Jagadish*
University of Michigan
jag@eecs.umich.edu

Nick Koudas
AT&T Labs–Research
koudas@research.att.com

Divesh Srivastava
AT&T Labs–Research
divesh@research.att.com

Abstract

As databases have expanded in scope from storing purely business data to include XML documents, product catalogs, e-mail messages, and directory data, it has become increasingly important to search databases based on wild-card string matching: prefix matching, for example, is more common (and useful) than exact matching, for such data. In many cases, matches need to be on multiple attributes/dimensions, with correlations between the dimensions. Traditional multi-dimensional index structures, designed with (fixed length) numeric data in mind, are not suitable for matching unbounded length string data.

In this paper, we describe a general technique for adapting a multi-dimensional index structure for wild-card indexing of unbounded length string data. The key ideas are (a) a carefully developed mapping function from strings to rational numbers, (b) representing an unbounded length string in an index leaf page by a fixed length offset to an external key, and (c) storing multiple elided tries, one per dimension, in an index page to prune search during traversal of index pages. These basic ideas affect all index algorithms. In this paper, we present efficient algorithms for different types of string matching.

While our technique is applicable to a wide range of multi-dimensional index structures, we instantiate our generic techniques by adapting the 2-dimensional R-tree to string data. We demonstrate the space effectiveness and time benefits of using the string R-tree both analytically and experimentally.

1 Introduction

Conventional databases, and the index structures defined on these databases, have been designed for business data. Over the years, and particularly now, on account of the rapid growth of the Internet and XML, there has been a growing need to manage, and index, string data. Several index structures for string data have been proposed, beginning with the classical work in [2, 15, 16]. However, all of this work, to our knowledge, has dealt with indexing a single string attribute.

Supported in part by NSF under grant IIS-9986030

Multi-dimensional indexing of string data is important in a variety of contexts. Conjunctive term queries on document sets are standard, and supported by almost every information retrieval system. As we move to build similar functionality in database systems, we must support string matching queries effectively. In many contexts where strings are used, supporting partial match queries, such as prefix and substring matching, which are more common and more useful than exact matching, is crucial. In XML databases, many attributes and elements tend to be string-valued. Almost any complex enough XML query involves selections specified on multiple such string-valued attributes and elements. Even in relational databases, one may need multi-dimensional string querying. For example, in a data warehouse, one can imagine queries that select on a prefix match of the supplier name and a substring match of the product name. Our own work was motivated by the need for such indexing in the context of LDAP directories [10, 13]. We often find queries such as "find a person whose name begins with Sri and a telephone number in the 973 area code". A single index search on the name attribute in the AT&T corporate directory would find matches amongst the entire AT&T population rather than the much smaller population in the 973 area code. A single index search on the telephone number would find everyone in the 973 area code, rather than just the ones with the matching name. A simultaneous index on both attributes could greatly speed up such a search.

The need for multi-dimensional indexes has been recognized in the business and scientific contexts for some time now, and there is a rich history of research in multi-dimensional index structures [19, 7]. However, this research has tended to assume numeric data. This work does not carry over directly to string data for a number of reasons. First, most of these structures require partitioning of an attribute space using spatial distance and volume metrics, whose meaning is not obvious in the context of string data. Second, traditional index structures store attribute values in index pages for comparison purposes during

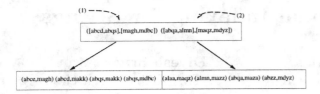

Figure 1: Applying R-tree concepts on a sample string data set

search, for page boundary demarcation, and so forth, implicitly assuming that these stored attribute values are small. This assumption is valid for most numeric attributes, which have values that can be stored in a small amount of space, frequently four bytes. Unfortunately, attributes with string values can often be very long: for instance, a 100 byte address field would not be unusual, nor would a 10,000 byte biography capsule. Storing such attribute values in index pages can be prohibitively expensive, leading us to search for special structures.

1.1 Contributions

In this paper, we present a generic technique for adapting a wide variety of multi-dimensional index structures for wildcard indexing of unbounded length string data. We choose to do so in this generic fashion because there is a plethora of structures that have been devised and little agreement on which is best, even in a well-specified application context [7]. Our generic technique addresses all of the issues raised in the foregoing. More specifically we make the following contributions:

- We map strings to a linear space in a manner that ensures strings that are extensions of a particular prefix are clustered, while preserving lexicographic ordering (Section 2).

  Such clustering is particularly important in a multi-dimensional context since one cannot, in multiple dimensions, use the well-known trick of keeping sideways pointers, as in 1-dimensional B-trees.

- We avoid storing long strings in index pages, and instead store only (small, fixed-length) references to the strings. To enable comparison during search, etc., *elided trie* (e-trie) structures, which are similar to Patricia trees [14], are used to organize these references on the index pages (Section 2).

  E-tries use space proportional to the number of string references stored in the index page, independent of the lengths of these strings.

- We present carefully designed index manipulation algorithms that exploit the e-tries on each index

page to minimize the necessity of fetching the full string for any index operation (Section 3).

- To render the entire discussion concrete, we instantiate our generic techniques in the context of the well-known R-tree [9] and present both an analytical and an experimental evaluation of the *String R-tree* (Section 4).

2 The Generic String Multi-Dimensional Tree

We wish to create an index structure for database objects, indexed on d string-valued attributes, and support indexed retrieval of objects with exact match or prefix match, on some or all of the d attributes. We would like to use standard multi-dimensional index structures (see, e.g., [7]) for this purpose to the extent possible. To this end, there are two basic problems we need to address. First, how best to map strings to a number line so that standard techniques can be used. Second, how to avoid storing possibly very long strings in index pages, and avoid performing possibly costly comparisons between very long strings. We tackle each problem in turn, and then, based on our solutions to these problems, suggest a generic string multi-dimensional index.

2.1 Numeric Mapping

Let strings be comprised of symbols drawn from an alphabet of size α. Then each string can be considered to be a (fractional) number between 0 and 1 written out in base $\alpha + 1$. In other words, one can map each symbol to an integer in the range 1 to α. Let a string of length n be $s_1 s_2 \ldots s_n$, with each symbol s_i mapped to an integer t_i. The string as a whole is then mapped to $t_1/(\alpha+1) + t_2/(\alpha+1)^2 + \ldots + t_n/(\alpha+1)^n$. It is easy to show that there is a one-to-one mapping from (possibly infinite) strings to rational numbers, using the above technique.

Through these means, we may appear to have mapped strings to rational numbers and thus solved the problem of performing string matching using standard numeric techniques. However, several challenges remain. First, the representation of a (long enough) string can require a very large precision representation for the corresponding rational number, certainly well beyond the commonly used four or eight byte representations. In dealing with "true" numbers (real or rational) we are usually willing to sacrifice a small amount of precision (beyond 15 significant digits or so) in return for fast processing. The rational numbers resulting from the above string mapping require substantially more bits per symbol since α is likely to be much larger than 10. Furthermore, to be able to support partial matches using this approach, we would need to keep the mapped numbers with high precision.

A second, and more subtle, problem has to do with the notion of distance. When numbers are drawn from a metric space, it is meaningful to speak of the distance between 10 and 12. It is also possible to use our intuition to estimate numbers of entries and numbers of queries that will fall within any numeric range, based upon reasonable distributions expected. These intuitions fall apart when dealing with strings. The difference between the numeric mappings of two strings represents some sort of lexicographic difference, and is not a very useful concept in terms of similarity or approximation. In particular, we would like the string az to be much closer to a than to b, for example, in a string domain with only the 26 Roman letters in the symbol alphabet.[1] This is because in a page partitioning, we would like to keep a and az together (along with ab, ac, etc.) to enable effective support for prefix match queries, rather than bundling az with b. We solve this problem next.

Distance Metric for Strings: Let the size of the alphabet be α, with an established lexicographic order on the symbols in the alphabet. Choose an integer $\beta > 2\alpha$. Let a string of length n be $s_1 s_2 \ldots s_n$, with each symbol s_i mapped to an integer t_i between 1 and α. The string as a whole is then mapped to $t_1/\beta + t_2/\beta^2 + \ldots + t_n/\beta^n$. Let us look at what is going on with an example, choosing β to be $2\alpha + 1$. In this case, let $[i, j]$ be the interval between two strings of some (equal) length that are adjacent to each other in the lexicographic ordering. Then, extensions of the first string by one character are equally placed in the open interval $(i, (i + j)/2)$. Thus, all extensions of the first string are still closer to i than to j in value. The role of β is to determine the "margin of victory". While it is technically sufficient to set β to be marginally greater than 2α, one can make absolutely certain of forcing page splits to occur only at desired points by choosing a much larger value of β. Our own belief is that a value of $\beta = 2\alpha + 1$ is sufficient.

Example 2.1 Consider an alphabet with 3 characters {a,b,c}. We have $\alpha = 3$ and choose $\beta = 7$. The mapping is shown in Figure 2. ∎

We are thus able to preserve the *prefix clustering property*: all strings that share a common prefix (of any length) occur within a numeric range that is smaller than the numeric distance between any string with this

---

[1]For convenience of exposition, we use an alphabet comprising just the 26 lower-case Roman letters in all our examples. Of course, any real system will have a larger alphabet, including upper case letters, numerals, punctuation symbols, and perhaps even control characters.

A	$\longrightarrow$	1/7
AA	$\longrightarrow$	1/7 + 1/49 = 8/49
AB	$\longrightarrow$	1/7 + 2/49 = 9/49
AC	$\longrightarrow$	1/7 + 3/49 = 10/49
B	$\longrightarrow$	2/7
C	$\longrightarrow$	3/7

Figure 2: Mapping Strings to Rational Numbers to Preserve Prefix Properties

prefix and any string without this prefix. Further, it is straightforward to verify that this metric obeys the triangle inequality.

Categorical Attributes: We have thus far considered strings and assumed clustering based on shared prefixes, and lexicographic ordering, as the most natural clustering likely to be queried. Whereas these assumptions are reasonable for most string objects in databases, one important context where this is not true is with category labels. In such a case, we typically have (or can construct, based on observed queries) a hierarchy of categories and sub-categories, with queries likely to ask for partial matches corresponding to subtrees in this hierarchy, and with no regard to any prefix or lexicographic ordering in the labels. The simple technique of prefixing each category label string with the full path from the root in the category tree solves this problem. All categories in any subtree of the category tree now share as a common prefix, the labels on the path from the root of the category tree to the root of the specified subtree. Thus subtree match is converted to prefix match. Of course, the lengths of the strings involved is now considerably more. But this is exactly the problem that we address in this paper so that no category label strings are stored in the index tree. Moreover, even for the external data storage, with the help of some simple data structures, one can obtain the full effect of the longer label while physically storing only the shorter category label (see [12]).

2.2 External Keys

The strings that need to be indexed can be long. As such, it is inefficient both in terms of storage as well as in terms of processing time for long string comparisons, to store string values in index pages. Yet, almost all index structures require comparands of some sort, and typically these are drawn from the set of values being indexed. For instance, page boundaries are marked in terms of the smallest and the largest (in some dimension) values that occur in the page. Parent index pages have to store the boundaries for each of their children index pages. One way to avoid storing long strings is just to store references to them. Thus, instead of storing strings, we store pointers to the actual strings

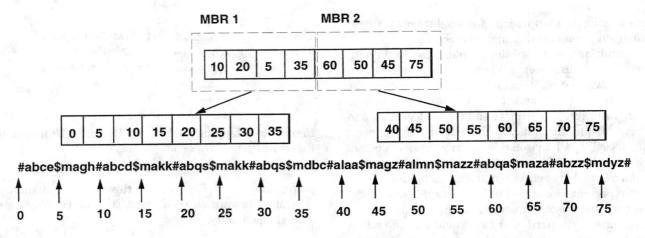

Figure 3: Using External Keys

stored elsewhere on disk. This idea has the virtue of providing us with the desired savings in memory, but now we have a challenge with respect to search (and other index operations).

Example 2.2 We illustrate the idea in Figure 3, using R-tree concepts. The original string data set, from Figure 1, is laid on disk. The representation has been enhanced with two characters '$' and '#' to denote boundaries between the elements of a 2-dimensional string pair and individual string pairs, respectively. The choice of the characters is arbitrary; any character can be used as long as it is not a member of the alphabet from which the strings were derived.

The index leaf pages contain references to individual string elements. This representation requires only a pointer (fixed size, usually 4 bytes) for each string. In each index leaf page, in this example, we store four 2-dimensional strings; we thus have two index leaf pages. In an index non-leaf page, we store the MBRs of the data elements of child index pages. The MBRs are also represented using offsets, not the actual strings, and take a fixed amount of space, that of storing 4 external offsets. ∎

2.3 Elided Tries

In most disk-based index structures, not much attention is paid to how one computes with the information on a page. Typically, one just performs a linear scan through the entries in a page to find the one(s) of interest. This is considered acceptable since most database applications are I/O bound, and the time required to scan a disk page linearly in memory is small compared to the time required to fetch a page from disk. However, with external keys we have a problem. Such a scan means that every pointer to an external key would have to be dereferenced, causing a horrendous amount of I/O. A solution that has been proposed to

this problem, in the 1-dimensional case, is to store a small in-memory structure: an *elided trie* [4, 6].

An elided trie for a set of strings is obtained as follows. First, construct a compacted trie on the strings in question [14]. Many edges in this trie will have multiple symbols, in situations where the first of these symbols determined the path to be taken down the trie, and there was no decision point associated with the rest. Obtain an elided trie (*e-trie*) by *eliding* (not recording in the trie) all but the first symbol in every such case, and instead just keeping a count of the elided symbols. The concept is similar to that used in Patricia trees [16, 14]. It is important that no string in an elided trie be a proper prefix of another string in the same e-trie. This can be ensured by appending to each string a character that does not occur in the alphabet. In our examples, we do not show this appended character, for simplicity, and make sure that our data sets satisfy the above property. It has been shown that an elided trie on n strings can be constructed to require only $O(n)$ space, irrespective of the lengths of the strings in question [6].

Example 2.3 Figure 4(a) shows a sample data set. Figure 4(b) shows a compacted trie constructed on this data set. Notice that strings need not be unique in the data set. Duplication is possible and the duplicate strings can be recorded (as references to the string collection) in the leaf nodes of the compacted trie. Figure 4(c) presents the elided trie after all but the first character on each edge has been removed and the count of the number of characters on the path from the root has been inserted at each vertex.

The structure in Figure 4 has a number of interesting properties. Consider the search for string $Q = $ abqe in Figure 4(d). Starting from the root, we can match the first character 'a'. The length of the string till the next node is 2; thus we visit this node and we test the third character 'q'. Following the branch for 'q' we reach a

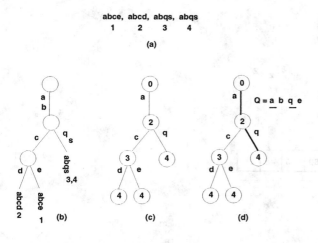

Figure 4: Elided Tries

node n, and we cannot branch further. Node n is the node in the elided trie where the maximal match of Q occurs. Let us choose a descending leaf l from the node n, in this case the node n itself, since it has no children. Leaf l has a very important property: it stores one of the strings that share the longest common prefix with Q [6]. We next retrieve that string. By testing it against Q, we can find Q's position in the collection of strings in the trie. The way to perform this test is to start again from the root of the e-trie and follow the correct path according to the values of the missing characters in the maximal match of Q. For the specific example, string Q should be located as a left child of node n. We can also test for Q's membership in the collection of strings in an e-trie in a similar way.

Consider now the problem of finding the positions of all strings having a given query Q, say ab, as a prefix. We can follow a similar procedure for this problem. The maximal match of Q on the e-trie matches only character 'a'. Then by retrieving any one of the strings corresponding to the leaves below, we can determine that (in this example) all the strings below share the prefix ab. ∎

We say that a string s is *maximally* matched in the e-trie if each character of s is matched with either elided or non-elided characters along a path in the e-trie. We say that a string s is *completely* matched in the e-trie if it is maximally matched with no elided characters. We say that a string s is *partially* matched in the e-trie if it is maximally matched with elided characters. E-trie structures can be efficiently stored, by linearizing them, and efficiently implemented to require minimal storage, independent of the string lengths [5].

The notion of a trie and a compacted trie can be extended to string-tuples in a multi-dimensional space [11]. Such multi-dimensional tries can also be elided in a manner similar to regular 1-dimensional

tries, and it was our first thought to use this data structure. However, it turned out that one could always do at least as well through keeping multiple 1-dimensional e-tries, one for each dimension. The reason is that any specified search predicate can be evaluated against all the tries, sets of candidate matches obtained from each, and then disk accesses performed only to verify candidates in the intersection. This is as good as multi-dimensional trie indexing could possibly get. As such, we focus on multiple 1-dimensional e-tries per index page in what follows.

In a multi-dimensional structure, we could have the same key value occur in multiple string tuples, in conjunction with different other strings each time. However, the e-tries are constructed on only one dimension at a time. As such, there could be multiple string tuples that match perfectly on the chosen dimension, and are all pointed to from the same e-trie leaf node. A property of these external references from a common node is that all the objects retrieved have exactly the same value for the string attribute of focus in the externally stored string tuple.

Example 2.4 We are now able to demonstrate the structure of a leaf index page (Figure 5(a)) and an index non-leaf page (Figure 5(b)) in the 2-dimensional string R-tree. E-tries are constructed for each dimension on the actual string representations. The e-tries in both the leaf and the index non-leaf pages point to the offsets in the index page, which point to the actual data on disk. Thus, the associations between the strings corresponding to the different dimensions in a string tuple are implicitly recorded as shared index page offsets. Similarly, the associations between the minimum bounding rectangles are also kept implicitly in the e-trie nodes of index non-leaf pages. ∎

Enhancing existing multi-dimensional index trees to effectively deal with strings essentially requires careful manipulation of elided tries, for the various index operations of search, insert, split, merge, etc. How to do so efficiently in multiple dimensions is the subject of the rest of this paper.

2.4 Distance Computation with Elided Tries

The mapping introduced in Section 2.1 can be used to compute the distance between any two strings, and hence determine the volume of any hyper-rectangle. The mapping assumes the exact string representation is available. However, with e-tries, the common case is that several characters have been elided. The mapping can, of course, always be computed by accessing the exact string representations from disk, and the distances and volumes subsequently determined. It turns out that one does not have to incur this cost if one

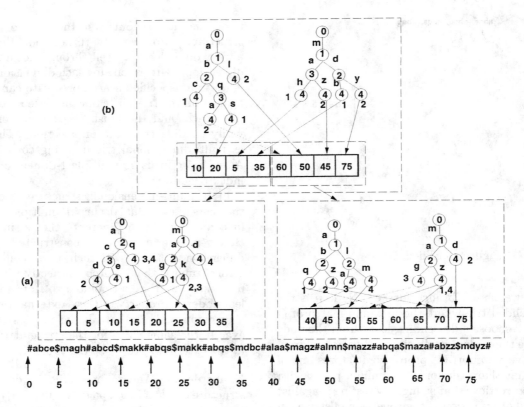

(b)

(a)

#abce\$magh#abcd\$makk#abqs\$makk#abqs\$mdbc#alaa\$magz#almn\$mazz#abqa\$maza#abzz\$mdyz#

0   5   10   15   20   25   30   35   40   45   50   55   60   65   70   75

Figure 5: String R-tree: Index Leaf and Non-Leaf Pages

is willing to accept *approximate* distances and volume measures, as illustrated below.

Example 2.5 Suppose we want to compute, using the e-trie in Figure 4, the distance between strings abcd (i.e., offset 2) and abqs (i.e., offset 4). From the elided representation of a string we have complete knowledge of the length of the string as well as the positions of the elided characters. Although we do not know the second character of the strings in the e-trie, it does not affect the distance between the two strings (since they are guaranteed to have the same second character), even though it affects the actual numeric values, under the mapping, of the two strings.

While the missing fourth character of the string at offset 4 does impact the exact distance, we can derive *lower* and *upper* bounds for this distance. The lower bound is obtained by assuming that the missing fourth character is 'a' (i.e., the string at offset 4 ends with qa), and the upper bound is obtained by assuming that this missing character is 'z' (i.e., the string ends with qz). An approximate distance between the strings can then be estimated as the average of the lower and the upper bounds. The error introduced in the approximate distance computation is very small. ∎

2.5 The Generic Index Structure

Based on the above ideas, we propose a generic string multi-dimensional index as follows:

- Build the multi-dimensional tree index of choice, partitioning either the attribute space or the data points in the manner selected.

- At each page in the index tree maintain d e-tries to describe the children pages, where d is the dimensionality of the index structure.

  The role of the e-tries is to establish partition boundaries that are $O(1)$ per partition, rather than using a possibly unbounded length string.

- Follow standard algorithms to search, insert, delete, and otherwise manage the index tree, with appropriate modifications on account of the changes discussed above.

The nature of these modifications is the subject of the next section.

3 The Algorithms

For reasons of space, update algorithms are not presented here. Algorithms for insertion and deletion, including page split and merge, as well as bulk-load, are available in the full version of this paper [12].

3.1 Indexed Data Access

We describe here modifications of the standard algorithms on multi-dimensional index structures to deal with prefix match queries on strings in 2-dimensions, for ease of exposition. Extensions to higher dimensions, and for exact match and range match queries can be derived analogously. Our presentation is in two parts. First, we describe search in index non-leaf pages. Then, we elaborate on search in index leaf pages.

Prefix Search In Index Non-Leaf Pages: As is common in all tree-based index structures, a search starts from the root of the index structure and proceeds down in the tree. The objective of this search in all multi-dimensional index structures is to obtain a list of pointers to lower level index pages, and proceed applying the same search procedure to each of these lower level index pages in turn, until we reach the index leaf pages. This is in contrast to search in 1-dimensional tree-based index structures that typically follow a single path down the index tree both for point and for range queries. We describe this generic step in terms of our modified index pages containing e-tries for each dimension. Let $Q = (s_x, s_y)$ be a 2-dimensional prefix query. Then the answer set of Q will contain all string-pairs (S_x, S_y) in the database that match (s_x*, s_y*). Let e_x and e_y denote the elided tries on the x and y dimensions respectively. Consider an index non-leaf page, I; searching I is algorithmically described in the full version of the paper [12]. Intuitively, we are interested in identifying the minimum bounding rectangles on index page I, such that the extent of the rectangles overlaps with the prefix match query (s_x*, s_y*). Clearly, this can be achieved by doing multiple disk accesses to retrieve all the strings corresponding to the boundaries of each of the minimum bounding rectangles stored on page I. However, this approach is unnecessarily expensive. Algorithm IndexNonLeafPagePrefixSearch shows how this set of MBRs can be identified with at most one disk access per dimension.

First, the query strings s_x and s_y are used to obtain the longest matches against the e-tries e_x and e_y. In extreme cases, $n1_x$ and/or $n1_y$ may be the roots of the elided tries. Note that these longest matches are not required to be maximal matches. To see why, consider the prefix match query Q1 = (abd*, makk*), and the index pages depicted in Figure 5. There is no maximal match for the query string makk against the e-trie of the y dimension in the index non-leaf page (b). However, there is a prefix match to this string in the first index leaf page, whose MBR's y range is [magh, mdbc]. Similarly, for the query string in the x dimension. In this example, node $n1_x$ is the parent of the left-most leaf of the elided trie e_x, and node $n1_y$ is the parent of the left-most leaf of the elided trie e_y.

Next, elided characters along the longest matching paths are determined, as described in Section 2.3. In our example, there is an elided character (the third character) in the longest matching path in the y dimension, which results in an external disk access; any of the strings beginning at offsets 5 or 45 may be fetched. Since the elided (third) character is 'g', $n2_y$ is the parent of $n1_y$ in e_y. No disk access is performed in the x dimension, since the query string abd in the x dimension is matched only against non-elided characters in e_x; in this case $n2_x$ is the same as $n1_x$.

Next, relevant minimum bounding rectangles along the x and the y dimensions are identified, by invoking Algorithm IdentifyOverlappingMBRs. In that algorithm, L_s identifies the MBRs whose left-endpoint is to the "left" of the query string s, and R_s identifies the MBRs whose right-endpoint is to the "right" of the query string s. Their intersection is the desired set. In our example, of the two minimum bounding rectangles stored in the index non-leaf page of Figure 5, $MBR_x = \{1\}$, and $MBR_y = \{1, 2\}$. We first illustrate the rationale for the x dimension. From the discovered elided characters, it can be determined that the x range of the first MBR is [abc_, abqs], and the x range of the second MBR is [abqa, al__], where '_' denotes an elided character. Independent of the values of the elided characters, prefix matches to query string abd can only fall in the first range. Next, consider the y dimension. From the discovered elided characters, it can be determined that the y range of the first MBR is [magh, mdb_], and the y range of the second MBR is [magz, mdy_]. Independent of the value of the elided character, prefix matches to the query string makk can fall in both the ranges. This rationale is algorithmically captured by Algorithm IdentifyOverlappingMBRs.

Finally, the intersections of the MBRs in the two dimensions are computed. In our example, the result is that only the left-most index leaf page will be searched subsequently for query matches.

Theorem 3.1 *Given an index non-leaf page I, and a prefix query Q in d dimensions, Algorithm IndexNonLeafPagePrefixSearch correctly identifies the minimum set of children index pages of I that need to be further searched to find answers to Q. Further, it does so using at most d external disk accesses.* ∎

Prefix Search in an Index Leaf Page: An index leaf page stores the offsets of the actual strings on disk as well as e-tries on each string dimension. Since no string ranges are present, the search on an index leaf page follows a different strategy. Algorithm IndexLeafPagePrefixSearch presents the approach.

Algorithm IndexNonLeafPagePrefixSearch$(I, Q = (s_x, s_y))$ {

1. Retrieve e-tries e_x and e_y from I.

2. Match s_x against e_x, and let $n1_x$ be the node in e_x corresponding to the longest match with s_x, based on elided and non-elided characters.

   Define node $n1_y$ analogously, based on matching s_y against e_y.

3. If there are any elided characters along the longest match path p_x from the root of e_x, then:

   (a) Choose any leaf l_x in the subtree rooted at $n1_x$.

   (b) Make an external disk access to retrieve the corresponding string in the x dimension, and determine all the elided characters along the path p_x.

   (c) Based on the known values of the elided characters along p_x, let $n2_x$ be the node along path p_x that has the longest match with s_x.

   If there are no elided characters along the path p_x, let $n2_x$ be the same as node $n1_x$.

   Define p_y, l_y and $n2_y$ analogously on the y dimension.

4. Determine the relevant minimum bounding rectangles in the x and y dimensions. $MBR_x =$ IdentifyOverlappingMBRs(I, e_x, p_x, s_x). $MBR_y =$ IdentifyOverlappingMBRs(I, e_y, p_y, s_y).

5. Let $MBR_{xy} = MBR_x \cap MBR_y$. For each of the child index pages I_c of I whose minimum bounding rectangle is included in MBR_{xy}, do either IndexNonLeafPagePrefixSearch(I_c, Q) or IndexLeafPagePrefixSearch(I_c, Q), based on where I_c is a non-leaf or a index leaf page.

}

Algorithm IdentifyOverlappingMBRs(I, e, p, s) {
/* p identifies the string, including both elided and non-elided characters, along the longest path in e that matches with s */

1. Insert string s into a local copy of e.

2. Let L_s denote the MBRs pointed to by trie nodes that precede s in a pre-order traversal of (the modified) elided trie e.

3. Let R_s denote the MBRs pointed to by trie nodes that succeed s in a post-order traversal of (the modified) elided trie e.

4. Return $L_s \cap R_s$.

}

Figure 6: Prefix Searching of an Index Non-Leaf Page

Algorithm IndexLeafPagePrefixSearch$(I, Q = (s_x, s_y))$ {

1. Retrieve e-tries e_x and e_y from I.

2. Maximally match s_x against e_x, and let n_x be the node in e_x corresponding to this maximal match, based on elided and non-elided characters. Define node n_y analogously.

3. If either s_x or s_y did not match maximally, there are no matches. Return $\emptyset$.

4. Let C_x and C_y denote the sets of string-pair offsets in the subtrees rooted at n_x and n_y.

   (a) If $C_x \cap C_y = \emptyset$, there are no matches. Return $\emptyset$.

   (b) If both s_x and s_y matched completely (i.e., no elided characters), no additional disk accesses are required. Return $C_x \cap C_y$.

   (c) Else, choose any string-pair in $C_x \cap C_y$. Perform a disk access to retrieve this string-pair. This can be used to determine the elided characters on the paths to n_x and/or n_y. If any of the determined elided characters does not match s_x or s_y, return $\emptyset$. Else, return $C_x \cap C_y$.

}

Figure 7: Prefix Searching of an Index Leaf Page

Essentially, maximal matches (not just longest matches, as in the case of Algorithm IndexNonLeafPagePrefixSearch) need to be performed against the elided tries. The intersection of the string-pairs in the two subtrees are the candidate matches. Essentially, the key property that holds is that either all of them are matches, or none of them are matches, depending on whether or not the elided characters along the maximal match paths agree with the query strings. Since the two components of a string-pair are assumed to be stored contiguously, either or both components of a string pair can be obtained using a single disk access, and the elided characters determined.

Consider, again, our example prefix match query Q = (abd, makk), and the left-most index leaf page. While there is a maximal match in the y dimension, there is no maximal match in the x dimension. Consequently, we can determine, without any additional disk access, that the query has no answers. If, instead, the prefix match query had been Q = (abc, makk), then the maximal match of abc with e_x in the left-most index leaf page would have determined that the string-pairs 1 and 2 are potential matches. Similarly, the maximal match of makk with e_y would have determined that string-pairs 2 and 3 are potential matches. Computing the intersection, the algorithm would have determined that only string-pair 2 is a potential match. Retrieving this string-pair, it is determined that it is indeed a query answer.

In general, if disk accesses are independently performed to determine the elided characters for each of the e-tries, one can perform as many disk accesses per index leaf page as the number of dimensions. However, we have the following result:

Theorem 3.2 *Given an index leaf page I, and a prefix query Q in d dimensions, Algorithm IndexLeafPagePrefixSearch correctly identifies the string-tuples that are answers to Q. Further, it does so using at most 1 external disk access, independent of the number of dimensions d.* ∎

Exact Match Search: Given an exact match query $Q = (s_x, s_y)$, we wish to retrieve all string-pairs from the database, that exactly match Q on each dimension. The search on an index non-leaf page proceeds in exactly the same way as in the case of prefix match on an index non-leaf page. The search on an index leaf page is similar to the case of prefix match, except that we search for exact matches in the e-tries, instead of searching for prefix matches.

4   Experimental Evaluation

We implemented string R-trees and string B-trees and we report preliminary experiments on their comparative performance. We evaluate the performance of prefix and range queries using real data sets, for a range of query selectivities.

4.1   Description of the Index Structures

In our implementation, the page size was 8KB. The e-tries in both data structures use a short (2 bytes) to represent the node counts. In addition we use char (1 byte) for the representation of the non-elided characters. In the case of string R-trees, we record the associations between the leaf nodes of the e-tries using short. Disk offsets and pointers to pages used long (4 bytes). A small fraction of the page size is used for auxiliary information (counts etc). The resulting fanout is 200 for the string R-tree and 400 for the string B-tree using the above values.

In each disk page, we pre-allocate size for the maximum size of an e-trie. E-tries are linearized with a traversal and stored on a page; they are reconstructed on demand.

4.2   Description of Data Sets

We used two real data sets, extracted from an AT&T data warehouse. Both data sets contain 200,000 2-dimensional strings. As in any access method, skew in the underlying data space is an important parameter in the evaluation of comparative performance. Let N be the total number of multi-dimensional strings. We divide the string domain into a number, n, of lexicographically equidistant segments. This results in n^2 lexicographic buckets, in 2-dimensional space. The expected number of strings in bucket i is $\hat{C}_i = \frac{N}{n^2}$. Let C_i be the real count of strings in bucket i. We then perform the χ^2 goodness of fit test:

$$\chi^2 = \sum_{i=1}^{n^2} \frac{C_i - \hat{C}_i}{\hat{C}_i} \tag{1}$$

The first data set, which we refer to as D1, contains last names in the first column and computer generated login id's in the second, and has a small value of χ^2, or inter-column correlation between strings in this data set. The second data set, which we refer to as D2, contains first names in the first column and last names in the second. D2 has a large value of χ^2, implying high inter-column correlation.

4.3   Query Description

We evaluate the performance of prefix, and range queries[2] on both data sets for low, medium and high selectivities. We generate prefix queries by uniformly selecting tuples from the data sets and uniformly (on

---

[2]Although we have not described the evaluation of range match queries in this paper, this evaluation can be performed by simple extensions of our evaluation strategy for prefix match queries.

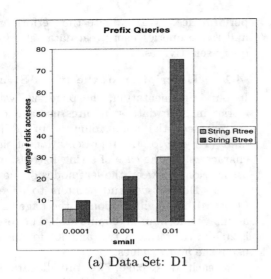

(a) Data Set: D1

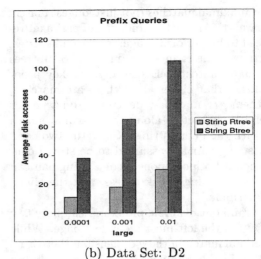

(b) Data Set: D2

Figure 8: Performance of Prefix Queries on String R-trees and String B-trees

the length of the strings) selecting the query size. For range queries, we uniformly choose the start and end ranges from the data sets.

We ask 100 queries of each kind and we report the average number of disk accesses (including both index non-leaf and leaf pages) performed in order to retrieve the query answer. High selectivity queries, medium selectivity queries and low selectivity queries retrieve fractions of approximately 10^{-4}, 10^{-3} and 10^{-2} of the database, respectively.

4.4 Experimental Results

Figure 8 presents the performance of prefix match queries on string R-trees and string B-trees that have been bulk loaded, using the the low-x bulk loading method for R-trees [18] and sorting on the indexed dimension for B-trees, for various selectivities for data sets D1 and D2. We report on their comparative performance using the metric of average number of disk accesses, which is the common metric of choice for the evaluation of index structures. For data set D1 and high selectivity the performance of the string B-tree is close to that of the string R-tree. This is somewhat expected as the number of strings retrieved is small and small inter-column correlation exists in D1. It is evident that as the selectivity increases, string R-trees show large performance benefits compared to string B-trees. The overhead of retrieving strings with common prefix per dimension is too high for string B-trees and it is the main reason for their poor performance. Figure 8(b) presents results of the same experiment, on data set D2. The gap between the performance of string B-trees and string R-trees increases even further, due to the higher inter-column correlation of D2.

Figure 9 presents the performance of range queries

on the data sets. The overall trends in performance are similar to prefix queries.

4.5 Space Considerations

One issue that is often overlooked in the performance of multi-dimensional versus 1-dimensional index structures is that of space. For example, the space required by two B-trees to index a 2-dimensional space is smaller than that required by an R-tree to index the same space. Thus, by using an R-tree we are essentially trading space for search time, since an R-tree can complete the search for most common queries much faster than querying two independent B-trees. We wish to carry out a similar evaluation in the case of string B-trees and string R-trees.

In the case of B-trees and R-trees over numerical domains, using 4 bytes per index entry and 4 bytes for a pointer, we expect a fanout of 400 and 1000 for an R-tree and a B-tree, respectively, for an 8KB page. Using a 16KB page, the numbers become 800 for an R-tree and 2000 for a B-tree.

In the case of string B-trees and string R-trees, an efficient implementation of e-tries is crucial, since e-tries are stored in index pages and their size limits the fanout of the index page. As mentioned earlier, in our implementation, we use short and char, where possible, for a concise encoding of the e-tries.

Let us compute the space requirements of the various entities in a string R-tree page. Assuming n minimum bounding rectangles, we require $16 * n$ bytes for their storage, since each offset is 4 bytes. We also require $4*n$ bytes for the pointer to index pages. For a single e-trie, using the encoding technique described above would require $2*n$ bytes for the storage of the characters and $4*n$ bytes for the storage of the node counts. Ideally,

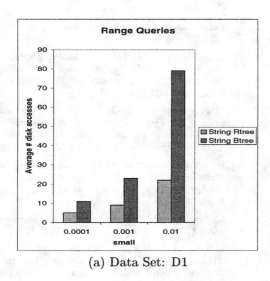

(a) Data Set: D1

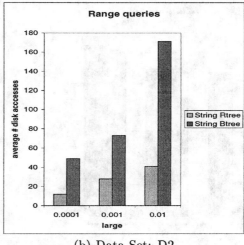

(b) Data Set: D2

Figure 9: Performance of Range Queries on String R-trees and String B-trees

only one of the tries would need an additional 4*n bytes for the storage of the trie associations. The complete storage requirements (for the case of a 2-dimensional string R-tree) is $36 * n$ bytes.

String B-trees, as defined in [6] require the index structure to store the start and the end offset (offset of minimum and maximum string in the page below) as opposed to the traditional B-tree approach of storing only the maximum key value in the child page. Carrying out a similar computation for the case of string B-trees, the total space requirements is $18 * n$ bytes.

Using these numbers we can obtain values of the fanout of the index pages for various disk page sizes. For example, with a page size of 8KB, we expect a fanout of 227 for a string R-tree and 455 for a string B-tree (202 and 449 in our "sub-optimal" implementation). Similarly, with a page size of 16KB, we expect a fanout of 455 for a string R-tree and 910 for a string B-tree (404 and 899 in our "sub-optimal" implementation).

The fanout ratio of the R-tree in the numeric domain and the B-tree in the numeric domain is 2.5. This ratio becomes 2 in the string domain. Figure 10 presents the average ratio of the space required by two B-trees and one R-tree for page sizes of 8KB and 16KB, for data sizes ranging from 10^4 to 10^7 elements. There are three categories, one for the ratio in the numeric domain, one for the ratio achieved by our implementation and one for the ideal ratio. It is evident that due to the design of the string B-tree, the space efficiency of R-trees improves when used in the string domain.

5   Related Work

The work presented in this paper is based on the idea of a string B-tree proposed in [6, 5, 4]. In

these papers, the authors introduce the notion of an index structure designed for unbounded length strings, and use elided tries in the leaf pages of a B-Tree for this purpose. However, the work described is very specific to a (1-dimensional) B-tree. Our contribution in this paper is to extend such a scheme to apply to a wide variety of index structures in multiple dimensions. Multidimensional indexing has a long history in database research [19, 7]. There are numerous proposals for indexing techniques in multiple dimensions. A very good recent survey can be found in [7]. There exist several structures for indexing strings in one dimension. Prefix B-trees [2] is a classic structure, capable of dynamically handling 1-dimensional variable length strings. String B-trees [6] provide better performance guarantees for variable length strings, than Prefix B-trees however. Suffix arrays [22] and PAT-arrays [8] allow for fast searches on strings but they are difficult to update in secondary storage. Suffix trees [15] are another classical index for strings; they have an unbalanced tree topology, which makes the dynamic maintenance in secondary storage difficult. We are not aware of any dynamic structures for multi-dimensional string indexing in secondary storage.

6   Conclusions

More and more frequently, databases have to index strings rather than numbers. It has been believed tacitly by many that well-understood index structures for numeric data can be adapted in a straightforward manner to deal with string data. In this paper, we have explored several of the pitfalls in this process, and proposed generic techniques that can be used to

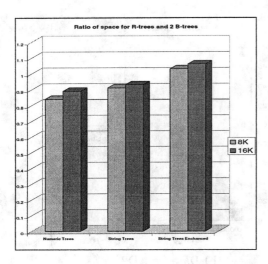

Figure 10: Average Space Ratios

adapt most multi-dimensional index structures to the string indexing problem. The proposed techniques, being generic, are open for various optimizations in specific application contexts. We have also evaluated the benefits experimentally through implementing the string R-tree. Several open problems remain. Foremost among them is effective support for substring match, rather than just the prefix match described in this paper. Of course, there is an obvious technique, of indexing all suffixes, rather than just the original strings, and indeed this is the basis of the well studied suffix-tree. However, we would like to believe that greater efficiency is possible in a multi-dimensional context, and this is the subject of our on-going research.

A second open problem worth mentioning is one of index structure choice. The use of our generic techniques to adapt index structures also changes the costs and performance of the structure. As such, any performance comparisons between multi-dimensional indexes in the numeric domain may not carry over directly to the string domain. Even for a given index structure, different algorithms may now become preferred for various index maintenance operations. Furthermore, we also have the possibility of multi-dimensional indexes with some dimensions being numeric and others string. A careful engineering assessment of the options is called for.

References

[1] L. Arge, P. Ferragina, R. Grossi, and J. S. Vitter. On Sorting Strings In External memory. *Proceedings of STOC, El Paso, Texas*, pages 540–548, June 1997.

[2] R. Bayer and K. Unterauer. Prefix B-trees. *ACM Transactions on Database Systems, 2,1*, pages 11–26, Jan. 1977.

[3] N. Beckmann, H.-P. Kriegel, R. Schneider, and B. Seeger. The R* - tree: An Efficient and Robust Access Method for Points and Rectangles. *Proceedings of ACM SIGMOD*, pages 220–231, June 1990.

[4] P. Ferragina and R. Grossi. A Fully Dynamic Data Structure For External Substring Search. *Proceedings of the 27th Annual ACM Symposium on the Theory of Computing*, pages 693–702, May 1995.

[5] P. Ferragina and R. Grossi. Fast String Searching In Secondary Storage: Theoretical Developments and Experimental Results. *Proceedings of the ACM SIAM Symposium on Discrete Algorithms*, pages 373–382, Jan. 1996.

[6] P. Ferragina and R. Grossi. The String B-Tree: A New Data Structure for String Search in External Memory and Its Applications. *Journal of ACM 46,2*, pages 237–280, Mar. 1999.

[7] V. Gaede and O. Günther. Multidimensional access methods. *ACM Computing Surveys*, 30(2):170–231, 1998.

[8] G. Gonnet, R. Baeza-Yates, and T. Snider. *New Indices for Text: PAT Trees and PAT Arrays*. Information Retrieval: Data Structures and Algorithms, Prentice Hall, 1992.

[9] A. Guttman. R-trees : A Dynamic Index Structure for Spatial Searching. *Proceedings of ACM SIGMOD*, pages 47–57, June 1984.

[10] T. Howes, M. Smith, and G. S. Good. *Understanding and deploying LDAP Directory Services*. Macmillan Technical Publishing, Indianapolis, Indiana, 1999.

[11] H. V. Jagadish, O. Kapitskaia, R. T. Ng, and D. Srivastava. Multi-dimensional substring selectivity estimation. In *Proceedings of the International Conference on Very Large Databases*, Edinburgh, Scotland, UK, Sept. 1999.

[12] H. V. Jagadish, N. Koudas, and D. Srivastava. On effective multi-dimensional indexing for strings. AT&T Labs–Research Technical Report, 2000.

[13] H. V. Jagadish, L. V. S. Lakshmanan, T. Milo, D. Srivastava, and D. Vista. Querying network directories. In *Proceedings of the ACM SIGMOD Conference on Management of Data*, Philadelphia, PA, June 1999.

[14] D. Knuth. *The Art of Computer Programming: Volume 3 Sorting and Searching*. Addison Wesley, Aug. 1998.

[15] E. M. McCreight. A Space-Economical Suffix Tree Construction Algorithm. *Journal of the ACM Vol 23.*, pages 262–272, Dec. 1976.

[16] D. R. Morrison. PATRICIA: Practical Algorithm to Retrieve Information Coded in Alphanumeric. *Journal of ACM, 15,4*, pages 514–534, Oct. 1968.

[17] J. Robinson. The K-D-B-Tree: A Search Structure for Large Multidimensional Dynamic Indexes. *Proceedings ACM SIGMOD*, pages 10–18, 1981.

[18] N. Roussopoulos and D. Leifker. Direct Spatial Search on Pictorial Databases Using Packed R-Trees. *Proceedings of ACM SIGMOD*, May 1985.

[19] H. Samet. *The Design and Analysis of Spatial Data Structures*. Addison Wesley, June 1990.

[20] T. Sellis, N. Roussopoulos, and C. Faloutsos. The R+ -tree : A Dynamic Index for Multi-dimensional Data. *Proceedings of VLDB 1987*, pages 507–518, Sept. 1987.

[21] K. C. Sevcik and N. Koudas. Filter Trees for Managing Spatial Data Over a Range of Size Granularities. *Proceedings of VLDB*, pages 16–27, Sept. 1996.

[22] M. U and G. Myers. Suffix Arrays: A New Method For Online String Searches. *SIAM Journal On Computing, 22,5*, pages 935–948, Jan. 1993.

Efficient and Cost-effective Techniques for Browsing and Indexing Large Video Databases*

JungHwan Oh   Kien A. Hua

Computer Science Program, School of EECS
University of Central Florida, Orlando, FL 32816-2362
E-mail: {*oh, kienhua*}*@cs.ucf.edu*

Abstract

We present in this paper a fully automatic content-based approach to organizing and indexing video data. Our methodology involves three steps:

- **Step 1**: We segment each video into shots using a Camera-Tracking technique. This process also extracts the feature vector for each shot, which consists of two statistical variances Var^{BA} and Var^{OA}. These values capture how much things are changing in the background and foreground areas of the video shot.

- **Step 2**: For each video, We apply a fully automatic method to build a browsing hierarchy using the shots identified in Step 1.

- **Step 3**: Using the Var^{BA} and Var^{OA} values obtained in Step 1, we build an index table to support a variance-based video similarity model. That is, video scenes/shots are retrieved based on given values of Var^{BA} and Var^{OA}.

The above three inter-related techniques offer an integrated framework for modeling, browsing, and searching large video databases. Our experimental results indicate that they have many advantages over existing methods.

KEYWORDS: Shot detection, Video indexing, Video browsing, Video similarity model, Video retrieval.

1   Introduction

With the rapid advances in data compression and networking technology, video has become an inseparable part of many important applications such as digital libraries, distance learning, public information systems, electronic commerce, movies on demand, just to name a few. The proliferation of video data has led to a significant body of research on techniques for *video database management systems* (VDBMSs) [1]. In general, organizing and managing video data is much more complex than managing text and numbers due to the enormous size of video files and their semantically rich contents. In particular, *content-based browsing* and *content-based indexing* techniques are essential. It should be possible for users to browse video materials in a non-sequential manner and to retrieve relevant video data efficiently based on their contents.

In a conventional (i.e., relational) database management system, the *tuple* is the basic structural element for retrieval, as well as for data entry. This is not the case for VDBMSs. For most video applications, video clips are convenient units for data entry. However, since an entire video stream is too coarse as a level of abstraction, it is generally more beneficial to store video as a sequence of shots to facilitate information retrieval. This requirement calls for techniques to segment videos into *shots* which are defined as a collection of frames recorded from a single camera operation. This process is referred to as *shot boundary detection* (SBD).

Existing SBD techniques require many input parameters which are hard to determine but have a significant influence on the quality of the result. A recent study [2] found that techniques using color histograms [3, 4, 5, 6] need at least three threshold values, and their accuracy varies from 20% to 80% depending on those values. At least six different threshold values are necessary for another technique using edge change ratio [7]. Again, these values must be chosen properly to get satisfactory results [2]. In general, picking the right values for these thresholds is a difficult task because they vary greatly from video to video. These observations indicate that today's automatic SBD techniques need to be more reliable before they can be used in practice. From the perspective of an end user, a DBMS is only as good as the data it manages. A bad video shot, returned as a query result, would contain incomplete and/or extra irrelevant information. This is a problem facing today's VDBMSs. To address this issue, we propose to detect shot boundaries in a more direct way by tracking the

*This research is partially supported by the National Science Foundation grant ANI-9714591.

camera motion through the background areas in the video. We will discuss this idea in more detail later.

A major role of a DBMS is to allow the user to deal with data in abstract terms, rather than the form in which a computer stores data. Although shot serves well as the basic unit for video abstraction, it has been recognized in many applications that *scene* is sometimes a better unit to convey the semantic meaning of the video to the viewers. To support this fact, several techniques have been proposed to merge semantically related and temporally adjacent shots into a *scene* [8, 9, 10, 11]. Similarly, it is also highly desirable to have a complete hierarchy of video content to allow the user to browse and retrieve video information at various semantic levels. Such a multi-layer abstraction makes it more convenient to reference video information and easier to comprehend its content. It also simplifies video indexing and storage organization. One such technique was presented in [12]. This scheme abstracts the video stream structure in a *compound unit, sequence, scene, shot* hierarchy. The authors define a *scene* as a set of shots that are related in time and space. Scenes that together give meaning are grouped into a *sequence*. Related sequences are assembled into a *compound unit* of arbitrary level. Other multilevel structures were considered in [13, 14, 15, 16, 17]. All these studies, however, focus on modeling issues. They attempt to design the best hierarchical structure for video representation. However, they do not provide techniques to automate the construction of these structures.

Addressing the above limitation is essential to handling large video databases. One attempt was presented in [18]. This scheme divides a video stream into multiple segments, each containing an equal number of consecutive shots. Each segment is then further divided into sub-segments. This process is repeated several times to construct a hierarchy of video content. A drawback of this approach is that only time is considered; and no visual content is used in constructing the browsing hierarchy. In contrast, video content was considered in [19, 20, 21]. These methods first construct a priori model of a particular application or domain. Such a model specifies the scene boundary characteristics, based on which the video stream can be abstracted into a structured representation. The theoretical framework of this approach is proposed in [19], and has been successfully implemented for applications such as news videos [20] and TV soccer programs [21]. A disadvantage of these techniques is that they rely on explicit models. In a sense, they are application models, rather than database models. Two techniques, that do not employ models, are presented in [11, 22]. These schemes, however, focus on low-level scene construction. For instance, given that shots, groups and scenes are the structural units of a video, a 4-level video-scene-group-shot hierarchy is used for all videos in [22].

In this paper, we do not fix the height of our browsing hierarchy, called *scene tree*, in order to support a variety of videos. The shape and size of a scene tree are determined only by the semantic complexity of the video. Our scheme is based on the content of the video. Our experiments indicate that the proposed method can produce very high quality browsing structures.

To make browsing more efficient, we also introduce in this paper a variance-based video similarity model. Using this model, we build a content-based indexing mechanism to serve as an assistant to advise users on where in the appropriate scene trees to start the browsing. In this environment, each video shot is characterized as follows. We compute the average colors of the foreground and background areas of the frames in the shot, and calculate their statistical variance values. These values capture how much things are changing in the video shot. Such information can be used to build an index. To search for video data, a user can write a query to describe the impression of the degree of changes in the primary video segment. Our experiments indicate that this simple query model is very effective in supporting browsing environment. We will discuss this technique in more detail.

In summary, we present in this paper a fully automatic content-based technique for organizing and indexing video data. Our contributions are as follows:

1. We address the reliability problem facing today's video data segmentation techniques by introducing a camera-tracking method.

2. We fully automate the construction of browsing hierarchies. Our method is general purpose, and is suitable for all videos.

3. We provide a content-based indexing mechanism to make browsing more efficient.

The above three techniques are inter-related. They offer an integrated framework for modeling, browsing, and searching large video databases.

The remainder of this paper is organized as follows. We present our SBD technique [23], and discuss the extensions required to support our browsing and indexing mechanisms in Section 2. The procedure for building scene trees is described in details in Section 3. In Section 4, we discuss the content-based indexing technique for video browsing. The experimental results are examined in Section 5. Finally, we give our concluding remarks in Section 6.

2 A Camera Tracking Technique for SBD and Its Extension

To make the paper self-contained, we first describe our SBD technique [23]. We then extend it to include new features required by our browsing and indexing techniques.

2.1 A Camera Tracking Approach to Shot Boundary Detection

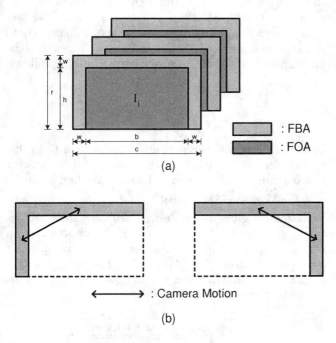

(a)

(b)

Figure 1: Background Area

Since a shot is made from one camera operation, tracking the camera motion is the most direct way to identify shot boundaries. This can be achieved by tracking the background areas in the video frames as follows. We define a *fixed background area* (FBA) for all frames as illustrated by the lightly shaded areas in Figure 1(a). The rationale for the ⊓ shape of the FBA is as follows:

- The bottom part of a frame is usually part of some object(s).

- The top bar cover any horizontal camera motion.

- The two columns cover any vertical camera motion.

- The combination of the top bar and the left column can track any camera motion in one diagonal direction. The other diagonal direction is covered by the combination of the top bar and the right column. These two properties are illustrated in Figure 1(b).

The above properties suggest that we can detect a shot boundary by determining if two consecutive frames

share any part of their FBAs. This requires comparing each part of one FBA against every part of the other FBA. To make this comparison more efficient, we rotate the two vertical columns of each ⊓ shape FBA outward to form a *transformed background area* (TBA) as illustrated in Figure 2. From each TBA, which is a two-dimensional array of pixels, we compute its *signature* and *sign* by applying a modified version of the image reduction technique, called *Gaussian Pyramid* [24]. The idea of 'Gaussian Pyramid' was originally introduced for reducing an image to a smaller size. We use this technique to reduce a two-dimensional TBA into a single line of pixels (called *signature*) and eventually a single pixel (called *sign*). The complexity of this procedure is $O(2^{\log(m+1)})$, which is actually $O(m)$, where m is the number of pixels involved. The interested reader is referred to [23] for the details. We illustrate this procedure in Figure 3. It shows a 13×5 TBA being reduced in multiple steps. First, the five pixels in each column are reduced to one pixel to give one line of 13 pixels, which is used as the signature. This signature is further reduced to the *sign* denoted by $sign_i^{BA}$. The superscript and subscript indicate that this is the sign of the *background area* of some frame i. We note that this rather small TBA is only illustrative. We will discuss how to determine the TBA shortly.

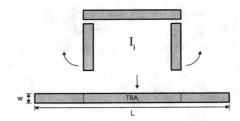

Figure 2: Shape Transformation of FBA

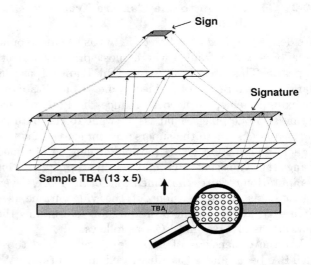

Figure 3: Computation of Signature and Sign

We use the signs and signatures to detect shot boundaries as illustrated in Figure 4. The first two stages are quick-and-dirty tests used to quickly eliminate the easy cases. Only when these two tests fail, we need to track the background in Stage 3 by shifting the two signatures, of the two frames under test, toward each other one pixel at a time. For each shift, we compare the overlapping pixels to determine the longest run of matching pixels. A running maximum is maintained for these matching scores. In the end, this maximum value indicates how much the two images share the common background. If the score is larger than a certain threshold, the two video frames are determined to be in the same shot.

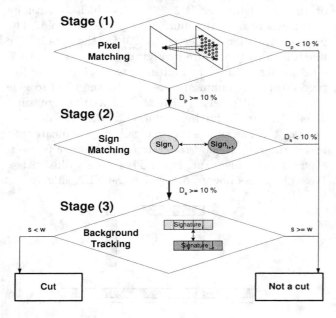

Figure 4: Shot Boundary Detection Procedure

2.2 Extension to the Camera Tracking Technique

We define the *fixed object area* (FOA) as the foreground area of a video frame, where most primary objects appear. This area is illustrated in Figure 1 as the darkly shaded region of a video frame. To facilitate our indexing scheme, we need to reduce the FOA of each frame i to one pixel. That is, we want to compute its sign, $sign_i^{OA}$, where the superscript indicates that this sign is for an FOA. This parameter can be obtained using the Gaussian Pyramid as in $sign_i^{BA}$. This computation requires the dimensions of the FOA. Given r and c as the dimensions of the video frame (see Figure 1), we discuss the procedure for determining the dimensions of TBA and FOA as follows.

Let the dimensions of FOA be h and b, and those of TBA be w and L as illustrated in Figure 1. We first estimate these parameters as h', b', w', and L',

respectively. We choose w' to be 10% of the width of the video frame, i.e., $w' = \lfloor \frac{c}{10} \rfloor$. This value was determined empirically using our video clips. They show that this value of w' results in TBAs and FOAs which cover the background and foreground areas, respectively, very well. Using these w', we can compute the other estimates as follows: $b' = c - 2 \cdot w'$, $h' = r - w'$, and $L' = c + 2 \cdot h'$.

In order to apply the Gaussian Pyramid technique, the dimensions of TBA and FOA must be in the *size set* $\{1, 5, 13, 29, 61, 125, ...\}$. This is due to the fact that this technique reduces five pixels to one pixel, 13 pixels to five, 29 pixels to 13, and so on. In general, the jth element (s_j) in this size set is computed as follows:

$$s_j = 1 + \sum_{i=2}^{j} 2^i \quad for \quad j = 1, 2, 3, ... \quad (1)$$

Using this size set, the proper value for w is the value in the size set, which is nearest to w'. This nearest number can be determined as follows. We first compute $j = 2 + \lfloor \log_2(\frac{w'+3}{6}) \rfloor$. Substituting this value of j into Equation (1) gives us the desired value for w. Similarly, we can compute L, h, and b. This approximation scheme is illustrated in Table 1. As an example, let $c = 160$. We have $w' = \lfloor \frac{160}{10} \rfloor = 16$. The corresponding j value is 3. Substituting j into Equation (1) gives us 13 as the proper value for w.

h', b', w' or L'	Nearest value	h, b, w or L
1, 2	1	1
3, 4, ..., 8	5	5
9, 10, ..., 20	13	13
21, 22, ..., 44	29	29
45, 46, ..., 92	61	61
...	...	...

Table 1: Approximate the dimensions using the nearest value from the size set.

In this section, we have described the computation of the two sign values $sign_i^{BA}$ and $sign_i^{OA}$, and provided the procedure to determine the video shots. In the next two sections, we will discuss how these shots and signs are used to build browsing hierarchies and index structures for video databases.

3 Building Scene Trees for Non-linear Browsing

Video data are often accessed in an exploring or browsing mode. Browsing a video using VCR like functions (i.e., fast-forward or fast-reverse) [25], however, is tedious and time consuming. A hierarchical abstraction allowing nonlinear browsing is desirable. Today's techniques for automatic construction of such structures, however, have many limitations. They rely on explicit models, focus only on the construction of low-level scenes, or ignore the content of the video. We discuss in this section our Scene Tree approach which addresses all these drawbacks.

In order to automate the tree construction process, we base our approach on the visual content of the video instead of human perception. First, we obtain the video shots using our camera-tracking SBD method discussed in the last section. We then group adjacent shots that are related (i.e., sharing similar backgrounds) into a *scene*. Similarly, scenes with related shots are considered related and can be assembled into a higher-level scene of arbitrary level. We discuss the details of this strategy and give an example in the following subsections.

3.1 Scene Tree Construction Algorithm

Let A and B be two shots with $|A|$ and $|B|$ frames, respectively. The algorithm to determine if they are related is as follows.

1. Set $i \leftarrow 1$, $j \leftarrow 1$.

2. Compute the difference D_s of $Sign_i^{BA}$ of shot A and $Sign_j^{BA}$ of shot B using the following equation. We use the number 256 since in our RGB space red, green and blue colors range from 0 to 255

$$D_s = \left(\frac{max. \ difference \ in \ Sign^{BA}s}{256} \right) \times 100(\%) \tag{2}$$

3. If D_s is less than 10%, then stop and return that the two shots are related; otherwise, go to the next step.

4. Set $i \leftarrow i + 1$.

   - If $i > |A|$, then stop and return that two shots are not related; otherwise, set $j \leftarrow j + 1$.
   - If $j > |B|$, then set $j \leftarrow 1$.

5. Go to Step (2).

For convenience, We will refer to this algorithm as *RELATIONSHIP*. It can be used in the following procedure to construct a browsing hierarchy, called *scene tree*, as follows.

1. A scene node SN_i^0 in the lowest level (i.e., level 0) of scene tree is created for each *shot#i*. The subscript indicates the shot (or scene) from which the scene node is derived; and the superscript denotes the level of the scene node in the scene tree.

2. Set $i \leftarrow 3$.

3. Apply algorithm *RELATIONSHIP* to compare *shot#* with each of the shots *shot#(i-2)*, $\cdots$, *shot#1* (in descending order). This sequence of comparisons stops when a related shot, say *shot#j*, is identified. If no related shot is found, we create a new empty node, connect it as a parent node to SN_i^0, and proceed to Step 5.

4. We consider SN_{i-1}^0 and SN_j^0. Three scenarios can happen:

   - If SN_{i-1}^0 and SN_j^0 do not currently have a parent node, we connect all scene nodes, SN_i^0 through SN_j^0, to a new empty node as their parent node.
   - If SN_{i-1}^0 and SN_j^0 share an ancestor node, we connect SN_i^0 to this ancestor node.
   - If SN_{i-1}^0 and SN_j^0 do not currently share an ancestor node, we connect SN_i^0 to the current oldest ancestor of SN_{i-1}^0, and then connect the current oldest ancestors of SN_{i-1}^0 and SN_j^0 to a new empty node as their parent node.

5. If there are more shots, we set $i \leftarrow i + 1$, and go to step 3. Otherwise, we connect all the nodes currently without a parent to a new empty node as their parent.

6. For each scene node at the bottom of the scene tree, we select from the corresponding shot the most "repetitive" frame as its *representative frame*, i.e., this frame shares the same sign with the most number of frames in the shot. We then traverse all the nodes in the scene tree, level by level, starting from the bottom. For each empty node visited, we identify the child node, say SN_m^c, which contains *shot#m* which has the longest sequence of frames with the same $Sign^{BA}$ value. We rename this empty node as SN_m^{c+1}, and assign the representative frame of SN_m^c to SN_m^{c+1}.

We note that each scene node contains a representative frame or a pointer to that frame for future use such as browsing or navigating. The criterion for selecting a representative frame from a shot is to find the most frequent image. If more than one such image is found, we can choose the temporally earliest one. As an example, let us assume that *shot#5* has 20 frames and the $Sign^{BA}$ value of each frame is as shown in Table 2. Since $Sign^{BA}$ is actually a pixel, it has three numerical values for the three colors, red, green and blue. In this case, we use frame 1 as the representative frame for *shot#5* because this frame corresponds to an image with the longest sequence of frames with the same $Sign^{BA}$ values (i.e., 219, 152, 142). Although, the sequence corresponding to frames 15 to 20 also has the same sequence length, frame 15 is not selected because it appears later in the shot. Instead of having only one representative frame per scene, we can also use $g(s)$ most repetitive representative frames for scenes with s shots to better convey their larger content, where g is some function of s.

Frames	Sign		
	Red	Green	Blue
No. 1	219	152	142
No. 2	219	152	142
No. 3	219	152	142
No. 4	219	152	142
No. 5	219	152	142
No. 6	219	152	142
No. 7	226	164	172
No. 8	226	164	172
No. 9	213	149	134
No.10	213	149	134
No.11	213	149	134
No.12	213	149	134
No.13	200	137	123
No.14	200	137	123
No.15	228	160	149
No.16	228	160	149
No.17	228	160	149
No.18	228	160	149
No.19	228	160	149
No.20	228	160	149

Table 2: Frames in the *shot#5*

Now, let us evaluate the complexity of the two algorithms above. The complexity of *RELATIONSHIP* is $O(|A| \times |B|)$. The average computation cost, however, is much less because the algorithm stops as soon as it finds the two related scenes. Furthermore, the similarity computation is based on only one pixel (i.e., $Sign^{BA}$) of each video frame making this algorithm very efficient.

The cost of the tree construction algorithm can be derived as follows. Step 3 can be done in $O(f^2 \times n)$, where f is the number of frames, and n is the number of shots in a given video. This is because the algorithm visits every shot; and whenever a shot is visited, it is compared with every frame in the shots before it. In Step 4 and Step 6, we need to traverse a tree. It can be done in $O(log(n))$. Therefore, the whole algorithm can be completed in $O(f^2 \times n)$.

3.2 Example to explain Scene Tree

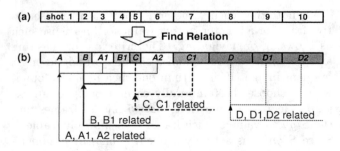

Figure 5: A video clip with ten shots

The scene tree construction algorithm is best illustrated by an example. Let us consider a video clip with ten scenes as shown in Figure 5. For convenience, we label related shots with the same prefix. For instance,

shot#1, *shot#3* and *shot#6* are related, and are labeled as A, $A1$ and $A2$, respectively. An effective algorithm should group these shots into a longer unit at a higher level in the browsing hierarchy. Using this video clip, we illustrate our tree construction algorithm in Figure 6. The details are discussed below.

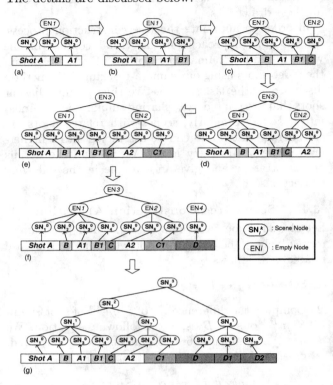

Figure 6: Scene Tree Building

- **Figure 6(a)**: We first create three scene nodes SN_1^0, SN_2^0 and SN_3^0 for *shot#1*, *shot#2* and *shot#3*, respectively. Applying algorithm *RELATIONSHIP* to *shot#3* and *shot#1*, we determine that the two shots are related. Since they are related but neither currently has a parent node, we connect them to a new empty node called *EN1*. According to our algorithm, we do not need to compare *shot#2* and *shot#3*. However, *shot#2* is connected to *EN1* because *shot#2* is between two related nodes, *shot#3* and *shot#1*.

- **Figure 6(b)**: Applying the algorithm *RELATIONSHIP* to *shot#4* and *shot#2*, we determine that they are related. This allows us to skip the comparison between *shot#4* and *shot#1*. In this case, since SN_2^0 and SN_3^0 share the same ancestor (i.e., *EN1*), we also connect *shot#4* to *EN1*.

- **Figure 6(c)**: Comparing *shot#5* with *shot#3*, *shot#2*, and *shot#1* using *RELATIONSHIP*, we determine that *shot#5* is not related to these three

420

shots. We, thus create SN_5^0 for *shot#5*, and connect it to a new empty node $EN2$.

- **Figure 6(d)**: In this case, *shot#6* is determined to be related to *shot#3*. Since SN_5^0 and SN_3^0 currently do not have the same ancestor, we first connect SN_6^0 to $EN2$; and then connect $EN1$ and $EN2$ to a new empty node $EN3$ as their parent node.

- **Figure 6(e)**: In this case, *shot#7* is determined to be related to *shot#5*. Since SN_7^0 and SN_5^0 share the same ancestor node $EN2$, we simply create SN_7^0 for *shot#7* and connect this scene node to $EN2$.

- **Figure 6(f)**: This case is similar to the case of Figure 6(c). *shot#8* is not related to any previous shots. We create a new scene node SN_8^0 for *shot#8*, and connect this scene node to a new empty node $EN4$.

- **Figure 6(g)**: *shot#9* and *shot#10* are found to be related to the immediate previous node, *shot#8* and *shot#9*, respectively. In this case, according to the algorithm, both *shot#9* and *shot#10* are connected to $EN4$. Since *shot#10* is the last shot of the video clip, we create a root node, and connect all nodes which do not currently have a parent node to this root node. Now, we need to name all the empty nodes. $EN1$ is named SN_1^1 because *shot#1* contains an image which is "repeated" most frequently among all the images in the first four level-0 scenes. The superscript of "1" indicates that SN_1^1 is a scene node at level 1. As another example, $EN3$ is named SN_1^2 because *shot#1* contains an image which is "repeated" most frequently among all the images in the first seven level-0 scenes. The superscript of "2" indicates that SN_1^2 is a scene node at level 2. Similarly, we can determine the names for the other scene nodes. We note that the naming process is important because it determines the proper representative frame for each scene node, e.g., SN_7^1 indicates that this scene node should use the representative frame from *shot#7*.

In Section 5, we will show an example of a scene tree built from a real video clip.

4 Cost-effective Indexing

In this section, we first discuss how $Sign^{BA}$ and $Sign^{OA}$, generated from our SBD technique, can be used to characterize video data. We then present a video similarity model based on these two parameters.

4.1 A Simple Feature Vector for Video Data

To illustrate the concept of our techniques, we use the same example video clip in Figure 5, which has 10 shots. From this video clip, let us assume that our

SBD technique generates the values of $Sign^{BA}$s and $Sign^{OA}$s for all the frames as shown in the 4th and 5th columns of Table 3, respectively. The 6th and

Shots	No. of start frame	No. of end frame	$Sign^{BA}$	$Sign^{OA}$	Var^{BA}	Var^{OA}
#1 (A)	1	75	$Sign_1^{BA}, ..., Sign_{75}^{BA}$	$Sign_1^{OA}, ..., Sign_{75}^{OA}$	Var_A^{BA}	Var_A^{OA}
#2 (B)	76	100	$Sign_{75}^{BA}, ..., Sign_{100}^{BA}$	$Sign_{75}^{OA}, ..., Sign_{100}^{OA}$	Var_B^{BA}	Var_B^{OA}
#3 (A1)	101	140	$Sign_{101}^{BA}, ..., Sign_{140}^{BA}$	$Sign_{101}^{OA}, ..., Sign_{140}^{OA}$	Var_{A1}^{BA}	Var_{A1}^{OA}
#4 (B1)	141	170	$Sign_{141}^{BA}, ..., Sign_{170}^{BA}$	$Sign_{141}^{OA}, ..., Sign_{170}^{OA}$	Var_{B1}^{BA}	Var_{B1}^{OA}
#5 (C)	171	290	$Sign_{171}^{BA}, ..., Sign_{290}^{BA}$	$Sign_{171}^{OA}, ..., Sign_{290}^{OA}$	Var_C^{BA}	Var_C^{OA}
#6 (A2)	291	350	$Sign_{191}^{BA}, ..., Sign_{350}^{BA}$	$Sign_{191}^{OA}, ..., Sign_{350}^{OA}$	Var_{A2}^{BA}	Var_{A2}^{OA}
#7 (C1)	351	415	$Sign_{351}^{BA}, ..., Sign_{415}^{BA}$	$Sign_{351}^{OA}, ..., Sign_{415}^{OA}$	Var_{C1}^{BA}	Var_{C1}^{OA}
#8 (D)	416	495	$Sign_{416}^{BA}, ..., Sign_{495}^{BA}$	$Sign_{416}^{OA}, ..., Sign_{495}^{OA}$	Var_D^{BA}	Var_D^{OA}
#9 (D1)	496	550	$Sign_{496}^{BA}, ..., Sign_{550}^{BA}$	$Sign_{496}^{OA}, ..., Sign_{550}^{OA}$	Var_{D1}^{BA}	Var_{D1}^{OA}
#10 (D2)	551	625	$Sign_{551}^{BA}, ..., Sign_{625}^{BA}$	$Sign_{551}^{OA}, ..., Sign_{625}^{OA}$	Var_{D2}^{BA}	Var_{D2}^{OA}

Table 3: Results from Shot Boundary detection

7th columns of Table 3, which are called Var^{BA} and Var^{OA}, respectively, are computed using the following equations:

$$Var_i^{BA} = \frac{\sum_{j=k}^{l}(Sign_j^{BA} - \overline{Sign_i^{BA}})^2}{l - k} \quad (3)$$

where k and l are the first and last frames of the ith shot, respectively. $\overline{Sign_i^{BA}}$ is the mean value for all the signs, and is computed as follows:

$$\overline{Sign_i^{BA}} = \frac{\sum_{j=k}^{l} Sign_j^{BA}}{l - k + 1} \quad (4)$$

Similarly, we can compute Var_i^{OA} as follows:

$$Var_i^{OA} = \frac{\sum_{j=k}^{l}(Sign_j^{OA} - \overline{Sign_i^{OA}})^2}{l - k} \quad (5)$$

$$\overline{Sign_i^{OA}} = \frac{\sum_{j=k}^{l} Sign_j^{OA}}{l - k + 1} \quad (6)$$

We note that Var^{BA} and Var^{OA} are the statistical variances of $Sign^{BA}$s and $Sign^{OA}$s, respectively, within a shot. These variance values measure the degree of changes in the content of the background or object area of a shot. They have the following properties:

- **If Var^{BA} is zero**, it obviously means that there is no change in $Sign^{BA}$s. In other words, the background is fixed in this shot.

- **If Var^{OA} is zero**, it means that there is no change in $Sign^{OA}$s. In other words, there is no change in the object area.

- **If either value is not zero**, there are changes in the background or object area. A larger variance indicates a higher degree of changes in the respective area.

Thus, Var^{BA} and Var^{OA} capture the spatio-temporal semantics of the video shot. We can use them to characterize a video shot, much like average color, color distribution, etc. are used to characterize images.

Based on the above discussions, we may be asked if just two values, Var^{BA} and Var^{OA}, are enough to capture the various contents of diverse kinds of videos. To answer this concern, we note that videos in a digital library are typically classified by their genre and form. 133 genres and 35 forms are listed in [26]. These genres include 'adaptation', 'adventure', 'biographical', 'comedy', 'historical', 'medical', 'musical', 'romance', 'western', etc. Some examples of the 35 forms are 'animation', 'feature', 'television mini-series', and 'television series'. To classify a video, all appropriate genres and forms are selected from this list. For examples, the movie 'Brave Heart' is classified as 'adventure and biographical feature'; and 'Dr. Zhivago' is classified as 'adaptation, historical, and romance feature'. In total, there are at least 4,655 (133×35) possible categories of videos. If we assume that video retrieval is performed within one of these 4,655 classes, our indexing scheme using Var^{BA} and Var^{OA} should be enough to characterize contents of a shot. We will show experimental results in the next section to substantiate this claim.

Unlike methods which extract keywords or keyframe(s) from videos, our method extracts (Var^{BA} and Var^{OA}) for indexing and retrieval. The advantage of this approach is that it can be fully automated. Furthermore, it is not reliance on any domain knowledge.

4.2 A Video Similarity Model

To facilitate video retrieval, we build an index table as shown in Table 4. It shows the index information relevant to two video clips, 'Simon Birch' and 'Wag the Dog.' For convenience, we denote the last column as D^v. That is $D^v = \sqrt{Var^{BA}} - \sqrt{Var^{OA}}$.

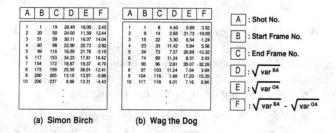

(a) Simon Birch   (b) Wag the Dog

Table 4: Index Information for the two Clips

To search for relevant shots, the user expresses the impression of how much things are changing in the background and object areas by specifying the Var_q^{BA} and Var_q^{OA} values, respectively. In response, the system computes $D_q^v = \sqrt{Var_q^{BA}} - \sqrt{Var_q^{OA}}$, and return the ID of any shot i that satisfies the following

conditions:

$$(D_q^v - \alpha) \le D_i^v \le (D_q^v + \alpha) \qquad (7)$$

$$(\sqrt{Var_q^{BA}} - \beta) \le \sqrt{Var_i^{BA}} \le (\sqrt{Var_q^{BA}} + \beta) \qquad (8)$$

Since the impression expressed in a query is very approximate, α and β are used in the similarity computation to allow some degree of tolerance in matching video data. In our system, we set $\alpha = \beta = 1.0$. We note that another common way to handle inexact queries is to do matching on quantized data.

In general, the answer to a query does not have to be shots. Instead, the system can return the largest scenes that share the same representative frame with one of the matching shots. Using this information, the user can browse the appropriate scene trees, starting from the suggested scene nodes, to search for more specific scenes in the lower levels of the hierarchies. In a sense, this indexing mechanism makes browsing more efficient.

5 Experimental Results

Our experiments were designed to assess the following performance issues:

- Our camera tracking technique is effective for SBD.

- The algorithm, presented in Section 3, builds reliable scene trees.

- The variance values Var^{BA} and Var^{OA} make a good feature vector for video data.

We discuss our performance results in the following subsections.

5.1 Performance of Shot Boundary Detection Technique

Two parameters 'recall' and 'precision' are commonly used to evaluate the effectiveness of IR (Information Retrieval) techniques [27]. We also use these metrics in our study as follows:

- *Recall* is the ratio of the number of shot changes detected correctly over the actual number of shot changes in a given video clip.

- *Precision* is the ratio of the number of shot changes detected correctly over the total number of shot changes detected (correctly or incorrectly).

In a previous study [23], we have demonstrated that our Camera Tracking technique is significantly more accurate then traditional methods based on color histograms and edge change ratios. In the current study, we re-evaluate our technique using many more video clips. Our video clips were originally digitized in AVI format at 30 frames/second. Their resolution

Type	Name	Duration (min:sec)	Shot Changes	Recall (H_r)	Precision (H_p)
TV Programs	Silk Stalkings (Drama)	10 : 24	95	0.97	0.87
	Scooby Dog Show (Cartoon)	11 : 38	106	0.87	0.75
	Friends (Sitcom)	10 : 22	116	0.88	0.75
	Chicago Hope (Drama)	9 : 47	156	0.96	0.84
	Star Trek(Deep Space Nine)	12 : 27	111	0.78	0.81
	All My Children (Soap Opera)	5 : 44	50	0.89	0.81
	Flinstone (Cartoon)	6 : 09	48	0.89	0.84
	Jerry Springer (Talk Show)	4 : 58	107	0.77	0.82
	TV Commercials	31 : 25	967	0.95	0.93
News	National (NBC)	14 : 45	202	0.95	0.93
	Local (ABC)	30 : 27	176	0.94	0.91
Movies	Brave Heart	10 : 03	246	0.90	0.81
	ATF	11 : 52	224	0.94	0.90
	Simon Birch	11 : 08	164	0.95	0.83
	Wag the dog	11 : 01	103	0.98	0.81
Sports Events	Tennis (1999 U.S. Open)	14 : 20	114	0.91	0.90
	Mountain Bike Race	15 : 12	143	0.96	0.95
	Football	21 : 26	163	0.94	0.88
Documentaries	Today's Vietnam	10 : 29	93	0.89	0.84
	For all mankind	16 : 50	127	0.90	0.81
Music Videos	Kobe Bryant	3 : 53	53	0.86	0.78
	Alabama Song	4 : 24	65	0.89	0.84
	Total	278 : 44	3629	0.90	0.85

Table 5: Test Video Clips and Detection Results for Shot Changes

is 160×120 pixels. To reduce computation time, we made our test video clips by extracting frames from these originals at the rate of 3 frames/second. To design our test video set, we studied the videos used in [28, 7, 9, 10, 29, 30, 2]. From theirs, we created our set of 22 video clips. They represent six different categories as shown in Table 5. In total, this test set lasts about 4 hours and 30 minutes. It is more complete than any other test sets used in [28, 7, 9, 10, 29, 30, 2]. The details of our test video set and shot boundary detection results are given in Table 5. We observe that the recalls and the precisions are consistent with those obtained in our previous study [23].

5.2 Effectiveness of Scene Tree

In this study, we run the algorithms in Section 3 to build the scene tree for various videos. To assess the effectiveness of these algorithms, we inspected each video and evaluated the structure of the corresponding tree and its representative frames. Since it is difficult to quantify the quality of these scene trees, we show one representative tree in Figure 7. This scene tree was built from a one-minute segment of our test video clip "Friends." The story is as follows. Two women and one man are having a conversation in a restaurant, and two men come and join them. If we travel the scene tree from level 3 to level 1, and therefore browsing the video non-linearly, we can get the above story. We note that

the representative frames serve well as a summary of important events in the underlying video.

5.3 Effectiveness of Var^{BA} and Var^{QA}

To demonstrate that Var^{BA} and Var^{QA} indeed capture the semantics of video data, we select arbitrary shots from our data set. For each of these shots, we compute its Var^{BA} and Var^{QA}, and use them to retrieve similar shots in the data set. If these two parameters are indeed good feature values, the shots returned should resemble some characteristics of the shot used to do the retrieval.

We show some of the experimental results in Figure 8, Figure 9 and Figure 10. In each of these figures, the upper, leftmost picture is the representative frame of the video short selected arbitrarily for the retrieval experiment. The remaining pictures are representative frames of the matching shots. The label under each picture indicates the shot and the video clip the representative frame belongs to. For instance, #12W represents the representative frame of the 12th shot of 'Wag the dog'. Due to space limitation, we show only the three most similar shots in each case. They are discussed below.

- **Figure 8** The shot (#12W) is from 'Wag the dog'. This shot is a close-up of a person who is talking. The D_{12}^v and Var_{12}^{BA} for this shot are 5.86 and 17.37, respectively, as seen in Table 4(b). The shot #102 from 'Wag the dog', and the shots #64 and #154 from 'Simon Birch' were retrieved and presented in Figure 8. The results are quite impressive in that all four shots show a close-up view of a talking person.

- **Figure 9** The shot (#33W) is from 'Wag the dog', and the content shows two people talking from some distance. The D_{33}^v and Var_{33}^{BA} for this shot are 1.46 and 9.37, respectively, as seen in Table 4(b). The shot #11 from 'Wag the dog', and the shots #93, and #108 from 'Simon Birch' were retrieved and presented in Figure 9. Again, the four shots are very similar in content. All show two people talking from some distance.

- **Figure 10** The shot (#76S) is from 'Simon Birch.' The content is a person running from the kitchen to the window. The D_{76}^v and Var_{76}^{BA} for this shot are -0.78 and 23.55, respectively, as seen in Table 4(a). The shot #87 from 'Wag the dog', and the shots #1 and #4 from 'Simon Birch' were retrieved and presented in Figure 9. Two people are riding a bike in shot #1S. In shot #4W, one person is running in the woods. In shot #87, one person is picking a book from a book shelf and walking to the living room. These shots are similar in that all show a single moving object with a changing background.

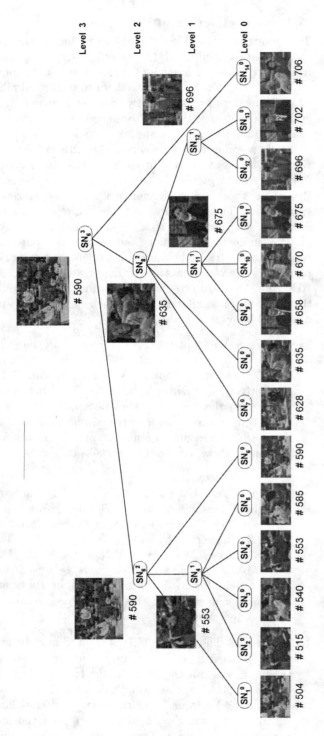

Figure 8: Shots with similar index values - Set 1.

#12W #102W
#64S #154S

Figure 7: Scene Tree of 'Friends'

#33W #11W
#93S #108S

Figure 9: Shots with similar index values - Set 2.

#76S #1S
#4S #87W

Figure 10: Shots with similar index values - Set 3.

6 Concluding Remarks

We have presented in this paper a fully automatic content-based approach to organizing and indexing video data. There are three steps in our methodology:

- Step 1: A Camera-Tracking Shot Boundary Detection technique is used to segment each video into basic units called shots. This step also computes the feature vector for each shot, which consists of two variances Var^{BA} and Var^{OA}. These two values capture how much things are changing in the background and foreground areas of the shot.

- Step 2: For each video, a fully automatic method is applied to the shots, identified in Step 1, to build a browsing hierarchy, called *Scene Tree*.

- Step 3: Using the Var^{BA} and Var^{OA} values obtained in Step 1, an index table is built to support a variance-based video similarity model. That is, video scenes/shots are retrieved based on given values of Var^{BA} and Var^{OA}.

Actually, the variance-based similarity model is not used to directly retrieve the video scenes/shots. Rather, it is used to determine the relevant scene nodes. With this information, the user can start the browsing from these nodes to look for more specific scenes/shots in the lower level of the hierarchy.

Comparing the proposed techniques with existing methods, we can draw the following conclusions:

- Our Camera-Tracking technique is fundamentally different from traditional methods based on pixel comparison. Since our scheme is designed around the very definition of shots, it offers unprecedented accuracy.

- Unlike existing schemes for building browsing hierarchies, which are limited to low-level entities (i.e., scenes), rely on explicit models, or do not consider the video content, our technique builds a scene tree automatically from the visual content of the video. The size and shape of our browsing structure reflect the semantic complexity of the video clip.

- Video retrieval techniques based on keywords are expensive, usually application dependent, and biased. These problems remain even if the dialog can be extracted from the video using speech recognition methods [31]. Indexing techniques based on spatio-temporal contents are available. They, however, rely on complex image processing techniques, and therefore very expensive. Our variance-based similarity model offers a simple and inexpensive approach to achieve comparable performance. It is uniquely suitable for large video databases.

We are currently investigating extensions to our variance-based similarity model to make the comparison more discriminating. We are also studying techniques to speed up the video data segmentation process.

References

[1] A. Elmagarmid, H. Jiang, A. Helal, A. Joshi, and M. Ahmed. *Video Database Systems - Issues, Products, and Applications.* Kulwer Academic Publishers, 1997.

[2] R. Lienhart. Comparison of automatic shot boundary detection algorithms. In *Proc. SPIE Vol. 3656, Storage and Retrieval for Image and Video Databases VII*, pages 290–301, San Jose, CA, January 1999.

[3] M. A. Smith and M. G. Christel. Automating the creation of a digital vidoe library. In *Proc. of ACM Multimedia '95*, pages 357–358, 1995.

[4] R. Lienhart, S. Pfeiffer, and W. Effelsberg. The moca workbench: Support for creativity in movie content analysis. In *Proc. of the IEEE Int'l Conf. on Multimedia Systems '96*, June 1996.

[5] M. Abdel-Mottaleb and N. Dimitrova. Conivas: Content-based image and video access system. In *Proc. of ACM Int'l Conf. on Multimedia*, pages 427–428, Boston, MA, November 1996.

[6] H. Yu and W. Wolf. A visual search system for video and image databases. In *Proc. IEEE Int'l Conf. on Multimedia Computing and Systems*, pages 517–524, Ottawa, Canada, June 1997.

[7] R. Zabih, J. Miller, and K. Mai. A feature-based algorithm for detecting and classifying scene breaks. In *Proc. of ACM Multimedia '95*, pages 189–200, San Francisco, CA, 1995.

[8] P. Aigrain, P. Joly, and V. Longueville. Medium knowledge-based macro-segmentation of video into sequences. In *IJCAI Workshop on Intelligent Multimedia Information Retrieval*, pages 5–14, 1995.

[9] H. Aoki, S. Shimotsuji, and O. Hori. A shot classification method of selecting effective keyframe for video browsing. In *Proc. of ACM Int'l Conf. on Multimedia*, pages 1–10, Boston, MA, November 1996.

[10] M. M. Yeung, B. Yeo, and B. Liu. Extracting story units from long programs for video browsing and navigation. In *Proc. of the IEEE Int'l Conf. on Multimedia Systems '96*, pages 296–304, Hiroshima, Japan, June 1996.

[11] D. Zhong, H. Zhang, and S-F Chang. Clustering methods for video browsing and annotation. Technical report, Columbia University, 1997.

[12] R. Hjelsvold and R. Midtstraum. Modeling and querying video data. In *Proc. of 20th Int'l Conf. on Very Large Database (VLDB '94)*, 1994.

[13] G. Davenport, T. Smith, and N. Pincever. Cinematic primitives for multimedia. In *Proc. IEEE Computer Graphics & Applications*, pages 67–74, July 1991.

[14] R. Hamakawa and J. Rekimoto. Object composition and playback models for handling multimedia data. In *Proc. of ACM Multimedia*, pages 273–281, Anaheim, CA, August 1993.

[15] R. Weiss, A. Duda, and D. Gifford. Content-based access to algebraic video. In *Proc. of IEEE Int'l Conf. Multimedia Computing and Systems*, Los Alamitos, CA, 1994.

[16] J. M. Corridoni, A. D. Bimbo, D. Lucarella, and H. Wenxue. Multi-perspective navigation of movies. *Journal of Visual Languages and Computing*, 7:445–466, July 1996.

[17] H. Jiang and A. K. Elmagarmid. Wvtdb - a semantic content-based video database system on the world wide web. *IEEE Transactions on Knowledge and Data Engineering*, 10(6):947–966, 1998.

[18] H. J. Zhang, S. W. Smoliar, and J. Wu. Content-based video browsing tools. In *Proc. of IS&T/SPIE Con. on Multimedia Computing and Networking*, 1995.

[19] D. Swanberg, C. F. Shu, and R. Jain. Knowledge guided parsing in video databases. In *Proc. of SPIE Symposium on Electronic Imaging: Science and Technology*, pages 13–24, February 1993.

[20] H. Zhang and S. W. Smoliar. Developing power tools for video indexing and retrieval. In *Proc. of SPIE Storage and Retrieval for Image and Video Database*, San Jose, CA, Jan. 1994.

[21] Y. Gong, H. Chua, and X. Guo. Image indexing and retrieval based on color histogram. In *Proc. of Int'l Conf. Multimedia Modeling*, pages 115–126, Singapore, Nov. 1995.

[22] Y. Rui, T. S. Huang, and S. Mehratra. Constructing table-of-cont for videos. *ACM Multimedia Systems*, 7(5):359–368, 1999.

[23] JungHwan Oh, Kien A. Hua, and Ning Liang. A content-based scene change detection and classification technique using background tracking. In *SPIE Conf. on Multimedia Computing and Networking 2000*, San Jose, CA, Jan. 2000.

[24] P. J. Burt and E. H. Adelson. The laplacian pyramid as a compact image code. In *IEEE Transactions on Communications V COM-31*, pages 532–540, April 1983.

[25] Kien A. Hua, W. Tavanapong, and J. Wang. 2psm: An efficient framework for searching video information in a limited-bandwidth environment. *ACM Multimedia Systems*, 7(5):396–408, September 1999.

[26] B. Taves, J. Hoffman, and K. Lund. The moving image genre-form guide. In *Motion Picture/Broadcasting/Recoreded Sound Division Library of Congress*, 1997.

[27] W. B. Frakes and R. Baeza-Yates. *Information Retrieval - Data Structures and Algorithms*. Prentice Hall, Englewood Cliffs, 1992.

[28] A. Hampapur, R. Jain, and T. Weymouth. Digital video segmentation. In *Proc. of ACM Multimedia*, pages 357–364, October 1994.

[29] S. Chang, W. Chen, H. J. Meng, H. Sundaram, and D. Zhong. Videoq: An automated content based video search system using visual cues. In *ACM Proc. of the conf. on Mutimedia '97*, pages 313–324, Seattle Washington, November 1997.

[30] Y. Rui, T. S. Huang, and S. Mehratra. Exploring video structure beyond the shots. In *Proc. of 98 IEEE Conf. on Multimedia Computing and Systems*, pages 237–240, Austin Texas, June 1998.

[31] H. D. Wactlar, M. G. Christel, Y. Gong, and A. G. Hauptmann. Lessons learned from building terabyte digital video library. *Computer*, pages 66–73, February 1999.

Efficient Algorithms for Mining Outliers from Large Data Sets

Sridhar Ramaswamy*

Epiphany Inc.
Palo Alto, CA 94403
sridhar@epiphany.com

Rajeev Rastogi

Bell Laboratories
Murray Hill, NJ 07974
rastogi@bell-labs.com

Kyuseok Shim*

KAIST[†] and AITrc[‡]
Taejon, KOREA
shim@cs.kaist.ac.kr

Abstract

In this paper, we propose a novel formulation for distance-based *outliers* that is based on the distance of a point from its kth nearest neighbor. We rank each point on the basis of its distance to its kth nearest neighbor and declare the top n points in this ranking to be outliers. In addition to developing relatively straightforward solutions to finding such outliers based on the classical nested-loop join and index join algorithms, we develop a highly efficient *partition-based* algorithm for mining outliers. This algorithm first partitions the input data set into disjoint subsets, and then prunes entire partitions as soon as it is determined that they cannot contain outliers. This results in substantial savings in computation. We present the results of an extensive experimental study on real-life and synthetic data sets. The results from a real-life NBA database highlight and reveal several expected and unexpected aspects of the database. The results from a study on synthetic data sets demonstrate that the partition-based algorithm scales well with respect to both data set size and data set dimensionality.

1 Introduction

Knowledge discovery in databases, commonly referred to as data mining, is generating enormous interest in both the research and software arenas. However, much of this recent work has focused on finding "large patterns." By the phrase "large patterns", we mean characteristics of the input data that are exhibited by a (typically user-defined) significant portion of the data. Examples of these large patterns include association rules[AMS+95], classification[RS98] and clustering[ZRL96, NH94, EKX95, GRS98].

In this paper, we focus on the converse problem of finding "small patterns" or *outliers*. An outlier in a set of data is an observation or a point that is considerably dissimilar or inconsistent with the remainder of the data. From the

above description of outliers, it may seem that outliers are a nuisance—impeding the inference process—and must be quickly identified and eliminated so that they do not interfere with the data analysis. However, this viewpoint is often too narrow since outliers contain useful information. Mining for outliers has a number of useful applications in telecom and credit card fraud, loan approval, pharmaceutical research, weather prediction, financial applications, marketing and customer segmentation.

For instance, consider the problem of detecting credit card fraud. A major problem that credit card companies face is the illegal use of lost or stolen credit cards. Detecting and preventing such use is critical since credit card companies assume liability for unauthorized expenses on lost or stolen cards. Since the usage pattern for a stolen card is unlikely to be similar to its usage prior to being stolen, the new usage points are probably outliers (in an intuitive sense) with respect to the old usage pattern. Detecting these outliers is clearly an important task.

The problem of detecting outliers has been extensively studied in the statistics community (see [BL94] for a good survey of statistical techniques). Typically, the user has to model the data points using a statistical distribution, and points are determined to be outliers depending on how they appear in relation to the postulated model. The main problem with these approaches is that in a number of situations, the user might simply not have enough knowledge about the underlying data distribution. In order to overcome this problem, Knorr and Ng [KN98] propose the following distance-based definition for outliers that is both simple and intuitive: *A point p in a data set is an outlier with respect to parameters k and d if no more than k points in the data set are at a distance of d or less from p*[1]. The distance function can be any metric distance function[2].

The main benefit of the approach in [KN98] is that it does not require any apriori knowledge of data distributions that the statistical methods do. Additionally, the definition of outliers considered is general enough to model statistical

*The work was done while the author was with Bell Laboratories.
[†]Korea Advanced Institute of Science and Technology
[‡]Advanced Information Technology Research Center at KAIST

[1]The precise definition used in [KN98] is slightly different from, but equivalent to, this definition.
[2]The algorithms proposed assume that the distance between two points is the euclidean distance between the points.

outlier tests for normal, poisson and other distributions. The authors go on to propose a number of efficient algorithms for finding distance-based outliers. One algorithm is a block nested-loop algorithm that has running time quadratic in the input size. Another algorithm is based on dividing the space into a uniform grid of cells and then using these cells to compute outliers. This algorithm is linear in the size of the database but exponential in the number of dimensions. (The algorithms are discussed in detail in Section 2.)

The definition of outliers from [KN98] has the advantages of being both intuitive and simple, as well as being computationally feasible for large sets of data points. However, it also has certain shortcomings:

1. It requires the user to specify a distance d which could be difficult to determine (the authors suggest trial and error which could require several iterations).

2. It does not provide a ranking for the outliers—for instance a point with very few neighboring points within a distance d can be regarded in some sense as being a *stronger* outlier than a point with more neighbors within distance d.

3. The cell-based algorithm whose complexity is linear in the size of the database does not scale for higher number of dimensions (e.g., 5) since the number of cells needed grows exponentially with dimension.

In this paper, we focus on presenting a new definition for outliers and developing algorithms for mining outliers that address the above-mentioned drawbacks of the approach from [KN98]. Specifically, our definition of an outlier does not require users to specify the distance parameter d. Instead, it is based on the distance of the kth nearest neighbor of a point. For a k and point p, let $D^k(p)$ denote the distance of the kth nearest neighbor of p. Intuitively, $D^k(p)$ is a measure of how much of an outlier point p is. For example, points with larger values for $D^k(p)$ have more sparse neighborhoods and are thus typically stronger outliers than points belonging to dense clusters which will tend to have lower values of $D^k(p)$. Since, in general, the user is interested in the top n outliers, we define outliers as follows: *Given a k and n, a point p is an outlier if no more than $n-1$ other points in the data set have a higher value for D^k than p.* In other words, the top n points with the maximum D^k values are considered outliers. We refer to these outliers as the D_n^k (pronounced "dee-kay-en") outliers of a dataset.

The above definition has intuitive appeal since in essence, it ranks each point based on its distance from its kth nearest neighbor. With our new definition, the user is no longer required to specify the distance d to define the neighborhood of a point. Instead, he/she has to specify the number of outliers n that he/she is in interested in—our definition basically uses the distance of the kth neighbor of the nth outlier to define the neighborhood distance d. Usually, n can be expected to be very small and is relatively independent of

the underlying data set, thus making it easier for the user to specify compared to d.

The contributions of this paper are as follows:

- We propose a novel definition for distance-based outliers that has great intuitive appeal. This definition is based on the distance of a point from its kth nearest neighbor.

- The main contribution of this paper is a *partition-based* outlier detection algorithm that first partitions the input points using a clustering algorithm, and computes lower and upper bounds on D^k for points in each partition. It then uses this information to identify the partitions that cannot possibly contain the top n outliers and prunes them. Outliers are then computed from the remaining points (belonging to unpruned partitions) in a final phase. Since n is typically small, our algorithm prunes a significant number of points, and thus results in substantial savings in the amount of computation.

- We present the results of a detailed experimental study of these algorithms on real-life and synthetic data sets. The results from a real-life NBA database highlight and reveal several expected and unexpected aspects of the database. The results from a study on synthetic data sets demonstrate that the partition-based algorithm scales well with respect to both data set size and data set dimensionality. It also performs more than an order of magnitude better than the nested-loop and index-based algorithms.

The rest of this paper is organized as follows. Section 2 discusses related research in the area of finding outliers. Section 3 presents the problem definition and the notation that is used in the rest of the paper. Section 4 presents the nested loop and index-based algorithms for outlier detection. Section 5 discusses our partition-based algorithm for outlier detection. Section 6 contains the results from our experimental analysis of the algorithms. We analyzed the performance of the algorithms on real-life and synthetic databases. Section 7 concludes the paper. The work reported in this paper has been done in the context of the Serendip data mining project at Bell Laboratories (www.bell-labs.com/projects/serendip).

2   Related Work

Clustering algorithms like CLARANS [NH94], DBSCAN [EKX95], BIRCH [ZRL96] and CURE [GRS98] consider outliers, but only to the point of ensuring that they do not interfere with the clustering process. Further, the definition of outliers used is in a sense subjective and related to the clusters that are detected by these algorithms. This is in contrast to our definition of distance-based outliers which is more objective and independent of how clusters in the input data set are identified. In [AAR96], the authors address the problem of detecting deviations – after seeing a series of

Symbol	Description
k	Number of neighbors of a point that we are interested in
D^k	Distance of point p to its kth nearest neighbor
n	Total number of outliers we are interested in
N	Total number of input points
δ	Dimensionality of the input
M	Amount of memory available
$dist$	Distance between a pair of points
MINDIST	Minimum distance between a point/MBR and MBR
MAXDIST	Maximum distance between a point/MBR and MBR

Table 1: Notation Used in the Paper

similar data, an element disturbing the series is considered an exception. Table analysis methods from the statistics literature are employed in [SAM98] to attack the problem of finding exceptions in OLAP data cubes. A detailed value of the data cube is called an exception if it is found to differ significantly from the anticipated value calculated using a model that takes into account all aggregates (group-bys) in which the value participates.

As mentioned in the introduction, the concept of distance-based outliers was developed and studied by Knorr and Ng in [KN98]. In this paper, for a k and d, the authors define a point to be an outlier if at most k points are within distance d of the point. They present two algorithms for computing outliers. One is a simple nested-loop algorithm with worst-case complexity $O(\delta N^2)$ where δ is the number of dimensions and N is the number of points in the dataset. In order to overcome the quadratic time complexity of the nested-loop algorithm, the authors propose a cell-based approach for computing outliers in which the δ dimensional space is partitioned into cells with sides of length $\frac{d}{2\sqrt{\delta}}$. The time complexity of this cell-based algorithm is $O(c^\delta + N)$ where c is a number that is inversely proportional to d. This complexity is linear is N but exponential in the number of dimensions. As a result, due to the exponential growth in the number of cells as the number of dimensions is increased, the nested loop outperforms the cell-based algorithm for dimensions 4 and higher.

While existing work on outliers focuses only on the identification aspect, the work in [KN99] also attempts to provide *intensional knowledge*, which is basically an explanation of why an identified outlier is exceptional. Recently, in [BKNS00], the notion of *local* outliers is introduced, which like D_n^k outliers, depend on their local neighborhoods. However, unlike D_n^k outliers, local outliers are defined with respect to the densities of the neighborhoods.

3 Problem Definition and Notation

In this section, we first present a precise statement of the problem of mining outliers from point data sets. We then present some definitions that are used in describing our algorithms. Table 1 describes the notation that we use in the remainder of the paper.

3.1 Problem Statement

Recall from the introduction that we use $D^k(p)$ to denote the distance of point p from its kth nearest neighbor. We rank points on the basis of their $D^k(p)$ distance, leading to the following definition for D_n^k outliers:

Definition 3.1: Given an input data set with N points, parameters n and k, a point p is a D_n^k outlier if there are no more than $n-1$ other points p' such that $D^k(p') > D^k(p)$.[3]
∎

In other words, if we rank points according to their $D^k(p)$ distance, the top n points in this ranking are considered to be outliers. We can use any of the L_p metrics like the L_1 ("manhattan") or L_2 ("euclidean") metrics for measuring the distance between a pair of points. Alternately, for certain application domains (e.g., text documents), nonmetric distance functions can also be used, making our definition of outliers very general.

With the above definition for outliers, it is possible to rank outliers based on their $D^k(p)$ distances—outliers with larger $D^k(p)$ distances have fewer points close to them and are thus intuitively stronger outliers. Finally, we note that for a given k and d, if the distance-based definition from [KN98] results in n' outliers, then each of them is a $D_{n'}^k$ outlier according to our definition.

3.2 Distances between Points and MBRs

One of the key technical tools we use in this paper is the approximation of a set of points using their minimum bounding rectangle (MBR). Then, by computing lower and upper bounds on $D^k(p)$ for points in each MBR, we are able to identify and prune entire MBRs that cannot possibly contain D_n^k outliers. The computation of bounds for MBRs requires us to define the *minimum* and *maximum* distance between two MBRs. Outlier detection is also aided by the computation of the *minimum* and *maximum* possible distance between a point and an MBR, which we define below.

In this paper, we use the square of the euclidean distance (instead of the euclidean distance itself) as the distance metric since it involves fewer and less expensive computations. We denote the distance between two points p and q by $dist(p, q)$. Let us denote a point p in δ-dimensional space by $[p_1, p_2, \ldots, p_\delta]$ and a δ-dimensional rectangle R by the two endpoints of its major diagonal: $r = [r_1, r_2, \ldots, r_\delta]$ and $r' = [r_1', r_2', \ldots, r_\delta']$ such that $r_i \le r_i'$ for $1 \le i \le n$. Let us denote the minimum distance between point p and rectangle R by MINDIST(p, R). Every point in R is at a distance of at least MINDIST(p, R) from p. The following definition of MINDIST is from [RKV95]:

Definition 3.2: MINDIST$(p, R) = \sum_{i=1}^\delta x_i^2$, where

---

[3]Note that more than n points may satisfy our definition of D_n^k outliers—in this case, any n of them satisfying our definition are considered D_n^k outliers.

$$x_i = \begin{cases} r_i - p_i & \text{if } p_i < r_i \\ p_i - r'_i & \text{if } r'_i < p_i \\ 0 & \text{otherwise} \end{cases} \quad \blacksquare$$

We denote the maximum distance between point p and rectangle R by MAXDIST(p, R). That is, no point in R is at a distance that exceeds MAXDIST(p, R) from point p. MAXDIST(p, R) is calculated as follows:

Definition 3.3: MAXDIST$(p, R) = \sum_{i=1}^{\delta} x_i^2$, where

$$x_i = \begin{cases} r'_i - p_i & \text{if } p_i < \frac{r_i + r'_i}{2} \\ p_i - r_i & \text{otherwise} \end{cases} \quad \blacksquare$$

We next define the minimum and maximum distance between two MBRs. Let R and S be two MBRs defined by the endpoints of their major diagonal (r, r' and s, s' respectively) as before. We denote the minimum distance between R and S by MINDIST(R, S). Every point in R is at a distance of at least MINDIST(R, S) from any point in S (and vice-versa). Similarly, the maximum distance between R and S, denoted by MAXDIST(R, S) is defined. The distances can be calculated using the following two formulae:

Definition 3.4: MINDIST$(R, S) = \sum_{i=1}^{\delta} x_i^2$, where

$$x_i = \begin{cases} r_i - s'_i & \text{if } s'_i < r_i \\ s_i - r'_i & \text{if } r'_i < s_i \\ 0 & \text{otherwise} \end{cases} \quad \blacksquare$$

Definition 3.5: MAXDIST$(R, S) = \sum_{i=1}^{\delta} x_i^2$, where $x_i = \max\{|s'_i - r_i|, |r'_i - s_i|\}$. $\blacksquare$

4 Nested-Loop and Index-Based Algorithms

In this section, we describe two relatively straightforward solutions to the problem of computing D_n^k outliers.

Block Nested-Loop Join: The nested-loop algorithm for computing outliers simply computes, for each input point p, $D^k(p)$, the distance of its kth nearest neighbor. It then selects the top n points with the maximum D^k values. In order to compute D^k for points, the algorithm scans the database for each point p. For a point p, a list of the k nearest points for p is maintained, and for each point q from the database which is considered, a check is made to see if $dist(p, q)$ is smaller than the distance of the kth nearest neighbor found so far. If the check succeeds, q is included in the list of the k nearest neighbors for p (if the list contains more than k neighbors, then the point that is furthest away from p is deleted from the list). The nested-loop algorithm can be made I/O efficient by computing D^k for a block of points together.

Index-Based Join: Even with the I/O optimization, the nested-loop approach still requires $O(N^2)$ distance computations. This is expensive computationally, especially if the dimensionality of points is high. The number of distance computations can be substantially reduced by using a spatial index like an R^*-tree [BKSS90].

If we have all the points stored in a spatial index like the R^*-tree, the following pruning optimization, which was pointed out in [RKV95], can be applied to reduce the number of distance computations: Suppose that we have computed $D^k(p)$ for p by looking at a subset of the input points. The value that we have is clearly an upper bound for the actual $D^k(p)$ for p. If the minimum distance between p and the MBR of a node in the R*-tree exceeds the $D^k(p)$ value that we have currently, *none* of the points in the sub-tree rooted under the node will be among the k nearest neighbors of p. This optimization lets us prune entire sub-trees containing points irrelevant to the k-nearest neighbor search for p.[4]

In addition, since we are interested in computing only the top n outliers, we can apply the following pruning optimization for discontinuing the computation of $D^k(p)$ for a point p. Assume that during each step of the index-based algorithm, we store the top n outliers computed. Let D_{nmin} be the minimum D^k among these top outliers. If during the computation of $D^k(p)$ for a point p, we find that the value for $D^k(p)$ computed so far has fallen below D_{nmin}, we are guaranteed that point p cannot be an outlier. Therefore, it can be safely discarded. This is because $D^k(p)$ monotonically *decreases* as we examine more points. Therefore, p is guaranteed to not be one of the top n outliers. Note that this optimization can also be applied to the nested-loop algorithm.

Procedure *computeOutliersIndex* for computing D_n^k outliers is shown in Figure 1. It uses Procedure *getKthNeighborDist* in Figure 2 as a subroutine. In computeOutliersIndex, points are first inserted into an R*-tree index (any other spatial index structure can be used instead of the R*-tree) in steps 1 and 2. The R*-tree is used to compute the kth nearest neighbor for each point. In addition, the procedure keeps track of the n points with the maximum value for D^k at any point during its execution in a heap outHeap. The points are stored in the heap in increasing order of D^k, such that the point with the smallest value for D^k is at the top. This D^k value is also stored in the variable minDkDist and passed to the getKthNeighborDist routine. Initially, outHeap is empty and minDkDist is 0.

The for loop spanning steps 5-13 calls getKthNeighborDist for each point in the input, inserting the point into out-Heap if the point's D^k value is among the top n values seen

---

[4]Note that the work in [RKV95] uses a tighter bound called MIN-MAXDIST in order to prune nodes. This is because they want to find the maximum possible distance for *the* nearest neighbor point of p, not the k nearest neighbors as we are doing. When looking for the nearest neighbor of a point, we can have a tighter bound for the maximum distance to this neighbor.

Procedure computeOutliersIndex(k,n)
begin
1. **for each** point p in input data set **do**
2.   insertIntoIndex(Tree, p)
3. outHeap := $\emptyset$
4. minDkDist := 0
5. **for each** point p in input data set **do** {
6.   getKthNeighborDist(Tree.Root, p, k, minDkDist)
7.   **if** (p.DkDist > minDkDist) {
8.   outHeap.insert(p)
9.   **if** (outHeap.numPoints() > n) outHeap.deleteTop()
10.   **if** (outHeap.numPoints() = n)
11.   minDkDist := outHeap.top().DkDist
12.   }
13. }
14. **return** outHeap
end

Figure 1: Index-Based Algorithm for Computing Outliers

so far (p.DkDist stores the D^k value for point p). If the heap's size exceeds n, the point with the lowest D^k value is removed from the heap and minDkDist updated.

Procedure getKthNeighborDist computes $D^k(p)$ for point p by examining nodes in the R*-tree. It does this using a linked list nodeList. Initially, nodeList contains the root of the R*-tree. Elements in nodeList are sorted, in ascending order of their MINDIST from p.[5] During each iteration of the while loop spanning lines 4–23, the first node from nodeList is examined.

If the node is a leaf node, points in the leaf node are processed. In order to aid this processing, the k nearest neighbors of p among the points examined so far are stored in the heap nearHeap. nearHeap stores points in the decreasing order of their distance from p. p.Dkdist stores D^k for p from the points examined. (It is ∞ until k points are examined.) If at any time, a point q is found whose distance to p is less than p.Dkdist, q is inserted into nearHeap (steps 8–9). If nearHeap contains more than k points, the point at the top of nearHeap discarded, and p.Dkdist updated (steps 10–12). If at any time, the value for p.Dkdist falls below minDkDist (recall that p.Dkdist monotonically decreases as we examine more points), point p cannot be an outlier. Therefore, procedure getKthNeighborDist immediately terminates further computation of D^k for p and returns (step 13). This way, getKthNeighborDist avoids unnecessary computation for a point the moment it is determined that it is not an outlier candidate.

On the other hand, if the node at the head of nodeList is an interior node, the node is expanded by appending its children to nodeList. Then nodeList is sorted according to MINDIST (steps 17–18). In the final steps 20–22, nodes whose minimum distance from p exceed p.DkDist, are pruned. Points contained in these nodes obviously cannot qualify to be amongst p's k nearest neighbors and can be

---
[5] Distances for nodes are actually computed using their MBRs.

Procedure getKthNeighborDist(Root, p, k, minDkDist)
begin
1. nodeList := { Root }
2. p.Dkdist := ∞
3. nearHeap := $\emptyset$
4. **while** nodeList is not empty **do** {
5.   delete the first element, Node, from nodeList
6.   **if** (Node is a leaf) {
7.   **for each** point q in Node **do**
8.   **if** ($dist(p,q)$ < p.DkDist) {
9.   nearHeap.insert(q)
10.   **if** (nearHeap.numPoints() > k) nearHeap.deleteTop()
11.   **if** (nearHeap.numPoints() = k)
12. p.DkDist := $dist(p$, nearHeap.top())
13.   **if** (p.Dkdist $\leq$ minDkDist) **return**
14.   }
15.   }
16.   **else** {
17.   append Node's children to nodeList
18.   sort nodeList by MINDIST
19.   }
20.   **for each** Node in nodeList **do**
21.   **if** (p.DkDist $\leq$ MINDIST(p,Node))
22.   delete Node from nodeList
23. }
end

Figure 2: Computation of Distance for k^{th} Nearest Neighbor

safely ignored.

5 Partition-Based Algorithm

The fundamental shortcoming with the algorithms presented in the previous section is that they are computationally expensive. This is because for each point p in the database we initiate the computation of $D^k(p)$, its distance from its kth nearest neighbor. Since we are only interested in the top n outliers, and typically n is very small, the distance computations for most of the remaining points are of little use and can be altogether avoided.

The partition-based algorithm proposed in this section prunes out points whose distances from their k^{th} nearest neighbors are so small that they cannot possibly make it to the top n outliers. Furthermore, by partitioning the data set, it is able to make this determination for a point p without actually computing the precise value of $D^k(p)$. Our experimental results in Section 6 indicate that this pruning strategy can result in substantial performance speedups due to savings in both computation and I/O.

5.1 Overview

The key idea underlying the partition-based algorithm is to first partition the data space, and then prune partitions as soon as it can be determined that they cannot contain outliers. Since n will typically be very small, this additional preprocessing step performed at the granularity of partitions rather than points eliminates a significant number of points as outlier candidates. Consequently, k^{th} nearest neighbor computations need to be performed for very few points, thus speeding up the computation of outliers. Furthermore, since the number of partitions in the preprocessing step is usually much smaller compared to the number of points, and the preprocessing is performed at the granularity of partitions rather than points, the overhead of preprocessing is low.

We briefly describe the steps performed by the partition-based algorithm below, and defer the presentation of details to subsequent sections.

1. **Generate partitions:** In the first step, we use a clustering algorithm to cluster the data and treat each cluster as a separate partition.

2. **Compute bounds on D^k for points in each partition:** For each partition P, we compute lower and upper bounds (stored in P.lower and P.upper, respectively) on D^k for points in the partition. Thus, for every point $p \in P$, $D^k(p) \geq P$.lower and $D^k(p) \leq P$.upper.

3. **Identify candidate partitions containing outliers:** In this step, we identify the *candidate* partitions, that is, the partitions containing points which are candidates for outliers. Suppose we could compute minDkDist, the lower bound on D^k for the n outliers. Then, if P.upper for a partition P is less than minDkDist, none of the points in P can possibly be outliers. Thus, only partitions P for which P.upper $\geq$ minDkDist are candidate partitions.

   minDkDist can be computed from P.lower for the partitions as follows. Consider the partitions in decreasing order of P.lower. Let $P_1, \ldots, P_l$ be the partitions with the maximum values for P.lower such that the number of points in the partitions is at least n. Then, a lower bound on D^k for an outlier is $\min\{P_i.\text{lower} : 1 \leq i \leq l\}$.

4. **Compute outliers from points in candidate partitions:** In the final step, the outliers are computed from among the points in the candidate partitions. For each candidate partition P, let P.neighbors denote the *neighboring* partitions of P, which are all the partitions within distance P.upper from P. Points belonging to neighboring partitions of P are the only points that need to be examined when computing D^k for each point in P. Since the number of points in the candidate partitions and their neighboring partitions could become quite large, we process the points in the candidate partitions in batches, each batch involving a subset of the candidate partitions.

5.2 Generating Partitions

Partitioning the data space into cells and then treating each cell as a partition is impractical for higher dimensional spaces. This approach was found to be ineffective for more than 4 dimensions in [KN98] due to the exponential growth in the number of cells as the number of dimensions increase.

For effective pruning, we would like to partition the data such that points which are close together are assigned to a single partition. Thus, employing a clustering algorithm for partitioning the data points is a good choice. A number of clustering algorithms have been proposed in the literature, most of which have at least quadratic time complexity [JD88]. Since N could be quite large, we are more interested in clustering algorithms that can handle large data sets. Among algorithms with lower complexities is the pre-clustering phase of BIRCH [ZRL96], a state-of-the-art clustering algorithm that can handle large data sets. The pre-clustering phase has time complexity that is linear in the input size and performs a single scan of the database. It stores a compact summarization for each cluster in a CF-tree which is a balanced tree structure similar to an R-tree [Sam89]. For each successive point, it traverses the CF-tree to find the closest cluster, and if the point is within a threshold distance ϵ of the cluster, it is absorbed into it; else, it starts a new cluster. In case the size of the CF-tree exceeds the main memory size M, the threshold ϵ is increased and clusters in the CF-tree that are within (the new increased) ϵ distance of each other are merged.

The main memory size M and the points in the data set are given as inputs to BIRCH's pre-clustering algorithm. BIRCH generates a set of clusters with generally uniform sizes and that fit in M. We treat each cluster as a separate partition – the points in the partition are simply the points that were assigned to its cluster during the pre-clustering phase. Thus, by controlling the memory size M input to BIRCH, we can control the number of partitions generated. We represent each partition by the MBR for its points. Note that the MBRs for partitions may overlap.

We must emphasize that we use clustering here simply as a heuristic for efficiently generating desirable partitions, and not for computing outliers. Most clustering algorithms, including BIRCH, perform outlier detection; however unlike our notion of outliers, their definition of outliers is not mathematically precise and is more a consequence of operational considerations that need to be addressed during the clustering process.

5.3 Computing Bounds for Partitions

For the purpose of identifying the candidate partitions, we need to first compute the bounds P.lower and P.upper, which have the following property: for all points $p \in P$, P.lower $\leq D^k(p) \leq P$.upper. The bounds P.lower/P.upper for a partition P can be determined by finding the l partitions closest to P with respect to MINDIST/MAXDIST such that the number of points in $P_1, \ldots, P_l$ is at least k. Since the partitions fit in main memory, a main memory index can be used to find the l partitions closest to P (for each partition, its MBR is stored in the index).

Procedure *computeLowerUpper* for computing P.lower and P.upper for partition P is shown in Figure 3. Among its input parameters are the root of the index containing all the

Procedure computeLowerUpper(Root, P, k, minDkDist)
begin
1.   nodeList := { Root }
2. P.lower := P.upper := ∞
3.   lowerHeap := upperHeap := $\emptyset$
4.   **while** nodeList is not empty **do** {
5.   delete the first element, Node, from nodeList
6.   **if** (Node is a leaf) {
7.   **for each** partition Q in Node{
8.   **if** (MINDIST(P,Q) < P.lower) {
9.   lowerHeap.insert(Q)
10.   **while** lowerHeap.numPoints() −
11.   lowerHeap.top().numPoints() $\geq k$ **do**
12.   lowerHeap.deleteTop()
13.   **if** (lowerHeap.numPoints() $\geq k$)
14. P.lower := MINDIST(P, lowerHeap.top())
15.   }
16.   **if** (MAXDIST(P,Q) < P.upper){
17.   upperHeap.insert(Q)
18.   **while** upperHeap.numPoints() −
19.   upperHeap.top().numPoints() $\geq k$ **do**
20.   upperHeap.deleteTop()
21.   **if** (upperHeap.numPoints() $\geq k$)
22. P.upper := MAXDIST(P, upperHeap.top())
23.   **if** (P.upper $\leq$ minDkDist) **return**
24.   }
25.   }
26.   }
27.   **else** {
28.   append Node's children to nodeList
29.   sort nodeList by MINDIST
30.   }
31.   **for each** Node in nodeList **do**
32.   **if** (P.upper $\leq$ MAXDIST(P,Node) **and**
33. P.lower $\leq$ MINDIST(P,Node))
34.   delete Node from nodeList
35. }
end

Figure 3: Computation of Lower and Upper Bounds for Partitions

partitions and minDkDist, which is a lower bound on D^k for an outlier. The procedure is invoked by the procedure which computes the candidate partitions, *computeCandidatePartitions*, shown in Figure 4 that we will describe in the next subsection. Procedure computeCandidatePartitions keeps track of minDkDist and passes this to computeLowerUpper so that computation of the bounds for a partition P can be optimized. The idea is that if P.upper for partition P becomes less than minDkDist, then it cannot contain outliers. Computation of bounds for it can cease immediately.

computeLowerUpper is similar to procedure getKthNeighborDist described in the previous section (see Figure 2). It stores partitions in two heaps, lowerHeap and upperHeap, in the decreasing order of MINDIST and MAXDIST from P, respectively – thus, partitions with the largest values of MINDIST and MAXDIST appear at the top of the heaps.

5.4   Computing Candidate Partitions

This is the crucial step in our partition-based algorithm in which we identify the candidate partitions that can potentially contain outliers, and prune the remaining partitions.

The idea is to use the bounds computed in the previous section to first estimate minDkDist, which is a lower bound on D^k for an outlier. Then a partition P is a candidate only if P.upper $\geq$ minDkDist. The lower bound minDkDist can be computed using the P.lower values for the partitions as follows. Let $P_1 \ldots, P_l$ be the partitions with the maximum values for P.lower and containing at least n points. Then minDkDist = $\min\{P_i.\text{lower} : 1 \leq i \leq l\}$ is a lower bound on D^k for an outlier.

The procedure for computing the candidate partitions from among the set of partitions PSet is illustrated in Figure 4. The partitions are stored in a main memory index and computeLowerUpper is invoked to compute the lower and upper bounds for each partition. However, instead of computing minDkDist after the bounds for all the partitions have been computed, computeCandidatePartitions stores, in the heap partHeap, the partitions with the largest P.lower values and containing at least n points among them. The partitions are stored in increasing order of P.lower in partHeap and minDkDist is thus equal to P.lower for the partition P at the top of partHeap. The benefit of maintaining minDkDist is that it can be passed as a parameter to computeLowerUpper (in Step 6) and the computation of bounds for a partition P can be halted early if P.upper for it falls below minDkDist. If, for a partition P, P.lower is greater than the current value of minDkDist, then it is inserted into partHeap and the value of minDkDist is appropriately adjusted (steps 8–13).

Procedure computeCandidatePartitions(PSet, k, n)
begin
1.   **for each** partition P in PSet **do**
2.   insertIntoIndex(Tree, P)
3.   partHeap := $\emptyset$
4.   minDkDist := 0
5.   **for each** partition P in PSet **do** {
6.   computeLowerUpper(Tree.Root, P, k, minDkDist)
7.   **if** (P.lower > minDkDist) {
8.   partHeap.insert(P)
9.   **while** partHeap.numPoints() −
10.   partHeap.top().numPoints() $\geq n$ **do**
11.   partHeap.deleteTop()
12.   **if** (partHeap.numPoints() $\geq n$)
13.   minDkDist := partHeap.top().lower
14.   }
15. }
16. candSet := $\emptyset$
17. **for each** partition P in PSet **do**
18.   **if** (P.upper $\geq$ minDkDist) {
19.   candSet := candSet $\cup$ {P}
20. P.neighbors :=
21.   {Q: $Q \in$ PSet and MINDIST(P,Q) $\leq P$.upper}
22.   }
23. **return** candSet
end

Figure 4: Computation of Candidate Partitions

In the for loop over steps 17–22, the set of candidate partitions candSet is computed, and for each candidate partition P, partitions Q that can potentially contain the kth

nearest neighbor for a point in P are added to P.neighbors (note that P.neighbors contains P).

5.5 Computing Outliers from Candidate Partitions

In the final step, we compute the top n outliers from the candidate partitions in candSet. If points in all the candidate partitions and their neighbors fit in memory, then we can simply load all the points into a main memory spatial index. The index-based algorithm (see Figure 1) can then be used to compute the n outliers by probing the index to compute D^k values only for points belonging to the candidate partitions. Since both the size of the index as well as the number of candidate points will in general be small compared to the total number of points in the data set, this can be expected to be much faster than executing the index-based algorithm on the entire data set of points.

In the case that all the candidate partitions and their neighbors exceed the size of main memory, then we need to process the candidate partitions in batches. In each batch, a subset of the remaining candidate partitions that along with their neighbors fit in memory, is chosen for processing. Due to space constraints, we refer the reader to [RRS98] for details of the batch processing algorithm.

6 Experimental Results

We empirically compared the performance of our partition-based algorithm with the block nested-loop and index-based algorithms. In our experiments, we found that the partition-based algorithm scales well with both the data set size as well as data set dimensionality. In addition, in a number of cases, it is more than an order of magnitude faster than the block nested-loop and index-based algorithms.

We begin by describing in Section 6.1 our experience with mining a real-life NBA (National Basketball Association) database using our notion of outliers. The results indicate the efficacy of our approach in finding "interesting" and sometimes unexpected facts buried in the data. We then evaluate the performance of the algorithms on a class of synthetic datasets in Section 6.2. The experiments were performed on a Sun Ultra-2/200 workstation with 512 MB of main memory, and running Solaris 2.5. The data sets were stored on a local disk.

6.1 Analyzing NBA Statistics

We analyzed the statistics for the 1998 NBA season with our outlier programs to see if it could discover interesting nuggets in those statistics. We had information about all 471 NBA players who played in the NBA during the 1997-1998 season. In order to restrict our attention to significant players, we removed all players who scored less then 100 points over the course of the entire season. This left us with 335 players. We then wanted to ensure that all the columns were given equal weight. We accomplished this by transforming the value c in a column to $\frac{c-\bar{c}}{\sigma_c}$ where $\bar{c}$ is the average value of the column and σ_c its standard deviation. This transformation normalizes the column to have an average of 0 and a standard deviation of 1.

We then ran our outlier program on the transformed data. We used a value of 10 for k and looked for the top 5 outliers. The results from some of the runs are shown in Figure 5. (findOuts.pl is a perl front end to the outliers program that understands the names of the columns in the NBA database. It simply processes its arguments and calls the outlier program.) In addition to giving the actual value for a column, the output also prints the normalized value used in the outlier calculation. The outliers are ranked based on their D^k values which are listed under the DIST column.

The first experiment in Figure 5 focuses on the three most commonly used *average* statistics in the NBA: average points per game, average assists per game and average rebounds per game. What stands out is the extent to which players having a large value in one dimension tend to dominate in the outlier list. For instance, Dennis Rodman, not known to excel in either assisting or scoring, is nevertheless the top outlier because of his huge (nearly 4.4 sigmas) deviation from the average on rebounds. Furthermore, his DIST value is much higher than that for any of the other outliers, thus making him an extremely strong outlier. Two other players in this outlier list also tend to dominate in one or two columns. An interesting case is that of Shaquille O' Neal who made it to the outlier list due to his excellent record in both scoring and rebounds, though he is quite average on assists. (Recall that the average of every normalized column is 0.) The first "well-rounded" player to appear in this list is Karl Malone, at position 5. (Michael Jordan is at position 7.) In fact, in the list of the top 25 outliers, there are only two players, Karl Malone and Grant Hill (at positions 5 and 6) that have normalized values of more than 1 in all three columns.

When we look at more defensive statistics, the outliers are once again dominated by players having large normalized values for a single column. When we consider average steals and blocks, the outliers are dominated by shot blockers like Marcus Camby. Hakeem Olajuwon, at position 5, shows up as the first "balanced" player due to his above average record with respect to both steals and blocks.

In conclusion, we were somewhat surprise by the outcome of our experiments on the NBA data. First, we found that very few "balanced" players (that is, players who are above average in every aspect of the game) are labeled as outliers. Instead, the outlier lists are dominated by players who excel by a wide margin in particular aspects of the game (e.g., Dennis Rodman on rebounds).

Another interesting observation we made was that the outliers found tended to be more interesting when we considered fewer attributes (e.g., 2 or 3). This is not entirely surprising since it is a well-known fact that as the number of dimensions increases, points spread out more uniformly in the data space and distances between them are a poor measure of their similarity/dissimilarity.

```
->findOuts.pl -n 5 -k 10 reb assists pts
          NAME    DIST   avgReb  (norm)  avgAssts  (norm)   avgPts  (norm)
 Dennis Rodman    7.26   15.000  (4.376)   2.900  (0.670)    4.700 (-0.459)
 Rod Strickland   3.95    5.300  (0.750)  10.500  (4.922)   17.800  (1.740)
 Shaquille Oneal  3.61   11.400  (3.030)   2.400  (0.391)   28.300  (3.503)
 Jayson Williams  3.33   13.600  (3.852)   1.000 (-0.393)   12.900  (0.918)
 Karl Malone      2.96   10.300  (2.619)   3.900  (1.230)   27.000  (3.285)

->findOuts.pl -n 5 -k 10 steal blocks
          NAME    DIST   avgSteals (norm)  avgBlocks (norm)
 Marcus Camby     8.44    1.100  (0.838)    3.700  (6.139)
 Dikembe Mutombo  5.35    0.400 (-0.550)    3.400  (5.580)
 Shawn Bradley    4.36    0.800 (-0.243)    3.300  (5.394)
 Theo Ratliff     3.51    0.600 (-0.153)    3.200  (5.208)
 Hakeem Olajuwon  3.47    1.800  (2.225)    2.000  (2.972)
```

Figure 5: Finding Outliers from a 1998 NBA Statistics Database

Finally, while we were conducting our experiments on the NBA database, we realized that specifying actual distances, as is required in [KN98], is fairly difficult in practice. Instead, our notion of outliers, which only requires us to specify the k-value used in calculating k'th neighbor distance, is much simpler to work with. (The results are fairly insensitive to minor changes in k, making the job of specifying it easy.) Note also the ranking for players that we provide in Figure 5 based on distance —this enables us to determine how strong an outlier really is.

6.2 Performance Results on Synthetic Data

We begin this section by briefly describing our implementation of the three algorithms that we used. We then move onto describing the synthetic datasets that we used.

6.2.1 Algorithms Implemented

Block Nested-Loop Algorithm: This algorithm was described in Section 4. In order to optimize the performance of this algorithm, we implemented our own buffer manager and performed reads in large blocks. We allocated as much buffer space as possible to the outer loop.

Index-Based Algorithm: To speed up execution, an R*-tree was used to find the k nearest neighbors for a point, as described in Section 4. The R*-tree code was developed at the University of Maryland.[6] The R*-tree we used was a main memory-based version. The page size for the R*-tree was set to 1024 bytes. In our experiments, the R*-tree always fit in memory. Furthermore, for the index-based algorithm, we did not include the time to build the tree (that is, insert data points into the tree) in our measurements of execution time. Thus, our measurement for the running time of the index-based algorithm *only includes the CPU time for main memory search*. Note that this gives the index-based algorithm an advantage over the other algorithms.

[6] Our thanks to Christos Faloutsos for providing us with this code.

Partition-Based algorithm: We implemented our partition-based algorithm as described in Section 5. Thus, we used BIRCH's pre-clustering algorithm for generating partitions, the main memory R*-tree to determine the candidate partitions and the block nested-loop algorithm for computing outliers from the candidate partitions in the final step. We found that for the final step, the performance of the block nested-loop algorithm was competitive with the index-based algorithm since the previous pruning steps did a very good job in identifying the candidate partitions and their neighbors.

We configured BIRCH to provide a bounding rectangle for each cluster it generated. We used this as the MBR for the corresponding partition. We stored the MBR and number of points in each partition in an R*-tree. We used the resulting index to identify candidate and neighboring partitions. Since we needed to identify the partition to which BIRCH assigned a point, we modified BIRCH to generate this information.

Recall from Section 5.2 that an important parameter to BIRCH is the amount of memory it is allowed to use. In the experiments, we specify this parameter in terms of the number of clusters or partitions that BIRCH is allowed to create.

6.2.2 Synthetic Data Sets

For our experiments, we used the *grid* synthetic data set that was employed in [ZRL96] to study the sensitivity of BIRCH. The data set contains 100 hyper-spherical clusters arranged as a 10×10 grid. The center of each cluster is located at $(10i, 10j)$ for $1 \le i \le 10$ and $1 \le j \le 10$. Furthermore, each cluster has a radius of 4. Data points for a cluster are uniformly distributed in the hyper-sphere that defines the cluster. We also uniformly scattered 1000 outlier points in the space spanning 0 to 110 along each dimension. Table 2 shows the parameters for the data set, along with their default values and the range of values for which we conducted experiments.

Parameter	Default Value	Range of Values
Number of Points (N)	101000	11000 to 1 million
Number of Clusters	100	
Number of Points per Cluster	1000	100 to 10000
Number of Outliers in Data Set	1000	
Number of Outliers to be Computed (n)	100	100 to 500
Number of Neighbors (k)	100	100 to 500
Number of Dimensions (δ)	2	2 to 10
Maximum number of Partitions	6000	5000 to 15000
Distance Metric	euclidean	

Table 2: Synthetic Data Parameters

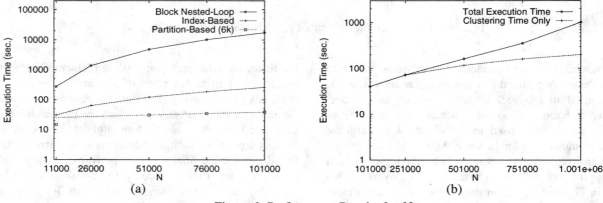

Figure 6: Performance Results for N

6.2.3 Performance Results

Number of Points: To study how the three algorithms scale with dataset size, we varied the number of points per cluster from 100 to 10,000. This varies the size of the dataset from 11000 to approximately 1 million. Both n and k were set to their default values of 100. The limit on the number of partitions for the partition-based algorithm was set to 6000. The execution times for the three algorithms as N is varied from 11000 to 101000 are shown using a log scale in Figure 6(a).

As the figure illustrates, the block nested-loop algorithm is the worst performer. Since the number of computations it performs is proportional to the square of the number of points, it exhibits a quadratic dependency on the input size. The index-based algorithm is a lot better than block nested-loop, but it is still 2 to 6 times slower than the partition-based algorithm. For 101000 points, the block nested-loop algorithm takes about 5 hours to compute 100 outliers, the index-based algorithm less than 5 minutes while the partition-based algorithm takes about half a minute. In order to explain why the partition-based algorithm performs so well, we present in Table 3, the number of candidate and neighbor partitions as well as points processed in the final step. From the table, it follows that for $N = 101000$, out of the approximately 6000 initial partitions, only about 160 candidate partitions and 1500 neighbor partitions are processed in the final phase. Thus, about 75% of partitions

are entirely pruned from the data set, and only about 0.25% of the points in the data set are candidates for outliers (230 out of 101000 points). This results in tremendous savings in both I/O and computation, and enables the partition-based scheme to outperform the other two algorithms by almost an order of magnitude.

In Figure 6(b), we plot the execution time of only the partition-based algorithm as the number of points is increased from 100,000 to 1 million to see how it scales for much larger data sets. We also plot the time spent by BIRCH for generating partitions— from the graph, it follows that this increases about linearly with input size. However, the overhead of the final step increases substantially as the data set size is increased. The reason for this is that since we generate the same number, 6000, of partitions even for a million points, the average number of points per partition exceeds k, which is 100. As a result, computed lower bounds for partitions are close to 0 and minDkDist, the lower bound on the D^k value for an outlier is low, too. Thus, our pruning is less effective if the data set size is increased without a corresponding increase in the number of partitions. Specifically, in order to ensure a high degree pruning, a good rule of thumb is to choose the number of partitions such that the average number of points per partition is fairly small (but not too small) compared to k. For example, $N/(k/5)$ is a good value. This makes the clusters generated by BIRCH to have an average size of $k/5$.

N	Avg. # of Points per Partition	# of Candidate Partitions	# of Neighbor Partitions	# of Candidate Points	# of Neighbor Points
11000	2.46	115	1334	130	3266
26000	4.70	131	1123	144	5256
51000	8.16	141	1088	159	8850
76000	11.73	143	963	160	11273
101000	16.39	160	1505	230	24605

Table 3: Statistics for N

k^{th} **Nearest Neighbor:** Figure 7(a) shows the result of increasing the value of k from 100 to 500. We considered the index-based algorithm and the partition-based algorithm with 3 different settings for the number of partitions— 5000, 6000 and 15000. We did not explore the behavior of the block-nested loop algorithm because it is very slow compared to the other two algorithms. The value of n was set to 100 and the number of points in the data set was 101000. The execution times are shown using a log scale.

As the graph confirms, the performance of the partition-based algorithms do not degrade as k is increased. This is because we found that as k is increased, the number of candidate partitions decreases slightly since a larger k implies a higher value for minDkDist which results in more pruning. However, a larger k also implies more neighboring partitions for each candidate partition. These two opposing effects cancel each other to leave the performance of the partition-based algorithm relatively unchanged.

On the other hand, due to the overhead associated with finding the k nearest neighbors, the performance of the index-based algorithm suffers significantly as the value of k increases. Since the partition-based algorithms prune more than 75% of points and only 0.25% of the data set are candidates for outliers, they are generally 10 to 70 times faster than the index-based algorithm.

Also, note that as the number of partitions is increased, the performance of the partition-based algorithm becomes worse. The reason for this is that when each partition contains too few points, the cost of computing lower and upper bounds for each partition is no longer low. For instance, in case each partition contains a single point, then computing lower and upper bounds for a partition is equivalent to computing D^k for every point p in the data set and so the partition-based algorithm degenerates to the index-based algorithm. Therefore, as we increase the number of partitions, the execution time of the partition-based algorithm converges to that of the index-based algorithm.

Number of outliers: When the number of outliers n, is varied from 100 to 500 with default settings for other parameters, we found that the the execution time of all algorithms increase gradually. Due to space constraints, we do not present the graphs for these experiments in this paper. These can be found in [RRS98].

Number of Dimensions: Figure 7(b) plots the execution times of the three algorithms as the number of dimensions is increased from 2 to 10 (the remaining parameters are set to their default values). While we set the cluster radius to 4 for the 2-dimensional dataset, we reduced the radii of clusters for higher dimensions. We did this because the volume of the hyper-spheres of clusters tends to grow exponentially with dimension, and thus the points in higher dimensional space become very sparse. Therefore, we had to reduce the cluster radius to ensure that points in each cluster are relatively close compared to points in other clusters. We used radius values of 2, 1.4, 1.2 and 1.2, respectively, for dimensions from 4 to 10.

For 10 dimensions, the partition-based algorithm is about 30 times faster than the index-based algorithm and about 180 times faster than the block nested-loop algorithm. Note that this was without including the building time for the R*-tree in the index-based algorithm. The execution time of the partition-based algorithm increases sub-linearly as the dimensionality of the data set is increased. In contrast, running times for the index-based algorithm increase very rapidly due to the increased overhead of performing search in higher dimensions using the R*-tree. Thus, the partition-based algorithm scales better than the other algorithms for higher dimensions.

7 Conclusions

In this paper, we proposed a novel formulation for distance-based outliers that is based on the distance of a point from its kth nearest neighbor. We rank each point on the basis of its distance to its kth nearest neighbor and declare the top n points in this ranking to be outliers. In addition to developing relatively straightforward solutions to finding such outliers based on the classical nested-loop join and index join algorithms, we developed a highly efficient *partition-based* algorithm for mining outliers. This algorithm first partitions the input data set into disjoint subsets, and then prunes entire partitions as soon as it can be determined that they cannot contain outliers. Since people are usually interested in only a small number of outliers, our algorithm is able to determine very quickly that a significant number of the input points cannot be outliers. This results in substantial savings in computation.

We presented the results of an extensive experimental study on real-life and synthetic data sets. The results from a

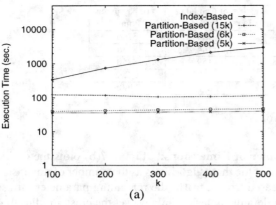 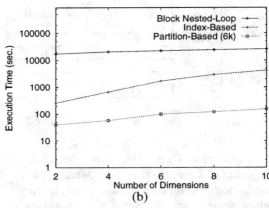

(a)　　　　　　　　　　　　　　　　(b)

Figure 7: Performance Results for k and δ

real-life NBA database highlight and reveal several expected and unexpected aspects of the database. The results from a study on synthetic data sets demonstrate that the partition-based algorithm scales well with respect to both data set size and data set dimensionality. Furthermore, it outperforms the nested-loop and index-based algorithms by more than an order of magnitude for a wide range of parameter settings.

Acknowledgments: Without the support of Seema Bansal and Yesook Shim, it would have been impossible to complete this work.

References

[AAR96]　A. Arning, Rakesh Agrawal, and P. Raghavan. A linear method for deviation detection in large databases. In *Int'l Conference on Knowledge Discovery in Databases and Data Mining (KDD-95)*, Portland, Oregon, August 1996.

[AMS+95]　Rakesh Agrawal, Heikki Mannila, Ramakrishnan Srikant, Hannu Toivonen, and A. Inkeri Verkamo. *Fast Discovery of Association Rules*, chapter 14. 1995.

[BKNS00]　Markus M. Breunig, Hans-Peter Kriegel, Raymond T. Ng, and Jorg Sander. Lof:indetifying density-based local outliers. In *Proc. of the ACM SIGMOD Conference on Management of Data*, May 2000.

[BKSS90]　N. Beckmann, H.-P. Kriegel, R. Schneider, and B. Seeger. The R^*-tree: an efficient and robust access method for points and rectangles. In *Proc. of ACM SIGMOD*, pages 322–331, Atlantic City, NJ, May 1990.

[BL94]　V. Barnett and T. Lewis. *Outliers in Statistical Data*. John Wiley and Sons, New York, 1994.

[EKX95]　Martin Ester, Hans-Peter Kriegel, and Xiaowei Xu. A database interface for clustering in large spatial databases. In *Int'l Conference on Knowledge Discovery in Databases and Data Mining (KDD-95)*, Montreal, Canada, August 1995.

[GRS98]　Sudipto Guha, Rajeev Rastogi, and Kyuseok Shim. Cure: An efficient clustering algorithm for large databases. In *Proc. of the ACM SIGMOD Conference on Management of Data*, June 1998.

[JD88]　Anil K. Jain and Richard C. Dubes. *Algorithms for Clustering Data*. Prentice Hall, Englewood Cliffs, New Jersey, 1988.

[KN98]　Edwin Knorr and Raymond Ng. Algorithms for mining distance-based outliers in large datasets. In *Proc. of the VLDB Conference*, pages 392–403, New York, USA, September 1998.

[KN99]　Edwin Knorr and Raymond Ng. Finding intensional knowledge of distance-based outliers. In *Proc. of the VLDB Conference*, pages 211–222, Edinburgh, UK, September 1999.

[NH94]　Raymond T. Ng and Jiawei Han. Efficient and effective clustering methods for spatial data mining. In *Proc. of the VLDB Conference*, Santiago, Chile, September 1994.

[RKV95]　N. Roussopoulos, S. Kelley, and F. Vincent. Nearest neighbor queries. In *Proc. of ACM SIGMOD*, pages 71–79, San Jose, CA, 1995.

[RRS98]　Sridhar Ramaswamy, Rajeev Rastogi, and Kyuseok Shim. Efficient algorithms for mining outliers from large data sets. Technical report, Bell Laboratories, Murray Hill, 1998.

[RS98]　Rajeev Rastogi and Kyuseok Shim. Public: A decision tree classifier that integrates building and pruning. In *Proc. of the Int'l Conf. on Very Large Data Bases*, New York, 1998.

[Sam89]　H. Samet. *The Design and Analysis of Spatial Data Structures*. Addison-Wesley, 1989.

[SAM98]　S. Sarawagi, R. Agrawal, and N. Megiddo. Discovery-driven exploration of olap data cubes. In *Proc. of the Sixth Int'l Conference on Extending Database Technology (EDBT)*, Valencia, Spain, March 1998.

[ZRL96]　Tian Zhang, Raghu Ramakrishnan, and Miron Livny. Birch: An efficient data clustering method for very large databases. In *Proceedings of the ACM SIGMOD Conference on Management of Data*, pages 103–114, Montreal, Canada, June 1996.

Privacy-Preserving Data Mining

Rakesh Agrawal   **Ramakrishnan Srikant**
IBM Almaden Research Center
650 Harry Road, San Jose, CA 95120

Abstract

A fruitful direction for future data mining research will be the development of techniques that incorporate privacy concerns. Specifically, we address the following question. Since the primary task in data mining is the development of models about aggregated data, can we develop accurate models without access to precise information in individual data records? We consider the concrete case of building a decision-tree classifier from training data in which the values of individual records have been perturbed. The resulting data records look very different from the original records and the distribution of data values is also very different from the original distribution. While it is not possible to accurately estimate original values in individual data records, we propose a novel reconstruction procedure to accurately estimate the distribution of original data values. By using these reconstructed distributions, we are able to build classifiers whose accuracy is comparable to the accuracy of classifiers built with the original data.

1   Introduction

Explosive progress in networking, storage, and processor technologies has led to the creation of ultra large databases that record unprecedented amount of transactional information. In tandem with this dramatic increase in digital data, concerns about informational privacy have emerged globally [Tim97] [Eco99] [eu998] [Off98]. Privacy issues are further exacerbated now that the World Wide Web makes it easy for the new data to be automatically collected and added to databases [HE98] [Wes98a] [Wes98b] [Wes99] [CRA99a] [Cra99b]. The concerns over massive collection of data are naturally extending to analytic tools applied to data. Data mining, with its promise to efficiently discover valuable, non-obvious information from large databases, is par-

ticularly vulnerable to misuse [CM96] [The98] [Off98] [ECB99].

A fruitful direction for future research in data mining will be the development of techniques that incorporate privacy concerns [Agr99]. Specifically, we address the following question. Since the primary task in data mining is the development of models about aggregated data, can we develop accurate models without access to precise information in individual data records?

The underlying assumption is that a person will be willing to selectively divulge information in exchange of value such models can provide [Wes99]. Example of the value provided include filtering to weed out unwanted information, better search results with less effort, and automatic triggers [HS99]. A recent survey of web users [CRA99a] classified 17% of respondents as privacy fundamentalists who will not provide data to a web site even if privacy protection measures are in place. However, the concerns of 56% of respondents constituting the pragmatic majority were significantly reduced by the presence of privacy protection measures. The remaining 27% were marginally concerned and generally willing to provide data to web sites, although they often expressed a mild general concern about privacy. Another recent survey of web users [Wes99] found that 86% of respondents believe that participation in information-for-benefits programs is a matter of individual privacy choice. A resounding 82% said that having a privacy policy would matter; only 14% said that was not important as long as they got benefit. Furthermore, people are not equally protective of every field in their data records [Wes99] [CRA99a]. Specifically, a person

- may not divulge at all the values of certain fields;

- may not mind giving true values of certain fields;

- may be willing to give not true values but modified values of certain fields.

Given a population that satisfies the above assumptions, we address the concrete problem of building decision-tree classifiers [BFOS84] [Qui93] and show that that it is possible to develop accurate models while respecting users' privacy concerns. Classification is one the most used tasks in data mining. Decision-tree classifiers are relatively fast, yield comprehensible models, and obtain similar and sometimes better accuracy than other classification methods [MST94].

Related Work There has been extensive research in the area of statistical databases motivated by the desire to be able to provide statistical information (sum, count, average, maximum, minimum, pth percentile, etc.) without compromising sensitive information about individuals (see excellent surveys in [AW89] [Sho82].) The proposed techniques can be broadly classified into query restriction and data perturbation. The query restriction family includes restricting the size of query result (e.g. [Fel72] [DDS79]), controlling the overlap amongst successive queries (e.g. [DJL79]), keeping audit trail of all answered queries and constantly checking for possible compromise (e.g. [CO82]), suppression of data cells of small size (e.g. [Cox80]), and clustering entities into mutually exclusive atomic populations (e.g. [YC77]). The perturbation family includes swapping values between records (e.g. [Den82]), replacing the original database by a sample from the same distribution (e.g. [LST83] [LCL85] [Rei84]), adding noise to the values in the database (e.g. [TYW84] [War65]), adding noise to the results of a query (e.g. [Bec80]), and sampling the result of a query (e.g. [Den80]). There are negative results showing that the proposed techniques cannot satisfy the conflicting objectives of providing high quality statistics and at the same time prevent exact or partial disclosure of individual information [AW89]. The statistical quality is measured in terms of bias, precision, and consistency. Bias represents the difference between the unperturbed statistics and the expected value of its perturbed estimate. Precision refers to the variance of the estimators obtained by the users. Consistency represents the lack of contradictions and paradoxes. An exact disclosure occurs if by issuing one or more queries, a user is able to determine the exact value of a confidential attribute of an individual. A partial disclosure occurs if a user is able to obtain an estimator whose variance is below a given threshold.

While we share with the statistical database literature the goal of preventing disclosure of confidential information, obtaining high quality point estimates is not our goal. As we will see, it is sufficient for us to be able to reconstruct with sufficient accuracy the original distributions of the values of the confidential attributes. We adopt from the statistics literature two methods that a person may use in our system to modify the value of a field [CS76]:

- *Value-Class Membership.* Partition the values into a set of disjoint, mutually-exhaustive classes and return the class into which the true value x_i falls.

- *Value Distortion.* Return a value $x_i + r$ instead of x_i where r is a random value drawn from some distribution.

We discuss further these methods and the level of privacy they provide in the next section.

We do not use value dissociation, the third method proposed in [CS76]. In this method, a value returned for a field of a record is a true value, but from the same field in some other record. Interestingly, a recent proposal [ECB99] to construct perturbed training sets is based on this method. Our hesitation with this approach is that it is a global method and requires knowledge of values in other records.

The problem of reconstructing original distribution from a given distribution can be viewed in the general framework of inverse problems [EHN96]. In [FJS97], it was shown that for smooth enough distributions (e.g. slowly varying time signals), it is possible to to fully recover original distribution from non-overlapping, contiguous partial sums. Such partial sums of true values are not available to us. We cannot make a priori assumptions about the original distribution; we only know the distribution used in randomizing values of an attribute. There is rich query optimization literature on estimating attribute distributions from partial information [BDF+97]. In the OLAP literature, there is work on approximating queries on sub-cubes from higher-level aggregations (e.g. [BS97]). However, these works did not have to cope with information that has been intentionally distorted.

Closely related, but orthogonal to our work, is the extensive literature on access control and security (e.g. [Din78] [ST90] [Opp97] [RG98]). Whenever sensitive information is exchanged, it must be transmitted over a secure channel and stored securely. For the purposes of this paper, we assume that appropriate access controls and security procedures are in place and effective in preventing unauthorized access to the system. Other relevant work includes efforts to create tools and standards that provide platform for implementing a system such as ours (e.g. [Wor] [Ben99] [GWB97] [Cra99b] [AC99] [LM99] [LEW99]).

Paper Organization We discuss privacy-preserving methods in Section 2. We also introduce a quantitative measure to evaluate the amount of privacy offered by a method and evaluate the proposed methods against this measure. In Section 3, we present our reconstruction procedure for reconstructing the original data distribution given a perturbed distribution. We also present some empirical evidence of the efficacy of the reconstruction procedure. Section 4 describes techniques for building decision-tree classifiers from perturbed training data using our reconstruction procedure. We present an experimental evaluation of the accuracy of these techniques in Section 5. We conclude with a summary and directions for future work in Section 6.

We only consider numeric attributes; in Section 6, we briefly describe how we propose to extend this work to include categorical attributes. We focus on attributes for which the users are willing to provide perturbed values. If there is an attribute for which users are not willing to provide even the perturbed value, we simply ignore the attribute. If only some users do not provide the value, the training data is treated as containing records with missing values for which effective techniques exist in the literature [BFOS84] [Qui93].

2 Privacy-Preserving Methods

Our basic approach to preserving privacy is to let users provide a modified value for sensitive attributes. The modified value may be generated using custom code, a browser plug-in, or extensions to products such as Microsoft's Passport (http://www.passport.com) or Novell's DigitalMe (http://www.digitalme.com). We consider two methods for modifying values [CS76]:

Value-Class Membership In this method, the values for an attribute are partitioned into a set of disjoint, mutually-exclusive classes. We consider the special case of **discretization** in which values for an attribute are discretized into intervals. All intervals need not be of equal width. For example, salary may be discretized into 10K intervals for lower values and 50K intervals for higher values. Instead of a true attribute value, the user provides the interval in which the value lies. Discretization is the method used most often for hiding individual values.

Value Distortion Return a value $x_i + r$ instead of x_i where r is a random value drawn from some distribution. We consider two random distributions:

- **Uniform**: The random variable has a uniform distribution, between $[-\alpha, +\alpha]$. The mean of the random variable is 0.

- **Gaussian**: The random variable has a normal distribution, with mean $\mu = 0$ and standard deviation σ [Fis63].

We fix the perturbation of an entity. Thus, it is not possible for snoopers to improve the estimates of the value of a field in a record by repeating queries [AW89].

2.1 Quantifying Privacy

For quantifying privacy provided by a method, we use a measure based on how closely the original values of a modified attribute can be estimated. If it can be

	Confidence		
	50%	95%	99.9%
Discretization	$0.5 \times W$	$0.95 \times W$	$0.999 \times W$
Uniform	$0.5 \times 2\alpha$	$0.95 \times 2\alpha$	$0.999 \times 2\alpha$
Gaussian	$1.34 \times \sigma$	$3.92 \times \sigma$	$6.8 \times \sigma$

Table 1: Privacy Metrics

estimated with $c\%$ confidence that a value x lies in the interval $[x_1, x_2]$, then the interval width $(x_2 - x_1)$ defines the amount of privacy at $c\%$ confidence level.

Table 1 shows the privacy offered by the different methods using this metric. We have assumed that the intervals are of equal width W in Discretization.

Clearly, for $2\alpha = W$, Uniform and Discretization provide the same amount of privacy. As α increases, privacy also increases. To keep up with Uniform, Discretization will have to increase the interval width, and hence reduce the number of intervals. Note that we are interested in very high privacy. (We use 25%, 50%, 100% and 200% of range of values of an attribute in our experiments.) Hence Discretization will lead to poor model accuracy compared to Uniform since all the values in a interval are modified to the same value. Gaussian provides significantly more privacy at higher confidence levels compared to the other two methods. We, therefore, focus on the two value distortion methods in the rest of the paper.

3 Reconstructing The Original Distribution

For the concept of using value distortion to protect privacy to be useful, we need to be able to reconstruct the original data distribution from the randomized data. Note that we reconstruct distributions, not values in individual records.

We view the n original data values $x_1, x_2, \ldots, x_n$ of a one-dimensional distribution as realizations of n independent identically distributed (iid) random variables $X_1, X_2, \ldots, X_n$, each with the same distribution as the random variable X. To hide these data values, n independent random variables $Y_1, Y_2, \ldots, Y_n$ have been used, each with the same distribution as a different random variable Y. Given $x_1+y_1, x_2+y_2, \ldots, x_n+y_n$ (where y_i is the realization of Y_i) and the cumulative distribution function F_Y for Y, we would like to estimate the cumulative distribution function F_X for X.

Reconstruction Problem *Given a cumulative distribution F_Y and the realizations of n iid random samples $X_1+Y_1, X_2+Y_2, \ldots, X_n+Y_n$, estimate F_X.*

Let the value of $X_i + Y_i$ be $w_i (= x_i + y_i)$. Note

that we do not have the individual values x_i and y_i, only their sum. We can use Bayes' rule [Fis63] to estimate the posterior distribution function F'_{X_1} (given that $X_1 + Y_1 = w_1$) for X_1, assuming we know the density functions f_X and f_Y for X and Y respectively.

$$F'_{X_1}(a)$$

$$\equiv \int_{-\infty}^{a} f_{X_1}(z \mid X_1 + Y_1 = w_1)\, dz$$

$$= \int_{-\infty}^{a} \frac{f_{X_1+Y_1}(w_1 \mid X_1 = z)\, f_{X_1}(z)}{f_{X_1+Y_1}(w_1)}\, dz$$

(using Bayes' rule for density functions)

$$= \int_{-\infty}^{a} \frac{f_{X_1+Y_1}(w_1 \mid X_1 = z)\, f_{X_1}(z)}{\int_{-\infty}^{\infty} f_{X_1+Y_1}(w_1 \mid X_1 = z')\, f_{X_1}(z')\, dz'}\, dz$$

(expanding the denominator)

$$= \frac{\int_{-\infty}^{a} f_{X_1+Y_1}(w_1 \mid X_1 = z)\, f_{X_1}(z)\, dz}{\int_{-\infty}^{\infty} f_{X_1+Y_1}(w_1 \mid X_1 = z)\, f_{X_1}(z)\, dz}$$

(inner integral is independent of outer)

$$= \frac{\int_{-\infty}^{a} f_{Y_1}(w_1 - z)\, f_{X_1}(z)\, dz}{\int_{-\infty}^{\infty} f_{Y_1}(w_1 - z)\, f_{X_1}(z)\, dz}$$

(since Y_1 is independent of X_1)

$$= \frac{\int_{-\infty}^{a} f_{Y}(w_1 - z)\, f_{X}(z)\, dz}{\int_{-\infty}^{\infty} f_{Y}(w_1 - z)\, f_{X}(z)\, dz}$$

(since $f_{X_1} \equiv f_X$ and $f_{Y_1} \equiv f_Y$)

To estimate the posterior distribution function F'_X given $x_1 + y_1, x_2 + y_2, \ldots, x_n + y_n$, we average the distribution functions for each of the X_i.

$$F'_X(a) = \frac{1}{n} \sum_{i=1}^{n} F'_{X_i} = \frac{1}{n} \sum_{i=1}^{n} \frac{\int_{-\infty}^{a} f_Y(w_i - z)\, f_X(z)\, dz}{\int_{-\infty}^{\infty} f_Y(w_i - z)\, f_X(z)\, dz}$$

The corresponding posterior density function, f'_X is obtained by differentiating F'_X:

$$f'_X(a) = \frac{1}{n} \sum_{i=1}^{n} \frac{f_Y(w_i - a)\, f_X(a)}{\int_{-\infty}^{\infty} f_Y(w_i - z)\, f_X(z)\, dz} \qquad (1)$$

Given a sufficiently large number of samples, we expect f'_X in the above equation to be very close to the real density function f_X. However, although we know f_Y,[1] we do not know f_X. Hence we use the uniform distribution as the initial estimate f^0_X, and iteratively refine this estimate by applying Equation 1. This algorithm is sketched out in Figure 1.

Using Partitioning to Speed Computation Assume a partitioning of the domain (of the data values) into intervals. We make two approximations:

---

[1] For example, if Y is the standard normal, $f_Y(z) = (1/\sqrt{(2\pi)})e^{-z^2/2}$.

(1) $\quad f^0_X :=$ Uniform distribution

(2) $\quad j := 0$ // Iteration number

`repeat`

(3) $\quad f^{j+1}_X(a) := \frac{1}{n} \sum_{i=1}^{n} \frac{f_Y(w_i - a)\, f^j_X(a)}{\int_{-\infty}^{\infty} f_Y(w_i - z)\, f^j_X(z)\, dz}$

(4) $\quad j := j + 1$

`until` (stopping criterion met)

Figure 1: Reconstruction Algorithm

- We approximate the distance between z and w_i (or between a and w_i) with the distance between the mid-points of the intervals in which they lie, and

- We approximate the density function $f_X(a)$ with the average of the density function over the interval in which a lies.

Let $I(x)$ denote the interval in which x lies, $m(I_p)$ the mid-point of interval I_p, and $m(x)$ the mid-point of interval $I(x)$. Let $f_X(I_p)$ be the average value of the density function over the interval I_p, i.e. $f_X(I_p) = \int_{I_p} f_X(z) dz \, / \int_{I_p} dz$. By applying these two approximations to Equation 1, we get

$$f'_X(a) = \frac{1}{n} \sum_{i=1}^{n} \frac{f_Y(m(w_i) - m(a))\, f_X(I(a))}{\int_{-\infty}^{\infty} f_Y(m(w_i) - m(z))\, f_X(I(z))\, dz}$$

Let $I_p, p = 1 \ldots k$ denote the k intervals, and L_p the width of interval I_p. We can replace the integral in the denominator with a sum, since $m(z)$ and $f_X(I(z))$ do not change within an interval:

$$f'_X(a) = \frac{1}{n} \sum_{i=1}^{n} \frac{f_Y(m(w_i) - m(a))\, f_X(I(a))}{\sum_{t=1}^{k} f_Y(m(w_i) - m(I_t))\, f_X(I_t)\, L_t} \qquad (2)$$

We now compute the average value of the posterior density function over the interval I_p.

$$f'_X(I_p)$$

$$= \int_{I_p} f'_X(z) dz \, / \, L_p$$

$$= \int_{I_p} \frac{1}{n} \sum_{i=1}^{n} \frac{f_Y(m(w_i) - m(z))\, f_X(I(z))\, dz}{\sum_{t=1}^{k} f_Y(m(w_i) - m(I_t))\, f_X(I_t)\, L_t} / L_p$$

(substituting Equation 2)

$$= \int_{I_p} \frac{1}{n} \sum_{i=1}^{n} \frac{f_Y(m(w_i) - m(I_p))\, f_X(I_p)\, dz}{\sum_{t=1}^{k} f_Y(m(w_i) - m(I_t))\, f_X(I_t)\, L_t} / L_p$$

(since $I(z) = I_p$ within I_p)

$$= \frac{1}{n} \sum_{i=1}^{n} \frac{f_Y(m(w_i) - m(I_p))\, f_X(I_p)}{\sum_{t=1}^{k} f_Y(m(w_i) - m(I_t))\, f_X(I_t)\, L_t}$$

(since $\int_{I_p} dz = L_p$)

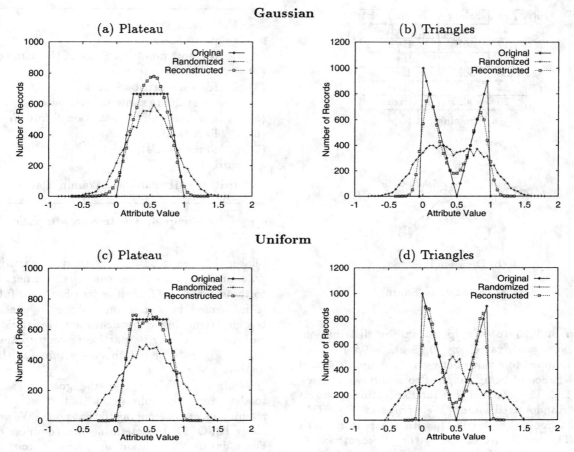

Gaussian

(a) Plateau

(b) Triangles

Uniform

(c) Plateau

(d) Triangles

Figure 2: Reconstructing the Original Distribution

Let $N(I_p)$ be the number of points that lie in interval I_p (i.e. number of elements in the set $\{w_i | w_i \in I_p\}$. Since $m(w_i)$ is the same for points that lie within the same interval,

$$f'_X(I_p) =$$
$$\frac{1}{n} \sum_{s=1}^{k} N(I_s) \times \frac{f_Y(m(I_s) - m(I_p)) \, f_X(I_p)}{\sum_{t=1}^{k} f_Y(m(I_s) - m(I_t)) \, f_X(I_t) L_t}$$

Finally, let $\Pr'(X \in I_p)$ be the posterior probability of X belonging to interval I_p, i.e. $\Pr'(X \in I_p) = f'_X(I_p) \times L_p$. Multiplying both sides of the above equation by L_p, and using $\Pr(X \in I_p) = f_X(I_p) \times L_p$, we get:

$$\Pr'(X \in I_p) = \qquad (3)$$
$$\frac{1}{n} \sum_{s=1}^{k} N(I_s) \times \frac{f_Y(m(I_s) - m(I_p)) \, \Pr(X \in I_p)}{\sum_{t=1}^{k} f_Y(m(I_s) - m(I_t)) \, \Pr(X \in I_t)}$$

We can now substitute Equation 3 in step 3 of the algorithm (Figure 1), and compute step 3 in $O(m^2)$ time.[2]

---

[2] A naive implementation of Equation 3 will lead to $O(m^3)$ time. However, since the denominator is independent of I_p, we can re-use the results of that computation to get $O(m^2)$ time.

Stopping Criterion With omniscience, we would stop when the reconstructed distribution was statistically the same as the original distribution (using, say, the χ^2 goodness-of-fit test [Cra46]). An alternative is to compare the observed randomized distribution with the result of randomizing the current estimate of the original distribution, and stop when these two distributions are statistically the same. The intuition is that if these two distributions are close to each other, we expect our estimate of the original distribution to also be close to the real distribution. Unfortunately, we found empirically that the difference between the two randomized distributions is not a reliable indicator of the difference between the original and reconstructed distributions.

Instead, we compare successive estimates of the original distribution, and stop when the difference between successive estimates becomes very small (1% of the threshold of the χ^2 test in our implementation).

Empirical Evaluation Two original distributions, "plateau" and "triangles", are shown by the "Original" line in Figures 2(a) and (b) respectively. We add a Gaussian random variable with mean 0 and standard

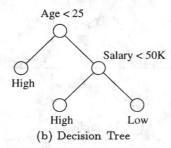

rid	Age	Salary	Credit Risk
0	23	50K	High
1	17	30K	High
2	43	40K	High
3	68	50K	Low
4	32	70K	Low
5	20	20K	High

(a) Training Set

(b) Decision Tree

Figure 3: Credit Risk Example

deviation of 0.25 to each point in the distribution. Thus a point with value, say, 0.25 has a 95% chance of being mapped to a value between -0.26 and 0.74, and a 99.9% chance of being mapped to a value between -0.6 and 1.1. The effect of this randomization is shown by the "Randomized" line. We apply the algorithm (with partitioning) in Figure 1, with a partition width of 0.05. The results are shown by the "Reconstructed" line. Notice that we are able to pick out the original shape of the distribution even though the randomized version looks nothing like the original.

Figures 2(c) and (d) show that adding an uniform, discrete random variable between 0.5 and -0.5 to each point gives similar results.

4 Decision-Tree Classification over Randomized Data

4.1 Background

We begin with a brief review of decision tree classification, adapted from [MAR96] [SAM96]. A decision tree [BFOS84] [Qui93] is a class discriminator that recursively partitions the training set until each partition consists entirely or dominantly of examples from the same class. Each non-leaf node of the tree contains a *split point* which is a test on one or more attributes and determines how the data is partitioned. Figure 3(b) shows a sample decision-tree classifier based on the training shown in Figure 3a. ($Age < 25$) and ($Salary < 50K$) are two split points that partition the records into High and Low credit risk classes. The decision tree can be used to screen future applicants by classifying them into the *High* or *Low* risk categories.

A decision tree classifier is developed in two phases: a growth phase and a prune phase. In the growth

Partition(Data S)
begin
(1)   **if** (most points in S are of the same class) **then**
(2)   **return**;
(3)   **for** each attribute A **do**
(4)   evaluate splits on attribute A;
(5)   Use best split to partition S into S_1 and S_2;
(6)   Partition(S_1);
(7)   Partition(S_2);
end
Initial call: Partition(TrainingData)

Figure 4: The tree-growth phase

phase, the tree is built by recursively partitioning the data until each partition contains members belonging to the same class. Once the tree has been fully grown, it is pruned in the second phase to generalize the tree by removing dependence on statistical noise or variation that may be particular only to the training data. Figure 4 shows the algorithm for the growth phase.

While growing the tree, the goal at each node is to determine the split point that "best" divides the training records belonging to that node. We use the *gini* index [BFOS84] to determine the goodness of a split. For a data set S containing examples from m classes, $gini(S) = 1 - \sum p_j^2$ where p_j is the relative frequency of class j in S. If a split divides S into two subsets S_1 and S_2, the index of the divided data $gini_{split}(S)$ is given by $gini_{split}(S) = \frac{n_1}{n}gini(S_1) + \frac{n_2}{n}gini(S_2)$. Note that calculating this index requires only the distribution of the class values in each of the partitions.

4.2 Training Using Randomized Data

To induce decision trees using perturbed training data, we need to modify two key operations in the tree-growth phase (Figure 4):

- Determining a split point (step 4).
- Partitioning the data (step 5).

We also need to resolve choices with respect to reconstructing original distribution:

- Should we do a global reconstruction using the whole data or should we first partition the data by class and reconstruct separately for each class?
- Should we do reconstruction once at the root node or do reconstruction at every node?

We discuss below each of these issues.

For pruning phase based on the Minimum Description Length principle [MAR96], no modification is needed.

Determining split points Since we partition the domain into intervals while reconstructing the distribution, the candidate split points are the interval boundaries. (In the standard algorithm, every mid-point between any two consecutive attribute values is a candidate split point.) For each candidate split-point, we use the statistics from the reconstructed distribution to compute gini index.

Partitioning the Data The reconstruction procedure gives us an estimate of the number of points in each interval. Let $I_1, ... I_m$ be the m intervals, and $N(I_p)$ be the estimated number of points in interval I_p. We associate each data value with an interval by sorting the values, and assigning the $N(I_1)$ lowest values to interval I_1, and so on.[3] If the split occurs at the boundary of interval I_{p-1} and I_p, then the points associated with intervals $I_1, ..., I_{p-1}$ go to S_1, and the points associated with intervals $I_p, ..., I_m$ go to S_2. We retain this association between points and intervals in case there is a split on the same attribute (at a different split-point) lower in the tree.

Reconstructing the Original Distribution We consider three different algorithms that differ in when and how distributions are reconstructed:

- **Global**: Reconstruct the distribution for each attribute once at the beginning using the complete perturbed training data. Induce decision tree using the reconstructed data.

- **ByClass**: For each attribute, first split the training data by class, then reconstruct the distributions separately for each class. Induce decision tree using the reconstructed data.

- **Local**: As in ByClass, for each attribute, split the training data by class and reconstruct distributions separately for each class. However, instead of doing reconstruction only once, reconstruction is done at each node (i.e. just before step 4 in Figure 4). To avoid over-fitting, reconstruction is stopped after the number of records belonging to a node become small.

A final detail regarding reconstruction concerns the number of intervals into which the domain of an attribute is partitioned. We use a heuristic to determine the number of intervals, m. We choose m such that there are an average of 100 points per interval. We then bound m to be between 10 and 100 intervals i.e. if $m < 10$, m is set to 10, etc.

Clearly, Local is the most expensive algorithm in terms of execution time. Global is the cheapest

---

[3] The interval associated with a data value should not be considered an estimator of the original value of that data value.

algorithm. ByClass falls in between. However, it is closer to Global than Local since reconstruction is done in ByClass only at the root node, whereas it is repeated at each node in Local. We empirically evaluate the classification accuracy characteristics of these algorithms in the next section.

4.3 Deployment

In many applications, the goal of building a classification model is to develop an understanding of different classes in the target population. The techniques just described directly apply to such applications. In other applications, a classification model is used for predicting the class of a new object without a preassigned class label. For this prediction to be accurate, although we have been able to build an accurate model using randomized data, the application needs access to non-perturbed data which the user is not willing to disclose. The solution to this dilemma is to structure the application such that the classification model is shipped to the user and applied there. For instance, if the classification model is being used to filter information relevant to a user, the classifier may be first applied on the client side over the original data and the information to be presented is filtered using the results of classification.

5 Experimental Results

5.1 Methodology

We compare the classification accuracy of Global, ByClass, and Local algorithms against each other and with respect to the following benchmarks:

- **Original**, the result of inducing the classifier on unperturbed training data without randomization.

- **Randomized**, the result of inducing the classifier on perturbed data but without making any corrections for randomization.

Clearly, we want to come as close to Original in accuracy as possible. The accuracy gain over Randomized reflects the advantage of reconstruction.

We used the synthetic data generator from [AGI+92] for our experiments. We used a training set of 100,000 records and a test set of 5,000 records, equally split between the two classes. Table 2 describes the nine attributes, and Table 3 summarizes the five classification functions. These functions vary from having quite simple decision surface (Function 1) to complex non-linear surfaces (Functions 4 and 5). Functions 2 and 3 may look easy, but are quite difficult. The distribution of values on age are identical for both classes, unless the classifier first splits on salary. Further, the classifier has to exactly find five split-points on salary: 25, 50, 75, 100 and 125 to perfectly classify the data. The width of each of these intervals is less

	Group A	Group B
Function 1	(age < 40) ∨ ((60 ≤ age)	otherwise
Function 2	((age < 40) ∧ (50K ≤ salary ≤ 100K)) ∨ ((40 ≤ age < 60) ∧ (75K ≤ salary ≥ 125K)) ∨ ((age ≥ 60) ∧ (25K ≤ salary ≤ 75K))	otherwise
Function 3	((age < 40) ∧ (((elevel ∈ [0..1]) ∧ (25K ≤ salary ≤ 75K)) ∨ ((elevel ∈ [2..3]) ∧ (50K ≤ salary ≤ 100K)))) ∨ ((40 ≤ age < 60) ∧ (((elevel ∈ [1..3]) ∧ (50K ≤ salary ≤ 100K)) ∨ (((elevel = 4)) ∧ (75K ≤ salary ≤ 125K)))) ∨ ((age ≥ 60) ∧ (((elevel ∈ [2..4]) ∧ (50K ≤ salary ≤ 100K)) ∨ ((elevel = 1)) ∧ (25K ≤ salary ≤ 75K))))	otherwise
Function 4	(0.67 × (salary + commission) − 0.2 × loan − 10K) > 0	otherwise
Function 5	(0.67 × (salary + commission) − 0.2 × loan + 0.2 × equity − 10K) > 0 where equity = 0.1 × hvalue × max(hyears − 20, 0)	otherwise

Table 3: Description of Functions

Attribute	Description
salary	uniformly distributed from 20K to 150K
commission	salary ≥ 75K ⇒ commission = 0 else uniformly distributed from 10K to 75K
age	uniformly distributed from 20 to 80
elevel	uniformly chosen from 0 to 4
car	uniformly chosen from 1 to 20
zipcode	uniformly chosen from 9 zipcodes
hvalue	uniformly distributed from $k \times 50K$ to $k \times 150K$, where $k \in \{0 \cdots 9\}$ depends on **zipcode**
hyears	uniformly distributed from 1 to 30
loan	uniformly distributed from 0 to 500K

Table 2: Attribute Descriptions

than 20% of the range of the attribute. Function 2 also contains embedded XORs which are known to be troublesome for decision tree classifiers.

Perturbed training data is generated using both Uniform and Gaussian methods (Section 2). All accuracy results involving randomization were averaged over 10 runs. We experimented with large values for the amount of desired privacy: ranging from 25% to 200% of the range of values of an attribute. The confidence threshold for the privacy level is taken to be 95% in all our experiments. Recall that if it can be estimated with 95% confidence that a value x lies in the interval $[x_1, x_2]$, then the interval width $(x_2 - x_1)$ defines the amount of privacy at 95% confidence level. For example, at 50% privacy, Salary cannot be estimated (with 95% confidence) any closer than an interval of width 65K, which is half the entire range for Salary. Similarly, at 100% privacy, Age cannot be estimated (with 95% confidence) any closer than an interval of width 60, which is the entire range for Age.

5.2 Comparing the Classification Algorithms

Figure 5 shows the accuracy of the algorithms for Uniform and Gaussian perturbations, for privacy levels of 25% and 100%. The x-axis shows the five functions from Table 3, and the y-axis the accuracy.

Overall, the ByClass and Local algorithms do remarkably well at 25% and 50% privacy, with accuracy numbers very close to those on the original data. Even at as high as 100% privacy, the algorithms are within 5% (absolute) of the original accuracy for Functions 1, 4 and 5 and within 15% for Functions 2 and 3. The advantage of reconstruction can be seen from these graphs by comparing the accuracy of these algorithms with Randomized.

Overall, the Global algorithm performs worse than ByClass and Local algorithms. The deficiency of Global is that it uses the same merged distribution for all the classes during reconstruction of the original distribution. It fares well on Functions 4 and 5, but the performance of even Randomized is quite close to Original on these functions. These functions have a diagonal decision surface, with equal number of points on each side of the diagonal surface. Hence addition of noise does not significantly affect the ability of the classifier to approximate this surface by hyperrectangles.

As we stated in the beginning of this section, though they might look easy, Functions 2 and 3 are quite difficult. The classifier has to find five split-points on salary and the width of each interval is 25K. Observe that the range over which the randomizing function spreads 95% of the values is more than 5 times the width of the splits at 100% privacy. Hence even small errors in reconstruction result in the split points being a little off, and accuracy drops.

The poor accuracy of Original for Function 2 at 25% privacy may appear anomalous. The explanation lies in

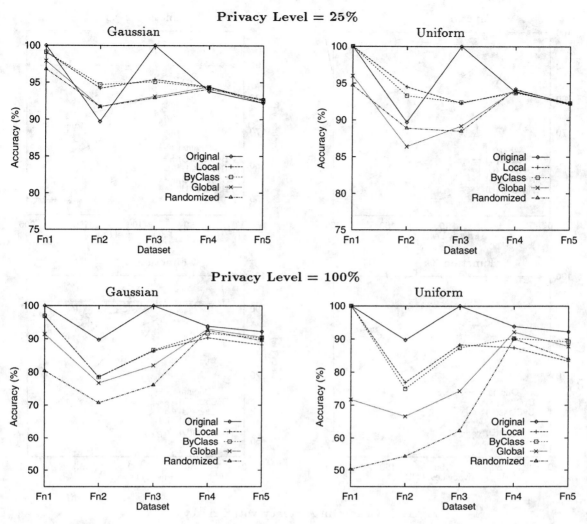

Figure 5: Classification Accuracy

there being a buried XOR in Function 2. When Original reaches the corresponding node, it stops because it does not find any split point that increases gini. However, due to the perturbation of data with randomization, the other algorithms find a "false" split point and proceed further to find the real split.

5.3 Varying Privacy

Figure 6 shows the effect of varying the amount of privacy for the ByClass algorithm. (We omitted the graph for Function 4 since the results were almost identical to those for Function 5.) Similar results were obtained for the Local algorithm. The x-axis shows the privacy level, ranging from 10% to 200%, and the y-axis the accuracy of the algorithms. The legend ByClass(G) refers to ByClass with Gaussian, Random(U) refers to Randomized with Uniform, etc.

Two important conclusions can be drawn from these graphs:

- Although Uniform perturbation of original data results in a much large degradation of accuracy before correction compared to Gaussian, the effect of both distributions is quite comparable after correction.

- The accuracy of the classifier developed using perturbed data, although not identical, comes fairly close to Original (i.e. accuracy obtained from using unperturbed data).

6 Conclusions and Future Work

In this paper, we studied the technical feasibility of realizing privacy-preserving data mining. The basic premise was that the sensitive values in a user's record will be perturbed using a randomizing function so that they cannot be estimated with sufficient precision. Randomization can be done using Gaussian or Uniform perturbations. The question we addressed was whether, given a large number of users who do this perturbation,

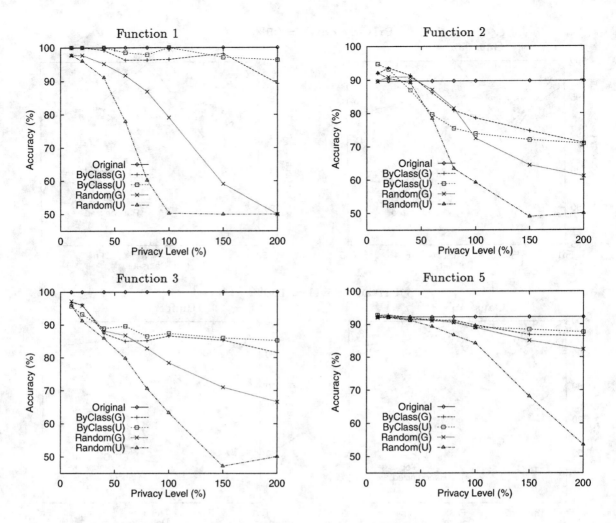

Figure 6: Change in Accuracy with Privacy

can we still construct sufficiently accurate predictive models.

For the specific case of decision-tree classification, we found two effective algorithms, ByClass and Local. The algorithms rely on a Bayesian procedure for correcting perturbed distributions. We emphasize that we reconstruct distributions, not individual records, thus preserving privacy of individual records. As a matter of fact, if the user perturbs a sensitive value once and always return the same perturbed value, the estimate of the true value cannot be improved by successive queries. We found in our empirical evaluation that:

- ByClass and Local are both effective in correcting for the effects of perturbation. At 25% and 50% privacy levels, the accuracy numbers are close to those on the original data. Even at 100% privacy, the algorithms were within 5% to 15% (absolute) of the original accuracy. Recall that if privacy were

to be measured with 95% confidence, 100% privacy means that the true value cannot be estimated any closer than an interval of width which is the entire range for the corresponding attribute. We believe that a small drop in accuracy is a desirable trade-off for privacy in many situations.

- Local performed marginally better than ByClass, but required considerably more computation. Investigation of what characteristics might make Local a winner over ByClass (if at all) is an open problem.

- For the same privacy level, Uniform perturbation did significantly worse than Gaussian before correcting for randomization, but only slightly worse after correcting for randomization. Hence the choice between applying the Uniform or Gaussian distributions to preserve privacy should be based on other considerations: Gaussian provides more privacy at higher confidence thresholds, but Uniform may be easier to explain to users.

Future Work We plan to investigate the effectiveness of randomization with reconstruction for categorical attributes. The basic idea is to randomize each categorical value as follows: retain the value with probability p, and choose one of the other values at random with probability $1-p$. We may then derive an equation similar to Equation 1, and iteratively reconstruct the original distribution of values. Alternately, we may be able to extend the analytical approach presented in [War65] for boolean attributes to derive an equation that directly gives estimates of the original distribution.

Acknowledgments A hallway conversation with Robert Morris provided initial impetus for this work. Peter Haas diligently checked the soundness of the reconstruction procedure.

References

[AC99]   M.S. Ackerman and L. Cranor. Privacy critics: UI components to safeguard users' privacy. In *ACM Conf. Human Factors in Computing Systems (CHI'99)*, 1999.

[AGI$^+$92]   Rakesh Agrawal, Sakti Ghosh, Tomasz Imielinski, Bala Iyer, and Arun Swami. An interval classifier for database mining applications. In *Proc. of the VLDB Conference*, pages 560–573, Vancouver, British Columbia, Canada, August 1992.

[Agr99]   Rakesh Agrawal. Data Mining: Crossing the Chasm. In *5th Int'l Conference on Knowledge Discovery in Databases and Data Mining*, San Diego, California, August 1999. Available from http://www.almaden.ibm.com/cs/quest/papers/kdd99_chasm.ppt.

[AW89]   Nabil R. Adam and John C. Wortman. Security-control methods for statistical databases. *ACM Computing Surveys*, 21(4):515–556, Dec. 1989.

[BDF$^+$97]   D. Barbara, W. DuMouchel, C. Faloutsos, P. J. Haas, J. M. Hellerstein, Y. Ioannidis, H. V. Jagadish, T. Johnson, R.Ng, V. Poosala, and K. Sevcik. The New Jersey Data Reduction Report. *Data Engrg. Bull.*, 20:3–45, Dec. 1997.

[Bec80]   Leland L. Beck. A security mechanism for statistical databases. *ACM TODS*, 5(3):316–338, September 1980.

[Ben99]   Paola Benassi. Truste: an online privacy seal program. *Comm. ACM*, 42(2):56–59, Feb. 1999.

[BFOS84]   L. Breiman, J. H. Friedman, R. A. Olshen, and C. J. Stone. *Classification and Regression Trees*. Wadsworth, Belmont, 1984.

[BS97]   D. Barbara and M. Sullivan. Quasi cubes: Exploiting approximations in multidimensional databases. *SIGMOD Record*, 26(3):12–17, 1997.

[CM96]   C. Clifton and D. Marks. Security and privacy implications of data mining. In *ACM SIGMOD Workshop on Research Issues on Data Mining and Knowledge Discovery*, pages 15–19, May 1996.

[CO82]   F.Y. Chin and G. Ozsoyoglu. Auditing and infrence control in statistical databases. *IEEE Trans. Softw. Eng.*, SE-8(6):113–139, April 1982.

[Cox80]   L.H. Cox. Suppression methodology and statistical disclosure control. *J. Am. Stat. Assoc.*, 75(370):377–395, April 1980.

[Cra46]   H. Cramer. *Mathematical Methods of Statistics*. Princeton University Press, 1946.

[CRA99a]   L.F. Cranor, J. Reagle, and M.S. Ackerman. Beyond concern: Understanding net users' attitudes about online privacy. Technical Report TR 99.4.3, AT&T Labs–Research, April 1999. Available from http://www.research.att.com/library/trs/TRs/99/99.4/99.4.3/report.htm.

[Cra99b]   Lorrie Faith Cranor, editor. *Special Issue on Internet Privacy*. Comm. ACM, 42(2), Feb. 1999.

[CS76]   R. Conway and D. Strip. Selective partial access to a database. In *Proc. ACM Annual Conf.*, pages 85–89, 1976.

[DDS79]   D.E. Denning, P.J. Denning, and M.D. Schwartz. The tracker: A threat to statistical database security. *ACM TODS*, 4(1):76–96, March 1979.

[Den80]   D.E. Denning. Secure statistical databases with random sample queries. *ACM TODS*, 5(3):291–315, Sept. 1980.

[Den82]   D.E. Denning. *Cryptography and Data Security*. Addison-Wesley, 1982.

[Din78]   C.T. Dinardo. *Computers and Security*. AFIPS Press, 1978.

[DJL79]   D. Dobkin, A.K. Jones, and R.J. Lipton. Secure databases: Protection against user influence. *ACM TODS*, 4(1):97–106, March 1979.

[ECB99]   V. Estivill-Castro and L. Brankovic. Data swapping: Balancing privacy against precision in mining for logic rules. In M. Mohania and A.M. Tjoa, editors, *Data Warehousing and Knowledge Discovery DaWaK-99*, pages 389–398. Springer-Verlag Lecture Notes in Computer Science 1676, 1999.

[Eco99]   The Economist. *The End of Privacy*, May 1999.

[EHN96]   H.W. Engl, M. Hanke, and A. Neubaue. *Regularization of Inverse Problems*. Kluwer, 1996.

[eu998]   *The European Union's Directive on Privacy Protection*, October 1998. Available from http://www.echo.lu/legal/en/dataprot/directiv/directiv.html.

[Fel72] I.P. Fellegi. On the question of statistical confidentiality. *J. Am. Stat. Assoc.*, 67(337):7–18, March 1972.

[Fis63] Marek Fisz. *Probability Theory and Mathematical Statistics*. Wiley, 1963.

[FJS97] C. Faloutsos, H.V. Jagadish, and N.D. Sidiropoulos. Recovering information from summary data. In *Proc. of the 23rd Int'l Conference on Very Large Databases*, pages 36–45, Athens, Greece, 1997.

[GWB97] Ian Goldberg, David Wagner, and Eric Brewer. Privacy-enhancing technologies for the internet. In *IEEE COMPCON*, February 97.

[HE98] C. Hine and J. Eve. Privacy in the marketplace. *The Information Society*, 42(2):56–59, 1998.

[HS99] John Hagel and Marc Singer. *Net Worth*. Harvard Business School Press, 1999.

[LCL85] Chong K. Liew, Uinam J. Choi, and Chung J. Liew. A data distortion by probability distribution. *ACM TODS*, 10(3):395–411, 1985.

[LEW99] Tessa Lau, Oren Etzioni, and Daniel S. Weld. Privacy interfaces for information management. *Comm. ACM*, 42(10):89–94, October 1999.

[LM99] J.B. Lotspiech and R.J.T. Morris. Method and system for client/server communications with user information revealed as a function of willingness to reveal and whether the information is required. U.S. Patent No. 5913030, June 1999.

[LST83] E. Lefons, A. Silvestri, and F. Tangorra. An analytic approach to statistical databases. In *9th Int. Conf. Very Large Data Bases*, pages 260–274. Morgan Kaufmann, Oct-Nov 1983.

[MAR96] Manish Mehta, Rakesh Agrawal, and Jorma Rissanen. SLIQ: A fast scalable classifier for data mining. In *Proc. of the Fifth Int'l Conference on Extending Database Technology (EDBT)*, Avignon, France, March 1996.

[MST94] D. Michie, D. J. Spiegelhalter, and C. C. Taylor. *Machine Learning, Neural and Statistical Classification*. Ellis Horwood, 1994.

[Off98] Office of the Information and Privacy Commissioner, Ontario. *Data Mining: Staking a Claim on Your Privacy*, January 1998. Available from http://www.ipc.on.ca/web_site.eng/matters/sum_pap/papers/datamine.htm.

[Opp97] R. Oppliger. Internet security: Firewalls and beyond. *Comm. ACM*, 40(5):92–102, May 1997.

[Qui93] J. Ross Quinlan. *C4.5: Programs for Machine Learning*. Morgan Kaufman, 1993.

[Rei84] Steven P. Reiss. Practical data-swapping: The first steps. *ACM TODS*, 9(1):20–37, 1984.

[RG98] A. Rubin and D. Greer. A survey of the world wide web security. *IEEE Computer*, 31(9):34–41, Sept. 1998.

[SAM96] John Shafer, Rakesh Agrawal, and Manish Mehta. SPRINT: A scalable parallel classifier for data mining. In *Proc. of the 22nd Int'l Conference on Very Large Databases*, Bombay, India, September 1996.

[Sho82] A. Shoshani. Statistical databases: Characteristics, problems and some solutions. In *Proceedings of the Eighth International Conference on Very Large Databases (VLDB)*, pages 208–213, Mexico City, Mexico, September 1982.

[ST90] P.D. Stachour and B.M. Thuraisingham. Design of LDV: A multilevel secure relational database management system. *IEEE Trans. Knowledge and Data Eng.*, 2(2):190–209, 1990.

[The98] Kurt Thearling. Data mining and privacy: A conflict in making. *DS**, March 1998.

[Tim97] Time. *The Death of Privacy*, August 1997.

[TYW84] J.F. Traub, Y. Yemini, and H. Woznaikowski. The statistical security of a statistical database. *ACM TODS*, 9(4):672–679, Dec. 1984.

[War65] S.L. Warner. Randomized response: A survey technique for eliminating evasive answer bias. *J. Am. Stat. Assoc.*, 60(309):63–69, March 1965.

[Wes98a] A.F. Westin. E-commerce and privacy: What net users want. Technical report, Louis Harris & Associates, June 1998. Available from http://www.privacyexchange.org/iss/surveys/ecommsum.html.

[Wes98b] A.F. Westin. Privacy concerns & consumer choice. Technical report, Louis Harris & Associates, Dec. 1998. Available from http://www.privacyexchange.org/iss/surveys/1298toc.html.

[Wes99] A.F. Westin. Freebies and privacy: What net users think. Technical report, Opinion Research Corporation, July 1999. Available from http://www.privacyexchange.org/iss/surveys/sr990714.html.

[Wor] The World Wide Web Consortium. *The Platform for Privacy Preference (P3P)*. Available from http://www.w3.org/P3P/P3FAQ.html.

[YC77] C.T. Yu and F.Y. Chin. A study on the protection of statistical databases. In *Proc. ACM SIGMOD Int. Conf. Management of Data*, pages 169–181, 1977.

DESIGNING AND MINING MULTI-TERABYTE ASTRONOMY ARCHIVES: THE SLOAN DIGITAL SKY SURVEY

Alexander S. Szalay, Szalay@jhu.edu, Peter Z. Kunszt, Kunszt@pha.jhu.edu, Ani Thakar, Thakar@pha.jhu.edu
Dept. of Physics and Astronomy, The Johns Hopkins University, Baltimore, MD 21218
Jim Gray, Gray@Microsoft.com, Don Slutz Dslutz@Microsoft.com
Microsoft Research, San Francisco, CA 94105
Robert J. Brunner, RB@astro.caltech.edu, California Institute of Technology, Pasadena, CA 91125

ABSTRACT

The next-generation astronomy digital archives will cover most of the sky at fine resolution in many wavelengths, from X-rays, through ultraviolet, optical, and infrared. The archives will be stored at diverse geographical locations. One of the first of these projects, the Sloan Digital Sky Survey (SDSS) is creating a 5-wavelength catalog over 10,000 square degrees of the sky (see http://www.sdss.org/). The 200 million objects in the multi-terabyte database will have mostly numerical attributes in a 100+ dimensional space. Points in this space have highly correlated distributions.

The archive will enable astronomers to explore the data interactively. Data access will be aided by multidimensional spatial and attribute indices. The data will be partitioned in many ways. Small *tag* objects consisting of the most popular attributes will accelerate frequent searches. Splitting the data among multiple servers will allow parallel, scalable I/O and parallel data analysis. Hashing techniques will allow efficient clustering, and pair-wise comparison algorithms that should parallelize nicely. Randomly sampled subsets will allow debugging otherwise large queries at the desktop. Central servers will operate a data pump to support sweep searches touching most of the data. The anticipated queries will require special operators related to angular distances and complex similarity tests of object properties, like shapes, colors, velocity vectors, or temporal behaviors. These issues pose interesting data management challenges.

Keywords

Database, archive, data analysis, data mining, astronomy, scaleable, Internet,

1. INTRODUCTION

Astronomy is about to undergo a major paradigm shift. Data gathering technology is riding Moore's law: data volumes are doubling every 20 months. Data sets are becoming larger, and more homogeneous. For the first time data acquisition and archiving is being designed for online interactive analysis. In a few years it will be much easier to download a detailed sky map or object class catalog, than wait several months to access a telescope. In addition, the online data detail and quality is likely to rival that generated by the typical telescopes.

Several multi-wavelength projects are under way: SDSS, GALEX, 2MASS, GSC-2, POSS2, ROSAT, FIRST and DENIS. Each is surveying a large fraction of the sky. Together they will yield a *Digital Sky*, of interoperating multi-terabyte databases. In time, more catalogs will be added and linked to the existing ones. Query engines will become more sophisticated, providing a uniform interface to all these datasets. In this era, astronomers will have to be just as familiar with mining data as with observing on telescopes.

2. THE SLOAN DIGITAL SKY SURVEY

The Sloan Digital Sky Survey (SDSS) will digitally map about half of the Northern sky in five spectral bands from ultraviolet to the near infrared. It is expected to detect over 200 million objects. Simultaneously, it will measure redshifts for the brightest million galaxies (see http://www.sdss.org/).

The SDSS is the successor to the Palomar Observatory Sky Survey (POSS), which has provided a standard reference data set to all of astronomy for the last 40 years. Subsequent archives will augment the SDSS and will interoperate with it. The SDSS project must not only build the survey hardware, it must also design and implement the software to reduce, calibrate, classify, index, and archive the data so that many scientists can use it.

The SDSS will revolutionize astronomy, increasing the amount of information available to researchers by several orders of magnitude. The SDSS archive will be large and complex: including textual information, derived parameters, multi-band images, spectra, and temporal data. The catalog will allow astronomers to study the evolution of the universe in great detail. It is intended to serve as the standard reference for the next several decades. After only a month of operation, SDSS found two of the most distant known quasars and several methane dwarfs. With more data, other exotic properties will be easy to mine from the datasets.

The potential scientific impact of the survey is stunning. To realize this potential, data must be turned into knowledge. This is not easy – the information content of the survey will be larger than the entire text contained in the Library of Congress.

The SDSS is a collaboration between the University of Chicago, Princeton University, the Johns Hopkins University, the University of Washington, Fermi National Accelerator Laboratory, the Japanese Participation Group, the United States Naval Observatory, and the Institute for Advanced Study, Princeton, with additional funding provided by the Alfred P. Sloan Foundation, NSF and NASA. The SDSS project is a collaboration between scientists working in diverse areas of astronomy, physics and computer science. The survey will be carried out with a suite of tools developed and built especially for this project – telescopes, cameras, fiber spectrographic systems, and computer software.

SDSS constructed a dedicated 2.5-meter telescope at Apache Point, New Mexico, USA. The telescope has a large, flat focal plane that provides a 3-degree field of view. This design balances the areal coverage of the instrument against the detector's pixel resolution.

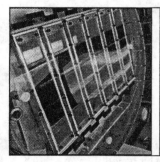

Figure 1: The SDSS photometric camera with the 5x6 CCD array contains 120 million pixels. The CCDs in each row have a different filter attached. As the earth rotates, images migrate across the CCD array. The array shifts in synchrony with this movement, giving a 55 second exposure for each object in 5 spectral bands.

The survey has two main components: a photometric survey, and a spectroscopic survey. The photometric survey is produced by drift scan imaging of 10,000 square degrees centered on the North Galactic Cap using five broad-band filters that range from the ultra-violet to the infra-red. The effective exposure is 55 sec, as a patch of sky passes over the focal plane with the earth's rotation. The photometric imaging uses an array of 30x2Kx2K Imaging CCDs, 22 astrometric CCDs, and 2 Focus CCDs. Its 0.4 arcsecond pixel size provides a full sampling of the sky. The data rate from the camera's 120 million pixels is 8 Megabytes per second. The cameras can only be used under ideal atmospheric conditions, but in five years the survey expects to collect 40 terabytes of data from its survey of the northern sky.

The spectroscopic survey will target a million objects automatically chosen from the photometric survey. The goal is to survey a statistically uniform sample of visible objects. Due to the expansion of the universe, the Doppler-shift in the spectral lines of the galaxies is a direct measure of their distance. This spectroscopic survey will produce a three-dimensional map of galaxy distribution, for a volume several orders of magnitude larger than current maps.

The primary targets will be galaxies, selected by a magnitude and surface brightness limit in the r band. This sample of 900,000 galaxies will be complemented with 100,000 very red galaxies, selected to include the brightest galaxies at the cores of galaxy clusters. An automated algorithm will select 100,000 quasar candidates for spectroscopic follow-up, creating the largest uniform quasar survey to date. Selected objects from other catalogs taken at different wavelengths (e.g., FIRST, ROSAT) will also be targeted.

The spectroscopic observations will be done in overlapping 3° circular "tiles". The tile centers are determined by an optimization algorithm, which maximizes overlaps at areas of highest target density. The spectroscopic survey uses two multi-fiber medium resolution spectrographs, with a total of 640 optical fibers. Each fiber is 3 seconds of arc in that diameter providing spectral coverage from 3900 - 9200 Å. The system can measure 5000 galaxy spectra per night. The total number of galaxy spectra known to astronomers today is about 100,000. In only 20 nights of observation, SDSS will double this.

Whenever the Northern Galactic cap is not accessible, SDSS will repeatedly image several areas in the Southern Galactic cap to study fainter objects and identify variable sources.

SDSS has also been developing the software necessary to process and analyze the data. With construction of both hardware and software largely finished, the project has now entered a year of integration and testing. The survey itself will take 5 to 7 years to complete, depending on weather.

2.1 The Data Products

The SDSS will create four main data sets: (1) a photometric catalog, (2) a spectroscopic catalog, (3) bitmap images in five color bands, and (4) spectra.

The photometric catalog is expected to contain about 500 distinct attributes for each of one hundred million galaxies, one hundred million stars, and one million quasars. These include positions, fluxes, radial profiles, their errors, and information related to the observations. Each object will have a bitmap "atlas image" in each of the five filters.

The spectroscopic catalog will contain identified emission and absorption lines, and one-dimensional spectra for one million galaxies, 100,000 stars, and 100,000 quasars. Derived custom catalogs may be included, such as a photometric galaxy cluster catalog, or quasar absorption line catalog. In addition there will be a compressed 1TB Sky Map. As shown in Table 1, the total size o f these products is about 3TB.

The SDSS will release this data to the public after a period of thorough verification. This public archive is expected to be the standard reference catalog for the next several decades. This long lifetime presents design and legacy problems. The design of the SDSS archival system must allow the archive to grow beyond the actual completion of the survey. As *the* reference astronomical data set, each subsequent astronomical survey will want to cross-identify its objects with the SDSS catalog, requiring that the archive, or at least a part of it, be dynamic with a carefully defined schema and metadata.

Table 1. Sizes of various SDSS datasets

Product	Items	Size
Raw observational data	-	40,000 GB
Redshift Catalog	10^6	2 GB
Survey Description	10^5	1 GB
Simplified Catalog	3×10^8	60 GB
1D Spectra	10^6	60 GB
Atlas Images	10^9	1,500 GB
Compressed Sky Map	5×10^5	1,000 GB
Full photometric catalog	3×10^8	400 GB

3. THE SDSS ARCHIVES

Observational data from the telescopes is shipped on tapes to Fermi National Accelerator Laboratory (FNAL) where it is reduced and stored in the *Operational Archive (OA)*, accessible to personnel working on the data processing.

Data reduction and calibration extracts astronomical objects and their attributes from the raw data. Within two weeks the

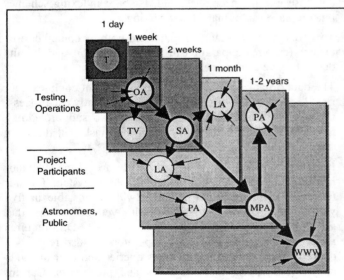

Figure 2. *A conceptual data-flow diagram of the SDSS data.* Telescope data (T) is shipped on tapes to FNAL, where it is processed into the Operational Archive (OA). Calibrated data is transferred into the Master Science Archive (SA) and then to Local Archives (LA). The data gets into the public archives (MPA, PA) after approximately 1-2 years of science verification. These servers provide data for the astronomy community, while a WWW server provides public access.

calibrated data is published to the *Science Archive (SA)* accessible to all SDSS collaborators. The Science Archive contains calibrated data organized for efficient use by scientists. The SA provides a custom query engine built by the SDSS consortium that uses multidimensional indices and parallel data analysis. Given the amount of data, most queries will be I/O limited, thus the SA design is based on a scalable architecture of many inexpensive servers, running in parallel.

Science archive data is replicated to many Local Archives (LA) managed by the SDSS scientists within another two weeks. The data moves into the public archives (MPA, PA) after approximately 1-2 years of science verification, and recalibration (if necessary).

The astronomy community has standardized on the FITS file format for data interchange [18]. FITS includes an ASCII representation of the data and metadata. All data exchange among the archive is now in FITS format. The community is currently considering alternatives such as XML.

3.1 Accessing The Archives

Both professional and amateur astronomers will want access to the archive. Astronomy is a unique science in that there is active collaboration between professional and amateur astronomers. Often, amateur astronomers are the first to see some phenomenon. Most of the tools are designed for professional astronomers, but a public Internet server will provide public access to all the published data. The public will be able to see project status and see various images including the 'Image of the Week'.

The Science Archive and public archives both employ a three-tiered architecture: the user interface, an intelligent query engine, and a data warehouse. This distributed approach provides maximum flexibility, while maintaining portability, by isolating hardware specific features. Both the Science Archive and the Operational Archive are built on top of Objectivity/DB, a commercial object oriented database system.

Analyzing this archive requires a parallel and distributed query system. We implemented a prototype query system. Each query received from the user interface is parsed into a query execution tree (QET) that is then executed by the query engine, which passes the requests to Objectivity/DB for actual execution. Each node of the QET is either a query or a set-operation node, and returns a bag of object-pointers upon execution. The multi-threaded query engine executes in parallel at all the nodes at a given level of the QET.

Results from child nodes are passed up the tree as soon as they are generated. In the case of blocking operators like aggregation, sort, intersection, and difference, at least one of the child nodes must be complete before results can be sent further up the tree. In addition to speeding up the query processing, this as-soon-as-possible data push strategy ensures that even in the case of a query that takes a very long time to complete, the user starts seeing results almost immediately, or at least as soon as the first selected object percolates up the tree.

We have been very pleased with Objectivity/DB's ability to match the SDSS data model. For a C++ programmer, the object-oriented database nicely fits the application's data structures. There is no impedance mismatch [18]. On the other hand, we have been disappointed in the tools and performance. The sequential bandwidth is low (about 3 MBps/cpu while the devices deliver more than 10 times that speed) and the cpu overhead seems high. OQL has not been useable, nor have we been able to get the ODBC tools to work. So we have had to do record-at-a-time accesses. There is no parallel query support, so we have had to implement our own parallel query optimizer and run-time system.

Despite these woes, SDSS works on Objectivity/DB and is in pilot use today. Still, we are investigating alternatives. We have designed a relational schema that parallels the SDSS schema. Doing this has exposed some of the known problems with SQL: no support for arrays, poor support for user-defined types, poor support for hierarchical data, and limited parallelism. Still, the schema is fairly simple and we want to see if the better indexing and scanning technology in SQL systems, together with the use of commodity platforms, can offset the language limitations and yield a better cost-performance solution.

In order to evaluate the database design, we developed a list of 20-typical queries that we are translating into SQL. The database schema and these queries are discussed in Section 4. Preliminary results indicate that the parallelism and non-procedural nature of SQL provides real benefits. Time will tell whether the SQL OO extensions make it a real alternative to the OODB solution. You can see our preliminary schema, the 20-queries, and the SQL for them at our web site: http://www.sdss.jhu.edu/SQL.

3.2   Typical Queries

The astronomy community will be the primary SDSS user. They will need specialized services. At the simplest level these include the on-demand creation of (color) finding charts, with position information. These searches can be fairly complex queries on position, colors, and other parts of the attribute space.

As astronomers learn more about the detailed properties of the stars and galaxies in the SDSS archive, we expect they will define more sophisticated classifications. Interesting objects with unique properties will be found in one area of the sky. They will want to generalize these properties, and search the entire sky for similar objects.

The most common queries against the SDSS database will be very simple - finding objects in a given small sky region. Another common query will be to distinguish between rare and typical objects, based upon their colors and sizes. Other types of queries will be non-local, like *"find all the quasars brighter than magnitude 22, which have a faint blue galaxy within 5 arcseconds on the sky"*. Yet another type of a query

is a search for gravitational lenses: *"find objects within 10 arcseconds of each other which have identical colors, but may have a different brightness"*. This latter query is a typical high-dimensional query, since it involves a metric distance not only on the sky, but also in color space. It also shows the need for approximate comparisons and ranked results.

We can make a few general statements about the expected queries: (1) Astronomers work on the surface of the celestial sphere. This contrasts with most spatial applications, which operate in Cartesian 2-space or 3-space. (2) Most of the queries require a linear or at most a quadratic search (single-item or pair-wise comparisons). (3) Many queries are clustering or top rank queries. (4) Many queries are spatial involving a tiny region of the sky. (5) Almost all queries involve user-defined functions. (6) Almost all queries benefit from parallelism and indices. (7) It may make sense to save many of the computed attributes, since others may be interested in them.

Special operators are required to perform these queries efficiently. Preprocessing, like creating regions of mutual attraction, appears impractical because there are so many objects, and because the operator input sets are dynamically created by other predicates.

3.3   Geometric Data Organization

Given the huge data sets, the traditional astronomy approach of Fortran access to flat files is not feasible for SDSS. Rather, non-procedural query languages, query optimizers, database execution engines, and database indexing schemes must replace traditional file processing.

This "database approach" is mandated both by computer efficiency (automatic parallelism and pipelining), and by the desire to give astronomers better analysis tools.

The data organization must support concurrent complex queries. Moreover, the organization must efficiently use processing, memory, and bandwidth. It must also support adding new data to the SDSS as a background task that does not disrupt online access.

It would be wonderful if we could use an off-the-shelf object-relational, or object-oriented database system for our tasks. We are optimistic that this will be possible in five years – indeed we are working with vendors toward that goal. As explained presently, we believe that SDSS requires novel spatial indices and novel operators. It also requires a dataflow architecture that executes queries and user-methods concurrently using multiple disks and processors. Current products provide few of these features. But, it is quite possible that by the end of the survey, some commercial system will be adequate.

3.4   Spatial Data Structures

The large-scale astronomy data sets consist primarily of records containing numeric data, maps, time-series sensor logs, and images. The vast majority of the data is essentially geometric. The success of the archive depends on capturing the spatial nature of this large-scale scientific data.

The SDSS data has high dimensionality - each item has thousands of attributes. Categorizing objects involves defining complex domains (classifications) in this N-dimensional space, corresponding to decision surfaces.

The SDSS teams are investigating algorithms and data structures to quickly compute spatial relations, such as finding nearest neighbors, or other objects satisfying a given criterion within a metric distance. The answer set cardinality can be so large that intermediate files simply cannot be created. The only way to analyze such data sets is to pipeline the answers directly into analysis tools. This *data flow* analysis has worked well for parallel relational database systems [2. 3, 4, 5, 9]. We expect that the implementation of these data river ideas will link the archive directly to the analysis and visualization tools.

The typical search of these multi-terabyte archives evaluates a complex predicate in k-dimensional space, with the added difficulty that constraints are not necessarily parallel to the axes. This means that the traditional indexing techniques, well established with relational databases, will not work, since one cannot build an index on all conceivable linear combinations of attributes. On the other hand, one can use the facts that the data are geometric and that every object is a point in this k-dimensional space [11,12]. Data can be quantized into containers. Each container has objects of similar properties, e.g. colors, from the same region of the sky. If the containers are stored as contiguous disk pages, data locality will be high - if an object satisfies a query, it is likely that some of the object's "friends" will as well. There are non-trivial aspects of how to subdivide the containers, when the data has large density contrasts [6].

These containers represent a coarse-grained density map of the data. They define the base of an index tree that tells us whether containers are fully inside, outside or bisected by our query. Only the bisected container category is searched, as the other two are wholly accepted or rejected. A prediction of the output data volume and search time can be computed from the intersection volume.

3.5 Indexing the Sky

There is great interest in a common reference frame for the sky that can be used by different astronomical databases. The need for such a system is indicated by the widespread use of the ancient constellations – the first spatial index of the celestial sphere. The existence of such an index, in a more computer friendly form will ease cross-referencing among catalogs.

A common scheme, that provides a balanced partitioning for all catalogs, may seem to be impossible; but there is an elegant solution, that subdivides the sky in a hierarchical fashion.

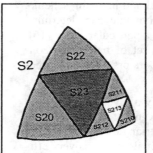

Figure 3. The hierarchical subdivision of spherical triangles, represented as a quad tree. The tree starts out from the triangles defined by an octahedron.

Instead of taking a fixed subdivision, we specify an increasingly finer hierarchy, where each level is fully contained within the previous one. Starting with an octahedron *base set,* each spherical triangle can be recursively divided into 4 sub-triangles of approximately equal areas. Each sub-area can be divided further into additional four sub-areas, ad infinitum. Such hierarchical subdivisions can be very efficiently represented in the form of quad-trees. Areas in different catalogs map either directly onto one another, or one is fully contained by another (see Figure 3.)

We store the object's coordinates on the surface of the sphere in Cartesian form, i.e. as a triplet of x,y,z values per object. The x,y,z numbers represent only the position of objects on the sky, corresponding to the normal vector pointing to the object. (We can guess the distance for only a tiny fraction (0.5%) of the 200 million objects in the catalog.) While at first this representation may seem to increase the required storage (three numbers per object vs. two angles,) it makes querying the database for objects within certain areas of the celestial sphere very efficient. This technique was used successfully by the GSC project [7]. The coordinates of other celestial coordinate systems (Equatorial, Galactic, Supergalactic, etc) can be constructed from the Cartesian coordinates on the fly.

Using the three-dimensional Cartesian representation of the angular coordinates makes it particularly simple to find objects within a certain spherical distance from a given point, or combination of constraints in arbitrary spherical coordinate systems. They correspond to testing linear combinations of the three Cartesian coordinates instead of complicated trigonometric expressions.

The two ideas, partitioning and Cartesian coordinates merge

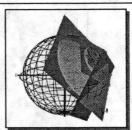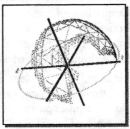

Figure 4. The figure shows a simple range query of latitude in one spherical coordinate system (the two parallel planes on the left hand figure) and an additional latitude constraint in another system (the third plane). The right hand figure shows the triangles in the hierarchy, intersecting with the query, as they were selected. The use of hierarchical triangles, and the use of Cartesian coordinates makes these spatial range queries especially efficient.

into a highly efficient storage, retrieval and indexing scheme. We have created a recursive algorithm that can determine which parts of the sky are relevant for a particular query [16]. Each query can be represented as a set of half-space constraints, connected by Boolean operators, all in three-dimensional space.

The task of finding objects that satisfy a given query can be performed recursively as follows. Run a test between the query polyhedron and the spherical triangles corresponding to the tree root nodes. The intersection algorithm is very efficient because it is easy to test spherical triangle intersection. Classify nodes, as fully outside the query, fully inside the query or partially intersecting the query polyhedron. If a node is rejected, that node's children can be ignored. Only the children of bisected triangles need be further investigated. The intersection test is executed recursively on these nodes (see Figure 4.) The SDSS Science Archive implemented this algorithm in its query engine [15]. We are implementing a stored procedure that returns a table containing the IDs of triangles containing a specified area. Queries can then use this table to limit the spatial search by joining answer sets with this table.

3.6   Broader Metadata Issues

There are several issues related to metadata for astronomy datasets. First, one must design the data warehouse schema, second is the description of the data extracted from the archive, and the third is a standard representation to allow queries and data to be interchanged among archives.

The SDSS project uses a UML tool to develop and maintain the database schema. The schema is defined in a high level format, and an automated script generator creates the .h files for the C++ classes, and the data definition files for Objectivity/DB, SQL, IDL, XML, and other metadata formats.

About 20 years ago, astronomers agreed on exchanging most of their data in a self-descriptive data format. This format, FITS, standing for the Flexible Image Transport System [17] was primarily designed to handle images. Over the years, various extensions supported more complex data types, both in ASCII and binary form. The FITS format is well supported by all astronomical software systems. The SDSS pipelines exchange most of their data as binary FITS files.

Unfortunately, FITS files do not support streaming data, although data could be blocked into separate FITS packets. The SDSS has implemented an ASCII FITS output stream, using a blocked approach. A binary stream is under development.

Figure 5. A typical complex object involving several nearby stars and a galaxy.

We expect large archives to communicate with one another via a standard, easily parseable interchange format. SDSS plans to participate in the definition of interchange formats in XML, XSL, and XQL.

3.7   Data Loading

The Operational Archive exports calibrated data to the Science Archive as soon as possible. Datasets are sent in coherent chunks. A chunk consists of several segments of the sky that were scanned in a single night, with all the fields and all objects detected in the fields. Loading data into the Science Archive could take a long time if the data were not clustered properly. Efficiency is important, since about 20 GB arrives after each night of photometric observations.

The incoming data are organized by how the observations were taken. In the Science Archive they are organized into the hierarchy of containers as defined by the multi-dimensional spatial index (Figure 3), according to their colors and positions.

Data loading might bottleneck on creating the clustering units—databases and containers—that hold the objects. Our load design minimizes disk accesses, touching each clustering unit at most once during a load. The chunk data is exported as a binary FITS file from the Operational Archive into the Science Archive. It is first examined to construct an index. This determines where each object will be located and creates a list of databases and containers that are needed. Then data is inserted into the containers in a single pass over the data objects.

4.   THE EXPERIMENTAL SQL DESIGN

4.1   SQL Schema

We translated the Objectivity/DB schema into an SQL schema of 25 tables. They were generated from a UML schema by an automated script, and fine-tuned by hand.

The SQL schema has some differences from our Objectivity schema. Arrays cannot be represented in SQL Server, so we broke out the shorter, one-dimensional arrays f[5] as scalar fields f_1,f_2,... The poor indexing in Objectivity/DB forced us to separate star and galaxy objects (for the 2x speedup), while in SQL we were able to merge the two classes and their associations. Object Associations were converted into foreign keys. Other than this, the schema conversion and data extraction and loading was remarkably easy. Detailed information about the data model can be found at (http://www.sdss.jhu.edu/ScienceArchive/doc.html).

The tables can be separated into several broad categories. The first set of tables relate to the photometric observations. A base table, called the *Photo* table, contains the basic photometric attributes of each object. Each record contains about 100 attributes, describing each object detected in the survey, its colors, position in each band, the errors of each quantity, and some classification parameters. The 30% least popular attributes, and a 5x15 radial light profile array are vertically partitioned into a separate *PhotoProfile* table. The array is represented as a BLOB with some user-

456

defined functions to access it.

In the same spirit, the 13 most popular attributes were split off into the Tag objects in the Objectivity/DB design, to make simple queries more efficient. In SQL the *Tag* table object is represented as one or more indexes on the *Photo* table. After this vertical partitioning we also segmented the data horizontally in the Objectivity/DB design. After an object classification, still performed by the pipelines, extended objects, classified as galaxies, and compact objects classified as stars are stored in separate object classes, since they will typically be queried separately most of the time. In SQL the design unifies the two tables, and assumes that clustering and partitioning will be done by the DBMS across the multiple disks and servers. We also created a few attributes from our internal spatial indices – these are the hash codes corresponding to a bit interleaved address in the triangular mesh or on the k-d tree.

There is a particular subtlety in dealing with merged objects. On the sky one often finds a nearby star superimposed over the image of a distant galaxy (see Figure 5). These can often be recognized as such, and deblended. This deblending process creates a tree of object relations, where a parent object may have two or more children, and so on. Also, about 10% of the sky is observed multiple times. All the detections of the same object will have a common object identifier. A unique *primary* selected by its sky position. Each *Photo* object record is marked as a primary or secondary, and all instances of the object have the same object-identifier.

Another set of tables is related to the hierarchy of observations and the data processing steps. The SDSS project observes approximately 130-degree long 2.5-degree wide *stripes* on the sky. Each stripe is actually two *runs* from two different nights of observation. Each run has six 5-color columns, corresponding to the six CCD columns in the camera (see figure 1) separated by 90% of the width of the CCDs. These columns have 10% overlap on each side, and are woven together to form a seamless mosaic of the 130x2.5 degree stripe. Each 5-color column is split into about 800 *fields*. Each field is a 5-color 2048x1489 2-byte per pixel image. There are separate tables with the metadata for stripes, runs, and fields. Each field carries about 60 attributes, consisting of its precise calibration data, and the coefficients of the transformation that maps pixel positions onto absolute sky coordinates. Chunks and Segments carry the observation date and time, the software version used during the data

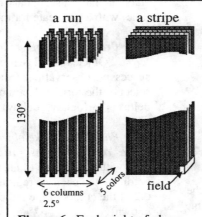

Figure 6. Each night of observation produces a 130 x 2.5 run of 5 colors. The columns of two adjacent runs have a 10% overlap and can be mosaiced together to form a strip. Stripes are partitioned into fields.

reduction process, and various parameters of the instruments during the observing run.

Another set of tables is related to the spectroscopic observations. They capture the process of target selection and eventual observation. There is a separate *SpectroTarget* table, corresponding to objects selected from the photometry to be observed with the spectrographs. Not all of them will be observed. The observed objects will then be classified as a galaxy, star, quasar, blank sky, and unknown. The observed objects have various attributes, a list of emission and absorption lines detected, estimated redshift, its errors, and quality estimate, stored in a *Spectro* table. Every object has a different number if lines, so the lines are stored in a *Lines* table. Each record has the object identifier, line type, (emission or absorption), lab wavelength, and rest-frame wavelength, line identifier, line width, and strength, and a few fitting parameters, and of course uncertainly estimates. There is also a *Plate* table describing the layout of a spectroscopic observation, since 640 objects are measured simultaneously.

Finally, there is a table to capture cross-reference information about SDSS objects also detected in other catalogs, if a unique identification can be made. This cross-reference table can evolve as the need arises.

4.2   SQL Queries

We developed a set of 20 queries that we think characterize the kinds of questions Astronomers are likely to ask the SDSS archives. This is much in the spirit of the Sequoia 2000 benchmark of [14]. We are in the process of translating these queries into SQL statements and evaluating their performance on a relational system.

Here follow the queries and a narrative description of how we believe they will be evaluated.

Q1: Find all galaxies with unsaturated pixels within 1 arcsecond of a given point in the sky (right ascension and declination). This is a classic spatial lookup. We expect to have a quad-tree spherical triangle index with object type (star, galaxy, …) as the first key and then the spatial attributes. So this will be a lookup in that quad-tree. Select those galaxies that are within one arcsecond of the specified point.

Q2: Find all galaxies with blue surface brightness between 23 and 25 mag per square arcseconds, and -10<super galactic latitude (sgb) <10, and declination less than zero. This searches for all galaxies in a certain region of the sky with a specified brightness in the blue spectral band. The query uses a different coordinate system, which ismust first be converted to the hierarchical triangles of Figure 3 and section 3.5. It is then a set of disjoint table scans, each having a compound simple predicate representing the spatial boundary conditions and surface brightness test.

Q3: Find all galaxies brighter than magnitude 22, where the local extinction is >0.75. The local extinction is a map of the sky telling how much dust is in that direction, and hence how much light is absorbed by that dust. The extinction grid is stored as a table with one square arcminute resolution – about half a billion cells. The query is either a spatial join of bright galaxies with the extinction grid table, or the extinction is stored as an attribute of each object so that this is just a scan of the galaxies in the Photo table.

Q4: Find galaxies with a surface brightness greater than 24 with a major axis 30"<d<1', in the red-band, and with an ellipticity>0.5. . Each of the 5 color bands of a galaxy will have been pre-processed into a bitmap image which is broken into 15 concentric rings. The rings are further divided into octants. The intensity of the light in each ring is analyzed and recorded as a 5x15 array. The array is stored as an object (SQL blob in our type impoverished case). The concentric rings are pre-processed to compute surface brightness, ellipticity, major axis, and other attributes. Consequently, this query is a scan of the galaxies with predicates on precomputed properties.

Q5: Find all galaxies with a deVaucouleours profile ($r^{1/4}$ fall-off of intensity on disk) and the photometric colors consistent with an elliptical galaxy. The deVaucouleours profile information is precomputed from the concentric rings as discussed in Q4. This query is a scan of galaxies in the Photo table with predicates on the intensity profile and color limits.

Q6: Find galaxies that are blended with a star, output the deblended magnitudes.
Preprocessing separates objects that overlap or are related (a binary star for example). This process is called deblending and produces a tree of objects; each with its own 'deblended' attributes such as color and intensity. The parent child relationships are represented in SQL as foreign keys. The query is a join of the deblended galaxies in the photo table, with their siblings. If one of the siblings is a star, the galaxy's identity and magnitude is added to the answer set.

Q7: Provide a list of star-like objects that are 1% rare for the 5-color attributes. This involves classification of the attribute set and then a scan to find objects with attributes close to that of a star that occur in rare categories.

Q8: Find all objects with spectra unclassified.
This is a sequential scan returning all objects with a certain precomputed flag set.

Q9: Find quasars with a line width >2000 km/s and 2.5<redshift<2.7. This is a sequential scan of quasars in the Spectro table with a predicate on the redshift and line width. The Spectro table has about 1.5 million objects having a known spectrum but there are only 100,00 known quasars.

Q10: Find galaxies with spectra that have an equivalent width in H_α >40Å (H_α is the main hydrogen spectral line.) This is a join of the galaxies in the Spectra table and their lines in the Lines table.

Q11: Find all elliptical galaxies with spectra that have an anomalous emission line. This is a sequential scan of galaxies (they are indexed) that have ellipticity above .7 (a precomputed value) with emission lines that have been flagged as strange (again a precomputed value).

Q12: Create a grided count of galaxies with u-g>1 and r<21.5 over 60<declination<70, and 200<right ascension<210, on a grid of 2', and create a map of masks over the same grid. Scan the table for galaxies and group them in cells 2 arc-minutes on a side. Provide predicates for the color restrictions on u-g and r and to limit the search to the portion of the sky defined by the right ascension and declination conditions. Return the count of qualifying galaxies in each cell. Run another query with the same grouping, but with a predicate to include only objects such as satellites, planets, and airplanes that obscure the cell. The second query returns a list of cell coordinates that serve as a mask for the first query. The mask may be stored in a temporary table and joined with the first query.

Q13: Create a count of galaxies for each of the HTM triangles (hierarchal triangular mesh) which satisfy a certain color cut, like 0.7u-0.5g-0.2 and i-magr<1.25 and r-mag<21.75, output it in a form adequate for visualization. This query is a sequential scan of galaxies with predicates for the color magnitude. It groups the results by a specified level in the HTM hierarchy (obtained by shifting the HTM key) and returns a count of galaxies in each triangle together with the key of the triangle.

Q14: Provide a list of stars with multiple epoch measurements, which have light variations >0.1 magnitude. Scan for stars that have a secondary object (observed at a different time) with a predicate for the light variations.

Q15: Provide a list of moving objects consistent with an asteroid. Objects are classified as moving and indeed have 5 successive observations from the 5 color bands. So this is a select of the form: select moving object where $\sqrt{((\text{deltax5}-\text{deltax1})^2 + (\text{delty5}-\text{delty1})^2)}$ < 2 arc seconds.

Q16: Find all star-like objects within DeltaMagnitde of 0.2 of the colors of a quasar at 5.5<redshift<6.5. Scan all objects with a predicate to identify star-like objects and another predicate to specify a region in color space within 'distance' 0.2 of the colors of the indicated quasar (the quasar colors are known).

Q17: Find binary stars where at least one of them has the colors of a white dwarf. Scan the Photo table for stars with white dwarf colors that are a child of a binary star. Return a list of unique binary star identifiers.

Q18: Find all objects within 1' of one another other that have very similar colors: that is where the color ratios u-g, g-r, r-I

are less than 0.05m. (Magnitudes are logarithms so these are ratios.) This is a gravitational lens query.
 Scan for objects in the Photo table and compare them to all objects within one arcminute of the object. If the color ratios match, this is a candidate object. We may precompute the five nearest neighbors of each object to speed up queries like this.

Q19: Find quasars with a broad absorption line in their spectra and at least one galaxy within 10". Return both the quasars and the galaxies. Scan for quasars with a predicate for a broad absorption line and use them in a spatial join with galaxies that are within 10 arc-seconds. The nearest neighbors may be precomputed which makes this a regular join.

Q20: For a galaxy in the BCG data set (brightest color galaxy), in 160<right ascension<170, 25<declination<35, give a count of galaxies within 30" which have a photoz within 0.05 of the BCG. First form the BCG (brightest galaxy in a cluster) table. Then scan for galaxies in clusters (the cluster is their parent object) with a predicate to limit the region of the sky. For each galaxy, test with a sub-query that no other galaxy in the same cluster is brighter. Then do a spatial join of this table with the galaxies to return the desired counts.

4.3   Analysis and Visualization

We do not expect many astronomers to know SQL. Rather we expect to provide graphical data analysis tools. Much of the analysis will be done like a spreadsheet with simple equations. For more complex analysis, the astronomers will want to apply programs written in Java, C++, JavaScript, VB, Perl, or IDL to analyze objects.

Answers to queries will be steamed to a visualization and analysis engine that SDSS is building using VTK and Java3D. Presumably the astronomer will examine the rendered data, and either drill down into it or ask for a different data presentation, thereby steering the data analysis.

In the spirit of the database query statements, here are a dozen data visualization and analysis scenarios.

VA1: Generate a 2D scatter plot of two selected attributes.
This is the bread and butter of all data analysis tools. The user wants to point at some data point and then drill down on it. It is also important to subset the data, do regressions, and other statistical tests of the data.

VA2: Generate a 3D scatter-plot of three selected attributes, and at each point use color, shape, size, icon, or animation to display additional dimensions.
This is the next step in visualization after VA1, handling higher dimensional data.

VA3: Superpose objects (tick marks or contours) over an image.
This allows analysts to combine two or more visualizations in one pane and compare them visually.

VA4: Generate and 2D and 3D plot of a single scalar field over the sky, in various coordinate systems.
Astronomers have many different coordinate systems. They are all just affine transformations of one another. Sometimes they want polar, sometimes Lambert, sometimes they just want to change the reference fame. This is just a requirement that the visualization system supports the popular projections, and allows new ones to be easily added.

VA5: Visualize condensed representations or aggregations.
For example compute density of objects in 3D space, phase space, or attribute space and render the density map.

VA6: 2D/3D scatter plots of objects, with Euclidean proximity links in other dimensions represented.
Use connecting lines to show objects that are closely linked in attribute space and in 3 space.

VA7: Allow interactive settings of thresholds for volumetric visualizations, showing translucent iso-surfaces of 3D functions.
This kind of visualization is common in parts-explosion of CAD systems; it would also be useful in showing the volumetric properties of higher-dimensional data spaces.

VA8: Generate linked multi-pane data displays.
In steering the computation, scientists want to see several "windows" into the dataset, each window showing one of the above displays. As the analyst changes the focus of one window, all the other windows should change focus in unison. This includes subsetting the data, zooming out, or panning across the parameter space. The http://aai.com/ Image Explorer is and example of such a tool.

5.   SCALABLE SERVER ARCHITECTURES

The SDSS data is too large to fit on one disk or even one server. The base-data objects will be spatially partitioned among the servers. As new servers are added, the data will repartition. Some of the high-traffic data will be replicated among servers. In the near term, designers must specify the partitioning and index schemes, but we hope that in the long term, the DBMS will automate this design task as access patterns and data volumes change.

Accessing large data sets is primarily I/O limited. Even with the best indexing schemes, some queries must scan the entire data set. Acceptable I/O performance can be achieved with expensive, ultra-fast storage systems, or with many servers operating in parallel. We are exploring the use of inexpensive servers and storage to allow inexpensive interactive data analysis.

As reviewers pointed out, we could buy large SMP servers that offer 1GBps IO. Indeed, our colleagues at Fermi Lab are using SGI equipment for the initial processing steps. The problem with the supercomputer or mini-supercomputer approach is that the processors, memory, and storage seem to be substantially more expensive than commodity servers – we are able to develop on inexpensive systems, and then deploy just as much processing as we can afford. The "slice-price" for processing and memory seems to be 10x lower than for the high-end servers, the storage prices seems to be 3x lower, and the networking prices seem to be about the same (based on www.tpc.org prices).

We are still exploring what constitutes a balanced system design: the appropriate ratio between processor, memory, network bandwidth, and disk bandwidth. It appears that Amdahl's balance law of one instruction per bit of IO applies for our current software (application + SQL+OS).

Using the multi-dimensional indexing techniques described in the previous section, many queries will be able to select exactly the data they need after doing an index lookup. Such simple queries will just pipeline the data and images off of disk as quickly as the network can transport it to the astronomer's system for analysis or visualization.

When the queries are more complex, it will be necessary to scan the entire dataset or to repartition it for categorization, clustering, and cross comparisons. Experience will teach us the necessary ratio between processor power, main memory size, IO bandwidth, and system-area-network bandwidth.

Our simplest approach is to run a **scan machine** that continuously scans the dataset evaluating user-supplied predicates on each object [1]. We are building an array of 20 nodes. Each node has dual Intel 750 MHz processors, 256MB of RAM, and 8x40GB EIDE disks on dual disk controllers (6TB of storage and 20 billion instructions per second in all). Experiments show that one node is capable of reading data at 120 MBps while using almost no processor time – indeed, it appears that each node can apply fairly complex SQL predicates to each record as the data is scanned. If the data is spread among the 20 nodes, they can scan the data at an aggregate rate of 2 GBps. This 100 K$ system could scan the complete (year 2005) SDSS catalog every 2 minutes. By then these machines should be 10x faster. This should give near-interactive response to most complex queries that involve single-object predicates.

Many queries involve comparing, classifying or clustering objects. We expect to provide a second class of machine, called a **hash machine** that performs comparisons within data clusters. Hash machines redistribute a subset of the data among all the nodes of the cluster. Then each node processes each hash bucket at that node. This parallel-clustering approach has worked extremely well for relational databases in joining and aggregating data. We believe it will work equally well for scientific spatial data.

The hash phase scans the entire dataset, selects a subset of the objects based on some predicate, and "hashes" each object to the appropriate buckets – a single object may go to several buckets (to allow objects near the edges of a region to go to all the neighboring regions as well). In a second phase all the objects in a bucket are compared to one another. The output is a stream of objects with corresponding attributes.

These operations are analogous to relational hash-join, hence the name [5]. Like hash joins, the hash machine can be highly parallel, processing the entire database in a few min-

utes. The application of the hash-machine to tasks like finding gravitational lenses or clustering by spectral type or by redshift-distance vector should be obvious: each bucket represents a neighborhood in these high-dimensional spaces. We envision a non-procedural programming interface to define the bucket partition function and to define the bucket analysis function.

The hash machine is a simple form of the more general dataflow programming model in which data flows from storage through various processing steps. Each step is amenable to partition parallelism. The underlying system manages the creation and processing of the flows. This programming style has evolved both in the database community [4, 5, 9] and in the scientific programming community with PVM and MPI [8]. This has evolved to a general programming model as typified by a river system [2, 3, 4].

We propose to let astronomers construct dataflow graphs where the nodes consume one or more data streams, filter and combine the data, and then produce one or more result streams. The outputs of these rivers either go back to the database or to visualization programs. These dataflow graphs will be executed on a **river-machine** similar to the scan and hash machine. The simplest river systems are sorting networks. Current systems have demonstrated that they can sort at about 100 MBps using commodity hardware and 5 GBps if using thousands of nodes and disks [13].

With time, each astronomy department will be able to afford local copies of these machines and the databases, but to start they will be network services. The scan machine will be interactively scheduled: when an astronomer has a query, it will be added to the query mix immediately. All data that qualifies is sent back to the astronomer, and the query completes within the scan time. The hash and river machines will be batch scheduled.

5.1   Desktop Data Analysis

Most astronomers will not be interested in all of the hundreds of attributes of each object. Indeed, most will be interested in only 10% of the entire dataset – but different communities and individuals will be interested in a different 10%.

We plan to isolate the 10 most popular attributes (3 Cartesian positions on the sky, 5 colors, 1 size, 1 classification parameter) into a compact table or index. We will build a spatial index on these attributes that will occupy much less space and thus can be searched more than 10 times faster, if no other attributes are involved in the query. This is the standard technique of *covering indices* in relational query processing.

Large disks are available today, and within a few years 100GB disks will be common. This means that all astronomers can have a vertical partition of the 10% of the SDSS on their desktops. This will be convenient for targeted searches and for developing algorithms. But, full searchers will still be much faster on servers because they have more IO bandwidth and processing power.

The scan, hash, and river machines can also apply vertical partitioning to reduce data movement and to allow faster scans of popular subsets.

We also plan to offer a 1% sample (about 10 GB) of the whole database that can be used to quickly test and debug programs. Combining partitioning and sampling converts a 2 TB data set into 2 gigabytes, which can fit comfortably on desktop workstations for program development.

5.2   Distributed Analysis Environment

It is obvious, that with multi-terabyte databases, not even the intermediate data sets can be stored locally. The only way this data can be analyzed is for the analysis software to directly communicate with the data warehouse, implemented on a server cluster, as discussed above. An **Analysis Engine** can then process the bulk of the raw data extracted from the archive, and the user needs only to receive a drastically reduced result set.

Given all these efforts to make the server parallel and distributed, it would be stupid to ignore I/O or network bottlenecks at the analysis level. Thus it is obvious that we need to think of the analysis engine as part of the distributed, scalable computing environment, closely integrated with the database server itself. Even the division of functions between the server and the analysis engine will become fuzzy — the analysis is just part of the river-flow described earlier. The pool of available CPU's will be allocated to each task.

The analysis software itself must be able to run in parallel. Since it is expected that scientists with relatively little experience in distributed and parallel programming will work in this environment, we need to create a carefully crafted application development environment, to aid the construction of customized analysis engines. Data extraction needs to be considered also carefully. If our server is distributed and the analysis is on a distributed system, the extracted data should also go directly from one of the servers to one of the many Analysis Engines. Such an approach will also distribute the network load better.

6.   SKY SERVER

Some of us were involved in building the Microsoft TerraServer (http://www.TerraServer.Microsoft.com/) which is a website giving access to the photographic and topographic maps of the United States Geological Survey. This website has been popular with the public, and is starting to be a portal to other spatial and spatially related data (e.g., encyclopedia articles about a place.)

We are in the process of building the analog for astronomy: SkyServer (http://www.skyserver.org/). Think of it as the TerraServer looking up rather than down. We plan to put online the publicly available photometric surveys and catalogs as a collaboration among astronomical survey projects. We are starting with Digitized Palomar Observatory Sky Survey (POSS-II) and the preliminary SDSS data. POSS-II covers the Northern Sky in three bands with arcsecond pixels

at 2 bits per pixel. POSS-II is about 3 TB of raw image data. In addition, there is a catalog of approximately one billion objects extracted from the POSS data. The next step will add the 2 Micron All Sky Survey (2MASS) that covers the full sky in three near-infrared bands at 2-arcsecond resolution. 2MASS is an approximately 10 TB dataset. We are soliciting other datasets that can be added to the SkyServer.

Once these datasets are online, we hope to build a seamless mosaic of the sky from them, to provide catalog overlays, and to build other visualization tools that will allow users to examine and compare the datasets. Scientists will be able to draw a box around a region, and download the source data and other datasets for that area of the sky. Other surveys will be added later to cover other parts of the spectrum.

7.   SUMMARY

Astronomy is about to be revolutionized by having a detailed atlas of the sky available to all astronomers, providing huge databases of detailed and high-quality data available to all. If the archival system of the SDSS is successful, it will be easy for astronomers to pose complex queries to the catalog and get answers within seconds, and within minutes if the query requires a complete search of the database.

The SDSS datasets pose interesting challenges for automatically placing and managing the data, for executing complex queries against a high-dimensional data space, and for supporting complex user-defined distance and classification metrics.

The efficiency of the instruments and detectors used in the observations is approaching 80%. The factor limiting resolution is the Earth atmosphere. There is not a large margin for a further dramatic improvement in ground-based instruments.

On the other hand, the SDSS project is "riding Moore's law": the data set we collect today – at a linear rate – will be much more manageable tomorrow, with the exponential growth of CPU speed and storage capacity. The scalable archive design presented here will be able to adapt to such changes.

8. ACKNOWLEDGEMENTS

We would like to acknowledge support from the Astrophysical Research Consortium, the HSF, NASA and Intel's Technology for Education 2000 program, in particular George Bourianoff (Intel).

9. REFERENCES

[1] Acharya, S. R. Alonso, M. J. Franklin, S. B. Zdonik, "Broadcast Disks: Data Management for Asymmetric Communications Environments." SIGMOD Conference 1995: 199-210.

[2] Arpaci-Dusseau, R. Arpaci-Dusseau, A., Culler, D. E., Hellerstein, J. M., Patterson, D. A. ,"The Architectural Costs of Streaming I/O: A Comparison of Workstations, Clusters, and SMPs", Proc. Fourth International Symposium On High-Performance Computer Architecture (HPCA), Feb 1998.

[3] Arpaci-Dusseau, R. H. , Anderson, E.,.Treuhaft, N., Culler, D.A., Hellerstein, J.M., Patterson, D.A., Yelick, K., "Cluster I/O with River: Making the Fast Case Common." IOPADS '99 pp 10-22, http://now.cs.berkeley.edu/River/

[4] Barclay, T. Barnes, R., Gray, J., Sundaresan, P., "Loading Databases Using Dataflow Parallelism." SIGMOD Record 23(4): 72-83 (1994)

[5] DeWitt, D.J. Gray, J., "Parallel Database Systems: The Future of High Performance Database Systems." CACM 35(6): 85-98 (1992)

[6] Csabai, I., Szalay, A.S. and Brunner, R., "Multidimensional Index For Highly Clustered Data With Large Density Contrasts," in *Statistical Challenges in Astronomy II*, eds. E. Feigelson and A. Babu, (Wiley), 447 (1997).

[7] Greene, G. et al, "The GSC-I and GCS-II Databases: An Object Oriented Approach", in *New Horizons from Multi-Wavelength Sky Surveys*, eds. B. McLean et al, Kluwer, p.474 (1997)

[8] Gropp, W., Huss-Lederman, H., *MPI the Complete Reference: The MPI-2 Extensions, Vol. 2,* MIT Press, 1998, ISBN: 0262571234

[9] Graefe, G., "Query Evaluation Techniques for Large Databases". ACM Computing Surveys 25(2): 73-170 (1993)

[10] Hartman, A. of Dell Computer, private communication. Intel Corporation has generously provided the SDSS effort at Johns Hopkins with Dell Computers.

[11] Samet, H., *Applications of Spatial Data Structures: Computer Graphics, Image Processing, and GIS*, Addison-Wesley, Reading, MA, 1990. ISBN 0-201-50300-0.

[12] Samet, H., *The Design and Analysis of Spatial Data Structures*, Addison-Wesley, Reading, MA, 1990. ISBN 0-201-50255-0.

[13] http://research.microsoft.com/barc/SortBenchmark/

[14] Stonebraker, M., Frew, J., Gardels, K., Meredith, J., "The Sequoia 2000 Benchmark." Proc. ACM SIGMOD, pp. 2-11, 1993.

[15] Szalay, A.S. and Brunner, R.J.: "Exploring Terabyte Archives in Astronomy", in *New Horizons from Multi- Wavelength Sky Surveys*, IAU Symposium 179, eds. B. McLean and D. Golombek, p.455. (1997).

[16] Szalay, A.S., Kunszt, P. and Brunner, R.J.: "Hierarchical Sky Partitioning," Astronomical Journal, to be submitted, 2000.

[17] Wells, D. C., Greisen, E. W., and Harten, R. H., "FITS: A Flexible Image Transport System," Astronomy and Astrophysics Supplement Series, 44, 363-370, 1981.

[18] Zadonic, S., Maier, D., *Readings in Object Oriented Database Systems*, Morgan Kaufmann, San Francisco, CA, 1990. ISBN 1-55860-000-0

Approximating Multi-Dimensional Aggregate Range Queries Over Real Attributes

Dimitrios Gunopulos
Univ. of California, Riverside
dg@cs.ucr.edu

George Kollios
Polytechnic Univ.
gkollios@milos.poly.edu

Vassilis J. Tsotras
Univ. of California, Riverside
tsotras@cs.ucr.edu

Carlotta Domeniconi
Univ. of California, Riverside
carlotta@cs.ucr.edu

Abstract

Finding approximate answers to multi-dimensional range queries over real valued attributes has significant applications in data exploration and database query optimization. In this paper we consider the following problem: given a table of d attributes whose domain is the real numbers, and a query that specifies a range in each dimension, find a good approximation of the number of records in the table that satisfy the query.

We present a new histogram technique that is designed to approximate the density of multi-dimensional datasets with real attributes. Our technique finds buckets of variable size, and allows the buckets to overlap. Overlapping buckets allow more efficient approximation of the density. The size of the cells is based on the local density of the data. This technique leads to a faster and more compact approximation of the data distribution. We also show how to generalize kernel density estimators, and how to apply them on the multi-dimensional query approximation problem.

Finally, we compare the accuracy of the proposed techniques with existing techniques using real and synthetic datasets.

1 Introduction

Computing approximate answers to multi-dimensional range queries is a problem that arises in query optimization, data mining and data warehousing. The query optimizer requires accurate estimations of the sizes of intermediate query results in the evaluation of different execution plans. Recent work also shows that top-k queries can be mapped to multi-dimensional queries [5, 9], so selectivity estimation techniques can be used to optimize top-k queries too.

The problem of approximating multi-dimensional range queries is also relevant for data mining applica-

tions. Answering range queries is one of the simpler data exploration tasks. In this context, the user defines a specific region of the dataset that is interested to explore, and asks queries to find the characteristics of this region (like the number of points in the interior of the region, the average value or the sum of the values of attributes in the region). Consider for example a dataset that records readings of different environmental variables, such as types of pollution, at various space locations. In exploring this dataset the user may be interested in answering range queries similar to: find how many locations exist for which the values of given pollution variables are within a specified range. The user may want to restrict the answers to a given geographical range too [3, 33]. The size of such datasets makes exact answers slow in coming, and only an efficient approximation algorithm can make this data exploration task interactive.

In data warehousing, datasets can be very large. Answering aggregate queries exactly can be computationally expensive. Instead, finding approximate answers to such queries efficiently, will allow the user to explore the data faster.

In this paper we address the problem of estimating the selectivity of multi-dimensional range queries when the datasets have numerical attributes with real values. The range queries we consider are intersections of ranges, each range being defined on a single attribute. In the multi-dimensional attribute space, the queries are then hyper-rectangles with faces parallel to the axes. Solving such a range query exactly involves counting how many points fall in the interior of the query. When the number of dimensions increases, recent results show [37] that the query time is linear to the size of the dataset.

Real domains have two important consequences. First, the number of possible queries is infinite in the case of real domains, but finite when considering a finite discrete domain. In the case of real domains, the number of possible query answers is still finite, since the dataset is finite, but depends on the size of the dataset. Second, with real domains it is unlikely that many attribute values will appear more than once in the database.

1.1 Our Contribution

There are three main contributions from this work:

First, we present a new technique, GENHIST, to find multi-dimensional histograms for datasets from real domains. The method has been designed to approximate the joint data distribution more efficiently than existing techniques.

Second, we show how to use multi-dimensional kernel density estimators to solve the multi-dimensional range query selectivity problem. Our technique generalizes in multiple dimensions the technique given in [4]. Kernel estimation is a generalization of sampling. Like sampling, finding a kernel estimator is efficient, and can be performed in one pass.

Third, we present an extensive comparison between the new techniques (GENHIST, multi-dimensional kernel density estimators), and most of the existing techniques for estimating the selectivity of multi-dimensional range queries for real attributes (wavelet transform [35], multi-dimensional histogram MHIST [27], one-dimensional estimation techniques with the attribute independence assumption, and sampling [13]). We include the attribute independence assumption in our study as a baseline comparison.

The experimental results show that we can efficiently build selectivity estimators for multi-dimensional datasets with real attributes. Although the accuracy of all the techniques drops rapidly with the increase in dimensionality, the estimators are still accurate in 5 dimensions. GENHIST appears to be the most robust and accurate technique that we tested. Multi-dimensional kernel estimators are also competitive in accuracy. An advantage of kernel estimators is that they can be computed in one dataset pass (just like sampling). However, they work better than sampling for the dimensionalities we tried. Therefore, multi-dimensional kernel estimators are the obvious choice when the selectivity estimator must be computed fast.

In the next section (Section 2) we formally define the problem. In section 3 we briefly describe the multi-dimensional histogram and wavelet decomposition approaches. We present a new multi-dimensional histogram construction in section 4. We describe how to use kernel estimators for multi-dimensional data in section 5. Section 6 includes our experimental results, and we conclude in section 7.

2 Problem Description

Let R be a relation with d attributes and n tuples. Let $\mathcal{A} = \{A_1, A_2, \ldots, A_d\}$ be the set of these attributes. The domain of each attribute A_i is scaled to the real interval $[0, 1]$. Assuming an ordering of the attributes,

each tuple is a point in the d-dimensional space defined by the attributes. Let V_i be the set of values of A_i that are present in R. Since the values are real, each could be distinct and therefore $|V_i|$ can be as large as n.

The range queries we consider are of the form $(a_1 \leq R.A_1 \leq b_1) \wedge \ldots \wedge (a_d \leq R.A_d \leq b_d)$. All a_i, b_i are assumed to be in $[0, 1]$. Such a query is a hyper-rectangle with faces parallel to the axes. The *selectivity* of the query $sel(R, Q)$ is the number of tuples in the interior of the hyper-rectangle.

Since n can be very large, the problem of approximating the selectivity of a given range query Q arises naturally. The problem is how to preprocess R so that accurate estimations can be derived from a smaller representation of R.

Let $f(x_1, \ldots x_d)$ be a d-dimensional, non-negative function that is defined in $[0, 1]^d$ and has the property that

$$\int_{[0,1]^d} f(x_1, \ldots x_d) dx_1 \ldots dx_d = 1.$$

We call f a *probability density function*. The value of f at a specific point $\mathbf{x} = (x_1, \ldots x_d)$ of the d-dimensional space is the limit of the probability that a tuple exists in volume U around $\mathbf{x}$ over the volume of U, when U shrinks to $\mathbf{x}$.

For a given f with these properties, to find the selectivity of query $(a_1 \leq R.A_1 \leq b_1) \wedge \ldots \wedge (a_d \leq R.A_d \leq b_d)$ we compute the integral of f in the interior of the query Q:

$$sel(f, Q) = \int_{[a_1, b_1] \times \ldots \times [a_d, b_d]} f(x_1, \ldots x_d) dx_1 \ldots dx_d.$$

For a given R and f, f is a good *estimator* of R with respect to range queries if for any range query Q, the selectivity of Q on R and the selectivity of Q on f multiplied by n are similar. To formalize this notion, we define the following error metrics (also used by [35]).

The *relative error* of a query Q is generally defined as the ratio of the absolute error over the selectivity of the query. Since in our case a query can be empty, we follow [35] in defining the relative error as the ratio of the absolute error over the maximum of the selectivity of Q and 1:

$$\epsilon_{rel}(Q, R, f) = \frac{|sel(R, Q) - n \, sel(f, Q)|}{\max(1, sel(R, Q))}.$$

To represent the error of a set of queries, we define the *p-norm average error*. Given a query workload $\{Q_1, \ldots, Q_k\}$ comprising of k queries, R, f, and an error metric ϵ that can be any of the above, the p-norm average error for this workload is:

$$\| \epsilon \|_p = (\frac{1}{k} \sum_{1 \leq i \leq k} \epsilon(Q_i, R, f)^p)^{\frac{1}{p}}.$$

We can also define different aggregate queries such as the sum on one attribute:

$$sum(R, Q, i) = \sum_{(x_1, \ldots, x_d) \in R \cap Q} x_i,$$

or the average

$$ave(R, Q, i) = \frac{\sum_{(x_1, \ldots, x_d) \in R \cap Q} x_i}{sel(R, Q)}$$

Following [31], we can approximate such a query using the density estimator f:

$$sum(f, Q, x_i) = \int_Q x_i f(x_1, \ldots, x_d) dx_1 \ldots dx_d.$$

3 Multi-Dimensional Density Estimators

In this section we briefly examine existing techniques to estimate the selectivity of a query. We group them into histograms (one- and multi-dimensional), discrete decomposition techniques, and statistical estimators.

3.1 One-Dimensional Histograms.

In system R [30], density estimators for each attribute are combined under the attribute independence assumption to produce a multi-dimensional density estimator. To estimate the selectivity of a multi-dimensional query as a fraction of the size of relation R, first the query is projected on each attribute and the selectivity of each one-dimensional query is estimated, and then the selectivities are multiplied. Typically one-dimensional histograms are used. This technique is still widely employed.

3.2 Multi-Dimensional Histograms.

Multi dimensional histograms were introduced in [24]. Multi dimensional histograms attempt to partition the data space into b non-overlapping buckets. In each bucket, the data distribution is assumed to be uniform [3, 17, 26, 33] or it can be approximated using parametric curve fitting techniques [19, 20].

[27] presents two new algorithms, PHASED and MHIST-2, the second being an "adaptive" version of the first. In PHASED, the order in which the dimensions are to be split is decided only once at the beginning and arbitrarily; in MHIST-2, at each step, the most "critical" attribute is chosen for partition. For a MaxDiff histogram, at each step, MHIST-2 finds the attribute with the largest difference in source values (e.g., spread, frequency, or area) between adjacent values, and places a bucket boundary between those values. Therefore, when frequency is used as a source parameter, the resulting MaxDiff histogram approximates the minimization of the variance of

values' frequencies within each bucket. Of the two techniques, MHIST-2 is shown to be more accurate and performs better than previous approaches [27].

Another very interesting alternative to multi dimensional histograms is the self-tuning histograms (STH) recently presented in [1]. However ST-histograms are less accurate than MHIST-2 for high dimensions and skewed data [1].

3.3 Discrete Decomposition Techniques

The d dimensional data distribution of a dataset R with attributes $A_1, \ldots A_d$ can be represented by a d dimensional array D with $\prod_{1 \leq i \leq d} |V_i|$ slots (recall that V_i is the set of distinct values of attribute A_i). The value in each slot is the number of times this value combination appears in R.

One approach to find an approximation of the joint data distribution is to approximate the array D directly. A number of decomposition techniques have been proposed in the literature to find such an approximation. These include the Singular Value Decomposition (SVD) [27], the wavelet transform [35], and recently the Discrete Cosine Transform (DCT) [22].

These techniques compute the transformation and keep the b most important coefficients, for a given input parameter b. The remaining coefficients are set to zero. This results in an array D'' with b non zero values (so we need $O(b)$ space to store it). To estimate a value of D we compute the inverse transformation on D''.

Of the three techniques we mentioned, SVD can only be used in two dimensions ([27]). Wavelets and, recently, DCT have been shown to give good results in high dimensionalities [35, 23, 22, 34]. In our comparisons we include the wavelet transform.

If the attributes have real values, the size of the array D can be n^d, where n is the size of R. Since each of these approaches involves operations on the array D, we cannot use the raw data, and therefore we perform a ξ *regular partitioning* of the data space first. Hence, we partition the domain of each attribute into ξ non-overlapping intervals. The width of each interval is $1/\xi$, so that we obtain an equi-width partitioning, resulting into ξ^d d-dimensional non-overlapping buckets that cover the entire data space. We denote the resulting ξ^d size array with D_ξ.

We can compute the wavelet decomposition of either D_ξ or the partial sum array D_ξ^s of D_ξ. In the partial sum the value of a array slot is replaced by the sum of all preceding slots:

$$D_\xi^s[i_1, \ldots, i_d] = \sum_{j_1 \leq i_1, \ldots, j_d \leq i_d} D_\xi[j_1, \ldots, j_d].$$

We ran experiments to determine which of the two methods should be used. The results indicate that wavelets on the partial sum array provide a more accurate approximation for our datasets. Also [35] suggests that partial sum method is more accurate because this operation smoothes up the data distribution.

3.4 Statistical Estimators

The simplest statistical method for selectivity estimation is sampling. One finds a random subset S of size b of the tuples in R. Given a query Q, the selectivity $sel(S, Q)$ is computed. The value $\frac{n}{b}sel(S, Q)$ is used to estimate $sel(R, Q)$. Sampling is simple and efficient, and so it is widely used for estimating the selectivity [30, 6, 10, 21, 25] or for on-line aggregation [14, 2]. Sampling can be used to estimate the selectivity of a query regardless of the dimensionality of the space, and can directly be applied to real domains.

More sophisticated kernel estimation statistical techniques [36, 7, 32] have rarely been applied in database problems.

One similar statistical technique is clustering the dataset and using a Gaussian function to model each cluster [31]. This technique can be quite accurate if the clusters themselves can be accurately modeled by multi-dimensional Gaussian functions. Even assuming that this is the case however, the technique requires clustering the dataset, a task that is much less efficient than simple sampling.

4 A New Multi-Dimensional Histogram Construction

In this section we present a new density estimation technique, GENHIST (for GENeralized HISTograms). As in other histogram algorithms, we want to produce a density estimator for a given dataset R using rectangular buckets. The important difference is that we allow the buckets to overlap.

Histogram techniques typically partition the space into buckets and assume that the data distribution inside each bucket is uniform (if uniformity within each bucket is not assumed, additional information about the data distribution must be kept, at a higher storage cost). The problem with partitioning the space into a fixed, small, number of buckets is that the volume of the space increases exponentially when the dimensionality increases, or alternatively, the number of buckets that are required to partition the space increases exponentially with the dimensionality. Even a partitioning scheme that partitions each attribute into 4 one-dimensional buckets, generates $4^5 = 1024$ 5-dimensional buckets. Since the data points become sparser in higher dimensions it is very likely that the actual data distribution deviates significantly from the uniform distribution within each of these buckets. The problem becomes severe in higher dimensions because the number of buckets a query can partially intersect increases exponentially with the dimensionality. For example, consider a ξ regular partitioning of a d dimensional space. A query that is the intersection of two $(d-1)$-dimensional hyper-planes intersects ξ^{d-1} buckets. In the 4 regular partitioning of a 5-dimensional space example above, such a query partially intersects 256 out of 1024 total buckets.

Clearly, to achieve acceptable accuracy a technique has to either ensure that the data distribution within each bucket is close to uniform, or ensure that each bucket contains a small number of points and therefore the error for each bucket is small. Note that non-overlapping partitions into b buckets allow only b different values for estimating the data density. To increase the number of values, one has to increase the number of buckets. This has conflicting results. The accuracy within each bucket becomes better, but the overall accuracy may decrease because a query can now partially intersect more buckets.

Our approach to solve this problem is to allow overlapping buckets. The intuition is the following. As in previous approaches, we assume that within each bucket the data distribution can be approximated by the average data density of the bucket. But when two buckets overlap, in their intersecting area we assume that the data density is the sum of the two densities. If more than two buckets overlap, the data density in their intersecting area will be approximated by the sum of the data densities of the overlapping buckets. Clearly, for our scheme to work, we have to be careful when we compute the average density within each bucket. In particular, if a tuple lies in the intersection of many buckets, we must count it in the computation of the average density of only one of the buckets.

A simple two dimensional example shows that we can achieve more using overlapping buckets (Fig. 1). In the example we partition $[0, 1]$ using four buckets. If the buckets are non-overlapping, this results into a partitioning into 4 regions. We have to assume that the data distribution is uniform within each region. If we use 4 overlapping buckets of the same size, we can partition $[0, 1]$ into a total of 9 regions. Although we again keep only 4 numbers, each of the 9 regions is the intersection of different buckets and its density is estimated differently. Moreover, if we use 4 rectangular buckets of different sizes, we can partition $[0, 1]$ into 13 regions, each with a different estimated density. The number of intersections increases exponentially with the dimensionality.

4.1 Heuristic for Finding Generalized Multi-Dimensional Histograms

Our heuristic approach partitions a d-dimensional space using b overlapping buckets of different sizes. The main idea of the algorithm is to iteratively compute

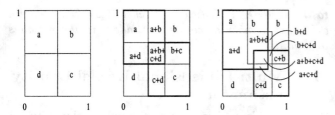

Figure 1: The same 2-dimensional space is partitioned first into 4 regions, using 4 non-overlapping buckets (average densities are a, b, c and d), then into 9 regions, using 4 overlapping equal-sized buckets (densities are a, b, c, d, a+b, b+c, c+d, d+a, a+b+c+d), and finally into 13 regions, using 4 overlapping buckets of different sizes.

an approximation of the density function using a grid. In each iteration, the algorithm tries to find and approximate the dense areas. Our approach for finding dense areas is to partition the space using a regular grid, and find which buckets have the larger average density. Buckets with high count are in areas where the density is large. However, instead of removing the entire dense buckets, we only remove enough points from each bucket so that the density of this bucket is approximately equal to its surrounding area. Tuples are removed at random to ensure that the density decreases uniformly to the level of the density of neighboring buckets.

The density of the entire dataset is now smoother, because the high bumps have been removed. In the successive iteration we have to approximate the new smoother data density in the entire data space.

Due to the overall smoothing effect, a coarser grid is used in each successive iteration. The buckets with the largest densities are kept in the estimator, along with their average density values set to the fraction of points removed from each. Clearly, buckets produced from different iterations can overlap. This ensures that the density of regions in the intersection of many buckets is correctly estimated by adding up the average densities of each one.

Thus GENHIST can be classified as a generalization of the biased histograms [28]. Biased histograms keep in singleton buckets the values with highest frequencies, and partition the remaining values in a number of buckets. Like biased histograms, GENHIST uses buckets to approximate the areas where the density is highest.

The possible bucket overlapping effectively partitions the data space into a much larger number of regions than simply the number of buckets. In this respect the technique is similar to the wavelet transform. Just as the wavelet transform provides more resolution in the areas where the variation in the frequencies is highest,

GENHIST provides more detail in the areas where more points are concentrated (the areas of higher density).

We next describe the algorithm in detail. There are three input parameters: the initial value of ξ, the number of buckets we keep at each iteration, and the value of α that controls the rate by which ξ decreases. We describe how to set these parameters after the presentation of the algorithm. The output of the algorithm is a set of buckets E along with their average densities. This set can be used as a density estimator for R. Figure 2 gives the outline of the algorithm.

Given a d-dimensional dataset R with n points and input parameters b, ξ, and α,

1. Set E to empty.

2. Compute a ξ regular partitioning of $[0, 1]^d$, and find the average density of each bucket (i.e., number of points within each bucket divided by n).

3. Find the b_ξ buckets with highest density.

4. For each bucket c of the b_ξ buckets with highest density:

   (a) Let d_c be the density of c.
   Compute the average density av_c of c's neighboring buckets.

   (b) If the density of c is larger than the average density av_c of its neighboring buckets:

      i. Remove from R a randomly chosen set of $(d_c - av_c)n$ tuples that lie in c.
      ii. Add bucket c into the set E and set its density to $d_c - av_c$.

5. Set $S = \sum_{c \in b_\xi} (d_c - av_c)n$ (S is the number of removed points).
   Set $\alpha' = \min((\frac{|R|}{|R|+S})^{\frac{1}{d}}, \alpha)$.
   Set $\xi = \lfloor \alpha' \xi \rfloor$.

6. If R is empty, return the set of buckets E.
   else if R is non empty and $\xi > 1$ return to Step 2.
   else if $\xi \leq 1$ add bucket $[0, 1]^d$ with density $\frac{|R|}{n}$ to E and output the set of buckets E.

Figure 2: The GENHIST algorithm

We use $\alpha = (1/2)^{1/d}$ to ensure that at each iteration we use roughly half as many buckets to partition the space as in the preceding operation (the new buckets have approximately twice the volume of the previous ones). Unless we remove more than half the tuples of R in each iteration, the average number of tuples per bucket increases slightly as we decrease the number of buckets. This is counterbalanced by the overall smoothing effect we achieve in each iteration. S counts the number of points we remove during an iteration. If this number is large ($\frac{|R|}{|R|+S} < \alpha^d$), we decrease ξ faster, and we do not allow the average bucket density to decrease between operations.

The number of buckets that we remove in each iteration is constant. Since ξ is replaced by $\lfloor \alpha\xi \rfloor$ in each operation, we expect to perform approximately $\log_{\frac{1}{\alpha}} \xi$ iterations, and in each iteration we keep approximately $\lceil b/\log_{\frac{1}{\alpha}} \xi \rceil$ buckets. The value of b is provided by the user.

The choice of ξ is important. If ξ is set too large, the buckets in the first iterations are practically empty. If ξ is set too low, then we lose a lot of details in the approximation of the density function. Since we have to provide b buckets, we set ξ so that in the first iteration the percentage of the points that we remove from R is at least $1/\log_{\frac{1}{\alpha}} \xi$.

4.2   Running Time

The running time of the algorithm is linear in the size of R. One pass over the data is performed each time the value of ξ changes. Since ξ is originally a small constant, the number of passes over the data is also small. In our experiments the number of passes was between 5 and 10. During each pass, to compute the number of points that fall in each bucket, we use a hashing scheme: non-empty buckets are kept in a hash table. For each point, we compute the slot it should be in and probe the hash table. If the bucket is there, we increment its counter, otherwise we insert it into the hash table.

Implementing step 4.b.i of the algorithm can slow down the process, because we have to designate that some points in the dataset are deleted, and to do so we have to modify the dataset.

The following technique allows us to estimate accurately, at each step of the algorithm, the number of remaining points that fall in each bucket, without having to write at the disk at all.

Assume that we are scanning the dataset D at the i-th iteration, and, in the previous $i-1$ iterations we have already computed a set of buckets that we will keep in the estimator. During the i-th scan of dataset D we want to determine the number of points that fall in the interior of each bucket in the grid, assuming that some points have been removed from the interior of each bucket in the estimator. For each such bucket B_j in the estimator we keep the total number dataset points that lie in its interior (let that number be $tot(B_j)$), and the number of points we would remove from B_j in step 4.b.ii (let that number be $r(B_j)$.

During the scan of D, if a point p lies in a bucket B_j that we have already included in the estimator, then, with probability $\frac{r(B_j)}{tot(B_j)}$, we do not use this point in the computation of densities of the grid buckets. The lemma follows from the discussion above.

Lemma 1 *The expected density of a bucket in the i-th iteration that is computed using this process is equal to the expected density of a bucket if we had removed the same number of points at random in the previous iteration.*

5   Multi-Dimensional Kernel Density Estimators

For the problem of computing the query selectivity, all the proposed techniques compute a density estimation function. Such function can be thought as an approximation of the probability distribution function, of which the dataset at hand is an instance. It follows that statistical techniques which approximate a probability distribution, such as kernel estimators, are applicable to address the query estimation problem. The problem of estimating an underlying data distribution has been studied extensively in statistics [29] [36].

Kernel estimation is a generalized form of sampling. The basic step is to produce a uniform random sample from the dataset. As in random sample, each sample point has weight one. In kernel estimation however, each point distributes its weight in the space around it.

A *kernel function* describes the form of the weight distribution. Generally, a kernel function distributes most of the weight of the point in the area very close the point, and tapers off smoothly to zero as the distance from the point increases. If two kernel centers are close together, there may be a considerable region where the non-zero areas of the kernel functions overlap, and both distribute their weight in this area. Therefore, a given location in the data space gets contributions from each kernel point that is close enough to this location so that its respective kernel function has a non zero value. Summing up all the kernel functions we obtain a density function for the dataset.

Let us consider the one dimensional case first. Assume that R contains tuples with one attribute A whose domain is $[0, 1]$. Let S be a random subset of R (our sample). Also assume that there is a function $k_i(x)$ for each tuple t_i in S, with the property that $\int_{[0,1]} k(x)dx = 1$. Then the function

$$f(x) = \frac{1}{n} \sum_{t_i \in S} k_i(x - t_i)$$

is an approximation of the underlying probability distribution according to which R was drawn.

To approximate the selectivity of a query Q of the form $a \leq R.A \leq b$, one has to compute the integral of the probability function f in the interval $[a, b]$:

$$\sigma(f, Q) = \int_{[a,b]} f(x) = \frac{1}{n} \sum_{t_i \in S} \int_{[a,b]} k_i(x - t_i).$$

As defined, kernel estimation is a very general technique. [29] shows that any non-parametric technique for estimating the probability distribution, including histograms, can be recast as a kernel estimation technique for appropriately chosen kernel functions.

In practice the functions $k_i(x)$ are all identical. The approximation can be simplified to

$$f(x) = \frac{1}{n} \sum_{t_i \in S} k(x - t_i).$$

To use kernels in d-dimensions we have to provide a d-dimensional kernel function.

For a dataset R, let S be a set of tuples drawn from R at random. Assume there exists a d dimensional function $k(x_1, \ldots, x_d)$, the *kernel function*, with the property that

$$\int_{[0,1]^d} k(x_1, \ldots, x_d) dx_1 \ldots dx_d = 1.$$

The approximation of the underlying probability distribution of R is

$$f(x) = \frac{1}{n} \sum_{t_i \in S} k(x_1 - t_{i_1}, \ldots, x_d - t_{i_d}),$$

and the estimation of the selectivity of a d-dimensional range query Q is

$$sel(f, Q) = \int_{[a,b]^d \cap Q} f(x_1, \ldots, x_d) =$$

$$\frac{1}{n} \sum_{t_i \in S} \int_{[a,b]^d \cap Q} k(x_1 - t_{i_1}, \ldots, x_d - t_{i_d}) dx_1 \ldots dx_d.$$

It has been shown that the shape of the kernel function does not affect the approximation substantially [7]. What is important is the standard deviation of the function, or, its bandwidth. Therefore, we choose a kernel function that it is easy to integrate. The Epanechnikov kernel function has this property [7]. The d-dimensional Epanechnikov kernel function centered at 0 is

$$k(x_1, \ldots, x_d) = (\frac{3}{4})^d \frac{1}{B_1 B_2 \ldots B_d} \prod_{1 \le i \le d} (1 - (\frac{x_i}{B_i})^2)$$

if, for all i, $|\frac{x_i}{B_i}| < 1$, and 0 otherwise. (Figure 3).

The d parameters $B_1, \ldots, B_d$ are the bandwidth of the kernel function along each of the d dimensions. The magnitude of the bandwidth controls how far from the sample point we distribute the weight of the point. As the bandwidth becomes smaller, the non-zero diameter of the kernel becomes smaller.

There are two problems that we have to solve before we can use the multi-dimensional kernel estimation method. The first is setting the bandwidth parameters and the second one is the boundary problem. Both problems have been addressed before in statistics

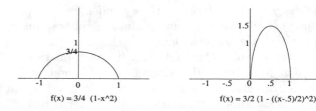

$$f(x) = 3/4 \ (1\text{-}x^\wedge 2) \qquad f(x) = 3/2 \ (1 - ((x\text{-}.5)/2)^\wedge 2)$$

Figure 3: The one-dimensional Epanechnikov kernel, with $B = 1$, centered around the origin, and, with $B = 2$, centered at 0.5.

[36]. No efficient solution exists for finding the optimal bandwidths. To get an initial estimate for the bandwidth we use Scott's rule [29] in d-dimensional space: $B_i = \sqrt{5} \ s_i \ |S|^{-\frac{1}{d+4}}$, where s_i is the standard deviation of the sample on the i-th attribute. This rule is derived using the assumption that the data distribution is a multi-dimensional normal and so it oversmoothes the function. To solve the second problem, we project the parts of the kernel function that lie outside $[0,1]^d$ back into the data space. The complexity of this projection increases with the dimensionality, because each d-dimensional corner of $[0,1]^d$ partitions $\mathcal{R}^d$ into 2^d quadrangles, and we have to find the intersection of the kernel function with each quadrangle.

5.1 Computing the Selectivity

Since the d-dimensional Epanechnikov kernel function is the product of d one-dimensional degree-2 polynomials, its integral within a rectangular region can be computed in $O(d)$ time. It follows that, for a sample of $|S|$ tuples, $sel(f, Q)$ can be computed in $O(d|S|)$ time.

5.2 Running Time

Computing a kernel density estimator with b kernels can be done in one dataset pass, during which two functions are performed:
1. Take a random sample of size b (where b is an input parameter.
2. Compute an approximation of the standard deviation for each attribute.

Therefore, the cost of computing a kernel estimator is comparable to the cost of finding a random sample. Moreover, for the dimensionalities we tried in our experimental study, it is always better to use a multi-dimensional kernel estimator rather that random sampling for selectivity estimation.

6 Experimental Results

In our experiments we compare the behavior of the different selectivity estimation on synthetic and real-life datasets with real valued attributes. There are three issues we want to address through the experiments.

First, one characteristic of the applications we have in mind (GIS, temporal and multimedia applications) is that attributes are also highly correlated. For example the precipitation and humidity readings in climatic data are definitely correlated attributes. Therefore, we create synthetic datasets that experienced significant correlations among attributes. In addition, our real-life datasets (Forest Cover and multimedia data) also have correlations among attributes.

Second, we want to evaluate the accuracy of the various methods as the dimensionality increases. We thus try datasets with 3, 4 and 5 dimensions. Interestingly, at 5 dimensions, accuracy dropped significantly for all methods in the correlated datasets we experimented with.

Third, we want to examine the behavior of the various methods when additional space for storing the estimator is available (in particular, how the accuracy of the approximation is affected by the extra space).

6.1 Techniques.

We compare the new techniques (GENHIST and multidimensional kernels) with the following existing techniques: random sampling, one-dimensional estimation with the attribute independence assumption, wavelet transform, and MHIST-2. Random sampling is a simple and widely used technique. In particular, we compare sampling against kernels, to measure the improvement we gain using kernels. We use the Attribute Value Independence (AVI) assumption as a baseline. We also consider the wavelet transform, since Vitter et al. [35] show that wavelets perform well for discrete valued attributes. Finally, we consider MHIST-2, as the current state of the art representative of multi-dimensional histogram approaches for density estimation.

6.2 Synthetic Datasets

We generate 3, 4, and 5 dimensional datasets with many clusters positioned in random locations in space. This produces significant correlations between the attributes (the attribute independence assumption does not work). In addition, the distribution is non-uniform in each attribute. We used 2 synthetic data generators:

Dataset Generator 1 creates clustered datasets (called Type 1). The number of clusters is a parameter, set to 100 in our experiments. Each cluster is defined as a hyper-rectangle, and the points in the interior of the cluster are uniformly distributed. The clusters are randomly distributed. They can overlap and create more complicated terrains. Datasets of Type 1 contain 10% to 20% uniformly distributed error.

Dataset Generator 2 is similar to the previous one, but the clusters we generate are in the $(d-1)$ or $(d-2)$-dimensional subspaces. This means that in datasets of Type 2 the d-way correlation is small. All datasets include 10^6 points.

6.3 Real Datasets

We use the Forest Cover Dataset from the UCI KDD archive[1]. This was obtained from the US Forest Service (USFS). It includes 590000 points, and each point has 54 attributes, 10 of which are numerical. We use subsets of three, four or five numerical attributes for our experiments (the projected datasets have the same number of points with the original). In this dataset the distribution of the attributes is non-uniform, and there are correlations between pairs of attributes. We have also used multimedia datasets which have shown similar results and therefore are not reported for brevity.

6.4 Query Workloads

To evaluate the techniques we created workloads of 3 types of queries. For each dataset we create a workload 1 of random queries with selectivity approximately 10%, and a workload 2, of random queries with selectivity approximately 1%. These workloads comprise 10^4 queries each. We also create a workload 3 of 20000 queries of the form $(R.A_1 < a_1) \wedge \ldots \wedge (R.A_d < a_d)$ for a randomly chosen point $(a_1, \ldots, a_d) \in [0,1]^d$.

For each workload we compute the average relative $\| e_{rel} \|_1$ error (experiments with other error metrics appear in [12]).

6.5 Experimental Comparison of the Accuracy of Different Methods

We implemented GENHIST algorithm as described in Section 4, using a main memory hash table, to maintain statistics for every bucket. In our implementation we only consider buckets that contain more than 0.1% of the remaining points. We vary the initial value of ξ between 16 and 20. For a given value of ξ, we can use only two numbers to store a bucket. We use one number to store the location of each bucket, and another one to keep the number of tuples in the bucket.

To implement the wavelets method we followed the approach presented in [35]. We used the Haar wavelets as our wavelet basis functions. In the first step we perform a ξ regular partitioning of the data space with ξ equal to 32, and then we compute the partial sum array D_ξ^s. We perform an one-dimensional wavelets transform on the first dimension and we replace the original values with the resulting coefficients. Then we do the same for the second dimension, treating the modified array as the original array, and we continue up to d dimensions. We perform thresholding after normalization, that is, first we weight the wavelets coefficients, and then we keep the C most important among them (with largest absolute value). To store a coefficient we used two numbers, one to store the bucket number and the other one to store its value. We run experiments both using partial sums and using

---

[1]available from kdd.ics.uci.edu/summary.data.type.html

the original array. Our datasets are not sparse, and the partial sum method performed better. Therefore, we report the partial sum results only. We obtained the code for wavelets from [15].

We ran MHIST-2, using the binary code provided by the authors [27]. We used MaxDiff as partition constraint, the attribute values as sort parameter, and frequency as source parameter in our experiments. We also tested the Area as source parameter, and obtained slightly worse results than for frequency. Therefore, we report the results obtained for frequency.

For the kernels method we used the Epanechnikov product kernel. We select a bandwidth using the Scott's rule [29]. The storage requirements of this method is the same as sampling. That is, we store for each sample the value of each attribute (thus for 5 dimensions we used $5t$ numbers to store t samples). The results we present in experiments for kernel and sampling are averages for five different runs with randomly chosen sample sets.

Finally, we used the Attribute Value Independence (AVI) assumption as a baseline. We did not use any particular method to keep statistics for each attribute separately, but we computed the selectivity of every query in each dimension exactly. Thus the results presented here are the optimal results for this method.

We performed an extensive study to evaluate the performance of different methods for 3-, 4-, and 5-dimensional data. For 3-dimensional datasets there were small differences in accuracy between the techniques. Interesting changes started appearing at 4 and then 5 dimensions and are described below. For brevity we present results only for two types of 4 and 5 dimensional datasets. Results for other datasets can be found in [12]. In particular, we show results for $DS1$ and Forest Cover dataset using query workloads 1, 2 and 3 on each one.

In Figures 4-11 we show the results. We plot the 1-norm average relative error for each method for different values of the available storage space to store the estimator. In Figures 4 and 5 we present the results for the 4-dimensional datasets. Figures 6 and 7 (10% queries) show the results for the two 5-dimensional datasets for query workload 1. Similarly, Figures 8-9 show the results for query workload 2 (1% queries) and Figures 10-11 show the results for query workload 3.

The results for query workloads 1 and 2 can be used to evaluate the impact of the query size on the accuracy of the selectivity estimators. Clearly the relative error rate increases when the query size decreases. This is to be expected from the definition of the relative error. Even a small difference in absolute terms between the estimated and the actual query size can lead to a large relative error if the actual query size is small. Thus the performance of all methods decreases significantly from workloads 1 to workloads 2.

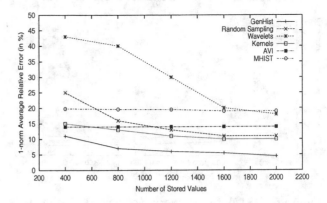

Figure 4: DS1 dataset, query workload 1, 4-dim.

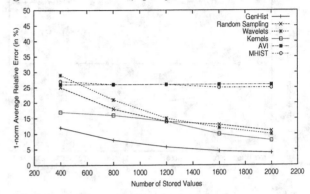

Figure 5: Forest Cover dataset, query workload 1, 4-dim.

It is clear that in 5 dimensions most methods do not offer very high accuracy, for small queries in particular. GENHIST, the most accurate of the methods we tested, offers an accuracy of 20% to 30% for queries of size 1%. In addition, the curves for all methods are rather flat, so accuracy is unlikely to increase a lot even if we allocate much more space.

However, all meaningful queries in high dimensions are likely to be small. For example, in six dimensions a range query of the form $(R.A_1 < 0.5) \wedge \ldots \wedge (R.A_6 < 0.5)$ only covers $\frac{100}{2^6}\% \approx 2\%$ of the space. We consider 5 dimensions to be close to the limit at which we can still expect an accurate estimation to the selectivity problem.

In another set of experiments we consider how the increase on the dimensionality affects the accuracy of GENHIST. In Figures 12 and 13 we plot the average relative error for GENHIST, for 3, 4 and 5 dimensions, as a function of the space used for dataset $DS1$ and workloads 1 and 3. The results, not surprisingly, show the significant degradation in the accuracy that accompanies the increase in space dimensionality.

Finally, when comparing the running times of the

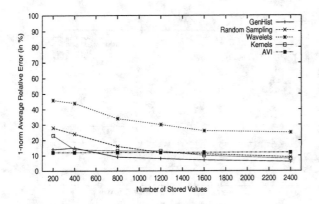

Figure 6: DS1 dataset, query workload 1, 5-dim.

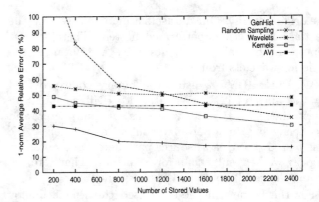

Figure 8: DS1 dataset, query workload 2, 5-dim.

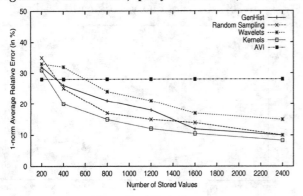

Figure 7: Forest Cover dataset, query workload 1, 5-dim.

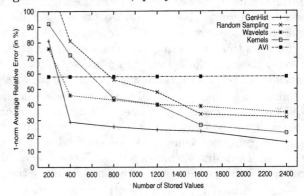

Figure 9: Forest Cover dataset, query workload 2, 5-dim.

technique, it is important to note that an important advantage of random sampling and kernels require only one pass through the data where other techniques are much slower. For example GENHIST requires 5 to 10 passes.

7   Conclusions

In this paper we have addressed the problem of estimating the selectivity of a multi-dimensional range query when the query attributes have real domains and exhibit correlations. In this environment each value appears very infrequently. Most of previous work considers only discrete-valued attributes with a small set of different values, which implies that the frequency of each value is high.

The contributions of the paper are: (1) We propose a new generalized histogram technique GENHIST to solve the problem. GENHIST differs from earlier partitioning techniques because it uses overlapping buckets of varying sizes. (2) For the same problem we generalize a kernel estimator technique to many dimensions. (3) We perform an experimental study to

evaluate and compare the GENHIST technique and the multi-dimensional kernel estimators over real attributes, with a number of existing techniques: attribute independence assumption, wavelet decomposition, MHIST-2 and sampling.

Conclusions we can draw from our experimental results include: (1) GENHIST typically outperforms other techniques in the range of space dimensionality (3 to 5) that we run experiments on. GENHIST can be thought as a multi-dimensional histogram that allows for overlapping partitioning. The experiments show that overlapping partitioning shows an improvement over non-overlapping partitioning. (2) Multi-dimensional kernel estimators offer good accuracy, and very fast construction time. The kernel estimator approach outperformed pure sampling in all our experiments. (3) For the real-valued and correlated datasets we have used, the accuracy of all techniques decreases when dimensionality increases. However some of the techniques we examine (and in particular GENHIST and the multi-dimensional kernels) can be used effectively in 5-dimensional spaces.

In future work we plan to perform experiments for

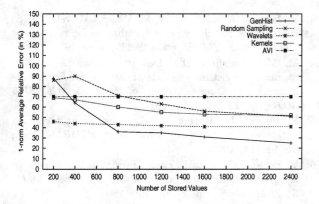

Figure 10: DS1 dataset, query workload 3, 5-dim.

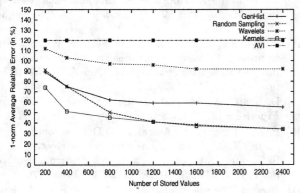

Figure 11: Forest Cover dataset, query workload 3, 5-dim.

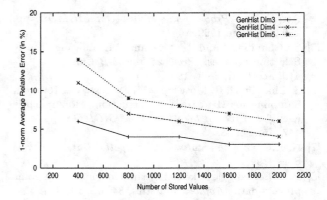

Figure 12: DS1 dataset, query workload 1, 3 to 5 dim, GENHIST.

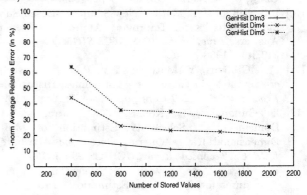

Figure 13: DS1 dataset, query workload 3, 3 to 5 dim, GENHIST.

higher dimensions. It is not clear how GENHIST, multi-dimensional histograms, wavelets and other decomposition techniques, and kernels will perform relative to each other or relative to sampling as the dimensionality increases. However we do not expect any technique to perform effectively when the dimensionality of the space approaches 10. As evidence for this, [36] reports that it is difficult to achieve good accuracy with kernel estimators when the dimensionality is larger than 5. We conjecture that sampling will outperform any of these techniques for dimensionality of around 10, but that the error will be too large to make the technique practical.

An interesting problem is to compare how the various query estimators are maintained under different update loads. Updating in random sampling can be achieved using techniques from [11]. Such techniques can be extended to apply to kernel estimators, too. Most work for maintaining histograms has concentrated on the one dimensional case [11], although recently [1] proposed a technique for maintaining multi-dimensional histograms. Maintaining GENHIST is similar to maintaining other multi-dimensional histograms: an

insertion or deletion will affect only one bucket. In particular for GENHIST if the updated point is in the interior of more than one bucket we chose to update the bucket that is the smallest in size.

8 Acknowledgement

We would like to thank Johannes Gehrke for providing the code of a dataset generator, and Vishy Poosala for providing the binary for the MHIST algorithm.

References

[1] A. Aboulnaga, S. Chaudhuri. Self-tuning Histograms: Building Histograms Without Looking at Data. *Proc. of the 1999 ACM SIGMOD*, pp. 181-192, June 1999.

[2] S. Acharya, P.B. Gibbons, V. Poosala and S. Ramaswamy. Join Synopses for Approximate Query Answering. *Proc. of the 1999 ACM SIGMOD*, pp. 275-286, June 1999.

[3] S. Acharya, V. Poosala and S. Ramaswamy. Selectivity Estimation in Spatial Databases. *Proc. of the 1999 ACM SIGMOD*, pp. 13-24, June 1999.

[4] B. Blohsfeld, D. Korus, B. Seeger. A Comparison of Selectivity Estimators for Range Queries on Metric

Attributes. *Proc. of the 1999 ACM SIGMOD*, pp. 239-250, June 1999.

[5] S. Chaudhuri and L. Gravano Evaluating Top-K Selection Queries. *Proc. 25th VLDB Conf.*, pp. 397-410, Scotland, Sept. 1999.

[6] S. Chaudhuri, R. Motwani, V.R. Narasayya. Random Sampling for Histogram Construction: How much is enough? *Proc. of the 1998 ACM SIGMOD*, pp. 436-447, June 1998.

[7] N. A.C. Cressie. *Statistics For Spatial Data*. Wiley & Sons, 1993.

[8] P.J. Digglediggle A kernel method for smoothing point process data. *Applied Statistics*, 34, pp. 138-147.

[9] D. Donjerkovic and R. Ramakrishnan. Probabilistic Optimization of Top N Queries. *Proc. 25th VLDB Conf.*, pp. 411-422, Scotland, Sept. 1999.

[10] P.B. Gibbons, Y. Matias. New Sampling-Based Summary Statistics for Improving Approximate Query Answers. *Proc. of the 1998 ACM SIGMOD*, pp. 331-342, June 1998.

[11] P.B. Gibbons, Y. Matias and V. Poosala. Fast Incremental Maintenance of Approximate Histograms. *Proc. of 23rd VLDB Conf.*, pp. 466-475, August 1997.

[12] D. Gunopulos, G. Kollios, V.J. Tsotras and C. Domeniconi. Selectivity Estimation of Multi-Dimensional Range Queries Over Real Attributes. *UCR CS Technical Report*, UCR-CS-99-02, 1999.

[13] P.J. Haas, A.N. Swami. Sequential Sampling Procedures for Query Size Estimation. *Proc. of the 1992 ACM SIGMOD*, pp. 341-350, June 1992.

[14] J.M. Hellerstein, P.J. Haas, H. Wan. Online Aggregation. *Proc. of the 1997 ACM SIGMOD*, pp. 171-182, May 1997.

[15] Imager Wavelet Library. www.cs.ubc.ca/nest/imager/contributions/bobl/wvlt/top.html

[16] Y. Ioannidis and V. Poosala. Histogram-Based Approximation of Set-Valued Query-Answers. *Proc. 25th VLDB Conf.*, pp. 174-185, Scotland, Sept. 1999.

[17] H. V. Jagadish, N. Koudas, S. Muthukrishnan, V. Poosala, K.C. Sevcik, T. Suel. Optimal Histograms with Quality Guarantees. *Proc. of 24rd VLDB Conf.*, pp. 275-286, August 1998.

[18] S. Khanna, S. Muthukrishnan, M. Patterson. On Approximating Rectangle Tiling and Packing. *Proc. of 9th SODA*, pp. 384-393, San Francisco, 1998.

[19] A. Konig and G. Weikum Combining Histograms and Parametric Curve Fitting for Feedback-Driven Query Result-size Estimation. *Proc. 25th VLDB Conf.*, pp. 423-434, Scotland, Sept. 1999.

[20] F. Korn, T. Johnson and H. Jagadish. Range Selectivity Estimation for Continuous Attributes. *Proc. of 11th SSDBMs Conf.*, pp. 244-253, July 1999.

[21] R.J. Lipton, J.F. Naughton. Practical Selectivity Estimation through Adaptive Sampling. In *Proc. of the 1990 ACM SIGMOD*, pp. 1-11, May 1990.

[22] J. Lee, D. Kim and C. Chung. Multi-dimensional Selectivity Estimation Using Compressed Histogram Information. *Proc. of the 1999 ACM SIGMOD*, pp. 205-214, June 1999.

[23] Y. Matias, J. Scott Vitter, M. Wang. Wavelet-Based Histograms for Selectivity Estimation. *Proc. of the 1998 ACM SIGMOD*, pp. 448-459, June 1998.

[24] M. Muralikrishna, D.J. DeWitt. Equi-Depth Histograms For Estimating Selectivity Factors For Multi-Dimensional Queries. *Proc. of the 1988 ACM SIGMOD*, pp. 28-36, June 1988.

[25] F. Olken, D. Rotem. Random Sampling from database Files:A Survey. *Proc. of 5th SSDBMs Conf.*, pp. 92-111, 1990.

[26] V. Poosala, V. Ganti. Fast Approximate Answers to Aggregate Queries on a Data Cube. *Proc. of 11th SSDBMs Conf.*, pp. 24-33, July 1999.

[27] V. Poosala and Y.E. Ioannidis. Selectivity Estimation Without the Attribute Value Independence Assumption. *Proc. of 23rd VLDB Conf.*, pp. 486-495, August 1997.

[28] V. Poosala, Y.E. Ioannidis, P. J. Haas, E.J. Shekita. Improved Histograms for Selectivity Estimation of Range Predicates *Proc. of the 1996 ACM SIGMOD*, pp. 294-305, May 1996.

[29] D. Scott. *Multivariate Density Estimation: Theory, Practice and Visualization*. Wiley & Sons, 1992.

[30] P.G. Selinger, M.M. Astrahan, D.D. Chamberlin, R.A. Lorie, T.G. Price. Access Path Selection in a Relational Database Management System. *Proc. of the 1979 ACM SIGMOD*, pp. 23-34, June 1979.

[31] Jayavel Shanmugasundaram, Usama Fayyad, Paul Bradley. Compressed Data Cubes for OLAP Aggregate Query Approximation on Continuous Dimensions *Proc of the 5th ACM SIGKDD Conf.*, pp. 223-232, August 1999.

[32] B.W. Silverman. Density Estimation for Statistics and Data Analysis. *Monographs on Statistics and Applied Probability*, Chapman & Hall 1986.

[33] Y. Theodoridis, T. Sellis. A Model for the Prediction of R-tree Performance. *Proc. of the 15th ACM-PODS*, pp. 161-171, 1996.

[34] J. S. Vitter and M. Wang. Approximate Computation of Multidimensional Aggregates of Sparse Data Using Wavelets. in *Proc. of the 1999 ACM SIGMOD*, pp. 193-204, June 1999.

[35] J.S. Vitter, M. Wang, B. R. Iyer. Data Cube Approximation and Histograms via Wavelets. In *Proc. of the 1998 ACM CIKM Conf.*, pp. 96-104, November 1998.

[36] M.P. Wand and M.C. Jones. Kernel Smoothing. *Monographs on Statistics and Applied Probability*, Chapman & Hall 1995.

[37] R. Webber, H.-J. Schek and S. Blott. A Quantitative Analysis and Performance Study for Similarity Search Methods in High-Dimensional Spaces. In *Proc. of 24rd VLDB Conf.*, pp. 194-205, August 1998.

Making B$^+$-Trees Cache Conscious in Main Memory

Jun Rao
Columbia University
junr@cs.columbia.edu

Kenneth A. Ross*
Columbia University
kar@cs.columbia.edu

Abstract

Previous research has shown that cache behavior is important for main memory index structures. Cache conscious index structures such as Cache Sensitive Search Trees (CSS-Trees) perform lookups much faster than binary search and T-Trees. However, CSS-Trees are designed for decision support workloads with relatively static data. Although B$^+$-Trees are more cache conscious than binary search and T-Trees, their utilization of a cache line is low since half of the space is used to store child pointers. Nevertheless, for applications that require incremental updates, traditional B$^+$-Trees perform well.

Our goal is to make B$^+$-Trees as cache conscious as CSS-Trees without increasing their update cost too much. We propose a new indexing technique called "Cache Sensitive B$^+$-Trees" (CSB$^+$-Trees). It is a variant of B$^+$-Trees that stores all the child nodes of any given node contiguously, and keeps only the address of the first child in each node. The rest of the children can be found by adding an offset to that address. Since only one child pointer is stored explicitly, the utilization of a cache line is high. CSB$^+$-Trees support incremental updates in a way similar to B$^+$-Trees.

We also introduce two variants of CSB$^+$-Trees. Segmented CSB$^+$-Trees divide the child nodes into segments. Nodes within the same segment are stored contiguously and only pointers to the beginning of each segment are stored explicitly in each node. Segmented CSB$^+$-Trees can reduce the copying cost when there is a split since only one segment needs to be moved. Full

CSB$^+$-Trees preallocate space for the full node group and thus reduce the split cost. Our performance studies show that CSB$^+$-Trees are useful for a wide range of applications.

1 Introduction

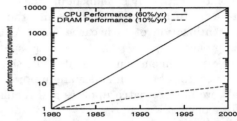

Figure 1: CPU-memory Performance Imbalance

As random access memory gets cheaper, it becomes increasingly affordable to build computers with large main memories. The recent "Asilomar Report" ([BBC$^+$98]) predicts: "Within ten years, it will be common to have a terabyte of main memory serving as a buffer pool for a hundred-terabyte database. All but the largest database tables will be resident in main memory." But main memory data processing is not as simple as increasing the buffer pool size. An important issue is cache behavior. The traditional assumption that memory references have uniform cost is no longer valid given the current speed gap between cache access and main memory access. [ADW99] studied the performance of several commercial database management systems in main memory. The conclusions they reached is that a significant portion of execution time is spent on second level data cache misses and first level instruction cache misses. Further more, CPU speeds have been increasing at a much faster rate (60% per year) than memory speeds (10% per year) as shown in Figure 1. So, improving cache behavior is going to be an imperative task in main memory data processing.

Index structures are important even in main

*This research was supported by a David and Lucile Packard Foundation Fellowship in Science and Engineering, by an NSF Young Investigator Award, by NSF grant number IIS-98-12014, and by NSF CISE award CDA-9625374.

memory database systems. Although there are no disk accesses, indexes can be used to reduce overall computation time without using too much extra space. Index structures are useful for single value selection, range queries and indexed nested loop joins. With a large amount of RAM, most of the indexes can be memory resident. In our earlier work [RR99], we studied the performance of main memory index structures and found that B^+-Trees are more cache conscious than binary search trees and T-Trees [LC86]. We proposed a new index structure called "Cache-Sensitive Search Trees" (CSS-Tree) that has even better cache behavior than a B^+-Tree. CSS-Trees augment binary search by storing a directory structure on top of the sorted list of elements. CSS-Trees avoid storing child pointers explicitly by embedding the directory structure in an array sequentially, and thus have a better utilization of each cache line. Although this approach improves the searching speed, it also makes incremental updates difficult since the relative positions between nodes are important. As a result, we have to batch updates and rebuild the CSS-Tree once in a while.

In this paper, we introduce a new index structure called the "Cache-Sensitive B^+-Tree" (CSB$^+$-Tree) that retains the good cache behavior of CSS-Trees while at the same time being able to support incremental updates. A CSB$^+$-Tree has a structure similar to a B^+-Tree. Instead of storing all the child pointers explicitly, a CSB$^+$-Tree puts all the child nodes for a given node contiguously in an array and stores only the pointer to the first child node. Other child nodes can be found by adding an offset to the first-child pointer. This approach allows good utilization of a cache line. Additionally, CSB$^+$-Trees can support incremental updates in a way similar to B^+-Trees.

CSB$^+$-Trees need to maintain the property that sibling nodes are contiguous, even in the face of updates. We call a set of sibling nodes a *node group*. There are several ways to keep node groups contiguous, all of which involve some amount of copying of nodes when there is a split. We present several variations on the CSB$^+$-Tree idea that differ in how they achieve the contiguity property. The simplest approach is to deallocate a node group and allocate a new larger node group on a split. "Segmented" CSB$^+$-Trees reduce the update cost by copying just segments of node groups. "Full" CSB$^+$-Trees pre-allocate extra space within node groups, allowing easier memory management and cheaper copying operations.

We compare the various CSB$^+$-Tree methods with B^+-Trees and CSS-Trees, both analytically and experimentally. We demonstrate that Full CSB$^+$-Trees dominate B^+-Trees in terms of both search and update times, while requiring slightly more space than B^+-Trees. Other CSB$^+$-Tree variants that take substantially less space than B^+-Trees also outperform B^+-Trees when the workload has more searches than updates.

It is now well accepted that many applications can benefit from having their data resident in a main memory database. Our results are significant for main memory database performance because index operations are frequent. Full CSB$^+$-Trees are the index structure of choice in terms of time performance for all workloads. For applications with workloads where there are more searches than updates, the other CSB$^+$-Tree variants also outperform B^+-Trees. Such applications include on-line shopping where the inventories are queried much more often than changed, and digital libraries, where the frequency of searching for an article is higher than that of adding an article.

The rest of this paper is organized as follows. In Section 2 we survey related work on cache optimization. In Section 3 we introduce our new CSB$^+$-Tree and its variants. In Section 4 we compare the different methods analytically. In Section 5 we present a detailed experimental comparison of the methods. We conclude in Section 6.

2 Related Work

2.1 Cache Memories and Cache Conscious Techniques

Cache memories are small, fast static RAM memories that improve program performance by holding recently referenced data [Smi82]. A cache can be parameterized by capacity, block (cache line) size and associativity, where capacity is the size of the cache, block size is the basic transferring unit between cache and main memory, associativity determines how many slots in the cache are potential destinations for a given address reference. Typical cache line sizes range from 32 bytes to 128 bytes.

Memory references satisfied by the cache, called hits, proceed at processor speed; those unsatisfied, called misses, incur a cache miss penalty and have to fetch the corresponding cache block from the main memory. Modern architectures typically have two levels of cache (L1 and L2) between the CPU and main memory. While the L1 cache can perform at CPU speed, the L2 cache and main memory accesses normally introduce latencies in the order of 10 and 100 cycles respectively. Cache memories can reduce the memory latency only when the requested data is found in the cache. This mainly depends on the memory access pattern of the application. Thus, unless special care is taken, memory latency will become an increasing performance bottleneck, preventing applications from fully exploiting the power of modern hardware.

Some previous work on cache conscious techniques were summarized in [RR99]. Recently, [BMK99] proposed to improve cache behavior by storing tables vertically and by using a more cache conscious join method.

2.2 Cache Optimization on Index Structures

B$^+$-Trees. We assume that the reader is familiar with the B$^+$-Tree index structure [Com79]. In [RR99] an analysis of the search time for B$^+$-Trees in a main-memory system was performed. The search times were not as good as CSS-Trees because at least half of each B$^+$-Tree node is taken up by pointers rather than keys. Compared with CSS-Trees, B$^+$-Trees utilize fewer keys per cache line, resulting in more cache accesses and more cache misses.

On the other hand, B$^+$-Trees have good incremental performance. Insertion and deletion are relatively efficient, and the requirement that nodes be half full bounds the size and depth of the tree.

In a main memory system, a cache line is the basic transferring unit (same as a page in a disk-based system). As observed in [RR99, CLH98], B$^+$-Trees with node size of a cache line have close to optimal performance.

CSS-Trees. CSS-Trees were proposed in [RR99]. They improve on B$^+$-Trees in terms of search performance because each node contains only keys, and no pointers. Child nodes are identified by performing arithmetical operations on array offsets. Compared with B$^+$-Trees, CSS-Trees utilize more keys per cache line, and thus need fewer cache accesses and fewer cache misses.

The use of arithmetic to identify children requires a rigid storage allocation policy. As argued in [RR99], this kind of policy is acceptable for static data updated in batches, typical of a decision-support database. However, there is no efficient means to update CSS-Trees incrementally; the whole index structure must be rebuilt.

Other Pointer Elimination Techniques.

[TMJ98] proposed a Pointer-less Insertion Tree (PLI-Tree). A PLI-Tree is a variant of a B$^+$-Tree. It allocates nodes in a specific order so that child nodes can be found through arithmetic calculations. As a result, PLI-Trees don't have to store child pointers explicitly. However, PLI-Trees are designed for append-only relations, such as backlogs where data is inserted in transaction timestamp order. All insertions are done in the rightmost leaf only and node splitting never occurs.

In [Ker89], the author mapped a binary search tree to an array in an unconventional way, calling the resulting structure a Virtual Tree (V-Tree). V-Trees can use a simple search procedure that uses implicit search information rather than explicit search pointers. Although V-Trees were shown to have better search performance (when the paper was published), they impose an upper bound on the size of the indices. Also, the maintenance cost starts to deteriorate when the area set aside for holding the index is nearly full.

To summarize, pointer elimination is an important technique in cache optimization since it increases the utilization of a cache line. The effect of pointer elimination depends on the relative key size. Keys of size much larger than the pointer size may reduce the impact of pointer elimination. If such is the case, we can put all distinct key values in a *domain* and store in place only the IDs as described in [RR99]. Thus, we assume that typical keys have the same size as integers. In the near future, we are going to have 64-bit operating systems. This means each pointer will be 8 bytes, instead of 4 bytes. Potentially, pointers can take more space than data. So pointer elimination will be even more important in the future. However, removing pointers completely often introduces some restrictions. For example, PLI-Trees require data to be inserted in order and CSS-Trees and V-Trees don't support incremental updates very well. As we will see shortly, we use a *partial* pointer elimination technique in CSB$^+$-Trees. By doing this, we avoid introducing new restrictions while at the same time being able to optimize cache behavior.

Finally, we don't address concurrency control and recovery in this paper. We'd like to investigate the impact of these issues on main memory indexing in the future.

3 Cache Sensitive B$^+$-Trees

Our goal is to obtain cache performance close to that of CSS-Trees, while still enabling the efficient incremental updates of B$^+$-Trees. We achieve this goal by balancing the best features of the two index structures. Our tree structure, which we call a CSB$^+$-Tree, is similar to a B$^+$-Tree in the way it handles updates. However, a CSB$^+$-Tree has fewer pointers per node than a B$^+$-Tree. By having fewer pointers per node, we have more room for keys and hence better cache performance.

We get away with fewer pointers by using a limited amount of arithmetic on array offsets, together with the pointers, to identify child nodes. For simplicity of presentation, we initially present a version of CSB$^+$-Trees in which a node contains exactly one pointer. Sometimes we simply use the term CSB$^+$-Tree to refer to this version when the context is clear. In Section 3.2 we will describe variants with more pointers per node. The number of pointers per node is a parameter that can be tuned to obtain good performance under particular workloads. We describe another variant of CSB$^+$-Trees that further reduces split cost in Section 3.3.

3.1 Cache Sensitive B$^+$-Trees with One Child Pointer

A CSB$^+$-Tree is a balanced multi-way search tree. Every node in a CSB$^+$-Tree of order d contains m keys, where $d <= m <= 2d$. A CSB$^+$-Tree puts all the child nodes of any given node into a *node group*. Nodes within a node group are stored contiguously and can be accessed using an offset to the first node in the group.[1] Each internal node in a CSB$^+$-Tree has the following structure:

nKeys   :number of keys in the node
firstChild :pointer to the first child node
keyList[2d] :a list of keys.

Each leaf node stores a list of <key, tuple ID> pairs, the number of these pairs, and two sibling pointers.[2]

Since a CSB$^+$-Tree node needs to store just one child pointer explicitly, it can store more keys per node than a B$^+$-Tree. For example, if the node size (and cache line size) is 64 bytes and a key and a child pointer each occupies 4 bytes, then a B$^+$-Tree can only hold 7 keys per node whereas a CSB$^+$-Tree can have 14 keys per node. This gives CSB$^+$-Tree two kinds of benefit: (a) a cache line can satisfy (almost) one more level of comparisons and thus the number of cache lines needed for a search is fewer; (b) the fan out of each node is larger, which means

---

[1][O'N92] also considers grouping nodes together in a disk-based B$^+$-Tree to improve I/O performance.

[2]see Section 5 for further discussion of how leaf nodes can be implemented.

it uses less space. Figure 2 shows a CSB$^+$-Tree of order 1. Each dashed box represents a node group. The arrows from the internal nodes represent the first child pointers. All the nodes within a node group are physically adjacent to each other. In this example, a node group can have no more than three nodes within it. Note that grouping is just a physical ordering property, and does not have any associated space overhead.

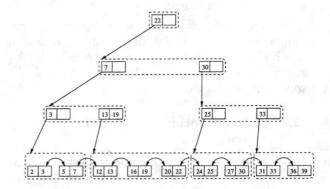

Figure 2: A CSB$^+$-Tree of Order 1

3.1.1 Operations on a CSB$^+$-Tree

In this section, we consider bulkload, search, insert and delete operations on CSB$^+$-Trees.

Bulkload. A typical bulkloading algorithm for B$^+$-Trees is to keep inserting sorted leaf entries into the rightmost path from the root. However, this method can be expensive if used for CSB$^+$-Trees since nodes in the same node group are not created sequentially. A more efficient bulkloading method for CSB$^+$-Trees is to build the index structure level by level. We allocate space for all the leaf entries. We then calculate how many nodes are needed in the higher level and then allocate a continuous chunk of space for all the nodes in this level. We then fill in the entries of nodes in the higher level by copying the largest value in each node in the lower level. We also set the first child pointer in each higher level node. We repeat the process until the higher level has only one node and this node is designated as the root. Since all the nodes in the same level are contiguous when they are created, we don't have to do any additional copying to form a node group.

Search. Searching a CSB$^+$-Tree is similar to searching a B$^+$-Tree. Once we have determined the rightmost key K in the node that is smaller than the search key, we simply add the offset of K to the first-child pointer to get the address of the child node. (For values less than or equal to the leftmost key, the offset is 0.) So, for example, if

K was the third key in the node, we would find the child using a C statement: `child = first_child + 3`, where `child` and `first_child` are pointers to nodes. There are several ways to search efficiently within a node; we defer further discussion until Section 3.1.2.

Insertion. Insertion into a CSB$^+$-Tree is also similar to that of a B$^+$-Tree. A search on the key of the new entry is performed first. Once the corresponding leaf entry is located, we determine if there is enough room in the leaf node. If there is, we simply put the new key in the leaf node. Otherwise, we have to split the leaf node.

When a leaf is split, there are two cases depending on whether the parent node has space for a new key. Suppose the parent node p has enough space. Let f be the first-child pointer in p, and let g be the node-group pointed to by f. We create a new node group g' with one more node than g. All the nodes from g are copied into g', with the node in g that was split resulting in two nodes within g'. We then update the first child pointer f in p to point to g', and de-allocate g.

A more complicated case arises when the parent node p is full and itself has to split. Again, let f be the first-child pointer in p, and let g be the node-group pointed to by f. In this case, we have to create a new node group g' and redistribute the nodes in g evenly between g and g'. Half the keys of p are transferred to a new node p', whose first-child pointer is set to g'. To achieve this split of p into p and p', the node-group containing p must be copied as in the first case above, or, if that node group is also full, we need to recursively split the parent of p. The parent node will then repeat the same process.

When there is a split, CSB$^+$-Trees have to create a new node group whereas B$^+$-Trees only need to create a new node. Thus when there are many splits, maintaining a CSB$^+$-Tree could be more expensive (we'll talk about how to reduce this cost in Section 3.2). On the other hand, CSB$^+$-Trees have the benefit of being able to locate the right leaf node faster. Potentially, we can reserve more space in a node group to reduce copying. We shall elaborate on this idea in Section 3.3.

Deletion. Deletion can be handled in a way similar to insertion. In practice, people choose to implement the deletion "lazily" by simply locating the data entry and removing it, without adjusting the tree as needed to guarantee 50% occupancy [Ram97]. The justification for lazy deletion is that files typically grow rather than shrink.

3.1.2 Searching within a Node

The most commonly used piece of code within all operations on a CSB$^+$-Tree is searching within a node. (The same is true for B$^+$-Trees.) So it's important to make this part as efficient as possible. We describe several approaches here.

The first approach, which we call the *basic* approach, is to simply do a binary search using a conventional while loop.

We can do much better than this approach through code expansion: As observed in [RR99], code expansion can improve the performance by 20% to 45%. Thus, our second approach is to unfold the while loop into `if-then-else` statements assuming all the keys are used. If we pad all the unused keys (`keyList[nKeys..2d-1]`) in a node with the largest possible key (or the largest key in the subtree rooted at this node), we are guaranteed to find the right branch. This approach avoids arithmetic on counter variables that are needed in the basic approach.

There are many possible unfoldings that are not equivalent in terms of performance. For example, consider Figure 3 that represents an unfolding of the search for a node with up to 9 keys. The number in a node in Figure 3 represents the position of the key being used in an `if` test. If only 5 keys were actually present, we could traverse this tree with exactly 3 comparisons. On the other hand, an unfolding that put the deepest subtree at the left instead of the right would need 4 comparisons on some branches. We hard code the unfolded binary search tree in such a way that the deepest level nodes are filled from right to left. Since keys in earlier positions have shorter paths, this tree favors the cases when not all the key positions are filled. We call this second approach the *uniform* approach because we use a hard-coded traversal that is uniform no matter how many keys are actually present in a node.

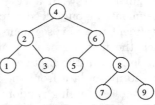

Figure 3: A Binary Search Tree with 9 Keys

The uniform approach could perform more comparisons than optimal. Consider Figure 3 again. If we knew we had only five valid keys, we could hard-code a tree that, on average, used 2.67 comparisons rather than 3. Our third approach is thus to hard-code all possible optimal search trees (ranging from

479

1 key to $2d$ keys). If we put all the hard-coded versions in an array of function pointers, we can call the correct version by indexing via the actual number of keys being used. Although this method avoids unnecessary comparisons, it introduces an extra function call, which can be expensive. Some C extensions (e.g., gcc) allow branching to a pointer variable that can be initialized via a program label. This trick allows us to inline the search code and jump to the beginning of the appropriate part and thus avoid the function call, paying just the cost of an extra array lookup and an extra jump at the end. This approach, however, increases the code size, which could be a problem when d is large. We call this approach the *variable* approach because the intra-node search method depends on the number of keys present.

3.2 Segmented Cache Sensitive B$^+$-Trees

Consider a cache-line of 128 bytes. Each node in a CSB$^+$-Tree can have a maximum of 30 keys. This means every node can have up to 31 children. A node group then has a maximum size of $31 * 128 \approx 4KB$. So every time a node split, we need to copy about 4KB of data to create a new node group. If the cache line were to get larger in future architectures, splitting a node would become more expensive.

One way to address this issue is to modify the node structure so that less copying takes place during a split. We divide the child nodes into segments and store in each node the pointers to each segment. Each segment forms a node group and only child nodes in the same segment are stored contiguously. For the sake of simplicity, we discuss only the two segment case in the rest of this section.

Our first thought is to fix the size of each segment. We start filling nodes in the first segment. Once the first segment is full, we begin to put nodes in the second segment. Now, if a new node falls in the second segment, we only need to copy nodes in the second segment to a new segment and we don't need to touch the first segment at all. However, if the new node falls in the first segment (and it's full), we have to move data from the first segment to the second one. Assuming random insertion, in the above example, the average data copied during a split will be reduced to $\frac{1}{2}(\frac{1}{2} + \frac{3}{4}) * 4KB = 2.5KB$.

Another approach is to allow each segment to have a different size. During the bulkload, we distribute the nodes evenly into the two segments. We also keep the size of each segment (actually, the size of the first segment is enough). Every time a

new node is inserted, we only create a new segment for the segment the new node belongs to. We then update the size of the corresponding segment. In this approach, exactly one segment is touched on every insert (except when the parent also needs to split, in which case we have to copy both segments). If a new node is equally likely to fall into either segment, the amount of data to be copied on a split is $\frac{1}{2} * 4KB = 2KB$. As we can see, this approach can further reduce the cost of copying. In the rest of the paper, this approach is the segmented CSB$^+$-Tree we are referring to. A segmented CSB$^+$-Tree (order 2) with two segments is shown in Figure 4 (we put only 2 keys per leaf node though).

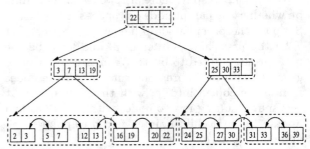

Figure 4: SCSB$^+$-Tree of Order 2 with 2 Segments

All tree operations can be supported for segmented CSB$^+$-Trees in a similar way to unsegmented CSB$^+$-Trees. However, finding the right child within each node is more expensive than the unsegmented case since now we have to find out which segment the child belongs to.

3.3 Full CSB$^+$-Trees

During a node split in a CSB$^+$-Tree, we deallocate a node group (say of size s) and allocate a node group of size $s + 1$. As a result, we pay some overhead for allocating and deallocating memory. If we were to *pre-allocate* space for a *full* node group whenever a node group is created, then we can avoid the bulk of the memory allocation calls. We need to allocate memory only when a node group (rather than a node) overflows. We call the variant of CSB$^+$-Trees that pre-allocates space for full node groups *full* CSB$^+$-Trees.

In full CSB$^+$-Trees, node splits may be cheaper than for CSB$^+$-Trees, even if one ignores the saving of the memory allocation overhead. In a CSB$^+$-Tree, when a node splits, we copy the full node group to a new one. In a full CSB$^+$-Tree, we can shift part (on average, half) of the node group along by one node, meaning we access just half the node group. Further, since the source and destination addresses for such a shift operation largely overlap,

Method	Branching Factor	Total Key Comparisons	Cache Misses	Extra Comparisons per Node
Full CSS-Trees	$m+1$	$\log_2 n$	$\frac{\log_2 n}{\log_2 (m+1)}$	0
Level CSS-Trees	m	$\log_2 n$	$\frac{\log_2 n}{\log_2 m}$	0
B^+-Trees	$\frac{m}{2}$	$\log_2 n$	$\frac{\log_2 n}{\log_2 m-1}$	0
CSB^+-Trees	$m-1$	$\log_2 n$	$\frac{\log_2 n}{\log_2 (m-1)}$	0
CSB^+-Trees (t segments)	$m-2t+1$	$\log_2 n$	$\frac{\log_2 n}{\log_2 (m-2t+1)}$	$\log_2 t$
Full CSB^+-Trees	$m-1$	$\log_2 n$	$\frac{\log_2 n}{\log_2 (m-1)}$	0

Table 1: Search Time Analysis

the number of cache lines accessed is bounded by s. In modern architectures, a cache write miss often requires loading the corresponding cache line into the cache (a read miss) first before writing the actual data. On average, full CSB^+-Trees touch $0.5s$ nodes on a split, whereas CSB^+-Trees touch $2s$ (s reads and s writes). Perfectly balanced 2-segment CSB^+-Trees and 3-segment CSB^+-Trees will touch s and $0.67s$ nodes respectively.

Thus we would expect full CSB^+-Trees to outperform CSB^+-Trees on insertions. On the other hand, pre-allocation of space means that we are using additional space to get this effect. This is a classic space/time trade-off.

4   Time and Space Analysis

In this section, we analytically compare the time performance and the space requirement for different methods. In particular, we want to compare B^+-Trees, CSS-Trees and CSB^+-Trees. To simplify the presentation, we assume that a key, a child pointer and a tuple ID all take the same amount of space K. We let n denote the number of leaf nodes being indexed, c denote the size of a cache line in bytes, and t denote the number of segments in a segmented CSB^+-Tree. The number of slots per node is denoted by m, which can be derived using $m = \frac{c}{K}$. We assume each node size is the same as the cache line size. Those parameters and their typical values are summarized in Figure 5.

Parameter	Typical Value
K	4 bytes
n	10^7
c	64 bytes
t	2
$m = \frac{c}{K}$	16

Figure 5: Parameters and Their Typical Values

Table 1 shows the branching factor, total number of key comparisons, number of cache misses and number of additional comparisons of searching for each method. B^+-Trees have a smaller branching factor than CSS-Trees since they need to store child pointers explicitly. CSB^+-Trees have a branching factor close to CSS-Trees as fewer child pointers are stored explicitly. This leads to different number of cache misses for each of the methods. The larger the branching factor of a node, the smaller the number of cache misses. For each additional segment in CSB^+-Trees, the branching factor is reduced by 2 since we have to use one slot to store child pointers and another to store the size of the additional segment. Also, when there are multiple segments in CSB^+-Trees, we need to perform additional comparisons to determine which segment the child belongs to. The numbers for B^+-Trees and CSB^+-Trees assume that all the nodes are fully used. In practice, typically a B^+-Tree node is about 70% full [Yao78] and we have to adjust the branching factor accordingly.

Method	Accessed Cache Lines in a Split	Typical Values (cache lines)
B^+-Trees	2	2
CSB^+-Trees	$(m-1)*2$	30
CSB^+-Trees (t segments)	$\frac{(m-2t+1)*2}{t}$	13
Full CSB^+-Trees	$\frac{m-1}{2}$	7.5

Table 2: Split Cost Analysis

Table 2 shows the expected number of cache lines that need to be accessed during a split. Full CSB^+-Trees have a smaller number since the source and destination overlap for copies. Note that the split cost is just part of the total insertion cost. Another part is the search cost for locating the right leaf node. The split cost is relatively independent of the depth of the tree since most of the splits happen on the leaves only. However, as the tree gets bigger, the search cost will increase in proportion to the depth of the tree. Although CSB^+-Trees have higher split cost than B^+-Trees, the total insertion cost will depend on the size of the tree.

Table 3 lists the space requirements of the various

Method	Internal Node Space	Typical Value	Leaf Node Space	Typical Value
B^+-Trees	$\dfrac{4nc}{0.7(m-2)(0.7m-2)}$	28.4 MB	$\dfrac{2nc}{0.7(m-2)}$	130.6 MB
CSB^+-Trees	$\dfrac{2nc}{0.7(m-2)(0.7m-1)}$	12.8 MB	$\dfrac{2nc}{0.7(m-2)}$	130.6 MB
CSB^+-Trees (t segments)	$\dfrac{2nc}{0.7(m-2)(0.7(m-2t)-0.3)}$	16.1 MB	$\dfrac{2nc}{0.7(m-2)}$	130.6 MB
Full CSB^+-Trees	$\dfrac{2nc}{(0.7)^2(m-2)(0.7m-1)}$	18.3 MB	$\dfrac{2nc}{(0.7)^2(m-2)}$	186.6 MB

Table 3: Space Analysis

algorithms, assuming all nodes are 70% full [Yao78]. We measure the amount of space taken by internal nodes and leaf nodes separately. We assume that each leaf node includes 2 sibling pointers. The internal space is calculated by multiplying $\frac{1}{q-1}$ (where q is the branching factor) by the leaf space. We do not include CSS-Trees in this comparison because CSS-Trees can never be "partially" full.

5 Experimental Results

We perform an experimental comparison of the algorithms on two modern platforms. The time we measured is the wall-clock time. We summarize our experiments in this section.

Experimental Setup. We ran our experiments on an Ultra Sparc II machine (296MHz, 1GB RAM) and a Pentium II (333MHz, 128M RAM) personal computer.[3] The Ultra machine has a <16k, 32B, 1> (<cache size, cache line size, associativity>) on-chip cache and a <1M, 64B, 1> secondary level cache. The PC has a <16k, 32B, 4> on-chip cache and a <512k, 32B, 4> secondary level cache. Both machines are running Solaris 2.6. We implemented all the methods including CSS-Trees, B^+-Trees, CSB^+-Trees, segmented CSB^+-Trees, and Full CSB^+-Trees in C. B^+-Trees, CSB^+-Trees, segmented CSB^+-Trees and Full CSB^+-Trees all support bulkload, search, insertion and deletion. We implemented "lazy" deletion since it's more practically used. CSS-Trees support only bulkload and search.

We choose keys to be 4-byte integers. For longer data types, we can put all distinct values in an order-preserving *domain* [Eng98] and use domain IDs as the keys. We also assume a TID and a pointer each takes four bytes. All keys are chosen randomly within the range from 1 to 10 million. The keys for various operations are generated randomly in advance to prevent the key generating time from affecting our measurements. We repeated each test three times and report the

minimal time. When there are duplicates, the leftmost match is returned as the search result.

The Ultra Sparc processors provide two counters for event measurement [Inc99]. We used *perfmon*, a tool provided by Michigan State University [Enb99], to collect certain event counts and then calculate the number of secondary level cache misses.

Implementation Details. As shown in [RR99], choosing the cache line size to be the node size is close to optimal for B^+-Trees. Thus we choose Ultra Sparc's cache line size to be the node size for all the searching methods. CSS-Trees have 16 keys per node. For B^+-Trees, each internal node consists of 7 keys, 8 child pointers, and the number of keys used. Each internal node for CSB^+-Trees consists of 14 keys, a first child pointer, and the number of keys used. Full CSB^+-Trees have the same node structure as CSB^+-Trees. We implemented segmented CSB^+-Trees with 2 segments and 3 segments. The 2-segment one has 13 keys and 2 child pointers per internal node whereas the 3-segment one has 12 keys and 3 child pointers per internal node (we use 1 byte to represent the size of each segment). For a 64-byte node size, it doesn't make sense to have more than 3 segments per node.

A leaf node in a B^+-Tree consists of 6 <key, TID> pairs, a forward and a backward pointer, and the number of entries being used. For CSB^+-Trees, all the nodes in a node group are stored contiguously. So, we don't really need to store sibling pointers for all the middle nodes in a group. For the first node and last node in a group, we need to store a forward pointer and a backward pointer respectively. As a result, we can squeeze 7 <key, TID> pairs in a leaf node. This optimization improves CSB^+-Tree's insertion performance by 10% and also reduces the amount of space needed.

For each method, we have three versions of the implementation corresponding to the basic, uniform and variable approaches described in Section 3.1.2. We use `#ifdef` in the code for the different code fragments among the versions. As a result, a lot of the code can be shared in the implementation.

During the bulkload, the higher level internal

---

[3]We omit the results for Pentium PC since they are similar to that for Ultra Sparc.

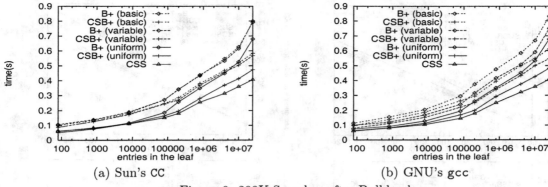

Figure 6: 200K Searches after Bulkload

nodes have to be filled with the largest keys in each subtree. We make this process more efficient by propagating the largest value in each subtree all the way up using the unused slots in each node. When building the higher level nodes, the last node could have only one child left from the lower level. In this case, we have no keys to put in the higher node. We address this problem by borrowing a key (and also the corresponding child) from the left sibling of the higher node. We implemented search and deletion iteratively to avoid unnecessary function calls. Insertion is still implemented recursively because of the difficulty of handling splits.

We implemented a simplified memory manager. Space is allocated from a large memory pool. Deallocated space is linked to a free pool. The space from the free pool could be used for other purposes although we didn't make use of it. We also didn't try to coalesce the free space since we expect this is done only occasionally and the cost is amortized.

Since cache optimization can be sensitive to compilers [SKN94], we chose two different compilers: one is Sun's native compiler CC and the other is GNU's gcc. We used the highest optimization level of both compilers. Since we can't get the address of a label in Sun's CC, we use function arrays in the variant version for Sun's compiler. For gcc, we use its C extension of "Label as Values" [Pro99] and thus can eliminate the function calls.

Our implementations are specialized for a node size of 64 bytes. We use logical shifts in place of multiplication and division whenever possible. All the nodes are aligned properly according to the cache line size. Again, this is done on all the methods we are testing.

Results. In the first experiment, we want to compare the "pure" searching performance of various methods. We vary the number of keys in the leaf nodes during bulkloading. We measure the time taken by 200,000 searches. For B^+-Trees

and CSB^+-Trees, we use all the slots in the leaf nodes and all the slots except one in the internal nodes. We tested all three versions of B^+-Trees and CSB^+-Trees. Figure 6(a) and 6(b) show the result using Sun's CC and gcc respectively. CSS-Trees are the fastest. Besides having a larger branching factor, CSS-Trees can put 8 <key, TID> pairs in the leaf nodes since it assumes the leaves are kept in a sorted array. CSB^+-Trees perform slightly worse than CSS-Trees. B^+-Trees are more than 25% slower than CSB^+-Trees. Among the three versions we tested, the uniform approach performs the best for both compilers. The variable approach using Sun's CC is actually a little bit worse than the basic one. This is because of the overhead introduced by functions calls. When function call overhead is removed, as shown in Figure 6(b), the variable version performs better than the basic one. However, the variable version is still worse than the uniform version. There are two reasons. First, there is an extra jump instruction in the variable version. Second, when the nodes are almost full, the variable version uses almost the same number of comparisons as the uniform version. Since the pattern among the versions is the same across all tests, we only present the result of the uniform version (using Sun's CC) in the remaining sections.

In our next experiment, we test the individual performance of search, insertion and deletion when the index structure stabilizes. To simulate that, we first bulkload 0.4 million entries followed by inserting 3.6 million new entries. We then perform up to 200,000 operations of each kind and measure their time. Figure 7 shows the elapsed time and the number of secondary level of cache misses.

For searching, CSB^+-Trees perform better than B^+-Trees as expected. CSB^+-Trees better utilize each cache line and thus have fewer cache misses than B^+-Trees as verified by our cache measurement. The larger the number of searches, the wider

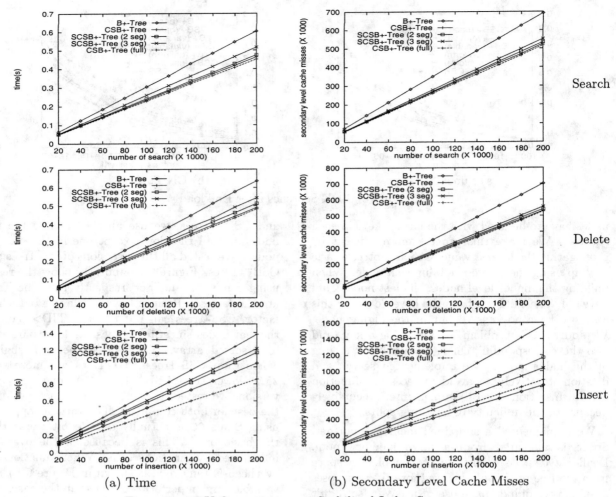

(a) Time   (b) Secondary Level Cache Misses

Figure 7: 200K Operations on a Stabilized Index Structure

the gap between the two. Segmented CSB⁺-Trees fall between CSB⁺-Trees and B⁺-Trees. There are two reasons why segmented CSB⁺-Trees search slower than CSB⁺-Trees. First, the branching factor for segmented CSB⁺-Trees is less since we have to record additional child pointers. This causes segmented CSB⁺-Trees to have slightly more cache misses than CSB⁺-Trees. Second, extra comparisons are needed to choose the right segment during tree traversal. Nevertheless, 2-segment CSB⁺-Trees perform almost as well as CSB⁺-Trees. Full CSB⁺-Trees perform a little bit better than CSB⁺-Trees and have fewer cache misses. We suspect this is because the nodes in full CSB⁺-Trees are aligned in a way that reduces the number of conflict cache misses. Unfortunately, we can't distinguish between a conflict miss and a capacity miss using the current counter events.

The delete graph is very similar to that of search. This is because in "lazy" deletion, most of the time is spent on locating the correct entry in the leaf.

Delete takes a little bit more time than search since we may have to walk through several leaf nodes to find the entry to be deleted.

CSB⁺-Trees are worse than B⁺-Trees for insertion. The insertion cost has two parts, one is the search cost and the other is the split cost. The split cost of CSB⁺-Trees includes copying a complete node group, whereas that of B⁺-Trees is creating a single new node. In our test, we observe there are about 50,000 splits (one every four inserts).[4] As a result, CSB⁺-Trees take more time to insert than B⁺-Trees. Segmented CSB⁺-Trees reduce the split cost. Now the copying unit is a segment. When nodes are relatively evenly distributed across segments, the copying cost is reduced. That's why we see 2-segment CSB⁺-Tree performing better than CSB⁺-Trees. The 3-segment CSB⁺-Tree is no better than the 2-segment one. The reason is that it's hard to distribute fewer than 12 keys

---

[4]This is consistent with the estimate of the average number of splits per insertion ($\frac{1}{1.386d}$) in [Wri85].

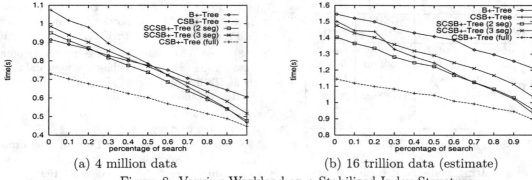

| (a) 4 million data | (b) 16 trillion data (estimate) |

Figure 8: Varying Workload on a Stabilized Index Structure

evenly among 3 segments. Large segments take more time to copy and are more likely to be selected for insertion. Additionally, more segments means extra comparisons during the search. An important issue is that while the split cost is relatively fixed (since most of the splits are on the leaves), the search cost depends on the size of the tree. The larger the data set, the higher the search cost. So the insertion cost will be different (favoring CSB$^+$-Trees) when the indexed data is much larger.

Full CSB$^+$-Trees perform insertion much faster than CSB$^+$-Trees. This observation was predicted in Section 3.3. What's even more interesting is that full CSS-Trees are even better than B$^+$-Trees on insert. The number of cache misses doesn't explain the difference since full CSB$^+$-Trees have more cache misses. It's likely that the explanation is that the allocation overhead for full CSB$^+$-Trees is lower. B$^+$-Trees have to allocate a new node on every split while full CSB$^+$-Trees make an allocation only when a node group is full.

Our last experiment tests the overall performance of all the methods. We first build the same stabilized tree as in the previous experiment and then perform 200,000 operations on it. We vary the percentage of searches and fix the ratio between inserts and deletes to be 2:1. The result is shown in Figure 8(a). Full CSB$^+$-Trees perform the best across the board. However, it uses somewhat more space than other methods. At the left end, B$^+$-Trees perform better than all but Full CSB$^+$-Trees. As more and more searches are performed, the cost of all the CSB$^+$-Trees decreases much faster than B$^+$-Trees. CSB$^+$-Tree starts to perform better than B$^+$-Tree when more than 45% of the operations are searches. 2-segment CSB$^+$-Tree is better than both CSB$^+$-Tree and B$^+$-Tree when the percentage of searches is between 25% and 90%.

To see how the cost of the methods scales with data size, we estimate the cost of all the methods under a much larger data set. The search cost

increases in proportion to the data size, while the split cost remains roughly the same. We separate the time in Figure 8(a) into two parts: search and split. We then scale the search time proportionally and combine it with the unchanged split time. Figure 8(b) shows the result when the search cost is doubled (corresponding to 16 Trillion of leaf entries). As we can see, all variants of CSB$^+$-Trees win across the board. Note that we're not claiming that trillions of data items is realistic for main memory in the near future. The point of Figure 8(b) is to show the limiting behavior, and to illustrate that as the data gets bigger, the performance of the various CSB$^+$-Trees improves relative to B$^+$-Trees due to the increased dependence of overall performance on search time.

5.1 Summary

Full CSB$^+$-Trees are better than B$^+$-Tree in all aspects except for space. When space overhead is not a big concern, Full CSB$^+$-Tree is the best choice. When space is limited, CSB$^+$-Trees and segmented CSB$^+$-Trees provide faster searches while still able to support incremental updates. Many applications, such as online shopping and digital libraries that we described in Section 1, have many more searches than updates (inserts, to be more accurate). For those applications, CSB$^+$-Trees and segmented CSB$^+$-Trees are much better than B$^+$-Trees. Depending on the workload, either of the CSB$^+$-Tree variants could be the best. We summarize the results in Table 4. Note that the ratings in the table are qualitative relative judgments. The precise numerical values for relative performance can be found in the previous section.

Our experiments are performed for 4-byte keys and 4-byte child pointers. Theoretically, B$^+$-Trees will have 30% more cache misses than CSB$^+$-Trees. As we have seen, our implementation of CSB$^+$-Trees has achieved most of the benefit. In the

	B$^+$	CSB$^+$	SCSB$^+$	Full CSB$^+$
Search	slower	faster	medium	faster
Update	faster	slower	medium	faster
Space	medium	lower	lower	higher
Memory Management Overhead	medium	higher	higher	lower

Table 4: Feature Comparison

next generation operating systems, if both the key size and the pointer size double (assuming the same cache line size), B$^+$-Trees will have 50% more cache misses than CSB$^+$-Trees and we'd expect more significant improvement by using CSB$^+$-Trees.

We close the presentation of the experiments by noting that many of the performance graphs are architecture dependent. Changes in compiler optimization methods or in architectural parameters may affect the relative performance of the algorithms. Nevertheless, the fundamental reason why the various CSB$^+$-Trees win is that they are *cache sensitive*, getting better utilization of each cache line. We expect cache sensitivity to be even more critical as CPU speeds continue to accelerate much faster than RAM speeds.

6   Conclusion

In this paper, we proposed a new index structure called a CSB$^+$-Tree. CSB$^+$-Trees are obtained by applying partial pointer elimination to B$^+$-Trees. CSB$^+$-Trees utilize more keys per cache line, and are thus more cache conscious than B$^+$-Trees. Unlike a CSS-Tree, which requires batch updates, a CSB$^+$-Tree is a general index structure that supports efficient incremental updates. Our analytical and experimental results show that CSB$^+$-Trees provide much better performance than B$^+$-Trees in main memory because of the better cache behavior. As the gap between CPU and memory speed is widening, CSB$^+$-Trees should be considered as a replacement for B$^+$-Trees in main memory databases. Last but not least, partial pointer elimination is a general technique and can be applied to other in-memory structures to improve their cache behavior.

References

[ADW99] Anastassia Ailamaki, et al. DBMSs on a modern processor: Where does time go. In *Proceedings of the 25th VLDB Conference*, 1999.

[BBC$^+$98] Phil Bernstein, et al. The Asilomar report on database research. *Sigmod Record*, 27(4), 1998.

[BMK99] Peter A. Boncz, et al. Database architecture optimized for the new bottleneck: Memory access. In *Proceedings of the 25th VLDB Conference*, 1999.

[CLH98] Trishul M. Chilimbi, et al. Improving pointer-based codes through cache-conscious data placement. Technical report 98, University of Wisconsin-Madison, Computer Science Department.

[Com79] D. Comer. The ubiquitous B-tree. *ACM Computing Surverys*, 11(2), 1979.

[Enb99] Richard Enbody. Permon performance monitoring tool (available from http://www.cps.msu.edu/~enbody/perfmon.html). 1999.

[Eng98] InfoCharger Engine. Optimization for decision support solutions (available from http://www.tandem.com/prod_des/ifchegpd/ifchegpd.htm). 1998.

[HP96] J. L. Hennessy and D. A. Patterson. *Computer Architecture: a quantitative approach*. Morgan Kaufman, San Francisco, CA, 2 edition, 1996.

[Inc99] Sun Microsystems Inc. Ultra sparc user's manual (available from http://www.sun.com/microelectronics/manuals/ultrasparc/802-7220-02.pdf as of oct. 16, 1999). 1999.

[Ker89] Martin L. Kersten. Using logarithmic code-expansion to speedup index access and maintenance. In *Proceedings of 3rd FODO Conference*, pages 228–232, 1989.

[LC86] Tobin J. Lehman, et al. A study of index structures for main memory database management systems. In *Proceedings of the 12th VLDB Conference*, 1986.

[O'N92] Patrick E. O'Neil. The SB-tree: An index-sequential structure for high-performance sequential access. *Acta Informatica*, 29(3):241–265, 1992.

[Pro99] GNU Project. Gun c compiler manual (available from http://www.gnu.org/software/gcc/onlinedocs/gcc_toc.html as of oct. 16, 1999). 1999.

[Ram97] Raghu Ramakrishnan. *Database Management Systems*. McGraw-Hill, 1997.

[RR99] Jun Rao and Kenneth A. Ross. Cache conscious indexing for decision-support in main memory. In *Proceedings of the 25th VLDB Conference*, 1999.

[SKN94] Ambuj Shatdal, et al. Cache conscious algorithms for relational query processing. In *Proceedings of the 20th VLDB Conference*, 1994.

[Smi82] Alan J. Smith. Cache memories. *ACM Computing Surverys*, 14(3):473–530, 1982.

[TMJ98] Kristian Torp, et al. Efficient differential timeslice computation. *IEEE Transactions on knowledge and data engineering*, 10(4), 1998.

[Wri85] William Wright. Some average performance measures for the B-tree. *Acta Informatica*, 21:541–557, 1985.

[Yao78] Andrew Yao. On random 2-3 trees. *Acta Informatica*, 9:159–170, 1978.

Congressional Samples for Approximate Answering of Group-By Queries

Swarup Acharya   Phillip B. Gibbons   Viswanath Poosala

Information Sciences Research Center

Bell Laboratories

600 Mountain Avenue

Murray Hill NJ 07974

{swarup,gibbons,poosala}@research.bell-labs.com

Abstract

In large data warehousing environments, it is often advantageous to provide fast, approximate answers to complex decision support queries using precomputed summary statistics, such as samples. Decision support queries routinely segment the data into groups and then aggregate the information in each group (*group-by* queries). Depending on the data, there can be a wide disparity between the number of data items in each group. As a result, approximate answers based on uniform random samples of the data can result in poor accuracy for groups with very few data items, since such groups will be represented in the sample by very few (often zero) tuples.

In this paper, we propose a general class of techniques for obtaining fast, highly-accurate answers for group-by queries. These techniques rely on precomputed non-uniform (biased) samples of the data. In particular, we propose *congressional samples*, a hybrid union of uniform and biased samples. Given a fixed amount of space, congressional samples seek to maximize the accuracy for all possible group-by queries on a set of columns. We present a one pass algorithm for constructing a congressional sample and use this technique to also incrementally maintain the sample up-to-date without accessing the base relation. We also evaluate query rewriting strategies for providing approximate answers from congressional samples. Finally, we conduct an extensive set of experiments on the TPC-D database, which demonstrates the efficacy of the techniques proposed.

1   Introduction

The last few years have seen a tremendous growth in the popularity of decision support applications using large-scale databases. These applications, also known as *on-line analytical processing* (OLAP) applications, analyze historical data in a data warehouse to identify trends that can be exploited in defining new business strategies. Often, this process involves posing several complex queries over

a massive database.[1] As a result, these queries can take minutes, and sometimes hours, to execute using even the state-of-the-art in data warehousing and OLAP technology.

A novel approach to address this problem, which has been receiving attention lately, is to provide *approximate answers* to the queries very quickly [HHW97, AGPR99, VW99, IP99]. This approach is particularly attractive for large-scale and exploratory applications such as OLAP. For example, a typical decision making process involves posing several preliminary queries to identify interesting regions of the data. For these queries, precise answers are often not essential. Similarly, for queries returning numerical results, the full precision of an exact answer may be overkill — the user may welcome an answer with just a few significant digits (e.g., the leading few digits of a total in the millions) if it is produced much faster. These approximate query answering systems give fast responses by running the queries on some form of summary statistics of the database, such as samples, wavelets and histograms. Additionally, the approximate answers are often supplemented with a statistical error bound to indicate the quality of the approximation to the user.[2] Because these statistics are typically much smaller in size, the query is processed very quickly. The statistics may either be generated on-the-fly after the query is posed, as in the *Online Aggregation* approach [HHW97], or may be precomputed *a priori*, as in the Aqua system [AGPR99] we have developed.

A popular technique for summarizing data is taking *samples* of the original data. In fact, this is the fundamental technique used by both the above-mentioned approaches to approximate query answering. In particular, *uniform random sampling*, in which every item in the original data set has the same probability of being sampled, is used because it mirrors the original data distribution. Also, by increasing the sample size, the system can provide more accurate responses to the user. Due to the usefulness of uniform samples, commercial DBMSs such as Oracle 8i are already supporting operators to collect uniform samples.

1.1   Limitations of Uniform Sampling

While uniform random samples provide highly-accurate answers for many classes of queries, there are important classes of queries for which they are less effective. This includes one of the most commonly occurring scenarios in

---

[1] A survey by the Data Warehousing Institute indicates that the average warehouse size is expected to exceed 400GB in the year 2000 and that a single decision process may involve more than ten fairly complex queries.

[2] In our discussion, *user* refers to the end-user analyzing the data in the warehouse.

decision support applications is to segment the data into groups and derive some aggregate information for these groups. This is typically done in SQL using the *group by* operation and hence we refer to them as group-by queries. For example, a group-by query on the U.S. census database containing information about every individual in the nation could be used to determine the per capita income *per state*. Often, there can be a huge discrepancy in the sizes of different groups, e.g., the state of California has nearly 70 times the population of Wyoming. As a result, a uniform random sample of the relation will contain disproportionately fewer tuples from the smaller groups (states), which leads to poor accuracy for answers on those groups because accuracy is highly dependent on the number of sample tuples that belong to that group [HHW97, AGPR99].[3] This behavior often renders the answer essentially useless to the analyst, who is interested in reliable answers for *all* groups. For example, a marketing analyst using the Census database to identify *all* states with per capita incomes above some value will not find the answer useful if the aggregates for some of the states are highly erroneous.

In fact, the inability of uniform random samples to provide accurate group-by results is a symptom of a more general problem with uniform random samples: *they are most appropriate only when the utility of the data to the user mirrors the data distribution*. Thus, when the utility of a subset of the data to the user is significantly higher relative to its size, the accuracy of the answer may not meet the user's expectation. The group-by query is one such case where a smaller group is often as important to the user as the larger groups, even though it is underrepresented in the data. A multi-table query is another example: a small subset of the data in a table may dominate the query result if it joins with many tuples in other tables [AGPR99, CMN99, HH99]. The flip side of this scenario is when different logical parts of the data have equal representation, but their utility to the user is skewed. This occurs, for example, in most data warehouses where the usefulness of data degrades with time. For example, consider a business warehouse application analyzing the transactional data in the warehouse to evaluate a market for a new line of products. In this case, data from the previous year is far more important than outdated data from a decade ago. Moreover, the user is likely to ask more finer-grained queries over the more recent data. This, in turn, means that the approximate answering system has to collect more samples from the recent data, which is not achieved with a uniform random sample over the entire warehouse.[4]

To address these inadequacies of uniform random samples, we consider non-uniform (i.e., *biased*) samples in this paper, which are discussed next.

1.2 Biased Sampling for Group-by Queries

In this paper, we propose a general class of techniques for obtaining fast, highly-accurate answers for group-by queries using (precomputed) biased samples of the data. We focus on group-by queries because they are among the most important class of queries in OLAP, forming an essential part of the common *drill-down* and *roll-up* processes [Kim96, CD97]. For example, of the 22 queries in Version 2.0 of the TPC-D benchmark [TPC99], 15 are group-by

queries. Our solutions, however, are more general and can be applied to a much broader set of problems wherever the limitations of uniform random samples become critical. Briefly, our techniques involve taking group-sizes into consideration while sampling, in order to provide highly-accurate answers to queries with arbitrary group-by operations (even none) and varying group-sizes. Our solutions apply and extend known techniques for subpopulation/domain/species sampling [Coc77] to the approximate answering of group-by queries. Our key extensions include considering combinations of group-by columns, construction and incremental maintenance, query rewriting, and optimizing over a query mix.

There are a number of factors affecting the quality of an answer computed from a sample, including the query, the data distribution, and the sample size. Of these, sample size is the most universal in improving answer quality across a wide range of queries and data distributions. Thus we focus in this paper on ensuring that all groups are well-represented in the sample. We consider single table queries; however, our techniques can be immediately extended to queries with foreign key joins, the most common type of joins (e.g., all joins in the TPC-D benchmark are on foreign keys), using the techniques in [AGPR99].

The techniques in this paper are tailored to *precomputed* or *materialized* samples, such as used in Aqua (see Section 2). Advantages of precomputing over sampling at query time include (1) queries can be answered quickly without accessing the original data at query time, (2) sampled tuples can be stored compactly in a few disk blocks, avoiding the overheads of random scanning, (3) no changes are needed to the DBMS's query processor and optimizer, and (4) data outliers such as small groups can be detected and incorporated into the sample. On the other hand, precomputed samples must commit to the sample before seeing the query, and are not well suited to supporting user-controlled progressive refinement [HHW97].

Our contributions are as follows:

- We introduce a hybrid union of biased and uniform samples called *congressional samples*[5], which provide statistically unbiased answers to queries with arbitrary group-by (including no group-bys), with significantly higher accuracy guarantees than uniform samples. Given a fixed amount of space, congressional samples seek to maximize the accuracy for all possible group-by queries on a set of columns. We also propose efficient strategies for executing queries on these samples.

- We develop a one pass algorithm for constructing a congressional sample without a priori knowledge of the data distribution. We use this technique to also incrementally maintain the sample as new data is inserted into the database, without accessing the base relation. This ensures that queries continue to be answered well even as the new data changes the database significantly.

- We show how congressional samples can be specialized to specific subsets of group-by queries. We also extend them to use detailed information about the data, such as variance, and to improve the answers for non-group-by queries.

---

[3] Based on this observation, the Online Aggregation approach employs an index striding technique to sample smaller groups at a higher rate [HHW97].

[4] Note that other common summary statistics such as histograms and wavelets suffer from this same general problem.

[5] As discussed in Section 4, the name *congressional* samples reflects an analogy to the U.S. Congress, which combines biased representation (two Senators per state, regardless of population) with more uniform representation (Representatives in proportion to a state's population).

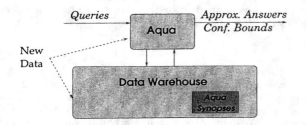

Figure 1: The Aqua architecture.

```
select l_returnflag, l_linestatus, sum(l_quantity)
from lineitem
where l_shipdate <= '01-SEP-98'
group by l_returnflag, l_linestatus;
```

(a) Original query

```
select l_returnflag, l_linestatus, 100*sum(l_quantity),
    sum_error(l_quantity) as error1
from bs_lineitem
where l_shipdate <= '01-SEP-98'
group by l_returnflag, l_linestatus;
```

(b) Rewritten query

Figure 2: Query rewriting in Aqua.

- We conduct an extensive set of experiments to establish the accuracy of congressional samples and identify an efficient execution strategy for running queries on them.

Map. The rest of this paper is as follows. In the next section, we describe Aqua, a system framework for approximate query answering. Then, we formulate the problem being addressed in this paper and in Section 4, we propose our novel sampling solutions. In Section 5, we highlight some implementation issues in using these new solutions in practice. Then, in Section 6 we propose efficient construction and maintenance techniques. The experimental study is in Section 7. In Section 8, we describe extensions of congressional samples that improve their accuracy for certain classes of queries. In Section 9, we present related work and in Section 10 we summarize the conclusions from this work.

2 Aqua System

This work is being performed as part of our efforts to enhance Aqua, an efficient decision support system providing approximate answers to queries [AGPR99, AGP99a]. Aqua maintains smaller-sized statistical summaries of the data, called *synopses*, and uses them to answer queries. A key feature of Aqua is that the system provides probabilistic error/confidence bounds on the answer, based on the Hoeffding and Chebyshev formulas [AGPR99]. Currently, the system handles arbitrarily complex SQL queries applying aggregate operations (avg, sum, count, etc.) over the data in the warehouse.

The high-level architecture of the Aqua system is shown in Figure 1. It is designed as a middleware software tool that can sit atop any commercial DBMS managing a data warehouse that supports ODBC connectivity. Initially, Aqua takes as an input from the warehouse administrator the space available for synopses and if available, hints on important query and data characteristics.[6] This information

---

[6]Work is also in progress to automatically extract this information from a query workload and adapt the statistics

l_returnflag	l_linestatus	sum(l_quantity)
A	F	3773034
N	F	100245
N	O	7459912
R	F	3779140

Figure 3: Exact answer.

l_returnflag	l_linestatus	sum(l_quantity)	error1
A	F	3.778e+06	1.4e+04
N	F	1.194e+05	2.6e+04
N	O	7.457e+06	1.9e+04
R	F	3.782e+06	1.4e+04

Figure 4: Approximate answer.

is then used to precompute a suitable set of synopses on the data, which are stored as regular relations in the DBMS. These synopses are also incrementally maintained up-to-date to reflect changes in the warehouse data.

When the user poses an SQL query to the full database, Aqua rewrites the query to use the Aqua synopsis relations. The rewriting involves appropriately scaling expressions in the query, and adding further expressions to the select clause to compute the error bounds. An example of a simple query rewrite is shown in Figure 2. The original query is a simplified version of Query 1 of the TPC-D benchmark. The synopsis relation bs_lineitem is a 1% uniform random sample of the lineitem relation and for simplicity, the error formula for the *sum* aggregate is encapsulated in the sum_error function. The rewritten query is executed by the DBMS, and the results are returned to the user. The exact answer is given in Figure 3. Figure 4 shows the approximate answer and error bound provided by Aqua when using this synopsis relation, and indicates that the given approximate answer is within error1 of the exact answer with 90% confidence[7]. The approximate answer for l_returnflag = N and l_linestatus = F is considerably worse than for the other combinations; this is the smallest group (a factor of 35 or more smaller than the others in the TPC-D database), and hence it contributes very few tuples to the sample bs_lineitem. This demonstrates a limitation of uniform random samples and motivates the need for the techniques proposed in Section 4.

To address the well-known problem of joins over samples [AGPR99, CMN99], Aqua collects special forms of samples, called *join synopses*, which can be viewed as uniform random samples on the results of all the interesting joins in the warehouse. In [AGPR99], we showed that join synopses are particularly effective on the *star and snowflake schemas* which are common in data warehousing [Sch97]. An interesting outcome of join synopses is that any join query involving multiple tables on the warehouse can be conceptually rewritten as a query on a *single join synopsis relation*. Due to this reason, in this paper, we restrict our discussion to queries on single relations.

3 Problem Formulation

In this section, we formulate the central problem being addressed in this paper, namely providing highly-accurate answers to group-by queries in an approximate query answering system. First, we present some relevant background on group-by queries.

---

dynamically.

[7]The confidence level is a parameter in Aqua.

3.1 Background

The central fact tables in a data warehouse contain several attributes that are commonly used for grouping the tuples in order to aggregate some measured quantities over each group. We call these the *dimensional* or *grouping* attributes. The attributes used for aggregation are called *measured* or *aggregate* attributes. For example, consider the central table (say, census) in a Census database containing the following attributes for each individual (the attribute names are listed in brackets): *social security number* (ssn), *state of residence* (st), *gender* (gen), and *annual income* (sal). In this schema, the grouping columns are st and gen, whereas the aggregate column is sal. A typical group-by query on census may request the average income of males and females in each state.

Of course, every query need not involve all the grouping columns in it, e.g., *highest income in each state*. For simplicity, we also consider a query with no groupings as a group-by query returning a single group. It is easily seen that for a relation containing a set G of grouping attributes, there are exactly $2^{|G|}$ possible groupings (the power set U of G) that can occur in a query. In the census relation, G is {st, gen} and U is {∅, (st), (gen), (st, gen)} (∅ is the empty set).

Next, we identify the typical requirements of approximate answers to a group-by query and describe natural metrics to quantitatively capture the errors in those answers.

3.2 Requirements on Group-by Answers

For queries returning a single numerical value (e.g., aggregate queries with no group-bys), it is straightforward to define the quality of the answer. It is simply the absolute or relative difference between the exact and approximate answers. However, since group-by queries produce multiple aggregates, one for each group, the metric is not so straightforward. The MAC error presented in [IP99] for quantifying the error in set-valued query answers works by matching the closest pairs in the exact and approximate answers and then suitably aggregating their differences. However, it is inadequate for our purpose because it does not necessarily match corresponding groups in the two answers. Hence, we develop here simple metrics specific to group-by queries.

At a high level, the user has two requirements on the approximate answer to a group-by query. First, the approximate answer should contain *all* the groups that occur in the exact answer, and second, as motivated in the introduction, the estimated answer for every group should be close to the exact answer for that group. We guarantee the first requirement, as long as the query predicates are not too selective, by ensuring that the schemes presented in the paper provide at least minimum-sized samples for every nonempty group in the relation across all grouping attributes.[8] Hence, in the remainder of the paper, we address the second requirement assuming the first to be true. Below, we formally describe simple metrics for capturing this requirement.

Let Q be a group-by query with an aggregate operation on one of the aggregate attributes C. Let $\{g_1, .., g_n\}$ be the set of all groups occurring in the exact answer to the query. Finally, let c_i and c_i' be the exact and approximate aggregate values over C in the group g_i. Then, the *error* ϵ_i

---

[8]The only way to ensure this requirement for highly selective queries is to sample nearly the entire relation. Otherwise, none of the sampled tuples may satisfy the predicate. This places a lower bound on the space allocated for samples, as a function of the number of groups and the target selectivity threshold.

in group g_i is defined to be the percentage relative error in the estimation of c_i, i.e.,

$$\epsilon_i = \frac{|c_i - c_i'|}{c_i} \times 100. \qquad (1)$$

For concreteness, we select a specific formalization, namely relative error, although other similar formulations (e.g., using absolute error) will not change the nature of the problem. We define the error in a group-by query as follows, considering three possible error metrics:

Definition 3.1 *The error ϵ over the entire group-by query returning a set of groups $\{g_1, .., g_n\}$ is defined to be either $\epsilon_\infty = MAX_{i=1}^n \epsilon_i$, $\epsilon_{L1} = \frac{1}{n} \sum_{i=1}^n \epsilon_i$, or $\epsilon_{L2} = \sqrt{\frac{1}{n} \sum_{i=1}^n \epsilon_i^2}$.*

Note that this definition applies even to the case of non-group-by aggregate queries, where the result is essentially an aggregate over a single group, in which case the three metrics are the same.

Using this definition as the basis, we can then informally define the primary goal to be one of minimizing one or all of the above errors for a mix of group-by queries.

4 Solutions

In this section we translate the general requirements of an approximate query answering system presented in the previous section to formal criteria on a sampling-based system. Then, we propose solutions for precomputing samples that optimize the criteria for various sets of group-by queries.

We first study individual groups in the answer and then the entire group-by query answer.

4.1 Sampling Requirements for Individual Groups

Here, we discuss the importance of the number of samples on which the aggregate is performed to the accuracy of a sampling-based result. Then, we show that among all possible sampling procedures, uniform sampling maximizes the expected value of this number.

Importance of Sample Size: The approximate answer provided from a sample is a random estimator for the exact answer, and we would like the estimates it produces to have small relative error (Eq. 1) with high probability. In the sampling literature, this quality is typically captured by the *standard error* of an estimator. Consider for example a column C in a relation of size N whose attribute values are $y_1, \ldots, y_N$, and let U be a uniform random sample of the y_i's of size n. Then the sample mean $\bar{y} = \frac{1}{n} \sum_{y_i \in U} y_i$ is an unbiased estimator of the actual mean $\bar{Y} = \frac{1}{N} \sum_{i=1}^N y_i$, with a standard error of

$$\frac{S}{\sqrt{n}} \sqrt{1 - \frac{n}{N}}, \qquad (2)$$

where

$$S = \sqrt{\frac{\sum_{i=1}^N (y_i - \bar{Y})^2}{N - 1}}$$

(see, e.g., [Coc77]). In general, the standard error depends on the sample size, the query (aggregate and predicate), and the variance of the expression on which the aggregate is taken. However, query information is usually not known a priori, and even where partial knowledge is available, optimizing for those queries may jeopardize the performance for other ad hoc queries. Because of this, short of sampling the entire relation, which is impractical, it is not possible to collect a single sample that works best for all queries. Hence, we first focus on techniques that are used when the aggregate, variance, and the predicate are unknown and later extend the techniques to use this information in Sections 4.7 and 8.

It is clear from the above equation that the standard error is inversely proportional to $\sqrt{n}$ for uniform sampling[9]. This is also true under other common quality measures such as Hoeffding and Chebyshev bounds, which when applied to AVG, COUNT, or SUM queries, are inversely proportional to $\sqrt{qn}$ or $q\sqrt{n}$, where q is selectivity of the predicate. Hence, a natural objective is to maximize the sample size for the group:

Objective: Let Q be an aggregate query with predicate P. In order to maximize the quality of an approximate answer for an aggregate in Q, we seek to maximize the number of sample tuples satisfying P.

Importance of Uniform Sampling: Here, we establish the need to use uniform random sampling for a single group by showing that it maximizes the expected sample size over all query predicates. First, we define some useful terms.

Let $\{t_1, t_2, \ldots, t_N\}$ be the set of N tuples in a relation R. We define a *sampling procedure* to be an assignment to each t_i of a probability p_i, the probability that t_i is selected for the sample. Let $\mathcal{C}_n$ be the class of all such sampling procedures such that $\sum_{i=1}^{N} p_i = n$, i.e., those with expected sample size n. Let $U_n \in \mathcal{C}_n$ be the uniform sampling procedure, i.e., $p_i = n/N$ for all i. A predicate P defines a subset $P(R)$ of R comprised of those tuples satisfying P. For a given predicate P and sampling procedure $C_n \in \mathcal{C}_n$, let $\mathrm{E}[n|P(R)]$ be the expected number of tuples satisfying the predicate in a sample produced by C_n, i.e., $\mathrm{E}[n|P(R)] = \sum_{i:t_i \in P(R)} p_i$. A natural goal, given the above objective, is to maximize the minimum $\mathrm{E}[n|P(R)]$ over all subsets $P(R)$ of a given size.[10] The next lemma shows that the uniform sampling procedure optimizes this goal.

Lemma 4.1 *For each subset size k, $0 < k < N$, the uniform sampling procedure U_n is the unique sampling procedure in $\mathcal{C}_n$ that maximizes the minimum $\mathrm{E}[n|P(R)]$ over all subsets $P(R)$ of size k.*

Proof. For U_n, the minimum $\mathrm{E}[n|P(R)]$ over all subsets $P(R)$ of size k is kn/N (all subsets have this same $\mathrm{E}[n|P(R)]$). For any other sampling procedure in $\mathcal{C}_n$, the reader can readily verify that the subset $P'(R)$ comprised of the k smallest p_i will have $\mathrm{E}[n|P'(R)] < kn/N$. ∎

In summary, we have established that it is important to collect as many uniformly sampled tuples as possible for any single group in query answer. Next, we extend our discussion to the multiple groups occurring in the group-by query answer.

4.2 Sampling Requirements for the Entire Group-by Answer

Recall from Definition 3.1 that the error in an approximate answer to a group-by query is the norm of the errors for the individual groups, for either the L_∞, L_1, or L_2 average norm. Hence, similar to the case of a single group, the quality of an estimator for a group-by query can be measured by the norm of the *standard error* for the individual groups. We seek to allocate a given sample space among the groups so as to minimize this norm.

Consider the L_∞ average norm (the other two norms lead to the same optimal strategy, as discussed in the full paper [AGP99b]). For this norm, and based on our objective, we seek to *maximize the minimum (expected) number of sample tuples satisfying the predicate in any one group*, which we denote by α. We extend our earlier notation and derive an expression for α as follows. Let g be the number of groups. For a relation R, let R_j be the set of tuples in R in group j. A predicate P defines a subset $P(R) = P(R_1) \cup \cdots \cup P(R_g)$. Let $\mathcal{A}_{n,g}$ be the class of all possible allocations of sample sizes to g groups, where the total size allocated is n. For a given predicate P, a sampling allocation $A_{n,g} \in \mathcal{A}_{n,g}$, and a sampling procedure $C_n \in \mathcal{C}_n$, α is given by:

$$\alpha = \min_{j=1,\ldots,g} \{\mathrm{E}[n_j|P(R_j)]\} \qquad (3)$$

where $A_{n,g}$ assigns sample size n_j to group j, and the sample within each group j is produced according to C_{n_j}.

For purposes of the analysis that follows, we restrict our attention to predicates that are independent of the groupings, i.e., the predicate's per-group selectivities are the same for all groups.[11] It is clear that our goal is to *maximize α*. Next, we present an optimal sampling strategy for realizing this goal.

Theorem 4.2 *Let T be a set of grouping attributes that partitions a relation R into g non-empty groups, and let X be the available sample space.[12] For each predicate of selectivity q, $0 < q < 1$, among all allocations in $\mathcal{A}_{X,g}$ and all sampling procedures in $\mathcal{C}_{n_j}$, the following strategy maximizes the α in Eq. 3 over all subsets $P(R)$ with per-group selectivity q:*

> *S1: Divide the available sample space X equally among the g groups, and take a uniform random sample within each group.*

Proof. It follows from Lemma 4.1 that uniform random sampling within each group maximizes α, for a given allocation strategy. With uniform sampling, each group R_j allocated n_j space has $\mathrm{E}[n_j|P(R_j)] = qn_j$. Hence α is determined by the smallest n_j. Allocating equal space to each group maximizes the smallest n_j, and hence maximizes α. ∎

In the remainder of this section, we consider mapping the strategy $S1$ to various classes of group-by queries, with arbitrary mixes of groupings. The difference between the resulting solutions can be shown by considering an example of grouping by U.S. states. The first solution we discuss would sample from each state in proportion to the state's population, whereas the second would sample an equal number from each state. Considering the two branches of the U.S. Congress, the former is analogous to the House

---

[9] While we do not analyze other kinds of sampling procedures within a group, it is intuitively clear that sample size will have a positive effect on their accuracy as well.

[10] Note that for all sampling procedures in $\mathcal{C}_n$, the *average* $\mathrm{E}[n|P(R)]$ over all $P(R)$ of a given size k is the same, i.e., $\binom{N-1}{k-1} \cdot n$.

[11] In general, it is not possible to tailor a strategy for a precomputed sample that works best for all predicates, if the per-group selectivities of a single predicate can vary widely. Although the assumption of predicate independence may not always hold in real life, the sample strategy we derive from this analysis works well even when the assumption does not hold.

[12] Throughout this paper, a unit of space can hold a single sampled tuple.

of Representatives while the latter is analogous to the Senate. The other techniques are hybrid extensions and combinations of these two, *a la* the U.S. Congress.

4.3 House

Consider applying the strategy $S1$ to the class of aggregate queries without group-bys. In this case, we have but a single group, so according to $S1$, we take a uniform random sample of size X of the entire relation, as is typically done in traditional sampling procedures. Next, we list two desirable trends of *House* (in general, uniform random samples) which coincide with a user's expectations on the quality of approximate answers.

1. *For the same aggregate operation, the quality of approximate answers increases with the query selectivity.* E.g., the standard error for an estimated average income over the entire nation is typically much smaller than the standard error for one of the states. (An exception would be if the variance among the incomes in a state was markedly smaller than the variance over all the states.)

2. *Answers to queries with the same aggregate and equal selectivities will typically have similar quality guarantees.* Thus assuming an equal number of men and women in the nation, the guarantees for the estimated average incomes for men are typically very similar to the guarantees for the women. (Again, an exception would be if the variances were markedly different.)

4.4 Senate

Consider applying the strategy $S1$ to the class of aggregate queries with the same set T of grouping attributes. For a given relation R, these attributes define a set, $\mathcal{G}$, of nonempty groups. Let m_T be the number of groups in $\mathcal{G}$. By following $S1$, for each nonempty group $g \in \mathcal{G}$, we take a uniform random sample of size X/m_T from the set of tuples in R in group g.[13] For example, if $T = state$ in a US census database, then $\mathcal{G}$ is the set of all states, $m_T = 50$, and we take a uniform random sample of size $X/50$ from each state.

Next, we illustrate a desirable characteristic of the *Senate* samples. *Given a Senate sample for group-by queries involving an attribute set T, we can also provide approximate answers to group-by queries on any subset T' of T, with at least the same quality.* This is because any group on T' contains in it one or more groups on T. Hence it will have at least as many sample points as any group in T, and correspondingly the same or better performance.

Problems with *House* and *Senate*: Note that using the samples from *House* here would result in very few sample points for small groups, and hence in a very small α. On the other hand, *Senate* allocates fewer tuples to the large groups in T than *House*. Hence, whenever queries are uniformly spread over the *entire* data, more of them occur in the large groups, and *House* will perform better than *Senate* for those cases. Next, we present techniques that perform well over larger classes of group-by queries.

4.5 Basic Congress

Here, we apply the strategy $S1$ to the class of aggregate queries containing group-by queries grouping on a single set T of attributes and queries with no group-bys at all. A natural solution is to simply collect both the *House* and the *Senate* samples (analogous to the U.S. Congress). However,

this doubles the sample space. Thus, we reduce this factor of 2 by the following strategy.

Let $\mathcal{G}$ be all the non-empty groups in the grouping on T, and let $m_T = |\mathcal{G}|$. Let g be a group in $\mathcal{G}$ and X be the available sample space. Let n_g be the number of tuples in the relation R in group g. Let h_g and s_g be the (expected) sample sizes allocated to g under *House* and *Senate* respectively. Then, under our new approach, we allocate the higher of these two (i.e., $\max(h_g, s_g)$) to g.[14] Of course, this may still result in a total space of X' that is larger than X (one can easily show that $X' \leq \frac{2m_T - 1}{m_T} X - m_T + 1 < 2X$). Hence, we uniformly scale down the sample sizes such that the total space still equals X. The final sample size allocated to group g is given by:

$$c_g = X \frac{\max\left(\frac{n_g}{|R|}, \frac{1}{m_T}\right)}{\sum_{j \in \mathcal{G}} \max\left(\frac{n_j}{|R|}, \frac{1}{m_T}\right)}$$

A *Basic Congress* sample is constructed by selecting a uniform random sample of size c_g for each group g in $\mathcal{G}$.

As an example, consider a relation R with two grouping attributes A, B. The different values in these attributes are depicted in the first two columns of Figure 5. Assume that the number of tuples for the groups $(a_1, b_1), (a_1, b_2), (a_1, b_3)$, (a_2, b_3) are $3000, 3000, 1500$, and 2500 respectively. The next two columns depict the space allocated by *House* and *Senate* with $T = \{A, B\}$ and $X = 100$. The fifth column depicts the space allocated by *Basic Congress* (before scaling down) by choosing the maximum of the *House* and *Senate* allocations for each group. The next column shows the allocation scaled down to fit the total available space. Note that while *House* allocates less space for the small group and *Senate* allocates less space for the large groups, *Basic Congress* solves both these problems. On the other hand, by considering only the extreme groupings, *Basic Congress* fails to address the sample size requirements of groupings on subsets of T. For example, grouping on A alone would require an optimal allocation of 50 and 50 samples to the two groups a_1 and a_2, whereas *Basic Congress* applied to T allocates 77.3 and 22.7 units of space respectively. Consequently, using *Basic Congress* to answer an aggregate query grouped solely on A would likely lead to a more inaccurate estimate on the group a_2.

We address this problem by our final technique, *Congress*, proposed next.

4.6 Congress

In this approach, we consider the entire set of possible group-by queries over a relation R, i.e., queries grouping the data on any subset (including $\emptyset$) of the grouping attributes, G, in R. Taking a naive approach of applying Strategy $S1$ using space X on each such grouping would result in a space requirement of $2^{|G|} X$. Hence, we perform an optimization similar to *Basic Congress* above, but this time over all possible groupings — not just G and $\emptyset$, as in *Basic Congress*.

---

[13] Recall that for simplicity we assume throughout this paper that each group is larger than the number of samples drawn from it. Handling scenarios when this is not the case is straightforward.

[14] We also consider an alternative approach, as follows. Let $Y = X/(\sum_{j \in \mathcal{G}} \max(\frac{n_j}{|R|}, \frac{1}{m_T}))$. Take a uniform sample of size Y of the relation R. Let x_g be the number of sampled tuples from a group g. For each group g such that $x_g < Y/m_T$, where m_T is the number of nonempty groups, add to the sample $Y/m_T - x_g$ additional tuples selected uniformly at random from the set of tuples in R in group g. Due to the choice of Y, the expected size of the resulting sample is X. In practice, the difference between the two approaches is negligible.

A	B	House $s_{g,\emptyset}$	Senate $s_{g,AB}$	Basic Congress (before scaling)	Basic Congress	$s_{g,A}$	$s_{g,B}$	Congress (before scaling)	Congress
a_1	b_1	30	25	30	27.3	20 (of 50)	33.3	33.3	23.5
a_1	b_2	30	25	30	27.3	20 (of 50)	33.3	33.3	23.5
a_1	b_3	15	25	25	22.7	10 (of 50)	12.5 (of 33.3)	25	17.7
a_2	b_3	25	25	25	22.7	50	20.8 (of 33.3)	50	35.3

Figure 5: Expected sample sizes for various techniques, for $X = 100$.

Let $\mathcal{G}$ be the set of non-empty groups under the grouping G. The grouping G partitions the relation R according to the cross-product of all the grouping attributes; this is the finest possible partitioning for group-bys on R. Any group h on any other grouping $T \subset G$ is the union of one or more groups g from $\mathcal{G}$. We denote each such g to be a *subgroup* of h. For example, in Figure 5, $G = \{A, B\}$, $\mathcal{G} = \{ (a_1, b_1), (a_1, b_2), (a_1, b_3), (a_2, b_3) \}$, and for the grouping $T = \{A\}$, the set of tuples in the group $h = a_1$ is the union of the tuples in the subgroups (a_1, b_1), (a_1, b_2), and (a_1, b_3) of h.

To construct *Congress*, we first consider applying $S1$ on each $T \subseteq G$. Let $\mathcal{T}$ be the set of non-empty groups under the grouping T, and let $m_T = |\mathcal{T}|$, the number of such groups. By $S1$, each of the non-empty groups in T should get a uniform random sample of X/m_T tuples from the group. Thus for each subgroup g in $\mathcal{G}$ of a group h in $\mathcal{T}$, the expected space allocated to g (from considering T) is simply

$$s_{g,T} = \frac{X}{m_T} \cdot \frac{n_g}{n_h}, \qquad (4)$$

where n_g and n_h are the number of tuples in g and h respectively. Then, for each group $g \in \mathcal{G}$, we take the maximum over all T of $s_{g,T}$ as the sample size for g, and of course scale it down to limit the space used to X. The final formula is:

$$\text{SampleSize}(g) = X \frac{\max_{T \subseteq G} s_{g,T}}{\sum_{j \in \mathcal{G}} \max_{T \subseteq G} s_{j,T}} \qquad (5)$$

For each group g in $\mathcal{G}$, we select a uniform random sample of size $\text{SampleSize}(g)$. Thus we take a stratified, biased sample in which each group at the finest partitioning is its own strata.

The space allocation by *Congress* for $G = \{A, B\}$ is depicted in the last two columns of Figure 5 before and after scaling. Each entry in the "before scaling" column is the maximum of the corresponding entries in the $s_{g,\emptyset}$, $s_{g,A}$, $s_{g,B}$, and $s_{g,AB}$ columns. These $s_{g,T}$ contain the optimal allocations according to $S1$ when considering grouping solely on T. By taking the row-wise maximum and then scaling down all values by the same amount

$$f = \frac{X}{\sum_{j \in \mathcal{G}} \max_{T \subseteq G} s_{j,T}}, \qquad (6)$$

we ensure that the sample size for *every* group across *all* combinations of group-by columns is within a factor of at most f of its target optimal allocation.[15] Thus *Congress* essentially guarantees that both large and small groups in all groupings will have a reasonable number of samples.

---

[15] The scale down factor f ranges from 1 (for a uniform distribution across all possible groups at the finest level of grouping G) to almost $2^{-|G|}$ (for a carefully constructed pathological distribution presented in the full paper [AGP99b]).

Key	Grouping Columns			Aggregate Column
K	A	B	C	Q
k_1	a_1	b_1	c_1	q_1
k_2	a_1	b_1	c_2	q_2

Figure 6: Relation `Rel` with two example tuples

```
select A,B, sum(Q)
from Rel
group by A,B;
```

Figure 7: User Query Q_2

4.7 Adapting to Query Workload

In the full paper, we discuss how to extend the previous strategies to handle preferences between groupings and/or between groups, whenever they can be determined.

5 Rewriting

In Section 2, we demonstrated how Aqua rewrites queries in the presence of uniform random samples. However, that approach does not apply to the biased samples presented in this paper. This section highlights some of the implementation issues that arise when using such samples. We first give some background on generating approximate answers from biased samples. Then, we present different strategies for rewriting queries in the presence of biased samples.

5.1 Approximate Answers from Biased Samples

Recall that query rewriting involves two key steps: a) scaling up the aggregate expressions and b) deriving error bounds on the estimate. The desired formulas for both steps can be derived using standard techniques. We illustrate by focusing on scaling. In Figure 2, the SUM operator was scaled by a factor of 100 since bs_lineitem was a 1% uniform random sample. We refer to this factor as the *ScaleFactor*. However, biased samples are not uniform samples — instead they are a union of different sized uniform random samples of various groups in the relation. Consider Figure 6. It shows a five column table on which the user poses the query Q_2 (Figure 7). Let SampRel be a biased sample of relation Rel, and let the groups $\langle A = a_1, B = b_1, C = c_1 \rangle$ and $\langle A = a_1, B = b_1, C = c_2 \rangle$ be represented in SampRel by a 1% and 2% sample respectively. Since both groups contribute to the group $\langle A = a_1, B = b_1 \rangle$ in the answer for Q_2, we have a non-uniform sample from which we must produce an approximate answer. This raises the concern that we may not be able to extract an unbiased estimator for the sum for this group.

However, using standard techniques for estimators based on stratified samples, we can generate an unbiased answer using all the tuples in the biased sample [Coc77]. For each tuple, let its scale factor *ScaleFactor* be the inverse of the sampling rate for its strata. For the SUM operator, we scale

493

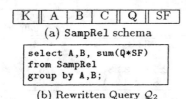

(a) SampRel schema

```
select A,B, sum(Q*SF)
from SampRel
group by A,B;
```

(b) Rewritten Query Q_2

Figure 8: *Integrated* Rewriting

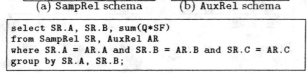

(a) SampRel schema   (b) AuxRel schema

```
select SR.A, SR.B, sum(Q*SF)
from SampRel SR, AuxRel AR
where SR.A = AR.A and SR.B = AR.B and SR.C = AR.C
group by SR.A, SR.B;
```

(c) Rewritten query Q_2

Figure 9: *Normalized* Rewriting

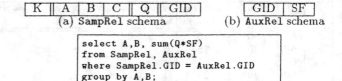

(a) SampRel schema   (b) AuxRel schema

```
select A,B, sum(Q*SF)
from SampRel, AuxRel
where SampRel.GID = AuxRel.GID
group by A,B;
```

(c) Rewritten Query Q_2

Figure 10: *Key-normalized* Rewriting

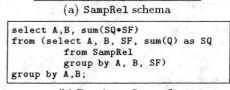

(a) SampRel schema

```
select A,B, sum(SQ*SF)
from (select A, B, SF, sum(Q) as SQ
      from SampRel
      group by A, B, SF)
group by A,B;
```

(b) Rewritten Query Q_2

Figure 11: *Nested-integrated* Rewriting

each value being summed by its *ScaleFactor*, and then sum the result. In query Q_2, for example, we would scale q_1 by 100 and q_2 by 50, and then add up the scaled sum. For the COUNT operator, we sum up the individual *ScaleFactors* of each tuple satisfying the query predicate. For the AVG operator, we compute the scaled SUM divided by the scaled COUNT.

Note that this approach is superior to subsampling all groups down to a common sampling rate in order to apply techniques for uniform sampling. For example, if the sampling rate for a group is j orders of magnitude smaller than the sampling rate for other groups, then the relative error bound for a COUNT operator using Hoeffding bounds can be $j/2$ orders of magnitude worse.

5.2 Rewriting Strategies

We now consider various strategies for rewriting queries to incorporate the scaling discussed above, using the example of the SUM operator. Rewriting strategies for other aggregate operators and error bounds can be derived similarly and are presented in the full paper [AGP99b].

Note that all sample tuples belonging to a group will have the same *ScaleFactor*. Thus, the key step in scaling is to be able to efficiently associate each tuple with its corresponding *ScaleFactor*. There are two approaches to doing this: a) store the *ScaleFactor* (SF) with *each tuple* in SampRel and b) use a separate table AuxRel to store the *ScaleFactors* for the groups. These two approaches give rise to three techniques described below.

The first approach is highlighted in Figure 8. The rewrite technique, called *Integrated*, incurs a space overhead of storing the *ScaleFactor* and a multiplication operation for *every tuple*. However, this approach incurs significant maintenance overhead — insertion or deletion of tuples from SampRel requires updating the *ScaleFactor* of all tuples in the affected groups.

The second approach addresses the maintenance problem by normalizing the SampRel table and is demonstrated in technique *Normalized* shown in Figure 9. It has only marginal maintenance overhead since the *ScaleFactor* information is isolated to AuxRel and thus, updates to SampRel requires updates only to AuxRel. Since the number of groups would very likely be much fewer than the number of tuples, AuxRel would have a lower cardinality than SampRel. However, this approach has an execution time penalty due to the join required between SampRel and AuxRel. Moreover, the join condition can be non-trivial if

there are many grouping attributes. The *Key-normalized* technique attempts to minimize this overhead. Since each group is specified explicitly by the attributes values of the grouping columns, they can be replaced by a unique *group identifier* (GID) as shown in Figure 10. Note that this optimization still limits changes to the smaller AuxRel relation during updates and also reduces the space overhead of AuxRel.

In each of the above approaches, the *ScaleFactor* multiplication operation was performed for every tuple. However, since all tuples belonging to a group have the same *ScaleFactor*, one can optimize further to first aggregate over each group and then scale this aggregate appropriately by the *ScaleFactor*. This approach, however, requires a nested group-by query. While applicable to all the three prior techniques, for space limitations we show this optimization in Figure 11 for *Integrated* rewriting and call it *Nested-integrated*.

In Section 7, we compare the query execution speeds of these four approaches.

6 Computation and Maintenance

In the full paper [AGP99b], we present one-pass algorithms for constructing the various biased samples presented in this paper. We also show how to maintain them in the presence of insertions of new tuples into the relation, without accessing the stored relation.

7 Experiments

We conducted an extensive set of experiments to evaluate the various sample allocation techniques and rewriting strategies. The sampling allocation schemes studied were *House*, *Senate*, *Basic Congress*, and *Congress* (Section 4). The rewriting strategies studied were *Integrated*, *Nested-integrated*, *Normalized*, and *Key-normalized* (Section 5). In this section, we present a representative subset of the results generated. They were chosen to show the tradeoffs among these schemes. First, we describe the experimental testbed. Then we perform experiments to measure the accuracy fo the various sample allocation scheme. Finally, we study the performance of the various rewriting strategies.

Attribute	l_id	l_returnflag	l_linestatus	l_shipdate	l_quantity	l_extendedprice
Data Type	int (1, 2, ..)	int	int	date	float	float
Role of Attribute	Primary Key	Grouping			Aggregation	

Figure 12: The `Lineitem` Schema Used in the Experiments

Q_{g2}	Q_{g3}	Q_{g0}
select l_returnflag, l_linestatus, sum(l_quantity), sum(l_extendedprice) from lineitem group by l_returnflag, l_linestatus;	select l_returnflag, l_linestatus, l_shipdate, sum(l_quantity) from lineitem group by l_returnflag, l_linestatus, l_shipdate;	select sum(l_quantity) from lineitem where $(s \leq l\_id \leq s + c)$;

Table 1: Queries studied

7.1 Testbed

We ran the experiments on Aqua, with Oracle (v7) as the back-end DBMS. Aqua was enhanced to use the proposed allocation schemes to compute its samples and also, the different rewriting strategies.

7.1.1 Database and Queries

In our experiments, we used the database and queries supplied with the TPC-D benchmark. The TPC-D benchmark models a realistic business data warehouse, with sales data from the past six years. It contains a large central fact table called `lineitem` and several much smaller dimension tables [TPC99]. As mentioned in Section 2, it is sufficient to consider queries on a single relation to evaluate the proposed techniques in Aqua. Hence, we restrict our discussion to queries on the `lineitem` table. The schema of this table is given in Figure 7,[16] along with the grouping (dimensional) and aggregation (measured) attributes. In all our experiments, the *Senate* technique computes the samples for the grouping on {l_returnflag, l_linestatus, l_shipdate}.

Next, we extended the TPC-D data to model several relevant aspects of realistic databases. Specifically, consider the groups obtained by grouping the above relation on all the three grouping attributes. In the original TPC-D data, these groups were nearly identical in size. The data in the aggregate attributes was also uniformly distributed. In our experiments, we introduced desired levels of skew into the distributions of the group-sizes and the data in the aggregated columns. This was done using the Zipf distribution, which is known to accurately model several real-life distributions. By changing the z-parameter of the distribution from 0 to 1.5, we are able to generate group-size distributions that are uniform (i.e., all sizes are same) or progressively more skewed. We fixed the skew in the aggregated column at $z = 0.86$, a commonly used z-parameter because it results in a $90 - 10$ distribution. Finally, we also varied the number of groups in the relation (from 10 to $200K$). For a given number of groups, we generated equal number of distinct (randomly chosen) values in each of the grouping columns. Since the total number of groups is the product of these counts, if the number of groups is n, the number of distinct values in each of these columns becomes $n^{1/3}$.

The different parameters used in our experiments are listed in Table 2. The size of the sample, determined by parameter SP, is given as a percentage of the original

---

[16] The original `lineitem` table has some other columns which are not relevant to this discussion. We introduced a l_id attribute to the table to use in the experiments.

Parameter	Range of Values	Default
Table Size (T)	$100K - 6M$ tuples	$1M$
Sample Percentage (SP)	$1\% - 75\%$ (% T)	7%
Num. Groups (NG)	$10 - 200K$	1000
Group-size Skew (z)	$0 - 1.5$	0.86

Table 2: Experiment Parameters

relation. In all our experiments, unless otherwise mentioned, the parameter takes its default value listed in the table.

Queries: We used queries with different number of group-by columns. They are listed in the Table 1 (the suffixes denote the number of group-bys in the queries). The first two queries are derived from Query 3 in the TPC-D query suite. The third query is parametrized to generate queries with desired selectivities on different parts of the data. Queries Q_{g0} and Q_{g3} represent two ends of the spectrum. The former poses the query over the entire relation whereas the latter causes the finest partitioning on three attributes. Q_{g2}, with two grouping columns, is in between the two extremes. The aim of this study is to identify a scheme that can provide consistently good performance for all the three classes and thus, the entire range.

For the current study, we chose parameter s for Query Q_{g0} randomly between 0 and $950K$ and fixed c at $70K$, and generated 20 such queries. Hence, each query selects about $70K$ tuples, i.e., 7% of the table when T is $1M$.

7.2 Accuracy of Sample Allocation Strategies

In this section, we first compare the accuracies of various sample allocation strategies for group-by and non-group-by queries. Then, we study the sensitivity of the various sampling schemes to size of the sample. In each case, we compute the exact as well as approximate answers for queries Q_{g2}, Q_{g3}, and each of the queries in the set Q_{g0}. For Q_{g2} and Q_{g3}, we define the error as the *average* of the percentage errors for all the groups. For the query set Q_{g0}, we define error as the average of the percentage errors for all the queries. In both cases, the error for a single group is computed using Eq. 1 (Section 3). We also measured the maximum errors and observed that the relative performance of all the techniques was identical to the above average error measures.

7.2.1 Performance for Different Query Sets

In this experiment, we fix the sample percentage at 7% and study the accuracy of various allocation strategies for the three classes of queries. Since each query set aggregates over

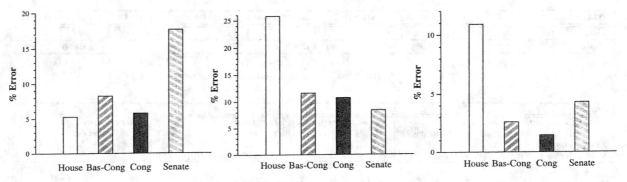

Figure 13: Query Q_{g0} Error   Figure 14: Query Q_{g3} Error   Figure 15: Query Q_{g2} Error

a different set of groups, intuitively, we expect the technique that allocates equal space to those groups to have the least error. Note that, when all the groups are of the same size (i.e., $z = 0$), all the techniques result in the same allocation, which is a uniform sample of the data. Hence, we discuss the results for the case of skewed group sizes (with $z = 1.5$) below.

Queries with No Group-bys (Q_{g0}) (Figure 13): Recall that Q_{g0} consists of queries selecting uniformly over the entire data. Since *Senate* allocates the same space for each group, it ends up allocating less space for the large groups than the other techniques. This results in a higher overall error for *Senate* because a large proportion of the queries land in the large groups. The other techniques perform better because one of their considerations is allocating space uniformly over the entire data. The result is that the space allocation mirrors the queries, and all queries are answered well. The relative performance of these three techniques is determined by the weight they give to this consideration — highest in *House* where it is the sole consideration to the least in *Basic Congress* whose space allocation is skewed towards the small groups. Surprisingly, *Congress*'s errors are low too and it is a good match for *House*.

Queries with Three Group-Bys (Q_{g3}) (Figure 14): Recall that Q_{g3} consists of aggregating over all groups at the finest granularity of grouping. This is precisely the grouping for which the *Senate* sampling was set up giving equal space to each of these groups. Hence, *Senate* has low errors for all the groups resulting in an overall good performance. On the other hand, *House* allocates a large part of the space to the few large groups and incurs high errors for the remaining smaller groups. Once again, *Basic Congress* and *Congress* perform in between these two ranges because they take into account small groups, but to a lesser extent than *Senate*.

Queries with Two Group-Bys (Q_{g2}) (Figure 15): This is the intermediate case of grouping on two attributes. Both *House* and *Senate* perform poorly since they are designed for the two extremes. The absolute magnitude of the error in this case, however, is significantly lower than the last two sets due to the larger size of the groups — both *House* and *Senate* contain enough tuples from each group to produce reasonable estimates. The *Congress* technique easily outperforms them because it is tailored for this case and explicitly considers this grouping in its allocation. Thus, its allocation is close to the ideal for this query set.

Conclusions: It is clear from the above experiments that only *Congress* performs consistently the best or close to best for queries of all types. The other techniques perform well only in a limited part of the spectrum, and thus, are not suitable in practice where a whole range of

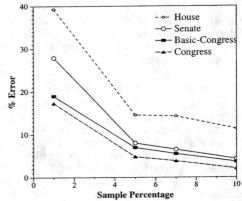

Figure 16: Sample Size vs. Accuracy (Query Q_{g2})

groupings may be of interest to the user during the roll-up and drill-down process. The *Congress* technique performs well because it is not optimized for a particular grouping set but instead takes into consideration all possible groupings (including no-groupings at all) in its space allocation. Thus, even in cases where it is not the best, it is extremely competitive. Consequently, we propose *Congress* as the sampling technique of choice.

7.2.2   Effect of Sample Size

In this experiment we perform a sensitivity analysis test by fixing the group-size skew at 0.86 and measure the errors incurred in answering Query q_{g2} by various allocation schemes for different sample sizes. The results are plotted in Figure 16. As expected, the errors drop as more space is allocated to store the samples. The errors for *House* flatten because it simply allocates more of the available space to the larger groups, which does little to improve the performance for the remaining groups. Overall, the behavior of *Congress* is very encouraging because its errors drop rapidly with increasing sample space. Consequently, it is able to provide high accuracies even for the arbitrary group-by queries.

7.3   Performance of Rewriting Strategies

In these experiments, we measure the actual time taken by each of the four rewriting strategies presented Section 5. We present the time in seconds for running Q_{g2} and writing the result into another relation. The experiments were run on a Sun Sparc-20 with 256MB of memory, and $10GB$ of disk space running Solaris 2.5. We focus on the effects of sample size and the number of groups because they almost entirely determine the performance of the rewrite strategies.

Technique	Sample Percentage		
	1%	5%	10%
Integrated	1.3	3.8	6.8
Nested-integrated	1.2	3.3	6.0
Normalized	1.7	14.0	27.3
Key-normalized	1.8	14.3	28.4

Table 3: Times Taken for Different Sample Percentages (actual query time = 40sec)

To mitigate the effects of startup and caching, we ran the queries five times and report the average execution times of the last four runs. We present our experiments on sample size; the experiments on the number of groups can be found in the full paper [AGP99b].

Effect of Sample Size on Rewrite Performance: In this experiment, we fix the number of groups at 1000 and vary the sample percentage. Table 3 shows the times taken by various rewrite strategies for different sample percentages. Running the same query on the original table data took 40 seconds on the average. The table makes two points: a) the *Integrated*-based techniques outperform the *Normalized*-based techniques and b) the rise in execution times are dramatic for the *Normalized*-based techniques with increasing sample sizes.

Normalized and *Key-normalized* perform poorly due to the join between the sample table and auxiliary table. Among them, the slightly better performance of *Key-normalized* is due to a shorter join predicate involving just one attribute (l_id), as against two (l_returnflag and l_linestatus) for *Normalized*. Among *Integrated* and *Nested-integrated*, quite surprisingly, the latter performed consistently better in spite of being a nested query. The fewer multiplications with the scalefactor performed by *Nested-integrated* (one per group) pays off over *Integrated* which does one multiplication per tuple. We explore this tradeoff in more detail in the full paper. Overall, solely from the performance viewpoint, these two techniques are still significantly faster than the normalized ones.

Summary of Rewriting Strategies: Our experiments show that *Integrated* and *Nested-integrated* have consistent performance over a wide spectrum of sample sizes and group counts and easily outperform the other two techniques. However, as pointed out in Section 5, they incur higher maintenance costs (which we do not study here). Hence, the choice of a technique depends on the update frequency of the warehouse environment. If the update frequencies are moderate to rare, *Integrated* (or *Nested-integrated*) should be the technique(s) of choice. Only the (rare) high frequency update case warrants for the higher execution times incurred by *Key-normalized* – note that as the warehouse grows larger relative to the sample, the probability of an update reflecting immediately in the sample shrinks significantly, making this an unlikely case in practice.

8 Extensions

In this section, we summarize some extensions to Congressional samples to use different biasing criteria derived from the data and to non-Group-by queries. Details are in the full paper [AGP99b].

Generalization to Multiple Criteria: One of the key features of congressional samples is its extensibility to different space allocation criteria beyond those studied in

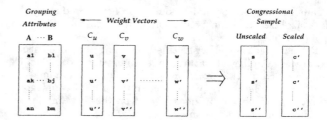

Figure 17: Congressional samples framework

this paper. Consider Figure 17. It shows a typical structure of the table that is used to determine space allocation in a congressional sample similar to that in Figure 5. Note that there are three classes on columns. The ones on the left are the attribute columns which contain the possible groups in some order. The columns in the middle, that we refer to as *weight vectors*, contain for some criteria, the relative ratios of space, or *weights*, to be allocated to each of the groups (e.g., in proportion to the variances of the groups). For example, in Figure 5, *House* and *Senate* strategies contributed a weight vector each. The last two columns aggregate the space allocated by each of the weight vectors to generate the final number of tuples assigned for each group.

Generalization to Other Queries: The Congressional Samples framework can also be extended beyond group-by queries. A group-by query simply partitions the attribute space based on specific attribute values. However, one may also consider other partitions of the space such as ranges of values, where the user has a biased interest in some of the partitions. For example, if a sample of the sales data were used to analyze the impact of a recent sales promotion, the sample would be more effective if the most recent sales data were better represented in the sample as opposed to older data. This can be easily achieved in the above framework by replacing the values in the grouping columns by distinct ranges (in this case on dates) and deriving the weight vectors that weigh the ranges appropriately with respect to each other.

9 Related Work

While statistical techniques based on samples, histograms, etc. have been applied in databases for a while now, they have been primarily used in selectivity estimation during query optimization [SAC+79, Olk93, PIHS96]. Approximate query answering using sampling has started receiving attention recently [Olk93, HHW97, GM98, AGPR99]. The closest work to ours is the *Online Aggregation* scheme proposed by Hellerstein *et al* [HHW97]. In their approach, the original data is scanned in random order at query time to generate increasingly larger random samples of the data, thus incrementally refining the approximate answer generated. Unlike Aqua, that work involves accessing original disk-resident data at query time; but it has the desirable feature of ultimately providing the fully accurate answer. However, both approaches encounter similar problems in answering group-by queries effectively. Their solution is to use the novel the *index striding* technique to control sampling rate among groups and thus ensure fairness among their qualities. Their approach is not suitable for the precomputed or materialized samples considered in this paper.

There have been several recent works using histograms [IP99] or wavelets [VW99] for approximate query answering.

Efficient processing and optimization of aggregate group-by queries has been addressed in [CS94, CS95]. Their techniques are orthogonal to our approach of reducing the data size itself and can be used in Aqua to further speed up group-by query processing.

Biased sampling (e.g., stratified sampling) has been studied in the sampling literature under many contexts [Coc77]. Most related is the work on subpopulation sampling, in which a population is partitioned into subsets (analogous to groups in a group-by query), and on-the-fly sampling is used to estimate the mean or other statistic over each subpopulation, as well as over the entire population. This paper is the first to consider the use of precomputed biased samples for approximate query answering of group-by queries, and extends the previous work by studying combinations of group-by columns, construction and incremental maintenance, query rewriting, optimizing over a range of possible queries, and performance on the TPC-D benchmark data.

10   Conclusions

The growing popularity of OLAP and data warehousing has highlighted the need for approximate query answering systems. These systems offer high performance by answering queries from compact summary statistics, typically uniform random samples, of the data. Needless to say, it is critical in such systems to provide reasonably accurate answers to the commonly posed queries.

In this paper, we showed that precomputed uniform random samples are not sufficient to accurately answer group-by queries, which form the basis of most of the data analysis in decision support systems. We demonstrated that, to be effective for group-by queries, the data should be sampled *non-uniformly*, and proposed several new techniques based on this *biased sampling*. We developed techniques for minimizing errors over queries on a set of possible grouping columns. We introduced *congressional samples*, which are effective for group-by queries with arbitrary group-bys (including none). Additionally, we proposed efficient techniques for constructing congressional samples in one pass over the relation, and for incrementally maintaining them in the presence of database insertions, without accessing the stored relation. We also presented efficient strategies for using the biased samples. The new sampling strategies were validated experimentally both in their ability to produce accurate estimates to group-by queries and in their execution efficiency.

All of the techniques presented in this paper have been incorporated into an approximate query answering system, called Aqua, that we have developed. By providing the ability to answer the important class of group-by queries, our new techniques have significantly enhanced the overall accuracy and usability of Aqua as a viable decision support system. Of course, the techniques themselves are applicable beyond Aqua, and even beyond group-by queries, and can be used wherever the studied limitations of uniform random samples become critical.

Acknowledgements

Sridhar Ramaswamy was one of the designers and implementors of the Aqua prototype. We also thank him for discussions related to this work.

References

[AGP99a]   S. Acharya, P. B. Gibbons, and V. Poosala. Aqua: A fast decision support system using approximate query answers. In *Proc. 25th International Conf. on Very Large Databases*, pages 754–757, September 1999. Demo paper.

[AGP99b]   S. Acharya, P. B. Gibbons, and V. Poosala. Congressional samples for approximate answering of group-by queries. Technical report, Bell Laboratories, Murray Hill, New Jersey, November 1999.

[AGPR99]   S. Acharya, P. B. Gibbons, V. Poosala, and S. Ramaswamy. Join synopses for approximate query answering. In *Proc. ACM SIGMOD International Conf. on Management of Data*, pages 275–286, June 1999.

[CD97]   S. Chaudhuri and U. Dayal. An overview of data warehousing and OLAP technology. *SIGMOD Record*, 26(1):65–74, 1997.

[CMN99]   S. Chaudhuri, R. Motwani, and V. Narasayya. On random sampling over joins. In *Proc. ACM SIGMOD International Conf. on Management of Data*, pages 263–274, June 1999.

[Coc77]   W. G. Cochran. *Sampling Techniques*. John Wiley & Sons, New York, third edition, 1977.

[CS94]   S. Chaudhuri and K. Shim. Including group-by in query optimization. In *Proc. 20th International Conf. on Very Large Data Bases*, pages 354–366, September 1994.

[CS95]   S. Chaudhuri and K. Shim. An overview of cost-based optimization of queries with aggregates. *IEEE Data Engineering Bulletin*, 18(3):3–9, 1995.

[GM98]   P. B. Gibbons and Y. Matias. New sampling-based summary statistics for improving approximate query answers. In *Proc. ACM SIGMOD International Conf. on Management of Data*, pages 331–342, June 1998.

[HH99]   P. Haas and J. Hellerstein. Ripple joins for online aggregation. In *Proc. ACM SIGMOD International Conf. on Management of Data*, pages 287–298, June 1999.

[HHW97]   J. M. Hellerstein, P. J. Haas, and H. J. Wang. Online aggregation. In *Proc. ACM SIGMOD International Conf. on Management of Data*, pages 171–182, May 1997.

[IP99]   Y. Ioannidis and V. Poosala. Histogram-based techniques for approximating set-valued query-answers. In *Proc. 25th International Conf. on Very Large Databases*, pages 174–185, September 1999.

[Kim96]   R. Kimball. *The Data Warehouse Tookit*. John Wiley and Sons Inc., 1996.

[Olk93]   F. Olken. *Random Sampling from Databases*. PhD thesis, Computer Science, U.C. Berkeley, April 1993.

[PIHS96]   V. Poosala, Y. E. Ioannidis, P. J. Haas, and E. J. Shekita. Improved histograms for selectivity estimation of range predicates. In *Proc. ACM SIGMOD International Conf. on Management of Data*, pages 294–305, June 1996.

[SAC+79]   P. G. Selinger, M. M. Astrahan, D. D. Chamberlin, R. A. Lorie, and T. T. Price. Access path selection in a relational database management system. In *Proc. ACM SIGMOD International Conf. on Management of Data*, pages 23–34, June 1979.

[Sch97]   D. Schneider. The ins & outs (and everything in between) of data warehousing. Tutorial in the *23rd International Conf. on Very Large Data Bases*, August 1997.

[TPC99]   Transaction processing performance council (TPC). *TPC-D Benchmark Version 2.0*, February 1999. URL: www.tpc.org.

[VW99]   J. S. Vitter and M. Wang. Approximate computation of multidimensional aggregates of sparse data using wavelets. In *Proc. ACM SIGMOD International Conf. on Management of Data*, pages 193–204, June 1999.

Counting, Enumerating, and Sampling of Execution Plans in a Cost-Based Query Optimizer

Florian Waas[1,2]
flw@cwi.nl

César Galindo-Legaria[2]
cesarg@microsoft.com

[1]CWI
P.O. Box 94079
1090 GB Amsterdam
The Netherlands

[2]Microsoft Corporation
One Microsoft Way
Redmond, WA 98052
U.S.A.

Abstract

Testing an SQL database system by running large sets of deterministic or stochastic SQL statements is common practice in commercial database development. However, code defects often remain undetected as the query optimizer's choice of an execution plan is not only depending on the query but strongly influenced by a large number of parameters describing the database and the hardware environment. Modifying these parameters in order to steer the optimizer to select other plans is difficult since this means anticipating often complex search strategies implemented in the optimizer.

In this paper we devise algorithms for counting, exhaustive generation, and uniform sampling of plans from the complete search space. Our techniques allow extensive validation of both generation of alternatives, and execution algorithms with plans other than the optimized one—if two candidate plans fail to produce the same results, then either the optimizer considered an invalid plan, or the execution code is faulty. When the space of alternatives becomes too large for exhaustive testing, which can occur even with a handful of joins, uniform random sampling provides a mechanism for unbiased testing.

The technique is implemented in Microsoft's SQL Server, where it is an integral part of the validation and testing process.

1   Introduction

Cost-based query optimizers typically consider a large number of candidate execution plans, and select one for execution. The choice of an execution plan is the result of various, interacting factors, such as database and system state, current table statistics, calibration of costing formulas, algorithms to generate alternatives of interest, and heuristics to cope with the combinatorial explosion of the search space. Normally, experimental

validation and testing of the query processor is limited to considering the one plan that was chosen by the optimizer for execution. This is a severe limitation, as this plan is only a minuscule fraction of the space of alternatives. In fact, during regular development and maintenance of a query processor, it has been our experience that some code defects can remain undetected for a long time, until the right combination of factors steer the optimizer to chose a plan that exposes the problem.

Rather than waiting for these problem scenarios to occur, or trying to manually influence optimizer choices towards "potentially problematic" cases, we generate alternative execution plans by enumeration and sampling, from the space of alternatives *considered* by the optimizer. The plans are generated independently from optimizer decisions and provide a large set of test cases for both the optimizer—are the alternatives considered really valid execution plans?—and the execution engine—do different but semantically equivalent plans produce the same output?

This approach to testing is similar to that taken by Slutz [11], in which a large number of random SQL statements are submitted to the database. Random statements can be generated quickly, and extensive coverage of the code can be achieved in a short time. Multiple execution plans for a given query test smaller system components; it shows the result of arbitrary combinations of optimization rules, and exercises execution algorithms in configurations that are less common. Starting from a query with that has specific properties, e.g. joins and outerjoins, or joins and aggregations, an "area" of the optimizer and execution code is targeted and exercised in a variety of combinations.

We develop a general approach based on *ranking* elements of a space, which allows enumeration and sampling of plans. The basic idea is to establish a one-to-one mapping between integers $0, \ldots, N-1$ and the N elements of a space. *Ranking* an element, e.g. an execution plan, means finding its number; *unranking* a number means constructing the corresponding plan. Once an unranking mechanism is available, uniform sampling of elements in the space reduces to random generation of numbers in the range $0, \ldots, N - 1$.

None of the known ranking and unranking techniques for tree structures apply to the current problem [10, 2], as the space of alternatives considered by industrial query optimizers is not restricted to an abstract combinatorial problem, such as join reordering. Multiple execution algorithms, index utilization, reordering of grouping operators, special-purpose physical operators, and heuristics to control the time spent on searching, all make up for an *actual* space that is hard to describe succinctly using abstract, regular structures.

The technique we devised achieves an unranking mechanism based on the compact representation of multiple alternatives, in the style of the MEMO structure of Volcano [7, 5], used in Microsoft's SQL Server and Tandem's NonStop SQL. Initially introduced in a transformation-based system, this data structure simply captures the multiple choices available to a cost-based optimizer, not necessarily constructed using transformation rules—a bottom-up enumeration approach implicitly uses a similar data structure.

After performing the regular optimization of a query, we modify this data structure to facilitate the counting of all possible plans and the subsequent generation of a particular plan. The overhead incurred by this kind of post processing is negligible for both, counting and extracting a certain plan. Furthermore, we extended the SQL syntax to allow the specification of a plan, i.e., the specification of a the plan's number, within the standard interfaces.

Its marginal overhead together with a simple and easy to use interface have made this technique a valuable tool and integral part of the testing process in the SQL Server development.

In addition to its immediate use for testing, we also used this mechanism to perform some experiments in a largely unexplored field of query processing: The cost distribution of query plans. Cost distributions are of interest, because they can be taken as obvious indicators of the stochastic difficulty of a problem, by simply considering the ratio of high quality to low quality plans [6].

The remainder of this paper is organized as follows. In Section 2, we briefly outline the optimizer framework and the MEMO structure. The counting and unranking schemes are introduced in Section 3. In Section 4, we report on the experience with using the tools in the ongoing development of Microsoft's SQL Server. We present initial results on cost distributions computed for TPC-H queries in Section 5. Section 6 concludes the paper.

2 Preliminaries

In this section we review the concept of a compact representation of the plan space in form of the MEMO structure. This concept was developed by Graefe and DeWitt in the context of transformation-based query optimization [4, 5, 1]. Independent of this development, a similar structure has been developed for bottom-up enumeration of join trees in Starburst [8]. Our technique is based on the MEMO but could be transferred easily to the Starburst enumerator.

We will briefly introduce the essential aspects of the MEMO and refer the interested reader to [3] for further reading.

A *query plan* determines the execution order of a set of relational algebra operators which implements a given, declarative query. Query plans are n-ary trees whose nodes correspond to algebra operators and are therefore referred to as operators too. Due to the tree structure, every operator represents a sub-goal of the plan, that is, the partial query evaluation done by the sub-tree rooted in it.

A cost function computes a *cost value* for a query plan which is for instance the time needed to execute the plan. The goal of the optimization is to generate the query plan with the least cost value, i.e. to solve the associated combinatorial optimization problem. Cost based query optimizers like the ones used in Microsoft's SQL Server, Tandem's NonStopSQL or IBM's DB2 generate partial query plans, cost them and—if a partial plan is a candidate to be part of the optimal plan—store them in a lookup table. The generation of sub-plans and their alternatives is guided by strategies and can be implemented for instance in a transformation-based framework or with dynamic programming.

In the following we outline the optimization process as implemented in SQL Server, which is similar to that of Volcano. We distinguish two kinds of operators: (1) *logical operators* that map to relational algebraic operators, e.g. join operator, and (2) *physical operators* that represent a particular implementation of a logical operator, e.g. hash join. Only physical operators may be used in the final query plan. Following Volcano, we call the aforementioned lookup table *MEMO structure*. It is a data structure that manages a system of *groups*, which represent different sub-goals of a query plan, i.e. every group corresponds to the root of a sub-plan.

We start out with an initial query plan that consists of logical operators only. This plan is a direct translation of a declarative query given in SQL. We map the initial query plan to the groups of the MEMO so that every operator is assigned to one group. The group that contains the initial plan's root operator is referred to as *root group*. We substitute the original references to an operator's children by references to the respective

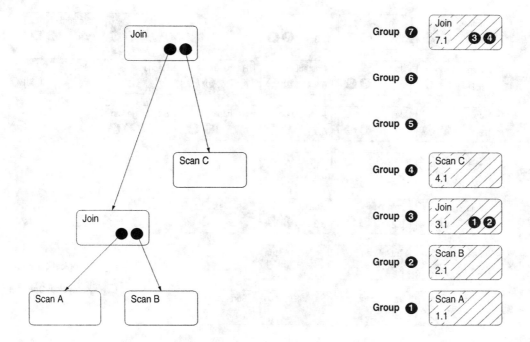

Figure 1: Copying the initial plan into the MEMO structure.

groups. Figure 1 shows an initial tree and its equivalent after copying it into the MEMO structure. Operators in the MEMO are depicted as rounded boxes with the references to the children's groups in the lower right corner and a unique identifier in the lower left corner. The references to the children's groups are ordered, that is, the left number represents the first child's groups, and if available, the right is the second child's. For simplicity, we use only unary and binary operators in the examples, however, the methods we present are not limited to any given degree. To avoid renumbering of groups at a later point in time we put the root operator immediately into group 7 in this example. Thus, group 7 becomes the root group. Notice, in the actual implementation, groups are not ordered but only referred to by their numbers. However, putting it directly into group 7 and maintaining an order makes this example more intuitive and easier to understand.

Once the initial plan is copied into the MEMO, we derive alternatives by applying transformations to the logical operators. A transformation rule can generate:

1. a logical operator in the same group, e.g. join(A,B) → join(B,A);

2. a physical operator in the same group, e.g. join → hash join;

3. a set of logical operators that form a connected sub-plan; the root goes to the original group, other operators may go to any group, including the creation

of new groups as necessary, e.g. join(A,join(B,C) → join(join(A,B),C).

In Figure 2, a partially expanded MEMO structure is depicted. The physical operators are shaded and an example plan is shown with darkened operators.

We do not apply rules to transform physical operators since everything that could be derived from a physical operator can also be derived from the logical one. A technicality that needs special attention is the fact that operators of the same group—i.e. with the same logical properties—may differ in physical properties. For instance, one operator may deliver a sort order whereas another operator of the same group does not, or it may deliver a sort order on a different attribute. In case the parent operator requires a sort order on a certain attribute, not all operators may be chosen as potential children.

The MEMO framework includes routines that analyze the results of a rule application and assign it to the groups, detect and eliminate duplicates, and create new groups. Furthermore, it also provides costing techniques that estimate and assign costs to each operator in the MEMO, that is, the costs of the sub-plan rooted in each operator. For every group we keep track of the best physical operator for a each set of physical properties. When costing a new operator we compute the costs using the children's best implementations. Moreover, the MEMO contains scheduler primitives that implement different strategies as to when to apply what rule. A

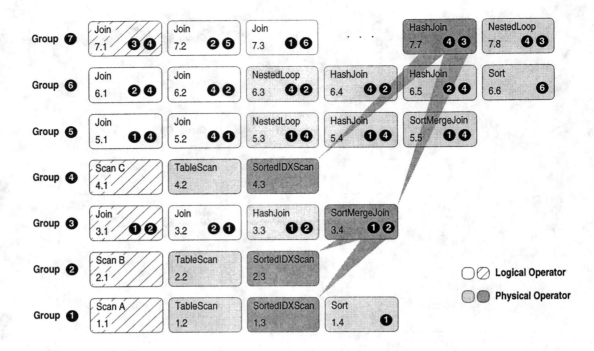

Figure 2: MEMO structure representing alternative solutions.

cost based pruning heuristic helps avoid expansion of very costly alternatives that, given the current state of optimization, cannot be a sub-plan of the optimal plan, and therefore need not to be explored.

The optimal query plan is the one rooted in the most cost effective operator in the root group. To extract this plan, we follow the references to the children's groups and select the most cost effective operator of each group, observing compatibility of physical properties. This step is repeated until we reach the terminal operators. Note, this plan was already implicitly used for costing the best operator in the root group.

Though we described the use of transformations to generate alternative sub-plans form an initial plan, also other techniques like bottom-up enumeration [8] could be used to populate a structure functionally equivalent to the MEMO. The methods developed in the following are independent of the algorithms to construct the MEMO structure, and simply rely on this structure as a compact representation of the candidate plans considered by the optimizer. Some optimizers by default discard suboptimal expressions. For our technique to be most effective, it is useful to have the optimizer keep each alternative generated, so they can be freely used, regardless of their cost.

3   Counting and Unranking Query Plans

Once all alternatives are generated, the MEMO structure contains all operators but does not keep track of how many combinations of operators there are, and only the optimal plan is completely assembled. That is, at the end of the optimization, the MEMO contains a concise and compact encoding of the complete search space that was considered during the optimization.

To illustrate the counting framework, let us assume a final state of the MEMO —after generation of alternatives is complete— as given in Figure 3.

3.1   Preparatory Steps

In order to facilitate later operations we extract all physical operators and materialize the links between operators and their possible children. In Figure 3, the materialized links for all children of the previous example's root (operator 7.7) are shown. The resulting structure describes all possible execution plans that can be rooted in this operator.

Due to the differences in physical properties some operators of a group may qualify as potential children while others do not. For instance operator 3.3 in Figure 3, can have any operator from group 1 and 2 as left and right child, respectively. Operator 3.4 however can use only the darkened operators 2.3 and 1.3 or 1.4.

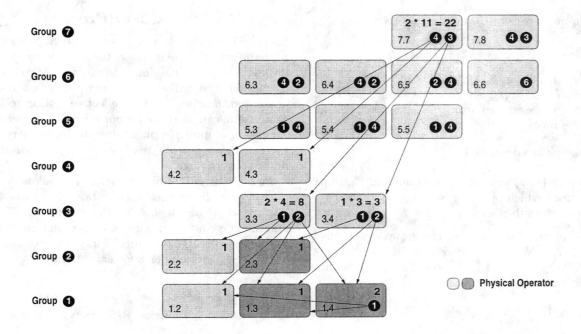

Figure 3: MEMO Structure with materialized links between operators and children, for possible plans rooted in operator 7.7.

3.2 Counting Query Plans

We compute the total number of possible plans bottom-up by computing the individual numbers of possible plans that can be extracted from each operator. We denote the number of children of operator v by $|v|$, and the j-th alternative for the i-th child of v by $w_{i,j}^{(v)}$. For example, in Figure 3, take $v = 7.7$, then $w_{1,1}^{(v)} = 4.2$, and $w_{2,2}^{(v)} = 3.4$.

To compute the number of plans $N(v)$ rooted in an operator v, we first determine the number of possible alternatives for each child i as

$$b_v(i) = \sum_j N(w_{i,j}^{(v)}).$$

Operator v will take any of the available alternatives for each child, independently, so the number of combined choices is given by a product. The numbers of plans we can generate using only the first k children is

$$B_v(k) = \prod_{i=1}^{k} b_v(i).$$

Hence, the number of plans rooted in v is

$$N(v) = \begin{cases} 1, & \text{if } |v| = 0 \\ B_v(|v|), & \text{otherwise} \end{cases}$$

In Figure 3, this process is illustrated for operator 7.7. The upper right corner of operators has the computation of the number of alternatives that can be extracted using it as a root.

The total number of plans is the sum of possible plans rooted in any of the root group's operators:

$$N = \sum_i N(v_i), \qquad v_i \in G_{root}$$

where G_{root} denotes the root group.

Computing the counts for operators takes linear time on the size of the MEMO, as each operator has to be visited exactly once.[1] In practice, the time needed for counting never exceeded 1 second even for large queries.

3.3 Unranking Plans

Before we describe the unranking mechanism in detail, it might be helpful to give a short outline of the idea:

Starting with the root group and the rank r, we choose an operator of the group to be the root of the tree. We then compute a *local rank* for this operator. This local rank for an operator v is in the interval $0, \ldots, N(v)$.

---

[1] For the number of logical operators for the problem of join reordering, see [8, 9]. There are a few physical operators for each logical joins, implementing different alternatives of hash join, merge join, and index lookups, so the number of physical joins is usually a small multiple of the count of logical joins.

Now, assume operator v has children alternatives

$$\{w_{1,1}^{(v)}, \ldots, w_{1,j_1}^{(v)}\}, \ldots, \{w_{n,1}^{(v)}, \ldots, w_{n,j_n}^{(v)}\},$$

with $n = |v|$. n *sub-ranks* are computed, and used in each child choice to recursively unrank a sub-plans. The resulting tree is assembled from unranked sub-plans, using v as the root.

Detailed steps are described next.

1. Given a pair (r, G) consisting of a rank and a group we determine which operator of this group becomes the root of the sub-plan.

   The first physical operator in the group covers the plans $0, 1, \ldots, N(v_1)-1$, the second $N(v_1), N(v_1)+1, \ldots, N(v_1)+N(v_2)-1$ and so on. Thus, the sought operator has index

   $$k = \max\{i | \sum_i N(v_i) \leq r\}.$$

   v_k becomes the root of the (sub-)plan. The local rank r_l of v_k is

   $$r_l = r - \sum_{i=1}^{k-1} N(v_i)$$

   The local rank is necessary to determine the sub-ranks for the children in the next step.

2. Using the concepts introduced in the previous section, we can write the sub-rank for the i-th child as

   $$s_v(i) = \begin{cases} R_v(i), & \text{if } i = 1 \\ \left\lfloor \frac{R_v(i)}{B_v(i-1)} \right\rfloor, & \text{else} \end{cases}$$

   with

   $$R_v(i) = \begin{cases} r_l, & \text{if } i = |v| \\ R_v(i+1) \bmod B_v(i), & \text{otherwise} \end{cases}$$

3. We add operator v_k to plan and repeat this step for each child, i.e. for the i-th child we unrank $(s_v(i), G_i)$ where G_i is the group for this child.

4. We repeat steps 1 through 3 recursively until we reach the terminal operators.

   Unranking is in $O(m)$, m being the number of operators in the tree which is limited by the number of groups in the MEMO. In terms of running time, unranking takes only a small fraction of the time needed for counting and is thus negligible.

4 Verifying Query Processors

In [11], Slutz presents a tool to generate SQL statements probabilistically, to increase the test coverage of the database engine. One simple advantage of this approach is the sheer speed at which new, different tests are generated, making it a very effective testing tool. The same claim can be made for our schema of selection and execution of multiple plans given a single query, which increases even further the coverage of query optimizer and execution logic.

In our current implementation in Microsoft's SQL Server, we extend the SQL syntax with an option to specify what plan to use for the execution. The SQL statement shown in Figure 4 causes the optimizer to build the MEMO structure, count the possible plans, and select plan number 8 for execution.

```
SELECT    *
FROM      Professors P, Students S, Enrolled E,
          Courses C
WHERE     S.Name = "Sam White" AND
          S.SID = E.SID AND
          E.Title = C.Title AND
          C.By = P.PID
OPTION    (USEPLAN 8)
```

Figure 4: Query with USEPLAN directive

Using scripting primitives, any given query can be extended easily with the OPTION clause and a loop construct that iterates over a deterministically or randomly selected set of possible plans. This way developers are able to generate test cases for specific queries, instantly extending existing test libraries substantially.

The main advantages of using these techniques in testing are:

1. It is easy to generate large test sets for the engine to scrutinize both correctness of the query execution and its performance.

2. The results are simple to verify since all plans should deliver the same outcome. The probability that an incorrect result is overlooked is rather small as opposed to conventional testing where each result requires manual verification.

3. It is possible to test operator implementations that the optimizer would not chose for the current state of the test database.

4. Optimizer decisions and correct assembling of plans by the optimizer can be easily verified. This point is of particular importance when extending the set of both operators and their implementations.

Query	#Plans	Min°	Mean°	In a sample of 10000		
				Max°	costs° ≤ 2	costs° ≤ 10
Q5	68572049	1.14	17098	4034135	0.47%	12.15%
Q7	228107572	1.15	3318	178720	0.11%	44.55%
Q8	20112521035	1.01	111	609	1.11%	14.7%
Q9	67503460	1.10	4107	109825	0.11%	4.08%
Q5*	455348910	1.23	105418	1287700	0.29%	5.70%
Q7*	3907373772	1.48	1793052	1523086611	0.03%	2.79%
Q8*	4432829940185	1.31	28159718	32595091399	0.06%	1.85%
Q9*	250657568	1.30	38363213	35866936219	0.02%	7.00%

°as factor of the optimum (=scaled costs); *including Cartesian products

Table 1: Parameters of search spaces of TPC-H join queries.

5. The verification and calibration of cost formulas is no longer restricted to one single plan per query but can also check cost values of sub-optimal plans.

6. The enumeration of complete search spaces for small queries helps check and analyze optimizer principles like cost-bound pruning and search strategies.

The features described are part of the routine testing in the development of Microsoft's SQL Server.

5 Cost Distributions

Besides their practical application to testing which was the driving force behind our efforts, the techniques presented are of importance for the experimental analysis of cost distributions, which we believe to be a promising area of research. Cost distributions capture the frequency of plans of certain costs, and they can be indicators of the difficulty of a query in that they show how many plans of what quality there are in the whole space.

Ioannidis and Kang were the first to report on cost distributions explicitly, i.e. they performed a sampling of the search space for the restricted problem of join ordering [6]. They pointed out that knowledge of the cost distribution helps understanding certain effects occurring in optimization, specifically needed for the tuning of probabilistic optimization techniques. They developed a search space model based on this analysis which provides useful insights into the working of randomized join ordering. The distributions they found were asymmetric and resembled Gamma-distributions implying certain topological structures in the search space. They attributed their findings to the particular cost model used.

However the question as to what degree do those results apply to the unrestricted, general case of query optimization is still open so far.

Using our framework we are able to perform a fair random sampling of costs in the search spaces that are not limited to join ordering only but may include arbitrary relational operators, various kinds of indexes and aggregates, and even cover parallel processing. We carried out numerous experiments with both standard benchmark queries like TPC-H and customer queries taken from various applications. Under the precondition that the queries were of sufficiently large size, i.e., involving more than 4 or 5 joins, the distributions obtained were characterized by a relatively strong concentration of costs relatively close to the optimum, asymmetric, and often resembling exponential distributions. These shapes correspond to Gamma-distributions with shape parameter close to 1, which were also observed by Ioannidis and Kang.

Figures presented here are the result of experiments with TPC-H queries 5, 7, 8, 9, which are the join-intensive queries of the benchmark, and have a larger search space. Table 1 summarizes some of the relevant values obtained. The first four rows consider a space of alternatives that does not allow cross products; while the last four rows allow cross products. Each experiment consists of a random sample of 10,000 plans from the space. All costs are normalized to the optimum plan found by the optimizer, which has cost 1.0.[2] The "min" column shows that with a relatively small sample from the space, it is possible to find plans that are pretty close to the optimum. In fact, the percentage of plans that are within twice the optimum cost is non-trivial. Also, it should be noted that the results are slightly different for the different queries, which vary in their selectivity and other properties. But the same trends can be seen in all the experiments.

Figure 5 shows histograms of the cost distributions discussed. All plots show that almost all plans are

---

[2]The measure of a very large number of plans in the space considered by the optimizer does not imply that a structure requires as many bytes—recall that the plans are obtained through composition and reuse of operators, from the compact encoding of the MEMO structure.

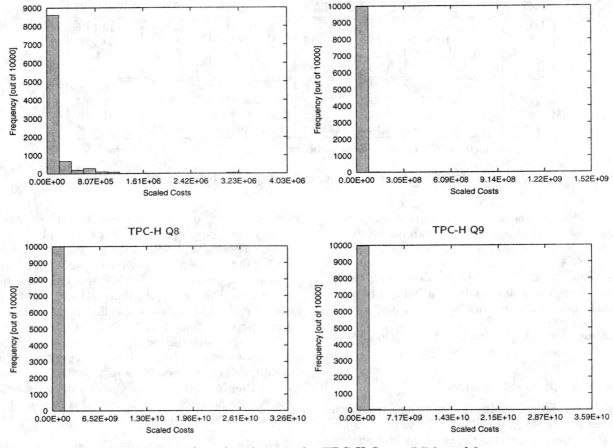

Figure 5: Cost distributions for TPC-H Query 5,7,8, and 9.

within the lower 10% of the entire cost range, suggesting a Gamma-distribution of costs. Figure 6 shows zoom-ins to the lower 50% sampled costs; that is, the part of the distribution that makes up for 50% of the space with the optimum as left edge. Still all four plots show a very strong resemblance with Gamma distributions. However, little disturbances are visible, particularly in case of Query 5.

Finally, Figure 7 shows a further zoom, to the points that are up to 50 times the cost of the optimum. In the "macro" view, we find that plans tend to be clustered to the left, close to the optimum solution. As we zoom in to the dense area, the histograms get less smooth, but they still seem to suggest Gamma distributions.

Our findings lend strong support to the assumption that cost distributions of the form detailed above are characteristic to query optimization and are of a much more general nature than first suspected by Ioannidis and Kang.

The distributions of queries that contained few tables were of no particular shape but consisted only of random noise (e.g. TPC-H 6). Although it is hypothetically possible to devise queries of arbitrary size where the cost distribution degenerates to a single point—e.g. the cross product of several instances of the same table, with a space restricted to be linear joins—we never observed any such tendency in practical instances or customer queries.

These results are only preliminary and further research is needed to investigate this subject. Besides the observation that cost distributions are generally of a certain shape, it would be particularly interesting to know what parameters are responsible in order to predict the distribution analytically.

6   Summary

Query optimizers select one execution plan out of a large number of alternatives considered, and traditional testing can verify only this one plan. In this paper we developed primitives to generate either the whole

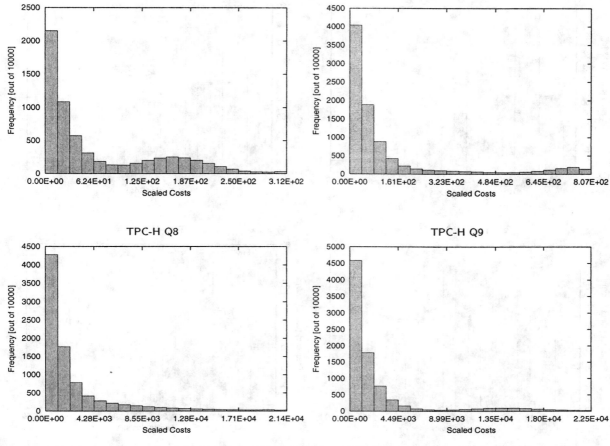

Figure 6: Cost distributions for TPC-H Query 5,7,8, and 9; lower 50% sampled costs.

space of alternatives, or a uniform random sample within that space. The problem is challenging because cost-based optimizers do not represent entire execution plans explicitly, but rather rely on data structures that maximize sharing of common expressions between candidate plans.

By opening up the space of alternatives to stocastic testing, we are able to validate the optimizer logic, and exercise the execution engine effectively. Unexpected interactions between different transformation rules can be seen, and execution iterators are tested in uncommon, but possible configurations. This provides a valuable tool to certify and increase the quality of a query processor, which would be difficult to match using only hand-crafted examples, either written by testers or obtained from customers.

Our validation tool is unintrusive to the workings of the optimizer, and it can be implemented separately, as long as it can access the table of alternatives constructed during optimization. A small extension to

the language provides access to the functionality, so it is easy to write scripts to do the extensive testing.

A further use of our enumeration and sampling primitives is the study of the search space itself. What was it all that the optimizer considered, and how does it compare with the actual optimal plan? We were able to obtain for the first time some initial results on cost distributions of *real* search spaces. Results on cost distributions are important for work on randomized query optimization, and we are also interested in their use to characterize the difficulty of particular problems —and the optimization effort required to solve them. This is a subject for future research.

References

[1] J. A. Blakeley, W. J. McKenna, and G. Graefe. Experiences Building the Open OODB Query Optimizer. In *Proc. of the ACM SIGMOD Int'l. Conf. on Management of Data*, pages 287–296, Washington, DC, USA, May 1993.

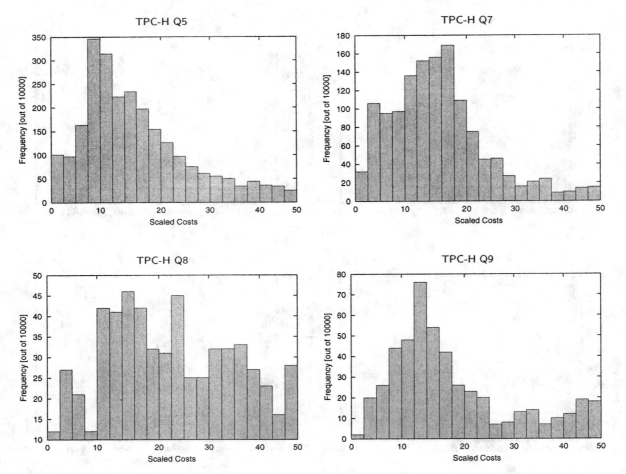

Figure 7: Cost distributions for TPC-H Query 5,7,8, and 9; blow-up of the interval $[0, 50]$.

[2] C. A. Galindo-Legaria, A. Pellenkoft, and M. L. Kersten. Uniformly-distributed Random Generation of Join Orders. In *Proc. of the Int'l. Conf. on Database Theory*, pages 280–293, Prague, Czech Republic, January 1995.

[3] G. Graefe. The Cascades Framework for Query Optimization. *IEEE Data Engineering Bulletin*, 18(3):19–29, September 1995.

[4] G. Graefe and D. J. DeWitt. The EXODUS Optimizer Generator. In *Proc. of the ACM SIGMOD Int'l. Conf. on Management of Data*, pages 160–172, San Francisco, CA, USA, May 1987.

[5] G. Graefe and W. J. McKenna. The Volcano Optimizer Generator: Extensibility and Efficient Search. In *Proc. of the IEEE Int'l. Conf. on Data Engineering*, pages 209–218, Vienna, Austria, April 1993.

[6] Y. E. Ioannidis and Y. C. Kang. Left-Deep vs. Bushy Trees: An Analysis of Strategy Spaces and its Implications for Query Optimization. In *Proc. of the ACM SIGMOD Int'l. Conf. on Management of Data*, pages 168–177, Denver, CO, USA, May 1991.

[7] W. J. McKenna. *Efficient Search in Extensible Database Query Optimization: The Volcano Optimizer Generator*. PhD thesis, University of Colorado, Boulder, CO, USA, 1993.

[8] K. Ono and G. M. Lohman. Measuring the Complexity of Join Enumaration in Query Optimization. In *Proc. of the Int'l. Conf. on Very Large Data Bases*, pages 314–325, Brisbane, Australia, August 1990.

[9] A. Pellenkoft, C. A. Galindo-Legaria, and M. L. Kersten. The Complexity of Transformation-Based Join Enumeration. In *Proc. of the Int'l. Conf. on*

Very Large Data Bases, pages 306–315, Athens, Greece, September 1997.

[10] R. Ruskey and T. C. Hu. Generating Binary Tree Lexicographically. *SIAM Journal of Computation*, 6(4):745–758, December 1977.

[11] D. Slutz. Massive Stochastic Testing of SQL. In *Proc. of the Int'l. Conf. on Very Large Data Bases*, pages 618–622, New York, NY, USA, September 1998.

Benchmarking Queries over Trees: Learning the Hard Truth the Hard Way*

Fanny Wattez†   Sophie Cluet,   Véronique Benzaken
INRIA, BP 105, 78153 Le Chesnay, France   U. Paris XI, LRI, 91405 Orsay, France
Fanny.Wattez@inria.fr   Sophie.Cluet@inria.fr   Veronique.Benzaken@lri.fr
Guy Ferran   Christian Fiegel
Ardent Software, 3 place de Saverne, 92400 Courbevoie, France
Guy.Ferran@ardentsoftware.fr   Christian.Fiegel@ardentsoftware.fr

1   Introduction

Hierarchical and graph structures are very popular nowadays, thanks to XML and object-relational systems that broadened their range of applications. They can be accessed in two fashions, depending on the applications: follow links from node to node (e.g., DOM-like [5]) or use associative accesses. A benchmark we ran on the O_2 system[1] showed, among other interesting things, that focusing on one kind of access may lead to overlooking the other, needlessly handicaping its performance. Not surprisingly, these results were not the ones we were looking for when we started benchmarking. Still, we believe they are relevant beyond this particular system and should interest any developer of a system dealing with objects, navigation and associative accesses.

In [8], we give some advice to would-be benchmarkers, explain why O_2 does not cope well with large associative accesses and give a performance analysis of queries against hierarchical structures in an object-oriented database featuring physical identifiers. This paper summarizes these three contributions.

2   Tips to Benchmarkers

The O_2 database management system [1] supports OQL [3, 2]. The current optimizer relies on heuris-

†This work was partially supported by the ANRT (French National Association for Technical Research)
†This work was done while the author was an employee of Ardent Software

tics. At the end of 1997, we benefited from an increase in manpower and considered implementing a cost-based search strategy. So, we started benchmarking in order to better understand what a good cost model should be. We understood that benchmarking could be tedious. Well, it was hard, long and very tedious. Most of the unpleasantness is certainly due to our inexperience. As a matter of fact, the advice we are about to give look incredibly obvious. Still, we did not find them in the litterature (e.g., [6]) and we wish someone had given them to us when we started.

Buy Big! We bought a 2G bytes disk. It looked large enough to store the largest of the databases we planned to test. Wrong arithmetic: when buying your disk think *sum*, not *max*. Each set of tests bring new questions and you need all your databases handy to answer them.

Get System Gurus Involved Soon. Alternatively, Read the Documentation Carefully. We now count two system gurus in our ranks, for nearly two years we had none and only benefited from a little guru tip once in a while. We were under the assumption that creating a large database was similar to creating a small one. Big mistake! Among the many problems that slowed our work considerably, let us simply mention this one. We had always heard that it is more efficient to create an index once the collection is populated, rather than to update one at each object insertion. This is usually true, but, as you can find out if you read carefully the O_2 system documentation, not for the first index. For various good reasons [8], the creation of a first index on a collection entails a physical move of all its objects and that takes some time.

Why Not Use a Database to store your results? We started storing results in files. On top of not being reliable, this is time consuming. You end up with files whose names are all but clear, have to use low level tools, etc. After messing around in this fashion for some time, we realized that a database was a very reasonable place to store information.

3 On Object Databases and Associative Accesses

O_2 provides functionalities that other object database systems do not. Notably: (i) the full ODMG model [2], including arbitrary complex values and persistence by attachement, (ii) indexes on arbitrary collections (i.e., not only extents), (iii) object versioning and (iv) dynamic class evolution. These various features and the fact that objects can be shared imply that some information be associated to each object. As an example, consider indexes. An object may belong to several collections, not all of which are extents, and that may be indexed or not. Thus, when an object is updated, there is a priori no way to know which index should be updated, unless the object has the appropriate information.

Thus, when O_2 loads an object into memory, it creates a structure called DV (for Dope Vector) that contains information about indexes, versions, types, etc. At some point in our experiments, we ran into results that clearly showed that DVs were large, considerably slowing down algebraic operations requiring some buffering (e.g., most join algorithms, grouping). We realized then that DVs had been growing over the years to reach 60 Bytes. At first, we thought it strange that no impact on performance was ever detected. But actually, DVs growed to improve performance. Indeed, large DVs are bad essentially for cold associative accesses requiring buffering. But, object benchmarks focus on applications requiring random navigation within objects residing in memory, applications which benefit a lot from a structure that allows to perform management tasks fast and without having to fix the object in memory. In [8], we propose various ways to solve this apparent conflict of interest.

4 On Join and Pure Navigation over Hierarchical Structures

We tested extensively a typical object query on collections of 1 to 3 million objects. The query is characterized by a dependency between variable definitions as in the following OQL **from** clause:

    from o1 **in** Collection1,
          o2 **in** o1.children

We compared algorithms relying on pure naviga-

tion (no intermediate structure but potentially random disk accesses) against hash-based ones, considering each time parent-to-child and child-to-parent accesses. The hash-join algorithm we used is a slight variation of the pointer-based join algorithm of [7] that allows sequential rather than randomized access to the outer collection.

Our tests indicate that, although pointer-based hash joins are certainly efficient, pure navigation is not bad, as usually believed. In a nutshell, when the number of children is large, child-to-parent pure navigation is always comparable to the best hash-join algorithms; it is better when the number is very large and worse when it is small. The second point indicates the need for hybrid hashing, which we did not test. In the parent-to-child direction, navigation beats hash-joins by far when the data is nicely clustered and is dreadful otherwise. This seems to indicate that object database systems should be natural candidates to provide DOM interface on persistent XML data [5]. Our results also seriously suggest that, given the appropriate manpower, object database systems could support OQL as efficiently as relational systems support SQL.

Acknowledgments

We would like to deeply thank Yves Lechevallier for helping us trying to make sense of our figures and Jérôme Siméon for giving us a hand in using YAT[4] to convert data from O_2 to Gnuplot.

References

[1] The O_2 database system. www.ardentsoftware.fr.

[2] R.G. Cattell. *The Object Database Standard: ODMG 2.0.* Morgan Kaufmann, 1997.

[3] S. Cluet. Designing OQL: Allowing Objects to be Queried. *Information Systems*, 23(5), 1998.

[4] S. Cluet, C. Delobel, J. Siméon, and K. Smaga. Your Mediators Need Data Conversion! In *Proc. ACM SIGMOD*, 1998.

[5] World Wide Web Consortium. The document object model. www.w3.org/DOM.

[6] J. Gray, editor. *The benchmark handbook for database and transaction processing systems.* Morgan Kaufmann, 1993.

[7] E. J. Shekita and M. J. Carey. A performance evaluation of pointer-based joins. In *Proc. ACM SIGMOD*, 1990.

[8] F. Wattez, S. Cluet, V. Benzaken, G. Ferran, and C. Fiegel. Benchmarking queries over trees: Learning the hard truth the hard way. www-rocq.inria.fr/~wattez.

Maintenance of Cube Automatic Summary Tables

Wolfgang Lehner
University of Erlangen-Nuremberg
Martensstr. 3, Erlangen, 91056, Germany
wolfgang@lehner.net

Richard Sidle, Hamid Pirahesh, Roberta Cochrane
IBM Almaden Research Center
650 Harry Road, San Jose, CA 95120, USA
{rsidle, pirahesh, bobbiec}@almaden.ibm.com

ABSTRACT

Materialized views (or Automatic Summary Tables—ASTs) are commonly used to improve the performance of aggregation queries by orders of magnitude. In contrast to regular tables, ASTs are synchronized by the database system. In this paper, we present techniques for maintaining cube ASTs. Our implementation is based on IBM DB2 UDB.

1. INTRODUCTION

ASTs are a well-known technique for improving the performance of aggregation queries that access a large amount of data while performing multiple joins in the context of a typical data warehouse star schema. Fully exploiting the power of the AST technique requires support from the database system in (a) picking the optimal set of ASTs for a specific application scenario and workload [1], (b) transparently rerouting user queries originally referencing base tables to those views [4], and (c) maintaining ASTs, i.e. synchronizing them with the base tables [2]. This paper focuses on techniques for maintaining cube ASTs.

2. DEFINITION OF ASTs

The example in Figure 1 defines a hierarchical data cube for location (city,state,country), product (group,lineitem), and time (month,year) dimensions further categorized according to marital status and income range of the customer. This example demonstrates that a complete OLAP scenario, providing data for 144 (4*3*3*4) grouping combinations at different levels of aggregation, can be specified as a single summary table.

Similar to a regular view, the content of an AST is defined by a SELECT expression. Additionally, an AST definition may contain an explicit specification of its physical layout similar to a regular base table, i.e. it can be partitioned, replicated, indexed, etc. Finally, each AST has a refresh mode. Declaring an AST as 'REFRESH IMMEDIATE' implies that all dependent ASTs are automatically synchronized when the underlying base data is modified. This is done optimally by applying the incremental maintenance strategy outlined in this abstract. If an AST is declared 'REFRESH DEFERRED' then no base table changes are propagated when a base table is modified. In lieu of sophisticated algorithms [3], refreshing a deferred AST implies full recomputation. While a deferred AST may be defined by any SELECT expression, the specification of an incrementally maintainable AST must adhere to the following rules:

- Grouping expression: The grouping expression may consist of single grouping columns or any valid combination of complex grouping expressions like CUBE(), ROLLUP(), or GROUPING SETS(). The evaluation of the grouping expression must not result in duplicate grouping combinations. For example, ROLLUP(a,b),a is not allowed, since it evaluates to ((a,b),a) = (a,b); ((a),a) = (a); and ((),a) = (a), resulting in the combination with (a) appearing twice.

- Aggregate functions: The set of aggregate functions is restricted to SUM and COUNT. Every AST must have a COUNT(*) column. If a column X is nullable and the AST computes SUM(X), a named COUNT(X) column is also required.

- Grouping functions: A GROUPING() function expression is required for any nullable grouping column that occurs in a complex grouping expression. This allows the system to differentiate between naturally occurring NULL-values and NULL-values that denote (sub-) totals. In the sample AST, the grouping columns "marital status" and "income range" are nullable. Since these columns may naturally produce NULL values, they require a GROUPING function column in the definition of the AST.

3. INCREMENTAL MAINTENANCE

The advantage of an incremental maintenance strategy is that the changes in the AST are computed directly from the changes of the base table. Consider an AST containing a join over several tables. Incremental maintenance can compute the changes to the AST using the joins of only the changes of the base tables (deltas) with all other tables of the AST definition. One unique feature of DB2 UDB's AST maintenance strategies is that its infrastructure naturally supports incremental maintenance for complex ASTs like hierarchical data cubes over a set of tables.

Maintenance of Automatic Summary Tables in IBM DB2/UDB

STEP I: Building the Raw Delta. All local deltas, i.e. the inserted, updated or deleted rows of all base tables are combined to generate the global raw delta stream. Multiple local deltas might be caused within the context of a single statement while maintaining database semantics, such as enforcing referential integrity constraints using 'ON DELETE CASCADE'. To synchronize an AST with an underlying update operation, the delta consists of the rows before and after the update extended with a numeric tag.

```
CREATE SUMMARY TABLE ast_demo AS (
  SELET   loc.country, loc.state, loc.city,
          pg.lineid, pg.pgid,
          c.marital_status, c.income_range
          YEAR(t.pdate) AS year, MONTH(t.pdate) AS month
          SUM(ti.amount) AS amount,
          COUNT(*) AS count,
          GROUPING(c.marital_status) AS grp_mstatus,
          GROUPING(c.income_range) AS grp_income_range
  FROM    transitem AS ti, transaction AS t, location AS loc,
          pgroup AS pg, account AS a, customer AS c
  WHERE   ti.transid = t.transid AND ti.pgid = pg.pgid
  AND     t.locid = loc.locid AND t.acctid = a.acctid
  AND     a.custid = c.custid
  GROUP BY ROLLUP(loc.country, loc.state, loc.city),
          ROLLUP(pg.lineid, pg.pgid),
          ROLLUP(YEAR(t.pdate), MONTH(t.pdate)),
          CUBE(c.marital_status, c.income_range)
) DATA INITIALLY DEFERRED REFRESH IMMEDIATE;
```
Figure 1: Sample AST Definition

STEP II: Aggregating the Delta. In this step, the delta stream is aggregated. If the underlying modification is an insertion or deletion, then the grouping specification contains all the combinations specified by the AST. For ASTs with complex grouping expressions, e.g. CUBE(), this step results in a complete delta cube with 'higher' delta aggregate values for all original delta changes. If the modification is an update, then the grouping specification contains all the combinations specified by the AST extended with the tag column. For updates, the resulting aggregate values are multiplied with the value of the tag, and a second delta aggregation step consisting of a simple aggregation over all grouping columns plus all grouping function columns is added to eliminate the tag column and compute the net aggregate changes (i.e. delta value) from the old to the new base table values.

STEP III: Pairing the Delta to the AST. After aggregation, the rows in the delta are paired with the current content of the AST using a left outer-join (the delta goes left) over the grouping and grouping function columns of the AST. Thus a delta group either matches with a single group of the summary table or no group at all. Delta groups that have matches cause the corresponding row in the AST to be modified; those that do not have matches are later added to the AST.

STEP IV: Aggregate Value Compensation. When a delta group has a corresponding group in the AST, then the new value for the group must be computed based on the value of the delta and the current value of the group. Since the AVG aggregation function can be mapped to an equivalent SUM/COUNT expression, '+' is the only aggregation value compensation function, required to support SUM, COUNT, and AVG.

For ASTs with complex grouping expressions (like CUBE(), ...), the overall summary value, or grand total, evaluates to NULL even if the number of contributing rows is zero and requires special treatment. The computation of the aggregate value SUM for non-nullable columns requires a COUNT(*) column to derive the new cardinality. If, however, the parameter column of the aggregate function is nullable, then the new cardinality is derived from the COUNT-values ranging over that nullable column.

STEP V: Applying the Delta to the AST-- Depending on the underlying base table operation, the delta stream is applied to the AST using the following operations:

- Base table insert: Already existing groups in the AST are updated, new groups are inserted into the AST.

- Base table delete: Groups of the delta with a new cardinality of zero are deleted, the remaining rows are updated with the new values of the delta stream. Note that in the case of ASTs with complex grouping expressions (like CUBE()), the grand total row is never be deleted.

- Base table update: This case may be considered a combination of base table insert and deletion resulting in a sequence of AST update, delete, and insert operation as described above.

4. FULL REFRESH

Although the incremental maintenance strategy provides an automatic synchronization for ASTs when the underlying base tables change, there are scenarios where 'DEFERRED' refresh is justified. For example, when incremental maintenance is becoming too expensive due to a high update frequency of the base tables and/or a high number of incrementally maintainable summary tables. In this case, ASTs can be fully refreshed.

5. SUMMARY AND FUTURE WORK

This paper outlines the current state-of-the-art in maintaining ASTs in the IBM DB2/UDB database system. The maintenance strategies provide a sound basis for a powerful data warehouse infrastructure within DB2.

6. REFERENCES

[1] Harinarayan, V.; Rajaraman, A.; Ullman, J.: Implementing Data Cubes Efficiently. In: SIGMOD'96, pp. 205

[2] Mumick, I.; Quass, D.; Mumick, B.: Maintenance of Data Cubes and Summary Tables in a Warehouse. In. SIGMOD' 97, pp. 100-111

[3] Beyer, K.; Cochrane, B. Lindsay, B.; Salem K.: How To Roll a Join. IBM research paper. In. SIGMOD'2000

[4] Zaharioudakis, M.; Cochrane, R.; Lapis, G.; Pirahesh, H.; Urata, M.: Answering Complex SQL Queries Using Automatic Summary Tables. In: SIGMOD'2000

i This work was done while author was visiting IBM Almaden Research Center.

Challenges in Automating Declarative Business Rules
to Enable Rapid Business Response

Val Huber

Versata

(No abstract was submitted for the proceedings.)

Expressing Business Rules

Ronald G. Ross
Business Rules Solutions, LLC
http://www.BRSolutions.com
rross@brsolutions.com

Business rules are formal statements about the data and processes of an enterprise. My overall approach to business rules is described in [1, 2]. Here, I will briefly discuss things we have learned about the expression of business rules in the last several years. This will shed light on where we stand in understanding business rules today.

First, it is clearly important to separate analysis-level expression of business rules from their design-level expression. Most of what I will say here is aimed toward the design level, but let me start with the analysis level.

Effective expression of business rules at the analysis level requires formative guidelines or Business Rule Statement Templates. Such language templates are now offered commercially (by my company and others). Think of these language templates as text or sentence patterns, to ensure higher clarity and consistency. These templates are important for making the business rule approach practical.

At the design level, how business rules are expressed to users must be cleanly separated from how they are represented inside the system. What is good for one is not good for the other.

For the *external* representation, at least several capture techniques are probably needed, each suited to different categories of rules. For example, each of the following techniques is probably well-suited to certain types of rules:

- Decision Tables for value thresholds, and perhaps certain types of computations.
- Point-and-Click Expression Builders, for instance limits and type consistency.
- Structured English, for more complex restrictions and logical inferences.
- Entity Life History or State Transition Diagrams, for both basic and more advanced state transition rules.
- Data Model or Class Model extensions, for basic property rules.

No matter how the rules are captured, there should be a single, unified *conceptual* representation "inside" of the man-machine boundary. "Inside" here means transparent to the specifiers, but

visible to analysis tools (e.g., for conflict analysis) and to rule engines or business logic servers (for run-time processing).

Inside, there may be still other representations. For processing and performance reasons, there might be many physical representations of the rules, optimized for particular tools or hardware/software environments.

The result is actually three layers of representation: external, conceptual, and internal. This is strongly reminiscent of the old ANSI/SPARC three-schema architecture for data. This should not be surprising since rules simply build on terms and facts, which can be ultimately represented by data.

Which technique is the best for each representation layer is a matter of great debate. All three layers are important, but clearly the ultimate power lies in the middle or conceptual layer. The important thing for this language layer is that the rules must be represented in a sufficiently rigorous form for automated (even if not very efficient) execution [1].

Alternative candidate representations for this level of language include the following.

- Predicate Logic (the baseline – any other representation must be at least this powerful.)
- Ross Method, featuring strong rule typing [1].
- Terry Halpin's work on Object Role Modeling (ORM) [2]
- The Object Constraint Language (OCL), from the OMG [3].
- Tutorial D in C.J. Date & H. Darwen's Third Manifesto [4]

These languages are not for the faint of heart, but point toward the technological future of business rules -- supporting higher-level automation schemes for user requirements.

In retrospect, I believe the main contribution of [1] is its highly organized scheme for the *conceptual* representation of all rules. This representation is based on rule typing (patterns), which I believe is a level above other approaches. The graphic notation might be useful for capturing *certain* types of rules at the external layer – especially using a point-and-click environment. However, this would certainly not be optimal for all rules.

Where is this research now? A new, more concise representation scheme is under development. One focus of this scheme is a formal expression of how non-atomic rule types are derived from atomic ones. This would allow reduction of rules to a common base of fundamental rule types, in order to support automatic analysis of conflict and overlap in systematic fashion.

This is opening exciting new avenues of research, and significant opportunities for those interested in getting involved.

REFERENCES

[1] Ross, Ronald G., *The Business Rule Book,* Business Rule Solutions, 2nd Edition, 1997.

[2] Ross, Ronald, G., *Business Rule Concepts*, Business Rule Solutions, 1998.

[3] Halpin, Terry, *Conceptual Schema and Relational Database Design*, 2nd Edition, Prentice-Hall, 1995.

[4] http://www.omg.org

[5] Hugh Darwen and Chris J. Date, *Foundation for Object/Relational Databases: The Third Manifesto*, Addison-Wesley, 1998.

Going Beyond Personalization: Rule Engines at Work

Eric Kintzer

Blaze Software

(No abstract was submitted for the proceedings.)

DLFM: A Transactional Resource Manager

Hui-I Hsiao

Inderpal Narang

IBM Almaden Research Center

San Jose, CA 95120

Email: hhsiao@almaden.ibm.com; narang@almaden.ibm.com

Abstract

The DataLinks technology developed at IBM Almaden Research Center and now available in DB2 UDB 5.2 introduces a new data type called **DATALINK** for a database to reference and manage files stored external to the database. An external file is put under a database control by "linking" the file to the database. Control to a file can also be removed by "unlinking" it. The technology provides transactional semantics with respect to linking or unlinking the file when DATALINK value is stored or updated. Further more, it provides the following set of properties: (1) managing access control to linked files, (2) enforcing referential integrity, such as referenced file cannot be deleted or renamed as long as it is referenced from the RDBMS, and (3) providing coordinated backup and recovery of RDBMS data with the file data.

DataLinks File Manager (DLFM) is a key component of the DataLinks technology. `DLFM is a sophisticated SQL application with a set of daemon processes residing at a file server node that work cooperatively with the host database server(s) to manage external files. To reduce the number of messages between database server and DLFM, DLFM maintains a set of meta data on the file system and the files that are under database control. One of the major decisions we made was to build DLFM on top of an existing database manager, such as DB2, instead of implementing a proprietary persistent data store. We have mixed feelings about using the RDBMS to build such a resource manager. One of the major challenges is to support transactional semantics for DLFM operations. To do this, we implemented the two-phase commit protocol in DLFM and designed an innovative scheme to enable *rolling* back transaction update after local database commit. Also a major gotchas is that the RDBMS' cost based optimizer generates the access plan, which does not take into account the locking costs of a concurrent workload. Using the RDBMS as a black box can cause "havoc" in terms of causing the lock timeouts and deadlocks and reducing the throughput of a concurrent workload. To solve the problem, we came up with a simple but effective

way of influencing the optimizer to generate access plans matching the needs of DLFM implementation. Also several precautions had to be taken to ensure that lock escalation did not take place; next key locking was disabled to avoid deadlocks on heavily used indexes and SQL tables; and timeout mechanism was applied to break global deadlocks.

We were able to run 100-client workload for 24 hours without much deadlock/timeout problem in system test. This paper describes the motivation for building the DLFM and the lessons that we have learned from this experience.

1. Introduction

IBM has focused on extensible database research for more than a decade. The results of many of these efforts have already appeared in IBM's DB2 family of relational database management systems (RDBMSs) [1]. To extend the reach of RDBMS functions even farther, IBM Almaden Research has now developed a new technology called DataLinks [2], which enables DBMS to manage data stored in external operating system files. DataLinks gives DBMS comprehensive control over external data and provides the following properties: referential integrity, access control, coordinated backup and recovery, and transaction consistency. DataLinks technology has now been deployed by several corporations and institutes, such as Boeing, Dassault, and automotive manufacturers, to provide database management of distributed scientific and engineering data stored in operating system files [2, 3].

The DataLinks technology comprises of the following major components: the DLFM, DLFF (DataLinks File System Filter), and an extension to the RDBMS engine (termed datalink engine hereafter). It also introduces a new DATALINK data type [4] to facilitate RDBMS to reference and manage externally stored data. The datalink engine is responsible for processing DDL requests to create datalink column(s) and for processing DML requests against the datalink column(s). On the other hand, the DLFM and DLFF components reside at file servers where the database managed external data are stored. The value of the datalink column in an SQL table is URL, which may reference files on the same or remote file server. A datalink column can be populated by an SQL insert statement or by a database load utility. Similarly, a record with datalink attribute can be deleted or updated through a standard SQL statement. Whenever a datalink value is selected or updated (or inserted or deleted), the datalink engine is invoked by the database engine to process the part of request specific to datalink. As part of the processing, a request to the DLFM residing on the file server as specified by the URL is sent to apply certain constraints in order to start (or stop) managing the file on that file server. DLFF helps to enforce these constraints when file system commands are executed against the linked files.

Database systems, in general, provide transactional semantics and ACID [5] property. To maintain the transactional semantics for SQL requests, operations performed at DLFM would have to be in the same transaction context as the one in the host database system (where the SQL requests of the application are processed). To satisfy this requirement, operations performed at the DLFM are treated as a sub-transaction[1] [6] of the transaction in host RDBMS and the two-phase commit protocol [7, 8] is used to atomically commit or rollback the operations done at both sides. Also to recover from a system failure, changes to DLFM data and state have to be both persistent and recoverable. One approach is to implement a proprietary persistent store as part of the DLFM. While this is not difficult to do technically, it is less portable and unnecessarily reinvents the technology available in all commercial database systems. As such, our design relies on a database server (DB2) for providing persistency and recoverability for DLFM data/state.

Figure 1 shows an example of the storage model of the DataLinks technology. In Figure 1, a DB2 database is used as a host RDBMS to store user's data and references to external objects via an URL in the datalink column. A DLFM residing with each file server is responsible for managing files stored in that server. System generated metadata for managing files and enforcing access control and integrity is stored in each DLFM. As previously mentioned, DLFM uses DB2 as a persistent store for all of its data. DLFM treats the DB2 as a black box and all requests to retrieve, insert, or update DLFM data/state are via standard SQL.

---

[1] By sub-transaction it is implied that the host DB2 always resolves the outcome of the transaction on the DLFM side. Standard 2-phase commit protocol is used between the host DB2 and the DLFM. Note that the host DB2 may or may not be the coordinator of the user initiated transaction. For example, the host DB2 can be a participant in an XA transaction that is initiated by a TP monitor, such as, CICS.

While this provides great flexibility and portability[2], it also poses significant challenge in enforcing transactional semantics and providing good system performance.

The rest of the paper is organized as follows. Section 2 gives an overview of the DataLinks technology and DataLinks application flow. Section 3 describes the functions and services provided by the DLFM component. Section 4 presents the experience and lessons we learned in building the DLFM and finally section 5 summarizes the paper.

DataLinks - DB Linkage withFilesystems
(Storage Model)

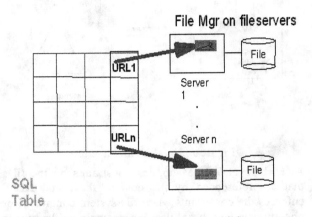

Figure 1: Datalink storage model

2. DataLinks Technology

DataLinks is a software technology that enables DBMS to manage data stored in external operating system files as if the data were stored directly in the database. By extending the reach of the DBMS to operating system files, DataLinks gives users flexibility to store data inside or outside the database as appropriate. To store and reference data outside of DBMS, a database application developer declares a column of DATALINK data type when creating an SQL table. The value stored in the datalink column is then used to represent and reference data in an external file. Figure 2 illustrates the architecture of the DataLinks technology. As shown in the figure, DataLinks comprises two components: datalink engine and Data Link Manager (ref. Figure 2). Datalink engine resides

---

[2] The DLFM can easily be ported to any RDBMS systems and/or any operating systems.

519

in the host database server and is implemented as a part of the database (DB2) engine code. It is responsible for processing SQL requests involving datalink column(s) such as table creation and select, insert, delete, and update of records with datalink column. Data Link Manager consists of 2 components, DataLinks File Manager (DLFM) and DataLinks File System Filter (DLFF).

DataLinks

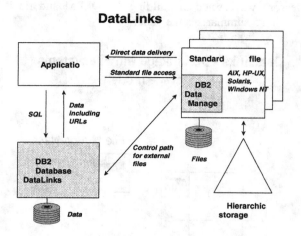

Figure 2: Datalink architecture

At high level, DLFM applies constraints on the files that are referenced by the host database and DLFF enforces the constraints when file system commands or operations affect these files. For example, a file rename or delete would be rejected if that file were referenced by the database. DLFF is a topic on its own and will not be described further in this paper. DLFM resides with the file server that can be local or remote to the host database server. DLFM provides a set of API's that the datalink engine uses to make requests for linking a file, unlinking a file, carrying out two-phase commit protocol, etc. Invoking the API's is through remote procedure call mechanism.

2.1 DataLinks Application

A datalink application is an application that manipulates datalink attribute (column) in an SQL tables and it is no different from a regular database application as far as the database is concerned. Before a datalink application can issue any requests, it must establish a database connection first. As part of the database connect request, a DB2 agent (process or thread) is identified to serve the application. After connection has been established, the application can start submitting SQL requests to the database engine. If an SQL request requires manipulating a datalink column, the datalink engine is invoked to process part of the request specific

to the datalink column. In turn, the datalink engine sends one or more requests to the DLFM to manipulate files and metadata stored at file server, if necessary.

Figure 3 illustrates how DataLinks works from an application perspective. In a DataLinks environment, a host database (e.g., DB2 UDB) provides the metadata repository for external data. Attributes and subsets of the data stored in external files are maintained in the host database tables along with the logical references to the location of the files (e.g., a server name and a file name). The application searches the host database via the SQL API to identify external files of interest. Examples would be finding the following: 50-day-moving-average chart of stocks that are tripled in price during the last 12 months; a video clip used in TV commercials within the last year that contains images of Michael Jordan; all of the email attachments received within the last six months that concern customer profiles; or employee who is older than 40 and has blue eyes and red hair. DB2 processes the request and returns the references (URL's) for selected files to the application. The application then accesses the file data directly using standard file-system API calls (file-open, etc.) Using standard file API's is very important for supporting existing applications without having to modify either the applications or the file systems.

DataLinks For Managing External Data

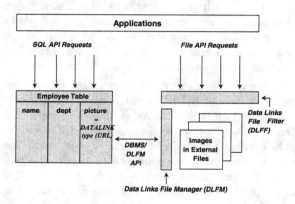

Figure 3: Managing external data with Datalinks

3. Datalink File Manager

The Data Links File Manager (DLFM) component of DB2 Data Links Manager plays a key role in managing external files. It is responsible for executing the link/unlink operations in the same transaction are linked to (referenced in) the database. When a file is initially linked to the database, the DLFM applies the constraints for referential integrity, access control, and backup and recovery as specified in the DATALINK column definition. If the DBMS controls read access, for example, the DLFM changes the owner of the file to the DBMS and marks the file "read only". All of these changes to the DLFM repository and to the file system are applied as part of the same DBMS transaction as the initiating SQL statement. If the SQL transaction is rolled back, the changes made by the DLFM are undone as well.

In order to support certain SQL operations, such as Drop SQL table, the concept of **File Group** was introduced. A File Group corresponds to all files that are referenced by a particular datalink column of an SQL table. This is so that it is possible to efficiently unlink all files associated with a column of an SQL table when it is dropped. The DLFM is also responsible for coordinating backup and recovery of external files with the database. When the DBMS transaction that includes a *Link File* operation commits, the DLFM initiates a backup of the newly linked file if DLFM is responsible for recovery of the file. This file backup is done *asynchronously* and is not part of the database transaction for performance reasons. In addition, by doing it this way, the database backup itself is not slowed down because the referenced file would typically have been backed up. This is particularly important in the case of very large files. Coordinated backup and recovery of external files with DB2 data can be done directly to disk or to an archive server supported by DLFM, such as IBM's ADSTAR Distributed Storage Manager (ADSM).

The DLFM tracks different versions of a referenced file and maintains the backup status of each in order to support point-in-time recovery. The DBMS also provides the DLFM with a "Recovery id" for a file whenever it is linked or unlinked to help synchronize recovery of files with data. This is important because a file with the same name but different content may be linked and unlinked several times. Without a separate "Recovery id" for each link operation, DLFM would not be able to restore the file to match the database state.

When the DBMS does a backup of its database, it communicates with the DLFM's to ensure that all of the necessary asynchronous copy operations for referenced files have completed before declaring that the database backup has been successfully completed. The DBMS backup utility has been extended to handle this level of communication and to keep additional information in the backup image about which file servers and file groups are involved in the backup. Backup copies of unlinked files may be kept for a specific number of database backup cycles, in case the database is restored to a point in the past in which the file was still linked to

the database. The DLFM is also responsible for "garbage collection" of backup copies of unlinked files that are no longer required by the DBMS.

3.1 Persistent Data Structure

The DLFM uses a local database to keep its metadata and state information. This information is stored in the following SQL tables.

1. Dbid Table: This table consists of registered entries for each host database that can connect to this DLFM. The *dbid* field in this table represents the unique combination of the host database name, instance name, and host machine name.

2. Group Table: This table consists of file group entries. Each group entry corresponds to a datalink column in an SQL table on the host database side.

3. File Table: This is the most accessed table that consists of the information of linked and unlinked files on the file server. Whenever a file is linked, a new entry is inserted into the file table. During the unlink operation existing file entry in linked state is marked as unlinked. This table retains the unlinked file entries if files need to be restored in the future via the host database restore utility. The columns of interest defined in this table are *dbid, filename, transaction_id, Recovery_id, file_status, entry_state*. Their usage will be described with the functional processing later.

4. Transaction Table: This table keeps track the transaction state of all the active DLFM transactions. Transaction state is maintained for each transaction as long as it is active. The transaction state information is first kept in an in-memory table when the transaction starts. The entry is inserted into the SQL table when the transaction begins the first phase of the commit processing. Once the transaction is completed, its entry is removed from the transaction table.

5. Archive Table: This table contains file and group entries that need to be archived to the archive server. When the load utility is used to insert a large number of files into a datalink column on the host database side, instead of replicating each file entry in the Archive table, only a group entry is inserted into the Archive table. The entry from the Archive table is processed to make copy of a set of files or just one file. After copy has completed, corresponding entry is removed from the Archive table.

3.2 Link and Unlink Operations

LinkFile and UnlinkFile are two most frequent operations that corresponds to insert and delete of the datalink value respectively from the host database. Whenever an application inserts a file entry into a datalink column the corresponding file on the server is linked by the DLFM. Linking involves applying certain constraints on the file such that subsequent rename and deletion of the referenced file, via normal file system API's (or commands), are prevented to preserve referential integrity from the host database. Furthermore, the access control mode of the datalink column determines the partial or full takeover of the file. In full access control file ownership is changed to "DB" (to the DLFM admin user) and the file is marked read-only. Also an access token assigned by the host database is needed to access such a file. All the files linked to the host database are guarded against unauthorized move / delete / rename operations by the DLFM and DLFF. During the LinkFile operation DLFM puts a new entry in the File table. This entry consists of dbid, transaction id, filename, and Recovery id among other things. Recovery id generated at the host database consists of dbid and a timestamp. It is guaranteed to be globally unique and monotonically increasing. For every LinkFile operation the DLFM makes the following two checks,

1. If a link entry already exists for the same file in the DLFM metadata table then it rejects the LinkFile operation as the file is already in the linked state.

2. If an unlink entry exists for the same file in the DLFM table whose unlink transaction has not committed (i.e. in in-flight or in-doubt state) then it rejects the LinkFile operation as the outcome of the unlink transaction is still unknown.

During an Unlinkfile operation, the table entry for the file is marked as unlinked. It also updates the unlink transaction id and unlink timestamp in the entry. At any given time the DLFM File table can have at most one linked entry for a given file while there can be multiple unlinked entries for a file because many successive link and unlink operations can take place for the same file. The unlinked entry is used in the coordinated backup-and-restore operation to identify the correct version of the file from the archive server, if needed. In this case, the unlinked file entry is later removed by the Garbage Collector daemon (described in Section 3.5) when it is no longer needed. If file recovery is not needed, the unlinked entry is deleted in the second phase of the commit processing. Note that we could not delete the entry earlier than the second phase of commit since we would not be able to undo the action if the transaction's outcome is abort after phase 1 (see Section 3.3).

During the link file operation, file entry checking and insertion **must** be an atomic operation (otherwise there is a small window where two DLFM agents can both check for and not find the linked entry for a file and then insert the two linked entries for the same file). To close the window for the race condition, a unique index

on the filename column and a new check-flag is defined.[3] During link file operation, the check-flag attribute is set to zero and during unlink file operation, the check-flag is set to Recovery id provided by the host database. This unique index prevents two linked entries but allows multiple unlinked entries for the same file.

During the forward progress of a transaction DLFM manipulates the entries in the File table as per link/unlink file operations. If the transaction needs to rollback, DLFM uses the recovery mechanism provided by the local database to undo the actions. The file server, on the other hand, does not support transactional semantics in general. Thus, actual takeover or release of the file from the file system is done during the second phase of the commit processing and is done by Chown daemon (described in Section 3.5). DLFM also supports unlinking of a file from one datalink column and re-linking of the same file to another datalink column within the same transaction. This is an important customer requirement where current and old versions of the file are maintained in separate SQL tables.

When an error occurs during regular link or unlink processing, DLFM reports the error status to the host database that will result in either statement level (savepoint) or transaction level rollback at the host database. If a link or unlink file request is initiated by a savepoint rollback at the host database, then any error reported by the DLFM local database will result in rolling back the full transaction at the host database. This is because DLFM treats local database as a black box and it is not possible to rollback a rollback. In addition, if a severe error such as deadlock occurs in the local database, the host database will rollback the full transaction. This is because the current transaction has already been rolled back in the local database. Also since DLFM does not write recovery log records for its own link and unlink file operations, it is not possible to do a database-style rollback. In our design, undoing link (or unlink) file operation is done by sending DLFM another link (or unlink) file request but with a special *in_backout* flag set to *true*. For a link file request with *in_backout* set, DLFM deletes the linked file entry that was inserted by current transaction. For an unlink request with the flag set, the unlinked file entry is restored back to linked state.

3.2.1 Performance Consideration
The File table has at least one entry for each file under database control. In a production environment, it would

---

[3] Note that for a given file name, there can be multiple entries in the File table and yet DLFM has to ensure that at most one entry is in the linked state. So a unique index on the filename alone is not sufficient.

be common to have hundreds of thousand or millions of entries in the File table. Since each link or unlink file operation needs to access the File table, efficiency in finding and retrieving entries from the File table is essential to provide good overall performance. The first thing we did was to avoid table scan by building several indexes, one for each access path. A side benefit of avoiding table scan is that the probability of triggering lock escalation is also reduced. When the table size (cardinality) is small, the optimizer could still pick table scan even when an index is available. To ensure that the optimizer always picks the access plan we want, the statistics in the database catalog are manually set before DLFM's SQL programs are compiled and bound. In a multi-user test, a different problem surfaced that was partially due to use of multiple indexes. When multiple insert and/or delete entry operations are being done concurrently, different DLFM processes may use different indexes to access the File table. This results in frequent deadlocks because of the next key locking [9] feature supported in the local database server. Since repeatable read is not really needed by the DLFM processes, that feature is turned off. With these enhancements, we were able to run 100-client workload for 24 hours without much deadlock/timeout problem in the system test. Also, the system achieved rates of 300 inserts per minute and 150 updates per minute.

3.3 Transaction Support

When a new transaction is started by the application, the host database assigns a new transaction id. In the case of an XA transaction, the host database also generates a local transaction id that is different from the global XA transaction id. A transaction id is associated with a particular database so that there is no problem with transaction id being the same from different databases. The transaction id generated at a specific database is guaranteed to be monotonically increasing, which is absolutely essential.[4] This id is passed to the DLFM in each of the API invocation. The DLFM associates the transaction id with each operation that changes DLFM metadata and state. The reason is that DLFM *does not* have logging services of its own, but uses a local database for persistence and logging. By associating the transaction id along with the operation, and storing them in the database tables, it can relate the actions performed by a particular transaction. This is important because a) the actions done by a DLFM for a particular sub-transaction may need to be undone if the

host transaction aborts after the sub-transaction completing the prepare phase (i.e., completed phase 1 of the 2 phase commit protocol) in the DLFM and b) certain actions on the file system have to be performed during phase 2 of the commit processing of the transaction.

DLFM uses the 2-phase-commit protocol to enforce the transactional semantics. Four API's are provided by the DLFM for this purpose: BeginTransaction, Prepare, Commit, and Abort. A sub-transaction starts when the host database makes BeginTransaction API call to a DLFM.[5] The transaction id generated at the host database is passed along with the BeginTransaction call. All subsequent API calls by the host database within the same transaction for linking and unlinking files are tagged with the same transaction id and are processed within the same transaction context by the DLFM. Once all operations are done under the present transaction, as a part of the commit processing on the host database, it sends a Prepare request to the DLFM. Prepare request processing on the DLFM makes sure that all the operations on the file server are made persistent by issuing an SQL commit to the local database. A separate transaction table is used for keeping the transaction id, its state, and other related information. The transaction entry for the current transaction is not made into the transaction table until the prepare request for the transaction has arrived. After the prepare transaction request is done successfully on all DLFM's, the host database sends a Commit transaction request to the DLFM's. On the other hand, if the prepare request fails, an Abort request will be sent to the DLFM's. It is important to note that, when multiple DLFM's are involved in a transaction, if one of the DLFM's fails to prepare the transaction, the host database sends Abort request to all the remaining DLFM's, even though they may have prepared successfully. Normally, prepare and commit/abort API's are invoked by the host database as part of an application's SQL commit. If the transaction is a branch of a global (distributed) transaction, the prepare request to the DLFM is invoked as part of global prepare processing and the commit/abort request is invoked when the outcome of the global transaction is known.

It is assumed that the commit transaction processing should not fail on the DLFM side if the prepare transaction processing has been successful. But that is not always true because there is a major difference

---

[4] DLFM records the transaction id as persistent information along with other information in the File table. Entries associated with a transaction are identified by this id during the commit processing.

[5] It is possible that files may be linked or unlinked to multiple DLFM's in a given host database transaction. This implies that a host DB2 transaction may involve sub-transactions on multiple DLFM's. In order to improve the readability of the paper we discuss the transaction management with respect to only one DLFM.

between database's SQL commit processing and DLFM's commit processing [ref. Fig 4]. The SQL commit processing does not acquire any new locks. It, in fact, releases all the locks acquired by the present transaction. On the other hand the DLFM uses the SQL interface to update the metadata and its state stored in its local database during commit processing. For a commit request, for example, DLFM retrieves entries from the File table and deletes an entry from the Transaction table. This, in turn, requires additional locks to be acquired by the DLFM. Since deadlocks are always possible when new locks are acquired, retry logic is included in the commit processing and it keeps retrying until it succeeds. However, if a deadlock forms among committing and/or aborting transactions, retry will not solve the deadlock. In our case, deadlocks have been found to form between a committing transaction and one of the DLFM daemons but not between two or more committing and/or aborting transactions. This is because table entries inserted or updated by two concurrent transactions are always disjoint[6]. Thus, our retry logic can solve deadlocks formed in the DLFM commit/abort processing.

SQL Transaction (Txn)

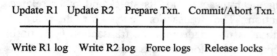

DLFM Transaction

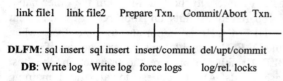

Figure 4: Commit processing

During a prepare transaction processing, DLFM inserts an entry into the transaction table and marks the transaction as prepared. If DLFM fails after the transaction has been prepared, then that transaction remains in an in-doubt state. It is the host database's responsibility for resolving the in-doubt transactions with the DLFM. Either host database restart processing does it, or if DLFM is unavailable at the restart, host database spawns a daemon whose sole purpose is to poll the DLFM periodically and resolve the in-doubts when the DLFM is up. In-doubt transactions are resolved based on the outcome of the parent transactions in the host database.

---

[6] This is enforced by the corresponding locking of the host database.

3.4 Coordinated Backup and Restore

The DLFM plays an important role in the coordinated backup and recovery of DBMS data along with the file data. When the transaction linking a file commits and the file group has recovery option[7] equals yes, DLFM starts archiving that file to the archive server such as ADSM.[8] The DLFM child agent (described in Section 3.5) puts an entry for the file into the Archive table and the Copy daemon picks up the entry from the Archive table and writes the file to the archive server. The main purpose behind the Archive table is to avoid contention in the main metadata table, the File table, and also to efficiently restart copying after recovering from any DLFM failure. Because multiple indexes are defined on the Archive table and size of the Archive table is small (entry gets deleted as soon as it is archived), deadlocks were encountered between child agent and the Copy Daemon while accessing the Archive table. Disabling the next key locking feature in DLFM's local database eliminated those deadlocks. Notice that phantoms may arise when the next key locking is not enforced. However, repeatable read property is not required for the DLFM to function correctly.

Note that the archiving of files is asynchronous when a transaction commits. DLFM does not hold any database locks while backup copy is being made. The asynchronous backup is possible because DLFM takes away the "write" permission of the file during commit operation. The Backup utility on the host database side makes sure that all the files linked since the last backup are archived to the archive server before declaring that backup is successful. In case archiving of some files is pending then it asks the Copy daemon to archive this set of files with high priority.

Restore utility restores the database from a backup image on the host database side. Whenever the host database is restored, DLFM may need to retrieve files from the archive server to match the database state if the linked files are not present in the file system. The database Recovery id at the time of backup is preserved in the backup image that is sent to the DLFM during restore to reconcile its metadata. Based on this Recovery id, all the files that are linked before the backup and unlinked after the backup are restored to the linked state. Similarly, files that are linked after the backup are removed from the linked state. All these actions (entry manipulation) are done via SQL calls to the local database in the DLFM side and we did not find it to be an issue.

---

[7] Recovery option is one of the properties of the datalink column.
[8] The DLFM also supports the option of backing up the files to a local disk.

The Reconcile utility is a new database utility introduced by DataLinks for synchronizing the host database state with the DLFM metadata information. After a database is restored to a point in the past, database state and DLFM state may be out of synchronization.[9] To bring the two sides back to a consistent state, the reconcile utility is invoked. When invoked, this utility goes through each datalink column, scans all entries for the column on the host database side, and then compares the information with the corresponding file status and metadata information on the DLFM side. It updates the information on either or both sides if necessary to bring the system back to a consistent state. Since the number of entries/records processed could potentially be very large, they are first stored in a temp table in the local database to reduce the number of file scans and the number of messages between the host database and DLFM. The processing on the DLFM side involves complex joins, sub-queries, and EXCEPT (difference) operation between the temp table and the File table, thus picking the right access plans is absolutely essential. To further optimize the performance, we handcrafted the table statistics to ensure that the database optimizer generates the best access plans.

3.5 DLFM Process Model

The DLFM is a concurrent server, i.e., it has a main daemon which spawns a child agent (or a process) when a connect request from a DB2 agent is received. The child agent then establishes a connection with the requesting DB2 agent. This child agent will serve all subsequent requests from the same connection. DLFM's main daemon then waits for another connect request from same or different host DB2. Applications on the host DB2 side will establish separate connections with DLFM, thus they are served by separate child agents on the DLFM side. Besides the child agent, DLFM provides several other services implemented as daemons and they are also spawned by the main DLFM daemon [ref. Figure 5]. This section describes the functionality and service provided by each of the daemons.

Delete Group Daemon

Whenever an SQL table is dropped on the host DB2 side then the corresponding file groups on the DLFM side, if any, will also need to be deleted. There can be lots of files referenced by the datalink column(s) in the dropped table and all those files need to be unlinked. So

---

[9] Restoring a database to the end-of-log (i.e. current state) does not require any reconciliation.

during the forward progress of the transaction, the file groups are marked deleted by the current transaction in the Group table. During prepare processing the child agent notes the number of groups deleted by this transaction and records it with the transaction entry in the transaction table. The commit processing checks if any group is deleted, by checking the deleted group count in the transaction entry, in the current transaction and if it is, it sends the transaction id to the Delete Group daemon. Using the transaction id the Delete Group daemon finds all the groups deleted in this transaction and then unlinks all the files in each group.

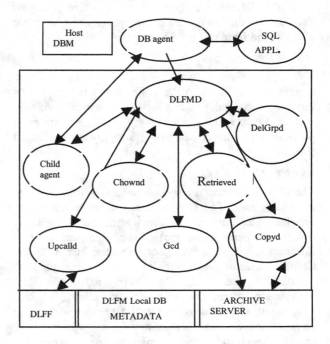

Figure 5: DLFM process model

The unlinking of the files by this daemon is asynchronous and the commit processing for drop table does not wait for it to complete. Note that the group entry is not deleted until all the files in that group have been unlinked. And as long as this transaction does not commit, the same file name is not allowed to be re-linked. Thus if DLFM fails before the Delete group daemon has completed unlinking all files from the deleted groups, then after DLFM restarts the Delete group daemon can still pickup all committed transaction entries from the transaction table and resume its work.

Garbage Collector Daemon

The Garbage Collector daemon is another asynchronous process, which does the cleanup of DLFM metadata. There are two types of cleanups; one is triggered by database backup while the other is to cleanup the deleted group whose lifetime has expired. The one by backup consists of cleaning up old backup entries according to the policy of keeping last N backups. So the last N+1 onwards backup entries and the corresponding unlink file entries from the File table are removed by the garbage collector daemon. It also removes the copies of those files from the archive server. The other one to cleanup deleted groups is based on their lifetime expiry. Each deleted file group is assigned a life span. Once the lifetime expires, the Garbage Collector daemon removes those deleted file group entries as well as associated unlink file entries from the DLFM metadata tables. If archive copies associated with the unlinked file entries exist, they are also deleted from the archive server.

Upcall Daemon

The Upcall daemon services requests from DLFF to determine if a file is in the linked state. If it is, user's request to delete, rename, or move the file via file system API's will be rejected by the DLFF. Its main purpose is to enforce referential integrity for the linked files.

Chown Daemon

The Chown daemon is a special process whose effective user id is *root*. The Chown daemon needs super user privilege as it manipulates attributes (such as ownership, permissions etc) of the files belonging to different users. A child agent communicates with the Chown daemon whenever it needs to get the file information, such as, file system id, inode, last modification time, owner, group etc. During commit processing, the child agent sends a request with a file name to the Chown daemon to take over the file, i.e. change owner and access permissions, or to release the file to the file system to restore original owner and access permissions. Since Chown daemon runs as super user, it is important to safeguard unauthorized requests. Thus, Child agent communicates with chown daemon with proper authentication.[10]

Copy Daemon

The Copy daemon is responsible for copying linked files from file system to an archive server or disk. When a file is linked, it will be copied asynchronously by the Copy daemon if DLFM is responsible for restoring the file after a database restore.

---

[10] The child agent encodes each message to the chown daemon with the specific signature. The chown daemon validates each message with the signature before doing any operation. The signature is a shared secret between the child agent and the chown daemon.

Retrieve Daemon

The Retrieve daemon is responsible for restoring files from archive server or disk. When the host database is restored to a point in the past, the file system state may be out of sync with the new database state. As part of re-synchronization, files are restored by the Retrieve daemon from the archive server, if necessary.

4. Lessons Learned in Building DLFM

As mentioned previously, we decided to use a DBMS (DB2) as a persistent store for storing DLFM metadata information. All changes to the DLFM metadata are written to the DB2 tables. Since standard SQL does not support two-phase commit between application and database, changes to metadata are hardened[11] during the prepare phase of the 2PC protocol. When something goes wrong in the host DB2 or in other DLFM's, the transaction will be aborted. In such cases, an abort request is sent to the DLFM in the second phase of the 2PC protocol and DLFM has to undo the changes even after they have already been committed in the local DB2. While schemes based on compensation application technique have been proposed for undoing committed transactions, it is extremely complicated to implement one in production systems. Consequently, our design takes a delayed update approach. With this approach, delete of any metadata information is marked as "deleted" while update creates a new entry in the database table with the old entry marked "deleted". When the transaction commits (second phase of commit), entries marked "deleted" in the current transaction are then deleted from the database. If the transaction aborts DLFM then changes these entries back to the normal state from the deleted state. This however, incurs a different problem. During both commit and abort processing, for example, locks will be acquired in the local database since these are normal SQL update/delete calls. This, in turn, may result in deadlocks or lock timeouts in both commit and abort processing. Since it is a sub-transaction and is not possible to change the outcome of a transaction in phase 2, DLFM will retry the commit/abort operation until it succeeds. Our experience has been that this was **not** a problem.

A set of indices is defined on the DLFM tables to improve search performance. We found that deleting a record from a table having index results in the next key locking. Since we have multiple indexes on some of the frequently accessed tables, the next key locking feature

---

[11] DLFM issues a commit to local DB2 to harden the changes before replying "yes" to a prepare request from the host DB2.

results in deadlocks frequently when multiple datalink applications are running concurrently. To maintain high performance and avoid such deadlocks, we turned off the next key locking in the DLFM database.

Load and Reconcile utilities tend to run for a long time and involve large number of link/unlink operations. Like any other long running transaction, there is a potential for running out of system resources such as log file or lock table entry. Since very long running transactions are always resulted from the database utilities that can be broken into pieces (i.e., undo of completed piece is not needed in case of a utility failure), we put intelligence in DLFM to recognize such transactions and to do local commit after finishing processing of each piece. A transaction entry is inserted into the transaction table in DLFM database when a local commit is issued for the first time for a given transaction but keep the entry marked as in-flight. The same mechanism is also applied to deleting entries in batch. For example, in the delete group daemon we unlink all the files under a deleted group. If a large number of files are linked under one group then unlinking them in a single DB2 transaction can cause the DB2 log full error condition. So we issue commits to local DB2 periodically after processing every N records (where N is implementation dependent).

We found that commit transaction API must be synchronous with respect to host database. Desire was to release the database locks on the host DB2 side while DLFM is doing the commit processing. However, this could lead to a distributed deadlock between the host database and DLFM as shown in the following scenario.

Transaction T1 is going through commit processing on DLFM side asynchronously. The host DB2 agent for T1 commits and starts a new transaction T11. T11 acquires an X lock on record *x* and then makes a LinkFile request to the DLFM. T11 is blocked on message send as the DLFM child is still doing the commit processing for T1[12] (and has not issued message receive). Assume that the commit processing of T1 on DLFM side is blocked waiting for lock *y* held by transaction T2. If the host DB2 agent for T2 happens to need to access record x, it will also be blocked. Now a deadlock cycle forms and it cannot be broken unless one of the transaction aborts. Since T11 and T2 are not involved in any local deadlock in the host DB2, they will not be aborted by the host DB2. On the DLFM side, T2 is not waiting for any locks and T1's request for lock y will eventually get timeout. But since it is in the phase two of the commit

processing, T1 will retry commit and later gets timeout again. This process will repeat forever as the deadlock cycle persists. By making commit request synchronous, distributed deadlock like the one above was avoided.

As in most distributed systems, identifying and breaking distributed deadlock is an important issue. While a distributed deadlock detector can be built in theory, it will add significant complexity and overhead to the system as host DB2 and DLFM database do not communicate directly. Instead, we take a simple approach and rely on the timeout mechanism to resolve potential distributed deadlock. The problem with the timeout mechanism is that it is difficult to come up with a perfect timeout period and some transactions may get rollback unnecessarily. In our case, we set the timeout to 60 seconds and it has performed reasonably well. Another problem related to locking is lock escalation. When a DLFM process holds lots of row level locks in a metadata table then it may result in a lock escalation to table level lock. The lock escalation for a high traffic table will result in timeouts for other applications. The rollback operations as a result of timeouts in turn add additional workload to the system. We observed that lock escalation in any of the metadata tables usually brings the system to its knees. Within our daemons, we are careful that they commit frequently enough so as to avoid any lock escalation. Also, applications should issue commit frequently to avoid holding a large number of locks and lock list size should be set sufficiently large to avoid forced lock escalation.

Cost based optimizer is the most advanced database optimizer and it has been used in most commercial database systems. We observed that Cost based Optimizer does not take locking cost (concurrent accesses) into account when choosing an index for access. In certain cases it also chose an index that was not only sub-optimal but also caused table scan, instead of index scan, to evaluate predicates. To get the desired access plan, we wrote a utility to set the statistics in the database catalog to force optimizer to select the plan we want. While this works in the lab, issuing a Runstat operation by any user will overwrite the handcrafted statistics and potentially result in sub-optimal plan being generated again. To prevent this from happening, additional logic is put into DLFM to check for changes in metadata statistics and re-invoke the utility to reset statistics and rebind access plans, if necessary.

5. Summary

In summary, DataLinks meets a very challenging application requirement that has existed for many years. DataLinks enables organizations to continue storing

---

[12] Recall that the same DLFM child is used to serve all requests for the same application on the host database.

data (particularly large files of unstructured or semi-structured data such as documents, images, and video clips) in the file system to take advantage of file-system capabilities, while at the same time coordinating the management of these files and their contents with associated data stored in an RDBMS.

DLFM is a key component of the DataLinks technology developed at the IBM Almaden Research Center. It plays a key role in enforcing access control, providing referential integrity, and supporting coordinated backup and restore. DLFM uses a DBMS as a persistent store for storing its data (metadata) and state change information that takes the advantage of existing database technology and at the same time offers excellent portability. Doing this, however, has its drawbacks too. Because the DBMS used is treated as a block box, one of the major challenges is to support transactional semantics for DLFM operations. To do this, we implemented the two-phase commit protocol in DLFM and designed an innovative scheme to enable rolling back transaction update after a commit to the local database. Also, a major gotchas is that the RDBMS' cost based optimizer generates the access plan, which does not take into account the locking costs of a concurrent workload. Using the RDBMS as a black box can cause "havoc" in terms of causing the lock timeouts and reducing the throughput of a concurrent workload. To solve the problem, we came up with a simple but effective way of influencing the optimizer to generate access plans matching the needs of the DLFM implementation. Also, several precautions had to be taken to ensure that lock escalation did not take place, that the next key locking was disabled to avoid deadlocks on heavily used SQL tables with multiple indexes, and that the timeout mechanism was applied to break deadlocks. In the system test, we were able to run 100-client workload for 24 hours, with a reasonably heavy update activity, without much deadlock/timeout problem.

Acknowledgement

Many people contributed to building DataLinks technology over the last few years. Major contributors include Suparna Bhattacharya, Karen Brannon, Kiran Mehta, Suhas Gogate, Mahadevan Subramanian, Ajay Sood, Parag Tijare, Dale McInnis, Lindsay Hemms, Jason Gartner, Nelson Mattos, Robin Williams, and last but not least Ashok Chandra. The authors would like to thank them for their dedication and contribution that made this paper possible.

References

[1]   E. F. Codd, "A Relational Model of Data for Large Shared Data Banks", CACM 13, p 377-387, 1970.

[2]   IBM, "DataLinks: Managing External Data With DB2 Universal Database", white paper prepared by Judith R. Davis, IBM corporation, February 1999.

[3]   M. Papiani, J. Wason, A. Dunlop, and D. Nicole, "A Distributed Scientific Archive Using the Web, XML and SQL/MED", ACM SIGMOD Record, Vol. 28, No. 3, Sept. 1999.

[4]   N. Mattos, J. Melton, and J. Richey, "Database Language SQL – Part 9: Management of External Data (SQL/MED)", ISO working draft, June 1997.

[5]   T. Hearder and A. Reuter, "Principal of Transaction Oriented Database Recovery", ACM Computing Surveys. 15(4), p287-317, 1983.

[6]   J. Moss, "Nested Transactions: An Approach to Reliable Computing." MIT, LCS-TR-260, 1981.

[7]   B. Lindsay, et al., "Notes on Distributed Databases", IBM San Jose Research Laboratory, RJ 2571, 1979.

[8]   G. Samaras, K. Britton, A. Citron, C. Mohan, "Two Phase Commit Optimization in a Commercial Distributed Environment", Distributed and Parallel Databases Journal, 3(4), 1995.

[9]   C. Mohan, "ARIES/KVL: A Key-Value Locking Method for Concurrency Control of Multiaction Transactions on B-Tree Indexes", 16th VLDB. P392-405, 1990.

Online Index Rebuild

Nagavamsi Ponnekanti   Hanuma Kodavalla

Sybase Inc.

1650, 65th street, Emeryville, CA, 94608

vamsi@sybase.com,hanuma@ieee.org

ABSTRACT

In this paper we present an efficient method to do online rebuild of a B+-tree index. This method has been implemented in Sybase Adaptive Server Enterprise (ASE) Version 12.0. It provides high concurrency, does minimal amount of logging, has good performance and does not deadlock with other index operations. It copies the index rows to newly allocated pages in the key order so that good space utilization and clustering are achieved. The old pages are deallocated during the process. Our algorithm differs from the previously published online index rebuild algorithms in two ways. It rebuilds multiple leaf pages and then propagates the changes to higher levels. Also, while propagating the leaf level changes to higher levels, level 1^1 pages are reorganized, eliminating the need for a separate pass. Our performance study shows that our approach results in significant reduction in logging and CPU time. Also, our approach uses the same concurrency control mechanism as split and shrink operations, which made it attractive for implementation.

1 INTRODUCTION

B+-trees [Comer79] are one of the main indexing methods used in commercial database systems. A primary B+-tree index has data records in the leaf pages while a secondary B+-tree index has only the index *keys* in the leaf pages, where a key consists of a key value and the ROWID of the data record. In this paper, we consider the rebuild of a secondary index[2]. We assume that the leaf pages of the index

---

1. Level 1 is the level immediately above the leaf level

are doubly linked and the non-leaf pages are not linked.

Over time, insertions and deletions may cause allocations and deallocations of index pages. As mentioned in [GR93], most practical implementations of B-trees do not merge index nodes upon underflow and the same is true for ASE. Index pages may become less than half full causing a drop in the space utilization and also an increase in the number of disk reads required to read the same number of index keys. Further, the index may become declustered (i.e. index keys within a key range may not be in contiguous disk space) thereby degrading the performance of range queries. To restore the clustering, users can drop and recreate the index. However, that typically requires holding a shared table lock on the table thereby making the table inaccessible to OLTP transactions, which may not be acceptable.

Online index rebuild restores the space utilization and clustering of the index with minimal blocking of readers and writers. It copies the index keys to fresh pages and deallocates the old pages. In this paper, we present an algorithm for online index rebuild that provides high concurrency, does minimal amount of logging, has good performance and does not deadlock with other index operations. Section 2 describes the concurrency control mechanisms in the index manager. Section 3, Section 4 and Section 5 describe the online index rebuild algorithm. Section 6 evaluates the algorithm with respect to some desirable properties. Section 7 compares it with related work in this area and finally, Section 8 gives the conclusions.

2 INDEX CONCURRENCY CONTROL

In this section, we describe the concurrency control mechanisms in the index manager.

We assume ***row level locking***. Insert, delete and scan operations acquire logical locks on rows as needed. Logical locks are meaningful only on rows at the leaf level. We do not discuss logical locking further, as split, shrink and rebuild operations do not acquire logical locks.

---

2. However, if the primary key value is used as data ROWID in the secondary indices, then the same algorithm can be used to rebuild a primary index as well.

Latches are used for physical consistency at the page level. To read or modify a page, an S (shared) or X (exclusive) latch is acquired on the buffer that contains the page. Latch deadlocks are prevented by requesting the latches in top down order or left to right order.

An insert may cause a split operation which consists of adding a new leaf page to the chain, possibly moving some keys to it and updating the parent and possibly higher levels. Shrink operation consists of removing a leaf page from the chain and updating parent and possibly higher levels. A page is shrunk when the last row is removed from it. Split and shrink operations are performed as *nested top actions* [GR93], which means that once the operation is complete, it is not undone even if the transaction performing it rolls back.

Now, we give an overview of insert, delete, split, shrink and scan operations. We also present the pseudocode for tree traversal routine. The deadlock issues are discussed in Section 6.5.

2.1 Insert and Delete

Insert and delete call traversal module to retrieve the appropriate leaf page X latched. If no split or shrink is needed, the latch is released after performing the insert or delete.

Traversal uses the familiar *crabbing* strategy [GR93] with latches. An S latch is sufficient, except at the leaf level, where an X latch is acquired. However, if a page in the path traversed is undergoing a split or shrink by another transaction, traversal *may* need to release its latches and block for the split or shrink to complete, as explained in the following sections (Section 2.2, Section 2.3 and Section 2.6).

2.2 Leaf Split

To split a leaf page P_0, both P_0 and the new page, say N_0, are *X latched* and *address-locked in X mode*. In addition, *SPLIT bits* are set on both of them. The X lock acquired by the split is called an *address-lock* to distinguish it from logical locks. For the rest of this paper, unless specified otherwise, a lock refers to an address lock. While the X latches are released soon after the modification of P_0 and N_0, the X locks and the SPLIT bits are retained till the end of the top action. The purpose of setting the SPLIT bit on a page is to block writes to that page by concurrent transactions after the splitter has released its X latch[3]. The writers block by releasing any latches held and requesting an unconditional instant duration S lock on the page[4]. Thus the writers are blocked till the top action is complete. However, readers can still access P_0 or N_0, if they have successfully acquired an S latch on it.

No locks or latches are held on higher level pages by the splitter when it is splitting the leaf page. They are acquired during the propagation phase, as explained below.

2.3 Propagation of Split to Higher Levels

The split is propagated *bottom up*. The latches held on the pages at the current level are released before moving to the next higher level. To propagate the split to level i, split calls traversal to retrieve the appropriate non-leaf page P at level i latched in X mode. (However, traversal may not start from root in this case. See Section 2.6.1.) The page returned by traversal is guarenteed not to have SPLIT (or SHRINK) bit set on it. Here is the action to be taken on P:

- If P needs a split, both P and the new page, say N, are X latched, X locked and SPLIT bits are set on them(just as in leaf split). Suppose that keys >= K are moved to N. The page P is also marked with OLDPGOFSPLIT bit and entry [K, N] is stored on page P as a *side entry*[5]. Once the side entry is established, both P and N are unlatched and the propagation continues to the next level. In case a concurrent traversal visits page P from its parent before the split propagates to the parent, the traversal uses the side entry to decide which of P or N is the correct target page.

- If no split is needed, no X lock or SPLIT bit is needed on P. The insert is performed, and the top action is completed and P is unlatched. The SPLIT bits and the OLDPGOFSPLIT bits are cleared and the X locks are released.

Recall that setting SPLIT bit on a page blocks writes to that page but not the reads. Thus a concurrent insert, delete, split or shrink operation that wants to traverse through P (or N) to a lower level page can access P (or N) after splitter has released its X latch on P (or N).

2.4 Shrink

Shrink is also performed as a nested top action and is propagated quite similar to split operation, except that SHRINK bits are set on the affected pages instead of SPLIT bits. Also, note that setting SHRINK bit on a page blocks both read and write operations on the page.

2.5 Scan

Scan calls traversal module to retrieve the starting page for the scan S latched. The scan qualifies the index keys under S

---

3. SPLIT bit does not block a writer that just wishes to modify its previous page link. This optimization allows two adjacent leaf pages to be split concurrently.

4. The SPLIT bit is similar to the SM bit in [MF92]. However, SM bit is accompanied with a tree latch (rather than an X lock on the page), which increases the likelihood of blocking. Also, in our approach, the bit is only an optimization of calls to the lock manager (checking for the bit can be replaced with a request for a conditional instant duration S lock).

5. Although the sidekey is similar to side pointers in B-link trees [LY81], it is valid only as long as the OLDPGOFSPLIT bit is set.

latch. The page is unlatched before returning a qualifying key to query processing layer and is latched again to resume qualification. Also, note that depending on the isolation level, the scan may need to acquire logical locks on qualifying keys.

2.6 Traversal Pseudocode

Here is the pseudocode for traversal. Note that a page is latched in X mode only if it is at the target level and the traversal was called in writer mode. In all other cases, the page is latched in S mode.

```
traverse(searchkey, searchmode, targetlevel)
{
retraverse:
    p = get root page latched;
    while (level of p > target level)
    {
        Search p to identify the child to chase;
        c = get child page latched;
        if (c has SHRINK bit set)
        {
            Unlatch c and p;
            Wait for instant duration S lock on c;
            goto retraverse;
        }
        if (OLDPGOFSPLIT bit is set in c)
        {
            if (searchkey >= key in side entry)
            {
                sibling = Get right sibling latched;
                Unlatch c;
                c= sibling;
            }
        }
        /* Now we are on the correct child */
        Unlatch p;
        p = c;
    }
    /* Target level is reached */
    if ((searchmode == writermode) and
        (p has SPLIT bit set))
    {
        Unlatch p;
        Wait for instant duration S lock on p;
```

```
        goto retraverse;
    }
    return p;
}
```

2.6.1 Retraversing

In the above algorithm, retraversal starts from the root page. However, ASE actually uses a more efficient strategy. While traversing down the tree, the pages encountered in the path are remembered. When there is a need to retraverse, rather than starting from the root, it starts from the lowest level page in the path that is *safe*. A page is safe if it is still at the same level as expected and the search key is within the range of key values on it. Same strategy is used by traversal during the propagation of split and shrink to avoid starting from root. Later, in Section 5.4.1, we will see that the propagation phase of online index rebuild also uses traversal and benefits from this strategy.

3 ONLINE INDEX REBUILD OVERVIEW

Online rebuild runs as a sequence of transactions, with each transaction performing a series of nested top actions and each top action rebuilding multiple contiguous leaf pages in the page chain. The top actions are called *multipage rebuild* top actions. The number of pages to rebuild in a single top action is denoted by **ntasize** and the number of pages to rebuild in a transaction is denoted by **xactsize.** Rebuilding multiple pages in a single top action reduces logging and CPU time. We chose an ntasize of 32 based on our performance study (Section 6.4). The significance of xactsize is explained below.

At the end of each transaction, the new pages generated in the current transaction are flushed to disk and then the old pages that were removed from the tree are made available for fresh allocations.

Flushing new pages to disk before making old pages available for fresh allocations allows rebuild not to log full keys during the key copying. Instead, the log records contain only the PAGEIDs and the timestamps of the source page and the target page and just the *positions* of the first and the last key that were copied. Redo may have to read the source page to redo the key copying. On the other hand, if the source page is made available for allocation before the target page is flushed to disk, then the new contents of the source page could reach the disk before the target page reaches the disk. If a crash occurs after the new contents of the source page reach the disk, but before the target page reaches the disk, the target page cannot be recovered.

While rebuilding several pages in a transaction has the advantage of delaying the forced write of new pages, it also delays the availability of the old pages for reuse. It is desirable to rebuild a few hundred pages in a transaction.

4 MULTIPAGE REBUILD TOP ACTION

Consider the rebuild of contiguous pages $P_1, P_2,..., P_n$ in a single nested top action. Suppose that PP is the previous page of P_1 and NP is the next page of P_n. The top action involves a copy phase and a propagation phase, which are explained below:

4.1 Copy Phase

The index keys are copied from $P_1, P_2,..., P_n$ to PP and zero or more newly allocated pages, say $N_1, N_2,..., N_k$, where k >= 0. Note that k could be > n if the user has specified that the new leaf pages be filled only upto a desired *fillfactor*, so that some space is left free for future inserts. Copy phase also includes fixing page linkages and deallocating the old pages.

4.1.1 Locking

X locks are acquired and SHRINK bits are set on PP, P_1, $P_2,..., P_n$ in that order. For i > 1, if P_i has SPLIT or SHRINK bit set on it, rebuild does not wait for lock. Instead, only pages $P_1, P_2,...,P_{i-1}$ are rebuilt in the current top action. On the other hand, if PP or P_1 has SPLIT or SHRINK bit set, then rebuild waits for the split or the shrink to complete.

4.1.2 Logging

Copy phase generates a *single keycopy* log record to capture *all* the key copying that has occurred from pages P_1, $P_2,..., P_n$ to PP and the newly allocated pages. It has multiple entries of the form [source pageno, target pageno, position of the first key copied, position of the last key copied]. It also generates allocation and deallocation log records and *changeprevlink* log record for NP.

4.1.3 Page Deallocations

A page can be in one of allocated, deallocated or free states. Only a page in free state is available for fresh allocations. When the page manager is called to deallocate a page, it logs a deallocation record and takes the page to deallocated state. The page manager has to be called again to free the page. The transition from deallocated state to free state is not logged by the page manager and it cannot be undone. In the event of a crash, after the redo and undo phases, recovery frees up pages that are still in deallocated state.

In the case of a shrink top action, deallocated pages are freed when the top action commits. However, in the case of multipage rebuild topaction, the deallocated pages are freed only when the current *transaction* commits. It uses log scan to determine what pages need to be freed up. Also, note that if rebuild needs to abort due to lack of resources or internal error or a user interrupt, during rollback, it needs to free up the pages deallocated in completed top actions. Before freeing up the old pages, the new pages need to be flushed to disk.

4.2 Propagation Phase

The changes are propagated to level 1 by deleting the entries for $P_1, P_2,..., P_n$ and inserting the entries for $N_1, N_2,..., N_k$ in the parent(s) of $P_1, P_2,..., P_n$. The propagation may continue above level 1. The propagation of split (shrink) can be thought of as passing of an insert (delete) command from one level to the next. The propagation of rebuild top action can be thought of as passing multiple commands from one level to the next, where each command could be an insert, delete or an update. At each level several pages could be affected. At a given level, the affected pages are modified in left to right order. Also, all modifications at the current level are finished before moving to the next higher level. For each affected non-leaf page, no more than one *batchdelete* log record and one *batchinsert* log record are generated. These log records contain the entire keys that were inserted or deleted. The propagation phase is described in detail in Section 5.

4.3 Advantages of Rebuilding Multiple Pages in a Single Top Action

Insert and delete log records in ASE have not only the key being deleted or inserted but also a lot of additional information such as transaction ID, old and new timestamps for the page, position of delete or insert etc. The amount of such additional information is as high as 60 bytes and is amortized by batching multiple inserts or deletes in a single batchinsert or batchdelete log record. Similarly, the overhead in other log records is amortized by rebuilding multiple pages in a single top action. Besides saving log space, rebuilding multiple pages in a top action reduces the number of visits to level 1 pages significantly, reducing the calls to lock manager, latch manager etc. Our performance study reflects this (Section 6.4).

5 PROPAGATION PHASE OF REBUILD

In this section, we discuss how the rebuild of multiple leaf pages is propagated to higher levels. The propagation is bottom up and the modifications to be done at the next higher level are specified in the form of *propagation entries*. Before describing propagation entries, we explain what an index entry is.

We assume that a nonleaf page in the B+-tree that has n child pointers has only n-1 key value separators. An index entry is of the form [key value, child pageid], except for the index entry for the first child, which does not have the key value. An index page having n children has n index entries $C_0, [K_1, C_1], [K_2, C_2],...,[K_{n-1}, C_{n-1}]$. For $0 < i <= n-1$, C_i has index entries greater than or equal to K_i and for $0 <= i < n-1$, C_i has index entries less than K_{i+1}.

Now, we define propagation entries and explain what propagation entries are passed from the leaf and the nonleaf pages. Then we describe how the propagation phase proceeds from one level to the next.

5.1 Propagation Entries

A *propagation entry* specifies the following:

- the page P that is sending the propagation entry.
- operation that must be performed at the next higher level. The possible operations are DELETE, UPDATE or INSERT of an index entry.
- INSERT propagation entry specifies the entry to be inserted at the next level. UPDATE propagation entry specifies the entry to replace the existing entry for that page. UPDATE and DELETE propagation entries do not specify the contents of index entry to delete (pageid P uniquely identifies the index entry).

5.2 Propagation Entries Passed From a Leaf Page

Consider the rebuild of leaf pages P_1, P_2,..., P_n in a single top action. Let PP be the previous page of P_1 and NP the next page of P_n. Here are the rules that determine what propagation entries are passed from a *single* page P_i:

- Suppose that k, where $k > 0$, new allocations are needed to accommodate the keys from P_i. The entry for P_i needs to be deleted from parent and entries for the k new pages need to be inserted in the parent. So an UPDATE propagation entry followed by k-1 INSERT propagation entries are passed.
- If all the keys from P_i could be copied into the last newly allocated page (i.e. *no new allocation* was needed to accommodate the keys from P_i), it passes DELETE propagation entry.

Thus, each page that was rebuilt passes one or more propagation entries. All the propagation entries from P_1, P_2,..., P_n are accumulated before the propagation proceeds to level 1.

5.3 Propagation Entries Passed From a Non-leaf Page

A non-leaf page P passes propagation entry(s) in the following cases:

- P is becoming empty (in this case P needs to be shrunk)
- P is split
- P is not becoming empty but there was some key movement from the subtree under P to the subtree under its left sibling.

These three cases are discussed in more detail below. Note that the last two cases are *not* mutually exclusive.

5.3.1 Shrink of P

If all children pass DELETE propagation entries, then page P needs to be shrunk[6]. It passes DELETE propagation entry. This means that *all* the leaf rows in the subtree under P have

been moved to the subtree under its left sibling.

5.3.2 Split of P

The inserts to be performed on page P (as a result of UPDATE/INSERT propagation entries coming from children of P) may cause P to be split. If so, P is split in such a manner that all the remaining inserts go to the old page or all of them go to the new page. Note that one split may not be sufficient to accommodate all such inserts. If the insertions cause k splits, then k siblings are generated for P and k INSERT propagation entries are setup for inserting entries for these new pages at the next higher level.

5.3.3 Key Movement Across Subtrees

Consider figure 1 shown below. P' is the parent of P and L is the left sibling of P. [K1, L] and [K2, P] are the entries for L and P in P'. Consider some key movement from the subtree under P to the subtree under L. If keys up to (but not including) K are moved to the subtree under L, then the entry for P in P' needs to be changed from [K2, P] to [K, P] to keep the index consistent. So P needs to pass an UPDATE propagation entry [K, P] to P'. Now let us look at how to detect such key movement and how to find the value of K.

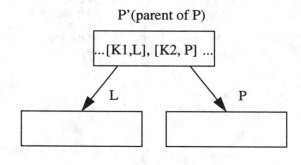

P'(parent of P)

...[K1,L], [K2, P] ...

L   P

Figure 1: Key Movement Across Subtrees

Let C_0, C_1,...,C_n be the children of P.

If C_0 did not pass DELETE or UPDATE propagation entry, then *no* key movement has occurred from the subtree under P to the subtree under L.

Otherwise, let C_i, where $0 <= i <= n$, be the leftmost child of P that did not pass DELETE propagation entry. (Such a child must exist. Else, all children must have passed DELETE propagation entries and it is the shrink case discussed in Section 5.3.1). Since the children C_0, C_1,...,C_{i-1} have passed DELETE propagation entries, it means all the keys in the subtrees under them have been moved and they have become empty. The entries for all of them on P need to

---

6. In this case, there is no need to perform the deletes. Page can directly be deallocated.

be deleted and C_i needs to become the first child of P.

- If C_i has passed an UPDATE propagation entry, say $[K_u, C_i]$, then keys $< K_u$ may have been moved from subtree under C_i to that under its left sibling. So, P passes UPDATE propagation entry $[K_u, P]$ i.e. $K = K_u$.
- Otherwise, C_i must have passed INSERT propagation entry(s) or no propagation entries. In either case, *no* key movement has occurred from the subtree under C_i to a subtree under its left sibling. If $[K_i, C_i]$ is the entry for C_i on P, then P passes UPDATE propagation entry $[K_i, P]$ to its parent i.e. $K = K_i$.

5.4 Propagation From Level i to Level i+1

An algorithm to apply a list of propagation entries passed from level i to level i+1 is described below.

5.4.1 Algorithm Propagate_to_level

Input: List $L = [E_1, E_2,..., E_m]$ of all propagation entries to be applied to level i+1 pages (these were passed from level i pages)

Output: List L_1 of propagation entries passed to the next higher level from level i+1 if any

Side Effect: The modifications specified by the input propagation entries are applied on level i+1 pages

propagate_to_level(L, i+1)

Initialize L_1 to empty list;

while (L is not empty)

{

e = first propagation entry in L;

C = page that propagated e;

K = *Any* key from page C;

/* Get the parent of C X latched. Note that
** traversal uses same strategy as described in
** retraversal section earlier to avoid starting
** from root (See Section 2.6.1).
*/

P = traverse(K, writer, i+1);

/* identify all the propagation entries that
** were sent by children of P (they are
** guaranteed to be contiguous in L).
*/

e' = last propagation entry in L that was
      passed by a child of P;

Delete propagation entries e through e'
      from L;

/* apply the propagation entries e through
** e' on P(See Section 5.4.2).
*/

Modify P;

Append the propagation entries passed by P
      if any to L_1

Release any latches held;

}

5.4.2 Modification of Page P

The propagation entries passed by the children of P are applied on page P in two phases, the delete phase followed by the insert phase. In the delete phase, the index entries for all the children that passed DELETE or UPDATE status are deleted. All such index entries will be contiguous. In the insert phase, the index entries specified by the INSERT/UPDATE propagation entries coming from children of P are inserted. The index entries inserted will also be contiguous.

Traversal would have retrieved page P latched in X mode. However, latch alone is not sufficient. The address locking mechanism used by split or shrink top actions is used here and the SPLIT and SHRINK bits are overloaded. P is locked in X mode. A SHRINK bit is set on P if traversals through P need to be blocked. If modifications to P need to be blocked but not the traversals through P, a SPLIT bit is set on it. The rules for deciding which bit needs to be set are mentioned below.

- If any delete is performed on a page (i.e. atleast one child passed a DELETE or UPDATE status), SHRINK bit is set.
- If only inserts are performed on a page (i.e. no deletes and no splits), then SPLIT bit is set.
- If P needs to be split, a SHRINK bit is set on it. The new page is also X locked and SHRINK bit is set on it. There is no need to establish a side entry as traversals through P are being blocked anyway. X latch needs to be retained only on the page where the rest of the inserts in the insert phase need to be performed.

These rules are very conservative. Traversals are being allowed through the page only in the insert-only case, as no keys in the subtree under the page would have been moved to the subtree under its left or right sibling in that case. (See Section 6.2 for a possible improvement).

5.5 Reorganizing Level 1 Pages

Consider the propagation from leaf level to level 1. In the propagation algorithm that has been described, while applying propagation entries on a level 1 page P, the insert phase inserts the index entries specified in UPDATE/INSERT propagation entries sent by the children of P. However, it is better to perform as many of those

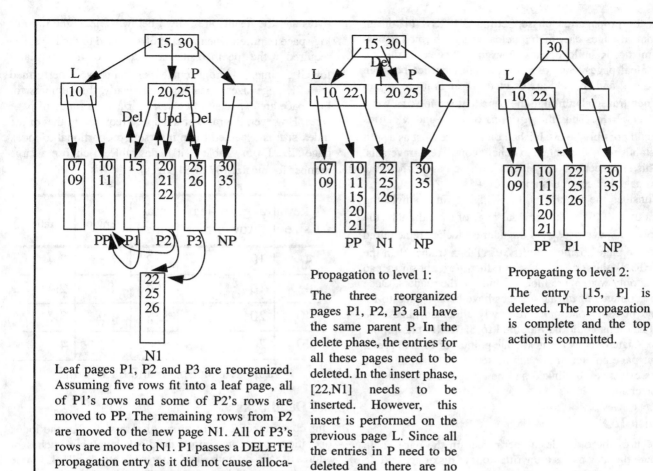

Leaf pages P1, P2 and P3 are reorganized. Assuming five rows fit into a leaf page, all of P1's rows and some of P2's rows are moved to PP. The remaining rows from P2 are moved to the new page N1. All of P3's rows are moved to N1. P1 passes a DELETE propagation entry as it did not cause allocations. P2 passes UPDATE propagation entry with [22, N1] as the index entry to replace the entry for P2 at the next higher level. P3 also passes DELETE propagation entry.

Propagation to level 1:

The three reorganized pages P1, P2, P3 all have the same parent P. In the delete phase, the entries for all these pages need to be deleted. In the insert phase, [22,N1] needs to be inserted. However, this insert is performed on the previous page L. Since all the entries in P need to be deleted and there are no inserts to perform on P, DELETE propagation entry is passed.

Propagating to level 2:

The entry [15, P] is deleted. The propagation is complete and the top action is committed.

Figure 2: Multipage Rebuild Top Action

inserts as permitted by space on the immediate left sibling of P that is not being shrunk in the current top action. Note that this can only be done if the first child of P is getting deleted in the delete phase (i.e. it passed a DELETE/UPDATE status). Otherwise, it would violate the index key ordering at level 1.

With this enhancement, level 1 pages are filled as much as possible without requiring a separate pass. An example of multipage rebuild top action with this enhancement is shown in figure 2.

6 EVALUATION

Here, we evaluate the algorithm with respect to some important metrics.

6.1 Restoration of Clustering

When online index rebuild begins, the page manager tries to allocate a new page from a chunk of large contiguous free disk space. After all the pages in the chunk are used up, it again looks for a chunk of large contiguous free disk space. As the index keys are moved to the newly allocated pages in the increasing key order, the new leaf pages are expected to be well clustered.

6.2 Concurrency

Although rebuilding multiple pages in a top action has the disadvantage of keeping many leaf pages locked at a given time, it significantly reduces the number of visits to a level 1 page and the total duration of exclusive access to it. It also significantly reduces the CPU time for the rebuild operation which in turn reduces the negative impact of the operation on the throughput of the system.

Here are some possible enhancements to reduce the impact on concurrent index operations:

- In the propagation phase, setting SHRINK bit on all nonleaf pages on which a delete was performed is pessimistic. Rebuild deletes contiguous index entries on nonleaf pages. Suppose that all index entries between $[K_i, C_i]$ and $[K_j, C_j]$ are deleted. There is no reason to block traversals through the page that are looking for $< K_i$ or $>= K_j$. Thus the *positions* of these index entries could possibly be established on the page (just as a split establishes a side entry) to benefit concurrent traversals. This enhancement only helps in those cases where the propagation continues above level 1.

- Consider the rebuild of P_1, P_2,..., P_n in a single top action. Let PP be the previous page of P_1 and NP be the previous page of P_n. As the address locks are acquired on the pages being rebuilt, SPLIT bits (rather than the SHRINK bits) could be set on them (except on PP) so that only writers are blocked and not the readers. Once the contents of *all* the n pages have been copied to PP and possibly one or more newly allocated pages, the SPLIT bits could be modified to SHRINK bits (under an X latch). Now the next page pointer of PP and previous page pointer of NP can be set so that the old pages are effectively unlinked and new pages are linked into the chain.

6.3 Disk I/O

One scan of the old index is performed in the page chain order and the new pages are written out to disk once. While the page size is 2KB, the buffer manager allows the user to configure buffer pools with 4K, 8K or 16K buffer sizes. Online rebuild requests buffer manager to use the largest size buffers available for reading old pages and for writing new pages to reduce disk I/O.

6.4 Logging and CPU Time

We performed some experiments to see how the log space used and the CPU time consumed vary with *ntasize*. Our experiments are performed under the following conditions

- The space utilization in the index being rebuilt is about 50% and the rebuild specified a fillfactor of 100%.
- The cache is cold (i.e. all pages had to be read from disk).
- The page size is 2KB but the buffer pool is configured with 16KB buffers so that 16KB I/O size is used for index page reads and writes as well as log writes.
- Sun Ultra-SPARC machine running SunOS 5.6 is used.

For a given number of leaf pages in the old and the new index, the log space required varies primarily with the average nonleaf row size. The index manager in ASE uses suffix compression which reduces the nonleaf row size especially when the index is on multiple columns or on wide columns. We experimented with index key size (i.e. sum of maximum column lengths of all index columns) of 4 bytes and 40

bytes and the results are shown below. L_{ratio} is the ratio of log space required when ntasize of 1 is used to the log space required at the specified ntasize. C_{ratio} is defined similarly for CPU time. Although our experiments were performed with 2K page sizes, speaking analytically, the numbers for log space are expected to be valid for a wide range of page sizes. However, the ratio of log space required to that of the index size is expected to be inversely proportional to index page size. From Table 1, it is desirable to choose a large number for ntasize (32 to 64 pages).

key size	avg non-leaf row size	nta-size	L_{ratio}	C_{ratio}
4	10	32	7.3	2.4
4	10	64	8	2.4
40	20	32	4.9	3.7
40	20	64	5.4	4

Table 1: Log Space and CPU Time

6.5 Deadlocks

Our concurrency control protocols are such that the index operations never get into a deadlock involving latches or address locks or both. The only possible deadlock is one that involves only logical locks. The following rules ensure this:

- While holding a latch, unconditional logical lock is never requested and an unconditional address lock is requested only on a page that is being allocated (and hence not accessible from the tree) or a page that does not have SPLIT/SHRINK bit set.
- Latches are requested only in left to right order at a given level and top down order across levels.
- Address locks are requested only in bottom up order across levels.
- Address locks within a nonleaf level are acquired only in left to right order.
- Address locks within leaf level: Shrink acquires address locks on two pages and they are acquired in *right to left* order. Split acquires address lock on the old page and then the new page. But since new page is not yet part of the tree, this sequence does not cause a deadlock with shrink. Rebuild acquires address locks in left to right order. However, as mentioned before, if rebuild needs to wait, it releases all the locks that are acquired already before waiting. After wakeup, it retries for all the locks again.

7 COMPARISON WITH RELATED WORK

The first published article on online rebuild is from Tandem [Smi90]. Our approach has the following advantages:

- In Tandem's approach, when the page split and merge operations are performed, the entire file is made inaccessible to the OLTP transactions where as in our method only access to the affected pages is restricted.

- Further, in Tandem's approach, although it is not explicitly stated, it seems all the moved keys are logged where as in our approach the key contents themselves are not logged.

A more recently published work in this area is [SBC97]. This paper describes a comprehensive scheme to reorganize a table and rebuild the associated indexes. That scheme has the following drawbacks:

- A separate copy of the table is made and the associated indexes are rebuilt thereby doubling the storage requirement.

- User transactions must be directed to use the new copy. If there are long-running user sessions (with opened cursors), reorg waits for them to complete.

- For the duration of the reorg, the log should not be truncated because the reorg relies on the log for any changes that need to be applied to the new copy.

- Incremental reorganization is difficult.

By doing inline reorganization, our scheme avoids the above problems.

[ZS96] gives a detailed description of an algorithm for rebuilding an index. We believe our algorithm has the following advantages over it:

- Our algorithm reorganizes level 1 pages without requiring a sidefile. The sidefile mechanism adds a lot of implementation complexity. It also adds overhead to splits and shrinks happening in the index during the rebuild of non-leaf levels.

- Logging is reduced in [ZS96] by assuming "careful writing" mechanism in the buffer manager. Our algorithm does not require such a mechanism in the buffer manager[7].

- Unlike [ZS96], our algorithm does only one pass of the index.

- In [ZS96], only one new page is rebuilt in each reorganization unit. However, we believe that it is important to build multiple new pages in each reorganization unit to reduce logging overhead and CPU time.

- In [ZS96], switching to the new B+-tree requires an X lock on the tree which may cause unbounded wait. It is

suggested that the transactions active in the tree be aborted if lock cannot be acquired after certain timeout interval. User transactions are never aborted in our algorithm.

Our algorithm has following drawbacks compared to [ZS96].

- During the propagation phase of multipage rebuild, pages above level 1 may need to be modified in which case X lock is acquired on the page being modified. [ZS96] does not X lock pages above level 1 in X mode (except for the X lock on the tree in the switching phase). However, since propagation is bottom up (as opposed to top down), the duration of X lock on non-leaf pages is expected to be small. This is because most of the time in the topaction is spent in reading old leaf pages and moving rows from old leaf pages to new pages.

- As mentioned before, to achieve good clustering, our algorithm needs a large chunk of contiguous free space on disk to begin with. However, since the amount of contiguous free space needed is small compared to the size of the index, this is not a significant problem.

- At the end of each transaction, new pages need to be flushed to disk. This disadvantage is alleviated to some extent by using large buffers and building a few hundred new pages in each transaction.

8 CONCLUSIONS

We have presented an industrial-strength algorithm for online index rebuild that provides high concurrency, does minimal logging and has good performance. By rebuilding multiple leaf pages in each top action, the updates to level 1 pages can be batched resulting in significant reduction in logging and CPU time. The level 1 pages are reorganized while propagating the leaf level changes thereby eliminating a separate pass for reorganizing level 1 pages.

9 ACKNOWLEDGMENTS

We thank our colleagues, Yang Wang, Sangeeta Doraiswamy, T. E. Raghavan and Shampa Chakravarty for reviewing the design and the implementation of this feature. We also thank Nageshwara Rao and Gopinath Chandra for their help in testing this feature.

10 REFERENCES

[Com79] Douglas Comer. The Ubiquitous B-Tree. *Computing Surveys*, Vol. 11, No. 2, June 1979.

[GR93] Jim Gray and Andreas Reuter. *Transaction Processing: Concepts and Techniques*, Morgan Kaufmann Publishers, Inc., 1993.

[LY81] Lehman, P. L., and S. B. Yao. Efficient Locking for Concurrent operations on B-Trees. *ACM TODS. Vol. 6, No.*

---

7. Note that we just assume "forced write", which is different from "careful writing". The former just requests the buffer manager to force a page to disk(without violating WAL), while the latter assumes a more involved mechanism of tracking the relative order in which a certain set of pages need to be written to disk.

4, pages 650-670, December 1981.

[MF92] C. Mohan and Frank Levine. ARIES/IM: An Efficient and High Concurrency Index Management Method using Write-Ahead Logging. *Proc. of ACM SIGMOD Conf,* pages 371-380, 1992.

[SBC97] Gary H. Sockut, Thomas A. Beavin and Chung-C. Chang: A Method for On-Line Reorganization of a Database. IBM Systems Journal. Vol. 36, No. 3, pages 411-436, 1997. Available at http://www.research.ibm.com/journal/sj/363/sockut.html

[Smi90] Gary Smith. Online Reorganization of Key-Sequenced Tables and Files. *Tandem Systems Review*, October 1990.

[ZS96] Chendong Zou and Betty Salzberg. On-line Reorganization of Sparsely-populated B+ trees. *Proc. of ACM SIGMOD Conf,* pages 115-124, 1996.

Indexing Images in Oracle8i

Melliyal Annamalai   Rajiv Chopra   Samuel DeFazio
Susan Mavris

Oracle Corporation
New England Development Center
One Oracle Drive, Nashua, NH 03062
{mannamal,rchopra,sdefazio,smavris}@us.oracle.com

Abstract

Content-based retrieval of images is the ability to retrieve images that are similar to a query image. Oracle8i Visual Information Retrieval provides this facility based on technology licensed from Virage, Inc. This product is built on top of Oracle8i interMedia which enables storage, retrieval and management of images, audios and videos. Images are matched using attributes such as color, texture and structure and efficient content-based retrieval is provided using indexes of an image index type. The design of the index type is based on a multi-level filtering algorithm. The filters reduce the search space so that the expensive comparison algorithm operates on a small subset of the data. Bitmap indexes are used to evaluate the first filter resulting in a design which performs well and is scalable. The image index type is built using Oracle8i extensible indexing technology, allowing users to create, use, and drop instances of this index type as they would any other standard index. In this paper we present an overview of the product, the design of the image index type, and some performance results of our product.

1   Introduction

The growth of the internet and multimedia technology has led to an increased demand in the market for content processing and management of image data. Some examples of applications that manage image data are e-commerce,

museum archives, art gallery archives, digital libraries, medical imaging, multimedia document archives, multimedia publishing, geographic information systems, etc. A large collection of images requires an efficient mechanism for search and retrieval. Keyword based retrieval, where some keywords are chosen to represent the image, does not satisfy the needs of all applications. *Content-based retrieval*, where a user can search for images that are *visually similar* to a given image, is a flexible and accurate method of searching images. The Oracle8i Visual Information Retrieval product provides this facility based on technology licensed from Virage, Inc. [Bac96, GJ97]. It additionally provides a new index mechanism for fast retrieval [Ovr97, Ora98c]. Matching images involves matching high dimensional vectors, and their indexing has been shown to be a difficult problem [Ang95, Fal94, Boz97, Fli95, Whi96].

The design of the index is based on a multi-level filter, where the filters operate on an approximation of the high dimensional data which represents the image, and reduces the search space so that the final computationally expensive comparison is necessary for only a small subset of the data. The reduction of the search space depends on selectivity of the filters. One way to increase the selectivity is to increase the number of dimensions used in the filters. Higher dimensions result in more accuracy of comparisons and hence better selectivity. Systems using the multi-level filter approach typically reduce the number of dimensions enough so that the filter can be based on an index structure such as an R-tree, KD-tree, SS-tree, X-tree etc [Fal94, Fli95]. In our approach we implement the first filter as a range query, one range per dimension, which enables us to use bitmap indexes to efficiently evaluate the query. Bitmap indexes are constructed on each dimension. The efficiency of indexing individual dimensions and combining results when using Oracle's bitmap indexes makes it possible to have a high dimensional (83 dimensions in this implementation) first filter which results in high selectivity and scalable performance. We present results for indexing and searching up to 100,000 images.

The extensible architecture of the Oracle server has enabled the addition of efficient and effective technology for the multimedia domain. A special image index type for content-based retrieval has been built using the Oracle8i extensible indexing framework [Ora98a]. This allows encapsulation of the index management routines in an index type schema object. It enables an index which is an instance of this index type to be created and used the same way as any other Oracle Server index. The index-based implementation of the SQL operators VIRSimilar and VIRScore can be used to search for images similar to a given query image. The operators can be used in SQL statements like any other operator.

The Oracle8i Visual Information Retrieval product is built on Oracle8i interMedia, which enables storage, retrieval and management of images, audios, and videos, and manipulation and format conversion of images. All the image functionality of interMedia is supported in this product. In this paper we first present a brief background and our terminology, followed by a description of the SQL interface of our product. We then describe the design of the index type and conclude with a section on issues related to performance.

2   Our Content-based Retrieval Model

The specifics of the content-based retrieval model chosen by Oracle is based on cooperation with Virage. Other technology can be incorporated into Oracle using similar concepts.

Each image in the Visual Information Retrieval product is represented by a high dimensional *signature*. The signature is an abstraction of the contents of the image in terms of its visual attributes. It is represented using 2000

bytes. Two images are compared by comparing their signatures. Comparison of signatures yields a *score* value between 0 and 100 which represents the degree of similarity between the two images. A value of 0 means a perfect match and a value of 100 means the two images are completely different from each other.

The signature contains information about the following visual attributes:

- *Global Color:* This attribute represents the colors in the entire image.

- *Local Color:* This attribute represents the spatial distribution of the colors in the image.

- *Texture:* This attribute represents the patterns in the image such as graininess and smoothness.

- *Structure:* This attribute represents the shapes that appear in the image, as determined by shape characterization techniques.

The user can assign a *weight* or importance measure to each of these visual attributes in a query. Each weight value indicates how sensitive the similarity computation should be to that visual attribute. The concept of weights gives the user flexibility in defining her search.

3   The SQL Interface

The Oracle8i Visual Information Retrieval product adds new operators and datatypes to Oracle's SQL interface.

3.1   Visual Information Retrieval Datatype

Object-relational extensions to Oracle8i can provide support for domain-specific applications. These extensions enable the provision of solution-oriented capabilities unavailable in the server. New datatypes can be defined which are integrated with the server engine so that the optimizer, query parser, indexer and other server components are aware of them. Data stored using these datatypes have access to all database services such as backup, recovery, transaction control, multi-user access etc. The Oracle interMedia product is such an extension that provides image, audio and video datatypes whose behavior is defined by the attributes and methods included in the product [Ora98b]. The object provided for storing images in interMedia is **ORDImage**. The Visual Information Retrieval product is layered on top of the interMedia product (Figure 1). **ORDImage** is extended to form the **ORDVIR** object by adding an attribute *signature* to the object. **ORDImage** contains the **ORDSource** object and content metadata such as height, width, content length, compression format, mime type of the image. **ORDSource** contains information about the location of the object - in the database, as an external file such as on a CD (but with the content metadata and the signature in the database), or as a URL.

The attributes of the **ORDVIR** object are:

> ORDImage
> signature

The attributes of the **ORDImage** object are:

ORDSource	height
contentLength	width
fileFormat	contentFormat
compressionFormat	mimeType

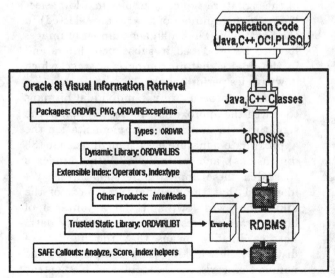

Figure 1: Architecture of the Visual Information Retrieval Product

3.2 Visual Information Retrieval Operators

Two new SQL level operators have been provided in Oracle8i:

1. VIRSimilar(signature_column, query_signature, weightstring, threshold, number).

   - **signature_column**: is the column of signatures in the table of images
   - **query_signature**: is the signature of the query image
   - **weightstring**: is the list of weights used to specify the importance of attributes used in the comparison
   - **threshold**: is a value which can be used by the user to specify the degree of similarity
   - **number**: is the parameter which matches the invocation of this operator with that of VIRScore.

   VIRSimilar returns 1 if two images match and 0 otherwise.

2. VIRScore(number)
   VIRScore is an ancillary operator that returns the score of similarity computed by VIRSimilar. It is used in conjunction with VIRSimilar.

   - **number**: is the parameter which matches the invocation of this operator with that of VIRSimilar.

The index type **ORDVIRIDX** enables the creation of the image index. The indextype encapsulates all the routines necessary for DDL, DML and query operations of an image index.

3.3 Examples of Usage

The following are examples of creating and using a Visual Information Retrieval index:

Create and populate a table:

CREATE TABLE images (id NUMBER, img ORDVIR);
INSERT INTO images VALUES (...);

Create index:

```
CREATE INDEX imgidx ON images(img.SIGNATU
INDEXTYPE IS ORDVIRIDX PARAMETERS(.....);
```

Query:

```
SELECT T.id, VIRSCORE(1) FROM images T
WHERE VIRSIMILAR(T.img.SIGNATURE,
querySignature, 'globalcolor=0.5, localcolor=0.0,
texture=0.5, structure=0.0',10,1) = 1;
```

Thus the user can avail herself of the image indexing technique through a straight forward SQL interface and can create and use the index in a manner similar to that of a standard index. Insert, delete and update operations on the underlying table are also performed in exactly the same way as with a standard index. From the user's point of view the usage and behavior of the image index which is an extensible index is the same as that of a standard index.

4   Design of Visual Information Retrieval Index

The Visual Information Retrieval index, unlike other database indexes, is not one single data structure but a collection of database schema objects. It consists of:

- *Feature Table:* Each image has a row in this internal table. Each row contains a set of numbers which are an approximate representation of the signature. (in this implementation there are 83 numbers).

- *Bitmap Indexes:* A set of bitmap indexes are created on columns in the above feature table.

The index lookup consists of three phases (Figure 2). The first two phases are filters, which reduce the search space, and the last phase is where the final matches are performed.

4.1   Phase 1: Evaluation of Filter 1

As we mentioned earlier, several systems use a multi-dimensional indexing structure such as an R-tree, KD-tree, SS-tree or X-tree to index the first filter [Fal94, Fli95]. For these index structures to be effective the number of

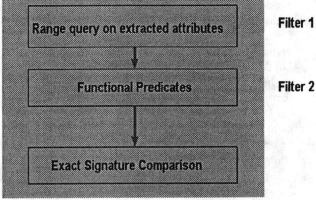

Figure 2: Query Execution Path

dimensions has to be low, in the range of 15-20. They do not scale well beyond these dimensions. QBIC [Fli95] is an example of an approach using the filtering technique. The dimensionality is reduced using K-L transform to get an approximate signature with dimensions as low as 2-3 which can be indexed using R^*-trees. Approximating the high dimensional signatures using low dimensional approximations of the signature typically results in a low selectivity (higher number of images are selected) in the first filter. Thus a higher number of images have to be processed in subsequent filters and in the final signature comparison stage which downgrades performance.

In our approach, we use individual bitmaps to search the approximate representation of the signature. In our current implementation the approximate signature has a high dimension (83 dimensions), and we create 83 bitmap indexes to search these approximate signatures. We identified that the cardinality of most of the dimensions was low, and the advantages of bitmaps are greatest for low cardinality data. Low cardinality means that the number of distinct values is low when compared to the number of rows in the table. This is true for many image attributes, where millions of images are represented by a fixed number of image attributes. Usage of multiple bitmap indexes is an efficient and scalable solution, because of the efficiency and scalability of Oracle's bitmap index implementation.

4.1.1 Bitmap Indexes

In a regular (B-tree) index a list of rowids for each key is stored. In a bitmap index a bitmap for each key value is used instead of a list of rowids. Each bit corresponds to a possible rowid, and if the bit is set, it means that the row with the corresponding rowid contains the key value [Ora98a].

Bitmap indexes are suitable when: (1) users primarily query the data rather than update it (2) the cardinality of the data is low (3) the data is involved in complex conditions in the WHERE clause in queries. Our design of the first filter satisfies all three conditions.

Queries with AND or OR conditions in the WHERE clause can be quickly resolved by performing the corresponding boolean operations directly on the bitmaps before converting the bitmaps into rowids [Ora98a], contributing to the scalability of the filter. The approximate signatures are stored in a feature table with 83 columns, with each column indexed by a bitmap. The first filter is executed by a query on the feature table. The query is a conjunction of range query terms, one range per column. The results of the individual bitmap index lookups are efficiently merged.

Another advantage of using bitmap indexes is that indexes on dimensions not used for execution of a particular query need not be accessed and used. The 83 columns are grouped according to the four attributes global color, local color, texture, and structure. If only global color and texture weights are specified in the query, only those bitmaps need to be used. This results in less data being read and fewer bitmaps being merged and thus improved performance for such queries. Such a selective dropping of dimensions is not easily possible with other index structures.

A detailed discussion on selectivity of the first filter is presented in the performance section.

4.1.2 Index Size

A typical application scenario would store images in an image table, one image in each row. Each row in the image table has an entry in the feature table. The feature table along with the bitmap indexes created on it has a total size that is not more than 30% of the original table size. The signature of each image in the image table is 2000 bytes, and each row in the feature table is not more than 300 bytes and the size of the bitmap indexes for each row is not more than 300 bytes.

4.2 Phase 2: Evaluation of Filter 2

The rows that pass the first filter in the previous phase are now passed through a second filter. This second filter is a distance measure computation that cannot be indexed or represented easily using SQL and is executed in C. The details are proprietary information to Virage, Inc.

4.3 Phase 3: Signature Comparison

The query signature is now matched with the signatures of the images that passed the second filter. A score is returned for each image and if the score is less than the user-specified threshold the image is returned as a match.

We can thus see that the index is in reality an assembly of database objects (Figure 3). Execution of a query involves execution of several steps accessing several database objects. First a range query which is a conjunction of several clauses is created from the query signature. This query is executed using the bitmap indexes on the feature table. The results of this query, which are the results of the first filter, are passed to the second filter. The final signature comparison using Virage's code is executed for the results of this filter.

4.4 DML Operations

Insert of a new signature is executed by extracting the approximate representation of the signature and adding that row to the feature table, which causes the bitmap indexes to be updated. Deletion of a signature is executed by deleting the row in the feature table which causes the bitmap indexes to be updated. Update of a signature triggers the regeneration of the approximate signature and update of the bitmap indexes.

4.5 Oracle and Virage

Oracle8i server and Virage software modules cooperate to execute the three phases. Virage routines execute in a process space separate

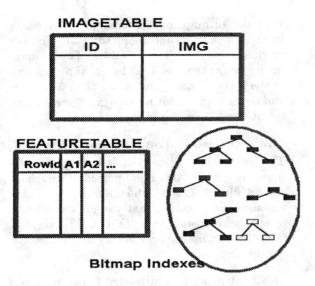

IMAGETABLE

ID	IMG

FEATURETABLE

RowId	A1	A2	...

Bitmap Indexes

Figure 3: Components of the Image Index

from that of the Oracle server. In phase 1, the range query terms are generated by a Virage function. In phase 3, the final signature comparison is executed by a callout to an external Virage function.

It has to be noted that while the implementation details of this product have been designed for successful interaction between Oracle and Virage, the same concept can be extended to other domain specific products such as face recognition, fingerprint matching, and region-based querying. Oracle's extensible architecture allows any specialized algorithm or product to be incorporated seamlessly in the server.

5   Performance Issues

It is interesting to investigate the various factors that affect the performance of the index. The performance is the combination of the performance of the three phases seen above. Obviously, in a multi-level filtering scheme, only the first filter can be indexed, and the performance of the following phases will be a factor of the number of images they process. The first filter design determines the scalability of the index and the bitmap index approach provides this scalability. The fact that we can drop dimensions which are not used in the match also influences performance.

The dominant factor influencing the performance of the index is the selectivity of the first filter. If the selectivity is high (number of rows returned is low), then the second and third phases operate on only a small percentage of the data, resulting in good performance. If the selectivity is low, performance deteriorates, though it is always linear with a slope less than 1. Some situations where the first filter selectivity is high are - low threshold indicating that the user is interested in only exact or near-exact matches, the query image being dissimilar to most of the images in the database, a selective attribute such as the texture attribute being the only one specified. Our index performs best in these situations, and in the worst case where selectivity crosses 50% the performance scalability is still linear with a slope less than 1.

In this section we present results on the variation of performance with threshold and specified attributes. To nullify the factors of distribution of data in the database and similarity of the image query with images in the database, we create a database populated with generic photographic images with a uniform distribution with respect to the four attributes.

5.1   Performance Setup

The experiments were conducted on a two CPU Ultra Enterprise Solaris machine running SunOS 5.6 and with 1 GB RAM. The image table size ranged from 10,000 rows to 100,000 rows.

Our experiments involved the following queries:

- Varying number of attributes specified: (threshold is 10)

  - ColorTex.sql: Nonzero weights for global color and texture only (the user wants to use only those attributes for the match).

  - Tex.sql: Nonzero weights for texture only.

  - TexStruc.sql: Nonzero weights for texture and structure only.

- Varying threshold: (attributes are global color and texture)

  - Thresh3.sql: The user is interested in only exact or near-exact matches.

  - Thresh10.sql: Threshold of 10.

- Thresh15.sql: Threshold of 15.

- Thresh20.sql: Threshold of 20. The selectivity of the first filter usually deteriorates.

In all our results disk I/O represents 10% of the total query time. CPU time is the dominant factor because of the bitmap merge phase and minimized I/O cost while accessing the bitmaps. The times represent measurements in our environment. The goal is to present the relative performance of the different queries rather than absolute numbers.

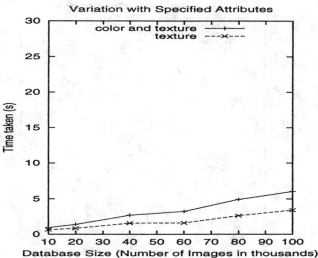

Figure 5: Variation with Number of Attributes

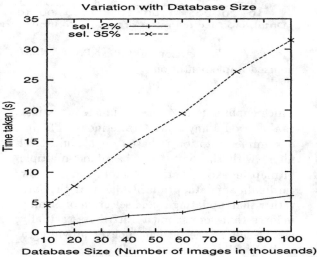

Figure 4: Variation with Database Size

5.2 Discussion

Figure 4 illustrates the performance of the query ColorTex varying with the size of the image table. It can be seen that the performance scales well with size. The figure shows the time taken for two queries each with different query images. The two queries have different first filter selectivities representing both ends of the spectrum - 2% selectivity and 35% selectivity. The time taken by the query with 35% selectivity increases more rapidly with size than the one with 2% selectivity. This is because with decreased selectivity the expensive signature comparison becomes the significant component of the total time, and that time grows more rapidly with time than the first filter time.

However, as indicated earlier, the slope is less than 1.

Figure 5 illustrates how performance varies with the attributes specified. The texture only query Tex has a higher selectivity than the ColorTex query resulting in better performance for such queries. The better performance is also because only the bitmaps corresponding to the texture attribute are accessed and merged, where as in the ColorTex query bitmaps corresponding to two attributes have to be accessed and merged.

Figure 6 illustrates how threshold affects performance. Queries Thresh3, Thresh10, Thresh15, Thresh20 are executed. When the threshold is 3, only exact or near-exact matches are retrieved. In this situation a large number of images are eliminated in the first filter. As the threshold increases the selectivity decreases and the time taken increases. The selectivity of the first filter when the threshold is 3 is less than 0.5%, when the threshold is 10 its 2%, when the threshold is 15 its 13% and when the threshold is 20 it jumps to 65%.

It has to be emphasized that these measures for time taken and selectivity could vary depending on the image data in a particular database. For instance, if all the images in the database are very similar to each other, these figures will change significantly.

The results clearly illustrate some of the

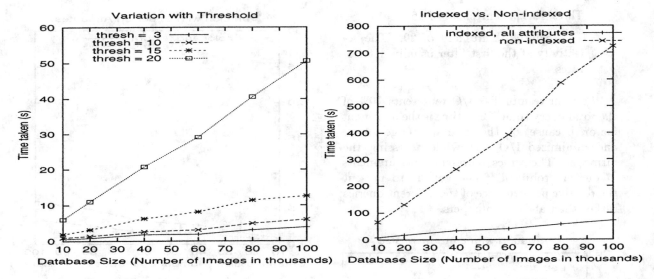

Figure 6: Variation with Threshold

Figure 7: Comparison of Indexed vs. Non-indexed implementation

advantages of our approach. When the user is not interested in certain dimensions, those are not used, leading to lesser bitmap indexes being read and merged, resulting in quicker execution of the query. Similarly when only the exact matches are required, efficient execution is possible. Determining that there are no good matches in the database is also very efficient. Users in some scenarios have a tremendous benefit, users in other scenarios might have a lesser benefit but still experience reasonable performance. These results give us some heuristics for using the index. For instance a large threshold results in a large result set and a linear scan might be better.

5.3 Indexed vs. Non-indexed

Figure 7 illustrates the tremendous improvement in using the index in Oracle. Even when all the attributes are used the indexed implementation outperforms the non-indexed implementation by an order of magnitude. When fewer attributes are used the improvement can be two or three orders of magnitude.

6 Conclusion

The Oracle8i Visual Information Retrieval Product provides for efficient content-based retrieval of images. It provides an image index type using Oracle8i's extensible indexing mechanism

which enables users to use an image index just as they would any other Oracle index. The index implementation is based on a multi-level filter, with the first filter based on multiple bitmap indexes. Various factors such as low cardinality of data, primarily querying the data rather than updating it and selection of bitmap indexes that correspond to attributes actually used result in the bitmap indexes providing a scalable solution.

7 Acknowledgements

We thank Jeff Bach and his colleagues at Virage, Inc. for their assistance during the design and implementation of this product.

References

[Ang95] Y. H. Ang, Z. Li, S. H. Ong, Image Retrieval based on Multidimensional Feature Properties, In *SPIE*, Vol. 2420, 47–57, 1995.

[Bac96] J. R. Bach, The Virage Image Search Engine: An Open Framework for Image Management, In *Proceedings of Storage and Retrieval for Still Image and Video Databases IV*, SPIE Vol. 2670, 76–87. 1996.

[Ber98] S. Berchtold, C. Bohm, H-P. Kriegal, The Pyramid-Technique: Towards Breaking the Curse of Dimensionality, In *Proceedings of the 1998 ACM SIGMOD*, 142–153, 1998.

[Boz97] T. Bozkaya, M. Ozsoyoglu, Distance-based Indexing for High-dimensional Metric Spaces, In *Proceedings of the 1997 ACM SIGMOD*, 357–368, 1997.

[Fal94] C. Faloutsos, R. Barber, M. Flickner, J. Hafner, W. Niblack, D. Petkovic and W. Equitz, Efficient and Effective Querying by Image Content, In *Journal of Intelligent Information Systems*, 3(3), 231–262, 1994.

[Fli95] M. Flickner, H. Sawhney, W. Niblack, J. Ashley, Q. Huang, B. Dom, M. Gorkani, J. Hafner, D. Lee, D. Petkovic, D. Steele and P. Yanker, Query by Image and Video Content: The QBIC System, *IEEE Computer*, 28(9), 23–31, 1995.

[GJ97] A. Gupta and R. Jain, Visual Information Retrieval, *Communications of ACM*, 40(5):70–79, May 1997.

[Ovr97] Leveraging Digital Image Assets Using the Oracle8 Image Cartridge and the Oracle8 Visual Information Retrieval Cartridge, *Oracle Business White Paper*, June 1997.

[Ora98b] *Oracle8i interMedia Audio, Image, and Video*, Oracle Corporation, February 1999.

[Ora98a] *Oracle8i Server Concepts*, Oracle Corporation, February 1999.

[Ora98c] *Oracle8i Visual Information Retrieval*, Oracle Corporation, February 1999.

[Whi96] D.A. White, R. Jain, Similarity with the SS-tree, In *Proceedings of the 12th International Conference on Data Engineering*, 1996.

Handling Very Large Databases with Informix Extended Parallel Server

Andreas Weininger
Informix Software
andreasw@informix.com

Abstract

In this paper, we investigate which problems exist in very large real databases and describe which mechanisms are provided by Informix Extended Parallel Server (XPS) for dealing with these problems. Currently the largest customer XPS database contains 27 TB of data. A database server that has to handle such an amount of data has to provide mechanisms which allow achieving adequate performance and easing the usability. We will present mechanisms which address both of these issues and illustrate them with examples from real customer systems.

1 Introduction

Most large databases are data warehouses or operational data stores. Therefore, we will concentrate in this paper on these types of database systems. Two different phases can be distinguished for data warehouses:

- A management phase during which data are inserted, updated, or deleted from the database and auxiliary structures like indices are created, and

- a query phase.

Traditionally, the management phase happned often during the night, and the queries were running during the day. However, for databases with web access and for databases in global companies, which have users in offices all around the globe, these two phases are more or less overlapping in time. Therefore, a database system must support this.

The following section discusses problems specific to the management phase of a very large data warehouse, and how these are solved by the Informix Extended Parallel Server (XPS). XPS is a shared nothing DBMS

with support for SMP machines, clusters, and MPP systems.

The next section considers problems and solutions for the query phase. After this, we look at a concrete example from a telecommunications company.

2 Problems and Solutions for the Management Phase

Loading and incremental loading of data is an important operation for data warehouses: It is the way how all the data gets into data warehouse. In some cases unloading/loading is used as a backup/restore solution.

Specific problems associated with loading are:

- Loads can be frequent and involve a large amount of data. For instance, one telecom company is loading daily 30 GB of data in a data warehouse.

- Normal queries are running during the load.

- The load often involved a lot of transformations and checks. For instance, unique and foreign key constraints have to be checked. Doing these checks via indices is usually too expensive.

- The queries executed by load jobs are often very complex. It is not untypical that these queries are the most expensive queries run against the data warehouse

Other problems during the management phase are:

- If old data is removed by delete statements, data is no longer stored as compact as before.

- Delete and update operations involve a large amount of data.

Some of these problems do also exist for smaller database but because of the amount of data, they become much more difficult to handle in very large databases.

There are several features in XPS which allow to solve the above problems efficiently:

- External tables provide an easy way of loading and unloading tables. They are created similar to regular database tables but describe the load/unload files. They can be used in the same way as internal database tables in insert and select statements. It is even possible to join internal and external tables.

- Hybrid fragmentation allows a two-dimensional partitioning of tables. Partitioning in one dimension (usually by hash) allows full use of parallelism while the second dimension provides a second criteria for reducing the amount of work per query by fragment elimination. The example in section 4 illustrates this in more detail.

- Hybrid fragmentation provides an mechanism for efficient incremental loading and deleting: A new table fragmented by hash in the same way as the target table can be loaded while the target table is still in use by other queries. After this, new table can be attached to the target table without any need for data movement. Old data can be removed by detaching the corresponding fragments.

- Update and delete joins provide statements, which handle mass updates and deletes efficiently.

- Constraint checks can be done by queries which use hash-based implementaions for operations. Thus random disk accesses are avoided.

3 Problems and Solutions for the Query Phase

There are two types of queries: Queries involving a large amount of data, which should be executed with intra-query parallelism and queries, which access only a small amount of data, which should get executed serially. For large queries to scale all operations must be executed in parallel: Insert, update, delete, select, update statistics, index builds, but even index checks have to be done in parallel in a very large database. In addition, the use of several coservers (which are logical nodes) on one SMP node in XPS allows to have several parallel instances of resources like the database log which would otherwise not exist in parallel.

For putting complex logic in SQL statements which are executed with intra-query parallelism by the engine, it is important to have a conditional expression like the SQL-92 CASE statements which can be used in any place where a column expression can be used.

4 Example

This examples shows how hybrid fragmentation is used in a data warehouse at a telecommunications company for the physical design of the largest table of the warehouse which contains the call detail records.

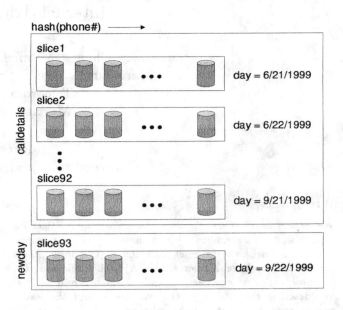

Figure 1: Fragmentation of calldetails table

This data warehouse contains three month of call detail records in a table called calldetails. Hybrid fragmentation is used for this table. By this way, the table is partitioned in so-called dbslices, which are a set of dbspaces, which are the database equivalent of disks. Within one dbslice, the data is distributed by a hash function on the column phonenumber. Therefore, queries involving all customers i.e. all phone numbers can use all the available parallelism while at the same time, the amount of work done by a query scanning calldetails can be reduced by fragment elimination, if the query restricts itself to a specific time interval.

Once a day, new call detail recoreds are loaded: First, these data are loaded into the table newday. Then, this table can be attached to the calldetails table without any effort. Deleting the oldest data from day 6/21/1999 can be done by detaching the corresponding dbslice from the table calldetails. Therefore, no delete has to run to achieve this.

5 Summary

This paper concentrated the discussion on topics related to the physical design of very large databases and the support provided by XPS. There are of course many other aspects which have to be considered when implementing large databases, like an efficient and scalable implementation of operations like join and group. However, these topics are beyond the scope of this paper.

Internet Traffic Warehouse

Chung-Min Chen   Munir Cochinwala   Claudio Petrone
Marc Pucci   Sunil Samtani   Patrizia Santa
Telcordia Technologies
Morristown, NJ, USA

Marco Mesiti
Universita' degli Studi di Genova, Italy

Abstract

We report on a network traffic warehousing project at Telcordia. The warehouse supports a variety of applications that require access to Internet traffic data. The applications include Service Level Agreement (SLA), web traffic analysis, network capacity engineering and planning, and billing. We describe the design of the warehouse and the issues encountered in building the warehouse.

1 Introduction

Service and network providers need access to and analysis of network traffic data for efficiency in management of network capacity and engineering, trouble-shooting faults, billing and conformance to service level agreements. Data collection is typically application specific with each application requiring parts of the data in a unique format. For example, a telephony billing application would require call detail records for each toll call [2].

Traditionally, network engineers collect traffic data in flat files as logs or dumps, and use special-purpose tools (such as `awk` and `perl` scripts) and custom programs for analysis [3]. These special purpose tools are generally not re-usable across data sets or for different analyses of the same data because they are customized for specific data formats and for a specific analysis goal.

Even for tools that adopt a DBMS, the data collected are usually "volatile", in the sense that they are thrown away soon after the statistics are computed. These detailed data, however, may contain useful information when gathered over an extended chronological interval. Typically, a catastrophic network backbone failure can be predicted by the presence of small, scattered network problems preceding the big crash.

In an attempt to help identify "root causes" of failures and forecast possible network catastrophes, as well as have a single data repository for multiple applications, we have taken the data warehousing approach. The warehouse also paves the way for data mining procedures that are designed to find such prediction rules. The warehouse is built from all the packets at particular collection points in the network. This includes header as well as payload information per packet. The data models allow users to query at the application level (e.g. number of sessions of duration greater than 10 minutes per user) as well as drill down to the packet level.

The rest of the paper is as follows: In Section 2 we give the motivation for using a warehouse; in Section 3 we describe the implementation including data models, cubes and the prototype; in Section 4 we explore two sample applications and in Section 5 we discuss the issues and limitation of the approach. Section 6 contains the status of the project and identifies future directions.

2 Motivation

The level of analysis available by capturing all of the packets used by an application is extremely powerful. Information such as what particular operations have been executed and how long responses took to be generated can be gleaned from the data stream. It can be argued that equivalent information can be generated directly by the end applications if they are sufficiently instrumented and record their behavior in log files. However, not all of the information that may be desired in subsequent analyses may have been anticipated by the instrumentor. For example, very few HTTP servers will include information about aborted downloads, even though this may be very useful in isolating performance bottlenecks or poor web design. Such information may be indirectly obtained from the packet traces. In addition, access to application source code in order to add instrumentation may be unavailable for proprietary reasons. In such cases, the packet trace may be the only

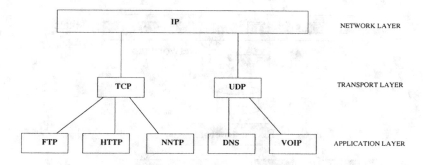

Figure 1: Hierarchical Data Model for Layered Protocols

way to obtain this knowledge. Direct instrumentation may also affect any time sensitivity of an application, or increase its load. Indirect measurement via packet trace analysis is non-intrusive.

Important applications that require access to application level data as well as packet level data are Service Level Agreements (SLA) [1] and Network Trouble Shooting. An SLA is a contract between the service provider and a (usually enterprise) customer on the level of service quality that should be delivered. An SLA may contain several "metrics". Each metric (e.g., available network bandwidth) is associated with a guaranteed performance (e.g., 1.2Mbps), the method of measurement (e.g., 90% of the time on 80% of the user nodes), and a penalty (e.g. $1000) to the provider if the agreement is not met. SLAs give providers a competitive edge for selling customized services into the consumer market and maintaining a high level of customer satisfaction. To track SLAs, the service provider must monitor application-specific performance metrics which generate per user reports on satisfaction/violation of the metrics. In addition, the provider must have the ability to drill down to detailed data in response to customer inquiries.

A warehousing approach to storing data combined with the flexibility of OLAP allows a single data repository and system to support diverse applications. An application can use the traffic warehouse by defining its view on the base tables. A warehouse also provides a "historical" perspective on network traffic and allows construction of data marts. These data marts can be used for determining network growth and hence forecasting of demand. Similarly data mining can be used to correlate faults and/or relation of traffic patterns at different time periods or in the presence of promotions that cause service overloads. Service overloads can also be caused by denial of service attacks.

3 Data Warehouse Implementation

The system requires a traffic data collection mechanism as well as methodology for populating that data into the warehouse. Data models for the different network

protocols also need to be defined. In this section, we describe the overall system with some insights into the complexity of the implementation.

3.1 Data Acquisition, Transportation and Integration

The data sources of our Internet traffic data warehouse exhibit some distinctive characteristics. First, the Internet traffic is a dynamic, ever-increasing data stream, as opposed to "static" data sources that are typically stored in relational databases or flat files [4]. We have written a suite of customized programs that read and filter data from the data collection routines into several output streams, each of which corresponds to a specific application such as a single HTTP or FTP operation. The input stream is reconstructed from the low level packet data contained in the trace. Protocol specific filter programs then parse this data and extract the data that has been identified as relevant for the given protocol. For example, an FTP session will record the name, size and transfer rate of the files it passes, while the HTTP filter will record the number and type of web objects contained in each page. The output is flushed to flat files and is further cleansed and correlated before they are imported into the warehouse.

Due to the continuous nature of traffic, we can only keep the data in a staging area for a limited period. The data must be processed (abstracted, cleansed, transferred, and imported into the warehouse) before the storage is re-claimed to hold the next batch of data. We have found no ETL (Extraction, Transformation, and Loading) tools that provide such capabilities.

Preserving the privacy expectations of the users of networks and applications is also of prime concern In particular, the full traces contain system passwords, private correspondence, proprietary documents and other sensitive data. Even the source and destination IP addresses of individual sessions convey information that may be considered private, especially since in today's computing arrangements, an IP address may uniquely identify a user.

While it is possible to completely obscure all of the

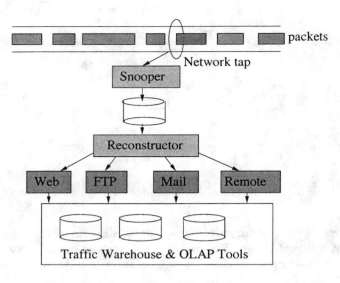

Figure 2: System Architecture

sensitive information in the header and payload of a packet stream, to do so would remove much of the valuable information. A balance must be found between the privacy requirements and analysis needs. While we want to conceal IP addresses so they cannot be used to identify specific sites, we also want to be able to detect multiple accesses to the same site, and therefore must use a consistent mapping scheme from original to obfuscated addresses.

3.2 Data Model

Logically, the warehouse is divided into two levels: the Network Layer (NL) and the Business Layer (BL). The Business Layer model consists of applications that can create their own views on the base relations in the NL model. Rules for materialization are defined under the control of the business application and based on business processes. For instance, billing applications will require views to be materialized at the end of a billing cycle, although they may choose to do it periodically or on demand for pay-as-you-go billing. With this design, new applications can be easily created. This enables service providers to deploy new or customized services based on market need.

The NL defines a data model for multi-layer network protocols (Figure 1). In our instance, the NL contains the network layer (with IP protocol), the transport layer (with TCP/UDP protocols), and the application layer (which models application-specific protocols such as HTTP, FTP, H.323). Each protocol in a layer is made of a set of entities that can be easily added or detached from the main schema. The multi-layer structure allows users to easily navigate and retrieve information at different levels of granularity. In our model, each protocol, such as HTTP, is identified by a port number. Any user-defined application that is similarly identified

can be integrated by adding appropriate custom filters to extract header and payload information.

3.3 Data Cubes

To facilitate OLAP queries, we have also created data cubes out of the base relations in the hierarchical network model. We chose to use an ROLAP data mart building tool for this purpose. Figure 3 shows an example data cube concerning Web access statistics. The fact table contains detailed IP records pertaining to HTTP that are selected from the base IP table. The dimension tables REQUEST_RESPONSE and URL are derived from the suite of HTTP base tables (to be described in Section 4.1).

With this data cube, we may answer questions related to Web page access easily. Consider the question: what is the total size of Web pages under domain www.research.telcordia.com that are accessed and transferred to users (customers) during the last month? This can be answered by slicing on the CUSTOMER, URL, and TIME dimensions, and computing the SUM aggregate on IP_PACKET.packet_length.

3.4 System Architecture

The system (Figure 2) consists of four phases: collection, re-construction, data loading and analysis. The overall process begins with low level access to the traffic data stream. There are several collection options available here. One technique is to use the tcpdump command available on most Unix systems to extract IP data directly from a computer attached to the network to be monitored. We have also used custom designed hardware that interfaces directly to T1 and OC-3c communications lines and copies traffic directly to tertiary storage. Depending on the data rates and duration

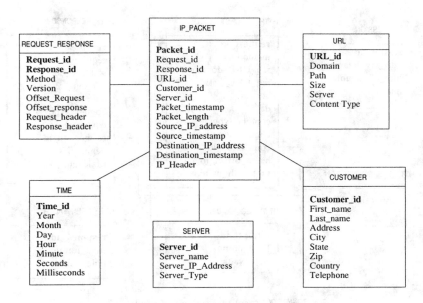

Figure 3: Star Schema for HTTP/IP data

of measurement, the required storage capacity can be enormous; terabyte sized data sets are to be expected.

The collected information represents the data that passes by on the physical communications link, not the data that an application would necessarily see. It also contains the interpersed traffic of hundreds or thousands of individual sessions whose data are interspersed across different applications. These data need to be reconstructed into the form that an application would encounter. This is done using a program that captures all the data embedded in the various protocol semantics in the 7-layer protocol stack. It takes as input a packet, parses the data in the stream (by identifying the port numbers of various application protocols), and generates data pertaining to the protocols (e.g. HTTP, FTP, TCP, IP). The program operates in the following manner: First, individual TCP and UDP sessions are identified in the data stream. Next, a sufficient number of packets are located to perform any necessary packet reassembly, duplicate detection and discard, and out-of-order corrections. Since both sides of a session need to be passed to the application filter, the packets traveling in each direction on the link need to be correlated and made available to the filter in the proper time sequence.

The port number found in the TCP or UDP header is used to select an appropriate application filter that will process the bidirectional traffic. Each filter is specialized to parse and analyze the stream information according to the behavior of the application. For example, the FTP filter will parse and record the commands and responses used in its file transfer protocol, but will skip over the bulk data involved in a file transfer.

The HTTP filter parses the HTTP protocol data,

including the use of persistent connections for multiple requests. It also decodes the HTML information contained within a request. It uses a regular expression parser to detect comments, URLs, scripting languages, embedded objects and other needed for the further analysis.

The output is staged into temporary files that are subsequently loaded into the warehouse. If one were loading HTTP data, the data would be parsed and multiplexed into four files: IP packets, TCP connections, HTTP requests and HTTP responses. This generates hundreds of MB of data to be loaded into the data warehouse per day. Once the files are generated in a staging area, they are loaded into the data warehouse as defined above.

4 Example Applications

We have actually collected data and analyzed multiple applications. In this section we describe two examples: Web Traffic Analysis and Voice over IP.

4.1 Web Traffic Analysis

We collect the data for Web traffic analysis from two sources: web server logs and an in-house developed network traffic filtering utility program as described above. The web server logs are readily available from most HTTP servers, in which they record some statistics about the HTTP requests. The logs we use come from a number of Apache HTTP servers. The data in web server logs contain information on every incoming HTTP request and the corresponding response, such as users (in terms of IP address or domain name) access patterns to pages (in terms of URL address).

553

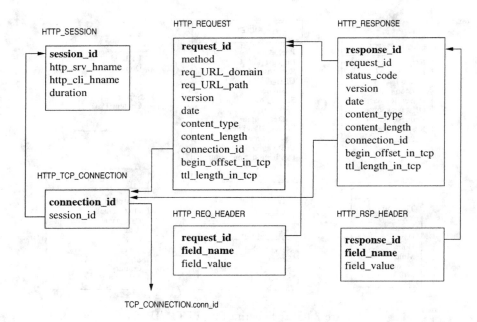

Figure 4: Schema of HTTP traffic data

While providing useful information, data contained in HTTP server logs pertains to the HTTP protocol layer only. This is not enough information for detailed analysis of HTTP traffic. (Recall, HTTP is built on top of TCP and IP protocols). In addition, some header information defined in the HTTP protocol is not captured by the server logs. This includes information such as content type, content length, HTTP version and correlation between the lower layers (TCP/IP) and the application layer (HTTP). This information is of crucial importance to system administrators responsible for system performance monitoring and resource planning.

Figure 4 shows the schema of the HTTP portion of the data model described in Figure 1. Primary keys are identified in boldface, whereas the arrowed lines indicate the foreign key relationships among the tables. All foreign key relationships are many-to-one except the one between HTTP_REQUEST and HTTP_RESPONSE, which is one-to-one. The HTTP_TCP_CONNECTION table identifies individual HTTP connection, which coincides with a TCP connection. Each such connection points to a corresponding TCP connection record in the TCP_CONNECTION table (which is not shown here).

An HTTP connection may contain several round trips of requests and responses (the so called "persistent" HTTP connection, as supported by HTTP version 1.1). Each record in the HTTP_REQUEST table represents a request from a browser. It is associated to a corresponding response in the HTTP_RESPONSE table. Each request/response is also associated with a number of HTTP headers. Finally, we create a table called HTTP_SESSION that introduces the fuzzy notion of "HTTP session", which is defined to be a sequence of requests from a visitor that are close in time.

On top of the base tables that host the protocol-wise data, we define star schema that facilitates analyses from different views. The star schema is the one described in Figure 3, and its purpose is to provide the appropriate structure for OLAP operations.

Figures 5, 6 and 7 give the look and feel of the OLAP output. Figure 5 shows the response time of requests made to various web sites. The first column lists the domain names of the web sites (consider this the "SERVER" dimension from Figure 3). Listed under each domain name are the individual HTTP connections and requests made to that site (consider these the "REQUEST_RESPONSE" dimension from Figure 3). For example, the bottom of the crosstab shows the first five connections (connection ID 912, 925, 926, 927 and 971) to cnn.com. Listed under each connection are individual HTTP requests (e.g. connection 971 contains three HTTP requests). The column "Content Length" indicates the total size of the file(s) getting transferred in each request, connection, and by each web site (during the observed period). The next column gives (total) round-trip response time of the transfers (computed from the "TIME" dimension of Figure 3). The last column measures the effective bandwidth which is computed by dividing the previous two columns. We note that the user can further drill down to TCP or even IP levels (omitted here) for more detailed analysis.

Figure 6 lists the number of different HTTP links embedded in the web pages accessed by individual browsers. These numbers are summarized at different levels: HTTP connection, HTTP request, content type,

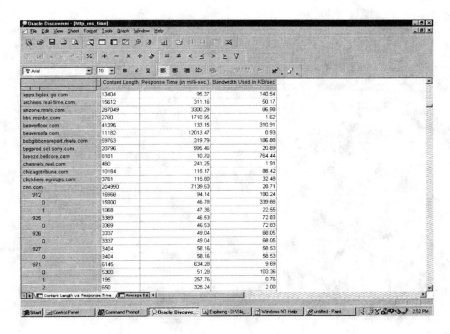

Figure 5: HTTP request response time

link type, and link address. For example, the first group of records indicate that 31 links are embedded in the web pages requested by connection 37. And the response to the fourth request (request 4) in the connection contains 12 embedded images and 7 hyperlinks. The number of links in a web page can be used by providers and caching server providers to determine the type of web page and thus use application specific information to cache.

Finally, Figure 7 gives the number of visits to various Web sites. One can also drill down to find out the visitors of the Web sites. The number strings in the first column under home.netscape.com are scrambled IP addresses of the visitors. The IP addresses are scrambled to maintain privacy.

4.2 Voice over IP

Many vendors are now attempting to emulate traditional telephony over the internet. However, to be competitive in the marketplace, the Quality of Service (QoS) of voice over IP should be equal to, if not better than traditional telephony. In traditional telephony (circuit switched network), a dedicated path between the two endpoints (callers) is set up with all required resources. The allocated resources are sufficient to handle continuous voice traffic from either endpoint. If a connection is made the quality of service is guaranteed. The call set-up time has real-time constraints so that either a connection is made in reasonable time (around 300 msecs) or not at all. If resources are not available either a fast busy or a voice recording is heard by the originating caller.

The packet world does not have the same QoS guarantees that a circuit switched world has. Thus, mechanisms for determining QoS need to be introduced. Voice quality is governed by jitter, loss and delay of packets and can be accurately quantified by data collection and monitoring. Call set-up time can be determined either by analyzing the log files generated by telephony "soft-switches" or examining the data traces.

Different paradigms exist today for setting up internet telephony calls. The most common protocols being used are ITU-T H.323, MGCP and SIP. In our study, we modeled the architecture based on IETF MGCP standard. The standard details call flows between different types of users. Based on the call flows, details about messages were extracted from the log files and stored in the data warehouse. In traditional telephony, call set-up delay is relatively simple to compute since a circuit switched network carries signaling over dedicated lines. However, in a packet switched network, where signaling packets can get multiplexed with other traffic this computation is not trivial. Also, the delay has more variance depending on the load in the network. This metric can be derived from the log files by associating the messages within a call context. The information from the logs had to be stored in the warehouse so that variances in call set-up time and hence variances in conformance to SLAs could be identified. The call set-up delay is a typical metric in user SLAs. Although we only looked at log files for call set-up delay, issues in reconstructing call set-up times arose due to the following issues:

- Log files are distributed and messages related to

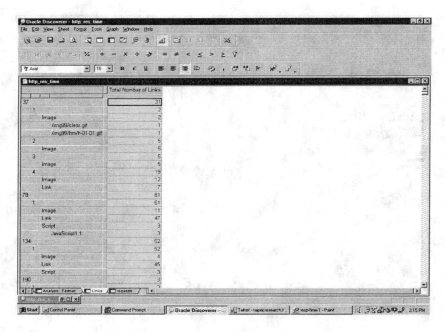

Figure 6: Number of Embedded Links

the same call are stored in multiple places and in different formats. We had to use our collection program and add parsing rules for log files just as we added parsing rules for http traffic.

- Log files are generated as static files and are overwritten after reaching the maximum file size. The copy needed to be placed into the warehouse before the maximum size was reached. We did not have the option of re-naming files and copy them at our convenience.

- Since the time stamps are stored in log files at different locations whose clocks are not synchronized, the time stamps need to be correlated when the logs are moved to the warehouse.

5 Issues and Limitations

5.1 Performance and Distribution

Traffic data can be extremely voluminous. A traditional warehouse approach requires sending all data to a central repository. This introduces problems such as: (1) the transmission of the data adds extra load to the network, and (2) the delay in the transmission results in longer update window of the data warehouse.

We are exploring the idea of implementing a "distributed" data warehouse, in which a number of data warehouses are connected to form a virtual warehouse. A data warehouse would be set up for each network region. All extracted traffic data are directed to and integrated into the regional data warehouses. Only a limited amount of data (e.g. data to correlate IP packets) needs to be exchanged among the data warehouses.

Since the data model is homogeneous among all nodes in the network, the same instance of schema can be used on each of the regional data warehouses.

This approach alleviates the problem of data transfer overhead and warehouse update delay. In addition, by harnessing the distributed computing power and storage capacity, it provides a scalable data warehousing architecture in presence of ever increasing traffic. The challenge, then, is how to efficiently process distributed queries and, in particular, OLAP queries.

Within a single warehouse, the IP packet table is the main source of performance bottleneck. We have chosen to cluster IP records on the timestamp attribute. This approach provides efficient performance to queries that analyze the IP traffic in chronological order, but adversely affects queries that analyze on other attributes. For example, consider queries that are related only to HTTP traffic or to the traffic load on a specific subnet. The IP records pertaining to HTTP or a subnet may be scattered throughout the physical table and subsequently incur substantial I/O access. One possible remedy to the problem is to maintain separate IP tables for each application protocol. While this approach provides adequate performance for application-specific queries, it incurs more indexing overhead and is more complicated in schemas and semantics. Another possible solution is to implement the packet table and indices in flat files, with associated operations implemented in specially tailored programs. The advantage is that, with proper implementation, much of the DBMS overhead can be avoided and the performance can be custom-tuned. The

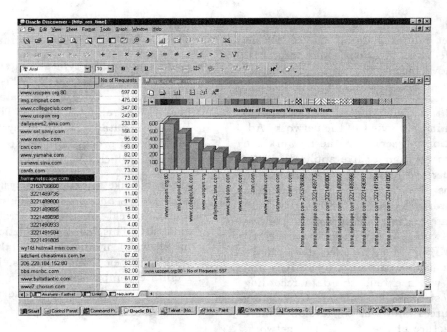

Figure 7: Web site visits

drawback is that we need an interface (APIs) through which we can query the flat files (semi- structured data) and integrate with other data that reside in the relational database. The feasibility of this approach is currently being investigated.

5.2   Historical Warehouse

One feature that is essential to our applications but has not been supported by commercials DBMSs is the incorporation of tertiary storage in the DBMS. Traffic data arrive at a speed that is several magnitudes faster than the data sources of traditional business data warehouses. Thus, secondary storage is saturated and data needs to be moved to a tertiary storage. This requires supports of the following:

- *Storage transparency*: The secondary and tertiary devices should be provided as a seamless storage system to the database users. Except for some configuration set-ups, the DBA or users must be able to run regular SQL queries without worrying about the location of the data across secondary and tertiary storage devices.

- *Efficient migration*: The DBMS must provide quick migration of data between the two-hierarchy storage system. This includes automatic eviction of data from the secondary to tertiary devices as they become "old", and fast retrieval/recovery of data from the tertiary storage to the disks when they are requested. A hybrid indexing technique to index data on both levels of storage is also needed.

- *Aggregates versus detailed data*: Packet data will typically be moved to tertiary storage at the end of a day or week. However, aggregate data derived from the packet data needs to be stored in secondary storage for a much longer time. Rules for deriving and constructing aggregate data as well as dependencies between packet data and aggregate data need to be maintained. The ideal case would be for the DBMS vendor to provide a mechanism for the user to design and build these rules in the warehouse configuration.

5.3   Protocols and Collection

Collection of data and modeling of protocols raise interesting issues for warehouse design. Some of these issues are:

- *Hierarchical structure of Internet protocols*: The layered network protocols suggest a hierarchical data model design. However, the design of the schemas (including base tables and materialized views/aggregates) so as to support efficient vertical drill down (through the protocol stacks) and horizontal traverse (cross-protocol analysis) remains an issue.

- *Data quality*: We have found that the location of the collector in a network can affect the quality of the collected data. Due to asymmetric routing in the Internet backbone, incoming and outgoing traffic may not travel on the same physical link. Collection at a single point in the network could result in observing only one side of a 'conversation'.

To alleviate this problem, we collect near the application to get re-united data. On collections from internal network locations, we preprocess the data to remove incomplete sessions. Further research is needed to deal with incomplete data.

- *What level to collect?* Collecting all the packets enables us to get an in-depth view of the network. Additional information not sent over the network can be gleaned from other sources like application logs such as those generated by web servers, firewalls or other applications. Information about the current state of the network can be obtained by periodically extracting appropriate measurement counters directly from network elements that have SNMP access to their MIBs. More detailed data can be found in the data fields maintained by RMON and RMON2 probes, which extend the data recording capabilities of most network elements. Correlating multiple data sources allows us to develop a more comprehensive picture of the state if the network. Additionally, some of the data source can be used to reduce the size of the data in the warehouse. The proper level and detail of data is an area of further research.

6   Project Status and Future Work

We have built the traffic warehouse and are currently using it to monitor SLAs within our local area network. The project is integrated with a traffic management IP telephony project where packet loss, jitter and delay can be experimentally controlled. We plan to introduce billing and other applications in this experiment to determine the feasibility of a warehouse.

Future work involves exploring issues identified in the paper as well as the following:

- A logical extension to this work involves capturing packet level information at multiple locations in a network. For example, probing at both the application and client processor network segments will enable the calculation of additional SLA parameters such as packet loss and packet delay. The amount of information needed to be stored in the warehouse would not increase substantially, since redundant information is eliminated. Only packets that do not appear in both traces would need to be added. In addition to SLA parameters, multiple correlated traces can be used to determine the location of packet loss in a large network. This can be used to verify or indicate suspected problem sources.

- Our goal is to allow end-users to monitor their own SLA if desired or monitor their own bills. This will require a web front end to end-users where customers can view their own information and aggregate information (patterns of customers like me) but not detailed information of other users.

- End-users are also typically interested in when their services will be activated. This requires access by end-users to service status databases that are not part of the traffic warehouse. This requires integration of the databases into our system, understanding the business processes of service activation, and figuring out which part to expose to end-users.

- We would like to extend the system to include real-time probes and populate the data into the warehouse for real-time network traffic monitoring and analysis. This real-time functionality is coincided in [2], which monitors and analyzes traffic data in traditional telephone networks. Real-time data also facilitate comparisons between historical and current data can be made to understand the state of the network.

References

[1] S. Aidarous, C. Rad, K. Smith, E. Bagnasco, and S. Desai. Service level agreements: can you deliver what you promised? In *Panel Session, Sixth IFIP/IEEE International Symposium on Integrated Network Management*, Boston, MA, May 1999. presentation slides avaialble at www.comsoc.org/confs/im/99/panel.html.

[2] Q. Chen, M. Hsu, and U. Dayal. A data-warehouse/OLAP framework for scalable telecommunication tandem traffic analysis. In *16th Intl. Conf. on Data Engineering*, San Diego, CA, Feb 2000.

[3] A. Erramilli and J. Wang. Monitoring packet traffic levels. In *Proc. IEEE Globecom*, pages 274–280, San Francisco, CA, 1994.

[4] R. Kimball. *The Data Warehouse Toolkit: Practical Techniques for Building Dimensional Data Warehouses.* John Wiley & Sons, 1996.

SQLEM: Fast Clustering in SQL using the EM Algorithm

Carlos Ordonez *
College of Computing
Georgia Institute of Technology
ordonez@cc.gatech.edu

Paul Cereghini
Retail Solutions Group
NCR Corporation
paul.cereghini@ncr.com

Abstract

Clustering is one of the most important tasks performed in Data Mining applications. This paper presents an efficient SQL implementation of the EM algorithm to perform clustering in very large databases. Our version can effectively handle high dimensional data, a high number of clusters and more importantly, a very large number of data records. We present three strategies to implement EM in SQL: horizontal, vertical and a hybrid one. We expect this work to be useful for data mining programmers and users who want to cluster large data sets inside a relational DBMS.

1 Introduction

1.1 Clustering

Clustering data is a well researched topic in Statistics [7, 13]. Unfortunately the proposed statistical algorithms are generally inefficient and do not work well with *large* data sets. Most of the work done on clustering by the database community attempts to make clustering algorithms more efficient in order to handle large data sets. Clustering algorithms can be broadly classified into distance-based and density-based; most of them work only with numerical data. BIRCH [17] is an important precursor in clustering for large databases. BIRCH is a distance-based algorithm based on the CF tree. It is linear in database size and the number of passes over the data is determined by a user-supplied accuracy, but it is sensitive to noisy data and is not designed to handle high dimensionality. CLARANS [14] and DBSCAN [10] are also important clustering algorithms that work on spatial data. CLARANS, using a distance-based approach, uses randomized search

and represents clusters by their medioids (most central point). DBSCAN clusters data points in dense regions separated by low density regions. CLIQUE [2] is a density-based clustering algorithm that can discover clusters in subspaces of multidimensional data and which exhibits several advantages with respect to performance, order of data and initialization over other clustering algorithms but is bad handling high dimensional data as it prunes most subspaces and finds only low dimensional embedded clusters. There is recent work on the problem of selecting subsets of dimensions being relevant to all clusters; this problem is called the projected clustering problem and the proposed algorithm is called PROCLUS [1]. This approach is specially useful to analyze sparse high dimensional data focusing on a *few* dimensions. An outstanding recent clustering algorithm is OptiGrid [11]. In this paper the authors develop a new technique that succesively partitions dimensions by hyperplanes in an optimal manner to discover dense regions. This algorithm effectively handles noisy data of high dimensionality and has a very good performance.

1.2 The EM clustering algorithm

EM is a well established clustering algorithm in the Statistics community. It was first introduced in the seminal paper [6] and there has been extensive work in Machine Learning and Computer Vision to apply it and extend it [4, 12, 15, 16]. EM is a distance-based algorithm that assumes the data set can be modeled as a linear combination of multivariate normal distributions and the algorithm finds the distribution parameters that maximize a model quality measure, called loglikelihood. EM was our choice to cluster data for the following reasons among others. It has a strong statistical basis, it is linear in database size, it is robust to noisy data, it can accept the desired number of clusters as input, it provides a cluster membership probability per point, it can handle high dimensionality and it converges fast given a good initialization. We must stress that EM does have some disadvantages. Sometimes the normal distribution assumption does not

---
*The first author was supported in part by grant LM 06726-02 from the National Library of Medicine

hold for some dimensions, given a poor initialization convergence can be slow, the algorithm may stop at a suboptimal solution, undefined computations may appear and interpreting results can be hard. All these issues will be addressed throughout the paper.

1.3 Motivation to implement EM in SQL

There are several reasons for which implementing EM in SQL turned out to be an interesting problem. One of the main points is that this task looked trivial at first sight, but it turned out to be challenging when we faced the problem of handling large data sets with high dimensionality. Here we list some of the reasons that motivated us to do this work:

- Most of the Database research papers on clustering concentrate on developing efficient algorithms in some high-level programming language, such as C++, but very few concentrate on the problem of actually deploying the solution inside a relational DBMS. Besides, many of those clustering algorithms lack a strong statistical foundation.

- Transferring data out of a large data warehouse for processing can be time consuming, error-prone and difficult. In our case transferring tables having more than 100 million records to a workstation to perform clustering uncovered many unexpected problems. The two alternatives to storing the data in a workstation were storing the data in a large text file, or in a database. First, having a big text file containing those 100 million records became a problem because of access speed (just sequential access) and susceptibility to read errors. So text files had to be limited in size in order to be used without errors. Second, we considered the problem of putting the data inside a local DBMS but that turned out to be a problem similar to just trying to cluster the data inside the data warehouse itself.

- SQL is a high-level data manipulation language available in most important DBMS's. SQL is well understood and standarized. Moreover, using SQL can save a great deal of programming.

- Data management is easier if one relies on the DBMS. A clustering program should be freed from managing data.

- In our case most of the times the access plan generated by the query optimizer was inefficient. Ideally, the EM implementation should run as fast as possible regardless of the order of the input data, the access plan produced by the optimizer, the dimensionality of the data and the presence of noise. In other words, the algorithm should have a guaranteed performance.

Having identified all these issues we decided to implement EM in SQL thinking it would be an easy task. However, we soon faced the following difficulties. SQL is based on the relational model and can execute relational operators but it does not support linear algebra operations. Inside a relational DBMS all the data is stored in tables; therefore there are no arrays. For the same reason there is no direct and efficient way to perform linear algebra operations which are required by the EM algorithm.

Any relational DBMS has practical limitations. Just to name a few, there is usually a maximum number of columns per table (as of today in the neighborhood of 1000), the string length of some SQL query cannot be more than a few kilobytes, many optimizations are only available internally. To handle high dimensional data table joins are required, and how the corresponding queries are formulated becomes critical to performance. A joinless solution was not feasible for the following reasons. There is a maximum number of columns per table and we required a number beyond that limit. There is a maximum length for a SQL expression that the SQL interpreter/parser can handle and some mathematical expressions were much longer. Lastly, in our case, the DBMS executes queries in parallel and results are returned in an unpredictable order.

Many times the DBMS becomes slower as record size and block size grow but that may vary depending on the particular DBMS. However, there is a tradeoff with the performance of indexes when these two numbers decrease as we shall see. Some operations have higher overhead than others. In some cases updates are better than inserts but in many other cases inserts are faster. Deletes turned out to be slow. Some database operations tend to be more efficient as the number of columns increases and some others tend to be faster as the number of records increases. The performance of the algorithm can degrade considerably if the SQL statement execution requires many joins and data needs to be sorted.

1.4 Contributions and outline of the paper

Our main contributions are the following:

- Explain how to create a simple SQL code generator to implement the EM clustering algorithm: SQLEM.

- Provide a solution that has good performace. Scale well with database size. Scale well with high dimensional data.

- Keep the basic behavior of the EM algorithm unchanged. This is important to check correctness and debugging.

- Prove that SQL can be used to perform complex mathematical calculations with a reasonable performance when queries are properly formulated.

- Provide a solution that does not require user-defined functions or external data structures (matrices, trees, hash tables). This improves portability and applicability.

- Produce SQL statements that can be easily optimized and executed in parallel by the DBMS.

- Perform most of the work inside the DBMS, having a small program in a workstation to control execution.

This work is organized as follows. Section 2 provides the basic background to understand our implementation. Section 3 describes in detail the three alternatives we came up with to implement EM in SQL and argues which was the best. Section 4 gives a detailed performance evaluation with synthetic and retail data to do customer segmentation. The paper ends with section 5; here we summarize our most important results and indicate directions for future research.

2 Statistical and database background

2.1 Mixture of Gaussians

EM assumes the data can be fitted by a linear combination (mixture) of normal (Gaussian) distributions. The probability density function (pdf) for the normal distribution on one variable x [8] is:

$$p(x) = \frac{1}{\sqrt{2\pi\sigma^2}} exp[\frac{-(x-\mu)^2}{2\sigma^2}].$$

This pdf has expected values: $E[X] = \mu$, $E[(x-\mu)^2] = \sigma^2$. The mean of the distribution is μ and its variance is σ^2. Samples from points having this distribution tend to form a cluster around the mean. The points scatter around the mean is measured by σ^2.

The multivariate normal pdf for p-dimensional space is a generalization of the previous function [8]. The multivariate normal density for a p-dimensional vector $x = x_1, x_2, \ldots, x_p$ is:

$$p(x) = \frac{1}{(2\pi)^{p/2}|\Sigma|^{1/2}} exp[-\frac{1}{2}(x-\mu)^t\Sigma^{-1}(x-\mu)],$$

where μ is the mean and Σ is the covariance matrix; μ is a p-dimensional vector and Σ is a $p \times p$ matrix. $|\Sigma|$ is the determinant of Σ and the t superscript indicates transposition. The quantity δ^2 is called the squared Mahalanobis distance: $\delta^2 = (x-\mu)^t\Sigma^{-1}(x-\mu)$. This formula will be our basic ingredient to implement EM in SQL.

Size	value
k	number of clusters
p	dimensionality
n	number of data points

Figure 1: Matrices sizes

Matrix	size	contents
C	$p \times k$	means (μ)
R	$p \times p$	covariances (Σ)
W	$k \times 1$	weights (w_i)

Figure 2: Gaussian Mixture parameters

EM assumes the data is formed by the mixture of k multivariate normal distributions on p variables. The Gaussian (normal) mixture model probability function is given by:

$$p(x) = \sum_{i=1}^{k} w_i p(x|i),$$

where $p(x|i)$ is the normal distribution for each cluster and w_i is the fraction (weight) that cluster i represents from the entire database. It is important to note that we will focus on the case that there are k different clusters each having their corresponding vector μ but all of them having the same covariance matrix Σ. However, it is not hard to extend this work to handle a different Σ for each cluster.

2.2 Outline of the EM algorithm

There are two basic approaches to perform clustering: based on distance and based on density. Distance-based approaches identify those regions in which points are close to each other according to some distance function. On the other hand, density-based clustering finds those regions which are more highly populated than adjacent regions. Clustering algorithms can work in a top-down (hierarchical [13]) or a bottom-up (agglomerative) fashion. Bottom-up algorithms tend to be more accurate but slower.

The Expectation-Maximization (EM) algorithm [16] is an algorithm based on distance computation. It can be seen as a generalization of clustering based on computing a mixture of probability distributions. It works by succesively improving the solution found so far. The algorithm stops when the quality of the current solution becomes stable; this is measured by a monotonically increasing statistical quantity called *loglikelihood* [6]. The goal of the EM algorithm is to estimate the means C, the covariances R and the

- Input: k, # of clusters. $Y = \{y_1 \ldots y_n\}$ a set of n p-dimensional points. ϵ, a tolerance for loglikelihood. *maxiterations*, a maximum number of iterations.

- Output: C, R, W, the matrices containing the updated mixture parameters. X, a matrix with cluster membership probabilities.

1. **Initialize.** Set initial values for C, R, W (random or approximate solution from sample)

2. **WHILE** change in loglikelihood llh is greater than ϵ and *maxiterations* has not been reached DO E and M steps

   E step

   $C' = 0, R' = 0, W' = 0, llh = 0$
   for $i = 1$ to n
      $sump_i = 0$
      for $j = 1$ to k
         $\delta_{ij} = (y_i - C_j)^t R^{-1}(y_i - C_j)$
         $p_{ij} = \frac{w_j}{(2\pi)^{p/2}|R|^{1/2}} exp[-\frac{1}{2}\delta_{ij}]$
         $sump_i = sump_i + p_{ij}$
      endfor
      $x_i = p_i/sump_i$, $llh = llh + ln(sump_i)$
      $C' = C' + y_i x_i^t$, $W' = W' + x_i$
   endfor

   M step

   for $j = 1$ to k
      $C_j = C_j'/W_j'$
      for $i = 1$ to n $R' = R' + (y_i - C_j)x_{ij}(y_i - C_j)^t$ endfor
   endfor
   $R = R'/n, W = W'/n$

Figure 3: Pseudo code for EM algorithm

mixture weights W of the Gaussian mixture probability function described above. The parameters estimated by the EM algorithm are stored in the matrices described in Figure 2 whose sizes are shown in Figure 1. The popular K-means clustering algorithm [16] is a particular case of EM when W and R are fixed: $W = 1/k, R = I$. It is trivial to simplify SQLEM to do clustering based on K-means and therefore we do not describe it.

The EM algorithm starts from an approximation to the solution. This solution can be randomly chosen or it can be set by the user (when there is some idea about potential clusters). A common way to initialize the parameters is to set $C \leftarrow \mu \, random()$, $R \leftarrow I$ and $W \leftarrow 1/k$; where μ is the global mean. It must be pointed out that this algorithm can get stuck in a locally optimal solution depending on the initial approximation. So one of the disadvantages of EM is that it is sensitive to the initial solution and sometimes it cannot reach the global optimal solution. Nevertheless, EM offers many advantages besides being efficient and having a strong statistical basis. One of those advantages is that EM is robust to noisy data and missing information. In fact,

EM was born to handle incomplete data as explained in [6].

2.3 The EM algorithm

The EM algorithm, shown in Figure 3, has two major steps: the *Expectation* step and the *Maximization* step. EM executes the E step and the M step as long as the change in global loglikelihood (called *llh* inside pseudo-code below) is greater than ϵ or as long as the maximum number of iterations has not been reached. Setting a maximum no. of iterations is important to guarantee performance. The global loglikelihood is computed as $llh = \sum_{i=1}^{n} ln(sump_i)$. The variables δ, P, X are $n \times k$ matrices storing Mahalanobis distances, normal probabilities and responsibilities repectively for each of the n points.

This is the basic framework of the EM algorithm and this will be the basis to do the translation into SQL. There are several important observations. C', R' and W' are temporary matrices used in computations. Note that they are not the transpose of the corresponding matrix. $||W|| = 1$, that is, $\sum_{i=1}^{k} w_i = 1$. Each column of C is a cluster; C_j is the jth column of C. y_i is the ith data point. R is a diagonal matrix in the context of this paper (statistically meaning that covariances are independent); that is, $R_{ij} = 0$ for $i \neq j$. The diagonality of R is a key assumption to make linear gaussian models work with EM [16]. Therefore, its determinant and its inverse can be computed in time $O(p)$. Note that under these assumptions the EM algorithm has complexity $O(kpn)$. The diagonality of R is a key assumption for the SQL implementation. Having a non-diagonal matrix would change the time complexity to $O(kp^2 n)$.

2.4 Simplifying and optimizing computations

The first important substep in the E step is computing the Mahalanobis distances δ_{ij} [6]. Remember that we assume R is diagonal. A careful inspection of the expression reveals that when R is diagonal the Mahalanobis distance of point y to cluster mean C having covariance R is

$$\delta^2 = (y - C)^t R^{-1}(y - C) = \sum_{i=1}^{p} \frac{(y_i - C_i)^2}{R_i}.$$

This is because $R_{ii}^{-1} = 1/R_{ii}$. For a non-singular diagonal matrix R^{-1} is easily computed by taking the mutiplicative inverses of the elements in the diagonal and being R^{-1} diagonal all the products $(y_i - C_i)R_j^{-1} = 0$ when $i \neq j$. A second observation is that R being diagonal can be stored as a vector saving space, but more importantly speeding up computations. So we will index R with just one subscript from now on. Since R does not change during the E step its determinant can be computed only once, making probability computations (p_{ij}) faster. For the M step since R is diagonal the covariance computation gets simplified. Elements off the diagonal in the computation $(y_i - C_j)x_{ij}(y_i - C_j)^t$ become zero. In simpler terms, $R_i = R_i + x_{ij}(y_{ij} - C_{ij})^2$ is faster to compute. The rest of the computations cannot be further optimized mathematically.

2.5 Dealing with null probabilities and null covariances

In practice $p_{ij} = 0$ sometimes, as computed in the E step. This may happen because $exp[-\frac{1}{2}\delta_{ij}] = 0$ when $\delta_{ij} > 600$; that is, when the Mahalanobis distance is big. There is a simple and practical reason for this: the numeric precision available in the computer. In most DBMS's and current computers the maximum accuracy available for numeric computations is double precision which uses 8 bytes. For this precision the $exp(x)$ mathematical function is zero when $x < -1200$.

A big Mahalanobis distance for one point can be the result of noisy data, poor cluster initialization or the point belonging to an outlier. So this problem needed to be solved in order to make SQLEM a practical solution. We must stress that this happens because the computer cannot keep the required accuracy, but not because EM is making a wrong computation. So we needed to have an alternative for δ_{ij} when the distances were big and we solved it like this:

$$p_{ij} = \frac{1/\delta_{ij}}{\Sigma_{l=1}^{k} 1/\delta_{il}}, j \in \{1 \dots k\}.$$

Note that this computation gives a higher probability to points closer to cluster j and is *never* undefined as long as distances are not zero. Also, if some distance δ_{ij} is zero then $exp(\delta_{ij}) = exp(0)$ is indeed defined (being equal to 1) and thus it can be used without any problem. In our current implementation this alternative computation solved the problem.

In many cases the individual covariance for some dimensions (variables) becomes zero in some clusters or more rarely in all the clusters. This can happen for a number of reasons. Missing information, in general, leaves numerical values equal to zero; clusters involving categorical attributes tend to have the same value on the corresponding column. Remember that the E step computes $p_{ij} = \frac{w_j}{(2\pi)^{p/2}|R|^{1/2}} exp[-0.5\delta_{ij}]$ for $i = 1 \dots n, j = 1 \dots k$. As we can see the computation for p_{ij} requires dividing by $\sqrt{|R|}$ and computing R^{-1} for Mahalanobis distances δ_{ij}. Therefore, the problem is really a division by zero which is undefined and computing R^{-1} which is also undefined. But our EM implementation uses only one *global* covariance matrix for all the clusters and then $R = \sum_{i=1}^{k} R^i$, where R^i

is the corresponding covariance matrix for cluster i. This can clearly be seen in the M step. In short, *one global covariance matrix R* solves the problem. We have found in practice that as k grows the chance of having $R_i = 0$ is very small, but it may happen. Having only one global covariance matrix R solves the problem in part, but there is a price to pay: we sacrifice cluster description accuracy a bit.

In the event that $\exists i$, s.t. $i \in \{1 \dots k\}$ and $R_i = 0$ we do the following to compute $|R|$ and R^{-1}. To compute the Mahalanobis distances we skip variables whose covariance is zero and then we avoid dividing by zero ($R_i = 0$). Having a null covariance means all the points have zero distance between them in the corresponding dimensions and then this does not affect δ_{ij}. In other words, we compute R^{-1} for the subspace in which covariances are not zero. To compute $|R|$ we do an analogous thing. Remember that noise independendence implies $|R| = \Pi_{i=1}^{p} R_i$ and then we can also skip null covariances. Therefore, $|R| = \Pi_{i=1, R_i \neq 0}^{p} R_i$. But again, there is a price to pay: loglikelihood computation is affected. Skipping null covariances solves the problem of undefined computations but we have observed that loglikelihood decreases sometimes. We believe this is the way to solve the problem but it requires further research.

2.6 Database background

The relational model represents data as relations, each having a primary key and a number of attributes. Each attribute has a simple data type. Arrays, for instance, are not allowed. This gets translated into SQL having tables with a number of columns. A subset of those columns will be the primary key. In general in a relational DBMS the primary key has a corresponding physical index to search data rows efficiently. Relation tuples become data rows in a table. Relational operations such as select, project and join get translated into SQL queries.

SQL is a standarized data manipulation language used in databases. SQL can save a considerable amount of programming and is effective to write high-level queries. However, SQL is neither efficient nor adequate to do linear algebra operations, but we managed to get around that problem by converting matrices to relational tables and using arithmetic operators (+-*/) and functions (exp(x) ln(x)) available in our DBMS. The most important SQL commands we used in our implementation were the following: CREATE TABLE, used to define a table and its corresponding primary index, DROP TABLE, to delete tables, INSERT INTO [table] SELECT, used to add data rows to one table from a select expression, DELETE, used to delete a number of rows from a table and UPDATE, to set columns to different values.

3 SQLEM: The EM algorithm programmed in SQL

This is the most important part of this work. The reader is referred to the EM description given in the previous section to understand the explanations given. Also, many optimizations and improvements to EM are assumed to be understood from the previous section.

3.1 Overview of alternatives

After analyzing and experimenting we discovered two basic strategies to implement EM in SQL: horizontal and vertical. These two strategies represent two extreme points to implement EM in SQL and there are tradeoffs regarding performance, flexibility and functionality. Experimental evaluation and practical constraints lead to a third hybrid approach.

The first challenge is to compute the k squared Mahalanobis distances for each point to each cluster. The next problem is to compute the k probabilities and k responsibilities. These are computed by evaluating the normal density function with the corresponding distance for each cluster. After responsibilities are computed we just need to update the mixture parameters; this requires computing several relational aggregate functions. Updating C and R requires several matrix products that are expressed as aggregate SQL sums of arithmetic expressions. Updating W requires only doing a SUM on computed responsibilities.

For the three approaches we will present we assume that in general $k \leq p$ (for high-dimensional data) and $p << n$. These assumptions are important for performance. In any case our solution will work well for big n as long as $p \leq 100, k \leq 100$. For the horizontal and vertical approaches we only show the SQL code for the E step. Since the hybrid approach turned out to be the best one it is analyzed in more detail and we show both the E and the M steps in SQL. The SQL statements required to create/drop tables and their indexes, to delete rows, and to transpose C, R are omitted for brevity.

Given a good initialization SQLEM converges fast; as seen before, we either initialize clusters to random values or better to parameters obtained from a sample (usually 5% for large data sets or 10% for medium data sets). Nevertheless, in some cases SQLEM does not converge soon because of noisy data or bad initialization. To avoid making useless computations we limit the maximum number of iterations to some fixed number. For large data sets we have found that 10 iterations is a good number. In some cases we may run SQLEM up to 20 iterations, but for large data sets we never let the program go beyond that limit. Otherwise, convergence can become a bottleneck for performance.

Table	PK	columns	#	Contents
Y	RID	y1,y2...yp	n	data points
YD	RID	d1,d2...dk	n	distances
YP	RID	p1,p2...pk,sump	n	probabilities
YX	RID	x1,x2...xk,llh	n	responsib's
C1..CK	-	y1,y2...yp	1	means
R	-	y1,y2...yp	1	covariances
W	-	w1,w2...wk,llh	1	weights
GMM	-	n,twopipdiv2	1	other
	-	sqrtdetR		parameters

Figure 4: Horizontal approach SQL tables

3.2 Storing data points and mixture parameters in tables

The data points and the Gaussian mixture parameters must be stored in tables. Following the notation we defined before we will add a few more conventions for naming columns in SQL. Column name i will indicate the cluster number, i.e. $i \in \{1 \ldots k\}$, column name v will indicate the variable number; that is, $v \in \{1 \ldots p\}$. val will be the value of the corresponding column. w_i will indicate the ith cluster weight. RID stands for row id and it is a unique identifier for each data point. Please refer to Tables 4,6 and 8 to understand these naming conventions.

All remaining parameters needed for computations are stored in the table called GMM. This includes all the matrix sizes p, k, n,the constant needed in the density function computation twopipdiv2$=(2\pi)^{p/2}$, the square root of determinant of the covariance matrix sqrtdetR$=\sqrt{|R|}$ and number of iterations. The table YX stores the loglikelihood for each point as well as a *score*, which is the index of the cluster with highest membership probability for that point; in our case *score* is used to classify/segment retail data.

3.3 Horizontal approach

The first way to solve the problem is called the *horizontal* approach. Here we compute the Mahalanobis distances in k terms of a SELECT statement. Each of the k terms is a sum of squared distances divided by the corresponding covariance as seen in the previous section. This is very efficient since all k squared Mahalanobis distances (δ^2) are computed in one table scan but has a major drawback: since there are no arrays in SQL the sum has to be expanded to a long string to sum the p terms. For high dimensional data we found that the parser of the SQL interpreter could not handle such long statements. Even having user-defined functions would not solve the problem because of expression size. For the same reason many computations required by EM have to be broken down into several simpler SQL statements.

```
INSERT INTO YD SELECT
  RID,(Y.y1-C1.y1)**2/R.y1+...+(Y.yp-C1.yp)**2/R.yp,
      (Y.y1-C2.y1)**2/R.y1+...+(Y.yp-C2.yp)**2/R.yp,
      ...
      (Y.y1-Ck.y1)**2/R.y1+...+(Y.yp-Ck.yp)**2/R.yp
  FROM  Y,C1,C2...CK,R;

INSERT INTO YP SELECT
  RID,w1/(twopipdiv2*sqrtdetR)*exp(-0.5*d1) AS p1,
      w2/(twopipdiv2*sqrtdetR)*exp(-0.5*d2) AS p2,
      ...
      wk/(twopipdiv2*sqrtdetR)*exp(-0.5*dk) AS pk,
      p1+p2+...+pk AS sump          FROM  YD,GMM,W;

INSERT INTO YX SELECT
  RID,p1/sump,p2/sump,...,pk/sump,ln(sump) FROM  YP;
```

Figure 5: Horizontal approach SQL for E step

The time/space complexity for computing the k Mahalanobis distances for each of the n points is $O(kp)$. This expression size can be a practical problem in almost any relational DBMS. Just to give an example think about computing parameters for 50 clusters for data having 100 dimensions ($k = 50, p = 100$). We need to compute squared differences on p terms, each being in the best case about 10 characters, add them p times, and then put k of those expressions in *only one* SQL statement. All in all, we end up with an expression having approximately $10 \times 50 \times 100 \approx 50,000$ characters. So far, we haven't seen any DBMS handling an expression this long.

The tables required to implement this approach in the most efficient way are given in Figure 4. It is important to note that C is stored in k tables to avoid having k different select statements to compute distances. This avoids launching k statements in parallel which would be slower, or doing the k selects sequentially. The code is shown in Figure 5.

To update mixture parameters C, R, W we proceed as follows. First of all, there is no need to create separate tables C', W', R' as seen on the pseudo code for EM; all temporary results are stored in the corresponding tables C, R, W. To update C we need to execute k select statements (updating C_j) each of them computing the product $y_i x_{ij}$ for $j = 1 \ldots k$ and then making a SUM over all n rows to update cluster means from cluster j: table C_j. These k SELECT statements join tables Y and YX by the primary key RID multiplying y_i by x_{ij}. Updating weights in W' is straightforward; first we have to sum the responsibilities and loglikelihood stored in YX and then dividing by n; this is done just by one SELECT statement using the SQL aggregate function SUM. Having computed C' and W' as described in the pseudo code for EM we can update $C_j = C'_j/W'_j$. Now since C is updated we can proceed to compute covariances R by launching k SELECT statements,

each computing $R' = R' + (y_i - C_j)x_{ij}(y_i - C_j)^t$ with $j = 1 \ldots k$. The last step involves updating R and W. We update covariances and weights: $R = R'/n$ and $W = W'/n$; n is stored in the table GMM.

3.4 Vertical approach

We call the second approach *vertical*. Here the n points are copied into a table having pn rows. And then the Mahalanobis distances are computed using joins. The tables used for this approach in the most efficient way are given in Figure 6. In this case C is stored in one table.

Note that we have to perform separate inserts to compute distances, probabilities and responsibilities because aggregate functions cannot be combined with non-aggregate expressions in the same SQL select statement. YSUMP.sump$= \sum_{i=1}^{k} p_i$ and it is computed using the SUM(column) SQL aggregate function. The code is shown in Figure 7. Note that the first SELECT statement computes distances. Once distances are computed we can obtain probabilities by evaluating the multivariate normal distribution on each distance; this is done in the 2nd SELECT statement shown. Finally, the 3rd SELECT statement shown computes responsibilities x_{ij} by dividing $p_{ij}/sump$ for $j = 1 \ldots k$. These responsibilities are the basic ingredient to update mixture parameters C, R, W.

To update mixture parameters C, R, W we proceed as follows. The first challenge is to compute the product $y_i x_i^t$. Each of the p coordinates for y_i are stored in one row in table Y, and each of the k responsibilities are in a different row in table YX. Therefore, to compute this matrix product $y_i x_i^t$ we need to perform a JOIN between Y and YX only on RID multiplying *value* by x . This JOIN will produce pk rows for each of the n points; the corresponding temporary table YYX will have kpn rows, in general a much bigger number than n. Then to compute C' we need to use the SUM function over all rows of YYX grouping by RID and inserting the aggregated pk rows into table C. To update weights we have to add responsibilities in YX. To that end, we

Table	PK	columns	#	Contents
Y	RID,v	value	pn	points
YD	RID,i	d	kn	distances
YP	RID,i	p	kn	probabilities
YX	RID,i	x	kn	responsib's
C	i,v	value	pk	means
R	v	value	p	covariances
W	i	w	k	weights
GMM	-	n,twopipdiv2	1	remaining
		sqrtdetR		parameters

Figure 6: Vertical approach SQL tables

```
INSERT INTO YD SELECT
    RID,C.i,sum( (Y.val-C.val)**2/R.val ) AS d
FROM      Y,C,R   WHERE  Y.v = C.v AND C.v = R.v
GROUP BY  RID,C.i;

INSERT INTO YP SELECT
    RID,YD.i,w/(twopipdiv2*sqrtdetR)*exp(-0.5*d) AS p
    FROM  YD,W,GMM  WHERE  YD.i = W.i;

INSERT INTO YX SELECT
    RID,C.I,p/YSUMP.sump
FROM  YP,YSUMP  WHERE  YP.RID=YSUMP.RID;
```

Figure 7: Vertical approach SQL for E step

use SUM on x grouping by RID on table YX inserting results into W. With these two summations we can easily compute $C_j = C'_j/W'_j$ (as specified in the pseudo code for EM) by joining tables C and W on column i, dividing $value$ by w. Once means C are recomputed we just need to recompute covariances R: we need to JOIN Y and C on v performing a substraction of their corresponding $value$ columns, and squaring the difference, storing results on temp table YC. Once these squared differences are computed we perform a JOIN with tables YC and YX on RID, multiplying the squared difference by x and then SUM over all rows. This will effectively recompute R. Finally, we just need to divide both W and R by n (stored in table GMM).

3.5   Solution: a hybrid approach

Here we combine the benefits from both the horizontal and the vertical approaches. The horizontal one is the most efficient since it minimizes I/O, while the vertical is the most flexible but has highest overhead in temporary tables created for joins. For each of the n points this solution computes the k distances vertically using SQL aggregate functions (SUM(column)) and computes probabilities, responsibilities and mixture parameters horizontally projecting expressions having p or k terms. The tables required for this approach are shown in Figure 8. The SQL code for the E and M steps is shown in Figures 9 and 10 respectively.

Before each insertion (in general INSERT INTO table SELECT exp.) the tables C, R, CR, W, YD, YP, YX are left empty; that is, their respective rows are deleted. These drop/deletion SQL statements are not shown to keep the SQL code understandable and shorter. The C and R matrices are transposed and copied into CR. This is currently done by launching several UPDATE statements in parallel but could be improved if there was a transposition statement available, similar to the SQL extensions to do Knowledge Discovery proposed in [5]. W stores the cluster weights as well as the loglikelihood. The first SQL statement in the E step computes $|R|$. The SQL code shown takes care of

Table	PK	columns	#	Contents
Z	RID	y1,y2...yp	n	points
Y	RID,v	value	pn	points
YD	RID	d1,d2...dk	n	distances
YP	RID	p1,p2...pk	n	probabilities
		sump,suminvd	n	
YX	RID	x1,x2...xk,	n	responsibil's
		llh,score		
C	i	y1,y2...yp	k	means
R	-	y1,y2...yp	1	global
				covariances
RK	i	y1,y2...yp	1	covariances/
				cluster
CR	v	C1,C2...Ck,R	p	C^t, R^t
W	i	w1,w2...wk	1	weights
		llh	1	
GMM	-	n,twopipdiv2	1	remaining
		sqrtdetR	1	parameters
X	RID,i	x	kn	responsibil's
				vertically
XMAX	RID	maxx	n	max(x) for/
				n points

Figure 8: Hybrid approach vertical tables

null probabilities by using the approximation $\frac{1/d_i}{suminvd}$ described before. Null covariances are handled by inserting a 1 instead of zero in the tables CR and R, but as we mentioned before this has an impact in loglikelihood accuracy and thus needs further research.

For this solution the computation of distances requires a join creating a temporary table with pn rows and k columns. The computation of probabilities and responsibilities requires joins with only n rows at any intermediate step. C and R are updated by inserting rows from k separate SELECT staments. This was necesary for two reasons: first expression size could be a problem again if we updated all parameters in one wide table and for high dimensional data we could easily exceed the maximum number of columns in our DBMS. shwon

Analyzing the query costs incurred by the hybrid approach we have the following. For each iteration the computation of distances requires scanning a table having pn rows. The computation of probabilities and responsibilites each require one scan on n rows. Updating C and R require k table scans on n rows each. Updating W requires only one scan on n rows. All other computation involve only scans on tables having less than p or k rows. Overall one iteration of EM requires $2k + 3$ scans on tables having n rows, and one scan on a table having pn rows. The theoretical minimum of table scans on n rows required by EM is only 4: two for the E step and two for the M step; the E step reads the input points Y and writes the responsibilities X, and the M step reads the input

```
UPDATE GMM SET detR=R.y1*R.y2*...*R.yp,
                  sqrtdetR=detR**0.5;
INSERT INTO YD SELECT
   RID,sum( (Y.val - CR.C1)**2/CR.R ),
       sum( (Y.val - CR.C2)**2/CR.R ),...
       sum( (Y.val - CR.Ck)**2/CR.R )
  FROM Y,CR WHERE Y.v=C.v AND C.v=R.v GROUP BY RID;

INSERT INTO YP SELECT
   RID,
   w1/(twopipdiv2*sqrtdetR)*exp(-0.5*d1) AS p1,
   w2/(twopipdiv2*sqrtdetR)*exp(-0.5*d2) AS p2,...
   wk/(twopipdiv2*sqrtdetR)*exp(-0.5*dk) AS pk,
   p1+p2+...+pk           AS sump,
   1/(d1+1.0E-100)+1/(d2+1.0E-100)+...+1/(dk+1.0E-100)
                              AS suminvd FROM YD,GMM,W;
INSERT INTO YX SELECT
   RID,
   CASE WHEN sump>0 THEN p1/sump ELSE (1/d1)/suminvd END,
   CASE WHEN sump>0 THEN p2/sump ELSE (1/d2)/suminvd END,
   ...,
   CASE WHEN sump>0 THEN pk/sump ELSE (1/dk)/suminvd END,
   CASE WHEN sump>0 THEN ln(sump) END, 0    FROM YP;
```

Figure 9: Hybrid approach SQL for E step

```
INSERT INTO C SELECT
   1,sum(Z.y1*x1)/sum(x1),sum(Z.y2*x1)/sum(x1),...
       sum(Z.yp*x1)/sum(x1)
FROM  Z,YX   WHERE Z.RID=YX.RID;
...
INSERT INTO C SELECT
   k,sum(Z.y1*xk)/sum(xk),sum(Z.y2*xk)/sum(xk),...
       sum(Z.yp*xk)/sum(xk)
FROM  Z,YX   WHERE Z.RID=YX.RID;

INSERT INTO W SELECT
   sum(x1),sum(x2),...sum(xk),sum(llh) FROM YX;
UPDATE W SET w1=w1/GMM.n,w2=w2/GMM.n,...,wk/GMM.n;

INSERT INTO RK SELECT
   1,sum(x1*(Z.y1-C.y1)**2),...,
       sum(x1*(Z.yp-C.yp)**2)    FROM Z,C,YX;
...
INSERT INTO RK SELECT
   k,sum(xk*(Z.y1-C.y1)**2),...,
       sum(xk*(Z.yp-C.yp)**2)    FROM Z,C,YX;
INSERT INTO R  SELECT
   sum(y1/GMM.n),sum(y2/GMM.n,...,
       sum(yp/GMM.n)                   FROM RK;
```

Figure 10: Hybrid approach SQL for M step

table Y as well as the responsibilities in the table X. This points out to several optimizations that can be made in the algorithm if scans can be synchronized and more computations are done in a single SELECT statement. The problem is that many optimizations happen automatically inside the DBMS and are not available through SQL commands.

Given current practical constraints found in the Teradata DBMS we expect this implementation to be useful for clustering problems having $n \leq 1.0E + 8$, $p \leq 100$, $k \leq 100$ and $pk \leq 1000$. These numbers clearly represent big problem sizes.

3.6   Important optimizations

Even though we used a parallel DBMS having a good query optimizer, several optimizations were needed to make our SQL code effective. The most important optimizations are the following.

Updates are slower than inserts. The reason for this is that updates involve 2 I/Os for each data block and inserts only one. Whenever there are two or more tables in one statement the access plan requires joins, even if some of the tables have only one row. This is particularly troublesome to compute distances because if Y is one table and C is stored in k tables with only one row then joins are performed anyway. To reduce the overhead of joins only one itermediate join produces pn rows: the SELECT statement to compute distances. All the remaining joins always produce intermediate tables having only n rows. Our DBMS uses a fast hash-based join approach and that is why times scale linearly as we shall see in the next section. As we have

pointed out before the Teradata DBMS returns rows in a normal query in an unpredictable order unless the user specifies that rows should be ordered (by primary key); this happens because queries are executed in parallel in several AMPS (processors) and results are assembled together in one processor. However, our solution does not require ordering results in any SELECT statements; this is crucial to keep the time complexity of EM unchanged. We accomplished this by joining tables always using the column RID.

For a big table, that is, a table storing n rows, it is faster to drop and create a table than deleting all the records. This is not true if the table is small (C, R, W) since the overhead to drop/create a table is greater than just deleting a few rows. As we mentioned the DBMS we used executes queries in parallel. One way to speedup the process is to make data block size smaller; in this way there is a finer grain for parallelism and the optimizer can better balance load among processors.

3.7   Practical considerations

EM offers many advantages besides having a strong statistical basis and being efficient. One of those advantages is that EM is robust to noisy data and missing information. In fact, EM was born to handle incomplete data as explained in [6]. SQLEM can be extended to cluster categorical data by converting each categorical value to a binary field. The cluster centroids C will then give the probability or percentage of points in some cluster having a particular categorical value. These findings can be further explained by looking at the covariance matrix R. The drawback is that this extension increases dimensionality.

A covariance matrix having entries equal to zero just affects the determinant $|R|$, R^{-1} and loglikelihood computation as explained before; zero entries are skipped to compute $|R|$ and loglikelihood is rescaled accordingly. Sampling can be used to obtain a good initial approximation to initialize the cluster centroids and the covariance matrix; note that sampling is not good enough to cluster the entire data set as standard error is proportional to the inverse of the square root sample size [9] and then such clustering results obtained from a sample are not reliable.

4 Experimental evaluation

We made our experiments on an NCR 4800 parallel computer running Unix MP-RAS (Unix System V). This machine has 2 nodes connected by a high speed interconnect network. Each node has 4 CPU's running at 400Mhz. The relational DBMS we used was NCR Teradata. The SQL code generator was written in the Java language and the connection to the DBMS was done using the JDBC library. We concentrated on benchmarking our hybrid solution.

4.1 Experiments with retail data

We used Market Basket data from a retailer involving sales for one month in several stores. We chose the number of clusters to be $k = 9$ based on customer's requirements. The data had the following characteristics: no categorical data; all numerical variables. Based on business requirements we focused on $p=6$ variables including: hour of the transaction, total sales per basket, total discount per basket, total cost per basket, distinct product quantity per basket, distinct categories of product per basket. The total number of baskets to analyze was $n=1,545,075$. SQLEM took around 31 minutes on 5 iterations to converge on a good solution. The EM algorithm uncovered the following as evidenced by the means and covariances found in the data.

This particular retailer had about 71% of its clientele in two clusters, that can be described as customers that would come into the store for an average of 1 to 3 low price products and would not take advantage of any discount promotions. The main discriminator between the two clusters was that one shopped around noon and the other shopped in the late afternoon, maybe after work. In other two clusters about 12% of the customers showed core behavior. These individuals had a tendency to have baskets that were higher in sales and not quite as low in discount. But the overriding characteristic was that they shopped for an average of 9 products from an average of 6 different sections in the store. These two clusters seemed to have shopping time

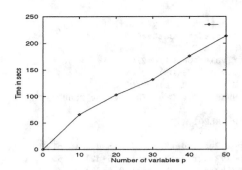

Figure 11: Time per iteration with varying dimensionality p, $k = 20$, $n = 10k$

as a main discriminator. Around 10% of the baskets were transacted by customers that seemed interested in lunch, since they shopped around noon time, yet they looked for possibly more than just lunch given the fact that they on average purchased 5 products from 4 different sections in the store. Maybe lunch was the main reason for their visit to the store but they realized that they needed something else while in the store.

A small cluster comprising 3% of the baskets showed the same characteristics as the 10% mentioned above except for the fact that these customers seemed to take advantage of promotions. The rest of the baskets show three distinct clusters. One that has convenience shoppers that like to shop later in the day. And two clusters that exhibited "cherry picking" behavior. High sales, high discounts due to promotions and low number of products per baskets.

With minimal analysis time we could start making some educated assumptions about customer behavior that with further analysis could turn into valuable data to a business. We were able to analyze a significant amount of data in a very short amount of time. As Data Warehousing becomes mainstream the availability of massive volumes of data for analysis will become more common place. We see SQLEM as a way to enable mining of large data volumes in Data Warehousing.

4.2 Experiments with synthetic data

We generated data by evaluating a mixture density of k Gaussian distributions on p variables. We varied the number of clusters k, the number of variables p and the number of points n to test scalability. We added 20% of n points as noise. The covariances were kept uniform across clusters.

We concentrated on benchmarking the time per iteration. To cluster big data sets in general we use sampling with about 10% of the data points to obtain several possible "good" initial solutions. With a good initial approximation EM usually converges in a few iterations (less than 10). In any case at each iteration EM always finds a solution that is guaranteed not to

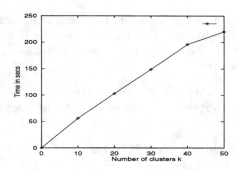

Figure 12: Time per iteration with varying no. of clusters k,$p = 20$,$n = 10k$

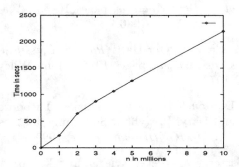

Figure 13: Time per iteration for different database sizes n,$p = 10$,$k = 10$

decrease loglikelihood from the previous one. Otherwise the classical version of the EM algorithm may not scale for a database having hundreds of millions of records. However, as our times show it may be feasible to cluster a data set with a few million records starting from a random initialization of mixture parameters.

As can be seen from the graphs 11,12,13 SQLEM scales linearly in the 3 dimensions we analyzed: p, k and n. It should be noted that the graph for p is not quite linear in data sets having lower dimensionality. A similar problem happens with database size n. This is because the execution overhead of the SQL statements is higher on smaller problem sizes. The times per iteration shown are at least as good as the times achieved by SEM [3]. However, a direct comparison is not possible since they compress the data and make most of the work in a workstation memory, whereas we rely heavily on using only efficient SQL code inside a relational DBMS. Another important note is that our times may vary in another relational DBMS if joins are not hash-based. A nested-loop join approach would definitely make our solution slower. Overall the execution time of SQLEM can be bounded by $O(p^2 n)$ if p and k are in the same order of magnitude since we do not change the complexity of the algorithm.

4.3   Related work

To the best of our knowledge the only other work that analyzes the problem of scaling EM to large data sets is [3]. Their clustering algorithm is called Scalable EM (SEM). However, this work was not inspired by SEM. It was not our intent to improve their solution since the performance results the authors report are very good and their approach is very different from ours. We just needed a clustering algorithm which had a strong statistical basis and EM was the choice. EM may not be the best clustering algorithm currently available but it offers advantages not available in other clustering algorithms published in the literature.

Here we give a brief summary of SEM. SEM can compute clusters in one database scan by updating several mixture models concurrently (usually around 10) and by doing data compression in two phases. Their solution relies on having special data structures to update the mixture parameters in memory. The algorithm makes iterations in memory, avoiding repeated table scans. It is important to note that our solution does not preclude incorporating some of the improvements proposed by SEM, but that requires further research.

5   Conclusions

We presented an efficient implementation of the EM algorithm in SQL to cluster large data sets inside a relational DBMS. The SQL statements presented are easy to optimize and to execute in parallel. Our implementation is fast and scalable. We used plain ANSI SQL which provides portability and applicability in most relational DBMS's.

We presented three basic approaches to solve the problem. A first *horizontal* approach was to project big arithmetic expressions and create SELECT statements involving k terms and returning n rows. This approach is very efficient but the Mahalanobis distance computation turned out to be a problem because of expression size: $O(kp)$. At the other extreme we developed a *vertical* approach in which the data points and the mixture parameters are stored in long tables having a compound key and only one data column. The table storing Y had pn rows. This is the most flexible approach, but also the most inefficient because the join to compute Mahalanobis distance produced a temporary table having kpn rows. The remaining joins produced tables having pn or kn rows slowing down EM even further. From these two approaches we devised a *hybrid* one that computes Mahalanobis distances vertically, but computes responsibilities and mixture parameters horizontally. This turned out to be a still flexible solution without seriously compromising performance. We explored general SQL query optimizations. Inserts are preferred over updates. Dropping/creating a table is preffered over deleting all its data rows for tables having n rows. A table having n rows and k columns is more efficient than a table having kn rows for join processing. The select operation to compute distances requires a join with pn rows in a temporary table. The remaining joins involve only n rows. Smaller block sizes give better granularity for parallel query execution.

Regarding performance. SQLEM scales linearly with dimensionality p, the number of clusters k, and more importantly with the number of data points n. The overall execution time makes clustering feasible for tables containing several millions of data rows and high dimensionality ($pk \leq 1000$). We presented experiments with synthetic and retail data to support our claims. Our clustering algorithm compares reasonably well with other approaches proposed in the literature as shown by our experiments.

In the future we would like to explore further improvements to make SQLEM more efficient and more robust to noisy data. This includes synchronizing operations to decrease table scans, avoiding computations that do not change mixture parameters in consecutive iterations, improving parallel execution and caching for small tables. We also want to apply SQLEM to a large collection of segmented images to continue our previous work on association rules obtained from an image collection [15].

Acknowledgements

The first author would like to acknowledge the support from NCR Corporation to accomplish this work. We thank the help provided by Scott Cunningham to understand the statistical concepts behind the EM algorithm. We thank Robert MacDonald, Ken Rhames and Roman Diaz for helping us improve the presentation of this paper. We thank the anonymous referees for their helpful comments. The first author would like to specially thank Edward Omiecinski, from Georgia Tech, for his encouragement to work on clustering algorithms.

References

[1] Charu Aggarwal, Cecilia Procopiuc, Joel Wolf, Phillip Yu, and Jong Park. Fast algorithms for projected clustering. In *ACM SIGMOD Conference*, 1999.

[2] Rakesh Agrawal, Johannes Gehrke, Dimitrios Gunopolos, and Prabhakar Raghavan. Automatic subspace clustering of high dimensional data for data mining applications. In *ACM SIGMOD Conference*, 1998.

[3] Paul Bradley, Usama Fayyad, and Cory Reina. Scaling clustering algorithms to large databases. In *ACM SIGKDD Conference*, 1998.

[4] Chad Carson, Serge Belongie, H. Greenspan, and J. Malik. Region-based image querying. In *IEEE Workshop on Content-Based Access of Image and Video Libraries*, 1997.

[5] John Clear, Debbie Dunn, Brad Harvey, and et. al. Non-stop sql/mx primitives for knowledge discovery. In *ACM SIGKDD Conference*, 1999.

[6] Arthur P. Dempster, Nan M. Laird, and Donald B. Rubin. Maximum likelihood estimation from incomplete data via the em algorithm. *Journal of The Royal Statistical Society*, 39(1):1-38, 1977.

[7] R. Dubes and A.K. Jain. *Clustering Methodologies in Exploratory Data Analysis*, pages 10-35. Academic Press, New York, 1980.

[8] Richard Duda and Peter Hart. *Pattern Classification and scene analysis*, pages 10-45. John Wiley and Sons, 1973.

[9] William DuMouchel, Chris Volinski, Theodore Johnson, and Daryl Pregybon. Squashing flat files flatter. In *ACM SIGKDD Conference*, 1999.

[10] Martin Easter, Hans Peter Kriegel, and X. Xu. A density-based algorithm for discovering clusters in large spatial databases with noise. In *IEEE ICDE Conference*, 1996.

[11] Alexander Hinneburg and Daniel Keim. Optimal grid-clustering: Towards breaking the curse of dimensionality. In *VLDB Conference*, 1999.

[12] Michael Jordan and Robert Jacobs. Hierarchical mixtures of experts and the em algorithm. *Neural Computation*, 6(2), 1994.

[13] F. Murtagh. A survey of recent advances in hierarchical clustering algorithms. *The Computer Journal*, 1983.

[14] Raymond Ng and Jiawei Han. Efficient and effective clustering method for spatial data mining. In *VLDB Conference*, 1994.

[15] Carlos Ordonez and Edward Omiecinski. Discovering association rules based on image content. In *IEEE ADL Conference*, 1999.

[16] Sam Roweis and Zoubin Ghahramani. A unifying review of linear gaussian models. *Journal of Neural Computation*, 1999.

[17] Tian Zhang, Raghu Rmakrishnan, and Miron Livny. Birch: An efficient data clustering method for very large databases. In *ACM SIGMOD Conference*, 1996.

Anatomy of a Real E-Commerce System

Anant Jhingran
IBM T.J. Watson Research Center
Hawthorne, NY 10532
anant@us.ibm.com

ABSTRACT

Today's E-Commerce systems are a complex assembly of databases, web servers, home grown glue code, and networking services for security and scalability. The trend is towards larger pieces of these coming together in bundled offerings from leading software vendors, and the networking/hardware being offered through service delivery companies. In this paper we examine the bundle by looking in detail at IBM's WebSphere, Commerce Edition, and its deployment at a major customer site.

Keywords

E-Commerce, Middleware, Web Applications, Databases.

1. INTRODUCTION

IBM's Websphere, Commerce Edition (henceforth called WCS) is an E-Commerce offering built mostly in Java that offers the ability for businesses to set up B2B (business-to-business) and B2C (business-to-consumer) sell-side focussed sites. It is being extended so that it can be deployed in the emerging E-marketplaces, by including dynamic pricing, catalog aggregation, workflow and approvals. In order to achieve this functionality, this software must offer the following capabilities in a bundle:

1.1 Commerce Functions

- User Management: In more complex B2B sites, this translates to roles, organization and access control (e.g. a "purchaser" from "acme corporation" cannot see an item "x") and associated workflow around that. In B2C scenario, this translates to authentication, and profile management.

- Content Management, as it relates to transactions (typically catalog management) including content aggregation for e-marketplaces and distribution hubs. The second part of catalog management is the browsing metaphors – shoppers, "Mr. Know-it-all", "comparison shoppers", "matchmakers etc."

- Merchandising: Ability to do up-sell and cross-sells, both through automatic data mining and rules generation , but more typically, through administrator managed rules. Typically, real estate on the pages is allocated to advertisements, promotions and recommendations to accomplish that, and this real estate is allocated to products based on some model of customer behavior.

- Negotiations: The fixed price model of yesterday is being replaced by negotiated deals typified by auctions, reverse auctions (also known as Request for Proposal/Request for Quotes or RFP/RFQ), and general exchanges. In addition, contract based pricing is becoming increasingly popular.

- Order Fulfillment, including taxation, shipping instructions, delivery instructions etc.

- Payment Processing, including B2B payment options such as purchase orders (P.O) and lines of credits.

- Service and Support: For follow through post sales.

Over time, many of these services could be outsourced (leaving the commerce site to be the prime driver of traffic, and not the prime catcher of transactions). Examples of these that are beginning to emerge is the outsourcing of credit, transportation, logistics etc.

1.2 Underlying Infrastructure

Underneath these functions are the following:

- Strong messaging layer that does protocol translation and service contracts (adherence to so-called Trading Partner Agreements, or TPA's)

- Websphere, which is an EJB application development environment with associated web servers. Typically, it also provides support for application/web page level caching (for repeated queries where database calls are too expensive) and other connection management tools.

- DB2 or Oracle, providing transactional support for the Commerce application. This support involves persistence store of all information (including catalogs, GIFs, videos, product specifications) and for all transactional pieces. In addition, decision Support through report generation, OLAP analysis (and rarely, as of now) and data mining is also provided.

- Asynchronous and synchronous connectivity to different back-end systems, including Enterprise Resource Planning (ERP) systems such as SAP/Baan/Peoplesoft, and other systems such as accounting, job floor scheduling, promotion management etc.

- Support for business rules – when "a value shopper shops, give him a 10% discount."

1.3 Typical Configuration

For 24x7 operations, elaborate efforts are made to handle load and failures. Load is typically handled at the application level (by creating more application threads) and by routing (using network dispatcher) to the free(er) nodes. In particular, care must be taken so that the "browsers/window shoppers" must not overrun the legitimate shoppers (who drive commerce transactions), and that implies quality of service within the application by keeping separate queues and priorities for different parts of the commerce

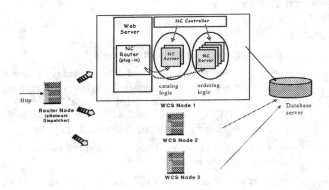

chain.

The size of the database is typically not very large, so the application model tends to be "parallel" application going against SMP based "database". Availability is typically handled through standard database techniques (replication, redundancy etc.) and fast restart at the application thread level.

In the figure above, we show a typical WCS installation, including the network dispatcher sending requests to different WCS server nodes (to balance load). Within a server node, different commerce functions (such as catalog browsing, order processing etc.) have a different degree of throughput requirements, managed by a controller process.

However, in addition to the application availability, sites need to maintain network availability. More robust web sites do that through elaborate set of routers and server nodes in front of the commerce site.

2. DATABASE ISSUES

Database is the repository of all information, and transactions. The transaction scope is typically the unit of recoverability. In the case of WCS, this translates to a "command" such as "add to shopping cart," "submit bid," "approve purchase order," etc. All higher level transactional semantics are maintained in the application (e.g., in the distributed transactional aspect, such as COYOTE [3]).

2.1 Information

Let us look at information at every level. A few months from now when XML support in relational databases becomes ubiquitous, this task might get simpler, but as of now, most commerce servers map information into relational tables one information at a time.

2.1.1 Catalogs

Catalogs are difficult to obviously map into relational tables. Not only are they hierarchical, but attributes vary considerably from node to node. Two obvious models exist: store in one relation, as name, value pairs (used in WCS); or store each category (with some uniformity of attributes within that category – after all men's shirts are likely to have similar attributes like collar size and sleeve length) in a separate relation. Text descriptions of products are entered in DB2 text extender, with appropriate efficient search techniques applied.

Search against these catalog entries is typically handled as a series of point queries against the database tables often resulting in over 10 – 15 SQL queries for a simple act of browsing. As a result, "caching" in the application is used often.

2.1.2 User Attributes

User attributes again tend to be hierarchical and extensible, since what is relevant to Macys.com's (a retailer) will be very different from SciQuest.com (a parts marketplace). LDAP is often used for membership information (backed by a relational database), but it unfortunately falls short of the customer/user model that the commerce server needs.

2.1.3 Promotion/Merchandising Information

See [1] for some details on how e-coupons get mapped into relational attributes. For other cross-sell and up-sell, implicit or explicit 2-ary relations are used. The concept of the value shopper is typically stored as a (derived) attribute of DB2, however the rules and actions do not use DB2 trigger mechanisms. We do not use DB2 trigger mechanisms, since most of the rules are so-called select rules (i.e. to be applied on selects), and it is deemed expensive to do a dummy insert to trigger a DB2 rule. Another reason for this is "portability" – the trigger and rule language of the database is just not standardized enough to be used.

2.1.4 Decision Support

Use of OLAP analysis built around transactional data is very common. A separate copy (denormalized) of the transactional tables is used for such analysis. What is becoming more common is that people do not want to view their ".com" storefronts as separate entities – they want to make more integrated decisions across their "click and mortar" enterprise.

2.2 Transactions

2.2.1 Negotiations

See [2] for details of the objects used in e-auctions within WCS. There are two requirements for real-time bid capture – one is simple, efficient insertion into a bid table (easy) and second is efficient computation of the max (or other details), on a per user basis, so that one can generate – "you have been outbid" message. The query for this can easily get very complicated, and we use elaborate in memory data structures to keep its performance bounded. There are considerable challenges in matchmaking and exchanges, including approximate search applied against traditional databases. Typically, the queries to execute a maximal bipartite matching are complex enough that WCS fetches the rows in memory and then executes these algorithms against them.

2.2.2 Order Fulfillment

This part is simple, transaction wise. Insert into a table; commit. Two-phase commit is not used.

3. REFERENCES

[1] "Sales Promotions on the Internet," Manoj Kumar, Anand Rangachari, Anant Jhingran and Rakesh Mohan, 3rd USENIX Workshop on Electronic Commerce, 1998

[2] "Internet Auctions," Manoj Kumar and Stuart I. Feldman, 3rd USENIX Workshop on Electronic Commerce, 1998

[3] "The Coyote Project: Framework for Multi-party E-Commerce," Asit Dan et al, ECDL 1998

From Browsing to Interacting: DBMS Support for Responsive Websites

Raghu Ramakrishnan
CTO, QUIQ, and Professor, UW-Madison
raghu@quiq.com, raghu@cs.wisc.edu

Abstract

Internet websites increasingly rely on database management systems. There are several reasons for this trend:

1. As sites grow larger, managing the content becomes impossible without the use of a DBMS to keep track of the nature, origin, authorship, and modification history of each article.

2. As sites become more interactive, tracking and logging user activity and user contributions creates valuable new data, which again is best managed using a DBMS. The emerging paradigm of *Customer-Centric e-Business* places a premium on engaging users, building a relationship with them across visits, and leveraging their expertise and feedback. Supporting this paradigm means that we not only have to track what users visit on a site, we also have to enable them to offer opinions and contribute to the content of the website in various ways; naturally, this requires us to use a DBMS.

3. In order to personalize a user's experience, a site must dynamically construct (or at least fine-tune) each page as it is delivered, taking into account information about the user's past activity and the nature of the content on the current page. In other words, personalization is made possible by utilizing the information (about content and user activity) that we already indicated is best managed using a DBMS.

In summary, as websites go beyond a passive collection of pages to be browsed and seek to present users with a personalized, interactive experience, the role of database management systems becomes central.

In this talk, I will present an overview of these issues, including a discussion of related techniques such as *cookies* and *web server logs* for tracking user activity.

Index Research: Forest or Trees?

Joseph M. Hellerstein
University of California, Berkeley
Berkeley, CA 94720-1776
jmh@cs.berkeley.edu

Indexes and access methods have been a staple of database research – and indeed of computer science in general – for decades. A glance at the contents of this year's SIGMOD and PODS proceedings shows another bumper crop of indexing papers.

Given the hundreds of indexing papers published in the database literature, a pause for reflection seems in order. From a scientific perspective, it is natural to ask why definitive indexing solutions have eluded us for so many years. What is the grand challenge in indexing? What basic complexities or intricacies underlie this large body of work? What would constitute a successful completion of this research agenda, and what steps will best move us in that direction? Or is it the case that the problem space branches in so many ways that we should expect to continuously need to solve variants of the indexing problem?

From the practitioner's perspective, the proliferation of indexing solutions in the literature may be more confusing than helpful. Comprehensively evaluating the research to date is a near-impossible task. An evaluation has to include both functionality (applicability to the practitioner's problem, integration with other data management services like buffer management, query processing and transactions) as well as performance for the practitioner's workloads. Unfortunately, there are no standard benchmarks for advanced indexing problems, and there has been relatively little work on methodologies for index experimentation and customization. How should the research community promote technology transfer in this area? Are the new extensibility interfaces in object-relational DBMSs conducive to this effort?

Panelists

The members of this panel provide a broad mix of research perspectives and real-world experience:

- Hans-Peter Kriegel, University of Munich
- Christos Papadimitriou, UC Berkeley
- David Lomet, Microsoft Research
- Christos Faloutsos, CMU
- Raghu Ramakrishnan, University of Wisconsin
- Paul Brown, Informix Corporation

Application Architecture: 2Tier or 3Tier?
What is DBMS's Role?

Anil K. Nori *(Moderator)*
Asera Inc.
600 Clipper Drive
Belmont, CA 94002
anori@asera.com

ABSTRACT

Experienced panelist will share their views on application architecture, specially, as it relates to database systems. The discussion will focus on what technologies and mechanisms are necessary for developing web applications, and where these mechanisms should reside.

Keywords

Databases, applications, world-wide web.

1. Background

Over the last few years, world-wide web has significantly elevated the role of Intra/Internet in an enterprise. Companies are beginning to use the web technology for Warehousing, Web Data Integration, Web Publishing, Electronic Commerce, Application Integration, etc. Typically, these features are implemented by pre-packaged or custom applications. Currently most of these applications use a 3-tier architecture and build some DBMS-like functionality (e.g. caching, querying), in the middle-tier, often under-utilizing the DBMS. On the other hand, database vendors are trying to subsume the application/business logic by building complete programming environments into their DBMSs. The question is, from an application development perspective, what should be the system architecture? Where should the business logic reside?

2. Discussion Topics

Following (but not limited to) are some discussion topics:

1. Components of a typical Internet application. What are the business requirements? What are the operational requirements? What are the technology requirements?

2. How should the business logic be developed? As middle-tier application? Or as a DBMS stored procedures?

3. Most middle-tier applications require caching and querying capabilities? Is this a reason to push application logic into the database? Or should the DBMS provide modular components for caching and querying that can be used in the middle-tier?

4. Often applications integrate other applications and data sources. Can a DBMS help?

5. XML is becoming popular in web applications. Business objects can be modeled as XML objects. Should databases natively support XML?

6. Should the DBMSs be componentized so that useful database technologies (e.g. cache, querying, queuing) can be used in the middle-tier applications?

7. Does Java support in the DBMS help application development?

Of XML and Databases: Where's the Beef?

Michael J. Carey *(Moderator)*
IBM Almaden Research Center
650 Harry Road, K55/B1
San Jose, CA 95120-6099
carey@acm.org

ABSTRACT

This panel will examine the implications of the XML revolution, which is currently raging on the web, for database systems research and development.

Keywords

Databases, XML, semistructured data, world-wide web.

1. PANELISTS

Adam Bosworth *(Succendo)*
Bruce Lindsay *(IBM Almaden Research Center)*
Michael Stonebraker *(Informix Software)*
Dan Suciu *(AT&T Shannon Laboratory)*
Jennifer Widom *(Stanford University)*

2. OBJECTIVES

The web and XML standards are capturing the attention of database system researchers and vendors alike. To hear some tell it, it may soon be impossible to get a database research paper published if its title lacks the acronym XML, or to sell a database management system product that doesn't provide XML as its primary interface. Is all this XML interest based on hype, or is XML truly the next great wave? How will XML *really* impact the database field in the long run? Is it our community's ticket to finally impacting the web in a big way? Those are some of the questions that will hopefully be discussed in this panel session.

3. XML + DATABASES = ?

Like all panels, this one will go wherever the panelists decide to take it, but some possible questions include:

1. Does the XML revolution mean that the days of structured database systems are now numbered and that we'll soon be rid of all those pesky schemas?

2. Should we be building new database systems specifically tailored for storing and querying native XML data? If so, what should such a system look like, what are the challenges, and what sorts of applications might it be used for?

3. Since XML is a derivative of SGML, it has a document legacy. For example, it has no binary data type, which makes it less than useful in non-text environments. What should our community be recommending to W3C about ways to make XML more useful for "real data"?

4. What role will XML most likely play with respect to database-based web sites? For example, will e-businesses use XML to publish their inventories on the web, providing XML-based query access to them? Or will XML just act as the transport mechanism for remote stored procedure calls?

5. Will XML and XML query facilities supplant object-relational database systems and standards (SQL99) before they ever really have a chance to succeed? I.e., are object-relational databases already dead?

6. Given that IMS is still widely used for mission-critical data, it seems likely that SQL databases (if not SQL99 databases) will survive the XML revolution. What must be done to XML to ensure that XML data sources can interoperate with SQL data sources?

7. Will XML make it possible to someday query the web as if it were one great big database?

4. RECOMMENDED READING

[1] T. Bray, J. Paoli, and C. Sperberg-McQueen (Editors), *Extensible Markup Language (XML) 1.0*, W3C Recommendation 10, http://www.w3.org/TR/REC-xml, February 1998.

[2] D. Lomet (Editor), Special Issue on XML, *Data Engineering Bulletin*, Volume 22, No. 3, IEEE Computer Society, September 1999.

[3] S. Abiteboul, P. Buneman, and D. Suciu, *Data on the Web: From Relations to Semistructured Data and XML*, Morgan Kaufman Publishers, San Francisco, CA, 1999.

Tutorial: Designing an Ultra Highly Available DBMS

Svein Erik Bratsberg
Clustra AS, 7485 Trondheim, Norway
svein.erik.bratsberg@clustra.com

Øystein Torbjørnsen
Clustra AS, 7485 Trondheim, Norway
oystein.torbjornsen@clustra.com

1 Introduction

Most database management systems available today are systems designed for general use. Certainly, some compromises have been done to satisfy the the most common users and the largest markets. One application which has been mostly ignored until now is the network equipment made for the telco operators.

The equipment used in the telco industry has requirements which have been quite different from the typical database applications, especially with respect to availability and real-time performance. This has caused the telco manufacturers to develop their own hardware, operating systems, programming languages and database management systems. There has been little standardization and co-operation causing a wide variety of solutions both between the vendors and within the vendors themselves. This has been possible because of high prices, long product development cycles and long product lifetimes.

Due to the deregulation of the market, increased competition, better price, quality and performance of standard products and an emerging Internet market with telco requirements, standard SW and HW products are becoming more and more fit for the telco market. Any database system trying to replace the proprietary solutions must satisfy the basic telco requirements: availability ($\geq$ 99.999%);

real-time response (1-10 ms.); scalable throughput (10 to 100,000 TPS); open interfaces (SQL, ODBC, JDBC); run on commodity HW/SW.

For today's mainstream database management systems several of these requirements are not satisfied. Although claiming high availability, the systems can only achieve an availability which is one or two orders of magnitude worse than the requirements. The main obstacles for this are system maintenance and long takeover times in the case of failures. Another requirement not satisfied by mainstream systems is the response times for update transactions. They all synchronously write the log to disk before committing. Combined with a group commit strategy, transaction response times are highly variable and in the range of 50 milliseconds or higher for update transactions.

2 Outline

This tutorial will present the design issues for a DBMS solving the specific problems addressed above. It will run through the state-of-the-art and focus on the *Clustra Parallel Data Server*. We will present basic software and hardware architecture for a high availability DBMS, including interconnect and disk solutions.

Special focus will be made on fault-tolerance mechanisms, including replication, take-over, recovery and repair. We will also go through methods for on-line system maintenance, including on-line backup and restore, software and hardware upgrades and schema changes. Testing and performance issues are treated as well.

This tutorial is aimed for designers and developers planning to use a DBMS in the telco or Internet domain, and for everybody interested in DBMS internals in general.

Data Management in eCommerce:
The Good, the Bad, and the Ugly

Avigdor Gal

Department of Management Science and Information Systems
Rutgers University
avigal@rci.rutgers.edu
http://www.rci.rutgers.edu/~avigal

1   Description

Electronic Commerce (eCommerce) is conceived as one of the major channels for performing commerce on a global scale, and the area is rapidly evolving. Electronic commerce is based on electronic transfer of data as a main vehicle of "doing business," while the usage of conventional methods (paper, telephone, etc.) is dramatically reduced in such an environment. In particular, electronic exchange of data becomes the most cost-effective channel of performing low-cost transactions.

Enabling the transfer of data, in and by itself, is hardly sufficient to support efficient and correct processing of transaction in an eCommerce environment. Especially in B2B, enterprises have evolved independently, creating different data ontologies, and thus giving rise to semantic heterogeneity. This problem, which has been investigated for a few decades now, have received a new vigour in a computerized environment that is constantly changing.

This tutorial is aimed at introducing the data integration problem in eCommerce and to discuss three types of solutions to it, namely the good, the bad, and the ugly. We start by reviewing the problem of data integration for distributed heterogeneous information sources. Next, we identify the bad and the ugly that is currently used in eCommerce. Finally, we identify the good, or rather, discuss the research role in this field.

Proceeding in a reverse order, we classify the use of glue code to connect ECommerce tools with enterprise databases (e.g., EDI-aware COTS) to be the ugly. The bad category includes half-baked, communication-based solutions (e.g., EDI and XML), deployed indiscriminately across the enterprise. Finally, we define the good to be well-integrated data management sys-

tem to support translation, integration, and coordination of data transfer, combining a global standard with local management systems. While such systems do not exist in any generic form (and glue coding them is considered to be ugly), a good basis for such systems exist in enterprises in the form of database and workflow management systems. Therefore, the last part of the tutorial provides some ideas as to the establishment of good data integration in eCommerce. These ideas come from the research areas of federated databases and inter-enterprise workflows.

The tutorial is based on a half-day seminar, given at CAiSE*99, and a full-day seminar, which was presented by the presenter at Twente University, the Netherlands on October 1999.

2   Instructor

Avigdor Gal is a faculty member at the MSIS Department at Rutgers University. He received his D.Sc. degree from the Technion-Israel Institute of Technology in 1995 in the area of temporal active databases. He has published more than 30 papers in journals (e.g. IEEE Transactions on Knowledge and Data Engineering), books (Temporal Databases: Research and Practice) and conferences on the topics of information systems architectures, active databases and temporal databases. Together with Dr. John Mylopoulos, Avigdor has chaired the "Distributed Heterogeneous Information Services" workshop at HICSS'98 and he was the guest editor of a special issue by the same name in the International Journal of Cooperative Information Systems. Avigdor is a member of the ACM and the IEEE computer society.

Avigdor has a practical, as well as academic, experience with Eeommerce. He worked as a consultant with MyZebra.com, a virtual enterprise specializing in customer service over the Internet. Also, he has conducted research in the area of data integration of federation of cooperative and non-cooperative databases, with applications to Web-based information services.

Tutorial: Data Access

José A. Blakeley
Microsoft Corporation
One Microsoft Way
Redmond, WA 98052-6399, USA
Phone: +1 (425) 936 5477

joseb@microsoft.com

Anand Deshpande
Persistent System Private Limited
Panini, 2A Senapati Bapat Road
Pune 411 016 India
Phone: +91 (20) 567 67 00

anand@pspl.co.in

ABSTRACT

With an explosion of data on the web, consistent data access to diverse data sources has become a challenging task. In this tutorial will present topics of interest to database researchers and developers building: interoperable middle-ware, gateways, distributed heterogeneous query processors, federated databases, data source wrappers, mediators, and DBMS extensions.

All of these require access to diverse information through common data access abstractions, powerful APIs, and common data exchange formats. With the emergence of the web, database applications are being run over the intranet and the extranet. This tutorial presents an overview of existing and emerging data access technologies. We will concentrate on some of the technical challenges that have to be addressed to enable uniform data access across various platforms and some of the issues that went into the design of these data access strategies.

Keywords

Data access, Database connectivity

1. Tutorial Outline

- *Overview, motivation, need for standards.*
- *Data Access Scenarios*
  - Client data access –from client-server applications
  - Middle-tier data access – from business objects, web servers etc.
  - Server-side issues such as stored procedures or functions.
- *Data Access Services*
  - Connection and resource management
  - Connected and disconnected sessions, local cache, connectionless updatability
  - Navigation (scrolling, filtering and ordering)
  - Bindings from programming languages
  - Distributed Queries
  - Distributed Transactions
- *Data access requirements* in the context of:
  - Internet, ERP, OLAP, and Document applications
- *Overview of technology offerings* and how they address the above requirements
  - Java Data Access
    - JDBC API, driver implementations (two-tier, three-tier), SQLJ
  - Microsoft Universal Data Access
    - Using OLEDB, ADO, and service components to integrate diverse data sources
  - XML in the context of data access
    - XML has rapidly become and important technology for data exchange. We will discuss key XML standards and their impact on business-to-business electronic data exchange.

Tutorial: LDAP Directory Services - Just Another Database Application?

Shridhar Shukla

Persistent Systems Private Limited
Panini, 2A Senapati Bapat Road
Pune 411 016 India

Email: shukla@pspl.co.in
Phone: +91 (20) 567 67 00 ext. 400

Anand Deshpande

Email: anand@pspl.co.in
Phone: +91 (20) 567 67 00 ext. 300

Abstract

The key driving force behind general-purpose enterprise directory services is for providing a central repository for commonly and widely used information such as users, groups, network service access information and profiles, security information, etc. Acceptance of the Lightweight Directory Access Protocol (LDAP) as an access protocol has facilitated widespread integration of these directory services into the network infrastructure and applications.

Both directory and relational databases are data repositories sharing the characteristic that they have mechanisms for dealing with schema and structure of information and are suitable for systematically organized data. This tutorial describes characteristics of directories such as schema information, query language and support, storage mechanisms required, typical requirements imposed by applications, etc. We then explain the differences between a directory and relational database, and show how the two are required to co-exist in a typical enterprise.

An essential characteristic assumed for information stored in directories is that it is relatively static and that the queries are mostly read only. We describe typical directory applications to validate this assumption and project the requirements imposed on them as these applications evolve. We then describe areas of overlap between traditional databases and directories, describe some database and directory integration solutions adopted in the market, and identify areas in which *directory deployment can benefit from the experience* gathered by the database community.

Tutorial Outline

Introduction to directory technology
- Hierarchical namespace
- Object classes, attributes, and indices
- Search filters and scope
- LDAP API

Directory application scenarios
- User/group management applications
- Using directories in security applications

Directory Design parameters
- Namespace design
- Storage implementations
- Constraint checking
- Server controls
- Replication

Databases and directories in perspective
- Top ten reasons why directories get deployed
- Top ten reasons why databases get deployed
- Challenges ahead for directory deployment
- Performance results for sample queries
- How the directory can benefit from present database technology

Duration: 1.5 hours

Tutorial: Research Issues in Moving Objects Databases

Ouri Wolfson

University of Illinois, Chicago

(No tutorial description was submitted for the proceedings.)

Self-Organizing Data Sharing Communities with SAGRES

Zachary Ives   Alon Levy   Jayant Madhavan   Rachel Pottinger
Ştefan Şaroiu   Igor Tatarinov   Shiori Betzler   Qiong Chen   Ewa Jaslikowska
Jing Su   Wai Tak Theodora Yeung

University of Washington

{zives,alon,jayant,rap,tzoompy,igor,shiorith,qiong,emjeden,jingsu,theodora}@cs.washington.edu

1   Introduction

An increasing number of devices (e.g., household appliances, PDAs, cell phones) have microprocessors and will soon be able to exhibit sophisticated behaviors and interactions with other devices: a home heating system will monitor its residents' alarm clocks and schedules to set the temperature optimally; a car's GPS system will use local traffic reports to optimize its driver's route based on road conditions. The SAGRES project at the University of Washington addresses the key issues of data sharing and management in the realm of invisible computing.

In the context of invisible computing, data exchange and computation occur in the background in response to cues from users. Devices are added and removed from the network on a regular basis, and they must be able to interoperate with little human intervention. The collection of devices that exist around a particular individual or in a particular location (e.g., a house, office building or virtual networked location) form a *data sharing community*. Ultimately, these devices must share data in a common format such as XML. Managing device interaction and the flow of such data is key to the operation of data sharing communities. We demonstrate the SAGRES system, which represents the first step in a large-scale project. Our ultimate goal is to develop a new programming paradigm and a scalable architecture for developing self-configuring devices under various user constraints and preferences. Issues we tackle include development of both a language and an environment for managing distributed, resource-sharing, concurrent device interactions and transactions.

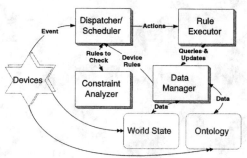

2   The SAGRES Architecture

Device functionalities and data must be represented within SAGRES (Fig. above), but the key to the system lies in our novel programming model. The rule-based DEVL language is event-driven, and combines semistructured data manipulation capabilities with constraints, synchronization, and message passing to facilitate seamless device interactions.

SAGRES data is stored in two graph structures: an Ontology, which represents the class/inheritance hierarchy of entities controlled by SAGRES, as well as rules, queries, and attributes; and a World State, which is a virtual view of the data present in the data sharing community.

As a device joins the system, it adds its class information to the Ontology and its data to the World State. Next, rules for the new device are analyzed by the Constraint Analyzer to verify they do not conflict with existing actions or constraints.

On an event, the Dispatcher looks up matching rules, tests their preconditions, and sends their actions to the Executor. The Executor performs the operations, querying and updating the World State and Ontology through a Data Manager. (Updates may initiate device actions.)

The vision of invisible computing encompasses nearly all subfields in computer science, and will require contributions from all of these communities to become a reality. SAGRES attempts to address the related data management issues, thereby representing the database community's contribution to this emerging area.

λ-DB: An ODMG-Based Object-Oriented DBMS*

Leonidas Fegaras[†]   Chandrasekhar Srinivasan[†]   Arvind Rajendran[†]   David Maier[‡]

The λ-DB project at the University of Texas at Arlington aims at developing frameworks and prototype systems that address the new query optimization challenges for object-oriented and object-relational databases, such as query nesting, multiple collection types, methods, and arbitrary nesting of collections. We have already developed a theoretical framework for query optimization based on an effective calculus, called the monoid comprehension calculus [4]. The system reported here is a fully operational ODMG 2.0 [2] OODB management system, based on this framework. Our system can handle most ODL declarations and can process most OQL query forms. λ-DB is not ODMG compliant. Instead it supports its own C++ binding that provides a seamless integration between OQL and C++ with low impedance mismatch. It allows C++ variables to be used in queries and results of queries to be passed back to C++ programs. Programs expressed in our C++ binding are compiled by a preprocessor that performs query optimization at compile time, rather than run-time, as it is proposed by ODMG. In addition to compiled queries, λ-DB provides an interpreter that evaluates ad-hoc OQL queries at run-time.

The λ-DB evaluation engine is written in SDL (the SHORE Data Language) of the SHORE object management system [1], developed at the University of Wisconsin. ODL schemas are translated into SDL schemas in a straightforward way and are stored in the system catalog. The λ-DB OQL compiler is a C++

preprocessor that accepts a language called λ-OQL, which is C++ code with embedded DML commands to perform transactions, queries, updates, etc. The preprocessor translates λ-OQL programs into C++ code that contains calls to the λ-DB evaluation engine. We also provide a visual query formulation interface, called VOODOO, and a translator from visual queries to OQL text, which can be sent to the λ-DB OQL interpreter for evaluation.

Even though a lot of effort has been made to make the implementation of our system simple enough for other database researchers to use and extend, our system is quite sophisticated since it employs current state-of-the-art query optimization technologies as well as new advanced experimental optimization techniques which we have developed through the years, such as query unnesting [3]. The λ-DB OODBMS is available as an open source software through the web at `http://lambda.uta.edu/lambda-DB.html`.

In our SIGMOD 2000 demo we will present the latest version of λ-DB . We will use a sample database that is simple enough for the audience to understand in few minutes but challenging enough to express some interesting queries for showing the basic features of our system. For a short demo, the audience will have the chance to submit a number of ad-hoc OQL queries either in text form or using our visual query formulator, VOODOO. For those in the audience interested in query processing and optimization, we will provide a visual interface to display the most important phases and results during the optimization of a query.

*This work is supported in part by the National Science Foundation under grant IIS-9811525

[2]The University of Texas at Arlington, CSE, 416 Yates Street, P.O. Box 19015, Arlington, TX 76019-19015

[3]Oregon Graduate Institute of Science & Technology, CSE, 20000 N.W. Walker Road, Portland, OR 97291-1000

References

[1] M. Carey et al. Shoring Up Persistent Applications. In *SIGMOD'94*, pp 383–394.

[2] R. Cattell et al. *The Object Database Standard: ODMG 2.0.* Morgan Kaufmann, 1997.

[3] L. Fegaras. Query Unnesting in Object-Oriented Databases. *SIGMOD'98*, pp 49–60.

[4] L. Fegaras and D. Maier. Towards an Effective Calculus for Object Query Languages. *SIGMOD'95*, pp 47–58.

An Approximate Search Engine for Structural Databases*

Jason T. L. Wang[†]   Xiong Wang[‡]   Dennis Shasha[§]   Bruce A. Shapiro[¶]

Kaizhong Zhang[‖]   Qicheng Ma[**]   Zasha Weinberg[††]

1   Background

When a person interested in a topic enters a keyword into a Web search engine, the response is nearly instantaneous (and sometimes overwhelming). The impressive speed is due to clever inverted index structures, caching, and a domain-independent knowledge of strings. Our project seeks to construct algorithms, data structures, and software that approach the speed of keyword-based search engines for queries on structural databases.

A structural database is one whose data objects include trees, graphs, or a set of interrelated labeled points in two, three, or higher dimensional space. Examples include databases holding (i) protein secondary and tertiary structure, (ii) phylogenetic trees, (iii) neuroanatomical networks, (iv) parse trees, (v) molecular diagrams, and (vi) XML documents. Comparison queries on such databases require solving variants of the graph isomorphism or subisomorphism problems (for which all known algorithms are exponential), so we have

*Work supported by NSF grants IRI-9531548, IRI-9531554, and by the Natural Sciences and Engineering Research Council of Canada under Grant No. OGP0046373.

[†] Dept. of Computer & Information Science, New Jersey Institute of Technology, University Heights, Newark, NJ 07102 (jason@cis.njit.edu).

[‡] Dept. of CIS, NJIT, NJ 07102 (xiong@cis.njit.edu).

[§] Courant Institute of Mathematical Sciences, New York University, New York, NY 10012 (shasha@cs.nyu.edu).

[¶] Experimental and Computational Biology Lab, National Cancer Institute, Frederick, MD 21702 (bshapiro@ncifcrf.gov).

[‖] Dept. of Computer Science, University of Western Ontario, London, Ontario, N6A 5B7, Canada (kzhang@csd.uwo.ca).

[**] Dept. of CIS, NJIT, NJ 07102 (qicheng@cis.njit.edu).

[††] Dept. of Computer Science & Engineering, University of Washington, Seattle, WA 98195 (zasha@cs.washington.edu).

explored a large heuristic space.

2   Prototype

We have two different search techniques: one based on topological relationships and the other based on physical position. In SIGMOD 2000 we will demo a search engine capable of answering the following queries on a structural database $\mathcal{D}$ containing 3D graphs:

(1) [nearest-neighbor query] Given a query object o, which items o' in $\mathcal{D}$ are "closest" to o? We have experimented with two different similarity scores. The score between a graph g_1 and a graph g_2 based on an alignment M is defined as the fraction of edges in g_1 (g_2, respectively) that are consistent in g_2 (g_1, respectively) based on M. Edge $\{i, j\}$ of g has a consistent edge in g' based on the alignment M if $\{M[i], M[j]\}$ is an edge in g'. The larger the score between g_1 and g_2, the closer g_1 is to g_2. We use this query to illustrate our search technique based on topological relationships.

(2) [discovery query] Which substructures approximately occur in all items in $\mathcal{D}$? A substructure may occur in a graph after allowing for an arbitrary number of whole-structure rotations and translations as well as a small number (specified by the user) of edit operations in the substructure or in the graph. (When a substructure appears in a graph only after the graph has been modified, we call that appearance "approximate occurrence.") The edit operations include relabeling a node, deleting a node and inserting a node. We use this query to illustrate our discovery technique based on physical position. We can search by physical position and discover by topological relationships.

For both queries, we will show the best alignment information in addition to graphically displaying the qualifying (sub)structures.

SERFing the Web: Web-Site Management Made Easy*

Elke A. Rundensteiner, Kajal T. Claypool, Li Chen, Hong Su, Keiji Oenoki
Department of Computer Science, Worcester Polytechnic Institute, Worcester, MA 01609
{rundenst|kajal|lichen|suhong|koenoki}@cs.wpi.edu

1 Introduction

In the era of electronic publishing, there is a need for a comprehensive Web Site Management System (WSMS) that provides an end-to-end solution ranging from integration of web sites to re-structuring and maintenance of new customized web views. Today, while many research efforts focus on generating diversified web sites, our Re-Web system [CRCK98] is the first to look at easing this process for end-users by providing *libraries* of pre-defined generic transformations for web re-structuring and *visual tools* for the generation and browsing of such transformations.

Re-Web translates web information to an OO schema and data, re-structures and integrates information at the OODB level (SERF [CR99]) and finally generates web pages from the information in the database. The Re-Web system uses JDK1.2, Java Swing, and PSE Pro6.0 as its persistent storage. We use LotusXSL and IBM's XML parser for the web generation module. Re-Web system (Figure 1) has been implemented and tested on WinNT and Solaris. It provides tools for generating, restructuring and maintaining web sites.

- **WebMap Subsystem.** Explicates a web site structure and captures it within an OODB system.

This work was supported in part by several grants from NSF, namely, the NSF NYI grant #IRI 94-57609, the NSF CISE Instrumentation grant #IRIS 97-29878, and the NSF grant #IIS 97-32897. Dr. Rundensteiner would like to thank our industrial sponsors, in particular, IBM for the IBM partnership award. Li Chen would also like to thank IBM for the IBM corporate fellowship. Special thanks also goes to the PSE Team at Object Design Inc. for providing us with a customized patch of the PSE Pro2.0 system that exposed schema-related APIs needed to develop our tool. The authors would like to thank students at the Database Systems Research Group at WPI for their feedback.

- **SERF Subsystem.** Applies re-usable transformation templates written in OQL with embedded schema evolution and view evolution primitives to enable powerful web site restructuring.

- **GUI Subsystem.** Allows easy visual generation and browsing of web transformations for the Re-Web Library.

- **WebGen Subsystem.** Provides the ease of web site generation and reformation by exploring web semantics in three tiers: ODMG, XML and HTML.

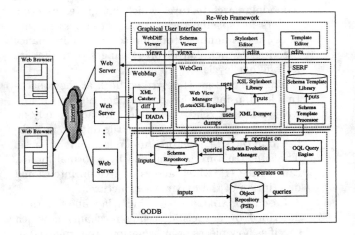

Figure 1: Architecture of Re-Web System.

References

[CR99] K. Claypool and E.A. Rundensteiner. SERF: Transforming your Database. In *IEEE Bulletin - Special Issue on Database Tranformation Technology*, pages 19–24, 1999.

[CRCK98] K. Claypool, E.A. Rundensteiner, L. Chen, and B. Kothari. Re-usable ODMG-based Templates for Web View Generation and Restructuring. In *WIDM'98*, pages 314–321, 1998.

HOMER: a Model-Based CASE Tool for Data-Intensive Web Sites

Paolo Merialdo [1], Paolo Atzeni [1], Marco Magnante [1],
Giansalvatore Mecca [2], Marco Pecorone [1]

[1] D.I.A. – Università di Roma Tre   [2] D.I.F.A. – Università della Basilicata

{merialdo, atzeni, magnante, mecca, pecorone}@dia.uniroma3.it

We present HOMER, a CASE tool for building and maintaining complex, data-intensive Web sites. In HOMER the processes of creation and maintenance of a Web site are completely based on the adoption of suitable models, to describe the various aspects of the site (content, navigation structure, presentation). The development of a site does not require any code writing activity: based on the results of the design process, the system automatically creates programs to implement the site, statically and/or dynamically, as needed; also, the system does not depend on any specific tool or language: it has a modular architecture, which integrates external servers for specific tasks; finally, the system supports site administrators for several maintenance activities, which can involve changes over the site at different levels.

The site content is described both at the conceptual level, using the ER data model, and at the logical level using relational tables. In fact, to rely on robust and effective technology, the data to be published in the site are stored in a relational database. The site structure is described by a formal model, called ADM [1], which allows to give an intensional description of the hypertext structure.

Based on ADM, the graphical layout of data is described by a specific styling mechanism, which specifies how pieces of information are formatted in a page.

The core of the system is the HOMER *Design Server* which manages the formal representations stored in the design repository, and generates algebraic expressions that map the database structures onto the site ones. These algebraic expressions, combined with the presentation directives, are used to automatically produce Java servlets (or Microsoft Active Server Pages) that implement the site.

Site designers and administrators access every functions of the system through a graphical user interface. A number of graphical primitives allow designers to draw the ER scheme, as well as the ADM scheme, in the site building process, and help administrators govern restructuring actions during the site life-cycle.

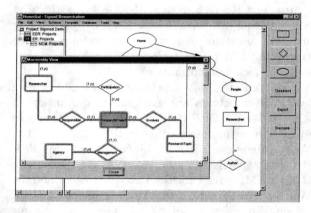

Figure 1: The HOMER GUI

The system is modular and scalable. HOMER can produce both static and dynamic sites, and is able to generate outputs for both HTML and XML/XSL formats. Also, it is worth noting that the system does not provide its own tool for designing the graphical layout of the site; on the contrary, it leaves designers free to handle graphics by their preferred tool (any WYSIWYG HTML editor).

Acknowledgments Work partially supported by MURST, CNR, and Università di Roma Tre.

References

[1] P. Atzeni, G. Mecca, and P. Merialdo. To Weave the Web. VLDB'97.

[2] P. Atzeni, G. Mecca, and P. Merialdo. Design and Maintenance of Data Intensive Web Sites. EDBT'98.

[3] G. Mecca, P. Merialdo, P. Atzeni, and V. Crescenzi. The (Short) ARANEUS Guide to Web-Site Development. WebDB'99.

FACT: A Learning Based Web Query Processing System

Songting Chen[2]   Yanlei Diao[1]   Hongjun Lu[1]   Zengping Tian[2]

[1]Computer Science Department
Hong Kong University of Science and Technology
Hong Kong, China

{diaoyl, luhj}@cs.ust.hk

[2]Computer Science Department
Fudan University
Shanghai, China

{stchen, zptian}@fudan.edu.cn

FACT (Fast and ACcuraTe) is a query processing system aimed at providing users with facilities so that they can get the query results from the Web in a database-like fashion. The system takes user queries in the form of keywords (free text) and returns segments of Web pages that contain the required information. It works as follows. The input from a user is passed to a general-purpose search engine to obtain a set of URLs of Web pages that may contain the required information. The system later locates the query results from the Web pages reachable from these URLs. Since queries expressed in keywords may be not able to express query requirements precisely or may not guarantee the discovery of required information inherently, the user is asked to first browse a few pages, during which the system learns from her/him about the exact query requirements and heuristics of finding the required information through a series of hyperlinks. The system will process the rest URLs and present the results in the form of segments of Web pages to the user.

We call the above approach a *learning-based* approach. As a result of the learning, the system is able to deliver to users the results that better match users' needs in a concise form. The novel features of FACT include:

(1) Different from most search engines that return URLs to users, FACT returns segments of Web pages, which releases users a great deal from the heavy burden of manually browsing pages and locating information.

(2) Though the query is posted in key words, the returned results contain exactly the information that the user is querying for, which may not be explicitly specified in the input query.

(3) The required information is often not contained in the Web pages whose URLs are returned by a search engine. FACT is capable of navigating in the neighborhood of these pages to find those that really contain the queried segments.

(4) The system does not require a prior knowledge about users such as user profiles [1] or preprocessing of Web pages such as wrapper generation [2].

A prototype system has been implemented using the approach. It learns and applies two types of knowledge, *navigation knowledge* for following hyperlinks and *classification knowledge* for queried segment identification. For learning, it supports three training strategies, namely sequential training, random training and interleaved training. *Yahoo!* is currently the external search engine. The URLs of Web pages returned by the external search engine are used in processing.

A range of queries that present different characteristics has been selected to evaluate the system. One query "*room rates of hotels in Hong Kong*" is used to represent the typical queries that have specific targets such as *price* and some indicators (e.g. $). Another query "*admission requirements on graduate applicants*" is selected to represent those queries with more general requirements such as *degree, GPA, test scores*, etc. Such results have larger variance compared with the query for prices. We even tested queries targeted at a concept. An example is "*data mining researcher*", for which the system is expected to extract segments as evidence that a person is a data mining researcher. The returned segments may talk about research interests, research projects or professional activity. It is rather subjective to determine whether a segment should be returned and effective learning is a must.

The preliminary results are encouraging. User query requirements and navigation heuristics can be reasonably well captured and stored in a rather simple form. For queries tested on the system, given a set of about 100 URLs and using interleaved training strategy, users need to browse no more than 10 of them to make the system capable of locating the queried segments or denying the irrelevant Web sites with the correctness rate higher than 80%. With respect to efficiency, to locate a queried segment, the system almost always navigates along the shortest path as human readers can find. In a Web site that does not contain the queried segment, it crawls no more than 2.5 pages to recognize the irrelevancy.

The demonstration will include the following items:
(1) A working system that can accept user queries and present segments as query results.
(2) A set of experiments that are designed to evaluate the system, and compare different implementations, such as knowledge representations and training strategies.

References

[1] R. Armstrong, D. Freitag, T. Joachims, T. Mitchell. WebWatcher: A Learning Apprentice for the World Wide Web. In *Proc. of the 1995 AAAI Spring Symposium on Information Gathering From Heterogeneous, Distributed Environments*, March 1995.

[2] N. Ashish, C. Knoblock. Wrapper Generation for Semi-structured Internet Sources. *SIGMOD Record*, 26(4): 8-15, 1997.

javax.XXL:
A Prototype for a Library of Query Processing Algorithms

Jochen van den Bercken   Jens-Peter Dittrich   Bernhard Seeger

Department of Mathematics and Computer Science
University of Marburg
35032 Marburg, Germany

{bercken,dittrich,seeger}@mathematik.uni-marburg.de

In our demo we present XXL (eXtensible and fleXible Library), a toolkit for rapid prototyping of query processing algorithms. XXL is a flexible, easy-to-use, platform independent Java-library. It provides a powerful collection of generic index-structures, query operators and algorithms facilitating the performance evaluation of new query processing techniques. Query algorithms in XXL use the same set of basic classes like I/O routines and improved (de)serialization methods. Therefore, XXL is an ideal testbed for experimental comparisons of new approaches to established ones. The most important packages in XXL deal with containers, cursors and index structures. The package *containers* consists of an interface and classes for implementing (persistent) sets of objects. A container is used to manage objects with respect to their identifiers generated by the container. This establishes an abstraction from the storage medium. Containers can be buffered by wrapping them with an instance of class *BufferedContainer* which provides an m:n-relationship between buffers and containers (Figure 1). Traditional storage manager like SHORE [2] support heterogeneous objects in a (distributed) repository. However, SHORE provides neither index structures nor query algorithms. The package *index-Structures* of XXL consists of both a framework of tree-based index structures and a set of implementations. Similar to GiST [5], this framework provides a skeleton implementation for a large class of index structures. In contrast to GiST, we also provide a wide range of generic query processing algorithms like the ones for joining [1] and bulk-loading. Index structures of XXL deliver the results of queries in a cursor-like fashion respecting the open-next-close interface (ONC) as it was proposed in Volcano [4]. Therefore, index structures can easily be used in queries. A typical example is a join cursor which consumes the outputs of two underlying cursors. Most of our work is however not dedicated to the area of relational databases, but mainly refers to spatial and temporal data. For spatial databases, for example, we provide several implementations of spatial join algorithms [3]. The cursor-based processing is however the major advantage of XXL in contrast to approaches like LEDA [6] and TPIE [7]. For more information on XXL see *http://www.mathematik.uni-marburg.de/DBS/xxl*.

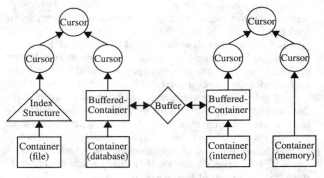

Fig. 1: Use-case of XXL

We will demonstrate the latest version of XXL using examples to show its core functionality. We will concentrate on three key aspects of XXL.

- *Usage:* We show how easily state-of-the-art spatial join-algorithms can be implemented in XXL using data from different sources.
- *Reuse:* We will demonstrate how to support different joins, e.g. spatial and temporal joins, using the same generic algorithm like Plug&Join [1].
- *Comparability:* We will demonstrate how XXL serves as an ideal testbed to compare query processing algorithms and index structures.

REFERENCES

[1] J. van den Bercken, M. Schneider, B. Seeger. Plug&Join: An easy-to-use Generic Algorithm for Efficiently Processing Equi and Non-Equi Joins. To appear in Proc. of EDBT 2000.

[2] M. J. Carey, D. J. DeWitt, M. J. Franklin et. al. Shoring Up Persistent Applications. SIGMOD Conference 1994: 383-394.

[3] J.-P. Dittrich, B. Seeger. Data Redundancy and Duplicate Detection in Spatial Join Processing. To appear in Proc. of ICDE 2000.

[4] G. Graefe. Volcano - An Extensible and Parallel Query Evaluation System. TKDE 6(1): 120-135 (1994).

[5] J. M. Hellerstein, J. F. Naughton, A. Pfeffer. Generalized Search Trees for Database Systems. VLDB 1995, 562-573.

[6] K. Mehlhorn, S. Näher. The LEDA Platform of Combinatorial and Geometric Computing. Cambridge University Press, 1999.

[7] D. E. Vengroff, J. S. Vitter. I/O-Efficient Scientific Computation using TPIE. Proc. Goddard Conference on Mass Storage Systems and Technologies, 1996, in NASA Conference Publication 3340, Volume II, 553-570.

i³: Intelligent, Interactive Investigaton of OLAP data cubes

Sunita Sarawagi   Gayatri Sathe

School of Information Technology, IIT Bombay, India.

{sunita,gayatri}@it.iitb.ernet.in

The goal of the **i³** (eye cube) project is to enhance multidimensional database products with a suite of advanced operators to automate data analysis tasks that are currently handled through manual exploration. Most OLAP products are rather simplistic and rely heavily on the user's intuition to manually drive the discovery process. Such ad hoc user-driven exploration gets tedious and error-prone as data dimensionality and size increases. We first investigated how and why analysts currently explore the data cube and then automated them using advanced operators that can be invoked interactively like existing simple operators.

Our proposed suite of extensions appear in the form of a toolkit attached with a OLAP product. At this demo we will present three such operators: DIFF, RELAX and INFORM with illustrations from real-life datasets.

The DIFF operator

One reason why analysts manually drill down to explore detailed data is to find causes for drops or increases observed at an aggregated level. For automating this task we propose the DIFF [Sar99] operator that can report a summarized difference between two values observed at aggregate levels. For example, a busy executive looking at the annual reports might quickly wish to find the main reasons why sales dropped from the third to the fourth quarter in a region. Instead of digging through heaps of data manually, he could invoke the new DIFF operator which in a single step will do all the digging for him and return the main reasons in a compact form that he can easily assimilate.

The RELAX operator

The RELAX operator is for automatically generalizing the scope of a problem case observed at detailed level.

Suppose a local branch manager notices a big drop in sales somewhere in detailed data. Often the next step is to check if this was an isolated case or is this drop part of a bigger problem. For this he rolls up to the next level and views the problem case in the context of combinations of other dimensions using a succession of selection, drill-down and pivot steps. The RELAX operator can be used to automate this search. The output is a set of maximal regions around the problem case with similar changes.

The INFORM operator

Here our goal is to provide an enhanced data exploration environment that is adaptive to a user's prior knowledge of the data [Sar00]. We capture the analysts context by continuously tracking the parts of the cube that a user has visited either through implicit monitoring or by explicit recording. The information in the scattered visited sections of the cube are pieced together to form a model of the user's mental picture of the unvisited parts. Finally, at any time, the user can invoke the INFORM operator that will output the most informative unvisited parts of the cube given his established context. This process of updating the user's context based on visited parts and querying for regions to explore further continues in a loop until the user's mental model perfectly matches the actual cube.

Integrating with OLAP products For each operator we designed fast algorithms that can be invoked *interactively* during cube exploration. They are tightly integrated with existing OLAP systems and ride on the servers' query processing capabilities through dynamically generated queries for all heavy duty processing.

References

[Sar99] S. Sarawagi. Explaining differences in multidimensional aggregates. In *Proc. of the 25th Int'l Conference on Very Large Databases (VLDB)*, 1999.

[Sar00] S. Sarawagi. User adaptive exploration of olap data cubes. Submitted for publication: http://www.it. iitb.ernet.in/~sunita, 2000.

AJAX: An Extensible Data Cleaning Tool

Helena Galhardas*
INRIA Rocquencourt, France
Helena.Galhardas@inria.fr

Daniela Florescu
INRIA Rocquencourt, France
Daniela.Florescu@inria.fr

Dennis Shasha[†]
Courant Institute, NYU
shasha@cs.nyu.edu

Eric Simon
INRIA Rocquencourt, France
Eric.Simon@inria.fr

Data quality concerns arise in order to correct anomalies in a single data source (e.g., duplicate elimination in a file), or to integrate data coming from multiple sources into a single new data source (e.g., data warehouse construction). In addition, the information handled may also need to undergo a formatting and normalization process so that the resulting data is structured and presented according to the application requirements.

Data quality problems usually arise when the same real object is modeled by different data representations (the "Object Identity Problem"). This may have several causes. First, data may contain *errors*, usually due to mistyping. Second, when data comes from different sources, different naming conventions may have been used. For instance, the same customer may be referred to in different tables by slightly different but correct names. Correcting the Object Identity problem and converting data formats is the job of software known as data cleaning and transformation tools. We will present such a tool: AJAX, whose main goal is to facilitate the specification and execution of data cleaning and transformation programs.

AJAX proposes a *framework* wherein the logic

---

*Founded by "Instituto Superior Técnico" - Technical University of Lisbon and by a JNICT fellowship of Program PRAXIS XXI (Portugal)

[†]Supported by National Science Foundation grant IRI-9531554

of a data cleaning program is modeled as a directed graph of data transformations starting from some input source data. Four types of data transformations are distinguished. The *mapping* transformation standardizes data formats when possible or simply produces records with a more suitable format. *Matching* finds pairs of records that most probably refer to the same real object. Records are compared via a matching criteria that can be arbitrarily complex. A similarity value representing the result of the matching criteria is attached to each matching pair of compared records. *Clustering* groups together matching pairs with a high similarity value by applying a given grouping criteria (e.g. by transitive closure). Finally, *merging* collapses each individual cluster into a tuple of the resulting data source. AJAX provides a *"declarative" language* for specifying data cleaning programs, which consists of SQL statements enriched with a set of specific primitives to express these transformations.

AJAX also offers a *graphical user interface*. It allows the user to interact with an executing data cleaning program to handle exceptional cases and to inspect intermediate results. Finally, AJAX provides a *data lineage mechanism* that permits users to determine the source and processing of data for debugging purposes.

We will present the AJAX system applied to two real world problems: the consolidation of a telecommunication database, and the conversion of a dirty database of bibliographic references into a set of clean, normalized, and redundancy-free relational tables maintaining the same data.

References

[1] http://caravel.inria.fr/~galharda/ajax.html.

Concept Based Design of Data Warehouses: The DWQ Demonstrators

M. Jarke[1], C. Quix[1], D. Calvanese[2], M. Lenzerini[2], E. Franconi[3], S. Ligoudistianos[4], P. Vassiliadis[4], Y. Vassiliou[4]

[1] Informatik V, RWTH Aachen, Germany, {jarke,quix}@informatik.rwth-aachen.de

[2] Dipartimento di Informatica e Sistemistica, Università di Roma "La Sapienza", Italy

[3] Dept. of Computer Science, Univ. of Manchester, United Kingdom

[4] Dept. of Electrical and Computer Eng., National Technical University of Athens, Greece

Abstract

The ESPRIT Project DWQ (Foundations of Data Warehouse Quality) aimed at improving the quality of DW design and operation through systematic enrichment of the semantic foundations of data warehousing. Logic-based knowledge representation and reasoning techniques were developed to control accuracy, consistency, and completeness via advanced conceptual modeling techniques for source integration, data reconciliation, and multi-dimensional aggregation. This is complemented by quantitative optimization techniques for view materialization, optimizing timeliness and responsiveness without losing the semantic advantages from the conceptual approach. At the operational level, query rewriting and materialization refreshment algorithms exploit the knowledge developed at design time. The demonstration shows the interplay of these tools under a shared metadata repository, based on an example extracted from an application at Telecom Italia.

1 Overview of the Demonstration

The demonstration follows roughly the 6-step process indicated in figure 1. In the middle of the figure, light-grey boxes indicate conceptual models which for the designer look like extended ER diagrams but are internally represented in a description logic formalism. The light-grey boxes represent logical (relational or semi-structured or multi-dimensional) schemata. The corresponding tools are organized around the DWQ metadata framework presented in [3] and implemented using the ConceptBase system.

Step 1 and 2: The DWQ approach to source integration is concept-centered, symmetric and incremental: Conceptual models of the sources and of the enterprise model are defined initially independently and related by explicit interschema assertions about which subsumption reasoning can be done. Thus, both a global-as-view and a local-as-view approach to data warehouse design can be suppored.

3. This conceptual modeling approach has been extended to the case where concepts are organized into aggregates along multiple dimensions [2]. Multi-dimensional views over the enterprise conceptual model can be defined to express the interests of DW clients, without losing the advantages of consistency and completeness checking as well as semantic optimization provided by the conceptual modeling approach.

4. These "conceptual data cubes" can be implemented by a MOLAP or ROLAP data model. We follow the

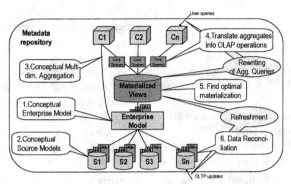

Figure 1: Structure of the demonstration

latter approach which requires a careful design of an OLAP relational algebra, together with the corresponding rewritings to underlying star schemata [5].

5. The mapping of multi-dimensional aggregates to ROLAP queries creates a set of view definitions. The materialization of these queries would be the optimal solutions in a query-only DW with hardly any updates. The direct mapping of the enterprise conceptual model to a relational database (ODS) would conversely be best for a very update-intensive DW. Typical DWs have less extreme usage patterns and therefore require a compromise between these two view materialization strategies. We demonstrate a combinatorial optimization algorithm for solving this problem [4].

6. The resulting optimal design is now implemented by data integration and reconciliation algorithms again derived from the conceptual perspective. The views to be materialized are initially defined over the ODS relations; there can be several qualitatively different, possibly conflicting ways to actually materialize these ODS relations from the existing sources which are generated by a further set of rewritings derived from steps 1 and 2 [1].

References

[1] D. Calvanese, G. De Giacomo, M. Lenzerini, D. Nardi, R. Rosati: A principled approach to data integration and reconciliation in data warehousing. *Workshop on Design and Management of Data Warehouses (DMDW'99)*, 1999.

[2] E. Franconi, U. Sattler: A data warehouse conceptual data model for multidimensional aggregation. *Workshop on Design and Management of Data Warehouses (DMDW'99)*, 1999.

[3] M. Jarke, M.A. Jeusfeld, C. Quix, P. Vassiliadis: Architecture and quality in data warehouses: An extended repository approach. *Information Systems*, 24(3), pp. 229-253, 1999.

[4] D. Theodoratos, T. Sellis: Data warehouse configuration. *23rd Conf. Very Large Databases (VLDB)*, pp. 126-135, 1997.

[5] P. Vassiliadis: Modeling multidimensional databases, cubes and cube operations. *10th Conf. Scientific and Statistical Database Management (SSDBM)*, pp. 53-62, 1998.

Towards Data Mining Benchmarking: A Test Bed for Performance Study of Frequent Pattern Mining

Jian Pei and **Runying Mao**

School of Computing Science

Simon Fraser University

Burnaby, BC, Canada

{peijian, rmao}@cs.sfu.ca

Kan Hu and **Hua Zhu**

DBMiner Technology Inc.

Burnaby, BC, Canada

{kanhu, hzhua}@dbminer.com

Performance benchmarking has played an important role in the research and development in relational DBMS, object-relational DBMS, data warehouse systems, etc. We believe that benchmarking data mining algorithms is a long overdue task, and it will play an important role in the research and development of data mining systems as well.

Frequent pattern mining forms a core component in mining associations, correlations, sequential patterns, partial periodicity, etc., which are of great potential value in applications. There have been a lot of methods proposed and developed for efficient frequent pattern mining in various kinds of databases, including transaction databases, time-series databases, etc. However, so far there is no serious performance benchmarking study of different frequent pattern mining methods.

To facilitate an analytical comparison of different frequent mining methods, we have constructed an open test bed for performance study of a set of recently developed, popularly used methods for mining frequent patterns in transaction databases and mining sequential patterns in sequence databases, with different data characteristics. The testbed consists of the following components.

- **A synthetic data generator**, which can generate large sets of synthetic data in various kinds of data distributions. A few large data sets from real world applications will also be provided.

- **A good set of typical frequent pattern mining methods**, ranging from classical algorithms to recent studies. The method are grouped into three classes: *frequent pattern mining, max-pattern mining*, and

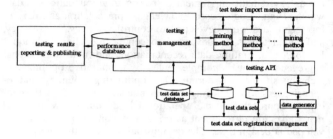

Figure 1: The architecture of the open test bed.

sequential pattern mining. For frequent pattern mining, we will demonstrate Apriori, hashing, partitioning, sampling, TreeProjection, and FP-growth. For maximal pattern mining, we will demonstrate MaxMiner, TreeProjection, and FP-growth-max. For sequential pattern mining, we will demonstrate GSP and FreeSpan.

- **A set of performance curves.** These algorithms, their running speeds, scalabilities, bottlenecks, and performance on different data distributions, will be compared and demonstrated upon request. Some performance curves from our pre-conference experimental evaluations will also be shown.

- **An open testbed.** Our goal is to construct an extensible test bed which integrates the above components and supports an open-ended testing service. Researchers can upload the object codes of their mining algorithms, and run them in the test bed using these data sets. The architecture is shown in Figure 1.

This testbed is our first step towards benchmarking data mining algorithms. By doing so, performance of different algorithms can be reported consistently, on the same platform, and in the same environment. After the demo, we plan to make the testbed available on the WWW so that it may, hopefully, benefit further research and development of efficient data mining methods.

Image Mining in IRIS: Integrated Retinal Information System

Wynne Hsu, Mong Li Lee, Kheng Guan Goh
School of Computing
National University of Singapore
Lower Kent Ridge Road, Singapore 119260
{whsu, leeml, gohkg}@comp.nus.edu.sg

Abstract

There is an increasing demand for systems that can automatically analyze images and extract semantically meaningful information. IRIS, an Integrated Retinal Information system, has been developed to provide medical professionals easy and unified access to the screening, trend and progression of diabetic-related eye diseases in a diabetic patient database. This paper shows how mining techniques can be used to accurately extract features in the retinal images. In particular, we apply a classification approach to determine the conditions for tortuousity in retinal blood vessels.

1. Introduction

Retinopathy is a common cause of blindness among the diabetic patients. Regular diabetic retinal eye screenings are needed to detect early signs of retinopathy so that appropriate treatments can be rendered to prevent blindness. With the large number of patients undergoing screenings, a tremendous amount of time and effort is required for the medical professionals to analyze and diagnose the fundus photographs.

In this paper, we will demonstrate how IRIS, an Integrated Retinal Information System, applies state-of-the-art data mining and image processing techniques on the retinal images to aid in the screening process.

2. Image Classification

An abnormal retinal image has one or more of the following signs of retinopathy (Figure 1):

1. Optic disc is not visible or not circular. The optic cup is disproportionately larger than the optic disc.
2. Blood vessels become tortuous, i.e. dilated and wavy.
3. Lesions of varying size and shape in the intervascular region.

Figure 1. Abnormal retinal images.

3. Tortuous Vessels

An early sign of diabetic retinopathy is the appearance of tortuous blood vessels. To determine whether the vessels are tortuous, we traverse the center (skeleton) lines of the extracted vessels and tabulate the curvatures of the outlines (using 12 attributes based on 4 curvature definitions). We extracted a total of 990 main vessel segments out of the 300 retinal images. Our initial study shows that no one single definition is able to give a reliable and consistent indication of the overall measure of tortuosity of the vessel segment under consideration. In IRIS, we combine all the 12 attributes extracted and feed them into an association based data mining classification tool, CBA [1]. The output of CBA consists of a set of classification rules that can accurately classify the input vessel segments as *Normal* or *Abnormal*. Figure 2 shows an example of the detected tortuous vessel by the system.

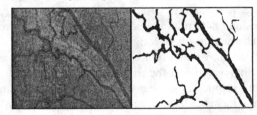

Figure 2. Detection of tortuous vessels (thicken portions).

Reference

[1] Liu B, Hsu W, Ma Y, 'Integrating Classification and Association Rule Mining.' *Proc. 4th Int. Conf. KD. and DM. (KDD-98, Plenary Presentation)*, New York, USA, 1998.

Acknowledgement

This project is funded by NUS research fund RP3991613.

MOCHA: A Database Middleware System Featuring Automatic Deployment of Application-Specific Functionality*

Manuel Rodríguez-Martínez , Nick Roussopoulos, John M. McGann,
Stephen Kelley, Vadim Katz, Zhexuan Song, Joseph JáJá
Institute for Advanced Computer Studies and Department of Computer Science
University of Maryland, College Park

Introduction

MOCHA[1] is a novel database middleware system designed to interconnect data sources distributed over a wide area network. MOCHA is built around the notion that the middleware for a large-scale distributed environment should be *self-extensible*. This means that new application-specific data types and query operators needed for query processing are deployed to remote sites in automatic fashion by the middleware system itself. In MOCHA, this is realized by shipping Java classes implementing these types or operators to the remote sites, where they can be used to manipulate the data of interest. All these Java classes are first stored in one or more *code repositories* from which MOCHA later retrieves and deploys them on a "need-to-do" basis. A major goal behind this idea of automatic code deployment is to fulfill the need for application-specific processing components at remote sites that do not provide them. MOCHA capitalizes on its ability to automatically deploy code to provide an efficient query processing service. By shipping code for query operators, MOCHA can produce efficient plans that place the execution of powerful data-reducing operators (filters) on the data sources. Examples of such operators are aggregates, predicates and data mining operators, which return a much smaller abstraction of the original data. In contrast, data-inflating operators that produce results larger that their arguments are evaluated near the client. Since in many cases, the code being shipped is smaller than the data sets, automatic code deployment facilitates query optimization based on data movement reduction, which can greatly reduce query execution time.

The architecture for MOCHA consists of four major components: **Client Application** - an applet, servlet or Java application used to pose queries to the system.; **Query Processing Coordinator** (QPC) - provides services such as query parsing, query optimization, query operator scheduling, catalog management and query execution, and is also responsible for deploying all the necessary functionality to the client and to those remote sites from which data will be extracted.; **Data Access Provider** (DAP) - provides the QPC with a uniform access mechanism to a remote data source, and executes some of the operators in the query, namely those that filter the data being accessed.; and **Data Server** - the server application that stores the data sets for a particular data site.

Description of the Demo

We have implemented MOCHA using Sun's Java Development Kit 1.2 and the system is operational at the University of Maryland. Our demo will showcase MOCHA interacting with an Earth Science client application. Users will be able run queries that extract satellite images and other GIS data (e.g. land features) from various sites, which will be combined and presented through a GUI. The client application and a QPC will be run from a computer located at the SIGMOD 2000 Conference venue. The QPC will connect over the Internet to the remote DAPs for two different data sources located at the University of Maryland. This demonstration shows the following unique aspects of MOCHA:

- Automatic deployment of the Java classes for the user-defined data types and operators used in a query to the client and remote data sites.
- Dynamic push of the code and computation of data-reducing operators (filters) to the remote data sites.
- Evaluation of data-inflating operators in a query near the client site.
- Easy and seamless specification and use of metadata for user-defined types and operators using XML and RDF.

In summary, our demo showcases a state-of-the-art database middleware system that is efficient, scalable and easy to maintain.

*This research was sponsored by DOD/Lucite Contract CG9815.
[1] Stands for **M**iddleware Based **O**n a **C**ode **SH**ipping **A**rchitecture.

A Goal-driven Auto-Configuration Tool for the
Distributed Workflow Management System Mentor-lite

Michael Gillmann, Jeanine Weissenfels, German Shegalov, Wolfgang Wonner, Gerhard Weikum
University of the Saarland, Germany
E-mail: {gillmann,weissenfels,shegalov,wonner,weikum}@cs.uni-sb.de
WWW: http://www-dbs.cs.uni-sb.de

1 System Overview

The Mentor-lite prototype has been developed within the research project "Architecture, Configuration, and Administration of Large Workflow Management Systems" funded by the German Science Foundation (DFG). It has evolved from its predecessor Mentor [1], but aims at a simpler architecture. The main goal of Mentor-lite has been to build a light-weight, extensible, and tailorable workflow management system (WFMS) with small footprint and easy-to-use administration capabilities. Our approach is to provide only kernel functionality inside the workflow engine, and consider system components like history management and worklist management as extensions on top of the kernel. The key point to retain the light-weight nature is that these extensions are implemented as workflows themselves.

The workflow specifications are interpreted at runtime, which is a crucial prerequisite for flexible exception handling and dynamic modifications during runtime. The interpreter performs a stepwise execution of the workflow specification according to its formal semantics. For each step, the activities to be performed by the step are determined and started.

Mentor-lite supports a protocol for distributed execution of workflows spread across multiple workflow engines. This support is crucial for workflows that span large, decentralized enterprises with largely autonomous organizational units or even cross multiple enterprises to form so-called "virtual enterprises". A communication manager is responsible for sending and receiving synchronization messages between the engines. In order to guarantee a consistent global state even in the presence of site or network failures, we have built reliable message queues using the CORBA Object Transaction Services.

For administration, Mentor-lite provides a Java-based workbench for workflow design, workflow partitioning across multiple workflow servers, and a Java-based runtime monitoring tool.

2 The Auto-Configuration Tool

A distributed configuration of Mentor-lite consists of different workflow servers (i.e., instances of the workflow engine), application servers, and one communication server (i.e., ORB). Each server of the first two categories can be dedicated to a specified set of workflow activities and invoked applications, resp., on a per type basis. Each of these dedicated servers and also the communication server can be replicated across multiple computers for enhanced performance and availability. Given this flexibility, it is a difficult problem to choose an appropriate configuration for the entire WFMS that meets all requirements with regard to throughput, interaction response time, and availability.

To this end, we have developed an auto-configuration tool that is driven by statistics on the workload from the monitoring tool of Mentor-lite. It can feed this information into its underlying analytic models [2] to assess a hypothetical configuration in a what-if analysis. By systematic variation of the parameters for such hypothetical configurations the tool is also able to derive the (analytically) best configuration, i.e., the minimum degree of replication of each of the involved server types to meet given availability and performance or performability goals, and recommend appropriate reconfigurations. The tool is largely independent of a specific WFMS, using product-specific stubs for its various components that need to interact with the WFMS. The components of the configuration tool and its embedding into the overall system environment are illustrated in Figure 1.

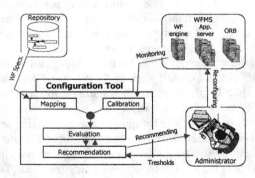

Figure 1 : Overview of the auto-configuration tool

References

[1] M. Gillmann, J. Weissenfels, G. Weikum, A. Kraiss, Performance and Availability Assessment for the Configuration of Distributed Workflow Management Systems, Int. Conf. on Extending Database Technology (EDBT), Konstanz, Germany, 2000

[2] P. Muth, D. Wodtke, J. Weissenfels, G. Weikum, A. Kotz Dittrich, Enterprise-wide Workflow Management based on State and Activity Charts, in: A. Dogac, L. Kalinichenko, M.T. Ozsu, A. Sheth (Eds.), Workflow Management Systems and Interoperability, NATO Advanced Study Institute, Springer, 1998.

TIP: A Temporal Extension to Informix*

Jun Yang   Huacheng C. Ying   Jennifer Widom
Computer Science Department, Stanford University

Our research in temporal data warehouses has led us to require a relational database system with full SQL as well as rich temporal support. Most commercial relational database systems today support only a DATE type (or its variants). A DATE attribute can be used to timestamp a tuple with a specific point in time (e.g., "this patient was taking Prozac as of September 1"). But for general temporal modeling, a timestamp should be able to consist of multiple time periods (e.g., "this patient was prescribed Prozac from January to April, and then from July to October"). Furthermore, the DATE type does not include NOW, a special symbol interpreted as the current (transaction) time with many uses in temporal modeling. Although it is possible to encode NOW and sets of time periods using DATE as the only type of timestamp, doing so can lead to cumbersome queries and inefficient implementations. An alternative is to use one of the available temporal database prototypes, but none of them fully meets the needs of our temporal data warehousing application, as we discuss in the extended version of this description.[1]

Recently the major relational database vendors have introduced technologies that allow their systems to be extended with software plugins developed by users or third-party vendors. Examples include *Informix DataBlades*, *DB2 Extenders*, and *Oracle Cartridges*. Some time-related extensions have been developed, such as time-series, spatiotemporal, and temporal index extensions. Unfortunately, they do not provide the general-purpose temporal support we need.

Hence, we built TIP (*Temporal Information Processor*), an extension to the Informix database system based on its DataBlade technology. The TIP DataBlade implements a rich set of datatypes and routines that support modeling and querying of temporal data. Once the TIP DataBlade is installed, TIP datatypes and routines become available to users as if they were built into the DBMS. Client applications connect directly to a TIP-enabled database through a standard API such as ODBC or JDBC, and they manipulate TIP datatypes using C and Java libraries provided by TIP. We have developed a Java client with a powerful graphical user interface for querying and browsing temporal data. The architecture and implementation of TIP are further described in the extended version,[1] which also includes screen shots from our temporal browsing interface.

The TIP DataBlade extends the Informix type system with the following datatypes related to time: (1) *Chronon* represents a specific point in time, like SQL's DATE type. (2) *Span* is a duration of time, which can be positive or negative. (3) *Instant* is either a Chronon or a NOW-relative time. A NOW-relative Instant is represented by an offset of type Span from the symbol NOW, whose interpretation changes as time advances. For example, "NOW-1day" denotes "yesterday." (4) *Period* consists of a pair of Instant's. The first one marks the start of the period and the second one marks the end. (5) *Element* is a set of Period's.

These datatypes allow complex temporal data to be modeled. Consider a table that records the prescription history for patients. We store a patient's date of birth as a Chronon, dosage frequency as a Span, and prescription periods as an Element. The following SQL creates the table:

```
CREATE TABLE Prescription
(doc CHAR(20),patient CHAR(20),patientDOB Chronon,
 drug CHAR(20),dosage INT,freq Span,valid Element)
```

TIP also defines an extensive collection of support routines for its datatypes, including casts, arithmetic operators (+, -, *, /) and comparison operators (=, <, >, etc.), TIP-defined routines (union, intersect, difference, overlaps, contains, length, etc.), and aggregate functions (group_union, group_intersect, etc.). For more details, please refer to the extended version.[1] With these support routines, we are able to express many temporal operations without adding new language constructs to SQL.

For example, the following query finds all patients who were prescribed Tylenol when they were less than w weeks old, for input parameter w. In the query, start is a TIP routine that returns the start time of the first period in an Element. The "::" is Informix's notation for explicit cast, needed here to convert the string into a Span.

```
SELECT patient FROM Prescription
WHERE drug='Tylenol'
AND start(valid)-patientDOB < '7days'::Span * :w
```

For another example, suppose we want to know who has taken Diabeta and Aspirin simultaneously, and exactly when. This temporal self-join query can be expressed as follows:

```
SELECT p1.*, p2.*, intersect(p1.valid, p2.valid)
FROM Prescription p1, Prescription p2
WHERE p1.drug='Diabeta' AND p2.drug='Aspirin'
AND overlaps(p1.valid,p2.valid)
```

Finally, we compute how long each patient has been on medication using the aggregate function group_union, which returns the union of a collection of Element's.

```
SELECT patient, length(group_union(valid))
FROM Prescription GROUP BY patient
```

Note that TIP does not introduce a new temporal query language, such as TSQL2. Instead, TIP enables temporal queries expressed in SQL by providing an extensive set of built-in datatypes and routines. See the extended version[1] for more discussion on related and future work.

---

* This work was supported by the National Science Foundation under grant IIS-9811947 and by an Informix Software Grant.

[1] http://www-db.stanford.edu/pub/papers/yyw-tipdemo.ps

AQR-Toolkit: An Adaptive Query Routing Middleware for Distributed Data Intensive Systems

Ling Liu, Calton Pu, David Buttler, Wei Han, Henrique Paques, Wei Tang

Georgia Institute of Technology
College of Computing
Atlanta, Georgia 30332-0280
{lingliu,calton,buttler,weihan,paques,wtang}@cc.gatech.edu

Overview. Query routing is an intelligent service that can direct query requests to appropriate servers that are capable of answering the queries. The goal of a query routing system is to provide efficient associative access to a large, heterogeneous, distributed collection of information providers by routing a user query to the most relevant information sources that can provide the best answer. Effective query routing not only minimizes the query response time and the overall processing cost, but also eliminates a lot of unnecessary communication overhead over the global networks and over the individual information sources.

The AQR-Toolkit divides the query routing task into two cooperating processes: query refinement and source selection. It is well known that a broadly defined query inevitably produces many false positives. Query refinement provides mechanisms to help the user formulate queries that will return more useful results and that can be processed efficiently. As a complimentary process, source selection reduces false negatives by identifying and locating a set of relevant information providers from a large collection of available sources. By pruning irrelevant information sources, source selection also reduces the overhead of contacting the information servers that do not contribute to the answer of the query.

In AQR-Toolkit, we develop a framework for building an adaptive query routing system. There are two important features of our approach. First, we use both the user query profile and the source capability profile as a measure of server relevance. By using user query profiles for query refinement, a well-focused query is produced to ensure the matching data sources selected have zero or minimized false positives. By using the source capability profiles and a multi-level progressive pruning algorithm, the result of source selection will have zero or minimized false negatives. Second, we allow different options for query refinements and source selection to be mixed and matched within a single application, and provide performance monitoring to allow a system developer to examine the impact of using different query routing mechanisms.

System Architecture. The system architecture of AQR-

Toolkit consists of a hierarchical network (a directed acyclic graph) with external information providers at the leaves and query routers as mediating nodes. The end-point information providers support query-based access to their documents. At a query router node, a user may browse and query the meta information about information providers registered at that query router or make use of the router's facilities for query refinement and source selection. The meta information about an information provider includes content summary, query capability description, and information quality of that provider, and is called the provider's source capability profile. A source capability profile contains a query that is true of all documents available from the information provider. The precise nature of source capability profiles is not specified by the query routing architecture, but left to the information providers and individual query routers themselves. A source capability profile may therefore be a simple predicate consisting only of the host name of the computer acting as the information server or a disjunction of all the terms in all the documents at the information server. It may also be a subset of the attributes derived from the indexed documents plus value-added attributes that describe the collection of documents but may not occur in the documents themselves. Readers may refer to our paper in the proceedings of the ICDE 1999 for further detail.

Description of Demo. The AQR-Toolkit is written in Java, running on both Windows NT and Solaris machines, and requires a Java-compliant web browser such as Netscape 4.0 or above. We demonstrate the latest version of our AQR-Toolkit, including the query refinement component, the source selection component, and the multi-level pruning strategies as described in the previous sections. Specifically we show the effectiveness and scalability of our AQR-Toolkit using a comparative shopping application, where multiple web-based information servers are used. The toolkit also includes facilities for performance monitoring, which allows a system developer to examine the impact of using different query routing mechanisms. In addition, we will use the execution monitoring capability of the AQR-Toolkit to show how the relevant information sources for a given query are dynamically discovered through the step-wise utilization of the user query profile and the source capability descriptions in the multi-level relevance pruning process, and how to ensure that each step considerably reduces the number of candidate rewritings considered in the next step.

Acknowledgement. This research is partially supported by DARPA contract MDA972-97-1-0016 and Intel.

SPIRE: A Progressive Content-Based Spatial Image Retrieval Engine

Chung-Sheng Li, Lawrence D. Bergman, Yuan-Chi Chang, Vittorio Castelli, John R. Smith

Data Management Department, IBM T. J. Watson Research Center, P. O. Box 704, Yorktown Heights, NY 10598

(914) {784-6661,784-7946,784-7327,945-2396,784-7320}

{csli,bergmanl,yuanchi,vittorio,jsmith}@us.ibm.com

ABSTRACT

In this demo, we will show the implementation of a content-based SPatial Image Retrieval Engine (SPIRE) for multimodal unstructured data. This architecture provides a framework for retrieving multi-modal data including image, image sequence, time series and parametric data from large archives. Dramatic speedup (from a factor of 4 to 35) has been achieved for many search operations such as template matching, texture feature extraction. This framework has been applied and validated in solar flares and petroleum exploration in which spatial and spatial-temporal phenomena are located.

Keywords

content-based retrieval, digital library, multimedia database.

1. INTRODUCTION

Despite the tremendous progress in the content-based retrieval systems during the recent decade, there still exists a number of outstanding issues: (1) Almost all of the content-based search engines are based on similarity matches on features extracted from a single data modality such as images or video. There still lacks a framework for performing similarity search across multiple modalities simultaneously. Combining fuzzy information from multiple systems has been investigated in the IBM Garlic project. However, only fuzzy conjunction or disjunction among attributes of the same data object has been considered. A more general framework that allows combining fuzzy information through spatial and temporal rules is still needed. (2) Scalability of the content-based search on a combination of raw data, features, semantics, and parametric data is yet to be investigated.

2. FRAMEWORK

In the SPIRE framework, a simple search object can be specified at different abstraction levels - raw data, feature, semantics, metadata, or a combination of the above. A composite search object can then be constructed from multiple simple objects with spatial, temporal, or Boolean relationships. During query processing time, the composite object query is transformed and processed sequentially using an algorithm based on dynamic programming. This algorithm eliminates the possibility of false dismissal of candidate combinations without having to perform an exhaustive search. The scalability of the proposed scheme is achieved by adopting a progressive framework, in which a hierarchical scheme is used to decorelates and reorganize the information contained in the images at all of the abstraction levels. Consequently, the search operators can be applied on a much smaller portions of the data and progressively refine the search results. This technique achieves a significant speedup as compared to more conventional implementations. The speedup factor for template matching (the search operator at the raw pixel level) and classification (the search operator at the semantic level) is more than 20 times. A 400% to 800% speedup has also been achieved for texture extraction and matching (the search operator at the feature level).

3. PROTOTYPE

Queries are constructed and parsed syntactically at the java-based client using a drag-and-drop interface in conjunction with an image navigation browser. This interface also allows the definition of new objects and features. After being specified and syntactically analyzed, the query is then sent to the server. A query usually involves both metadata search and potentially multi-modal search on both images and time series. Based on the progressive framework and the SPROC algorithm, the search engine works in conjunction with the query parser to parse the query string into a script consisting of a set of SQL statements and content-based search operators. The IBM DB2 database engine performs search on the metadata, while the image content search is performed by the content search operators scheduled and sequenced by the search engine. Usually the metadata search serves as a pruning mechanism, to achieve maximum reduction of the search space during the first stages of the query execution process. The content-based search engine also accesses the feature descriptors as well as the raw pixels of an image region in order to compute the final results. The results of the search are rendered by the visualization engine.

In the demo, we will show a reservoir modeling scenario that often arises in the oil/gas exploration and production environments. A simple object for *laminated sandstone* based on the texture feature is defined through the drag-and-drop java interface with both examples and counter examples. The query results from a dataset consisting of 1000 feet of resistivity measurement of borehole and well log data are then displayed. This scenario allows the capture of geologist's knowledge of definitions of various geological structures, and thus facilitate interpretation of vast amount of oil/gas exploration data.

Integrating Replacement Policies in StorM: An Extensible Approach

Chong Leng Goh, Beng Chin Ooi, Stephane Bressan, Kian-Lee Tan
Department of Computer Science
National University of Singapore
3 Science Drive 2, Singapore 117543
email: {gohcl,ooibc,steph,tankl}@comp.nus.edu.sg

1 Java-based *Storage Manager*

StorM is a storage manager, consisting of a set of classes and objects for the development and tuning of non-standard data intensive applications in Java. It is entirely written in Java (JDK 1.2), and hence it does not require a special compiler or a special abstract machine or a set of (possibly OS specific) native methods. Exploiting the serialization properties of Java objects, StorM offers support for persistence for almost any Java object, and support for an independent notion of persistent homogeneous collection of Java objects. Since StorM aims at providing suitable support for a wide range of applications, it has been designed with an emphasis on extensibility.

2 StorM's Extensible Buffer Manager

The buffer manager of StorM is extensible. Supporting extensibility at the buffer management level is essential for the following reasons. First, extensions made at one level of a DBMS require extension support at other levels as well. For example, having a new data type extension typically requires making extensions to both the access method and query optimizer. With buffer replacement extensibility, it becomes possible to custom-tailor a smart buffer replacement policy to manage buffer replacements intelligently by exploiting the reference behavior of new access methods or transactions. Second, the emergence of more complex applications also provides more opportunities for exploiting domain specific semantics to improve system performance at the buffer manager level. Finally, supporting buffer level extensibility facilitates the evaluation and fine-tuning of new

buffer replacement policies for domain specific operators, algorithms or applications. Buffer extensibility in StorM is achieved using a hierarchical buffer pool model and a priority scheme. A buffer replacement policy is modeled by a collection of types (buffer group types, local selection policy types, and abstract selection policy types) and mapping among the types (among buffer group types, and between buffer group types and selection policy types). Using a priority scheme allows us to set priorities for the various group types, so that the page to be replaced will come from group types with the lowest priority. The separation of a replacement policy into the abstract selection and local selection policies not only supports flexibility, reusability, but also allows us to design new replacement policies by different combinations of existing or new local and abstract selection policies. In summary, StorM provides a generic interface for specifying buffer replacement policies in which introduction of a new policy into StorM requires registering only five methods with the buffer manager.

In order to concretely demonstrate the effectiveness of the incorporation of a new replacement policy into the buffer manager, a visualization interface was purposely built to show the B^+-tree traversal for the concurrent queries as well as the actions (page accessed, page flushed, page fetched, etc.) taking place in the buffer pool. In this demonstration, we will show how a customized replacement policy based on [1] that exploits the access patterns of indexes to increase hit ratio, can be easily coded and incorporated into our buffer pool model on the fly. We also coded various replacement policies and used various access traces to demonstrate the extensibility provided by the system and the benefit of supporting them.

References

[1] C.Y. Chan, B.C. Ooi, and H.J. Lu. Extensible buffer management of indexes. In *Proceedings of the 18th Very Large Data Bases Conference*, British Columbia, 1992.

DISIMA: A Distributed and Interoperable Image Database System

Vincent Oria,* M. Tamer Özsu, Paul J. Iglinski, Shu Lin and Bin Yao
Department of Computing Science - University of Alberta
Edmonton, Alberta, Canada T6G 2H1
{oria, ozsu, iglinski, shulin, yao}@cs.ualberta.ca

1   Introduction

DISIMA (Distributed Image Database Management System) is a research project under development at the University of Alberta. DISIMA implements a database approach to developing an image database system. Image contents are modeled using object-oriented paradigms while a declarative query language and a corresponding visual query language allow queries over syntactic and semantic features of images. The distributed and interoperable architecture is designed using common facilities as defined in the Object Management Architecture (OMA).

2   Modeling and Querying Images

In DISIMA [OÖL+97], an image is composed of a set of physical salient objects (*PSO*) which are regions of this particular image with some syntactic features such as shape, color, and texture. The meaning of a PSO is given by an LSO (logical salient object), an abstraction of all the PSOs, referring to the same real world concept.

The colors in the images are organized in a hash-like index structure for color similarity searches. The entire image is divided into 4 quadrants, and each quadrant is recursively divided into 4, and so on. Each image is then represented by a quadtree that stores the color histograms corresponding to the quadrants. The dimensions of the colors histograms are then reduced and the result is stored in a multidimensional hash structure for a filtering step in similarity searches before using the color histograms for a refinement step.

The syntactic and semantic features are used in MOQL (Multimedia Object Query Language) to query images. MOQL is an extension of the standard OQL language. We also defined an equivalent visual query language (VisualMOQL [OÖX+99]) and a translator to translate a visual query into an MOQL query.

The distributed architecture is based on CORBA which provides transparencies at the platform and the communication levels. At the image database level, different data models (different schemas) can be found, necessitating homogenization of the semantics of these schemas and any associated image content descriptions. The distributed architecture involves both homogeneous and heterogeneous systems although the first distributed prototype is built for DISIMA sites only.

3   Conclusion

Most image database systems are built around a multidimensional index and focus on similarity queries. In DISIMA, data are manipulated through algebraic operators, and indexes (if any) are used to speed up the query processing. This conference demonstration augments the on-line version (http://www.cs.ualberta.ca/~database/DISIMA/Interface.html) with distributed features and a novel indexing facility for multi-precision color-similarity searches.

4   Acknowledgments

This research is supported by a strategic grant from the Natural Science and Engineering Research Council (NSERC) of Canada.

References

[OÖL+97] V. Oria, M. T. Özsu, X. Li, L. Liu, J. Li, Y. Niu, and P. J. Iglinski. Modeling images for content-based queries: The DISIMA approach. In *Proceedings of Visual'97*, pages 339–346, San Diego, California, December 1997.

[OÖX+99] V. Oria, M. T. Özsu, B. Xu, L. I. Cheng, and P.J. Iglinski. VisualMOQL: The DISIMA visual query language. In *Proceedings of the 6th IEEE ICMCS*, volume 1, pages 536–542, Florence, Italy, June 1999.

---

* Current address: Computer and Information Science Department, New Jersey Institute of Technology, University Heights, Newark, NJ, 07102-1982, oria@cis.njit.edu.

The MLPQ/GIS Constraint Database System*

Peter Revesz, Rui Chen, Pradip Kanjamala, Yiming Li, Yuguo Liu, Yonghui Wang
Dept. of Computer Science, University of Nebraska, Lincoln, NE 68588

MLPQ/GIS [4,6] is a *constraint database* [5] system like CCUBE [1] and DEDALE [3] but with a special emphases on spatio-temporal data. Features include data entry tools (first four icons in Fig. 1), icon-based queries such as ∩ **Intersection,** ∪ **Union,** **Area,** **Buffer,** **Max Max** and **Min Min,** which optimize linear objective functions, and **Q** for **Datalog queries**. For example, in Fig. 1 we loaded and displayed a constraint database that represents the midwest United States and loaded two contraint relations describing the movements of two persons. The query icon opened a dialog box into which we entered the query which finds (t, i) pairs such that the two people are in the same state i at the same time t.

MLPQ/GIS can animate [2] spatio-temporal objects that are linear constraint relations over x, y and t.

Users can also display in discrete color zones (isometric maps) any spatially distributed variable z that is a linear function of x and y. For example, Fig. 2 shows the mean annual air temperature in Nebraska. Animation and isometric map display can be combined.

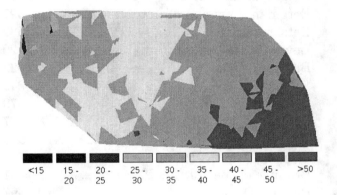

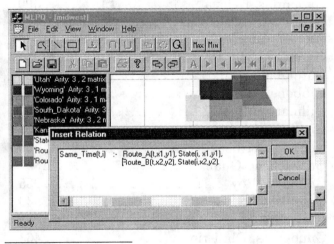

References

[1] A. Brodsky, V.E. Segal, J. Chen, P.A. Exarkhopoulo, The *CCUBE* Constraint Object-Oriented Database System. *Proc. ACM SIGMOD*, p. 577-579, 1999.

[2] J. Chomicki, Y. Liu, P. Revesz, Animating Spatiotemporal Constraint Databases. *Proc. STDBM*, p. 224-242, 1999.

[3] S. Grumbach, P. Rigaux, L. Segoufin, The DEDALE System for Complex Spatial Queries. *Proc. ACM SIGMOD*, p. 213-224, 1998.

[4] P. Kanjamala, P. Revesz, Y. Wang, MLPQ/GIS: A GIS using Linear Constraint Databases. *Proc. COMAD*, p. 389-392, 1998.

[5] P. Kanellakis, G. Kuper, P. Revesz, Constraint Query Languages, *JCSS*, 51(1):26-52, 1995.

[6] P. Revesz, Yiming Li, MLPQ: A Linear Constraint Database System with Aggregate Operations. *Proc. IDEAS*, p. 132-137, 1997.

*Supported by NSF grants IRI-9625055, IRI-9632871 and a Gallup Research Professorship.

Author Index